A NOTE ON THE AUTHOR

DAVID KYNASTON was born in Aldershot in 1951. He has been a professional historian since 1973 and has written eighteen books, including *The City of London*, a widely acclaimed four-volume history, and *WG's Birthday Party*, an account of the Gentleman v. Players match at Lord's in July 1898. He is the author of *Austerity Britain, 1945–51* and *Family Britain, 1951–57*, the first two titles in a series of books covering the history of post-war Britain (1945–79) under the collective title 'Tales of a New Jerusalem'. He is currently a visiting professor at Kingston University.

MODERNITY BRITAIN

1957–62

David Kynaston

BLOOMSBURY

NEW YORK · LONDON · NEW DELHI · SYDNEY

Bloomsbury Paperbacks
An imprint of Bloomsbury Publishing Plc

50 Bedford Square
London
WC1B 3DP
UK

1385 Broadway
New York
NY 10018
USA

www.bloomsbury.com

BLOOMSBURY and the Diana logo are trademarks of Bloomsbury Publishing Plc

British Library Cataloguing-in-Publication Data
A catalogue record for this book is available from the British Library.

ISBN: HB: 978-1-6204-0809-4
PB: 978-1-4088-4438-0
ePub: 978-1-6204-0810-0

2 4 6 8 10 9 7 5 3 1

Typeset by Hewer Text UK Ltd, Edinburgh
Printed and bound in Great Britain by CPI Group (UK) Ltd, Croydon CR0 4YY

MIX
Paper from
responsible sources
FSC® C020471

To find out more about our authors and books visit www.bloomsbury.com. Here you will find extracts, author
interviews, details of forthcoming events and the option to sign up for our newsletters.

Contents

OPENING THE BOX

Author's Note

Tales of a New Jerusalem is a projected sequence of books about Britain between 1945 and 1979. The first two books, *A World to Build* and *Smoke in the Valley*, are gathered together in the volume *Austerity Britain*; the next two books, *The Certainties of Place* and *A Thicker Cut*, in the volume *Family Britain*. This present volume, *Modernity Britain*, covers the years 1957 to 1962 and comprises the fifth book in the sequence, *Opening the Box*, and the sixth book, *A Shake of the Dice*.

OPENING THE BOX

This book is dedicated to Lucy

PART ONE

I

Isn' 'e Smashin'?

'Council tenants and potential council tenants are today a much more typical section of the population at large than ever before,' declared a junior housing minister, Enoch Powell, to the annual conference of the Society of Housing Managers on Thursday, 10 January 1957 – at almost exactly the moment that Harold Macmillan was calling at the Palace to succeed Sir Anthony Eden as the new Conservative prime minister. Later that afternoon, discussion turned to the nonconformists. 'I find that, generally speaking, there is no cause for complaint about the standard of decoration of those tenants who "defy regulations" and do their own,' conceded Lambeth's director of housing, Mr C. C. Carter. 'They carry out the decorations to a standard which is usually very satisfactory. I am not sure whether the day has not arrived when you might well let tenants do their own internal decorations.' Next day's main address was given by Mrs E. Denington, vice-chairman of London County Council's Housing Committee. 'I think that the natural way for people to live is in houses,' she insisted. 'I should like to sound a word of warning to authorities which are thinking of building flats. I believe that no more than 5 per cent of the population want to live in flats. Do not build them unless you have to, and if you have to then do make provision for children, because if you do not you have no right to grumble if they are a nuisance.'

Judy Haines as usual was at home in Chingford on Saturday the 12th. 'Fed up,' she noted flatly. 'Girls went to pictures, John [her husband, earlier known as Abbé] to London, and here I am. Decided to please myself and blow housework. Therefore I enjoyed some needlework – Pamela's frock and curtains.' Another diarist, Allan Preston, the

25-year-old son of an English teacher, went to Burnden Park in the afternoon. 'The first half was very entertaining,' he recorded of the home team's First Division clash with Leeds. 'Both sides attacked crisply and at half time Bolton were winning 4–2. The second half was more dismal. Two goals only were scored and there were one or two unpleasant incidents.' Stay-at-homes could have watched Percy Thrower's *Gardening Club* and *The Lone Ranger* on BBC television, while 7.30 saw another favourite, *Dixon of Dock Green*, back for his third series. 'The whole family has been eagerly waiting for the return of Dixon,' reported a viewer, 'and judging by this edition [characteristically called 'Give a Dog a Good Name'] this series is going to be every bit as good as the last.' *Hancock's Half Hour* by this time was on both radio and television, and on Sunday evening the Light Programme broadcast 'Almost a Gentleman', episode 14 of the fourth radio series: overlooked once again in the New Year's Honours List, the anti-hero of 23 Railway Cuttings, East Cheam is persuaded he needs etiquette lessons, with predictably disastrous results. Perhaps revealingly, Philip Larkin seems never to have evinced any interest in, let alone enthusiasm for, Tony Hancock. 'An utterly lonely Sunday, spent indoors except for the usual excursion to the pillar box,' Larkin wrote from his flat in Hull later that evening to Monica Jones in Leicester. 'I have sat doing nothing since about 4 o' clock, & am now slightly drunk on rum and honey & hot water. The usual revolting insufficient meals – an awful tinned steak pudding, like eating a hot poultice, & sausages ... I can't ever remember being so dead since about 1947.'[1]

'Top People Take *The Times*' was a new poster from Monday the 14th, as the PM sought to finalise his administration. 'Many considerations had to be borne in mind,' the Old Etonian (like his predecessor) would reflect after a difficult process. 'The right, centre & left of the party; the extreme "Suez" group; the extreme opposition to Suez; the loyal centre – and last, but not least, U & non-U (to use the jargon that Nancy Mitford has popularised), that is, Eton, Winchester, etc. on the one hand; Board school & grammar school on the other.' Top people also had to face the cameras, and Macmillan on the 17th found himself on fraught terms with the new-fangled teleprompter as he gave a ministerial broadcast. Reactions were mixed. 'In its *extremely* clear intimation that we were neither a second-rate power nor a satellite [i.e. of the USA], it gave me a lift of the heart such as I had never hoped to experience again,' wrote the once-Marxist novelist Patrick Hamilton to his brother. But a 67-year-old housewife in Barrow, Nella Last, was appalled to read next morning in her *Daily Express* about Macmillan's apparent promise to move decisively towards what she called 'free trade with Europe': 'I'm not either clever or well read, I don't – can't – decide the issues of such a step, BUT I *do* disagree utterly with one man coming to a T.V. screen, & calmly announcing such a step . . . As I tidied round I thought that many cleverer heads than mine would feel the same sense of "shock"!' Labour's television guru Anthony Wedgwood Benn was abroad, but heard disturbingly favourable reports on his return. 'His television performance was evidently a very dramatic one,' Benn noted. 'His call for an "opportunity state" has created interest and discussion just when things looked so soggy in his own Party.' The Edwardian actor-manager was indeed not someone to underestimate, though Malcolm Muggeridge soon afterwards had a bit of fun in *Life*. 'The lean, sinewy neck pulsates,' he told his American readers, 'the tired grey features wear a smile; the voice, soft and sibilant, emerges from the drooping moustache. A publisher? No. A civil servant? No. A Prime Minister.'[2]

Modelled on the Parisian jazz club Le Caveau, the Cavern opened in Liverpool the evening before Macmillan's broadcast. Nearly 2,000 people queued outside, only 600 were able to get in, and (reported a local paper in a brief story about 'Liverpool's New Jazzy Club') 'dressed in jeans, skirts and sweaters, they filled every corner of the club, standing packed between the bricked arches', as they listened to 'various jazz bands' plus the Coney Island Skiffle Group. The foreign influence was spreading. 'The snack bar near Kew Gardens station was crowded out,' noted the solipsistic, emotionally impenetrable civil servant Henry St John on Saturday the 19th. 'There seem no times or seasons for anything now; people seem to fill cafés day and night, whereas they used to be almost deserted except at meal times.' The old insularity was also starting to go in football, with Manchester United the first English team to take part (in defiance of the football authorities) in the European Cup and soon afterwards – on 6 February – beating Bilbao 3–0 to reach the semi-finals. Next day's *Listener* reviewed Lawrence Durrell's novel *Justine*, the first volume of what would become an exotic literary phenomenon, *The Alexandria Quartet*. 'Less fiction than incantation,' reckoned Ronald Bryden, 'beautifully conceived, only too consciously beautiful in the writing.' Durrell himself lived in Provence and was fond of calling England 'Pudding Island', a view that in certain moods the young American poet Sylvia Plath (recently married to Ted Hughes) shared. 'It is often infuriating to read the trash published by the Old Guard, the flat, clever, colorless poets here,' she wrote back home a few days earlier. Little was as unashamedly English as *At the Drop of a Hat*, the musical revue by Michael Flanders and Donald Swann playing since 24 January to packed houses at the Fortune Theatre. 'None of their songs are very melodious and not all of them are really amusing,' grumbled Anthony Heap, local government officer in St Pancras and inveterate first-nighter, but Harold Hobson in the *Sunday Times* relished the 'kindly satire' and 'the crisp, neat, elegant, cultured jokes about gnus, bindweed, the monotonous lot of the umpire in the Ladies' Singles at Wimbledon, the very contemporary furniture of his flat, and the disastrous season of 1546 in the English theatre'. Flanders (bearded and in a wheelchair) had, Hobson added, 'an inner merriment which, when he is not speaking, communicates itself to the audience'.[3]

The day after Flanders and Swann opened in the West End, five shop stewards at Briggs Motor Bodies, the Ford Motor Company's body-making plant at Dagenham, were suspended – one of them, an extrovert, free-speaking Cockney from West Ham called Johnny McLoughlin, indefinitely. His offence was that, during working hours, he had defied the wishes of his foreman by ringing a handbell in order to call a meeting in his toolmaking 'shop' to discuss possible strike action, following the suspension of two fellow shop stewards for unauthorised absences. Within days the 'bellringer' incident had led to a walk-out by some 8,000 employees. 'The workers of Briggs know very well that the Company is trying to exploit the situation of unemployment and short time which exists in Dagenham at the present time,' declared the Strike Committee, in the larger context of continuing post-Suez petrol rationing causing problems for the motor industry as a whole. 'They are trying to force a return to the bad old days when "Fordism" was a by-word for non-trade unionism, low wages, and bad working conditions.' Talks to reinstate McLoughlin broke down, with the man himself declining to look for another billet. 'What chance would I have after all the publicity this has brought me?' he explained on 12 February to the

Daily Mail. 'Wherever I go I am known as "the man who tolled the bell".' That same day, the Tory MP for Hornchurch, Godfrey Lagden, told the Commons that Briggs had 'the most unfortunate collection, above-average collection, of shop stewards who are practically Communists', adding that generally for the workers there 'it is extremely dangerous not to come out when they ring the bell'. Dagenham's Labour MP, John Parker, spoke of how at Ford (including Briggs) 'no attempt is made to treat individuals as live men and women, but to just take them as industrial cogs'. Two days later, Amalgamated Engineering Union (AEU) members at Briggs voted decisively for further strike action, though leaving time for government intervention. Through it all, there had been something else on the collective Briggs mind: the home tie (on 9 February) for the company's football team against the Amateur Cup holders, mighty Bishop Auckland. At a packed Rush Green, the visitors squeaked home by the only goal – 'very lucky', according to the *Barking Advertiser*'s 'Onlooker', against 'the motor boys . . . firing smoothly on all eleven cylinders'.[4]

Almost everywhere, whether in Dagenham or County Durham, the shared daily reference points were shifting from sound to vision. 'Mrs Atkinson keeps asking when we are coming in to see the Television,' Nella Last noted on the last Wednesday of January about her persistent neighbour, '& I'd a rather difficult task of explaining how my husband would never stay up to see any play.' Radio that evening included a road-and-housing-development storyline in *Educating Archie* and some typical by-play in *Take It From Here.* Standing outside the house he shares with his father, Ron Glum is kissing his girlfriend Eth good-bye when he realises he is locked out. He rings the bell to wake up Mr Glum senior, who opens the door:

> *Mr Glum:* Eth? What you coming round this time of night for?
> *Eth:* I'm going.
> *Mr Glum:* You mean you got an old man like me out of a hot bed just to tell me you're going? Oh, I dunno what's come over this generation. It's all them Elvis Parsley records.

Most people's focus that Wednesday, though, was on *Double Your Money*, in particular whether Lynda Simpson, a 13-year-old schoolgirl from Sutton Coldfield, would take the £500 she'd already won through her spelling prowess or try to double it. 'It's your decision, my girl,' her father was reported in the *Daily Mirror* as having told her, while Lynda herself calmly announced at the start of the programme, 'I think I'll disregard everybody's advice and go on.' So she did, entering the see-through box and successfully spelling five words: *manoeuvre, connoisseur, reconnoitre, chlorophyll* and *hypochondriac*. 'What are you going to do with the money?' asked compère Hughie Green. 'I'm going to buy a tape recorder and put the rest in the bank,' Lynda replied. 'I hope to go to a university and it'll help to pay for that.'[5]

Lynda had presumably passed her 11-plus, but that was not the case for the majority of the nation's children. Two days later, on 1 February, the BBC showed a largely reassuring television documentary about the exam, presented by the Canadian political analyst Robert McKenzie and featuring a secondary modern in north London. A chemist noted disapprovingly that 'there appeared to be no expense spared in this school to buy every bit of modern equipment possible', but a teacher's wife preferred to accentuate the positive: 'How wonderfully the children behaved. There was no glancing at the cameras, etc, which is so apt to distract the viewer.' This proved a relatively uncontroversial programme – unlike the following Monday's *Panorama*, which included a clip from a film by Dr Grantly Dick-Read (whose work had inspired the recently founded Natural Childbirth Association, later National Childbirth Trust) showing a natural childbirth through relaxation. Only two people rang in to complain, but the headline in the right-wing tabloid *Daily Sketch* was 'REVOLTING', its columnist 'Candidus' condemning the film as 'part of the exhibitionism that is the growing weakness of our day and age'.[6]

Between those two programmes, on the evening of Sunday the 3rd, Britain's first rock 'n' roll star, Tommy Steele, and his band were giving two performances (each lasting barely 20 minutes) in Leicester. 'The act itself is simple enough,' wrote Trevor Philpott in *Picture Post*. 'It's ninety per cent youthful exuberance. There is not a trace of sex, real or implied. The Steelemen, bass, drums, saxophone and piano, all writhe around the stage with their instruments – even the pianist doesn't have a stool. All the antics they, as professionals, freely admit have nothing to do with music. As Tommy would put it: "We do it for laughs."' As for the audience, it was 'happy – hysterically so', reported the *Leicester Mercury*. 'They were saying (in rock 'n' roll jargon): "Isn' 'e smashin'?" "Isn' 'e a luvly colour?" "Isn' 'e berrer than that other feller?" and "Aren't you glad you came, Elsie?" Others didn't say a word. They just shouted.' In fact not everyone was entirely happy. 'I felt rather ashamed of my sex on Sunday night,' an 18-year-old from Kibworth wrote to the paper: 'I'm no square, but it was shocking. Silly girls go to make fools of themselves by screaming and shouting, the whole of the show through. I attended the show but have no idea what he sang. I'm a great fan of Tommy's, but I like to listen not scream.' An immediate riposte came from Diane, Judy and Pat of 212 Wigston Lane, Leicester: 'We think he is the mostest and the best recording artist Britain has ever produced. THE WAY HE DIGS ROCK 'N' ROLL SENDS US ALL SCREAMING WITH DELIGHT.'

In spite of the attendant noise and hysteria, there was little dangerous about the 20-year-old Steele – a former merchant seaman called Tommy Hicks who was, in Philpott's words, 'an ordinary, likeable British kid who obviously gets a kick out of life' – nor was there about the appreciably older, rather podgy Bill Haley, who arrived in England with his Comets two days later. Besieged by fans at Waterloo station, Haley remarked, 'I'd rather the kids would show more restraint.' Over the next few weeks, for all the audiences' jiving in the aisles, his underlying middle-of-the-roadness was epitomised by his regular, benign refrain to journalists that 'all young people have a certain amount of vim and vigour and they like to let off steam and I really don't see too much harm in that'. Still, especially with Steele, *something* – just for a moment – was going on. 'There was a croak in his voice like he meant the words,' recalled Ray Gosling about walking down East Street market in south London around this time, as his latest hit, 'Singing the Blues', sounded out from the record trestles on the market stalls, 'and there were photographs of him bulldog-clipped to the stalls and Tommy Steele looked like us – cheeky British youth with tousled hair and pouting lips and a cockney so-fucking-what look.'[7]

There would be all too few market stalls in the Stepney–Poplar Comprehensive Development Area (CDA). 'Poplar will have its 19-storey skyscraper' was the *East London Advertiser*'s main headline on 8 February, having learned that the Minister of Housing, Henry

Brooke, had just given his approval to the London County Council's scheme for Tidey Street – thereby overriding the wishes of the local council, whose leader had recently described the scheme as a 'monstrosity'. Indeed, the considered view of the council was that high blocks of flats were 'just a load of trouble'. The *Architects' Journal* in its next issue disagreed: 'Tidey Street is unlikely to prove the best advertisement for tower blocks: but it is a great deal the better for having one, and may even convince the Poplar Borough Council that some of the objections of their tenants to high blocks can be overcome by improved design.' Brooke's was not the only approval, for on the 8th the Secretary of State for Scotland signalled the green light for the Hutchesontown/ Gorbals CDA. 'That guarantees an end to the dingy squalor that is Gorbals' was the unambiguously welcoming response of the *Glasgow Herald*. Accompanying photographs showed on the one hand a model of the new Gorbals with its 'spacious layout' and on the other a squalid back court in Florence Street, 'an example of the conditions which will be eliminated by the Glasgow Corporation plan'.

Of the human aspect of what would be involved in 'comprehensive development', not a word. A few days later, Wilfred Pickles was in the East End to present a live edition of radio's still very popular *Have a Go!*. One contestant was Sam Ward, a council park attendant living in Dagenham: 'I'd sooner be back in old Poplar; you can't beat the neighbours.'[8] One can perhaps exaggerate the neighbourliness of those neighbours, but (as in the Gorbals and, in due course, many other rundown inner-city areas) they were about to be cast to the four winds, as their intimate, intensely human world disappeared for ever.

Other issues, reported the *New Statesman*'s Norman MacKenzie from the 'slightly dingy dormitory area' of North Lewisham, were on voters' minds ahead of the by-election there on Valentine's Day:

I liked that Gaitskell until he started running down our boys [i.e. British troops during the Suez crisis]. It isn't right for Labour to do that. They should get on with doing something for the old people. That's their business. *(Housewife)*

I thought Macmillan would be different. But he's giving in to the Yanks, too. He should go on and teach those Egyptians and Indians a lesson. *(Shopkeeper)*

I don't care about foreign policy. If anything I've always believed
Eden. But I'm going to retire next year, and they tell me that this Rent
Bill will put my rent bill up 15 shillings a week. I won't be able to afford
it on my pension. I know it sounds selfish but I'm going to vote for
myself. *(Teacher)*

The Blues have always come and fetched me, and I've put one in for
them. But they can find someone else this time. The doctor told me it was
Mr Butler who put that money on my medicine, and I don't see why I
should go out and catch my death for him. *(Pensioner)*

I don't like what Labour did over Suez. But that isn't what the voting
is about, is it? They're against the Tories, and so am I. *(Busman)*

Hugh Gaitskell's Labour Party duly took the seat from the Tories, the
latter's 'most positive set-back since the 1945 General Election' according to the *Sunday Times*. The three most obvious reasons were the Suez
debacle, inflation and the legislation under way to defreeze private-
sector rents, but for respectable 'middle England' people – natural Tory
voters – something else was increasingly agitating them: excessive taxation and the unacceptably high cost of maintaining the welfare state. 'We
have worked hard and saved all our lives, and the worry of modern
conditions may yet drive us into a mental institution,' a couple in their
sixties from West Bromwich wrote to the *Birmingham Mail* on the day
of the by-election. 'Can't the Government, who do everything for the
lazy and extravagant, do something for the thrifty and careful? They'll take
most of what we have left when we die, anyhow.' So too in Barrow earlier
in the week. 'Mrs Atkinson was in a "militant" mood,' recorded Nella
Last. 'She said "Welfare State" – time it got working smoother & not
throwing money about.' Mrs Atkinson then proceeded to tell Last about a
woman 'in a nearby road' who was 'never economising', became widowed,
and was now getting her rent and rates paid. 'It's a queer world,' the diarist
reflected later. 'No wonder there's unrest & discontent, no one seems to
have the idea of standing on their own! I hear grumbles from OAPs &
mothers drawing allowances, as if they feel there's a bottomless purse for
the Govt to draw on, & it's their *right* to have an increasing share!'[9]

Another matter of state was vexing Last that Monday the 11th. 'I
often say nowadays, though with ever lessening frequency, "nothing
would surprise me nowadays",' she noted, but

the guarded hints on the front page of the *Express*, of differences between the Queen & Duke of Edinburgh, was a bombshell ... I felt *sick* with pity for the Royal Family, with 'spies' & 'disloyalty' in those near to them. I hope there's no foundation in the rumour, but they don't have a *lot* of shared interests on the whole. The Queen has horse racing, & he the sea. They don't seem to 'give and take'.

With Philip in Gibraltar near the end of his four-month world tour, the couple not due to be reunited until the following Saturday (in Portugal at the start of a joint visit there), and stories in the American press leading to official denials of any 'rift', the *Daily Mirror* was especially strident. 'FLY HOME, PHILIP!' it demanded on Monday, followed on Tuesday by 'DUKE – WHY NO ACTION?'. The Palace remained unmoved, and briefly the focus switched to the Queen's younger sister. 'When is Princess Margaret going to be her age (which is 26) and behave like a member of the Royal Family instead of a half-baked jazz mad Teddy Girl?' another royal-watcher, Anthony Heap, asked himself on Friday. 'For what should be reported in this morning's papers but that last night she went to see the latest trashy "rock 'n' roll" film [*The Girl Can't Help It*] at the Carlton – she never goes to an intelligent play or film – and, taking off her shoes, put her feet up on the rail round the front of the circle and waved them in time with the "hot rhythm".' Next day the Queen duly flew out in a Viscount, the Duke (with hearts on his tie) went into the plane at Montijo airfield for some private minutes, and when they emerged together he had, the *Sunday Express* was able happily to report, 'a tiny smear of lipstick on his face'.[10]

The couple missed a notable few days on the small screen, not least the controversial end of the so-called 'Toddlers' Truce'. This was the government-enforced ban on television programmes between 6 and 7 in the evening, to make it easier for parents to get younger children to bed, a ban that the commercial television companies had found increasingly irksome. 'Keep the Toddlers' Truce!' insisted the *Sketch*'s 'Candidus' in December 1956. 'The most docile children who are taken away from a fascinating programme will be tearful and deprived, and will lie awake thinking of what they are missing.' But the Postmaster General, Dr Charles Hill, was adamant that 'it was the responsibility of parents, not the State, to put their children to bed at the right time', and

16 February was set as the date for the start of hostilities. The BBC's new Saturday programme to fill that slot would be, explained the *Radio Times*, 'designed for the young in spirit who like to keep abreast of topical trends in the world about them', with 'plenty of music in the modern manner'.[11]

On the 16th itself, following a news bulletin, the *Six-Five Special* came down the tracks right on time, with a catchy signature tune ('over the points, over the points') and two definitely non-teenage presenters, Pete Murray and Josephine Douglas, doing the honours:

> *Pete:* Hi there, welcome aboard the *Six-Five Special*. We've got almost a hundred cats jumping here, some real cool characters to give us a gas, so just get with it and have a ball.
>
> *Jo:* Well, I'm just a square it seems, but for all the other squares with us, roughly translated what Peter Murray just said was, we've got some lively musicians and personalities mingling with us here, so just relax and catch the mood from us.

What followed over the next 55 minutes included rock 'n' roll from the King Brothers, jazz from Kenny Baker and his Dozen, ballads from Michael Holliday, a group of youngsters from Whitechapel singing a couple of folk songs, an interview with the film actress Lisa Gastoni, an exercise demonstration by the former boxer Freddie Mills and two muscular Hungarian refugees, an extract from a Little Richard film – and, a gloriously Reithian touch, the concert pianist Leff Pouishnoff playing a movement from Beethoven's 'Pathétique' Sonata and then, 'just to show that we, too, can play fast and loud', Chopin's Prelude in B flat minor.

'There was plenty of evidence to show that the older the viewer the less he (or she) enjoyed this programme,' was the predictable conclusion of BBC audience research, adding that though some older viewers were tolerant ('Of course we must cater for youth,' said one), others found it 'utterly trashy' and 'quite intolerably noisy'. As for teenage viewers, there were two perhaps representative responses, the first by an apprentice panel beater: 'I am what is known as a "square" so how could I enjoy this? And why do we have to have so much Rock 'n' Roll lammed at us?' 'This is what many of us have wanted for a long time and I just cannot say how much I enjoyed it. But my dad was grumbling all the time. He said it was "just a lot of noise".' The *News Chronicle* critic tended to agree with Dad – 'a noisy, clanking special' – while the *Daily Telegraph*'s L. Marsland Gander confirmed all the instinctive prejudices of his readers: 'A hundred "cats" were let loose on unsuspecting viewers. Grim-faced, many of them oddly dressed in tight trousers, they jived and did their dervish dances to loud brassy noises.' But it was arguably the shrewd, level-headed Peter Black, the *Daily Mail*'s TV critic, who called it right: Murray was 'jaunty', Douglas was 'arch', and 'the whole thing smelled fragrantly of bread and butter'.[12]

Next day, Sunday, BBC programmes were set out in the *Radio Times* with television coming before radio, for the first time, while Monday saw the arrival of lunchtime television in the shape of *Lunch Box* on ITV. 'People now eat from trays,' presenter Noele Gordon said in advance, 'so they can watch the show and pick up our catch phrases.' The show itself, focusing on viewers' birthdays and wedding anniversaries as well as plenty of baby snapshots sent in by mothers, drew some predictable flak – 'the most folksy, matey, cuddly programme yet', reckoned Maurice Wiggin in the *Sunday Times* – but again Black was perceptive, describing Gordon as 'absolutely first-class, an elegant chum who catches perfectly the desired blend of charm and class-war neutrality'. Yet it was not for *Lunch Box* that 18 February 1957 has gone down in television history, but for the launch of the BBC's weekday evening programme to replace the Toddlers' Truce. '*Tonight*', promised the *Radio Times*, 'will be kaleidoscopic but it will not be superficial; it will be entertaining but it will also be intelligent.'[13]

The first edition of this current affairs magazine, presented by the avuncular, unflappable Cliff Michelmore, featured 12 items over 40 minutes. These included the FA Cup draw, a survey of the morning's papers, a topical calypso by Cy Grant ('Future sociologists may well speculate/On the impact of *Tonight* on the welfare state'), a nude statue of Aphrodite that was causing consternation in Richmond-upon-Thames, an interview with the Dame of Sark, a humorous sketch by a young Jonathan Miller about Charing Cross Road shops, an interview by Derek Hart with the veteran American broadcaster Ed Murrow on the subject of post-Suez Britain, footage of conductor Arturo Toscanini's funeral in Milan earlier in the day, and Cy Grant again, this time singing 'Kisses Sweeter than Wine'. The critics were qualifiedly positive: 'kept on repeating itself', but 'I applaud the programme's attempt to develop a free-and-easy topical programme' (Raymond Bowers, *Mirror*); 'had variety, some spice and reasonable pace but lacked compelling interest and gaiety' (L. Marsland Gander); 'a promising start', though Miller's sketch 'invaded the territory that Johnny Morris has made his own and was duly slaughtered by the comparison' (Peter Black). Viewers themselves gave largely favourable feedback about the first week's editions as a whole, with Grant's up-to-the-minute calypsos (sometimes written by the journalist Bernard Levin) 'particularly enjoyed' and 'the "personality" interviews' holding 'pride of place in viewers' estimation'. For Michelmore as anchorman, praise was almost unanimous: 'Viewers on all sides commended him as "a good mixer", friendly and informal in his approach to participants in the programme, and a clear and relaxed speaker, with the ability to cope quickly (and effectively) with any contretemps.'

Tonight was a breakthrough moment. For almost a year and a half, since its launch in September 1955, commercial television had been trouncing BBC in the ratings and, more generally, exposing it as stuffy, unimaginative and deeply paternalistic. *Tonight* – the inspiration of a brilliant, difficult 33-year-old Welshman, Donald Baverstock – was different. 'The aim would be to get on to a level of conversation with the viewers which means that the presentation and the manner of the people appearing in the programme would be very informal and relaxed,' he had written in early January to a BBC superior (Grace Wyndham Goldie), and over the next few years that was what, working closing with Alasdair Milne (a future director-general), he drove through. The tone was deliberately light, even irreverent, news mixing seamlessly with entertainment. Pioneering use was made of vox pop material, and above all the programme consciously placed itself on the side of the citizen and the consumer rather than the minister or the official. 'A kind of national explosion of relief' was how Goldie herself would contextualise *Tonight*'s impact. 'It was not always necessary to be respectful; experts were not invariably right; the opinions of those in high places did not have to be accepted.'[14] None of this happened overnight, not least in the field of planning and architecture, but a broad,

unstoppable process was under way, and *Tonight* – for all its prepon-
derant middle-classness – was an indispensable outrider.

For truly mass audiences, however, television's future lay elsewhere,
and Tuesday the 19th saw a final new programme in this rather breathless sequence. Originally entitled *Calling Nurse Roberts* and set in the
fictitious hospital Oxbridge General, *Emergency—Ward 10* was ITV's
first high-profile, twice-weekly soap opera. 'Should run for ever,'
Maurice Wiggin confidently predicted, adding:

> It is bound to delight all who gulp in euphoric draughts of an atmosphere
> of iodoform and bedpans. It has just about everything: a flawless blonde
> probationer nurse, and a dedicated brunette one, and a rather sleazy
> doctor, and a martinet sister, and a crotchety 'character' patient with a
> heart of gold. All it needs is for Dan Archer to be wheeled in by Gran
> Grove and operated on by Dr Dale, and that's the millennium, folks.[15]

2

A Lot of Mums

'It was reading Hoggart forty years ago,' recalled Alan Bennett in his preface to *The History Boys* (2004), 'that made me feel that my life, dull though it was, might be made the stuff of literature.' Or, as David Lodge characterised the impact of Richard Hoggart's *The Uses of Literacy* (published in February 1957, going into Pelican paperback in 1958 and reprinted four times in the next seven years), 'In those days it was a kind of Bible for first-generation university students and teachers who had been promoted by education from working-class and lower-middle-class backgrounds into the professional middle class.' From the start, the chorus of critics' adjectives revealed this to be the right book for a particular cultural moment – 'challenging' (*Daily Herald*), 'invigorating' (*Daily Telegraph*), 'urgent' (*Observer*), 'required reading' (*TLS*) – while the *Manchester Guardian* devoted an editorial to Hoggart's 'moving and thoughtful' work:

> The first part is an exquisitely drawn picture of the urban working-class life in which the author (now an extra-mural tutor at Hull University) grew up; hard, sometimes harsh, conventional, gregarious, mother-centred, with an outlook limited in range but realistic within its limits. The second part describes the erosion of some old landmarks by the irrupting new media of popular culture – the cheap magazine with its sex and 'bittiness', the cheap novel with its sex and violence, the juke-box, some radio, much television, all 'full of a corrupt brightness, of improper appeals and moral evasions', and all leading to a broad and shallow condition of mind, a hazy euphory, and an increasingly ready response to (a significant phrase) 'sensation without commitment'.

Hoggart himself (born in 1918) had grown up in the Hunslet district of Leeds, the *locus classicus* of the book's wonderfully vivid, often very autobiographical opening half. The cultural historian Richard Johnson has offered perhaps the most acute assessment of why, over and above those who identified with the 'scholarship boy' theme, *Uses* had such appeal: 'It was surely the fact that working-class culture was described intimately, from within, that made the book so powerful. For the middle-class reader, it was a solvent of assumed cultural superiorities or a lesson, at the very least, in cultural relativities.'[1]

Two months later in 1957, another, more explicitly sociological, study (also in due course a best-selling Pelican) likewise hit the mark. 'I suppose that, having in our various ways in our previous jobs been on the fringes of the Establishment, we are in revolt against it,' Michael Young had reflected the previous year about himself and his colleagues at the recently founded Institute of Community Studies. 'We feel,' he continued,

> that our former associates in the Cabinet's Ministries and Parties were in a strange way out of touch with the ordinary people whom they so confidently administered, and we feel that we want to put them right. For this purpose a mere first-hand description of what people's lives are like seems to us justified ... We pin our faith on our powers of observation and our more or less literary skill in describing the results. Then too we are in protest against the contemptuous attitude which the intellectual department of the Establishment seems to have towards the working classes ...

In the event, *Family and Kinship in East London*, co-written by Young and Peter Willmott, had an even greater initial impact than Hoggart's *Uses*. During the last eight days of April, the *Star* (one of London's three evening papers) ran a five-part serialisation ('Londoners under the microscope'); there were major stories on the book in the *Herald*, the *Mirror*, the *News Chronicle* ('Strangers in a Council Paradise') and the *Telegraph* ('East Enders Dislike Spacious New Estates: Family Links Are Missed'). *The Times* had a long leader ('The Ties that Matter') endorsing the housing aspect of the central argument that most Bethnal Greeners preferred to stay in their familiar local community rather than move out to the less friendly new LCC estate in 'Greenleigh' (in fact Debden), while the *Daily Mail* ran a big feature story ('The wife-beater doesn't live here any more') highlighting the claim that Bethnal Green husbands were becoming increasingly domesticated:

It is a refreshing change from the deluge of treatises on problem families, Teddy Boys, juvenile delinquency, broken homes, and child neglect which have created an impression that working-class families are dis-united, unsocial, and unhappy.

Mr Willmott lived in Bethnal Green for two years during the researches with his social-worker wife, Phyllis, and two young children. He enjoyed the rich, down-to-earth, companionable life so much that he left only because he wanted a garden for the children.

The reviews themselves were largely positive, typified by the conclusion of George Bull's in the *Financial Times*: 'This shrewd – and in places extremely amusing – book combines warmth of feeling with careful sociological method. It should make us look at the new towns and estates with a keener eye.'[2]

One avowedly left-wing critic (whose own Fabian pamphlet *Socialism and the Intellectuals* had made a mini-splash at the start of the year) took on both books. 'The main trouble with Mr Hoggart's diagnostics is that they are as thin in illustrations as his reminiscences are rich' was Kingsley Amis's negative reaction to the second half of *Uses*:

He sees his 'mass publications and entertainments' from the outside. He tells us in a note that ballroom dancing is the second-largest entertain-ment industry in the country with its 500-odd ballrooms, but he might never have been in one of them for any sign he gives of understanding the part they play in their patrons' world. His account of modern popular songs is evidently based upon an exiguous, ill-chosen sample and is riddled with precarious intuitions about such imponderables as the kind and degree of self-consciousness displayed. He does not know what tele-vision programmes are like or how people behave while they watch them; he does not know that *Astounding Science Fiction* prints some of the best works in its genre despite its name and cover which are doubtless all he has seen of it; he does not even know that there is more than one kind of comic strip.

Amis's final sentence was a disdainful flick of the wrist from someone who had himself come a long way in barely three years: 'It would be pleasant to say of the book written out of such obvious earnestness and decency of feeling that it represented an achievement, but it is only an attempt.' He was on the whole warmer towards *Family and Kinship*, praising Young and Willmott as 'observant, tactful, sympathetic, humorous – and able to write'. But he did wonder about the key element in their treatment of community in Bethnal Green:

> The central figures of this network are the mums, educators, providers of the family meeting-place, non-technical obstetric consultants, child-care advisers, regular lenders of that vital ten-bob note. I hope I can say without undue disrespect that if I were a working-class girl in Bethnal Green I should probably find somewhere like Holyhead or Wick a handy place to conduct my relationship with Mum after marriage, but then I am not, and on the evidence here presented I cannot doubt that my feelings are shared by few. Or I would not doubt it if I were certain that the authors never confused seeing Mum every day and liking it with seeing Mum every day and being too pious, too timid or too lazy to complain.

'Anyhow,' as he added with a certain weariness, 'a lot of Mums are seen a lot of the time.'

Other readers also had their reservations, with undoubtedly the spikiest intervention coming in May from Leonard Cottrell, a BBC producer who for several months had been researching the New Towns clustered around London (including Stevenage, Bracknell, Crawley and Hemel Hempstead). Declaring himself 'sick of middle-class reviewers and sociologists who persist in sentimentalising the working class', he continued in a riposte in the *Listener* to its recent favourable review (by an academic psychologist) of *Family and Kinship*:

> 'Mum' is a monster . . . In my investigations I have found, time and time again, that working-class wives are happy and relieved to put thirty miles between themselves and 'Mum'; that she is no longer there to interfere

with her aboriginal warmth, her glutinous, devouring affection. Young wives who had been dominated throughout childhood, adolescence, and marriage by these stupid, arrogant, self-pitying matriarchs have suddenly found that they can do without them, to the benefit of their own happiness and that of their husbands.

Strongly suspecting that the same was true in 'Greenleigh', and lamenting that Young and Willmott 'will not face up to the fact', Cottrell went on:

In my experience a small minority of New Town residents long for the pubs, the fish-and-chip shops, the 'chumminess' of the crowded streets; perhaps three or four per cent, not more. The rest are extremely glad to have, for the first time in their lives, a home of their own, with fitted carpets, 'contemporary' furniture, and a washing-machine – all the middle-class trimmings over which middle-class social investigators shake their heads but which working-class people value, when they can get them.

The trouble is that some middle-class people, such as authors and book-reviewers, will persist in romanticising aspects of working-class life of which they themselves have had no direct experience – 'neighbourliness', 'kinship', etc., and the stifling, claustrophobic intimacy of crowded tenements, which have been forced upon working people by sheer economic circumstance.

That autumn, in *Encounter*, Tosco Fyvel called 'surely too romantic' the authors' 'sweeping conclusion' that 'Bethnal Greeners should be rehoused on the spot so that their family ties could be kept intact', arguing from their own evidence that at 'Greenleigh' the 'significant answer was that given to the investigators even by discontented families: that they would not think of returning to Bethnal Green because of the undisputed advantage of the new Estate for their children'. Soon afterwards, a damning-with-faint-praise review in the *TLS* ('their field work was reasonably careful') took particular issue with how 'the authors deplore the fact that workers moved to Essex developed middle-class, particularly lower middle-class, ways':

The fact is that in Bethnal Green these families were isolated from those social patterns increasingly characteristic of Great Britain. It was rather in Essex that they encountered the current face of things for the first time. The authors regret the destruction of working-class traditions, but their own remedies will hardly alter the larger movement of British society.

Perhaps the most suggestive review was in the obscure pages of *Case Conference*, 'A Professional Journal for the Social Worker and Social Administrator'. Justifiably praising the book's many-sidedness, and Young and Willmott's 'ear for language', the young housing expert David Donnison thought aloud about whether 'Greenleigh' itself (depicted by the authors as cold, non-communal, materialistic, etc.) was *really* the prime culprit for the feeling of loss and helplessness among many Bethnal Greeners newly or recently settled there:

> Could the *old* community also be to blame – a community with so sheltered a social life that its warm human relationships are all ready-made for children to grow into without ever consciously 'making' a friend? It may be that the cosy neighbourliness of our traditional, long-settled working-class areas has been achieved at the cost of a dangerous isolation from the outside world: people may feel surrounded with friends and relatives in neighbouring houses and streets, yet look with suspicion on those who live the other side of the main road, or in the next borough; people may achieve a warm sense of comradeship with other working men, and nurse an unreasoning hostility towards foremen, managers, clerks and professional workers.

'Communities such as Bethnal Green have many strengths which our society needs to preserve,' Donnison concluded, 'but in other ways they may be as unfitted to the modern world as the streets that are scheduled for clearance.'[3]

For Young himself – the driving force in what was a fruitful, complementary partnership with Willmott – the appearance of *Family and Kinship* was the justification of his decision some six years earlier to move away from party politics and into sociology and social policy. 'Yours is a study of *living* people, who come and go, all through,

– rather like a novel, and at times like scenes from a play,' his benefactress and co-dedicatee Dorothy Elmhirst wrote to him from Dartington Hall after receiving her copy:

> I feel I know the individuals, – they seem to come right out to greet me. Surely this is a new method, – I mean the interweaving of charts, statistics, factual statements with the spontaneous, individual voices of human beings speaking their thoughts and feelings. The effect is vivid and exciting. And how well you bring out the contrasts between Bethnal Green and Greenleigh! The implications of migration are quite startling, aren't they? – the shift in the whole balance of family roles, the class distinctions that arise, the importance of possessions, and that dreadful competitive struggle to keep up with the neighbours. And yet surely the only answer can't be to improve conditions in Bethnal Green. Will you be challenged, I wonder, in that conclusion?
>
> Michael, – this is an important book – and it achieves something that Chekhov used to talk about – the art of saying serious and profound things in a light vein.

Essentially a shy, reserved man who had known relatively little love in his life, Young replied with a deeply revealing letter:

> It is certainly true that B. Green is somewhat idealised. Some days, walking through the streets, I see it all in a different way, cramped, grey, dirty, with all the beauty pressed out of it into the pitiless flag-stones; and that vision is perhaps as true as the one that I usually have, which is not of the place but of the people, who live with such gusto and humour, are earthy although there is little of it there, and who are admirable (& maybe have much character) just because they have imposed life upon such a terrible city environment. The people of an Indian village even, have more cultural resource in their surroundings. I hardly dare talk about the people, & tried not to make judgements on them in the book, except obliquely, because when I get away from the description, I become sentimental. My unconscious engages gear. The secret of why I am so attached to these working-class people lies buried there, and has remained inviolate even to the analysis.

'It is disconcerting, but somehow exciting (if one could bring it out),' he finished, 'to recognise that the book is not about Bethnal Green but Michael Young.'[4]

Whatever the psychodramas involved, the two books – *Uses* and *Family and Kinship* – bequeathed, taken together, three significant legacies.

The first was the way in which they decisively moved the working class into the centre of the cultural frame, after 12 post-war years of what seems in retrospect almost perverse marginalisation. In 1955, in his coruscating *Encounter* essay on British intellectuals, Young's American friend and colleague Edward Shils had forcefully made the point that the absence of the working class – at least two-thirds of the population – was the glaring, seldom-discussed elephant in the room of British intellectual life, whether in terms of treatment or of the personal backgrounds of the intellectuals themselves. From the late 1950s on, this would no longer be the case, at least as far as subject matter was concerned. There were, however, two problems, both owing at least something to *Uses* and *Family and Kinship*. One was that the working class now at last getting proper attention tended to be the *traditional* working class – just as that very class was starting to fragment, not least through the devastating impact of huge slum clearance programmes. The other problem was the implicit exaltation of working-class over middle-class ways of life and values – an exaltation that in time would influence not only the unnecessarily brutal destruction (irrespective of the underlying rights and wrongs) of the grammar and direct grant schools but also the disastrous emergence by the 1970s in the Labour Party (and on the left generally) of what the commentator David Marquand has helpfully called 'proletarianism'.

The second legacy also had political implications. This was the profound, puritanical mistrust of modern, commercial culture and American-style, TV-watching materialism – that 'Candy-floss World' vehemently denounced by Hoggart, that competitive acquisitiveness in 'Greenleigh' described by Young and Willmott with understanding but without warmth or approbation. By the late 1950s the Labour Party's relationship with affluence was becoming increasingly tortured – theoretical acceptance of its desirability combined with visceral dislike of its manifestations – and these two much-read, undeniably moralistic books (especially *Uses*) played their part in delaying for over three decades a resolution of this troubled relationship.

Finally, especially with *Family and Kinship*, there was the bittersweet (but for many years mainly bitter) 'urbanism' legacy. If the main thrust of 1940s-style planning had been towards dispersal, epitomised by the New Towns programme, by the late 1950s the prevailing mood – at least amongst the 'activator' intelligentsia – was the other way, and undoubtedly Young and Willmott, with their powerful, emotionally charged exposition of the virtues of community in traditional urban settings like Bethnal Green, helped to fuel it. Yet there were two fundamental ironies involved: not only did most Bethnal Greeners of the 1950s and after, especially younger ones, have a much greater desire to leave the area and move upmarket than *Family and Kinship* suggested (as the authors would explicitly concede in their introduction to the 1986 edition); but in the climate of the time, 'urbanism' inevitably meant the wholesale demolition of rundown (if often homely) Victorian terraced 'cottages' and, in their place, the large-scale erection of high-rise blocks of flats – this *despite* Young and Willmott's adamant insistence that such blocks were at best only a partial solution to the housing problem. 'One of the most extraordinary aspects of this sorry affair is that in practice the new flatted estates had little in their favour,' they would ruefully reflect in 1986, in relation to inner-city areas all over the country, not just Bethnal Green, during that fateful, transformative period between the late 1950s and early 1970s.[5] It was a sad legacy for an inspiriting, life-enhancing book.

―――――

Even if they underestimated its attraction, Young and Willmott were absolutely right to pinpoint the importance of 'Greenleigh', emblematic of many other dispersed estates and settlements that had been built since the war and mainly housed manual workers. Indeed, one commentator, Charles Curran, claimed in the *Spectator* in 1956 that, in the context of the full-employment welfare state, these estates had been responsible for creating a new class in the shape of those living there: 'They have been lifted out of poverty and also out of their old surroundings. Now they form the bulk of the inhabitants on the municipal housing estates that encircle London and every other urban centre. They are the New Estate of the realm.' The rest of his piece was mainly derogatory, especially about the culture of this 'New Estate' – 'a place of mass-production comfort, made easy by hire-purchase . . . ideas of furnishings are derived from the cinema and from women's magazines . . . books are rare, bookshelves rarer still' – as also was a radio talk given by June Franklin not long before the publication of *Family and Kinship*, about the experience of living in Crawley New Town with her family. Emphasising that they had given it every chance – 'we have joined local organisations, two of our children attend local schools, and last year my husband was a candidate in the parish council election' – she now admitted defeat: 'The social life is simply that of a village. I tried, but I found it difficult, to work up enthusiasm for an endless round of whist drives, beetle drives and jumble sales. It bored me. I feel my life shrinking. And I don't think it's really a good way to make friends, in spite of the official advice handed out to us to "join something".' Almost certainly middle class, Franklin was looking forward to moving to a place into which she could get her 'roots' – and 'bury the memories of five years in Subtopia'.[6]

Debden itself, aka 'Greenleigh', has not yet been the subject of a systematic historical study, but we do have contemporary surveys of comparable places. When Margot Jefferys in 1954–5 interviewed housewives at South Oxhey, an LCC out-county estate in Hertfordshire, she found three-quarters of those transplanted Londoners 'on the whole' glad to have made the move, with only one in twelve 'entirely sorry'. Perhaps predictably, those who had found the transition difficult, causing loneliness and even mental illness, tended to be older women. In the late summer of 1958 it was explicitly with the Young/Willmott findings in mind that Manchester University's J. B. Cullingworth conducted a detailed survey of 250 families who had moved to an overspill estate at Worsley, eight miles from the centre of Salford. A common pattern emerged: a six-month honeymoon (i.e. the vastly improved living conditions), a year of disenchantment (often relating to lack of external facilities) and then a pragmatic acceptance of the new environment, which did indeed tend to be less 'communal' (fewer pubs and clubs) and more home- and TV-centred. 'Although nearly half said that they had not wished to move to Worsley,' he reported, 'only 17 per cent wanted to return to Salford. The majority of families seemed to have settled down to their suburban way of life whether or not they wished to leave Salford.' The following summer, Cullingworth conducted a survey in Swindon – in other words of overspill from London – and found broadly similar results, with improved housing conditions again being the single most important criterion for most people.

A particularly judicious, well-informed overview of the whole question was provided by Hilary Clark, deputy housing manager at Wolverhampton, who in December 1958 gave a paper to the Royal Society for the Promotion of Health on 'Some Human Aspects of Overspill Housing'. Observing at the outset that building flats in central areas was not *the* answer – 'houses are preferred because they are more suitable for family life – people cannot be conditioned on a large scale to believe that flats are as good' – and that therefore overspill housing was necessary, she confronted the pessimistic 'Greenleigh' version: 'In my experience, a new estate is thought of as remote and unknown at first, but as it grows and brothers and sisters of potential residents move there, it becomes less forbidding to the families who are deciding whether to go.' Overall, she had found, 'a high proportion of local authority overspill tenants seem to settle down well after the first few years'.[7]

By this time four of the biggest concentrations of new or recent settlers from the inner city were Glasgow's peripheral estates: Pollok, Drumchapel, Easterhouse and Castlemilk. During 1957, the year of *Family and Kinship*, the sociologist Maurice Broady conducted a series of interviews with tenants on the huge Pollok estate, mainly members of tenants' associations. Their general, not necessarily representative, view was that things were improving and that such blights as vandalism and sectarianism were on the decrease, though more shops would be appreciated, as well as such facilities as children's playgrounds. Not everyone, though, was happy, among them Mrs Stewart, living in the Craigbank district:

She complained very sorely about the rough people on the buses and about the noise made by the people upstairs. There was invariably a rough family in each block. She was particularly concerned that her little boy, who goes to a private school, should not pick up bad habits by associating with the other children in the scheme. As the local children were coming out of school she took me to a window to show me what was apparently an every-day occurrence: several little boys standing urinating in a circle. Many of the local children also swore badly. If you went to see a mother to complain about the children stealing things, for instance, she would ask the children whether they had done it, and if they said no, would defend her children against you . . .

Mrs Stewart had been an active member of the Craigbank Tenants' Association since its start in 1951, but, as she was compelled to admit about those around her, being a law-abiding tenant was one thing, being an active citizen quite another:

Two complaints particularly were made: that South Pollok should be at the entrance to the scheme, giving the area as a whole a bad reputation, and secondly that the houses were noisy. One young couple whom Mrs Stewart knew, who had been badly troubled by the noise made by a neighbour, had been told by Paton, the local factor, that if they could produce a petition with six signatures complaining about this neighbour he would be prepared to take some action. In the event however, although many complained, only one signed.[8]

3

Never Had It So Good

'The first-floor gallery, known to our regular visitors as "gadget gallery", is maintaining its high standard this year,' reported L.E.W. Stokes-Roberts, organiser of the *Daily Mail* Ideal Home Exhibition. 'But because gadgets and labour-saving notions are so popular we have also originated another section for them, called "That's a Good Idea".' Stokes-Roberts was writing in the *Mail* on 4 March 1957, the day the Queen and Prince Philip were due to visit Olympia for a special preview, and the exhibition was opening the following morning for four weeks, with visits scheduled from Princess Margaret, the Duchess of Kent and other house-proud royals. A highlight this year at the Village of Progress was 'The *Woman's Hour* House', furnished by Jeanne Heal according to the results of a *Radio Times* questionnaire relating to her 'Castle in the Air' broadcasts. 'The front has a pillared porch, wooden shutters, and a balcony reminiscent of an American colonial-style house,' noted the *Mail* about this expression of listeners' taste. 'But inside, the rooms are modern with doors which fold back to make an open-plan living area and an eating bar which seats seven between the dining-room and the kitchen.' The exhibition itself – some 600 stands across 14 acres as well as a range of display houses, flats and shops – was its usual roaring success, but Anthony Carson in the *New Statesman* could only sound a regretful note, comparing the whole thing to 'a sort of florid uncle with endearingly excruciating taste'. As for the thousands flocking there, 'Where do the Ideal people come from? They come from the smaller columns of the evening newspapers, from television competitions, from public libraries beyond Hither Green. They are the untroubled, the stolid backbone, the beloved floating voters.'

Forty-one per cent may in a recent Gallup poll have expressed the
wish to emigrate if they could (the highest figure since 1948), the Bank
of England's new £5 note may have been (in *Punch*'s words) 'rather
like a Victorian sampler as seen in a nightmare by the Council of
Industrial Design', but the Ideal Home Exhibition was the annual
sign that spring was in the air, even in Glasgow. There, a huge municipal campaign began on 11 March, involving over the next five weeks
the X-raying of 87 per cent of the city's population in order to identify carriers of TB. 'Wonderful new treatments have greatly improved
the outlook for patients with tuberculosis,' declared the Medical
Officer of Health in an advance letter to all households, adding reassuringly that 'there will be no undressing, and all results will be
entirely confidential'. Poverty as well as disease existed in all sorts of
pre-gentrified places. Later in March, the then unpublished writer
John Fowles went with his wife-to-be Elizabeth to Kentish Town and
Camden Town 'to scout round for old furniture' for their flat in
Hampstead. 'Peeling, pitted, endlessly dirty houses; children playing
in the streets,' he recorded. 'The people all poor, or flashy; junk-shops,
cheap grocers. E remarked that when she asked for half a pound of
cheese they cut it and cut it again till it weighed exactly what she
wanted; not as here, where nobody minds paying for a two-ounce
miscalculation.'[1]

A month later, the Wednesday after Easter, the 22-year-old Brian
Epstein – a student at RADA and living alone – was not so far away, in
Finchley Road, when he found himself being arrested for 'persistent
importuning' earlier in the evening in the public lavatory at Swiss
Cottage tube station. 'The damage, the lying criminal methods of the
police in importuning *me* and consequently capturing me, leaves me
cold, stunned and finished,' he wrote immediately afterwards. Next
morning, however, on the advice of a detective, he pleaded guilty at
Marylebone Magistrates' Court and was fined rather than being
imprisoned.

For Manchester United's 'Busby Babes' it was the cruellest of
springs: that same Thursday they went out of the European Cup, after
a pulsating 2–2 draw against Real Madrid in front of a raucous, bellow-
ing Old Trafford crowd, prompting the *Manchester Guardian*'s 'An
Old International' (Don Davies) to reflect that 'Bedlam after this will

hold no terrors.' Nine days later, on 4 May, the unfairest, most unre-constructed of Cup Finals saw United lose their goalkeeper Ray Wood to a cynical assault by Aston Villa's Peter McParland ('one of those things that can happen in football', the TV commentator Kenneth Wolstenholme reassured the nation), play most of the match with effectively ten men and eventually go down 2–1, with a brace for McParland. For one spectator, Harold Macmillan, 'the Cup-Tie Final' was the end of 'a particularly tiresome week', but 11 days later he welcomed petrol coming off the ration after five post-Suez months. Hull University's librarian could muster at best only two springtime cheers. 'This institution totters along, a cloister of mediocrities isolated by the bleak reaches of the East Riding, doomed to remain a small cottage-university of arts-and-science while the rest of the world zooms into the Age of Technology,' Philip Larkin wrote to a friend near the end of May. 'The corn waves, the sun shines on faded dusty streets, the level-crossings clank, bills are made out for 1957 under bill-heads designed in 1926.'[2]

'1926' indeed, for it was a spring of industrial troubles. 'When it's a question of capital and labour there's no such thing as impartiality' was the reaction of the 'bell-ringer' Johnny McLoughlin to the news in late February that the Minister of Labour, Iain Macleod, was appointing a court of inquiry under Lord Cameron to investigate the dispute at the Ford-owned Briggs plant in Dagenham. McLoughlin was talking to *The Economist*'s 'special correspondent', who also listened to some of the men as they had a smoke outside the factory gates. 'I reckon an inquiry's what we want,' said one. 'What this plant needs is a dose of salts, and not just for the management either.' Some six weeks later, Cameron came down almost wholly on the side of management: it had been justified in not reinstating McLoughlin, who was characterised as 'glib, quick-witted and evasive', with 'a considerable capacity' for 'agitation and propaganda'. More generally, the shop stewards at Briggs were described as a Communist-influenced 'private union within a union enjoying immediate and continuous contact with the men in the shop, answerable to no superiors and in no way officially or constitu-tionally linked with the union hierarchy'. Even so, if those were the headline findings – summed up by *The Times*'s ensuing castigation of the Briggs shop stewards as 'a cancer on the body of trade unionism'

– Cameron did also note 'a certain insensitivity in the mental attitude of the Company towards those whom they employ' and 'a desire to impose, rather than agree by negotiation'. The episode as a whole left at least one lasting legacy: McLoughlin was reputedly the ultimate inspiration for Fred Kite, the character so memorably played two years later by Peter Sellers in *I'm All Right, Jack*.[3]

That satirical film would accurately reflect the increasing national focus on the unions and labour relations, with the spring of 1957 seeing a palpable ratcheting-up. 'The *shipbuilding strike started*,' recorded Marian Raynham in Surbiton on 16 March. 'And there are 900 million pounds of orders at stake. I think it is wicked.' Anthony Heap agreed, and on the 20th, with the shipbuilders out and a national engineering strike imminent, he reflected that 'Union bosses have got too big for their boots. Meanwhile the more intelligent and industrious Germans and Japanese will continue to capture our world markets by competing with manufactured goods at much keener prices – and good luck to them!' At about the same time, Malcolm Muggeridge discussed the 'strike situation' with the radical journalist Claud Cockburn: 'Thinks, as I do, that we may now really be for it – strikes becoming general strike, possibly civil war. On the other hand, perhaps not. Anyway, sooner or later, crack-up inevitable.'

To gauge the mood among the strikers themselves, the journalist John Gale went to the Cammell Laird shipyard at Birkenhead, where 'a slim man with floppy brown hair, faint sidewhiskers and big eyes' told him: 'Myself, I'm dead against the strike. Honestly, 75 per cent don't want it, but they are behind the unions . . . A lie-in for two days is all right but I'll be definitely relieved when the strike is over. I don't like painting the house. I haven't got to wheeling the pram yet. My wife isn't very pleased. All the women blame the top union men.'

As for government, Macmillan talked a tough game to himself, expressing determination not to repeat the 'industrial appeasement' of 'the Churchill–Monckton regime'. But in practice, as events unfolded, he let Macleod have his head, and that highly capable minister was unwilling to fight a battle he was far from sure he could win, not least with sterling fragile and public opinion overall marginally more sympathetic to the strikers than the employers. 'The only possibility is some form of arbitration' had been his view from the outset, and over these weeks he applied considerable pressure on the employers, to ensure that by early April (with over six million working days already lost) it was possible to appoint a court of inquiry, to be chaired by Professor Daniel Jack. 'The news that the grave shipbuilding and engineering strikes had been called off caused an enormous wave of public relief here,' the writer Mollie Panter-Downes told her *New Yorker* readers on the 4th, adding however that 'most people seem to feel cautiously that the situation is not as yet anything better than a truce in the bitter industrial battle – a battle of which the country as a whole is heartily weary and critical'. Four weeks later, Jack gave the unions more or less what they wanted, leaving the employers (above all the Engineering Employers' Federation) bitterly frustrated and the government looking rather impotent. But as Macleod had already explained to Macmillan while awaiting the Jack findings, 'there is no short cut to the problem of making men get on better with each other and there is little we can do, either by government exhortation or by legislation'.[4]

Another vexed area, ripe for re-evaluation, was defence. On 4 April the *Evening Standard* covered the continuing trial at the Old Bailey of Dr John Bodkin Adams, the Eastbourne doctor accused (but eventually acquitted) of hastening rich old ladies on their way, and slipped in an item about the retirement of a stockbroker called Herbert Ballard, known for many years on the Stock Exchange as 'the Mayor of Tooting' even though he had never lived in Tooting and never been a mayor. The main story, though, made a particularly direct appeal to the nation's youth: 'Call-Up Planned To End By 1961'. The phasing out of National Service was part of *Defence: Outline of Future Policy*, a White Paper presented by Duncan Sandys, son-in-law of Winston Churchill and nicely evoked by Ferdinand Mount as 'that formidable slab of old red sandstone'. Other key elements included a general reduction in overseas forces, in the explicit context of Britain's reduced economic means, and a pivotal role for the nuclear deterrent, with the *Standard* quoting Sandys: 'Development of the hydrogen bomb and of rocket weapons with nuclear warheads has fundamentally altered the whole basis of military planning.' The White Paper was a cardinal document, and the historian Jim Tomlinson has helpfully elucidated the driving political-cum-economic motives: not only would a nuclear strategy 'free trained manpower for the civilian sector' but it would 'reduce the claims of conventional weapons development and production on economic resources which could better be used to raise the standard of living'. In short, 'nukes would replace guns to allow more resources for butter'.

For the British aircraft industry this was a major hit, leading to the cancellation of many projects and much downsizing, while more broadly the White Paper fitted into a post-Suez narrative of national decline. 'England is now too olde to have reason to be merrie' was the motion put before the Cambridge Union a month later, though the undergraduates voted defiantly against, 96 to 68. Not long afterwards, Churchill's physician, Lord Moran, asked Sir Oliver Franks, distinguished civil servant and now chairman of Lloyds Bank, whether he was gloomy about the future. 'I think the period 1945 to 1975 may be like 1815 to 1845,' Franks replied.

> We have a good many old men at the top living in the past. Macmillan tells how he was in Darlington in 1931 at the time of mass unemployment, and he was horrified by what he saw. There is a Labour leader [presumably Frank Cousins of the Transport and General Workers' Union], too, who says bitter things to the TUC because for ten years his father was out of employment, and tramped up and down the Great North Road, looking for a job. They think more about this than of the last war. Nothing much will happen until a new generation takes over; we need younger men who are not obsessed with the past, men who are thinking over where they want to go.[5]

Six days after the Sandys White Paper saw a notable opening night. It was a sell-out, so when (recalled Colin Clark, Alan's younger brother and PA to the star) Princess Margaret arrived late demanding the best seats in the house, 'some unfortunate couple had to be kicked out'. During the interval, 'a large red-headed actress' sat naked on the stage 'draped in a Union Jack, with a trident and a helmet, in the pose of Britannia on a penny coin' – of course 'not allowed to move a muscle, otherwise the theatre would be shut down' (i.e. by the Lord Chamberlain). Inevitably, Anthony Heap was there:

Those of us who went to the Royal Court tonight to scoff at John Osborne's successor to the excruciatingly boring and ridiculously over-rated 'Look Back in Anger' had, perforce, to rapidly revise our opinion of this controversial young actor-playwright and stay to bray as 'The Entertainer', with no less distinguished a play jockey than Sir Laurence Olivier up, romped home an easy winner ... It has wit, irony, humour and pathos in plenty and, despite Tony Richardson's much too slow production, the acting to match. Olivier's vital virtuoso performance as the flashy, facetious, irrepressible and irresponsible music hall comic dazzles and delights at every turn.

'I shall, in sooth,' he concluded, 'be very surprised if "The Entertainer" doesn't prove to be the play of the year, and Olivier's the performance.'

The audience agreed, but most of the critics were less wholeheart-edly enthusiastic, with few bringing out the state-of-the-nation character of the play, above all the clapped-out music-hall comedian Archie Rice as symbol of the declining power that Suez had so starkly revealed. The partial exceptions were Kenneth Tynan and John Wain: the former, in the *Observer*, acclaimed Osborne's ambi-tion ('the big and brilliant notion of putting the whole of contempo-rary England on to one and the same stage'); the latter, in a review on the Third Programme, emphasised the play's theme of surrender to 'the transatlantic invasion', quoted Archie's vaudevillian father looking back on the great Edwardian days ('We were English – and we spoke English'), and noted that 'crudely daubed' on the 'hideous backcloth showing three blousy nudes', against which Archie performed, was 'not, as it used to be, the Eiffel Tower and the Seine but New York harbour'. Of course, *The Entertainer* was also nota-ble because of Olivier, the greatest living English actor, now so publicly embracing the theatrical new wave – an astonishing moment. Yet for Olivier himself it was *au fond* a marriage of convenience. Within two days of the opening he was demanding cuts to 'all that anti-Queen shit', and after Richardson demurred he successfully insisted, as part of his contract for the West End transfer, that the most offensive line ('the gloved hand waving at you from the golden coach') be taken out, along with some others. 'They didn't make that much difference to the play,' Richardson would reflect, 'but Larry felt he'd bravely defended the Queen.'[6]

The legacy of the previous autumn was Hungary as well as Suez, and at least one biographer has speculated that it was the Soviet invasion that helped give Kingsley Amis a significant rightwards push. 'I think the best and most trustworthy political motive is self-interest,' he had asserted soon afterwards in his Fabian pamphlet *Socialism and the Intellectuals*. 'I share a widespread suspicion of the professional espouser of causes, the do-gooder, the archetypal social worker who knows better than I do what is good for me.' Indeed, he claimed, one 'edge' that the Tories had over the socialists was that 'they at least are not out to do anybody any good except themselves'.

Amis would never be part of the post-Hungary New Left, starting to take firm shape by spring 1957. 'Those who feel that the values of a capitalist society are bankrupt, that the social inequalities upon which the system battens are an affront to the potentialities of the individual, have before them a problem, more intricate and more difficult than any which has previously been posed,' declared the editors in the first number of *Universities and Left Review*. 'That is the problem of how to change contemporary society so as to make it more democratic and more egalitarian, and yet how to prevent it degenerating into totalitarianism.' Their solution was 'the regeneration of the whole tradition of free, open, critical debate' – partly through the magazine itself, partly also through the Universities and Left Review Club, due to hold fortnightly discussion meetings in the 'comfortable and informal surroundings' of the Royal Hotel, Woburn Place. All four editors were in their twenties, three of them (including Stuart Hall, a West Indian Rhodes Scholar) were Oxford-based, and the fourth, Ralph (later Raphael) Samuel, was researching London dockers' history at the London School of Economics. A strong line-up in this spring issue included G.D.H. Cole, Eric Hobsbawm (still a member of the Communist Party), E. P. Thompson ('parts of Mr Amis's recent pamphlet bristle with inhibitions against the affirmation of positive, humanist values'), film critic and director Lindsay Anderson ('Commitment in cinema criticism') and David Marquand (then an Oxford undergraduate).

The *ULR*'s second issue (Summer 1957) featured a symposium (including a rather cagey Raymond Williams) on Hoggart's *Uses*, while by then the first issue of the *New Reasoner* had appeared, co-edited by Thompson and his fellow historian John Saville. 'We have no desire to break impetuously with the Marxist and Communist tradition in Britain,' they insisted – a rather different stance to the broader-based pluralism of the *ULR*. The longest piece, by Thompson himself, was characteristically called 'Socialist Humanism: An Epistle to the Philistines'. This was mainly an attack on Stalinism, accused of 'anti-intellectualism, moral nihilism, and the denial of the creative agency of human labour'. But in the last few pages Thompson turned specifically to the British situation, arguing that the working class had, following its considerable '1945' achievement with the establishment of the modern welfare state, 'got no further because, being pragmatic and hostile to theory, it does not know and feel its own strength, it has no sense of direction or revolutionary perspective, it tends to fall into moral lethargy, it accepts leaders with capitalist ideas'. And he had a pop at the Labour politician Anthony Crosland, quoting the 'more open-air cafés, brighter and gayer streets at night' passage from Crosland's recent *The Future of Socialism* and declaring it an inadequate vision:

> Men do not only want the list of *things* which Mr Crosland offers; they want also to change themselves as men. However fitfully and ineffectively, they want other and greater things: they want to stop killing one another; they want to stop this pollution of their spiritual life which runs through society as the rivers carried their sewage and refuse through our nineteenth-century industrial towns.[7]

The British Communist Party itself lost some 7,000 of its 33,000 members as a result of Hungary, but the Scottish poet Hugh MacDiarmid decided that this was the moment to rejoin. Even if all the accusations made by 'the enemies of Communism' were accurate, he declared in the *Daily Worker* in late March, 'the killings, starvings, frame-ups, unjust judgements and all the rest of it are a mere bagatelle to the utterly mercenary and unjustified wars, the ruthless exploitation, the preventable deaths due to slums, and other damnable consequences of the profit motive, which must be laid to the account of the so-called "free nations of the West".' A Party Congress held at Hammersmith Town

Hall over the Easter weekend overwhelmingly endorsed Soviet Russia's action and its own executive's unambiguous support. Among those speaking was a 19-year-old Yorkshire delegate, the miner Arthur Scargill, who told a spirited story of youthful industrial militancy in his own pit and accused the party of 'criminal neglect' of the Young Communist League, given that 'the young people of Britain alone can determine the future of socialism in this country'. A particularly key vote was the heavy defeat for a minority report on party democracy that sought to open up debate. 'There is an authoritarian tendency in the party, a tendency to distrust the rank and file and keep down discussion' insisted one of the report's authors, the historian Christopher Hill. 'We have been living in a world of illusions. That is why the 20th Congress and the Hungarian events came as a shock to so many party members. We have been living in a snug little world of our own invention.' Hill resigned from the party immediately afterwards, while a co-author, Malcolm MacEwen, was soon expelled. His offence was refusing to resign from the editorial board of the *New Reasoner*, high on the party's index of prohibited publications. 'The chairman of the panel that heard my case at a perfunctory but perfectly friendly hearing was Johnny Mahon,' recalled MacEwen about one of the party's leading apparatchiks and the driving force behind the closing-down-debate majority report. 'Had we been in a "people's democracy" I think he would have shaken my hand before firmly despatching me to the gallows.'[8]

It was about this time that L. Ely of Barnes had a Hoggartian letter in the *Daily Worker* castigating jazz, rock and skiffle as 'nearly the No. 1 bore in Great Britain', claiming that 'for everyone who finds relaxation and pleasure there are the many whose fostered interest is of a blasé, moronic character', and calling on the paper to 'make a stand against commercialism, against candy-floss and juke-box deterioration of our working-class culture'. In fact, at least two aspects of popular culture were now coming under serious threat, one in the long term, the other more immediately. The first was smoking, as a result of the Medical Research Council publishing in June a report that found a causal relationship between it and cancer, thereby cementing Richard Doll's groundbreaking study seven years earlier. Attitudes did not change overnight: the government kept a careful distance from the report, denying that it had a specific duty to warn the public; Chapman Pincher in the *Daily Express* inveighed against 'interfering' medics; and the *Manchester Guardian* cautioned that any anti-smoking legislation would 'run counter to British susceptibilities', adding that since there was 'no evidence that smokers harm anybody but themselves . . . an act forbidding smoking in public places would have no more moral validity than one prohibiting it altogether'.

The aspect of popular culture far more imminently endangered in 1957 was the cinema. 'The standard of films today is not big enough to merit more than one run,' lamented a cinema manager, Leonard Caton, in March. 'We have no answer to television.' Caton's cinema was the Olympia in Irlams o' th' Height, Salford, and it had just closed its doors, with the building sold to a local radio and TV dealer. 'I intend to open it as a showroom where people can come in to see sets working,' announced the new owner. 'The atmosphere is ideal for people to sit down and watch TV.' Elsewhere, cinemas under threat were resorting to all sorts of gimmicks and promotions to try to retain their once loyal audiences. 'During the three weeks that *The Curse of Frankenstein* played,' remembered the New Zealand writer Janet Frame about her 'tiring and depressing' month later this spring working as an usherette at the Regal in Streatham, 'vampires, stakes, silver bullets, a model of Frankenstein, all in a mixture of horror folklore, were displayed in the foyer' – as 'all the while the manager, a short middle-aged man with an upward gaze and sandy hair, looked increasingly anxious.' Still, the cinema kept its traditional uses: one Friday afternoon in May the weather in London was 'so horrid' that the middle-aged, highly respectable Madge Martin and her Oxford clergyman husband went to 'the small Cameo Royal' to see 'a naughty French film', namely *And God Created Woman* with 'the kitten-like Brigitte Bardot'.[9]

On the small screen, 14 March saw the launch of the most celebrated advertising magazine (or admag), *Jim's Inn*, with Jimmy Hanley as the genial landlord in the village of 'Wembleham' and everyday brands popping up in surprising places. Next day, the historian Hugh Trevor-Roper (shortly to pip the less establishment A.J.P. Taylor for the Regius Professorship at Oxford) appeared live on *Tonight* talking about the Ides of March. 'When that dreadful couple sang their lower-class music-hall turn and ended in each others' arms before the camera, I felt like walking out,' he complained afterwards. 'Nothing I could seriously say on the subject of Julius Caesar, or indeed on any subject, could be worth saying to the same audience as theirs . . . I felt that the whole programme was simply a succession of knock-about turns in which I would rather not take part . . . I cannot appear again.' Just over a fortnight later – on the same day that the *News Chronicle* reported that homework standards had not been adversely affected by the end of the Toddlers' Truce, with a grammar school head 'glad to say parents here belong to the better classes and know how to control television' – came a memorable *Panorama*. 'It isn't only in Britain that spring this year has taken everyone by surprise,' was how Richard Dimbleby began the last item, going on to deliver a deadpan commentary about the spaghetti harvest in Switzerland, with accompanying footage apparently showing spaghetti cultivation in progress. 'And that,' he concluded, 'is all from *Panorama* on this first day of April.' The BBC telephone exchange in Lime Grove was inundated with calls – 'mainly', recalled Leonard Miall, 'to settle family arguments: the husband knew it must be true that spaghetti grew on a bush because Richard Dimbleby had said so and the wife knew it was made with flour and water, but neither could convince the other'.[10]

BBC executives needed something to smile about. '*Hey, Jeannie!* [a benign sitcom] is surely a much better, more attractive and more intelligent programme than *The Buccaneers* [a pirate series starring Robert Shaw],' Cecil McGivern wrote in March to Robert Silvey, head of audience research, about the respective BBC and ITV programmes that had been up against each other on the early evening of Saturday, 9 February. 'Yet its audience was only 9 [i.e. 9 per cent of a panel of almost 500 with access to both channels] as against *The Buccaneers* 29 . . . This really is discouraging!' To which Silvey replied: 'I am tempted to say that if you altered the word "yet" in your comment to "hence" it might have been nearer the truth. Seriously, what warrant have we for assuming that "the best" of a given kind of material will assuredly draw the majority?' He went on: 'Surely ITV's Saturday programme represents a single-minded pursuit of the admass; whereas our schedule looks more like a BBC-type attempt to entertain a wide spectrum.' Other BBC programmes that evening had included *Dixon of Dock Green*, *Billy Smart's Circus*, *The Dave King Show*, *Twenty Questions* and a play called *Aunt Mary*, while among ITV's attractions were *Wyatt Earp*, *The 64,000 Question* (an American-style game show) and *Val Parnell's Saturday Spectacular*. As Silvey conceded about Saturday evenings, 'the ITV has the reputation now, so for many it's a case of switching on to ITV unless there is an overwhelming reason not to'.

Altogether, some 45 per cent of all households had a TV set by the end of May; just over half of those sets transmitted commercial television, so far available only in London, Birmingham and the North. In homes where both channels could be viewed, the audience share was roughly 35 per cent for the BBC and 65 per cent for ITV, with the latter doing even better among young people and the more prosperous part of the working class. Soon afterwards, on 19 June, ITV unveiled a big new comedy hit with Granada's *The Army Game* about duty-dodging conscripts. Barely a week later, the Corporation's troubled fortunes were epitomised by the sudden end after three years of its pioneering soap *The Grove Family*. 'This programme is going down and down,' the *Spectator* had recently grumbled. 'All the naturalism it once had has disappeared. Even Grandma seldom gets a good line.' Understandably, the father-and-son writing team of Roland and Michael Pertwee had asked for a break, and by the time they were ready to return, the jobbing builder Bob Grove and his north London family were a television memory.[11]

On unfashionable radio, a durable innovation was ball-by-ball commentary on the Test matches, starting at Edgbaston on 30 May. Commentators included John Arlott and Rex Alston, with magisterial summaries by E. W. Swanton. The contrast was stark with television (commentators Brian Johnston and Peter West), which that day covered less than an hour and a half's play, with intruders including *Mainly for Women*, *Watch with Mother* ('Rag, Tag and Bobtail') and *Champion the Wonder Horse*. The Test itself featured on the final two days an epic partnership of 411 between Peter May and Colin Cowdrey, leaving West Indies to scramble a draw at the death. 'Yes, wasn't the Test splendid,' Larkin wrote afterwards to Monica Jones. 'I heard of it only through periodic bulletins from the switchboard operator, but about 5 I could stand no more & cleared off home to listen to the last 1½ hours ball by ball. I revelled in the very *facts* of the score – the 500 plus for 4 wickets: it took me back to 1938 & 1934.' For all that resonance, the eight-hour partnership by the two amateur batsmen involved a huge amount of cynical pad play, tacitly supported by the home umpires, to counter the magical West Indian spinner Sonny Ramadhin. 'I could have wept for him,' remembered his fellow spinner Johnny Wardle, England's twelfth man. 'If he appealed 50 times, at least 30 were plumb out lbw even from the pavilion. It was a great partnership in its way, but an utter scandal really.'

Pad play was part of what was increasingly felt to be cricket's over-defensive, slow-scoring malaise. Three weeks later, the writer C.L.R. James – West Indian and Marxist – launched an assault on 'the long forward-defensive push, the negative bowling' as 'the techniques of specialized performers (professional or amateur) in a security-minded age', and called those cricketers 'functionaries in the Welfare State'. His piece in the *Cricketer* coincided with the second Test at Lord's, where among MCC members watching in the pavilion was a retired Eton teacher, George Lyttelton. 'Weekes was good; so was Cowdrey,' he reported to his old pupil and regular correspondent Rupert Hart-Davis. 'I passed him and Bailey as they went in on Friday morning. I murmured "Good luck". Cowdrey said "Thank you, sir"; Bailey said nothing. In five balls Bailey was out and in five hours Cowdrey had made 152.'[12]

The Edgbaston match was still in progress when soon after 9 a.m. on Saturday, 1 June at Lytham St Anne's, one Ernie (Ernest Marples, the energetic Postmaster General) set in motion a rather larger ERNIE (Electronic Random Number Indicator Equipment, a machine the size of a small van) to make the first Premium Bonds draw. Since November, the public had bought 49 million bonds; some 23,000 prizes were available, and there were 96 winners of the £1,000 top prize. Later that day, Harold Macmillan, godfather of Premium Bonds, was in his old constituency, Stockton-on-Tees. 'It was strange to drive down the old High St, now so modern & smart & prosperous, then so drab (but more beautiful),' he noted, adding that 'the old Georgian houses have had their fronts "Woolworthed"'. 1 June was also the date of the final issue – after 19 years – of *Picture Post*. 'What will the one-eyed monster devour next?' wondered Anthony Heap, and indeed television was doubtless the major cause of the magazine's demise, though as one of its journalists, Katherine Whitehorn, has pointed out, *Picture Post* by the end had 'completely lost its sense of who it was aiming at', with no coherent character running through its pages, quite unlike the great days. Still, its death was a blessing for *Tonight*, with Fyfe Robertson, Trevor Philpott and Kenneth Allsop all moving in due course on to Donald Baverstock's talented, diverse team.

Three days later, on Tuesday the 4th, the leaving students at the Central School of Speech and Drama, including Judi Dench and Vanessa Redgrave, gave the customary job-touting public matinee at Wyndham's. Among those watching was the wife of the manager of the Frinton Summer Theatre; later that day she wrote to Redgrave offering a summer engagement at Britain's most staid resort. There was also a surprise in the post for Kenneth Barrett, who ran the John Hilton Bureau, in effect a citizen's advice bureau subsidised by the *News of the World*. On Friday he received a typed letter, addressed to the bureau, that had been found – almost torn in two – in a gutter in Soho. The writer was a 17-year-old who had left school two years earlier and since worked 'as Comis waiter' in a London hotel (its name missing, as was the writer's name and address):

Every day when I was on time off I used to go over to Hyde Park for a walk etc because I did not want to stay indoors and as it was summer the Park was the best attraction. But constantly I was followed by men who kept on either sitting near me or trying to make up conversation. I did not realise what they wanted till one day one of these men asked me to go to his flat. I was so scared I got up and ran. This also happened at the tables I used to serve at. The men used to say such things as 'Come out with me when you have time off'. So I told my friend who I thought appeared to be my friend. But instead of helping me he said that I should go about with these men. These incidents were not only happening in the Park but in the Hotel. Staff rooms etc. So I left that job. I am scared at going to the pictures by myself because nine times out of ten a man always comes up next to me and I suppose you would call it assault me. I go about with a group of friends . . . one of these invited me to his house for a records evening. Well when I got there we played a few records and his mother and father went out to the pictures leaving us in the house. He then asked me to have a friendly wrestle and then after about five minutes fighting I realised that he was constantly pressing himself so close to me that I just could not help myself. You may say to yourself 'Well why didn't I try to stop him'. Well you see I like to think of sex doings but I would never let any man go that far. You see that is why I have always let these men and boys do this to me. In other words to put it point blank to you I would never go with a man or boy for money or otherwise. But only do the fairly harmless things. Please do not let my parents know or I would leave home for good. I have just had to let some one know. Please just advise me what to do.[13]

'Modernity' may have meant different things to different people, and the pace of change varied considerably from place to place, but by 1957 it was unmistakeably becoming the dominant (albeit top-down) zeitgeist – a spirit of the age epitomised by the desire in relation to the built environment to dump the past, get up to date and embrace a gleaming, functional, progressive future. This spring, in at least three major provincial cities, the modernity drive was under way.

In Birmingham, work began on the city's Inner Ring Road, for which the earliest plans dated back to 1917 but as it would now take shape very much the creation of the City Engineer, Sir Herbert Manzoni. Meanwhile in Sheffield, preliminary work also started on the streets-in-the-sky Park Hill development, destined to become emblematic, and in Bradford, reported the *Yorkshire Post*'s John Bland, 'bulldozers are creating miniature mountains of rubble, demolition squads are battering down rows of abandoned offices, and yawning potholes, worthy of Ingleborough, gape in the roadway'. The 'man of vision' behind Bradford's Development Plan was the City Engineer and Surveyor Stanley Wardley. Bland interviewed him in his office, where a scale model showed 'a modern centre spaciously laid out around the civic precincts', a centre in which 'few present-day buildings are recognisable except for the Town Hall, the Wool Exchange, Britannia House and a cinema or two'. Wardley was in confident mood – 'This is not just a plan that may happen. It is on its way' – while Bland, after noting that new blocks of flats had been built or were being built to replace slums, concluded: 'Bradford will certainly be one of the first cities in Britain to be not only worthy of the 20th century but also proud to look the 21st in the face.'

Elsewhere, the rhetoric was similarly being cranked up. In London's East End, the tenth anniversary of the inauguration of the Stepney–Poplar comprehensive development area not only came soon after the LCC's decision to press ahead with two new housing schemes (Clive Street and Mountmorres Road) involving four 17-storey blocks of flats but was the cue for 'an exhibition, a lantern lecture, and a bus tour' that, explained the *Architects' Journal*, 'made it possible in a morning to glimpse the "grand design" which is being put together piece by piece "to make the East End a very beautiful place," as the LCC Planning Committee's chairman put it'. In Liverpool, a strongly pro-modernity local journalist, George Eglin, had a three-part feature in the *Liverpool Daily Post* about the wonders of Rotterdam, an almost entirely rebuilt city that had 'banished the higgledy-piggledy development ideas of the old city, the conglomeration of dwellings, shops, offices and workshops that had grown up together', and was instead now becoming 'a city with room to breathe, where people can live, work and play in pleasant and efficient surroundings' – in stark contrast to Liverpool's 'archaic, stultified approach to post-war civic problems'. A youngish, idealistic architect-cum-planner, Graeme Shankland, was a fair representative of progressive opinion. 'One cannot avoid the impression that at present we are frightened of the new scale of the city,' he declared in the spring issue of *Universities and Left Review*. 'This fear, masquerading as "the avoidance of monotony", is false. The real danger is muddle – than which nothing is more monotonous.' And he insisted that because 'social demands' were now greater – whether of business or housing or education or traffic – so must 'the scale of the mid-twentieth-century city therefore be larger'. In short, it was time, more than time, to replace 'the present small-scale patchwork city pattern'.[14]

Did all this inevitably mean a substantial and increasing proportion of future new housing being in the form of flats and high-rises? Quite a strong pro-flats consensus had already emerged by the mid-1950s, but in 1957 itself – during which year there were almost 73,000 local authority approvals for new houses, compared with almost 32,000 for flats and just over 10,000 for high-rises – the debate was still surprisingly

lively, with the way led that spring by the resolutely individualist architectural journalist Ian Nairn. 'People are being driven from the centre
not by congestion but by the wrong sort of redevelopment,' he declared.
'Elizabeth Denby [a well-known, much-respected housing consultant]
has plenty of unpublished evidence to show that what working-class
families really wanted was the type of building they had before – a
house and garden, cosily planned and near their work . . . If you rehouse
entirely with flats, then naturally the big families will want to leave.'
Denby herself confirmed soon afterwards that 'the form of high-flat
redevelopment is unacceptable to many English families', calling it an
approach 'in which architects delight' even though 'I have still to find
one who lives in such a block himself!' Significantly, she added that her
analysis of 'four London squares' had shown that '*family houses* with a
reasonably large common garden and good private gardens can be
grouped at the same density as *family flats*, costing less and giving
greater human satisfaction'.

Later in March there was a sharp squall in Birmingham: David
Eversley, a university lecturer, flatly stated in the local *Mail* that 'people
like their own front door and a garden', that in fact 'the whole social
tradition in the Midlands is against flats and tenements', and cited 'the
barracks on the cliffs at Rubery' as a prime example of 'cramped and
noisy and ill-ventilated' flats. To this Dennis Thomas, chairman of the
City Council's Planning sub-committee, replied that most flats were
much better than those at Rubery, adding: 'In a city of houses and
gardens, it is understandable that people cling to the old idea of things.
However, if we build flats with properly developed open spaces around,
we shall overcome this prejudice.' And in May, in the letters page of
The Times, Michael Young and Peter Willmott, fresh from the success
of *Family and Kinship*, noted that 'the overwhelming majority' of their
East End interviewees wanted 'a house rather than a flat', preferably in
a familiar location, and called on architects to 'apply their ingenuity to
designing decent terraced houses with small gardens at high densities'.

The sociologists, however, were divided. A riposte came from John
Westergaard, who on the basis of research at the recently built Lansbury
estate in Poplar argued that 'the antipathy towards flats, although
strong, is not immutable', and that indeed, more generally, 'the success
of the new tall blocks suggests that the traditional attitude is not

permanent'. As Patrick Dunleavy has observed, it would take the sociological profession as a whole until the 1960s to tackle 'the social dimensions of high-flat living' and, as a result, 'slowly come round to a better-founded and generally more critical appraisal of the implications of the high-rise boom'.[15]

Even so, the sense of it not being an open-and-shut question – or at least involving potentially awkward sensibilities – continued in the early summer. Analysing why Manchester had not tried to solve 'the overspill problem' by 'building so high that as many families are rehoused on the site [i.e. of slum clearance] as living on it before demolition', the *Manchester Guardian*'s local government correspondent noted (as if it was a given): 'There are, of course, social objections to compelling families with young children to live in high flats, and economic objections to a form of housing that costs over twice as much, in labour and materials, both to build and to maintain, as the two-storey dwelling which the vast majority of tenants prefer.' Later in June, Birmingham's City Architect A. G. Sheppard Fidler explained to the Housing Centre in London that it was his council's current policy to provide 30 per cent of new housing in tall blocks, with most of the rest in four-storey maisonettes. He showed slides demonstrating how, since his arrival in the city five years earlier, great care had been taken in deciding what buildings should be placed close to tall blocks in order 'to bring the scale down to the ground and humanise the whole scheme', as well as generally 'producing the feeling of enclosure so familiar and popular in Birmingham'. The Housing Minister was the solid, well-intentioned, cricket-loving Henry Brooke, who soon afterwards, at a slum clearance conference, felt compelled to defend the high-rise approach. 'High flats do not always lead to heaven,' he conceded, 'but they are certainly not the housing hell some of their opponents seem to think.'[16]

Even one of the most-publicised redevelopment schemes failed to generate unalloyed enthusiasm. 'A clean sweep' of the Hutchesontown/ Gorbals area was 'necessary', Ninian Johnston reckoned in 'Miracle in the Gorbals?' (published in the spring issue of a Scottish architectural magazine), 'not only because of the existing conditions, but also to achieve an integral plan which will not suffer intrusion and infiltration by through traffic and undesirable development'. However, Johnston could not help noting wistfully that 'many of the buildings have been substantially built to sound individual designs, and it appears that if they had not been neglected and allowed to fall into disrepair, some might have been incorporated in new planning proposals'. The *Architects' Journal* was somewhat more sceptical. Although 'in general the proposals would transform the area out of all recognition, and completely for the better', nevertheless 'it seems questionable whether the layout at the density adopted ... provides either the necessary community open space, or contrasting small-scale intimacy and large-scale openness, that one would like to see'.

A particularly informed, telling critique came from Glasgow University's Tom Brennan in the June issue of the *Scottish Journal of Political Economy*. Pointing out that 'during a survey of what were reputed to be the two worst blocks in the Comprehensive Development Area it was found that nine households out of ten had made fairly substantial improvements', so that 'less than five per cent were dirty or in a poor state of decoration', he dared to ask the fundamental question 'whether adaptations could not be made to improve conditions sufficiently in the present area at something less than the cost [an estimated £13 million] of tearing the whole place down'. And he pressed on:

> Is it really impossible to make these buildings fit at reasonable cost if the problem is examined simply as a technical one and restrictions which might be imposed by out-of-date bye-laws and regulations are ignored? To the layman it certainly looks as if the roofs could be repaired, not for a few pounds but well within the limits of cost of the alternative which has been put forward. Informal enquiry of one or two people with the right kind of technical experience suggests that it would also be possible to design a free-standing toilet cabinet with a shower bath and lavatory which could be installed easily ...

Bearing in mind these and other practical possibilities, and characterising the Gorbals as an area where 'a large proportion of the population' had already 'adapted themselves very well' in spite of overcrowding, Brennan nevertheless at the last implicitly accepted that the larger argument was likely to go the other way. 'If the planners still say that the property in the scheduled area is in such poor condition that it has to be

pulled down now, that it has no useful life left and would fall down in
any case, then that is the answer.'[17] And in truth, this particular debate
was by that time effectively over, with perhaps the two most distinguished British architects of the time, Robert Matthew and Basil Spence,
already appointed as consultants for the detailed designing work of the
new Gorbals.

'For the Planned as well as the Planners' was by now the motto of the
Town and Country Planning Association's magazine, and the historical
challenge is to recover the often ignored views of the planned. At this
stage they could as easily be positive as negative. When in March the
Star ran a front-page story about the problems of damp on the LCC's
high-rise Ackroydon estate on Wimbledon Common – 'The Shame of
London: Woman grows cress on damp armchairs in flats that are the
wonder of the world' – and even compared it to 'rat-ridden dockland',
tenants quickly spoke up. 'I could not wish to live anywhere better,'
one woman told the *Architects' Journal*, another that 'this is the finest
estate in London, and anybody here will tell you so'. Or take (talking
to a Liverpool paper around the same time) the tenants of Coronation
Court, a ten-storey block on the East Lancashire Road:

> It takes some getting used to at first, but once you've convinced yourself
> you are not dreaming, it is like being on a permanent holiday. The central-
> heating scheme is marvellous. We really wanted a house, but until we
> came here we didn't know how comfortable a flat could be. (*Mrs Joan
> Dutton, who with her husband had lived with her mother for the previ-
> ous sixteen years*)
>
> We don't want any publicity, we just want to say a very big thank you
> to the Corporation for bringing us together after seven terrible years
> apart. It's like starting married life all over again. (*Couple on seventh floor
> who had been living apart with their respective parents*)
>
> I've no complaints at all. My wife and I waited 18 years for a place of
> our own. Now that we've got it, we're happy. What more can I say? I
> know the terrible conditions some unfortunate folk are living under . . .
> Yes, we are very lucky indeed. (*Middle-aged man on fourth floor*)

It was very different, reported the *Coventry Standard* not long afterwards, on Charter Avenue in the low-rise estate at Canley on the

city's outskirts. Mrs E. Whitehead, a pensioner, complained that her flat was damp and cold and 'smells like a graveyard', while Mrs Beryl Stamper, living next door with two young children, was also suffering from the dampness, had nowhere nearby to hang her washing, was worried that the children had nowhere to play in safety and crisply announced that 'whoever told the planners to go ahead didn't look at it from a woman's point of view'. Meanwhile in Barking, the local council had announced 'Operation Clearance', a 15-year plan to demolish 2,000 houses in the middle of the town and replace them with modern homes. 'We have bought this house and kept it spic and span for 20 years or more,' a housewife in St Paul's Road told the local paper. 'I've worked hard to keep it in good condition. Why should they come and pull it down? This is our home.' Mr W. Garland, also living in St Paul's Road, was equally outraged: 'Go along London Road and look at the new Council flats. They look lovely from the front – but at the back the conditions are beyond description. There is more justification to call them "slums" than our homes. And that is what they want to build here.'[18]

It is not quite true that the planners never listened to the planned. The LCC, for example, employed a sociologist, Margaret Willis, who during these months produced two typically painstaking surveys: one on how tenants in flats and maisonettes used their balconies, which in practice usually depended on how privately they were situated; and one on the wishes of old people living in flats and bungalows on the council's estates, with the great majority expressing reluctance to live any higher (up to eight or ten storeys) even if there was a lift. Yet overall – and on the part of 'activators' generally, not just planners – it is hard not to feel that, in this whole area of urban development and the often rapidly changing built environment, there existed a yawning gulf between those making the pronouncements (on whichever side of the argument) and those being pronounced upon. An increasingly active activator was John Betjeman. 'I cannot believe,' he declared in the *Spectator* in May, 'that the London County Council decision to reconstruct the Albert Bridge, Chelsea, means that it is to be destroyed and that we will never see its graceful outline again. Shining with electric lights to show the way to Festival Gardens, or grey and airy against the London sky, it is one of the beauties of the London river.' In the event, the Albert Bridge was saved – aesthetically a happy outcome, but not necessarily what would have happened if, say, there had been a referendum on the matter in south-west London. Or, as an anonymous verse in *Punch* put it, parodying Macaulay:

> When the driver inches slowly
> Through motor-darkened squares;
> When the traffic-cop stands helplessly
> In trackless thoroughfares;
> With weeping and with gnashing
> Still is the story told
> How Betjeman saved the Albert Bridge
> In the brave days of old.[19]

'A sweltering day!' recorded Judy Haines in Chingford on 6 July. Elsewhere that Saturday, Florence Turtle in Wimbledon Park went with the Wandsworth History Circle on a coach trip to Blenheim, 'conducted round the ground floor rooms by an educated young man who spoke well'; Madge Martin in Oxford travelled the other way, to 'the last of the Light Festival Concerts' in the 'serene, cool atmosphere' of the Royal Festival Hall; Nella Last in Barrow accompanied her husband to Ulverston, where 'I *never* saw so much "dripping" ice cream'; and Philip Larkin in Hull 'yielded to the temptation of buying an antiperspiration atomiser, partly for the fun of squirting it about, but whether it will be of any use or not I don't know'. In Liverpool, 12-year-old Patricia Buckley of Bootle Grammar School for Girls was crowned Bootle's Carnival Queen; long queues formed at the pier head for boats to New Brighton and the Isle of Man; and, reported the *Liverpool Echo*, 'Corporation buses bound for Woolton, Aigburth Vale, and other outlying districts of the city were full, many people carrying picnic hampers.' Did some of those Woolton-bound passengers picnic on the field behind St Peter's Church? There, as part of the annual church fête ('tickets 2/-, refreshments at moderate prices') and standing on a makeshift stage, the Quarry Men Skiffle Group performed that afternoon, led by a tousled 16-year-old wearing a checked shirt and tight black jeans. 'Paul met me the first day I did "Be-Bop-a-Lula" live onstage,'

John Lennon would remember 23 years later, just hours before his death.

> A mutual friend brought him to see my group. And we met and we talked after the show and I saw he had talent and he was playing guitar backstage and doing 'Twenty Flight Rock' by Eddie Cochran and I turned round to him right then on first meeting and said do you want to join the group and he said um hmm you know hmm de hmm and I think he said yes the next day as I recall it.[20]

The heatwave was over by Thursday the 18th, the date of the next *Vauxhall Mirror*, monthly house magazine of Vauxhall Motors in Luton. 'One more Victor rolls off the track and then the family is off on holiday,' declared the caption to the front-page photo of the assembly line. 'It's good to be beside the seaside and it's good to know that the Victor – like all our products – is going swimmingly. And that is our insurance of happy holidays in the years ahead.' The monthly '20 Questions' slot featured C. Bradbury of Div 70, whose answers might have been those of any respectable, decently paid working man:

What characteristic do you most dislike in other people? – *Unreliability.*

What would you like to be other than yourself? – *Stanley Matthews, because he is my idea of a true sportsman.*

If you had three wishes, what would you wish for? – *A little more money for the old folks, continued good health, peace in our time.*

If you could meet anyone living today, whom would you choose? – *Her Majesty the Queen.*

If you could do any job at all, other than the one you have now, what would you do? – *Pilot a jet airliner.*

What is your secret ambition? – *To go on a world tour with my family.*

If you could do something unconventional without let or hindrance, what would you do? – *Level off the hill I have to climb to get home to lunch.*

Is Rock 'n' Roll a vice, a habit, a passing craze, a good expression of high spirits, a form of hysteria, or a mere racket? – *Not enough space allotted to express my opinion.*

Which is the stronger sex? – *No doubt about it – man!*

The back page was an advertisement for Taylor Woodrow houses. 'IT'S YOUR WELCOME HOME – never before at so low a cost, has such streamlined home luxury been offered' (in this case at £2,175 freehold on the Skimpot Estate, Hayhurst Road, Luton). 'Many features have been incorporated to bring you new pleasure, new comfort. It has spacious rooms, an ultra-modern kitchen, including refrigerator, luxury bathroom, ample space for a garage, good sized garden and – above all – it is designed to a plan which makes for gracious living, and built to make the housewife's work easier and happier.'

That evening's performance at Frinton Summer Theatre was Gerald Savory's comedy *A Likely Tale*. 'The atmosphere of the play is brilliantly created by the two dear old sisters who talk of their past beaux over their crochet and tea cups,' appreciatively noted the *East Essex Gazette*'s critic of this latter-day *Cranford*. 'Pauline Murch and Vanessa Redgrave succeed in playing admirably these two characters.' Two days later, on Saturday the 20th, Stirling Moss at Aintree in a green Vanwall became the first British driver to win a world championship grand prix in a British car; Anthony Heap by contrast 'came nowhere in the fathers' eat-a-dog-biscuit-before-starting race' at his son's sports day in Great Missenden; Judy Haines's husband treated her and the children to a matinee at the Royal Ballet ('He bought us a pound box of Mackintosh's Week-End Assortment'); and miners and their families gathered for the annual Durham Miners' Gala. Poor weather and the start of a national bus strike badly depleted numbers, but, added the *Durham Chronicle*, 'the spirit of the gala was unimpaired', with boating 'as usual a popular pastime', while 'crowds spent liberally at the "fun of the fair" on the high ground'. Tellingly, 'while thousands listened to the speeches,' including one from the Labour leader Hugh Gaitskell, 'still more thousands spent their time in other ways.'[21]

By six o'clock much of the younger part of the TV public was settling down for *Six-Five Special* – Josephine Douglas and Pete Murray still in charge but the concert pianist long gone, with this evening's stars including the crooner Dennis Lotis and the up-and-coming British rock 'n' roller Terry Dene. In Bedford there was more serious business, however. Amidst rain, some 3,000 assembled at Bedford Town's football ground, the Eyrie, to listen to the Prime Minister. All seats were

under cover at 10s and 2s, covered standing room was free, and most of
the intermittent heckling came from League of Empire Loyalists,
though right at the start as Macmillan rose to speak, there was a piercing yell of 'Up the Eagles!' Resting his notes on a locally made oak box
presented to him for the occasion by four Bedfordshire Conservative
Associations, the long-sighted speaker, too vain to wear glasses, was
about halfway through his speech when, having listed some of the
economic progress since 1951, he peered at his typewritten text and
read the immortal passage:

> That is all to the good.
> Indeed,
>> let's be frank about it;
>> most of our people
>>> have never had it so good.
> Go around the country,
>> go to the industrial towns,
>> go to the farms,
> and you will see a state of prosperity
>> such as we have never had
>>> in my lifetime –
> nor indeed ever in the history
>> of this country.

Much of the rest of Macmillan's speech was about the dangers of inflation, but the five words 'never had it so good' would soon become
inextricably linked with – even come to define – the main thrust of his
premiership. For Macmillan himself, ultimately a moralist, this would
prove understandably frustrating; and for a different, less materialistic
gauge of satisfaction, he might have appreciated 'The Letter of the
Week', from Mrs M. S. of Tayport, in the issue dated that day of the
homeliest of magazines, the *People's Friend*:

> I love to read the letters page every week. How many interesting people
> write to you!
>   But isn't it a good thing that people aren't all alike and don't all do
> spectacular things?

I am just an ordinary housewife with a husband and family to look after. My day is a busy full one. I'm happy doing my work and knowing my family need me.

I think I have one of the most satisfying jobs in the world, and it's not everyone who can say that. I wouldn't change it for anything.[22]

PART TWO

4

Catch a Falling Sputnik

'The main change that has taken place in the last few years is that customers no longer seem as price-conscious as they were,' the *Financial Times* noted about Marks & Spencer some four months after Macmillan's speech. 'Ninety-five-shilling dresses are found to sell better than 65s models.' Yet none of M&S's 237 stores had fitting rooms, and, more generally, in terms of the apparently inexorable shift into a shiny new consumerist world, there were by 1957 at least three significant areas of continuity.

Starting with consumer durables, ownership figures for the second half of the year showed that their penetration was far from total: 56 per cent of adults owned a TV set, 26 per cent a washing machine and only 12 per cent a refrigerator (the figure for the working class specifically being just 5 per cent). In addition, only 21 per cent of adults had a telephone, while even in Colin Shindler's home in Prestwich, Manchester, where his businessman father kept a Humber Hawk in the drive and a Hotpoint washing machine had recently arrived, they still used a mangle on wash day.

Nor, a further continuity, were supermarkets anything like ubiquitous. The *Liverpool Echo*'s 'Onlooker' reckoned in September that they 'seem to have made much more of a mark in the South of England than so far they have in the North. Motoring in London and the Thames Valley, I was surprised to find them in quite small towns and suburbs.' Would they spread? 'I suspect,' added Onlooker, 'that in the North we may be more reluctant than the Southerners to forgo our cross-the-counter courtesies.' In fact, there was a total of almost 4,000 self-service shops in Britain, but the great majority were relatively small, at around

1,000 square feet. And although supermarkets were undoubtedly on
the rise – Sainsbury's with nine so far, Fine Fare (part of the Allied
Bakeries Group) with 15 and planning to open another 15 in the next
12 months – these were still, in the long sweep of things, the Dark Ages.
'The out-of-town supermarket, based on the North American pattern
of the out-of-town shopping centre in the open country, has not yet
been attempted,' the *FT* pointed out around the time of Onlooker's
southern tour. 'The obvious reason is the comparatively small number
of cars owned in Britain [only 24 per cent of the population had a car].'
Moreover, existing high-street supermarkets 'as yet provide no parking
accommodation' – and thereby 'probably miss much potential trade
which goes to the neighbourhood grocer, the shop at the corner, the
grocer who still delivers (which supermarkets do not) and the grocer
who brings his shop to the house'.

The third continuity, helped by a shopping environment in which
only 2 per cent of all food products sold were pre-packed, was thrift.
Radio and television repairs; the hire and repair of gas appliances;
matches, soap and cleaning materials – all featured strongly in 1957's
pioneer annual household expenditure survey. 'A really tasty dish, and
economical too!' was the headline in *Woman's Own*, two days before
Macmillan's speech, for Philip Harben's recipe for cold pigeon pie,
while Mrs H. had revealed earlier in the summer in the same magazine
that 'I cut my loofah into slices – some for cleaning pans, others for
bases to hold flowers steady in a vase.'[1] Economical hints from readers
remained a staple of many popular publications.

Even so, there was plenty new on the market in 1957, often being
aggressively pushed through the recently available medium of television advertising. Fry's Turkish Delight, the scientifically devised (by
Lyons) instant porridge known as Ready Brek, 'the new, exciting taste
of Gibbs SR', the original aftershave (Old Spice), the Hoovermatic twin
tub, Wash and Spin Dry machine – all were fresh entrants, while in
general two trends stood out. One was towards home-centredness,
epitomised by the rapid growth of sales of canned beer, up from 1.5
million cans in 1954–5 to 70 million by 1957–8. 'It's nice to watch television but it's even nicer when you've got a drink in your hand,'
Gregory Ratcliffe, a Birmingham shopkeeper, told *Reynolds News*.
'Makes it more intimate somehow. Gives you the feeling that you're in

a posh cabaret.' The outspoken textile manufacturer Cyril Lord was already plugged in to the home, manufacturing and selling tufted carpets that made use of new man-made fibres and were aimed squarely at the mass market, often replacing linoleum in working-class homes. Soon there would be a TV jingle – 'This is luxury you can afford by Cyril Lord', a jingle accurately described by his biographer as 'relentless' – and his carpets were set to become a byword for the gathering consumer boom. The other trend, though far from invariable, was towards going upmarket. The launch of Camay soap involved a series of mildly risqué Norman Parkinson photographs in the more superior women's magazines, with Parkinson himself claiming elsewhere that he used Camay for shaving in the bath. In the autumn Van den Berghs heavily promoted a new soft-blend luxury margarine, Blue Band, with distinctive gold-coloured packaging. And about the same time, faced by a falling market share, the British Patent Perforated Paper Company decided that it needed a new approach if its cheap, traditional, notoriously non-absorbent toilet paper, Bronco, was to thrive against more yielding competitors like Andrex.[2]

Inevitably, the pleasure and excitement of new possessions could come tinged with regret, as when shortly before Christmas the parents of 13-year-old Subrata Dasgupta, living in Derby, 'bought a Bush electric record player'. Admittedly he could now buy records (LPs and EPs) that he had 'only handled wistfully in Dixons', but it was still 'with a great deal of sadness I put away our mechanical, wind-up gramophone', whose 'thick, metal-shiny playing arm which held the needle, curled up like a contented kitten, looked clumsy and prehistoric, compared to the lightweight "pick-up" arm on the new player'. The older teen, though, was probably melancholy-free if he or she acquired a Dansette: brightly coloured (usually a mixture of blues, creams, reds and turquoises) and unashamedly lo-fi, it still had the volume to get partygoers dancing.[3]

How to choose between competing goods and services? The first *Egon Ronay Guide* to restaurants appeared in 1957, but the event making greater waves came in October with the first issue of *Which?*, the magazine of the Consumers' Association. The CA itself had been started the previous year by a young American graduate, Dorothy Goodman, who on returning to the States had passed it over to Michael

Young. For Young, as he recalled some 20 years later, there was a direct, potentially fruitful link with the work he had been doing for *Family and Kinship*:

> In Bethnal Green we were able to reconstruct what was happening in the 19th century. It was clear that men's lives were very much centred on their work; they kept a large proportion of the family income for themselves and spent it quite separately from their wives in pubs and gambling and smoking. Partly they did it because the home was such a bloody uncomfortable place to be.
>
> What we saw was the beginning of a change. The younger men, although interested in their work, were giving more interest to their homes, having something more like a partnership with their wives in building up their homes. And this was symbolised by the material goods that people bought.
>
> They had a terrific pride, an emotional investment in these material goods, and it seemed that they would be more satisfied if they could feel that the things they were buying were efficient and functional. Anything, we thought, that could tell them that, would strike a chord. It struck much more of a chord with the middle classes than it did with the working classes.

The unfortunate class differential was no doubt inevitable, but perhaps less so was the dramatic whoosh of *Which?*'s early life. 'At 10 a.m. on Tuesday morning,' Young wrote on Friday the 10th to his benefactors the Elmhirsts, 'when we opened the doors of this office which we have rented for 10s a week, a special messenger arrived from Sir Simon Marks [chairman of M&S] with a standing order for 20 copies; and ever since then the letters have been pouring in.'[4]

Press response was initially cautious – no doubt on account of anxiety about advertising boycotts by upset manufacturers – but a favourable article and editorial in *The Times* helped ignite interest, as did an item by Marghanita Laski on the 11th in *Woman's Hour*, and within a month there would be some 10,000 members of the CA, few agreeing with the electrical retailer who told the *Electrical Times* that 'all these well-meaning but voluntary unofficial watchdogs are making much ado about nothing'. Among those do-gooders, the key editorial figure from early on was the hugely capable, clear-sighted Eirlys Roberts, fairly described on her death in 2008 as 'the mother of the modern British consumer movement'. Meanwhile *Which?* itself focused in its first issue – after a bold declaration that its mission was to supply 'the information, impartial, accurate and thorough, which will enable people to get better value for their money' – on electric kettles (the Russell-Hobbs failing one of the insulation tests), sunglasses, aspirin, cake mixes, scouring powders and pastes (Mirro, Vim and Ajax as the top-rated three, followed by Chemico and Gumption), and no-iron cottons, with additionally the results of Swedish tests of two popular British cars, the Austin 35 and the Standard 10 Saloon. 'Somehow it seems to belong quite well to a "classless middle-class" society,' Young wrote a week after the launch to the anthropologist Geoffrey Gorer, thanking him for his subscription. 'From now on everyone can have the same article, "the best".'

Sadly, what one does not get in the pages of *Which?* – undeniably imbued, for all its sterling work, with a whiff of paternalistic puritanism – are the voices of the consumers themselves. For those one can still turn occasionally to Mass-Observation (albeit by now an organisation devoted to market research rather than sociological enquiry), specifically to its Detergent Survey of late 1957 and early 1958. Among 40 housewives interviewed in London, Liverpool and Manchester, a headmistress said she would 'rather pay for a good all-rounder' and was 'old-fashioned enough to want to see the bubbles'; a part-time shop assistant declared herself 'very sensitive to smell' and thought 'they scent them too much, especially Daz'; and a Liverpool docker's wife, who went 'to the wash house to do the big wash', explained how 'I used to use Persil quite a lot' but had 'changed to Fairy Snow' because 'Persil is very hard on the hands'. One of the interviewees, in a small, untidy Paddington flat, was a childless 38-year-old who worked as a part-time researcher and was married to an *Encyclopaedia Britannica* sales rep. Not exactly a bright, bushy-eyed consumer, she described her washing routine:

Always on Sunday morning after I read the Sunday papers. It has to be very much of an emergency to wash any other time. I often find my husband's things on my chair or my ashtray, for me to wash up, if my

husband wants anything done he'll follow me about with them, put them
on my bed, my pillow and so on till I wash them. I can't wash things
while I'm running the bath, because the bath looks too tempting. My
terylene curtains, it's essential to wash them once a fortnight – I go on
with mine till people mention it, but I don't care personally if they're
black, and if my dog could speak, he'd ask for his bedding washed. In
other words you can gather I don't like washing.[5]

'Some of the methods used to prevent coaches not involved in the stoppage from carrying on were far removed from the peaceful picketing
allowed by law,' reported the *Manchester Guardian* on Tuesday, 23 July
(three days after Macmillan's Bedford speech), about the ongoing
national (outside London) busmen's strike. 'Drivers were attacked and
beaten, tyres were slashed and windows broken – sometimes to the
danger of passengers as well as crew.' Later that week at Headingley the
West Indies were again on the rack, with the England fast bowler Peter
Loader celebrating his hat-trick by dancing a fandango, very different
to cricket's still customary low-key displays of emotion. But Philip
Larkin on the Friday was more interested in *The Archers*. 'Don't you
adore Carol Grey's voice when Toby S. [Toby Stobeman] is making
love to her?' he asked Monica Jones. 'It quite broke me up over my
leathery tinned tongue tonight: she goes all small & unconfident. She's
the only woman on the programme I've ever liked. I'm getting to the
point where I want to bang a skillet on Prue's [Pru Harris, later Forrest]
head.' A less inveterate grumbler, Florence Turtle, spent the weekend in
Suffolk, and on the train back to London 'a passenger remarked that he
thought Liverpool St Station must be the dirtiest station in the world, a
remark that I must agree with'. Harold Macmillan was more satisfied
when his Monday audience with the Queen turned to the question of
where the eight-year-old Prince Charles was to go to boarding school
next term: 'She has chosen Cheam – a good preparatory school, solid
but not smart.'[6]

In fact the royals and those around them were in for a tricky few
months. 'A pain in the neck' was young Lord Altrincham's memorable
description of the Queen's voice, in a trenchant article on the monarchy
in the August issue of the *National & English Review*; he added that the

unfortunate impression she gave in her speeches was of 'a priggish schoolgirl, captain of the hockey team, a prefect and a recent candidate for Confirmation'. Altrincham (the future John Grigg) largely blamed the monarch's 'tweedy' entourage – a 'tight little enclave of English ladies and gentlemen' – rather than Elizabeth herself, but that did not stop a torrent of abuse. The *Daily Express* inevitably led the way; in the *Daily Mail* the political commentator Henry Fairlie accused the peer of 'daring to put his infinitely tiny and temporary mind against the accumulated experience of the centuries'; Altrincham received some 2,000 letters of complaint and a punch in the face from a member of the League of Empire Loyalists; and Macmillan noted his luncheon guest Churchill as 'splendidly indignant'. Even so, a poll of *Daily Mail* readers found that as many as 35 per cent agreed with Altrincham, compared to 52 per cent disagreeing – and that among younger readers the split was actually 47–39 in his favour. Summing up 'this unofficial national debate' later in August, Mollie Panter-Downes wrote in the *New Yorker* that there were indeed 'many loyal and thoughtful English' who would be 'glad to see a bit of fresh air blown into the stuffier recesses of palace protocol'; she pinned her hopes on the 'forceful ventilating influence' of the Duke of Edinburgh, 'whose breezy common sense and intelligence make short work of red-tape trimmings'. The Queen's first minister was less convinced. 'After luncheon, a sharp little discussion with Prince Philip,' recorded Macmillan at Balmoral on 1 September. 'He is *against* our having a nuclear power. The tone of his talk confirms me in the view that he will try to play up to the Left. He may honestly think this to be in the Queen's interest. But I don't altogether like the tone of his talk. It is too like that of a clever undergraduate, who has just discovered Socialism.'[7]

One month later, and the controversy was still alive. 'Mr [Geoffrey] Howe is the chairman of the Bow Group, and as impertinent a young whipper-snapper as ever needed his breeks dusting,' was how the *Spectator*'s new Westminster correspondent 'Taper' (Bernard Levin) described the launch of that Tory pressure group's magazine *Crossbow*. 'He spent a good deal of his speech insulting Lord Altrincham in a particularly offensive, ham-fisted and naive manner.' A *Sunday Dispatch* photo caption a few days later about Princess Alexandra was a reminder of the royals' increasingly fish-bowl world – 'a princess plays tennis

– in slacks' – before news broke that, to coincide with the Queen's North American tour, New York's *Saturday Evening Post* was publishing a critical piece on the royals and their great cheerleader, Richard Dimbleby. The *Sunday Express* headline provided a pithy if not a balanced summary – 'MALCOLM MUGGERIDGE RIDICULES ROYAL FAMILY IN USA. ASTOUNDING ATTACK ON THE QUEEN. SHE IS CALLED DOWDY, FRUMPISH, BANAL' – and one of its readers, Nella Last in Barrow, reflected that 'after listening to his prim, waspish voice on "Any Questions"' she had pictured Muggeridge as an 'ageing Peke'. The *People* also weighed in, a front-page piece calling his article 'ruthless' and 'tasteless'. Next day he was banned from appearing on that evening's *Panorama*, and later in October the BBC's board of governors not only disinvited Altrincham from *Any Questions?* but decided not to renew Muggeridge's contract. 'This chap will never go on the air as long as I am director-general,' declared Lieutenant General Sir Ian Jacob, and, as a military man, he was as good as his word.[8]

'You go too flamin' far when you criticise our Queen, who does more good than you if you lived to be 5,000 . . . signed, Eight (loyal to the Queen) Teddy Boys.' So read one of the many patriotic letters to Altrincham back in August, but not everyone felt reassured by the nation's youth. 'We did not enjoy the horrid crowds of Leicester Square, Coventry Street and Piccadilly Circus,' recorded Madge Martin that month after an evening in London to see Anna Neagle in *No Time for Tears*. 'Surely these were exciting, gay places to be in at night, but now filled with the lowest type – Teddy boys with their friends of both sexes, etc. We had a cup of tea at Fortes – once the dear old Criterion – feeling tired and disgusted with this side of our dear London.' In September a series run by the *Liverpool Echo* about widespread vandalism on Merseyside culminated with readers expressing their views. Mrs M. Green of 10 Bower Road, Huyton blamed working mothers – 'when her day is spent largely outside her home, the pivot is removed and the family, as such, just disintegrates' – but for most there was a single, unambiguous line of thought:

We won't get anywhere until the punishment fits the crime. It is scandalous that if one catches a delinquent in the act and cuffs his ear, one is liable to be hauled up for assaulting a juvenile. (*M. Temple, 10 Abergele Road, Stanley, Liverpool 13*)

They ought to bring the cat in again: a few strokes with that would soon put an end to it. Teachers should be able to use the cane again to show children which is right or wrong. (*Mrs White, Parkgate Road, Neston*)

Why not bring back the birch like the Isle of Man? (*'Disgusted' (OAP)*)

Mrs K. E. Lee of 32 Barnsbury Road, Liverpool 4 also had a question, or rather two: 'What sort of homes do these little vultures come from and what kind of citizens are they going to be?'[9]

The young themselves were bothered by neither issue. On 7 August, a month and a day after the Woolton church fête, the Quarry Men (not yet with McCartney) played for the first time at the Cavern in Liverpool. 'We did some skiffle numbers to start off with but we also did rock 'n' roll,' recalled the drummer Colin Hanton. 'John Lennon was passed a note and, very pleased, he said to the audience, "We've had a request." He opened it up and it was from Alan Sytner [the club's cantankerous owner] saying, "Cut out the bloody rock 'n' roll."' Elsewhere these summer holidays, the 11-year-old Helen Shapiro first met the 10-year-old Mark Feld (later Marc Bolan), 'this chubby kid' whose 'quiff would cover his face when he combed it forward'. Another 11-year-old, Bob Harris, was on holiday with his parents in Cromer when he passed an amusement arcade and heard the American singer Paul Anka's 'Diana' coming from the jukebox ('There was a magic to it that made me want to be a part of the world it came from'), while the 14-year-old Lorna Stockton (later Sage) went with a friend to Southport:

Gail and I spent all our time and pocket money dashing from one juke-box to another to make sure that Pat Boone's chaste hit 'Love Letters in the Sand' would be drowned out all over the windswept town by 'All Shook Up'. The one was sweetness and light, the other inarticulate, insidious bump-and-grind . . . All the Elvises groaned and whimpered at once, and the waves rushed in and obliterated Pat Boone. And we clung to each other in a shelter smelling of orange peel and piss on the promenade, and shrieked with glee, like the Bacchae who dismembered Orpheus.

Skiffle was by now at its apogee, with the catchy (especially for this six-year-old boy) 'Last Train to San Fernando' by Johnny Duncan and the Blue Grass Boys steaming through the charts. But a curmudgeonly Welshman, Frank Lewis, was less enamoured when on 2 September he saw 'the Mountaineering Skiffle group' play at the Globe pub in Barry: 'The skiffle place was jammed with young people. Too many tunes all in one key. It begins to boredom [*sic*] after a while.'[10]

Two days later, HMSO published a blue paper-bound volume, 155 pages long and priced at five shillings. This was the Wolfenden Report – or *Report of the Committee on Homosexual Offences and Prostitution* – and its initial 5,000 print run sold out within hours. 'It is a fine, thorough, dispassionate piece of work, which uses words more clearly than many best-sellers do,' found Mollie Panter-Downes. Its two key recommendations were that prostitutes should be punished much more severely for accosting and that, more controversially, private homosexual relations between consenting adults should be decriminalised. 'It is not, in our view, the function of law to intervene in private lives of citizens, or to seek to enforce any particular pattern of behaviour,' declared the report about the latter aspect. 'It follows that we do not believe it to be a function of the law to attempt to cover all the fields of sexual behaviour.' Importantly, Wolfenden made clear that 'this limited modification of the law should not be interpreted as indicating that the law can be indifferent to other forms of homosexual behaviour, or as a general licence to homosexuals to behave as they please'. The following evening on ITV, a programme on the report – preceded by a warning to viewers that it was unsuitable for children and might distress some adults – featured an anonymous doctor (his back to camera), who was asked by the interviewer, 'Would you prefer to be normal?' 'Oh yes,' he replied, 'I would – if there was a guaranteed cure – a hope – that I could become an ordinary normal person I would certainly welcome it. I think all homosexuals would like to be cured and marry and have children.'[11]

Press reaction to the decriminalisation proposal was predictably mixed. Only two national dailies came out unambiguously against, namely the *Daily Mail* ('leaving perverts free to spread corruption') and the *Daily Express* ('cumbersome nonsense'); *The Times*, the *Manchester Guardian* and the *News Chronicle* were almost wholly supportive; the

Daily Telegraph worried that legalised homosexuality might spread like an infection; and the *Daily Mirror* initially sat on the fence, but eventually backed Wolfenden. Among the Sundays, the *Observer* was positive, but the *Sunday Times* warned against the undermining of the 'basic national moral standard', while in the *Sunday Express* the resolutely homophobic John Gordon wrote about 'degraded men' with 'bestial habits' and called the report 'The Pansies' Charter'. As for the weeklies, the *Spectator* asserted that 'whatever feelings of revulsion homosexual actions may arouse, the law on this point is utterly irrational and illogical'. Most provincial papers were hostile, and the *Scotsman* declared flatly that it was 'no solution to any public problem to legitimise a bestial offence'.

The *Mirror* took a poll of its largely working-class readers. Within a week there were nearly 7,000 votes in, overwhelmingly wanting prostitutes cleared off the streets but narrowly against decriminalisation of private homosexual behaviour. As further votes came in, those overall preferences stayed constant, while it became apparent that there were significant regional variations: roughly 1 in 2 in the south of England wanting decriminalisation, compared to 3 in 7 in the north and only 1 in 6 in Scotland. A more authoritative opinion poll (though broadly in line) was Gallup's, published later in September. This revealed that 81 per cent had heard about the report; that 42 per cent saw homosexuality as 'a serious problem', compared with 27 per cent 'not very' and 31 per cent 'don't knows'; and that 38 per cent agreed with decriminalisation, as against 47 per cent disagreeing. 'Considering all things,' commented Panter-Downes on Gallup's figures, 'this hardly represents the wave of scandalized indignation that many people thought would follow.'[12]

The issue rumbled on through the autumn, with one Oxford undergraduate, Dennis Potter, reflecting in *Isis* that 'inevitably the natural reaction of all of us who find the thought of homosexual behaviour repulsive or difficult to comprehend will be a troubled one'. Politically, the Home Secretary, Rab Butler, was inclined initially to legislate for decriminalisation, but soon found that he was out of line with mainstream Tory opinion and pushed the issue into the longish grass. The House of Lords did debate the question in December, with Lord Denning speaking for many when he condemned unnatural vices and insisted that the law should continue to punish homosexual conduct, albeit 'discreetly'. Meanwhile, for homosexuals themselves, the secrecy and gnawing anxiety continued – perhaps typified this autumn by how Brian Abel-Smith, arguably the most gifted social scientist of his generation, felt unable to apply for a safe Labour seat (the retiring Hugh Dalton's, in Bishop Auckland) for fear of public humiliation if his homosexuality was discovered. Earlier in the year there had been a sign of the Victorian permafrost starting to melt (with the Homicide Act, which restricted the use of the death penalty for murder), but for the moment this remained a right little, tight little island.[13]

'What the British people are waiting for,' Macmillan reflected privately on 17 September with an alert reference to an ITV game show, 'is the answer to the 64,000 question – how to stop rising prices & fall in value of money. They will (perhaps) accept measures to deal with these problems.' In the context of sterling under severe pressure, he went on: 'But they regard an exchange crisis (which they do *not* understand) as some kind of a swindle organised by foreigners.' Two days later the *Evening Standard* included a review of *Hamlet* at the Old Vic: 'Ophelia is played by a girl called Judi Dench, whose first professional performance this only too obviously is. But she goes mad quite nicely and has talent which will be shown to better advantage when she acquires some technique to go with it.' Homeward-bound commuters, though, could not avoid the front-page headline: 'Bank Rate Shock – Up To 7 per cent: Thorneycroft's H-bomb shakes the City'. Peter Thorneycroft was Chancellor, and he had gone for a 2-per-cent hike heavily under the influence of the Governor of the Bank of England, Cameron (Kim) Cobbold, whose spokesman was quoted in strikingly robust language: 'There has recently been a good deal of speculative pressure against the pound. People have been selling sterling. This will show them "where they get off".' The démarche temporarily did its job, confounding the instant, apocalyptic prediction of the cerebral merchant banker Siegmund Warburg (made privately to the Shadow Chancellor Harold Wilson and recorded in the diary of Wilson's colleague Richard Crossman) that 'it was a gamble which would not come off and we were in for a 1931 crisis, but this time with rising unemployment and rising prices simultaneously', yet it still generated plenty of scepticism.

The *Spectator*'s Keynesian economic commentator Nicholas Davenport was appalled, calling the move 'the crowning folly', while the more measured *FT* argued that unless there was real 'determination in extending restraint to wages', which in practice meant the government standing up to the unions, then 'nothing will have been gained, and much will have been lost'.[14]

There were two piquant consequences of this sharp tightening of policy. 'It is alleged that there was a "leak" about the intention of the Government to raise the Bank Rate,' Macmillan noted the following week, adding that 'careful enquiries' had found 'no trace of any irregularity'. The ambitious Wilson, however, was on the case, and by October he was publicly demanding a formal inquiry – a request eventually acceded to by a very reluctant Macmillan. The other consequence, barely noticed at the time, concerned the implications of an accompanying measure, the temporary forbidding of London banks to use sterling to finance third-party trade. Dollar deposits had already been mounting in Paris and London – in part reflecting the Cold War reluctance of Soviet and East European banks to trust their dollars to New York – and it was these dollars that some of London's banks now sought to use in order to go on doing their business of financing international trade. Such were the origins of what would become known as the Eurodollar market. One of its pioneers was the visionary Sir George Bolton, a former Bank of England man but now chairman of the Bank of London and South America (BOLSA). In his pitch for the job earlier in 1957 he had asserted, 'London has barely succeeded in maintaining its international banking system following the loss of political influence by the UK, the weakened position of sterling and the incapacity of the London Market to increase its foreign investment net.' Accordingly, those London banks, like BOLSA, 'whose main business is to maintain and develop a position in the foreign field will have to adapt their structure to meet the needs of the time'.[15] The Euromarkets, starting with the Eurodollar market, would be the means of that adaptation – and a first, long step towards London returning to its pre-1914 glories as an international financial centre.

Judi Dench's was not the only debut that autumn. 'Mr Ted Hughes is clearly a remarkable poet, and seems to be quite outside the currents of his time,' wrote the august critic Edwin Muir in the *New Statesman*, reviewing *The Hawk in the Rain*. 'His distinguishing power is sensuous, verbal and imaginative; at his best the three are fused together. His images have an admirable violence.' The very different poet Robert Conquest generously agreed in the *Spectator* – 'not just promising but very promising' – though his friend Kingsley Amis held his counsel, perhaps mulling instead over the tepid critical response to the just-released Boulting brothers' version of *Lucky Jim*. 'The film has taken what was farcical in the book and turned it into a rowdy, slap-happy, knockabout comedy in which all that was social, significant, representative, etc., etc., is kept firmly out,' reckoned Isabel Quigly, while Lindsay Anderson was even less forgiving: 'The characters have been flattened, simplified and vulgarised. The temptations of realist shooting have been consciously resisted, and the story has been wholly abstracted from reality.'

Elsewhere, Florence Turtle went to the Ambassadors to see *The Mousetrap* (almost six years in) and recorded that 'it was a Comedy Thriller, somewhat tripey but quite entertaining'; Anthony Heap 'walked down to Drury Lane Theatre and back in early evening to make enquiries about First Night seats for "My Fair Lady" seven months hence', discovering that 'booking for the first year commences next Tuesday!'; and the third series of *Hancock's Half Hour* on the small screen began at the end of September. 'I can't remember when I laughed so much at a comedy show on television,' declared a viewer. One cultural phenomenon largely passing under the radar was that of the cartoon character Andy Capp getting into his work-shy, beer-swilling, cigarette-dangling groove. Created by a Hartlepool man, Reg Smythe, he had first appeared in August in northern editions of the *Daily Mirror* and would soon go national, becoming an emblematic, wholly unreconstructed working-class figure. 'Look at it this way, honey,' Andy says in one of the early strips, leaning nonchalantly against the wall as his wife Florrie sits battered on the floor, 'I'm a man of few pleasures and one of them 'appens to be knockin' yer about!'[16]

'Forward with the People' was the slogan on the *Mirror*'s masthead, and on Thursday, 3 October the people's party, gathered on the south coast, experienced a day of high drama. Some six months after Muggeridge had noted Gaitskell telling him that the Labour Party was 'hopelessly split' over the H-bomb issue and that it was 'impossible to have sensible or coherent policy', and some five months after a British nuclear test in the Pacific, this was the day of decision – played out, recorded Panter-Downes with her novelist's eye, 'on the boarded-over ice rink of Brighton's Sports Stadium in a haze of cigarette smoke and Asian flu heated to the combustion point by strong television lights'. The pivotal figure was Aneurin Bevan: the rebel of 1951, by now shadow Foreign Secretary and in increasingly visible, if ultimately uneasy, partnership with Gaitskell. 'Already every inch a statesman in his dark suit, with his distinguished silvery thatch of hair,' noted Panter-Downes, 'he sat on the platform frowning over horn-rimmed spectacles at the *Times*, as though lifted intact from the bow window of a St James's Street club.' The quondam unilateralist also spoke, with that compelling oratory which few if any politicians of the era came close to matching:

> If you carry this [unilateralist] resolution and follow out all its implications and do not run away from it you will send a Foreign Secretary, whoever he may be, naked into the conference chamber. Able to preach sermons, of course; he could make good sermons. But action of that sort is not necessarily the way in which you can take away the menace of this bomb from the world.

A minute or two later, being heckled from the floor, he was provoked into dismissing unilateralism as 'an emotional spasm' – at which words, reported James Cameron next day in the *News Chronicle*, 'something like an emotional spasm did indeed go through that stark, crowded arena'. For Bevan's disciple and future biographer Michael Foot, and for others on the Labour left, it was a moment of deepest betrayal. Yet, Foot would insist in later years, the widely bruited idea that Bevan had 'entered into a cynical compact' – in other words, that his speech was the price of becoming Foreign Secretary in a future Labour government – 'was not merely deeply repugnant to his nature, but is utterly confounded by any study of the facts'.

At the conference itself, the unilateralist motion was crushingly defeated, with the leader of the Transport and General Workers' Union, Frank Cousins, unable to persuade his block-voting delegation to support it. Bevan's stance was no doubt electorally necessary, but arguably this was the fateful post-1945 moment when Labour and radical sentiment as a whole started to become increasingly detached from each other. 'People like himself had lost interest in the Party after Nye's Brighton speech,' Crossman (in 1961) would record the playwright Wolf Mankowitz telling him. 'That was the turning point. Since then they couldn't care less about the Parliamentary leadership or see any great distinction, indeed, between Gaitskell, Wilson and Crossman intriguing against each other.'[17]

In any case, another event – also science-related – quickly stole Bevan's thunder. 'Russians first to launch satellite,' noted Judy Haines on Friday the 4th, in an increasingly rare mention of current affairs. 'It is circling the earth at a fast rate and emitting signals.' This was Sputnik, the world's first man-made satellite and, amidst considerable popular enthusiasm, tracked from Britain by the new Jodrell Bank observatory. As early as the 5th the *FT* placed a dot by the globe on its normally staid front-page news summary; that same day Frances Partridge on behalf of 'Bloomsbury' welcomed the satellite as a news story for once 'something purely interesting and pleasant'; and Doris Lessing was one of many staying up all night hoping 'to catch a glimpse of it bowling past overhead'. On the 7th the *Evening Standard*'s headline was 'Thousands See The Blip', which had passed over London that morning at just after 7.07 a.m., and by the 11th the *FT*'s dot had transmuted into a satellite-like shape.

What were Sputnik's implications? 'The satellite is not an isolated breakthrough on a narrow front,' claimed the *New Statesman*. 'It merely crowns the growing pyramid of evidence that over a wide sector of scientific knowledge the Russians are advancing further and faster than the West.' Bevan agreed, asserting in *Tribune* that the satellite was evidence of Russia's 'technically dynamic society'. For Churchill 'the disconcerting thing', as he told his wife, was not 'the satellite itself' but 'the proof of the forwardness of Soviet Sciences compared to the Americans'. Gallup duly sounded public opinion: 36 per cent felt an increased respect for the Russians, 27 per cent could not understand why the Americans had been beaten to it, and only 14 per cent said that Sputnik had made them more frightened of Russia. Inevitably, the fascination eventually abated. 'As the week progressed and the satellite continued, after a panicky interval of doubt and speculation, to transmit its signals, the BBC allowed a note of boredom to creep into its bulletins,' Bernard Hollowood was recording in *Punch* by the 23rd.

'The satellite became "it". "Well," the announcer began, "it's still up there and going strong." The thing was proving rather a disappointment: it hadn't burned itself out, it hadn't landed on Washington, it wasn't quite playing the game. It was threatening to clash with the royal visit to Canada.'[18]

Six days into Sputnik's flight – and seven months after the announcement by the Paymaster-General, Reginald Maudling, of the tripling of the civil nuclear power programme – it was discovered that one of the nuclear reactors at Windscale (later renamed Sellafield) was on fire. That was early on Thursday the 10th. Over the next two days, as makeshift hoses delivered water into the reactor, enormous bravery was displayed, above all by the deputy works manager Tom Tuohy. 'I went up to check several times until I was satisfied that the fire was out,' he recalled. 'I did stand to one side, sort of hopefully, but if you're staring straight up the core of a shut-down reactor you're going to get quite a bit of radiation.' Or, as he also put it, 'I'm glad I was there, but I'd rather not do it again.' From the start the official line was to downplay the seriousness of the situation and its potential dangers: the BBC's six o'clock radio news bulletin on the 11th stressed that no public hazard was being caused because the wind was blowing from the east and carrying radioactivity out to sea, while next day the ban on the sale of locally produced milk covered only 14 square miles. Nevertheless, reflected Nella Last that Saturday after reading about the fire, 'I often have wondered about "fall" of atomic tainted dust from Windscale, or Calder'; she called the prospect of it being blown down the coast to Barrow '*not* a happy thought'.

Monday saw the ban being significantly extended – to 200 square miles, thereby including a further 500 farms – but the Atomic Energy Authority was adamant that 'people in the new area need have no apprehension about milk they have already drunk'. As for the undrunk milk, thousands of gallons were now being tipped into the sea, but it was too late to prevent what Panter-Downes soon afterwards described as 'a wave of national disquiet' not only about the 'alarming leak of radioactive iodine' into west Cumberland's milk supplies but, more generally, about 'what went wrong, why the Atomic Energy Authority was so slow in saying that anything had gone wrong, why the safety measures were fumbled – and slow off the mark, too'. This was probably an accurate assessment, to judge by Nella Last's chat on the 17th with her friend Mrs Higham. 'Like myself she has had "qualms" about these big atomic works,' Last noted, adding they were both agreed that 'there's bound to be downright ignorance of effects & results, with something so utterly new'. In fact the government had already commissioned an inquiry by the AEA's Sir William Penney, but on its completion later in the month Macmillan – deeply concerned not to endanger Anglo-American nuclear collaboration – was willing to release only a relatively anodyne version. 'On the whole, reassuring,' was the *News Chronicle*'s response to the ensuing White Paper on the accident, though in regard to Britain's ambitious atomic energy programme, the paper highlighted the 'radiation risks about which we still know far too little', plausibly asserting that 'it is this mystery, this sense of vague and ill-understood menace, which worries the public'.

And the locals? 'As an inhabitant of West Cumberland, the accident at Windscale has naturally been an unpleasant shock,' a woman wrote to a local paper in the almost immediate aftermath. 'The fact, however, that heightens the shock is that we were given no warning until the situation was under control. Why not? Suppose the situation had "run away"? What then? Surely people have a right to be given enough warning either to move their children out of the vicinity, or, at least, to keep them indoors if any severe accident is expected.' Accordingly, 'until we can rely on a more immediate warning of irradiation or even a threatened explosion, we shall remain dissatisfied and anxious'. Even so, the most authoritative historian of the episode, Lorna Arnold, reckons that 'Cumberland remained remarkably calm', and she points to the fact that Windscale, since the start of its construction ten years earlier, 'had brought employment and considerable prosperity to a severely depressed area'.

Jenny Crowther (later Uglow) was at school next to the plant and lived three miles up the coast at St Bees. 'People were told not to eat anything from their allotments,' she remembers. 'But the allotments were their pride and joy, and as the word "fallout" was used they assumed the ban only applied to vegetables above ground, as if rain had fallen on them, not radiation. They just ate the carrots and beetroot and potatoes without giving it a thought.'[19]

'I have discovered another August pleasure in London, and that is to walk in the evening light around the new council estates,' John Betjeman announced in his *Spectator* column a few weeks after Macmillan's Bedford speech.

> Some of the latest are magnificent, and when one compares their open-ness, lightness, grass and trees, and carefully related changes of scale from tall blocks to small blocks, with the prison-like courts of artisans' dwellings of earlier ages, one realises that some things are better than they were. 'The awful equality of it all is frightening,' a friend said to me. And that is true. If you are lucky enough to have one of these new work-ers' flats, there is not much chance of showing individuality . . . But there are compensations. There are light and air, and the shrieks of children, instead of echoing against brick walls, are dispersed in open space.

Betjeman singled out for praise Brixton's Loughborough estate ('tall concrete and glass blocks turn out to be two-storey houses built on top of one another'), the Cremorne estate near World's End ('provides a quiet walk among grass and houses which are of pleasant texture and to human scale') and in particular the vast Churchill Gardens estate by the river. 'It is hygienic, egalitarian and frightening, but it has a beauty and can never deteriorate into the squalor of the parts of Pimlico it has replaced,' he declared. 'Maybe it has no place for someone like me, but it gives one hope for modern architecture.'

Increasingly, though, Betjeman was in embattled mode about the forces of modernity. In October, soon after he had lamented how 'the majority of building projects today in Britain are ones of vast bulk' (as typified by the City of London's Bucklersbury House, 'that monster now dwarfing everything between the Monument and St Paul's'), he was campaigning vigorously to save John Nash's Regent's Park terraces from the wrecking ball. And in December, responding to an MP who wanted to see Tower Bridge demolished, he argued in his column that 'the reason why people dislike the word "planning" and those connected with it is not because they object to new towns or to flowering cherries and civic centres, but because in their minds planning is associated with destruction'. 'Bombing we can take,' he went on. 'It is part of the fortunes of war. Fire may be carelessness. But the deliberate pulling down of a familiar street or building with associations, the felling of timber in a village and the destruction of old cottages is really playing about with part of ourselves. They are roots and home to somebody.' He ended with a caustic personal observation: 'I have always noticed that progressive architects and planners and, no doubt, the chief share-holders in those sinister development trusts which are buying up London and ruining it with oblong-ended packing cases, live in old houses and go to a good deal of trouble to protect their views.'[20]

Yet for the planners themselves – but *not* the architects or developers – the unpalatable truth in 1957 was that their high tide had already passed. 'One of the expressions of bewilderment that is most commonly heard in the profession,' the once highly influential town planner Thomas Sharp told his peers that spring, 'is that to most people plan-ning has now become just a colossal bore and that to many others it is something actually to dislike with an active hostility.' He added, not implausibly, that 'what is most disliked about us, I think, is that control which we exercise over other people's activities with so little obvious and acceptable result'. Peter Self of the Town and Country Planning Association tended to agree: 'Town planning questions ... seldom figure in party manifestos or wireless debates, and they arouse hardly any political controversy – more as a result of indifference than agree-ment. Planning controls are coming to be viewed as necessary evils, rather than as instruments for forging lasting benefits. A dead hand grips the spirit of planning.'

In late July the Institute of Contemporary Arts staged a highly charged meeting on the subject of 'planning controls' in London. Among architects speaking, Lionel Brett insisted that the case for control was ultimately to prevent 'the spivs' (i.e. presumably the devel-opers) from wrecking the environment; the ultra-modernist Peter Smithson was for complete abolition of aesthetic controls; and the equally modernist Ernö Goldfinger concurred. For the planners, Hertfordshire's County Planning Officer E. H. Doubleday spoke in unashamedly paternalistic vein about the value of planning control for 'arrogant young architects'. In a subsequent Third Programme talk, Brett astutely identified how on the part of younger architects there existed an increasing feeling that the post-war planners are out of touch with the real world of 1957, that our New Towns, neighbourhood centres, shopping precincts, national parks, etc, are not what is wanted and lack some essential thing that our old towns and neglected counties had, presumably spontaneity, so that nobody would ever want to paint a picture in Harlow or Bracknell . . . planners waste their time controlling elevations in Watford and Redhill when they should be concentrating their minds on Liverpool and Glasgow.

1960s-style urbanism, in short, was where the exciting future action lay, not 1940s-style planned dispersion. Brett added that, at the recent ICA meeting, 'the people on the platform in favour of planning control wore suits and ties and the people against it wore open shirts or turtle-necked jerseys'.[21]

In Liverpool itself, as in other major cities, the key players by this time were neither planners nor architects, nor yet developers or construction companies, but instead local politicians. 'It is already apparent that the eleven-storey blocks now going up are really insignificant when considered against their backgrounds and we are investigating very closely the possibility of going much higher,' stated Alderman David Nickson, Labour chairman of the Housing Committee, in early September, in the context of tower blocks rising on Everton Heights. 'This form of development is obviously the only answer to sprawl.' Later in the month he continued to insist that 'the Housing Committee take the view that there is no reason why the 20-storey mark should not be passed', adding that 'we regard this as important a step in the construction of domestic dwellings as was the breaking of the sound barrier in the world of aeronautics'. Soon afterwards the *Liverpool Echo*'s Municipal Correspondent wrote suitably portentously of time and the city:

Slowly but surely the face of Liverpool is changing and its terraced skyline, so familiar to travellers by sea arriving in or leaving the Mersey, is gradually taking on new features. Already Everton Brow is crowned with a mammoth block of flats [i.e. the ten-storey Cresswell Mount, opened in 1956], the symbol of the new Liverpool, and just below it, on the sweeping seaward slope, new twin blocks [i.e. The Braddocks], with the skeleton fingers of mammoth cranes reaching for the sky in close attendance, are fitting themselves into the landscape.

Just in case there were any doubters, he emphasised that the two new blocks were 'rising on a site that not so long ago was occupied by count-less mean cottages of uniform drab brick separated by narrow ditches of streets'.

Even so, when Nickson at the end of September reported on the Housing Committee's annual inspection of building developments, and set out again its aspirations for new blocks of up to 21 storeys, he was revealingly anxious about working-class families being housed high: 'They have always been used to the more ordinary type of dwelling, and we shall have to convince them of the advantages of this type of construction. If we can persuade the people to accept this type of build-ing as a reasonable type of home, then we will have achieved something worthwhile.'

At a City Council meeting in early October, the Tory councillor J. Maxwell Entwistle declared himself as supportive as the Labour group of high-rise blocks, and as opposed to unnecessary future over-spill to such places as Skelmersdale, Ellesmere Port or Widnes. 'Dislike flats as they might, the people of Liverpool would sooner stay, even in multi-storey buildings, than go to outlandish areas where there was little industry and the cost of getting back to the city was great.' Was that in fact a fair reflection of the wishes of Liverpudlians living in decaying inner-city areas? Easily the best evidence we have is the 1956 survey of residents of the Crown Street district: on the one hand, 61 per cent did indeed want to stay where they were, whether or not they were rehoused; on the other hand, in terms of those specifically living in houses *already* scheduled for slum-clearance demolition, almost half wished to move away entirely. Or, put another way, the survey's Liverpool University authors helpfully noted, 'variety, confusion and conflict prevailed both in the district as a whole and its sub-areas'.[22]

Across the Pennines, November 1957 saw the opening of a ten-storey block of flats about three-quarters of a mile from the centre of Leeds. This was the start of the Saxton Gardens development – hailed by the *Yorkshire Post* as 'one of the biggest post-war housing schemes of its kind in the Provinces' – with six further blocks, between five and nine storeys each, to be completed over the next year, altogether housing some 1,460 people on land that had been cleared of slums just before the war. That was when the nearby Quarry Hill estate had been opened, and its office now took on the additional management of Saxton Gardens. Indeed, with almost 4,000 people to be rehoused in due course in the York Road redevelopment scheme, which Saxton Gardens overlooked to the east, and a further 6,000 or so also to be rehoused in the Burmantofts area east of York Road, this meant, declared the *Post*, that 'Saxton Gardens will form part of a new central township with a population of more than 15,000 people.' On the day of the opening ceremony, the *Yorkshire Evening News* trumpeted loud and hard: 'With its central heating and domestic hot water in all dwellings, its gas or electric wash boiler with clothes drying cabinet in each flat; its 30 lifts and Garchey system of refuse disposal, Saxton Gardens reaches the heights of modern amenities.' At the ceremony itself, the major reported speech was given by Alderman F. H. O'Donnell, who had spent his boyhood on the Saxton Gardens site, then known as The Bank. 'To the people outside, The Bank was a place where policemen walked about in pairs. But, he pointed out, the people there 50 years ago worked hard for long hours and were as industrious, intelligent, and respectable as any in the country.' And O'Donnell ended by looking ahead: 'He hoped that the people of Saxton Gardens would be as good as the people of the old Bank, and that there would be not only 448 units of accommodation but 448 homes.'

Even the politicians of Bognor Regis had their dreams, as this autumn the possibility emerged of an apparently attractive deal with Billy Butlin, by means of which he would be permitted to build a holiday camp close to the town in return for knocking down his tatty funfair on the Esplanade and giving the land to the council. 'Not often does opportunity knock in so decisive a manner as it does in Bognor Regis today,' declared its chairman J. C. Earle.

> Facing, as they do, the finest sandy beach on the South Coast, the opportunities for really bold and imaginative architecture are immense. Tall, modern buildings in the style of Basil Spence, Corbusier or the many other gifted architects practising today are what I hope to see. Nothing pseudo, nothing shoddy, we must not tolerate drab brick boxes. This is

our chance to have beautiful architecture reflecting our day and age, and
we must seize it with firm hands. Fine hotels, luxury flats, a solarium,
shops, theatres and conference halls, and civic buildings can and should
arise, fronted by a broad, impressive seaway.

With only one dissenter, who argued that a Butlin's holiday camp would
be disastrous for Bognor's image, the deal was overwhelmingly
approved.[23]

Almost everywhere, but above all in the major conurbations, the
greatest engine of physical change was of course the slum-clearance
programme. Slum clearance in 'the atomic age' was the theme of an
address by Dr Ronald Bradbury (Liverpool's City Architect) to a
national housing conference in September, which included the estimate
that almost two-thirds of the 850,000 unfit dwellings in England and
Wales were concentrated in about one hundred industrial towns, headed
by Liverpool itself (88,233), followed by Manchester, Birmingham,
Leeds, London, Hull, Sheffield, Salford, Stoke-on-Trent, Oldham,
Bradford and Bristol – 'all of which', noted Bradbury, 'have very
considerable slum problems'.

In third-placed Birmingham, it was around this time that demolition
began in the Ladywood district, a process of slum clearance that from
the start seems to have been carried out in a horribly flawed way, at
least to judge by the subsequent *cri de coeur* of Canon Norman Power
of St John's, Ladywood – *not* an opponent of slum clearance in principle. 'In all this redevelopment, during which I saw a living community
torn to pieces by the bulldozers and scattered to the four corners of the
city,' he recalled in 1965 in his short, devastating book *The Forgotten
People*, 'there was no consultation with the people most affected and
concerned. Neither was any opinion sought from local teachers, social
workers, organisation-leaders or clergy.' Crucially, Ladywood's demolition started not with the worst housing, but instead with some of the
better; Power surmised that 'probably the need to clear a space for the
new Inner Circle Road was one motive'. Overall, he went on, 'The
heart of our community was destroyed. A living, corporate personality
was crushed by the bulldozers. There were some extraordinary and
inexplicable side-effects. The new Waste Land was left waste for seven
years. But it was not cleared. It was left a wilderness of brick-ends, tin

cans, broken bottles and even half-demolished buildings.' In short, 'It
was the best school of vandalism I have ever seen.'

Elsewhere, the *Salford City Reporter* announced towards the end of
1957 that '"HANKY PARK" AREA WILL SOON DISAPPEAR' –
the district which, back in the 1930s, 'gained notoriety in Walter
Greenwood's *Love on the Dole*' – while in Bristol some 10,000 houses
were identified as needing to be cleared in the next five years, including
among the steeply sloping Georgian terraces of Kingsdown, thus leading to protests from Betjeman downwards. In London the ongoing
development of Notting Hill Gate (already involving considerable
demolition ahead of planned road-widening, the replacement of the
two existing underground stations on opposite sides of the road by a
single station under it, and the construction of two tall slab blocks of
flats as well as many new shops and offices) was likewise a source of
unhappiness. 'The Village Behind The "Gate"' was the title of some
verses that J. F. Adams of Bulmer Place sent in November to the local
paper:

> Once we were happy the whole day through,
> With neat gardens where our flowers grew;
> There's not many left, sad to relate,
> In the Village behind the 'Gate' . . .

> We'll dig up our roots and home ties,
> Remember those welcomes and final goodbyes
> Of loved ones passed on early and late
> In the Village behind the 'Gate'.

> But there will be no friendship in skyscraper flats
> Or leaning on garden fence for chats,
> And help your neighbour in this new estate,
> Like we did in the Village behind the 'Gate'.

As it happened, it was not so far away, in the Kensington drawing
room of the Victorian artist Linley Sambourne, that (a few days earlier)
the Countess of Rosse had acted as hostess at a meeting to form the
preservationist Victorian Group (later Society). Betjeman was present,

as was the leading architectural journalist of the day, that qualified modernist (and suburb-loving, but New Town-hating) J. M. Richards. 'On the whole,' Richards suggested in vain soon afterwards, 'it had better avoid calling itself "Victorian" – the word now has overtones of funniness.'[24]

The Victorian era seemed remote enough when in due course the *Architects' Journal* ran its feature 'Buildings of the Year: 1957'. Presenting 'the uncensored opinions' of the users of a dozen or more newly completed buildings, the tone was largely positive. 'Smashing!' declared James Loft, a 52-year-old worker who had spent ten years in the dust of a cement factory before coming to the Bowater-Scott Tissue Mill, producing Andrex toilet rolls, at Northfleet, Kent. 'You don't know what the weather's like outside: it's practically always the same temperature in here.' Generally there,

> The workers, when asked what they like, find it difficult to put in words. Sally Donoghue, the shop steward in the converting department, said the girls liked the press button machinery. 'It's very modern, isn't it?' she said. Could she suggest any improvements? The answer was a simple, 'No.' Beryl Duff, a pretty Irish girl who was packing, said 'It's a good place to work in: it's modern, isn't it?' And pressed to say what she means by 'modern', she says it's light, airy and colourful. The very high quality of the toilet accommodation was mentioned by everybody who was interviewed, and Mr Morley [assistant manager] has found that it is appreciated by the staff and properly treated.

Elsewhere, Sir Vincent Tewson, General Secretary of the TUC, praised its new headquarters in Great Russell Street as 'a piece of contemporary architecture our eight million members can be proud of'; recently married Daphne Jones on the 14th floor of Great Arthur House, on the Golden Lane estate just north of the City of London, loved the 'feeling of being out in the open', with the balcony being 'like sitting in a garden', while in Basterfield House, one of the estate's four maisonette blocks, Angela Hobday, a nurse at Bart's, found it all 'exciting, so new and different, and such fun to be living in'; at Dunn's in Bromley (specialists in selling modern furniture), the managing director Geoffrey Dunn was almost entirely happy with his quasi-brutalist new premises, noting that he had had 'letters from perfect strangers, and not from such high falutin' addresses either, congratulating us on adding this shop to the town'; and at a primary school in Amersham, two small boys with caps askew, Geoffrey Magee and Garry Livemore, offered a spontaneous volley of praise – 'Super!' 'Smashing!' 'Supersonic!' – with the magazine reckoning that 'what appeals to the children most is the colour, the glass, the wallpapers, the lighting, in a word the bright modernity of the interior, as much as the practical arrangements'. The feature, though, did include a couple of grumblers. On the Claremont estate in West Ham, Mrs Nellie Richardson (living with her bus-conductor husband and four small children) was adamant that a flat 'isn't really a place for a family', adding that 'most of the time you have to say to the children, "keep it down a bit"'. And at the factory-like Churchfields Comprehensive (845 pupils in six completely isolated blocks) in West Bromwich, the headmaster Mr Hobart not only found the use of glass 'quite excessive', especially in south-facing rooms like his own study, but called the sound insulation 'downright disgusting'.

There were mixed feelings, too, in a vox pop survey late in 1957 of Britain's most emblematic city of post-war reconstruction. 'Generally, it is the older Coventrians who are least happy,' found the *Sunday Times*. '"Horrible ugly boxes!" they rail, as the new blocks go up. But the youngsters, with no nostalgic memories of the old town, are delighted. "The new cathedral," exclaimed a young typist with real fervour, "is going to be *beautiful* – lovely and bright, you know, not a gloomy old place like they usually are."' Even so, it was probably not all that aged a waitress who, in the Civic Restaurant, 'gazed wistfully across the new Broadgate at an isolated block of pseudo-Tudor beyond', and said, 'I'd have liked little black-and-white buildings really, but the foreign visitors all say this is wonderful.' The piece's accompanying photographs (including of the vast, glass-sided Owen Owen's depart-ment store) provoked a cross letter from a reader in the south-east. 'I see nothing admirable in the new Coventry,' he asserted. 'The large buildings illustrated last week might do for a prison or a boot factory, but I don't think they would do for the patrons of Nash and Wren. The style is ungentlemanly.' To which John Hewitt, the Ulster poet who had recently become curator of Coventry's new Herbert Art Gallery and Museum, replied a week later that the new centre of Coventry is built to a human scale . . . Coventry is not a capital city with the necessity for State architecture, impressive to visitor and reassuring to citizen. It does not belong either to the age of Wren or Nash. It is an industrial city, where motor-cars and aeroplanes and machine tools are manufactured. Having lived here for six months any other industrial town depresses me with the heavy pomposity and grimy insincerity of its architecture.

Meanwhile, one footloose, hard-to-please Londoner was finding everything disagreeable. 'On the whole a dull, disappointing tramp,' recorded Anthony Heap in November after a Sunday inspection of Denmark Hill, Herne Hill and Camberwell. 'Pleasantly picturesque this hilly part of South London may have been fifty years ago. Today it's just a dreary wilderness of uniform blocks of drab new council flats, and dilapidated old Victorian villas. And I'm not sure which look the most depressing.'[25]

'John went to football,' noted Judy Haines in Chingford on Saturday, 12 October, the day after the Windscale fire had been put out. 'I mowed the lawn. So much to do.' That same day the Tory conference (in Brighton, like Labour's) ended, with the party's new chairman, Lord Hailsham, the undoubted star and doing much to boost flagging, mid-term, post-Suez morale. Early each morning he appeared on the seafront in a blue dressing gown, bathing trunks and bedroom slippers, ready to take a chilly dip; his oration one evening to the Conservative Political Centre, containing a fierce, uninhibited attack on the conduct of the trade unions, was, according to Mollie Panter-Downes, 'rapturously hailed next day, over the conference coffee cups and cocktail glasses, as being "as good as one of Winston's wartime speeches"'. On the Saturday morning itself, winding up the conference, 'that stocky, rumpled figure' with a 'cherubic, aggressive face' (as she described Hailsham) found a prop and let himself go. 'At the end of his speech,' reported the *Sunday Times*,

he stretched out his hand and gripped the large handbell which Mrs Walter Elliot, the chairman, had used during the conference. Holding it above his head and ringing it with enthusiasm he said: 'Let it ring more loudly. Let it ring for victory.' As the delegates rose to their feet and cheered and stamped, Lord Hailsham shouted: 'Let us say to the Labour Party "Seek not to inquire for whom the bell tolls. It tolls for thee."'

At least one commentator, Francis Williams, was viewing the 50-year-old Hailsham by the end of the week as 'a potential prime minister', but Hailsham himself was quick to reassure Macmillan of his 'unqualified loyalty and support', adding, 'I am not quite such an ass as I seem.' Macmillan himself, just before the conference, had privately pondered his government's position. 'At the moment, the whole thing is swinging *away* from us,' he readily conceded. 'If we cannot bring back the traditional strength of the Party to the fold – small shopkeepers, middle class, etc., – we have no chance. But we also need at least three million trade union votes. We have a war on two flanks.' Over and above such tactical considerations was the increasingly asked question of what was to be done about national decline, relative though it may have been. Or, as a youngish *Daily Express* journalist with misplaced political ambitions, the future historian Maurice Cowling, put it from a particular perspective in a letter to the *Listener* later in October,

Many people in Britain – not only tories, not only tories of the right, and not only members of the middle-class – fear that an infernal conjunction of inflation, excessive taxation, trade-union irresponsibility, governmental interference and governmental timidity have in the recent past been undermining Britain's social stability and may in the future destroy her economic prosperity.[26]

It was a different kind of decline that the contributors to *Declaration*, published the same month, mostly addressed. Edited by an ambitious 24-year-old publisher, Tom Maschler, the book was a gathering-up of those more or less connected with the 'Angry Young Men' (AYM) phenomenon, his only two refuseniks being Kingsley Amis and Iris Murdoch. Among the eight essayists, Doris Lessing (at 37 the oldest contributor and only woman) expressed her frustration at the 'kindly, pleasant, tolerant' British people, 'apparently content to sink into ever-greater depths of genteel poverty because of the insistence of our rulers on spending so much of the wealth we produce on preparations for a war against communism'; Colin Wilson went 'beyond the Outsider'; John Osborne, writing late and furiously, took scattergun aim, including at the Royal Family – 'the gold filling in a mouthful of decay'; Kenneth Tynan observed that 'the trouble with most Socialist drama, and with much Socialist thinking, is its joylessness'; and Lindsay Anderson coined the phrase 'chips with everything' (about the culinary ordeal of returning to Britain from abroad), called the absence of working-class characters from British films 'characteristic of a flight from contemporary reality', and claimed that Amis would 'rather pose as a Philistine than run the risk of being despised as an intellectual'.

Critical reaction was largely negative. J. W. Lambert in the *Sunday Times* was particularly hard on Anderson, not least his 'curiously old-fashioned worship of what he calls the "working-classes"', having failed to 'notice that the very nature of this stratum of society is changing'. So too Angus Wilson, at 44 possibly not unjealous of the AYM. 'We have rhetoric, exhortation, apocalyptic spine-chilling, smart-aleckry – each and all rather earnest and repetitive – but the total content is trivial,' he asserted in the *Observer*. And soon after, on the Third Programme, the middle-aged critic Alan Pryce-Jones frankly accused the eight of contempt for the public: 'They dislike it for one set of reasons if they are materialists. In that case, other people seem dull, gullible, and snobbish. If on the other hand they are transcendentalists, they accuse the public of lack of purpose, torpidity, unawareness.' Still, *Declaration* sold some 20,000 copies, made a lot of noise and put Maschler firmly on the map.[27]

Also in October, on Saturday the 19th, an undeniably authentic working man, Billy McPhail, scored three second-half headed goals in Celtic's 7–1 trouncing of Rangers in the Scottish League Cup Final, which was played with the usual heavy, laced ball. A third of a century later, long after the end of his professional career, McPhail would lose his claim in the courts for compensation, even though he had been suffering from pre-senile dementia since his thirties. Twelve days after his hat-trick, another Scottish working man, Lawrence Daly, attended a meeting at Glencraig Colliery, Fife – where there had been a plethora of unofficial stoppages over the past year – between National Coal Board management (including G. Mullin, Area General Manager) and

National Union of Mineworkers' officials (including Daly himself as local branch delegate). 'The position at Glencraig is very serious,' insisted Mullin. 'We spent money on this pit and the output should improve. Unless there is improvement, I may be compelled by circumstances to recommend to the Divisional Board to consider whether it is worthwhile carrying this pit on or not.' To which Daly riposted, 'You have refused to listen to the complaints from Glencraig for 15 years.' But Mullin was adamant: 'I would say to you people here, let a man examine himself – and you Mr Daly are talking about a manager being to blame – I think you are just as much to be blamed for the atmosphere at this pit. That is the impression I get from your manner and demeanour at this meeting.'

Towards the end, after Mullin had referred to an under-official being recently threatened by a miner, Daly baldly asserted that 'if men are treated as human beings that is not likely to happen'. Daly – an articulate, even charismatic man in his early 40s – had left the Communist Party the previous year and was starting to become the New Left's emblematic working-class representative. 'I can see how to carry on our cultural and intellectual work all right, and perhaps how to deepen and extend it,' E. P. Thompson wrote to Daly earlier in the month after staying at Glencraig with him and his wife Renée. 'But in the practical organisational side I am puzzled and depressed. I think there is a 50/50 chance that a new left party may in the end get formed, because I don't see how the broader labour movement will be transformed without an electoral threat being presented on the left of the official LP.'[28]

Daly, with a fine tenor voice, enjoyed singing Scottish and Irish folk songs, but like many in the New Left had little enthusiasm for commercial pop music. Top of the charts at the start of November were the Crickets with 'That'll Be The Day' – the vocal style as well as spectacles of their leader, Buddy Holly, an inspiration to the short-sighted John Lennon, by now at art college, while on Saturday the 16th, *Six-Five Special* was broadcast live from the 2i's coffee bar in Soho. The line-up included the pink-haired rocker Wee Willie Harris, seen calling Gilbert Harding (an improbable presence) 'daddy-o'; comedians Mike and Bernie Winters; and the Worried Men, whose Terry Nelhams would go on to become Adam Faith. The 2i's' most famous alumnus, Tommy Steele, was also present in a co-hosting role, just 48 hours before topping the bill at the Palladium's Royal Variety performance, a bill that featured (among others) Gracie Fields, Judy Garland, Tommy Cooper, Vera Lynn and Alma Cogan. That night, the week after his ninth birthday – marked by an unprecedentedly informal, hand-in-the-pocket official photograph by Cecil Beaton's usurper, the more modern-minded Antony Armstrong-Jones – there was no place in the royal box for Prince Charles, confined to quarters at prep school; but the Crazy Gang, lining up to meet the Queen, wore blue Cheam blazers and caps, with a large 'C' badge. Steele himself, reported the *News Chronicle*, initially struggled:

> His first number, 'Rock With The Caveman', ended in dull silence from an icy audience. The young Rock and Roll King started on 'Hound Dog'. Still the audience did not respond.
>
> Then, from the Royal Box high up on the right, somebody was heard clapping in rhythm. It was the Queen Mother.
>
> Once she turned to her daughter as if to say: 'Come on, dear,' but the Queen refrained. After a little, the Duke of Edinburgh started, rather half-heartedly, and off-beat.

Within weeks 'The Pied Piper from Bermondsey' was the subject of an *Encounter* profile by Colin MacInnes, who saw in Steele ('every nice young girl's boy, every kid's favourite elder brother, every mother's cherished adolescent son') the harbinger of a possible English challenge to the dominance of American songs and performers. Coming from whichever side of the herring pond, all this youth culture largely passed Gladys Langford by. In poor health in her late 60s, living alone in a room in Highbury Barn, she kept her diary going despite severe bouts of depression. 'Waiting to cross Highbury New Park,' she recorded on the last Thursday of November, 'I was amazed by the chivalry of the lorry-driver's mate, a handsome Teddy boy who leapt from the cabin and led me across the road like a courtly knight errant.'[29]

Other diarists this month focused on the unfolding Space Age. 'The 2nd Russian Satellite launched with a dog on board,' noted Gladys Hague, living with her sister in Keighley, on 3 November. 'Protests voiced from all over the world.' Or, as Macmillan wryly put it two days later, 'The English people, with characteristic frivolity, are much more exercised about the "little dawg" than about the terrifying nature of these new developments in "rocketry."' The dog, popularly known as Laika, 'obsessed the public imagination', wrote Mollie Panter-Downes. And when she was officially pronounced dead, recorded Frances Partridge on the 15th, 'the *Daily Mirror* came out with a wide border of black, and a great deal about soft noses and velvety eyes up there in the stratosphere'.

As for the satellite itself, degrees of excitement took several forms. 'It is far more momentous than the invention of the wheel, the discovery of the sail, the circumnavigation of the globe, or the wonders of the industrial revolution,' Anthony Wedgwood Benn reckoned in his diary on the 5th; at a Church Assembly meeting in London on the 12th, one speaker declared the Church should send a Sputnik into outer space with a bishop inside it, given that 'the present generation, founded on technology and science, is more interested in the "bleep, bleep" of the satellite than the "bleep, bleep" of the preacher'; and for almost a fortnight satellite-like shapes could again be spotted on the front page of the *FT*.

The canine aspect apart, perhaps the most striking thing about the episode was, a year after the USA had brutally pulled the plug on Eden's war against Nasser, the extent of the pleasure taken in America's technological humiliation – or what Panter-Downes tactfully described to her *New Yorker* readers as 'the slight chuckle with which a man might note the discomfiture of the rich neighbor across the way whose Cadillac has suddenly refused to start'. A few weeks later, the failure of an American rocket provoked some almost gleeful headlines from Fleet Street ('US calls it Kaputnik', 'Ike's Phutnik', 'Oh, What a Flopnik!'), while by the following spring schoolchildren were chanting the rhyme

Catch a falling sputnik,
Put it in a matchbox,
Send it to the USA
They'll be glad to get it,
Very glad to get it,
Send it to the USA

to the tune of Perry Como's 'Catch a Falling Star'.[30]

On Monday the 11th, Armistice Day, John Sandoe opened his

high-class bookshop in Chelsea, despite his grandmother's shock about
the absence of shutters to cover the windows on Sundays. Next day, Sir
Robert Fraser, director general of the Independent Television Authority
(ITA), gave a press conference robustly criticising the BBC and defending commercial television, while *Woman's Hour* had at least one irritated listener. 'That wretched "know all" Ruth Drew took part in telling us "how",' noted Judy Haines. 'Another was telling us "how" in
regard to fish, and another "how" in regard to washing, but Ruth *loves*
housework. She takes a duster in *each* hand so that she doesn't waste
time with the odd hand! Of course, I only hate her because she's not
good for my conscience.' That same day, the Post Office's announcement of plans to introduce postal codes was neatly balanced by the
Advisory County Cricket Committee's decision at Lord's to shelve yet
again a proposed knockout competition. Arguably, though, the overall
mood was for change, for two days later Buckingham Palace let it be
known that after 1958 debutantes would no longer be presented at
court, a decision effectively ending 'the Season' and perhaps reflecting
Princess Margaret's reputed disgust that 'every tart in London can get
in'.[31]

'The conventional characters of "good BBC" and "bad ITA"
belong to the land of myth and fable,' Fraser had asserted at his press
conference, responding to disparaging remarks by the head of BBC
television. 'We are often told we have audiences of morons: we think
we have an audience of men and women . . . What some regard as the
herd, we respect as the human family.' Fraser was certainly talking
from a continuing position of strength, having the day before given
the key facts to Wedgwood Benn. 'In 4.5 million homes with choice,
75 per cent prefer ITA, 25 per cent preferring BBC if you include
children,' the Labour MP duly noted. 'Excluding children the figures
are 70/30.' Later in the week he lunched with the BBC's Mary
Adams: 'She said they were absolutely defeated and in a complete
dither.'

Still, the original television channel had its undoubted glories, not
least the scriptwriters Ray Galton and Alan Simpson. 'There's a bite to
Hancock's Half Hour,' observed the critic John Metcalf soon afterwards, 'a willingness to accept the worst in all of us, to make social and
human observations that belong to the satirist rather than the clown.'

So too *Tonight*, soon to move to a 6.45 start and increasingly addictive to members of the Viewers' Panel:

> The whole programme is good from beginning to end. It also has the essence of surprise – you don't know what to expect next (which is the very thing that makes it hold you, I believe).
>
> I would sooner miss my evening meal than miss this harmonious three (Cliff Michelmore, Derek Hart and Geoffrey Johnson Smith).

There had also been a sharpening-up in a key area. 'The BBC, inspired by ITV News, has improved the manner of its news presentation,' reckoned the *Spectator*'s John Cowburn in his end-of-year TV review, 'so that it is no longer the voice of the Establishment talking to the poor gammas.' Even so, for the medium as a whole, paternalism remained the order of the day: not only did the Postmaster General, Ernest Marples, refuse in December to allow an extension of viewing hours ('It is not only quantity but general quality and balance which has to be borne in mind') but many among the progressive intelligentsia disdained to acquire a set, so that, as Doris Lessing recalled, 'One could more or less work out someone's political bias by the attitude he took towards television.' Of course, there were variations. At the end of January, Michael Young was informing the anthropologist Geoffrey Gorer that his co-author Peter Willmott had become 'a real television addict': 'He says that he has not been to a cinema since December 16th when he acquired his new set.'[32]

Young passed on this titbit in the context of Gorer having been engaged since the autumn on a detailed investigation of television-watching habits. Adults were surveyed in November, leading to some suggestive statistics: 59 per cent of the upper middle class never had the set switched on while they were eating, compared to an overall average of 46 per cent; 22 per cent, mainly from the working class, always had the set on during meals; and, in answer to the question 'How important is television in your daily conversation?', 52 per cent overall replied, 'not at all important' (66 per cent in the case of the upper middle class). One of Gorer's 'greatest surprises' from the study was 'the apparent almost complete absence of emotional involvement of the viewers with "TV personalities"', while in general he reckoned that 'although TV will help somewhat to identify people who appear on the screen fairly

frequently its influence as a form of political education and enlightenment is practically non-existent'.

Two months later it was the turn of children to give their views:

> I would rather go out really; go down to the coffee bar or stay with a
> friend, we have the records on. Yes, records are more important. *(Jean
> Milner, 14, girls' grammar, Stoke-on-Trent)*
>
> Everyone sits down and watches it; you don't talk as much as you used
> to. If anyone came in, you used to talk – now you watch the television.
> *(Elaine Bate, 14, girls' grammar, Stoke-on-Trent)*
>
> I don't think some programmes it is a timewaster but with others it is.
> Such as these cowboy Westerns – I can't see what use you get from them
> but I watch them just the same. *(Peter Sockett, 14, secondary modern,
> Sheffield)*
>
> I ask if we can have it on and if my brother wants the BBC, there is
> always a row going on. *(Janet Slack, 10, primary, Sheffield)*
>
> I think I have learned a lot from it – Panorama and Tonight, these
> specially I like. Some of the comedy programmes haven't taught me
> much. *(D. J. Bettany, 15, boys' grammar, Newcastle-under-Lyme)*
>
> Westerns – you get sick of them. *(David Wise, 14, secondary modern,
> Crawley)*

Gorer's conclusion was that television had only two major effects on
young people: it made them stay at home more, and it made them go to
bed later. The *Manchester Guardian*'s television critic, in a swingeing
attack just before Christmas on ITV's fare for children, was much less
inclined to ignore the moral dimension. 'There is a certain amount of
crime and violence in these programmes,' he complained, 'but almost as
disturbing is the tawdry and trashy character of the incessant films and
series.' And he instanced *The Buccaneers* – 'a sort of pseudo-Stevenson
tale, in which, as in all ITV serials, neither character nor dialogue matter
one jot; action, crude, abrupt, and almost mechanical, is all that matters'.
Even *Robin Hood*, 'which I had thought passable when commercial
television began, now seems to have deteriorated into the same perfunctory, empty bustle as all the rest of the film serials'. In fact, the only
saving grace was *Rin-Tin-Tin*, 'the most humane of these affairs,
perhaps because this handsome dog can neither talk nor shoot'.

Radio's principal innovation this autumn was the coming of *Today* on the Home Service, in effect as the sound equivalent of *Tonight*. It began as two 20-minute strands, either side of *Lift Up Your Hearts* and the eight o'clock news; its debut on 28 October featured Petula Clark, interviews with a pilot and plane passenger, record reviews, Robert Morley on a first night, Eamonn Andrews on boxing, and an item about an auction of Napoleon's letters – a miscellany with not a hint of politics, let alone a bruising interview. It was not until the following summer that the raffish Jack de Manio, with his gin-and-tonic voice, became the main presenter, and another five years before *Today* more systematically focused on news and current affairs. *The Archers* remained the favourite radio programme, with some 18 million listeners. In late November a survey was conducted, and many fans 'paid tribute to the authentic atmosphere of the Ambridge community', as in the words of a police sergeant's wife: 'The characters – foolish, kind, wise and occasionally spiteful – make a very realistic programme.' A salesman's wife, however, found the female characters less plausible. 'Why are all the women rather crudely drawn? They whine, they nag, they grumble, they are usually very silly and demanding; and when they *are* good, they are very, very dull.'[33]

The run-up to Christmas began for Judy Haines on the last day of November. 'Had an enjoyable but exhausting time in Gamage's,' she recorded. 'Girls got pencil cases from Father Christmas and enjoyed the Animal Show. I ordered four articles to be sent home.' The following Wednesday afternoon, in dense fog near Lewisham, the 4.56 steam express from Cannon Street to Ramsgate crashed into a stationary electric train, bringing down a bridge carrying a loop line over the track path and altogether killing 90 people. 'Bodies shrouded in blankets and coats lay in a long row beside the track,' reported the *Manchester Guardian*. 'Alongside were strewn handbags, gloves, shoes, and gaily wrapped Christmas parcels.' That was a disaster, down to human error as well as the weather, but later in the month three scandals began to unfold. On the 7th, in Thurso, a police officer was provoked by a foul-mouthed 15-year-old grocer's boy ('you think you're a smart fucker') into hitting him, leading to complaints which the police dismissed before the local MP eventually forced a public inquiry, amidst considerable parliamentary disquiet about a cover-up. On the 9th, the former and future right-wing Labour MP Woodrow Wyatt exposed on *Panorama* the gerrymandering practices of the Communist-led Electrical Trades Union, most recently its cynical blackballing of Les Cannon, the union's gifted Education Officer who had resigned from the CP over Hungary. And on the 19th, the Commons debated the recently exposed abuses at Rampton Mental Hospital near Retford, Nottinghamshire, where the mentally ill rubbed shoulders with violent criminals. Amidst all this, the critic Hilary Corke (in the *Listener* on the 12th) ferociously attacked Doris Lessing (a writer 'of absolutely no importance'); the 14-year-old future critic, Lorna Stockton, went to her first, dismal school dance in Whitchurch, Shropshire and met Vic Sage ('temples glistening with sweat and Brylcreem'); and on the 16th, in a live TV transmission of *Hancock's Half Hour*, much of the scenery fell prematurely apart, leaving Hancock to play an entire scene holding up a table. But at least the audience was laughing – unlike for the most part at *Barnacle Bill*, the final Ealing comedy, released just before Christmas to a critical panning summed up by Isabel Quigly's three words, 'a big flop'. It was comic cuts, though, at a cold, wet Valley on Saturday the 21st, as ten-man Charlton Athletic came from 5-1 down to beat the visitors Huddersfield Town 7-6, leaving their manager, Bill Shankly, for once speechless until the train back reached Peterborough.[34]

A running subplot during December was the 'Bank Rate Tribunal'. Reluctantly granted by Macmillan under political pressure, and sitting at Church House, Westminster under Lord Justice Parker, its brief was to determine whether there had been a 'leak' that accounted for the heavy selling of gilt-edged stocks just before the 2-per-cent rise in the Bank Rate on 19 September. The individuals under most suspicion were two of the Bank of England's non-executive directors, Lord Kindersley of Lazards and W. J. ('Tony') Keswick of Mathesons. Keswick's cross-examination on the 6th, conducted by the Attorney General, Sir Reginald Manningham-Buller, included the question of what he and his brother had discussed five days before the rise. 'It is difficult for me,' he observed in a memorable phrase that would be much cited, 'to remember the exact timing of conversation on a grouse moor.' Overall, Macmillan was privately reflecting by the second week that the evidence to the tribunal, 'tho' not really damaging, does the Capitalist system as a whole no particular good', while the following week the City establishment's increasing vexation with the proceedings was encapsulated by Kindersley's angry missive to the banker George Bolton about Manningham-Buller's 'offensive' winding-up speech: 'If he was the next gun to me tomorrow I would certainly use my cartridges in a different direction to the pheasants!!!' Even so, for outsiders it was a fascinating spectacle, watching (as Panter-Downes put it) 'a succession of spruce, pink-joweled City gentlemen easing themselves and their briefcases into the witness chair' and speaking a 'totally different language' about '"comparatively small"' deals of a million or so pounds. 'It has all been a revealing glimpse into a special, jealously guarded world,' she added, and 'many Conservatives are wondering what the average hard-up voter is going to make of it'.[35]

Christmas Day was marked by the Queen's first Christmas television broadcast, live from the Long Library at Sandringham. 'That it is possible for some of you to see me today is just another example of the speed at which things are changing all round us,' she observed. 'Because of these changes, I am not surprised that many people feel lost and unable to decide what to hold on to and what to discard, how to take advantage of the new life without losing the best of the old.' Viewers were predictably delighted:

> Her Majesty was so natural and her message must surely have moved and inspired many viewers. The innovation of TV in the Queen's home made us feel, as she herself said, that she is really our friend and not a removed figure.
>
> Her Majesty's relaxed, sincere and charming approach was captivating. It seemed in contrast to her former style of speaking, which always struck me as slightly aloof.
>
> A real thrill to see the Queen so clearly and so close.

It was a prosperous-feeling Christmas in Chingford. 'Had a picnic lunch in the lounge, which was most enjoyable,' Judy Haines noted two days later. 'Now we have electric fires in both dining and lounge we can use both rooms at a moment's notice.' Another diarist, Dennis Dee, was just starting out. A farm worker and horse breaker turning himself into a horse, pig and poultry breeder, he was 31 and had recently acquired a smallholding in the East Riding village of Winestead. A countryman of few words, he began his journal at the start of 1958 as economically as he intended to go on:

> *1 January.* Keen frost today. W [his wife Wendy] went to Hedon to see her mother. I am working for Mr Patchett at 'Westlands Farm', Winestead.
> *2 January.* More frost. I punctured George's car today.
> *3 January.* Frosty again today. Mowing the big ditches out at Westlands.
> *4 January.* Milder weather. Started to cut the large rough hedge round the paddock. A big job and a hard one.

That same day, Saturday the 4th, fellow diarist Madge Martin went to the Old Vic to see *A Midsummer Night's Dream*, in which 'Frankie Howerd, the comedian from the music-halls and radio, was a good, but quiet Bottom', playing alongside (she did not mention) Ronald Fraser as Flute and Judi Dench as First Fairy; next day, Anthony Heap visited his mentally unstable wife Marjorie at Friern Barnet, to which she had recently returned and where the doctors were going to try 'electric shock treatment' again. The weekend also saw, amidst stirring scenes, the last passenger train run between Abergavenny and Merthyr Tydfil. 'I have lived in a house where the back garden adjoins the line,' Graham Jones of 36 Rhyd-y-cae, Rassau wrote soon afterwards to the *Merthyr Express*.

> The trains passing by have formed part of our lives. Last Monday was so quiet and then we realised that no longer would those grand ladies of the steam track pass by again. To many on-lookers we may seem perhaps sentimental and a little foolish, but that sad last train with its even sadder whistles as it graced the track for the last time was to me and many others the end of something in our lives which will never be replaced.[36]

5

Not a Matter of Popularity

On Monday, 6 January 1958 a disgruntled housewife in Paddington gave her Detergent Survey interview to Mass-Observation; Dennis Dee in Winestead did 'hedging and ditching at the farm' amidst 'heavy rain nearly all the day'; Madge Martin in Oxford went to *Barnacle Bill* at the Ritz ('amusing enough, but a little too farcical'); Judy Haines in Chingford took her daughters as a pre-school treat to Norman Wisdom's *Just My Luck* at the Odeon ('no indication as to where queues should form until opening time and there was a great reshuffle in the wind and rain'); the Queen took Charles and Anne to the Bertram Mills Circus at Olympia ('both the Royal children bounced up and down in their seats with excitement');[1] and all three Treasury ministers resigned – a unique event in twentieth-century British political history.[2]

The story had begun a year earlier when Macmillan, as the new prime minister, had chosen his Treasury team: Peter Thorneycroft as Chancellor of the Exchequer, Enoch Powell as Financial Secretary and Nigel Birch as Economic Secretary. The 47-year-old Thorneycroft, president of the Board of Trade since 1951, was a capable, seasoned politician whose main quirk was dropping into fashionable 1930s' Cockney twang at the end of sentences, and Macmillan had deployed him as campaign manager in the post-Eden succession battle with Rab Butler. Few doubted Thorneycroft's free-market instincts. 'No system of social security, no schemes of unemployment insurance,' he had written ten years earlier, 'are a substitute for enterprise, hard work, modern methods and up-to-date machinery,' adding that Keynesian 'remedies for unemployment still remain in the realm of theory'. And at the Board of Trade, his implacable opposition to import controls to protect the Lancashire textile industry had earned him the sobriquet 'the hangman of Lancashire' from Cyril Lord. Thorneycroft's instincts were shared by his two junior ministers: Powell, fresh from steering through legislation to decontrol rents in the private housing sector, and Birch, an acerbic operator who had made his fortune as a stockbroker. In Powell's case, though, there was a paradox, namely the juxtaposition of a classical free-market approach (including, later in 1957, pushing fruitlessly for an extensive denationalisation programme) with a deep-dyed English nationalism. As William Rees-Mogg would put it after Powell's death, 'his two big ideas were not entirely compatible with each other'. For Powell himself in 1957, his new post – requiring uncompromising Gladstonian parsimony resting upon unbending will-power and unassailable grasp of detail – felt like destiny calling. 'As frigid as any spell woven by some ice maiden of a Nordic saga', noted one parliamentary sketch writer of his performance in May. 'Under his chilling touch the Finance Bill was laid out like a fish on a slab.'[3]

Within weeks of his appointment in January 1957, Thorneycroft was taking a hard, unyielding, non-Keynesian line. The government, he told his Cabinet colleagues at the end of the month, 'spends too much, drifts into inflation, then seeks to cure the situation by fiscal and budgetary measures'. And in case anyone misunderstood, he reiterated: 'We shrink from the measures necessary to cut expenditure, and inflation starts again.' His Budget in April was avowedly 'disinflationary', emphasising the indispensable 'maintenance of a satisfactory budget balance'; the next month he wrote to Macmillan insisting that government not 'spend more than we are spending already', asking for his support to help counter the inevitable pressure from spending ministers, and claiming there was a 'real danger' of 'an economic crash – or at any rate a suffi-cient stumble to throw the Conservatives out of office for quite a considerable time'.

During July, Thorneycroft's analysis of what needed to be done to slay the inflationary dragon developed significantly. On the 17th (three days before Macmillan's Bedford speech sought to highlight the dangers of inflation) he told the Cabinet that 'we should lose no opportunity of making it clear in public that the source of our inflationary disease is wages increasing out of all proportion to increases in production' – an understandable enough approach in the wake of the unions' victory in the engineering and shipbuilding strikes that spring. But by the 30th, his line to Macmillan was that 'the only resolute action which is really within the power of the Government' was 'to restrict the supply of money to the point where cost and price increases were checked by severe unemployment' – a strategy, he accepted, that 'would involve cuts in public investment and checking private investment by a savage credit squeeze'. In short, it was an embryonic form of monetarism, though the term itself had yet to be coined, and almost certainly, moreover, monetarism of a less full-blooded kind than that embraced by either Powell or Birch.

Then came September's sterling crisis, largely caused by 'hot money' speculators. A Keynesian economist, J.C.R. Dow, subsequently reflected that what was 'remarkable' about Thorneycroft's view of the crisis was 'the way in which he accepted rising prices at home as the cause of the run on the reserves'. Or, as the historian Ewen Green has suggested, it was an emergency that – for all Thorneycroft's undoubted, deeply sincere wish to protect the currency – also provided him 'with one more stick to belabour his colleagues into accepting his deflationary strategy'. Accordingly, the measures announced on 19 September included not only a 2-per-cent rise in the Bank Rate but also a two-year standstill in public-sector investment, and in his statement Thorneycroft stressed that, given his determination 'to maintain the internal and external value of the pound', there could be 'no remedy for inflation' that was 'not founded upon a control of the money supply'. Soon afterwards, at the IMF's annual conference in Washington, he loudly banged the same drum, prompting *The Economist* to observe that a British politician had, for the first time since 1945, 'openly offered to face unemployment, should that be the price of beating inflation and defending the pound'.[4]

There was another, highly symbolic aspect to the economic debate this autumn. Back in April, in his Budget speech, Thorneycroft had pointed out that the British economy was facing particular problems as a result of what he called 'our function as banker for a large part of the world', i.e. the sterling area. That in itself was a breakthrough, bringing the issue out into the open. Siegmund Warburg would recall that when he told people soon after the war that sterling's reserve currency status no longer made sense for what had become a debtor country, he had been chastised by the governor of the Bank of England for breaking ranks from the general view, while when – in the immediate aftermath of the Suez crisis – Eden and Macmillan swapped notes on the burden of being bankers for the sterling area (with the latter noting laconically that 'we must either carry on the business with all its risks, or wind it up and pay 5s in the £'), it was very much a private exchange of views. But now, in the autumn of 1957, following the September measures that had placed in sharp focus the domestic implications of sterling's international role, the issue definitively broke cover. Two left-inclining figures, the economist A.C.L. Day and the economic journalist Andrew Shonfield, led the way in November. 'What Price the Sterling Area?' was the title of Day's Third Programme talk in which he asserted that 'the only sensible policy for the United Kingdom is to withdraw from our over-extended commitments to the sterling area', adding that it was 'extremely easy to exaggerate the importance of the financial services [i.e. invisible earnings] provided by the City'. As for Shonfield, a trenchant *News Chronicle* piece ('We should stop playing fairy godmother') claimed that the sterling area contributed nothing 'except a warm feeling that we still count for something pretty important in the world of international finance', accused it of 'taking away British capital for investment abroad, which we badly need to build more factories at home', and argued that internationally it put Britain 'in the position of a kind of buffer at the end of a long line of trucks'.

The orthodoxy, though, remained firmly the other way, and Shonfield quoted Thorneycroft himself stating recently in the Commons that the sterling area 'brings us a great deal in the way of wealth, strength and prestige'. Such was also the line, in a lengthy analysis entitled 'What Is At Stake', taken by *The Economist* shortly before Christmas: 'A major retreat from sterling's present responsibilities, whether on capital account or on current account, cannot possibly be represented as an unequivocal advantage to this country. It would create a new set of troubles.' Either way, the issue was live – much to the displeasure of the Bank of England's deputy governor, Humphrey Mynors, who soon afterwards privately referred to the wartime gunner and intelligence officer in the British Army as 'Andrew Shönfeld'.[5]

Meanwhile, a political crisis was coming to a head. On 22 December, after a long talk with Thorneycroft, Macmillan noted that 'the

Chancellor wants some swingeing cuts in the Welfare State expenditure
– more, I fear, than is feasible politically'. The timing of the denouement
was determined by Macmillan's long-planned departure on Tuesday,
7 January on a lengthy Commonwealth tour. At Cabinet on Friday the
3rd, Thorneycroft found himself isolated over his demand that, in addition to an agreed £100 million of cuts in estimated civil and defence
expenditure for 1958–9, a further £50 million of savings be found,
including through abolishing family allowances for the second child.
An aggrieved Macmillan wrote next day, 'Thorneycroft behaved in
such a rude & "cassant" way that I had difficulty in preventing some of
the Cabinet bursting out in their indignation.' Increasingly over the
weekend he came to the view that 'Nigel Birch & especially Enoch
Powell' were 'egging him on', with the former appraised by Macmillan
as 'a cynic', the latter as 'a fanatic'. By the end of Sunday's lengthy
Cabinet meeting, Thorneycroft was still refusing to give significant
ground, while Macmillan for his part was adamant that the abolition of
the second child's allowance was 'neither politically nor socially desirable – it would be contrary to the tradition of the Conservative Party'.
It is tempting but probably mistaken to accept Macmillan's picture of
Thorneycroft as a pawn of Powell and Birch. Not only was Thorneycroft
a substantial politician in his own right, with firm convictions, but
Powell himself was insistent in later years that he and Birch were only
'minor partners' in the Chancellor's decision. Tellingly, once
Thorneycroft had taken the decision to resign, he told Powell and
Birch, 'that doesn't mean you have to go too'.[6] Both men, however,
were just as determined to draw an unequivocal line in the sand.

In his resignation letter of the 6th, Thorneycroft flatly stated that 'the
Government itself must in my view accept the same measure of financial discipline as it seeks to impose on others' and referred to the need
for 'politically unpopular courses' – an implicit accusation that
provoked Macmillan into replying: 'This is not a matter of popularity.
We have never shrunk from unpopular measures. This is a matter of
good judgement.' Birch's resignation letter to the PM stressed even
more emphatically than Thorneycroft's that government expenditure
must be reduced. 'These reductions are certainly painful and distasteful,' he declared, 'but the electorate is more likely to forgive us for
taking painful and distasteful measures which they will know in their

heart are right than for lacking in courage and clear thinking.' Macmillan himself, on a busy Monday, not only fulfilled the constitutional requirement of one Old Etonian (Thorneycroft) at No. 11 being replaced by another (Derick Heathcoat Amory), but found time to rehearse what he would say at London Airport the next day. Practice paid off. 'I said a few words to the BBC, TV etc.,' he duly noted, 'about the Commonwealth trip and "our little local difficulties". This will annoy a lot of people, but I think it will give them a sense of proportion.'⁷ 'A little local difficulty' passed into political folklore, a triumph of style over substance.

In its reaction to this almost wholly unanticipated turn of events, the Tory-supporting press was largely disinclined to add to the government's troubles. The *Telegraph* argued that there had been 'a touch of the prima donna' about Thorneycroft's wish 'to dictate Government policy', that under Macmillan there would be 'no taking of the hand from the anti-inflationary plough', and that overall the episode was 'no economic Munich'; the *FT* criticised Thorneycroft's stance as unduly 'rigid'; for the *Express*, he was a 'stiff-necked' finance minister 'carrying fiscal purity to excessive lengths'; and for 'Candidus' (on behalf of the *Sketch*), not only was there 'not the least suggestion that the Government is wavering in its resolve to strengthen the value of the pound', but the crux of the 'disagreement' was 'whether rigid doctrine should prevail over common sense and flexibility'. With the *Mail* and the *Spectator* sitting it out, and the *Sunday Times* slightly pro-Macmillan ('the Government is not like a business'), support for Thorneycroft came only from *The Economist* and *The Times*. Even then, the former's backing was qualified – describing Thorneycroft as two-thirds 'a man of rare resolution', but one-third 'of peculiar punctilio' – so it was left to 'The Thunderer' (under the moralising editorship of Sir William Haley) to provide the heavy guns. 'Flinching' was the unambiguous title of its leader on the 7th, beginning: 'So Mr Macmillan has not, in the end, supported his courageous Chancellor of the Exchequer. All those who have felt that the battle for Britain's economic security is still in the balance must have hoped that that support would be forthcoming.' Next day saw a follow-up editorial on 'A Principle', that of keeping a lid on government expenditure: 'If, as we believe, a principle is at stake, the smallness of the amount involved becomes an argument for strict observance of the principle, not an argument that it does not really matter anyway.'[8]

Elsewhere, the provincial press was more instinctively inclined than the nationals to support the resigning trio – they 'have set an example in resolute adherence to the principle of an all-out economy drive and a standstill in Government expenditure which wholly commends itself to all who are honestly realistic in regard to the future', acclaimed the *Kent & Sussex Courier* – but there was still a widespread reluctance to follow those instincts through, especially if it meant rocking the Tory boat. 'To insist upon drastic Governmental economies, even to the extent of striking at the structure of the social services which Conservatives and Socialists alike have helped to build up, might seem an heroic policy, well attuned to the necessities of the times,' declared the *Yorkshire Post*. 'But,' it went on less than heroically, 'would it serve the national interest if it set the trades union movement by the ears?'

One commentator had no doubts about the merits of Thorneycroft's case or its importance in the big post-war picture. This was Harold Wincott, editor of the *Investors Chronicle* and contributor each Tuesday to the *FT*, with a defiantly homely, non-Oxbridge column that enjoyed a considerable following in the City and even beyond. 'I have yet to discover what the modern Conservative really believes in,' he wrote on the 14th.

At least, stupid as I am, I have yet to discover that he believes in the things I expect him to believe in as a member of the party which is in opposition to Socialism. I expect the Socialists to introduce Excess Profits Taxes, to break records in the number of council houses they build, to perpetuate a profits tax which discriminates against distributed profits, to do nothing to foster the property and share-owning democracy which they know will destroy them if it really gets rolling, to go on depreciating the currency. I don't expect Conservatives to do these things.

Wincott then applauded Thorneycroft for having publicly thrown overboard at least 'one aspect of the Keynesian doctrine', namely that 'internal policies take precedence over the external value of the currency'. After a reference to 'the realities of our position in 1958', he concluded: 'In the ultimate resort, if Mr Amory is not to be as expend-able as Mr Thorneycroft was, it is the attitude of mind in the Conservative Party which has got to change. For over six years now, that attitude has been the "Dear-Mother-I-am-going-to-save-7s 6d-but-not-this-week" attitude. It still is. But the supply of weeks is running out.'[9]

From the other end of the political spectrum, the *New Statesman* had little sympathy for what it called 'The Silliest Chancellor', but did fore-see that he would receive significant rank-and-file Tory support, given that 'the political mood of the suburban middle-class Tory, who forms the backbone of the local Associations, is a characteristic expression of social and economic insecurity: angry, reckless and greedy'. One provincial middle-class Tory sympathiser, Kenneth Preston in Keighley, was certainly on Thorneycroft's side. 'A new Chancellor has been appointed,' he noted on the 7th, 'and presumably now all these wage claims that have been refused will be granted. Politics are a sad busi-ness.' When Gallup in due course produced its opinion-poll findings, they showed that 42 per cent of all voters sided with Thorneycroft, 20 per cent with Macmillan, and the rest a mixture of 'neither' and 'unde-cided'. As for specifically Tory voters, 36 per cent plumped for Macmillan, compared with 33 per cent for Thorneycroft. Yet among those same voters, confronted by the proposition that government expenditure, including defence and social services, should be cut back in order to fulfil the government's first duty of fighting inflation and preserving the value of the pound, 69 per cent agreed and only 13 per cent disagreed.[10] How to explain the difference between the two Tory sets of figures? Perhaps it was a combination of personal faith in Macmillan, tribal loyalty to the party leadership and a certain innate reluctance to think things through.

An important subset of Tory support was broadly in Thorneycroft's camp. Oscar Hobson, doyen of City journalists, early on detected in the Square Mile 'very strong support for, and sympathy with' the former Chancellor, while soon afterwards the *Spectator* noted that the resignations had been regarded in the City as 'a loss of nerve by the Government at a particularly vital moment', as the 'disinflationary policies were just beginning to be successful'. Even so, the probability was that many practical City men did not quite see it as a black-and-white issue. Rab Butler, temporarily in charge of the government, reported to his absent master what a leading broker had told him: 'I would like to see the Government cutting every penny off expenditure. But if it is a matter of political judgement I would prefer to trust Macmillan rather than Thorneycroft.'[11] And of course, peculiarly important in the City, there was also the unquantifiable tribal factor.

Predictably, the Tory MPs closed ranks. So far from 'Flinching', one outraged backbencher, Robert Cary, wrote to *The Times*, 'the Prime Minister has faced courageously the issue of not only maintaining the stability of sterling, but, equally important, of sustaining social peace at home'. The same day his letter appeared, the 8th, the *Daily Express* published its poll of 58 Tory MPs, revealing only 6 open (if unnamed) supporters of Thorneycroft, 30 supporters of Macmillan and the rest of the Cabinet, 11 hedgers and another 11 refusing to comment. By the following week, the Tory chief whip Edward Heath was able to report reassuringly to Macmillan in Pakistan: 'Our members now seem to have settled down again and are waiting until the House resumes before passing final judgement. The party as a whole remains loyal to the Government but is still somewhat perplexed about the reasons for the resignations.' Parliament was due to reassemble on the 21st, and 'from all the signs', as Mollie Panter-Downes had already perceptively noted, 'Mr Thorneycroft will not receive much support in public in the House of Commons, whatever it may say in private'. She was in a crowded press gallery for the politically crucial economic debate on the 23rd, which, prior to a vote of confidence on the government's declared policy of keeping the pound strong and controlling inflation, included Thorneycroft's resignation speech:

The Government, displaying some anxiety over possible abstentions on the Tory benches when it came time to vote, had reportedly drummed up Conservative absentees who were on holiday or away convalescing, and had got them to come along – sunburnt or wan or in any shape at all – to make the result look really heartening for home-and-abroad consumption. As it turned out, the Government need hardly have bothered, since there were no recriminations from Mr Thorneycroft, and the Party, cheering him to the echo, voted solid [i.e. for the government], in a glow of enthusiasm for the principles on which he had apparently insisted to the point of resignation. If this sounds bewildering, that was just about the way it seemed.

Or as Panter-Downes also put it, this 'demonstration of the gentle-manly oddities of the British political system' was 'enough to baffle foreign observers and make lots of Britons, too, feel somewhat confused as to who was hitting whom among all the congratulatory Conservative handshakes'.

In fact, the content of Thorneycroft's gravely delivered, 11-minute speech – a 'personal triumph', according to the *FT* – was far from anodyne. Since the war, he asserted, Britain had sought to combine a full-scale welfare state with a large defence programme, not to mention discharging its onerous responsibilities to the sterling area. He went on to offer his analysis of the consequences and implications of this not ignoble attempt: 'It has meant that for twelve years we have slithered from one crisis to another. Sometimes it has been a balance of payments crisis and sometimes of exchange but always it has been a crisis. It has meant the pound sinking from 20s to 12s. It is a picture of a nation in full retreat from its responsibilities. It is the road to ruin.' And he went on: 'The simple truth is that we have been spending more money than we should . . . It is not the sluice gate which is at fault. It is the plain fact that the water is coming over the top of the dam.' His conclusion was stirring: 'I believe there is an England that would prefer to face these facts and make the necessary decisions now. I believe that living within our resources is neither unfair nor unjust, nor perhaps, in the long run, even unpopular.'[12]

In the fullness of time, Thorneycroft and his co-resigners would be portrayed as proto-Thatcherite martyrs. And so in an obvious sense they were – despite the temptation to exaggerate the Macmillan of the mid-1950s (whether at No. 11 or No. 10) as a Keynesian spendthrift, and despite Edward Heath's characteristic insistence three decades later, in a radio interview about the episode, that 'the only way in which it was historic was that it showed that some people who wanted to get rid of Harold Macmillan as Prime Minister failed to do so'. Yet in truth, by 1958 itself, not only had the small-state free-marketeers barely joined battle, let alone started to win it, but the assumptions of a rising genera-tion of 'activators' were almost wholly pointing the other way. 'In economics he was, like the rest of our generation, under the influence of the Keynesian revolution,' William Rees-Mogg would recall about a fellow bright young graduate on the *FT*'s staff, Nigel Lawson. 'We looked on the neo-classical Treasury mandarins as dangerous old fuddy-duddies.'

Even so, the small but purposeful organisation that would do much to lay the intellectual ground for Thatcherism was by now in existence: the Institute of Economic Affairs, under the leadership of the extrovert Ralph Harris and the more cerebral Arthur Seldon, both from working-class backgrounds. The latter's first publication for the IEA, *Pensions in a Free Society*, had recently appeared. 'The philosophy underlying this paper is that most of us are now adult enough to be left, or to be helped, to live our own lives according to our own lights,' Seldon wrote. 'The transition from dependence to independence must be gradual; that is all the more reason for beginning soon.'[13] As long as collective memories remained strong of the slump of the 1930s, and of the appalling human misery that had accompanied it, it was a message that would struggle to win either emotional support or political traction.

6

A Worried Song

On Saturday, 11 January, five days after Thorneycroft's resignation, the BBC experimented by televising two race meetings, at Newbury and Haydock Park, on the same afternoon. Most viewers thought it 'a very good idea', saving 'a lot of boring twaddle about the horses that are to appear in the next race', but 11 per cent found it 'unsettling' and 'hard to keep up with'. That evening Florence Turtle went to the Wimbledon Theatre to see Elsie and Doris Waters in *Cinderella* – 'it was good fun & especially for the many children' – while the Youngs and the Willmotts travelled to Little Cox Pond Farm, outside Hemel Hempstead. 'We dined in the usual baronial Fienburgh manner,' recorded Peter Willmott's wife Phyllis, by now keeping a regular diary. Their host Wilfred Fienburgh was 38, a Labour backbencher, intelligent, amusing, somewhat louche, with 'good looks and big brown eyes' that (recalled Denis Healey) 'often led him astray'. He told his guests 'the Parliamentary gossip: that Macmillan's youngest daughter is really Robert Boothby's; that Princess Margaret still carries a torch for Peter Townsend; that the Cabinet want Elizabeth to have another child; that Philip has a Wren officer for a mistress'. The guests stayed on after dinner. 'Michael [Young] is deaf to the sound and the pull of modern, popular music,' continued Phyllis. 'He looked almost uncomfortable as we listened to Wilf's records. Disconcerted, unsure.' The Youngs left at about midnight. 'The rest of us went on rousting until 2 a.m. We played records and ended up dancing and jiving. Wilfred pretends to be very up to date on it all. He probably is more than we are. I can't help feeling that it is more dignified to sit back and watch the youngsters caper.'[1]

Next day another perceptive woman living in north London, Jill Craigie, had a question or two for the film producer Michael Balcon. 'Can you honestly say that any of our directors gets under the skins of their women characters?' she asked him. 'Has your wife or daughter said anything to you about British films – I mean in the last six or seven years – "that is me, that is how I would have felt under those circumstances"?' Judy Haines in Chingford was more concerned about her daughters' moral and educational well-being. 'I suggested they both pay as much attention to "Children's Newspaper" as to "School Friend" and "Girl",' she wrote on the 16th. 'Pamela said oh she most certainly did read C.N.; she knows *all* about Tommy Steele. I roared. She meant to be funny.' As it happened, the first issue of *Bunty* was just hitting the newsagents ('Ladybird Ring Free Inside!' announced the front page), with *Roxy* shortly on the way for Steele fans ('Tommy's Lucky Little Guitar Brought Marcie Luck In Love'). But arguably the most signal publishing event of early 1958 was the coming of *Woman's Realm*, launched by Odhams in February with a blizzard of advertising, including a four-page inset in *Radio Times*. 'On this, our birthday, we greet Her Gracious Majesty, the Queen, and with her all our readers,' began the editor's message in the first issue. 'We promise to serve them both loyally, and with all our hearts.' And she went on:

> Our country today *is* literally a woman's realm – ruled over by our young and beautiful sovereign and containing in itself those other realms in which all women are supreme.
>
> In the home and in the heart of her husband and her family, every woman finds happiness and fulfilment, as well as duty. This need never be a narrow domain, bounded though it often is by kitchen, nursery and household chores. Indeed, if she chooses to make it so, it can be the widest and most wonderful and the most rewarding realm in the whole world.

Items on later pages included Susan King's 'Favourite Family Puddings' (cherry apple flan, golden peach tart, magic mousse, topsy-turvy pineapple, chocolate chiffon, butterscotch pie), a pull-out booklet of 'NEW knitting patterns', a special offer for 2/6 of 'Four Lovely Lipsticks for You!', a report called 'Can a husband want too much love?' by a founder of the Marriage Guidance Council, stories with titles like 'The Waiting Game' – and, almost throughout, a relentless domestic-cum-family focus. The editor was Joyce Ward, and she had a conscious aim, brilliantly realised, of seeking to increase the enjoyment of home life for women who did not go out to work and were often rather older than the readers of the two market leaders, *Woman* and *Woman's Own*. 'From the very first issue the magazine "went like a bomb" and has achieved considerable popularity in the North of England,' noted the historian of women's magazines Cynthia White a decade later. 'Judging by its correspondence, it draws the bulk of its readers from amongst home-bound housewives, as well as attracting a large number of lonely women in bedsitters.'[2]

One elderly woman living alone in a bedsitter was Gladys Langford. 'Depression deepening,' she wrote on the very Tuesday that the first *Woman's Realm* came out. 'Conversation nil.' By this time there was compelling testimony available in Peter Townsend's *The Family Life of Old People*, the offshoot of Young and Willmott's *Family and Kinship* that was likewise a study of Bethnal Green and also widely reviewed. 'Those who are afraid of an isolated old age will find no consolation in these pages,' noted an already apprehensive Kingsley Amis. But although Townsend pointed to serious deficiencies in provision for the elderly, it was not (with perhaps the exception of pensions) an area high on the political agenda. This same year in Glasgow, in a chronic ward of what had been a Poor Law hospital, the future geriatrician Bernard Isaacs encountered an utterly grim, twilight world:

> The dayroom was not a large room, perhaps six metres square. Its main item of furniture was a great grimy black stove, which stood in the centre of the room. It emitted very little heat, but evil-smelling wisps of smoke escaped from cracks and seams in its structure, blackened the walls and ceiling, and set the inhabitants of the room coughing and spluttering.
>
> Bunched around this stove, sitting on rickety wooden kitchen chairs, were some thirty or forty old men of terrifying appearance. Their countenances expressed a kind of dying rage, a wrath that had been replaced by despair, now become lifeless, unmoving, as though carved out of cold, grey stone.
>
> The bunch of cracked, unmoving bodies, silent apart from the occasional wracking cough or the switch of spittle into the stove, were dressed

in what answered for blue jackets and blue trousers . . . The jackets were
shrunken, crumpled, shapeless, devoid of all buttons, thickly stained
with dried soup, saliva, caked tobacco. The trousers, unsupported by
belt or braces, devoid of all fly buttons, remained in position only by
virtue of a chance fit between the circumference of the garment and that
of the wearer's waist. This piece of good fortune was rare . . . The blue
jacket and trousers were virtually all that the patients wore. There were
no vests, no shirts, no ties, no underpants, no pullovers and cardigans.

Many of these neglected, ill-treated elderly people had, Isaacs in time
came to realise, grown up in appalling, brutalising slums and then gone
on to ill-treat their own children. Accordingly, 'the result was that
when the parents reached old age, the children did not feel the recipro-
cal bond expected of them'.[3]

––––––––––

It was a world away from the money men in the City of London. 'There
is no justification for allegations that information about the raising of
the Bank Rate was improperly disclosed to any person,' roundly
asserted Lord Justice Parker's Tribunal report, published on 21 January,
about the rumoured 'leak' the previous September. As for those in
receipt of advance warning of the rise, 'in every case the information
disclosed was treated by the recipient as confidential and . . . no use of
such information was made for the purpose of private gain'. For the
government, the Bank of the England and the City, the dominant reaction was relief – the *FT* declaring the report had 'utterly vindicated the
reputation of the City of London for financial integrity' – though
considerable indignation persisted that the Labour opposition, and
specifically Harold Wilson as Shadow Chancellor, had foisted the
inquiry on them in the first place. In early February there followed,
again at Labour's request, a two-day Commons debate on the episode,
with Wilson himself giving an unabashed, virtuoso performance, not
least with his cricket analogy for the City, where 'merchant bankers are
treated as the gentlemen and the clearing bankers as the players using
the professionals' gate out of the pavilion'. Left unspoken, and there-
after hanging in the air for many years, was the question of whether the
two main suspects, Keswick and Kindersley, had got away with it. The

Bank of England's most recent historian, Forrest Capie, suggests that the latter anyway may have done so, pointing to how the British Match Company (on whose board he sat) had for several years faithfully held around £250,000 of gilts – until it abruptly got rid of them the day before the Bank Rate hike was announced. 'They sold that stock,' a leading gilts broker, Sir Nigel Althaus, would recall almost half a century later, 'and that seemed to me the absolute clincher, and I think Lord Kindersley was very lucky.'[4]

On Saturday, 1 February, two days before the Commons debate got under way, London witnessed two resonant sporting moments: at Highbury a crowd of over 60,000 watched the 'Busby Babes' beat Arsenal 5–4 in a pulsating encounter on a mud heap, among them a 15-year-old Spurs supporter, Terry Venables, there specially to see the Manchester United powerhouse left-half Duncan Edwards, only six years older, while at Twickenham there was rare booing when Australia had one England rugby player carried off and another concussed, before at the death Coventry's Peter Jackson scored a memorable jinking, swaying try to clinch the match 9–6. The following evening saw the launch of BBC TV's arts programme *Monitor*, fronted by Huw Wheldon, its very name indicative of the Reithian paternalism that still permeated the Corporation's culture. 'Lean, eager, sardonic and compelling,' was one critic's view of Wheldon, who would later be heard to remark off-screen, 'We can't have someone who's overtly queer on the programme.' As for viewers, 'upstage', 'highbrow' and generally 'stodgy' was the early, unenthusiastic verdict. Next day, Monday the 3rd, the trial began at the Old Bailey of three senior Brighton police officers on charges of conspiracy – a trial that eventually led to the town's Watch Committee dismissing the chief constable – while that evening Wilfred Fienburgh died after his car had collided on Saturday night with a lamp post at Mill Hill. Tuesday featured the first nudity on British television (an excerpt on ITV from the Windmill Theatre's current non-stop revue), while on Wednesday a 3–3 draw at Red Star Belgrade saw Manchester United through to the semi-finals of the European Cup shortly before Anthony Heap went to the first night of Graham Greene's *The Potting Shed* at the Globe ('more of a parable than a play, and a pretty preposterous one at that'). And on Thursday the 6th, Dennis Dee encountered 'keen frosts and winds' on his East Riding smallholding as he spent the day 'riddling spuds'; 14-year-old George Harrison met the Quarry Men; and Captain James Thain's twin-engined Elizabethan-class plane, chartered by Manchester United and having refuelled on the way back from Belgrade, failed to get full lift-off on the slushy runway at Munich airport.[5]

The news started to come through late that chilly afternoon: some 21 feared dead, including seven players, with both Duncan Edwards and the manager Matt Busby gravely injured, and the 20-year-old Bobby Charlton among the survivors. One of the eight journalists killed was the *Manchester Guardian*'s Don Davies. The sports editor had originally assigned John Arlott to cover the match, but in the event 'An Old International', as Davies was invariably bylined, had taken Arlott's place. That evening much of the nation was in a state of disbelieving grief, but a Keighley diarist focused on the practicalities. 'Manchester United were to have played Wolverhampton on Saturday,' noted Kenneth Preston. 'That match has had to be cancelled. That will throw the League games out of gear. Then Manchester were in the running for some sort of European Cup. That will be upset.' He drew two lessons: 'If the aeroplane had been carrying troops we should not have heard as much about it. These accidents only go to show that man has not mastered the forces he thought he had mastered.'

Next day, Nella Last in Barrow 'thought with sadness of the Manchester people who died in the plane crash', reflecting how 'this time yesterday, wives would be shopping & planning a "welcome" meal', while in Manchester itself a young teacher, Vincent Walmsley, recorded in his diary that 'going through town this morning the one topic on the buses, in the streets, where people queued for papers, was yesterday's tragedy which has, because of its unique character, shocked the world; and Manchester to the core'. Brian Redhead, at the time a youthful journalist in Manchester, would remember people 'frozen' in the streets on learning the news, and generally it seems to have been stoicism – the legacy of two world wars – that marked the next few days. If so, that was little thanks to the press. 'One of the most distressing consequences of a catastrophe like the recent aeroplane accident in Munich,' complained Malcolm Muggeridge soon afterwards, 'is the manner in which the newspapers play it so hard that it is soon drained of all emotion, and even becomes positively repugnant.'

The bodies were flown back to Manchester on the evening of Tuesday the 11th and taken in solemn procession to Old Trafford. In cold and rain, thousands lined the 11-mile route – many, according to a local paper, with 'a bewildered look about them'. Eight days later a patched-up United, including emergency signings, played Sheffield Wednesday in the FA Cup and won 3-0; but although Busby was starting to pull through, the man who had been expected to captain England for much of the 1960s, Duncan Edwards, died in the early hours of the 21st.[6]

Just up the road from Manchester, a historic by-election campaign had been taking place either side of the crash. 'We do not intend to depart from our usual practice in by-elections that we do not influence voters nor report the campaigns in news bulletins,' ran the BBC's pompous announcement ahead of the Rochdale contest, with polling set for Wednesday the 12th, but the local commercial television station, Granada, boldly broke ranks. For the first time on British screens, it (together with ITN's bulletins) offered something approximating full-bodied political coverage. The seat was a Tory marginal, under threat from a Labour candidate whose agent was a young local councillor, Cyril Smith, while the Liberals' (now led by Jo Grimond) candidate was the articulate, not unglamorous Ludovic Kennedy, until recently an ITN newscaster. Granada's first election broadcast, on the 5th, was watched by over a third of the local electorate, with Kennedy coming out best in the eyes of those viewers. 'We shall lose Rochdale, I fear, by a lot,' privately predicted Macmillan (in Australia) on the 10th. 'The Liberal intervention in all these by-elections is very annoying.' Next day, eve of polling, Richard Crossman paid a visit. 'Though the centre of Rochdale is rather fine,' he noted, 'the rest of it is the usual ghastly Lancashire town, with its slummy streets running up and down the hills.' As for Granada's big debate that evening, with 'three journalists interrogating the three candidates' live in the Council Chamber, he reckoned Labour's Jack McCann was 'easily the best', followed by Kennedy.

'I'd have liked to sit up & hear the Rochdale Election results,' Nella Last wrote on the Wednesday evening itself before reluctantly going to bed. 'I don't share my husband's optimism that the Tories will hold the seat – the Liberal will *very* much split the votes.' She was right: the Tories lost to Labour, and were pushed into a bad third place, with many of their votes going to the Liberals, who enjoyed their biggest by-election vote for over 20 years. Macmillan landed at London Airport on Friday, and was soon being defended by Gerald Nabarro on *Any Questions?* ('he's an experienced tactician, an able politician, an outstanding statesman, and he'll handle the situation, and the Tory Party will still win the next election, and by a good majority ... LAUGHTER'), but the real story lay elsewhere. 'The televoter is born,' declared Kenneth Allsop that day in the *Daily Mail*. 'Rochdale has changed the nature of democratic politics. Theorizing may now end. Television is established as the new hub of the hustings.'[7]

Macmillan and the fellow Conservative whom he had vanquished for the keys to No. 10 were about to have a weekend of contrasting fortunes. 'As Mr Butler entered the hall, he was welcomed by a jazz band, the bangs of exploding squibs, shouting and singing,' reported the *Evening Standard* about a lively occasion on Friday the 21st at Glasgow University, where Rab Butler was due to be installed as rector and address the students. Whereupon:

> The first missiles began to fly. A tomato hit him square in the back. A flour bomb hit him full in the face.
>
> The barrage of missiles and noise continued throughout the ceremony and during Mr Butler's speech. Often he stood silent, waiting a rare chance to make himself heard.
>
> Finally the platform party stood and bravely sang 'God Save the Queen'. As they departed, fire extinguishers and water showered all over them.

The Home Secretary was already being strongly criticised by many Tories for his apparent softness towards crime, and it did not help his cause when the next day's papers featured photos of him covered in flour and soaked in foam. 'I understand youth,' Butler vainly protested. 'I have children of my own and I like to feel I haven't lost touch.'

Macmillan meanwhile was preparing to take his chance, on Sunday the 23rd, with the first live, one-on-one television interview with a prime minister. 'As the cameras were being lined up he derived considerable amusement from the seating arrangement,' recalled his inquisitor, ITN's Robin Day. 'He complained that whereas he was sitting on a hard upright seat, I was enthroned behind the table in a comfortable swivel chair with well-padded arms. This, said the Prime Minister, seemed to symbolize the new relationship between politician and TV interviewer. He felt as if he were on the mat.' In the 13-minute interview, Macmillan was at his relaxed, confident best, offering early on the characteristic post-Rochdale reflection that 'at home you are a politician, abroad you are a statesman' and later giving a calm, effective reply when Day asked him about the position of the Foreign Secretary, Selwyn Lloyd, who was facing even more Tory criticism than Butler: 'I do not intend to make a change simply as a result of pressure. I don't believe that that is wise. It is not in accordance with my idea of loyalty.' Should Day, though, have had the nerve even to raise the issue? The *Telegraph* ('Who is to draw the line at which the effort to entertain stops?') and the *Manchester Guardian* ('This may be judged a good or a bad development, according to taste, but it is certainly new') were unsure, but the *Mirror*'s 'Cassandra' had no doubts: 'The Idiot's Lantern is getting too big for its ugly gleam.' As for Macmillan, his private verdict later that evening was eloquent enough: 'I think it went well, altho' the questions were of the *Daily Mirror* type – brash & impertinent.'[8]

The Liberal revival would continue in late March with Mark Bonham Carter's dramatic by-election gain from the Tories at Torrington in north Devon. 'A splendid meeting in a kind of barn lit by paraffin lamps,' recorded his mother Lady Violet during a strongly rural campaign, 'full of enthusiastic horny-handed supporters.' Given the negative effects of the credit squeeze following the September measures, rising unemployment and the USA slipping into recession, any mid-term government was likely to be unpopular. For Macmillan, with the recalcitrant Thorneycroft gone and Heathcoat Amory likely to prove somewhat more malleable, the question was not whether to reflate but when to do so. This was certainly the case after 13 March. 'Roy Harrod to luncheon (alone),' the PM noted after a visit from his favourite – and loyally Keynesian – economist. 'He is very keen that we should start to take "anti-deflationist" measures. According to him, the slump is now the enemy, not the boom. I rather share his view.' For the moment, though, Macmillan was prepared to be cautious, knowing he had at least one pre-election budget up his sleeve.

Nor perhaps would he have been surprised if he had been present a few weeks earlier at a small dinner at the Garrick Club that included Gaitskell and an inveterate diarist. 'Hugh listed the reasons why those disillusioned with Toryism are not voting Labour,' recorded Richard Crossman.

> Labour is a high taxation party, Labour is a trade union party, Labour is a nationalization party and Labour is not as sound as the Tories on the foreign issues. When asked what he would do to change this hostility to Labour, he said there was a very limited amount one could do. He himself would play down the nationalization of steel but, after all, we are a trade union party, with these views.

Macmillan might also this spring have noted the first-quarter figures for the sales of domestic fridges: 57,000, up from 34,000 for the same period in 1957. A fridge, observed *The Times*, was increasingly viewed 'as a necessity rather than a luxury', but only one of the two main parties was psychically conditioned to be the white-goods party, the party of acquisitive consumerism, and that was not the still puritanical, producer-oriented people's party.[9]

On Friday, 14 March, the day after Harrod's lunch at No. 10, a viscerally non-Keynesian was at Maidstone, making her third attempt since returning to the political fray – after a phase of serious disenchantment in the mid-1950s – to land a winnable Tory seat. 'Mrs Thatcher went straight into politics, leaving only a very short time at the end of her talk for her tactics in nursing the seat,' reported the Area Agent to Central Office. 'She was asked about her ability to cope as a Member, having in mind the fact that she had a husband and a small family, and I do not think her reply did her a lot of good. She spoke of having an excellent nanny.' The twins' mother duly lost out to a 'very pleasant, ebullient' Old Etonian, John Wells – and, as Thatcher's biographer John Campbell nicely puts it, 'naturally the fact that Wells had four children under ten was not an issue'. That evening at the Woolwich Granada featured two performances by a touring package that had been on the road for the past fortnight: Buddy Holly and the Crickets; an English crooner, Gary Miller, who before the tour had been entertaining the troops in Cyprus; the Tanner Sisters, in effect the poor woman's

Beverley Sisters; the 13-piece Ronnie Keene Orchestra; and, supplying the gags and linking the acts, the relatively unknown Des O'Connor (billed as 'Comedian with the Modern Style'). Among those at the 6.45 show was a 14-year-old from Dartford, attending his first concert, still known as 'Mike' and accompanied by a classmate, Dick Taylor. 'Finally the Crickets appeared,' records his biographer Christopher Sandford.

> They plugged in; they tuned up. Jagger at this stage gave one of his world-weary sighs. What, he seemed to ask, was all the fuss about? Just then Holly announced 'That'll Be The Day', followed by 'Peggy Sue' and 'Rave On'. By the last Jagger was clapping along. During 'Not Fade Away' he was out of his seat, hair puffing over his eyes, miming the lyrics, showing incredible levity for one whose precept was at all times to 'stay cool'. Leaving the cinema he went as far as to announce to Taylor, 'That was a gas.'[10]

Thatcher and Jagger: their destinies would be linked far more closely than either ever imagined.

        '———————

The package tour had ended the previous Tuesday at the Hammersmith Gaumont when on Saturday the 29th, Dennis Dee's diary made its first reference of the year to an external event. 'Grand National day,' he noted. 'Won by "Mister What" ridden by Freeman.' Two days later Philip Larkin, back from a London trip and starting work again on 'The Whitsun Weddings', told Monica Jones how he had been 'impressed afresh by the enormous cleanliness & efficiency of Southern region trains'. And on Tuesday the 1st the BBC's Radiophonic Workshop began at Maida Vale, the brainchild of Daphne Oram, who however would soon leave in protest at the Corporation rule that people could stay there for only three months, lest working with experimental sound lead to brain disturbances or even madness. Later that same day, *Hancock's Half Hour* on the radio included Hancock responding to a policeman's commonplace pronunciation of 'garage' by giving his own, posher version, with the second 'a' drawn out.[11]

Two notable new books were around at the start of April. 'This deadly analysis of managerial humbug in modern society', was Eric

Keown's approving summary of *Parkinson's Law* by C. Northcote Parkinson, with his *Punch* review calling it 'a book to make the ordinary down-trodden citizen hug himself with pleasure'. The other was Ian Fleming's *Dr No*, a year after *From Russia With Love* had catapulted him into the commercial big time. His latest provoked some severe criticism, above all from a young left-wing journalist, Paul Johnson. 'I have just finished what is, without doubt, the nastiest book I have ever read,' began Johnson's *New Statesman* piece, which argued that *Dr No*'s three basic ingredients, 'all unhealthy' and 'all thoroughly English', were 'the sadism of a schoolboy bully, the mechanized, two-dimensional sex-longings of a frustrated adolescent, and the crude, snob-cravings of a suburban adult'. *Dr No* was expected to sell half a million copies, prompting Johnson to reflect that 'our curious post-war society, with its obsessive interest in debutantes [their last season just beginning], its cult of U and non-U, its working-class graduates educated into snobbery by the welfare state, is a soft model for Mr Fleming's poison'. He might have added that a fourth key element in Fleming's thrillers by this time was the sharp sense of regret about – and defiance against – British decline, especially following Suez. 'At home and abroad,' lamented 007 in *From Russia With Love*, 'we don't show any teeth anymore, only gums.' Rapid decolonisation, moreover, was looming, and as Simon Winder puts it with pardonable exaggeration in his study of James Bond, *The Man Who Saved Britain*, 'as a large part of the planet slipped from Britain's grasp one man silently maintained the country's reputation'.[12]

For some, there was a different route to restoring national greatness.[13] 'The British of these times, so frequently hiding behind masks of sour, cheap cynicism, often seem to be waiting for something better than party squabbles and appeals to their narrow self-interest, something great and noble in its intention that would make them feel good again,' wrote J. B. Priestley on 'Britain and the Nuclear Bombs' in the *New Statesman* in November 1957. 'Alone, we defied Hitler; and alone we can defy this nuclear madness into which the spirit of Hitler seems to have passed, to poison the world.' The nuclear issue had had increasing salience since the Defence Review the previous April, followed soon after by Britain's H-bomb test at Christmas Island ('*OUR* H-BANG!', *Daily Express*) and then, in October, by Bevan's renunciation of unilateralism, the direct provocation for Priestley's much-read article. Private meetings ensued, before (on 17 February 1958) a public one took place at the Methodist Central Hall in Westminster, proving so popular that five overflow meetings had to be arranged. Priestley, Bertrand Russell, Michael Foot, A.J.P. Taylor and Alex Comfort were among the speakers; the rhetoric was fierce and inspiring, epitomised by Taylor's shouted claim that 'Any man who can prepare to use those weapons should be denounced as a murderer!' Thus the Campaign for Nuclear Disarmament (CND) was born as a new political and social reality – though a reader of the next morning's *Times* would not have been aware of the fact.

'What difference to the deterrent does our contribution make?' Robin Day asked Macmillan the following Sunday. 'Well, I think the independent contribution is a help,' he replied. 'It gives us a better position in the world, it gives us a better position in the United States, and it puts us where we ought to be, in a position of a great power.' Soon afterwards Anthony Wedgwood Benn resigned from the Labour front bench – not a unilateralist, yet morally unable to endorse the potential use of nuclear weapons – while Priestley by the end of March was complaining of how over the past few weeks the anti-CND establishment had been 'hurling wild accusations, making a personal issue of it from the word Go', with 'emotional' and 'hysterical' the two most favoured derogatory epithets. Among CND's many well-known supporters was John Arlott. 'So long as atomic weapons are competitive everybody is going to want them,' he told the *Any Questions?* audience at Bournemouth Town Hall on 4 April. 'I reckon in the end everybody will get them and sooner or later if that happens, one hot-headed maniac will drop one and that will be the end.'[14]

The programme went out on Good Friday, and that morning some 4,000 had gathered in Trafalgar Square for the start of a four-day, 45-mile protest march (organised from the offices of *Peace News*) to the Atomic Weapons Research Establishment at Aldermaston in Berkshire. 'This can be the greatest march in English history,' declared Michael Foot from the plinth on Nelson's Column, while among those on the first stage was Kenneth Tynan, 'cigarette authoritatively held at the ready' according to the *Manchester Guardian*, which went on to quote Mrs Anne Collins of Gillingham, pushing her small daughter in a pushchair: '"I've been thinking about this for ten years," she said, a humble yet fixed light in her eyes. "If I become a grandmother I don't want a bomb to drop on her and her children – I don't want to drop bombs on the Russians, either. I'd rather let the Communists take over." A trifle falteringly she walked on.' There were still 2,000 marching by the end of the day, but numbers thinned to 700 or fewer during a miserably cold, wet, even snowy Saturday. 'We came down the Bath Road to London Airport in the rain under the dripping skeletons of trees,' reported John Gale in the *Observer*. 'But we were mighty cheerful' as 'a scratch band played "It Takes a Worried Man to sing a Worried Song," and the notes of the clarinet floated clearly'. Among those at the front were the Rev. Donald Soper, the march's organiser Pat Arrowsmith ('astonishingly young, with black hair, a bright face, a pack on her back, a pale mauve raincoat and red luminous socks'), and 'a spruce-bearded figure with grey hair, cap and a fur-lined tank jacket, a master from Tonbridge School'. Generally, noted Gale, there were 'a lot of girls with long hair and earnest expressions'.

Two days later, on Easter Monday, the numerically reinforced marchers – still singing 'Don't you hear the H-bomb's thunder/Echo like the crack of doom?', the opening lines of a song for the march by the young science-fiction writer John Brunner – were met on a field outside the research station by a large band of waiting supporters. Tynan had been an early drop-out, but he now arrived by taxi, joining Christopher Logue and Doris Lessing for an impromptu picnic, while in the background a loudspeaker proclaimed the march's message: 'Lift up your heads and be proud. The lead has been given to the English people. Britain must take up that lead in the world. "England arise! The long, long night is over."' Inspiriting, patriotic words (quoting Edward Carpenter), but soon afterwards a rival megaphone, manned by the right-wing twins Norris and Ross McWhirter, boomed out an alternative message from the roof of their Mercedes: 'Each one of you is increasing the risk of nuclear war. You are playing Khrushchev's game. Moscow is making use of you.' Enraged marchers attacked the car, causing £150 worth of damage before they were forcibly removed by stewards.[15]

The emergence of CND did nothing for Labour unity. 'At sixes and sevens', was Wedgwood Benn's post-Aldermaston assessment of where the party stood over the nuclear issue, while Aneurin Bevan as shadow Foreign Secretary – his head and his heart facing in opposite directions – now had to perform (as Denis Healey later put it) 'prodigious acrobatics in a vain attempt to straddle the divide between unilateralist and multilateralist'. Constituency parties were far from unanimous in following Gaitskell's firmly multilateralist lead: in Greenwich one ambitious would-be MP, Richard Marsh, secured the nomination through wearing a prominent CND badge at his selection meeting. Either way, many CNDers were instinctively reluctant to have their cause identified too closely with Labour, let alone taken over – even though, realistically, unilateralism could only become British policy if Labour was converted to it. There was a telling moment when the march stopped in Reading: after a collection had been taken, a local party official announced that the proceeds would be divided between CND and Labour, but this produced such outrage that instead all the money went to CND. This attitude reflected in part the movement's strongly youthful composition, certainly in terms of marchers (one of whom was a cloth-capped student from Bradford College of Art, 22-year-old David Hockney). Indeed, the grass-roots membership as a whole would never be susceptible to central control, but was instead, as Stephen Woodhams has illuminatingly argued, 'the expression of individual desires and beliefs' – an individuality that 'might be seen to parallel the drive toward personal expression in wider social patterns ranging from consumer capitalism to modes of school learning'. CND was, in short, a precursor to the counterculture of the 1960s, with all of that phenomenon's diverse political implications and legacies.

'"Nuclear Disarmament" seems to be a purely middle-class show,' commented one observer of the pre-march gathering in Trafalgar Square, observing that banners came from districts like Hampstead or Finchley, while 'the only banner from a less bourgeois area – Woolwich – was borne by the local National Union of Teacher's. A.J.P. Taylor came reluctantly to agree. 'The Campaign is a movement of eggheads for eggheads,' he reflected in June, after several weeks of addressing crowded meetings around the country. 'We get a few trade union leaders, themselves crypto-eggheads. We get no industrial workers.' It was somehow emblematic that Pat Arrowsmith herself was a product of Cheltenham Ladies College, albeit a serial rule-breaker while there. Moreover, even within the progressive middle class (and not just the Labour Party), there were divided views. 'They would take what loot they wanted, set up their bases and leave the population to rot,' was Kingsley Amis's prediction about what the Russians would do if there was no nuclear deterrent, adding that 'they would simply suppress the BBC and the Press, not to mention shooting half a million chaps out of hand', while in north London during the march, recorded Phyllis Willmott, Michael Young 'went on Good Friday and Saturday, coming back each night to sleep in his bed'. But she and Peter 'could not decide whether his protest was good or useful or not'.

How did people at large view the unilateralist cause? 'All recent Gallup Polls seem to show,' noted Mollie Panter-Downes a fortnight after the march, 'that while the British public's heart may have its reasons for sympathizing with the Aldermaston marchers, solid British reason has not forgotten the lesson of the disarmament of the thirties.' Generally, the evidence was of around three opponents of unilateralism to every supporter. 'Interested silence' was, according to John Gale, the main characteristic of people watching the march, and he ended his report with a haunting question: 'People mainly watched and thought and wondered at the children in the rain. "Look at them there, those little children. But it won't make any difference. There'll be a war if there's going to be one." But will there?'[16]

––––––––––

'You can hear people banging doors – it is like guns going off,' declared Mrs Grace to the *Coventry Standard* in its January 1958 profile of Bell Green, one of the recently built council housing estates on the city's outskirts. Complaining about theft and inadequate drying facilities, and predicting that the estate would become 'another slum area', she announced that she and her husband were 'saving up to move as soon as we can'. Next week it was the turn of the Willenhall estate, where, as in Bell Green, the blocks of flats, mainly four storeys, prompted consid-erable dissatisfaction:

> I have a small baby. I can't get her outside at all unless I push her right round the back of the flats, where I can leave the pram under the window.
> (*Mrs M. Lennon*)

I can't do any washing – there is no boiler at all. It's awful to have to
pay so much money for a place like this. I would sooner be in a little
cottage than this place. *(Mrs Amy Spencer)*

Among the well-intentioned activators, Michael Young continued to
insist that the problems on such relatively low-density estates, mainly
peopled by tenants transplanted from high-density inner-city areas,
went far beyond an absence of physical amenities, even if the housing
itself was satisfactory. 'Migration of this particular kind gives rise to
great problems of mental health,' he had recently told a conference,
adding that 'it would be almost fair to talk of a new disease – housing
estate neurosis – because it is in some parts of the country assuming
such dimensions that it is worthy of a name of its own'. In May 1958,
his Home Service radio programme with Peter Willmott, 'Families on
the Move', so starkly contrasted warm, tight-knit Bethnal Green with
cold, atomised Debden that, as the *Observer* put it, 'the narrator's
conclusion, that resettlement is a great thing but not at the expense of
the old neighbourliness, sounded powerful and incontrovertible after
the recordings'.

Three months later, in August, the first families moved on to a new
estate on Oxford's eastern outskirts, Blackbird Leys. Many tenants
came from areas of the city lately cleared of slums, notably St Ebbe's, to
the vexation of those tenants who had come to Oxford to work at
Cowley's prosperous, expanding car plants. 'I don't like it up here
getting all the tail end,' insisted one. 'It's a disgusting place. Putting all
the backend up here won't give people like us a chance to make this a
decent place to live.' Stigmatised from the start, and utterly remote
from the dreaming spires, Blackbird Leys would suffer acutely from
vandalism while it was being completed. 'For four years,' recorded a
local paper in 1962, 'acres of unlit buildings sites, inadequate police
supervision, parental apathy and the provision of a public house catering mainly for young people, has provided a perfect setting for the idle,
the mischievous, and the more sinister night people.'[17]

For those who, unlike Young, were pushing hard for dispersal and
low density, the jewels in the crown were of course the New Towns –
which, by 1958, were starting to change significantly. Take Stevenage,
becoming not only more urban (with the first shops around the

belatedly developed Town Square opening in June) but also more individualistic. The AGM of the Stevenage Residents' Federation attracted
only 30 people, representing 0.1 per cent of the town's population; the
Stevenage Echo, a seemingly well-established campaigning forum,
closed; campaigns themselves became increasingly social rather than
political, typified by the start of the Stevenage Nursery Association;
and it was reported that 'gossip fences (or anti-gossip fences) six-feet
high are being erected [by the Development Corporation] at the request
of tenants who want privacy', with these fences 'being built around all
the gardens'. There was also the thorny question of class. In Crawley
the Development Corporation reluctantly accepted that it had no alternative but to give developers a freer hand if professionals, wanting
appropriate private housing, were to be permanently attracted – an
acceptance that in effect led to the town being divided into separate
zones of public and private housing, as opposed to the previous policy
of 'pepper-potting' private, unsubsidised houses through the estates.
Much the same was happening in Harlow. 'When the town began they
had this idea of mixing the executive-cum-business-man type of houses
with those of the workers,' the *Harlow Citizen*'s editor explained to the
Daily Mail. 'Human nature being what it is, the policy hasn't really
succeeded. Now the house-building trend is towards segregation.' Or,
as Mrs Ferguson, the wife of a local security officer, put it, 'In our
neighbourhood, one side of the road is working-class and the other is
rather middle-class. When the children come out to play you find they
keep to their own sides of the street, as if a line were drawn down the
centre.'

At this stage the only second-generation New Town in the offing was
Cumbernauld, near Glasgow. Preliminary planning proposals appeared
in May, and tellingly all the major facilities were to be concentrated in
the central, hilltop area – an implicit abandonment of the neighbourhood planning, with its socially balanced neighbourhood units, that
had dominated the idealistic thinking behind the first-generation New
Towns.[18]

More generally in the built environment, 1958 was the year when
modernism indisputably entered the mainstream. '"Modern" architecture of second and lower degrees of originality is now so universally
accepted that even planning officers approve it,' rather sardonically

noted the *Architects' Journal* in March, before asserting flatly that
'"Modern" architecture is now the accepted style.' Over the next few
months, three new buildings helped to validate this claim: Coventry's
Belgrade Theatre, a municipal venture hailed by Kenneth Tynan as 'a
beautiful box of steel and glass and timber'; Gatwick Airport's steel-
and-glass terminal building, according to the ultra-modernist Reyner
Banham 'so up-to-date it shames the tatty old BEA Dakotas on the
tarmac'; and, at fusty Lord's, the gently modern, nicely curving Warner
Stand, which according to Sir Pelham Warner himself avoided being
one of those 'huge skyscraping stands which would turn the ground
into something approaching a cockpit'. An increasingly ripe modernist
target was the expanding world of higher education. In April the
Architects' Journal found it 'encouraging' that the design for a new
lecture block at Manchester College of Science and Technology was
'uncompromisingly modern', but not long afterwards lamented how
the almost completed Nuffield College in Oxford would 'stand as lasting evidence of a great industrialist's fear of progress in architecture'.
And from June the process was under way of drawing up a shortlist of
potential architects for the massive rebuilding of Leeds University, with
only modernists being seriously considered.[19]

The pursuit of modernity was quickening everywhere, it seemed. In
Westminster a pilot scheme for parking meters was trialled, 23 years
after they had first been used in America; near Luton the M1 began to
be built, eventually by some 7,000 workers, mainly from Ireland; in
Nottingham the city began to 'inflict on itself', in Simon Jenkins's
words, 'the absurd Maid Marian Way, cutting the old centre from the
castle mound and destroying, among a warren of streets, an exquisite
set of Queen Anne almshouses'; in Ilford there was the first move
towards a comprehensive redevelopment of the central area, above all
to upgrade the shopping facilities; on Tyneside a local paper applauded
how 'out of the jumble of small shops and Arab-owned coffee bars, the
new and ultra-modern South Shields Market Place has begun to emerge',
with 'the hotch-potch of buildings along the north-west corner' being
'swept away to make room for a concrete and glass office block'; in
Birmingham the decision to demolish the Market Hall, splendid and
Victorian, opened the way for an ambitious redevelopment of the city
centre; across England and Wales over 55,000 houses were demolished

in slum clearance areas, often in northern cities; in Edinburgh three young local architects won the competition for a major housing development at the Port of Leith, where the two resulting 21-storey towers (Cairngorm and Grampian Houses) would dominate the huge Leith Fort estate; and in Bethnal Green the new, high-rise Dorset estate, the borough's largest, was named after the Tolpuddle Martyrs. Bethnal Green was also host to Denys Lasdun's pioneering, controversial 'cluster' blocks: an 8-storey one in Usk Street and a 16-storey one (Keeling House) in Claredale Street, with the latter being topped out in August, as the Union Jack was flown, the mayor and mayoress looked on benignly, and the 200 workers celebrated with a pint. 'The thing was radically broken up, this building, into four discrete connected towers, each semi-d on a floor, each a maisonette, so that they were moving into homes not so very different from what they were used to, updated on sanitary stuff,' Lasdun would recall about his explicitly social purpose. 'It was an attempt to get some of the quality of life retained as distinct from being treated like a statistical pawn in a great prism.'[20]

By 1958 London was in the relatively early stages of a phenomenal office boom – one that would soon spread into the provinces. It had begun in the City with three buildings that went up in the mid-1950s: the Bank of England's New Change (just to the east of St Paul's), condemned by Pevsner in 1957 as a 'vast pile' that was 'shockingly lifeless and reactionary', but half a century later defended by Gavin Stamp as 'a stodgy but well-made classical design which made no attempt to upstage Wren', in contrast to the 'arrogant, irrational, vulgar' One New Change shopping centre that was replacing it; the more modern, 14-storey Bucklersbury House, which according to Ian Nairn had 'no virtues and no vices . . . it is the null point of architecture'; and Fountain House in Fenchurch Street, a 12-storey tower (on a low horizontal podium) that had an all-glass curtain wall and which became the prototype for what the architectural historian Nicholas Bullock has called 'commercial modernism'. Whatever the architectural style, the conditions were propitious by the late 1950s for a speculative property boom, not only in offices but also in shops and other development schemes. The Conservative government in November 1954 had abandoned the building controls of the previous 15 years; resourceful, clear-eyed property developers like Charles Clore, Jack Cotton and Max Rayne were fully aware of the potential financial jackpot; and the local authorities (whether in London or elsewhere) were usually no match for their ambitions, even if they did want to thwart them, by no means always the case.[21]

One architect above all – in every sense – was switched on to the possibilities. The planners 'feared me more than I feared them', the shrewd, unassuming, pipe-smoking Colonel Richard Seifert would accurately recall about his remarkable skill in exploiting loopholes in planning laws, thereby enabling the maximum lettable space from a site. Seifert ran his architectural practice (motto: 'Prestige Without Vulgarity') with all the focus and discipline of a military operation, befitting his army past. The imposing Woolworth House on Marylebone Road (1955) was his first major London building, and several hundred office blocks lay ahead as well as hotels and high-rise housing. 'Seifert was the antithesis of the image of the architect as bohemian artist,' noted an obituary. 'His solid businessman-like approach won him few friends in the architectural Establishment, which tended to dismiss his work as "development architecture".'[22]

During 1958 it became almost a cliché that London's skyline was changing dramatically. 'Skyscraper London' was the title in March of an enthusiastic piece in the *Star*, and soon afterwards Barbara Hooper painted a word picture on *Radio Newsreel*. After describing the visual effect of the tall blocks that had gone up, and were going up, in the City, she went on:

> Look north along Fleet Street, for instance. Not long ago the only square-topped white building was the *Daily Telegraph* office; now there is also Hulton House, eight storeys high, and St Bride's House, much the same height. Stand on the banks of the Serpentine in Hyde Park: a few months ago you could not see a building above the treetops, and now at least four storeys of the central tower on a huge building rear high above the trees. In and around Oxford Street at least two new shopping blocks are going up, some eight storeys high. If you go up the tower of Westminster Cathedral, as I have done, the view over that part of the West End is changing, too. Above the cluster of old dark roofs and chimneys you can pick out new office buildings in Whitehall, an engineering

block behind Buckingham Palace, twelve- and fourteen-storey blocks of flats near Paddington Station, and others down in Pimlico, and the tower of the massive London Transport headquarters by St James's Park. Soon, if you walk through St James's Park towards The Mall, 200 feet and more of the not-yet-built New Zealand House will partly block the view up Haymarket.

'If planning permission is given,' she concluded, 'there may be hotels in Park Lane and Lancaster Gate that are more than 300 feet high, and over on the South Bank of the Thames work has already begun on an office block [the Shell Building] 330 feet high – nearly as high as St Paul's.'

Not everyone was thrilled by London's new skyline. The same week in April that Hooper's evocation appeared in the *Listener*, a letter to the *New Statesman* from a professed layman, Arthur Kemsley of 106 Finchley Road, disparaged the 'infinite number of up-ended matchboxes' that now littered the London scene. 'The reason, it seems, is that a cube is the most economical structure to build . . . Every square inch of floor space is financially productive. And to hell with what it looks like.' His letter was probably read by John Fowles, who the following Sunday took a walk round a new estate in St Pancras:

The Regent Square area is now a postwar development scheme – gaunt blocks, cheap, shoddy. They reminded me of the Dartmoor prison blocks. High, rectangular, imprisoning. One great slab pitted like a cliff with red and mauve and blue square balcony-caves. Nearby were flats of a slightly earlier period – with ribbed corners, tired balconies and windows. None of them look as if they will last; the horror is that they will.

For the architectural historian Alec Clifton-Taylor, responding to Hooper in the following week's *Listener*, the time had arrived when 'we have got to decide, once for all, whether we are going to abandon the human values which are to the fore in London and launch out towards the creation of another megapolis, or not'; he hoped 'fervently' that the LCC would refuse permission for 'skyscraper hotels' in Park Lane and Lancaster Gate. Frainy Heap was probably on the other side of the argument. 'Every evening,' recorded Anthony in June about his nine-year-old son, 'he wanders across to trespass in the new 11 storeys high block of council flats over in Regent Square, ride up and down in its lift, and look over London from its roof.'

Soon afterwards, J. M. Richards in the *Architectural Review* offered his overview on the prospects for 'High London'. Although pleased that the very tall office block planned for Millbank had just received planning consent – 'it will provide the London landscape with a vertical punctuation mark just where it is needed' – his larger case was that 'it is unfortunate in the extreme that, with a few honourable exceptions, the new high buildings planned for London fall far below the best of what our architects are capable'. His explanation might have been written with Colonel Seifert in mind: 'The average property developer is not in touch with the best architectural advice, the kind of architect he favours, understandably from his point of view, being the kind with most experience of extracting the greatest profitable floor area from a given plot-ratio and of circumventing most speedily the rules and regulations that stand in his way.' Richards, a moderate modernist and a man of huge common sense, was disinclined to underestimate the significance of this historical moment:

> In accepting high buildings we are accepting nothing less than a revolution in the visual character of London, which has always been a horizontal city. But are we also aware of another revolution that follows? There were vertical elements in the old horizontal London, but these deserved their place because of their symbolic significance. They were the spires of churches and the towers of imperial institutions and the like; they were among the dignified furnishings proper to a capital city. The new vertical elements, dominant in the skyline, will instead be anonymous commercial blocks with no civic significance . . .

'How', he asked, 'are we going to reconcile the civic pride of a city confident in its ability to control its own future with the fact of its most conspicuous monuments being where they are simply because it was to some individual's profit to put them there?'[23]

Redevelopment generally remained a perhaps surprisingly contested process. In January it was reported that 'more than 14,000 council house tenants have decided to stay where they are rather than accept the offer of moving into luxury flats in an eight-storey block being built at Wolverhampton', with 'only 40 willing to change'. On the refuseniks being quizzed by housing officials, it emerged that their main objections to moving were that 'flats lack privacy, they have no gardens, children have to be penned in or sent into busy streets to play, and rents are higher', while 'some tenants think that noise would carry too easily in the flats and a few just don't like anything new'. In February in a talk in Bristol on that city's post-war planning and architecture, Ian Nairn castigated the apparent willingness to allow Kingsdown's demolition as 'frightening', observed of the Kingsmead shopping centre that he could not 'imagine so many buildings designed by so many different architects with the same level of mediocrity', and called the new Prudential building in the insensitively developed Lime Street area a 'monster'. Writing to the *Salford City Reporter* in March, 'Disgusted Citizen' implicitly questioned the very rationale of slum clearance: 'Having had the opportunity over many years of visiting people in their homes week after week, in every part of Salford and Manchester, I have arrived at the firm conclusion that slums are caused by the people themselves, not by the state of the buildings in which they live.' And soon afterwards, in a lecture to the Royal Institution of Chartered Surveyors, the architectural historian John Summerson almost as daringly wondered whether the current 'wave of curiosity and expanding interest' in old buildings, a nod perhaps to the recently formed Victorian Society, had 'something to do with our lack of success in producing a contemporary architecture which is warmly and instinctively loved'.[24]

Nairn was back in the fray in early April, one of some 700 people attending on a cold night another meeting at Kensington Town Hall to discuss the Notting Hill Gate scheme. 'Why was not the public asked their opinion at an earlier stage?' he asked, and a motion expressing dissatisfaction with the scheme was passed by a large majority. Back in Salford, local elections in early May highlighted the issue, according to a local journalist, of 'the general unsightliness of our clearance areas, extending over months and in some cases years', so that 'there never seems to be a clean sweep anywhere', while in Surbiton in June, the rumour that a block of flats was to go up near her brother's house prompted grim reflections from Marian Raynham: 'Awful things for families to live in. Every available space is being built on, & the planners *never* do anything to make a neighbourhood look prettier.' July saw Nairn commenting balefully on changes, partly in the context of road-widening, in a Cambridgeshire town – 'Wisbech is settling down, with complacent phrases all round, to a bit of self-destruction just as effective as the H-bomb' – and Lady Morris, retiring president of the National Federation of Community Associations, bemoaning how housing estates were still being built without adequate amenities, so that 'the people for whom they are intended are forced to choose between a home without a neighbourhood and a neighbourhood without a home'. The next month in Coventry, the councillor most responsible for that city's remarkable post-war reconstruction, George Hodgkinson, reluctantly conceded in an interview that retrenchment was becoming unavoidable, given that it was now increasingly difficult to receive public support 'for schemes which seem remote from their point of view'. But Hodgkinson himself was one of four Coventry councillors (including the chairman of the Housing Committee) who that August, according to a local MP soon afterwards, 'spent a week at the Edinburgh Festival at the cost of Wimpeys', which 'had so far done £8,000,000-worth of housing at Coventry, most of it without tenders'. Richard Crossman added that Wimpeys had also 'thrown some tremendous parties'.[25]

Ultimately, though, a combination of the spirit of the age and seemingly inescapable practical necessity was irresistible. '15-storey Flats Next?' ran a Salford headline in March, followed by news about plans for St Matthias No. 2 Clearance Area, where demolition was proceeding apace. 'As we go on,' explained the Housing Committee's Councillor N. Wright, 'we find that, because many people are loath to go from slum clearance areas into the overspill districts at Little Hulton and in Cheshire, we are more or less tied down to the high-flats type of density housing.' A week later another Salfordian, Mrs K. Mountney of Ewart Street, itself in a proposed clearance area, stoutly insisted that 'every available piece of land in this hemmed-in city must be used to its fullest advantage and if that means eight-storey flats on one's doorstep that's just one of the hazards of living in Salford'. Just along the road, Manchester had long been known for its scepticism about high rises, but that spring a delegation of councillors visited blocks of flats in

Berlin, Hamburg and Amsterdam. 'The Germans and the Dutch have learned to live in flats,' stated their admiring report in due course. The lesson for Manchester was that, provided 'great care' was 'exercised in the selection of tenants to occupy multi-storey development', then such development could 'provide good housing and a colourful and interesting development worthy of our city'. For most progress-minded activators, clearance and redevelopment was a black-and-white issue. 'We still have too many slums – both to live in and to work in,' declared T. Yates, chairman of the General Council of the TUC, when he formally opened the Dorset estate. 'To be rid of them we need more than bricks and mortar; more than men and women. We need courage and vision. In Bethnal Green, in their social development scheme, I believe they have shown this courage.'

So too with reconstruction more generally – with Coventry still a compelling emblem of modernity at its best. 'So much more like a city of the world than many other four or five times its size,' declared Stanley Baron in April in the first of his *Reynolds News* series on 'The Changing Face of Britain'. Soon afterwards, Coventry was also the obligatory first stop for the *News Chronicle*'s Sarah Jenkins in her 'So This Is England' series, as she praised its 'air of looking forward and not back'. An architect certainly not looking back was Peter Smithson. At about this time, in his capacity as a tutor at the Architectural Association, he received an essay from a fourth-year student on the current work of the Italian architect Ernesto. 'The essay spoke warmly of this new, softened modernism,' records the biographer of Richard Rogers, 'but it was anathema to Smithson who dismissed it all as romantic nonsense and demanded that the essay be rewritten. Similarly, a housing scheme by Rogers for Richmond Park, which displayed the same romantic tendencies and which derived in part from the neo-liberty revival in Italy, received the same response. It even had bow windows.'[26]

Back in the early 1950s, an unsuccessful entry by Smithson and his forceful wife Alison in the City of London's competition to design new housing at Golden Lane had done much to launch the concept of 'streets-in-the-air', usually known later as 'streets-in-the-sky' – in effect, an attempt to recreate, off the ground, the communal aspect of the working-class street. The first place where it came into being, rapidly attracting huge international attention, was the new Park Hill estate in Sheffield, on

a hillside overlooking the railway station and city centre, designed by
Jack Lynn and Ivor Smith for the go-ahead City Architect, Lewis
Womersley. 'Out of ugliness we are to create something of beauty and
utility,' declared the lord mayor on the last Friday of April 1958, as –
amidst the rubble of 800 condemned houses in the process of being
demolished – two veteran councillors (one Labour, one Tory) were
handed a souvenir trowel and laid the foundation stone. Soon afterwards,
ahead of the local elections, Labour's party political broadcast featured
the area's MP, George Darling, telling a housewife that Park Hill would
be 'a quiet, self-contained community, with its own shops and schools,
and other amenities'. Later in the broadcast, Councillor Harold Lambert,
vice-chairman of the Housing Committee and the driving force in pushing through Sheffield's new housing developments (not only Park Hill),
explained to Darling how while smaller children would be able to play,
under their mother's eye, on the 'large sheltered balcony' that each flat
would have, for older children there would be playgrounds at ground
level. 'The type of equipment we have in mind,' he added, 'is not only
entertaining, it is of an educational value for the kiddies, too.'[27]

Womersley himself was adamant, as he told a housing conference
two months later at London's County Hall, that 'the opportunities
which were missed for comprehensive redevelopment prewar are not to
be allowed to escape again'. By this time a similar spirit was starting to
imbue many of Glasgow's activators, especially in relation to the
Gorbals. There, the biggest redevelopment commission had been given
to the Scottish architect Basil Spence, best known for the new Coventry
Cathedral that was rising up and who was now acclaimed by the
Architects' Journal (in July 1958) as 'The Popular President', i.e. of the
Royal Institute of British Architects. 'Brilliance describes the man,'
declared the magazine's admiring profile. 'He designs fluently, speaks
fluently, is capable, sincere and almost too tender-hearted.' Following
his commission from Glasgow Corporation, Spence had visited Le
Corbusier's famous, hard-modernist *Unité d'Habitation* in Marseille
and been much impressed, not least by its nautical flavour; this summer,
on presenting to the Housing Committee his plans for ten 20-storey
blocks raised on stilts and with inset communal balconies, he enthusiastically claimed that 'on Tuesdays, when all the washing's out, it'll be
like a great ship in full sail!'

The Housing Committee itself, on giving its approval in late August to not only the blocks but also the whole layout for the development area (including shops, restaurants and much else), called Spence's scheme 'a new method of living in cities at high densities without loss of humanity', while the *Glasgow Herald* had no qualms about what would become 'the Queenies': 'The special feature is the provision of small garden or patio for each house, no matter at what height . . . By this perpetuation of the familiar tenement "green", it is hoped to create a community spirit.' A few days later, in a piece on 'The Hanging Gardens of the Gorbals', the *Architects' Journal* expressed the hope that Spence 'succeeds in his enterprising attempt to civilize the tenement'. In the words soon afterwards of the almost legendary journalist Hannen Swaffer (who back in 1950 had written powerfully in 'I have Ascended into Hell' about the overcrowded, rat-ridden tenements of the Gorbals) this was a scheme to ensure that in five years' time the Gorbals would have 'one of the finest community centres in the world'.

Swaffer was writing, in his column in the *People*, the week after claiming that London was 'gradually becoming a monstrosity of utilitarian architecture', typified by how the first sight on coming out of Paddington station was 'a beehive of offices – one block is almost 20 storeys high! – which is ugly beyond belief'. He added that he had recently expressed his views 'to Authority' (unnamed) and been blandly informed: 'That is the modern style.' Swaffer's attack on modern architects provoked a riposte, printed in the paper. 'They are not the inhuman, callous Big Brothers that Mr Swaffer would have us believe,' declared a young architect from Hull. 'The majority are working thoughtfully and sincerely, in face of complex and difficult problems. Many are succeeding.' Calling them 'the envy of the world', Alan Plater cited the LCC housing estates: 'They have brought fresh air and light to people who previously knew only backyards and smoky squalor. All great architecture was once "modern".'[28]

7

Stone Me

On Friday, 11 April – four days after the end of the Aldermaston march and just as *Balthazar*, the second instalment of Lawrence Durrell's projected 'four-decker novel', left the literary critic Walter Allen 'eagerly awaiting the next shake of the kaleidoscope' – Accrington Stanley's vice-chairman, Charles Kilby, heard about the imminent sale, at an army depot in Aldershot, of the double-decker stand previously used for the Aldershot Military Tattoo. It seated 4,700, was on offer at a give-away £1,450 and seemed the heaven-sent answer to the perceived need to increase Peel Park's meagre seating capacity of 800. On Monday he and the chairman, Bob Moore, inspected the stand, and by Tuesday the club had successfully bid for it. Even allowing for the £10,000 cost of dismantling, conveyance and re-erection, Stanley were on course, reported an enthusiastic *Accrington Observer*, to save something like £25,000. Moore explained his rationale: 'The whole future of football is in the melting pot. There is a possibility in seasons to come of a super-European League, and with Stanley's ambitions as high as the sky we wish to be "in" on the ground floor and make Accrington one of the centres of football.' Sadly, there were three snags. Spending even £11,450 would push an already financially troubled club into further debt; it was completely the wrong type of stand for a football ground; and the notion of Stanley, never yet in one of England's two top divisions, as part of a European super-league was, to put it mildly, a stretch. 'We'll never fill it,' the cash-strapped, departing manager Walter Galbraith commented bluntly to a supporter, 'and I could have had three new players with the money.' As it happened, the Football League itself was about to be restructured, with Divisions Three and Four as national divisions replacing Third Divisions North and South. Stanley would be in Division Three, so a touch of nobility characterised the club's veteran director Sam Pilkington successfully pleading in May at a Football League meeting that there should be four-down and four-up between the two new divisions. 'Remember the Fourth Division clubs,' he urged. 'Give them a chance to rise again.'[1]

The week after Stanley sealed the fateful deal, Tony Hancock explored the infinite boredom of 'Sunday Afternoon at Home'. The opening lines, with their unscripted pauses and sighs, took a full 48 seconds to deliver:

> *Tony: (Yawns)* Oh dear! Oh dear, oh dear. Cor dear me. Stone me, what a life. What's the time?
> *Bill [Kerr]:* Two o'clock.
> *Tony:* Is that all? Cor dear, oh dear, oh dear me. I don't know. *(Yawns)* Oh, I'm fed up.

A few lines further on, Sid James put the Sunday feeling into global perspective: 'Look, so am I fed up, and so is Bill fed up. We're all fed up, so shut up moaning and make the best of it.' Making the best of it . . . Sundays were still Sundays, the Victorian age was still alive, and for children especially it could be an endurance test.

Even so, for all the ennui, a Gallup poll a few weeks after Hancock's radio episode revealed almost two-fifths of people not wanting places of entertainment to open on Sundays as on weekdays, 41 per cent disapproving of the idea of professional sport on Sundays, and 44 per cent favouring the existing shorter opening hours for pubs on Sundays. To each of those questions there were about 15 per cent of 'don't knows', so overall it was hard to discern an overwhelming desire for change.[2]

The 32-year-old Paul Raymond, hitherto best known for his nude touring revues, was probably not a sabbatarian. Raymond's Revuebar, opening on 21 April in Soho, had a conscious strategy: being a members' only club would get round censorship problems; the striptease would be appreciably more sexually explicit and 'Continental' than at the nearby, by now rather old-hat, Windmill Theatre; and altogether it would, as the historian Frank Mort puts it, 'evoke a world of contemporary metropolitan leisure'. This child of affluence was a success from the start. 'Already he has enrolled 10,000 half-guinea members,' recorded the *People*'s roving reporter Arthur Helliwell on the first Sunday after opening, 'and all last week they were queuing up in the bright afternoon sunshine for tables around the raised floor on which 20 beautiful girls appear in various degrees of nudity.' Raymond himself reassured Helliwell: 'I have never put on an indecent show in my life. In fact, I won't engage any girl with a bigger than 36 bust because I wouldn't like to embarrass my customers.'

Raymond's Revuebar had its first police raid on the evening of Friday, 2 May. The clientele found there included military men, impeccably middle-class gentlemen from the Home Counties, foreign tourists – and, noted the police statement, a party that had 'come down' from Stockport 'with their pals' for next day's Cup Final and had, via a local tour operator, booked tickets for Soho as well as Wembley. They were probably supporting Manchester United, as indeed was most of the country, only three months after Munich. Their opponents were Bolton Wanderers. 'We went down to London three days before the game,' remembered Bolton's captain Nat Lofthouse, 'and we all got a suit from Burtons, two pounds ten shillings – we all looked well.' Matt Busby was present, frail and with a walking stick, but an emotionally drained United were never really in it. The defining moment, with Bolton one-up, occurred not long after half-time. 'This shot came across,' Lofthouse recalled in 1992, 'and their goalie palmed it up, and before he caught it I went in and shoulder-charged him, and the ball, Harry Gregg and me finished in the back of the net, and the referee gave a goal. If that had've happened now I would have been sent off.' But in 1958 it was still a self-consciously man's game and there were no hard feelings from the United players, though next day, as the Bolton coach travelled through Salford on the way home with the cup, 'there were Manchester United supporters waiting with flour bombs in little packets, and they bombarded us'.[3]

The following evening, the middle-aged Labour frontbencher Richard Crossman encountered the youthful New Left, in the form of a Universities and Left Review Club meeting at a hotel in Monmouth Street, where 'a certain Raymond Williams' was giving a lecture on which Crossman had been asked to comment afterwards. 'I found it absolutely packed with some 300 young people, mostly under 30 and mostly, I fear, open-necked, swarthy and ugly,' he recorded. 'I noticed it was a bit of a dumpy atmosphere and I was slightly surprised when nobody, on an appallingly hot evening, welcomed me or offered me a drink at the bar.' The 50-minute lecture by Williams, an adult education tutor, was 'very competent, not at all stupid, but read in a dull, competent, dreary voice'; its theme was that 'there was not a good, high-class press and a bad, popular press, but various presses appealing to various audiences and catering for various tastes'. Crossman in response explained the difference between writing for the *New Statesman* and the *Daily Mirror*, before his evening then deteriorated: during the interval barely anyone spoke to him, while afterwards in the discussion an 'entirely humourless' attack on him 'consisted of disagreeing with things I had written in the [*Mirror*] column'. Watching was the tyro playwright Arnold Wesker. 'Boy!' he wrote next day to his future wife Dusty (about to do a stint as a waitress at Butlin's holiday camp in Skegness),

> He just did not know where he had come. He thought he could toss a few humorous crumbs to the crowd and a couple of observations and they would be satisfied. He didn't even prepare anything. Beside Williams he was a loud showman. And when the discussion came – Jesus! he didn't know what hit him. The boys stood up and lambasted him in clear, precise terms. How could he, as a socialist, support a paper [i.e. the *Mirror*] which, for its vulgarity, was an insult to the mind of the working class; a paper which painted a glossy, film-star world. The smugness left his face, he evaded every direct question and even in winding up said nothing except 'Well, you high-class people are just as easily led up the garden path in your papers!' Which may be true – but that does not justify him leading the working class up the garden path in their papers!

Crossman's own take on the evening was rather different. These 'ex-Communists who broke away during the Hungarian crisis' were now, he concluded, 'creating a Chapel for themselves with an even more sectarian atmosphere'.

There was undeniably a cultural turn to the New Left. 'A reportage and critique of the "culture" of post-Welfare Britain' was one of the *ULR*'s central aims, stated an editorial soon afterwards, adding that 'we

want to break with the view that cultural or family life is an entertaining
sideshow, a secondary expression of human creativity or fulfilment';
while later in the summer David Marquand, still an undergraduate at
Oxford, stated in the *Manchester Guardian* that Oxford's socialist
intelligentsia were far more concerned with 'culture' than 'politics as
usually understood', and he quoted one prominent university left-
winger as having shouted at him recently, '*Look Back in Anger* is a
more important political document than anything the Labour Party has
said since 1951.'[4] Arguably, moreover, this was not just true of Osborne's
play. For by the summer of 1958 the British theatre was in the middle
of an extraordinary year, among other things taking the '1956' revolution to a whole new place and level, if not necessarily always immediately appreciated.

Ann Jellicoe's uninhibited *The Sport of My Mad Mother* at the Royal
Court in February had set the ball rolling – Anthony Heap dismissing
it as 'putrid piffle', but Kenneth Tynan acclaiming 'a play of spectacular
promise and inspiring imperfection' and especially enjoying the
'raucous and lissom' Wendy Craig as 'the gang's symbolic mother' –
before an intense theatrical sequence, lasting barely two and a half
months, began at the Saville on 23 April with the musical *Expresso
Bongo*. Principally the creation of Wolf Mankowitz (who via a scholarship had journeyed from East Ham Grammar School to being taught at
Cambridge by the literary critic F. R. Leavis), and essentially a Steele-
inspired satire on callow youths being discovered in Soho coffee bars
and turned into pop stars by ruthless managers, it was warmly greeted
as a latter-day *Beggar's Opera*. Heap was among the first-night admirers, praising 'a caustic and devastating wit that is no less effective for
being essentially good-humoured', finding the songs 'engagingly bright
and lively', and singling out Millicent Martin's 'excellent
performance'.

Then, a week later, three days before the Cup Final, came the long-
awaited *My Fair Lady* at Drury Lane, with Heap present again.
'Handsomely and colourfully staged,' he conceded, and 'ambles agreeably through a variety of scenes', but overall 'far from being the wonderful show we'd been led to expect, and what all the fuss was about in
New York I can't imagine'. The paid critics were on the whole kinder:
'perfectly delicious' declared Derek Granger in the *Financial Times*,

while Harold Hobson in the *Sunday Times* thought it a 'near-miracle' that, after all the endless publicity, the musical was 'not merely as good as we had been told, it is better' (though he added that Julie Andrews's performance as Eliza Doolittle had 'no interest whatever', and that Alan Jay Lerner's book and lyrics had 'foisted on to the most piercing and unsentimental intellect of the English theatre [i.e. George Bernard Shaw's] the outlook of a Berta Ruck)'. The following week's *Any Questions?* picked up that theme. Should 'musical comedy writers', asked Mrs Carter at the Memorial Hall in Ludgershall, Wiltshire, be 'prevented from making a musical out of a straight play after the author's death when he has expressly forbidden this during his life?' 'Well,' answered Harold Wilson, 'I belong to one of the large majority in this country that's absolutely sick to death of all this ballyhoo about *My Fair Lady*.' Wilson went on to express himself worried about what would happen when the copyright expired of Gilbert and Sullivan ('of which we in this country are very rightly proud'). 'Heavens,' he continued, 'if those are going to be turned into New York musical comedies, or ice shows, or for that matter rock 'n' roll popular classics, I shall be extremely upset, and I think so will the majority of decent-minded people in this country.' This puritanical, old-fashioned, selectively modernising Yorkshireman ended by pointing out that 'as with anyone of us here who's been in the Boy Scout movement or Girl Guide movement knows very well, quite a large proportion of the new popular songs, jazz hits and so on, are old songs we used to sing round the camp fire a few years ago, that have been pinched by some Tin Pan Alley spiv and turned into a very big money-making racket'.[5]

The evening before Wilson's outburst, 8 May, saw the London opening at the Globe of Terence Rattigan's new play, *Variation on a Theme*, about a rich woman (played by Margaret Leighton) who had taken up with a young ballet dancer. It was the evening when Rattigan, in his biographer's words, 'finally realised the changes that had been taking place in the London theatre'. An unenthusiastic Heap was typical of the audience, while next day the critics let rip, with even W. A. Darlington, usually very pro-Rattigan, regretfully noting in the *Telegraph* that this time he was 'out of form'. Even so, for all this being the unmistakeable start, four years after the triumph of *Separate Tables*, of what would become a long, painful retreat in Rattigan's reputation, the theatrical revolution as a whole was still far from complete. 'Who will put Life into our theatres?' beseeched Alex Atkinson, a 42-year-old playwright and journalist, in the *News Chronicle* on the 10th about what he regarded as a lamentable failure to follow up the Osborne breakthrough almost exactly two years earlier:

> The Royal Court Irregulars are fighting almost unaided against the forces of reaction and twaddle, and unless a few more enthusiasts will rally to the cause, we may go down in the history of the Drama as the country in which a leg show never closed throughout the Second World War, and the longest-running play was a who-dun-it by a lady whose more serious dialogue has been known to make even seasoned actors giggle . . . Have we no longer the courage to blast the commercial Upper Circle out of its moonstruck reverie? Who will follow Shaw? Did we ever have even the ghost of an O'Neill? Where is our Arthur Miller?[6]

Nine days later, on the evening of Monday the 19th, a chronicler of the Drama needed to be in three places at once. Bernard Kops's enjoyable if sentimental *The Hamlet of Stepney Green* was having a generally well-received premiere at the Oxford Playhouse; the Bob Mitchell Repertory Company was starting a week-long run of *Jane Eyre* at Crewe Theatre, with 22-year-old Glenda Jackson in her first major role as the heroine ('does well', noted the *Crewe Chronicle*); and Heap was taking his seat at the Lyric, Hammersmith. He soon discovered he was in for 'just the sort of lunatic stuff they love to inflict on us at the Court':

> All its characters are clearly insane, all its dialogue completely irrational, and what the whole thing is supposed to convey or signify is beyond understanding. I wouldn't go so far as to call it tedious or boring, for its young author, who is probably just trying to cash in on the stupid contemporary cult for avant-garde obscurity, has at least the knack of somehow holding one's attention. But its utter incomprehensibility becomes irritating, its calculated idiocy, embarrassing, and not even the excellent acting of John Slater, Richard Pearson and Beatrix Lehmann as the three craziest crackpots gathered together in the dingy seaside boarding-house that comprises the setting, can redeem its lack of sense and sensibility.

The 'young author' of *The Birthday Party* was Harold Pinter, who as a jobbing actor called David Baron had written this, his first profession-ally produced play, during a tour of *Doctor in the House*. The next morning, few if any of the critics dissented from Heap's unfavourable verdict. 'The author never got down to earth long enough to explain what his play was about,' complained the *Telegraph*'s Darlington, bemoaning the lot of critics 'condemned to sit through plays like this'. Alan Dent in the *News Chronicle* ('Mr Pinter Misses His Target') declared, after outlining the plot, that 'the moral would seem to be that every man-jack of us is a raving lunatic'. And for the *Mail*'s Cecil Wilson, though not denying Pinter's 'wit that gleams through his mist of a play', it was altogether a 'baffling mixture'. Pinter himself, some forty years on, recollected in tranquillity the emotion of that Tuesday morning. 'I went out at 7.30 a.m. to get the morning papers, went to a café and had a cup of tea and read them. Each one was worse than the last. I thought I might give the whole thing up and go and write a novel. But my wife at the time, Vivien [Merchant], said, "Come on, you've had bad notices as an actor, pull yourself together."' There was still the *Evening Standard* headline to endure – 'Sorry, Mr Pinter, you're just not funny enough' – but by then the decision had already been taken to pull the plug at the end of the week. Audiences for the rest of the six-day run were desultory, and by the time a eulogising review by Harold Hobson appeared in the *Sunday Times* – 'Mr Pinter, on the evidence of this work, possesses the most original, disturbing, and arresting talent in theatrical London' – it was too late.[7]

Just two days afterwards occured another London debut. Shelagh Delaney, a Salford teenager, had gone to Rattigan's *Variation on a Theme* during its pre-London tour and been so infuriated by what she saw as its insipidness that she had rapidly written her own, locally set play, *A Taste of Honey*. Joan Littlewood at the Theatre Workshop responded positively and, with the Lord Chamberlain agreeing to turn a blind eye so long as the gay character was called an 'art student' and things generally were not made too explicit, it had its first night at the Theatre Royal, Stratford East, on Tuesday the 27th. That morning the *Daily Mail*'s gossip column included a friendly item about Delaney. She was 19, lived with her parents in a council house and had worked as a photographer's assistant. 'It's drawn from my observations and some experience,' she told Paul Tanfield as she sipped lemonade and refused a cigarette. However, the *Mail* giveth, the *Mail* taketh away, and next day's review by Edward Goring was a stinker. After observing that the play 'tastes of exercise books and marmalade', he went on: 'Once, authors wrote good plays set in drawing-rooms. Now, under the Welfare State, they write bad plays set in garrets.' And after giving a plot summary, he concluded: 'It hardly amounts to a play, and for all the shouting it says little. It has a few touching moments, but those stem from the touching quality sometimes found in immaturity . . . If there is anything worse than an Angry Young Man, it's an Angry Young Woman.'

For the most part, however, critical opinion was positive. *The Times* praised it as 'tough, humorous, and close to the ground'; J. W. Lambert in the *Sunday Times* enjoyed the 'curt, quick, funny' dialogue and Delaney's 'wonderfully non-committal attitude' towards 'the grubbier aspects of life'; and Tynan in the *Observer*, while conceding there were 'plenty of crudities' in the play, acclaimed its 'smell of living' and called her 'a portent'. That was also the take of the *Spectator*'s Alan Brien, who reckoned that 'even five years ago, before a senile society began to fawn upon the youth which is about to devour it, such a play would have remained written in green longhand in a school exercise book on the top of a bedroom wardrobe'. A vigilant Wesker went during the second week of the run. 'They shout at each other, interrupt each other, talk to the audience,' he observed of the characters in his appraisal for *Dusty*. 'This seems to be on the way to the real theatre, not quite there but an eye-opener.'[8] *A Taste of Honey* was an important play not only in theatrical history, and not only in relation to social issues (illegitimacy, race, homosexuality), but also in terms of the north of England. So long off the metropolitan cultural radar, it was now just starting to move on to it – a process that had been begun the previous year by John Braine's best-selling novel *Room at the Top*.

For the unknown Wesker, the hour was almost at hand. 'I suppose I'll be branded an angry young man for it,' the 26-year-old told the *Coventry Standard*'s 'Thespis' over coffee at the start of July, ahead of *Chicken Soup with Barley*'s one-week run at the Belgrade Theatre before going straight to the Royal Court for another week, as part of its Repertory Festival. 'My limitation is that I can only write about things

that happen to me – but it is also a strength.' Calling his play 'one of a
trilogy', he also elaborated on his politics. 'An ardent Socialist,' duly
noted his interviewer, 'Arnold Wesker sees Socialism as an attitude to
life rather than a political quality. He considers present-day values
topsy turvy, producing people in a kind of "rat race". He has strong
views on education, and sees much of his art in terms of education.' The
week beginning the 7th presented Coventry's theatregoers with strongly
contrasting attractions: on the one hand, at the brand new civic theatre,
the Belgrade Theatre Company (including Frank Finlay) performing
Wesker's semi-autobiographical episodic chronicle of a Jewish – and
Communist – family in London's East End between 1936 and 1956,
culminating in the anguish of Hungary; on the other, at the long-
established, commercial Coventry Theatre, a comedy called *The Bride
and the Bachelor* by the future Tory speechwriter Ronald Millar, starring three old warhorses in Cicely Courtneidge, Robertson Hare and
Naunton Wayne. Conceivably, some may have stayed at home to watch
Ask Me Another and the *Phil Silvers Show* on BBC, or *Wagon Train*
followed by *Free and Easy* (starring Dickie Valentine) on ITV.

Wesker won on points in the local reviews. According to the *Standard*,
the Millar farce 'failed to evoke more than a titter for the whole of the
first act' and was 'a misfire', while *Chicken Soup* was 'full of life and
colour and detail', and was 'quite moving', but ultimately left 'deeply
etched outlines that form an unsatisfactory whole'. The *Evening
Telegraph* was equally scathing about the 'feeble farce', whereas the
Wesker was 'the stuff of life' and 'never fake, never touched up with
sentimentality'. On that first night there were cheers and applause at
the end, and even the shout of 'Author!', though Wesker preferred to
stay in the wings. He was less satisfied on the second evening. 'The
audience laughed in all the wrong places, and displayed such stupidity
it was unbelievable,' he told Dusty. 'They are so used to seeing corny
films and drawing-room comedies that when they come up against a
little real-life drama it embarrasses them and they have to treat it as a
joke.'

Then came the Royal Court. Not everyone went overboard – a play
'built for pygmies' thought Alan Brien; 'a documentary rather than a
play' reckoned Eric Keown; while Harold Hobson found it 'often
impressive' but was more interested in *Five Finger Exercise* at the

Comedy by Peter Shaffer ('may easily become a master of the theatre') – but the general tone was positive. 'John [Dexter, the play's director] and I stayed up all night walking from Sloane Street in order to get the papers as they came out,' Wesker reported to Dusty. 'The *Daily Mail* calls me a playwright of "rare ability and even rarer promise". The *Standard* says I have "rare understanding . . . passion and urgency". Even *The Times* and *Telegraph* are favourable.' The longer wait was for the increasingly influential Tynan, who on Sunday heralded *Chicken Soup* as an 'intensely exciting play' and asserted that if Wesker could 'survive the autobiographical stage', he was 'potentially a very important playwright'.[9] Tynan called it right: if there was one dramatist over the next few years who would command the most intense attention, and simultaneously capture and chase the moment, it was undoubtedly Wesker.

Tonight continued this summer to consolidate its hold as television's most popular current affairs programme. Henry Turton in *Punch* rounded up some of the 'splendid' team under its unflappable MC: 'high-pitched, querulous' Fyfe Robertson; 'neat and impish' Derek Hart; 'smooth' Geoffrey Johnson Smith; 'crisp and alert' Polly Elwes. The leading soap remained *Emergency—Ward 10* – 'the interminably incident-packed saga of that nice hospital full of photogenic nurses and terribly British doctors', noted Turton, but 'well done according to the soap-opera conventions' – while *Take Your Pick* and *Double Your Money* were the two dominant quiz shows. 'Last week's star,' recorded John Braine in May about the latter, 'was Plantagenet Somerset Fry, who decided to keep the £500 he'd already won but just out of curiosity asked what the £1,000 question would have been. He could have answered it.' That same week, *Take Your Pick* (hosted by Michael Miles, with Alec Dane on the gong) was the second-most-watched programme on either channel, but the most popular (viewed in 4.17 million homes) was *The Army Game*. 'These slapdash proceedings arouse feelings in me which verge on the sadistic,' recorded Turton, who saw it as a particular waste of the talents of Alfie Bass, 'that subtle and delicate droll'. Such was the show's popularity, however – reflecting in part the widely shared experience of National Service – that in June its signature tune went to number 5 in the charts, as, a few months later, did Bernard Bresslaw, aka Private 'Popeye' Popplewell, with an in-character rendition of 'Mad Passionate Love'.

At this stage the BBC's main weapon against *The Army Game* in the comedy stakes was Benny Hill at least as much as Tony Hancock. 'Benny Hill is the king of comedians,' acclaimed one viewer after his show on 26 April; 'he never fails to amuse, is never monotonous and abounds with natural fun and humour.' A rare telerecording of that show survives, revealing a still traditional Variety format – fillers include a glee group, Alma Cogan and a circus double-act – while Hill himself sings two suggestive faux-medieval songs and is the central figure in a series of quick-fire, inventive sketches, with one in drag. The show ends, in his biographer's words, 'with Benny stepping out of character and, for just fifteen seconds, appearing as "himself", accepting the applause of the studio audience, waving, winking at the camera and – for the only time in the entire hour – looking a little uncomfortable'. For straight-up-and-down, middle-of-the-road music, few programmes beat *The Billy Cotton Band Show*, with the good-looking Russ Conway by this time as resident pianist and the host himself one evening remarking to applause that 'skiffle' rhymed with 'piffle'. Cotton would not have enjoyed *Oh Boy!*, ITV's new pop show (masterminded by Jack Good), which made its bow late at night on Sunday, 14 June and, noted an appreciative Tom Driberg, 'crowds more bands and girls and vocal groups on to the stage than you'd think possible and is faster and more frantic than *Six-Five Special*'. The determinedly *au courant* Labour politician went on to express himself especially partial to 'the wonderfully Dadaist Marty Wilde'. Most adults preferred to look elsewhere. 'One of the few singers who sings modern songs pleasantly and quietly, and doesn't fling himself about while performing – such a relief,' declared one such viewer later in the summer after *The Perry Como Show* had ended its series, adding that 'his quiet natural charm and delightfully unassuming manner are most endearing'. Such was the residual dislike among many BBC viewers of almost anything American that another conferred still higher praise on Como: 'Perhaps the least offensive of the all too many imported American show business personalities.'[10]

Was it all too much? 'I have been reading your long article on Television in our lives, sitting out in the warm sun overlooking the sea,' Enid Blyton wrote in April from the Grand Hotel, Swanage to the anthropologist Geoffrey Gorer. 'It was time that someone gave us a clear view of TV and all its implications!' 'I myself,' she added, 'do not watch TV very much but love the things I *do* watch – Peter Scott's programmes, some plays – Dr Bronowski's programmes – good talk – & really *funny* programmes.' Gorer himself was a man of broad human sympathies, but in his *Sunday Times* series he came down hard on working-class viewers. Not only did they eschew 'topical programmes, discussions and brains trusts, serious music and ballet', instead obstinately preferring 'films and serials, variety, and quizzes', but almost half of them were 'addicts' (defined as watching for at least four hours a night), with as a result 'all sense of proportion lost in their gross indulgence, and their family life, if not wrecked, at least emptied of nearly all its richness and warmth, their children's education often imperilled by the absence of any quiet place to do homework'. Even worse, whereas five years previously the owner of a TV set had been likelier to be middle class than working class, now 'there are approximately three owners of a set from the working classes for every two from the middle classes', with every prospect of that trend intensifying. One reader cautioned against exaggerated alarm. 'The article is rather terrifying,' William Empson wrote to Gorer from Hampstead. 'All the same, the race of man is not destroyed so easily; it seems clear that, in the end, if they have time, they will manage to acquire a "tolerance" for their new poison.'[11]

Children naturally were a particular concern. 'I once asked a child,' Blyton related to Gorer, 'why he preferred watching TV to going to the cinema, and he said he liked its "nowness."' As it happened, the most extensive, authoritative survey would appear later in 1958 – namely, *Television and the Child* by the academic Hilde Himmelweit and colleagues, the fruit of several years of research and analysis. 'Television is not as black as it is painted,' she found, 'but neither is it the great harbinger of culture and enlightenment which its enthusiasts tend to claim for it,' adding that 'its capacity for broadening a child's horizons is not spectacularly different from that of any other of the mass media', not least because 'television stimulates interests, but only fleetingly'.

Four of Himmelweit's findings had a particular piquancy: that as many as 60 per cent of the children in the survey said that the TV was left on all evening in their homes; that three out of four 10–11-year-olds viewed until nine o'clock; that middle-class children were glued to the box just as much as their working-class peers; and that almost all children seemed wholly blasé about onscreen violence. Gorer, reviewing Himmelweit's book in the *Listener*, disputed the worth of her overtly paternalistic recommendations about programme content, but was otherwise of a similar mind. 'In so far as television has any influence,' he argued, 'it is as a leveller; it makes the dull brighter, and the brighter duller.'

Himmelweit's was a rather bloodless survey, but fortunately the writer and secondary modern teacher Edward Blishen took charge of a study conducted earlier in the year on behalf of the Council for Children's Welfare. Some 700 parents (weighted a little towards the middle class) spent at least a fortnight watching children's programmes with their offspring, and parental positives were more than counterbalanced by negatives:

- It has quietened him down, as he will now sit and watch.
- It helps to keep them indoors in the evenings.
- Lost his fear of dogs, thanks to Lassie.
- Too much violence. It was a sorry day when ITV began.
- It is difficult to get him to bed.
- They don't want to go to the Scouts or any other movement because there is always something they want to watch.
- Had four books for Christmas, and hasn't read them yet.

As for the opinions of the children themselves, Blishen provided a helpful summary of their favourite programmes generally. 'The boys all plumped for *Zoo Time, Zoo Quest, Look, Lone Ranger, The Silver Sword* and *Little Rascals*,' he found, 'with, not far behind, *Circus Boy, Crackerjack, Sports View, Criss Cross Quiz, Studio E, Onion Boys, Sir Lancelot, Billy Bunter, Popeye, Robin Hood, Rin-Tin-Tin* and *Lassie*. Invited to let themselves go on their dislikes, the boys proved to be very highly satisfied with everything.' For their part, the girls 'liked most of all *Sooty, Emergency—Ward 10, Zoo Quest, Zoo Time, Look*, the quiz programmes and *Little Rascals*'. And they were, he added 'far more disgruntled than the boys, most of them expressing a round feminine displeasure at the many films full of shooting'.[12]

There was at this time no set in the Haines home in Chingford, where instead Judy, after the family's return in early June from half-term week at a Brixham holiday camp (The Dolphin), concentrated on matters at hand. 'Have decided to work to a routine as from tomorrow,' she noted on Sunday the 1st. 'Hope that will get the housework done.' All went satisfactorily to plan over the next few days, and on Friday the 6th she invited Win, from across the road, 'to afternoon tea as my routine doesn't allow of an hour's coffee time', but something more exciting was on her mind: 'I have bought John a summer jacket for our Anniversary. He has bought me a Morphy-Richards steam iron! It is beautifully light and effective.'

By now the World Cup was about to start in Sweden, but even though all four home nations were represented it was far from an all-consuming event, with few mentions in diaries. Quite apart from the sad legacy of Munich, England's campaign under Walter Winterbottom was blighted from the start. Fulham's Johnny Haynes was under attack from the northern press as an overrated 'glamour boy'; the gifted Bobby Charlton was replaced, amidst widespread criticism, by the dogged but lumbering Derek Kevan; and the *Daily Express* published, with censorious commentary, a love letter from captain Billy Wright to the divorced singer Joy Beverley (his future wife). England were knocked out on the 17th, beaten 1–0 by Russia. 'They fought until there was nothing left but heavy hearts and legs wearied to the point of torture,' proudly reported the *Express*'s Desmond Hackett. But the match, he went on, 'unhappily emphasised how wrong England were, from the first kick of this world campaign, to insist that fighting hearts can replace football'. At the end, 'there was something intensely sad about the shirts stained with sweat from their courageous, but unskilled, labours'. Or, as an *Observer* headline bluntly put it: 'Industry Without Skill'. England's early exit provoked a storm of discontent, prompting Haynes to remark that 'everyone in England thinks we have a God-given right to win the World Cup'. Nevertheless, one Englishman did get to the final. George Raynor, a miner's son from Barnsley who coached the Swedish team that lost to Brazil, had previously been in charge at

Juventus and Lazio in Italy, and was renowned for his meticulous, 'scientific' methods. After the tournament he sought a coaching post in England, but the only work he could secure was with Skegness Town, part-timers in the Midland League. British teams, he asserted mildly but unequivocally two years later in his memoir *Football Ambassador at Large*, were 'not yet equipped to win world competitions'.[13]

This was also the summer of the great London bus strike, with Frank Cousins, left-wing leader of the Transport and General Workers' Union, as central protagonist.[14] 'People hearing Cousins in action for the first time are usually struck by the remarkable way he combines a donnish clarity of analysis with the fervour of a demagogue,' noted an *Observer* profile earlier in the year of this 53-year-old miner's son who had become General Secretary of the giant T&G in 1956 and rapidly emerged as 'a national figure' through television and radio appearances. 'His speed of thought and dialectical gifts are familiar to every viewer, so are his watchful eye, his swift changes from evident suspicion to candour and confidence, and the way his relaxed good-natured bearing suddenly stiffens into cold hostility.' As a union leader, continued the profile, his approach could be summed up as 'militancy to be kept high at all times, action to be taken only through the established machinery'. As for his broader politics, 'He is a Socialist consciously, if at times slowly, working to shape a society from which one day the private profit motive will have been eliminated.' About the same time, Julian Symons for the *Daily Mail* interviewed Cousins at his spacious office in Transport House, to which he had driven from Epsom in his Ford Zephyr. Symons observed to him that, sitting behind his large desk, he looked like a big business executive. To which, with a 'pleasant, faintly smiling expression', Cousins replied: 'Yes, you might say that. Of course, I get here earlier [8.30] than most business men seem to do, and I leave a good deal later, and while I'm here I don't do the same sort of thing. There are differences, don't you think?' By 1958 he was undoubtedly the best-known trade unionist, and equally undoubtedly he was in the sights of a Tory government still smarting from its defeat by the engineers and shipbuilders the previous year and now increasingly committed to a policy of wage restraint.

'A London bus strike', noted Macmillan in his diary on 29 April, 'now seems inevitable'. This followed the failure of protracted negotiations over wages between the busmen and the London Transport Executive, and he added that 'it may be salutary'. At a rally of 6,000 London busmen at the Empress Hall in Earl's Court on Friday 2 May, Cousins in effect said that, left to himself, he would not have been pushing for a strike that might well prove very hard to win, but that he honoured the busmen's determination to pursue their just cause and was proud to be leading them. The busmen themselves were virtually solid. 'A strike's deadly action, really, but we want what's right,' one of them told the journalist John Gale. 'Take my own case. The rent's just gone up 15s; National Health's gone up; coal's gone up about a shilling a quarter ton; my wife says she wants more money. Well, what can you do?' Another agreed: 'The job's not what it was. We were the second best paid on the industrial list; now we're fifty-seventh.'[15]

The strike duly began on the 5th, with most of the national press (including the *Manchester Guardian*) hostile, the *Mirror* neutral and the *Express* soon unashamedly demonising Cousins. From the start it failed to be more than an inconvenience. 'John doesn't mind,' recorded Judy Haines in Chingford on the 11th. 'He can park at Turnpike Lane and then by underground to Piccadilly. It has also proved that Central London is far better off without great buses blocking the traffic. I feel sorry for busmen's wives having to feed their families just the same.' Then within days came the major blow of the government settling with the strike-threatening railwaymen, leaving the busmen isolated. Cousins himself, moreover, was equally isolated within the trade union leadership as a whole. 'They wanted Cousins taken down a peg,' recalled Iain Macleod, the tactically brilliant Minister of Labour. 'They didn't like him. They wanted to ensure that the Government didn't cave in to him, because it would have made their job that much more difficult.' 'TUC,' noted Macmillan by the end of the month, 'are obviously pressing Cousins to settle the bus strike somehow. I fear, however, that he is in a sort of Wagnerian–Hitlerian mood. "Fight to the last penny, & bring the whole nation crashing down."'

'Very depressed,' lamented Gladys Langford on 1 June. 'Continued 'bus strike imprisons me in this one room.' Indeed, the public mood now began to harden against the busmen, not least as it turned out to be the wettest June for half a century. 'To blazes with Cousins and his followers,' declared Mrs C. Cheesman of Salisbury Road, Manor Park to the *Evening News* on the 3rd. 'I blame union members for not standing on their own feet. I know who has the biggest worry – the housewife.' Cousins by this time knew that he had either to end the strike or to extend it, with the latter option involving bringing out the oil-tanker drivers, but it was an option that the TUC General Council, told by Macmillan that he would not hesitate to use troops if need be, flatly refused to countenance. The end eventually came after seven weeks. 'The buses start running again tomorrow,' noted an unsympathetic Anthony Heap on the 20th. 'And precious little the fools have gained by it.' Indeed, with Londoners having got accustomed during the strike to using alternative forms of transport, the dispute marked the moment – in London anyway – when gradually declining bus use (with the rise of the private car) turned into headlong fall. 'What is clear to anyone roaming around London is that the buses look strangely empty,' observed Mollie Panter-Downes in early July, and she anticipated the 'sad' day 'when the only note of scarlet on the London streets will turn out to be a fire engine'.

'One of the good things that came out of that dispute,' Cousins would remark many years later about the bus strike to his biographer Geoffrey Goodman, 'was an awareness of the importance of trade unionism: an awareness that had not been there for some time previously.' Arguably, that awareness already existed. 'At the present time the power of the Trade Unions is such that you have a dictator state within a democratic state,' the farmer-writer A. G. Street had declared in February on *Any Questions?*, in the context of a controversial – three men alleged to be in the wrong union – National Union of Toolmakers stoppage; he added (to applause) that 'every time the law of the country is flouted by anybody, even Trade Unions, this nation is going one step nearer to Fascism with all its horrors'. During the bus strike itself, *Punch* (then serialising Alan Hackney's satirical *I'm All Right, Jack*, featuring a Communist shop steward, Mr Kite) ran a full-page cartoon by Illingworth depicting the unions as anti-democratic. Florence Turtle in Wimbledon Park probably spoke for most of the diarists when she reflected, 'What a lot of silly sheep members of trade unions are

– haven't got the guts to say they don't want to strike, do so at the behest of extremists.'[16]

Among Tories generally, a significant element wanted a wholly uncompromising response to almost all wage claims by the unions. 'Of course,' somewhat wearily recorded Macmillan on 11 May shortly before his decisive offer to the railwaymen, 'some ministers & a lot of the Party want a "showdown".' Determined though both men were to see off the London busmen, a relatively soft target, that was instinctively not his or Macleod's approach. 'I am very anxious that the Govt, while firm, sh^d not seem to be obstinate,' Macmillan had noted a month earlier in relation to the railwaymen. 'Above all, we must not "challenge" the T. Unions (as people like Lord Hinchingbrooke w^d like). We must appeal to the Unions, & try to take ourselves some constructive initiative.' Next day, returning to the subject, he observed that 'the middle class' were 'so angry' that needless confrontation with the unions would lead to 'bitterness' and 'class war'. Unsurprisingly, neither man was enthused when in June the Inns of Court Conservative Association published a report, co-authored by Geoffrey Howe and called A Giant's Strength, which asserted that the unions had become 'over-mighty subjects' and argued for ending their long-established legal privileges. Macleod sent a senior Ministry of Labour official to warn off the authors from publicising their pamphlet, while Macmillan, with an election in the not too distant offing, saw no reason to revise his conclusion the previous year that the Tories would not have won in 1951 or 1955 without a sizeable trade unionist vote, and that therefore it 'would be inexpedient to adopt any policy involving legislation which would alienate this support'.[17]

Macmillan's principal domestic concern during 1958 was to get the political and economic cycles roughly aligned, which in practice meant keeping as tight a lid as possible on unemployment through starting to reflate the economy – a process helped by having a largely amenable Chancellor in Heathcoat Amory. His Budget in April was broadly neutral, still targeting inflation and keeping in place the restrictive measures of the previous September. But during the summer, the Bank Rate started steadily to come down, and crucially, in early July, credit controls (particularly in relation to bank lending) were lifted. 'It is now generally agreed that measures to expand the economy are desirable,' purred the *FT*, 'and that a moderate increase in demand for goods and services would not add to the dangers of rising prices; nor would it endanger the position of sterling.' For Macmillan, the Treasury storm of six months earlier seemed a blessedly distant memory. 'The Chancellor of Ex is really handling the economy with great skill,' he reflected at the end of July. 'Cautious where necessary, but not afraid of bolder action. He is worth 20 Thorneycrofts!'[18]

The political mood music did much to inform his buoyant assessment. Back in mid-June, five by-elections 'turned out very well indeed for us'; soon afterwards, the bus strike collapsed, amidst much praise for the government's firmness; by late June the Tories were only 3½ points behind Labour in the latest opinion poll; and on 9 July, Gallup revealed the two parties level pegging at 47½ per cent each, with the brief Liberal bubble having seemingly burst. Altogether it had been, commented the *New Statesman*, a 'breathtaking' swing to the Tories. Five days after that most recent Gallup poll, at a selection meeting for the Finchley constituency, an unaccompanied Margaret Thatcher (with Denis in South Africa) narrowly saw off three men, all of whom had been to public school and all of whom had their wives with them. 'Tories Choose Beauty' was the *Evening Standard*'s headline, but she still had a final hurdle to jump: the acceptance of the whole local Association, meeting on 31 July. This she did with élan. 'Speaking without notes, stabbing home points with expressive hands,' reported the *Finchley Press*,

> Mrs Thatcher launched fluently into a clear-cut appraisal of the Middle East situation, weighed up Russia's propagandist moves with the skill of a housewife measuring the ingredients in a familiar recipe, pinpointed Nasser as the fly in the mixing bowl, switched swiftly to Britain's domestic problems (showing a keen grasp of wage and Trade Union issues), then swept her breathless audience into a confident preview of Conservatism's dazzling future.

As he watched his once-commanding lead being wiped out, these were difficult days for Hugh Gaitskell. On 27 June the *Daily Herald* gave a small private lunch for him in St Ermin's Hotel. The Labour leader, remembered the paper's Geoffrey Goodman, was in 'a passionate mood' as he analysed his party's slippage:

Why, he enquired, aren't the public reacting against the Conservatives? He believed it was because the Labour Party had not departed sufficiently from its old 'working-class attitudes'. People in Britain, he reflected, were in the main 'radical' but not socialist; they wanted a 'left of centre radical party' which would make social changes without being revolutionary or authoritarian. More and more, he believed, the 'Keir Hardie image was becoming a dim and distant feature of the past'. The Labour Party had to find some more modern image if it was to be a successful force. There was now a feeling of prosperity among the working class, he observed, and this was turning the British electorate into a largely middle-class vote.

A fortnight later, lunching at the Athenaeum with Richard Crossman, Gaitskell pursued the theme again. 'Working-class people,' he insisted, 'are week by week becoming less working class, less class-conscious and more allergic to such old appeals as trade union solidarity or class loyalty. Anything we say which can be used as being merely class interest loses us votes.' Did this mean that Labour was inevitably doomed to lose? 'We've got to win the next Election,' Gaitskell kept repeating to Crossman, but a few days later the diarist noted that 'even' Roy Jenkins, 'who was one of the great addicts of the theory that we were bound to win, now admits that we are faced with a possibility of defeat'.[19]

As if on cue, two very different working-class archetypes were on display this month. 'The year was 1957, the morning bright and gay/ On the ninth of February John Axon drove away,' began *The Ballad of John Axon* on the Home Service at 10 p.m. on 2 July – the story of an engine driver who the previous year in a railway accident near Buxton had died heroically to save many others, and the first of the celebrated *Radio Ballads*. Created by the folk singers Ewan MacColl and Peggy Seeger, and produced by Charles Parker, these were pioneering programmes: not only did they celebrate working-class lives, but in a potent blend of music and recorded speech they told their stories through the voices of ordinary people, not professional actors. 'This really was some of the characteristic poetry of the idiom of the people,' declared W. L. Webb next day in the *Manchester Guardian*, being especially struck by the 'gentle reminiscing Northern voices', while Tom Driberg in the *New Statesman* called it 'this superb piece of radio'.

Even so, the programme's Appreciation Index of 61 was five below the Home Service average, and the reaction of individual listeners was at best mixed. 'Unconventional, untraditional, but all completely *right*, nothing jarred,' noted one, another that 'it was refreshing to hear songs which have some relationship with everyday working-class existence, rather than the moon/June noises of tin-pan alley'; but a third listener reckoned that the treatment 'smothered and almost buried the story of a gallant man hurtling to his death', and a fourth that 'John Axon deserved something better than this pseudo-American Annie-get-your-gun-Calypso nonsense'.

'Pop' Larkin's life was not the sort that MacColl et al were ever likely to celebrate. H. E. Bates's new novel *The Darling Buds of May* was, noted Penelope Mortimer in her *Sunday Times* review on the 13th, about 'the family of Larkins – six children, Pop and Ma – who make a fortune out of market-gardening and rather dubious deals, and live in a state of blissful Rabelaisian squalor'. Whereupon: 'A weedy young tax inspector arrives with the absurd intention of trying to get Pop to make an income-tax return. He is persuaded to stay and, transformed by Pop's eccentric taste in drink and by the lovely Mariette, remains to become Pop's son-in-law and partner in future piratical schemes to outwit the Welfare State.' Mortimer, although not much enjoying the book on her own account, had little doubt about its likely popularity, claiming that Bates had 'reached the zenith of his talent for creating life as millions of readers wish it could be'. It was a perceptive assessment of the author's intentions. 'The Larkin philosophy,' Bates himself would recall,

> is all *carpe diem* and the very antithesis of the Welfare State. The Larkins' secret is in fact that they live as many of us would like to live if only we had the guts and nerve to flout the conventions. Pop and Ma demonstrate that they have the capacity by indulging deeply in love and champagne before breakfast, passion in the bluebell wood and encouraging their enchanting daughter to a life of wilful seduction.

Modesty, however, forbade him to quote the novel's most arresting piece of dialogue: 'Pass me the tomato ketchup. I've got a bit of iced bun to finish up.'[20]

Of course, most people (including working-class people) were neither selfless Axons nor look-after-number-one Larkins; and most people naturally enjoyed the rising, if unevenly rising, sense of prosperity and widening range of material goods. Anthony Crosland was on the right side of the historical curve when in May he produced a highly critical report on the Co-operative movement, including its many shops. 'In many areas the word "co-operative" is associated with a drab, colourless, old-fashioned mediocrity,' with 'too many societies' being run 'complacently and unimaginatively'. This, he insisted, was 'not good enough for the consumer in 1958'; indeed it betrayed 'a somewhat patronising and insulting attitude to the wants and expectations of the ordinary co-operative member', whose tastes were 'changing and rising rapidly'. The reaction from Labour's left was predictably negative ('Why,' wondered *Tribune*, 'should Co-ops ape the capitalists?'), as it was from the Co-operative movement itself, and to Crosland's intense frustration his report – recommending fundamental change, including a drastically slimmed-down structure to the whole unwieldy organisation – largely gathered dust. Instead, the consumer future lay elsewhere. 'Our many outlets make it possible for us to take advantage of bulk buying to the full and we are constantly on the look-out for new lines and new ideas,' declared an unblinking champion of private enterprise, Jack Cohen, at Tesco's AGM in July, as he announced trading profits up by more than 50 per cent. 'Our policy is to give the best possible value.' Looking ahead, he promised a 'programme of constant modernisation of branches'.[21]

By this time some 4,250 self-service grocery shops were doing around 17 per cent of the UK's grocery trade, with those shops including 175 supermarkets (i.e. self-service with a sales area of at least 2,000 square feet) – of which 83 were owned by the Co-op and 75 were in London and the south-east, though Ken Morrison was getting going in Bradford (with all of three checkouts). Even so, a Gallup survey this summer of housewives' shopping preferences revealed that small independent shops were still much preferred, often involving considerable residual loyalty and/or conservatism, with 65 per cent buying their groceries from the same shop, and 75 per cent from the same butcher. 'Their main criticism against large multiple stores [preferred by only about 17 per cent of housewives] is that they are unfriendly,' reported the *News Chronicle*. 'They complain that the self-service stores encourage them to buy too much; then that lack of over-the-counter warmth pops up again.' Increasingly, though, supermarkets (led by Tesco and, from July, followed by Sainsbury's) were significantly reducing their prices on branded goods, especially foods. 'I am not cutting prices,' an independent grocer in a well-to-do London suburb so far reasonably free of supermarkets defiantly told the *Mail*. 'My customers want delivery and monthly bills. I need big margins to give this service.'

The problems for that business model would become increasingly apparent, while in 1958 other signs of change were the start of Green Shield Stamps (begun by Richard Tompkins, who had seen trading stamps in action in a flourishing petrol station near Chicago) and of another phenomenon, cash-and-carry (pioneered by a Huddersfield wholesaler, Lawrence Batley). The multiples, meanwhile, were offering an increasingly attractive shopping experience. Florence Turtle, a stationery buyer for British Home Stores, visited in Birmingham 'our Super Duper new Store which really is a store to be proud of', while a full-page advertisement in the *Kentish Mercury* for Lewisham's 'beautiful new C&A' set out its wonders:

- Great modern arcades of superbly lit windows – you can window-shop to your heart's content!
- Big, modern showrooms, beautifully decorated and arranged so that you can reach out anywhere and touch a bargain
- Twice as many self-contained fitting rooms, where you can try things on in comfort and privacy

Importantly, there also seems to have been a greater willingness on the part of shoppers to buy on credit. A survey in August found that 58 per cent of people (and 65 per cent of those under the age of 45) approved in principle of the practice, and that 23 per cent of all adults were at that time making payments. It was an area of life that could cause domestic tensions. 'Your father and me were talking about TV Friday night,' Tom Courtenay's mother Annie wrote to him earlier in the summer from working-class Hull. 'He seems to think he can get one that gradually reduces to 1/- a week. So we nearly ended up arguing.'[22]

Advertising roared on, in 1958 for the first time since the war regaining its pre-war proportion of 2½ per cent of all consumer expenditure, as naturally also did commercial television. 'Three in every four viewers affirm that the advertisements on television interest them,' noted a survey in June. 'Cartoons with jingles continue to lead the popularity stakes. The most popular advertiser in 1958 to date: Sunblest. The least popular advertiser in 1958 to date: Omo.' New brands on the market this year included Blue Daz and Tango (heavily promoted through the 'Tango Wobbly Ball' offer), while successful rebranding campaigns included Kattomeat (hitherto struggling, in a pre-Whiskas world, behind the market leader Kit-E-Kat) and the continuing Bronco story, with first a 'gay' wrapper pushing up sales and then the testing in Tunbridge Wells of the toilet paper itself in pastel shades of pink, blue and green demonstrating a clear public preference for colour. Two new television advertisements, meanwhile, had particular resonance, becoming in their way classics: 'Go to work on an egg' (contrary to myth *not* devised by the copywriter and future novelist Fay Weldon but by a colleague of hers at Mather & Crowther) and the creation of the impeccably middle-class, long-running Oxo family, with the young, attractive housewife Katie (played by Mary Holland) happy to 'give a meal man appeal' – virtue that husband Philip would occasionally reward with a patronising 'good girl'.[23]

So much was new in 1958, such as stereo 'hi-fi' equipment and discs, throwaway Biros, and eye-level grills on gas cookers. For teenage girls there was now, in shocking pink and peacock blue, the 'Pink Witch' bicycle, produced by Triumph and recommended by Jackie Collins: 'My, if you'd gone round asking girls what they wanted it couldn't have been nicer. It's so *vivid* – and so *gay* – and so marvellously *sensible* too.' The Continental influence was becoming ever more apparent. Italian Lambrettas and, to a lesser extent, Vespas dominated the motor-scooter market; for the young Howard Jacobson and friends, the moment when 'the first Italians opened up a coffee bar on Oxford Road in the centre of Manchester' around this time 'changed our lives'; and even in a 'poorish suburb' of Bournemouth with 'nothing in the least imaginative in the shopping line', related an amused Frances Woodsford in April to her American correspondent, there was a new shop which was 'all frills and flounces, and they have called it "Mes Petits"'.[24]

Yet as always there were limits to the appetite for the new. 'Confident and distinctly modernist' is how Terence Conran's biographer describes his 1958 furniture catalogue, but the range flopped commercially. Nor, owing presumably to lack of consumer demand, was the sandwich revolution even remotely in the offing, with the travel writer Arthur Eperon lamenting in July how he had 'recently been charged 3s in pubs for a sandwich consisting of dry scrapings from an old chicken carcase between hunks of cardboard bread'. Instead, 1958 saw in Reading the first of a chain that would become the reliable home of the unreconstructed breakfast fry-up: an 11-seater Little Chef, modelled on an American roadside diner.[25]

On 26 July, at the close of the Empire and Commonwealth Games in Cardiff, the Queen's recorded voice announced that Prince Charles, future hammer of the modernists, was to be known as the Prince of Wales – surprise news that, noted Mollie Panter-Downes, 'seems to have caused emotion among the middle-aged and over, for whom it revives memories'. Over the next few days three other stars were born or at least sighted. From nearly 3,000 talking budgerigars from across Europe, the winner of the BBC's Cage Word Contest was revealed as Sparkie, a budgie not only possessing a wide vocabulary and capable of singing in Geordie but also soon to become a household name and, almost half a century later, to inspire a Michael Nyman opera. 'Look, an original comic!' was the *Mirror*'s 'Telepage' headline above praise for Bruce Forsyth's appearance on the *The Frankie Vaughan Show* as that of 'an original performer who takes trouble with his material, has a deft delivery, and tops it with a personality which, though assured, is not in the least cocky or big-headed'. And also in the *Mirror*, Patrick Doncaster's weekly column on new records looked ahead to the release on 29 August of the first single by 'a 17-year-old dark-haired dark-eyed singer and guitar twanger from Cheshunt Herts', reckoning that Cliff Richard had 'a personality that shines through the grooves' and 'could succeed in discland'.[26]

Kenton and Shula Archer were born on 8 August, and the Australian novelist Patrick White, staying in London, might have preferred to be in Ambridge. 'It is so terribly dirty, ugly, the people so drab – also ugly

and dirty – the women like uncooked dough, the men so often suggestive of raw veal,' he informed a friend on the 12th, adding that during a
recent lunch with his English publisher he had been struck by Douglas
Jerrold's 'habit of chewing his words in the best English manner – as if
they were a difficult and unpleasant meat'. On the 23rd the BBC finally
consented to give starting prices with its racing news; two days later
Midland announced it would be the first high-street bank to offer
personal loans; and on Wednesday the 27th Madge Martin went to a
matinee of *My Fair Lady* ('well-nigh perfect'), Gladys Langford treated
herself to a long ride on the 179 bus to Grove Park (where, with female
toilets 'conspicuously missing', she 'had to take a 2d platform ticket,
find someone who would unlock lavatory & found it smelly, cistern
chain not working'), Ted Hughes had a selection of his work read on
the Third Programme ('It is not often that one is so excited by the work
of a new poet,' said the *Listener*), and Philip Larkin boldly predicted to
Monica Jones that the England cricket team ('swollen with pride') that
had been selected to tour Australia would 'come a cropper'.[27]

These were not the all-time-best summer holidays. 'Wakes week'
may have been the episode that on 14 July finished the first series proper
of radio's *The Clitheroe Kid*, but such was the seriousness of the down-
turn in the Lancashire cotton trade that, as the *Rochdale Observer*
gloomily reflected about this time, some would have no alternative but
to 'regard the annual holiday as a luxury which will have to be sacrificed this year'. Nor did the weather help, with Macmillan himself
noting on 20 August that 'it has now rained, practically without ceas-
ing, for 6 weeks in every part of the country'. Still, there was always
plenty to see and do in 'The Most Magnificent Gardens In The British
Isles'. An advertisement itemised the attractions of Staffordshire's
Alton Towers:

Fully Licensed Bars and Catering – Boating – Children's Paddling Pool
– Miniature Railway, and many other amusements for all ages – Unrivalled
Woodland Walks – Flag Tower – Chinese Temples, etc., etc.

   Also the world's largest 'oo' Gauge Model Electric Railway.

   Celebrated Bands Sundays and Bank Holidays. (The Jaguar Car Works
Band will play in the Gardens on Sunday, August 17th.)

Judy Haines spent a Sunday morning in early August in Littlehampton. 'Butlin's have a place there right on the front,' she noted. 'But for that it's very pleasant.' The Butlin's in question was only an amusement park; for the real Butlin's experience she should have gone to the holiday camp at Clacton-on-Sea, where soon afterwards Cliff Richard and the Drifters began a residency at the Pig and Whistle Bar. 'Campers used to go for a knees-up and a sing-song,' recalled a Redcoat, Stan Edwards. 'They thought Cliff's music was a racket and nobody went in there when he was playing. Cliff only knew about eight numbers at the time, and they were all Elvis Presley songs. He used to look like Elvis, and wiggle in the same way. You can imagine the campers who wanted a sing-song liking that sort of music!' It transpired that Cliff had been put in the wrong bar; on transferring to the recently opened South Seas Coffee Bar, 'he went down well' and also did afternoon sessions in the Rock 'n' Roll Ballroom. One night towards the end of the season a terrific thunderstorm left the top end of the camp completely flooded, including the South Seas. 'It had glass tables with live goldfish, and was really sprauncey,' remembered another Redcoat, Roy Hudd. 'The place was three feet deep in water, and the drains couldn't take any more. We were all woken up at three in the morning, and told to get up there.' A less than gruntled Hudd reluctantly did so. 'About 2,000 campers were there, baling out the water, cleaning the tables, checking everything was OK as if they were employed by Butlin's. One of them wading in the water turned to me and said, "Marvellous, isn't it? Just like the Blitz."'[28]

On Saturday, 30 August, while a teenage Jimmy Greaves scored five at Stamford Bridge against the usually formidable Wolves defence, the Empire Theatre in Portsmouth prepared for its last performance. Variety theatres around the country were by this time closing down at a rapid rate, and a supermarket was to be built on the site. That evening, for the second house, there was standing room only to watch Terry (Toby Jug) Cantor's 'Folies à la Parisienne', with others on show including the Hungarian acrobats the Great Alexis troupe and the double-jointed comedian Dale Robertson. After it was all over, and the audience had departed, some stagehands took to the stage and started to sing. Whereupon, according to the local *Evening News*:

Someone opened a side door, just as 63-year-old Mrs Lilian Salmon was going by on her way home. She paused as the noise flooded out into the almost deserted Edinburgh Road, and went inside. Through the maze of passages and stairways she found her way to the stage – and took command.

This was no longer Mrs Salmon, of 21 Sommerville Road, Southsea. This was Lilian Ravenscroft, 'Lancashire's Singing Mill Girl' of World War I, when the theatre was in its heyday.

On that same stage she made her professional debut in 1914 as one of The Six Red-heads. Another member of the group was Gracie Fields . . . A pianist joined in, and soon the theatre was ringing with The Singing Mill Girl's rich contralto voice.

Song after song she sang, and before long there was a small gathering at the open side door, including a police sergeant and two constables. Their interest was not surprising, since it was long past midnight.

Eventually, a stagehand announced that everybody had to go home. The Singing Mill Girl led 'Auld Lang Syne', and the Empire Theatre was dead.[29]

8

Get the Nigger

Just after closing time on the evening of Saturday, 23 August, exactly a week before the curtain came down on the Portsmouth Empire, a 21-year-old blonde, Mrs Mary Lowndes, and her miner husband were leaving a pub in the rundown St Ann's district of Nottingham, to go back to their two small children, when she was apparently punched in the back by a black man. 'The next thing I knew,' she related afterwards, 'my husband was being punched from one side of the road to the other by a group of coloured men. I heard bottles being smashed and everyone started screaming and shouting.' Things rapidly escalated. There were knife attacks on several white men; a crowd of some 1,500, mainly white, rapidly gathered; counter-attacks began against blacks; and it took the police an hour and a half to restore order. Over the next day or two it emerged that the initial events had been a reaction against the previous fortnight's series of assaults by white Teddy boys on the area's heavy concentration of black residents – assaults mainly fuelled by an atavistic dislike of black men having white girlfriends and eventually leading to some West Indians taking the law into their own hands. The following Saturday, the 30th, Teds and others turned up in St Ann's en masse, a milling mob of up to 4,000, with revenge on the agenda amidst cries of 'Let's lynch them', 'Let's get at them' and 'Find some niggers', but with their targets almost all staying prudently at home, they fought instead with the police, resulting in 24 arrests. 'This was not a racial riot,' insisted the Chief Constable, Captain Athelstan Popkess. 'The coloured people behaved in a most exemplary way by keeping out of the way. Indeed, they were an example to some of our rougher elements.'

Between the two Saturdays, the *Manchester Guardian* had on Wednesday the 27th an optimistic headline: 'Other cities not perturbed about Nottingham: It-couldn't-happen-here feeling'. Even so, the accompanying report did note that in the Notting Hill Gate–Shepherd's Bush area, where 'between three and five thousand West Indians are living, mostly in poor housing conditions, among a white population largely composed of people who are themselves not Londoners and have little community life', the previous three weeks had been 'unsettled', including 'fights and attempts to run down pedestrians with cars on Saturday nights'. Meanwhile the Hammersmith area had witnessed 'a recent outburst by gangs of Teddy boys said to be cruising the streets on week-end evenings, looking for Africans or West Indians', with those gangs 'said to choose streets where only the occasional coloured person is to be seen, and then attack in the ratio of half a dozen to one'. In fact, there had been a particularly vicious episode the previous Saturday night – just an hour or two after the first Nottingham battle – when a gang of nine white youths, mainly from Shepherd's Bush, had gone out 'nigger-hunting' (their term) and, armed with iron bars and other weapons, had wantonly indulged in unprovoked attacks, injuring five black men, including three seriously. On Friday the 29th the *Kensington News and West London Times* noted more broadly that 'Nottingham must be a warning to North Kensington' (aka Notting Hill), where almost 7,000 'coloured' people lived, approaching a tenth of the population.[1]

Taking place in increasingly warm weather at the fag-end of what had been a dismal summer, the 'Notting Hill Riots' – by some distance the most serious civil unrest of the decade – began shortly before midnight on Saturday the 30th. 'A bottle bomb was thrown through a basement window of a house in which coloured people rent rooms,' reported the *Daily Express*, and over the next few hours other 'coloured' houses were attacked, as were random black men as well as white women known to be going with blacks, often by roaming white gangs with, according to another report, 'iron railings, choppers and in some cases bicycle chains'. It was worse on Sunday night, with threatening, violent crowds of some 500 or 600 on the streets, and 17 arrests made after, noted the *Kensington News*, 'West Indians had been savagely assaulted and petrol bombs had been thrown by the mobs into the homes of coloured people'. For four hours, stated the ensuing police evidence, 'there were running fights continuously between coloured and white people and, at times, the two opponents were ganging up against the police'.[2]

Monday, 1 September was the climax. 'I have seen nothing uglier, or nastier, than this,' declared one reporter, Merrick Winn, about an incident that became emblematic:

> A young man, coloured, a student, walks alone in the middle of a shabby road, Bramley Road, Notting Hill, London. It is three in the afternoon. He carries a brown bag, for he has just come to the area. He looks about him, jumpily, wondering about the silent people, white people, crowding the pavements. He has not heard about the race riots.
>
> The people watching, violently. Suddenly a voice yells: 'Get him.' Other voices yell: 'Get the nigger.' The people sweep after him. Middle-aged people, but most of them young people. And many are children.
>
> They hit the student. A youth flings his cycle at him. He pleads and cries out, then breaks away, into a greengrocer's shop. The greengrocer locks the door. The student stands trembling and says: 'They'll kill me.'
>
> Then police cars come and a police van with a dozen policemen. They take the student to safety and the greengrocer says to me: 'They'd have murdered him.'

The man running for his life was Seymour Manning, a 26-year-old African student living in Derby, who had come down to London for the day to see friends; the greengrocer's wife who bravely let him in and kept the pursuers at bay was Mrs Pat Howcroft. 'I was one of the three that first got 'im,' an angry white boy in a red shirt told another reporter. 'I half-twisted his leg off anyway. We'd have tore 'im apart if it hadn't been for the police.'

That evening, as darkness fell, huge, rampant mobs of white youth – shouting 'Kill the niggers!' and estimated as up to 2,000 strong – smashed their way through a large swathe of Notting Hill. By this time the local blacks, supplemented by Jamaicans from Brixton (itself in a highly volatile state), were fighting back, including an all-out pitched battle in Powis Terrace, with the philosophy being, recalled one, 'In for

a penny, in for a pound'. A *Daily Express* reporter caught something of
the flavour of a chaotic, violent night:

> Youths surged from the Bramley Road area, through Oxford Gardens
> into Blenheim Crescent. They shattered windows of a Jamaican woman's
> home with palings torn from the garden fence of her English neighbour.
>
> A Fascist meeting in Barandon Street nearby lost its audience as youths
> marched away to Blenheim Crescent. A bottle containing lighted petrol
> was hurled among them from the roof of a four-floor tenement. A rain of
> milk bottles followed. The road was littered with broken glass. An old
> lamp-lighter going his rounds on a bicycle was felled by a brick. Two
> more petrol bombs followed, sending sheets of flame up from the road.

Early next morning a politician, living in nearby Holland Park, toured
the battle zone. 'I saw the debris and the corrugated iron up behind the
windows of the prefabs where the coloured families live,' recorded
Anthony Wedgwood Benn. 'The use of petrol bombs and iron bars and
razors is appalling. There is a large area where it is not safe for people to
be out.' That Tuesday afternoon he toured again – 'even at 5 o'clock
there was an ugly atmosphere and people hurried along the streets' –
and indeed another night of trouble lay ahead, with 55 people (mainly
white) arrested, often for possession of offensive weapons such as
broken milk bottles and loaded leather belts. 'In one street where some
of the ugliest fighting has taken place your Correspondent found a
group of men in a public house singing "Old Man River" and "Bye
Bye Blackbird", and punctuating the songs with vicious anti-Negro
slogans,' noted *The Times*. 'The men said that their motto was "Keep
Britain White", and they made all sorts of wild charges against their
coloured neighbours.' Rain at last arrived on Wednesday to damp
things down, and though Thursday was another hot, tense day with
some disturbances, a degree of normality began to return from Friday
onwards.[3]

It was hardly news, of course, that not all whites in Britain viewed
the 165,000 or so non-white immigrants with unalloyed enthusiasm. 'I
have been living in Hartington Street for over 30 years and I have seen
the deterioration which has been caused by the coloured people,' Mrs
F. L. Greenwood, a widow from Moss Side, Manchester, told a local

paper the previous autumn. 'We are all made by the same Creator, but I think the coloured folk should live together in one district, as they do in Birmingham.' Or from Paddington, take the views (as elicited in April 1958) of some of the white residents of Oakington Road:

- I've got nothing against them, but they should have a place of their own like Maida Vale. I was brought up prejudiced against them.
- There's 10 people sleeping in a room over there.
- They should not be allowed to flood here. They must be stopped. They give white girls babies.
- They blow their nose as they pass you.
- Their windows and curtains are filthy. They are noisy.
- God made black as well as white, but if you see all the black prostitutes in Piccadilly, it's awful.
- They don't interfere with me. I don't like them around. I don't know why.

Two months later it became a national story when local magistrates renewed the licence of the Scala ballroom in Wolverhampton even though it was operating a colour bar. 'The fact is people don't want them,' the manager, Michael Wade, explained. 'They have said to me: "We have to work with them; some of us even have to live next to them. We want to get away from them sometimes."' So too elsewhere in the West Midlands. 'Are there too Many Coloured Folk in Coventry?' was the title at the start of August of an editorial in the *Coventry Standard* – noting how 'each day a stream of them wends its way down Grey Friars Lane to the Employment Exchange, and most of them have savings accounts at the banks' – while later in the month the *Birmingham Mail*'s industrial correspondent, Clem Lewis, argued that, in the context of 'no longer enough jobs to go round', the time had come for action: 'The problem is one of people coming from impoverished countries to a country with standards and a way of life that they cannot immediately understand or accept. For their sake and our own it has to be faced honestly, fairly, and imaginatively – NOW.'[4]

For their part, non-white immigrants undoubtedly continued to encounter significant prejudice and discrimination – but the question is to gauge how much. A glance at the small ads for furnished apartments in the *Kensington News* on 22 August, just before the troubles began, is suggestive, being full of phrases like 'English only', 'Europeans only', 'White business people only', 'No coloured people' and, regretfully, 'Sorry, no coloured'. Moreover, as the sociologist Ruth Glass found not long afterwards, the omission of such a phrase was no guarantee of an open door. Only one in six of 'neutral' private advertisers in the *Kensington Post* were in practice, on being rung up, willing to countenance West Indian tenants. With council housing almost out of the question in the context of the ongoing housing shortage – 'It would be quite unrealistic,' frankly stated a housing minister, Reginald Bevins, in November 1957, 'to expect local authorities to give priority to immigrants over other local families who have often been on the waiting-list for several years' – the most common recourse was to dilapidated housing owned by fellow immigrants, too often far from scrupulous about issues of sanitation and overcrowding. As for employment, where non-whites by now were often doing the menial or ill-paid jobs that whites no longer wished to do, it was a more mixed picture: the colour bar virtually gone in sectors like the NHS and public transport, but explicitly or implicitly often present elsewhere, not least through local branches of trade unions operating colour quotas with the tacit consent of employers. 'We do not get past the factory door because we are told "No coloured workers wanted" as soon as they see us,' a Jamaican in Birmingham told a journalist in March 1957. 'Even when we know there are jobs vacant we are told, "Sorry, there is nothing." Sometimes they are very polite, but politeness and rudeness mean just the same thing.'[5]

One should not exaggerate the general severity of the prejudice. 'Wherever there are tensions, these tend to be subdued,' reckoned Ruth Glass about the customary workplace situation. 'West Indians sometimes complain that they have been slighted or insulted by their workmates. More often they tell stories of incomplete "integration": they say that all goes well at work, but once it is done, the white workers do not mix with them in the canteen or on their way home, nor do they ask them to come along to the local pub.' That is probably right: incomplete integration as typical rather than, say, the more dramatic experience in 1958 of the future actor Delroy Lindo, living in Eltham as the six-year-old son of Jamaican parents, and one day terrified out of his skin when a Teddy boy got his attention in the street and then drew a finger across his throat. Either way, it was piquant timing for the singalong smiliness of the BBC's *The Black and White Minstrel Show*, which, complete with The Television Toppers and Kenneth Connor as MC, had its first outing on 14 June and was an instant hit. 'Very much to my taste,' applauded *Punch*'s Henry Turton in pregnant late August. 'I am glad that most of the creaking conventions of the old-time minstrel-show have been dispensed with. George Mitchell's merry men black up, certainly . . . otherwise little pretence is made at reproducing the rather flat-footed routine of the genuine burnt-cork-and-tambourine troupes.'[6]

Inevitably, whatever the prior rumblings, the lurid events of Nottingham and Notting Hill came as a considerable shock to activators. Ten years after *Windrush*, and with non-white Commonwealth immigration during 1955–7 running each year at well over 40,000 (compared to 2,000 in 1953 and 11,000 in 1954), the question naturally arose of whether 'the emigration of coloured people to this country should be limited' – as the opening questioner put it at the Leisure Hall in Mere, Wiltshire, on the return of *Any Questions?* on 12 September from the programme's summer break. The panel's response was unanimously negative. The Tory MP Ted Leather said there could be 'no possible excuse for intolerance and mob violence of any kind'; the Labour MP Anthony Greenwood insisted it would be 'morally wrong' to impose such a limitation; the would-be Liberal MP Jeremy Thorpe declared that 'if the brotherhood of man means anything, well then let's share what we have got'; and the farmer-writer A. G. Street was likewise against restrictions ('to stop immigration would wreck the Commonwealth'), though he observed that 'this coloured thing is very difficult, it is based on physical repulsion, if you like on sex jealousy'. A last word went to the chairman, Freddie Grisewood, who added that 'as a corollary to what has been said it wouldn't be a bad moment just to pay a tribute to the police in the way they have handled these shocking riots'.[7]

That all sounded more or less fine, dandy and liberal, but for both the main political parties the reality this autumn was more complex. In the immediate wake of the troubles, only *The Times* of the Tory-supporting national dailies came out unequivocally against immigration controls, declaring in a leader on 'A Family of Nations' that such a policy would 'almost certainly have unforeseen and harmful effects', was 'a counsel of despair' and 'should not be countenanced'. With an election probably only a year away, however, the last thing Macmillan wanted was a major, divisive furore, and on 8 September – two days after Butler as Home Secretary had asserted in a speech at Maldon that it would need 'considerable force of argument' to alter the 'right of British citizenship to come in and out of the mother country at will' – the Cabinet was entirely in agreement that it was 'important to avoid, if possible, any major pronouncement on Commonwealth immigration'.

Over the next few weeks most Tories adopted a measured tone – 'faults on both sides' was the overriding theme of the analysis in the *Smethwick Telephone* by that constituency's prospective Tory candidate Peter Griffiths, before he dropped in the assertion that 'it would seem reasonable to restrict immigration into this country to healthy people who have jobs to go to' – but it became increasingly clear that there was a divide between on the one hand the party leadership, on the other hand some backbench MPs and the bulk of the party membership. In October the party conference was at Blackpool, where (despite Butler's insistence that 'we should maintain the long and respected tradition of allowing citizens of the Commonwealth to come here'), delegates endorsed by a large majority a motion calling for immigration controls. No backbencher was keener on those restrictions than Cyril Osborne, who later that month in the Commons declared that 'it is time someone spoke for this country and for the white man who lives here', and expanded upon what he claimed to be the idleness, sickness and crime that coloured people brought to the country. Few other Tory backbenchers openly supported him, however, and at a meeting of the 1922 Committee he was humiliated and indeed reduced to tears. One backbencher watching it all, and keeping his counsel, was the MP for Wolverhampton South West, Enoch Powell, who 35 years later would tell his biographer Simon Heffer that he had felt ashamed ever since of staying silent during the attacks on Osborne.[8]

It was not wholly different in the Labour and Labour-supporting ranks, from where in early September there were four significant interventions. 'The Government must introduce legislation quickly to end the tremendous influx of coloured people from the Commonwealth,'

North Kensington's MP George Rogers told the right-wing *Daily Sketch*. 'Overcrowding has fostered vice, drugs, prostitution and the use of knives. For years the white people have been tolerant. Now their tempers are up.' Another Labour MP, the usually liberal-minded Maurice Edelman, wrote a fairly balanced but ultimately pro-control piece for the *Daily Mail* that was given the exaggerated headline, 'Should we let them keep pouring in?' – a piece that earned him praise for his 'courage' from the *Daily Mirror*, which itself did not just declare that Commonwealth citizens should only be allowed to come to Britain if they already had a job and home lined up but also called for greater powers of deportation: 'Some of the coloured people who have settled here are no-goods. As Commonwealth citizens, they cannot be deported. That is ludicrous.' The fourth intervention came from the TUC, meeting at Bournemouth, where its General Secretary, Sir Vincent Tewson, spoke in favour of immigration control, asserting that 'there should be gates in their land of origin and here through which people must pass'.

Nevertheless, the majority opinion among Labour MPs was almost certainly the other way, with Benn on the 7th expressing it in a *Reynolds News* article which claimed that the introduction of immigration controls would in effect be 'the start of apartheid', given that the object of such controls could only be 'to keep out coloured people'. For many on the Labour side, including the leader Hugh Gaitskell, haunted by memories of the 1930s, the much-publicised presence of Sir Oswald Mosley's fascist followers during the Notting Hill troubles was probably a decisive consideration in their determination to brook no compromise. Later in the month, just before its conference, the party issued a statement unambiguously rejecting immigration controls and promising that the next Labour government would 'introduce legislation making illegal the public practice of discrimination'.[9]

What of public opinion? It is easy enough to locate individual viewpoints – 'It's high time the growing resentment felt in the country against the black invasion of Britain was thus made violently and forcibly manifest,' noted an approbatory Anthony Heap on 1 September about the 'racial riots', while letters received by Edelman after his *Daily Mail* article were largely supportive – but the only reliable representative guide is the Gallup poll conducted nationwide on the 3rd and 4th.

The key findings included: 55 per cent wanting restrictions on non-white immigration from the Commonwealth; 71 per cent disapproving of 'marriages between white and coloured people'; 54 per cent not wanting 'coloured people from the Commonwealth' to be 'admitted to council housing lists on the same conditions as people born in Britain'; and 61 per cent definitely or possibly moving 'if coloured people came to live in great numbers' in their district. These were striking enough figures – with the first especially at variance with the broad party political consensus – but need to be set against others: only 9 per cent definitely moving, and 21 per cent possibly, 'if coloured people came to live next door'; and only 7 per cent objecting 'if there were coloured children in the same classes as your children at school'.

Altogether, as Ruth Glass dryly put it, the poll showed that 'the veneer of racial tolerance is a rather thin one'. But at the same time, at least that thin veneer existed, and arguably owed at least something to a widespread underlying decency on the part of a socially still very conservative population. 'Discussed the Colour problem, Jewish problem, & agreed that the 4 years sentence on the Teddy Boys who beat up the Colour chap was just,' noted Florence Turtle after lunch with a friend on the 17th, in the context of the recent deliberately punitive sentences given to the nine white thugs who had presaged the Notting Hill troubles. Not dissimilarly, speaking in some sense for Middle England, there was the Giles cartoon of the 7th, showing three Teds walking out of a surgery where the battle wounds they had brought on themselves had been treated by a black nurse and doctor. Even on the part of averagely decent whites, though, a strict limit applied to their appetite for the whole issue. As BBC Television's autumn schedule unfolded, members of the viewers' panel found it 'a pleasure to watch such an artist' when Harry Belafonte was on, but not so with *The Untouchable*, a worthy-sounding Sunday-night drama about an impoverished widow taking an Indian law student into her home as one of her lodgers. 'To a good number,' noted the report, 'this play about the colour bar seemed "ill timed" – there was "too much talk and controversy" already and they were "sated with the subject".'

Probably for many anyway, it was still a rather academic question, given that only 49 per cent of those polled by Gallup had actually ever known a non-white person.[10] But for those living in the areas of non-white settlement it was far from academic, and in three of them there were some particularly strong reactions during these charged days and weeks.

Starting in Notting Hill itself, so much in the national spotlight that on 5 September the nine o'clock news on the radio had five minutes shaved off in order to include a special report on the area that featured the views of white people living there. 'Some of those interviewed, after disavowing any racial prejudice, agreed,' noted the *Listener*,

> that 'This here trouble with the blacks' as one of them called it, all started by coloured men forcing white girls into prostitution and living handsomely on their earnings and often drawing national assistance as well. Others alleged that coloured immigrants bought up houses in the area, evicted the original tenants and then filled them up with their friends, five and six to a room, when they further outraged the feelings of the local inhabitants by rowdy parties lasting all night.

Three days later, nearly fifty teenagers (almost certainly all white) attended the newly opened Dale Youth Club to take part in a subsequently reported discussion:

> They felt that it has been a small minority of the coloured population that has provoked the white people in the area. The general consensus of opinion was that mixed marriages were wrong and that there was a certain amount of feeling against white girls who married coloured men. During the discussion many of the teenagers quoted actual cases of their own experience, of the appalling low standards of living, among the coloured people. As regards the housing problem, they were annoyed that 'West Indians could come here and get houses when white people are overcrowded and have not got houses'. They agreed that some sort of immigration restriction should be imposed particularly in their area.

Finally, these four dozen white youths were asked whether the riots had been justified. 'They would give no definite answer,' the club leader, Mr Hale, told the local paper, 'but they would rather say yes than no.'

Up in the West Midlands (which had the second-biggest concentration after London of non-white immigrants) there had been no serious disturbances, with the partial exception of Dudley, but that did not prevent some uninhibited correspondence in Wolverhampton's *Express and Star*:

> I do not advocate an inhospitable attitude towards foreign elements within our midst, but surely we have the undeniable right to choose our guests and 'weed out' the sick, the lame and the lazy? Our outraged intellectuals would do well to visit their local pubs where more common sense is aired than in many a Parliamentary gathering. *('Geordie')*
>
> Jobs are scarcer, rent and rates higher, yet people are entering this land and going straight on to public assistance. It is completely wrong. Friction in such circumstances is inevitable, regardless of colour or creed. If common sense and less sentiment were employed, everyone would stand to gain. *(Florence Beamand, 49 Butts Road, Penn, Wolverhampton)*
>
> We dread the summer or any nice weather, as a crowd of Jamaicans gather in the next-door gardens to play cards, and make the neighbourhood hideous with their noise . . . It is useless for Cabinet ministers or anyone else to attempt to whitewash. They should live amongst these coloured immigrants and suffer as we have done. *('Long-Sufferer')*

Colin Quayle of Himley Road, Dudley also had West Indian neighbours. 'The lines of clean washing which hang above their well-tended gardens testify to their cleanliness and industry,' he insisted. 'They are good neighbours, who wish to interfere with my way of life as little as I wish to interfere with theirs.'

The third place was Kentish Town in north London, where a local by-election was due to be held on 25 September. The Conservative, Labour and Communist candidates all agreed to keep race issues out of it, but a fourth candidate stood as an independent specifically on a 'Keep Kentish Town White' platform. He was William Webster, a 51-year-old publican and former boxer at whose pub, the Black Horse in Royal College Street, only whites were admitted. 'My platform is primarily a moral one,' he explained. 'The so-called Teddy boy era is the most healthy reaction we have had to date. Even if the coloured people were acceptable biologically there is neither work nor accommodation for them in this area.' And to another journalist about his opposition to a multiracial society: 'It is a matter of racial survival and

I can see in this a lowering of standards. The Negro is on a lower evolutionary plane so far as I can see.' As for his policy at his pub, Webster maintained that 'if I did not keep coloured people out of my house I should have no customers at all'. Shortly before polling day, the brewers Watney, Combe and Reid gave him a year's notice to quit, and the chairman of the Central Panel of the Brewing Trade wrote to *The Times* making it 'abundantly clear' that 'this trade dissociates itself entirely from all forms of racial discrimination', prompting in turn a letter from Webster's wife Emmeline, who claimed that all her husband was trying to do was 'to keep the area in which his wife and children reside, and the house wherein he earns his living, morally and socially respectable'. The voters (predominantly white) duly gave their verdict: 479 votes for Webster, out of a total of almost 6,500 cast.

In other words, the non-white immigrants – of which there were by now a critical mass – were here to stay. Including Sylvester Hughes, who in his early thirties had sailed from Antigua on Christmas Eve 1957, started in London as a kitchen porter in Lyons Corner House, and over the next 15 years would work as a carpenter (rising to foreman) before turning himself into a self-employed stallholder, eventually becoming in the early 1980s the first-ever West Indian stallholder in the Portobello Road fruit-and-veg market. Year-round, on stall 109, he wore the same outfit, recalled his obituarist Emily Green in 1991:

> Tweed hat, pressed cotton shirt, knotted tie, wool jumper. He never hawked. There was no easy familiarity. He addressed others as 'Miss', 'Missus' or 'Mister' – never 'Love', 'Lovey' or 'Darling'. And he was known locally, even by those who knew him well, as 'Mr Hughes'.
>
> His produce, too, was an exercise in contrast . . . Jamaican peppermint, white and yellow yams, plantains, ackee, limes, several types of root ginger, a good variety of chillies, coconuts, smooth Jamaican avocadoes and the exotic squash *chayote*.

On the day of Hughes's funeral, at All Saints' Church, Notting Hill, 'stall 109 was heaped with bouquets from shoppers and neighbouring stallholders, who had grown quite fond of the quiet man with the queer fruit'.[11]

'Today the Do-It-Yourself Exhibition opens at Olympia,' noted the *Evening Standard* on 4 September, adding that 'in no section has there been such a boom as in sailing craft'. Marinas and suchlike, however, were not on the minds of those gathered at Bournemouth that week for the Trades Union Congress, with Frank Cousins an increasingly vexed participant. 'The general atmosphere of apathy & display of unreadiness to enter into a real examination of major problems was increasingly apparent,' he privately reflected after it ended, and went on:

> It seems we have too many men in the Council of the T.U.C. who either do not believe fully in the principles of public ownership or do not understand it in relationship to the control of the country's economy . . . Even subjects such as security in employment, mobility of Labour, social services, full employment, productivity & the like appear to be matters of no concern . . . Many of the leaders seem to have no forward purpose except to maintain their individual status. Not a solitary lesson was learned from the Bus Strike of May 1958 & every one seemed satisfied to have reached a position where no one was wrong & no one was right on the issues involved.

Even more disenchanted, though, was Les Cannon, the ex-Communist trade unionist who was by now in bitter dispute with his union, the Communist-dominated Electrical Trades Union, over its shameless ballot-rigging practices. On the eve of the TUC he gave a high-profile press conference. But in the event he received precious little support (Vic Feather an honourable exception), with the sympathy of the capitalist press, together with the ETU's vehement line that an attack on one union was an attack on the movement as a whole, probably having the effect of turning many trade unionists against his cause, or at least just wishing it would go away.

In terms of employer–employee relations it was in many ways still a paternalistic world. Take the giant ICI, whose Billingham sports club, the Synthonia (a portmanteau of Synthetic Ammonia), had a new ground, superbly appointed for both football and athletics, officially opened by the Earl of Derby on Saturday the 6th. 'I must express on behalf of the members our sincere and grateful thanks to the Company

for yet one more act of supreme generosity towards us,' declared the
club's president at the ceremony. Paternalism was also usually the order
of the day in the many small or medium-sized family-run firms that
largely comprised the City of London. The merchant bank Antony
Gibbs & Sons was one such, holding this autumn for family, partners,
staff and pensioners a cocktail party at the Grocers' Hall to celebrate its
150th anniversary. 'Mac', the recently retired Stanley McCombie, naturally received an invitation after 44 years' service, but, stricken with
dermatitis, he warned 'Mr Antony' he might be unable to attend. 'So
far I don't consider my retiring to be an unqualified success,' he wrote
on the 20th from his home in Leytonstone, 'and my wife is threatening to send me back to the office as a washout so far as home is
concerned . . . I miss you very much, but I'm sure all goes on as usual
without me.'[12]

By this time *Sunday Night at the London Palladium* had a new host,
following Lew Grade's abrupt sacking of Tommy Trinder, possibly for
telling a racist or anti-Jewish joke. This was the 30-year-old Bruce
Forsyth, who a year before had talked of giving up comedy to run a
tobacconist's. Clifford Davis on the *Mirror*'s 'Telepage' charted
Forsyth's early progress. In his first show, 14 September, 'a likeable
personality – without being too forceful'; a fortnight later, 'packed in
some topical material' but 'will have to stop overworking the word
"wonderful" every time he interviews contestants for "Beat the Clock"';
and a week later, 'managed to hold this rather indifferent show
together . . . versatile . . . tailor-made for the job . . . gets better each
week'. The *Mirror* in September also gave its appraisal of a new British
film. 'Unabashedly relies on beating customers over the head with a
bladder of lard,' reckoned Dick Richards, adding 'the jokes come thick
and fast' and that, although 'sometimes the comedy sags', this was 'only
while the cast is getting its second breath'. *Carry On Sergeant* owed a
fair bit to television's *The Army Game*, not only being similarly set
amongst a bunch of National Service squaddies but also featuring three
of its stars in William Hartnell, Charles Hawtrey and Norman
Rossington, who helped out Bob Monkhouse, Dora Bryan, Kenneth
Connor and Kenneth Williams. In any case, it was such an instant hit
that at the Last Night of the Proms a huge banner proclaiming 'Carry
On Sargent' was waved behind the unwitting conductor, Sir Malcolm.

At the outset the film had been conceived by producer Peter Rogers and director Gerald Thomas as a one-off, but within weeks *Carry On Nurse* was in production.[13]

On a damp Thursday four days after Forsyth's debut, an American professor of genetics, George W. Beadle, arrived in Oxford with his wife Muriel and son Red to take up a visiting professorship. Their brisk, matter-of-fact landlady showed them round their rented house – small and cluttered – in Headington and, as recalled by Muriel in her nicely humorous memoir of an often baffling year, offered some local guidance: '"Thursday is early closing," she said, "and if you wish to lay on supplies you must get to the shops before one." The butcher shops shut their doors on Monday and Saturday afternoons, in addition, she told us; and the wine merchant was open (for the purchase of spirits) only during "hours", which I later found out meant during the same hours the pubs were open.' Umbrellas in hand, they set out for some immediate groceries:

> At Berry's, the bakery, I bought a small round loaf of bread, receiving it with a piece of thin paper loosely wrapped around part of it. At Murchison's the Headington greengrocer, I added newspaper-wrapped potatoes, carrots, and a limp head of lettuce to the bundles in Red's arms. Our final stop was H. E. Weaver's Quality Meats, and there I made a mistake. Walking along, I had made a quick calculation as to what might be the simplest menu to prepare, and I had answered myself: a good Irish stew. So I asked Mr Weaver for 'a pound of beef for stew', expecting the succulent squares of chuck that the same request would have produced at home. I don't know what he gave me, because I never ordered it again.

That evening at 8.30, with a fork still unable to penetrate the meat despite four hours of cooking on top of the Rayburn, Muriel's patience snapped:

> I said, 'Let's eat it. If we cut it into small enough pieces, we won't even have to chew it.' I *did* chew one piece of mine to see what it tasted like, and it didn't have any taste.
>
> Red, sensing my distress and doing his best to relieve it, said, 'The potatoes are awfully good, Mom.'

'I'm glad you like them,' I said with savage politeness, and burst into tears.

Later, she lay awake for hours, listening to the rain. 'I let my thoughts drift back to the electric range in my California kitchen, and to the furnace we lit by pressing a button, and to the big living-room in our Spanish-style house.'

One of John Bloom's washing machines would probably not have made the difference. 'Britain's Greatest-Ever Washing Machine Value!' boasted an advertisement on the back page of the *Mirror* six days later for the 'Electromatic Washing Machine and Spin Drier'. 'From 49 [in huge type] Gns. A Brand New Combination ... A Complete home laundry for 1/3rd deposit and only 7/3 a week for 2 years!' A remarkable story was under way. The 26-year-old Bloom was the son of a Polish-born tailor and had grown up in the East End before leaving school at 16. By 1958 he had tried his hand at various things (salesman at Selfridge's, running a road-haulage business, selling paraffin door-to-door), but not got very far in any of them. But that year, in quick succession, he started selling cut-price washing machines imported from Holland, grew a beard to make himself look older, and now, in September, took a punt by advertising in Britain's best-selling daily paper – so successfully that more than 8,000 readers sent off the coupon requesting details about the Electromatic. It was a propitious moment. Hire-purchase controls were about to be abolished, washing machine sales for 1958 would be 44 per cent up on the previous year, the market leader (Hotpoint) largely eschewed price reductions, and at this point Bloom was one of only two entrepreneurs who saw the gap in the market for (to quote the historian of domestic electrical appliances) 'really cheap and less indestructibly durable appliances, using high-pressure salesmanship to sell them', mainly to 'working-class homes, still so understocked with many appliances'. Bloom's rival was the Manchester-based A. J. Flatley, who in the course of the year began to make clothes dryers and gave his name to the advertising jingle 'Mum deserves a Flatley'.[14] History, however, would remember Bloom.

These were still early days after Nottingham and Notting Hill, and, quite apart from issues of immigration and race relations, there were the implications to be considered of the Teddy boys' violent behaviour.

The industrialist Sir Halford Reddish, appearing on a *Brains Trust* television panel just before Forsyth's Palladium debut, had no doubts: 'I would like to see corporal punishment brought in and these young thugs given a good thrashing.' A few weeks later, at the Tory conference, Butler managed to fend off vociferous demands to restore flogging, though at the price of promising harsher youth detention centres to 'de-Teddify the Teddy Boy', while also in October the government set up a committee under Lady Albemarle to consider the youth problem, including the question of facilities. Phyllis Willmott, meanwhile, offered a beady perspective. 'The Committee members absolutely appalled me at first sight,' she wrote after attending in late September her first meeting as a member of the Managing Committee of Westlea Hostel for the aftercare of teenage girls. 'They seemed very middle-aged, rather frumpish, and overpoweringly middle class.' Next day she and other committee members visited Dixcot Hostel, a large Edwardian house near Tooting Common that catered for 'difficult' girls of 11–15:

> The hostel is ridiculously spic & span for a *children's* home. Poor little dears, no wonder they spend all their free time out on the Common. The Warden seemed a very stiff person. I should think most children would feel immediately uneasy with him . . . It was like a hotel not a home . . . 'Not a single scribble on the wall' as one handsome well-dressed Tory woman said. One can't help wondering in such a place whether the hostel is run for the children or the adults supposed to be caring for the children . . .[15]

'The publisher who accepted the manuscript told me that it was the sort of book he liked to have on his list, a very reputable work, but of course very few people would want to read it,' recalled Raymond Williams. 'He said: "I've got another book called *The Uses of Literacy*, of which I would say the same."' The publisher was Ian Parsons of Chatto & Windus, and Williams's *Culture and Society, 1780–1950* eventually appeared in September 1958, a year and a half after Hoggart's book and four months after Crossman's disconcerting evening listening to him speak at a New Left meeting. *Culture and Society*, like *Uses*, hugely exceeded expectations: some 200,000 copies sold by 2005, and over the years it has often been identified as the start of 'cultural studies'. Williams was 37, the son of a Welsh railway signalman; via Abergavenny Grammar School, he had gone to Cambridge – for a time falling, like so many, under the influence of the powerfully moralising F. R. Leavis – before (in 1946) becoming an adult education tutor in East Sussex. *Culture and Society* was not his first book, but it was his breakthrough into a much wider readership, and over the next three decades he emerged as arguably the leading British public intellectual.

At the heart of *Culture and Society* was its sympathetic recapitulation of the views of those English writers (including Coleridge, Carlyle, the 'Condition of England' novelists, Mill, Morris, Lawrence and Orwell) who, according to Williams's reading, had reacted, whether from a conservative or a more socialist standpoint, *against* the utilitarian assumptions of laissez-faire industrialism – the phenomenon that in his eyes, looking back over the previous two centuries, was the worm in the Enlightenment bud. Williams wrote with particular warmth, and clear personal empathy, about D. H. Lawrence:

> He had the rich experience of childhood in a working-class family, in which most of his positives lay. What such a childhood gave was certainly not tranquillity or security; it did not even, in the ordinary sense, give happiness. But it gave what to Lawrence was more important than these things: the sense of close quick relationship, which came to matter more than anything else. This was the positive result of the life of the family in a small house, where there were no such devices of separation of children and parents as the sending-away to school, or the handing-over to servants, or the relegation to nursery or playroom . . . in such a life, the suffering and the giving of comfort, the common want and the common remedy, the open row and the open making-up, are all part of a continuous life which, in good and bad, makes for a whole attachment.

'A whole attachment': that was the ideal. Raphael Samuel would write illuminatingly after Williams's death of how 'the socialism which he advocated was not a utopian blueprint, but rather the recovery of a lost wholeness . . . a matter of age-old solidarities reasserting themselves, in conditions of difficulty, and complexity'.

Where lay that wholeness in the third quarter of the twentieth century? In an ambitious, more explicitly personal concluding chapter, Williams seemed to pin his hopes on 'working-class culture', a culture which he (like Hoggart) contrasted with the inexorably rising, commercialised mass culture, but which he (unlike the pessimistic Hoggart) saw as having an intrinsic, deep-rooted strength that would carry the day. This culture, he insisted,

> is not proletarian art, or council houses, or a particular use of language; it is, rather, the basic collective idea, and the institutions, manners, habits of thought and intentions which proceed from this ... [it] is primarily social (in that it has created institutions) rather than individual (in particular intellectual or imaginative work). When it is considered in context, it can be seen as a very remarkable creative achievement.

Citing Edmund Burke's fear of the 'swinish multitude' trampling down learning, Williams ended this passage by comparing the historical record of collective working-class culture favourably to that of individualistic bourgeois culture: 'This, indeed, is the curious incident of the swine in the night. As the light came, and we could look around, it appeared that the trampling, which we had all heard, did not after all come from them.'

Culture and Society was reviewed widely if not always favourably. John Jones in the *New Statesman* noted 'a generosity of temperament which gives moral stature to his work', but Denys Harding, an out-and-out Leavisite, charged Williams in the *Spectator* with failing to 'squarely face the fact that vast numbers of people want, and pay for, rather low-quality work, and only a small public wants work of the quality discriminatingly appraised in this book', while the *TLS* called his approach 'at times suffocatingly abstract'. A typically shrewd, balanced verdict came in *Encounter* from the rising literary critic Frank Kermode. While admiring the book's intelligence, candour and seriousness, he was sceptical about the exaltation of working-class culture – 'I do not feel that it retains the value that Mr Williams allows it. Specially, I think the harm being done by television advertising is catastrophic.' In due course two of the strongest critiques came from a pair of historians much more deeply embedded in the Marxist tradition than Williams himself was at this stage. 'The prime requisite for any study of cultural history is a firm framework of historical fact – economic, social, political ... The one great deficiency of the book is the lack of just this,' declared Victor Kiernan the following summer in the *New Reasoner*. Then later, in its successor journal, E. P. Thompson wrote disparagingly (if fairly) of the book's 'procession of disembodied voices' whose 'meanings' had been 'wrested out of their whole social context'; he particularly mourned the apparent absence of 'struggle', especially class struggle, in Williams's cultural tradition. For most readers, though, in the book's early life, any reservations were far outweighed by a sense of excitement. Williams's first biographer, Fred Inglis, put it best: 'It was a life-changer for young-ish readers in 1960 or so (including me). Its large, never-quite-grasped purpose was to find and recharge the lost veins of English romantic socialism, to make them glow again in the body politic.'[16]

Within a week or two of *Culture and Society*'s publication, an essay by Williams appeared in *Conviction*, a collection edited by Norman MacKenzie. Entitled 'Culture is Ordinary', the piece argued forcibly that, for 'the Socialist intellectual', there were 'no masses to save, to capture, or to direct, but rather this crowded people in the course of an extraordinarily rapid and confusing expansion of their lives'. A year after the Angry Young Men had made their *Declaration*, this was generally a more sober gathering, with the contributors – again, all under 40 – generally on the left of the Labour Party but for the most part at some distance from the New Left. They included the Labour politician Peter Shore, the journalists Paul Johnson and Mervyn Jones, the historian Hugh Thomas and Richard Hoggart, the last with a piece characteristically called 'Speaking to each other', a plea for what he called 'a decent classlessness'. Two essays that attracted particular attention were on welfare issues: Brian Abel-Smith sought to demonstrate that the middle class was benefiting disproportionately from the welfare state, and Peter Townsend, shaping up for what would become almost a lifetime's work, attacked the myth that poverty had been abolished. But arguably the most striking essay was the last, and the only one by a female contributor: 'A house of theory' by Iris Murdoch. Starting with a comprehensive demolition job on the inadequacies of current and recent British philosophy, she then demanded not only a more rigorous, systematic theory of socialism but a return to the ideals of William

Morris – without which, in the alienating conditions of modern industrial life, the 'proletariat' would remain 'a deracinate, disinherited and excluded mass of people'.

It was stirring if *de haut en bas* stuff, but in the event Murdoch's subsequent, mainly understated political journey would be to the right, as ultimately was the trajectory of the collection's already sceptical reviewer in *Socialist Commentary*. 'I detect in this book a condescension to the goodness of ordinary people, as opposed to the radicals whom they philosophically admire, or the careless submerged, whom they envy but dare not emulate,' wrote John Vaizey. 'I detect a reluctance to live their own ideals.' And he asked:

> What is the socialist vision today? I strongly suspect – much as I detest it – that it has more to do with the kind of hunger for achievement that we see in the New China than with any Scandinavian arcadia. Either that, or the socialist vision is now a private vision; a turning-away from public causes; a decision to live one's own life concerned with one's relationship with other human beings and with oneself, in which socialism is the political equivalent of turning down the neighbour's noisy wireless because it interferes with our children's sleep.

Vaizey in 1958 was a young, leftish economist specialising in education, but in the end he would be the intellectual par excellence who, in Noel Annan's words about this 'mercurial, erratic, ingenious' man, 'declared that he [i.e. Vaizey] and his generation had got it wrong and they should shake out a reef and sail on a new tack'.[17]

Sadly, neither *Declaration* nor *Conviction* took a line on the rapidly changing built environment, but towards the end of September the *Architects' Journal*'s 'Astragal' (probably J. M. Richards) described his recent visit to the almost completed, already part-occupied showpiece of public housing. 'If you drive across Richmond Park towards the towering slabs and point blocks of the LCC's Roehampton estate,' he began, 'you will feel that this is what the approach to a city ought to be like – open country leading to rolling parkland punctuated by buildings.' Admittedly there were faults – 'the access balconies are sordid bleak places, and there isn't any relief from the spartan *matières brutes* once you get inside the maisonettes' – but overall these were 'faults that are easy to forget when you look at the scheme as a whole and compare it with any other local authority work in this country'. Around this time, one Sunday afternoon, Florence Turtle also had a look:

> We toured Richmond Park & the Roehampton LCC Estate – this latter a terrible eyesore from Richmond Park, it resembles seven or eight tall piles of matchboxes surmounted by a drum, and at some angles it looks like a giant industrial plant. Letters in the 'Telegraph' praising it & others the contrary. I suggest the 'pros' don't have to live in sight of it. The occupants of the flats complain about travel, shopping, & entertainment facilities, during the bus strike they were cut off. They have some justification, many of them rehoused from the East End. To us who appreciate the amenities of the district it is 'The Murder of a Neighbourhood', it used to be one of the loveliest districts in London.

There had indeed been a vigorous correspondence in the *Daily Telegraph*, and a few days later the last word went to W. R. Atherton, who had moved in February into one of the estate's new high-rise flats. 'I found myself at home,' he said, despite not being a natural modernist. 'I hate rock 'n' roll, toneless music, abstract painting, and all sculpture after Jacob Epstein. I am a Cockney in exile. And yet I am content.'

So too in Bristol this autumn, where one sky-blue Saturday morning a local MP inspected Barton House, a new 14-storey block. 'We went right to the roof and visited various flats,' recorded Anthony Wedgwood Benn. 'To see the bright airy rooms with the superb views and to contrast them with the poky slum dwellings of Barton Hill below was to get all the reward one wants from politics. For this grand conception of planning is what it is all about. The people were happy, despite the grumbles about detail.' Up in Sheffield, it was a less grand outlook for Mrs Mary Slinn, who since 1899 had lived at 50 Woodside Lane, Pitsmoor, in a small but comfortable house due to be demolished as part of the Corporation's Burngreave redevelopment scheme. 'Nobody is going to shift me away to some estate outside the town,' she told the *Sheffield Telegraph* a few days before her 90th birthday. 'I am too old to put roots down somewhere else now . . . It doesn't look much, but it is a friendly street. You couldn't ask for nicer neighbours and that means a lot at my age.' In Hertfordshire a whole town, Ware, was seemingly being demolished. 'A holocaust of antiquity', with 'medieval timbers and kingpost roofs, Elizabethan wall-paintings, a Regency assembly room, all gathered round a handsome red-brick Georgian Inn, swept away', was a local description in October of what had been taking place in recent years, with this letter-writer to an architectural magazine adding despairingly of how 'the homeliness of brick and tile is replaced by carpets of concrete dotted with municipal bedding plants'.

In the City of London a wonderful Victorian building by now under threat was the Coal Exchange, recommended for demolition as part of a road-widening proposal. On 25 October *The Times* published a plea from Betjeman, repudiated a few days later by David Young of Sloane Avenue, Chelsea: 'The Coal Exchange may be "a pioneer building in cast iron", to quote Mr Betjeman, but it is in bad repair, cold, dirty, and no longer of any use to the coal industry. We must not be sentimental about buildings of this type.' Would J. B. Priestley have agreed? The day after Betjeman's letter, the BBC broadcast *Lost City*, showing the crusty Yorkshireman making a rare return trip to Bradford, his boyhood city, still strikingly Victorian in character and appearance despite the redevelopment recently under way. For the most part nostalgia ruled, but at the end, as the London train prepared to pull out, he offered his considered verdict on present-day Bradford and how it needed fully to embrace the second half of the twentieth century: 'It's not as good as it promised to be once. It's not bad, but it's not good enough for the real Bradfordians.'

T. Dan Smith had no doubts that the Newcastle of 1958 was not good enough for Geordies. 'I talked a different language,' he recalled about his failure (only 14 votes out of 60) to be elected leader of the city's Labour Party after it had won power in the local elections in May. 'My arguments were about inner cabinets in local government, efficiency as a complement to caring, and planning as the handmaiden of a civilised life. Their talk was of drains and majorities and rates. These were important things, but not priorities in a city which was being strangled by traffic, humiliated by lack of opportunity and murdered by mediocrity.' Instead, he had to make do with the chairmanship of the Housing Committee, where he put new drive into the existing slum-clearance programme and, faced with nearly 10,000 families on the waiting list and no spare building land within the city boundaries, saw no alternative but to build high.

Smith's immediate focus was on Newcastle's rundown West End, including the Scotswood Road area, and that autumn he wrote a long poem about his hopes and ambitions for it that began by emphasising the determination to clear the 'horrid slums'. Smith was an intelligent, rounded man, whatever his flaws, and the poem's most interesting passage conveys a certain ambiguity – even regret – about the process, often a brutal one, that was now starting to unfold:

> Here and there a gable wall
> Exposing papers to us all –
> Flowered, plain, in stripe or check
> Silent parchments watch men wreck
> As building after building falls
> Leaving exposed those few odd walls;
> Wherein once sheltered windows clean,
> Now only broken glass is seen.

Ultimately, though, he believed there was no alternative, and the final lines looked ahead to that glorious day almost four years thence, the centenary of the Blaydon Races:

> Old Scotswood Road must live again
> To carry further still its fame.
> We're soon to have a celebration –
> Let Tynesiders rise in jubilation
> A century has marched along
> Since first we heard that Tyneside song.
> On June the 9th in '62
> We will tell the world anew –
> Together with the sculptors' art,
> A Festival to play its part.
> We'll make Tyneside thus loud proclaim
> How just and right its shout of fame –
> Tomorrow, then, we all will see
> That Scotswood's making history.[18]

In the early days of October, 18-year-old Ronnie Wycherley was audi-
tioned in Birkenhead by the impresario Larry Parnes and would soon
be known as Billy Fury; *Saturday Skiffle Club* on the Light Programme
transmuted into *Saturday Club* (introduced by Brian Matthew in a
non-BBC, cross-class voice); and the first single by Harry Webb (aka
Cliff Richard) entered the Top Twenty. 'So rock 'n' roll is dead, is it?'
the jazz critic Steve Race had asked in *Melody Maker* in June. 'My
funeral oration consists of just two words: good riddance.' An incensed
young songwriter, Ian Samwell, had seen Cliff perform at the 2i's coffee
bar in Soho and then penned for him an authentic rock 'n' roll number,
'Move It', inspired musically by Chuck Berry. Released in late August,
the song was taken up by Jack Good, the strong-minded TV producer
who had become disenchanted with the BBC's antiseptic *Six-Five
Special*, started *Oh Boy!* on late-night commercial television during the
summer, and in September was able to get his fast-paced, cutting-edge
show directly competing on Saturday evenings against Pete Murray et
al. Good's trump card was Cliff, and vice versa. 'It was Jack who created
the beginnings of Cliff Richard,' recalled the singer half a century later.
'He didn't want an Elvis lookalike, so off came the sideburns, away
went the guitar, and in came the sneer, the curled lip, and that sultry
look up at the camera. I was 100% directed by him but, oh boy, did he
know what he was doing.' Not that, even on the pop scene, the pouting
young Cliff was everyone's cup of tea. 'Violent hip-swinging and crude
exhibitionism', the *New Musical Express* would call his performing
style, adding tartly that 'Tommy Steele became Britain's teenage idol
without resorting to this form of indecent, short-sighted vulgarity.'[19]

The start of *Saturday Club* on 4 October coincided with the return
of a national champion. Back in 1952 the De Havilland Comet had
inaugurated the jet age, but three crashes in less than a year meant that
all Comets had been grounded from 1954. Four years on, two wholly
redesigned Comet IVs now flew the BOAC flag from London to New
York – the world's first transatlantic passenger jet service, beating
(amidst considerable national satisfaction) Pan Am's Boeing 707 by a
little over three weeks. A momentous occasion in the wider transport
sense, with 1958 the last year in which more passengers crossed the
North Atlantic by sea than by air, it did not in the event signal a lasting
British triumph. The process of getting Comet IV into service had been

too slow to secure decisive first-mover advantage, the plane's seating capacity was only half that of the 707 or the Douglas DC-8, and it was only a few years before BOAC was looking to Boeing for its long-haul needs. Symbolically, within days of the initial moment of glory, BOAC found itself beset by an unofficial strike of 4,000 maintenance men – a strike overseen by a rising trade unionist, the supremely self-confident and articulate Clive Jenkins. 'While the Comet IV is a delightful aircraft in which to fly,' he observed soon afterwards in his analysis of the dispute, 'it represents a marginal commercial operation. This is easy to see when it stands alongside the large Boeing 707 on the apron at London Airport.' And as for 'the Tories and their plans for hobbling the unions in civil aviation and further traffic-diversions to the under-cutting private operators', he quoted a Spanish proverb: 'Have patience and you will see your enemy's funeral procession.'[20]

Two days after the Comet soared was 'Decontrol Day' – the coming into operation, after a 15-month standstill, of the government's contro-versial Rent Act. Around six million dwellings were owned by private landlords, with some 40 per cent of London's population living in the private rented sector. The purpose of the legislation was to give those landlords an adequate return after many years of rent control and generally to try to restore the forces of supply and demand to the hous-ing market, which ultimately – ministers believed – would help to reduce the dire housing shortage. Many middle-class tenants, enjoying the genteel advantages of protected tenancies and rents, were appalled by the prospect. 'Why should a wicked act be passed?' Mrs Philips Guise in January 1958 asked the Housing Minister, Henry Brooke – an act that allowed 'unscrupulous landlords' to 'put up rents more than double, causing misery and distress to thousands of people who have fought for their country & have always strived to live within their means'. The novelist Ivy Compton-Burnett was especially wrathful. 'The Rent Act is looming over everything here, and it has fallen on me with thunderous force,' she wrote from South Kensington to a friend abroad in September 1957. And again, some nine months later: 'It would be of little good to move as the same thing is happening every-where and there is nothing to be done but suffer it, though in my case not in silence.' To a cousin indeed, she was positively apocalyptic, declaring that 'these are hard days and we are the doomed class'.

Unforeseen by its creators, and presumably not affecting Dame Ivy, the Rent Act would through reducing security of tenure also give birth to 'Rachmanism': in essence, the systematic, often brutal use of intimidating methods by landlords – usually slum landlords – to induce or coerce sitting tenants to leave, so that with vacant possession they could either sell the property at a handsome profit or pack it with new tenants (often West Indian immigrants) paying inflated rents. Perec (Peter) Rachman himself was an immigrant from Poland in his late thirties who by this time had already built up a slum empire of some 70 or 80 houses, mainly in Paddington and North Kensington, by unsavoury means; the new legislation played into the hands of this 'short, chubby-faced, plump and balding' man, who, adds a biographer, 'dressed in silk shirts, cashmere suits and crocodile shoes', as well as always wearing 'dark glasses and a gold bracelet which was locked to his wrist and inscribed with serial numbers of his Swiss bank accounts and safe-combinations'.[21]

Tenants rather than owner-occupiers gathered at White Hart Lane on Saturday the 11th to see Tottenham, with Bill Nicholson as new manager, run out 10–4 winners against Everton (Albert Dunlop in goal). It was not a final score that BBC television's new rolling sports programme, making its debut that afternoon, could immediately bring. *Grandstand*, introduced by Peter Dimmock (who had wanted to call it 'Out and About'), started at two o'clock and featured golf, horse racing and show jumping, but at 4.45 had to give way to *The Lone Ranger* followed by *Jennings at School* before, at 5.40, *Today's Sport*, introduced by Kenneth Wolstenholme, at last gave the football results, read by Len Martin. Elsewhere this Saturday, Philip Larkin in Hull bought a new tie – 'black, with gold horizontal stripes: *nearly* Teddy Boy but not quite, at least I hope not quite', as he informed Monica Jones – and in London Paul Robeson gave a half-hour recital, singing spirituals, during Evensong at St Paul's, with a crowded congregation of 4,000, including many non-whites, watching a significant, reconciling moment some six weeks after Notting Hill.[22]

Culturally, though, the defining event of the weekend was the reviews in the two upmarket Sundays of Alan Sillitoe's first novel, *Saturday Night and Sunday Morning*. 'The rowdy gang of singers who sat at the scattered tables saw Arthur walk unsteadily to the head of the stairs, and though they must all have known that he was dead drunk, and seen the danger he would soon be in, no one attempted to talk to him and lead him back to his seat,' began this story by a working-class Nottingham man of a working-class Nottingham anti-hero, the cynical, hedonistic, newly affluent young Arthur Seaton. 'With eleven pints of beer and seven small gins playing hide-and-seek inside his stomach, he fell from the topmost stair to the bottom.' It struck an immediate chord, with Richard Mayne in the *Sunday Times* praising its 'authenticity, bolshie anarchism' and John Wain in the *Observer* welcoming the realistic characterisation of Seaton, 'not . . . a displaced intellectual but a genuine working man, who doesn't hanker for a dimly glimpsed world of books and ideas, but differs from his mates only by being more rebellious'. A few days later, Peter Green in the *Telegraph* was even more complimentary, calling it 'that rarest of all finds: a genuine, no-punches pulled, unromanticised working-class novel'. An alternative type of literary exotica was available this month, though, in the form of Lawrence Durrell's *Mountolive*, the third of his *Alexandria Quartet*, now starting to be provisionally judged as an entity. 'Not much more than an Arabian Nights Entertainment,' was the sceptical view of fellow novelist Pamela Hansford Johnson, who deemed it 'an entrancing, odorous maze without a centre'.[23]

'Looked in at Television, such a lot of it is drivel,' Florence Turtle noted on Thursday 16 October. 'Hughie Green's double your money is quite a good programme, but what a lot of illiterate people they get on it.' In retrospect, though, the main TV event that day had already happened, at five o'clock on the BBC. 'Toys, model railways, games, stories, cartoons' was the subtitle given in the listings for *Blue Peter*, 'a new weekly programme for Younger Viewers, with Christopher Trace and Leila Williams'. He was a handsome 25-year-old actor, she was Miss Great Britain 1957 (and also an active Young Conservative). The under-11 target audience soon gave their verdict:

Almost without exception they found this programme very enjoyable to watch. For the small boys, of course, Christopher Trace's demonstration of toy trains and model railways was an especial attraction . . . The demonstration of mind reading passed almost without comment, but a number of young viewers (boys and girls alike) seem to have found the cartoon – 'Sparky and the Talking Train' – very appealing.

Children over 11 mainly dismissed the programme as 'babyish', though a few girls 'reacted favourably to the doll collection item' as presented by Williams, who also talked about their trousseaux.

Three days later a daredevil, good-time motor racer from Farnham, 29-year-old Mike Hawthorn, became world champion, courtesy of an act of the utmost sportsmanship by Stirling Moss, who, following a controversial incident at the Portuguese Grand Prix earlier in the season, had given testimony that allowed his rival to keep second place. Hawthorn on becoming champion immediately retired, but for Tommy Steele the next career move was a change of direction, with his manager announcing next day, 'He wants to get away from rock 'n' roll,' in the context of Steele signing a film contract to play a British seaman who gets involved in a Spanish bullfight. By this time, Monday the 20th, the president of the German Federal Republic, Dr Theodor Heuss, had begun a state visit. 'The sight of Germany's black, red, and gold flying alongside the Union Jack on government buildings has given many Londoners a mighty queer feeling,' commented Mollie Panter-Downes, adding that along the Mall 'most of the crowds watched silently when he drove past them in the open royal carriage'. No doubt some had been reading the *Mirror*'s 'Cassandra', who that day categorically called Germany 'the cause of the greatest bloodshed and misery the world has ever known' and insisted that 'Papa' Heuss, for all his 'good manners', would be unable to 'wash away the nature of the nation that he represents'. Two days later the unforgiving columnist reprised, arguing that 'the ageing professor has successfully been sold to an amiable but significantly silent British public, as a benign and scholarly man', though in reality 'a skilful apologist for the German people'; he signed off with a reference to 'the stench of the gas ovens still in the air'.[24]

That same day, Wednesday the 22nd – three weeks after being 'tremendously heartened' by how on his tour of the West Midlands 'everyone seemed very cheerful & very friendly', and four days after noting that 'the Socialists are working up a "slump" scare', with unemployment having tipped over the then politically invidious half a million mark – Macmillan recorded a cardinal moment in the pre-election cycle:

I had a good talk today with the Chancellor of the Ex^r on the 64,000 dollar question – is it a boom? is it a slump? is it slack water? If the last, will the tide go in or out? The people have now a pathological fear of even a little unemployment. Yet 1% means *over*-employment and a financial crisis. 3% means almost a political crisis . . .

It is a great pleasure to talk with Heathcoat Amory, after having dealt with Thorneycroft. The former is *very* intelligent, flexible, & courteous. The latter was fundamentally stupid, rigid, & 'cassant'. We agreed on the things we *might* do to 'reflate' the economy.

Five days later, on the 27th, the government announced the end of the remaining restrictions on hire purchase and the renting of goods: no longer would it be compulsory to make a minimum deposit of one-third or to pay in advance for the first four months' rental. 'We can give this extra bit of freedom because the credit squeeze and the other stern measures we took a year ago have worked,' declared the president of the Board of Trade, Sir David Eccles, though the *Manchester Guardian* observed cautiously that 'no Chancellor can lose sight of the balance of payments' and that the government was bound to be criticised for having 'favoured consumption before investment'. The public, however, was willing to take the risk: a Gallup poll soon afterwards revealed 58 per cent approval for this green light and only 26 per cent disapproval.[25]

Tuesday the 28th saw the state opening of Parliament being televised for the first time, with two commentators in direct competition. As 'Her Majesty returns to the Robing Room and thence to Buckingham Palace,' solemnly intoned the BBC's Richard Dimbleby near the end, 'she leaves behind in all of us, a memory of a state occasion at its most magnificent.' Over on ITV, Robin Day was altogether crisper and more informal: 'The crown will go back to the Tower of London. All the scarlet and ermine robes will go back to wherever they came from. And Parliament will go back to work.' In the afternoon, Gladys Langford again 'went 'bussing': 'Finsbury Park – Golders Green – Victoria – Green Park – Highbury Barn. But my world is gone. Cliff-like flats, girl children in colourful pants, old women raddled & "permed".' That evening Anthony Heap dutifully attended the Royal Court for the first night of Samuel Beckett's *Krapp's Last Tape* and *Endgame* ('these dreary sleep-inducers'), and Dr Bronowski's guests on ITV's *New Horizon* programme, discussing the good and bad effects of science, were Aldous and Julian Huxley. 'Move It' was meanwhile moving up the charts – number 3 by the end of the week, tucked behind Connie Francis's 'Stupid Cupid' and Elvis's 'King Creole' – while on Saturday 1 November *Grandstand*-watchers noted a changing of the guards, with Dimmock now co-presenting with an unknown face, 32-year-old David Coleman. Then from the 8th it was Coleman on his own.

The new man was, in Frank Keating's apt words, 'smart, street-wise and regional', having previously been the first non-international athlete to win the Manchester Mile and played for Stockport County reserves as well as working on the *Stockport Express* and in the BBC newsroom in Birmingham. The time was ripe for a new, non-public-school approach to covering sport. 'Out,' as Jim White puts it, 'went the clipped, detached, patronising dinner-jacket style inherited from radio presentation, and in came a much more engaged manner.' It was an elevation that undoubtedly owed much to *Grandstand*'s producer, the fiercely driven 31-year-old Bryan Cowgill, who had been to grammar school in Clitheroe and was at this stage convinced that his lack of a university education would block his progress at the BBC.[26] Coleman and Cowgill: part of a fresh breed – call them meritocrats – whose hour was seemingly at hand.

9

Parity of Esteem

Just as Coleman was preparing to take the hot seat (and a peasant's son was being elected Pope John XXIII), the first reviews started to appear of Michael Young's *The Rise of the Meritocracy* – the book for which he would be remembered even more than *Family and Kinship*. Contrary to subsequent assumptions, Young did not in fact coin the term *meritocracy*: two years earlier, writing in *Socialist Commentary* (a magazine to which Young contributed), the sociologist Alan Fox had put the word in quotation marks and defined it as 'the society in which the gifted, the smart, the energetic, the ambitious and the ruthless are carefully sifted out and helped towards their destined positions of dominance, where they proceed not only to enjoy the fulfilment of exercising their natural endowments but also to receive a fat bonus thrown in for good measure'. But it was certainly Young who popularised it.

The book itself – in which 'Intelligence and effort together make up merit $(I + E = M)$' – is set in 2034 and comprises two parts. The first traces the rise, well under way by 1958, of a meritocratic elite chosen largely through intelligence-testing and educational selection; the second relates the disturbing consequences, as those deemed unmeritorious become an increasingly alienated underclass, with the threat looming by the 2030s of a 'Populist' revolution. Although the first part reveals Young as far from unsympathetic to the meritocratic case, ultimately the book is a dystopian warning against a rampant, self-serving, IQ-driven, intolerant meritocracy. 'Were we to evaluate people, not only according to their intelligence and their education, their occupation, and their power, but according to their kindliness and their courage, their imagination and sensitivity, their sympathy and generosity, there could be no classes,' asserts the 'Chelsea Manifesto', issued by a local group of the Technicians Party (as the Labour Party has been rebranded) in 2009. 'Who would be able to say that the scientist was superior to the porter with admirable qualities as a father, the civil servant with unusual skill at gaining prizes superior to the lorry driver with unusual skill at growing roses?'[1]

The notices were respectful rather than wholly enthusiastic. The *Financial Times* waited 'in vain for the sound of a human voice or a glimpse of earthy people'; the *TLS* reckoned the final revolt 'too sketchily contrived to be convincing'; and in the *Spectator* the literary critic Boris Ford regretted that Young's satire 'operates at a comparatively simple debating level', with 'little command of the undertones of irony, let alone of the verbal compression, that one associates with Swift'. On the substance of the satire, Young was attacked from both directions. 'He seems to think that if we now chose comprehensive schools, with a common curriculum for all children, the cleavage in society would never take place,' observed *The Times*. 'But in a country whose economic survival depends on discovering and promoting the best brains, even such schools would still be selective instruments. There is no getting away from the rise of the meritocracy in a scientific world.' By contrast, reviewing in the *Manchester Guardian*, Raymond Williams was unconvinced by the reach of the new meritocracy: 'I see no evidence, in contemporary England, of *power* being more closely connected with merit, in any definition. The administrators, professional men and technicians are increasingly being selected on educational merit, but the power is still largely elsewhere, "and no damned merit about it".'

Perhaps the most searching critique, looking ahead and similarly sceptical, came from Charles Curran in *Encounter*, arguing that Young was 'guilty of a gross over-simplification' in assuming that 'the road to Meritocracy' lay wide open without obstacles. Instead, he contended, 'the British masses', far from seeking a meritocracy, 'want a society that protects and cares for the untalented many', and he identified 'three great barriers to the attainment of Meritocracy in Britain', which collectively were 'impregnable': first, an increasingly elderly electorate, who had 'outlived their competitive years' and were now 'social pacifists, against change and struggle'; second, the power of the family unit, involving parents 'caring fiercely, irrationally, instinctively, combatively' for their offspring, so that the family was 'the historic fortress of favouritism, the nest of nepotism, the protective shell that guards the dull, the timid, the slow, the non-competitive weakling'; and third, the deep roots in British history of status being 'fixed by inheritance and tradition, rather than achieved as a prize in competitive struggle'. In short, Young had constructed a meritocratic straw man. And, he added, 'the lower classes need not start advertising for a Spartacus just yet'.[2]

But undoubtedly, even if their numbers and potency were exaggerated, the meritocrats – advancing largely by dint of their own endeavours, as opposed to socio-economic background and connection – were on the march in the course of the 1950s, and Young's analysis was tapping into a real trend.

'Lucky Jim Dixon is the first hapless hero to climb from the crib of the Welfare State,' Philip Oakes wrote in the *Evening Standard* in September 1957, almost four years after Kingsley Amis had given birth to a literary-cum-social phenomenon. 'His bones are reinforced by Government dried milk. His view of the world is through National Health spectacles. And he looks back – not in anger – but with surprise, that he has been allowed to barge through the privileged ranks of bores and phonies, towards some kind of success.' In short, 'he is the man most likely to move into the room at the top'. The last four words had a particular resonance, just six months after the publication of John Braine's instantly best-selling novel *Room at the Top*, the story of the aspirational, socially climbing, lower-middle-class (like Braine himself) Joe Lampton, newly arrived in a prosperous northern provincial town. 'A callous, ambitious, sexy L-cky J-m,' declared John Davenport in his *Observer* review. 'He is a ruthless rather than an angry young man.' Over the summer, Richard Crossman read this 'nauseating new vulgarized Lucky Jim book' and pondered its success. 'It is lower middle-class, anti-working-class, describing the working classes as dirty, smelly people, eating fish and chips and favouring the upper class as people who have tiled bathrooms and beautiful voices.' Only a Wykehamist, of course, could fail to appreciate the allure of tiled bathrooms, and over the next few years Joe Lampton increasingly replaced Jim Dixon as the symbol of new, meritocratic social forces dynamically and hungrily on the move.

'GRAMMAR SCHOOL BOYS DID IT' was the *Daily Sketch*'s exultant headline in January 1958 after the Atomic Energy Authority announced that a team of young British scientists at Harwell had produced the world's first controlled fusion reaction. This was ZETA, the Zero-Energy Thermonuclear Assembly, 'a 120-ton yellow and black painted reactor' that was a man-made sun on earth and held out the promise of limitless fuel. Sadly, that promise flattered to deceive, but the emphasis on 'a team of grammar school and scholarship boys' was a reminder of how the scientific and technological thrust of grammar schools and red-brick universities was an increasingly frequent element in the advance of the new men. Two of engineering's notable new men by the late 1950s were James Drake and Denis Rooke. Drake, Accrington-born and spiky, was Britain's first great motorway creator, with a vision of roads like 'sculpture on an exciting, grand scale', carving and moulding 'earth, rock and minerals into a finished product'; the lantern-jawed, no-nonsense Rooke, in his mid-thirties and the son of a south London commercial traveller, had recently joined the North Thames Gas Board to explore the crucial possibility of importing natural gas. In 1959 he was in charge of the technical team aboard the *Methane Pioneer*, as it transported liquefied gas from the Gulf of Mexico to Canvey Island on a storm-tossed, 23-day voyage.[3]

The meritocratic businessman was also afoot, with a trio poised around the end of the 1950s for great things. For the implacably rational Arnold Weinstock, son of Jewish refugees from Poland, the start of a remarkable career in electronic manufacturing was the 30-year-old's arrival in 1954 at the firm of his father-in-law Michael Sobell, who made radio and television sets. 'With colossal self-confidence he immediately took charge, largely ignoring his 63-year-old father-in-law, who was suffering from prostate problems,' records a biographer. 'Weinstock concentrated on producing – efficiently and profitably – basic products that worked, in contrast to his competitors, dominated by engineers who did not believe as did Weinstock that "the customer is king".' By 1958, when the firm was floated under the name of Radio and Allied, Weinstock was 'established as among the most formidable operators in the whole electrical sector'. At the textile manufacturers Courtaulds, the rising star was Frank Kearton, whose way to the top was blocked

by the ageing, indeed failing, Sir John Hanbury-Williams. The thrusting Kearton had been educated at Hanley High School, the gentlemanly
Hanbury-Williams at Wellington College, and the former's 'barely
concealed contempt' was reciprocated by the latter's 'active dislike'.
There were no tantrums at the merchant bank Schroders, where Gordon
Richardson was on a rapid upward curve. The son of a Nottingham
provision merchant, he had become a successful barrister before in 1955
trying his luck in the financial world, going to the Industrial and
Commercial Finance Corporation (the future 3i). There he was
unhappy, according to a mole, because 'it is not the kind of business nor
does he in general meet the sort of people which he hoped for when he
left the Bar'. But by 1957 this handsome, imposing, intelligent man,
vanity his only Achilles heel, was ensconced among the City's crème de
la crème, just as the post-war revival of the Square Mile was at last
getting under way.[4]

Inevitably, the meritocrats – almost all of them male – would flourish especially in the media and the arts. Robert Robinson, a product of
Raynes Park County Grammar School under the famed headmaster-
ship of John Garrett, wrote sardonic radio criticism for the *Sunday
Times* and from 1959 was the astringent presenter of television's *Picture
Parade* about current films. The *Manchester Guardian*'s features editor
Brian Redhead, son of a Newcastle printer, would also make the transition to the small screen, though in his inveterately loquacious case
radio ultimately loomed. Another northern journalist, Harold Evans,
son of a railwayman, was a wiry, energetic assistant editor of the
Manchester Evening News; meanwhile Jean Rook, Hull-born daughter of an engineer and an usherette, was gearing up on the *Sheffield
Telegraph* to take on the world. Keith Waterhouse, whose father
walked about Leeds selling produce from a barrow, was on the *Daily
Mirror* and by 1958 writing his second novel, about an undertaker's
assistant (as he himself had been) who was a habitual fantasist; another
young novelist, Malcolm Bradbury, first-generation grammar school
let alone university, debuted in 1959 with *Eating People is Wrong*,
about the dilemmas of a red-brick university professor. The as yet
unpublished B. S. Johnson, undergraduate at King's College London
and son of a stock-keeper, threw a party at his parents' home in Barnes,
but not before taking down from the wall of the lounge the three

horribly tell-tale flying ducks, unfortunately leaving marks that provoked amused comments. John Carey, accountant's son and from a grammar school in East Sheen, had his first teaching job at Christ Church, Oxford, full of window-smashing public schoolboys, and spent his time 'totting up how much more their clothes had cost than I earned'; a more attractively self-possessed Oxford undergraduate, Ian Hamilton, launched the literary magazine *Tomorrow*, having already at grammar school in Darlington started *The Scorpion* and got Kingsley Amis, Angus Wilson and Cecil Day Lewis among others to contribute. Two young, already well-established theatre directors, Tony Richardson (son of a pharmacist) and Peter Hall (son of a stationmaster), were facing the future with high artistic ambition and seemingly inexhaustible drive, while John Thaw, son of a Mancunian lorry driver, arrived as a 16-year-old at RADA in 1958 'dressed like a typical teddy boy', whereas 'the other kids all looked so bloody superior, I've never felt so alone in all my life'. Stanley Baker, from the Rhondda Valley and close to rivalling Dirk Bogarde as Britain's leading male film star, brought working-class machismo and sexual arrogance to Joseph Losey's 1959 *Blind Date*; that same year Terence Donovan, from the Mile End Road, set up his own studio, just before Leytonstone's David Bailey, while the third of what Cecil Beaton would ruefully call 'The Terrible Three' of fashion photographers, East Ham's Brian Duffy, was already shooting for *Vogue*, 'an easy way to make money'. A defiantly non-fashion photographer, Don McCullin, whose Finsbury Park childhood had been dominated by weekly trips to the pawn shop, had his picture of a gang posing on an old bombed-out building published by the *Observer* in 1959 and suddenly was in demand ('that little thing inside me knew this was the only hope of having a life'). The artist Peter Blake, son of a Dartford electrician, was starting to embrace, in a contemporary yet nostalgic way, the popular culture of postcards and pin-ups. The self-educated, self-made Bryan Robertson, who had had a hard childhood in Battersea, was several years into the directorship of the Whitechapel Art Gallery and becoming the witty, generous presiding spirit of the British art world. Zandra Rhodes, her mother a fitter at a fashion house, was at Medway College of Art; Lionel Bart, son of an East End tailor, wrote his first songs for Tommy Steele and enjoyed claiming he could not tell the difference between A flat and a council flat; and Joe Meek, whose father had run a fish-and-chip shop on the edge of the Forest of Dean, was the engineer on 'Last Train to San Fernando' and, by 1958, was writing home that 'I'm sure your Son is going to be famous one day Mum, as things are going I am very well known in the whole record world and have a very good name too.'[5]

Few if any of that gallery, though, were classic meritocrats – 'classic' in the sense of passing the triple historical test of (a) being born in 1933 or later, (b) being working-class and (c) going to grammar school as a direct beneficiary of the 1944 Education Act and using that education as a ladder for further advancement. It was those meritocrats who were, par excellence, 'Britain's New Class', as sharply described in *Encounter* in February 1958 by Frank Hilton, himself from a grammar school (though born in 1929) and now a teacher:

> Our underdogs are on the move today . . . In some ways everything and anything is possible. But they don't know where to start. They have no background that could have nursed their talents and trained them how to use them. They have only their intelligence, their energy, and too much choice. So they have no confidence and approach everything with suspicion. They loathe the scullery, the kitchen, and the front room they've left behind, and most of them – whatever they may care to say to the contrary – look upon their mums and dads as semi-prehistoric creatures, evolutionary missing links between the gin-and-work-sodden 19th-century working-class ape-man and the modern Grammar School-Redbrick university-Sergeants'/Officers' Mess working-class 'cream'.

This arguably overheated depiction prompted Joe Lampton's creator to respond from Bingley. 'As for the New Men,' predicted Braine, 'they will be quite content with a little house, car, wife, TV, and a bottle of gin in the sideboard. And if they work hard enough they will get them. And what on earth is wrong with that? Only a tiny minority, thank God, ever wants power.'

Dennis Potter was undeniably a classic meritocrat. The son of a coal miner in the Forest of Dean, he went to Bell's Grammar School in Coleford and then, in 1956, to New College, Oxford, richly populated with Wykehamists and Etonians. 'The few other grammar-school boys were creeps, adopting as many mannerisms of Oxford as they could and distancing themselves from their past,' he recalled. 'I took to being aggressive and making an issue of it.' Part of that aggression was keeping his accent intact, and he rapidly began to make a university name for himself as both a debater and an actor, as well as writing for *Isis*, with a first article unashamedly describing his personal background. 'There's nothing more terrifying than a young man on the make,' he conceded many years later. 'And of course I was feeling these things, but at the same time I was manipulating the very feelings that I was in a sense enduring. Therefore I went out of my way [to say] "My father is a miner." Which of course is a slightly more complicated sort of betrayal.' Potter's second year featured an acrimonious spat with fellow undergraduate Brian Walden, an article in the *New Statesman* on being torn between two worlds and a book contract for a state-of-the-nation tract, culminating in August 1958 in a lengthy interview on a BBC television documentary about class. 'Do you want to become classless, Mr Potter?' asked Christopher Mayhew. 'No,' he replied. 'Well, I did at one stage, I think, like most people from the working classes want to get away from the working class, but I certainly want to keep a sense of identity, as it were, with that background.' Yet, as Potter went on to explain, that sense of identity was far from untroubled:

By now my father is forced to communicate with me almost, as it were, with a kind of contempt, now and again. It is inevitable. I mean, he does everything he can possibly do to get through to me, and I to him, but it is just that our circumstances make this communication rather difficult. I mean, he is likely to ask me a question through my mother, for example. And a little thing like the allocation of radio time – it might seem small, petty. If I want something on which is likely to be – in fact very often is – very different from what the rest of the family want, then, well, this is likely to spotlight the tensions. The little petty things like that. I mean, I have a row with my sister, inevitably, over whether we should have something like *Life with the Lyons* on, or not. And, well, I – it's at times like this that I think, oh darn, why does one have one way of life, and you just can't come to terms with it ever again?

Potter by his last year was an established star at the Oxford Union – 'in a slashing peroration he denounced the Tory chrome-plated coffee-bar civilization,' reported Peter Jay in November 1958 – and, after taking an undistinguished Second (having barely worked) he slipped into a BBC traineeship in July 1959.

Two other 'classics' began at Oxford in 1957, a year after Potter. 'My room in Somerville was on the ground floor of the library block, a large, square, high-ceilinged room with a mullioned window overlooking a lawn shadowed by a huge cedar tree,' remembered Margaret Forster, daughter of a fitter at the Metal Box factory in Carlisle. 'It was easily four times the size of any room at home and the sheer space thrilled me.' Writing essays about medieval history proved less thrilling – 'it was such an unreal task, so removed from my mother's life' – but Forster loved being pulled into a different social and political world. 'I'd thought political allegiances were according to class and money but now I saw they could not be – it was as odd that my working-class mother voted Tory as that my Somerville friends voted Labour. They were all upper middle class, all from wealthy (to me) homes, and yet they all passionately wanted to align themselves with the working class.' In the more traditional (and right-wing) culture of a men's college, her contemporary Melvyn Bragg, son of an RAF sergeant and (later) publican, was making a largely cautious transition from Wigton in Cumberland to Wadham College. 'I took it all on "their" terms,' he reflected many years later. 'I was trying to learn the secrets of those in the educational and social citadel.' Significantly, this did not lead to chippiness:

> I knew an awful lot they didn't, but I sort of thought it didn't count. I mean, at breakfast in college they'd have really detailed conversations about Africa or Malaysia. Some of these men had led people into battle. But I'd been to places like Manchester and Blackburn about which they knew nothing. I knew about a whole range of life that simply didn't appear on their agenda. It was as if your past was locked away at the age of 18, as if they were saying 'put that away, you won't need that for the journey, dump that over the side of the stagecoach'. I didn't resent it, frankly, I just thought 'that's the way it is.'[6]

Crossing the Lines would be the title of Bragg's subsequent novel about his Oxford experience. Probably for most meritocrats, certainly including him, they were at this point not enemy lines.

———

For Potter, Forster and Bragg, as also for Ian McKellen, Trevor Nunn, Tom Courtenay, Alan Plater, Alan Bennett, Alan Bates, Glenda Jackson, Hunter Davies, Joan Bakewell, Neil Kinnock, Tim Bell, David Hockney, Roy Strong, Dudley Moore and many other meritocrats starting (or about to start) to come through by the late 1950s, the grammar school had been the formative, indispensable education. 'What is the most important factor in getting to the top?' a *Sunday Times* survey into teenage aspirations asked in 1959. Specifically, was it hard work or personality? Among public school boys, 48 per cent plumped for hard work and 45 per cent for personality. Among grammar school boys, the respective figures were 80 per cent and 16 per cent. Going to a grammar was of course a variable experience, both within the school and between schools. But a trio of retrospective accounts for these years is particularly suggestive about an educational world where for the most part charm was not the name of the game.

Anton Rippon's recollections of Bemrose School, Derby (1956–61) are largely benign. He enjoyed the daily morning assembly (Victorian hymns accompanied by the magnificent school organ) and was appreciative of the general lack of bullying; his only real complaints were over the 'silly rules', especially the regulation school cap to and from school, and the house system, 'particularly because of its obsession with cross country running', an obsession that once caused him to be 'spectacularly sick' at the top of Rykneld Rec hill 'not long after I'd enjoyed two helpings of treacle pudding and custard on the second sitting for school dinner'.

Mary Evans's take on her unnamed girls' grammar (1957–64) in her trenchant memoir-cum-essay *A Good School*, is markedly more critical – though with a similar exasperation about the petty rules, such as 'never going upstairs on buses (since they were apparently dens of iniquity, or more precisely men smoking cigarettes), always wearing our school hats in the streets, never walking along a pavement more than two abreast, never, ever, eating in the street, never going outside in our indoor shoes and never bringing into the school either sweets or books or magazines that were not part of our school work'. During these years, she notes, 'pupils were still sufficiently intimidated by the authority of their teachers to believe that school rules had the force of absolute law'.

It was the first year, though, that set the tone, a year in which Evans not only had her posture continuously assessed (with the reward of a posture stripe, to be sewn into her navy-blue tunic, if she proved herself not to be a sloucher), but spent all the domestic-science lessons on smocking a pinafore – seemingly futile and pointless, but 'we were quite explicitly told that our performance at this task would be taken as a measure of our "patience" and our ability to do something called "work steadily".' Indeed, the emphasis throughout was on diligence and steadiness, with Aesop's fable of the hare and the tortoise 'much favoured as an illustration of the virtues of plodding away'. With the academic work, teachers imparted the inflexible virtues of what she calls 'the conventional sandwich essay' (defined as 'beginning with a proposition to examine, examine it and then reach a conclusion'), and where 'to have an essay returned as "badly organised" was the greatest shame'. Was it an ultra-competitive environment? Evans's answer is interestingly nuanced: yes, in the sense that there was rigorous streaming from the start, and at one level the dominant ethos was all about individual achievement, yet at the same time, by sixth form anyway, 'our civics classes were weekly exercises in being taught that individuals were not allowed to act merely for themselves'. Altogether, she reckons, 'a reliable product, the grammar school child, emerged at the end of a seven-year education, and the product was reliably well schooled in writing legibly, writing grammatically, being punctual and having at least the appearance of respect for authority'. *A Good School*, written in the early 1990s, ends with a thought as double-edged as its title: 'We emerged into the adult world with extensive and authoritative evidence of our ability to carry out given tasks and to live a disciplined and sober life. Little wonder that many people still dream fondly of the institutions that apparently created us.'

Roy Greenslade is the most negative of the three. Looking back on his time (from 1958) at Dagenham County High School (very far from one of the country's top-rated grammars), he highlights 'the communication barrier' between the middle-class staff and mainly working-class pupils; the widespread disaffection and divisiveness, caused in his analysis by a mixture of the streaming system, the pressure of exams and differences in home status; the general absence of classroom discussion, with teachers 'preferring instead the these-are-the-facts-now-go-away-and-learn-them approach'; and the prevailing conformity, with 'dissent the school's dirtiest word'. Caustically, Greenslade describes the education that he received as 'simply a five-year course in how to succeed without understanding why':

> At school the propaganda was subtle, but it combined well with the thrust from home. 'Pupils, you are in a privileged position; take your chances while you can; don't fall behind; don't end up like the secondary modern layabouts; there really is room at the top.' Classroom competition was fostered with the front-runners constantly exhorted to do better; and those at the bottom put under pressure to do much, much better. I hardly need add that the sports field was another element in the same indoctrination.

Accordingly, 'the boys of County High emerged into the adult world bursting with enthusiasm for little more than money', a long way removed from 'the once-favoured ideal that grammar schools would carry on the public school tradition of training for community service'. And when Greenslade interviewed many of his contemporaries in the mid-1970s, he was dismayed by their apathy and complacency towards the wider world – characteristics that he largely attributed to the narrow, reductive efficiency of their grammar-school training.

Ashby-de-la-Zouch Boys' Grammar School was almost certainly of a higher standing than Dagenham County High, perhaps somewhere in the middle range. The report in the school magazine for 1957–8 about the activities of the Literary and Debating Society, written by a sixth-former, nicely conveys the grammar culture – not least its ineradicable whiff of priggishness – in this its final classic phase:

> *3rd October, 1957*
> In two embryo debates, we considered the relative merits of BBC and Commercial Television *and* the advisability of continuing experiments

with nuclear weapons. The eloquence and humour elicited by the former discussion was soon surpassed by the zest with which the scientists defended their colleagues' activities, to the great joy of the members.

17th October, 1957
The House debated the motion 'That gambling is socially and morally indefensible'. Impassioned appeals to our conscience earned little but scorn and eventually the suffrage of precisely half our number: the Chairman's casting vote alone preserved the Society's reputation for moral rectitude, while the need for it left room for grave doubts.

20th February, 1958
Candidates ranging from *Machiavelli* to *Gilbert Harding* were proposed to fill the last place in Heaven; every speaker had cogent arguments for his protégé, and it is doubtful whether the final choice of *Babyface Nelson*, the notorious American gangster, reflects genuine anarchical sympathies, or merely the eloquence of his advocate.[7]

Of course, these debaters were only there because they had passed the 11-plus. The exam itself was usually taken in January and often at the actual grammar school, with masters invigilating. 'Even I feel nervous,' wrote one in 1957 about the experience of superintending a classroom of excited hopefuls:

The starting bell makes one sallow child visibly start, but only for a second. Immediately all are at work: their fingers nervously nicked to their pens, their lips pursed or tacitly murmuring as they do their sums. Somehow they looked years older than when they came in; already on their foreheads frowns are beginning to appear which time will etch more deeply. Ten minutes have passed; according to my instructions, I remind them that there are more questions on the other pages of their answer books. Some have already started on them. Some have finished five minutes before the end of the fifty-minute paper.

After a ten-minute interval they get down to English ('Do not forget to put your number on the top of the paper'). Now I begin to see them more clearly. There is little difference in their size although the two largest boys are already in long trousers. Only two of the thirty wear glasses.

Some are in their Sunday suits, others wear cardigans and sweaters, sometimes with a watch (Dad's or Uncle's?) fastened over the sleeve. Somehow it seems that the most poorly dressed have the grandest fountain pens.

One boy upsets his ink-well; I help him to mop up the ink which has divided his answer book into blue and white sections. I notice that his hand shakes. Another boy absorbed in work sits on his own leg and rather dirty shoe. Yet another picks his nose and then puts his finger in his mouth. I feel embarrassed that he has noticed that I have noticed; he probably thinks that I will take a mark off!

I wonder if it is possible to estimate their intelligence from their physiognomy. Surely that intense boy with the tousled hair is intelligent? I walk up the aisle only to discover that he not written down anything. His vacant-looking neighbour who has at least half a dozen badges on the lapels of his green blazer has half-finished the paper.

At the end of English they go out to break, and I warn them to use the toilets before returning to the classroom. In the Common Room where I go for coffee they are discussing the illiteracy of some of the candidates and the foolhardiness of some of the examiners. Somebody says that even the Parliamentary Secretary to the Ministry of Education has not been able to do some of the questions that have been set. No wonder that two candidates have been sick and one has had a fit.

Back to the classroom for the General Paper ('Put your examination number . . .') and then English Composition ('. . . at the top of the paper'). Some children have their own personal spelling ('cushion' for 'cousin'; 'duck' for 'Dutch'; 'arrisen' for 'horizon'), others write very creditable conversation passages in idiomatic prose. Only two write in italic hand; their penmanship creates a very favourable impression when contrasted with the others. One boy in describing 'An Enjoyable Outing' describes a trip to France; in another row a boy describes 'the flicks and fish an chips and sweets.'

At last, at 12.30, the final bell shatters the silence. I collect in the papers and tell them to be careful crossing the road. They become young again, and some even say 'Ta-ta, sir!' as they leave the room. It is over. Some parents are already at the school gates to take their offspring home after what for most will be their one and only visit to a grammar school.

So much, in every sense, depended. Jacky Aitken (later Jacqueline Wilson), from Kingston in Surrey, sat the exam that year and had 'one of those head-filled-with-fog colds, when you can't breathe, you can't hear, you can't taste, you certainly can't *think*'. The result was a nightmare ('I'd never felt so frightened in my life'), especially the arithmetic test ('I couldn't calculate in my bunged-up head, I had to use my ten fingers, like an infant') and the number sequences in the intelligence test. A year later, on a Friday morning in January 1958, it was the turn of Ione Haines at Chingford. 'I feel sick,' noted an apprehensive Judy, but Ione herself 'awoke happily and tucked in to a three-course breakfast'. They set off for the High School, Ione taking with her the '"success" cards' she had received and 'many lucky charms, including 3*d* bit from Daddy'; nearing their destination, 'the children poured off buses and along to the school in the snow'. An anxious few hours followed, before Ione returned at lunchtime, 'eyes shining, and saying she had had a lovely time', with 'questions not too bad', and that 'she enjoyed using my fountain pen'.

Then came the waiting. Eventually, Jacky was informed by her primary teacher, in front of the class, that she had failed and ought to be ashamed of herself, leaving the poor girl to tell her parents. As for Ione, her mother's diary recorded the outcome:

> *24 April.* Gwen had told me 11+ results would be out today and I waited and waited for post. Suddenly I wondered if a tearful Ione would come home from school. Relieved this was not so and nobody appears to have heard anything.

> *25 April.* No post.
> Ione came rushing home from school with the good news that she *has passed General Admission Examination*. What a thrill! We 'phoned Daddy, me in tears . . .
> By the way, the official card came at mid-day.

A year or so later, in the Cheshire village of Bunbury, there was elation too at the Blakemore home after a little brown envelope popped through the door:

I'd come downstairs to get some breakfast and found Mum waiting for
me in the hall, smiling. And then something totally unexpected happened.
With a whoop of joy she held me round the middle and danced around
the hall with me.

It was one of those moments that stay with you forever. The fresh
green summer morning, sunlight dappling through the windows, the
threadbare carpet on the stairs, the press of my mother's apron against
my face, the giddy feeling as she swept me off my feet. And all this from
a mother who'd rarely put her arm around me. For those few seconds I'd
been grabbed and returned to early childhood.

When she stopped I smiled, embarrassed. It felt good, though the
evident relief and joy in her face led me to wonder whether my parents
had really expected me to fail. From Dad I just got a cheery smile and a
'well done' as he sat at the breakfast table neatly polishing off his bacon
and tomato.

Ken Blakemore then went to school, where he found that though two
of his friends had passed, the one who had really wanted to, Clive
Bevan, had failed: 'He was sullen, red-faced with anger and disappointment, and couldn't bring himself to talk to us.' Several months later, in
September after Ken had started at the grammar, he decided to go round
to see Clive at his home, a little bungalow. 'It was an attempt to ask
whether we could still be friends. We couldn't. He couldn't wait for me
to leave.'

Passing the exam did not necessarily clinch the deal. A quite common
impediment was financial, despite the 1944 Act, and revolved round the
purchase of a uniform and other expensive, compulsory accoutrements.
'They felt exploited by having to go to the school's selected outfitters
and paying prices they, rightly or wrongly, felt were higher than elsewhere,' recalled Roy Greenslade about Dagenham's working-class
parents. 'For some it was undoubtedly a financial burden and a real
sacrifice. For a few, it was an impossibility and their children were never
equipped in County High's sombre black, blue and white.' Another
possibility was that the child might demur. In May 1958, for instance,
Kent Education Committee notified John Jones that his son David (the
future Ziggy Stardust) had, having passed his 11-plus, a choice between
Bromley Grammar and the new Bromley Technical School, due to open

in the autumn. Mr Jones initially preferred the former but David strongly the latter, and so it was – though not before the council's education officer had interviewed the 11-year-old about his career plans.[8]

The Britain of the late 1950s was not conspicuously characterised by equality of either outcome or – rising meritocrats notwithstanding – opportunity. In terms of the former, despite some redistribution during the 1940s, not only did the richest 5 per cent own some 75 per cent of total wealth, but also the share of incomes (both before and after tax) enjoyed by the different occupational strata was not yet fundamentally different from what it had been shortly before the First World War. In terms of the latter, some eloquent detail peppered Tom Bairstow's analysis of 'The Establishment' in the *News Chronicle* in April 1958. All but two of Macmillan's Cabinet had been educated at public school, including almost one-third at Eton; all but four had gone to Oxbridge; the two Opposition leaders, Gaitskell and Grimond, had backgrounds of (respectively) Winchester and New College, Eton and Balliol. The top three ambassadors had all gone to Eton or Winchester, while in the City, the governor of the Bank of England was an Etonian, and the chairmen of the Big Five banks included two Etonians, one Harrovian and one Wykehamist.

Bairstow did think, though, that the power of the old school tie was perhaps waning in industry at large, and he cited Sir Alexander Fleck, head of ICI, 'who came up the hard way from an elementary school'. Or as one industrialist, A. D. Bonham-Carter, had recently put it in a radio talk on 'The Way to the Top in Industry': 'Social and educational backgrounds are now immaterial. What matters is the way in which a man uses his qualities and knowledge, not how he acquired them.' Yet almost certainly this was a gross exaggeration, to judge by the statistical evidence of a trio of surveys conducted between 1955 and 1958 into the backgrounds of Britain's business leaders. 'These three studies agree that, while some men have managed to get to the top without special advantages, the odds were heavily against them,' concluded Roy Lewis and Rosemary Stewart in their 1958 book *The Boss*. 'The men who were most likely to succeed were those with family connections in business, although this was less important in the larger firms, and those who had been to public school. Most likely of all were the Old Etonians.'[9]

Of course, by the late 1950s the effects of the 1944 Act had not yet started to work through into these sort of surveys. What is striking, though, is the extent to which – even in the new dispensation – the working class as a whole was still seemingly being shut out of the meritocratic race. Take the key question of social composition of the grammar schools, systematically investigated by Jean Floud and colleagues in their much-quoted *Social Class and Educational Opportunity* (1956), based on grammar admissions in 1953 in two contrasting parts of the country. The following were the percentage chances, from the parents' occupational groups, of their sons being selected for admission:

	South-West Hertfordshire	Middlesbrough
Professional workers, business owners and managers	59	68
Clerical workers	44	37
Foremen, small shopkeepers, etc.	30	24
Skilled manual workers	18	14
Unskilled manual workers	9	9
All social classes	22	17

It is unlikely that these figures changed markedly during the second half of the decade, and in late 1959 the Crowther Report, *15 to 18*, was unequivocal that in secondary moderns – overwhelmingly the most common destination for those who had failed to pass the 11-plus and thereby get into a selective school (usually a grammar) – 'the children of non-manual workers are much under-represented, and the children of semi-skilled workers over-represented'.

In theory, there was 'parity of esteem' between the roughly 1,200 grammar schools and 3,800 secondary moderns. In practice, not only did most people view the secondary moderns as vastly inferior but there was a shocking relative shortfall in their resourcing. 'It is likely,' noted John Vaizey in his 1958 treatise *The Costs of Education*, 'that the average Grammar school child receives 170 per cent more per year, in terms of resources, than the average Modern school child.' Teachers at secondary moderns were paid less, only about a fifth were graduates, and even by the end of the 1950s barely 10 per cent of the buildings they worked in were new and purpose-built.

The gulf in expectations was even greater. Surveying in 1961 that year's school-leavers from a semi-skilled and unskilled background at five Leicestershire schools (two grammars and three secondary moderns), William Liversidge found that 93 per cent of the grammar boys anticipated moving into a higher class of employment than their parents – whereas only 18 per cent of the secondary modern boys did. 'The general conclusion that emerges from this study,' he reflected, 'is one of startlingly accurate appraisal of life chances by the children, and a shrewd appreciation of the social and economic implications of their placing within the educational system.' Not long before, in 1959–60, another sociologist, Michael Carter, had sampled 200 boys and girls (overwhelmingly from working-class homes) who were about to leave, or had just left, secondary moderns in the Sheffield area. Among those still at school, three-quarters 'expressed their satisfaction that they would soon be workers – independent, recognised as grown-up, no longer "school kids"', while half the overall sample, including those who had left, 'objected strongly' to the very idea of raising the school-leaving age to 16. 'I don't think I could have lasted,' said one girl, and a boy was equally adamant: 'It is not fair; we left at 15, so the others should be able to.'[10]

Social class was not just relevant to grammars vis-à-vis secondary moderns; it also did much to determine outcomes *within* grammars. In 1954 an official report on *Early Leaving* found that whereas children from the semi-skilled and unskilled working class represented over 20 per cent of grammar school intakes, by the sixth form that proportion was down to barely 7 per cent. Given which figures, it was unsurprising that by the mid-1950s a middle-class child who had been to a grammar was five times as likely to go on to a university as was a child from an unskilled working-class background who had also been to a grammar. Why was this? Towards the end of the decade, Eva Bene sought part of the answer by surveying 361 boys from the Greater London area who were in the third year at their grammars; she revealed by social class the percentages of replies to various suggestive statements such as 'If he had a chance he would like to go to university'. There was a telling

20-per-cent gap between that working-class minority wanting to stay on after the age of 16 (45 per cent) and that working-class majority wanting to go to university (65 per cent).[11]

The university system itself was gradually expanding – 50,000 university places just before the Second World War doubling to some 107,000 by 1960–61 – and plans were afoot by the end of the 1950s for a clutch of new universities, including what would become Sussex, York, East Anglia, Essex, Kent and Warwick. 'The elite of tomorrow' was the *Observer*'s headline in 1960 for an article by Mark Abrams on the 1.6 per cent of the adult population – some 570,000 people – who were university graduates or who had comparable professional qualifications. 'Since the war the graduates have not looked back,' he declared. 'Today they are still far from having completely supplanted the pre-war elite, but by the end of the 1960s they will be well on the way towards doing so.' And, according to Abrams, 'the rise of the graduates has been resisted only in trade union leadership, industrial management, popular journalism and the entertainment industry'. It was heady, Whiggish stuff, but Abrams did not pretend it would be a wholly open elite. 'Where yesterday's elite was based on birth and wealth, tomorrow's will rest largely on education and wealth. And because of this difference the gap between the elite and the rest of society will surely be just as great as it was in the past.' Indeed, in 1960 itself, only 2.6 per cent of 18-year-olds from working-class homes went to university – compared with 16.8 per cent from middle-class homes. At the pinnacle of the university system, Oxbridge, the public schools continued to dominate: 56 per cent of the 1955 intake at Cambridge came from there; two years later, 70 per cent of scholarships and exhibitions awarded at Oxbridge men's colleges went to public schoolboys; and Abrams in his 1960 article cited a recent survey of the latest Cambridge graduates, showing that a majority still came from public school and only 9 per cent from the working class.[12]

There were many reasons – including institutional bias, going back to primary school – why most working-class children failed to thrive in a largely middle-class educational system, but arguably the most important revolved round parental attitudes and expectations. Floud et al found in their study of grammars in South-West Hertfordshire and Middlesbrough in the early-to-mid-1950s that over half the working-class parents 'either desired no further education for their children or were uncertain in the matter', while when Abrams in 1956–7 interviewed some 200 married couples in London, mainly from the skilled working class, he seldom encountered 'that degree of personal ambition which is likely to carry them socially upward'. This also applied to their aspirations for their children, even though a majority hoped they would go to either a grammar or a technical school (the latter thin on the ground, but viewed as good for learning skills and job security), and only 15 per cent positively wanted a secondary modern – where, of course, most of their children would in the event go. As Abrams reflected:

> For most people in the sample, 'education' is something provided by the authorities for which parents do not have to pay but over which, correspondingly, they can exercise no control . . .
>
> It is difficult to persuade oneself, from the general tone of the results of this enquiry, that the majority of working-class parents or children yet regard education as being so important that the frustration of their hopes is a major disaster. The system is still new, still imperfectly understood, and its possibilities are still rather vaguely glimpsed. The parents themselves, almost without exception, left school at 14 or 15, and most of them see no reason why they should be unduly disturbed if their children have to do the same, provided that after they leave school they can get decent jobs which they are unlikely to be thrown out of.

So too with other studies. Interviewing working-class couples in Dagenham (mainly in 1958–9, on the LCC's huge inter-war Becontree estate), Peter Willmott 'found some support for the view that most parents on the estate are not educationally ambitious for their children, and do not take a keen interest in their schooling', typified by a trio of vox pops:

> I've never really thought about it. I've always taken it for granted he'll leave school at 15 unless he turns out brilliant and goes to College.
>
> I don't care a lot myself. The main thing is for the children to be happy.
>
> It's immaterial to us. If he wants to go in for the 11-plus, we wouldn't stand in his way.

The classic, most nuanced account of this whole charged area is by Brian Jackson and Dennis Marsden, whose *Education and the Working Class* (1962) was a groundbreaking survey, conducted in about 1959–60, of 88 young working-class people who had been to grammar school in Huddersfield during the 1950s. Coming out of the Institute of Community Studies (run by Young and Willmott), and combining sociology with anthropology, it gave a detailed, moving picture of the social, cultural and psychological pressures faced by working-class pupils – especially over such matters as sport, uniform and friendship groups – and their often baffled, frustrated parents. Jackson and Marsden identified on the part of those parents a familiar pattern. Initial pleasure at their child's 11-plus success and, during that child's early terms at grammar school, flickers of intellectual excitement for themselves, were followed, by the third year, by 'a growing sense that the child was out on its own, moving into worlds to which the parents had no access'. At this point many of those parents, usually the fathers, 'sought to reassert control over their children's education by demanding some clear statement about the kind of job this was leading to'. They quoted one: 'I always wanted education for myself, and then I thought our lad would have it. But what I thought was the technical side, something that I could understand. That was what I thought education would be. I never thought about that Arts side, literature and language and all that stuff. That was new to me; that didn't come into my reckoning about education at all.' There was also, explained another parent, the problem of the neighbours:

> Many a time you'd be out and the neighbours would say, 'Eeh, is your lad still at school? What's he going to be then?' And I'd have to say, 'I don't know what he's going to be yet.' And they'd say, 'Doesn't *he* know yet?' . . . I hadn't got an answer and I felt soft. They'd look at you as much as to say, 'Staying on at school all that time and don't know what he's going to be, well!'

The obvious solution was for the parents to talk to teachers about courses and choices, but, suffused by a sense of 'them' and 'us', they seldom did, even if their children were in the A stream and there was no shame involved. Altogether, noted the authors, 'by the time the leaving age was reached and the General Certificate taken, many wondered whether there was much to be gained by leaving their child at school'. Or, as one father put it about the whole unsettling experience: 'Tha can't *afford* to send t'lasses to t'grammar schools. Tha sends 'em and when they come back they're no good to y'. They don't want a mucky job even if that's where t'brass is. They won't look at it!'

Still, it was sometimes the teacher who thwarted a parent's aspirations. From Sheffield in about 1960 is this emblematic account of a leaving pupil's interview with the headmistress of a secondary modern and the Youth Employment Officer:

The YEO enquires – with a smile designed to put mother and child at ease, but standing no chance of overcoming the suspicion which mother feels for officials – what job the girl would like to do. Before the girl has a chance to speak, mother jumps in, saying with a determination made more formidable by the certain knowledge that she will shortly be contradicted, 'she ain't going to work in a warehouse.' The head teacher disregards mother and turning to the girl says 'What do you want to do?' The girl blurts out that she wants to be 'one of them shorthand-typewriters'. The YEO now has something to work on, and enquires of the girl whether she is good at spelling. There is a dull silence, broken by the head teacher, who says in a significant tone, 'One out of ten'. An enquiry about English Composition leads to the comment 'Four out of twenty'. The head teacher is becoming impatient, and tells the girl that this is a waste of time: that there is no likelihood of her getting an office job: that she would not be happy doing office work: and that she *would* be happy doing packing work in a warehouse. Mother has by this time reached 'the sniffing stage'. The head teacher turns her attention to her and says, 'Look here, Mrs So-and-so, things have changed since you and I were children. Lots of valuable things are packed nowadays. It is an important job. Factories have good conditions, girls can earn good wages, wear nice clothes and be happy doing the work.'[13]

On 31 July 1958 the Yorkshire professional cricketer Johnny Wardle was, reported the *Daily Mail*, 'cheered all the way to the wicket by the Sheffield crowd' – the day after the club had announced it would be dispensing with his services from the end of the season. He had fallen out badly with Yorkshire's new amateur captain – 39-year-old Ronnie Burnet, who had never played first-class cricket before this season – and though in the rest of the match he performed brilliantly, taking eight wickets at fewer than ten runs each, he never played for Yorkshire again. The following week he was back in the pages of the *Mail* with two prominently displayed articles, 'Why I Was Sacked' and 'We're Carrying the Captain', claiming that Burnet's 'lack of experience' had made it 'desperately hard for the key men of the side'. Later in August, offended by Wardle's trenchant criticism of the Yorkshire committee, the MCC (which still ran English cricket) withdrew his invitation to tour Australia.

The amateur-professional divide continued to run deep: an amateur, Surrey's Peter May, would be captaining the English tourists, and, earlier in the year, an MCC committee chaired by the club's president, the Duke of Norfolk, had concluded that 'the distinctive status of the amateur cricketer was not obsolete, was of great value to the game and should be preserved' (though at the same time, in terms of the financial recompense of those nominally unpaid performers, the committee admitting to being 'disturbed by the apparent over-liberal interpretation of the word "expenses" in certain cases that had come to their notice'). The hypocrisy was rank, with a range of different methods being found to pay the socially more prestigious, so-called amateurs. Ahead of the tour, England's other spinner, also a Yorkshireman, gave George ('Gubby') Allen, chairman of the selectors, stockbroker and a pillar of the Lord's Establishment, a bad quarter of an hour. 'I told Gubby that I was considering becoming an amateur and I wondered how he would feel about this,' recalled Jim Laker. 'He asked me if I'd given it serious consideration and said that, if I had, he thought it was absolutely splendid but wondered why I wanted to do this. He didn't look best pleased when I told him that I thought I would be better off in financial terms playing as an amateur in the England team in Australia with expenses rather than drawing professional pay.'[14]

The Wardle Affair, the introduction of life peerages (Sir Eric James, High Master of Manchester Grammar School and arch-meritocrat, on an early list), satire about the complacent incompetence of the traditional ruling class (the Boulting brothers' film *Carlton-Browne of the*

FO, with Terry-Thomas as the bumbling diplomat), Basil Bernstein's pioneering study ('Some sociological determinants of perception') of the different affective and cognitive equipment of working-class children compared to middle-class, even some daring cross-dressing (the fashion photographer Antony Armstrong-Jones taking a riverside room in Rotherhithe, the metropolitan intelligentsia starting to form Sunday morning soccer teams) – one way and another, quite apart from the celebrated new wave of plays and novels, class and related issues were bubbling away strongly in the late 1950s.[15]

'Despite (and sometimes because of) the Welfare State,' declared the *Radio Times* in August 1958 in its preview of Christopher Mayhew's television series 'Does Class Matter?' (including the Dennis Potter interview), 'we British are still one of the most class-ridden peoples in the world.' Produced by Jack Ashley, this was a notable examination of a ubiquitous but seldom overtly discussed subject, and, noted BBC's audience research, 'many viewers found it an enjoyable and interesting experience to be looking at themselves "from outside", though some questioned the wisdom of stressing class distinctions'. Not long afterwards, in January 1959, Tom Lupton and C. Shirley Wilson published their pathbreaking analysis 'The Social Background and Connections of "Top Decision Makers"', taking as their starting point the recent evidence given to the Bank Rate Tribunal. This detailed with unambiguous clarity the narrow social and educational background of the City elite, as well as its multiple interconnections, and, though appearing in an obscure academic journal, it received considerable publicity. So much so that four months later, at the City of London Society's annual luncheon at the Mansion House, that body's chairman (the self-made Harley Drayton) was compelled to declare, boldly if unconvincingly, that 'if a young man has talent, integrity and courage, not only is there nothing to stop him going to the top, he will almost be kicked there'.[16]

Among those watching 'Does Class Matter?' were Florence Turtle and Tom Driberg. 'He is a Socialist & somewhat prejudiced against Public Schools,' Turtle noted unenthusiastically of Mayhew, but the Labour politician (and regular TV reviewer for the *New Statesman*) was struck by how '95 per cent of those questioned put education as the first determinant of class', reflecting further that it was 'hard to

believe that most people will acquiesce for much longer in an educational system which artificially reserves so many of the best jobs for
those with a particular kind of education, identified by a particular
accent'. Two years earlier Anthony Crosland in *The Future of Socialism*
had had strong words about the existing 'system of superior private
schools' – 'open to the wealthier classes, but out of reach of poorer
children however talented and deserving . . . much the most flagrant
inequality of opportunity, as it is cause of class inequality generally, in
our educational system' – while there was a degree of unease even
among some Tories. After referring in 1957 to 'the almost comically
overwhelming predominance of Old Etonians in the Conservative
Party', the writer and former MP Christopher Hollis went on in the
Spectator: 'I think that the time has come when it would be for the
advantage of the nation that the Conservative Party should be somewhat less "U" in its higher personnel and when a party which pays
lip-service to equality of opportunity should in practice treat at least
(shall we say?) a Rugbeian as the equal of an Etonian.' The next year,
more seriously, the Education Minister Geoffrey Lloyd (Harrow and
Trinity College, Cambridge) privately expressed some sympathy with
'elements on our side, e.g. The Bow Group, which thinks that basis for
entry should be widened, and not restricted, as for all intents it is, to
those who can meet the heavy cost of a preparatory, as well as of a
public school education'. But, anxious about charges from elsewhere
in his party that direct government subvention to enable 'deserving'
children to take up places would threaten the independence of the
schools, he opted for a policy of masterly inaction. And those institutions themselves? 'You Can't Write Off the Public Schools' was a *Daily
Mail* headline in May 1958, with the article revealing that numbers had
increased since the war from 50,000 to 80,000 and that many had no
vacancies until 1966 or 1967.[17]

Although their academic superiority over the better grammars was
now questionable, they were continuing to deliver the goods where it
mattered, and when the *New Statesman* later in 1958 published statistics definitively revealing their dominance of Oxbridge entrance, a
flurry of letters ensued. It was all 'simple enough', insisted the constitutional expert Ivor Jennings, Master of Trinity Hall, Cambridge: 'It is
that the number of applicants from public schools is more numerous

– in this college much more numerous – than the number of applicants from other schools: and all are meritorious because they are supported by the schools, which are familiar with Cambridge standards and help us enormously in our selection.' Other correspondents were unconvinced, with some (including John Vaizey) calling for the integration of the public schools into the state system, while a youngish Oxford historian, Lawrence Stone, conceded there were 'too many' public-school men at Oxbridge 'who in a world of equal opportunity would not be there at all'. About the same time, another Oxford fellow, J. R. Sargent of Worcester College, elucidated in *Socialist Commentary* the three 'ineluctable factors' at work:

> First, there is the classical tradition of the public schools, combined with the large number of classical scholarships offered at Oxford or Cambridge. Secondly, there is the fact that public school masters are old hands at the complex procedure for getting admission. They make less mistakes than grammar school masters with less experience, and this does not simply mean that they are better at 'nobbling'. Thirdly (let's face it), there is the fact that many public schools provide very good teaching and can do so because many people are willing to pay large sums in order to get it.

There was an Oxbridge coda the following spring, when scientists at both universities led campaigns to get the Latin exam dropped from admission requirements. Cambridge agreed to relent, but Oxford narrowly not, before eventually permitting those with a maths or science A level to be exempted.

'I have never been able to understand,' declared Crosland in *The Future of Socialism*, 'why socialists have been so obsessed with the question of the grammar schools, and so indifferent to the much more glaring injustice of the independent schools.' Yet it was clear which issue had the greater traction in the popular mind. Certainly, the BBC television documentary in February 1957 on the 11-plus, featuring a secondary modern in north London, engendered no shortage of viewer response:

> The answer is, Eleven Plus is bad, comprehensive schools not the remedy. The remedy is better teachers and less crowding of classes. Look at that

nondescript lot of stuff you showed us tonight. No wonder you chose a powerful commentator, otherwise we may have dozed off. *(Technician)*

There is a good standard of education in these schools [i.e. secondary moderns]. It would be a poor sort of world peopled with academic types only. We must have practical men and women. *(Engineer's Wife)*

I feel too much pressure is brought to bear on the children at this age and they are far better left alone, with a natural interest in their work being shown by the parents. *(Correspondence Clerk)*

The 'do-or-die' attitude of many parents towards their children – pass and so win a place to a grammar school or else . . . – has as its basis near snobbishness. *(Cashier)*

Despite all that has been written and spoken about those children who do not gain Grammar School status, in attempting to alleviate their feelings at having *failed*, failure is in fact the cold clear truth, and nothing can now change this. *(Architect)*

Hard words, and a teacher (unstated at which sort of school) could offer only another cold, clear truth: 'The Grammar Schools can only take a certain number of pupils, and in most parts of the country there are not enough Grammar Schools.'[18]

In fact, by the late 1950s the dynamics of this whole inter-related cluster of issues – 11-plus, grammar schools, secondary moderns, comprehensives – were changing quite rapidly. Above all, it was becoming increasingly apparent that the future of the widely admired grammars was being threatened by deep dissatisfaction with two things beyond their control: the 11-plus and the secondary moderns.

A significant part of the 11-plus problem was that a child's chances of passing the exam hinged to an alarming extent on where he or she lived, depending on the availability of grammar-school places. Those chances were as high as 35 per cent in the south-west, 33.5 per cent in Wales, and 31.6 per cent in London and the south-east, but as low as 24.1 per cent in the Midlands, 22.4 per cent in the north-east, 18.9 per cent in the south and, in one particularly ill-favoured city, Nottingham, a mere 10.1 per cent. More generally, beyond that, there was the key question of misallocation. In practice, 11-plus failures had relatively few opportunities to transfer across at a later stage to a grammar, yet even in 1954 the *Early Leaving* report was revealing, on the basis of 1951 O-level results, that whereas 45 per cent of those who had been at state grammars since the age of 11 got five or more passes, the comparable figure for those who *had* subsequently been transferred from secondary moderns was 45.7 per cent.

But the first real heavy lifting in the debate on intelligence testing and selection came from a committee of leading psychologists led by the Institute of Education's Professor Philip Vernon. In their 1957 report, *Secondary School Selection*, they declared, in contradiction to the theories of genetic determination popularised by Cyril Burt, that

> psychologists should frankly acknowledge that completely accurate classification of children, either by level or type of ability, is not possible at 11 years, still less on entry to the junior school at 7 [a reference to the prevalent streaming at primaries], and should therefore encourage any more flexible form of organisation and grouping which gives scope for the gradual unfolding and the variability of children's abilities and interests.

Moreover, they added, 'only among the top 5% or so and the bottom 50% do we consider that allocation to grammar, technical and modern schools can be made automatically from test scores and scaled estimates', with 'all intermediate pupils' to be 'regarded as border-zone'. Later that year, a detailed report on how selection worked in practice (*Admission to Grammar Schools*, commissioned by the National Foundation of Educational Research and written by Alfred Yates and D. A. Pidgeon) found that, even if all possible improvements were made in the selection process, there would still be an ineradicable misallocation of at least 10 per cent. 'Whether a 10% error for all the country at large, involving 60,000 children per annum,' reflected Professor Ben Morris in his preface to the report, 'is to be regarded as reasonable or intolerable of course depends upon what particular educational values are regarded as most important.'

Nevertheless, what in most people's eyes ultimately did for the 11-plus was its inherent cruelty and divisiveness – prompting even a Tory minister, the liberal-minded Sir Edward Boyle (the Parliamentary

Secretary at the Ministry of Education who had apparently struggled with some of the questions), to refer publicly in 1957 to its 'evil effect' and to how it 'casts a shadow over the classroom'. Understandably, many parents voted with their feet, it being estimated at the time that nearly half that year's eligible children were not in the event sitting the test. And when, soon afterwards, a *Daily Express* poll asked whether the 11-plus should be left as it was or replaced by an assessment based on the child's general school record, only 25 per cent opted for the status quo, with little difference between Tory and Labour voters.[19]

As for the other Achilles heel of the existing system, a bald statement in the *Manchester Evening News* in April 1956 said it all: 'With shock and disbelief many parents have learned this week that their own son or daughter will be going to a Secondary Modern school next September.' A year later, Manchester's recently retired, strongly pro-selection chief education officer, Norman Fisher, accepted that 'even where there are secondary modern schools in first-rate buildings, it has seldom been possible to persuade parents or children that they offer a reasonable alternative to the grammar school'. And in June 1957 the *Spectator* published a stark piece by Colm Brogan based on the experience of a female teacher he knew who had recently worked in a co-ed secondary modern on a housing estate near London. 'Nearly all the teachers devote time, labour and anxious care,' he concluded, but in the end it was 'the apathy and the negative attitude of the pupils', from a working-class East End background, that prevailed, including a total lack of discipline and corporate spirit:

The school had nothing to offer them that they believed to be of any value whatever. Educationists may talk of deepening the aesthetic experience, rounding the personality and enriching the lives of secondary modern pupils, but these words are as thorns crackling under the pot for the pupils themselves. With the exception of the minority who have agreed to stay on, the sole aim and object of the children is to get out the instant the law releases them. The world outside is Eldorado, to which their eyes and thoughts are ever straining.

The negative depictions continued. 'Run away to sea rather than go to a secondary modern,' was the sage advice of A.J.P. Taylor later in 1957;

in 1960, in his manual *Secondary Modern Discipline*, Richard Farley called secondary moderns 'the focal point of the duller, less responsible, maladjusted and potentially criminal young people', so that as a result 'ninety per cent of the work in a Secondary Modern School is control and discipline'.

Inevitably, among those teaching in the secondary moderns, a deep defensiveness prevailed. 'Why is it that when I go into your secondary modern schools the teachers are so apologetic?' a visiting educationalist from abroad was quoted as asking in 1956. '"You must remember," they tell me, "that these are not the brightest children. You must realise that we do not have the best." And so they warn me not to be disappointed. They make excuses for the work I shall see.' But it could hardly have been otherwise, as the *Times Educational Supplement* (still strongly pro-selection) went on in its report: 'The visitor was surprised that the teachers expected him to judge the secondary modern school by the grammar school. The teachers, of course, could have told him that the public as yet had seldom done anything else. This was not an apology the teachers were offering the visitor. It was seasoned self-defence.'[20]

Yet for all this – including (not least) press treatment of secondary moderns in which, as one observer wearily put it, 'the stress is upon physical violence and the threat of the adolescent' – the larger reality was perhaps not quite so bleak. In implicit riposte to Brogan, the *New Statesman* in September 1957 ran a five-page survey by Judith Hubback in which she did not deny that the 59,000 secondary modern teachers, almost half of them taking classes of over 30, were often mediocre, so that 'most of the dull classrooms will go on witnessing dull, overcrowded, incompetent and undisciplined lessons for the next few years'. But, she stressed, 'the majority of classes do not get out of control, the majority of children are moderately well taught and most of the regular teachers do not have discipline problems'. A more whole-hearted defence came the following year from Harold Dent (educationalist and former editor of the *TES*) in his *Secondary Modern School: An Interim Report*. By his calculations, over half the secondary moderns were doing good work, almost half sound work and only 5 per cent bad work; vocational courses, tailored to a wide range of aptitudes and interests, were giving 'a lively sense of purpose and reality'; and altogether, the 'incontestable fact' was that 'hundreds of thousands of girls and boys in secondary modern schools' were now 'being given a much better, much more genuinely secondary education than were even their elder sisters or brothers who attended the self-same schools only a few years previously'. The picture was positive too in 1959 in E. R. Braithwaite's *To Sir, With Love*, his justly celebrated account of a black teacher at a secondary modern in the East End – drawn from his real-life experience at St George's-in-the-East Secondary Modern, located amidst the grimness and periodic violence of Cable Street, Stepney, but where a remarkable, inspiring head, Alex Bloom, made every child feel counted and created a real sense of school community.

Even so, this was undoubtedly the exception rather than the rule. More representative – but still positive in its own terms – was the experience of Julia Gunnigan, teaching in 1959 in the secondary modern at Pimlico and encountering an atmosphere that was rough but friendly. 'The boys queuing to hand over their lunch money would sometimes pause at the head of the line and demand: "Fulham or Chelsea, Mam?",' relates her son John Lanchester. 'The wrong answer would get a scowl and sneer; the right answer would be met with "Buy ya dinner."' And, relevant not just to the typical working-class secondary modern, he also describes what his mother found during her London sojourn:

> No one would ever admit it, but people were happy where they were. They were especially happy with the level of complaint and grumbling, which often seemed one of life's most important pleasures. A few of her brightest pupils had passed the eleven-plus and been offered a place at grammar school, but their parents had not allowed them to take it up. She raised the question with one of the parents and they shuffled and looked shifty and embarrassed and eventually admitted to her – as they perhaps wouldn't have if she hadn't been Irish – 'We didn't want him to think he was better than us.'[21]

Middle-class parents, alarmed by the possibility (however statistically slight) of their children failing the 11-plus, felt very differently. 'In some of the Home Counties and other areas where there is a large middle-class dormitory population, the abolition of entry to the County Grammar schools by payment of fees has caused a great deal of bewilderment and intense public pressure upon the authorities to provide some outlet of comparable value,' noted F. S. Marston in the *Journal of Education* as early as 1954. 'Indeed, it may be that parents with this social background will, despite their preference for the Grammar school, join with others having very different ideas to replace it by the comprehensive [i.e. non-selective] school unless some other acceptable solution is forthcoming. It is only too probable that the unilateral Modern school is engaged in a race against time.' In practice, this race against time meant not an 'education for life', the vocational model upon which the secondary moderns had originally been conceived in the 1940s, but instead something more akin to grammar school lite, through the provision of exam-tested extended courses. 'The knowledge that others in such a [secondary] modern school are succeeding and going to college or a student apprenticeship is the greatest educational tranquilliser for parents and is worth 1,000 pamphlets describing the methods of selection!' declared Rhodes Boyson, head of a secondary modern in Lancashire's Rossendale Valley and a Labour councillor, in a letter to the *Sunday Times* in February 1958. 'What parents fear in the 11+ is not technical error, but an alternative choice which will cut their children off from later educational opportunities.' Progress along these lines, however, was relatively slow, and by 1960 there were still only 21,680 secondary modern pupils staying on after 15 to take GCE exams.

From Tory politicians, for the most part viscerally committed to the grammars, mere boosterism of the ill-favoured but indispensable secondary moderns was no longer enough. In late 1958, Geoffrey Lloyd unveiled the government's White Paper *Secondary Education for All: A New Drive*, promising among other things a five-year £300 million programme of new school building, mainly for the secondary moderns, as well as a greater emphasis at the secondary moderns on supplying examination courses for academically abler pupils. Altogether, reckoned *The Economist*, 'it embodies the Conservative tactic for grasping the political thistle of the eleven-plus: to level up educationally without seeking to stamp flat socially; to overbid the comprehensive school with the new-style secondary modern (renamed high school); to put the really big money behind a practical "parity of esteem" which will alone take the sting out of selection'.[22]

From this perspective, there was no doubt about the identity of the elephant – or potential elephant – in the room. 'Have you heard about what are called comprehensive schools?' asked Gallup earlier in 1958, a reasonable question given that there were still fewer than a hundred – one of which, Holland Park, started in September that year under reassuringly traditional lines (uniforms with school crest, house system, streaming). By a narrow majority, most people *had* heard of comprehensives; by a much larger majority, 58 to 19 per cent, those who had heard of them thought they were 'a good idea'. Accordingly, it was an urgent political context in which Lloyd's White Paper served, in *The Economist*'s sympathetic words, 'blunt warning' that the Conservative government 'will not approve attempts by local authorities to "comprehensivise" schools if they would damage existing grammar schools'– a warning designed to ensure that 'the grammar schools can be left to get on with their essential job of training the country's upper quartile of intelligence for the major academic and scientific skills'.[23] Grammars and selection on the one hand, comprehensives on the other: by the late 1950s a national debate was gathering steam.

There were already some predictable anti-compers. 'Greater equality of opportunity is not to be attained easily by some administrative reorganisation of our schools,' but rather by 'the civilising effects of extended education on the homes and on the whole community', warned Eric James of Manchester Grammar School, reviewing Floud et al; 'a veneer of confidence is being spread about the comprehensive school which has no substance to support it', claimed the *TES* soon afterwards, in February 1957, in a fierce attack on the LCC's determination to push ahead with more comprehensives; and later that year *The Economist* visited one (probably Kidbrooke in south-east London) and worried not only about 'too ready a flight in the new schools from academic subjects into pottery and cookery and dressmaking' but also whether the staff was 'so "comprehensive-minded" that duty to the majority is all and a special effort with the bright ones thought rather unfair'. In his sceptical response to Lloyd's White Paper, which he interpreted as the government trying 'to catch votes by buttering up the secondary modern schools rather than by thinking out what is their purpose', Christopher Hollis in the *Spectator* declared that selection went with the grain of the fundamental human reality that there were many children who were 'simply of the type that learns by doing rather than by reading', whereas at a comprehensive, 'if the non-academic boy is to leave school at fifteen and the academic boy to stay on till eighteen, then the non-academic can never in the nature of things attain to a position of prominence and responsibility and is likely to feel more frustrated than if he stayed in a school [i.e. a secondary modern] of his own kind'.

Another seemingly entrenched anti-comper was Harry Rée, liberal-minded head of Watford Grammar School, who in his 1956 book *The Essential Grammar School* rejected the comprehensive alternative as requiring huge, unwieldy schools and strongly defended the grammars as ladders of social mobility and as the democratic alternative to what he saw as the dying public schools. So too a promising playwright, who had taught at a grammar, in his letter to the *New Statesman* soon after Hubback's survey of the secondary modern. 'The fact is that if a child has failed his 11-plus he is probably stupider, or lazier, or both, than the child who has passed,' wrote Robert Bolt. 'Socialists don't quite like to say this because it seems to imply second-class citizenship, but a human being has his citizenship, not in virtue of his attainments, but in virtue of his mere humanity.' And, Bolt continued, it was the 'special style and *panache*' of a grammar sixth form 'which enables children of ability from moneyless homes to compete on a footing of absolute equality with the sprigs of the upper class', thereby making 'a Grammar school sixth the only wholly successful intrusion of democracy into the special reserve of the rulers'. A starker warning still, also from a leftish perspective, came in the same magazine a year later (October 1958) from B. Laslett:

Unhappily, these schools [comprehensives] are too new to have the confidence of many parents who care about education, and many, given a choice, will feel unable to take a risk, and will struggle to find money for fees in a misguided effort 'to buy the best' for their own children. Among grammar school teachers there is at present strong prejudice against comprehensive schools, and many will get out, if they can, into fee-paying schools.

The comprehensive threat to grammars would, in short, 'make it more certain than ever that fee-paying schools will flourish'.

Two heads of new comprehensive schools naturally on the other side of the argument were Miss Margaret Miles of Mayfield in Putney and Mrs Harriet Chetwynd of Woodberry Down in Stoke Newington. The comprehensive principle, claimed Miles in a Third Programme talk in 1957, recognised through its heterogeneity that pupils had 'widely varying interests and abilities and long- or short-term objectives', whereas in the avowedly homogeneous grammar 'the average girl' was 'often regarded as a dud'. As for the assumption that, in order to provide courses for all abilities, comprehensives by definition would be too big, she asserted that 'size can give dignity to an institution and it can give stimulus and a sense of adventure'. Chetwynd, writing in the *New Statesman* in February 1959 to counter an 'Against the Comprehensive' article by Rée, impatiently summarised the familiar anti-comp negatives ('size, chaos, teachers will not mix, children will not mix, parents will not mix, the most able will be neglected, the least able will suffer, schools will be sausage machines, there will be no room for the individual, leadership will go only to the academic seniors') before setting out her credo:

> The Comprehensive school exists to develop a new conception of secondary education based on a positive moral philosophy – that it is right for all children (or at any rate a full cross-section) who will be the next generation's adult society to spend their adolescent years together; that it is right for their education to be concerned not only with the brain, important though that is, but with the mind and character, the body, the spirit, the standards of judgment – both personal and to the community; that it is right for the individual to have the means to grow to his full stature and yet to discipline himself as a member of the society in which he will live, with its obligations, its rights and limitations.

Others onside included two tireless educationalists, Brian Simon and Robin Pedley, the latter writing the influential *Comprehensive Education: A New Approach* (1956) and declaring soon afterwards that the abolition of the 11-plus would be 'a giant stride towards the achievement of national prosperity and individual happiness'; Professor Vernon and his fellow psychologists, arguing that 'on psychological grounds there would seem to be more to be said in favour of comprehensive schools than against' while not denying that 'it would be unwise to ignore the strength of tradition and parental prejudice'; and of course Michael Young, so alert to the dangers of a meritocratic elite.

But what about the ladder for the working class? Raymond Williams did not specifically refer to grammar schools, yet – even though he had been to one himself – they were surely in his sights in a passage towards the end of *Culture and Society*. Arguing that the ladder was essentially a 'bourgeois model' that had 'produced a real conflict of values within the working class itself', he claimed that it was especially 'objectionable' because 'it weakens the principle of common betterment, which ought to be an absolute value' and 'sweetens the poison of hierarchy'. Williams concluded with unshakable moral certainty: 'In the end, on any reckoning, the ladder will never do; it is the product of a divided society, and will fall with it.'[24]

Increasingly the debate would be played out also at local level, nowhere more pertinently than in Leicestershire. There, a *Conservative*-controlled authority sanctioned in 1957 the ingenious, attention-attracting 'Leicestershire experiment', initially applied to two areas of the county and inspired at least in part by the Leicester-based Pedley. 'It is the county's boast,' explained the educational journalist Dinah Brook, 'that it is not only the first education authority to abolish eleven-plus but also the only one to give parents the freedom to choose a grammar school for their children if they want it.' Essentially, it was a two-tier approach: 'All children go from primary school at the age of eleven to a new version of the secondary modern school, called the high school. At fourteen, children whose parents undertake to keep them at school until they are sixteen can transfer to grammar school.' The *TES*'s response to the announcement of the scheme was scathing – 'a wholly needless abdication of leadership' – but on the ground the early signs were positive, to judge by the reports of the headmaster (Rev. E.S.C. Coggins) of Oadby Gartree High School, one of the county's new-style secondary moderns. 'I have not received a single parental objection to the Scheme,' he reported to his governors in September 1957. As for the open meetings held that term for parents, some of whose children might have been admitted directly to grammar school under the previous system, 'I did not encounter any feelings of injustice or snobbery. The parents of children in the less academic streams were equally enthusiastic.'

Ironically, in Labour-controlled Leicester itself, selection and the traditional ladder-climbing 11-to-18 grammar remained the order of the day, though from 1959 the external 11-plus examination did give way to what the city's director of education reassuringly called 'a standardised junior school assessment of each child's ability'.[25]

Passions ran higher in Bristol, and along somewhat more orthodox party lines. 'If the babblement of confused voices demanding the destruction of grammar schools – and the latest one is that grammar schools breed Tory voters – showed less envy and prejudice and more hard thought about what is to replace them if they are destroyed, they might convince us that they care something about education and less about playing politics,' declared the headmaster John Garrett at Bristol Grammar School's prize-giving in October 1957. 'At a time when trained minds are more than ever necessary to enable the nation to skirt the edge of the abyss of bankruptcy; at a time when men unafraid of doing a hard day's work are desperately needed, is it wise to gerrymander with schools which have shown they can produce both?' This was too much for Alderman St John Reade, before the war a teacher at the local public school (Clifton College) but now Labour chairman of Bristol Education Committee and pushing hard for comprehensivisation, including of Garrett's 425-year-old grammar school: 'We must, I suppose, expect that our future leaders, now being trained at Bristol Grammar School, will be stout supporters of the "separate but equal" principle advocated by Mr Garrett and Governor Faubus and Little Rock.' Readers of the *Western Daily Press* would have picked up the allusion to American bigotry; even so, another letter-writer chose to distance himself from Reade's structural ambitions. 'Generalisations about a whole class of school are rash,' reflected an anonymous Labour Party member who was also a teacher. 'A really first-rate school of its kind, be it Grammar, Technical, Secondary or Comprehensive, is as different from most of its kind as from quite another kind of school. Where such a school exists, it should be cherished and preserved for the sake of the whole community.'

Up in the north-east in autumn 1958, educational ferment seized Darlington after the town council narrowly voted, despite a split in the ruling Labour group, to establish a comprehensive school at Branksome. 'We believe every child in this town has the right to a proper education and proper standard,' declared Councillor Whelan, while Councillor O'Brien was more emollient: 'We want to absorb the Grammar Schools, not supplant them. We hope the best traditions of these schools will be carried over into the new.' There ensued a flurry of mainly hostile letters to the *Northern Despatch*, typified by L. Davis writing sarcastically that 'when Coun. Whelan has demolished our Queen Elizabeth Grammar School and our sons are receiving their diplomas for rock 'n' roll at the comprehensive schools, he may turn his attention to other ways in which he can promote our community's welfare'; that grammar's Old Boys' Association took out a half-page ad on 'YOUR CHILD'S FUTURE' ('If Comprehensive Schools are set up in Darlington, no child will have the opportunity of the best education now available ... Grammar School education requires special gifts and great application ... It would be harmful to force it on children who are not really fitted for it'); early in 1959 both Macmillan and Gaitskell paid visits to Darlington, touring respectively the grammar and a secondary modern; and finally, in April, the minister, Lloyd, refused permission for the new school to go ahead as proposed, a decision confirmed in June largely on the basis of 2,500 local objections, mainly parental.[26]

Or take Bradford, whose City Council was bitterly divided during 1957–8 about a seemingly innocuous proposal from the controlling Labour group to build a new secondary school in Flockton Road in the south of the city, next to Bolling Girls' Grammar School. 'It must have a disturbing effect on the teachers of that school, knowing that they were going to be integrated into a comprehensive school,' claimed Councillor J.E.B. Singleton for the Tories in December 1957. 'What effect would it have on the pupils? They were going to lose the grammar school environment ... It was all very well saying: "Put them under one roof" but it did not work out in education practice. They had to have a certain amount of environment and they could not bring the clever ones down to the level of the dull ones.' This provoked, later in the meeting, a telling Tory–Labour exchange:

Coun. Audrey Firth said she did not want a comprehensive school in Bradford. There would be some sort of remote control and it would be a great barrack-like place where the child was not going to be an individual. It could not be with 2,000 children in the same building. Someone mentioned environment, and someone called 'snobbery'. Surely there was nothing wrong in giving a child environment and background. They should be proud to provide it.

Coun. J. T. Tiernan said the mention of snobbery brought back memories to him. He went to an ordinary elementary school and had to pass a grammar school. The children there told them: 'My mother has told me we haven't to play with you.'

Almost a year later the issue was still unresolved, with Labour's Alderman R. C. Ruth, leader of the anti-selection, pro-comprehensive lobby within the Labour group, giving the larger picture:

Ald. Ruth said it was proved over and over again that children with brains were being denied an opportunity to go to University because of the test made at the age of 11-plus. Was it suggested because they were building a Secondary School near a Grammar School that it was going to reduce the social status of the Grammar School because of the adjacency of boys and girls who fail to pass the 11-plus examination?

Singleton refused to yield ground. 'Alderman Ruth appeared to have forgotten that in Bradford they had a transfer system between Secondary and Grammar Schools, and no pupil was denied the possibility of going forward to Grammar School and then to University,' insisted the councillor. 'It was known in educational circles that schools of a smaller population had a better opportunity of encouraging pupils than had the larger schools. Alderman Ruth had accepted the fact that all children had the same educational attainment. That was not so . . . They could not all be put in one school and attain the same standard at the end.'

Muriel Beadle, wife of the visiting professor of genetics at Oxford in 1958–9, despaired. This keen-eyed American came – after immersing herself in educational debates, visiting several schools of each type and following the 'hot controversy' in the spring of 1959 over whether north Oxford should get a comprehensive – to 'the inescapable conclusion' that 'England's educational problems are not likely to be solved as long as schooling and social status remain so inextricably entwined'. And, like the Bristol letter-writer, she drew a parallel between racial segregation in the USA and educational segregation (whether private/state or grammar/secondary modern) in England:

> The sad thing is that secondary education, as education, is so much better overall than it was before 1944. A pity it had to get mixed up with social class, and the business of having a proper accent. That hopeful phrase, 'parity of esteem', is as hollow as our 'separate but equal'. The main difference is that we discriminate against a minority and the English against a majority.[27]

Amidst the swirling controversies, Labour's challenge by 1957 was to forge a coherent education policy ahead of the next general election. The Study Group on Education that met for the first time in March comprised mainly MPs, including two Wykehamists in Gaitskell and Crossman, Anthony Greenwood (Merchant Taylors) and Michael Stewart (Christ's Hospital). Soon afterwards, Stewart was in public conversation with Edna Healey, who chaired the managers of a group of schools in London, and they touched on the issue of whether and how comprehensives needed to build a 'tradition' of good reputation in order to compete with established schools:

> *EH* – It is true that we don't want to create a mystique of tradition, but neither do we want to throw the baby out with the bath water. The grammar schools understandably take the view that since they are doing a good job already, why interfere with them . . .
>
> *MS* – The question that matters is: what is the whole education system turning out? Is it doing the best for the average as well as the clever pupil? History gives no instance of a civilization collapsing because it neglected its élite; but it tells of many which perished because they paid insufficient attention to the mass and allowed a gap to yawn between the élite and the ordinary citizen. Is there not a lesson here for modern England?

Throwing the baby out with the bath water: Healey's understandable fear reflected a party still deeply conflicted about the grammars, though ultimately it would be Stewart's take-no-prisoners line that spoke the loudest.

Over the rest of the year the Study Group considered a series of memos and submissions. 'Our real enemy is, surely, not the examination of children but the *separation* of them at 11,' argued Stewart in tandem with Margaret Cole, while on the other key front, it was 'an illusion' that 'if the Labour Party leaves the public schools alone and concentrates on creating comprehensive schools, these latter will become "Everyman's Eton", and the special advantages enjoyed by those parents who can pay public school fees will disappear'. For his part, Crossman did not deny the socially pernicious consequences of the old boy network, but warned against policy 'actuated by motives of envy' and was adamant about the need to recognise 'one basic human right – the right of the parent to pay twice for the child's education'. The great historian and radical R. H. Tawney advocated 'establishing not a small percentage of free places at a large number of schools, as the Fleming Committee recommended [in 1944], but a large percentage of free places at a smaller number of schools', claiming that 'nothing would do more to knock on the head the boarding school social snobbery of today than the existence, side by side with the one-clan Eton, Harrow and the rest, of equally successful boarding schools recruited from all sections of the nation'. And, in another memo, Eric James solemnly stated that grammars had been 'the strongest solvents of class divisions', given that 'Manchester Grammar School, and a few others like it, represent probably a wider social cross-section than almost any other schools, not in England alone, but in the whole Western world (this is literally true), and an academic standard which challenges the very best independent schools.'

The Study Group also heard evidence in December from Mark Abrams, commissioned to survey parental attitudes to education. In terms of working-class parents and the maintained sector, a predictable enough set of findings emerged: that most were 'quite happy to leave things as they are'; that 'while emphatic that children with good brains should be given every chance to develop, most parents seemed convinced that their own children were unlikely to obtain this opportunity because of lack of ability'; that 'they did not feel that their own children were likely to benefit particularly from any improvements in education'; and that 'the idea of the comprehensive school had made practically no impact upon them'. As for private education, Abrams noted that his survey had revealed 'an overwhelming majority of parents', including working-class ones, 'in favour of private spending on education', with 'the general feeling' being that 'if parents wanted to send children to private schools there was no reason why they should not do so'. Accordingly, concluded Abrams, 'any attempt' to abolish private education 'or even to stir up hostility against private education would probably only seem curious to the electorate'.

In February 1958 the Study Group decamped to Clacton-on-Sea for a weekend conference, listening to the views of some 18 outside experts. 'There was no criticism of Labour's proposals for reorganisation of secondary education on comprehensive lines,' recorded the official summary of the proceedings, 'provided that these were submitted in terms of a 15/20-year plan and full provision was made for flexibility in implementing the new system.' Crossman, however, privately recorded that 'everybody emphasised how impossible it was to go too fast towards a comprehensive system'.

Gaitskell looked in on the Sunday session and expressed his preference for 'Flemingism', in effect the extension of free places, chosen by intellectual ability, in about 30 public schools, but this was dismissed by Crossman as 'totally impractical', an opinion that most of the Study Group apparently shared. Altogether, noted the official summary of the session, 'the discussions were largely inconclusive but seemed to indicate the view that under present circumstances the public schools were best left alone'. Next day, writing up his diary, Crossman reflected wryly how 'at the conference there was almost universal bewilderment and amazement at the idea, and all for the right reasons – that to attack Manchester Grammar School, while leaving Eton, is the act of a zanie'.[28] The syntax was confusing, but the sense was dismayingly clear.

Learning to Live, Labour's policy document on education (largely drafted by Stewart), was published in mid-June. Under a future Labour government, all local authorities would be required to produce plans ending selection at 11; but at the same time, there was an acceptance that, in terms of the precise mechanics, local circumstances would demand a degree of flexibility. What about the public schools? The document yielded nothing in its ferocious denunciation of the current system – 'damages national efficiency and offends the sense of justice . . . all who desire equality of opportunity and social justice will agree that the existence of this privileged sector of education is undesirable' – but the nub, it insisted, was the question of priorities:

> There is a risk that argument over this question may give it an importance which, in proportion to the whole field of education, it does not possess. Compare, today, the free national system of education and the private fee-paying system. It is the national system which provides the greater variety and attempts the most difficult tasks. Despite all its present inadequacies, it is vigorous and capable of great advances. To make the nation's schools fully worthy of the nation will be an immense achievement. Smaller classes, better-qualified teachers, better equipment and a higher proportion of sixth formers in our own schools will open the door of opportunity and steadily reduce the influence of the privileged fee-paying schools in public life. We believe that the next Labour Government should concentrate its educational endeavours on this work.

And 'therefore', as Mollie Panter-Downes not long afterwards informed her *New Yorker* readers, 'Eton, Harrow, and the others will be left as they are'.

The document inevitably provoked some strong criticism. 'We are afraid to tackle the public schools to which the wealthy people send their sons,' lamented the working-class 'Manny' Shinwell (a former Labour minister) in *The Times*, 'but at the same time are ready to throw overboard the grammar schools, which are for many working-class boys the stepping stones to the universities and a useful career – I would rather abandon Eton, Winchester, Harrow and all the rest of them than sacrifice the advantage of the grammar school.' The journalist Geoffrey Goodman, in a letter to the *New Statesman*, was equally appalled: 'It is almost inconceivable that a party dedicated to the concept of greater equality (to say nothing of Socialism) can argue that privilege of any kind will wither away in an acquisitive society, provided you offer "suitable" alternatives.' And in the same magazine, the Cambridge literary critic Graham Hough offered a caustic prediction: 'There will remain to the Labour Party the glory of messing up the grammar schools, the oldest and best of English educational institutions; and of continuing the nineteenth-century public school system for the very few who can afford to pay for it.'[29]

The party conference was at Scarborough at the end of September. In the same debate that endorsed the anti-11-plus aspect of *Learning to Live*, Fred Peart, a dissenting member of the Study Group, moved a resolution calling for the integration of public schools into the state system. In support, Gillingham's delegate, the young Gerald Kaufman, declared that 'a progressive measure of this sort would be advancing Socialism and gaining middle-class support', while for Frank Cousins the issue was that something needed to be done about the fact that 'this country's economic, international, political and industrial affairs are in the hands of a privileged group who hand the privileges on from place to place, whether it is in the Tory Party or in our Party'. On the other side, Alice Bacon (also of the Study Group) argued that the practical problems of integration were too great and its immediate relative importance too limited, but promised that the 'scandal' of public schools getting 'priority of entry into Oxford and Cambridge' was 'something we can stop', while Stewart dismissed Peart's resolution as irrelevant: 'Ask yourselves how many members of your own constituency party want to send their children to public schools.' The outcome, on a card vote, was a defeat for Peart by 3.54 million votes to 3.07 million. 'Some day,' reflected the *New Statesman* soon afterwards, 'Labour must clearly make away with the fee-paying public schools; but it had better choose its own time, which will not be until the comprehensive schools have been firmly established in sufficient numbers and have had time to show their merits.'

A range of reasons had contributed to Labour's unwillingness to take on the public schools – not least an honourable dislike of interfering with people's liberty, a dislike felt as much by Bevan as by Gaitskell and Crossman. But perhaps the last word should go to Sir Richard Acland, reviewing Michael Young's *The Rise of the Meritocracy* in 1959. According to this singular man – Rugby and Balliol, from 1935 a Liberal MP, then founding member during the war of the socialist Common Wealth Party, later a Labour MP until in 1955 resigning from the party over its support for nuclear weapons – Young's optimistic forecast that by the end of the 1970s the public-school question would be (in Acland's paraphrasing words) 'quietly and effortlessly eliminated' as a result of vastly increased educational expenditure on the state system was 'almost wholly divorced from reality':

> The privilege of public school education has little to do with better teachers – man for man I doubt if they are very much superior to grammar school staff. Still less has it anything to do with some subtle atmosphere distilled from the spirit of Matthew Arnold hovering in the quads. It is based on something far more material which I very seldom see mentioned. Having them under their hands all day long *the public schools can give their pupils many more hours of education per week*.
>
> At a typical public school known to me the boys have 38 hours of organised instruction per week, including all games, and 1½ hours prep. per night in quiet study or under discipline in hall. The corresponding figure for Wandsworth School (comprehensive) where I taught last year is 28 hours, including 1 hour's prep. in a home where there may be no escape from the tele. The other material factor is size of class – averaging about 22 compared with 32 at Wandsworth.
>
> Speaking to a sixth form at a public school recently I had to say to them: 'Of those at Wandsworth who will seriously try to reach university this year and will fail, two-thirds would succeed if they could work under your conditions; of you who will succeed in entering university, two-thirds would fail if you worked under Wandsworth conditions.'
>
> *This* is the measure of the educational privilege which the rich can buy. *This* is the reason why no wealthy socialist can do other than send his son to public school – he cannot face the vision of his own son, aged 21 and perhaps by then a keen Conservative or Liberal, saying to him: 'You had the means of giving me the best chance, and for your blasted political humbug you didn't do it.'
>
> And *this* is the reason why the Labour Party, in the present temper of the nation, does not and dare not propose to end public schools. Putting it quite brutally, they know that against such an appalling invasion of privilege and inequality, the rich would 'go on strike' in one way or another and bring the economic life of the community to chaos in which (once again in the present temper of the nation) the government would

not receive such zestful backing from workers and middle-classes as would win from the chaos a government victory over the rich.

Therefore, let it be perfectly clear, we are not going to have Michael Young's Meritocracy or anything like it merely by accentuating our present tendencies.[30]

PART THREE

10

Unnatural Practices

Pinky and Perky, not yet sundered by musical differences, starring on *Sunday Night at the London Palladium*; a television critic laying into the fake bonhomie of ITV's 'Show Biz Corps' ('Mr Michael Miles's awful relish . . . Mr Hughie Green's twangy transatlantic archness . . . Mr Bruce Forsyth's twinkle-toes and strident congratulations'); *Grandstand* starting to show rugby league (commentator, Eddie Waring); Cliff Richard's 'Move It' peaking at number 3, 'Hoots Mon' by the novelty act Lord Rockingham's XI climbing to number 1; Walter Allen praising Stanley Middleton's first novel *A Short Answer* as 'a sharp and fruitful picture of middle-class provincial life'; reading Angus Wilson's *The Middle Age of Mrs Eliot* feeling for Pamela Hansford Johnson like being 'hobbled with the author in a sort of three-legged race'; Arnold Wesker issuing his first major blast ('Let Battle Commence!') on the need to bring art to the masses ('It is the bus driver, the housewife, the miner and the Teddy Boy to whom I should like to address myself'); Philip Larkin admiring a newspaper photo of London Zoo's Guy the Gorilla ('I felt considerable kinship with him'); John Fowles, on his way to the Whitechapel Gallery's Jackson Pollock exhibition, walking through the 'eighteenth-century streets' of Spitalfields, 'full of Indians, Jews, poverty, beautiful door-ways painted in tatty varnish, dirty, ragged children'; a Gallup poll finding 81 per cent had a favourable view of the Royal Family, 71 per cent of the House of Commons, 52 per cent of the House of Lords and 51 per cent of the trade unions; Marian Raynham in Surbiton rebelling one Saturday ('Why should I spend all morning making cakes & scones? Seem to be spending all my life doing these foolish things. I

just won't . . .'); Judy Haines's younger daughter Pamela doing an old
11-plus paper at home one evening ('Nearly screamed when I found
she had gone wrong in two of the simplest sums . . . Must get her a
tonic. This swotting for 11+ is getting on her nerves'); and Anthony
Heap citing 'the latest craze' among girls and young women – 'rotating
an old fashioned child's wooden hoop (now called a "hula-hoop")
around one's waist as long as possible without letting it drop' – as
further evidence it was 'a mad world' . . .[1] Yet nothing mattered more
in November 1958 than the fact that on the 26th the House of Commons
at last openly debated the issue of homosexuality – almost fifteen
months after the Wolfenden Report, six months after the founding of
the Homosexual Law Reform Society and by chance just a few days
after a high-profile episode had thrown the whole issue into uncomfortably stark relief.

On the night of Wednesday the 19th Ian Harvey – rising Tory MP,
junior minister at the Foreign Office, married with two daughters –
was walking along the Mall shortly after 11 o'clock. 'A young guardsman in uniform passed me at a slow pace and I knew what that meant,'
he recalled in his memoir *To fall like Lucifer*. 'I turned and caught up
with him and we went together into the Park.' There they were 'caught
by a park official accompanied by a policeman', taken (not without a
struggle on Harvey's part) to a police station, and, next morning, stood
side by side in the dock at Bow Street Court, each charged with
'committing an act of gross indecency with another male person' and
'behaving in a manner reasonably likely to offend against public
decency', with both men being remanded until 10 December. It was
the end of Harvey's political career. 'If (as I fear) he is guilty, it means
that he must resign his post in the Govt *and* his seat in Parl¹,' recorded
Macmillan on the Friday. 'I saw him this morning, & did my best to
comfort him. But it [is] a terrible thing & has distressed me greatly.' In
the event, Harvey resigned both post and seat on Monday the 24th,
well aware that in his constituency association at Harrow East there
were 'many people who, whilst they were my supporters, regarded
what I had done as unspeakable'. On 10 December each man was
found guilty and fined £5 – with Harvey paying not only for the
guardsman but also, as his counsel accurately predicted, for the rest of
his life. He found himself rapidly being cut off by former colleagues in

politics and advertising, with one remarking that 'the only thing for
Ian Harvey to do is to change his name and go to Canada'; the Carlton
Club accepted his resignation without comment; the Junior Carlton
Club hoped he would retain his membership, but asked him to promise not to enter the premises for two years; and the War Office had to
be persuaded not to have this former lieutenant colonel in the Territorial
Army cashiered. 'I remember him,' wrote Matthew Parris in 2002
(15 years after Harvey's death), 'a sad old man, living alone and forgotten in a small flat.'[2]

The proposed decriminalisation of homosexual relations was of
course only one part of Wolfenden; on the other part – the recommendation that prostitutes be outlawed from the streets – Rab Butler as
Home Secretary made it clear, opening the thinly attended debate, that
he was fully in accordance, leading in due course to legislation to that
effect. The story goes that an uncertain Butler had sought the opinion
of the stationmaster in his Saffron Walden constituency, who had told
him that people did not mind prostitutes, but had no wish to see them
in public places. As for the more contentious question, Butler's unyielding line, on behalf of the government as a whole, was that 'there was at
present a very large section of the population who strongly repudiated
homosexual conduct and whose moral sense would be offended by an
alteration of the law' – a no-change policy backed by a narrow majority
of the speakers, among them Labour's Fred Bellenger. 'I can well understand the pleas of those who say that those who practise this cult in
private are inoffensive citizens,' he conceded. 'Perhaps they are, if it is
meant that they do not break windows or behave riotously. Nevertheless,
they are, in my opinion, a malignant canker in the community and if
this were allowed to grow, it would eventually kill off what is known as
normal life.' A Tory backbencher, William Shepherd, agreed: 'I think
there is far too much sympathy with the homosexual and far too little
regard for society . . . I believe that it is our duty as far as we can to stop
this society within a society. I believe that to a great extent, perhaps 90
per cent of the cases, these men could be deviated from their path . . .'
Perhaps the most emphatic speaker was his colleague Cyril Black, an
inveterate campaigner for traditional morality. 'These unnatural practices, if persisted in, spell death to the souls of those who indulge in
them,' he declared. 'Great nations have fallen and empires been

destroyed because corruption became widespread and socially acceptable.' On the morning of the debate *The Times* had contended that
though it was 'a foregone conclusion that the homosexual laws will not
be reformed yet', it was 'equally a foregone conclusion that reform
must come eventually', given that 'the majority of well-informed people
are now clearly convinced that these laws are unjust and obsolete'. But
for the moment, as Butler accurately indicated, public opinion as a
whole continued to run the other way, and a few weeks later a Gallup
poll revealed only 25 per cent wanting decriminalisation, as opposed to
48 per cent favouring the laws staying as they were. Ironically, it was in
Shepherd's own constituency – at Bilston in Staffordshire – that a fortnight after the debate two men (aged 66 and 41) gassed themselves to
death, having been questioned by police in connection with (consenting) 'indecent actions between men'.

More bleak years lay ahead. *A Minority: A Report on the Life of the
Male Homosexual in Great Britain* was produced in 1960 by Gordon
Westwood (pseudonym for Michael Schofield), based on a survey of
127 'self-confessed' homosexuals. 'It is impossible to work on a research
of this kind,' noted the book's first sentence, 'without becoming immediately aware of the repugnance with which homosexuality is regarded
by many people.' And Schofield itemised how 'all sorts of difficulties
were put in the way of the research', not least by 'the Medical
Committees of some hospitals', which 'refused to allow doctors on
their staff to help'. Inevitably, the interviewees themselves spoke
eloquently of the attitude of heterosexuals:

> They think it's disgusting. The kind of remarks I get are, 'Be a man,' or
> 'You're not a proper man.'
>
> It's very difficult for a normal to understand. There are no expressions
> they would not use to show their disgust. It's horrifying how men or
> women who in every other way are decent and sensible can lose their
> sense of proportion on this subject.
>
> The normal men I work with simply don't understand. They say,
> 'Why do they have to do such things when there are plenty of women
> about?'
>
> Many people – like my brother, for example – think it's all a huge joke
> and just don't take it seriously.

Inevitably it affects your social life. I always seem to go on holidays alone and sometimes I get a pitiful feeling, knowing that I'll live the rest of my life in solitude.

A homosexual cannot relax in ordinary company.

The effect of acting a part can be exhausting. I envy people in jobs where they haven't got to act a part. In the business world one spends a lot of time taking care – making sure one doesn't give oneself away.

But of course, it all depended. 'If you are a failure in the world, they look down on you if they know you are queer. But if you are successful and queer, you become rather quaint.'[3]

Even so, to an extent sometimes under-appreciated, there were clear signs by the late 1950s of the hold of 'respectable' morality starting to break up. Specifically, three pieces of essentially liberal legislation had been enacted – not without difficulty – by the end of the decade. The Mental Health Act, by abolishing the categories of moral defectiveness and feeblemindedness, made it impossible to lock up in Victorian mental institutions women deemed promiscuous or otherwise troublesome; the Legitimacy Act significantly extended the legitimisation of children born illegitimate; and the Obscene Publications Act, piloted through by Roy Jenkins, greatly reduced the powers of censorship over the printed word.[4] Significantly, this last piece of legislation was not yet enacted when in spring 1959 Vladimir Nabokov's controversial *Lolita* was at last published in Britain, by Weidenfeld and Nicolson – who were not subjected to prosecution. A battle had seemingly been won.

———

Two key industrial announcements were made in the closing months of 1958. The first, on 18 November, concerned steel strip mills: the expectation had been that the government would back the construction of a huge new continuous one at Llanwern, near Newport in South Wales; but instead, in the general context of worryingly high unemployment in the old 'depressed areas', political pressure from Scotland was such that Macmillan decided – exercising what he called 'the judgement of Solomon' – to back *two* smaller, semi-continuous new mills, namely one at Llanwern and another at Ravenscraig in Lanarkshire. This call, justly comments the historian Peter Scott, 'resulted in neither being

sufficiently large to obtain the economies of scale achieved in continental plants'. But at least at this point there was not a problem of inadequate demand, quite unlike the ominous, rapidly developing situation
in the coal industry. There, total consumption during 1957 had abruptly
fallen by over 6 million tons, followed in 1958 by a drop of a further 13
million tons, as coal found itself being brutally undercut by oil. 'Coal is
still our main source of power – and a vital part of our natural inheritance,' proclaimed a full-page National Coal Board advertisement in
November 1958, exhorting 'young men' to become 'the next generation
of managers, engineers and scientists' in the coal industry. Soon afterwards, on 3 December, the NCB announced that 36 pits would have to
close (including 20 in Scotland and 6 in South Wales), most of them in
the next few months, with some 4,000 mineworkers to be made redundant. Still, from a Tory point of view, this would hardly lose votes,
whereas another sector in deep trouble, the Lancashire cotton industry,
was a different, more troubling matter. The upshot was not only detailed
negotiations to reduce Commonwealth imports but, in summer 1959,
the passing of the Cotton Industry Act, in effect a state-supported
scrapping scheme designed to eliminate excess capacity as painlessly as
possible. 'A sop to Lancashire,' the historian of the Lancashire cotton
industry brusquely calls this politically motivated, taxpayer-funded
piece of government interventionism that did little to equip the industry for challenges ahead that might anyway have proved impossible to
overcome.[5]

The housing trends by the late 1950s had an even more significant
political dimension, as is suggested by the annual breakdown for permanent dwellings built in England and Wales:

	Local authorities	Private builders
1956	149,139	119,585
1957	145,711	122,942
1958	117,438	124,087
1959	102,905	146,476

Macmillan was fully alert to the potential dividend of stimulating the
number of owner-occupiers, and during 1958 (the year that Lawrie
Barratt formed a house-building company in Newcastle, initially

focusing on first-time buyers) he overrode Treasury objections and pushed his Housing Minister into developing the concept of 100-per-cent, government-supported mortgages, as enshrined in due course in the House Purchase and Housing Act of 1959. 'Whatever the Opposition may say now,' declared the junior Housing Minister Reginald Bevins in the Commons debate on the Bill in December 1958, 'the fact of the matter is that the Labour Party has always been secretly, not publicly, contemptuous of the conception of a property-owning democracy. [HON. MEMBERS: "Nonsense."] Of course, they have. Indeed, from their own point of view, they are probably right, because it is not part of the Socialist mission in this land to manufacture Conservatives.'[6]

Nevertheless, those Hon. Members opposite were by and large in an optimistic frame of mind during the winter of 1958–9, notwithstanding the recent tightening in the polls and an instantly celebrated Vicky cartoon in the *New Statesman* in November dubbing the PM as 'Supermac'. Rising prices, rising unemployment (up by February 1959 to 620,000, the highest level since 1947), a deteriorating balance of payments – no wonder that, in Geoffrey Goodman's words, 'both Left and Right wings of the Labour Movement felt that 1959 would bring a Labour Government to power with Gaitskell as Prime Minister'. Admittedly the temporary accord between Left and Right was paper-thin – 'Gaitskell's piddling all the time for fear of losing the Election,' Nye Bevan scornfully told Dick Crossman in December – but at least it existed. There was even a glossy new policy document in place, *The Future Labour Offers You*, launched during the autumn in tandem with a notably effective party political broadcast. Yet two indicators this winter might have given pause for thought. In November a detailed analysis in the *Financial Times* concluded that 'the long post-war decline in the economic position of the middle class has now been halted'; and in January the publication of weekly averages of shop sales for 1958 revealed that a sharp drop in the early months had given way, following the end of the credit squeeze, to a steep rise between August and the end of the year. Bevan, though, was adamant. 'We shall win the Election,' he informed Crossman, 'and the trouble will come very soon afterwards.'[7]

One direction in which Labour did not look for lessons was from the New Left. On the same evening as Bevan's predictions, Brian

Abel-Smith read a paper to the Fabian Society, with Anthony Wedgwood Benn among those present. In it he advocated that the Fabians become more like the *Universities and Left Review*, which (in Benn's words, reporting Abel-Smith) 'got five or six hundred to their meetings', whereas 'we were completely missing young people'. Abel-Smith further urged the Fabians to 'meet in a coffee house instead of in large bare halls'. Whereupon: 'Tony Crosland opened the attack. He said that he could see nothing of interest in the *ULR* except that "there's a man who seems to be able to run a coffee house". He thought that political activity under the age of thirty-five was not of great interest to the Fabians ... All this was said in a most bored and offensive way.' The others who spoke 'agreed with Tony to a greater or lesser extent', except for Benn himself, who argued that 'the question we had to face was whether we had anything relevant to say in the modern world'.

The coffee house that Crosland so disdainfully referred to was the Partisan at the *ULR*'s premises at 7 Carlisle Street in Soho – a place not only for food and drink ('Bill of fare includes Farmhouse Soup ... Borscht ... Irish Peasant Stew ... Liver dumplings ... Boiled Breconshire Mutton with caper sauce ... Apple dumplings with hot lemon sauce ... Whitechapel cheese-cake and pastries ... Vienna coffee ... café filtre ... Russian tea') but also chess, music and debate. The venture was run by the ebullient, charismatic, hopelessly disorganised young historian Ralph (later Raphael) Samuel, by this time based at the Institute of Community Studies. 'He obviously has tremendous faith in people and in his beliefs,' reflected Phyllis Willmott after talking to him at a Christmas party. 'I find his earnest idealism most wonderfully touching.' In January, intrigued, she visited the Partisan and found 'mostly odd cranks and broken-down "artists"', often 'sporting beards or berets', as well as serious-looking young students. 'Girls in duffle coats and black stockings, young boys in old jackets. A coloured man began to play the guitar more or less spontaneously as I could judge. I felt very sophisticated and elegant by comparison, although I wasn't.'[8]

Benn's 'modern world' was coming on apace. On the morning of 5 December, two days after the pit-closures announcement, Macmillan inaugurated the 8.5-mile Preston Bypass, Britain's first stretch of motorway and, subsequently, part of the M6. 'In the years to come,' the

PM declared, 'the county and country alike may look at the Preston Bypass – a fine thing in itself but a finer thing as a symbol – as a token of what is to follow'; pressing a button, he cut the traditional tape by remote control; and then, watched by 200 cheering schoolchildren from what *The Times* called 'one of the futuristic-looking bridges that straddle the motorway', he was driven along in a Rolls-Royce Landau. On another front, though in public call boxes it was still a case of insert four pennies and press button A, there was major progress too, for later that day the Queen visited Bristol telephone exchange and directly dialled an Edinburgh number (031 CAL 3636), thereby inaugurating the new subscriber trunk dialling (STD) system. 'Those present then heard an amplified voice reply: "The Lord Provost of Edinburgh speaking," to which the Queen replied: "This is the Queen speaking, from Bristol. Good afternoon, Lord Provost."' Back in Preston, the AA in the evening reported traffic flowing at 400 vehicles an hour at an average speed of 70 mph, with excellent lane discipline and 'exemplary' signalling, though it did regretfully add that 'the speed and density of the traffic' would probably make a traditional salute from their patrols 'impracticable'.

Literary tastes – like many other tastes – remained for the most part defiantly unmodern. 'Mr and Mrs Brown first met Paddington on a railway platform,' began Michael Bond's *A Bear Called Paddington*, inspired by a stocking-filler bear he had bought for his wife at Selfridges the previous Christmas Eve. The *TLS* was only cautiously enthusiastic about Bond's creation ('it must be said that a 6-year-old to whom the book was read laughed himself sick over some of the slapstick'), but the entire first print run rapidly sold out. So too did John Betjeman's *Collected Poems*, though not without the odd dissenting note amidst the general enthusiasm. 'I wish he wouldn't appear to be writing off some millions of his fellow humans because they say "Pardon",' reflected Janet Adam Smith in the *New Statesman*, while K. W. Gransden in the *Listener*, after acknowledging the poet was 'in the rare position of being both chic and popular', teased out the implications of how Betjeman's 'own emotions enter into everything he writes':

He really feels it and means it. Does class matter? By jove, yes. Down with vulgar new rich City men; down with suburban pseudo-gentility;

down with supercinemas, neon, fish and chips, chromium; down with the phoney picture-postcard England of the brewers' advertisements. Up with romantic Baker-street buffet; up with churches; up with the Home Counties and horses. Down, in short, with the century of the common man, and up with the past from about 1880 to 1914.

And of course one sometimes agrees. Mr Betjeman is an extraordinarily accurate observer and recorder of middle-class manners and prejudices, some of which are endearing and even good. But at times the exclusiveness and triviality of this point of view seems ignoble and, like all rearguard actions, rather pathetic. It is all very funny; but how seldom one laughs without a pharisaic snigger; and how unscrupulously Mr Betjeman beguiles and flatters us into accepting his values along with his verbal felicities. We may feel cleverer, 'nicer', or even more U after reading him; we rarely feel better.

Shortly before Christmas, at the Hyde Park Gate home of Enid Bagnold, Betjeman was presented with the Duff Cooper Prize by Princess Margaret. 'A really thrilling moment of triumph,' Betjeman wrote afterwards to his publisher Jock Murray, while another publisher present at the ceremony, Rupert Hart-Davis, told his old schoolmaster, 'My dear George, she is exquisitely beautiful, very small and neat and shapely, with a lovely skin and staggering blue eyes.'[9]

Tom Driberg's swoon of choice was Cliff Richard. 'Though he is said to be in private life a modest and likeable Hertfordshire lad,' the politician noted about this time following his latest performance on *Oh Boy!*, 'he has been taught to assume just the right look of delinquent fretfulness: his eyes have the smouldering but fixed glare of a sulky basilisk; his coiffure is mountainously upswept. A menacingly one-sided Ozymandias curl of the lip reveals strong incisors.' A few days later, the *New Musical Express* reported that Cliff now had a new manager (the tough-minded impresario Tito Burns, keen from the start to turn him into 'an all-round entertainer'); that his parents, with whom he still lived in Cheshunt, had been promised for Christmas 'a 17 in. console television set'; and that his plan for Christmas Eve was to go for 'a bumper Chinese spread' at Edgware Road's Lotus House (London's first upmarket Chinese restaurant, run by John Koon). Elsewhere in pop-land, Tommy Steele was now

already taking his first step on the primrose path to all-round entertainer, starring at the Coliseum as Buttons in *Cinderella*, alongside
the 'handle-bar moustached comedian' Jimmy Edwards (of current
Whack-O! fame) and 'Television glamour girl Yana', an altogether
'odd, not to say outlandish conglomeration of talents'. The descriptions were by Anthony Heap, present of course at the first night (18
December) and his usual implacable self: the 'rock 'n' roll idol'
brought 'to his first stage acting part little but an atrocious cockney
accent', while Edwards 'seldom contrives to be funny, least of all in
his long-winded trumpet-playing solo act'. Alan Brien in the
Spectator agreed about Steele's deficiencies ('his timing is embarrass-
ingly erratic and he moves as stiffly as a stilt-dancer'), with the
panto's only redeeming feature being Kenneth Williams as a 'campy
sister'.

   In the days after Christmas, two faces of the future were sighted on
the small screen. On ITV's *Small Time* for younger viewers, Muriel
Young read 'Little Rocky: The rocket who was afraid of heights', and
on the BBC, the quiz game *Ask Me Another* (produced by Ned Sherrin)
included Ted 'Farmer' Moult, praised by viewers for his 'wonderful
good humour' and treating the programme 'certainly seriously, but as a
game, and not as a grim contest'. There were plaudits too for the chairman Franklin Engelmann – 'firm, fair, friendly, quick-witted and always
very natural', noted an insurance agent – while a marine fitter called the
whole thing 'not only instructive, but also very interesting and entertaining'. Even so, the show captured only 16 per cent of the working-
class audience, with 36 per cent opting instead for *Emergency—Ward 10*
on the other channel.[10]

The trade unions may have trailed far behind the Royal Family in terms
of the public having a 'favourable' attitude, but with 51 per cent they
did better in Gallup's November poll than the City and Stock Exchange,
which managed only 44 per cent, though with a high 'neutral' (in practice indifferent?) rating of 40 per cent. 'The City must often to foreign
eyes seem deceptively sleepy; it does not take fleets of lawyers to reach
an agreement; it often likes to pretend that it is more old-fashioned than
it is,' the *Financial Times* complacently reflected a few weeks later. 'At

Christmas we can allow ourselves the favourite English pastime of congratulating ourselves on being a lot shrewder than we are taken for. Let other people be "too clever by half" so long as we can be "not such fools as we look."' But as it happened, two stories at the end of the year and going into 1959 suddenly put the City unusually and at times uncomfortably in the national spotlight.

Shortly after Christmas the government announced the full convertibility of sterling held by non-residents. 'Pound Flies High' (*Sunday Express*), 'This Proud, Free £' (*Daily Express*) and 'The £ Stands Firm on Freedom Day' (*Evening Standard*) was the patriotic chorus of the Beaverbrook press, while the *FT* declared that sterling's convertibility, following on from the end of credit controls, meant that 'now, for the first time, it is possible to claim that the post-war period, with all its artificial pressures and constraints, is over and done with'. *The Economist*'s line on 'An Act of Bravery?' was altogether more cautious: 'The main meaning of the move is that Britain, as the world's leading short-term banker, will now be more formally (and therefore possibly more forcefully) committed to take the strain upon its gold reserves whenever any other currency in the world is regarded as temporarily more desirable to hold than sterling.' And, accepting that 'to voice these misgivings is just another way of saying that Britain is, for better or worse, in the international banking business', it concluded: 'Sterling sets sail on a long voyage in a fair weather ship at a moment when the weather forecast is favourable. Let us hope, indeed everybody must hope, that it will remain favourable. But it is rash to bet that it will do so for ever.'

What were the domestic implications of what one economic historian calls 'Britain's new cosmopolitanism'? Although the announcement itself provoked no great controversy, Anthony Crosland would state the potential downside forcibly in a Third Programme talk in early February. Claiming (probably correctly) that the 'strongest pressure' behind the decision had come from the Bank of England and the City, wanting convertibility 'in order to enhance the position of London as a world banker and financial centre', he called it 'a disastrous approach' – given not only that 'the financial earnings of the City from overseas business are trivial in relation to our balance of payments' but that 'every step in the direction [i.e. of financial liberalisation, ultimately leading to the end of exchange controls] increases our vulnerability to speculation'. And:

> The really serious thing about all this is that our *domestic* policies are increasingly dictated by the holders of sterling – by bankers in Zurich and London, by speculators all over the world, and by traders using sterling as an international trading currency. These people are not, unfortunately, as the City likes to think they are, highly rational and sophisticated judges of the true state of the British economy. On the contrary, they are often naive, volatile, and ill-informed – as they were, for example, when they caused the sterling crisis of 1957; or else they are plain incompetent, as the City syndicate was in the recent British Aluminium dispute. Yet the fear of what they may do to sterling increasingly influences our Bank rate policy, our rate of economic expansion, our wages policy, and now – to judge from a recent leading article in *The Economist* – even what taxation policy we are allowed to pursue. Heaven alone knows – or rather I can easily guess – what their attitude would be to the policies of a Labour Government.

In short, in characteristic Crosland tones (and, no doubt, drawl): 'All this seems to me an intolerable derogation of British sovereignty; the more tiresome since bankers and speculators are all natural deflationists and their influence is invariably against a rapid rate of growth.'[11]

The 'British Aluminium dispute' to which Crosland referred was the other story.[12] In essence it was a disputatious, high-profile City setpiece arising out of the contested takeover of British Aluminium (BA), an ailing company whose chairman was Viscount Portal of Hungerford, Chief of Air Staff during the war and now president of the MCC. The rival bidders were on the one hand the Aluminium Company of America, favoured by BA, and on the other hand an alliance of an American company, Reynolds Metals, and a British one, Tube Investments (TI). The prestigious, ultra-respectable merchant banks Hambros and Lazards were advising BA, while for the other side the principal adviser was Warburgs, a recently created Jewish merchant bank headed by Siegmund Warburg that was still regarded with considerable suspicion by the City Establishment. 'Rather a "Gentleman v.

Players" affair' was how Macmillan privately characterised the Aluminium War (as it became known), and the whole episode would prove richly symbolic.

Amidst considerable acrimony between the two camps, the dramatic denouement began in the last few days of 1958 when Hambros and Lazards formed a City consortium of the great and the good (including Morgan Grenfell, Brown Shipley and Robert Fleming) to protect BA from the attentions of Reynolds/TI, a grand alliance prompted less by a dispassionate analysis of what was best for BA than a visceral dislike of hostile takeover bids, still a relative rarity. Kim Cobbold, governor of the Bank of the England, tried to arrange a truce between the two parties, which in practice meant persuading them not to engage in further buying of BA shares. But during the early days of 1959, while the City consortium heeded Cobbold's wishes, Warburgs did not, deploying the black arts of what Cobbold himself crisply called 'monkey business'. Put simply, one side played cricket, the other did not. By 6 January, Reynolds/TI had achieved majority control; the following week, *The Times* published an extraordinary letter by Olaf Hambro, claiming that the wishes of the City had been violated.[13]

The Aluminium War was the making of Warburgs, ushered in an era of contested takeover battles and generally struck a blow – though not a fatal one – at the City's traditional ethos of gentlemanly capitalism. For Portal, it was part of a distressing winter, with his MCC tourists taking a pounding down under against a notably uncompromising Australian side. 'Cowdrey,' noted Philip Larkin on 27 December shortly before the Second Test, with England already one down, 'is clasped in some cloudy private inhibition: Bailey is like the old horse in *Animal Farm* – "I will bat slower"; Dexter, well, don't know much about Dexter: *pas sérieux*, I'd say. Fenner's playboy.' All three were amateurs, the team's captain (Peter May) was an amateur, and of course the dissenting professional, Johnny Wardle, had been left behind. Things failed to improve at Melbourne, with the visitors being rolled over in their second innings for a miserable 87. 'Never can I remember such a dismal batting display,' declared one old salt, Alec Bedser, while Frank Rostron in the *Sunday Express* blamed May and the manager Freddie Brown (yet another amateur) for 'their staggeringly slack attitude and complacence from the beginning of the tour'. It got still worse. England eventually went down 4–0, and in one match the supremely professional off-spinner Jim Laker, pausing as was his habit to check his field before coming in to bowl, noticed that down at deep square leg the young Cantab Ted Dexter was ... practising his golf swing.[14]

11

Morbid Sentimentality

A suburban vignette, and an ill-natured turn against a sporting hero, helped mark the start of 1959. At Finchley Central on the evening of the 2nd, a Friday, passengers travelling on the Northern Line – for so long 'the misery line' – refused to leave their carriages when 'all change' was called. Holding the doors open to prevent the train from moving, they wanted, according to eyewitness Ernest Lindgren of 57 Ventnor Drive, N20, 'to know what the reason was'. Eventually most got out, after the police had been summoned, but Lindgren in his letter to *The Times* was adamant that 'this sudden, spontaneous demonstration was not provoked by one incident or one official, but by the accumulated resentment of rational people at being treated habitually and consistently as unreasoning cattle'. The mood was also dark the next afternoon at Old Trafford, where, after winning a penalty for his visiting Blackpool team, Stanley Matthews found himself being booed for the first time in his 28-year career.

Three days later, on 6 January, Anthony Heap took his nine-year-old son to the King's Cross Gaumont to see Norman Wisdom's latest, *The Square Peg*, with the star taking a 'gratifying – and well seized – opportunity to get away from his customary cloth capped "little man" character'; on the 8th the *Daily Express* exposed in 48-point type the double life of Edwin Brock ('PC 258 CONFESSES I'M A POET . . . THE THINGS HE THINKS UP AS HE POUNDS THE PECKHAM BEAT'), after he had had some poems published by the *Times Literary Supplement*; and at Earl's Court on the 12th, Bellingham's Henry Cooper became British and British Empire heavyweight champion by outpointing Blackpool's Brian London over 15 gruelling rounds – 'an extraordinary fight!' declared Philip Larkin, as he listened on the radio to what one reporter called Cooper's 'superbly judged' performance against the 'bull-like rushes' of his opponent, left at the end looking like 'an over-grown schoolboy receiving a caning'. Macmillan meanwhile was heading for the north-east, for a three-day tour that included a series of factory visits, largely convincing him that, with order books still thin, it would be sensible to postpone the general election until the autumn. In Sunderland on his final morning, the 15th, he toured the North Sands shipyard of Joseph L. Thompson and Sons. 'There was Mr Macmillan, in a nest of girders, watching the workmen watching him,' recalled an accompanying journalist, Alan Brien. 'Then the noon-day hooter gave its bronchial blast. The motionless men sprang to life and poured past him in a hurrying, preoccupied flood. His eyebrows twitched in surprise and he muttered something to his wife. Lady Dorothy was quicker on the uptake. "When the whistle blows," she explained, "they all go off for their luncheon."' That evening in Newcastle was the first night of Tyne Tees Television, and Macmillan gave an interview. 'They are rather like fish, the further north you go the better they get,' he said of the people of the north-east. And, after noting how impressed he had been by the sight of workers and employers pulling together, unlike in the old days, he added: 'It has given me a tremendous inspiration – even a few days like this. In London you really don't see what is going on.'[1]

The weather during much of January and February was miserable – peasoupers, a flu epidemic carrying chesty complications, and, as Mollie Panter-Downes put it, 'every theatre, train, and bus crowded with customers barking like a vaudeville dog act'. Frost damage caused the famed Preston Bypass to be closed for over a month, but the weather was probably not responsible for the death on 22 January of the recently retired motor-racing champion Mike Hawthorn, racing his customised Jaguar against a friend's Mercedes on the Guildford by-pass. 'About ten minutes of the fifteen minutes was wholly concerned with it,' grumbled Kenneth Preston after the six o'clock news on the radio. 'It is a comment on the time that so much should be made of a young man for travelling fast in a car. What sort of values have we got nowadays?' A week later in Chingford was the eve of Pamela Haines's 11-plus exam. 'I set her

hair and got clean blouse, cardigan, etc, ready for tomorrow,' recorded
Judy. 'Cleaned shoes, too, as I intend going to school with her, even
though she's taking the exam at her own school.' Next day: 'I went
down with her. She looked lovely and at this eleventh hour – relaxed. I
am so grateful . . .' And even better: 'Pamela came home radiant (as did
Ione last year) saying she had had a lovely time.' By now it was almost
exactly five months since the Notting Hill riots, and late on Friday the
30th the BBC showed live from St Pancras Town Hall half an hour of
the first Caribbean Carnival. Its stars included Cleo Laine, The
Southlanders and The Mighty Terror; a Carnival Queen beauty contest
was won by the very black Faye Craig; and decorative palms from Kew
Gardens gave a suitably tropical feel. The presiding spirit of the event
(direct forerunner of the Notting Hill Carnival) was Claudia Jones, a
Trinidadian Communist who had been deported in 1955 from the
United States and who in March 1958 had founded the *West Indian
Gazette*. 'West Indians newly transplanted to British soil,' she wrote in
the souvenir brochure, 'strain to feel and hear and reflect their idiom
even as they strain to feel the warmth of their sun-drenched islands and
its immemorable beauty of landscape and terrain,' while the events of
the previous summer had been 'the matrix binding West Indians in the
United Kingdom together as never before', so that 'those who have
filled St Pancras Hall' were 'determined that such happenings should
not recur'.[2]

Most politicians spent the first week of February reading with horrified fascination Labour MP Wilfred Fienburgh's posthumous novel *No
Love for Johnnie*, accurately acclaimed by Bernard Levin as 'a modern
Fame is the Spur . . . a dagger-sharp observation and a deep understanding of the itch that bites at a politician'. Among public condemnations,
Richard Crossman in the *Daily Mirror* called it a 'nauseating caricature
of Labour politics', and J.P.W. Mallalieu in the *New Statesman*
complained that Fienburgh had 'almost totally excluded' from his
hero's character (apparently based in part on James Callaghan) 'any
trace of integrity or any real feeling for the movement of which he is a
member'. Privately, George Wigg thought the book an epitaph not only
for social democracy but for the parliamentary system itself, and
Macmillan reflected that if Fienburgh 'hadn't died, the other Labour
MPs would have killed him'.

The latest death in the news, though for the most part far from banner headline, was Buddy Holly's. Four days after the plane crash, early in the morning on Saturday the 7th, the eight-year-old Brian McHugh heard 'a loud scratching' from the particularly squalid Glasgow tenement next to his rather better one and looked across:

A window was open, and the ragged remnants of a curtain were pulled to one side. A young man was standing gazing out of the window. Suddenly, the loudest noise I thought possible exploded from the window. It was Buddy Holly singing 'That'll Be the Day'.

I can still remember [in 2011] the look of sad but bewildered ecstasy on the man's face. The music was blaring from a brand new portable Dansette record player. As the music finished there was commotion in the further recesses of the room; I could make out a young woman and two small, semi-clad children scurrying about.

The window was closed and there was more noise – wailing, arguing, someone crying . . .

The noise was more decorous that evening, as the married couple Pearl Carr and Teddy Johnson zestfully performed 'Sing, Little Birdie' to become the British entrants for the Eurovision Song Contest. How would they fare the next month in Cannes? 'Although it has a catchy tune,' reckoned one viewer, 'I can't imagine it having much chance on the continent.'³

Undeniably there was a whiff of the Continental about Jack Clayton's film of the bestselling John Braine novel *Room at the Top*, and not only because of Simone Signoret's starring role. 'Its camera-work has an unheightened truth so foreign to our feature films that one often drifts into looking for the subtitles,' noted an admiring Penelope Gilliatt in the February issue of *Vogue*. 'Casually and baldly, as Fellini would, it states what a Northern town is like: cobbled streets, smudged views of chimneys, women cooking at ranges, wet slaps of washing to be dodged by children playing in the street.' The film also involved – despite the British Board of Film Censors insisting that words like *lust* and *bitch* be removed – a serious examination of sex and social class, and altogether marked the start of the British New Wave in the cinema. 'So moving, so raucous, so pertinent', wrote the *Spectator*'s Isabel Quigly; 'a British film that shatters the pattern', agreed the *New Statesman*'s William

Whitebait; and even in the *Sunday Express*, Derek Monsey praised its 'sheer, blatant honesty', claiming that 'in this case at least, and at last, the X certificate [introduced in 1951 for adult-only films] looks like a badge of honour'. Inevitably, there was the odd facetious snicker. 'Now Britain joins the BEDROOM BRIGADE ... and adds a slice of Yorkshire pudding,' was the *Daily Herald*'s headline; 'By gum,' declared *Picturegoer*, 'this scorching analysis of bed and brass in a Yorkshire town rates its X certificate.' *Room at the Top* deservedly proved a considerable commercial success. 'Only once before in the history of the Plaza cinema [in London] has more money been taken by a film,' noted the *Birmingham Mail* at the end of February, shortly before its local opening, 'and that was *The Ten Commandments*, which ran at increased prices.' For any Brummie doubters, the paper applauded the movie for being 'up-to-the-minute in its audacious frankness'.[4]

A more British type of frankness characterised the year's most popular film, hitting the nation's screens during March. 'Mr Bell?' asks the nurse, a glamorous Shirley Eaton. 'Ding dong, you're not wrong,' replies the patient, an urbane Leslie Phillips. *Carry On Nurse* begins with an ambulance hurtling to hospital, the crew urgently wanting to hear the latest racing results; Matron is criticised for her pettifogging rules; and throughout there is a mildly subversive streak. The critics were divided. 'Script and director rely for laughs on nurses' endeavours to undress men and supervise their baths,' complained the *Manchester Guardian*, but for Dilys Powell in the *Sunday Times* this hospital farce brought 'a welcome breath of good, vulgar music-hall fun'. In due course Anthony Heap took his son to the Century. 'Something of a sequel to that surprising box office hit of 1958, "Carry On, Sergeant",' he noted, finding that 'the humour – mainly, as one might expect, anatomical – is on much the same broad, unsophisticated level'. Even so, *Carry On Nurse* is now generally viewed as the first authentic Carry On film, and in Charles Hawtrey, Kenneth Williams, Joan Sims, Hattie Jacques and Kenneth Connor the nucleus was in place for what would become a rolling – and in its early years still fresh – national institution.[5]

Following that astonishing burst between the previous April and July, the theatrical revolution continued in early 1959 to cause ripples and occasionally waves. *The Long and the Short and the Tall*, opening at the Royal Court on 7 January, was the title that the director Lindsay Anderson gave to Willis Hall's claustrophobic anti-war play about young working-class British soldiers in the Malayan jungle. Hall himself was from Hunslet, as was the 26-year-old Peter O'Toole, praised by Alan Brien for 'the arrogant casualness of his performance', having 'exactly the right blend of sardonic irreverence and aggressive satire for the unspoiled Jimmy Porter from the Lower Depths'. Perhaps 'not a great play', conceded Brien, but it was still 'a great portent . . . another one of the trail-blazers towards a live British theatre'. The following Monday, at the Birmingham Theatre Centre, saw the first performance of Harold Pinter's *The Birthday Party* since its Hammersmith debacle. It was performed by Stephen Joseph's pioneering theatre-in-the-round Studio Theatre – based in Scarborough and aimed, as Joseph told the *Birmingham Mail*, at getting audiences 'to take part in the actual excitement of creation, of imagination at work' – and the playwright had travelled to the resort for pre-tour rehearsals. 'He was in a very defensive, not to say depressed state,' recalled Alan Ayckbourn, then a 20-year-old actor charged with playing the part of Stanley. 'I remember asking Pinter about my character. Where does he come from? Where is he going to? What can you tell me about him that will give me more understanding? And Harold just said, "Mind your own fucking business. Concentrate on what's there."' In the event, the *Mail*'s critic found it 'a profitless form of playmaking' for all Pinter's technical adroitness, whereas the *Post* reckoned it 'not a pleasant play' but 'impossible to dismiss lightly'; among those providing 'its tautly theatrical effect' was Ayckbourn's 'tormented pianist'. A month later, Joan Littlewood's Theatre Workshop had another new play, in fact a quasi-musical, to present at the Theatre Royal, Stratford East. This was *Fings Ain't Wot They Used T'Be*: music and lyrics by Lionel Bart, book by five-time former convict Frank Norman and the whole, heavily cockneyfied performance set in a gambling den. 'Matter-of-fact, jocular, argumentative, and optimistic', noted Brien about what became an instant hit; in addition to Littlewood's 'slap-up, street-party production', he had especially warm words for Yootha Joyce, 'surely genuine star material', as one of the three whores: 'She looks like a leopardess – beautiful, intelligent and terrifying, all in one feline glance.'[6]

Fings appeared the week after Littlewood's most acclaimed production of 1958, *A Taste of Honey* by Shelagh Delaney, began a much-publicised run in the West End. 'Just because we have some big money now, we have no plans to leave our council house,' her 43-year-old widowed mother, down from Lancashire with the rest of the family, told the press shortly before the curtain went up at Wyndham's on 10 February. 'What has happened has made no difference between us and the neighbours.' The play got eight curtain calls (though Delaney herself declined to take a bow), Michael Foot called it 'absolutely first class', and among those in the audience were Margot Fonteyn, David Niven and Vivien Leigh. A local government official from St Pancras presumably did not join in the applause. 'How the censor came to pass this first crude play-writing effort of Shelagh Delaney, a 19-year-old Salford ex factory worker, is as much of a mystery as why any reputable management should have brought it to the West End from the East End where it first got presented under the odious auspices of the communist Theatre Workshop,' wrote Anthony Heap that night. 'A squalid and thoroughly obnoxious story of a gormless teen age slut who, neglected by her whoring mother, has a baby by a nigger seaman and is befriended and nursed through her pregnancy by an equally half-baked young homosexual, it is about as savoury as a sewer and as edifying as a dung-hill.' Next morning, Alan Dent in the *News Chronicle* tended to agree. Condemning the play's 'all-pervading murkiness', and deploring the West End succumbing to 'the kitchen-sink', his review declared it 'an odd sort of evening altogether when the one likeable character is the young coloured sailor' who 'at least knows what he wants, gets it, and gets out'.

It was the start of a short but intense storm, further fuelled by a front-page letter in the same paper on the 13th. Attacking Dent's 'air of patronage and insensitivity', John Osborne declared that the critic had 'an image of Britain which seems to be derived principally from the pages of the daily newspapers, Jane Austen, and glossy magazines devoted to gun dogs and girls at point-to-point meetings' – whereas, he went on, 'Miss Delaney has written an acutely sensitive play about a group of warm, immediately recognisable people.' Dent the next day flatly dismissed her play as 'squalor, impure and simple ... the latest example of the Lavatory School of drama', adding that 'Miss Delaney has a gift for pungent natural low dialogue, and no other discernible talent as yet.' On the 15th the Sunday heavies came to her defence – 'a dramatist born, not one manufactured by study', insisted Harold Hobson in the *Sunday Times*; 'a very intelligent, moving and original play', asserted Angus Wilson in the *Observer* – but Derek Monsey in the *Sunday Express* took no prisoners: 'It has its few moments of truth, but it also has acres of hooey, whole slices of sheer incompetence, and long stretches of boredom.' Next day the *News Chronicle* published an avalanche of letters – including one from Correlli Barnett, author of *The Hump Organisation*, calling Osborne 'a Welfare State Byron without a Missolonghi' – and by Thursday, when the editor called stumps, opinion was running three to one in Dent's favour.

T. C. Worsley in the *New Statesman*, meanwhile, frankly expressed the hope that, now the English play had shown it could 'break through the class barrier at will', its 'period of intoxication' with working-class plays would be 'short'. Worsley's hope led to an equally frank riposte from 15 Clapton Common, E5:

> So, we 'prole' playwrights must make the most of it, must we? We've been given our little say and now the hierarchy is a bit tired and we must finish amusing them, is it? . . .
>
> Now, listen to me, Mr T.C.W., I've been waiting for twelve years and it's only in the last year that I've been given my chance. I didn't write *Chicken Soup with Barley* simply because I wanted to amuse you with 'working-class types' but because I saw my characters within the compass of a personal vision. I *have* a personal vision you know, and I will not be tolerated as a passing phase. You are going to see my next play soon, and I am going to write many more and you are going to see them as well, *not* because I'm a young '*primitive*' writer out on a leash for a bit of airing but because I'm a *good* writer with a voice of my own!

A fellow playwright not quite yet in Arnold Wesker's camp was in London a couple of months later. 'I went to *A Taste of Honey*,' recorded Noël Coward, 'a squalid little piece about squalid and unattractive people.'[7]

Television was doing its bit for the revolution. There would be 'no costume dramas, no classical plays, nothing of a contemplative nature', Sydney Newman, a forceful Canadian producer who looked like a Mexican, had promised after taking over *Armchair Theatre* the previous autumn on Sunday nights on ITV, with a new emphasis on plays by British writers. By March he was declaring his ambition 'to marry the intellectual idea to the requirements of a mass audience'. Some two-thirds of Britons now had a set, with no programme still more consistently popular in early 1959 than the farcical comedy *The Army Game*. Tony Hancock continued to ride high. 'What *can* one say further than my small son's remark: "He's so funny even when he's not"?' rhetorically asked a viewer in January after the latest episode (including Rolf Harris as a sailor) of Hancock's fourth series. But for another gifted comedian, Tyneside's 'Little Waster', the small screen proved a disaster. *The Bobby Thompson Show* began on Tyne Tees in March, with a sketches format quite unsuited to his stand-up talents, and, after a reasonably promising start, the series bombed, almost wrecking Thompson's life and career.[8]

The highbrow critics could be harsh. *The Black and White Minstrel Show* may have been a viewers' favourite ('a grand show, wonderful songs, wonderful singing, great comedy and bags of talent all round'), but the *Listener*'s Ivor Brown saw 'no point in white singers (and fine ones) putting on a grotesque make-up, which has nothing to do with the natural good looks of an African, in order to sing popular songs which have nothing to do with the coloured world'. Tom Driberg found Huw Wheldon's presentation of *Monitor* – for which 'Kenneth' Russell directed on 1 March a filmed portrait of Betjeman – 'too arch for my taste and too mannered in his emphases and pauses: the upper-middle-brow's Pete Murray'. And Henry Turton compared Richard Dimbleby's fronting of *Panorama* ('almost uncomfortably polite . . . a holy attitude to the rich and glittering things of life . . . pronounces most words elaborately . . .') unfavourably to Ludovic Kennedy's of *This Week* ('achieves his atmosphere of urgency by crisp reading or a stern expression'). Turton also had it in for the anchorman of *Sunday Night at the London Palladium*. 'I understand that he has won a great following (much of his own act was devoted to telling us so), and I am glad for him,' he wrote in March. 'At the same time I cannot believe that a compère should fluff quite so often when announcing the names of performers.' Even more unkindly, Turton referred to Forsyth's 'vague resemblance to Tommy Trinder, a trickle of lame gags, a strange London accent and a matey grin'. Hughie Green, star of *Double Your Money* (in which the footballer Bobby Charlton appeared in January and won £1,000, promising to buy a car for his father, a miner), put it all in perspective. 'Highbrow – low rating,' he crisply told an interviewer.

> I'm not interested in the people who live in Mayfair and Westminster, but those in Wigan and Bermondsey ... We like people at home to feel that they might be able to answer some of the questions. That's why some of the first questions are not too hard. It's a matter of audience participation nowadays. People like to see someone like themselves on the screen. They like to feel that it might be themselves up there.[9]

It was 'The Miner-Author', a regular columnist on the *Neath Times*, who bitterly anticipated St David's Day. 'Where are our harps in these days?' asked B. L. Coombes.

> Where are the small orchestras which used to be in every village? Where are our first-class instrumentalists, or our really top-class singers? Yes, and dramatists also who can truly depict the life of our folk? How many of our choral singers can read music? No! The land of song is a comforting piece of ballyhoo to make our folk feel they can do one thing at least better than other nations.

On 1 March itself, television had two more victims, as Universal and Gaumont closed down their cinema newsreel operations; next day in Leeds, Holbeck Working Men's Club voted that members' wives should be permitted to become lady members; and on the 4th, Bertrand Russell was John Freeman's second interviewee on *Face to Face* (following on from the celebrated lawyer Norman Birkett), while in the *Romford Times* a 'quick-witted, fast-talking' would-be magnate had his first newspaper profile ('money rolls in faster than John Bloom ever dreamed it would a year ago as he tramped streets, persuading housewives to buy washing machines'). On Monday the 10th, the notoriously divisive Cutteslowe Walls in north Oxford at last came down, having according to a local journalist become not only pernicious but also illogical, given that 'the size of a wage packet may now be higher in a council home than in an owner-occupied home'. Next day, Florence Turtle visited the recently much-extended Woolworths in Dundee ('a really fine store'); Ernest Marples announced that telephone operators were to have greater freedom to be themselves and sound like human beings; and Britain's Pearl and Teddy came second at Cannes to Teddy Scholten's '*Een Beetje*'.[10]

The following day was the last *Take It From Here* written by Frank Muir and Denis Norden (though the programme limped on for a final series); Muriel Young in *Small Time* on Friday the 13th was inviting young viewers 'to meet Joan, Angelica and Jeremy the Cat'; and by the end of Saturday the last three left in the FA Cup comprised an improbable trio. 'I don't mind about Norwich particularly,' Philip Larkin conceded graciously enough about a Third Division club that had overcome Manchester United, Cardiff, Tottenham and Sheffield United. 'I can't say I want any of them to win the cup – in *my* day Luton were 3rd Div[n], Nottingham Forest, oh, 2nd I'd say, & Norwich didn't exist. None of them seems quite serious to me.' In the event the Canaries went out 1–0 in a replay against Luton the following Wednesday, the same day that 19 students from Hatfield Technical College secured a world record by piling into a telephone kiosk and two days before Madge Martin had 'a horrible shock' lunching in the Grill Room at the Regents Palace Hotel: 'Gone the old-fashioned, comfortable ordinary surroundings, gone the attentive familiar waiters, gone the large extensive menu. Now given place to harsh modern décor, colouring, lighting. Small, uncomfortable plastic tables, "floozies" as waitresses, fresh from school, paper "serviettes", food served all on one plate, wines in ugly jugs.' Still, it was better than being a horse at Aintree, where at next day's Grand National only four finished out of 34 starters, and among the 14 fallers at Becher's Brook one had to be destroyed after breaking its back. A 'disgusting, bloody circus', complained the League Against Cruel Sports, but the course's managing director, the formidable Mirabel Topham, yielded no ground: 'They don't know what they are talking about. How dare they talk of banning the race!'[11]

On the 18th, the political terms of trade changed significantly. 'Mr Iain Macleod, the immensely able Minister of Labour, unexpectedly rose in the House to announce – with obvious enjoyment, and minus notes to help him with the complicated statistics that he reeled off to the silent benches opposite and to the cheering ranks behind him – the first significant drop in unemployment figures,' reported Mollie Panter-Downes. 'He got a relieved ovation from his party, which now feels that its major election worry has been removed.' This was hardly cheering news for Gaitskell, who had something else weighing on his mind. 'Hugh made one observation to me which he had got from Mark Abrams,' recorded Crossman next day.

> One of our long-term problems, he said, is that the kind of emotions and behaviours which held the Party together in the past were all based on class. Yet, since the war, progress has all been such as to weaken these senses of class loyalty upon which the Labour Party is based. More and more the younger people don't feel class-conscious in that sense of the word, and they are actually repelled by what they feel to be the fusty, old-fashioned, working-class attitudes of the people who run the Labour Party.

The perception was probably not inaccurate: 'tired, grizzled men and grey-haired careworn women', was how a *Times* journalist had described Labour workers at the recent Southend West by-election.

Ultimately, of course, the question for the left as a whole was whether it would be able to grasp – let alone empathise with – the larger social and economic forces now at work. John Vaizey for one was sceptical. 'Surely the problem for socialists is to understand the life of the suburbs, the problems of the semi-detached society – attached in part to the working class in its origins, but to the middle class by aspiration,' he argued in that month's *Socialist Commentary* in a swingeing attack on the backward-looking romanticism of the Bethnal Green school of sociology (i.e. Young and Willmott's *Family and Kinship*, supplemented by Peter Townsend's *The Family Life of Old People*).

> These are the people who are becoming articulate, who provide the new social problems – lonely life, ambitious life, but a secure life, and a life with often surprisingly broad horizons and directed by a serious

intelligence that has enabled its people to rise into the ranks of the skilled and the white-collar people. These people call beer beer [a dig at George Orwell's preference for calling it 'wallop'], and prefer babycham. To do otherwise voluntarily is dangerously near sentimentality.

Women's magazines pointed in the same direction. Old-fashioned, unglossy, non-aspirational ones like *Home Chat* and *Everybodys* had recently folded, but to glance at an issue (14 March) that spring of the hugely successful *Woman* is to be struck by a world of colour, of burgeoning consumerist modernity, of apparent classlessness – and of a seemingly total disconnect with current affairs of any sort, let alone politics as such. Instead, jostling with 'My Strange Life' by the Duke of Bedford and 'Learning to Wait' by Anna Neagle (a regular columnist), 'The Wooden Spoon Club' assembled this week at the Brighton home of reader Eileen Timms, who with six other 'keen cooks' chatted to the magazine's cookery editor about 'everyday eating':

Pat Taylor: Half our trouble is that families are so conservative about food. I'm so tired of all this cooking a Sunday joint, but my husband and children don't like anything else.

Eileen Timms: They will if you make it sound exciting. Every now and then I promise my family a continental dish as a special Sunday treat. We call it 'going travelling'. The favourite, up to date, is Hungarian Goulash.

Mary Carter: That sounds most exciting, but isn't it terribly difficult to make?

Eileen Timms: Not really, it's only another name for veal stew . . .

Elizabeth Taylor: High tea is my problem. My children are tired of eggs.

Jane Fraser: It's mine, too. My husband likes something savoury to eat in the evening.

Pat Taylor: I find the new condensed soups and packet soups used half-strength like sauce are good for quick snacky dishes. You can make all sorts of egg, fish and meat dishes with them. I often use two kinds of soup mixed together.

The last, robustly sensible word went to Mary Carter: 'My standby for all occasions is Irish stew. It cooks itself and there's only one saucepan to wash up.'[12]

And the young, those objects of Gaitskell's special concern? They were not yet voters, but about the same time some 2,000 'candid' teenagers were surveyed for the *Woman's Mirror*. Four in five said they would bring up their own children in an organised religion; 35 per cent intended when they were 21 to vote Conservative, 35 per cent Labour, and 20 per cent were 'don't knows' or would refuse to vote; and half the girls thought it wise to marry before they were 21, their favourite dream was to be a model (no longer an air hostess), and 68 per cent said that parents were right to disapprove of premarital sex (compared to 40 per cent of the boys in the sample). The girls' favourite TV stars were Robert Horton of *Wagon Train* and Clint Walker of *Cheyenne*, while the boys plumped for Tony Hancock and Popeye; on the big screen, the respective favourites were Dirk Bogarde and Brigitte Bardot; and the majority had no favourite politician, though among those who did, Churchill was 'easily' the front-runner. What about work? Two-thirds of Britain's youth were in employment by the time they were 16. Soon afterwards, the Industrial Welfare Society published recently written, unedited essays on 'What I expect from work' by a cross-section of school-leavers:

> I have chosen to be a scientist because I have always felt a sense of vocation for this type of work. I know that society should, and will, provide me with a job suited to my capabilities. *(Norman, 18)*
>
> One thing I hope to gain is really a combination, poise, self-confidence and good taste. *(Patricia, 14¾)*
>
> I dont suppose I will have much choice of work, but I will just have to be satisfied with the Job I get and hang on to it. I will not expect high wages at first, and will learn to respect the manager. I know most of my libities will be cut out a little when I am earning my living, but theres always the feeling you get that you'r no longer a child and wish to be treated as a grown up. *(Frank, 14¼)*
>
> The Civil Service offers security which forms the basis of any man's life especially if he intends to marry. *(Raymond, 17½)*
>
> Every one wants a well decorated house with all the modern

conveniences fridge, washing and so on. I am sure a dustman could not afford this. *(Peter, 14)*

I would like to work in a shipping office, where you have a full Navel dress, shoes, shirts, tie and be well respected with all the office workers. *(Maurice, 15)*

At the moment, I have doubts about being a shipping magnate or head of an atomic power station. *(Leonard, 14)*[13]

'Seems to be leaving realism further and further behind and developing only in the direction of an atomic, sophisticated Sapper,' was Maurice Richardson's verdict in the *Observer* on 22 March on Ian Fleming's *Goldfinger*, with Bond himself becoming 'from a literary point of view ... more and more synthetic and zombie-ish'. The villain was almost called 'Goldprick', after the hot-tempered, left-wing architect Ernö Goldfinger had threatened to sue; indeed, back in the 1930s, Fleming had been among those protesting against the demolition of cottages in Willow Road, Hampstead to enable the building of Goldfinger's modernist house. Neatly enough, the book's publication almost coincided with the outcome of another Hampstead run-in, this time over Goldfinger's plans for an ultra-modern four-storey block of flats, resting on pillars over a car port, to be built in the Vale of Health. One nearby resident, Anthony Greenwood, Labour MP and chairman of the Hampstead Labour Party, claimed that it would 'help to make us a Mecca for students of architecture from other parts', but 53 other local residents disagreed, signing a petition that described the proposed development as 'out of keeping'. At the two-day public inquiry in November 1958, Goldfinger's expert witness, the recently knighted John Summerson, described 'the greater part' of the Vale of Health's architecture, full of 'dreadful little Victorian villas', as 'rubbish chaotically arranged', while Goldfinger himself not only was equally adamant that the surrounding buildings had 'neither architectural nor aesthetic merit, nor any charm in their own right' but insisted that working-class people in the Vale were fully behind him. In the event, the Housing Minister (and Hampstead MP) Henry Brooke deliberately sat on the decision so long that by the time consent was given, in early March 1959, the architect's client had gone elsewhere. 'It was Goldfinger's misfortune in the

The Bradford Empire just before demolition, 1957

Birmingham, May 1957: Aston Villa players and mascot parade the FA Cup at Villa Park

Unrationed sweets: London, 1957

Clarendon Crescent, Paddington, 1957

Notting Hill at night, 1958

Fishermen carry coracles to the River Teifi in Cardiganshire, March 1958

Cherry-picking: West Malling, Kent, July 1958

Redevelopment in Everton Heights, Liverpool, 1959

AUS

Youth club float, New Malden, Surrey, July 1959

St George's Day parade, St Helier Estate, South London, 1959

Harold Macmillan (*right*) in the north-east, January 1959

Hugh Gaitskell (*left*) at the Midland Area Miners' Gala, June 1959

Election night, October 1959

1950s,' his biographer would reflect in 2004, 'to have come up against a succession of proto-Prince Charles figures with their ill-thought-out conservative mantras of "local character" and "fitting in".'[14]

It had been a triumph for 'the Hampstead preservationist lobby', as the *Architects' Journal* noted crossly, but of course Hampstead was not London. 'Whichever party won the next election there would be an enormous amount of work for them to do,' Lord Stonham, who until recently had been Shoreditch's MP as Victor Collins, reassured the London Master Builders' Association at a luncheon in December 1958. 'Some people said that it was a shame to pull down some of the old buildings,' replied the Association's president, 'but each generation must build for its own needs and many of the new buildings were very fine indeed.' By this time work was under way on what would become the Stifford Estate – three 17-storey towers dominating the Stepney Green skyline, replacing (in Paul Barker's words) 'low terraces, built by the Mercers' Company in the early 19th century, which had lasted satis-factorily for about 130 years' – while a few months later *The Times* surveyed Bethnal Green, where 'from Spitalfields to Victoria Park the whole face of the borough is being changed'. No fewer than 15 blocks of 10 storeys or more had been built or were being built in the square mile of Bethnal Green alone; by the end of the process, a third of the borough's 50,000 inhabitants would have moved into new flats built since the war. Walking round the borough's eastern end, between Roman Road and Old Ford Road, the special correspondent observed that 'whole streets have already been demolished in the Cranbrook Street scheme', adding how 'again and again someone has chalked on the shattered walls "I lived here", with the dates'.

Not so far away, but a world apart, the City of London's redevelop-ment was moving up a gear by early 1959. The City Corporation was poised to give approval to the Paternoster scheme, with that precinct (just to the north of St Paul's) envisaged as London's premier modern shopping centre; the impending construction of large new office blocks was necessitating the widening of historic Cheapside; and between Aldersgate and Moorgate, the construction of the urban motorway that was Route 11 was pushing ahead, notwithstanding the contractors having to build a covered pit to store the 200 or so skulls and other bones they had accidentally disturbed beneath the old Barber-Surgeons'

Hall – a pit that children managed to get into at weekends, using the skulls for games of Cowboys and Indians. So too in the capital at large, but for almost the first time with a whiff of controversy that went beyond merely nimby-ism. 'All of a sudden,' noted Mollie Panter-Downes in March, 'Londoners seem to be looking around at the new London that is rising out of the bombed or demolished areas and to be asking critical questions.'[15]

What sort of questions? The LCC had just given the go-ahead to a 31-storey building on Millbank, it was negotiating with the property developer Harry Hyams a deal by which it would consent to the Seifert-designed 35-storey office tower (the future Centrepoint) at St Giles Circus in return for Hyams 'giving' it £1.5 million of adjacent land on which to build a roundabout (which never happened), and the unlovely 17-storey Bowater House had just gone up in Knightsbridge. But for the briefly much-publicised Anti-Uglies – students mainly from the Royal College of Art but also from the Architectural Association – the villain of the piece was dreary neo-Georgianism, above all in the City. Two particular targets were Sir Albert Richardson's defiantly non-modernist Bracken House (the new home of the *Financial Times*), on which the Anti-Uglies marched, and the elephantine new Barclays head office in Lombard Street, with the RCA's duffle-coated but glamorous Pauline Boty photographed outside scattering rose petals on the coffin of British Architecture. Far from a modernist in most things, Panter-Downes tended to sympathise, while like 'most Londoners' she found the LCC's housing projects 'something to be proud of' – not least 'the enormous Roehampton Estate of small skyscrapers, which you can see glittering in the sun these spring mornings as you motor in from Kingston, and which are brilliantly sited among the cedars of the Victorian suburban mansions they have replaced'.[16]

Outside London, it was Birmingham that now set the pace. On 25 February a Corporation spokesman reiterated to the local press that the Market Hall (1828), in the way of the Inner Ring Road and the redevelopment of the whole Bull Ring area (which already included 'The Big Top', the giant, 160-foot City Centre House shop-and-office block erected by the rising local and increasingly national property developer Jack Cotton), was to be demolished 'as soon as possible'. Next day, opening the British Road Federation's exhibition ('Town Roads for

Today – and Tomorrow') at the Civic Centre, Alderman Frank Price, about to step down after five years chairing the Public Works Committee, declared that people who advocated banning cars from city centres were like 'ostriches' and expressed the hope that the city's Inner Ring Road, due for completion in 1969, would give a lead to the rest of the country. And on the 27th the *Birmingham Mail* issued a 'Progress Report on the New Birmingham', accompanied by a photograph of the broad sweep of the showcase first section of the Inner Ring Road, starting to take shape in Smallbrook:

> In and around the city centre, building work totalling some £65,000,000 is now in progress. Enormous changes have been made in the past five years. But this is only the beginning.
>
> Ugly old buildings are being wiped away. The city centre changes almost daily. The visitor returns to find white new buildings mushrooming amid the architectural debris of the past. The city's list of post-war new buildings, either completed or proposed, covers no fewer than 45 substantial projects.

Price himself – Labour, mid-30s, from Birmingham's slums, previously a toolmaker, now a public relations officer – was quoted: 'In 20 years from now the future citizens of Birmingham will look back on this period of their city's history and will say: "This was Birmingham's finest and most courageous period."' But soon afterwards the *Mail* asked this 'tough, ambitious realist with more than a touch of the visionary' whether any mistakes had been made in the city's redevelopment plans. 'Obviously we have made some,' he replied. 'At times I think we should stand still and try to get into perspective what we are attempting to do. I think certain buildings in the city could have been improved upon. But, by and large, I think a magnificent effort has been made.' At this stage almost the only detectable opposition to all this came from small traders. 'Ask any local retailer [in Smallbrook] for his views on this wonderful city of the future,' wrote F. D. Walkley to the *Mail*. 'He will reply in words not usually found in the dictionary.' J. F. Munro agreed: 'Moderate redevelopment in any city is welcome, but wholesale bulldozing is another matter. Small traders, after years of service to city and citizens, are being indiscriminately turned out

– many to face ruin and the end of all their efforts.' Still, a city's pride
was at stake, and in April the pedestrian subway under Smallbrook
Ringway opened – the first in the country.

Alderman Price featured prominently in *Who Cares? A New Way
Home*, a BBC documentary about slum clearance in Birmingham
broadcast on 24 February. Calling the slums 'caves' and 'holes in the
wall', he argued that young families moving to new blocks of flats
would benefit from the open space around, opposed mews-type development, conceded that the lack of the extended family on the new
estates was a problem – and claimed that Birmingham was on the way
to becoming 'one of the most beautiful cities in Europe'. The TV
programme as a whole was relentlessly upbeat. 'One must admire the
drive and enthusiasm of the Housing Department,' declared the
presenter, Douglas Jones, who at one point asked the city engineer, Sir
Herbert Manzoni, about the 'comprehensive manner' of the slum-
clearance programme and, specifically, whether people were enthusiastic. 'Of course it's difficult for those who are being disturbed,' Manzoni
replied, adding that he usually found them 'getting enthusiastic' once
they were in their new homes.[17]

The documentary was transmitted barely a fortnight after BBC television's *Second Enquiry*, in which (after an interval of over six years)
Robert Reid paid a return visit to Glasgow and its housing issues,
including the redevelopment of the Gorbals. 'This programme didn't
mince matters,' noted one impressed critic. 'Years of neglect have
created a colossal problem; it may be twenty years before Glasgow
clears the last of its tenements. But one felt it would be done; and that
this time the citizens of this "no mean city" will not have to leave Britain
as their fathers did to find a decent life, but will receive their birthright
in their own country.' Reid's programme won from the Viewers' Panel
a notably high Reaction Index of 78. 'Without seeing, who would
believe that people had to live in such awful surroundings in Britain
today?' asked a housewife, while a chemical worker's wife declared,
'Surely slum clearance which is needed as obviously as this demands
tip-top priority above everything else.' Even so, the odd comment did
query whether Glaswegian slum-dwellers possessed a high-enough
quota of the self-help ethos. From a research engineer's wife: 'These
people seemed quite content to put their names on a list for council

houses and then sit back and wait. My husband and I have struggled to buy our house.' Perhaps inevitably, several viewers took exception to the 'mournful and monotonous mouth organ music'.

By this time the Sub-Convener of Glasgow's Housing Committee was David Gibson, an idealistic, high-energy left-winger (and former Independent Labour Party stalwart) described by Miles Glendinning and Stefan Muthesius, historians of the tower block, as 'arguably the most remarkable of Western Europe's postwar municipal housing leaders'. Gibson's passion was to rehouse Glasgow slum-dwellers in the city itself, not to banish them to overspill estates on the periphery; his means was the high-rise flat. 'Gibson,' they note,

> intuitively grasped that, if the multi-storey blocks proposed by the planners for mixed development use in the CDAs [Comprehensive Development Areas] were instead built by the Committee *outside* those areas on gap-sites, much higher blocks would be possible, unfettered by planning restrictions and acquisition delays. This would allow a cycle of decanting within the city, without resorting to overspill.

There ensued during 1958–9 'much agonised discussion' on the Housing Committee, but for the moment its natural conservatism prevailed.

One approach, though, that lamentably failed to produce any worthwhile discussion was Tom Brennan's in his book *Reshaping a City*, published in early 1959. Focusing especially on Govan (run-down centre of the shipbuilding industry and home to Glasgow Rangers) and Pollok (site of a huge peripheral estate), his 'arresting conclusion', as the *TLS* reviewer fairly summarised it, was that 'the process of decanting people to the outskirts and radically rebuilding the centre may have gone far enough and is not the true answer to the situation as it now exists', especially given that 'overcrowding in the central districts is no longer serious and the dispersal of industry and services has not kept pace with the dispersal of population'. What was the true answer? For 'the majority' of Govan's population, Brennan himself argued, 'the obvious solution, if it could be managed, would be to make available to them the components for a better life – not in a new town in ten or twenty years' time, but in Govan now. The idea should be one of repairing, reviving, and thereby renewing Govan rather than waiting until it has deteriorated sufficiently to be replaced altogether.' It was an analysis backed up by detailed evidence of how in Govan's older properties the occupants (who revealed little wish to move to new towns or overspill estates) were already using their new prosperity to upgrade their living conditions, and backed up also by a call for 'a judicious combination of commercial, public and private enterprise' to stimulate renovation – a very different route to Glasgow becoming, through local-authority demolition and local-authority redevelopment, 'Corporation-owned and Corporation-managed'.[18]

If a similar diagnosis had appeared at this time about any other large British city, it would almost certainly have received an equally nugatory response from the activator class. 'It will be of particular interest to the residents of 375 of Liverpool's darkest acres, those 39,000 people living in the forest of 90 to 130-years-old terraces of the municipal wards of Netherfield, Vauxhall, St Domingo and Westminster,' promised the *Liverpool Echo* in November 1958 about a new exhibition, *Liverpool of the Future*, on the Everton Heights Redevelopment Scheme, in which some 6,500 houses were to be replaced by mixed development, including 21-storey blocks of flats. 'They will see what the future holds for the dreary, narrow streets and blackened houses which have been their familiars for so long.' The paper went bullishly on about this 'attempt at creating a closely-knit community':

Already the new North Liverpool skyline is taking shape, with the majesty of Creswell Mount crowning the slope on which are huddled the mean and narrow streets of the old Liverpool.

The two new blocks, The Braddocks, already have nestling near them a number of modern buildings, colourful and fresh in contrast to the black dreariness surrounding them. They are the forerunners of what is to come.

It is a brave project, charged with imagination, but well capable of realisation.

The old Everton Heights had one shop for every 65 people, and when 'a brains trust composed of four leading council officials, with a senior lecturer in social science at Liverpool University as chairman, answered questions on the scheme, the audience's main concern, after the question of the housing, was what would be the fate of the little shops'.

Little shops were not on Anthony Wedgwood Benn's mind when, the following February, he took Boris Krylov, a Russian academic, on a tour of Bristol. This featured 'the worst slums' plus 'an old smoky school with overcrowded classes and no proper playground' plus 'the prefabs' and 'the horrible, dull red brick pre-war council houses', before 'finally the new housing':

> I took him to Barton House, the 16-storey block of flats in the centre of the Barton Hill redevelopment. We went to the roof and then knocked on a flat door and were shown round by a railwayman and his wife. It was lovely and they were very happy.
>
> Then we went out to Hartcliffe estate – a 50,000-people new suburb. It really is a lovely place, well laid out and planned with different types of houses and the finest school I have ever seen anywhere in the world. I spotted it in the distance, not knowing what it was. But we walked in the front door bravely and asked if we could look round. It was Withywood Comprehensive School and the headmaster insisted on taking us on a tour. We started by going up in the lift to the top and walked down and through the beautifully equipped laboratories and classrooms. The school has enormous playing fields, two gymnasia and lovely design in aluminium and glass.

'It really knocked Boris sideways,' concluded Benn.[19]

So too in Newcastle, where in March – not long after reports about the local authority's intention to demolish Dobson's Royal Arcade and replace it with a roundabout – the City Council decided to proceed with T. Dan Smith's recommendation, as chairman of the Housing Committee, to build high-rise blocks of flats (12 to 15 storeys) in the slum-cleared or to-be-cleared areas of Heaton Park Road, Shieldfield and Cruddas Park. This last was just off the Scotswood Road in Newcastle's West End and near to Rye Hill, a particularly rough area where in the mid-1950s the Tory-run council had been responsible for erecting the much-criticised Noble Street flats: five storeys, no lifts, badly designed, done on the cheap, a slum before the first tenants moved in. The new breed of flats, insisted Smith, would be wholly different. 'The Council need have no fear at all about this scheme,' he declared after listing in great detail all the mod cons and suchlike (including gas water-heater, gas-heated clothes-drying cabinet, full-size bath and centralised aerial system) that would be available. 'The external is as attractive as any block of flats I have seen built anywhere else, and more attractive than most. The flats will make a tremendous contribution not only to the housing problem but to the brightening up of areas which hitherto have been depressing.' The female perspective came from a fellow councillor, Mrs Wynne-Jones. 'It has always surprised me that flats have not been popular in this part of the world, and we hear people say "I would rather have a proper house," she observed. 'Here, quite obviously, the architect and the people responsible have not forgotten that it is the ordinary, practical running of a house that is going to matter so tremendously to the women who are to live there.'

Manchester since the war had been rather slow to embrace the modern high-rise, but no longer. 'Albert Bridge House shows signs of blowing some of the cobwebs away, but they have been there a long, long time and it looks as if a howling gale will be required finally to dislodge them,' was the somewhat grudging appraisal by the *Architects' Journal* in April of a newly completed 18-storey block to house Manchester's tax officials. Elsewhere in the city centre, work had just started or was about to start on not only the Co-operative Wholesale Society and Co-operative Insurance Society cluster of buildings (including the 25-storey CIS tower modelled on Chicago's Inland Steel Building) but also Piccadilly Plaza, described by a latter-day Pevsner as 'a huge commercial superblock' that 'completely fails to take any account of its surroundings', though 'the sheer confidence and scale impress'. The residential nettle was also being grasped. News that an 11-storey block was to be built in Chorlton-on-Medlock once 54 acres had been cleared was welcomed in November 1958 by the *Manchester Evening News*, which 'has campaigned for years for multi-storey flats blocks, well designed and equipped, to be built near the city centre for people who wish to stay in Manchester'.

In nearby Salford, such good progress was being made in major multi-storey building programmes that by April 1959 the slum-clearance schedule there was expected to speed up – with most of Walter

Greenwood's 'Hanky Park' (now in the Ellor Street Clearance Areas) likely to be cleared by the end of the year. 'It is a district of people whose roots are firmly embedded in the hard ground, and there is every sign that they are not going to take kindly to the sudden upheaval,' observed a visiting reporter. 'There was a sense of uneasiness around, which is in many cases hidden by a joke or a resolution to face the new life – the sort of resolution one reaches when facing a visit to the dentist to have that worrying tooth removed. The jokes take the form of suggestions that the Royal Oak Hotel [i.e. a pub] should be removed en bloc as it is and put down in the new area of habitation, a joke obviously based on a feeling of lack of security.' Some were happy to move – 'mostly women who see in the new life a chance to throw the kids into a bath at night-time with the steaming hot water coming out of a tap instead of a kettle' – but tellingly, 'everybody in the area' wanted 'to go to Southgarth [likely to be Salford's last new council estate built of houses] and don't want to be on the eighth floor of any flats'. 'They all know they are going,' concluded the reporter, 'but to where, and to what, they do not know.' Later in the month, the Housing Committee announced plans for 15-storey blocks in the St Matthias Clearance Area – Salford's highest yet.[20]

Modernity did not try to spare the town of the crooked spire. 'Chesterfield's old, cobbled Market Place, which for centuries has been the hub of the town's shopping area, seems doomed to disappear,' began the *Derbyshire Times*'s story in early 1959, with the Labour-run Town Council expected on 3 February to agree to move the market area some 400 yards, demolish the old Market Hall, and instead develop a modern shopping centre in the Market Place. At the meeting, discussion was predictably 'stormy', as was the 23–11 vote in favour of the plan. 'A lot of this is sentimentality,' was the (ultimately unsuccessful) opposition-quashing line of Councillor H. C. Martin, chairman of the Town Planning Committee. 'I have had the same feeling. I was reared in Chesterfield. It is my town. I don't like to see the Market Place developed, but am I to allow morbid sentimentality to prejudice the future development of the town?'

A few weeks later, in the city of the dreaming spires, a local paper endorsed John Summerson's charge that Oxford was too timid in its attitude to new buildings, but chose not to blame the Planning Committee. 'The fact is that there is still a large body of public opinion which is a great deal more timid than the Committee seems to be,' argued the *Oxford Mail*. 'These people, to whom high buildings and modern design are the Devil's works, make the noise that frightens Committees – be they City, college or University – and ensure that new buildings in public places must be either archaic or tame.' Even so, the *Mail* was pleased that Arne Jacobsen, 'the greatest Danish architect', had been invited to design the new St Catherine's College, while Sir William Holford had been asked to scrutinise the plan for the redevelopment of St Ebbe's: 'They, and more like them, must be encouraged to do their finest and boldest work here. Only in this way can a modern Oxford be created worthy to stand beside historic Oxford.'

Soon afterwards, in Lancashire, the fourth estate was even more trenchant. 'I shudder to think what posterity will say about us when they see the buildings we are handing down to them,' claimed Councillor S. Preston about 'Picasso-like buildings' at the monthly meeting of Orrell Council, in the context of a new school being built in the district. 'I do not see anything picturesque in them, but there is apparently little we can do about it.' Other councillors seemingly agreed, but not the *Wigan Examiner*: 'The architects who design these schools are professional men who have spent a lifetime learning their business. Their designs are fundamentally good and reflect the mood and character of the age we live in. That laymen don't like them, is a point in their favour, for laymen have never liked advances in the arts.' After a pop at local authorities' penchant for 'neo this and neo that' in the tradition of the 'revolting imitation Gothic which our Victorian grandfathers have inflicted on us in such vast and nauseating quantities', the paper went on:

> From our new schools, our children will derive considerable benefit of an unobtrusive kind. They will subconsciously learn to appreciate the beauty of unfussy, functional design. They will benefit from the light and space which modern methods and modern materials allow the designer to incorporate in his conceptions and, since they will not be surrounded by clutter, let us hope their minds will be uncluttered too.

In short: 'More power to the modern architects say we.'[21]

So also, unsurprisingly, said the architects themselves. 'A battle has to be fought against public ignorance and apathy, and sometimes aggressive retrogression,' declared Basil Spence in November 1958 in his inaugural presidential address at the Royal Institute of British Architects. He made clear his particular target:

> If ever an objective of the lowest common denominator of ignorance and bad architecture had to be achieved, the planning committee precisely fits the bill. That is my own personal conviction . . .
>
> We are in an adventurous new period of architectural development, and architects must be helped, not hindered, by this form of bureaucracy if we are to allow our native genius to flourish in the future.

It had of course to be native genius of a particular type: around this time Quinlan Terry, a student at the Architectural Association, was submitting classical designs, only to be informed he would fail if he continued to do so. Yet though the supremely arrogant example of Le Corbusier still bewitched, at least some rising architectural stars were showing a degree of critical detachment. 'Graeme Shankland felt that Le Corbusier's tendency to make man in his own image, to project this image on society and often to impose a formal pattern regardless of circumstances, in some degree vitiated his contribution,' noted in February a listener to a Third Programme appraisal of the exhibition *Le Corbusier and the Future of Architecture* at the Building Centre. 'James Stirling expressed the opinion that the spatial luxury which was necessary to all his achievement was now beginning to detract from the viability of his forms, and proposed that in the post-Corbusier world a more down-to-earth empiricism was to be desired.' Soon afterwards Peter ('Joe') Chamberlin – of Chamberlin, Powell & Bon, which had recently won the commission for a massive reconstruction of Leeds University and would soon be tackling the Barbican – gave a lecture at the Housing Centre on 'High Density Housing' that seems to have been modernism at its best:

> His general approach was to analyze the qualities that could make life in a closely-packed urban environment enjoyable, and then to suggest how these qualities could be achieved in new developments.

People had fled to the suburbs, not because they disliked high density as such, but because of the negative qualities of the central areas as they knew them – noise, smoke, smell, dirt, dangerous traffic and a general restrictiveness as to the detail of daily life: there was nowhere to potter around and 'do it yourself,' pets were often prohibited and so on. These negative qualities were not essential to high density living, it was our job as architects to get round them, and offer many 'plus' qualities to set against them. A dazzling slide of a Van Gogh pavement café night scene – intensely evocative of the excitement of eating out together – suggested the sort of quality he had in mind.

Other specific, attainable, with-the-grain recommendations followed, prompting a revealing reflection at the end of the admiring report in the *Architects' Journal*: 'The approach to high density housing from the humanist angle of "how can we make city life as enjoyable as possible" ought not to be unusual – but it certainly is, and how.'

Ian Nairn was surely in sympathy. 'The Antiseptic City' was the title of a typically trenchant recent *Encounter* piece, in which he argued that the missing dimension in too many projects, however good they looked as architectural models, was 'ordinary people in all their idiosyncrasy and variety of temperament'. As a result, the new urban pattern taking shape in London (including much-vaunted Roehampton) was 'chopped-up, monotonous, inhuman yet overcrowded – and this in a city whose outstanding virtue is in its contrasts and sudden incongruities and irrepressible vitality'. Nairn went on to explain his credo – one that 'so few' modern architects were 'prepared to accept in practice' – namely, that 'buildings ought to fit the people who will use them':

There should be no building for a mean, but simultaneous building for every kind of extreme; and everybody is extreme in one way or other. On a larger scale the city should be a place for everyone – tarts as well as good girls, spivs as well as model husbands and honest men . . . You can no more separate good and evil to create a clean, rational, social-minded city than you can separate the poles of a magnet.

Condemning 'use-zoning' (i.e. zoning by function) as 'a disaster for the vitality of a city, which makes its impact from the multiplicity of things all thrown together', and emphasising the need for 'some continuous change for the eye to hook on to', as opposed to 'separate staccato impressions, however grand', Nairn summed up his advice to architects 'in nine words: look at people, look at places, think for yourselves'. The alternative, he signed off, was that 'we will rapidly build ourselves an inhumane, cliché-ridden, and antiseptic nut-house'.[22]

The search for the right kind of urbanism was fuelled in part by a degree of deepening disenchantment – arguably much exaggerated by commentators and observers – with the post-war trend of dispersal to new, outlying estates. Take Coventry, where early in 1959 not only did a survey of Tile Hill reveal a huge gap between planned and actual amenities (no community centre, youth centre, branch library, day nursery, swimming baths or cinema) but a report by the local Labour Party found generally that 'the tenant feels that the centre of authority is too remote from him', with the council being 'too big and impersonal, despite the best efforts of the elected representatives and officers concerned'. In Birmingham the *Mail* soon afterwards focused on Kingshurst, an overspill estate (out past Castle Bromwich) with almost 9,000 residents. Eyes and ears told different stories: the reporter 'saw pleasant homes, with bright paint and neat curtains, wide roads, rural street names, grass and the wide, wide vista of winter sky that no central area can offer', but he 'heard, as I talked to people who live there, a tale of bewilderment, disinterest, loneliness and dislike'. Lonely, bored young wives, almost nothing for young people to do ('they hang around together, talking and daring each other,' said a mother, adding that 'wickedness is sure to happen'), old people cut off from their Birmingham roots left 'to wilt and pine in their new homes', poor and expensive public transport – the litany was becoming increasingly familiar. 'In solving the problem of homes and city overcrowding by "spilling" into the country, have we raised a host of subtler problems which will be much harder to solve?' wondered the reporter. 'Can we form a community from people who still persist in feeling that they are exiles from somewhere else?'

By this time, moreover, relatively few – certainly relatively few activators – believed that the New Towns were necessarily the answer. *Socialist Commentary* in April featured a coruscating analysis by Nottingham University's Geoffrey Gibson of 'New Town Ghettos', in which he argued that the planners had got it fundamentally wrong – above all through their misguided concept of the self-contained neighbourhood unit, which had almost completely failed to foster community spirit. A *cri de coeur* came soon afterwards from Nicholas Hill, who had lived for the past 15 months in the new town at Hemel Hempstead. 'There is no imagination or planning behind the lay-out of the community,' he wrote to the *Spectator*.

> The houses are jerry-built ... The few shops are built and look like matchboxes. They are situated at the edge of the community rather than in the middle, and sell a meagre selection of second-rate goods ... The community resembles a modern chicken farm, every chicken alone in its identical box ... Let someone who loves people, and not uniformity – beauty, and not drabness – build the next town.[23]

'I proceeded to Turnham Green (10.30 a.m.) and watched some of the marchers move off, split into contingents by the police, presumably to inconvenience the traffic less,' recorded a non-committal Henry St John on 30 March. 'There were several hundred of them, average age about 20, of the intellectual type, hardly a hat among them.' It was Easter Monday, and whereas the pioneer 1958 march for nuclear disarmament had gone from London to Aldermaston, this time (under CND's auspices) it was the other way round, an implicit recognition that direct action was not going to close down the Atomic Weapons Research Establishment. Later that day, the march – with architecture the only profession to be represented by its own banner – was some four miles long as it approached Trafalgar Square, and, according to another, more sympathetic observer, 'the vast majority were quite ordinary young men and women, serious, politically minded and indistinguishably working and middle class'. Up on the Ayrshire coast (Glasgow's 'lung'), the first sunny weather of the holiday weekend attracted thousands of 'flu-wearied, smog-ridden' city-dwellers. 'At Ayr railway station where 14 special trains brought around 3,000 visitors, it was the good behaviour of the crowd that caught the attention of the staff,' noted a local paper. '"The best-behaved holiday crowd we've had in years," said one official. "Not a rowdy among them."'[24]

Further down the west coast, Nella Last in Barrow had at last succumbed to the urgings of her children and neighbours by acquiring a television set. 'Knowing my husband's love of an old time Variety show I tuned in to the Bob Monkhouse Show on ITV – a really good show & to see & hear my poor dear chuckle and laugh was a real pleasure,' she wrote on the first Saturday of April. Even so, caution still prevailed:

> An hour, or one & a half hours at most, is quite enough, & I will have to vet programmes on TV as closely – no, more so, than on wireless. Last week in Emergency Ward 10, a man died under a serious operation & it did upset my husband – lingered the next day – while any violence or 'savage' grimaces make him dream he says. A Quiz programme is his delight – we both grieved for that 'Double or Quits' contestant, who so gallantly tried to turn £500 into £1,000 – & lost the lot. I've *no* courage like that!

Nella was never a likely candidate for *Drumbeat* – debuting that evening as BBC's latest hopeful riposte to *Oh Boy!*, with Adam Faith and the John Barry Seven among the regulars – while on the radio she missed 'Faces in the Crowd', a Third Programme talk in which Asa Briggs regretted how social history lacked the 'academic prestige' of political history. Next evening, also on the Third, *New Poetry* included a reading of Philip Larkin's as yet unpublished 'The Whitsun Weddings' ('any supercilious note should be rigorously excluded', insisted the poet in advance) – presumably not listened to by Jean Bird, receiving several doses of pethidine that day at a maternity hospital before on the Monday, under general anaesthetic, giving birth to her son James through a complicated high-forceps delivery:

> When I came round, the baby had already been taken away. It seems quite shocking now [1996], but it was par for the course in those days. He'd had a difficult start, and the drill in those days was 'cot nursing', which meant the baby wouldn't be touched any more than was absolutely necessary for 48 hours. He was kept in the nursery, so I didn't even see him until he was nearly two days old. I remember they brought him along in his cot and left him by my bed just before the 48 hours was up.

Of course I was desperate to look at him and hold him, so I picked him up and put him to the breast. He was ravenous – he'd only had a bottle of half-strength milk – and latched on straightaway.

'But then,' she added, 'the curtains were pulled back and I got a real ticking off for getting him out of his cot too soon.'[25]

During the interim, on Tuesday the 7th, the year's seminal economic event had taken place, one with powerful political resonance. 'Budget statement was very effective,' recorded a satisfied Macmillan, who for many months had been pushing Heathcoat Amory hard to do exactly what at last he now delivered. 'The C of Ex[r] got rather tired at the end of his 2 hour speech & we thought he was going to faint. But he got through.' Amory himself was sufficiently recovered to give a television interview in the evening, reassuringly calling it a 'Steady Ahead' Budget, but in reality it was far more expansionary than that: ninepence off the standard rate of income tax, cuts in purchase tax, twopence off a pint of beer, and altogether, as the *FT* approvingly noted, 'a Budget of large concessions', designed to 'restore economic confidence' and 'combat recession'. Even *The Times* – temporarily forgetful of its earlier, anti-Keynesian sternness at the time of Thorneycroft's resignation, but instead mindful that this was almost certainly an election year – was similarly positive, after managing with a certain amount of legerdemain to satisfy itself that consumers were 'not getting more than their share' of Amory's largesse. Among the politicians, Reginald Maudling in the Budget debate robustly insisted that disapproving talk by the Shadow Chancellor, Harold Wilson, of 'a consumers' spree' was a 'particularly silly' way of describing what was in practice 'leaving more money in the pockets of the public to spend as they wish', but it was Wilson's colleague Richard Crossman who really – albeit privately – let the cat out of the bag. 'My first reaction, I am afraid, was that I had saved about £100 on my new Humber Hawk by postponing delivery until after the Budget,' he wrote. 'In fact, as far as I can calculate, I shall also get nearly £200 in reduced income tax.' On more mature reflection, the following week, he would call it 'a selfish, egotistical Budget', but his rival diarist had already had the right of it on the 9th: 'Budget has been *very* well received in the country & by the Press,' noted Macmillan. And he added: 'The 64,000 dollar question remains – When? I am feeling more & more *against* a "snap" election.'[26]

There were few complaints about the Budget in middle-class Woodford, which was not only Churchill's constituency but also the subject this spring, two years after *Family and Kinship*, of intensive study by Peter Willmott and Michael Young. They found, further out on the Central Line but not as far as Debden, an utterly different world from Bethnal Green – from where (or thereabouts) many upwardly mobile Woodfordians had come over the years. 'How few people there seemed to be in Woodford, and how many dogs!' they wrote in their subsequent *Family and Class in a London Suburb* (1960). 'In Bethnal Green people are vigorously at home in the streets, their public face much the same as their private. In Woodford people seem to be quieter and more reserved in public, somehow endorsing [Lewis] Mumford's description of suburbs as the apotheosis of "a collective attempt to lead a private life."' Almost two-thirds of their general sample were middle class, roughly reflecting Woodford's composition: a typical middle-class house had 'thick pile carpets, rooms fashionably decorated with oatmeal paper on three walls and a contrasting blue on the fourth, bookcases full of Charles Dickens, Agatha Christie and *Reader's Digest* condensed books, above the mantelpiece a water-colour of Winchelsea, VAT 69 bottles converted into table-lamps, French windows looking out on to a terra-cotta Pan in the middle of a goldfish pond, the whole bathed in a permanent smell of Mansion polish'. And Willmott and Young were struck by the district's 'general adoption of middle-class standards', with electricians and bank clerks (and their respective wives) wearing 'the same sort of clothes', driving 'the same sort of cars' and inside their homes watching 'the same television set from the same mass-produced sofa'.

Yet for all this, much of the middle-class vox pop – gathered while the authors held glasses of sherry 'gingerly in the left hand while unchivalrously scribbling notes with the right' – revealed keen status anxieties and resentments:

> There's all this emphasis on material possessions. People seem to think that if they've got something you haven't got they're better than you are. And they're not really what I would call well-educated people. They're

people who've got the money but not the educational background to go with it.

As soon as next door knew we'd got a washing machine, they got one too. Then a few months later we got a fridge, so they got a fridge as well. I thought all this stuff about keeping up with the Joneses was just talk until I saw it happening right next door.

The working class is better off, which is a good thing *if* they know how to use their money. Which they don't, I'm sorry to say.

I think the richest class today is the working class, and they don't know how to spend their money. They waste money on fridges, washing machines, TVs and cars. It's the old tale – the person born to money knows how to use it, the person new to getting it doesn't.

Those people from the East End are good-hearted folk, but you couldn't make friends of them. Sounds a bit snobbish, I know, but we've got nothing in common with them.

Unsurprisingly, the working-class interviewees were far from oblivious to this censorious disapproval:

In Woodford they haven't got much, but they're what I class as jumped-up snobs. They think they're better than what you are.

The middle-class people here are snobs. They put on airs and graces. They are all out for show – nothing in their stomachs but nice suits on.

Some people here are more classy – or they try to be. They're just the same as we are, but they try to be something different.

'Inside people's minds,' concluded Willmott and Young about this Essex suburb, 'the boundaries of class are still closely drawn. Classlessness is not emerging there. On the contrary, the nearer the classes are drawn by the objective facts of income, style of life and housing, the more are middle-class people liable to pull them apart by exaggerating the differences subjectively regarded.' In short, there were 'still two Woodfords in 1959, and few meeting-points between them'.

Such sociological concerns, though, were not the stuff of parliamentary debates – unlike the question of the moral state of the nation, on its way to becoming a hardy perennial. 'The disease is in the body politic itself,' declared Lord Denning in the House of Lords the day after the

Budget. 'It is a loosening of moral standards, a decay of religion. It is up to us, each of us, to do our part in leading our country to a strong and healthy opinion, condemning wrongdoing and upholding the right.' Perhaps he should have visited Gardenstown in Banff, a male-dominated fishing village (population 1,200) that was a stronghold of the Plymouth Brethren. From there, earlier in April, the national press reported not only the disapproval directed towards 'fair-haired' Mona Tennant (manager's wife in the solitary pub) for wearing slacks, but also the case of Diana Norman, the only girl to wear make-up. 'I find the Lord is sufficient,' replied a Plymouth Brethren girl, her long hair tied in a bun, when asked her views. Elsewhere in Scotland, at almost the same time, the *Weekly News* (from the hugely successful D. C. Thomson stable in Dundee) published a letter by Miss A. F. of Maryhill, Glasgow in which the 17-year-old complained how she found it 'very humiliating' to be spanked with a slipper by her mother after she had returned from a dance after midnight, and asking what other readers thought. 'Miss A.F. should be thankful her mother uses only a slipper on her,' reckoned 18-year-old Miss J. S. of Dundee. 'My aunt keeps a tawse, and regularly warms my fingers and posterior with it.' And among 'dozens' of other letters, 19-year-old Miss A. Davidson of Drongan spoke for the majority: 'I'm always home by 10.30. As long as she is under her parents' roof, they have a right to spank her, whether she is 17 or 37.'[27]

It all depended. Few had a bad word to say about Russ Conway – twinkle-eyed pianist, regular on *The Billy Cotton Band Show*, favourite of the Queen Mother, his honky-tonk 'Side Saddle' topping the charts in early April – but the troubled rock 'n' roll singer Terry Dene (former bicycle messenger, timber-yard labourer, plumber's mate and odd-job boy in a clock factory) was another matter. 'DENE DRINKS CHAMPAGNE – to the Army that found he was unfit,' announced the *Daily Mirror* on Easter Saturday, two days after his discharge from National Service after only eight weeks, most of them spent in psychiatric wards. 'The Army has made a new man of me,' he told the press from his 'luxury flat' in Gloucester Place, Marylebone. 'I was a crazy, mixed-up kid. Now I have been straightened out. I hope my public will stay loyal to me. It will be several months before I can even think of going back to the stage.' In fact, less than three weeks later, the manager of a cinema in Burnley went on stage to test audience reaction to the news that Dene had been booked as part of a forthcoming Dickie Valentine bill touring mainly northern cinemas. 'The response was shocking,' a Star circuit executive revealed. 'They booed. But during the interval we talked to teenagers individually and discovered they were anxious to welcome Terry.' On 20 April the *Derby Evening Telegraph* broke the news to locals that the following Sunday, the 26th, would be the start of Dene's comeback, at the Majestic on the outskirts of Derby. 'He is able to make the Chaddesden stage appearance at short notice because he recovered from his breakdown earlier than expected.'

Coming hard on the heels of Marty Wilde's exemption from National Service on account of flat feet, a week of controversy ensued. 'In view of the fact that he is a "rock and roll" expert, has the War Office consulted the Admiralty as to whether he would be suitable for sea service?' asked Herbert Morrison in the Commons, while Gerald Nabarro promised, 'I would have smartened-up Terry Dene's parade for him.' And in Derby itself, not only were there hostile letters in the local paper – 'I wonder what the veterans of two wars are thinking of it' and 'In my opinion the only emotional strain Terry Dene suffered was the fact that his wages dropped from hundreds of pounds per week to a mere 17*s* 6*d* and he wasn't man enough to take it' – but anti-Dene slogans (such as 'GET ON PARADE!' and 'GET YER 'AIR CUT') were daubed overnight in yellow on the Chaddesden Majestic. On Saturday, despite protest letters to the BBC, Dene appeared on *Drumbeat*, and then on Sunday evening came the big test:

> As soon as he appeared cheers were mingled with a storm of booing. Some of his songs were completely drowned by the din as the barrackers jeered, booed and chanted: 'LEFT RIGHT LEFT RIGHT.' As the boos reached a crescendo so his fans cheered even louder . . . right through his 16-minute act.
>
> And while the uproar raged, Terry Dene sang and quivered, oblivious to the noise. His show went on.

'That was good,' he told a journalist afterwards. 'I think they still like me.' Sadly, they did not. Dene's next single, 'There's No Fool Like a Young Fool', failed to trouble the charts, and by the end of the year he was a forgotten man.[28]

'M still looking pretty grim with no top teeth and it seems likely to remain so since they won't make her an upper denture unless she has all her lower teeth out as well,' related Anthony Heap on Sunday the 26th after a second visit to his mentally unwell wife Marjorie (who during the winter had gone missing) at Horton Hospital, Epsom. 'To which, of course, she won't agree and I don't blame her ... Why *must* these dentists be so damned awkward?' Three days later, 11-year-old Gyles Brandreth, at a prep school near Deal, bought Rolos at the tuck shop ('They don't have Aeros or Spangles, but can order them if enough people want them') and Accrington Stanley had their last match of the season, going down 5–0 at Reading, barely a week after a 9–0 drubbing at Tranmere. 'It is now very strongly rumoured that 11+ results come out next Tues,' noted Judy Haines on Thursday. 'I fluctuate between quiet confidence in a satisfactory result to agonies in case it isn't.' Friday, 1 May was a suitable date for the consecration service of the leftish Mervyn Stockwood at Southwark Cathedral (Princess Margaret present 'in a grey two-piece velvet suit and a pink hat'), while elsewhere the local comedian Arthur English crowned the Fleet Carnival Queen ('Gor blimey, there are some real smashers up there'), Nella Last watched 'that moronic Army Game', Richard Crossman addressed Labour's annual rally at Grantham ('just over 100 people, stolid and totally apathetic, all of them waiting for the dance to begin'), and, in the small hours, the plucky but limited Brian London was knocked out by world heavyweight champion Floyd Patterson in Indianapolis, despite the support of 'a party from the north of England, who had flown over, complete with bowlers and umbrellas'.[29]

Next afternoon, Marian Raynham in Surbiton took a walk along the Ewell Road ('How everywhere is changing, flats going up everywhere'); Crossman joined Betty Boothroyd to speak to 38 people at Stamford Labour Club, before 'we went across the passage to the bar, where some 50 people had been sitting throughout the meeting!'; Ted Dexter got married at Bray to the model Susan Longfield, with the Bishop of Gibraltar officiating; in South Wales, Briton Ferry Town's first home match of the cricket season was 'an uninspiring display' drawing 'only a handful of people', with the visitors from Clydach recovering to win after losing three early wickets (G. Davis c. Mainwaring b. E. Jones 2, Will Jones b. D. Jones 0, Eifion Jones c. N. Jones b. E. Jones 0); and

Arthur English was in Ash (near Aldershot) to crown the May Queen
at the Red Cross May Fair. 'I was going to Wembley for the Cup Final,
but I wouldn't let the Red Cross down. They do such a lot of wonderful work. I'll see the last few minutes of the game on the TV at home.'[30]

He was in time to watch Luton Town doggedly but uninspiringly
trying to equalise against Nottingham Forest, down to ten men after
Roy Dwight (uncle of Reg Dwight, later Elton John) had been carried
off with a broken leg. 'Syd Owen ran up towards the end,' wrote Alan
Hoby in his *Sunday Express* match report about Luton's veteran
defender playing his last game, 'and even vaulted the rails when the ball
went loose.' But Hoby, like almost every other neutral observer, agreed
that Forest deserved their 2–1 triumph. Both TV channels covered the
match, though neither lingered: by 5.05 on BBC it was children's TV,
by 5.10 on ITV it was (appropriately enough) *The Adventures of Robin
Hood*, with Richard Greene as Robin and Richard O'Sullivan as Prince
Arthur, Duke of Brittany. One more football issue still needed resolv-
ing, and that evening the visitors at Dulwich Hamlet won 3–1 and
thereby clinched the Isthmian League title. 'Although they take some
stopping,' noted *The Times*, 'Wimbledon are not a graceful side.'

Crossman's dispiriting jaunt ended on Sunday afternoon in rain-
swept Nottingham. 'The May Day procession was about half a mile
long, with 15 big floats and 4 bands,' he recorded of a downbeat occasion, 'but I should guess that not more than 1,200 people were marching.' At the ensuing rally he referred in his speech to 'the shameful
Budget', but the bigger cheer came when John Silkin, prospective
Labour candidate for Nottingham South, declared, 'Look what we
brought you – we brought you the Cup!' In fact, everyone had to wait
until the next evening to see the trophy itself, when the homecoming
heroes made a memorable tour along seven miles of the city's roads. As
the *Nottingham Evening News* reported:

At every point were gathered crowds to see the coach carrying the players with skipper Jack Burkitt waving aloft the FA Cup, and in the old
Market Square there gathered the biggest crowd (some 50,000) ever seen
in that arena. The thousands who had come to see Forest bring back the
Cup, cheered and screamed themselves hoarse and sang 'Robin Hood' as
vociferously as it had ever been sung. Bells were played and rattles were

plied as the seething sea of red and white demonstrated its appreciation of the team's achievement.

No royal visit has ever brought out the tumultuous turn-out on this occasion.[31]

12

A Merry Song of Spring

'There's gold in them there stock markets – and how it shines this bright May morning!' proclaimed the brazenly pro-Tory tabloid the *Daily Sketch* on the 5th, the day after Nottingham's loving cup:

> These are great days for anyone who has a stake in Britain's drive for prosperity. Share values are UP yet again. From TV to textiles . . . radio to rubber . . . banks to breweries – the markets sing a merry song of spring.
>
> Car sales – always the best index of a boom – are hitting new heights. And the peak season is still to come.
>
> *Can we keep it up? Yes – and yes again.*

Indeed, only one thing was missing from the feel-good prospectus: '*All we want now is for the summer to follow the market's example – and get in the golden groove, too!*'

Two families this Tuesday had unashamedly local preoccupations. 'I'm afraid Essex is a very competitive county,' a Woodfordian had recently admitted to Willmott and Young about parental anxieties concerning the 11-plus, and Judy Haines in Chingford would probably not have pretended to be any different. Happily, a year after Ione's success, it turned out fine again: 'At 9.30 (as I was trying to concentrate on ironing) a loud rat-a-tat-tat came on the front door, and there was Pamela with Cynthia Gayton. "I've passed," she cried. What joy. I pinched myself to make sure I was awake and then kissed them both.' Up on Humberside, the preoccupation was with Hull's imminent appearance in the Rugby League Cup Final. 'I shall be pleased when it's all over,' Tom Courtenay's mother frankly wrote to him in London. 'There seems to be an atmosphere all the time.' Tom's father wrote also, making plans for his 10.15 arrival at King's Cross on Saturday morning: 'I am looking forward to a real good day. Our programme will be a drink to give us an appetite then a good feed so I'm hoping you know where a good pint and a meal can be had. We shall have plenty of time. I think if we get to Wembley Stadium by 2.30 we should be in clover.' But for John Osborne, it was thorns all the way on Tuesday evening. The first night at the Palace Theatre of his satirical, anti-Establishment musical, *The World of Paul Slickey*, featured booing during the show, more booing at the end, and afterwards Osborne being chased up the Charing Cross Road. Heap reckoned it 'crude, tawdry, puerile and putrid'; in Noël Coward's eyes, it was a case of 'bad lyrics, dull music, idiotic, would-be daring dialogue', the whole thing the work of 'a conceited, calculating young man blowing a little trumpet'. Reviews were almost unanimously hostile, Larkin noting with bipartisan pleasure that 'it got a bashing in *both* the *D. Telegraph* & the *M. Gardener*', and when Mollie Panter-Downes a few weeks later attended a matinee performance, 'the seat holders in the stalls huddled together like shipwrecked mariners in a sea of red plush'. Of course, the conceited Osborne had had it coming, and *Slickey* was clearly a second-rate (or worse) piece. But Michael Billington also has a point when he argues that the way in which it was 'elevated from a resounding flop into an instrument of generational revenge' – John Gielgud among those booing at the curtain calls – revealed the 'cultural chasm' across which 'mutually hostile groups' were now glaring.[1]

This was not the only chasm. On Thursday the 7th, two days after Osborne's debacle, C. P. Snow gave the Rede lecture at Cambridge, taking as his theme 'The Two Cultures and the Scientific Revolution'. It did not come out of the blue – Snow himself almost three years earlier had written in the *New Statesman* about 'The Two Cultures', i.e. literary and scientific, while Richard Crossman more recently had lamented how 'the preservation of an anachronistic elite educational system', in the form of public-school-dominated Oxbridge, had created 'an Establishment with a set of cultural values hostile to technology and applied science, and with an arrogant belief that a mind trained in mathematics, classics or pure science can solve any problem to which it gives attention'. But it was this celebrated lecture, almost instantly printed as a book, that crystallised public attention around the subject. Ostensibly, Snow was the meritocratic (son of a Leicester clerk), Olympian, dispassionate observer – on the one hand an accomplished novelist who would coin the phrase 'the corridors of power', on the other hand Scientific Adviser to the Civil Service Commission – but in reality, although of course he called for a better mutual understanding between the two cultures, his principal target was men of letters.

'If the scientists have the future in their bones,' Snow declared, 'then the traditional culture responds by wishing the future did not exist. It is the traditional culture, to an extent remarkably little diminished by the emergence of the scientific one, which manages the western world.' He continued with an attack on what he saw as the elitist guardians of that Luddite, anti-scientific culture:

> They still like to pretend that the traditional culture is the whole of 'culture', as though the natural order didn't exist. As though the exploration of the natural order was of no interest either in its own value or its consequences. As though the scientific edifice of the physical world was not, in its intellectual depth, complexity and articulation, the most beautiful and wonderful collective work of the mind of man. Yet most non-scientists have no conception of that edifice at all. Even if they want to have it, they can't. It is rather as though, over an immense range of intellectual experience, a whole group was tone-deaf. Except that this tone-deafness doesn't come by nature, but by training, or rather the absence of training.

Almost inevitably, a year and a half after Sputnik had apparently revealed the Soviet lead in the global power game, he looked east for the solution. 'I believe the Russians have judged the situation sensibly,' boomed Snow.

> They have a deeper insight into the scientific revolution than we have, or than the Americans have. The gap between the cultures doesn't seem to be anything like so wide as with us. If one reads contemporary Soviet novels, for example, one finds that their novelists can assume in their

audience – as we cannot – at least a rudimentary acquaintance with what industry is all about.

At the end, he issued a ringing call for education to become more scientific, more technological, more progressive, more *modern*:

All the arrows point the same way. Closing the gap between our cultures is a necessity in the most abstract intellectual sense, as well as in the most practical. When those two senses have grown apart, then no society is going to be able to think with wisdom. For the sake of the intellectual life, for the sake of this country's special danger, for the sake of the western society living precariously rich among the poor, for the sake of the poor who needn't be poor if there is intelligence in the world, it is obligatory for us and the Americans and the whole West to look at our education with fresh eyes.[2]

This sunny Thursday was also the day of local elections. Labour overall sustained some 200 losses – 'the Tories have got in!' exalted Kenneth Williams in St Pancras, adding 'so that's got rid of all those Red Flag merchants who have queened it so arrogantly & for so long' – but soon afterwards a cautious Macmillan definitively confirmed that there would be no general election before the autumn. 'On a hot summer night,' wondered a Labour agent about the poor turnout, 'was Diana Dors or Bob Monkhouse more important than exercising the long-fought-for right to vote?' Results were still coming in when on Friday morning, at Pentonville Prison, a 25-year-old scaffolder, Ronald Marwood, was hanged for stabbing to death a policeman outside a dance hall in Seven Sisters Road, Holloway. 'Cassandra is out of touch with public opinion when he suggests that the case against Marwood was prejudiced because the victim was a policeman on duty,' a letter to the *Daily Mirror* asserted earlier in the week after the paper's star columnist had vainly called for a reprieve (as had 150 MPs, almost all of them Labour). 'The reverse is the case, for the public, in the main, do not like policemen.' A few weeks later, an opinion poll showed over half of British adults believing that '*all* murderers should be liable to the death penalty', with barely a tenth wanting outright abolition. On the evening of Marwood's execution, *Frankly Howerd*, the new TV sitcom starring Frankie Howerd, had its

second outing, and it was already clear it was shaping up to be a humiliating flop. Whereas 'we never quite know how Hancock will respond,'
observed *Punch*'s Henry Turton, the Howerd character was 'entirely
predictable'; soon afterwards an unforgiving BBC executive privately
called him a 'neurotic performer unable to make up his mind whether he
wants to be a slapstick comedian or a comic actor'. For Howerd himself,
as with Bobby Thompson up on Tyne Tees, it seemed a career-destroying
moment. Next morning, Saturday the 9th, Tom Courtenay's father duly
caught the 5.45 from Hull and the duo made it to Wembley, but the
RADA student was distracted by the prospect of performing in Chekhov
that evening at Senate House and had to leave shortly before half-time.
Hull crashed 30–13 to a Wigan outfit spearheaded by Billy Boston –
powerful, Welsh and black.[3]

Dealing 'tactfully' with 'all shades of opinion in a controversial issue',
was how *The Times*'s film critic the day before had praised Basil
Dearden's London-set whodunit, *Sapphire*. The issue in question was
race, and Oswald Mosley – veteran fascist and now the Union
Movement's prospective parliamentary candidate for North Kensington
– spoke on the Sunday for an hour in Trafalgar Square, undaunted by
continuous chanting of 'Down with Hitler', '*Sieg Heil*' and 'Gestapo',
as well as being struck on the shoulder by an orange. 'Mosley is back,
here in London, and anyone who thought Fascism was dead in 1945 is
a fool,' Alan Sillitoe wrote soon afterwards to his brother. 'He and his
thugs are on the streets, organising meetings, stoking hatred.' Then, in
the early hours of the following Sunday, the 17th, a young black carpenter from Antigua, Kelso Cochrane, was attacked and murdered in
Notting Hill by white youths, as he walked back – bespectacled, with
hand in bandages – from Paddington General Hospital after going there
for tablets to ease the pain of his broken thumb. That Sunday evening,
with the news of the murder having rapidly spread, the local reporter
Colin Eades toured North Kensington. 'Young white boys walked the
streets in twos and threes giving an occasional whistle and jeer at known
coloured men,' while in West Indian clubs 'the general attitude was one
of patience and determination – a determination not to be pushed
around'. Two days later, with the police insisting to general disbelief
that the murder had no racial significance, Mosley issued a statement,
describing as 'nonsense' the suggestion that he had contributed to racial

tension and thus Cochrane's death. Would the murderers be found? 'Notting Hill has closed its eyes and its ears to this crime,' conceded the *Kensington News and West London Times* on Friday the 22nd. Indeed they never were tracked down – at least in part a reflection of how deeply and impermeably there ran in the police culture at this time what perhaps one can already call institutional racism.

That Friday evening, the journalist John Gale stood outside a youth club in Notting Hill and found out what a handful of white youths thought about the blacks:

> With the white women and that. The birds. Whores, like. Buying up all the houses. Riding around in big cars. Layabouts.
>
> Well, they do jobs you don't like. You wouldn't like to work in the gasworks or the sewers, would you?
>
> They don't like to work. They're lazy. I've worked with them. Metal polishing. Do they work? Do they nothing!
>
> Between you and me, as long as there are coloured blokes in this district there'll be trouble. Giving the area a bad name. If you're on holiday, and you say you're from Notting Hill no one wants to know you. We was in Southend and a copper picks us up and we was in the nick all night.

Altogether, Gale discerned in the youths 'a reflection of the environment: of the peeling stucco, littered newspapers, festering basements'.[4]

Next day, Colin Jordan – a 35-year-old Coventry schoolteacher, visiting North Kensington at weekends in his capacity as national organiser of the recently founded, pro-repatriation White Defence League – spoke to the press. 'We are reflecting an opinion,' he insisted. 'It may be that it goes unspoken most of the time, but it is held by the overwhelming majority of people in this country.' Parading the banner 'Keep Britain White', the League held a meeting in Trafalgar Square on the Sunday, as students chanted in riposte, 'No Colour Bar in Britain' and 'Who Killed Kelso Cochrane?' In the event, contrary to some expectations, Notting Hill did not blow up as a result of the Cochrane murder – on the 26th, Eades walked at dusk around 'a troubled area' and found 'emptied streets' and a 'deathly hush', with 'people watching the streets below from open windows, or, more cautiously, from behind curtains' – but after Cochrane's packed Ladbroke Grove funeral on 6 June, some 1,200 mourners formed a procession a quarter of a mile long from there to Kensal Green cemetery. 'I was pregnant with my second child and I stood in line feeling the shame of my colour,' remembered (many years later) Maureen, an Irishwoman who earlier in the decade had married a black musician called Ozzie. 'Those near me were all white, all feeling that it was our fault for not stopping the poison. Ozzie changed from that day. He was so carefree when we met. I was a singer. He became dark, afraid, and sometimes he took it out on me. He saw me as white, not the woman he had fallen in love with. When he died [in 1970], I was the only white woman at his funeral.'

Racial harmony, let alone racial integration, seemed a distant prospect in the summer of 1959. 'The immigrants are living in tight pockets turning inwards to themselves and it would seem intent on creating a "little Jamaica" or the like within the City,' reported Mr A. Gibbs, Birmingham's Liaison Officer for Coloured People, to the City Council at around the time of Cochrane's killing. After spelling out some salient facts – 35,200 non-white immigrants in Birmingham occupying only 3,200 houses; those immigrants including 24,000 West Indians, 7,000 Pakistanis and 2,000 Indians – most of the well-meaning, deeply paternalistic report was a plea for a properly resourced home-visiting service, on the grounds that by the time immigrants reluctantly visited his office it was usually too late to help: 'They talk things over with each other, follow suggested courses of action which are ill-conceived and doomed to failure, and they finish up talking "colour bar" when they finally come to the office.' Situations where a home-visiting service would be able to help, went on Gibbs, included child welfare when mothers went out to work, complaints by tenants, domestic troubles, health issues, employment problems and voluntary repatriation. Such situations were epitomised by (in a local paper's summary of the report) 'the prostrate mother of a murdered girl; the father in Jamaica asking for news of his son – last address Birmingham; the West Indians who lost their house deposits "through criminal activities of certain estate agents"; the West Indian who wrote to the Queen asking for help'. And Gibbs himself solemnly (though in the event to little avail) made his case:

The normal outside influences which are brought to bear within the homes of white people are absent because there is no way open at the moment to introduce them. Unless the apparent mistakes of the present are rectified, neither integration nor a stable community will be achieved. There will exist a coloured quarter made up of people who wish to have the best of both worlds yet are not prepared to accept the moral obligations of either. Very few people will have access and very little information will leak to the outside.

He might have wished, though, for a rather different headline in the *Birmingham Mail*: 'White Women Who Live With Coloured Men'.[5]

————

During the second half of May, intense scorn was directed at the England football team for losing successive friendlies in such minor outposts as Peru and Mexico; the days of the Aldershot Show seemed numbered after disappointing attendances despite Princess Margaret's presence; the first Commonwealth Day (replacing Empire Day) was marked in a low-key way; Dame Margot Fonteyn appeared on *Sunday Night at the London Palladium*; Gladys Langford lamented how 'boys & girls, tiny or adolescent, wear gaudy trousers, long or short, plastic hair slides, multi-coloured, plastic rings for horse-tail hair styles'; and the property developer Charles Clore provoked virulent opposition by bidding for Watneys. 'I disapprove of take-overs,' declared A. P. Herbert soon afterwards. 'It's simply not right for someone to reap the benefits of other people's work just by offering a ridiculous amount of money. What does this Mr Clore know about pubs, anyway?' The two great emerging Marxist historians were in contrasting modes. E. P. Thompson declared in the *New Reasoner* that the New Left of the future would 'break with the administrative fetishes of the Fabian tradition, and insist that socialism can only be built from below, by calling to the full upon the initiatives of the people', just as Eric Hobsbawm (no friend of the New Left) was publishing, as 'Francis Newton', his survey *The Jazz Scene*. Larkin's *Observer* review was respectful enough – though 'there are times when, reading Mr Newton's account of this essentially working-class art, the course of jazz seems almost a little social or economic parable'. He added that 'Mr Newton has little charm as a writer'.[6]

Class could not be avoided. Ian Rodger's radio column in the *Listener* besought the writers of *Mrs Dale's Diary* to create 'something more than permanently ignorant "proles" and continually omniscient middle-class managing women', while the release of the film version of Osborne's *Look Back in Anger* (by now 'easily digestible and mildly dated', according to Leonard Mosley in the *Daily Express*) prompted discussion about whether Richard Burton had become too grand to play an authentic working-class anti-hero. On Saturday the 30th, *Oh Boy!* – live from the Hackney Empire, as usual – bowed out with a Cliff Richard/Marty Wilde duet, and two days later pop music on television took a decisive 'family' turn with the first *Juke Box Jury*. The impeccably smooth David Jacobs was in the chair, and – in addition to 'Britain's number one Dee-Jay', Pete Murray – the pioneering panel comprised 'the popular songstress' Alma Cogan, 'popular recording star' Gary Miller and, almost *ex officio*, 'a typical teenager' in Susan Stranks. The programme was immediately followed by the first British showing of *Bronco*, with the BBC trusting to Ty Hardin as the roving cowboy to challenge the dominance of a hugely popular genre that ITV had established through *Cheyenne*, *Gun Law* and above all *Wagon Train*.

These TV developments coincided with the piquant case of Eftihia Christos. 'SCANDAL OF THE HARD WORKING MOTHER' was the *Sketch*'s indignant front-page headline on Friday the 29th after Mrs Christos, from the council estate at Dog Kennel Hill, East Dulwich, had been sentenced by the Lambeth magistrate to two months' imprisonment, waking up this morning (her 39th birthday) in Holloway Prison. She was a widow, her husband having died six years earlier of TB; three of her four children had TB; and her crime was concealing the fact that on various occasions in the past four years she had supplemented a National Assistance allowance by earning two or three pounds a week at home – mainly by sewing hooks and eyes on clothes, with the two shillings per dozen garments set aside for the benefit of her children. The *Mirror* was similarly indignant, fiercely attacking the magistrate, 69-year-old Geoffrey Rose, for his lack of compassion; next day it was able to report that over a thousand London dockers had not only signed a petition calling for Christos's release but were collecting money for the children. The double denouement came on Monday, 1 June, as

Christos was released on bail and Rose was taken ill at his Oxfordshire farmhouse, dying hours later. Even-handedly, the London dockers sent a telegram of condolence to the magistrate's widow.[7]

The rest of June was the time of part of Southport Pier burning down (machines crashing apart on the beach, people instantly gathering to pocket still-warm pennies); of the Minister of Supply, Aubrey Jones, going to Paris to propose the joint building of a supersonic civil aircraft; of Vanessa Redgrave appearing in Peter Hall's production of *A Midsummer Night's Dream* ('played Helena in the tradition of that fine old English schoolgirl, Joyce Grenfell', observed Al Alvarez); and, in Madge Martin's words, of 'such a spell of lovely weather', though on another day 'hotter and more trying than ever'. On the 8th, Nigel Pargetter was born and George Lyttelton in Suffolk hosted his old pupil John Bayley and his wife Iris Murdoch ('I liked the tousled, heelless, ladder-stockinged little lady'); on the 9th, Heap took his son to Littlehampton, where 'in a dingy café alongside the Funfair' tea was served in 'small cardboard cartons at 5*d* a cup!'; on the 15th, Macmillan recorded with satisfaction ('the crowds were enormous, & very enthusiastic') the first time the Trooping of the Colour had been on a Saturday; on the 17th, Liberace won £8,000 damages plus costs after the *Mirror*'s Cassandra had strongly implied that the pianist, a 'slag-heap of lilac-covered hokum', was homosexual; and on the 19th, Charles Clore bowed to the hostile mood music by reluctantly withdrawing his bid for Watneys. The following week, some five dozen miners at the Devon Colliery near Alloa in Clackmannanshire spent 52½ very cold hours underground – 'singing, playing card games and draughts', with local people sending down food at regular intervals – in protest at the colliery's announced closure (along with 15 others). Eventually, recalled one of them, 'the pit committee called us up. The Coal Board had agreed to meet a delegation of miners in Edinburgh to discuss the closures. But the net effect was that the pit still closed.'[8]

The collapse in the demand for coal, the sunshine blazing, a national printers' strike under way that affected magazines, local papers and book publishers (including delaying the last volume of Lawrence Durrell's *Alexandria Quartet*), the Tories ahead in the polls – June would have been a difficult time for Labour even without the start of a major defence row, particularly unhelpful just as Gallup was about to show only 15 per cent in favour of unilateralism. 'I have led more controversies and rebellions than anyone else here,' Nye Bevan as shadow Foreign Secretary admonished the unilateralist Frank Cousins at a heated meeting on the 23rd between Labour Party leaders and the TUC, 'but whenever Elections approach I call for unity against the common foe.' Eventually a form of wording was temporarily agreed, causing Macmillan to worry that Labour's '"compromise" policy on the H Bomb' might 'have a rather spurious success'. But a lengthy private letter to Gaitskell on the 26th made it clear that Cousins would continue to press for a pledge that Britain not only would not use the nuclear bomb first but would suspend production of it – 'in the firm belief', he helpfully explained, 'that ambiguity on any aspect of our defence policy would be the most damaging thing in our approach to the electorate'. Gaitskell's even lengthier reply to Cousins on the 30th gave little ground, insisting that if Labour won the election he did not want to find himself in the position 'in a year or two hence unable to do something which I believed to be right for the country because of some commitment I have made now'. He ended by pointedly expressing confidence that 'you will appreciate the great importance of presenting, as far as we are able, a united front at the moment'.[9]

Also on the 30th, Arnold Wesker's *Roots*, his second play of a projected trilogy that had begun with *Chicken Soup with Barley*, had its London opening. Joan Plowright (about to become Lady Olivier) starred as Beatie Bryant, 'an ample, blonde, healthy-faced young woman' who had returned to impoverished rural Norfolk after living in London, and Heap that first night called it 'an exceeding well written and richly rewarding play, frequently funny, occasionally moving and never in the least dull', all of which made Wesker 'a far more promising playwright than John Osborne'. Reviews were mixed, but most were favourably struck by Wesker's full-frontal, unsentimental treatment of the working class. 'Even in the Welfare State,' reflected Alan Brien,

a large section of the population still lives on a hostile and unmapped planet where the invisible dragons of disease and loneliness and poverty wait outside the light of the camp fire. Conversation is the interchange of ritual, repetitive magic formulas which dull the edge of their fears. *Roots* not only captures the occasional surface eruptions of humour and anger but also exposes the banked fires beneath the surface.

He added that, although a left-wing dramatist, Wesker (unlike most such) 'does not start off with the assumption that the working class are noble victims of a selfish conspiracy'.

Phyllis Willmott was unconvinced. 'I hated the points where he seemed to be saying to the audience "Look at the funny, ludicrous ways of these clods!"' she noted after going to the Royal Court a week or two into the run. 'And even more the amusement of the audience in response.' So too Charles Parker, middle-class producer of the *Radio Ballads*, who in early July complained directly to Wesker that his portrayal of the gracelessly boorish agricultural labourer had all too easily enabled 'an intellectual Royal Court audience' to 'hug to themselves the comfortable feeling that these uncouths did not significantly touch their own humanity at any point'; 'corrupt and moronic though the common people are seemingly becoming,' he added, 'only in the common people can the true work be rooted, the true tradition rediscovered and re-informed.' Wesker's unapologetic reply was suggestive of how much his play had been influenced by the challenging, largely pessimistic implications of Hoggart's *The Uses of Literacy*: 'I come from the working class and I know all their glories but I know their faults also, and this play was written *for* them . . . It was aimed at the muck-pushers for pushing the third-rate and at them for receiving it. It must have been obvious that I saw these people as warm and worthwhile.'

It was a more nuanced, complicated perspective than another playwright's. 'Graham [Payn] and I have taken a great shine to the East End,' recorded Noël Coward shortly before *Roots* opened, 'and we drive down and go to different pubs, where we find the exquisite manners of true cockneys, all of whom, men and women, are impeccably dressed and none of whom is in the least "look back in angerish", merely cheerful and friendly and disinclined to grumble about anything.'[10]

During a long, memorable summer, the new world continued, especially in London, to come inexorably into being. In the City, central

London's first new highway since the war, Route 11 (now named London Wall), was formally opened, with a car park beneath for 250 cars, while just to the north the City Corporation was preparing to give the go-ahead to Chamberlin, Powell and Bon's hugely ambitious Barbican proposals, hailed by the architect-planner Graeme Shankland as 'Britain's most imaginative scheme for big-scale central area redevelopment'. In the West End, Basil Spence's 14-storey Thorn House was completed ('somehow the human scale of the St Martin's Lane area has been preserved', thought the *Architects' Journal*), designs appeared for the towering New Zealand House at the foot of Haymarket, and Richard Seifert lodged the formal planning application for Centre Point, crisply informing the City of Westminster that 'we shall be glad to discuss any amendments, but it is most important that the bulk of the building should not be reduced'. South of the river, Ernö Goldfinger won the LCC's competition for office development at Blitz-ravaged Elephant and Castle, for what became the Ministry of Health's Alexander Fleming House – more popular (concedes even Goldfinger's biographer) with architects than with occupants and eventually infamous for 'sick building syndrome'. And in the East End, the LCC announced that Chinatown, in the Pennyfields district of E14, was to be wholly demolished, while officials of the LCC and the British Transport Commission met to discuss a proposed reconstruction of the whole of Euston station, with its famed Doric arch to be moved to Euston Road.[11] Elsewhere, Croydon's first major new office block, Norfolk House, was approaching completion – the start of 'Croydonisation'; Coventry decided to liven up its new shopping centre by building blocks of residential flats above it; the highest block in the Midlands, 16 storeys in the Lyndhurst estate on the outskirts of Birmingham, was almost finished, giving 'an unrivalled vista over green-belt Warwickshire'; and in Hull, the new university library was ready by the end of the summer to receive books. 'Some bits are awful: others are not bad,' the hard-to-please librarian informed Monica Jones. 'It is a clumsy, rather graceless building, lacking intelligence at all levels, but not without a certain needless opulence in parts.'[12]

Understandably, few if any activators denied the need for pressing on with at least a substantial measure of slum clearance. 'At Anderston Cross, built in the middle of the last century, I visited the worst slums I have ever seen,' wrote John Betjeman in June in a *Telegraph* piece about Glasgow.

> Enter one of the archways to the court-yards which they enclose, and you will see the squalor. Small children with no park or green space for miles play in rubbish bins with dead cats and mutilated artificial flowers for toys. Spiral stone stairs, up which prams and bicycles have to be carried, lead to two-storey tenements with one lavatory for four families. One such tenement I saw housed five children and the parents. The coal and the marmalade and bread were in the same cupboard. There was one sink with a single cold tap. There was a hole in the roof and a hole in the wall, and the only heat was from an old-fashioned kitchen range on which was a gas ring for cooking.
>
> Yet these people, though they complained, were not bitter and I was told that there were 150,000 such houses in Glasgow . . .

That city's housing problems were of course unique, but by 1959 in England and Wales only some 18 per cent of the 850,000 dwellings estimated four years earlier as unfit for human habitation had been demolished or closed. The Housing Minister, Henry Brooke, declared later in June during an inspection of slum clearance in Bethnal Green that 'many of these mothers and fathers are putting up a splendid fight in the surroundings they have to put up with. It is libellous to dub them slum dwellers. They may have just a tap and a sink in a black hole under the stairs, and a tumble-down closet shared with their neighbours in an open yard at the back, but they are trying to keep decent standards in their homes all the same.' He added: 'We are going to win this battle. I am determined to get all slums down.'

Among architects by this time, if Basil Spence firmly represented the acceptable face of the modernist push – 'he belongs to the modern school', noted an *Observer* profile, 'yet he and his buildings have a charm well calculated to mollify the feelings of those who are normally affronted by modern architecture' – then Alison and Peter Smithson were still defiantly uncuddly. 'The use of traditional forms in traditional ways is sentimentality,' they bluntly informed students at the Architectural Association. 'It is possible that a future architecture will be expendable, and that an urban discipline of few fixed points and the

pattern of change will be developed. In such an architecture the short-
ness of life can allow of solutions in which the first process is the last
process. There would be no problem of maintenance. At present most
buildings are assumed to be permanent.' Many of those students continued to be bewitched by Le Corbusier, and by this time the high-profile,
high-rise, Corb-inspired, hard-modernist estate at Roehampton was
finished. Among those making the pilgrimage to it were members of
Dundee's Housing Committee and the young, über-modernist architect
Rodney Gordon (future partner of Owen Luder), profoundly shocked
to witness the unreconstructed taste of the early tenants: 'The windows
were covered with dainty net curtains, the walls were covered with pink
cut-glass mirrors and "kitsch", and the furniture comprised ugly three-
piece suites, not even the clean forms of wartime Utility furniture.' The
estate's special eminence was recognised in a lengthy piece by Nikolaus
Pevsner in the July issue of *Architectural Review*. Admiring its 'pride in
béton brut', its 'delight in chunky shapes' and its 'instinctive refusal to
compromise with sentimentality', he approvingly asserted that altogether the estate was a 'vast, yet not inhuman, composition'.[13]

In many towns and cities, the juggernaut – which some dared criti-
cise, or even resist – was still only revving up, but in September the
Shrewsbury Chronicle printed a heartfelt letter ('Stop knocking
Shrewsbury about') from B. Dodd of 9 Combermere Drive:

The Crown Hotel is to be knocked down and replaced by shops. The
Raven Hotel may be demolished and its place taken by more shops. On
the old Smithfield site – a splendid setting for a public garden – there is
to be more 'development' in the form of a large block of shops. Next
April, the market clock is to be knocked down and a characterless
modern structure is to be erected in the place of that charmingly ugly
piece of Victoriana, so essentially a part of the Shrewsbury skyline.

Can nothing be done to halt this maniacal 'progress'? . . .

We can see the kind of proposed 'improvements' in any of a hundred
other towns. There is, sir, at present, only one Shrewsbury. Has not the
time come to cry halt and keep it that way? Or is it already too late?

Lurking increasingly by this time was the sometimes barely visible
hand of the property developer. 'We knew nothing about the matter;

nobody has approached us and the suggestion that someone can come along and pull down our property like that is quite laughable,' declared (in August) the indignant managing director of the down-at-heel Tolmer Cinema in Tolmer Square, just north of Euston Road, after St Pancras Borough Council rejected a planning application to demolish the cinema and redevelop the island site:

> This cinema is regarded with a great deal of affection locally and many of our elderly patrons come along three and four times weekly and they like us because we do not hustle them out; if they want to stop for three or four hours, they are welcome. I am certainly looking further into this matter because I want to know if it is really possible for someone to seek planning consent in respect of property that they do not even own.

The Hippodrome at Golders Green was also under threat, with Hallmark Securities Ltd seeking to have the theatre demolished and turned into a 13-storey block of flats, but during September some 25,000 people signed a protest petition, stars of stage and screen attended crowded 'Save the Hippodrome' meetings ('If I were in charge,' announced Bruce Forsyth, 'this would never have happened'), and eventually Hendon Council unanimously recommended to Middlesex County Council that the application be rejected.[14]

Two situations this summer highlighted the gulf between planners and planned. 'Pit Village Preferred to New Town' was the *Manchester Guardian*'s story in June after over 1,700 of the 2,000 adults in the Durham mining village of South Hetton had signed a petition protesting against the rehousing of 620 of them in the new town of Peterlee. The county's planning department could not understand, observed the special correspondent, why they did not want 'good new houses' in Peterlee in preference to the back-to-backs in South Hetton scheduled for demolition. The answer, he went on, was partly the six miles between new town and pit head, but also 'the community spirit built up through 120 years of living and working together', making South Hetton 'a large, close-knit family'. Accordingly, 'its new and handsome miners' institute is not an experiment in social living, it is an elegantly painted roof over a thriving social life to which the happiest citizens of new towns may sometimes look back in wistfulness'. In another mining area, South Wales, the conflict in Aberdare, running for almost two years, was between the Labour-run council supporting Glamorgan County Council's town plan – one-third of the buildings (including over 3,000 houses) to be demolished, with instead comprehensive development areas releasing the townspeople from an 'outworn environment' – and the many local residents who bitterly opposed it. 'They will have to get the bloody army to get me out,' declared one. 'Whether they want my house for a bus station or a car park, I just don't intend to go.' Ralph Samuel wrote up the case in August in the *New Statesman*. 'The Glamorgan planners did not set out to destroy a community,' the young historian reflected. 'They wanted to attack the slums and give to the people of Aberdare the best of the open space and the amenities which modern lay-out can provide. It did not occur to them that there could be any opposition to a scheme informed by such benevolent intentions; and, when it came, they could only condemn it as "myopic".' In the spirit of the New Left, he concluded: 'When bureaucracy is at work in the institutions of welfare, its intentions are quite frequently benevolent, and its face is always bland. As a result, its sway is generally unresisted and its assumptions rarely challenged. But the people of Aberdare have shown that its advance need not be inexorable.'

Overwhelmingly, the sense in 1959 was of being on the eve of not only a new decade but also of urban change of a fundamental nature with unknowable consequences. 'This is a very ambitious project and one can only wish its sponsors luck,' John Osborn, a prospective Conservative candidate in Sheffield, told the local *Telegraph* in June after touring show flats among what the paper called 'the giant honeycomb of future homes' at Park Hill, just a few months before the first residents were due to arrive. 'It is indeed a social experiment and the architects have given a lot of thought to the problems involved,' he went on. 'This trend for building upwards is new to the city and it is something we have got to accept.' Osborn was asked if high-rise development was the answer to the problem created by the huge Sheffield housing list. 'We shall know that only in the future,' he replied. 'When, in fact, people have the choice of living on estates or in multi-storey blocks. I would like to walk around these flats – which I consider very good – in five years' time. Then we shall know how successful the project has been.'

Or take the thoughts of a clergyman, observing at close quarters the whole fraught process of slum clearance and subsequent development. Norman Power, occupant of about-to-be-demolished Ladywood Vicarage, wrote in the *Birmingham Post* of Ladywood's 'strange appearance', as 'besides the shells of the condemned back-to-back houses, the new flats rise in hygienic, impersonal majesty'. He did not pretend to be regret-free. 'I do think it is very tragic that some fine old roads, with real charm and character, should also be swept away. Surely a civilised city would wish to preserve roads like Calthorpe Road, Hagley Road, and Beaufort Road? Surely its citizens would insist that it should?' He found it impossible too to quell his doubts about 'the great, American-looking blocks of flats' that were making up the new Ladywood. 'Splendid as they look, there is something very cold and impersonal about the new flats. And each block seems curiously separate – here are people without any community where once thrived the intense social life of a city centre.'

Yet overall, Power's glass was at least half full. 'On the whole, it is impossible not to rejoice. I have seen too much of what living in "back-to-back" does to the third or fourth generation to have many regrets.'[15] A perceptive witness with humane concerns, he was still travelling hopefully. And so, to a greater or lesser extent, were most people.

13

We're All Reaching Up

'I turned on BBC Television – so often hopeless, & we were agreeably surprised to find it as clear as ITV,' reported Nella Last about her reception on 3 July, the same day that the three reassuring words *Sing Something Simple*, as performed by the Adams Singers (directed by Cliff Adams), were first heard on the Light Programme. 'Morecambe area, like up on the East Coast, often has a poor "shimmering" screen,' Last continued. 'We hope for better results when the new receiving station is built in this district.' She had always been preoccupied by her listening habits, and now she and her neurasthenic husband had to juggle the viewing too. 'I like Tuesday night – The Flying Doctor & Twenty Questions & little or no Television,' she wrote four days later.

> Far from 'becoming a fan' as friends told me, we seem, now the 'novelty' has worn off, to be as 'choosy' as over sound transmission, & as our watching time can only begin when my husband has heard The Archers & finishes at 9 o'clock – except Sunday night, if he is enjoying a Variety show from 8.30 to 9.30 – & he won't have cowboy, Emergency Ward 10 or 'crime' shows where there is shooting or killing, it's a bit restricting. I'm often wryly amused at his attitude of 'nothing to interest *me*'.

The following Friday, 'doing several little jobs at once' in the 'kitchenette', Last heard on the radio (from the adjoining sitting room?) the Adams Singers, so she 'sat down & listened to the gentle, "sweet" voices, as they sang the years away for me'.

Predictably, Frances Partridge had not yet yielded to the box in the corner, but soon afterwards, visiting Robert Kee in his London flat, she had no choice but to give *Tonight* a try. 'It certainly riveted one's attention in a horrid, compulsive sort of way, yet I was bored and rather disgusted, and longed to be able to unhook my gaze from this little fussy square of confusion and noise on the other side of the room,' she recorded. '"Ah, here's one of the great television personalities – the best-known face in England!" said Robert, and a charmless countenance [presumably Cliff Michelmore's] with the manner of a Hoover-salesman dominated the screen.' Yet among the millions who did watch regularly, there were perhaps signs of changing taste. 'He is vulgar and gives the rest of the country a horrible impression of Northerners,' noted one among several critical viewers later in July in response to the BBC's *Blackpool Show Parade* featuring a well-known, long-established variety comedian. 'Dave Morris is still doing the same act he did twenty years ago . . . His usual "bar" or "club" humour does not work on a stage, or on television.' And perhaps most damningly: 'Probably OK for those on holiday there and out for the evening, but not for a television audience.'

Reporting this month, under the BBC's auspices and chaired by Antony Jay (the future co-writer of *Yes Minister*), was TICTAC, acronym for Television's Influence on Children: Teenage Advisory Committee. 'Teenagers,' it found, 'are bored by politics.'

> This is rather a bald statement, but it does seem to be true of an astonishingly large proportion of them. 'It's all talk', 'it's boring', 'I don't know what they're talking about'. Again and again all of us came across these comments and others like them. Western Germany, steel nationalisation, the constitutional future of Rhodesia and Nyasaland, the Singapore elections – nearly all of them seem incapable of the slightest interest in, let alone enthusiasm for, any of these topics. The reason seems to be that they cannot see how 'politics' impinge on them, or what they have to do with their lives . . .
>
> We found a widespread disenchantment with politicians. 'It's sort of corrupt'. 'They're too dogmatic'. 'It's all fixed'. 'They're just keeping to the party line'. At the back of it seemed to be the feeling that their views were conditioned by their party allegiance; they didn't honestly believe what they said, or at least you couldn't be sure they did; and that discussion between, say, Labour and Conservative was pointless since neither was open to persuasion by the other.

Other findings were that teenagers were more interested than adults in 'the large issues of ethics and morality' such as 'the colour bar, crime, punishment, marital fidelity, social justice, religion, the H-Bomb'; that they were highly observant of television techniques, criticising 'bad cueing, unconvincing studio exteriors, fake props and set dressing, bad camerawork, etc'; that they were often 'outraged' by insincerity in a speaker or programme; and that particular dislikes included the quiz games watched by their parents (seeing 'if some bloke was going to go on and win £3 2s'), period drama ('I can't bear all those "'pon my soul's" and overacting') and slow-paced BBC programmes ('Victor Sylvester and all that'). Altogether, concluded TICTAC, 'the more we talked to teenagers about television, the clearer it became that for them it was solely a source of entertainment. They never volunteered this fact, because it had clearly never occurred to them that it might be anything else. Its function in the home was that of Court Jester: to pass the time, to keep boredom at bay, to hold the attention, to interest, to amuse, but always to entertain.' Or, put another way, 'neither they nor their parents looked to the television set to serve as private tutor, chaplain, woodwork instructor, occupational therapist or Youth Leader'.[1]

Nor were Cousins or Gaitskell in the entertainment business. 'I have never believed that the most important thing in our times was to elect a Labour Government,' declared the T&G's leader in early July at his union's conference on the Isle of Man, shortly before it voted unilateralist. 'The most important thing is to elect a Labour Government determined to carry out a socialist policy.' The press gave him a predictable lashing – 'COUSINS LOSES THE ELECTION' (*Daily Sketch*); 'COUSINS GOES WRONG' (*Daily Mirror*); 'IS COUSINS A DANGER TO BRITAIN?' (*Sunday Express*) – and shortly afterwards a poll conducted for Labour found almost half the electorate agreeing with the proposition that the party was 'severely split by disagreement', an impression presumably confirmed when Gaitskell on the 11th, speaking at Workington, repudiated unilateralism and insisted that 'the problems of international relations' would not be 'solved by slogans, however loudly declaimed, or by effervescent emotion, however genuine', but by 'very hard, very clear, very calm and very honest thinking'. By now, everyone was expecting an autumn election, and Labour's anxieties were compounded by industrial troubles, especially in the motor industry, while the printers' strike dragged on until early August.

'I am sure your sensitive adolescent souls will burn with righteous indignation when you read that some poor motor car builders simply had to go out on strike because they were earning only £30 a week,' Dr J. E. Dunlop, rector of Bell Baxter High School at Cupar, Fife sarcastically surmised on 3 July at senior prize-giving. 'Try to rise above this horrible example set by your elders,' he urged the school-leavers, 'and you will gain what they have missed, the greatest prize in the world – a tranquil soul.' Within a fortnight, in a different dispute, a major, almost month-long strike had started at Morris Motors (part of the British Motor Corporation) in Cowley, following the instant dismissal of chief shop steward Frank Horsman – 'because', according to management, 'of a continuous and deliberate policy of obstruction, insubordination and insolence over a period of many years, culminating in the incident of July 14, when he instructed certain men to stop work'. Mrs W. Lawrence, a farmworker's wife and mother of three, was unimpressed. 'What must other countries think of England?' she asked in a letter to the *Oxford Mail*, shortly before Cousins managed to settle an increasingly invidious dispute by arranging for Horsman to be transferred to Pressed Steel. 'Is it *Great* Britain when it seems the unions try their best to stop workers' efforts by these constant strikes?' A few weeks later, in early September, Gallup found that those viewing trade unions as on the whole 'a good thing' had declined from 67 per cent in 1955 to 60 per cent now; given the overwhelming press hostility, arguably the surprise was that the figure was as high as that.

Not only the press was hostile. The Boulting brothers (John and Roy) had been making low-to-medium-strength anti-Establishment comedies for several years, and now, with *I'm All Right, Jack*, they hit the jackpot. Set in a munitions factory, and in theory attacking equally both sides of industry (with Terry-Thomas playing the useless, pompous manager, Major Hargreaves), in reality the film had as its principal target hypocritical, self-serving trade unionism, as embodied by the shop steward Fred Kite (played – indeed created – by Peter Sellers with cruel brilliance, including short-back-and-sides haircut, Hitler moustache, ill-fitting suit, waddling walk). 'All them corn fields and ballet in the evening,' is how he imagined his beloved Soviet Russia. As for concepts of economic efficiency: 'We do not and cannot accept the principle that incompetence justifies dismissal. That is victimisation!' Crucially, most reviewers from the left portion of the political spectrum found little to object to. The *Manchester Guardian* on 15 August reckoned it 'not so far from the reality as told in the daily news of strikes', while the day before, Dick Richards in the *Mirror* gave 'full marks' to the 'witty, irrepressible' Boultings for their 'latest thumb-to-the-nose mickey-taking piece of gaggery', in which they 'shrewdly, and with very little malice, poke fun at every phase of industrial life'. 'Maybe,' conceded Richards at the end, 'it's not an accurate picture of 1959 factory life, but it's splendid comedy.' Splendid enough for the Queen, who watched it while on holiday at Balmoral – apparently in the company of Macmillan. 'If that doesn't win you the election,' said someone to the PM, 'nothing will.'[2]

Macmillan himself had spent the last Thursday of July at his Sussex home, Birch Grove. 'Butler, Heathcoat Amory, Hailsham, Macleod, & a lot of TV experts to luncheon,' he noted. 'We then did about 50 minutes discussion (to be cut to 15 minutes) wh. it is hoped w^d do to open the election campaign . . . We did it in the Smoking Room & the whole house was in confusion, with 40–50 electricians, technicians & what-not who made havoc of the place.' The following week he toured three new towns (Basildon, Stevenage and Harlow, with a 'good' or 'very good' reception everywhere), while on the 7th came a feel-good announcement from the Palace. 'The Queen is to have another baby in January or February,' recorded Harold Nicolson. 'What a sentimental hold the monarchy has over the middle classes! All the solicitors, actors and publishers at the Garrick were beaming as if they had acquired some personal benefit.'

Nothing, though, improved the national mood more this summer than the heady cocktail of sun and affluence. 'For week after week, the skies have been deeply blue and cloudless every day, followed by warm, starry nights in which people have sat out in pavement cafés and on their own doorsteps and in every slip of a back garden to enjoy the rare, un-English balminess,' wrote Mollie Panter-Downes.

Though the old idea of London in August is of empty streets becalmed in a dead season, the city has never appeared more lively and booming, with the hotels, restaurants, and theatres all packed; the chauffeurs waiting beside their Rolls-Royces and Jaguars at West End curbs; the television masts seeming to sprout thicker each day over the suburban housing-estate roofs; and crowds from the provinces, dressed in their holiday best and with money to burn obviously smouldering in their pockets, happily lounging along Shaftesbury Avenue and Regent Street.

She did not need to spell out the political import: 'This is also the summer when the country's prosperity – coming so suddenly after the long, bleak series of governmental exhortations to cut down on spending that many citizens are inclined to pinch themselves rather sharply – can be felt on the skin along with the sunshine.'[3]

———

The prospective Labour candidate for Grimsby was far from the metropolis. 'So now this most gifted political problem-child, this all-but-statesman already at 40, so outstandingly able, astringent, brave, integral, quick, gay – such fun to have about – is on the high road up,' a delighted, ever-admiring Hugh Dalton had written to Gaitskell in February after the local party had chosen the undeniably gifted, undeniably arrogant Anthony Crosland, out of the Commons since 1955. 'Great success, given a flick of luck, is easily within his powers.' His constituency was of course synonymous with fishing, and during August the author of *The Future of Socialism* spent a fortnight on the Grimsby trawler *Samarian*. As he docked, wearing his wartime red paratrooper beret and an old sweater, Crosland informed the *Grimsby Evening Telegraph* that the fishermen were 'the most hard-working and cheerful people I have met in a long time'.

Gaitskell would have approved the sentiments. He had confided to Richard Crossman (a fellow Wykehamist) earlier in the month, apropos Crosland's friend and rival, Roy Jenkins,

He is very much in the social swim these days and I am sometimes anxious about him and young Tony ... We, as middle-class Socialists, have got to have a profound humility. Though it's a funny way of putting it, we've got to know that we lead them because they can't do it without

us, with our abilities, and yet we must feel humble to working people.
Now that's all right for us in the upper middle class, but Tony and Roy
are not upper, and I sometimes feel they don't have a proper humility to
ordinary working people.

It may have been around this time that Nye Bevan added his perspective. If Gaitskell won the election, someone speculated to him, there
would probably be a good job for Jenkins, albeit he was said to be a
little lazy. 'Lazy? *Lazy?*' reputedly exclaimed Bevan. 'How can a boy
from Abersychan who acquired an accent like that be lazy?'

August bank holiday was still on the first Monday of the month, and
that day questions of class were high on the agenda in a recorded
conversation between Richard Hoggart and Raymond Williams, above
all the increasingly vexed question of whether the new affluence was
de-proletarianising the working class. Williams was inclined to be
sceptical – claiming that, through for instance the universal use of the
welfare state, it was as much a case of the middle class becoming working class as the other way round, and he stressed the continuing relevance of 'the high working-class tradition', defined as 'the sense of
community, of equality, of genuine mutual respect'. Hoggart did not
deny that tradition, but – with a nod to *Family and Kinship* – argued
that whereas 'living together in a large industrial district' produced a
sense of solidarity, 'if you spend some time on a new housing estate
you are aware of a kind of break, of new pressures and tensions'. And
he went on:

> I'm not surprised that working-class people take hold of the new goods,
> washing-machines, television and the rest (this is where the statement
> that they have become middle class is a statement of a simple truth). This
> is in line with working-class tradition and isn't necessarily regrettable or
> reprehensible – what one does question is the type of persuasion which
> accompanies these sales, since its assumptions are shallower than many
> of those people already have.
>
> A lot of the old attitudes remain, but what one wants to know is how
> quickly these new forces – steady prosperity, greater movement, wives
> going out to work – will change attitudes, especially among younger
> people. I've talked to a lot of working-class adolescents recently and

been struck not only by the fact that they didn't see their industrial and political situation in the way their fathers did at their age (one expected that), but by the difficulty in getting any coherent picture of their situation out of them. Everything seemed open, and they seemed almost autonomous.

But by the time they've married and settled in with commitments a great many forces encourage the picture of a decent, amiable but rather selfish, workable society – the New Elizabethan Age.

Towards the end, the conversation turned to politics. 'The emphasis the Conservatives put is quite strong and attractive,' conceded Williams.

That the competitive society is a good thing, that the acquisitive society is a good thing, that all the style of modern living is satisfying and a real aim in life. They seem to believe these things a lot more strongly than the Labour Party believes in anything. Labour seems the conservative party, in feeling, and it's bound to remain so unless it really analyses this society, not to come to terms with it, but to offer some deep and real alternative, of a new kind.[4]

As Williams and Hoggart were speaking, the Hague sisters – Frances and Gladys, unmarried, living together in Keighley – were on the third day of their week's holiday at Bridlington. 'We began with a dash for the bus, as the taxi we ordered never came, so we only just caught our train,' recorded 62-year-old Gladys about the Saturday, when public transport was its usual crowded self at the start of a bank holiday weekend.

What a crush in Leeds as all were rushing to the far end of the station for the East-coast trains. Porters need some patience as some travellers need so much reassuring about their train. We were lucky to get in a comfortable coach and sat back to enjoy the scenery . . . Bridlington station with its wooden foot bridges could do with a more modern look but at any rate we had arrived. After a good welcome and tea at our lodge we spent our first evening enjoying the air and watching the players on the putting and bowling greens. After working hard it is nice to watch others playing hard.

Sunday featured a walk on the South Sands, the afternoon on the beach, a salmon salad tea, and church in the evening ('about 300 in the congregation, very good singing'), while on bank holiday Monday itself the clerk of the weather again obliged:

> The sun was hot all morning so deck chairs were in great demand . . . Fathers on holiday seem to have more fun than the mothers who are left in chairs to keep an eye on the family's possessions, perhaps they would rather watch the cricket and football than take part. Races and other games organised by representatives of a children's comic paper attracted many of the younger children and there were plenty of prizes for lucky winners. Donkeys weren't in the mood for trotting and needed some coaxing.

That evening in Glasgow, Willis Hall's *The Long and the Short and the Tall*, by now on its post-London tour, opened for a week at the King's Theatre. The main actors from the original production had all left, so instead the *Glasgow Herald*'s reviewer singled out Michael Caine (26, working-class, this his first major role) as 'the remorselessly jocular cockney', Private Bamforth, with his performance 'taking (with no small success) the easy way on all occasions to raise a laugh'. The not wholly pleased Christopher Small continued: 'He does it, it must be owned, with considerable charm; nevertheless, the effect, which brings a complaisant audience almost to the point of finding funny the enforced slaughter of a prisoner, is a little odd.'

Next Saturday the Hagues set off home. 'Such large crowds at the station that it was 3 hours before we left,' noted Gladys. 'The earlier trains came in full of Butlins campers from Filey. The Boys Brigade came on the platform in very orderly style being accompanied by the band playing. Had a very restful and enjoyable holiday. All gone well.' The 18-year-old Joe Brown had been performing at Butlin's in Filey earlier in the season, but the group he was in were so wretched, and he was so fed up with being made as a gimmick to have his head shaved à la Yul Brynner, that by the start of the month he had dropped out. Meanwhile at Butlin's in Pwllheli, the 23-year-old Glenda Jackson did stick it out as a Blue Coat – 'having', she remembered rather sourly, 'to tell all the happy holidaymakers who wanted to be in York House that they were in Windsor House' – and took the opportunity to dye her hair peroxide-blonde, wear mauve and generally try to become Jeanne Moreau, in the hope of kick-starting her stagnant acting career. The ubiquitous soundtrack this August was Cliff Richard's number 1 hit 'Livin' Doll' – a single that, observes Pete Frame, 'conferred unimaginable respectability on Cliff, smoothing out all the bumps in his reputation' – and the film was *South Pacific*, on record-breaking runs all across the country. For her family, recalled Trina Beckett half a century later, it was as usual Southbourne in Dorset, even though in an old Austin Seven it was two days' drive from their Wolverhampton home. The drill was familiar – an unbendingly strict landlady ('No dinner for late arrivals'), no choice about what you had to eat, four families of four competing for the bathroom – and 'each day started with the 8.30 non-negotiable breakfast of cornflakes followed by bacon, fried egg and baked beans'. Whereupon, with no one allowed in the house after 9.30 a.m.,

> Come rain or shine, we would trail down the cliff path to our beach hut, No 2,378, with a plastic beach bag stuffed with sliced white bread, margarine, meat paste, a couple of Lyons individual fruit pies and, on the last day, a pack of Kunzle cakes.
>
> Once news got round our digs that we had a hut, other guests would often 'just happen' to pass by. 'Could we just dry our Jenny out of the wind?' A tricky one to refuse, so a cuppa would be offered, which generally extended into lunch. By the end of the week, our four-seater hut was accommodating a dozen interlopers most days.
>
> 'Look at the time!' my father would say each day at precisely 5.10 p.m., followed by a mad dash up the path to the digs, seconds after the hallowed 5.30 p.m. unbolting of the front door.
>
> After dinner, still hungry, we would stroll out to our favourite Forte's café and tuck into vanilla slices and mugs of Horlicks.

And then, with the sky dark, the final ritual of piling into the Austin, which 'chugged along the seafront between Boscombe and Bournemouth piers, as we oohhed and aahed at fairy lights on lamp posts and the moon shimmering on the sea'.[5]

On Sunday 16 August, eight days after the Hagues left Bridlington and the day after the East Riding smallholder Dennis Dee dropped off his wife and four children for a week's caravan holiday there, the Street Offences Act 1959 came into action, immediately driving prostitutes off the street. Three days later it was the end of trolley buses on the East End's Mile End and Bow routes; two days after that, Princess Margaret's 29th birthday was marked by the release of an official portrait (photographer: Antony Armstrong-Jones); and on Saturday the 22nd (Dee fetching the family from Brid, 'all looked fit & brown, good weather') the *Manchester Guardian* announced that from Monday it would be known as the *Guardian*, reflecting the fact that two-thirds of its 183,000 circulation (72,000 behind its 'chief competitor' *The Times*) lay outside the Manchester area. The following Tuesday evening, Everton played away at Burnley and lost 5–2, bad news for the football special back to Liverpool. 'The train's return route was marked by broken glass and various missiles hurled from windows,' reported a local paper, 'and the trip was punctuated by halts as passengers pulled the communication cord.' Altogether, 20 coach windows were smashed, and many electric light bulbs removed from their fittings and smashed, but a British Railways spokesman opted for the laconic: 'Two policemen travelled with the train and they had their hands full.' Four days later the Toffeemen were at Bolton, lost again, and the home goalie Eddie Hopkinson was 'pelted with broken glass, sticks, apple cores and other missiles by hooligan fans behind the goal'.

In Liverpool itself that Saturday evening, the opening night of the Casbah Coffee Club, in the cellar of a large Victorian house in the West Derby district, starred the Quarry Men, the start of a welcome residency after treading water. They got a warm reception from almost 300 – the more troublesome Teds kept out by a bouncer – but Paul McCartney's brother Mike vomited after swallowing hair lacquer from a bottle claiming to be lemonade. The weekend's big story, though, was the mass break-out from Carlton Approved School in Bedfordshire. Over 80 boys absconded on Sunday, but by next day, after a police search with tracker dogs, only 11 were still free. 'It is not true that we are allowed too much freedom at the school – it's just the opposite,' a non-absconder told the press. 'Although we know an approved school is for punishment, the discipline is much too harsh. Our only recreation is a film show on various occasions, and otherwise we work hard in our different trades. Only the other night one member of the staff smashed our portable radio, and another took the pick-up arm from a record-player.' 'I am sorry,' he added, 'to see all this rioting happen, but some good may probably come out of it.'[6]

The weather was at last getting a little cooler, and Madge Martin on the 31st detected in Oxford even 'a real autumnal nip in the air', albeit short-lived. That Monday the British Home Stores head office in Marylebone had a telling absence. 'Frankie [a much younger colleague] not in,' noted Florence Turtle, 'her sister in law had had a baby, & Frankie had to mind the baby boy aged two. I should never have dreamed of staying from work for such a reason. Jobs are so easy to come by nowadays.' The presence of the day was Ike's, as Macmillan, only six months after the publicity coup of a summit in Moscow, now stage-managed President Dwight D. Eisenhower's visit to London, including a live television conversation – full of mutually warm bromides – between the two men, both in dinner jackets, direct from No. 10. The American's 'simplicity and directness came over rather better, most Londoners seemed to think, than the Prime Minister's urbane style, which appeared a shade uneasy', Mollie Panter-Downes informed her readers.

That same evening, 825 men reported for work at Morris Motors' first night shift at Cowley, as the company sought to boost production to meet ever-growing demand, while down the road a new revue, *Pieces of Eight*, opened at the New Theatre. Peter Cook, still at Cambridge, wrote most of the sketches ('warm, human, topical and spot on the mark', according to the *Oxford Mail*), additional material came from Harold Pinter with 'several bright sketches', and the senior member of a youthful ensemble was the 'quite irrepressible' Kenneth Williams, 'this small, cherubic bundle of high spirits'. The cherub himself recorded his mixed emotions: 'I hang above flies while cast do the opening & then descend on a wire. It was unadulterated agony. The audience was wonderful. They behaved charmingly throughout. There were quite a few vultures from London but I didn't care reely.'[7]

Two distinctive new novels were up for scrutiny in the *TLS* in early September. 'Low-life pastoral' was the reviewer's unenthusiastic tag for Colin MacInnes's *Absolute Beginners*, a novel about teenagers two years after his *City of Spades* about black immigrants. 'Sarcastic and facetious rather than humorous', an 'unsuccessful mixture of picaresque invention and knowing "copy"', a 19-year-old narrator who was not only a 'pornographic photographer' but 'an extremely sententious young man' – there was praise only for the 'vivid' London (mainly Notting Hill) descriptions, though even they were 'largely written in a sort of up-to-date Runyonese'. D. J. Enright in the *Spectator* was also unconvinced – 'Mr MacInnes himself can hardly be a teenager, and much of his "teenage *thing*" rings false' – but the *New Statesman*'s critic was far more positive. 'Although the decade is almost over, there are few novelists writing about the late nineteen-fifties,' he declared, whereas this 'sings with the vitality and restlessness that is seeping out of the glass skyscrapers and the crowded streets'. He quoted with pleasure how the novel's hero looks around him and says, 'My lord, one thing is certain, and that's that they'll make musicals one day about the glamour-studded 1950s.' Altogether, MacInnes had done 'a first-class reporting job' on 'a generation that has more money, leisure and independence than any of its predecessors', a generation instinctively impatient of class distinctions.

The reviewer was a 30-year-old *Daily Mirror* journalist, Keith Waterhouse – whose own new novel, *Billy Liar*, was the other one being appraised by the *TLS*. There, enthusiasm for the subject was muted, the reviewer calling Billy Fisher, the undertaker's clerk, 'a hapless welfare-state Yorkshire chap'; but the novel as a whole was acclaimed as 'a brilliantly funny book, rich in absurdities and beautifully edged writing'. Other critics also dished out the plaudits, with Maurice Richardson in the *Statesman* applauding how 'Billy's daydreams, with their amalgam of telly-formed consciousness and literary ideas and juke-box sex, and his dialogue, with its scriptwriter's wisecracks and puns, are contemporary right up to the minute'. A long, multimedia life lay ahead for Waterhouse's creation. But in retrospect, arguably what is most striking is not so much the contribution that *Billy Liar* made to the cultural northern drift, but more Waterhouse's delight in guying the crusty, stolid, narrow-minded northern stereotype, whether in Billy's uncomfortable encounters with Councillor Duxbury or in his fantasy conversations with the *Stradhoughton Echo*'s columnist 'Man o' the Dales'. One reviewer, John Coleman, referred to 'that humorist's playground, the grim North', but this was humour with a sardonic albeit half-affectionate twist.[8]

Yorkshire's cricketers did their bit on Tuesday the 1st by winning the county championship – 'one in the eye for J. Wardle', noted Larkin – and thereby ending Surrey's remarkable seven-year run. The following weekend included a section of the West Ham crowd starting a slow handclap and chanting 'Take him off' after the visiting goalkeeper was knocked out; *Juke Box Jury* (Murray and Stranks joined this week by Eric Sykes and Cleo Laine) in its now regular Saturday early evening slot; the death of Kay Kendall, only 32; and a one-off performance at the Royal Court of Wesker's early play, *The Kitchen*. Too many characters becoming 'People, and then Ideas', reckoned Brien, but Alvarez called it, 'without any qualifications at all, the best play of the decade'. Next day, Monday the 7th, saw the unveiling in Bethnal Green – in the new Roman Road market square adjacent to the fairly recent Greenways housing estate – of a group of modernist bronze statues. Depicting the borough's traditional 'Blind Beggar and Dog', this was the work of 29-year-old Chelsea sculptress Elisabeth Frink, who calmly told a local paper, 'I never worry about people's reactions to my work.' The mayor, Alderman Bill Hart, did the honours, but among those watching, one woman apparently spoke for most. 'It's disgusting,' she said angrily. 'I can't see how it has cost £1,000. Fancy spending money like that. The council ought to have their heads examined.' A youngster got hold of one of the blind beggar's legs, which swayed slightly before he was told to stop by a man who then said, 'It's very frail. I bet it won't be there after Saturday.' There was more vox pop next morning when the TV cameras visited. 'It looks all right,' remarked 69-year-old George Biggs, 'and if I knew what it was it would be even better.' But Councillor G. A. Hadley, chairman of the Housing Committee which had commissioned it, was adamant: 'It's typical Bethnal Green. Put a fence round to keep people away? Certainly not. People will like it when they get used to it.'[9]

These were challenging, invigorating days for Edward Thompson. During August he signed a contract to write a textbook of 60,000 words on working-class politics between 1759 and 1921 – a commission that ultimately came out in 1963 as the rather different *The Making of the English Working Class*. More pressing, though, was the organising and supporting of the New Left's only candidate in the almost certainly imminent general election. This was the highly intelligent miner

Lawrence Daly, who after leaving the Communist Party had founded the Fife Socialist League and was now about to stand in West Fife. 'Brother, I cannot produce a loudspeaker & van,' Thompson wrote from his Halifax home to Daly at the end of August. 'It is just possible we might lay hands on a speaker, but not a van. People just don't have vans to lend around.' More missives followed:

> Look. This Ernest Rodker lad is a first-class lad. He is, what a young socialist comrade ought to be, heart soul and body in the cause. He has initiative and good ideas. He is willing to listen and learn. He has proved himself as an organiser – did most of the publicity in London for the first Aldermaston. It would be good for him. The only problem? A beard. I have written to him and suggested to him he takes off his beard. If he does, I am telling you Bro. Daly, you will damn well have him for your campaign, and you will thank us all afterwards. (*2 September*)
>
> I think Ernest Rodker has been choked off with the beard business; but he might be up for a weekend . . . In my view you ought to send an address to every elector, since I think there will be arguments inside families, especially between young voters and their parents. (*8 September*)

The 8th itself was yet another warm, sunny day; Gallup put the Tories 5½ points ahead; and Macmillan at last fired the starting gun, with polling day to be exactly one month hence.[10]

———

Galaxy, Picnic, Caramac ('Smooth as chocolate . . . tasty as toffee . . . yet it's *new all through*!'), Knorr Instant Cubes, Bettaloaf, Nimble, New Zealand Cheddar ('Now I'm sure they'll grow up firm and strong'), Jacob's Rose Cream Marshmallow Biscuits, Sifta Table Salt ('Six Gay Colours'), Player's Bachelor Tipped, Rothmans King Size, wipe-clean surfaces, Sqezy ('in the easy *squeezy* pack'), coloured Lux ('four heavenly pastel shades of blue, pink, green and yellow, as well as your favourite white'), Fairy Snow, new Tide with double-action Bluinite, Persil ('washes whiter – more safely'), Nylon, Terylene, Orlon, Acrilan, Tricel, Daks skirts, Jaeger girls, 'U' bra by Silhouette ('Gives You the Look that *He* Admires'), Body Mist, Mum Rollette, Odo-ro-no, Twink ('The Home Perm that Really Lasts'), Pakamac, Hotpoint Pacemaker, Pye

Portable, Philips Philishave, 'Get Up to Date – Go Electric!'[11] Irrefutably, 1959 was the year of consumption: refrigerator sales up from 449,000 (in 1958) to 849,000; washing machine sales up from 876,000 to 1.2 million; vacuum cleaner sales up from 1.1 million to 1.5 million; radio and electrical equipment sales up by 21 per cent; motor-car sales (including exports) up from 1.05 million to 1.19 million; jewellery sales, ladies' underwear sales, money spent on eating out – all up by significant percentages. Even so, there still remained a considerable way to go in the consumer durables revolution: TV sets may have been in roughly two out of three British homes by the summer of 1959, but the ratio for telephones was one in two, for washing machines one in four and for refrigerators only one in ten.[12]

Integral to the *FT*'s analysis in July of the 'Consumer Boom' – fuelled by the end of hire-purchase restrictions, reductions in purchase and income tax, and a 'general feeling of buoyancy and optimism' – was 'the rising trend in sales of radio and television sets, records, cameras and photographic equipment'. Soon afterwards, in late August, the National Radio and Television Exhibition at Earl's Court (heavily plugged by the BBC, including on *Saturday Club*) featured not only the technological breakthrough (and Anthony Heap's future nightmare) of the transistor radio, but also the latest TV sets, whose sales as a whole had almost doubled during the first half of 1959. Hitherto the great majority of sets had been 17-inch, but by now there were signs (noted the *FT* in its exhibition preview) that the 21-inch set was 'at last beginning to make some headway', with 'the new wide-angle cathode ray tube' making it 'possible to design a far slimmer model reducing the 21-inch set to more manageable dimensions'. Up in Liverpool, to chime in with Earl's Court, the prominent local retailer T. J. Hughes held its own Radio and Television Exhibition, with the sets on display still the smaller screen size but with plenty else to compensate, such as the Philco Slender Seventeener II:

- Takes up only a fraction of the space that older bulkier sets needed
- Biggest possible picture from 17" tube
- Finest full circuit gives perfect clarity and definition
- Finely proportioned in the contemporary style
- Rich walnut veneers with *scratch-resistant* finish

Ekco still had the largest market share among set manufacturers, but Bush, Pye, Ferguson, Murphy, Philips and Sobell were all pushing hard. 'Elegant slim cabinet covered in simulated pigskin with matching mouldings and carrying handle', promised a recent ad for the Ferguson Flight 546, while a rival made creative use of its name: 'Touch of genius! BUSH BUTTON channel change TV . . . With this exclusive Bush feature, you can change channels instantly. Once you're switched on, you have BBC or ITA at your fingertips – accurately, instantaneously!'[13]

In the kitchen – itself transformed by the mass arrival of light plastics, whether (itemises the historian Jan Boxshall) in the form of washing-up bowls or bins or laundry baskets or storage jars or tablecloths – two of the keenest marketing wars during 1959 were over soups and breakfast cereals. Heinz Tomato still accounted for one in every four tins of canned soup, and chicken and mushroom soups were still stalwarts. But, noted the *FT*, 'green pea and spinach are not what they were, and the present tendency is towards lighter or "cream" soups, and those with a meat content', while Knorr-dominated packet soups, 'almost negligible five years ago', now made up over 20 per cent of UK soup sales. As for breakfast cereals, their production some 33 per cent up since 1953, 'the latest arrivals on the market have been for the most part sugared, or pre-sweetened, cereals, almost all of which have contained some kind of free gift and have been carefully packaged to appeal to children', though the pink paper did not deny that 'brand loyalty is fairly strong among the old-established brands – Cornflakes (Kellogg Company of GB), Shredded Wheat (Nabisco Foods) and Puffed Wheat (Quaker Oats) for instance'. In terms of trends more generally, the National Food Survey carried out this year found that convenience foods (i.e. already cooked and canned, quick-frozen or dehydrated) were increasingly popular, taking around a quarter of total food expenditure on the part of younger housewives; that old-fashioned staples like potatoes, tea, herrings and kippers were being consumed less, while relatively expensive commodities like poultry, coffee (especially instant) and fresh citrus fruit were being consumed more; that housewives had lost much of their appetite for turning fat into dripping; and that, among regional variations, the people of the north-west ate the most carrots and onions, Midlanders the most canned and bottled tomatoes, and the Welsh the most pickles and sauces.[14]

If dripping's halcyon days were over, so too were tripe's. In July the *Manchester Evening News* ran a large, rather desperate, front-page ad for UCP tripe ('EVERY-NIGHT supper dish – because it is LIGHT, TASTY and NOURISHING . . . and ensures a good night's REST . . . with plenty of ZEST for tomorrow') that convinced few, just days before, in the same paper, Mary Murphy's feature 'NOW TRY THAT SALAD THE FRENCH WAY' included a recipe for French salad dressing. Other signs of Continental influence in 1959 were the popu-larity not only of Italian motor scooters but also of three-wheeler bubble cars like Isettas and Messerschmitts; the opening in Soho of the informal, modestly priced La Terrazza, 'the Trat'; and at Burton's, the arrival of the Italian suit (lighter, brighter, slimmer). The American influence had of course been spreading through the decade, but it was in 1959 that the Hungarian-born rag-trade salesman Willi Gertler won the UK distribution rights for Levi's jeans. Further straws in the wind pointing away from the rigidities of the black-and-white past and towards a more relaxed, easeful, sophisticated future included electric razors becoming increasingly available, Colston marketing its first dishwasher, sales of untipped cigarettes dropping but those of filter-tipped rising fast, and Bronco's coloured toilet paper successfully going national, with pink the most popular, followed by blue and green – perfect accompaniments for the new coloured bathroom suites.[15]

Continental influence was at work in a classic car launched in April 1959. 'The first small, affordable British car actually to look chic,' claims an obituarist of Harry Webster, designer of the Triumph Herald, whose 'sharp, sleek lines came from Italy' and which 'was available as a racy coupé and a stylish convertible, as well as a two-door saloon'. In fact, 'there was nothing else quite like it, especially at the £702 price'. Yet after only four months, in late August, the Herald was overshadowed by the launch of a car that rapidly became not only a classic but an icon. 'IT'S WIZARDRY ON WHEELS AND "QUALITY FIRST" ALL THROUGH,' proclaimed a full-page, dots-filled advertisement for the Morris Mini-Minor, made at Cowley:

> Who would have thought it possible . . . Four adults travelling in comfort in a car just 10 feet long . . . with heaps of luggage . . . at up to 70 m.p.h. and 50 miles per gallon? But today Morris make it possible! With one

stroke of genius they have turned the engine East-West *across* the car – and created the Mini-Minor, the roomiest high-performance small saloon in the whole history of motoring!

Known from almost its earliest days as the Mini, the car's origins lay in the petrol rationing caused by the Suez Crisis, prompting the BMC's Leonard Lord to demand that his chief designer, the brilliant, implacable Alec Issigonis (creator of the Morris Minor), come up with a new small car with low fuel consumption. Reaction in the national press to its unveiling was not far short of ecstatic – 'obviously destined to meet with world-wide success' (*Times*), 'the most sensational car ever made here' (*Daily Express*), 'a new era in democratic motoring' (*Daily Telegraph*) – while the bluff, handlebar-moustached John Bolster tested it for *Autosport*. 'At first sight,' he acknowledged, 'the car is not beautiful to look upon, its very short bonnet, small wheels on each corner, and lack of an overhanging nose or tail perhaps offending convention. Yet, one soon grows used to it, and the sheer good sense of its design appeals enormously.' A detailed, almost wholly positive technical appraisal followed, including a reference to how 'quite the most outstanding feature is the suspension', before Bolster ended 'on a slightly personal note':

I have for long deplored the old-fashioned design of the typical British small car, and have had to go to the Continent for acceptable transport. Now, Britain has produced a really modern vehicle which can teach the Continentals a thing or two. I am so happy that at last patriotism may be combined with enjoyable motoring, and I have expressed my appreciation by signing an order form.

Unsurprisingly, the Mini – fatally underpriced at just under £500, including purchase tax – attracted enormous attention from the start, with an unofficial strike at Cowley in early September merely stoking up demand even more. 'No beauty to look at, certainly,' readily conceded Mollie Panter-Downes on the 3rd of the squat newcomer; but she warmed to its 'astonishing' leg room as well as parking-in-London possibilities, adding that 'every day, the BMC showrooms on Piccadilly are packed with family parties waiting their turn to hop in and out of these obliging midgets.'[16]

Even at that price, and despite their significantly enhanced disposable income (real wages up by 50 per cent since 1938, compared to 25 per cent for adults), few 'teenage consumers' could afford a Mini. The term itself was coined in July 1959 in a pamphlet by Mark Abrams, who defined the group as unmarried people aged 15–24. Clothing, footwear, drink, tobacco, sweets, soft drinks, slacks, pop records, gramophones, romantic magazines and fiction paperbacks, the cinema, the dance hall – these, according to Abrams, were the things on which *The Teenage Consumer* spent his or her money, a pattern of 'distinctive teenage spending for distinctive teenage ends in a distinctive teenage world'. Insisting that 'the teenage market' was 'almost entirely working-class', given that middle-class teenagers were 'either still at school or college or else only just beginning on their careers', Abrams offered other nuggets: fewer than 4 per cent of young women did not use cosmetics; at least two-thirds of all teenage spending was in male hands; over 60 per cent of teenagers visited the cinema at least once a week; the *Daily Mirror* was easily the most-read paper; and among young (under-25) working-class housewives, the majority used the same brands as their mother and largely stuck to traditional working-class foods (bread, potatoes, margarine), avoiding 'modern' foods like fresh milk, eggs, and fresh fruit and veg.

Around this time, interviews in Sheffield with those about to leave school, or who had just left it, revealed a little more about teenage spending habits:

> Bus fares for leisure alone take a lot of money. Dancing costs 3s 0d and 2s 0d for fares and a drink. I go to the cinema about once a week, but a boy friend pays about two out of three times. I buy two hair shampoos a week at 7d or 9d each. And I have to buy combs and hair grips. My mother buys my nylons, but they are supposed to last for two weeks. If I ladder a pair soon after getting them, I have to pay for a new pair.
>
> I go [to the cinema] with my friend three times a week. We don't go to the Ambassador, because it is full of coloured people. And we don't go to the Regent, because not many people go there, and it is usually old people who do. We like the Victoria best – it's people of your own age more, there.

'While you have the money,' fairly typically remarked a third teenager, 'you might as well spend it and enjoy yourself.'[17]

Inevitably, across the age range, not all shopping trends pointed in the same direction. Woolworth's opened in 1959 its 1,000th store (at Portslade in Sussex), though would soon be losing its way; another expanding multiple chain, Littlewoods, took over Oxford's long-established Grimbly Hughes; British Home Stores paid £140,000 for the huge Trinity Methodist Church in Scunthorpe High Street, so that it could be demolished and have a BHS store put up in its place; Edwin Jones of Southampton, one of the Debenhams group of department stores, opened what was claimed to be 'the most up-to-date store in the South', including 'high local intensity' lighting, Formica plastics 'on counters, table tops, walls and doors', and, in the large self-service food hall, 'Sweda Speeder moving belt check-out counters, designed to smooth out rush-hour peaks and eliminate queues and delays'. Self-service generally was by now reckoned to produce a 30-per-cent increase in a shop's turnover within six months of conversion, but the roughly 5,000 self-service stores still represented only about 3 per cent of grocery outlets. In Northampton, the entrepreneurial Frank Brierley opened the first of his cut-price discount stores, which rapidly spread across the East Midlands, and, befitting the self-confessed 'Pirates of the High Street', adopted the skull and crossbones as their logo. At Burton's menswear shops, the tone was becoming both more upmarket and less relentlessly masculine, with wives actually encouraged to be present, or at least on hand, during the fitting ritual, while at another multiple tailor, John Collier (formerly known as the Fifty Shilling Tailors), the emphasis was on younger customers and new fabrics, with heavy promotion from 1959 of the John Collier 4 Star Policy, each of the stars (gold, blue, white and silver) representing a particular cash price for a range of suits, overcoats and waterproofs. Anywhere and everywhere, meanwhile, there was potentially the American-imported attraction – or threat – of Muzak, as pioneered by a company called Readitune, which by this time boasted the availability of over 5,000 'unobtrusive and relaxing' melodies, thereby creating 'in shop, store or showroom an atmosphere of goodwill and the background for better and increased business'.[18]

In prosperous Coventry, the recently built shopping centre in the city's heart was becoming particularly busy on Saturdays, as shoppers flocked there from the new estates, where local shops supplied food and essentials, to buy bigger items like furniture, radio and TV sets, kitchen equipment and larger items of clothing. 'They like to have a lie-in and then a good breakfast,' one retailer told a journalist about customers' Saturday habits, 'driving in at about 10.30 to do their shopping and make a day of it.' What did the shoppers want? 'Coventry people, say retailers, are quality and brand conscious, partly because of television advertising. Attractive prices are not enough; shoppers want selection, and the increasing popularity of the city as a shopping centre is due partly to the greater choice that shops are able to give.' Even so, and perhaps especially in rather more typical working-class areas, a strong counter-trend was towards mail-order shopping, the total sales of which virtually tripled during the 1950s. 'Slowly chipping away at the fixed-price structure', according to the *Daily Mail* in March 1959, and dominated by three major players (Littlewoods, Great Universal Stores, Grattan Warehouses), it was a type of shopping 'largely done on a friends-and-neighbours basis in industrial areas' – i.e. involving local organisers who received a commission – 'and only recently have there been signs that it is now spreading to suburbia also'. One such organiser was Mrs Isabel Stewart, a compositor's wife living in Battersea. 'I have 20 members, mostly neighbours, and with £25 in hand I can order goods worth £125,' she told the *Mail*. 'I usually manage to make enough commission for the family holiday, and enjoy meeting the friends it has brought me.' Was a possible third way, though, the development of planned shopping centres away from established town centres? Later in 1959, A. D. Spencer of Boots addressed the Multiple Shops Federation on this nascent trend. Delegates were generally sceptical, with a speaker from the British Shoe Corporation adamant that 'the women shoppers who provided the greater part of retailers' business preferred the congestion, the bright lights, the noise and the traffic of the High Street.'[19]

Television advertisements were of course on the front line of the consumer boom, but there were indications, with commercial TV almost four years old, that viewers were starting to tire. In March, shortly after Gallup had revealed 81 per cent expressing irritation about adverts *in* – as opposed to *between* – programmes, the Rev. R. G. Bliss, living near Midhurst, wrote to Geoffrey Gorer (who in a letter to *The Times* had played down the menace): 'These breaks so madden all my household that we now just cannot look at ITV even when the programme is excellent. We live deep in the countryside, without other evening entertainment, apart from what we make ourselves, which makes it all the more infuriating.' Beverley Nichols disagreed. 'During those two minutes in which the screen is filled with the rival claims of the detergent giants, one can leave the set in order to powder one's nose, replenish one's glass, and let out the cat. This is impossible during the chaste, non-commercial productions of the BBC. One must sit it out to the bitter end.' And, argued this veteran, versatile writer in his letter to the *New Statesman*, 'though some of the advertisements are admittedly idiotic, many of them – particularly the cartoons – are brilliant little cameos, worthy of Disney'. Predictably, the diarists sided with the grumblers. 'Now we are "settling down" to Television,' reflected Nella Last in July, 'I find much of the Commercial advertising irritating.' After citing the ads for two soaps, Camay and Knights Castille, as particularly 'distorted' and 'misleading', she added: 'I always take the chance of the advertisement "breaks" to let the dog out, or in, lay breakfast in the front room – any little needed job.' So too from a less house-proud perspective, that of John Fowles. 'The Roman putridness of ITV,' he declared in August during a spell of enforced television-watching at his parents' home at Leigh-on-Sea. 'Advertisements for detergent and budgerigar seed – why so many?'[20]

Plenty of activators may have worried in 1959 about the working class being swept along in a degrading consumer frenzy. The Labour politician Christopher Mayhew, for instance, launched another campaign against commercial television; *Shopper's Guide* (published by the Consumer Advisory Council) described as 'fit only for the nursery' the language of 'magic new formulas' and 'exclusive ingredients' used to sell Omo, Daz et al; and *I'm All Right, Jack* included cheerful, mindless jingles for 'Num-Yum' and 'Detto'. But around this time two sociologists were uncovering salutary evidence. 'I don't need one, my wife is my washing machine' and 'My wife wouldn't have it' were frequent responses when Ferdynand Zweig asked working men in different parts of the country whether they had a washing machine. Regarding the material possessions they did have, and the general home comforts they enjoyed, gratitude and a degree of pride predominated over acquisitive greed, with remarks like 'I have many things which would be unthinkable to my father' and 'I have achieved something which I thought would have been impossible for me'. As for burgeoning automobile ownership, Zweig found that a car was prized less for status reasons than as 'a toy, a tool for pleasure', and he quoted one man: 'It is my main luxury; others spend £2 or more on beer, I spend it on a car and have something to show for my money.' Peter Willmott's relevant fieldwork was concentrated on heavily working-class Dagenham, where 'the overwhelming impression' he gained from his interviewees was that 'the improvement in material standards has generated very little tension or anxiety'. He quoted some:

> There's more pride – when you buy something now, you go out to buy the real thing. But that's not because of the green-eyed monster, or keeping up with the Joneses. It's because we're all reaching up for the same sort of thing at the same time.
>
> These things like washing machines have become necessities for working-class people. It's not a matter of copying other people. It's everybody wants them when they can get them.
>
> I was telling the young woman over the road about the Marley tiles my husband had just put down in the scullery. She seemed interested, so I said, 'Why don't you come over and look at it?' Now she's seen it she'll tell her husband about it. I gave her a sample, as a matter of fact. I expect her husband will put some down for her in their scullery. We don't mind about that. Why should we?

'There's not a bit of jealousy about these things, as far as I can see from people round here,' another wife observed to Willmott. 'People seem to be glad if someone else gets something. They don't grudge it. They say, "Good luck to them."'

As so often, it is the brief, suggestive fragment that tells the larger story. Towards the end of August 1959 the *Hampstead & Highgate Express* ran a front-page story on the 'storm of protest' that had broken out in Hampstead Village about the Tastee-Freez (i.e. ice cream) and Wimpy Bar that had opened in Heath Street a month earlier. The result was a petition to the paper, signed by over 150 residents, calling on it to mount an investigation into 'how and why this particular tasteless design complete with mock mosaic pillars of different patterns, diamond-shaped multi-coloured facia, and the lettering Tastee-Freez, was passed'. The *Ham & High* seems to have declined to do so, instead quoting the proprietors – brothers Tony and Brian Burstein – of this, the first combined Tastee-Freez and Wimpy Bar in London. 'It is our policy,' they simply stated, 'to try to please the majority.'[21]

14

Beastly Things, Elections

'In my belief the Socialist Party in its present form cannot survive a third successive defeat,' declared the Conservative candidate for Southall on Saturday, 12 September at the North Hanwell Conservatives' annual garden party. 'We have,' insisted Michael Underhill, a barrister, 'the opportunity of dealing it a death blow.' It was yet another glorious day, and before everyone returned to the other attractions – a cake stall, a 'white elephant' stall, a flower display, a demonstration of square dancing by the Foot and Fiddle Dance Club – he added that he was just back from the seaside, where 'the remarkable prosperity being enjoyed at all social levels was visible on every hand'. Five days later at Grimsby Town Hall, 350 people attended Wilfrid Pearson's adoption meeting as Crosland's Conservative opponent. 'I would suggest to the working man,' said this local fish merchant, 'that he puts his faith in the Government which puts money in his pocket. Surely his loyalties lie first with his family.'

Both men were on message. The Tories had been engaged in an unprecedentedly expensive press and poster advertising campaign for the past two years, but since the spring there had been a single dominant slogan – 'Life's Better with the Conservatives; Don't Let Labour Ruin It' – accompanied by visuals showing either a family gathered round a well-laden table or a family washing its new small car. Now, in the campaign itself, few opportunities were lost to emphasise Labour's ruinous capacities, typified by Macmillan on radio on the 26th condemning as retrogressive 'the old socialist system of controls, nationalization, extravagant expenditure and all the rest of it'. Macmillan himself – barely a year after Mollie Panter-Downes had reflected that he 'has always seemed a politician's Prime Minister', being 'popular and admired in the House but leaving the general public oddly cold' – was by this time undeniably an electoral asset. The self-confident member of the governing class, the courageous war veteran, the Keynesian sympathiser, the businessman, the loyal churchman, the unflinching patriot: altogether, notes his biographer D. R. Thorpe, he 'appealed to a remarkably broad cross-section of British society'. To which were added not only a flair for publicity (the fur hat on his Moscow trip) and remarkable phrase-making ('a little local difficulty') but that delightful, conspiratorial sense, conveyed by twinkling eye and urbane manner, that we were all in on the joke together. Doubtless there was a degree of acting involved – 'Beastly things, elections,' he muttered to one young candidate, Julian Critchley, as they toured the Medway Towns – but *The Times* got it right. 'Labour will do well to take the true measure of Mr Macmillan,' observed the paper at the start of the campaign. 'They are in the ring with a consummate politician.'[1]

Voters found it harder to warm to the more obviously cerebral Hugh Gaitskell, even though in private life it was Macmillan who was the roundhead and Gaitskell the cavalier, fond of parties, of dancing, of extramarital activity. Such was the strength and obvious appeal of the Tories' relentless focus on material gains that it proved impossible for Labour to shift the focus to an alternative central battleground. 'We hear of prosperity, but it is not what it should be if you really want a government which planned expansion in this country,' declared Gaitskell at Peterborough on the 26th, speaking on behalf of 29-year-old Betty Boothroyd. 'The fact remains that millions of our fellow citizens are still living under conditions of hardship and poverty which the rest of us ought not to tolerate any longer.' Of course, Labour tried: in a magazine-style radio broadcast the day before, in addition to Barbara Castle promising that Labour would 'protect the housewife' against 'hire-purchase ramps and shoddy goods', Harold Wilson inveighed against Tory-blessed 'City deals based purely on get-rich-quick gains for a few', Aneurin Bevan promised that a Labour government representing Britain would not be 'tainted' at a diplomatic summit 'with the poisons of the Suez adventure', and the author Compton Mackenzie flatly said of the Tories that 'as I approach advanced old age, I feel my mind cannot be at the mercy of these boneheads'. Wilson in particular

– quick-witted and starting to develop just a hint of the cheeky chappie – was emerging as a campaign star. Accusing the Tories of selling the prime minister 'like a packet of tablets' and of turning the Stock Exchange into 'a casino', his speech at Luton on the 20th was typical. 'Thirteen Old Etonian ties!' he exclaimed of the Cabinet in his homely Yorkshire accent. 'They believe they were born to rule, as the Prime Minister's favourite expression, "Masters and Men", shows. They see the country divided into first- and second-class citizens. Their only problem is to get the second-class citizens to go on voting them their privileges and their perks.'[2]

It was not an easy campaign for Wilson's one-time master. 'He looks tired and weary,' privately noted (early on) the *Daily Herald*'s Geoffrey Goodman, who was accompanying Bevan on his campaign. 'Oppressed by the scale of the problems inside the Labour movement and outside in the wider political arena. Still bitterly critical of Gaitskell whom he regards as "sincere enough in his own beliefs – but no Socialist".' Soon afterwards, Goodman described for *Herald* readers how, on 'a draughty corner in grey and smoky Blackburn', outside the gates of the Mullard radio factory and listened to 'in attentive silence' by a thousand workers, the shadow Foreign Secretary 'stood on a rickety chair beside an ageing car, speaking political poetry into a small microphone', claiming among other things that the Tories if returned to power would at last get their wish and wreck the principle of a free National Health Service. More private gloom followed in more hotel rooms, as the late-night whisky flowed. 'I am heartily sickened by the Parliamentary Labour Party,' Bevan told Goodman at Llangollen on the 24th. 'It is rotten through and through; corrupt, full of patronage, and seeking after patronage; unprincipled.' Two days later, in Coventry, he was described by Goodman as 'angry, frustrated, like a fenced tiger', yet at the last – although probably already seriously ill – refusing to yield to defeatism. 'There is always the unknown factor,' he insisted. 'You must carry on on that, if there is the chance of winning or at least doing something. If you forget that, you might as well commit suicide.'[3]

Altogether, 1,536 candidates – including 76 women, only one more than in 1955 – were contesting 636 seats. At North Devon a rising Liberal, Jeremy Thorpe, did much doffing of his brown bowler; at Epping and Falmouth two cricket-minded broadcasters, John Arlott and Alan

Gibson, also stood for the Liberals; for the Tories, Finchley of course had Margaret Thatcher ('A vote for any other person is a vote for a Socialist Government. Do not shirk this issue') and Gower had the embryonic magazine publisher and property developer Michael Heseltine ('I'm a young man looking to the future, not an old man grumbling about the past'). Labour's ranks included, at Hampstead, a charismatic black GP, Dr David Pitt; at Southampton Test the 29-year-old Shirley Williams (promising 'long-overdue provisions' for the NHS, including a plan to encourage doctors to see patients by appointment); and, at Buckingham, the 36-year-old publisher Robert Maxwell, who had only recently become a party member and spent much of the campaign fending off accusations about his business reputation, military record and even racial origins. Another Labour candidate, Anthony Crosland, made at his adoption meeting a particular pitch to the young ('They are bored by the Victorian restrictions we still maintain, by the stuffed-shirt and fuddy-duddy atmosphere of so much of life in Britain, by the lack of gaiety and opportunity open to them'), while at West Fife the Fife Socialist League's Lawrence Daly continued to receive well-meaning advice from Edward Thompson in Halifax ('You have got somehow or other to introduce more urgency and more sense of constructive politics into the campaign . . . Pit-head meetings are a "must", whatever the difficulties') and wore a full miner's outfit, including pit boots and protective helmet, when he arrived at Dunfermline Sheriff Court to lodge his nomination. In its unpleasant way the most resonant candidacy was at North Kensington, where Sir Oswald Mosley stood for the Union Movement. 'More sound and fury than anything else,' recalls Bernard Bergonzi of 'a rhetorical mode that was already becoming obsolete'. But Paul Barker remembers how, at a meeting in the Golborne Road, 'that barking voice, those clutching gestures, were impossible not to rise to' – so that eventually he 'called out in protest' at 'the drip, drip, drip of innuendo', leading to one of Mosley's henchmen turning round and inaccurately shouting, 'Go back to Jerusalem, sheenie!'[4]

In theory this was the first 'TV election', in the sense that a majority of voters now had sets, but in practice there were no interviews with party leaders (and of course no debates between them), while *Tonight* was taken off the air and *Panorama* told to ignore the contest. In any case, quite a few in the political class wished that the small screen had never been invented. A former Tory MP, Christopher Hollis, lamented in the *Spectator* that politicians were having to address the electorate in its own, debased language; Bevan claimed it was turning them into 'pure salesmen – like American politicians'; and, addressing one evening a meeting of barely 50 people in a chilly hall, Labour's candidate for North Kensington, George Rogers, lamented that 'nowadays it is hopeless for a political candidate to compete with *Wagon Train*'. It was unlikely, moreover, that the television revolution significantly enhanced or deepened political engagement – even from the comfort of voters' own homes. Audiences for the BBC's *Hustings* programmes, involving candidates in generally rather sterile, formulaic debate, were found to be 'very much less than might have been expected had the normal programme, *Tonight*, been broadcast'. Only 30 per cent of the viewing public watched party political broadcasts, and whereas normally the TV audience dropped by about one-sixth at 10 p.m., during the election (with the PPBs being broadcast simultaneously on both channels, at the parties' insistence) the drop was over a quarter. Tellingly, that precipitous fall was 'entirely due to the behaviour of ITV viewers', barely half continuing to watch, whereas 'the proportion of BBC viewers who continued to view actually rose somewhat'.

No one disputed which party took most of the PPB honours. 'When I sat down to watch the first programme, it was absolutely catastrophic – awful,' recalled the government's chief whip, Edward Heath, about the first Tory effort, broadcast on the 19th and showing (as filmed in late July) Macmillan at his country home in discussion with Butler et al:

It was meant to be a report on our term in office, and there was Mr Macmillan sitting very comfortably in an armchair with his senior Cabinet colleagues around him. And Harold said: 'Well now, Rab, I think we've done very well, don't you?' And Rab said, 'Oh yes, I think we've done awfully well, particularly the things I've been doing.' And Iain Macleod then said, 'Yes, well, I've done awfully well and we've all done very well indeed.' After we'd had a quarter of an hour of this we were driven absolutely up the wall.

By contrast, the techno-savvy Anthony Wedgwood Benn was masterminding Labour's efforts, assisted by *Tonight*'s Alasdair Milne, and the first one was unveiled two evenings later. Fronted by Benn himself – 'a nice, intense *jeune premier*', thought a critic – it consciously adopted a topical, *Tonight*-style approach, including Gaitskell direct to camera, film profiles of several contrasting Labour MPs, a report on the inadequate level of pensions (focusing on the Kingston upon Thames constituency of the pensions minister), and an attack on government waste and inefficiency. 'Nearly every visual device was employed in a rapidly changing mélange of cartoon, diagrams, film shots, and direct interview,' praised *The Times*. Other papers largely agreed. Altogether, reflected Benn, 'we have scored a tremendous advantage'. The PM reluctantly concurred. 'The Socialists had a very successful TV last night – much better than ours,' noted Macmillan on the 22nd. 'Gaitskell is becoming very expert.'[5]

Helped also by continuing fallout from the 'Jasper Affair' (a City scandal involving takeover malpractice and the misuse of building-society funds), Labour at this point appeared surprisingly buoyant, and Gaitskell in particular a plausible prime minister. Within days of the election being called, he had given a virtuoso performance at the TUC at Blackpool, making it impossible for Cousins to cause difficulties during the rest of the campaign, while his promise – highlighted in almost all his speeches – to raise pensions by ten shillings and thereby 'once and for all abolish poverty in old age' gave him the moral high ground. 'He has suddenly become a television star, a political personality in his own right – confident, relaxed, a Leader,' reflected Crossman on the 22nd, adding two days later, as opinion polls showed the Tory lead starting to narrow, that 'the Gaitskell boom has been rapidly swelling'. On Saturday the 26th, the sage of Hull took pessimistic stock. 'I shouldn't be surprised if Labour did better than people expect,' Larkin informed Monica Jones. 'I am sure that elections go by purely irrational factors such as are we tired of having a Conservative government & w$^{dn't}$ it be more fun to have a change, rather than any considerations of record or programme, and the "innate British sense of fair play" may well give them a go, despite their farcical front line & jumbled policies.' He was also worried about the threat of a serious Liberal revival, predicting that 'Laughing Boy Grimond will get many votes by his a-plague-on-both-your-houses line.'

That evening on television was Labour's second PPB, with Gaitskell 'coming over', according to the *Spectator*'s Peter Forster, 'charming and persuasive as Older Brother rather than Big Ditto, the hysterical grace-notes of his Suez appearance on TV quite gone'. That same evening, Gaitskell predicted to Roy Jenkins that he would win. Next day, spending Sunday in bed, a temporarily exhausted Macmillan (finding comfort in 'Miss Austen's *Mansfield Park*') did not rule out the possibility. 'If everyone keeps calm, it will be all right,' he reckoned. 'If our people begin to panic, the result might be serious.' The following morning, Monday the 28th, the poll in the *Daily Mail* had the Tory lead down to 2 per cent; according to Walter Terry, the paper's political correspondent, Gaitskell had 'won hearts not with emotional gestures and cries but with economics and figures'. And although the latest jobless numbers showed a further fall (taking the unemployment rate down to only 1.9 per cent), Crossman at Labour's HQ at Transport House described the mood there as 'on top of the world'. So too Benn. 'The tightest, slickest show we have done,' he wrote in his diary that evening after his third television PPB, with John Osborne and Ted Willis (creator of *Dixon of Dock Green*) among those giving reasons for voting Labour. In short: 'We have definitely got the Tories on the run.'[6]

Occasionally the election seemed to pervade everything. 'Your reviewer of Miss Compton-Burnett's new novel describes its characters as "upper-middle-class",' Evelyn Waugh wrote to *The Times*. 'They are in fact large landowners, baronets, inhabiting the ancient seat that has been theirs for centuries. At this season, when we are celebrating the quinquennial recrudescence of the class war, is it not desirable to be more accurate in drawing social distinctions?' Nella Last, though, was more typical. Her diary during September kept its running preoccupation with matters televisual – even a letter back from Hattie Jacques ('such a nice one, as warm as her beautiful voice') after Last had sent her a fan letter – before this on the 27th: 'We settled to read till the Flying Doctor on ITV & then the Palladium Show. I suddenly realised today how near the General Election is – not a fortnight, & we both agree we never knew less excitement – even interest.' About this time, Mollie Panter-Downes took the pulse in a Tory marginal and found neither leaflets nor posters, nor loudspeakers from 'slowly cruising cars', managing to disturb 'the equanimity of the local inhabitants, who plod along on their daily rounds as though October 8th were no special date in their minds'. Indeed, 'the very atmosphere of Wandsworth Central sunning itself on a fine September afternoon, with the men out at work, the front doors shut tight, and only a non-political cat or two dozing on the railings, is marginally mum'. For another writer, very much an expat, these weeks were an eye-opener. 'In justice I must say that England was *marvellous* this time,' Lawrence Durrell informed Henry Miller after a lengthy autumn visit. 'You really would have been startled to see what three months of solid sun (first time in 200 years) can do to my compatriots; such humour, kindness, serviceability, exquisite manners, rugged laughter. It was uncanny! It was like a real move forward. People were sparkly, alive, forthcoming, devil may care; and all as brown as berries. Food's improved too.'[7]

It was not all sunshine, though. Scotland had its worst mining disaster for 70 years when on the 18th almost 50 miners died in Lanarkshire's Auchengeich Colliery; that day the *Romford Recorder* devoted a full page to a comprehensive round-up of the latest exam results, with no hiding place for low achievers – though surnames only for those at secondary moderns, unlike private schools and grammars; and on the 28th the musician, artist and humorist Gerard Hoffnung died at only 34 of a cerebral haemorrhage, less than a year after his 'Bricklayer's Lament' to the Oxford Union. The literary event was Alan Sillitoe's *The Loneliness of the Long-Distance Runner*, a collection of stories with a working-class setting that, according to one critic, resembled 'a war correspondent's reports from some fantastic front which although it is all round us, is only sometimes visible'. On the stage, *Pieces of Eight*'s arrival on Shaftesbury Avenue earned mixed notices ('Bernard Levin in the *Express* gives it an absolute stinker!' recorded Kenneth Williams. 'O dear o dear. I'm so depressed – this pile trouble is back again'), and on the small screen, the welcome start of *The Saga of Noggin the Nog* (created by Peter Firmin and Oliver Postgate) was offset by how Robert Robinson in *Monitor* interviewed T. H. White in his Alderney home and, according to a TV critic, 'took it upon himself to treat Mr White not merely as an equal but as an intellectual inferior, attempting to browbeat him, snub him, correct him'. Larkin meanwhile inspected the newly released *Carry On Teacher* ('just about the unfunniest "comedy" I've ever seen') and read the most recent Iris Murdoch. '*The Bells* [in fact *The Bell*] is balls,' he pronounced. 'It's dotty stuff, with a faint whiff of the most creepy & pretentious scenes of *Women in Love*, and I wouldn't give it room on my shelves, let alone money to have it there.'

It was a notable Saturday the 19th in East London. That morning, despite a waist-high metal fence having just been erected, Elisabeth Frink's controversial 'Blind Beggar' statue was found lying horizontally across its concrete base and, later in the day, was moved to a council depot for repairs and restoration. 'We are certain it is the work of irresponsible young hoodlums,' insisted Bethnal Green's Deputy Town Clerk, Mr E. Woolf. 'Many people said they didn't like it, but I don't think they would stoop to this sort of thing.' A mile or two away, at about six o'clock, All Saints' Hall, Haggerston Road saw the arrival of the celebrity to present the prizes at the annual show of the East London Budgerigar and Foreign Birds Society. This – at the suggestion of the secretary's nine-year-old son, having read in a magazine that she was fond of birds – was Jayne Mansfield, currently filming *Too Hot to Handle* at Borehamwood Studios and who had recently switched on the Blackpool illuminations. The hall, reported the *Hackney Gazette*, was 'besieged by youngsters who climbed to windows to get a glimpse', but 'smiling Jayne enjoyed every minute of it'. An organiser declared, 'She's lovely, absolutely charming, and a good sport to come here.'[8]

Elsewhere, an election campaign did nothing to halt the tide of progress. Shell-Mex and BP launched a huge advertising campaign ('Mrs 1970') to promote the spread of oil-fired domestic central heating; the imminent demolition was announced (for the usual redevelopment reasons) of the Victorian central colonnade at Cleethorpes; 'First Look at £1m Shopping Centre Plan for Shrewsbury' was the front-page headline in the local *Chronicle*; Madge Martin 'on top of a dear old 13 bus' saw the new Finchley Road, 'where great blocks of flats have replaced the small, pretty houses, many of which were destroyed in the Blitz'; and *The Times* published a photograph of demolition in progress at 145 Piccadilly, the Queen's childhood home. The latter's purpose was a road-improvement scheme for Hyde Park Corner, and at the start of October the *Architects' Journal* brought out a special issue, 'Motropolis:

A study of the Traffic Problem'. This included a lengthy analysis ('Can we get out of the jam?') by Malcolm MacEwen, advocating huge investment in both public transport and the large-scale reconstruction of city centres, but not the building of roads for their own sake. 'My approach was essentially technological rather than humanistic or ecological,' he conceded many years later. 'I was looking for a top-down professional solution rather than a bottom-up democratic one.' The same issue featured a full-frontal attack by a Birmingham architect, Leslie Ginsberg, on that city's under-construction Inner Ring Road, which 'unhappily looks like being the greatest traffic and town design tragedy yet to afflict an English city'; even more damningly, he dubbed Herbert Manzoni's brainchild as the native equivalent of 'those "highwaymen" across the Atlantic who are destroying the souls of the American cities with their monstrous routes'.

Still worse perhaps was the spectre – raised a fortnight earlier at Margate at the annual conference of the Association of Public Health Inspectors – of 'a new slumdom' emerging from the housing projects that were replacing the old slums. 'The condition of common staircases, passageways and refuse disposal arrangements, not being any particular individual's responsibility, soon deteriorate and foul conditions develop,' noted Liverpool's Mr W. H. Wattleworth. 'Although it may be possible to provide a caretaker in a tower block, it may not be an economic consideration in the three- and four-storey flats, and in any case the attention of the attendant must be mainly concerned with any lift provided.' For William Amos, writing in the *Liverpool Daily Post*, Wattleworth's remarks raised three 'disquieting questions': 'Should it be necessary for the public to clean up after people whose accommodation is already being heavily subsidised? Is it not time that the tenement litterlouts were given a sharp administrative rap over the knuckles by the Corporation? And is Liverpool in fact building modern slums?' John Betjeman for his part was finally through with high-rise. 'Walking about in new LCC estates as I have been doing lately,' he told John Summerson, 'convinces me that the low blocks and the two-storey and single-storey houses are what we really need. I have found no large blocks I have visited either liked or inviting – they are just plot ratio buildings.'[9]

Betjeman was writing on 28 September, the day of Benn's confident diary entry – and, probably about the same time, of Gaitskell's speech at Newcastle. 'You can be assured of this,' he told the 3,000 present that evening. 'There will be no increase in the standard or other rates of income tax under the Labour Government so long as normal peacetime conditions continue.' The *Daily Herald* reported that 'a terrific cheer' greeted this unexpected tax pledge, but *The Times*'s political correspondent was immediately on the money when he called it 'extraordinary' and 'a significantly strong reaction to the massive Conservative attack that is being directed to the cost of the Labour programme'. Among politicians, two instant reactions were recorded: Hailsham's, telling a meeting in Doncaster that 'The Lord hath delivered them into our hands'; and Bevan's, turning to Geoffrey Goodman and angrily saying, 'He's thrown it away. He's lost the election.' The problem was perceived – however unfairly – as one of credibility, putting Labour firmly on the back foot, and Macmillan next evening, speaking in Glasgow, called Gaitskell's promise 'a very queer one for a professional economist and an ex-Chancellor of the Exchequer'. That same evening, 'amidst applause and cheering', Mosley was strutting his stuff in Notting Hill. Warning against 'the cheap coloured labour that is being imported into Britain', he told his white listeners that 'no matter how skilled you may be, you can't compete with a man who is prepared to live on a tin of Kit-E-Kat a day.' He added: 'In the whole of my political career I have never been so disgusted as I am now at what is happening in North Kensington. Why should English women suffer this sort of thing? Meanwhile, the police are told to look the other way.' In short: 'There is one law for the blacks and one for the whites.'[10]

On Wednesday the 30th, the opening of the much-delayed Chiswick Flyover, London's first major two-level highway to be built since the war, had a double twist: the presence – following the unavailability of Harold Watkinson (Minister of Transport), Stirling Moss and Donald Campbell – of the almost inevitable, scarlet-dressed Jayne Mansfield to cut the ribbon, as to a chorus of wolf-whistles she blew kisses to 600 admirers before announcing, 'It's a sweet little flyover'; and, a few streets away, a vehement open-air speech from the local Conservative candidate, Dudley Smith, denouncing it as 'thoroughly irresponsible to turn a fine British achievement into a stunt for a film star who is not even British'. The flyover itself stood up admirably to its first rush hour. 'A brilliant success,' claimed the AA. 'Some motorists even went back for another go.' That evening, Bevan was at a packed school in nearby Ealing, speaking on behalf of Smith's Labour opponent. Early on, a slight commotion at the back of the hall prompted Bevan to remark, 'Perhaps Jayne Mansfield has arrived,' while later, after he had called the Suez expedition 'immoral and inept', a shout of 'Why was it immoral?' prompted him to rap out to cheers: 'It was immoral because by armed might we tried to impose our will on a weaker country. We would never have done it if Nasser had had bombs to drop on London. It was the act of a coward and a bully.' The place for bullies that evening, though, was Hampstead Town Hall. There, for nearly 20 minutes, David Pitt struggled to make himself heard above shouts of 'Keep Britain white' and 'We don't want England a dumping ground for niggers,' before a running fight broke out between members of the White Defence League and Labour Party stewards. Chairs were broken, glass showered everywhere, even an old water-colour of Hampstead was smashed on the wall. Whatever his inner feelings, Pitt 'remained', observed the *Ham & High*, 'calm and smiling throughout the mêlée'.[11]

October arrived with the political outlook more uncertain than the meteorological. 'First signs of the Election – got our voting cards,' noted Nella Last on Thursday the 1st. 'I was surprised to find both Mrs Atkinson & Mrs Higham think Labour will win.' But at Transport House the mood had changed. 'We feel the Tories have now got us on the defensive,' reflected Benn, and that evening Macmillan sententiously if effectively declared at Nottingham that 'elections are very severe tests and Mr Gaitskell has managed to destroy in a week a reputation he had built up over a number of years'. Bevan meanwhile was speaking at the Co-operative Hall in Upper Tooting Road, Wandsworth – 800 inside, 500 outside listening via a loudspeaker – where most of the heckling came from League of Empire Loyalists, but a man with a large ginger beard shouted out that perhaps Bevan would join up in the next war. 'Obviously you have worn a beard to hide your weak mouth,' retorted Bevan, who later in his speech claimed that Labour had a 'moral stature' that the Tories could not possibly reach. Next morning he was conclusively down with flu and cancelled the rest of his campaign tour.

The *Spectator* now announced that it could not support the Conservatives (a party that seemed 'ready to sacrifice almost anything to stay in office') and published various voting intentions. Wolf Mankowitz and Angus Wilson were unenthusiastic backers of Labour; Evelyn Waugh hoped to see the Conservatives return 'with a substantial majority' and recalled his 'bitter memories of the Attlee-Cripps regime when the kingdom seemed to be under enemy occupation', but added that he did not personally intend to vote, since 'I do not aspire to advise my Sovereign in her choice of servants'; and Kingsley Amis, though calling Labour 'sinister as well as fatuous and revolting', conceded he would 'just about rather see a Labour Government in office than another Conservative one', given that 'Labour had an idea in its head once, even though it is now almost forgotten', whereas 'Conservatism never had an idea at all, except to hold on to its wallet'. Another novelist, Keith Waterhouse, undertook some reportage in a suburban pub on the Friday evening:

> The television lounge was populated by a crowd of youths, just touching voting age [21], who had spent a comfortable evening sipping lager and lime and watching Hancock [on BBC from 8.30 to 9, at which point they had presumably switched to ITV]. They were genuinely affronted when [at 10] the election programme came on. One minute they were singing contentedly, 'The Esso sign means happy motoring,' and the next they were on their feet shouting abuse. Four adults, sitting with their backs to the television set, turned round idly to see what the row was about, then resumed their drinking. A man came to the door carrying a glass of stout in each hand, called, 'It's only the television mention' over his shoulder, and went out again. The youths switched over to the other channel and then, seeing the same blank politician's face, pulled the plug out of its socket.

The theme of the party political broadcast was 'Britain Overseas', the main politicians featured were Alan Lennox-Boyd (Colonial Secretary) and Selwyn Lloyd (Foreign Secretary), and Waterhouse added that 'so far as those youths in the pub were concerned, the Tories might as well have put on an old film of Neville Chamberlain'.[12]

'Last day of "summer time" and light evenings,' recorded Anthony Heap on Saturday the 2nd. 'But with afternoon temperatures still soaring well up in the seventies there's no sign yet of any end to this golden summer.' Next day, speaking in Grimsby's Alexandra Hall, Anthony Crosland allowed himself a touch of exasperation. 'Who has never had it so good?' he asked. 'I am sick and tired of hearing the Tories trot out this little party piece.' Among those not having it so good, he identified not only the sick, old-age pensioners and widows but also railway workers, teachers and nurses; while those who *were* having it so good were Stock Exchange speculators (getting away tax-free) and businessmen who indulged in the 'expense account racket'. It was the last weekend before polling day, and on Sunday the psephologist David Butler – who in mid-September had privately predicted a heavy Tory victory – rang Wedgwood Benn to tell him the outcome was 'wide open'. Indeed, Gallup on Monday had the two parties level-pegging – perhaps the provocation for Lord Montgomery, hero of El Alamein, to declare publicly that anyone who voted Labour 'must be completely barmy, absolutely off his rocker' – though Richard Crossman privately reflected 'I still don't, in my inmost heart, believe in victory.' Not so Gaitskell. That evening he made his final television appeal, commending Labour's 'fine, modern, new, realistic programme', which was in tune with the British people's 'special qualities' of 'kindliness, tolerance, decency, a sense of fair play'; later, unable to sleep, he drew up a list of his Cabinet. Nella Last's preoccupation this Monday, though, was rather different. 'I was interested in & rather against character in Double Your Money – with an outstanding knowledge of Opera,' she recorded. 'When she got her £500 I sighed with relief, hoping she didn't risk it to reach out for £1,000. £500 *can* make her dream of going to New York Opera House come true. I feel Hughie Green would contact friendly people to help her. To read his life story of all his different activities and struggles, sounds like fiction rather than fact, & he seems to have a gift for making friends.'[13]

On Tuesday the 6th the election's scariest scare story turned up on the front page of the *Daily Sketch*'s later editions. 'If you vote the Socialists into power on Thursday,' it claimed entirely groundlessly, 'you can say good-bye to commercial television,' adding for good measure that abolition would take place within six months. Everywhere, the campaigning continued. 'A monstrous infringement' was the reaction of Peter Tapsell, Conservative candidate for West Nottingham, to the news that council-house tenants had been told by the Labour-run local authority to take down election posters and window bills. At lunchtime in Luton, heckled by Vauxhall workers that the Tories were the party of privilege, Charles Hill (one-time 'Radio Doctor' and now a minister) countered that his origins were 'just as humble as many of you here' and that he was 'not ashamed' he had 'made a bit of progress and worked hard'. Shirley Williams at Southampton Test put in her usual 17-hour day, driven around by her husband Bernard in a 'zippy green sports car', while in Bristol, after a similarly hectic day of loud-speakers and meetings (including at Robertson's jam factory), Wedgwood Benn privately conceded that 'there is not quite as much enthusiasm here as I had expected and the number of workers has not been as great as I had hoped', that indeed 'frankly, the campaign has lost some of its impetus'. That evening, Macmillan made his final television pitch and solemnly quoted Churchill: 'To build is the laborious task of years. To destroy can be the foolish act of a single day.' In the broadcast's immediate aftermath, the pro-Conservative members of the BBC Viewers' Panel noted that he had been 'in excellent form . . . relaxed . . . calm . . . convincing', but the anti-Conservative ones found the 'Old School Tie' atmosphere 'out of key with modern times'.

Four different opinion polls had been appearing regularly, and on Wednesday the *Telegraph* published its final throw, which unlike the others was restricted to marginal seats and now gave the Tories a 2.5-point edge. That lunchtime, Gaitskell was in Leeds (where his constituency was), speaking at an open-air meeting for factory workers. 'Don't let the telly keep you from the poll,' he urged. 'Leave the kids at home to watch *Rawhide*. They can tell you what has happened when you get back.' That evening, just as the 200th edition of *Educating Archie* on the Light Programme had Bruce Forsyth taking over from Max Bygraves as Archie's new tutor, Michael Foot, trying to wrest back Plymouth Devonport from Joan Vickers, ended his campaign at the city's newly built Guildhall. 'The Tories haven't got any dreams or ideals for the future,' he told an audience of some 1,500. 'They want the nation to stay as it is. They don't want anything better.' As ever, Kenneth Preston in Keighley was tirelessly writing up his diary. After a passing reference to how 'Spain has latterly become very popular as a Continental holiday place,' he pondered the situation: 'It has not been a very exciting election, as far as one can judge. We take things more calmly here than in other lands. The Socialists must be particularly anxious for if they do not win this time their future will be dark indeed.'[14]

'A perfect day' (Benn in Bristol), 'another glorious day' (Preston in Keighley), 'another marvellous autumn day' (Phyllis Willmott in Highgate) – the weather on polling day declined to deviate from the Tory script. 'Shares Reach New Peak on Election Hopes' was the head-line in *The Times*, and indeed the three new opinion polls in that morn-ing's papers all put the Tories ahead, by between 1.5 and 3.6 points, with Benn gloomily noting how 'the Gallup poll suggests that the enormous "don't know" group may be inclining to the right'. But for some there was no room for complacency. 'Finchley's attractive Conservative candidate, Mrs Margaret Thatcher, started canvassing at 8 a.m. in a blaze of blue,' reported a local paper. 'She wore a glamorous royal blue silk suit with matching shoes and handbag, and was driven round by her husband in a blue Jaguar.' Churchill too – wearing black overcoat, black homburg and white muffler, as well as sunglasses – was out and about, going on a 12-mile tour of his Woodford constituency in a yellow open car. 'At one of his stops,' it was reported, 'Christine Truman, the tennis star, who is helping out at the committee rooms, leant over and took Sir Winston's hand and then had a word with Lady Churchill.' The elec-torate largely performed its democratic duty – 'Have been & voted – wish it were for draught beer,' noted Philip Larkin, while Frank Lewis in south Wales voted despite telling himself he had 'absolutely NO interest in politics' – amidst widespread concerns about the impact of the TV set on potential evening voters. 'Let's make it the BIGGEST POLL EVER' the Labour-supporting *Daily Mirror* that morning had urged its several million working-class readers. '*Your* X Can Make The Difference Today. To Hell with the telly until we've all voted.' Indeed, the *Mirror* even declined this Thursday to list programmes before nine o'clock, when the polls closed, though presumably it was an open secret that the BBC was showing *The Black and White Minstrel Show*, and ITV not only *Rawhide* but also *Dotto* ('turns dots into pictures and pictures into pounds'). 'With The Archers, Top of the Form (sound) &

Dotto & This Wonderful World on ITV,' recorded Nella Last, 'the evening seemed to pass quickly.'[15]

Then came her inevitable wifely disappointment – 'I'd have liked to stop up awhile & listened to the Election results, but knew it was useless to suggest it' – though 59 per cent of the adult population did stay up to watch or listen. Television was overwhelmingly the medium of choice, and over twice as many watched BBC's coverage fronted by Richard Dimbleby ('the firmest base on which any such programme could rest,' noted one critic, 'and a most jolly, even skittish, jumbo he became as the night wore on') as ITV's under Ian Trethowan. Even so, 'the usual cheerful election-night crowds jammed into Piccadilly Circus and Trafalgar Square to watch the returns flashed on screens', observed Mollie Panter-Downes, including 'parties of young people bobbing along with Tory-blue balloons and shouting that they wanted Mac'.

Alma Hatt, ambitious Clerk of Basildon Council, was determined that Billericay should declare first, and through meticulous organisation and a 400-strong army of volunteers he succeeded – despite losing eight minutes after a ballot box had been left behind in a car – at almost exactly 10 p.m. This was the moment of truth, including for the Labour veteran Hugh Dalton:

> From the start the results went wrong. No. 1 Billericay, containing the New Town of Basildon, recruited by good Labour voters from West and East Ham. Surely a Labour gain. But no, held by Tories with 4,000 majority. True we held the two Salford seats but then came a stream of disappointments. Battersea South and Watford both held by Tories, and a Tory gain from Labour at Acton. And so, on and on.

In fact the first Tory gain was Holborn and St Pancras, where the handsome, personable television journalist Geoffrey Johnson Smith overcame Lena Jeger by 656 votes. Among those helping at the count was Anthony Heap, who – 'much bucked' by these 'joyous tidings' – then headed home for a 'night of gladness'. 'Election results coming in thick & fast,' recorded Kenneth Williams. 'All v. exciting. Tory gains all the time. Labour is going to be crushingly defeated.' Shortly after midnight, Crosland squeaked through in Grimsby by 101 votes; half an hour later, Thatcher swept home in Finchley ('the cheers, always more controlled from Tory than from Liberal or socialist lips, rose', she remembered); and shortly before one o'clock at Leeds Town Hall, a dignified Gaitskell conceded defeat, promising that 'the flame of democratic socialism still burns bright'. Bevan at every level was dismayed – 'I would never concede,' he told those around him at Ebbw Vale, 'I would wait until the last vote was properly counted' – while for Benn in Bristol it suddenly seemed a long time since those triumphant magazine-style PPBs. 'The count is very depressing with the crowing Tories and our people very dejected,' he noted. And, after retaining his seat with a sharply reduced majority, 'back to the Grand Hotel too depressed to watch TV'.[16]

The eventual outcome, on a 78.7 per cent turnout, was an overall Conservative majority of 100 – an astonishing triumph for a government already almost eight years old. The shares of the popular vote were 49.4 per cent for the Conservatives and 43.7 per cent for Labour, a wider margin than predicted by any of the final opinion polls, while the Liberals more than doubled their share, up to 5.9 per cent, but were still stuck on six seats. Strikingly, the Conservatives fared particularly well in newly prosperous areas like Dagenham and Coventry (where Labour lost a seat for the first time since the war) and in new working-class housing developments, such as at Borehamwood or Birmingham's outer estates, as well as (of course) at Basildon. By contrast, a mixture of unemployment and pit closures gave Labour a 3-per-cent swing in Scotland, though that country still produced plenty of Tory victors, including Sir Colin Thornton-Kemsley at Angus North and Mearns and Sir William Anstruther-Gray at Berwick and East Lothian, not to mention Lord John Hope at Edinburgh Pentlands. Elsewhere, winners included Julian Critchley, Charles Hill, Jeremy Thorpe, Dudley Smith and Peter Tapsell; losers included Michael Heseltine, Michael Underhill, Lawrence Daly (though securing almost 5,000 votes), Michael Foot, Shirley Williams, John Arlott, Alan Gibson, David Pitt and Betty Boothroyd (congratulated by her opponent Harmar Nicholls on being 'a bonny fighter'). There were two particularly outraged losers. Robert Maxwell at Buckingham declined to shake the victor's hand, claiming he would have won 'had the Tories fought cleanly'; and, in arguably the election's single most important – and heartening – result, Oswald Mosley in North Kensington simply refused to accept that he had lost his deposit.

Early reactions included frantic trading on Friday morning on the floor of the Stock Exchange, now it was clear the steel industry would not be renationalised; Graham Greene hearing about Labour's defeat while on a plane over Canada and celebrating with a slug of whisky; and Larkin in Hull observing 'some long faces in the University on Friday, haw haw', while expressing his own hope that 'the present crowd don't do anything silly in their mad flush of victory'. A quartet of female observers had their own takes. 'Now we can have Stable Government for another 4½ years,' reflected Florence Turtle; for Nella Last, notwithstanding her satisfaction with the outcome, it was 'the gallant attitude of Mr Gaitskell' that she thought would remain with her, '& his courageous smile as he spoke of the defeat as a "set-back" only'; Tom Courtenay's mother in Hull wrote to him that she felt 'very sorry for the Labour people, mainly Welsh and Scottish, and I'm sure they will hate clever buggers English mainly non-industrial South'; and Mrs B. K. of Camberwell announced in the *Daily Sketch* how glad she was, 'as a woman', that the election was finally over: 'It will be so good to have our menfolk peacefully at home again – without having to endure their arguments with neighbours over the garden fence. Or having to listen to them laying down the law to their wives and families, who apparently aren't expected to have minds of their own!'[17]

Why had the Conservatives won so conclusively? Some emphasised Gaitskell's tax-pledge blunder, some the Conservatives' much greater advertising spend during the long run-up to the election, some their greater organisational capacity in the decisive weeks. For Richard Crossman, writing up his diary on the Friday, one 'simple truth' had 'dogged' his party's efforts: 'Tory voters are far more afraid of another Labour Government than Labour voters are afraid of another Tory Government. The Tories were able to exploit fear of nationalization, inflation, flight from the pound, trade unions, and so on.' Ultimately, though, the most common – and surely correct – perception was that, whatever the attractions or otherwise of Labour's case, the electorate just did not want to change horses at a time of such welcome prosperity. 'He votes for his stomach, or not at all,' was the view of a 'furious' John Fowles about the typical voter, while the young David Owen, just starting as a medical student, was equally jaundiced. 'Can any party ever have won an election on a more immoral slogan, a positive disgrace and a sign of the moral depravity of our life?' he asked himself. 'People seem to vote solely on their bellies.' And famously, Trog drew a wonderful cartoon for the *Spectator*, showing Macmillan sitting in best Edwardian manner opposite an array of consumer durables (fridge, car, washing machine, TV set) and saying, 'Well, gentlemen, I think we all fought a good fight . . .'

There was one other dimension to this instant analysis. 'A prosperous, mainly middle-class Britain cannot be stampeded by the crude old cries of under-privilege,' declared *The Times* on Saturday the 10th. Macmillan himself fully agreed, composing that day a letter to the Queen that finished with a paragraph he must have known was destined for the history books:

> The most encouraging feature of the Election from Your Majesty's point of view, is the strong impression that I have formed that Your Majesty's subjects do not wish to allow themselves to be divided into warring classes or tribes filled with hereditary animosity against each other. There was a very significant breakdown of this structure of society which, in spite of its many material advantages, was one of the chief spiritual disadvantages of the first industrial revolution. It will be curious if the second industrial revolution, through the wide spread of its amenities of life to almost every home in the country, succeeds in destroying this unfortunate product of the first. At any rate, anything that makes Your Majesty's subjects more conscious of their unity and of their duty to each other seems to me to be a real gain.

Macmillan had probably not read (despite its address) a letter that had appeared in late August in the *Viewer*, the TV magazine covering the Tyne Tees area. 'Every time the quiz show *Concentration* comes on, it annoys me to death,' complained G. Barraclough of Lincoln Grove, Albany Estate, Stockton-on-Tees. 'I have never yet seen an ordinary working-class person on it, they are always middle-class – and most of them, no doubt, already have the prizes which they win. I might add that my friends and neighbours think the same!'[18]

A SHAKE OF THE DICE

This book is dedicated to the memory of Deborah Rogers

PART ONE

I

Sure as Progress Itself

'Met a most charming young married woman on underground,' recorded Judy Haines on Friday the 16th, just over a week after Harold Macmillan's October 1959 election triumph. 'We put her right for Marshall & Snelgrove's.' The Chingford diarist was on a shopping trip with her neighbour opposite, and after lunch at D. H. Evans (soup and tomato juice respectively, 'then heaps of steak and kidney pie and veg', followed by ice cream and coffee) they got down to business. 'I bought blue with white circles for Pam, red with white spots for Ione and yellow Viyella for me. Win bought black organza and blue blouse material (sort of Broderie Anglaise). She wanted a hat but hadn't the difficult-to-match winter coat on (it is very fine and warm still) so daren't chance it. I bought a sort of "lamp shade" and was thrilled.' That evening's television featured Tony Hancock in full rhetorical flight as foreman of the jury in 'Twelve Angry Men' ('Does Magna Carta mean nothing to you? Did she die in vain?'), clashing with *Any Questions?* on the Light Programme. 'What were the team's reactions,' asked Harold R. Marr from the audience at the Town Hall, Eastleigh, 'on hearing that the guardsman on sentry-go at Buckingham Palace had to retreat behind the railings?' Following an episode in August when a guardsman had been confined to barracks after a woman complained of being kicked, it had recently been announced that from the 17th the sentries would be mounted in the forecourt in front of the building. 'It is a bad show,' declared Enoch Powell. 'I hope it will be reversed and that they will be brought outside again. It seems to me to be one of those comparatively rare lapses from the British sense of humour.'

The British sense of humour struggled also, post-Suez, to embrace national decline. 'I have been struck as, of course, any observer must have been, by the efforts to build up British achievements and hail them as being in some way superior to those of the United States and Russia,' Michael Young privately reflected later in October. And referring to his sociological study (with Peter Willmott) of largely middle-class Woodford in suburban Essex, he added, 'These people were by no means leaders of the elite. They did not seem to register the decline in British power, and were defensively touchy at the suggestion that there had been any.' Soon afterwards, the Queen's Speech promised independence for Cyprus and Nigeria, but attitudes remained largely Podsnappian – not least in relation to the English football team, despite severe recent disappointments. 'Storm Dooms the Swedes' was the *Daily Mirror*'s confident headline on the 28th, ahead of that afternoon's match at Wembley, with Bill Holden explaining how 'the storm which lashed Britain has swept fear into the hearts of Sweden's Soccer stars,' whereas their English opponents 'couldn't care less if it snows – THEY'LL KEEP GOING'. No doubt they did, but Sweden won 3–2, as Middlesbrough's Brian Clough in his second (and last) England outing hit the woodwork twice but failed to score, leaving Holden to rue 'the blackest day' in England's 'once-proud Soccer history'. 'England,' he declared, 'didn't resemble an international team. They lacked method, fight and control. Name any attribute a team should have had – AND ENGLAND JUST HADN'T GOT IT.'[1]

The theatrical revolution continued. *Serjeant Musgrave's Dance* by John Arden would ultimately become an anti-colonial classic, but it opened on the 22nd at the Royal Court to largely negative notices, mainly on the grounds of incomprehensibility, followed by gapingly empty houses. Al Alvarez in the *New Statesman* had a particular gripe with Lindsay Anderson's direction. 'Having used Dudley Moore's music so effectively to create a background of emotion,' he noted, 'it is a pity he did not bring it in where most needed: to set off the bits of doggerel with which Mr Arden studs his text.' More immediately, the greater impact was made by Alun Owen's *No Trams to Lime Street*, shown four days earlier in ITV's pioneering *Armchair Theatre* slot on Sunday evenings. 'A strikingly successful piece of work,' acclaimed *The Times*, 'catching with unobtrusive skill the cadence of everyday speech but heightening, concentrating and shaping to make each line tell.' The plot concerned three sailors (played by Alfred Lynch, Jack Hedley and Tom Bell) going ashore in Liverpool one evening – 'never degenerating into the slapdash regional caricatures which often take the place of characterisation in television drama' – while 'Miss Billie Whitelaw's Liverpool widow was a brilliantly observed piece of acting'. Such plaudits did not stop a blizzard of angry letters and phone calls to the *Liverpool Echo*. 'I thought it was sordid, nasty, cheap,' complained one local woman. 'You get that sort of thing in any seaport, and to bring Liverpool into the picture with a public house of drunks was absolutely deplorable. I am proud of my city, and I thought the play was a definite aspersion.' Owen, himself Liverpool-Welsh, was unabashed. 'I have fought for two years now to get plays performed in the Liverpool accent,' he informed the paper. 'I was told the accent was ridiculous, comical, absurd and very ugly . . . I could quite easily have set this play in some never-never land of the north with everybody talking like Gracie Fields . . .'

The fiction title of the autumn was undoubtedly Vladimir Nabokov's *Lolita*, while for non-fiction the accolade went to *The Lore and Language of Schoolchildren* by Iona and Peter Opie, an astonishing exercise in retrieval that included, as one reviewer put it, 'rhymes, riddles, nicknames, catch-phrases, counting-out chants, and the whole *lingua franca* of the playground'. It made an immediate mark, including a lengthy review on the leader page of *The Times*, and was further evidence of an increasing appetite for 'ordinary' voices and faces. Contributions came from some 5,000 children attending over 70 schools, none of them private, and it included some of the names that those at secondary moderns directed at their neighbourhood peers: 'Grammar grubs', 'Grammar-bugs stinking slugs, dirty little humbugs', 'Grammar School Slops', 'Grammar School Spivs', 'Grammar School Sissies', 'Filthy twerps' and, naturally, 'Slaps'. The Prime Minister, however, still preferred the non-ordinary, noting at the start of November that he was reading Anthony Powell's 'The House of Acceptance' – ie, presumably *The Acceptance World* – and that he was finding it 'witty but pointless'.[2]

The election had come and gone, but the whirlwind of urban development remained relentless. During these weeks, the model was unveiled for the 'ultra modern' new Co-op building in the centre of

Basingstoke, replacing 'a whole string of small shops' and billed as 'the
first major step towards a bright, modern shopping centre for the town';
the property developer Jack Cotton revealed his latest plans for transforming Piccadilly Circus's north-east corner (the Monico site) into a
brightly illuminated 13-storey building with what the *Daily Mirror*
admiringly called a 'space-age look'; Madge Martin in Oxford took a
walk through 'the queer devastated slums of St Ebbe's', then in the
process of being cleared; a single issue of the *East London Advertiser*
reported on the housing scheme in Locton Street, Limehouse (to
include a 16-storey block of flats), the rehousing in Poplar of more than
230 families in the Rowsell Street area under an LCC clearance plan, the
compulsory purchase of several acres of rundown housing in Stepney's
Cayley Street neighbourhood, and, in Canning Town, 'on the site of the
famous Trinity Church, Barking Road', the erection of a large block of
flats in West Ham Corporation's new Ascot estate; the *New Yorker*
profiled 'Metamorphosis in the Gorbals', where the comprehensive
redevelopment scheme then under way would 'result in the disappearance of the existing Gorbals, or most of it, and the creation of a new
community, which promises to bear no resemblance to the old except in
name'; and, some 7 miles away in Paisley, the locals contemplated not
only the first of six 15-storey blocks of flats but also plans for the
complete redevelopment of the town centre – plans which, according to
the *Paisley Daily Express*, would turn that centre into 'a show-place and
a cynosure for years to come' (though the paper conceded that 'so
futuristic' were the models that 'people have had difficulty in grasping
all that it means'). Frederic Osborn, a long-ago founder of Welwyn
Garden City and still a passionate advocate of dispersal and New
Towns, looked on with horror. 'The architects,' he wrote in late October
to Lewis Mumford, 'want to go up into the air . . . They are supported
by the lucky people in country houses and parks who don't want their
Arcadia invaded. They have succeeded to some extent, owing to the
structure of our democracy. But they are overriding the inarticulate yet
vast majority . . .'[3]

Occasionally the voices of those most intimately affected did break
through. When, around this time, A.W. Davey, housing manager for St
Pancras Council, publicly contrasted the 'good-hearted fun, laughter
and happiness' of the old slums with 'the atmosphere of worry, tension,

slobbishness, and all that goes with these things which are immediately obvious on any modern housing estate', the *Evening Standard* took the pulse in the multi-storey flats of the big new Regent's Park estate behind Euston Station. Two young housewives were adamant that Davey was wrong, with 21-year-old Barbara Pike, married to a lorry driver and with three small children, praising the friendliness of her neighbours and saying that, after getting out of her leaking Kentish Town slum, she had never been so happy in her life; but 79-year-old George Phelps agreed with Davey and spoke of how 'the people are nosy, there are too many snobs and the children are badly behaved and rude.' Or take Liverpool soon afterwards, where Dr Ronald Bradbury, the City Architect, complained that 'the stay-putters are one of our biggest problems' – ie slum-dwellers refusing to move. Whereupon a local paper found in Toxteth some evidence backing Bradbury – 'When you have lived here this long you don't want to move just anywhere, do you?' said Teresa McVeigh, living at 241 Beaufort Street with her aged mother – while other slum-dwellers waited impatiently for a move to new housing: 'People like 30-year-old Mr Albert Lee, his wife and two children, Shirley (8) and Albert (3), who live in a damp, cramped cellar at 41 Park Street with only one living room. They wash in a converted air-raid shelter and sleep in the one room upstairs.' The paper also quoted Mr Lee, a motor driver suffering from congestion of the lung and frequent attacks of bronchitis: 'We have been living here for six years. They keep telling us it will only be another 18 months before we are re-housed but that 18 months is the longest I've ever come across.'

Feelings were mixed too in Sheffield, where the Park Hill development was still being built but was about to receive its first tenants. 'Some people, particularly the elderly, had no wish to move at all,' recalled Mrs J. F. Demers, who that October moved in as assistant estate manager and welfare officer. 'Inadequate, uneconomic and unhygienic as their old houses were, they were familiar and had spelled home to them for many years. Not only were they worried about the impending move, they were naturally concerned over increased costs, who their new neighbours might be, whether they would get used to "living in the sky" and so on.' Life in the sky indeed, but a local paper was meanwhile reassuring potential residents that 'THE PLANNERS HAVE GONE

TO GREAT LENGTHS TO MINIMISE THE NECESSARY ADJUSTMENTS', and that 'the deck system' (providing 'on every third floor a 10 feet wide "street"') would enable 'neighbours to chat' and 'small children to play'. Soon afterwards, on the 22nd, two well-attended public meetings included 'varied reactions' to the announcement that no dogs or cats would be allowed, with some prospective tenants 'obviously distressed at the prospect of having to part with loved pets when they move from clearance areas to the new flats'. However, Councillor George Cooper, chairman of the Housing Management Committee, took the larger view, insisting that Park Hill would become 'the finest modern housing estate in Europe', adding, 'The scheme has the finest contemporary features. Semi-detached houses are "square" in comparison and forward-looking people should look forward to living there. These are almost perfect dwellings. It is now up to you, the would-be tenants, to make this a really worthwhile community which is not just technically correct but also socially correct.' Just over a fortnight later, on 7 November, at a ceremony presided over by the Lord Mayor, a key was handed over to 61-year-old Helen Jackson, who with her husband Fred lived in a condemned house in nearby Duke Street and were due to move into Park Hill on the 11th. 'A historic occasion,' Councillor Harold Lambert, chairman of the Housing Development Committee, predictably called it, acclaiming Park Hill as 'a tribute to public enterprise in its best form'.[4]

There were two other notable beginnings that autumn. On 30 October, in a Soho basement at 39 Gerrard Street, Ronnie Scott's Club was born. 'Too many clubs seem to degenerate into "jiving palaces",' claimed Scott in advance, whereas 'here, there will be plenty of room to dance, but also plenty of room to sit and listen – to the musicians.' Opening night featured not only the Tubby Hayes Quartet but also (noted the *Melody Maker* ad written by Scott himself) 'a young Alto Saxophonist PETER KING, an old Tenor Saxophonist RONNIE SCOTT, plus first appearance in a Jazz Club since the Relief of Mafeking, of JACK PARNELL'. The other opening was three days later, on Monday, 2 November. 'Today is the beginning of a new era,' proclaimed a quarter-page ad for the Caterpillar Tractor Co in that morning's *Times*:

But only the beginning. Our highways will reflect the Nation's prosperity, save the Nation more than they cost to build, benefit each and every one of us – and we need them NOW.

Caterpillar has contributed much towards these new avenues of progress and opportunity – and will contribute more. For Caterpillar earth-moving equipment is as reliable and sure as progress itself.

The highway starting that day was the first completed stretch, some 55 miles, of what at this stage was usually referred to as the London–Birmingham Motorway, subsequently the M1. It had taken only 19 months (helped by 1959's glorious weather), and anticipation was particularly keen in Luton, close to the southern end (where the opening ceremony was to be) and itself a car-manufacturing town. 'The Police will have their work cut out patrolling the road – not for speedsters but for cars and other vehicles going too slow, and holding up the pace of the road,' predicted the *Luton News*. 'Every motorist will be calling it his Dream Road, for he will be king of his own little realm as he speeds down this vast Motorway.' And the front-page article ended with a roll of the drums: 'The whole world will be looking to this Motorway. And to Luton falls the honour of knowing it was in on the start of a revolution.'

The new Minister of Transport, the energetic, self-promoting Ernest Marples, duly did the business at nearby Pepperstock, from where he gave a radio signal to police along the route to open the motorway's approaches, before himself walking a few hundred yards to a bridge spanning the new road, from where he watched the pioneering traffic. 'I was frightened when I watched the first users of this road today,' he frankly told a celebratory luncheon in London a few hours later. 'I have never seen anybody going so fast and ignoring the rules and regulations. Of the first four cars, three were not in traffic lines and one broke down ... People must learn to master these great roads. Otherwise there will be many grave accidents.' In fact, seven cars broke down in the first half-hour – overheating (two), out of petrol (two), punctures (two), out of oil (one) – while an AA patrolman also admitted to being unimpressed: 'There is a fair amount of motorists trying out the old bus to "see what she'll do" – and often hugging the outside lane at 60 mph, not thinking of the car behind doing 80 or 100.' But should the speedometers even be hitting three figures? 'We are keeping an open mind at the moment on the question of speed limits,' observed Marples. 'We will see what happens.'[5]

The decade was drawing to an end, including for four very fifties people. 'A real master in making comedy of everyday situations' was a typically enthusiastic viewer reaction to Tony Hancock's current television series, but Hancock himself spent a week in October at a nursing home. 'I was doing my nut,' he explained afterwards to a sympathetic journalist. 'Got a bit strained. Couldn't remember my lines.' Gilbert Harding at the same time was endorsing Macleans new double-action indigestion tablets. 'I could write a treatise on indigestion,' he told newspaper readers. 'I know. I get it. I get indigestion because I like good food; because I worry about totally unimportant things; because I rush around much more than I should.' These tablets, though, 'always do the trick'. Princess Margaret spent 28 October at the opening in Old Bethnal Green Road of St Jude's Church of England Secondary School, destroyed by enemy action in 1940 and now rebuilt in the shadow of a modern housing estate. 'In these days, a plethora of material pleasures are constantly being offered as ideal goals for prosperity and happiness, and we need the inspiration of our Christian faith to maintain our spiritual resources to help us over our problems,' the Princess, wearing a full-length sable coat, told her audience. 'It is no good,' she added with reference to the latest Soviet satellite, 'for man to seek escape in luniks and rocketry and to leave his soul morally earthbound among the television sets and espresso bars.'

A week or two later, an even more glamorous figure, accompanied by her tiny Pekinese dog Powder Puff, was also in East London. 'It's been so exciting,' announced Jayne Mansfield after a visit to The George in Glengall Grove, Millwall, where she pulled pints of bitter, sang and played the piano, as well as scoring 45 points with her first three darts. 'I love the pub, the drink and atmosphere.' As for the tough dockers crowded admiringly round the bar: 'They are so sweet.'[6]

2

A Real Love Match

Harold Macmillan may in the immediate flush of electoral victory have declared the class war dead, but it was class that fuelled a couple of episodes in November 1959. In one, Kingsley Amis, in the course of making an advertisement in the company of the photographer Antony Armstrong-Jones, happened to comment unfavourably on the intelligence of Princess Margaret, before being offered by him a lift to Staines. En route, they stopped at Slough for an apparently cordial drink, after which Armstrong-Jones abruptly left Amis and his wife standing on the pavement to make their own way to Staines. 'He's upper-*class*,' a friend helpfully explained afterwards. 'Which means he doesn't end up one down to the likes of fucking you.' The other episode featured sardonic treatment by the *Daily Express* society gossip columnist 'William Hickey' directed at an Old Etonian, Jeremy Sandford, and his heiress-wife, Nell Dunn. Their crime was daring to move from their 'fashionable, bow-windowed flat' in Cheyne Walk, Chelsea to 'a block of condemned houses' on the other side of the river – from where he was 'anxious to experience life "with real people", so he tells his friends', while she, 'carrying his philosophy to the extreme, has taken a job in a local chocolate factory'. The payoff came a week or so later when 79 Lavender Road, Battersea was burgled. 'The Sandfords get their first real taste of low life,' exalted Hickey, who, after giving details of what had been stolen, slipped in the killer touch: 'They are particularly upset because the new pink bath which they have had specially installed – theirs is the only bathroom in the street – has been badly scratched.'[1]

Largely unconcerned – at least on the surface – with questions of class, the musical flow continued. On 15 November the Light Programme launched Alan Keith's *The 100 Best Tunes in the World* (shortened before long to *Your Hundred Best Tunes*), a Sunday-night staple, especially with female listeners, for over four decades; five days later, at Bruce Forsyth's 'I'm in Charge' show at the Palace Theatre, Manchester, Sam and Kitty Lunn were summoned to the stage as that evening's longest-married couple (51 years), where they sang 'My Old Dutch' before she had a heart attack and died in the host's arms; late in November, mainly favourable reviews started appearing of the film version of Wolf Mankowitz's satire on Tin Pan Alley, *Expresso Bongo*, including a cameo role for Gilbert Harding (as himself) complaining about 'plastic palm trees' and 'teenage rebellion' – though the part of the teenage idol was played so straight that one critic, Isabel Quigly, was 'left with the disturbing feeling that here is Cliff Richard in person, as credulous and as nice as Bongo, as simple and as duped'; by early December, Adam Faith's unanswerably of-the-moment 'What Do You Want (If You Don't Want Money)', arranged by John Barry, was settling in at the top of the charts; and on the 11th, Bernard Manning's Embassy Club opened in Manchester, with his mother on the till and the 29-year-old Manning singing 'High Hopes'. 'A barely prettified working men's club, with harsh lighting, formica-topped tables and hard-working, white-jacketed waiters sweating under the weight of trays of brimming pint glasses' is how his biographer describes the Embassy, while a day or two later, across the Pennines in Huddersfield, the sociologist Dennis Marsden was at the bar of the Scape Goat Hill Band Club, taking notes:

> Talk about TV which they'd all been watching earlier in the evening. 'Ah like that Billy Cotton Show. He's a wonderful turn is that. He can make that band sound real good – just like a brass band.' 'Ah like that little fat chap,' said another. 'What's his name, Eric something or other. He gets some real good singers on his programme, opera singers' . . . Somebody else said, 'Vic Oliver's a good turn an' all tha knows. He allus conducts a bit on his show. Just at t'beginning he conducts t'full orchestra.'

'And,' to clinch the case, 'he never gets any o'these, what d'you call him, Bing Crosbies on his programme.'[2]

Most cinema-goers would surely have endorsed Anthony Heap's diary lament in November about the 'total disappearance of newsreels from cinema programmes' – because of television – and how 'in their place we usually get short "interest" films that, as often as not, are of no interest whatever.' For radio listeners, though, there was always the comfort of Ambridge. 'The Archers to me are completely real – I worry about them all, talk about them, and plan for them,' a typical addict told the BBC that autumn. 'I *never* miss an episode if I can help it,' affirmed another. 'I should be very sad indeed to see this programme ended, and would feel I had lost a lot of friends.' Even so, the accompanying audience-research report noted quite a widespread view that 'in recent months events have been altogether too sensational – escaped criminals, international gangs of thieves with Interpol on their tail, and the mysterious and sudden disappearance of Madam Garonne do not fit with Ambridge, while on the domestic scene we are "now reaching a point where a man can't climb a ladder without falling off or get on a horse without taking a toss."' To judge by Nella Last's diary comment a few months later ('The Archers – getting further from reality'), this melodramatic trend would continue, while a further vexation was the possibility – as yet unconfirmed – that Jill Archer was pregnant again:

Several thought this showed Phil had no sympathy with or understanding of his wife, some considered it quite disgusting ('As an ex-nurse and a Mother I know it is never easy and sometimes fated to have babies. She should not have had intercourse at all yet, let alone conceived') and some thought Jill much too placid if it were true ('If I were having babies like a machine (one out – one in) I'd be very, very irritable'). All those who raised the matter were united in feeling that it should not be allowed to happen, and it was suggested that Phil and Jill should get in touch with the Family Planning Association immediately.

As always, Walter Gabriel provoked a 'very sharp division of opinion'. Some regarded him as a 'miserable old curmudgeon' with a 'stupid cackle', but almost twice as many enjoyed this 'loveable old rascal'. In London, the run-up to Christmas featured as usual the Regent Street decorations – 'the best yet', reckoned Madge Martin, with 'glittering chandeliers' and 'festoons of lights', given the full Richard

Dimbleby treatment in a live outside broadcast on *Panorama*. 'I kept hoping he might be led in his solemn enthusiasm to refer to "this great street",' recorded *Punch*'s Henry Turton. 'When at last he did, my festive season was made.' And it was in Regent Street, at Burberry's on a dank December day, that a young Canadian writer, Leonard Cohen, now bought a not-yet-famous blue raincoat. Meanwhile, in theatreland, Cliff Richard found himself at the Globe in Stockton-on-Tees, performing in the panto *Babes in the Wood* in white trousers and a cropped jacket, but for the capital's small children nothing beat *Noddy in Toyland* at the Prince's Theatre. 'Can no one convince Miss Enid Blyton,' asked Alan Brien in vain, 'that in this day and age, before audiences which include coloured children, it is displaying the crassest insensitivity to portray the golliwogs as idiot victims of toyland *apartheid*, with the parallel made quite explicit by a nasty song and dance by three of them called "I'm Golly, I'm Woggy, I'm Nigger"?' On Christmas Day itself, almost the biggest Home Service audience was for the nostalgic *The Tommy Handley Story*, though it was an unmistakable sign of increasingly TV-oriented times that four days later marked the end of the sixth and final radio series of *Hancock's Half Hour*.[3]

At about the same time, Gallup's regular end-of-year poll had 60 per cent looking back on a good 1959 and only 6 per cent expecting 1960 to be a worse year. Probably neither David Blunkett nor Tony Garrett was in the majority. Blunkett's father was a highly respected foreman at a water gas plant, but in early December he fell, owing to the incompetence of a fellow-worker, into a giant vat of boiling water, dying an agonising death a month later. Blunkett's widowed mother in Sheffield was left in poverty after the East Midlands Gas Board behaved in a manner (in her son's unforgiving words) 'more reminiscent of the worst private employer than a publicly owned industry'. As for Garrett, he was living with the writer Angus Wilson in the Suffolk village of Felsham Woodside and working locally for the Probation Service. But malicious gossip spread, and a few weeks before Christmas he was informed by the Chief Probation Officer that he could continue in the Service only if he stopped living with Wilson and moved 40 miles away – a compromise that Garrett refused, resigning in January. 'The offer was distressing on many levels,' notes Wilson's biographer Margaret

Drabble, and Garrett himself, for whom his job had been a vocation, developed a stammer in consequence.[4]

A trio of reports this winter considered different aspects of the welfare of the young. The Crowther Report of December 1959, entitled *15–18*, argued cogently in favour of raising the school-leaving age from 15 to 16 and of making part-time attendance at county colleges compulsory, but, despite being well received, it failed to sway ministerial minds. The following month, a QC's report into the previous summer's disturbances at Carlton Approved School pinned much of the blame on what *The Times* in its summary called 'the emergence of a small but exceedingly difficult hard core of anti-authority young people'. Soon afterwards, in early February, a committee chaired by the 'youthful grandmother' Lady Albemarle issued a report on the Youth Service that found it failing to reach at least one person in three and urged a ten-year development plan. 'All this preoccupation with youth, with teenagers is so high-minded,' reflected John Vaizey in an overview of Crowther and Albemarle. 'Is there *really* a teenage problem? Do they want or need to be done good to?' These were pertinent questions, and indeed a survey of youth clubs in Cardiff in 1960 encountered 'considerable distrust of "missionary" activity in many of them', as well as more generally observing, on the part of that city's teenage population without contact with youth clubs, an entirely qualm-less preference for 'more individual and more passive uses of leisure, with a heavy emphasis on television viewing and cinema going'.

Certainly one teenager in 1960 – 14-year-old Jacqueline Aitken (later Wilson), living in Kingston-upon-Thames and going to school in New Malden – had plenty of her own fish to fry. 'We got some smashing bargains so I'm jolly glad I went,' she wrote in her new diary on 2 January after going to the Bentalls' sale with her mother, and over the coming weeks a succession of rather breathless entries followed:

9 January. I did the shopping with Dad and you'll never guess what we bought! A RECORD PLAYER! ... It is an automatic kind and plays beautifully. We bought 'Travelling Light' by Cliff Richard and Dad chose a Mantovani long player ... I've been playing them, and all our old 78 records, all the afternoon.

18 January. In Latin we had 28 vocabs to learn! Not homework, mind you, but just to be done in our spare time! Honestly, isn't it ridiculous? I'm just dying to leave school.

22 January. In the evening I went to see 'Expresso Bongo' with Carol at the Regal. We saw tons of girls from school there, all dressed up pretending to be sixteen.

8 February. We had chips, corned beef and American salad and mince and apple tart for dinner today, not bad for school dinners.

9 February. Dinner was steak pie, greens and mashed potato, and semolina and jam for pud. Pretty awful, n'est-ce pas?

12 February. In the evening I went dancing. Sue didn't come or Judith, but Carol and Jill did. I wore my new nail varnish and new flatties which were lovely for dancing in. We did a lot of complicated Samba steps and I had Peter for a partner. After Ken I think he's terribly ordinary.

13 February. Mum said she wanted to see the film 'The Reluctant Debutante' so we went together. On the way we went into the Bentalls' record department. I saw P. Wilson and Y. McCarthy in turquoise duffle coats, extremely tight jeans and cha-cha shoes being cuddled by a group of horrible spotty teddy boys.

Just over a week later, she was at Kingston's Granada cinema for her first pop concert. 'I've never experienced anything like it, you don't feel at all self conscious, just madly *hep*,' she recorded. 'Of course Adam was wonderful. Honestly, I've never believed girls could scream so loud! Adam looked ever so handsome though!' And on another page of her diary she stuck in a photo of him with the words – in green biro – 'Adam for Always!' and 'Faith Forever'.[5]

The Goon Show in effect bowed out with 'The Last of the Smoking Seagoons', but there were plenty of beginnings during the early weeks of 1960. From New Year's Day, the BBC had a new director-general in Hugh Carleton Greene, who was determined (as he later put it) 'to dissipate the ivory tower stuffiness'; on 8 January, at Portishead in Somerset,

Margaret Thatcher made her *Any Questions?* debut, was asked in the first question about show-business personalities being used to advertise products, and replied that her usual reaction was 'Hmm, I wonder what they're being paid for this'; on the 21st a literary career was launched when the Wintersons adopted baby Jeanette and took her home to 200 Water Street, Accrington; two days later, a 17-year-old red-headed Scot, Billy Bremner, was blooded for Leeds United in a 3–1 win at Chelsea; next day in the *Observer*, Bridget Colgan (real name Lydia James) started a monthly 'Within the Family' column, probably the first in a British newspaper to give parenting and child-care advice; on the 25th, American-style ten-pin bowling reached Britain, as Sir John Hunt of Everest fame sent down the first bowl at an old ABC cinema in Stamford Hill, with boxing's Henry Cooper among those in attendance; two evenings later at London's Conway Hall, 'an audience of 70 sat transfixed with gloom' (according to someone present) as the young avant-garde composer Cornelius Cardew gave 'a concert of really stunning boredom'; on BBC TV on the 29th, up against *The Army Game*, Eric Sykes and Hattie Jacques were together for the first time in *Sykes And A. . .*; a week later, on 5 February, Thatcher delivered a well-organised maiden speech in the Commons, earning the compliment from a Labour MP that she had hardly needed to refer to her notes; next afternoon, 'a vaunted figure in school football', 17-year-old Terry Venables from Dagenham, made his league debut for Chelsea in a 4–2 defeat at West Ham; and the following week another early-vaunted figure, Dennis Potter, had his first book published, *The Glittering Coffin*, fairly described in the *Sunday Times* on the 14th as 'a wordy but eloquent plea for a Socialist Britain, for an end to what the author considers the inertia, mortmain and commercialisation that are cankering our society'. But beginnings could also be endings, and around this time there appeared on billboards and television a memorable advertisement for a new brand of cigarette: a man in a trench coat, standing on the Albert Bridge at night and lighting up, with the accompanying slogan 'You're never alone with a Strand'. The unfortunate assumption was widely made that to smoke a Strand was to be lonely and therefore a loser; the cigarette itself proved too hot for smokers' fingers; and the campaign, along with the brand itself, was rapidly pulled.[6]

It was almost fifteen years since the war, and the war-film boom was at last over. But on 11 February, the Duke of Edinburgh and Admiral of the Fleet the Earl Mountbatten of Burma were among those at the Odeon, Leicester Square attending the premier of *Sink the Bismarck!*, starring Kenneth More as the Director of Naval Operations. 'To my mind it seems stupid to have shown the Bismarck crew as oafs and simpletons, and their commander, the distinguished Admiral Lutyens, as nothing better than a bully and a Hitler toady,' commented the *Observer*'s Caroline Lejeune, while *Films and Filming* found it 'an incredibly old-fashioned film, almost as if one were watching a 1940 piece of flag-waving instead of a 1960 piece of drama'. But these and similar strictures failed to prevent *Sink the Bismarck!* becoming the year's top-grossing film in Britain. That same evening saw a rather different West End first night, of the Cockney musical *Fings Ain't Wot They Used T'Be*, which since its initial production a year earlier at the Theatre Royal in Stratford East had been given a major revamp and upgrade by Joan Littlewood. The result was considerable critical acclaim – predictably not shared that first night by the diarist Anthony Heap ('low life squalor on the stage') – and a two-year run at the Garrick. 'This tough and virile musical has been improved out of all recognition,' declared Harold Hobson, while Eric Keown praised the cast's 'enormous comic gusto', including particular mentions for Miriam Karlin as the gangster's moll ('a coarse brilliance') and Barbara Windsor as the prostitute ('asking in a baby voice where little birds go in the winter'). Who came to *Fings*? When a book version was published some months later, Littlewood asserted in her introduction that the Garrick had been 'packed night after night with Cockney people', a claim that one reviewer flatly denied. 'Chuck it, Miss Littlewood!' expostulated John Bowen in *Punch*. 'Even at Stratford East it wasn't Cockney people, on the night I saw *Fings*, who drove away in their posh cars or took the tube back to Chelsea.' The other *Fings* tailpiece came soon afterwards, in October 1960, when the 23-year-old Barbara Windsor – from Hackney Road, Bethnal Green, but now sitting in her dressing-room at the Garrick – was interviewed by the *East London Advertiser*. Would 'The Dish', as the article repeatedly called her, eventually be returning to the East End, to act again at the Theatre Royal? '"Are you kidding?" she shrieked. "I'm finished with all that ten quid a week lark. I'm not in this business for art's sake, you know – I'm in it for the money. Besides, I've got too many expenses to keep up. I've just bought a telly."[7]

Fings was merely one example of a broader trend. *Clea*, the final part of Lawrence Durrell's *The Alexandria Quartet*, was published in February to a mixed reception, but the landmark novel that month, starting to mark out 1960 as 'The Year of the North', was David Storey's unsparingly realistic *This Sporting Life*, set in the world of rugby league. The reviews were largely positive, though tending to suggest a gulf between reviewer and subject matter. 'A piece of field work in darkest Yorkshire' was the *TLS*'s characterisation, while Karl Miller informed *Observer* readers that 'the whole team plays a very grim kind of Rugby and there is none of the complexity, none of the loveable dramatic appeal, which there is in soccer.' Just as Storey's novel was being published, the *TLS* sought to offer a larger perspective on the phenomenon in a leading article called 'Roots'. 'It is rather ironical,' reflected the paper, 'that, at a time when the British working classes seem to be growingly conservative in their political views and growingly middle-class in their tastes and habits, we should be enjoying for the first time in many years something like a renaissance of working-class literature.' Obvious examples were cited – including the work of Arnold Wesker, Shelagh Delaney, Alan Sillitoe and Keith Waterhouse – and the point made that 'what is called "the New Left" in politics is very much concerned with breaking down the dominance in our cultural life, in our literary monthlies and weeklies, for instance, of what is often called "the genteel tradition".' Yet inevitably the *TLS* entered a reservation: 'One has an uneasy feeling that any novel or play with a working-class setting and with a note of protest about it, is setting off, perhaps for the next five years or so, with a flying start' – in other words, irrespective of literary merit. Even so, not every working-class novelist was flying in 1960. *The Big Room* was Sid Chaplin's first novel in a decade, but in February it got the treatment from Keith Waterhouse in the *New Statesman*. 'Something has gone seriously wrong,' Waterhouse reckoned, before expressing the wish that the author had 'stuck to the ordinary, dreadful lives of this ordinary, dreadful family in this great room'. Chaplin himself, though, was stoical. 'It's been nice,' he wrote from Newcastle to a friend, 'to see another one launched after all these weary years', adding hopefully that the novel he was completing 'may be better for them to understand'.[8]

On far more people's lips in early 1960 were the titillating 'My Confessions' being peddled by Diana Dors each Sunday in the *News of the World*. Arguably the first authentic kiss-and-tell, and earning her some £35,000, they began on 24 January with an attempt on the front page to soften criticism: 'I know I've been a naughty girl. I know they call me the film star with a lurid past. But today I'm a happy wife. Soon I hope to become a devoted mother.' A week later, another message: 'Thank you, all of you, for writing. I'm delighted you are finding my story so exciting. Forgive me for not replying personally, but it's impossible just now as my baby is expected any moment.' And on 7 February: 'Well, he's arrived. He's in my arms now, my wonderful 7lb son Mark Richard. I'm so proud and so happy.' Nella Last, not a *News of the World* reader, tried to keep up. 'Dear me,' she noted that day, 'I am intrigued about the articles about Diana Dors life – Mrs Salisbury [her cleaner] was very censorious but vague, but for it to be mentioned in Parliament & John Gordon thought it of enough "news" value to include in his "jottings," make me wonder, what exactly she did write.' John Gordon was the habitually censorious *Sunday Express* columnist on 'Current Events', and Last had just read this: 'I would like to have congratulated Miss Diana Dors on achieving motherhood. Instead I extend my sympathy to an innocent baby born at a time when his mother is publicly degrading herself as few women have done before.' 'Poor Diana,' reflected the kindlier Last, 'she will perhaps welcome such publicity now – but knowing little boys pretty well, her "punishment" for such, is to come . . .'

That same evening, Tony Hancock was the subject of John Freeman's *Face to Face* – a compelling half-hour, with Hancock chain-smoking and deeply uneasy, that left many viewers at the time dissatisfied:

I'd prefer to think of Mr Hancock as a character in 'H—ancock's Half-Hour'.

Seemed unable to cope with the stringent demands of the programme.

Lost without a script.

Hancock's utterings seemed to be the outpourings of a confused mind.

I failed to understand them all and wonder if he did himself, e.g. on religion.

I thought John Freeman hit below the belt and was at times impertinent.

Does it really matter whether Hancock wants children or how much the BBC pays him? These are the sort of questions one would expect from a Sunday newspaper reporter.

Punch soon afterwards noted that Freeman 'sometimes overdoes it and causes an uprush of sympathy for the victim, as in the Hancock programme', but for Hancock himself it was a fateful turning point. 'It was the biggest mistake he ever made,' his brother Roger would reflect. 'I think it all started from that, really. Self-analysis – that was his killer.' As for Freeman, barely a fortnight later on *Panorama* he conducted another controversial interview, in this case going a long way to demolish the credibility of Frank Foulkes, President of the Communist-run Electrical Trades Union, recently accused again of ballot-rigging. Whereupon, five prominent Labour figures (none remotely pro-Communist) wrote to *The Times* complaining about 'trial by television'; dissenting letters followed from Malcolm Muggeridge and Christopher Chataway, among others; but a future Tory MP, John Stokes, agreed with the Labour five. 'Indeed,' he declared, 'I would go further; why must the Prime Minister, the Foreign Secretary, and other important persons of the day be constantly badgered, e.g. when getting into or out of aeroplanes, &c., to give their views at a moment's notice on grave issues?'[9]

The other union in the news that February was the National Union of Railwaymen, threatening strike action from the 15th. 'There is undoubtedly much sympathy for the most cruelly underpaid railwaymen,' Mollie Panter-Downes on the 10th told her *New Yorker* readers, but next day the diarist Florence Turtle was probably more representative of opinion, certainly of middle-class opinion: 'The Rail Strike seems inevitable, a complete deadlock. Blackmail by the Unions it seems, they are the curse of this country. All they seem to want is more pay for less work & less efficient work. The First Class carriage I travelled in last week was filthy.' In the event, the government blinked first, conceding a 5-per-cent wage increase. 'Irresponsibility has been made respectable,' complained *The Times*, but as ever there was also a general sense of relief, prompting the *Sunday Times* to praise the new Minister of Labour, Edward Heath, for his 'diplomacy and powers of gentle persuasion'. Almost everyone knew, though, that the underlying issue was the industry itself. 'British Railways must be taken in hand,' insisted the *Daily Mail* in the immediate wake of the settlement. 'They must be rationalised and streamlined.' The *Economist* concurred: 'The only possible economic future for the railways of this country is to become much smaller in scale (and staff) and vastly more efficient in organisation and more specialised in operation.' It was an unsentimental prospect that dismayed the writer Sylvia Townsend Warner. 'We still have some very sweet little branch-lines,' she wrote to a friend on the 14th from her home in Dorset.

> There is one from Taunton to Castle Cary which ten years ago I used very often, coming back from visiting my poor witless mother in her nursing-home. I caught its last journey of the day; and at each little station the guard got out, locked up the ticket office, looked round like a mother to see that everything was as it should be, put out the lights, and no doubt said God Bless You to it. This idyllic artless journey ended at Castle Cary, the train took itself off to sleep in a siding, and I waited half an hour for the express to come dashing & flashing in like something of a different breed. There is also a God-fearing train from Yeovil to Taunton that doesn't run on Sundays, and our own local pet from Maiden Newton to Bridport that has the best blackthorn brakes I know, and trots like a horse under the neolithic fort of Eggardon, & crosses a quantity of narrow bridges with screams of apprehension.

'As for the primroses along the cuttings,' she added, 'you can lean out of the window and smell them.'[10]

The week after the railway strike was called off was dominated by one subject: the imminent prospect of the first child born to a reigning monarch for over a century. 'Kept listening yesterday & today to the hourly news on Light Programme about the Queen, & Doctors coming & going,' noted Marian Raynham in Surbiton on Thursday the 18th. That afternoon, the left-wing Janet Hase – 'fed to the teeth with all the sentimental crap and shoddy sentiment being spewed forth by the press and radio, but disguised for the occasion as a bland Australian journalist' – interviewed nearly 50 people out of the crowd of several hundred (mainly middle-aged, middle-class women) waiting outside the gates of Buckingham Palace. 'She's an example to us all – a wonderful wife and mother – such a happy family – I'm so interested because my daughter is her age and has a little girl almost the same age as Princess Anne,' said one woman. Hase was generally struck by the high degree of personal identification. 'I think she'd *like* to know that we're out here, wishing her well,' said another. 'I've got three children myself – boy, girl and another boy. That's why I hope her third's a boy.' Next day, Judy Haines in Chingford was also on the *qui vive*: 'After lunch heard that the Queen's doctors were in attendance on her. Listened to all news bulletins. Then just after 4 o'c John Snagge announced: "The Queen has had her baby. It's a boy."' Among other diarists, Mrs Raynham switched the radio back on just in time to hear the news, Madge Martin (on holiday in Brighton) saw the newspaper placards announcing 'The Queen's Baby – A PRINCE', and Nella Last missed the first announcement but after hearing the news wondered 'if the fact there's another "direct" heir will change Princess Margaret's life a little – make her choice a bit less "rigid"'. Most of the diarists, and presumably most people, were pleased by the news (the baby not yet named Andrew), while in the press next day the *Sketch* and the *Mirror* ('OH BOY!') devoted six pages each to the story, the *Mail* only five.

Constitutional continuity was further assured the following Wednesday when David Dimbleby (undergraduate) and Jonathan Dimbleby (schoolboy) made their TV debuts on Richard Dimbleby's *No Passport* holiday programme, with the pair going to the Lakes for a fortnight. 'They went by car, stayed in hotels costing up to £3 per day for each of them, and presented papa on return with a bill for between £70 and £80,' noted Hilary Corke in the *Listener*. 'Surely this was an appalling example? If this was intended as a sample holiday for young persons, then it should have been adjusted to a normal young persons's economy, with stays in youth-hostels and so on. If it was intended as a sample holiday for adults, then adults should have been sent on it.' But the week's big constitutional moment was still to come – a secret known only to a few, including the PM. 'I fear,' Macmillan had reflected on the 16th, 'it will not be very popular, but I think nevertheless that people will feel that the Princess has been very unlucky. So long as the young man is (as he appears to be) a gentleman, *not* divorced, & a Protestant,

I cannot see that the Queen or Ministers have any right (still less duty) to interfere under the Act of 1772.'[11]

It all went public on Friday the 26th, succinctly recorded by Jennie Hill, living near Winchester: 'T.V. Gardener's Club was interrupted to announce Princess Margaret engaged to be married to Tony Armstrong-Jones.' Judy Haines for her part was 'staggered' but 'thrilled' to hear the news, Madge Martin was 'delighted' for the Princess ('she had seemed so lost, somehow'), and Kingsley Amis in Swansea had a particular interest as he watched the television in his kitchen: 'There was the oleaginous Godfrey Talbot, always kept on hand for these do's, mouthing, "And everybody's so delighted because this is so obviously a real love match."' A love match perhaps, but Florence Turtle's immediate comment was 'not a particularly good match I would think', while next day Nella Last (herself 'glad') was 'pegging out some tea towels on the line' when her neighbour Mrs Atkinson called over: 'She was *shocked* at Princess Margaret's engagement to a common photographer – for once, not asking me what I thought before she began . . . She said "Why, she will be Mrs Armstrong-*Jones*." I said, "Oh no, she is a princess & will keep her title – perhaps they will give her husband a title." She said "I hope they *do*."' The press of course went to town: not just the fulsome guff from the usual suspects, but even the *Guardian*, extolling as it did 'a fairy-story romance of the young man working for his living, like countless other young men, who has won the hand of a princess', though managing to refrain from following the example of the *Mirror* and the *Herald* by calling the Old Etonian a 'working lad'. Altogether, it was, as Anthony Heap noted soon afterwards, an 'awful lot of gush and ballyhoo' about the whole thing. As for the Princess herself, Heap offered the thought that 'maybe marriage will help her to acquire a little more dignity and decorum.'[12]

———

'The building sites are damp,' John Berger wrote in November 1959 about Frank Auerbach's latest London paintings. 'The mud clings. The tarpaulins are heavy with moisture. The light in the sky is far less comforting than a cup of tea.' But the pace of urban change was insufficient for the influential, left-wing architectural-*cum*-design writer Reyner Banham. 'Our city centres, untouched by even piecemeal redevelopment since 1939, are now at least twenty years out of date, clogged with inefficient buildings in the wrong places,' he declared soon afterwards. 'Simply as physical equipment our urban hubs are intolerable and must be replaced . . .' Architecture was becoming an increasingly fashionable topic, and in March 1960 a three-part television series by Sir Kenneth Clark, *The Art of Architecture*, was the occasion for *TV Times* to commission a piece ('Building for Beauty') by the best-known architect of the day, Basil Spence, that offered an uncompromising defence of the modern idiom:

> Not all this newness will succeed. But it is far better that some of it should fail and people should *try* than we should continue copying past styles paradoxically called traditional. Modern architecture is as exciting as any adventure in history for it looks straight into the future, not backwards.
>
> We have new materials, new techniques to apply. Modern architecture is sweeping in like the tide. The future is bright.

It wasn't bright for all, though, as witnessed by the destruction of the solid, red-bricked Victorian barracks at Aldershot, where E. S. Turner had recently observed that 'today the demolishers are cutting a great swathe across the Camp', with for instance 'a new military housing estate' rising 'on the site of the old Waterloo Barracks'. Turner's sympathies were clear, and he found one source of consolation: 'In the town those curious shops which call themselves military stores have made few concessions to modern taste. In one window I saw an array of tea cosies, elaborately worked in bright regimental colours, like inflated Valentines.'[13]

London's rapidly evolving skyline remained on the front line of urban change and debate. In the *Spectator*'s last Christmas number of the 1950s, John Betjeman issued a blast devoid of festive cheer:

> A few solemn pundits, but very few Londoners, praise the new tall office blocks and regimented flats which are choking the city and mucking up the skyline in what once were countrified suburbs . . . In the office blocks of the City and West End, the idea is to make as much money as possible for their promoters out of the rents. In Council

blocks of flats the idea is to pack in as many people as possible at a minimum cost to the rates and regardless of the fact that London is a horizontal city and that Londoners have always preferred living in streets
with their own back gardens . . .

The march of the vertical was undeniable: Marylebone Road's Castrol
House and St Martin's Lane's Thorn House ('London's townscape has
been greatly enriched,' declared the town planner Walter Bor about
them in March 1960); Berwick Street's 18-storey block of shops, offices
and flats rising by this time in otherwise intimate Soho; London Wall's
Moor House, the first of an intended cluster of tower blocks there, to
be linked together by pedestrian walkways ('pedways') in the air; and,
in Camberwell, the newly completed Sceaux Gardens estate, dominated
by two 15-storey blocks and set amid the district's Georgian and
Regency buildings (but, insisted the *Architects' Journal* in January 1960,
'the architects have succeeded admirably in continuing this tradition').
One of the more balanced architectural writers, Kenneth Robinson,
wondered in April about the long-term consequences. 'Will discretion
be used, or will we make as much of a mess with vertical slashes across
the skyline as we have done with ribbons across the landscape?' he
asked. 'I'm appalled to find that the LCC has no policy about the siting
of high buildings: it considers each case on its merits.' The LCC itself
had recently stated explicitly that it had 'no intention of turning London
into New York', but Robinson was not satisfied: 'We wouldn't mind
the invigorating skyline of a Manhattan. What we fear is the crudeness
of a Shanghai waterfront.'[14]

The great *cause célèbre* of these months was Jack Cotton's proposed
scheme for the Monico site at Piccadilly Circus, as opinion rapidly
hardened after his naive if hubristic unveiling in late October 1959 of
what the *Architects' Journal* dismissed as 'a clumsy office block on a
crude podium of shops, using neon advertisements in the most obvious
manner'. An effective campaign – including the dubbing of it as
'Chewing Gum House' – rapidly led to a public enquiry being
announced for mid-December. The enquiry lasted several weeks, the
bow-tied Cotton 'beamed on all and sundry as though he were playing
host at an amusing party that could only end with the guests thanking
him and going quietly' (Panter-Downes), the architectural profession

stood almost four-square behind the Civic Trust in condemning the vulgar design, and Osbert Lancaster declared that 'the present level of advertising in the Circus was acceptable, but the unrestricted vertical space on the proposed tower would encourage the worst excesses of Times Square, New York.' The eventual upshot was the blocking of Cotton's scheme. But already a new *cause célèbre* was taking shape: the Great Arch at Euston, which British Railways proposed to demolish. The two best-known architectural critics (and rivals) now had their public say, with John Betjeman demanding the arch's reconstruction in the Euston Road itself, and Nikolaus Pevsner adamant that 'if the Euston Arch were destroyed, that would be the worst loss to the Georgian style in London architecture since most of Soane's Bank of England fell shortly before the war.'

That outcome remained uncertain, but one development definitely set to happen was the brutalist Barbican, narrowly endorsed in principle by the City authorities in December 1959. 'The intention underlying our design is to create a coherent residential precinct in which people can live both conveniently and with pleasure,' declared the architects Chamberlin, Powell and Bon. 'Despite its high density the layout is spacious; the buildings and the space between them are composed in such a way as to create a clear sense of order without monotony.' Denys Lasdun's Bethnal Green cluster blocks, meanwhile, were now complete, with the Claredale Street scheme (one 14-storey cluster block and two 6-storey blocks at right angles to each other) complementing the earlier Usk Street blocks. Accompanied by plenty of glamorous-looking photos, the *Architectural Review* (in May 1960) applauded the new scheme as more 'decisive' and 'authoritative', explained that the 14-storey block was 'intended to be read as a type of vertical street of stairs, lifts, services and public spaces', and generally perceived the best of all worlds: 'The cluster concept offers a viable alternative on the visual side by creating tower accents without visually destroying the existing grain; on the human side it shows promise in possessing domestic scale in the component parts of these towers and maintaining something like the pre-existing sociological groupings of the streets that gave the original urban grain to the district.'[15]

Outside the capital, Birmingham remained at the forefront of change. Early in 1960 the Corporation accepted a design (from the

London-based Laing Development Co) for the Bull Ring Centre, in effect to be a covered shopping centre operating on five levels – a scheme that, reckoned the *Architects' Journal*, had 'much to commend it'. Traffic was by now flowing on the first completed section of the Inner Ring Road, the 400-yard stretch known as Smallbrook Ringway (later Smallbrook Queensway) that was officially opened by Ernie Marples in March. Shortly before the opening, the *Liverpool Daily Post*'s admiring George Eglin was shown round the ring road – 'the equivalent of driving the M1 through the heart of the city' – and reflected ruefully how, while Liverpool had been 'sitting tight and thinking that nothing else mattered but building houses', Birmingham had been 'boldly and imaginatively planning for the future'. Eglin also had a word with Frank Price, 'a vital, bubbling volcano of a man', until recently chairman of Birmingham's Public Works Committee. 'The central fringes of all our older cities are ill-planned, overcrowded and insanitary,' asserted the vertically minded alderman. 'Birmingham is no exception. The street pattern is out of date, there is a shortage of open space, and land is used in a most uneconomic fashion.' Rather touchingly, Price added, 'When I see all that's going on in the city I feel frightened myself . . .'

There tended to be less Price-like drive among Edinburgh's staid city fathers, but at 6 Beaumont Place on a rainy night in late November 1959 the final collapse and evacuation of what became known as the 'Penny Tenement' dramatically highlighted the Scottish capital's festering slum problem. Questions were asked in the House, while when officials and councillors toured one of the city's worst slums, Greenside, tenants shouted angrily at them from windows. Two key Edinburgh developments, meanwhile, now got the green light. In December the city administration's 'big five' (town clerk, city chamberlain, town planning officer, city engineer, city assessor) all publicly agreed to the 'bold implementation' of a scheme to develop the St James Square slum area at the eastern end of Princes Street – a scheme having at its heart what would become the unloved 'sprawling grey concrete leviathan' of the St James Centre. Three months later, and after many years of controversy, the Secretary of State for Scotland endorsed Robert Matthew's plan (based in part on an earlier one by Basil Spence) to destroy George Square's south-east corner with a 15-storey Arts Tower for the university – a square full of eighteenth-century domestic architecture that was, according to the *Architects' Journal*, 'of great charm and historic interest but only modest architectural distinction'. As for Glasgow, the momentous decision of these months was the Corporation's to approve in principle, as the *Glasgow Herald* reported in February 1960, 'plans for the building of a multi-lane highway which will encircle the city for about four and a half miles', involving the demolition of 'thousands of houses' and to 'be built in conjunction with the comprehensive redevelopment of seven areas bordering the route'. The planning convenor, Bailie William Taylor, was adamant that such was the increasing traffic congestion in central Glasgow that only an inner ring road could prevent it dying 'of slow strangulation'. The *Herald* itself unambiguously backed both 'the timing and the logic', considered that 'redevelopment of the central areas provides the opportunity for road building on the boldest lines', and proudly praised the 'local initiative' that had led to Glasgow having 'produced a blueprint for the first urban motorway in Britain, probably in Europe', albeit for the moment forgetting Birmingham's already roaring lanes.[16]

Glasgow Corporation took its decision on the same day – the 18th – that Salford City Council approved by thirty-six votes to five the ambitious Broad Street Redevelopment Scheme. 'The scheme,' summarised the *Guardian*, 'entails the construction of 2,652 homes in multi-storey flats and maisonettes; the demolition of all the main road shops and their rebuilding as a shopping precinct; and major improvements to Broad Street, which is part of the A6 highway.' In the debate itself, Councillor Albert Jones, chairman of the Planning and Development Committee, inevitably referred to Walter Greenwood's famous Salford novel of the 1930s, *Love on the Dole*, and went on: 'We may be 30 years late but we are trying now to obliterate Hanky Park as it was known and propose to make the area something of which we can be proud . . .' Nearby, the demolition men were almost on the doorsteps of the 70 small shopkeepers in the Ellor Street Clearance Area. 'They are having to hang on and lose money while their customers are being moved out of the area,' noted the local paper in April, for 'if they move now they lose compensation rights.' And, the reporter added, 'the general impression one gets from the shopkeepers is of complete uncertainty.' 'The way in which the Council have gone about the whole thing,' complained Mr E. Clarke, a dyer and cleaner, 'has been dictatorial and they have not considered us in any way.' But Mr H. W. Hartley, general storekeeper, was reflective rather than bitter: 'Although we cannot stand in the way of progress I will be very sorry to leave, for I came to Ellor Street in 1912.'

Over in Sheffield, keys had been given by the end of 1959 for 400 of the new flats at Park Hill. 'At one time, there was a certain amount of prejudice against flats, but now, thanks to publicity in the local Press and the development of Park Hill and other schemes, people have begun to want them,' confidently asserted an official in the Housing Department at the start of 1960. 'They now realise the many advantages the flat-dweller has, particularly in a scheme such as Park Hill where tenants have shopping facilities on the doorstep, covered roadways, central heating, easy refuse disposal, and other benefits not available to people living in traditional houses.' All the more troubling, then, were the findings of 'a sociological report' for the City Council's Housing Management Committee that the *Sheffield Telegraph* revealed in March, as the streets in the sky continued to be filled as soon as they were ready. 'Life in Sheffield's new multi-storey Park Hill flats is becoming a nightmare for many tenants,' the paper began bluntly, and some details from the report followed: canvassers, selling everything from washing machines and electric razors to laundries and indoor photographs, 'clutter up hallways of dwellings with handbills of all descriptions – and worse, repeatedly ply their wares at house doors'; 'lifts have been a magnet for children of all ages and continue to be so', causing frequent breakdowns; 'a more dangerous and harmful "game" is that of throwing objects – milk bottles, saucepans, open knives, steel etc, off the decks and roof'; and 'there have been many instances of violence among teenage groups gathered round the coffee bar.' The report itself reached a sombre conclusion, far removed from all those feel-good sentiments that had so liberally – and understandably – been wafted around the previous autumn:

> If the central part of Park Hill is already unsafe for residents, this may prove to be a vital factor of the success or failure in building up an effective community. They need all possible support to help them achieve as high a standard of community pride as possible. The estate on its side must foresee and avert dangerous and socially disintegrating trends.

Or, as the *Telegraph* put it, preferring at this delicate stage to focus on the early troubles of one particular age group, 'the move to Park Hill seems to have been a great strain for many old people, even those fortunate enough to have the support of relatives and friends.'[17]

Generally, 1960 was the year when 'high-rise' became 'higher', with work starting (or authorised to start) on blocks of flats of 20 storeys or more in, among other places, Southampton, Edinburgh, Newcastle, Smethwick and Liverpool. Undoubtedly the concept had its glamour, or at the least a curiosity value: when in January the Scottish Special Housing Association opened its first high-rise block in Dundee, of a mere ten storeys, some 25,000 people inspected the flats. Harder evidence of attitudes, though, came that spring from Leeds and Merseyside. In the former, S. I. Benson, a senior figure in the Housing Department, frankly informed the Housing Committee in March that, in terms of placing families, 'our experience shows that it is far better to avoid larger dwellings in multi-storey development', not least given that the average family still wished to be rehoused 'in a semi-detached two-storey house, with a second choice of a terrace-type house'. The 'traditional objections' to flats, he went on, remained strong, including in relation to internal layout, noise, general appearance and lack of privacy, while 'many families from clearance areas wish for a private garden, especially where young children are concerned.' In short, he reiterated, for those 'thousands of families from the clearance areas' facing compulsory rehousing, their 'aspirations do not include rehousing in tall storey blocks or, indeed, in flats/maisonettes of any kind'. Instead, 'these people are looking for dwellings which will enable them to "spread" and enjoy open space – with privacy – immediately around their homes.' Benson's uncompromising message was anathema to Karl Cohen, dynamic chairman of the Housing Committee and wholly committed to the high-rise solution to Leeds's housing problems; a few weeks later, he read out to his fellow-councillors an unsolicited letter from a Mr Ryan, a new tenant in a recently opened multi-storey block, Beevers Court: 'I must admit that I never relished the idea of living in a flat until I saw this "Point" block. The Housing Department are to be congratulated on this design which gives ample privacy with all amenities. If you have any more "doubters" on your waiting list I can honestly say that they would be well advised to accept one of these flats.'[18]

About the same time in Bootle, where opinion was apparently divided by the sight of two 11-storey blocks of flats being built in Marsh Lane (involving the demolition of 'little Wales', a cluster of streets named after Welsh towns and counties), the *Liverpool Echo* obtained some representative-sounding vox pop from those living nearby:

> I like them. I like their appearance. I think it would take some time, however, to get used to living in them, but once you were accustomed, everything would be all right. (*Mrs Eleanor Tanner*)
>
> I think these flats are an eyesore. If there was more space surrounding them, it would not be so bad. This kind of development of large blocks of flats needs a lot of open space and we have not got that here. (*Mr Samuel Wood*)
>
> The main thing is that they will give homes to so many people. I like them because when they are finished, it will put an end to the no-man's land we have looked at for so long. They will at least look tidy and that is a big thing. (*Mrs Edna Traynor*)
>
> I am the mother of seven children and I need fresh accommodation badly. I like the flats and I would go anywhere if I could find accommodation for my family. (*Mrs Teresa Flynn*)

One should not exaggerate the high-rise phenomenon at this stage. Local authorities in England and Wales during 1960 gave tender approvals to 58,256 houses and 36,372 low-rise flats, compared to 15,685 high-rise flats (five or more storeys), and it would not be until the mid-1960s that the real spike came in high-rise, especially the taller blocks. Predictably, then, the new or newish low-rise estates still tended at the start of the decade to be the main focus of attention, as in a cluster of stories in the *Evening News* about London County Council's 'out-county' estates. At Borehamwood, the Rev. J. W. Larter claimed that young families were always 'looking back to London' instead of settling down, with too many parents 'guilty of putting personal pleasures above showing an interest in their children's hobbies'; at Sheerwater near Woking, the chairman of the Community Association complained that 'if the present apathy and lack of interest in our activities continues there is no point in continuing the association'; and at Belhus in Essex, a Hungarian refugee, Zoltan Glotter, who was an art teacher, likened the estate to 'the Wild West' and lamented how it was 'so segregated from culture'.[19]

A particularly authoritative – because from the inside – assessment of life on a mixed-development council estate came from J. L. Hayes, for nine years a tenant on the Churchill Gardens estate in Pimlico and now chairman of the fairly recently formed London Standing Conference of Housing Estate Community Groups. 'Very few housing managers, housing assistants, or even chairmen of housing committees are actually council tenants,' he pointedly observed at the outset in an address in January to the Society of Housing Managers. Arguing that 'it is basically a feeling of insecurity that wrecks the idea of community,' and adamant that 'the majority of council tenants are proud of their homes, feel fortunate, and are very grateful to have them,' he noted that the philanthropic days of Octavia Hill (a Victorian pioneer of social housing) had gone: 'Standards of living are higher, social aspirations are greater, and what is required today is good housing, with efficient and sympathetic management – not charity. The paternal approach is definitely out. The burning problem on many estates today is not to provide more wash-houses but to provide garages or car-parks.' Nothing, though, vexed Hayes more than what (according to him) were usually called 'Conditions of Occupation and General Rules for Housing Estates' – ie the tyrannical, often nit-picking lists of do's and don'ts. 'I often wonder just how many private tenants would stomach such a list of fifty to sixty regulations designed to cover every aspect of their home life,' he reflected. 'The council tenant, for example, agrees "not to keep any animal in the dwelling" or any bird "except as may be authorised in writing by the housing manager." "No singing, dancing or playing musical instruments is allowed after 11 pm," not even at Christmas, apparently!'

Of course, it all depended, and the variables were enormous – whether between person and person or between place and place. Nevertheless, there was a ring of authenticity about the findings of a study published in March on the early collective experience of the thousands of Londoners who in recent years had settled in Swindon's new housing estates:

Many of them have lived in rooms in London and are longing for a home of their own. When they move into their new house the reaction is one of delight. They are building a nest, settling in.

After the first few weeks have passed, the man finds he has to keep on overtime to cope with extra expenses, and his wife is left alone. The novelty begins to wear off and the wife feels lonely and a little homesick.

Then she goes back and sees the place she has come from with new eyes. She sees the drab houses and the smoky street, and the reaction is, 'Oh, let me get back to my own home, quick.'

Certainly there were plenty of smoky streets on Liverpool's Everton Heights, where a local journalist, William Amos, listened in January to some of the women facing demolition of the houses that had been their homes for most of their lives:

You can do and do and do, and it never gets clean. My sister's got a brand new house and she has half the work I've got in this place.

The smog's terrible. You can't have the windows open – those, that is, that will open. Unless you have the back door open you don't get a breath of air in the house.

Some walls are so damp you have to keep the wallpaper up with drawing pins.

Four of my five married sons have modern homes. When I go to see them and then come back to this, I could scream.

'Each of the women I spoke to,' reckoned Amos, 'was looking forward to the move' – ie, out of the district, and 'their only regret was that they would lose their neighbours.'

Among the many thousands on the move were Tom Courtenay's parents, in December 1959 leaving their home in Harrow Street near the Fish Dock in Hull and going to what his mother Annie called a 'Corporation house', on the new Longhill estate on the city's outskirts, where the fresher air might improve her health. 'I went through the back door and into the kitchen,' recalled their son (poised for breakthrough as an actor) about going there for the first time on Christmas Eve. 'It was much bigger than its Harrow Street equivalent. Likewise the sitting room, which doubled as the front room. It had a small square hallway rather than a passage, and upstairs were three bedrooms and, glory of glories, a bathroom.' Even so:

> It wasn't so homely and it wasn't what Mother had been used to all her life. And two bus rides for Dad to get to work. He would sometimes come home at lunchtime in Harrow Street, but not any more. Nor Ann [Tom's sister]: Longhill was too far from her office in the city centre. Aunt Alice was there, true. But she was the only one. No kindly Mrs Hinchcliffe next door, or Annie Brooks' shop alongside us. No Mrs Hales' beer off shop for a natter. No Aunt Phyllis calling in for a sub till Friday, and no Grandma Quest to sit there and get on her nerves. Full though I was of my coming opportunity, I had the ominous feeling that she would be very lonely out at Longhill.

On Monday, 2 May, Tom spent the day with his mother: 'I tried to reassure her that they had been right to move, especially with summer coming. But I wasn't at all convinced. It just wasn't as homely as mucky, scruffy Harrow Street.' Next morning his eyes filled with tears as he left to get the bus to Paragon Station: 'She looked so lost and lonely waving from the front door of 20 Duddon Grove.'[20]

Saturday early evening was as usual *Dixon of Dock Green* time. 'Continues to be tremendously popular,' noted a BBC report on reaction to the episode on 27 February, the day after Princess Margaret's engagement. 'In fact, it might almost be said that *Dixon of Dock Green* is now an institution. Time and again viewers insisted that this was one programme they "*never* missed – for whatever reason."' Or, as an engineer put it, 'It's hard to think of old Dixon and company as actors now. They are all just perfect.' Distinctly imperfect in some viewers' eyes was *Living for Kicks*, an ITV documentary four days later investigating teenage life in London, Brighton and Northampton. 'The probe is gentle, sympathetic,' promised *TV Times*, but in the event the 'misrepresentation of modern youth' left three apprentices at Cranfield's College of Aeronautics unable to contain their indignation: 'We are fully aware that the sensation value of these programmes attracts a wide audience, but we feel moved to point out that there is also a considerable number of teenagers who possess a modicum of intelligence whose existence seems to be denied.' Jacqueline S. Wicks of Sevenoaks was similarly impelled to write to the magazine: 'I reassure those who are beginning to fear for the future of England that all over the country there are teenagers in thousands who, in spite of liking jazz, coffee-bars, and the society of the opposite sex, are both intelligent and well-mannered.' To which the editor appended a note that 'many other readers have written expressing similar views on this programme.'

Next morning, on Thursday, 3 March, a DC-7 on its way from Germany to New Jersey stopped briefly for refuelling at Prestwick Airport, and the 26-year-old Elvis Presley, about to be discharged from the US Army, set foot for probably the only time on British soil. *The Times* that day, attuned to the rather different preoccupations of its core readership, was in Trollopian mode. 'To be either Prime Minister of England or Chancellor of Oxford University is each sufficient for any one man without his being also the other,' it asserted on the first day of voting at Oxford in a head-to-head between Macmillan and the distinguished mandarin-*cum*-banker Sir Oliver Franks. Among those voting for the former was Isaiah Berlin, largely on the negative grounds that he considered Franks 'a planner, a puritan & over energetic'. With voting in abeyance on the Friday, the press looked elsewhere. 'There has been a revolution in the savings habits of Britain,' explained the *Daily Mirror* about its decision to launch a regular column on stocks and shares, adding that 'no longer is The City the exclusive domain of Big Money'; while at the strait-laced *FT*, a feature on the new oral contraceptive just announced by British Drug Houses led to agonised editorial discussion about what to call the piece, before eventually hitting upon 'Limiting the World's Population'. Saturday saw a second day of voting for the Oxford chancellorship, with in due course Haroldus Macmillanus declared the winner by 1,976 votes to Oliverus Frankus' 1,697. 'He got most of the *women* MAs & a lot of the Oxford dons,' reflected the victor that evening. 'But Trevor-Roper (Professor of Modern History) ran a brilliant campaign on my behalf, & lots of friends all over the country rallied to my support. It was quite a gamble for me. There was little to gain, & much to lose. But it came off.'[21]

Macmillan's day job, with the post-election honeymoon over, had its strains by that spring. 'Governor of Bank and Chancellor are suddenly very pessimistic about the future – inflation, too much imports, balance of payments difficulties, loss of gold and dollar reserves etc. etc. – the same old story,' he privately observed in late February. 'So they want violent disinflationary measures and a fierce Budget . . .' Over the next few weeks, he applied the full weight of his office and personality to ensure that his Chancellor, Derick Heathcoat Amory ('fundamentally, he lacks nerve'), presented an essentially neutral – as opposed to deflationary – Budget in early April. 'I have won this battle quite definitively,' recorded the expansion-minded PM on the 4th, hours after the dandyish Leo Abse had offended some fellow Welsh Labour MPs by attending his first Budget day in a grey top hat. Across the floor, a group of free-market, tax-cutting Tory MPs, headed by the almost equally flamboyant Gerald Nabarro, was even more dismayed. 'Whose side does he think he's on?' asked one after Amory had announced a higher profits tax and measures against dividend stripping, while the luxuriantly moustached Nabarro accused Amory of 'practising Socialism' and returning the country to 'the dreariest period of the post-war years characterised by Butskellism'. The Chancellor himself, unsurprisingly, soon cut an increasingly disenchanted figure. 'Nasty about the threatened resignation of Mr Amory!' noted Philip Larkin, in economics a man of the right, soon afterwards. 'But I fancy they have been getting at him to produce "popular" measures wch no doubt feeds him up.'

Notwithstanding growing consumer prosperity, the underlying relative health of economy was now an increasing cause of legitimate concern. 'In terms of economic expansion and production and so on,' declared Anthony Crosland on *Any Questions?* a few days after Amory's budget, in a vein that did not seem particularly outlandish to the Wiltshire audience in the village hall at Winsley, 'this country has recently been falling very badly behind, not merely Soviet Russia, which we're falling catastrophically behind, but also all the leading countries in Europe.' Ian Fleming's analysis of post-Suez decline was military and diplomatic rather than economic, but in one of the James Bond stories published later in April in *For Your Eyes Only* he had an American millionaire condescendingly describe England as a 'pleasant little country' (with 'old buildings and the Queen and so on') that had 'gone broke'. It was not difficult to find symbols of decline, but arguably the creaking railway system was as resonant as anything. 'The industry must be of a size and pattern suited to modern conditions and prospects,' Macmillan told the Commons in March, before Marples in early April announced the composition of an advisory body to examine its structure and finances. Two of the four chosen members were rising, middle-aged industrialists, Frank Kearton of Courtaulds and Dr Richard Beeching of ICI. 'I get "absolutely first-rate" from very relia-ble sources,' the Bank of England's Cameron (Kim) Cobbold subse-quently reported on the latter to a Treasury mandarin. 'One of the few first-rate scientists who is also a first-rate administrator and business man: top-level quality.'[22]

Easter that year fell in mid-April – and the long weekend by now included a new ritual. 'Gathering strength all the way along its route through London,' reported the *Guardian* about the Easter Monday climax, 'the Aldermaston anti-nuclear march quickly developed into a column roughly six miles long and 40,000 strong':

> At three o'clock, after a stately progress up Whitehall, its only music the plod of this multitude of tired feet and the tattoo of a single drummer at the head, it began to overwhelm Trafalgar Square. A crowd of spectators – also estimated at 40,000 – awaited them in the square. At first it seemed there would be no room for the marchers, but, somehow, space was made as unit after unit, banners flying, came trooping up towards Nelson's Column.
>
> Within an hour the police had conceded that the Aldermaston pilgrims had staged the biggest demonstration ever held in Trafalgar Square ... Supporters were jubilant and so were the many speakers from the plinth. One after another they stepped to the microphone to say, in so many words, 'Nobody can ignore us now.'

'Weirdies and beardies, colonels and conchies, Communists and Liberals, vegetarians and alcoholics, beauties and beasts' was Alan Brien's assessment of the heterogeneous composition of his fellow-marchers, while according to Sylvia Plath, proudly taking her recently born baby to watch the lengthy column enter Trafalgar Square, '40 per cent were London housewives.' 'The Aldermaston march,' already reckoned Anthony Wedgwood Benn on Easter Sunday, 'is a stupendous triumphant success and is getting massive and sympathetic publicity' – and to a large extent that indeed seems to have been the case. The *Daily Express*, though, declined to waver from outright hostility, with René MacColl depicting Trafalgar Square as full of 'the sort of hairy horrors who think it intellectual not to wash more than once every three weeks'. So too the crusty farmer-writer A. G. Street, still an *Any Questions?* fixture. 'I personally,' he informed a probably sympathetic audience the following Friday at the British Legion Hall in Middle Wallop, 'do not fear now annihilation, instant annihilation, half as much as I should fear to live the rest of my life under the rule of either the Communists or the Aldermaston Marchers.'[23]

Anti-apartheid was the other great cause in the air by spring 1960, but Larkin for one remained unmoved. 'Seven pounds ten if you don't mind,' he had written to Monica Jones in early February – the day after Macmillan's famous 'wind of change' speech in Cape Town had, among other things, unequivocally condemned apartheid – in the wake of applying for tickets for South Africa's Test at Lord's in June. 'Still,' he went on, 'we may not get the best seats, though we shall if people decide to boycott the tour!' March saw a month-long boycott (backed by the Labour Party, the TUC and Christian Action) of South African goods and produce, a boycott that, to the pleasure of Anthony Heap, was reported as a failure by the *Express* on the 14th. 'So much,' he observed, 'for the mischievous efforts of our nigger-supporting reds to undermine the white supremacy in South Africa.' Exactly a week later came the massacre at Sharpeville, leaving 67 dead, and soon afterwards Gallup found that, of countries from which the British people would prefer not to buy goods, South Africa ranked second only to Japan. How would this affect the impending South African cricket tour? 'Large numbers of British feel strongly that politics ought to be kept out of sport,' noted Mollie Panter-Downes on 12 April, a view not shared by the cricketing parson, the Rev David Sheppard, who about this time let it be known that he would refuse to play against the tourists so long as the colour bar operated in the selection of their team.

Among those who should on merit have arrived with the tourists on Easter Sunday was a 28-year-old 'Cape-coloured' cricketer, Basil D'Oliveira. Instead, the following Saturday, the 23rd, he made his first appearance on English soil for a Central Lancashire League club,

Middleton. The cricket writer and broadcaster John Arlott had played a key role in securing this berth for D'Oliveira as the club's new professional, and though he took a while to settle to English conditions, it was clear by the end of the summer that this was a gifted cricketer of high but hitherto thwarted potential. Arlott himself, Liberal in politics and liberal-minded in most aspects of life, pondered three days after D'Oliveira's debut on the rights and wrongs of the South African tour. 'Some of the many British people who have been roused to indignation by Sharpeville and all it represents are now – in the absence of anyone at hand more immediately culpable – prepared to make McGlew's cricketers the object and sounding board of their disapproval,' he reflected. 'It is to be hoped – but is by no means certain – that common sense will show the cricketers to be an inappropriate target.' Arlott added that 'if their tour were to collapse', then 'English cricket would find itself in a very awkward financial position.'[24]

'Another City Cinema Closing', announced the *Sheffield Telegraph* on 22 March, bringing the total there to 16 in the previous five years, while for one distinguished film director, Michael Powell, the spring was also more or less terminal. 'It's a long time since a film disgusted me as much as *Peeping Tom*,' declared Caroline Lejeune in the *Observer* about this study of a psychopathic photographer; 'stinks . . . muck . . . peculiarly nauseous . . . morbidity . . .' caught the tone of William Whitebait in the *New Statesman*; and in Bristol a young journalist, Tom Stoppard, writing in the *Evening World*, called it 'a loathsome, mawkish, barely excusable, out-and-out commercial and thoroughly sickening piece of horror for horror's sake', in short 'a nasty, unwholesome, catchpenny picture'. The distributors rapidly took fright, the film disappeared from sight, and Powell's reputation would take decades to recover. No such problems, though, for *Carry On Constable* – 'the successful mixture of rather blue jokes and not very subtle slapstick as before,' approvingly noted Heap – while on TV the great news was that, as one critic put it, 'Hancock is back and the streets lie deserted on Friday evenings.' Around this time, when the Labour politician Aneurin Bevan was reported as 'depressed and horrified' by the current low standard of TV programmes, he identified *Hancock's Half Hour* as almost the only exception.

The teenage pound, meanwhile, continued on the march. 'It is no secret,' wrote Katharine Whitehorn in April, 'that *Vogue*, by dropping to 2s 6d, coming out oftener and filling its pages with things like jazz, little-girl dresses and young male models, is aiming at the vast teenage spending potential for its advertising.' The same month saw the launch of *Honey*, with Jacqueline Aitken devoting an hour and a half to reading the first issue 'solidly'; and in Chingford, Judy Haines recorded Ione wearing 'Jeans' and Pamela a 'Top Ten sweater'. Number 1 in that Top Ten between late March and late April was Lonnie Donegan's 'My Old Man's a Dustman'. But the iconic moment occurred around midnight on Easter Saturday at Chippenham in Wiltshire, where a Ford Consul crashed, the American singer Eddie Cochran was killed, his fellow passenger Gene Vincent was seriously injured – and among the first to arrive on the scene was an 18-year-old police cadet, Dave 'Dee' Harman, who retrieved Cochran's guitar from the wreck and subsequently enjoyed 'a good strum' before returning it to the family.[25]

That spring one play sought to nail the zeitgeist by focusing on Coventry, boom city of the West Midlands. *Never Had It So Good*, by a young South African called John Wiles, opened at the Belgrade Theatre on 29 February and attracted national attention, with the *Daily Mail*'s reviewer recording how 'one long litany of protest sounds throughout the play – at false values bred by bursting wage packets, the creed of greed and "I'm all right, Jack", the scramble for bigger T.V. screens and glossier veneers, trade unions ("they are there to protect the worker from his own inefficiency"), failing churches, Coventry Corporation, and "the technicolour plastic boxes" of contemporary architecture with the emphasis on "temporary".' Local dignitaries were broadly unimpressed – 'a one-sided, cynical picture' (Bishop of Coventry); 'a very harsh caricature' (Councillor H. Richards); 'very exaggerated' (Alderman Mrs P. M. Hyde) – while the *Coventry Evening Telegraph* called it 'not a portrait of Coventry', but instead 'a collection of unflattering glimpses of some of us who live in Coventry, as seen by a visitor'. The following week, *Panorama* featured an item on the controversy surrounding the play, including some Coventrian vox pop from shoppers in the Precinct, a place that, according to the reporter, Ludovic Kennedy, was 'dedicated to household gods':

> I'm having a marvellous time. I like to buy clothes and go a lot to the pictures. (*Young married woman*)
>   It has changed for the better. You have to move with the times. (*Older woman*)
>   Yes, I've never had it so good. I spend money on everything I want. You can't spend the money when you are dead. (*Married woman*)

'The people of the city are largely indifferent to their critics,' summed up Kennedy. 'They can afford to be. They have never had it so good and they mean to have it better.'

Two rather more distinguished playwrights were experiencing contrasting fortunes. 'A work of far less clarity and dramatic energy than its two predecessors' was the verdict of *The Times* on Arnold Wesker's *I'm Talking About Jerusalem*, the last of his trilogy, after the first performance at Coventry in early April. A local paper agreed, calling it 'on the whole an anti-climax', being 'long and too drawn-out'. But for Harold Pinter, these were life-changing times. On Tuesday, 22 March, an ITV production of his once-scorned *The Birthday Party* attracted 11 million viewers, a figure no doubt helped by the fact that the counter-attraction on BBC was a performance of Mendelssohn's Violin Concerto in E Minor. Indeed, most of the letters subsequently published in *TV Times* were negative, as with Miss M. Taylor of Middle Lane, N8: 'The only reason I suffered until the end was in the hope that I might get some explanation. But, alas, no!' Then, a month later, on 24 April and again on ITV, almost immediately following *Sunday Night at the London Palladium*, Pinter's relatively realistic, conventional play *A Night Out* was showcased by *Armchair Theatre*, where it usefully clashed with the arts programme *Monitor*, preceded the western *Cheyenne* and attracted 14 million viewers. But Pinter's real breakthrough came three days later on the 27th, with the first night at the Arts Theatre of *The Caretaker*, starring Donald Pleasence as the tramp. Tumultuous cheers and 12 curtain calls preceded a round of mainly enthusiastic reviews, typified by Cuthbert Worsley's assertion in the *FT* that the play was not only 'immensely funny' and 'rich in observation', but 'below that level a disturbing and moving experience'. Al Alvarez in the *New Statesman* declined to join the chorus – 'it is bitty, haphazard, too long by about a third' – but Noël Coward went along on about the third night and, despite himself, was gripped ('squalor, repetition, lack of action, etc – but somehow it seizes hold of you'). Within a few weeks *The Caretaker* had transferred triumphantly to the Duchess in the West End. Although Anthony Heap was an unforgiving first-nighter there ('oh what a depressingly melancholy evening à la Godot it all amounts to'), a more typical reaction was probably that of the young Richard Eyre. 'It was the first really modern play that I'd seen in a theatre,' he recalled, 'and it seemed to me that the author had a way of looking at the world that was completely singular . . . partly that it was about working-class people, partly that the play didn't seek to explain itself . . . It was as original and striking as when I first saw a Francis Bacon.'[26]

On Saturday, 30 April, three days after the unveiling of Pinter's meditation on power, Yorkshire's season began at Lord's, with that proud county playing for the first time in the twentieth century under a professional captain, Vic Wilson. On the same day down at Arundel, the Duke of Norfolk's XI had to make do without their usual captain, David Sheppard, and lost to the South Africans by five wickets, while up at Deepdale the much-loved, ultimate one-club footballer, Tom Finney, made his final league appearance for Preston North End, at home to Luton Town. 'The band played "Keep Right On to the End of the Road," followed by "For He's a Jolly Good Fellow," in which the crowd joined,' reported the *Lancashire Evening Post* about the moving pre-match scene. 'After a pause for cheering to subside, this unique ceremony concluded with "Auld Lang Syne," in the singing of which match officials and the players of both sides joined hands in the traditional fashion, to the accompaniment of continued applause.' At nearby Burnley there was little room for sentiment, as that unfashionable club moved within reach of the league championship title – eventually attained on Monday, 2 May with a 2–1 win at Manchester City. Harry Potts was Burnley's understated manager, the beating heart of the team was the staunchly loyal hometown wing-half Brian Miller, and the unexpected outcome was a direct reflection of how the maximum wage of £20 a week continued to make the top division a not wholly unlevel playing field. The following evening, the still badly injured Gene Vincent reluctantly dragged himself on stage at Liverpool Stadium, top of a bill that also included Gerry and the Pacemakers (already singing 'You'll Never Walk Alone') and other Merseyside acts – but not the Beatals, as the former Quarry Men were now briefly known, John Lennon instead being photographed watching proceedings with, in his biographer's words, 'envy and longing in his eyes'. Next day, Wednesday the 4th, Larkin informed Monica Jones that he had given his niece 'My Old Man's a Dustman', adding that he hoped it was driving her parents 'insane, in their house they built to be so U in'; while 6.30 in the north-east saw the Tyne Tees TV debut of *Young at Heart*, billed as 'a teenage programme with Mum-and-Dad appeal'. The studio was set up to resemble a coffee bar, the guest artiste recorded a song live on a disc-cutting machine that became a competition prize, the compère was Jimmy Savile (each week his hair a different colour), and, in one of the turning-points of history that failed to turn, he very nearly got the sack for continually saying, 'How's about that, then?'[27]

This was also the week of Princess Margaret's wedding, with every serviceman having sixpence docked from his pay to contribute to a present (a marble-topped commode). The major hiccup between engagement and nuptials concerned the best man. Jeremy Fry of the chocolate family was originally chosen, before in early April he (as Mollie Panter-Downes nicely put it) 'cancelled for the highly unusual reason, as reported in the press, that he expected to be ill between now and May', reference being made to recurrent attacks of jaundice. The real backstory was that the press had become aware that, eight years earlier, Fry had been fined £2 for homosexual importuning, and it seemed too risky. The youngish Liberal politician Jeremy Thorpe was briefly in the frame as Fry's replacement, but in the end Armstrong-Jones settled on the impeccably heterosexual Roger Gilliatt, son of the Queen's gynaecologist and himself a consultant neurologist. Anticipation was rising by the start of May – and on Monday the 2nd, Kingsley Amis let himself go. 'Such a symbol of the age we live in,' he wrote to American friends, 'when a royal princess, famed for her devotion to all that is most vapid and mindless in the world of entertainment, her habit of reminding people of her status whenever they venture to disagree with her in conversation, and her appalling taste in clothes, is united with a dog-faced tight-jeaned fotog of fruitarian tastes such as can be found in dozens in any pseudo-arty drinking cellar in fashionable-unfashionable London. They're made for each other.' Two days later the Queen gave a huge ball for the couple at Buckingham Palace. Joe Loss and his band played tunes from *Fings Ain't Wot They Used T'Be*, but the evening ended unhappily when the Duchess of Buccleuch discovered she had lost a £2,700 brooch, inevitably with some of the photographer's loucher friends high on the list of suspects. Noël Coward, who was among those attending, found Armstrong-Jones 'a charmer . . . easy and unflurried and a sweet smile'.[28]

Friday, 6 May was a working day, but in glorious sunshine the streets of London were crowded, while across the country 54 per cent of the population aged five or over (schoolchildren had the day off) saw the wedding on BBC television. 'For one moment,' ran a typical part of Richard Dimbleby's commentary, 'we see the bride now as she looks about her at the Abbey in this lovely gown of white silk organza, with the glittering diadem on her head, the orchids in her hand, and the comforting, tall, friendly, alert figure of the Duke of Edinburgh on whose right arm she can rely . . .' Guests at the Abbey included Winston Churchill, John Betjeman and Antonia Fraser (wearing a white shepherdess's bonnet), while among diarists watching were Judy Haines ('Queen looked heavy, almost scowling'), a Derbyshire schoolteacher called May Marlor ('Queen looks a bit down in the dumps'), Madge Martin ('Princess Margaret looked enchanting') and Nella Last ('our first experience of seeing a "big" event on Television, & memory will never fade', but disappointed by 'the bridegroom's *awful* pants, like a pair of compressed flannel, emphasised by his queer "knock kneed" stance'). Another diarist, Florence Turtle, was appalled by the thought that Margaret's new father-in-law had 'two ex-wives & is now married to an Air Hostess! half his age!' Macmillan was altogether more relaxed, taking pleasure in 'the slightly "raffish" element' present at the ceremony. Later in the day, the couple inched their way through a packed City of London, en route to Tower Pier, the Royal Yacht and a Caribbean honeymoon:

> For all but the newly married it was fiesta gaiety [wrote Patrick Keatley in the *Guardian*], a marvellous change from the grinding sameness of a

working day in the City. High overhead, while Princess Margaret fought back tears and exhaustion and managed a brave smile, a fur broker leaned out of his suite of third-floor offices, telephone in hand, gaily describing the scene of heat and paralysis below. A trunk call to New York (perhaps) or Leningrad? A thrill for those at the other end to hear the roar of the London crowds? This was glamour, perhaps, on the international scale, but for one small Englishwoman down below in Cannon Street it was sheer, plain agony.

'Yet,' concluded Keatley, 'the Princess fastened on still another brave Bowes-Lyon smile and saw it through to the end. Her mother would have been proud of her.'

In Barrow that evening, Nella Last 'made supper while my husband watched *The Army Game*. It makes him laugh & I appreciate it for that – but not to the extent of watching it.' If the reception had been better, they probably would have been watching the BBC, where Tony Hancock and Sid James made one last appearance together in what was the final *Hancock's Half Hour*, the end of Railway Cuttings – a decision to call time on their partnership (after 12 series on radio and television) that was entirely of Hancock's volition. The episode was 'The Poison Pen Letters', with Tony found to have been writing hate mail to himself in his sleep. 'You see, boy, you've been over-working,' kindly explains Sid. 'You're all strung up. Your nerves are like violin strings, and secretly, underneath it all, you don't like the life you've been living, so your subconscious mind has revolted. I mean, you're like everybody else, really. *You* don't like you either . . . all you need is a bit of rest, a long break.'[29]

3

To the Rear of the Column

'Never before has a party won three elections in succession with an increased majority each time,' reflected a triumphant Conservative supporter, Anthony Heap, on 9 October 1959, the day after polling. One predictable consequence was Labour's most profound existential crisis since the harrowing experience of 1931.[1] 'Hugh Cudlipp's *Daily Mirror* in the 1940s and 1950s was the voice of postwar popular social-ism, of the factory workers in the factory age,' William Rees-Mogg would accurately recall; but that age now seemed to be passing. Within days of the election, the *Mirror* not only ruthlessly dropped both its celebrated masthead 'Forward With The People' and its even more celebrated strip-cartoon heroine Jane (indelibly associated with wartime solidarity) but it pointed the way to a different sort of future by starting a regular 'petticoat page' and explicitly putting the emphasis on 'youth', 'fun', 'gaiety' and 'finding the girl with the smartest autumn sparkle'. Politics were temporarily off the agenda, the Labour frontbencher Richard Crossman lost his column, and the *Observer* commented sourly that the tabloid's new slogan should be 'Forward With The Shareholders'.[2]

———

Within the Labour Party itself, the revisionist wing – whose key text was Anthony Crosland's *The Future of Socialism* (1956) – moved rapidly into action. 'Douglas Jay started off with a great oration on the moral of the election defeat,' noted the veteran Hugh Dalton about a gathering on the 11th at the Hampstead home (18 Frognal Gardens) of the Labour leader, Hugh Gaitskell. 'He wanted (1) to drop "nationalisation", (2) drop the trade unions, (3) drop the name "Labour Party" . . . Otherwise, he said, we should never win.' Others were 'more cautious', and Gaitskell himself 'said little', but later that day he repeated several times to Anthony Wedgwood Benn (then a fairly centrist figure in the party), 'I'm not prepared to lose another Election for the sake of nationalisation.' The next evening, one of Gaitskell's key allies, Roy Jenkins, warned on *Panorama* about the dangers of advocating further nationalisation, before dropping in on Benn on the way home. 'We had a flaming row,' recorded his host. 'As a matter of fact I was very calm and collected and he got into a semi-hysterical state. Usually it's the other way round. "We must use this shock to drop nationalisation entirely at this forthcoming Conference" he said, and I concentrated on the dangers to our integrity if we were to be so reckless.'

The post-election conference was in the event to be held at Blackpool during the last weekend of November, and – among those who cared about these matters – passions ran high during the weeks leading up to it, especially after Jay published an article insisting that Labour was condemned to further defeats unless it adopted a more socially up-market image and scaled back its commitment to public ownership. 'They got so heated that they yelled (and booed) at each other,' noted the 'Bloomsbury' diarist Frances Partridge in early November about two friends, both of them left-leaning public intellectuals. 'Philip [Toynbee] thought that if one believed one's principles were right one shouldn't scrap them just because of failure, but consider how to persuade one's adversary more forcefully; Robert [Kee] that we must beat the Conservatives, and use any means to that end.' 'The Labour Party,' reckoned the almost invariably shrewd Mollie Panter-Downes soon afterwards, 'has arrived at a critical moment of truth and choice, in which the arguing protagonists are its middle-class intellectuals – the clever chaps, the dons and journalists and economists of the Gaitskell stamp, who think they know what is wrong with the movement and often burst into print to say so – and the old trade union Party faithful, who act like pious widows reluctant to change a thing in the house that has been set up by some revered departed hand.'[3]

By this time it was clear that the crux of the argument concerned nationalisation – specifically, whether the leadership would dare to attempt to scrap or revise the commitment, as embodied in Clause 4 of the party's constitution, to achieving 'the common ownership of the means of production, distribution and exchange'. That cause had of course been significantly advanced by Clement Attlee's 1945–51 government, when the electricity, gas, coal and railway industries had all been nationalised, as had the steel industry before being denationalised in 1953 by the Conservative government. Even on the left, it was by the mid-to-late 1950s no longer a policy, or indeed a subject, that aroused huge enthusiasm. 'Of course we had to wait 3 days for the Elect. Board! Nationalisation!!!,' the moderate-minded writer Sid Chaplin, who himself worked for the National Coal Board, told a friend after moving house in 1957. That same year, from the other end of the left spectrum, the South Wales miners' leader Will Paynter declared that a decade of public ownership had 'shattered' the idea that nationalisation was 'a half-way step to socialism and an ally in the struggle to end private enterprise', given that in practice there had been only marginal improvement in wages and conditions, that the same people remained in charge, and that 'the relationship of master and servant still operates'. Those and other criticisms of the nationalised industries were cogently made, from a left-wing perspective, by the ambitious trade unionist Clive Jenkins in his book *Power at the Top*, published shortly before the 1959 election. 'Let's face it, comrades, nationalisation is a boring subject,' began the review by the socialist, definitely non-revisionist, intellectual Ralph Miliband, who fully conceded the difficulty of making the nationalised industries 'islands of socialist virtues' in 'a sea of capitalist impulses'. 'Ultimately,' he went on, 'there is only one way of giving the public corporations a different character, and that is by an extension of nationalisation to the point where the public sector [currently some 20 per cent of the economy] is overwhelmingly more important and powerful than the private one. Even then, a socialised base will not amount to socialism, or resolve all the problems attendant upon a socialist organisation of industry. But it will constitute the essential beginning, for this, and for much else. Without it, any talk of socialism must remain a poor joke.'

The whole question played a significant part in the election itself, not least through the much-publicised results of a survey – mainly funded by steel companies, anxious about Labour's renationalisation pledge – revealing 63 per cent of people 'favouring no more nationalisation' and only 18 per cent favouring more. 'As for public ownership, it has certainly proved a liability in the election,' admitted the strongly pro-nationalisation Barbara Castle in the immediate wake. 'So conditioned has the public mind become as a result of the Tory advertising campaign, that even the announcement right in the middle of the election campaign that the nationalised electricity industry had made a profit of £27 million last year made not the slightest impact on the general belief that all nationalised industries are losing money.' Soon afterwards, the replies to questionnaires sent to 600 Labour candidates and organisers confirmed that nationalisation had been the single most damaging issue. What, then, would Gaitskell say at Blackpool? 'Hugh feels that Nationalisation was a vote loser at the Polls,' noted the most prominent trade unionist of the day, the left-wing Frank Cousins of the Transport and General Workers' Union, after a pre-conference dinner at the Euston Hotel attended by several union leaders as well as Gaitskell and his famous deputy. 'Nye [Bevan] thinks it was a vote winner when tackled boldly.'[4]

The weather at Blackpool was suitably miserable for a fractious weekend by the sea. 'We regard public ownership,' Gaitskell told the conference on Saturday afternoon, 'not as an end in itself but as a means – and not necessarily the only or the most important one – to certain ends, such as full employment, greater equality and higher productivity. We do not aim to nationalise every private firm or to create an endless series of state monopolies.' The problem, he went on, was that the continued existence of Clause 4 laid Labour open to damaging misrepresentation: 'It implies that we propose to nationalise everything, but do we? Everything? – the whole of light industry, the whole of agriculture, all the shops – every little pub and garage? Of course not. We have long ago come to accept a mixed economy ... Had we not better say so?' At this point there were hostile interruptions, and when Gaitskell's speech ended a few minutes later, one observer was struck by 'the thinness of the applause'. 'A ghastly failure,' reckoned Benn, who thought it had been too negative and added that 'he is quite incapable of inspiring people.'

There followed soon afterwards (in the words of the watching Bernard Levin) a 'violent attack on the leadership' by Michael Foot, showing 'nothing but contempt and hatred for those who would bring the Labour Party up to date, and a fine, mad arrogance for those who abated a jot of the ancient faith'. This produced 'hysterical cheers', and over the rest of the weekend most other speeches were highly critical of any attempt to revise or scrap Clause 4. Among those relatively few who made 'sensible and moderate speeches', Levin identified such rising figures as Denis Healey, Merlyn Rees, Dick Taverne and Shirley Williams, the last 'one of the brightest of all the bright hopes'. Given the scale of dissent from his initiative just weeks after a crushing election defeat, was Gaitskell's very leadership threatened? Much would depend on Bevan, who in what proved to be his final major speech disappointed some by going out of his way on Sunday afternoon to be a unifying figure and seeking to square the circle. On the one hand, he insisted on 'a planned economy' and described 'the so-called affluent society' as 'an ugly society' in which 'priorities have gone all wrong'; on the other, he explicitly accepted Gaitskell's argument that public ownership should not 'reach down into every piece of economic activity', because, as Bevan put it, 'that would be asking for a monolithic society'. 'In manner,' appraised Levin, 'one of the most splendid orations I have ever heard, and in matter a pitiful succession of threadbare attitudes and windy platitudes.' It only remained for the *Spectator*'s political correspondent to catch the train back to London. This took seven hours and twenty minutes to travel 226½ miles; much of the way 'seemed to be calling regularly, every hour on the hour, at Sheffield'. Finally, at journey's end, 'a trainload of tired, sick, filthy, bruised, late travellers were formed up on arrival at Marylebone into a huge, heaving mob and forced in single file through a narrow gate so that their tickets could be examined again.' Obviously, Levin reflected, the nationalised British Railways had been bribed by Gaitskell.[5]

Foot was unamused. 'Like it or not, one of the most spectacular events of our age is the comparative success of the Communist economic systems,' he wrote in Levin's magazine in early 1960. 'Khrushchev,' he went on,

> tells the Russians quite as plainly as Macmillan tells the English, that they never had it so good. Considering the tumultuous forty years through which the Russians have lived, the achievement by any reckoning is stupendous. Or does the *Spectator* dissent from that judgement? And

does the *Spectator* really ask us to suppose that public ownership and the allocation of resources it makes possible are irrelevant to those achievements? Do not tell us, please, as the clinching, specious argument in reply to the challenge of nationalised sputniks and the Soviet industrial revolution, that British Railways do not always run on time or that they sometimes serve cold soup in the dining cars.

For the anti-revisionists – call them the fundamentalists – the apparent Soviet success story was the trump card in the rhetorical battle for the retention of Clause 4. 'In terms of military power, of industrial development, of technological advance, of mass literacy and, eventually, of mass consumption too, the planned Socialist economy, as exemplified in the Communist States, is proving its capacity to outpace and overtake the wealthy and comfortable Western economies,' declared Richard Crossman that spring in a Fabian pamphlet on *Labour in the Affluent Society*. He concluded (with truly Wykehamist confidence): 'We can predict with mathematical certainty that, as long as the public sector of industry remains the minority sector throughout the Western world, we are bound to be defeated in every kind of peaceful competition which we undertake with the Russians and the Eastern bloc.'

Among others in the fundamentalist camp was the *New Statesman*, which now had firmly in its sights the Labour MP whom it called 'the cup-bearer of the revisionist draught'. 'Though he has a general sympathy for equality,' noted its profile of the 42-year-old (and undeniably arrogant) Anthony Crosland, 'it rarely leads him to the tea-room of the House of Commons and the company of its trade union members . . . He specialises in insolence with a smile – a special charm in an only son which tends, however, to wear a little thin when the chin thickens.' Crosland himself had just sought to explain, in a lengthy *Encounter* article on 'The Future of the Left', that Gaitskell's Blackpool speech had essentially been about the pursuit of clarity, to end the 'series of very confused noises' that had bedevilled Labour through the 1950s. 'The leadership, both Left and Right, tended to speak with two voices – one for the electors and another for the Party militants,' he explained. 'The Left-wing leaders, especially, were schizophrenic on the subject of nationalisation; intellectually they accepted a mixed economy, emotionally they still clung to the dogma of wholesale public ownership.'

Damagingly, therefore, 'the extremist phraseology of the Party's formal aims bore no relation to the moderate, practical content of its short-term programme.' Ultimately, reckoned this champion of Keynesian managed capitalism with a liberal-*cum*-egalitarian twist, the great problem was psychological. 'Revisionism destroys the simplicity, the certainty, and the unquestioning conviction that come from having clear-cut crusading objectives to fight for,' Crosland reflected (condescendingly or sympathetically according to taste). 'It makes everything complicated and ambiguous; it is an explicit admission that many of the old dreams are either realised or dead. No wonder it is resented – especially in the moment of defeat.'[6]

The revisionists never stood a chance, especially once the trade union leaders – even the right-wing ones who usually supported Gaitskell – made a dead set against any attempt to tamper with Clause 4. The whole issue was, the *New Statesman* jubilantly proclaimed in March after a key meeting of Labour's National Executive Committee, 'now water under the bridge'. Three months later, after another party meeting, Benn noted how 'the trade unionists' were 'strongly critical of Gaitskell and particularly attacked his assault on Clause 4 and "his little coterie of friends"'. None more critical than Cousins, in whose private view the revisionists were 'reformists with a main purpose to secure political power for themselves, quite satisfied to maintain the existing structure of society with kindly alterations'. The foot soldiers seemingly agreed. On the day in early July that Bevan died of cancer, the National Union of Mineworkers agreed at their annual conference that there should be no modifying of Clause 4, let alone jettisoning of it, which out of the six major unions made it the fifth to adopt that adamantine stance. The trade union movement as a whole was by this time beginning its long march leftwards. Ralph Miliband observed with satisfaction, in his scathing indictment of *Parliamentary Socialism* (published in 1961 but written in 1960), that a Labour leadership 'whose purpose it is to reduce the Party's commitment to socialist policies' could 'no longer rely on the trade unions to help it in achieving its aims'.

The role of sentiment had been, as Crosland identified, undoubtedly crucial to the outcome. 'The present constitution and statement of objects, adopted so long ago [1918], has a place in our hearts and in our traditions that makes it quite impossible to delete or rewrite it,' George

Brown, a leading member of the Gaitskellite wing, told a meeting in his Belper constituency. There was also the question of Gaitskell's tactical wisdom in deciding at Blackpool to make so much of the Clause 4 issue. It would, Crosland had already told him, 'start a battle in the Party that will cause far more trouble than the thing is worth'. As post-Blackpool played out, the revisionists, as a result of these reservations, arguably lacked a certain collective fire in their bellies. The class element was a further negative aspect, with the gulf now painfully visible between the habits of mind and lifestyles of the Hampstead (or Frognal) set of intellectuals around Gaitskell on the one hand and the trade unionist backbone of the Labour movement on the other. Even trade unionists on Labour's right, including many members of the Parliamentary Labour Party, 'remained attached', to quote the labour historian David Howell, 'to the view that the party was fundamentally, if cautiously, committed to the ending of capitalism'. Or, as Cousins succinctly put it from Labour's left, 'We can have nationalisation without socialism – we cannot have socialism without nationalisation.' The most celebrated verdict on the episode came from the non-revisionist, broadly Bevanite Shadow Chancellor, Harold Wilson. 'We were being asked,' he told an interviewer a few years later, 'to take Genesis out of the Bible. You don't have to be a fundamentalist to say that Genesis is part of the Bible.' At the time, though, Wilson did have a typically astute view about how Gaitskell should have gone about the job of selling abolition of Clause 4 to an essentially tribalist party if as leader he really felt there was no alternative but to try. 'Comrades, in our deliberations on what this great party of ours must do next, let us never forget one undeniable fact: the Tories are a bunch of bastards,' began Wilson's mock speech (as delivered over dinner at the Athenaeum to a trio of *Guardian* journalists including John Cole). 'But as we consider the future of public ownership, let us not leave ourselves open to the slanders and lies our opponents will throw at us. For never forget, comrades, that the Tories are a bunch of bastards. But do we really want the state to take over every corner sweet-shop or petrol station? Of course we don't, but that's what the Tories will say about us, because the Tories are a bunch of bastards . . .'[7]

Yet that, of course, was hardly Gaitskell's style, and Labour by the second half of 1960 still remained 'spiritually enfeebled because of its continued refusal to resolve the issue once and for all', in the despairing words (the previous autumn) of the gifted left-of-centre economic commentator Andrew Shonfield. 'Until capitalism is explicitly accepted by the Labour Party as a permanent, proper, and indeed superior form of organisation for the overwhelming bulk of industry,' he had added, 'it will be hard to remove the doctrinal confusion which at present impoverishes the thinking of the British Left.' Yet during that very autumn of 1959, not only was an election resoundingly lost by the Labour Party, but a month later in West Germany, its counterpart, the Social Democrats, agreed at Bad Godesberg, following a run of election defeats, a Basic Programme that, as an understandably envious Crosland put it soon afterwards, 'accepts categorically the doctrine of the diminished importance of ownership' – in effect turning the SDP into a modern social democratic party, by the mid-1960s under the leadership of Willy Brandt. Elsewhere, the Dutch Labour Party, the Swedish Social Democratic Party and the Swiss Social Democratic Party were all by 1960 moving to an explicitly pragmatic, mixed-economy position over the issue of public ownership. 'No doubt it is usually pointless to urge the example of continental Europe on the insular British,' reflected Crosland in *Encounter* that spring. 'But at least to the internationalists on the British Left, the example may bring some comfort.' Was the Labour Party even trying to march in step with the others? Crosland diplomatically claimed it was, but, as he conceded with some understatement, it was doing so 'a bit to the rear of the column'.[8]

Labour's Clause 4 debate coincided with the launch of the *New Left Review*. The term 'New Left' seems to have become current in 1959, three years after the defining event of the Soviet invasion of Hungary. Shortly before Christmas, the new magazine – an amalgam of the *New Reasoner* and the *Universities and Left Review* – was launched on a chilly Monday evening at St Pancras Town Hall. 'Not everyone was young, amongst the 700 or so present at this public meeting,' noted W. John Morgan. 'Lawrence Daly, a Fife miner, made a very moving speech; Mrs Jeger [the left-wing Labour MP Lena Jeger] spoke very pertinently; Raymond Williams and Stuart Hall said the kind of things, sensible, imaginative and modest, which suggest that the enterprise may well succeed.' The 27-year-old Hall, who had come from Jamaica earlier in the decade and been one of the *ULR*'s founding editors, would be the *NLR*'s first editor. In a 'soft, compelling voice' he emphasised his hope that the *NLR* would help to break down the wariness between intellectual and industrial workers. The meeting lasted from 8.00 p.m. to 10.40 p.m., at which point many adjourned to The Partisan, the New Left's Soho coffee house, where Morgan observed 'grave faces considering grave events and the problems of post-capitalist society'.

'The humanist strengths of socialism – which are the foundations of a genuinely popular socialist movement – must be developed in cultural and social terms, as well as in economic and political,' insisted the editorial in issue number 1, dated January–February 1960. 'The task of socialism is to meet people where they *are*, where they are touched, bitten, moved, frustrated, nauseated – to develop discontent and, at the same time, to give the socialist movement some direct sense of the times and ways in which we live.' The bimonthly's first issue (circulation around 9,000) included Ralph Miliband on 'The Sickness of Labourism', concluding that it 'has now all but spent itself', but that 'the battle for socialism has barely begun'; a study of the working-class Tory voter by Ralph (later Raphael) Samuel, based on preliminary surveys in Clapham and Stevenage; an 'open letter to the British Comrades of the New Left, Victory for Socialism, Tribune etc' by the young London-based American writer Clancy Sigal, claiming that 'the launching of a genuine Youth and Student movement in Britain, owing allegiance to a socialist picture of life, can ensure not only the substance of the Labour Party but may provide a truly important touchstone for the whole country'; and 'Something Rotten in Denmark Street' by Brian Groombridge and Paddy Whannel, who, while trying to avoid 'the tyrannical asceticism' of the Communist states ('we read that keeping it groovy with Elvis Presley is an indictable offence in East Germany'), nevertheless argued that heavily commercialised pop music was offering up 'a surfeit of mediocrity' and that 'the teenage culture does not only consist of coffee bars and juke boxes.' The early issues were inevitably of mixed quality, but to an impressive degree the *NLR* at this stage fulfilled its original prospectus, with one youthful reader, Fred Inglis, warmly recalling two decades later 'the tabloid format, the grainy social realist photography, the instantly intelligent commentary on the world of the times' – in short, a seductive mixture of 'pace and immediacy' and 'large-hearted left eclecticism'. Not every item, admittedly, was large-hearted. The May–June issue featured a review by Colin Falck of Dennis Potter's hot-tempered tract *The Glittering Coffin*; Falck, clearly irked by the assumption in earlier, more mainstream reviews that 'here at last is the authentic voice of the New Left', did not refrain from putting the boot in. Potter's 'too liberal recourse to second-hand vision' meant that his rhetoric began 'to wear thin'; he had 'never really focussed and reflected for himself' on the problems of 'working-class culture and the new affluent society'; and, perhaps most damningly, 'the contradiction between his strictures on Labour politicians and his professed ambition to become one himself remains unresolved.'[9]

The dominant figure in the New Left of the late 1950s and early 1960s was the historian Edward (E. P.) Thompson – handsome, charismatic, difficult and, from his Halifax fastness, inherently suspicious of metropolitan modishness. The New Left's first book, *Out of Apathy*, was published in spring 1960, and although it included pieces by Samuel on '"Bastard" Capitalism', by Hall on 'The Supply of Demand' ('Has the Labour Movement come through the fire and brimstone of the last fifty years to lie down and die before the glossy magazines?') and by Alasdair MacIntyre on 'Breaking the Chains of Reason' (calling on philosophers to make 'a decisive break with utilitarianism'), the leading voice was Thompson's. 'How much longer,' he asked in his introduction 'At the Point of Decay', 'can the Labour Movement hold on to its defensive positions and still maintain morale? Is the aim of socialism to recede forever in the trivia of circumstances? Are we to remain forever as exploited, acquisitive men? It is because the majority of Labour politicians have ceased to hold any real belief in an alternative to capitalism that their kind of politics has become irrelevant.' A second essay, 'Outside the Whale', in large part a meditation on W. H. Auden and George Orwell, put the question, 'Can a new generation, East and West, break simultaneously with the pessimism of the old world and the authoritarianism of the new, and knit together human consciousness into a single socialist humanism?' A third piece, 'Revolution', ended the book and saw Thompson laying into Crosland's recent *Encounter* article on 'The Future of the Left'. He accused him and Gaitskell of bowing down before 'the permanent Cold War', and condemned both 'the permanent dependence of Labour upon "afflu-ent" capitalism' and 'the permanent defensive ideology of defeatism and piecemeal reform'.

The essay's last section addressed the question of revolution itself. There, Thompson rejected the two usual models – on the one hand, 'the evolutionary model' of 'gradual piecemeal reform in an institutional continuum', and on the other, 'the cataclysmic model' with its 'aroma of barricades and naval mutinies in an age of flamethrowers' – before offering a third way. Essentially, this was non-violent and extra-parliamentary, involving in effect a rainbow coalition. 'Alongside the industrial workers, we should see the teachers who want better schools, scientists who wish to advance research, welfare workers who want hospitals, actors who want a National Theatre, technicians impatient to improve industrial organisation.' Together, deploying 'constructive skills within a conscious revolutionary strategy' and asserting 'the values of the common good', they would build 'the socialist community' and thereby progressively undermine capitalism's stranglehold. Finally, after noting how 'it is the greatest illusion of the ideology of apathy that politicians make events' ('Did *Lord Attlee* really free India? Did *Lord Morrison of Lambeth* wrest the pits from the coal owners?'), he ended with a passage about 'the long and tenacious revolutionary tradition of the British commoner' that was distilled essence of Thompson:

> It is a dogged, good-humoured, responsible, tradition: yet a revolution-ary tradition all the same. From the Leveller corporals ridden down by Cromwell's men at Burford to the weavers massed behind their banners at Peterloo, the struggle for democratic and for social rights has always been intertwined. From the Chartist camp meeting to the dockers' picket line it has expressed itself most naturally in the language of moral revolt. Its weaknesses, its carelessness of theory, we know too well; its strengths, its resilience and steady humanity, we too easily forget.

'It is a tradition,' in short, 'which could leaven the socialist world.'

Reactions were mixed. David Caute in the *New Statesman* praised the collection's 'verve and confidence', but doubted whether 'the hope that the patient educational activity of left clubs and trade union groups will bring the people to socialist maturity' truly comprehended 'the lessons of twentieth-century history'; A. J. Ayer in the *Spectator* described as 'exaggerated' the authors' picture of a society 'dominated by a business outlook and by business values', found their solutions 'disappointingly vague', and concluded that 'moral indignation is not enough'. The *TLS* (which had given Thompson such a hard time over his Marxist biography of William Morris five years earlier) was surprisingly sympathetic in tone, but ultimately unconvinced:

> How can we know that a community of equals, rather than a world of I'm-all-right-Jacks and kept-up-with-Joneses, is what the average free man would choose? May he not prefer material goods to hospitals, lavish Hollywood epics to documentaries, television commercials to Shakespeare? And how much difference would more education and more communication make? It is quite possible that, if the capitalist system did not exist, the vast majority of people would want to invent it. At any rate, it is hardly possible to assume the opposite . . .
>
> The New Left put their faith in the community and the mutual interests it contains, demanding a standard of clear thinking and unselfishness that the ordinary man cannot bear. They overrate people in their social behaviour. And in doing so they run the risk of overrating themselves, both by demanding so high a standard of idealism that they reject even the most satisfactory compromise, and by imagining that their own recipe for the future is the only right one.

The most hostile critique of *Out of Apathy* came from the young politics lecturer (and Labour supporter) Bernard Crick. 'All is denunciation and sectarian polemic,' he wrote in the *Political Quarterly*. 'It is, brothers, the revolution or nothing; damn your mess of potage and God bless mine.' Orwell's future biographer was generally a controversialist who took few prisoners, and 'the ranting near-hysteria, the self-righteousness, the good old Marxist style of souped-up violence' was as little to his taste as its 'wind of rhetoric'.[10]

The New Left's relationship with the Labour Party, and indeed the broader labour movement, was of course fraught. 'What we need is a living movement of people, battering away at the problems of socialism in the mid-Twentieth century, pooling their experiences, yet, at every point, breaking back into the Labour Movement, thrusting forward like so many uninvited guests into Constituency Parties and Trade Union branches, pushing within CND, picking up the quick tissues in the society, sloughing off the dead,' proclaimed the *NLR*'s first editorial. The quite rapidly growing Left Clubs were seen as the vanguard of this broadening strategy, and in the next issue an open letter to readers in them spoke of how what was needed was 'the *consciousness* that the constituency worker, fighting to get the Conference floor, and the duffle-coated jazz fan on the Aldermaston March are both *running* in the same direction', thereby breaking down 'mutual hostility and suspicion'. Yet if these were conciliatory words, the editorial in the May–June issue had all guns blazing in its attack on Gaitskell ('incapable any longer of understanding what a popular, democratic movement of people would be like ... a bourgeois politician') and the Labour right ('sheer dishonesty when facing the implications of the facts about our society'). 'I am convinced that in order to progress towards socialism the British labour movement must ultimately find a way of accommodating within itself the radical idealism and dynamic impulse to action characteristic of the New Left,' reflected Jay Blumler (a lecturer at Ruskin College, Oxford) soon afterwards in the revisionist-friendly *Socialist Commentary*. 'But the New Left must not make this accommodation impossible. From this point of view its addiction to Marxist tenets is unfortunate, and the increasing shrillness of its attack upon those in the labour movement who do not share its outlook is quite ominous.' Or, as an *SC* reader, Ronald Parker of Middlesbrough, put it in October 1960 (some six months after the purportedly anti-cataclysmic Thompson had privately invoked the memory of Russia in 1917 and foreseen 'a new kind of revolution lying around in Britain in 1969 or 1974'), although '*New Left Review* is an organ of dissident Marxism and would avoid the errors committed by Stalin, its authors have the same quite disconcerting sense that history is with them which characterised the Stalinists, the theological certainty of latter-day saints and a touching feeling that the second coming is at hand'.[11]

Only half the 1959 electorate old enough to have voted in a pre-war general election, one family in every six moving between 1948 and 1958 into a newly built house or flat, the industrial worker's average real earnings rising by over 20 per cent between 1951 and 1958, rapidly growing consumption (especially on durable 'white goods') and hire-purchase credit, the living room and the TV set displacing the pub and the cinema, family life increasingly focused on the newly acquired car, the number of white-collar workers up by over a million between 1951 and 1959, manual workers falling in the same period by half a million, the Butler Act of 1944 enabling working-class children to advance via grammar schools to become middle-class adults – one way and another, reflected David Butler and Richard Rose in their instant but authoritative account of the 1959 election, 'the last ten years have eroded some of the traditional foundations of Labour strength.' 'Social changes,' they went on, 'have been weakening traditional working-class political loyalties; simultaneously the middle classes have become more prosperous and more self-confident. Full employment and the welfare state have made the well-paid worker much less dependent on his trade union or on the Labour party than before the war. At the bench a man may still be plainly working-class, but in his new home, in his car, or out shopping, his social position may be more difficult to assess. He may well think of himself as a consumer first and only secondly as a worker.' Moreover, they added, 'television, women's weeklies, and the popular press have on the whole emphasised values which foster any inclinations people may have to identify their interests with the more prosperous part of the nation – which, in political terms, means voting Conservative.'

Unsurprisingly, Anthony Crosland and his fellow-revisionists tended to agree with this pessimistic (from a Labour standpoint) analysis. 'The scales today are weighted against the Labour Party,' he told a Fabian audience in April 1960, 'so long as it preserves its one-class image.' Further grist to the revisionist mill soon followed with the celebrated Abrams survey. This was conducted by the Labour-sympathising sociologist-*cum*-market-research expert Mark Abrams, published by *Socialist Commentary* between May and August, and, that autumn, turned into a Penguin Special, *Must Labour Lose?* On the basis of 724 in-depth interviews (including with 255 Labour supporters) in the first two months of 1960, Abrams sought 'to establish those attitudes and social values which have led the electorate to turn away steadily from the Labour Party over the past ten years and to reject it decisively at the latest General Election'.

Perhaps his most striking finding was that whereas an overwhelming majority agreed with the proposition that Labour 'stands mainly for the working class', 50 per cent of non-Labour supporters who were in fact working-class nevertheless perceived themselves as middle-class. Indeed, among the unskilled working-class respondents who did not vote Labour, 'three-quarters of them rejected their "objective" social status of "labouring working class".' Unsurprisingly, and whatever their self-selected social status, working-class non-Labour supporters agreed particularly strongly (67 per cent) with the statement that the Conservatives 'would make the country more prosperous', a criterion that only 7 per cent believed to be applicable to Labour. Abrams also turned to the much-publicised question of youth (defined as 18 to 24) and politics, at a time when 21 was still the minimum voting age. '35 per cent of all working-class young people are ready to identify themselves with the Conservative Party,' he found, 'and only 10 per cent of middle-class young people support the Labour Party.' He added that 'young people were much more emphatic than their elders in seeing Labour as overwhelmingly the party which stands mainly for the working class, as out to help the underdog and to abolish class differences.' Unfortunately for Labour, though, 'none of these traits seemed of much significance to young people when they indicated the most important features of a good political party', with five times more choosing 'out to raise standard of living' than 'out to help the underdog'. 'They are,' concluded Abrams about the nation's youth in the first year of the 1960s, 'highly optimistic about the future, and very satisfied with their jobs. They know very little about the Labour Party's programme, and where their own interests are concerned they are convinced – by an almost 2 to 1 majority – that Conservative policies would suit them best.'

Ralph Samuel was unimpressed. 'Dr Abrams and the End of Politics' was the title of his *New Left Review* piece in September, attacking Abrams for having succumbed to 'a species of status determinism, supported by a behaviourist psychology of opinions and informed by the assumptions of motivational and market research'. It was, according to Samuel,

a gloomy characterisation of contemporary British man; one which allows him no core of conviction or steady centre, but only a moral vacuum in which the fast-flowing streams of status deposit their sediment. He sees people as *consumers* of politics, behaving in politics much as they would – in the motivational research imagination – when confronted with mass-market commodities: they 'buy' political labels and allegiances as they would any brand-image – because of the pleasurable associations it promises to afford . . . These associations may have an organic or only an accidental connection with people's desires; they may bear a real or only a fancied relation to people's genuine needs; but for this political philosophy, it does not matter at all.

There followed some detailed criticism of Abrams's methodology, not least his 'cavalier' treatment of young people – 'Teds and Mods, Beatniks and Ravers, Aldermaston Marchers and Nuclear Campaigners, they all disappear amidst the whirrings of his Hollerith machines, to re-emerge on his Punch Cards, an almost undifferentiated mass' – before the inevitable uplifting peroration in dark times: 'Behind the image scores, and the identity tables which here encapsulate them, there are real living, breathing, thinking, feeling people: Tredegar steel workers and Cannock miners, Blackheath teachers and Suffolk farmers, Kentish Town mothers and Wythenshawe clerks: the common people; not all of them with Labour, and not as many as in the past, but still, Radical England, *us* and not *them*.' And 'if the Labour Movement,' concluded Samuel, 'were finally to abandon its traditional way of thinking about people – and that alone is truly fundamental – to lose its faith in the power of the word to move people, and of the idea to change them, if it were to let go its conviction in the capacity of human beings rationally to choose between the alternatives which face them, and purposefully to re-shape the society in which they live, then it would be finished, and would find itself trapped in that limbo of the political imagination whose features Dr Abrams has so meticulously outlined.'[12]

Just for a moment in 1960 there appeared to be a chance of a whole new political flank opening – with little or nothing to do with the New Left – in the wake of the crushing election defeat for the two progressive parties, Labour and Liberal.

'Real tea is so welcome at Dover,' Michael Young had written back in January 1958 (soon after starting the instantly successful *Which?* magazine),

> you hardly notice the cracked cup it comes in. Corpses of ham sandwiches may arouse a kind of affection for the archaism of England. But what about the people? How polite we are compared to foreigners! How gentle the swearing of the porters! How sedate and how safe!
>
> Too sedate, too quiet, too safe – where has the vitality gone? We all seem such willing victims of oppression. Are we all terrified of authority? In restaurants, bars, shops we put up with cold food, warm beer and the icy look. We seem to be a nation that has ceased to protest. We accept housing estates, smoke, British Railways, external pipes, rockets, and shoddy shoes as though everything was so royally blessed as to be beyond criticism.

The consumer as king (or even queen)? It seemed a preposterous thought amidst such a deeply entrenched culture of passivity and uncomplaint. But by November 1959, weeks after the election, Mark Abrams was giving a talk on the Third Programme about 'The Home-centred Society' (a phrase that now entered the mainstream) which analysed changing habits of spending, especially the rapid rise of household goods, and noted not only how women's magazines were increasingly geared to appeal to 'the housewife as a consumer' but also how in industry it had become marketing directors, 'buttressed by sales managers and advertising experts', who had become 'today's innovators and risk-bearers', poised to 'earn the largest managerial salaries and dominate the boardrooms of the future'. In short, concluded Abrams about society at large, the unmistakable trend was towards 'the supremacy of the consumer'.

The politics were tantalising. 'Chris is really out of sympathy with the Party as it now exists and thinks we must gradually break loose of the trade unions and become a consumers' Party,' recorded Anthony Wedgwood Benn in June 1960 about Christopher Mayhew, the Labour politician and resolute opponent of commercial television. That same month, a Gallup poll revealed that 25 per cent would be willing to vote for a consumers' party, not in the pocket of either the unions or big business, at a new general election, with 37 per cent undecided. Four months later, Young published a pamphlet – turned down by the Fabian

Society as anti-Labour – with the title *The Chipped White Cups of Dover*, explicitly projected as 'a discussion of the possibility of a new progressive party'. At the heart of his case was the argument that henceforth 'politics will become less and less the politics of production and more and more the politics of consumption'. Accordingly, he envisaged a reforming party that, among many other things, would 'mount an attack on the monopolies and restrictive practices by which Britain is more ridden than any other country in the world', and he cited such major irritants as resale price maintenance, the absurdly restricted opening hours permitted by the Shops Act, and the lofty disregard of the user prevalent in the public services (whether health, education, housing or social security). He then specifically considered the reforming credentials of the Labour Party – whose manifesto he himself had written in 1945 – and found them wanting, largely because of that party's umbilical link with the trade unions, which 'to consumers seem too small-minded about their own sectional interest as producers'. Altogether, wrote Young near the end, after a nod to the television age as a political game-changer, 'I do not think a new party would find itself at a disadvantage if it was a much less elaborate affair than the old parties, with less ponderous headquarters than the one where I worked, with a less tight discipline, with less insistence on conformity, with less subordination of members to the national office, and above all with more plain speaking by MPs emancipated from the Whips.'

It was probably never a runner. 'It all sounds very reasonable,' reflected Benn after his conversation with Mayhew. 'But politics is about power and if we are not firmly linked to the working-class movement, then we shall never be anything at all except a lot of Liberals with bright ideas.'[13] Yet arguably the indissolubility of that link (in effect with the unions) was not just a question of power. To have accepted the new reality that many working-class people were starting to become, in their self-image and even their way of life, relatively classless consumers at least as much as they were class-conscious producers would have required for middle-class socialists like Benn a profound recasting of a heroic, moralistic mythology. In the event, it would take a full three decades before Labour had a leader who was not sentimental about the working class and who finally – more or less – persuaded his party to accept that chipped cups were no longer good enough.

4

Some Fearful Risks

On Saturday, 7 May the newly wed Princess Margaret was on her way to Mustique as Wolverhampton Wanderers comfortably beat Blackburn Rovers 3–0 in yet another no-substitutes Cup Final marred by injury, this time a broken leg for the Rovers defender Dave Whelan. 'Not a moment of beauty or of transcendent football to cherish,' regretted John Arlott, while in Blackburn itself the outcome merely compounded the sense of grievance already fuelled by an unfair system of ticket allocation that had prevented life-long supporters from going to Wembley. Next day saw *Bonanza*'s debut – the 'painfully familiar juvenile melodramas', according to *Punch*'s Henry Turton, of 'yet another Western series bought from American TV for our delight' – before on Monday a great moment in the Heap household. 'Glory be!' recorded a relieved diarist. 'Frainy has passed his 11 Plus exam!' There followed next evening the promised (if he passed) 'celebration dinner' at the Chicken Inn, Leicester Square: 'A wing of chicken with thin "French fried" chips each, plus a "knickerbocker glory" and orangeade for F, a sherry trifle and lager for me'.

A week later the Cold War took a chilly turn with the comprehensive failure of the Paris summit. Most people blamed the Russians – 'Kruschev a menace', bluntly noted the middle-aged Jennie Hill – but a younger diarist, Kate Paul, castigated 'pig-headed, proud individuals' across the board. 'I want to grip these maniacs by the shoulders and shout: "Don't you dare destroy me!" How can I live on probation like this? How can anyone? But we do.' Next day, the 18th, the first and last act of corporal punishment ('2 on seat') took place at Risinghill School, a newly opened co-educational comprehensive in Islington under the progressive leadership of Michael Duane; that evening, in the European Cup Final at Hampden Park, Real Madrid's sumptuous 7–3 thrashing of Eintracht Frankfurt lit the European flame for at least one of the 135,000 awed Glaswegians, the 18-year-old part-time professional Alex Ferguson; on Thursday, 14-year-old Jacqueline Aitken had dinner at a friend's house ('liver, baked beans, cauliflower and new potatoes', followed by 'rhubarb and evaporated milk', altogether *very nice!*'); soon afterwards, Penelope Gilliatt, in her *Spectator* review of Doris Lessing's sociological *In Pursuit of the English*, argued that, 'with post-Orwellian insight, she knows in her heart that for a middle-class intellectual like herself the idea of the working class is essentially talismanic and unattainable'; simultaneously, an emerging giant among middle-class intellectuals, Eric Hobsbawm, deplored in the *New Statesman* (in his capacity as jazz critic 'Francis Newton') the 'present vogue' among the young for Miles Davis, describing him as not only 'of surprisingly narrow technical and emotional range' but also as unhealthily close to 'self-pity and the denial of love'; on the 25th the hitherto jazz-oriented Cavern in Liverpool had its first all-beat session; and, three days later, Gateshead were dropped from the Football League in favour of Peterborough United, a decision not implausibly attributed by the *Newcastle Evening Chronicle* to a conspiracy by 'a cosy clique of southern clubs'.[1]

There was hardly a youthquake yet in 1960 Britain, but older people that May continued to resent even the relatively early tremors. 'I was deeply shocked,' noted Nella Last on the 22nd after the first-ever televising of the Royal Variety Performance, 'when that queer neurotic youth Lonnie Donegan forgot his lines – wondered how he got on the bill . . .' About the same time, the *East London Advertiser*'s Tom Duncan interviewed the actor Jack Warner, 'a Bow boy for a great chunk of his life' and now of course best known as PC George Dixon. The interview took place as Warner drove the journalist round central London in his new car, starting off at Broadcasting House:

> We were just beginning to infiltrate into that part of the West End which is occupied by the weirdies, and Jack pulled my attention to a couple of misguided delinquents who were lounging in front of a café. 'Look at them,' he insisted, a tone of disgust ricocheting through his voice.

'They're beatniks,' I murmured.

'What do they do?' he replied.

'I can tell you what they don't do,' I answered. 'They don't wash and they comb their hair once every other month.'

'Bring back the birch,' Jack scowled, commandeering his car through a thin gap in the traffic.

Another local paper had been rather more tolerant, but was now half-regretting it. 'Our picture page last week, featuring impressionistic views of 'teen-age dancing in the Northern Meeting Rooms, aroused some controversy,' apologised the Inverness-based *Highland News* on the 20th about a vivid full-page photo feature that had been headed 'LET'S GO MAN GO!' and had included the caption 'A little relaxation is a good thing' for the photo of a couple in a tight clinch away from the dance floor. 'Certainly there was no intention to impute laxness of conduct on the part of the management ... The page was intended to be a study in *joie de vivre*, and if the, necessarily, contrasting tones had an element of sensationalism about them, the effect intended was to present an ensemble of youthful motion and emotion in a particular setting.'

Northern Border Dances held their nerve and, the following evening, Saturday the 21st, proudly presented something for everyone: downstairs, 'Old Thyme Dancing to Lindsay Ross and His Famous Broadcasting Band'; upstairs, 'Modern Dancing to THE BEAT BALLAD SHOW', starring 'T.V. and Decca Recording Star JOHNNY GENTLE and his Group'. Gentle's backing group were in fact the Silver Beetles, as they were now briefly known; and this date in Inverness was the second of seven on an ill-planned Scottish tour that also included St Thomas' Hall in Keith, the town hall in Forres and the Regal Ballroom in Nairn, eventually leading a hungry John Lennon to place a desperate reverse-charges phone call to the promoter, demanding, 'Where's the bloody money?' Everyday life along the north-east coast went on sweetly oblivious. Forres Junior Farmers' Club held a stock-judging competition, with three classes of pigs and two of sheep; the monthly meeting of the Altyre Women's Rural Institute featured 'an interesting demonstration of floral arrangements' as well as a talk on 'what one would do to protect one's home and family in the case of nuclear warfare'; Glen Urquhart, with seven of its 12 players either Mackintoshes or Macdonalds, won a junior shinty championship; and in Keith the greatest buzz was around the third-placed appearance of the Keith Townswomen's Guild team in the final at the Royal Albert Hall of a national quiz sponsored by the Electricity Development Association.[2]

Fame still lay some way ahead for Lennon et al, completing their tour at Peterhead on Saturday the 28th, but for the 25-year-old and very left-wing Dennis Potter a degree of celebrity was already becoming familiar. The following Friday, the BBC showed *Between Two Rivers*, about Potter returning to his native mining village in the increasingly affluent and consumerist Forest of Dean after three years at Oxford. 'Seemed bitter and full of rancour,' thought one viewer. 'He was the odd man out, refusing to recognise the signs of the times.' Certainly he was never likely to be one of the angels in marble – those working-class Conservatives (so cherished by Disraeli) whom the political scientists Robert McKenzie and Allan Silver were now trying to tease out, especially after the hat-trick of Tory election victories. Their interviewees in late May and early June lived in council flats off the Edgware Road in London W2:

You've got to have people with money to run the country. That's my feeling. (*Housewife, 51*)

I suppose there's only really two classes – the people with the real money . . . I don't think anyone is really in the poor class today . . . It's the middle class and as near to it as they could ever be. I don't think anyone is really bad off – in a poor class. (*Self-employed man delivering paraffin, 37*)

You'll always find the upper dog and the under dog, no matter which party is there . . . (*Housewife, 45*)

The Conservative Party I think are run by people that know a bit, and are more sensible and classy . . . They keep the country better than what a Labour man would . . . They keep the country decent, sort of thing . . . When we had these Labour in, things don't go so nice . . . They just want Dick, Tom and Harry to have the money all the time, and they forget that there's other people in the country to keep going . . . I do like it when the Conservatives are in . . . They always do their best and do things for both sides . . . They've done no end of buildings since they've been in, flats and things . . . I think Unions cause a lot of trouble in the country . . . I think they cause more strikes and everything . . . (*Housewife, 59*)[3]

'Some silly people on the right nowadays wish the sixties hadn't happened because that was when people discovered sex and pot-smoking,' observed Alan Bennett three decades later. 'I wish the sixties hadn't happened because that was when avarice and stupidity got to the wheel of the bulldozer. They called it enterprise and still do, but the real enterprise would have been if someone in 1960 had had the clout and the imagination to say, "Let us leave this city much as it is, convert it perhaps, replumb it, but nothing else."' 'If they had,' he added regretfully about the city he had grown up in, 'Leeds today would have been one of the architectural showpieces of the kingdom, a Victorian Genoa or Florence, on the buildings of which many of its banks and commercial properties were modelled. Instead it's now like anywhere else.' Many other British cities and towns, and indeed the built environment generally, also changed fundamentally during the 1960s. In this respect at least, the '1960s' were well under way by 1960 itself; for by that summer and autumn, the pace of change in the urban built environment – whether actual change or planned change for the future – was becoming as rapid as at any time since the Industrial Revolution.

In hitherto sleepy Basingstoke, for example, the town centre was turned into a cluster of one-way streets; in Birmingham, the construction of the Inner Ring Road continued to devour everything in its way (including Smallbrook's Scala cinema, bowing out with *Teenage Loves*), and work started on the landmark Rotunda, with the projected height of the circular tower now doubled from 12 storeys to 24; in Coventry, the City Arcade of 1932 began to be replaced by a concrete version; in Derby, the Coliseum cinema (previously a Congregational church) was demolished with the construction of Bradshaw Way; in the Great Parndon neighbourhood of Harlow New Town, a brutalist 'casbah' housing project won an architectural competition and would prove, in Lionel Esher's words, 'a fish out of water in the arcadian scene'; in Leeds itself, the completion of the Saville Green 10-storey flats, part of the Ebor Gardens scheme in York Road, was the latest addition to the city's skyline, now (as a local paper put it) 'quite dwarfing the gigantic mill chimneys of our youthful recollection'; and in Liverpool, the headline was 'City's soaring skyline' as the city council signed contracts for a range of multi-storey schemes, while the university's just completed physics building, on a site 'still surrounded by condemned slum property', was the latest tower block by the newly knighted Basil Spence. In London, meanwhile, amid much else, new buildings included the BBC's gleamingly modern Television Centre at White City and Sir Giles Gilbert Scott's 325-foot-high Bankside Power Station (the future Tate Modern); buildings under construction included the massive *Daily Mirror* headquarters in Holborn Circus and the London County Council's highest block of flats yet (19 storeys, in Stepney); demolition work was in hand, courtesy of the developer Charles Clore, on the site for Park Lane's London Hilton ('this long-awaited, much-discussed addition to London's roster of super-hotels'); Spence got the go-ahead to design a tower block at Knightsbridge Barracks; and the winning design for the Elephant and Castle Shopping Centre featured a cruciform glass-roofed arcade rising through two floors and laid out with planting, fountains and pavement cafés. In Newcastle, the Scandinavian-style Civic Centre began to be built, while nearby there was a green light for Northumberland County Council to redevelop Killingworth, in due course becoming (in Elain Harwood's words) 'the most comprehensive megastructure in Britain . . . a whole town centre and flanking housing conceived as a single unit with walkways over the main roads'; in Oxford, the demolition of rundown St Ebbe's continued apace, with the Gas Works no longer the first glimpse of the city from the train, while on the Blackbird Leys estate work started on a 15-storey block of flats, Windrush Tower; in Plymouth, the local paper's year-end progress report gave pride of place to the newly extending inner ring road ('progress should be as rapid as the rehousing of displaced families permits'); and in Sheffield the last of Park Hill's 995 dwellings was handed over to tenants shortly after the city's trams headed for the breaker's yard. It was much the same in Scotland, above all in the two biggest cities. In Edinburgh, demolition started in historic George Square, and the massive Leith Fort redevelopment began (including two 21-storey point blocks); while in Glasgow the latest Development

Plan envisaged the comprehensive demolition and rebuilding of 29 areas (more than a third of the city) over the next 20 years, and the Corporation – stimulated by Wimpey's rapid completion in Royston Road (amid a tangle of railway lines and a canal) of three 20-storey blocks, Scotland's tallest so far – moved decisively in favour of high-rise flats within the city boundaries.[4]

One way and another, 1960 was undoubtedly a 'moment', not just because it was the start of a decade. That autumn, the *Yorkshire Post*'s Harry Franz sought to capture it in a piece called 'New brick, concrete, steel and glass . . . AMONG THE ALIEN BLACK OF BRADFORD STONE':

> Bradford's £5,000,000 facelift continues at breakneck pace with old buildings in the former congested central area disappearing as swiftly as snow in a sudden thaw. Towering modern office and shopping blocks are creeping skyward in their place. This expensive and expansive building project is going hand in hand with the Corporation's new road plans, which will eventually open up the city centre with an inner ring road . . .
>
> Above the traffic's roar comes the distinctive note of the pneumatic drill, biting clearly and cleanly into some hard tough object. The rasping circular saw shrills out a higher pitch as its teeth tear into timber and plank. The lighter duller noise of hammer and chisel break through occasionally under the rhythmic movement of the master craftsman's hands . . .

'Bradford is indeed a progressive city these days,' declared Franz. And he added, with just possibly a nod to J. B. Priestley, who on television two years earlier had urged his home city to advance into the twentieth century: 'Exiles returning to it will hardly know it in its modern shape . . .'

'In the long run it is enlightened public opinion that matters most,' a government minister, Lord Craigton, told the Town and Country Planning summer school. How to make that public opinion sufficiently enlightened? Politicians themselves sometimes expressed views – 'with much greater vigour,' urged Labour's Patrick Gordon Walker, 'we must rebuild our whole environment of working and living in terms of the motor car' – while modernist architects (and not only Spence) were naturally not shy in coming forward. 'In 10 years London could be a beautiful skyscraper city,' Ernö Goldfinger explained to the *Sunday Times*, 'and the view from the river could be as it was in Wren's London, except that instead of churches you would have skyscrapers towering over the lower buildings.' But what strikes one about the state of play in 1960 is the key cheerleading role played by the still much-read local press. When in July, for instance, the winning design was unveiled for Dumbarton's fundamental redevelopment, including a new main road through the town to be raised on pillars, the *Lennox Herald*'s response was unambiguously positive, declaring that 'the whole scheme hangs together effortlessly'. Later that month it was the turn of south London, with the *Peckham & Dulwich Advertiser & News* trumpeting the news that 'the Elephant and Castle is to have the most fabulous, up-to-date shopping centre in Britain . . . perhaps in Europe.'

Ultimately, perhaps it all came down to zeitgeist, to a certain something in the air. 'There is about such buildings more than the excitement of unaccustomed height and variety of scale,' reflected the middle-aged landscape painter William Townsend in a radio talk inspired by the Golden Lane flats just north of the Barbican and by Denys Lasdun's cluster blocks in Bethnal Green. 'I cannot help feeling a sense of relief at seeing them there, as though they were something we should not be without, something one has to have these days, like nylon and neon signs and television; and this not to make sure we do not feel inferior to the United States or Brazil [a reference presumably to embryonic modernist Brasília], but because they stand in a special way, like abstract painting, good or bad, for where human societies have really got to.'[5]

One local figure, leader from early 1960 of the Labour group in Newcastle and in effect that city's boss, was poised to become emblematic of the new spirit of the age. 'A Practical VISIONARY' was the title in March of a local paper's profile of T. Dan Smith – the start of the mythologising of the sixties man who, as Martin Linton would aptly put it in the 1970s, 'came to sort out local government with a strong belief in business efficiency and a burning social purpose'. Describing him as 'more than six feet tall' with 'a powerful though sympathetic personality', the *Evening Chronicle* heralded Councillor Smith as 'the first man since the war with the dedicated enthusiasm, ability and perseverance to tackle the problem of re-building the city'. As Smith himself told the interviewer, 'So little has been done in the past, we are painting a new canvas as it were.' That spring, amid facing down the City Engineer and securing the appointment of Newcastle's first City Planning Officer (Wilfred Burns), Smith spoke at the annual meeting of the Town Planning Institute (held in Newcastle), and outlined in his usual fluent and expansive way what would become familiar themes. His city needed to be at the heart of a region (serviced by a regional planning authority) creating 'a compelling interest to forward-looking industrialists to come North'; the city's slums would be cleared within five years; in terms of what replaced them, 'increasing standards of amenity', including 'new parklands, adequate community buildings, modern shopping centres and children's playing centres', would be 'sought after all the time'; and as for the city centre itself, the aim was to make Newcastle 'the most outstanding provincial capital in the country'. In passing, Smith noted: 'I oppose the traffic "Canutes" – the modern city needs as much traffic as possible and it must deal with tomorrow's traffic problems today.' At this stage, the aspect of redevelopment closest to his heart was Cruddas Park, a cleared 5-acre site where work was under way on erecting a cluster of 15-storey point blocks. Cruddas Park, Smith told the conference, not only would be 'the focal point of the Scotswood Road Development Area' but also – through the quality of the modern, well-equipped blocks themselves, together with 'landscaping and other features' (including a sculpture to be unveiled on the centenary of the Blaydon Races in June 1962) – would 'contribute locally to the stimulation of the arts on Tyneside and nationally to a wider appreciation of the cultural and industrial potentialities of the Tyneside of tomorrow'.

Not everyone fell tamely into line. 'Our life is dominated by television programmes which we do not wish to hear,' wrote a malcontent flat-dweller, Norman Lingham, to the *Sunday Times* – a fortnight after Goldfinger's high-rise vision – from his 'cacophonous pigeon-hole' in London SE15. So too with Park Hill in Sheffield. 'THE VERDICT: It's "SMASHING" living right up IN THE SKY' was the *Star*'s headline in May. However, a few months later a letter to the paper from 'New Sheffield' disparaged 'the whole dismal, slablike mass' of 'the city's newest eyesore', while a local businessman, Anthony Greenfield, expressed himself 'certain' that 'within a quarter of a century' the flats would be 'regarded as slums'. Slum clearance also had its critics. 'All these houses were well cared for and I think they would still have been in good condition in 50 or a 100 years,' complained E. Macdonald, 'a Middletonian of the Fourth Generation', to his local paper in Lancashire about a recent spate of demolition, while in Bristol the newly elected, anti-socialist 'Citizen' councillors tried unsuccessfully to persuade the Conservative housing minister, Henry Brooke, to allow a more selective approach in that city. Or take one of the areas of most intense clearance. 'Living as the *City Reporter* does on the boundary of the Ellor Street slum clearance area,' noted Saul Reece in his column in August, 'we are visited almost daily by residents, indignant, angry, or just plain sarcastic, complaining about the chaotic progress (or lack of progress) of the demolition. One or two large areas have been cleared around Hankinson Street, but street after street of houses stand empty in various states of ruin . . .' Ellor Street, in short, 'now looks like the worst kind of blitzed area on the morning after the raid, a disgrace to Salford in its death as it has been for half a century in its life'.[6]

The juggernaut was rolling, albeit with varying speed and efficiency, and usually it seemed irresistible. In Glasgow, Councillor Derek Wood declared that 'what disturbed him most' about that city's radical Development Plan was that 'they were treating people like cattle' in the sense that 'the proposals were being imposed from the planner's point of view without regard to other considerations.' Almost certainly during this complicated process, what one might call a regretful fatalism was widely felt, if not always by the majority of people, who may well have been largely indifferent or perhaps even mildly positive. It was an indifference that might have puzzled the Vale of Leven's David Stevenson. 'Demolishing old buildings and erecting others in their place,' began his ponderously eloquent letter to the local paper about the early-Victorian settlement in Bonhill known as 'the Wee Field' and its almost complete destruction, 'is in these days always keeping up a steady pace in endeavouring to meet the demands of this age of progress and speed, wiping out with one fell blow, changing completely old familiar landscapes which have been in existence for many a long year, becoming part and parcel so to speak of succeeding generations as they lived and moved and had their being.'

One of the more contested cities – though only ever with one outcome

– was Birmingham, site of arguably the most rapid and fundamental change anywhere in urban Britain. 'Dramatic surgery – but it may well kill a city' was the *News Chronicle* headline in September for a powerful critique by the young and bearded architectural writer Peter Rawsthorne, who argued that Birmingham's officials were, in their understandable attempt to solve the traffic problem, 'tearing their city apart' and making it 'alarmingly impersonal'. The villain of the piece was of course the Inner Ring Road, 'slicing' its way 'across the cosy tangle of old streets and buildings'; soon afterwards, in an architectural magazine, Rawsthorne called this 'massively ambitious' project 'a menacingly misguided colossus that may well overpower the withering vestiges of informality altogether'. In October the *Birmingham Mail* helpfully published a large map showing the new central Birmingham (within the still-under-construction Inner Ring Road) that was taking, or planned to take, shape. The accompanying article by the chairman of the City Council's Public Works Committee was the usual stuff – 'outdated, overcrowded . . . being reborn . . . huge, clean, new concrete buildings . . . modern and comprehensive . . . tremendous redevelopment . . .' – while on another page the blurb for an artist's impression of the future Bull Ring expressed complete satisfaction with how 'clean, flowing lines and a 20th century symmetry' would be replacing 'the old untidy jumble and bustle of the city's traditional market place'. Two self-styled 'old Brummies' responded on the letters page. Although conceding that 'long acquaintance, and a measure of sentiment, may cause regret over the disappearance of familiar buildings and landmarks', T. Austin of Birmingham 24 reckoned that 'the Ring Road scheme, and vast rebuilding, considered as a whole, will give Birmingham a status it has lacked'; by contrast, 'I do not see anything of beauty in it – only some copy of Continental ideas,' was the view of Birmingham 23's 'Citizen', who, after adding that 'putting huge blocks of offices and skyscrapers – some call them houses – is not sufficient', declared himself 'utterly disgusted'.

Perhaps the most resonant charges came from a former Lord Mayor, Norman Tiptaft. 'Second Thoughts on the New Look in Birmingham' was the title in November of his trenchant *Daily Telegraph* piece, arguing that – far from it being the case of 'a few nostalgic old fogies' having qualms – in reality there had grown up 'a deep, underlying resentment'. Partly this was about 'handing over to developers more concerned with financial profits than with building the city beautiful of the future'; partly it was about 'the type of city being constructed'. Noting that high-rise flats had 'never been asked for by Birmingham citizens', Tiptaft went on:

> In the new city, we shall be housed in 16-storey flats, shop in brick or concrete boxes, and be segregated in zones – some for houses, some for shops, some for factories. The little shop on the corner or in the side street will disappear, along with the self-employed boot repairer or tobacconist or little grocer ... Never mind how convenient the odd building would be. The planners and the zoners and the believers in monotony and in everybody being exactly alike won't allow it.

Altogether, the new Birmingham was, concluded Tiptaft, 'the vision of "1984"'.[7]

They did things differently in Bury St Edmunds. 'COUNCIL HEARS REVOLUTIONARY PLAN TO DEVELOP THE TOWN CENTRE' announced the *Bury Free Press* back in November 1959, as the essence of an audacious deal emerged: a cluster of handsome old buildings (Corn Exchange, public library, School of Art) to be demolished, the site to be sold to developers, a large block of shops and offices to be built. 'It will make Bury St Edmunds one of the best shopping centres in East Anglia,' noted the paper, but over the following nine or so months opposition to the scheme steadily increased. 'Why the sudden craze to speed up the tempo of change, to make revolutionary developments which must tear the guts out of the old place?' asked Colonel Sidney Rogerson, who had lived near Bury for 25 years. When the councillors eventually came to vote in October 1960, the Corn Exchange was saved for posterity; altogether, the scheme had seemingly been, as the *Bury Free Press* put it, 'strangled to death by public opinion'. Yet what is striking is that, in the only systematic test of what Bury's residents actually wanted (a postal referendum in Northgate Ward shortly before the decisive meeting), the voting went 933 for the scheme, 922 against. Perhaps the last word should go to 'Winkle Picker', who in a letter to the local paper declared that the outcome had been 'a victory to a bunch of elderly barnacles on the backside of progress'.

The trenchant architectural critic Ian Nairn, who would presumably have been on the side of the angels, was in any case still travelling more or less hopefully during these months on a tour of some of the major provincial cities. In Birmingham he was nervous about the effect of the Inner Ring Road, though overall he reckoned that it would be 'all right' despite 'some fearful risks' having been taken; Newcastle had the potential to be 'one of the great cities of Europe', but all depended on the Corporation's quality of patronage; in Manchester the crux was whether 'public and private enterprise' could combine in the central area, currently dead after the working day, to achieve 'not only "urban renewal" (which so often means replacing lively old dirt by dead new cleanness) but urban awakening'; and in Glasgow, Nairn focused mainly on the Gorbals, where some parts were undeniably 'past repair' but others 'could easily be salvaged, not as a stop-gap or cut-rate measure, but because of the innate qualities of the buildings' (adding that 'all over Glasgow' there were 'similar terraces in a similar condition'). Yet over and above the individual fates of individual cities, there existed in Nairn's eyes a more fundamental problem:

> Very few people are really trying to find out what a city is like to be in, not only in terms of their own life but for every kind of person who uses it ... Does any planner in Birmingham or Liverpool or Manchester know how the corporation dustmen live, what they enjoy in the city centre and what they abhor? The problem is at least as important as plot ratio, daylight angles and sight lines. To take one related example, most Cockney families like to live in the kitchen. The architect's job is not to ask why, nor to persuade Cockneys to live like young married architects, but to build big kitchens in the specific proportion that they are needed, as far as can be assessed. But do they? – not on your life ...

'Choice, or multiple use, is one key to a happy city,' he concluded. 'Humanity, or care with the details, is perhaps the other.'[8]

But of course, for all the obvious importance of long-established cities, the fact was that a rapidly increasing number of people – probably at least several million – were now living in a wide variety of new (or newly expanded) towns and housing estates on the periphery of those cities, or even well outside them. One such fast-growing settlement, in effect a new town without the advantages of being an official new town, would come during the 1960s to embody that trend for better or (usually) worse: Kirkby.

'On the drearily flat, wet plain of South-West Lancashire, it repeats many of the less pleasing features of similar developments elsewhere,' observed the sociologist John Barron Mays in 1963 about a place, some 6 miles north-east of Liverpool, whose population had mushroomed from 3,000 in 1951 to 52,000 only ten years later. 'There are the usual long avenues of similar houses, some taller buildings and blocks, but little architectural elegance. An atmosphere of organised anonymity prevails throughout its length and breadth; a new raw, hardly-lived-in place, unsoftened by time and unrelieved by local colour.' A dip into the *Liverpool Echo* for the autumn of 1960 suggests that Kirkby had already become a byword for undesirability. 'Kirkby is still being troubled by gangs of young vandals who leave a weekly trail of havoc' ran a story about how the vicar of St Chad's could take it no longer and was moving to genteel Southport. Moreover, although Southdene (the oldest part of the Kirkby estate) had 'settled down', elsewhere there was 'no sign of improvement', and householders were 'alarmed by the gangs and hesitant of taking action'. The local MP was Harold Wilson, Labour's Shadow Chancellor; in September he officially opened Kirkby County Comprehensive School, the first comp in the county, declaring that 'only the best is good enough for Lancashire girls and boys.' The headmaster, Mr S. Bury, was more modestly optimistic. 'I think Kirkby is settling down,' he told the press. 'We attach great importance to training for citizenship and we are proud of the progress we have made. The children are loyal and keen to help every good cause.'[9]

The great majority of Kirkby's windswept residents had previously lived in Liverpool – usually in slum or rundown areas, one of which had been the subject of Liverpool University's 'Crown Street' survey in 1956. Four years later, during the summer of 1960, the Department of Social Science returned to the fray and investigated the process of social adjustment in Kirkby. There they found a young town in every sense (half the population under 15, only 3 per cent over 60); the inevitable chronic shortage of facilities; a marked dislike of living in blocks of flats (at this stage mainly four storeys or under); and, overall, though often with negative exceptions, a reluctant acceptance by residents of their new situation. 'For the majority of ex-inner city dwellers the new estate is desirable or at least adequate,' claimed the cautiously positive Mays. 'Certainly the residents interviewed did not seem to be unusually isolated. Only 29 per cent found their neighbours less friendly in Kirkby than they had found their neighbours in Crown Street.' 'In the end,' he hoped and even predicted, that 'long trek from the dingy, cramped back-streets of central Liverpool' would prove for Kirkby's newcomers 'a step towards a happier and fuller life'.[10]

The voices of the interviewees themselves come through in the surviving fieldwork. Perhaps inevitably the brickbats tended to outnumber the bouquets:

> The accommodation was no good [ie, in 'Crown Street'], but we were a sight happier there ... Atmosphere not same – nowhere to go ... I'd rather live among foreigners than live among this lot. (*26-year-old housewife with four children*)
>
> You can hear people eating celery next door. (*Married couple in thirties living in flat with seven-year-old daughter*)
>
> The only friend I have made is the neighbour next-door ... I'm just a bit lost for somewhere to go – can't belong to the club because not an RC and I don't like to depend on people – I would like to get out ... I've been to the Woolworths – and got lost. (*32-year-old wife of brewery driver, three children*)
>
> They should have put the roughs in flats and the respectable ones in houses to look after gardens. (*Machinist's wife, two daughters*)
>
> With having children it's very difficult in a flat, we're always worried in case the children make a noise. (*Married couple in twenties, husband a rigger, four children*)
>
> There's nothing for teenagers – they started a Youth Club. Then there was complaints from neighbours. They spoil it for themselves. (*29-year-old docker's wife, two children*)
>
> Don't get on with children – they smash windows. I deal with that! (*75-year-old retired handyman at trams depot*)

Did this first generation of Kirkby newcomers ever feel like guinea pigs? 'A clear example of failure to settle in K – and of psychological distress because of it', began the interviewer's rather clinical report on a

40-year-old housewife who was married to a butcher and had five children of 11 or under:

> Her doctor is reinforcing her application to the Housing Department for
> transfer back to the centre. She is not very bright – some of her 'don't
> know' responses may be the result of apathy but the I.Q. here may be no
> more than 80–85. The place is not particularly well kept but is 'passable'.
> She has very little to do with neighbours, suffers from depression includ-
> ing crying fits. She lost a baby (before birth?) recently . . . She has no
> contact with any church, nor have the children. She is rather vaguely
> 'Protestant'.[11]

'In a week's time I shall leave Cambridge for good,' recorded Margaret
Drabble on Saturday, 4 June. 'Everything seems to be making a deliberate attack on my capacity for regret and nostalgia; the weather is
perfect, exams are over forever, Pimm's is flowing, and people are
surrounded by a halo of curious sunset charm.' So too in Oxford this
first summer of the 1960s, where Peter Jay (son of the Labour politician Douglas Jay and already engaged to the daughter of James
Callaghan) was going down with the treble of President of the Union,
a First in PPE and passing first into the Civil Service. Golden lasses,
golden lads . . . Not so in Yeovil, where, also on the 4th, a sensitive
young diarist, Kate Paul, went into town with a friend. 'It was terrible,' she wrote. 'We slunk into Woolworth's the back way, masses of
slowly shifting morons, passing rows of greasy faces, wafting smells.
Great bunches of odious spotty youths chewing gum, staring at white
pimply girls in sloppy thin dresses, exposing their pink spotted backs.'
Jacqueline Aitken that same Saturday was dutifully shopping with her
mother ('a pair of cream flatties' in Richmond, 'very soft and comfortable'), while on the other side of the park a week later, the carnival
procession as usual marked the start of Malden's Youth Week. The
theme that year was 'Scenes from Television': first and third prize
went to 'Captain Pugwash' floats; second prize to Malden Methodist
youth club for its 'Black and White Minstrel' float (including 'banjo-
strumming black-faced "coons"'); and fourth prize to 4th Malden
senior air scouts for their moralistic 'Emergency-Ward 10' ('the float

was apparently the scene of a traffic accident and bore a large poster warning viewers to "Honour their (highway) code"'). The small dormitory borough of Malden and Coombe had as many as 56 different youth organisations, and one journalist lingered to take the pulse of this 'pleasant residential corner' of suburban Surrey. 'There are no cinemas and the only sign of life of an evening in the tree-lined main shopping street [in New Malden] is the solitary milk bar. It is a quiet place with a first-rate youth record.'[12]

Later in June, the singer Jimmy Young made a career-changing move by presenting *Housewives' Choice* for a fortnight; the publisher Rupert Hart-Davis spent a broiling day in Oxford among 'bearded youths naked to the waist, negresses and other exotics, all sweating and jostling'; the Queen Mother opened Hull University's new library and responded, 'Oh, what a lovely thing to be' when told, 'This is Mr Larkin, our poet-librarian'; the Conservative government, eight months after its Keynesian election triumph, felt compelled to raise the Bank Rate in response to inflationary pressures and was rebuked by the *Financial Times* for having 'allowed its own expenditure to rise this year in a reckless way'; Princess Margaret carried out her first post-wedding public engagement, with Judy Haines noting that 'Tony', so far titleless, 'doesn't fancy office life and wants something "arty"'; Evelyn Waugh appeared on John Freeman's *Face to Face* ('a magnificent interrogation', thought the Manchester doctor Hugh Selbourne), confessing to irritability as his major fault, the same Sunday evening that a short television film on *The Patience of Job* featured the comic actor Deryck Guyler as the voice of God; and Thomas Dibble, a letter-writer to the *Glasgow Herald*, dismissed any sentimentality about the impending disappearance of that city's trams, asserting that 'we have endured their inconvenience, clankings, and groaning for too long.' That was on Thursday the 28th, destined to be one of the sombre dates in the collective memory of South Wales, as an explosion at the Six Bells Colliery outside Abertillery killed 45 miners. 'There is hardly a house in the street which has not lost a relative,' Mrs Joyce Frampton of Arrael Street, just a hundred yards away from the colliery gate, told the *South Wales Echo*. 'We are so dazed that none of us is doing housework in the normal way. We just want to stand around and think for a while.' One of those killed, Danny Bancroft, had lived in nearby Griffin Street; his son-in-law mused, 'It's an awful price to pay for coal, and people don't realise it.'[13]

The following evening, the 29th, the House of Commons discussed for the second time the Wolfenden recommendation of 1957 to decriminalise homosexual conduct between consenting adults. 'I fully appreciate that this subject is one which is distasteful and even repulsive to many people,' began the Labour MP Kenneth Robinson, who was proposing early action. 'I have no wish to suggest that I regard homosexuality as a desirable way of life.' The ensuing debate followed broadly predictable lines. Some wholly unreconstructed speakers were typified by Godfrey Lagden, Conservative MP for Hornchurch, who described homosexuals as 'people with warped minds who have little self-control', adding that 'in the general run the homosexual is a dirty-minded danger to the virile manhood of this country'. The middle position, elegantly put forward by Rab Butler as Home Secretary, was that there was 'a very great deal of work still to be done', including in terms of educating public opinion, before it would be possible to decriminalise. For the reformers, Roy Jenkins urged MPs not to be 'too eager to stand out as an island against the general current of civilised world opinion'. Robinson's motion to decriminalise was defeated 213–99 on a free vote. The former camp included well over 150 Conservative MPs as well as 41 Labour MPs (including the robustly commonsensical Fred Peart and Ray Gunter); the latter camp included 75 Labour MPs, the handful of Liberal MPs (including Jeremy Thorpe) and 22 Conservatives (including Enoch Powell, Margaret Thatcher and a solitary minister, Richard Wood). Those not voting – of whom there were many – included Harold Macmillan, Harold Wilson, Jim Callaghan and Edward Heath.

'The battle was not yet conclusively won,' insisted the Sheffield *Star* next day, arguing that 'the strong pressure group which demands social recognition for homosexuals' would soon prepare 'a new attack', being determined 'to have the public believe that the real "queer" is he who is intolerant of moral laxity'; therefore, it all depended on 'the moral fibre of the nation' to resist them. What in truth motivated those who had voted in favour of early decriminalisation? 'The proponents of reform,' acutely notes the historian Richard Davenport-Hines about the larger debate, 'repudiated not only homosexuality, but also homosexuals.

They argued that the existing law degraded or corrupted the police charged with enforcing it, that it facilitated blackmail, that it was ineffective, that its severity compared with equivalent laws on the European mainland reflected poorly on Britain's reputation for tolerance or justice. Almost no one spoke positively of homosexuality.' And he quotes the society lady to her friend in Osbert Lancaster's *Daily Express* cartoon two days afterwards: 'What I particularly admired about the debate was the way that every speaker managed to give the impression that he personally had never met a homosexual in his life.' One Labour MP who had declined to vote was the redoubtable Bessie Braddock, and a Liverpool constituent wondered in the *Spectator* why not. 'Perhaps she prefers,' replied her agent on her behalf, 'to devote her considerable energies to helping the helpless rather than the self-pitying.'[14]

Twenty-four hours after the people's tribunes had done their worst, Anthony Heap was at the New Theatre for the first night of *Oliver!* – 'the overwhelming, rip-roaring success of which firmly establishes Lionel Bart as the foremost writer and composer of musicals in Britain today'. 'Small wonder,' Heap added, 'that the reception was the most rousing, ecstatic and prolonged since the memorable First Night of "Oklahoma" thirteen years ago. It could scarcely have been *better* deserved.' Bart, son of an East End tailor, was still in his twenties; the cast included Barry Humphries, who had arrived from Australia the previous summer; and most critics were similarly enthusiastic. 'This is the first time we have seen that it is possible to combine the *milieu* of Beckett and Pinter with the verve of *Oklahoma!*,' declared Harold Hobson in the *Sunday Times*; he was particularly struck by 'the fog, the gloom, the gin, the darkness and corruption of early industrial England evoked by Sean Kenny's settings'. Gusto amid grimness did not do it, though, for Alan Brien. 'This tasty strip-cartoon fillet of Dickens by the composer-lyricist of *Fings* is served with a thin, sugared gruel of words and music,' he wrote in the *Spectator*; it relied 'almost entirely on ingratiation and insinuation as techniques for courtship of its audience', and, altogether, the result was 'a safe, cosy, comfortable evening out'. Either way, it was an indisputable smash hit for a mercurial, self-taught talent justly remembered by an obituarist as 'one of the few composers' of the time 'to deal uncondescendingly with the working classes, transposing their life styles and vernacular to the stage'. That was also, in a somewhat different genre, the purpose of Arnold Wesker, whose recently completed trilogy (*Chicken Soup with Barley*, *Roots* and *I'm Talking About Jerusalem*) was performed that summer at the Royal Court. A key theme of the last of the three plays was a caustic reappraisal of the achievements of the post-war Attlee government, and this was also a moment for reappraisal of Wesker himself. Kenneth Tynan remained supportive – 'one of the few Western dramatists,' he asserted in the *Observer*, 'who can write about political idealists without mockery or condescension' – but for the most part there was now a marked degree of scepticism. Hobson found himself listening 'with growing impatience' to 'the tedious repetitions of the most ordinary forms of illiterate speech'; Al Alvarez in the *New Statesman* noted that whereas 'in *Roots* the characters were alive, in *Jerusalem* they merely talk endlessly about the *idea* of being alive'; and Brien dismissed the whole thing as 'a Forsyte Saga of the Left'. Bart and Wesker: one at his zenith, the other getting his first glimpse of the other side of the hill.

The latter anyway was now not just a playwright. 'Wesker wants to lead unions to culture' was the *Daily Mail* headline at the end of June, after he had called a press conference to explain how he was actively urging trade unions to build theatres in industrial cities without one and – in order no longer to be 'at the mercy of the cultural cheapjacks and easy entertainment boys' concocting 'travesties like *I'm All Right, Jack*' – to sponsor film productions. But, he emphasised, his campaign was not just about money; it was even more about getting the unions 'to accept the principle that the Arts are as important as bread and butter'. 'It will take a long time,' he concluded. 'There is union machinery to go through, but our first aim is to establish the principle that the Arts are not just for the nobs.' And, one novelist might have added, not just about the nobs. 'Working men and women who read do not have the privilege of seeing themselves honestly and realistically portrayed in novels,' declared the working-class Alan Sillitoe in a *cri de coeur*, 'Both Sides of the Street', that appeared in the *TLS* barely a week later. Then, after noting how 'novelists of the Right', if they did try to portray the working class, were able to 'delineate only stock characters', he called on novelists of the left to emerge capable of 'encouraging ordinary people to think of themselves not as a mass but as individuals and ridding themselves of narrow patriotic attitudes'. As it happened, a new and rather different working-class novelist was just appearing. The life of what he called 'a "lace-curtain" working-class family' – respectable to the core – was Stan Barstow's subject, and the result was *A Kind of Loving*, published in July to mainly warm reviews. Maurice Richardson in the *New Statesman*, for instance, found this story of 'white-collared subtopians' in a West Riding industrial town 'satisfyingly up to the minute without being overstrained'; altogether, Barstow was 'a scrupulous naturalist' who had produced something 'seductively readable'. The mandarin *TLS* dissented. 'Flatly realistic', regretted its brief review, with 'much repetitive dialogue of the semi-illiterate kind', while – still worse – 'the interesting material in this monotonously styled fiction is all but swamped by its dreary preoccupation with sex.'[15]

Kingsley Amis was by now shifting decisively to the mandarin side of the broader socio-cultural argument. Writing in *Encounter* that summer, the focus of his critique was what he called, from his vantage-point as a decade-long lecturer at Swansea University, 'the pit of ignorance and incapacity into which British education has sunk since the war'. The ever-more-nominal socialist went on:

> The trouble is not just illiteracy, even understanding this as including unsteady grasp of the fundamentals of the subject as well as unsteadiness with hard words like *goes* and *its*. But for the moment I want to drum the fact of that illiteracy into those who are playing what I have heard called the university numbers racket, those quantitative thinkers who believe that Britain is *falling behind* America and Russia by not producing as many university graduates per head, and that she must *catch up* by building *more* colleges which will turn out *more* graduates and so give us *more* technologists (especially them) and *more* school-teachers. I wish I could have a little tape-and-loudspeaker arrangement sewn into the binding of this magazine, to be triggered off by the light reflected from the reader's eyes on to this part of the page, and set to bawl out at several bels: MORE WILL MEAN WORSE.

More will mean worse . . . 'One of the most eloquent defences of a hierarchical society that I have ever read,' commented the right-wing columnist Henry Fairlie. 'I agree with all he says: but to find Mr Amis in 1960 protesting against democratic values is well worth noticing, and even thinking about in one's bath.'

A charismatic, egalitarian politician who sometimes despaired of the mediocrity of popular taste passed away on 6 July, twelve years and a day after his creation of the National Health Service. 'ANEURIN BEVAN DIED NO FRIEND OF MINE "STILL GOD REST HIS SOUL",' wrote Florence Turtle in her diary. What was striking over the next few days was 'a rush of deep national emotion', as Mollie Panter-Downes put it, 'that the departure of no other statesman, bar Winston Churchill, would evoke' – a 'sense of acute loss' not only 'among the admiring millions of Labour's rank and file' but also 'among large numbers of the far from adoring sections of the community that had suffered at one time or another from his reckless invective'. The Tory press led the way, with the *Daily Mail* calling Bevan's early death 'one of the biggest political tragedies of our times'; Churchill himself made a rare appearance in the Commons to listen to the tributes; and the memorial service in the Abbey later in the month was a suitably grand affair. 'I know that it was impossible to be with him without quarrelling, that he was a leader with feet of clay and that sometimes he was selfish and unrewarding,' mused his on-off ally Richard Crossman during it. 'Nevertheless, oh dear, oh dear, oh dear . . .'

Bevan's service on the 26th came shortly after Crossman had spent a thought-provoking weekend in Pembrokeshire at a Fabian summer school:

> In the discussion a comrade got up and complained, 'What's the good of your saying you're progressive in social problems? On capital punishment the Party doesn't have a line and concedes a free vote. The same with the Wolfenden Report. Anything really difficult you funk.' And then another one got up and said, 'And what about your attitude to fee-paying schools? How can we believe in the Party when its leaders send their children there?' I made the usual reply about admitting the democratic principle that one has the right to pay fees, and to this I got the annihilating reply, 'Of course that applies, Mr Crossman, to everyone, except to you. Other people, who don't set themselves up as Socialist leaders, can pay fees. You can't.'

The coda came a month later, when the diarist gave dinner at the Athenaeum to Harold Wilson. 'He talked a good deal, and I was pleased that he did,' noted Crossman, 'about the need to revive some kind of Puritanism in the Party, some self-dedication, and he was careful to remind me twice that he couldn't tell the difference between hock and burgundy.' Afterwards, as Wilson dropped him off at Vincent Square, Crossman told him about the problems he was having deciding what to do about his son's education. 'Suddenly Harold said, "It was the worst mistake of my life when I sent my boys to [the private] University College School. You're right that we can't afford to sacrifice our principles".'[16]

———————

'Shocking Summer weather,' recorded May Marlor, in Swadlincote, on 16 July. 'Heavy showers, an odd gleam of sun, then a depressingly cool dull evening – not cold enough for a fire but not warm enough to settle down with a book indoors in comfort.' The following weekend, the *People* featured a double-page exposé ('THIS IS THE BEATNIK HORROR') of the squalid living conditions of a flat rented by Liverpool art students, one of them John Lennon; on Wednesday the 27th, the day that a young Australian, Carmen Callil, arrived in England and was struck by how low the skies were as well as by the immediately visible difference between rich and poor, a government reshuffle saw the dogged Selwyn Lloyd going to No. 11, amid hopes that he could restore optimism to economic policy; two days later, Madge Martin and her husband arrived in Scarborough for their annual holiday ('down to the Spa, and enjoyable Max Jaffa concert'), while elsewhere in Yorkshire the industrious East Riding smallholder, Dennis Dee, borrowed a friend's boar for the white sow, 'but he was tired out, a bit like me'; and on Saturday the 30th in Sussex, the Bluebell Line was re-opened by volunteers three years after being closed by British Railways, and in Dorset the sun mercifully shone on the church fete at Loders – with 'the thing that really made the husbands sit up', according to the Rev. Oliver Willmott in his Parish Notes, being 'the parade of the Women's Institute wearing home-made hats that had cost no more than a shilling'.[17]

In retrospect, the book of the moment, though not a bestseller until its Penguin edition five years later, was *The Divided Self* by a radically minded 32-year-old Glaswegian psychoanalyst, R. D. Laing. The *New*

Statesman's hard-working critic Maurice Richardson praised this 'study of schizophrenia from the existentialist point of view', in particular how some of Laing's case histories were 'remarkable for the way he is able to preserve an integrated view of the patient as a person'. But Edward Glover in the *Listener* was unimpressed by Laing's sprinkling of 'existential arcana' and concluded, loftily enough, that 'his theoretical presentation of "subject–object" relations does not provide sufficient recompense for the sacrifice of most of the laboriously acquired analytical insights of the past seventy years.' Richardson surely called it right. Demystifying madness, demonstrating a continuum between the sane and the insane, providing an understanding of 'mad' behaviour – 'It made,' recalled Anthony Clare after Laing's death, 'an immense impact on me', and Clare was far from alone.

Top of the charts at the end of July was Cliff Richard's 'Please Don't Tease', but with 'Tie Me Kangaroo Down Sport' by Rolf Harris and 'Apache' by Cliff's backing group The Shadows both on their way up. It was the start of the Shadows phenomenon, defined by Hank Marvin's echo-laden vibrato on his Fender Stratocaster with tremolo arm. 'As the evening drew to a close and the live band was playing a Shadows tune, we would form lines,' recalled Yvonne Wilson about teenage Saturday-night dances in small-town Kendal. 'There'd be row after row of us doing the Shadow walk. The atmosphere was electric!' A more male constituency attended the Beaulieu Jazz Festival on August Bank Holiday (still early in the month), when outright, bottle-throwing warfare broke out between the 'traddies' loyal to the New Orleans tradition and the modernists inspired by Charlie Parker's bebop. The traddies tended to be bearded and wear long sweaters (frequently under duffel-coats), were often members of CND, and saw the modernists as not only betraying jazz's roots but as unacceptably close to American consumer culture, while the modernists deplored the increasing commercial popularity of trad jazz. Acker Bilk, definitely on the trad side of the fence, played for over an hour in an attempt to calm what he called the 'phoney imitation beatniks'. Jazz wars in Hampshire were complemented by Prom wars in South Kensington. 'There is really no "old" or "new" music – only music, good or bad,' rather nervously noted the *Radio Times* about the 'New Look' for that year's Proms, as BBC's new Controller of Music, William Glock, put the emphasis on the modern. 'Many, though they thought the

BBC right to broadcast new music, had not listened to any of it them-selves,' reported Audience Research after the Proms were over; a minor-ity declared their outright hostility to '"psychopathic muck" masquerad-ing as music'. Thea Musgrave's *Triptych* won an Appreciation Index rating of only 39 (out of 100), but the evening of Gilbert and Sullivan excerpts proved 'very popular'. 'The Proms,' complained an accountant after watching Glock defend his policy on *Monitor*, 'have been ruined by this compulsory listening to modern music. In fact one would rather not attend them now as the programmes are spoiled – the new music is not even placed that one can leave the hall conveniently.'[18]

Two diarists, neither of them Prom-goers, had rather different Augusts. 'It was very good in beautiful colour; moral: count your blessings,' recorded Judy Haines on Tuesday the 2nd after taking her daughters up to town to see Hayley Mills in *Pollyanna* at Studio One. 'I acceded to Ione's request to see it through again. Came away at 5.45 and what a rush hour! Queued in long line for tickets but we soon got seats in the train. Ione felt ill and Pamela had splitting head-ache. I was just weary.' Next week, Friday the 12th, a perhaps even wearier Prime Minister spent the day in bed at Chequers 'dozing, reading, & doing a little work'. The work involved regular updates on a threatened power strike, with a settlement reached late that night; the reading was Trollope's *Orley Farm*, 'a fine story'. Three days later it was an unofficial shipping strike that concerned Macmillan – 'doing a great deal of harm, & a great loss of money' – while the following day Judy Haines took the girls to Kew Gardens (by boat from Westminster Pier). 'Queue for Cafeteria, but pleasant people. However, we passed through to the tea pavilion and how we enjoyed that delightful 3/- set tea. So fresh and plentiful.' On Thursday the 18th, having heard the welcome news that the *Queen Elizabeth* had managed to sail, thus signalling the imminent end of the shipping strike, the PM set off to Yorkshire for some shooting. 'Outside Leeds there was anti-H Bomb demonstration of a dozen or so youths with placards. The only good one was "I'm not a Grouse. I want to live"!' A day later, and for one mother in Chingford, as presumably for many elsewhere by this time, the summer holidays suddenly seemed endless: 'It is a lovely morning and I was irritated that the children were frowsily indoors instead of out treasure-hunting or something.'[19]

5

An Act of Holy Communion

'Full of silly pseudo-intellectual jokes,' pencilled the Lord Chamberlain's Office – still the theatre's censor – on the original script. More or less unbutchered, but to a sparse and initially puzzled audience, *Beyond the Fringe* debuted on 22 August 1960 as part of the Edinburgh Festival. Earlier in the evening at the Lyceum, a young working-class actor from Hull, Tom Courtenay, had been making his name in *The Seagull*; now in the same theatre it was the turn of four Oxbridge graduates, two of them working-class.

A national newspaper critic who got it immediately was the *Daily Mail*'s Peter Lewis. Hailing 'the funniest, most intelligent, and most original revue to be staged in Britain for a very long time', he noted how *Beyond the Fringe* disregarded 'all the jaded trimmings of conventional sketches, production numbers, dancing, and girls', instead getting down to 'the real business of intimate revue, which is satire and parody'. So too *Punch*'s Eric Keown and, inevitably, the *Spectator*'s Alan Brien. Between them they described Peter Cook (writer of most of the material) as 'brilliant wearing Mr Macmillan's teeth' and 'a little man whose ambition to be a judge was thwarted by lack of Latin'; Jonathan Miller as 'a lanky, tow-haired, staring-eyed disciple of St Vitus with the face of an aggrieved unicorn'; 'gig-lamped, square-faced' Alan Bennett as not only a 'preternaturally old schoolboy giving an anti-intellectual pi-jaw' but a 'strangulated' Anglican clergyman ('Life's like a tin of sardines, we're all looking for the key . . .'); and Dudley Moore (providing the music) as 'a born jester' who was 'at his most hysterical as a pianist who couldn't finish'. Houses were packed from the second night onwards for these 'four young men in fluorescent shirts', a West End run was soon being planned, and in the convincing judgement almost half a century later of Michael Billington (present at the 'slightly shambolic opening performance'), this moment – even more than the first night of *Look Back in Anger* four years earlier – 'marked a genuine cultural turning point', launching as it did 'a whole era of snook-cocking disrespect'.[1]

Full houses too that August at the Queen's in Blackpool, where a rather different sort of revue, *The Time of Your Life*, starred George Formby, Jimmy Clitheroe and Yana – 'a busty, sultry-voiced chanteuse' famous, according to Formby's biographer, for her fish-tail dresses and 'huge gay following'. Elsewhere it was a less happy seaside picture. At Southend, the local paper complained about the absence of 'the Carnival spirit' at that town's 1960 Carnival. 'Where were the streamers, balloons and the wavers? Crowds on long stretches of the route watched the procession pass by with hardly a clap or a cheer. Far too many of Saturday's crowd were television-conditioned. They had seen just about all there was to see . . .' Apathy was not the problem at Porthcawl, where a European heavyweight championship fight between Newport's Dick Richardson and Blackpool's Brian London finished with a full-scale brawl in the ring, while at Whitby, an American visitor found her brief stay there 'depressingly mucky', all too typical of English seaside resorts. 'Of course,' explained Sylvia Plath in her letter home, 'the weather is hardly ever sheer fair, so most people are in woollen suits and coats and tinted plastic raincoats. The sand is muddy and dirty. The working class is also dirty, strewing candy papers, gum and cigarette wrappers.'[2]

The resort where the TUC gathered in early September was Douglas on the Isle of Man. In its preview, the *Daily Herald*, in effect the paper of the trade union movement, urged support for a resolution – put forward by the Association of Cine, TV and Allied Technicians, and inspired by Arnold Wesker – calling on unions to participate more actively in the arts. 'Perhaps it is an idea that takes a little getting used to,' conceded the *Herald*, before declaring that 'the heritage of music and plays and films and books and painting and fine buildings is the heritage of everyone.' 'We do not accept,' the ACTT's Ralph Bond told Congress on the 8th, 'that culture is the preserve of an enlightened intelligentsia and that any old rubbish is good enough for the masses.'

After noting that the only difference between tap water and TV was that 'tap water is purified before we get it', he argued that 'our spiritual heritage, its culture, its songs, its living drama, its poetry is dying away, distorted and vulgarised by the purveyors of mass-production entertainment.' Resolution 42 was carried – but, significantly, against the wishes of the General Council, for whom Wilfred Beard insisted that 'unions have enough difficulty in raising subscriptions high enough to pay for their industrial work, without the additional expense of encouraging culture.'

Next day, Macmillan had a fatherly chat at Balmoral with the 'very sensible' Antony Armstrong-Jones about his career ('he realises that the Stock Exchange, or an advertising firm, or even photography of fashion models will not do'); on Saturday the 10th, the civil servant Henry St John took a train to Dorset ('opposite me sat a girl in light blue trousers, no stockings, sandals, with lacquered toe nails and long straight straw-coloured hair'), while that evening's sequence on ITV included the short-lived experiment of the second half of a live league match (Blackpool v Bolton, no Stanley Matthews, one goal) and debuts for *77 Sunset Strip* (an American import) and *Candid Camera* ('nothing very clever', thought the *Daily Mail*'s Peter Black, about 'making fools of simple feelings'); over the next two days, an inexorable pull to the capital was suggested by the *Guardian* for the first time printing in London, though *Woman's Hour* ran a special East Anglian edition featuring 'Allan Smethurst, postman' singing 'one of his own Norfolk songs'; on the 14th, Florence Turtle visited the packed but 'horrible' Picasso exhibition at the Tate ('Talk about Whistler's Chucking a Paint pot at the Public. Picasso chucks a dust bin!'); and, the following Saturday, the even sterner Hugh Selbourne watched on his set the 'farrago of nonsense' that was the Last Night of the Proms, including 'a poor speech' by Sir Malcolm Sargent.[3]

But September's main cultural event was a first night – that of *Billy Liar*, adapted for the stage from the Keith Waterhouse novel, directed by Lindsay Anderson and starring an aspiring Salford actor. 'For all the commendable efforts of Albert Finney,' reckoned Anthony Heap on the 13th, 'young Billy remains an unamusing, uninteresting and unappetising clod throughout,' with indeed the whole piece 'trashy, tedious and totally unfunny', reducing the diarist to 'counting the

number of "bloody's" uttered by the foul-mouthed father'. Other critics, though all praising Finney, were rather more nuanced. Keown likewise wanted 'to throttle the father', but admired how the 'unattractive
delinquent' Billy became 'an extraordinarily complete character', by
turn 'shambling, cunning, cowardly yet childishly eager'; Brien regretted that, despite its wonderfully convincing depiction of Billy's working-class northern family ('a milieu too often cartooned on the stage'),
the play ultimately degenerated into 'over-stuffed emptiness like the
aftermath of a cream bun feast', largely because of 'Billy's isolation
from the complicated confusions of the world outside'. For Kenneth
Tynan, an admirer of the 'exuberant' original, the shame was that its
'broader implications' had been 'skirted or ignored', with instead an
emphasis on 'pure farce'. 'The present state of the English theatre is one
of deadlock,' he more broadly argued in his *Observer* review of the
18th. 'Its audience is still predominantly conservative, wedded by age
and habits to the old standards; its younger playwrights, meanwhile,
are predominantly anti-conservative, irretrievably divorced from the
ideological *status quo*.' And, he concluded, 'the only general assumption in which Mr Wesker, his colleagues and their audiences seem to be
substantially agreed is that the lower strata of English society deserve a
more central place on the English stage.'[4]

The cover of the current *Radio Times* featured the 53-year-old
Gilbert Harding, thus accurately reflecting his broadcasting ubiquity:
on the panel of television's *What's My Line?*, chairman of radio's *Twenty
Questions* and *Round Britain Quiz*, and – that particular Sunday evening – subject of John Freeman's *Face to Face*. The programme would
always be remembered for Harding coming close to breaking down as
he referred to watching his mother die, though at the time there seems
to have been as much controversy about his confession that he would
prefer to be dead himself. 'A brilliant piece of interviewing, but painful
to watch' was the general consensus among the Viewers' Panel, with
many agreeing with the opinion that 'unexpected exposure of grief is
not for public exhibition'. Older viewers were especially disconcerted,
one describing 'publicly prying into personal private lives' as 'not viewers' business', another feeling 'terribly uneasy when John Freeman
probes into a man's soul'. As for the subject, famously the rudest man
on television, there was considerable sympathy. 'The personality of

"Old Grumpy" certainly came over well,' thought the wife of an arma-
ture winder, 'and proved him to be a most kind and gentle man for
whom we now have much feeling', while a teacher's wife found herself
'terribly sorry for Harding – not because of the interview itself, but
because of what it revealed of the man'.

'These changes do not mark the end of an old era; in a sense they are
the beginning of a new one,' unconvincingly explained the same issue
of the *Radio Times*. 'They are the extension and adaptation of the past
to provide a service which is suited to the needs of listeners today and
adjusted to the tempo of modern life.' The key change, announced a
few months earlier and about to take effect on the 19th, was the decision to move the late evening news on the Home Service from 9.00 to
10.00 – and, crucially, to truncate Big Ben's chimes before the bulletin
to only one. 'Ever since November 1940,' noted W. Tudor Pole, founder
of the Big Ben Council, in a letter to the *Radio Times* after the announcement, 'the chiming and striking of Big Ben has signalled a Minute of
Prayer and Remembrance at nine each evening':

> This observance has spread across the world, and is now widely kept by
> men and women of good will, both here and overseas, including those
> who live behind the 'Iron Curtain' . . .
>
> Following consultation with our members and supporters at home
> and abroad, the Big Ben Council has decided to recommend that the
> 'Silent Minute' shall continue in future to be kept at nine each evening as
> in the past. To switch the observance from 9.0 to 10.0 pm would prove
> unsuitable for the very many who value and keep this evening tryst in
> hospitals, nursing homes, and in family circles, the latter hour being too
> late for the purpose.

Eventually, after a sustained campaign to reinstate the chimes, involving
thousands of letters to the BBC, the governors accepted a compromise
by which they would gradually fade away as the 10 o'clock bulletin
began to be read. Irrespective of the Big Ben issue, at least one listener
was already welcoming the change of schedule. 'I am busy at 6 o'clock
in the evening and in bed by 10,' Mrs J. M. Woodward of Tunbridge
Wells told the *Radio Times*. 'As long as there was a nine o'clock News
one felt impelled to listen to it and then to go to bed seething with the

world's problems. What a relief now to be able to leave it all until tomorrow, and think of something else!'[5]

The cultural plates continued to shift in the closing days of September. *Monitor* featured what one critic called 'the brilliant meeting with Shelagh Delaney and the vision through her lucid eyes of the restless, slate-grey, black-brick spirit of Salford', while earlier in the evening not only did ITV show Alun Owen's *Lena, Oh My Lena* – concluding his trilogy of working-class realist plays, this one starring Billie Whitelaw and set, according to the script, 'on the East Lancs Road . . . between St Helens and Salford' – but the BBC initiated a major weekly series of newly commissioned plays by contemporary dramatists, starting with John Whiting's *A Walk in the Desert* (about a disabled man in a provincial town, with music by Bert Weedon). The Sunday heavies and the weeklies were by now giving a mixed reception to Kingsley Amis's fourth novel, *Take a Girl Like You* – 'nasty & bad', commented Larkin on the 26th after reading it. Arguably as resonant an event was ITV's launch on the 23rd of *Bootsie and Snudge*. Written by Marty Feldman, Barry Took and John Antrobus, it related the fortunes in Civvy Street of two of *The Army Game*'s now demobbed characters: Montague 'Bootsie' Bisley (Alfie Bass), handyman and general dogsbody at a Pall Mall gentleman's club, the Imperial, and Claude Snudge (Bill Fraser), the commissionaire who tormented him. Infused by class and a love-hate relationship with authority, the show was, claimed Simon Callow half a century later, 'an account of postwar Britain as acute as anything from the pen of John Osborne or Arnold Wesker, and rather funnier'.[6]

———

'Three party conferences,' noted John Fowles on 8 October. 'The Liberals – children playing at kings and queens; the Socialists, passionate, sincere, adult but sadly unfascinated; the Tories, hollow platitudes, the village hall. Even the *Telegraph* admits that there is no Tory enthusiasm – "rows of empty seats". The only party that seems real, contemporary, adult and alive, is the Socialist.' Alive perhaps, but alive with discord: Labour had by now put aside Clause 4 as its great contentious issue, replaced since the summer by that of unilateralism – a cause embraced by Frank Cousins, leader of the Transport and General Workers' Union, and increasingly by unions generally. Ahead of

Labour's defence debate on the 5th, the expectation was that Hugh Gaitskell, unyieldingly not a ban-the-bomb man, would be defeated on the issue. 'All the speakers,' reflected Mollie Panter-Downes, present that Wednesday at Scarborough's smoke-filled Spa Hall, 'were so much in earnest that what they had to say, however badly expressed or haltingly delivered, seemed to take abstract shape beside them on the rostrum'.

They spoke of fears that had become a familiar part of everyone's daily life, which maybe is the worst thing of all – fear of instant annihilation or mass destruction from the pressing of a button by a Russian or an American finger, fear of trigger-happy accidents, fear of American patrol flights from Britain, fear for children and homes. 'If the mad groups in the world want to have a go at each other, let us have no part of them!' shouted Mr Cousins. 'Let us stop being an expendable base for the Americans,' urged someone else. Last year's winner of the Nobel Peace Prize, Mr Philip Noel-Baker, a gray-haired, distinguished man with a gentle face, came to the rostrum like an anxious father, to warn the children that if they changed their views on the urgency of working for collective disarmament they would never win the country to their side. A lady whose name I did not catch but who sounded like Joyce Grenfell imitating a games mistress roared brusquely that the scientists were now killing goats by rays, and that she would rather be blown up, thanks very much . . .

At last Gaitskell took to his feet:

It was a magnificent performance. He hammered home his intention of continuing as leader until the Parliamentary Labour Party decided otherwise, and of fighting neutralism to the last ditch. He stated the clear choice for the Labour voter – to be inside the NATO alliance and pressing for collective disarmament, or to be outside, 'defenceless and alone.' The part of the speech that particularly infuriated the nuclear-disarmers and caused many angry, gesticulating young men to rise, as though they intended to rush the platform, was his asking, also in anger, 'Do you think we can simply accept a decision of this kind, become overnight the pacifist unilateralists and fellow-travellers that other people are? How wrong can you be?', and adding bitingly, 'As wrong as you are about the attitude of the British people.' At the end, the conference and some – though noticeably not all – of his colleagues on the platform rose to cheer him loudly . . .

In the event, union block votes ensured that the somewhat vague unilateralist motion was carried, albeit far more narrowly than anticipated.

'Wanted: a Leader', demanded the next issue of the anti-Gaitskell, pro-unilateralist *New Statesman*; the most plausible candidate, inevitably coming from the left, was Harold Wilson, who stayed seated, vigorously striking matches for his pipe, during Gaitskell's standing ovation. 'Frankly all he's interested in is turning the situation to his own advantage,' Anthony Wedgwood Benn had observed during pre-conference manoeuvres. 'He thinks Gaitskell can be dislodged. My opinion of him drops the more I see of him.' There were two other pointers to the future. One was the state of public opinion, where Gaitskell's confidence was justified to the extent that Gallup evidence suggested only about a third of the electorate holding unilateralist views. The other was the development of the nuclear disarmament movement itself, where the emerging key figure was a dynamic, charming young American, Ralph Schoenman, studying at the London School of Economics. Increasingly disenchanted by the CND's lack of urgency, typified in his eyes by the fact that it had formed a Campaign cricket team, Schoenman successfully detached Bertrand Russell from the organisation and formed that month the Committee of 100, embracing direct action and civil disobedience. The danger was obvious, and by the end of October the *Guardian* was warning how law-breaking would 'alienate the British public, especially the sweet young suburban wives who form an important part of the movement'.[7]

On all this, as on so much else, Henry St John in Acton had no comment to make or record. But on Sunday, 16 October he did spend fourpence buying the *Empire News*, prior to its being absorbed by the *News of the World*, which 'led to a few remarks by the shopkeeper on the high costs of producing newspapers, especially for labour'. Next morning, the mid-market *News Chronicle* – 'unsmart, inefficient, non-hip, elderly', but also, noted soon afterwards one of its journalists, Philip Purser, 'kindly, concerned, occasionally courageous and in its own way cultured' – appeared as usual. An editorial called on Gaitskell to continue to 'STAND FIRM'; Purser reviewed the previous night's play on the BBC, praising 'an enormously vital young actor called Anthony Booth'; Greta Lamb's dieting tips included 'have a tin of no-sugar biscuits by your bed' so 'you won't get up and raid the larder'; a reader, Mrs D. M. Todd of Streatham Hill, shared her method of countering claustrophobia on the London tube ('I find that sucking a boiled sweet helps to relieve that awful tension'); and the subject of Big Chief I-Spy's column was the 'new special lamp fixed to the beacon poles' of zebra crossings, with the first report of it being spotted coming from Redskin D. G. Jackson of Warrington, thereby winning him a tie. Rumours about the paper's uncertain prospects had been circulating for months if not years, and in the course of that Monday the owner, Laurence Cadbury, finally decided that, for all its fine liberal traditions and heritage, enough was enough: the *Chronicle* would be sold to the *Daily Mail*, and its sister London evening paper, the *Star*, to the *Evening News* – in both cases, to be swallowed virtually whole by Lord Rothermere's Associated Newspapers, with immediate effect. The announcement was made in the evening, and reputedly the *Chronicle*'s drama critic only found out next morning when the *Mail* unexpectedly came through his front door instead. Even by the standards of Fleet Street it had been a brutal death. Still, Peter Pound perhaps had a point, commenting in the *Listener* on TV interviews with journalists from the defunct papers: 'In all their accusations about whose fault it was – the owners', trade unions', advertisers' – I did not detect the slightest hint of a still, small voice asking "Was it also perhaps partly our fault for not producing better newspapers?"'

On Tuesday the 18th, the *Mail* sought to reassure its new former *Chronicle* readers: not only had the *Mail* 'consistently supported progressive Conservatism', but 'its outlook is liberal in the true sense of the term'. Two days later, readers had their say. 'For many years I have taken the *Daily Mail* and have admired the modern, forthright, and vital manner in which the news has been presented,' declared C. Knight of Southend-on-Sea. 'The first mongrel edition filled me with disgust.' By contrast, J. W. Tapper of Worthing, a *Chronicle* reader for over 50 years, offered his congratulations on 'the joint issue'. 'I hope however,' he added, 'you will not be too critical of the Labour Party.'[8]

'The inevitable is happening on a large scale,' an anonymous white man told a Manchester paper in August 1960. 'Moss Side is not large enough for these immigrants. Now they are spreading to other areas. Wherever they set foot, property values tumble; white people move out as soon as possible in the stupid belief that they will escape the invaders' tentacles. My own area, Rusholme, has undergone a drastic change in the last two years. Everywhere I look there are Jamaicans, West Africans, Pakistanis . . .'

Net immigration from the New Commonwealth was certainly accelerating: 21,600 in 1959, 57,700 in 1960, with the West Indian component in those two years 16,400 and 49,650 respectively. The pull was essentially economic – the demand for labour – and the political response for the time being largely static: neither legislation to control numbers (with Rab Butler at the Home Office skilfully heading off the Tory right, unable even to bring up the issue at the autumn party conference) nor legislation to outlaw racial discrimination (blocked in the summer by an all-party group of MPs). But noises off were getting louder, not least from Colin Jordan, who taught at a primary school in Coventry and ran the White Defence League. 'Our greatest national asset and treasure is our Anglo-Saxon blood,' he insisted to a journalist, adding that the influx of non-whites would inevitably breed 'a mulatto population'. Jordan's WDL specialised in 'Keep Britain White' demonstrations, including one on 1 September when protesters – mainly white youths – gathered at Waterloo Station to meet three boat trains from Southampton carrying West Indian immigrants; amid angry scenes they were successfully dispersed by police.

That day the ten-year-old Floella Benjamin, joining her parents in London, was on one of those trains – 'so unlike the smaller wooden ones back in Trinidad that I almost didn't recognise it as one'. For a few weeks she was at school in Chiswick – teacher treating her like an idiot, children taunting her – before the family moved to Penge. 'I hated the rejection,' she remembered. 'Even going shopping was an ordeal. Sandra [her older sister] and I would stand at the counter waiting to be served but would be ignored, treated as though we were invisible . . . I came to England feeling special, like a princess, but was made to feel like a scrounger.' One Sunday the family went to church. 'I see they are letting in that kind now,' she heard a group of white parishioners complain after the service. 'Is no place sacred?' So too for Mandy Phillips, arriving from Dominica that year in her late twenties and settling in Notting Hill. 'They used to say "go back home",' she recalled. 'You know, Black this, Black that. White people did not want black people. They did not want dogs. They did not want the Irish. I can remember walking past a church on a Sunday and then these children started throwing bottles. It was a shock.' How many white people did not want black people? 'Is like that Stork on television,' V. S. Naipaul heard a disenchanted West Indian immigrant say 'in a slow, negligent way' on a boat train to Southampton a few days after Benjamin's arrival. 'Three out of five can't tell the difference from butter. Three out of five don't care for you.'

It was almost certainly at least three out of five in Birmingham, emerging that autumn as a focal point of white opposition to uncontrolled immigration. 'My own view,' declared a local councillor for multi-racial, overcrowded Sparkbrook, 'is that immigration must be slowed up so that the people who are already here can be integrated into the life of Birmingham.' Later in October saw the formation of the Birmingham Immigration Control Committee, headed by a Conservative shopkeeper-*cum*-councillor, Charles Collett, who was at pains to distance his committee from explicitly racist (or even neo-fascist) pressure groups, while publicly highlighting 'the menace of coloured infiltration and a piebald population'. A student living that autumn in digs in Balsall Heath, one of the city's rougher areas, was the liberal-minded diarist Kate Paul, recording what she saw in the non-judgemental, documentary detail of a stranger. 'Now I'm in the flat in the notorious Varna Road, street of tarts and unsavoury stabbings,' she noted in late September. And a few days later, on a Sunday:

> The people on this street live on their sexual instincts and fear. It's a street of brothels and men hanging about on corners. To be white is exceptional. I have just been out for cigarettes. The street was scattered with Jamaicans and Indians, standing in small groups, or wandering in and out of houses. A few old women, no longer of any interest, walk slowly up the street carrying shopping bags.
>
> There is suspicion and fear, eyes shift from one face to another, black,

bloodshot ones and pale shifting ones . . .

Men in cars kerb-crawl and raise their fingers, leaning forward, eager, their faces drawn with lust. I hate these, not the street-walkers.

As for them, I think they're mad to be in such a losing business. It's really terrible in the street. They have cock-fights and stabbings and the police come up here in twos or on motor bikes.

At night it's really grim, men melting into doorways, beckoning. The endless crawl of cars, the slamming of doors, the women's shrill voices. Old men being insulted by young tarts . . .

The old couple upstairs, us and two of the tarts are the only whites. The old people, Leopold and his wife, are ancient, amazingly kind and straight from a Balzac novel.

'I've just been to the front room,' the appalled but fascinated diarist added. 'The street is alive with prostitutes and pimps in spivvy suits, spilling out of doorways. I daren't let them catch me watching. One avoids other people's eyes. It's grim.'⁹

Ultimately, despite everything, the future would be more or less multicultural; it would also, less controversially but not always welcomed, be consumerist.

The new in 1960 included the stripe in Signal toothpaste; the spectacularly successful launch of Blue Gillette Extra (the blade touted as a scientific 'break-through' in shaving); 'ready-salted' crisps from Golden Wonder, an ingenious riposte to the familiar blue bag of salt in Smith's Crisps; the arrival of Lego; plastic carrier bags and refuse sacks; the transformation of the Kenwood mixer through a stylish blender attachment; the first automatic dishwasher (Miele); and Hoover's manufacture of the Keymatic washing machine, a fully automatic model. Keeping a watchful eye on this last development was the young washing-machine entrepreneur John Bloom, who early in the year had acquired his own production facility by effectively taking over Rolls Razor, a staid, loss-making company based in Cricklewood that had diversified from razors into washing machines. Typically, Bloom was much attracted by the word *Rolls*, whose deluxe connotations would, he thought, speak to his target working-class market.¹⁰

There was still a long way to go, not least in terms of mod cons. Figures for the first half of 1960 reveal 79 per cent of adults owning a

television set, but otherwise possession of major consumer durables as
the preserve of a minority: 40 per cent owning a washing machine, 31
per cent a car, 22 per cent a telephone and 21 per cent a fridge. Even
among the middle class, barely half had a car or a washing machine, and
only two out of five a fridge. Jacqueline Aitken's family in Kingston,
living in a respectable block of council flats, had by this time only just
acquired a car and a phone:

> We still didn't have a washing machine or a fridge and owned just a very
> small black and white television. We went for a holiday once a year but
> we hardly ever went out as a family otherwise.
>
> We had the special treat on Sundays of a shared bottle of Tizer and a
> Wall's family block of raspberry ripple ice cream after our roast chicken.
> This was High Living as far as we were concerned. The flat was still
> furnished with the dark utility table and chairs and sideboard bought just
> after the war, with a gloomy brown sofa and two chairs filling up the rest
> of the room . . .

Nor did older people in particular necessarily plunge headlong into the
new. 'He said my old machine was not worth repairing,' noted Florence
Turtle about the visit of 'the Singer man' in September. 'Recommended
the electric one I tried in the shop. Said I would think about it.' Even so,
the regretful but predominantly excited experience not long before of
the Haines family in Chingford was perhaps emblematic. 'John took
Pamela to collect 8948 VW,' recorded Judy on a Saturday in June.
'Beautiful! but so sad leaving 825 CEV.' Then next day came the second
afternoon drive in their 'lovely grey' new Triumph Herald. 'Parked in a
glade near the Owl, where we could decently have a good look at her,
particularly in the Boot which is accessible from outside as well as in . . .
We have heater and blower, nine pockets, and wonderful windows in
the TH. Doors like horse box. Girls have grand view from back seats.'
One last initiation ceremony remained: 'As the car has been described
as "Fabulous Triumph Herald," we've named her Faith.'[11]
Persil, Tide, Omo, Daz, Stork, Guinness, Nescafé, Surf, Maxwell
House, Ford – these (in descending order) were the ten most heavily
advertised products in 1960. As for TV commercials specifically,
research in August revealed that the two most popular ads were for

Esso and Sunblest, while the most irritating were for Daz, Omo, Tide and Surf, each incessantly repeated through the evening, leaving the viewers the main victim of the apparently never-ending detergent war. It was more than irritation, though, that the *Spectator*'s Peter Forster continued to feel for 'that intolerably coy couple' Philip and Katie 'whose love-life is dedicated to proving that "Oxo gives a meal Man-appeal".' The selling was a shade more nuanced in *Jim's Inn* – ITV's weekly advertising magazine – which, based in Jimmy Hanley's pub at 'Wembleham', was still going strong. Hanley continued to play himself as 'Mine Host', accompanied by his wife Maggie; regulars included Jack the burly farmer, the absent-minded Ron (manager of the village's hardware and electrical store), the commuting Dennis with a job in the City and an army-style moustache, and Roma, who ran the local beauty salon.

Food consumption steadily increased, by 1960 perhaps around one-fifth more per person per week than in 1950. The changes were qualitative as well. Sheila Hutchins in the *News Chronicle* argued that the advent of the Danish open sandwich, or *smörrebröd*, along with the rapidly growing popularity of coffee, wine, spaghetti and Chinese restaurants, was proof that 'the typical Englishman' was 'no longer conservative' about his food and drink; Marguerite Patten's lavishly illustrated *Cookery in Colour* – seeking, according to the publishers, 'to match the gay, practical kitchens of today and bring a sense of adventure into cooking' – included a recipe for prawn cocktail and accompanying pink sauce; American-style steak houses, led by the Angus chain, were now flourishing; and Anthony Heap, eating his regular café lunch, overheard 'one old gaffer' say to another, 'You never hear of mutton nowadays, always lamb.' The inexorable march of convenience foods continued. Sales of deep-frozen food, having doubled between 1955 and 1957, doubled again by 1960, while one evening in Hull a suspicious Philip Larkin tried what might well have been a Vesta forerunner. 'I had a peculiar reconstituted beef curry for supper – enough for two, it said!' he reported to Monica Jones. 'Not on your life: I ate it all. The rice, prettily done up in a separate packet, was nice (how do you dry rice?), but the beef curry was awful – dark fibrous acrid syrup, not nearly hot enough.'[12]

Following on from a similar survey three years earlier, Market

Investigations Ltd that autumn interviewed 2,000 housewives at the door about their grocery-shopping habits. Some 40 per cent now shopped once a week (compared with 35 per cent in 1957), and Friday was the main shopping day for 40 per cent. Whereas 52 per cent had always gone to the same grocer in 1957, only 27 per cent now did so, with 'loyal buyers found to a greater degree among the older, working-class sections of the community'. Where did housewives shop? 'Of every ten regular customers, five use the Independent grocer, three go to a shop belonging to a Co-operative Society, while two buy their groceries regularly at a Multiple outlet' – ie, with ten or more branches. Predictably, Co-ops were especially favoured by 'the working class, older women over 45, and in the North and Scotland', whereas independent grocers had 'a slight bias towards upper-income families'. As for supermarkets, these were now used by one in ten as their main grocer, usually in the south, where most were located. Significantly, in four out of five categories – clean shops, fresh stocks, economical, best range of stock – the interviewees ranked the multiples (including the supermarkets) highest, with the independents favoured for friendly service and the Co-ops winning none of the categories. Across all grocers, self-service was on the rise – one in ten grocers in 1957, now one in four – and a substantial minority of housewives saw no advantage in it, with 'antagonism somewhat higher among the higher income groups, among housewives over 45, and in the North-East'. Interviews were also conducted with 2,000 housewives as they left their grocer, always on a Friday. These revealed that the average spend was 10s, though often above that for those with ITV at home; that four in five did not take a shopping list with them; and that 'almost half the housewives who claimed to have a regular grocer were, in fact, coming out of *another* grocer's shop when they were interviewed'. In short, solemnly concluded the report, 'shopping around is rife indeed'.

About the same time, Katharine Whitehorn inspected the facelift at Bentalls of Kingston and noted that it was part of the trend among big department stores to 'cover in the well, do away with daylight, smarten up and get modern', with Bentalls following the example of Bourne and Hollingsworth while anticipating Liberty's. Among the major multiples, modernisation increasingly involved larger-than-normal retail space, as in a huge 12,000-square-feet Bradford example. 'We went to the new Super Duper [W H] Smith's shop & spent some time there,' recorded Florence Turtle in July. 'It is a lovely store with various new ideas in selling. I particularly admired the electric signs suspended from the ceiling indicating departments, Cash desks etc.' By contrast, she added, she had also visited in Bradford 'a most antiquated Woolworths with steps up to it very badly lit', as well as 'a very old Victorian enclosed Market'.[13]

Overall, it was indisputable that the multiple retailers were on the up, with their total share of the distributive trades rising (by value of sales) from 22 per cent in 1950 to 29 per cent by 1961, while in the food trade specifically, their turnover grew by 42 per cent between 1957 and 1961, compared with 11 per cent for independent retailers and a mere 3 per cent for co-operative societies. Increasingly it would be supermarkets that spearheaded the multiples: by mid-1960, American-owned Fine Fare was leading the way with 40 stores – '100s and 100s of BRANDED GROCERIES at PERMANENT CUT PRICES!' shrieked one opening soon afterwards in Rayleigh, Essex – followed by Sainsbury's on 27 and Victor Value on 23, with the more upmarket Waitrose lagging on 6. Madge Martin for one preferred a different type of therapy. 'We had a fascinating time in the Portobello Market,' she noted after a Saturday jaunt. 'It is entrancing – the *amount* of things to buy at the stalls, or in the cavern-like shops, with their many tables of silver, china, jewellery, "Victoriana", pictures, "objets d'art" in wild profusion – and the strange people buying and selling.'

Arguably the emblematic consumer experience that autumn was in Southend-on-Sea. 'Shopping was never, *never* so good!' exclaimed the headline for an advertorial in the local paper marking the launch of Super-Save, until recently the Essoldo Cinema. Fifteen thousand square feet of floor space, 15 wide aisles, 38 displays, 10 counters – the key stats for Britain's first American-style no-frills self-service discount store were as expansive as the prose:

SUPER-SAVE is a new kind of store – the only one of its kind in Britain. At SUPER-SAVE you can buy everything – but everything! – food, clothes, cosmetics, shoes, kitchen utensils, toys, ironmongery – the lot under one great roof. You wander round with a little cart helping yourself. And when you think you've spent enough, you go through a sort of gate, where a pretty young mother of a cashier tots up your bill – and you find you haven't spent nearly as much as you thought!

'We're building up a huge turnover and we buy in bulk,' the manager explained. 'So we can afford a very small profit margin because it all adds up. We're all right, Jack. And Jill – the housewife, our customer – she's all right, too.' To the local paper's reporter, after walking round the store shortly before it opened on 30 September, it felt like a landmark moment. 'I thought back to the days of rationing – a dozen years ago now – when shopping was purgatory. I remembered the queues, the harassed, terse assistants, everything you wanted "under the counter." To those of us who remember those grim days, SUPER-SAVE is a shoppers' paradise.' Southenders mainly agreed – despite disapproval of the new venture by the local Chamber of Trade, protective of small shopkeepers – and on the first Saturday the crowds trying to get in were so large that the doors had to be closed after a quarter of an hour. Especially thrilled were the Keddies, the two youngish brothers behind Super-Save; Peter Keddy was perhaps not being vainglorious when he expressed the belief that Super-Save, with its wide range and its low prices, would 'create a new shopping public – that it will give people what they've always wanted and never been able to afford before'.[14]

'Nasty, malicious, warped, banally snobbish, and, in its affectation of chic cynicism, as rancidly unpleasant to the palate as gone-off *paté de foie gras*' ran Kenneth Allsop's *Daily Mail* review on 20 October 1960, adding that 'the lower classes' were 'caricature proles, viewed with sneering contempt'. That Thursday, though, it was not Auberon Waugh's *The Foxglove Saga* that made the main headlines, but a novel already three decades old. 'LADY C. IN THE DOCK TODAY' announced a newspaper placard, as the trial began at the Old Bailey that in effect tested the limits of the recent liberalising Obscene Publications Act – and, specifically, whether Penguin Books could publish, as a mass-market paperback, an unexpurgated edition of D. H. Lawrence's *Lady Chatterley's Lover*.

Mervyn Griffith-Jones – with, noted a watching Mollie Panter-Downes, 'the sort of neat, well-boned good looks that you often see in

eighteenth-century family portraits of country squires and their span-
iels regarding each other with mutual satisfaction' – opened for the
Crown. After calling it a novel that 'sets upon a pedestal promiscuous
and adulterous intercourse' and commended sensuality 'almost as a
virtue', he asked the nine men and three women on the jury a trio of
questions, the third of which, apparently ad-libbed, became instantly
quotable: 'Would you approve of your young sons, young daughters –
because girls can read as well as boys – reading this book? Is it a book
that you would have lying around in your own house? Is it a book that
you would even wish your wife or your servants to read?' Griffith-
Jones then itemised the novel's thirteen 'episodes of sexual intercourse',
as well as lavish use of 'fuck', 'fucking', 'cunt', 'balls', 'shit', 'arse', 'cock'
and 'piss' – all part of the prosecution's larger case that it was a dangerously depraving piece of work. For Penguin in defence, Gerald Gardiner
– 'a big, cheerful-looking man', observed Panter-Downes – argued in
his opening address that Lawrence's book was not obscene, would not
deprave, and possessed genuine literary merit. The day ended with Mr
Justice Byrne giving jurors a week to read the novel before resumption
of the case.[15]

By then a further moral front had opened up, with the premiere on
the 26th at the Warner, Leicester Square of *Saturday Night and Sunday
Morning*. Based on Alan Sillitoe's 1958 novel (by then a bestselling
paperback) and vividly shot in Nottingham, Karl Reisz's film definitively launched the British New Wave. 'Don't let the bastards grind you
down,' declares at the outset the young machine operator Arthur Seaton
(in a part wonderfully played by Albert Finney that Dirk Bogarde had
originally wanted). 'I'd like to see anyone grind me down. All I'm out
for is a good time. All the rest is propaganda.' It was, reflect the film
historians Sue Harper and Vincent Porter, 'the first time in British
cinema' that 'the working class were shown *not to care* about the disapproval of their betters, and to have a culture of their own – hedonistic,
abrasive, volatile – which was perfectly competent for the job in hand.'
Perhaps the most interesting review was by the *FT*'s David Robinson.
He praised the film as 'completely free of excess ornament, self-indul-
gence or pyrotechnic' and noted how 'working-class life – the telly and
cheap furniture, the casual love-making on a thin hearthrug – is depicted
truthfully and without condescension', while recording that at the

press show he had been 'distressed' to find some of his colleagues attacking the film 'as amoral, if not immoral'. Olga Franklin was not a film reviewer, but by the end of a week in which 'all the praise went to Alan Sillitoe' she was using her regular *Daily Mail* feature to launch a frontal assault on 'The Cad Makers' – into whose ranks Sillitoe through his creation of 'the thoroughly unpleasant' Seaton now joined Kingsley Amis (Jim Dixon), John Osborne (Jimmy Porter) and John Braine (Joe Lampton). Accordingly, Franklin called on her female readers 'to inspire an uncivil disobedience campaign and say quite plainly that we're sick of cads'. At least two instantly agreed. 'It is about time we stopped putting the so-called Angry Young Men on pedestals,' declared Marguerite Lovejoy of Cheshunt, Herts. 'Also, let us cut down on radio and TV interviews with layabouts and beatniks.' As for Eve Braby of Alverstoke, Hants, she conceded that the old type of hero could be 'rather smug', but was adamant that at least he had (or professed) 'certain standards for which the loutish cads have a contempt which only betrays their abysmal shallowness'. Like Franklin, she was 'thoroughly nauseated with the Jims and Jimmys, Arthurs and Joes of present-day fiction'.[16]

Back at the Old Bailey, 18 witnesses had appeared for the defence during Thursday the 27th and Friday the 28th. Rebecca West stated that much of *Lady C* was 'ludicrous', though it was still of 'undoubted literary merit'; the Bishop of Woolwich, the free-thinking John Robinson, claimed that Lawrence portrayed sex as 'in a real sense an act of holy communion', prompting the judge to gaze at him and twirl his pencil; and E. M. Forster, half a century after *Howards End*, connected Lawrence to Bunyan, both of whom 'believed intensely in what they preached'. Everyone agreed, though, that the star defence witness was Richard Hoggart, working-class author of *The Uses of Literacy*, a senior lecturer in English at Leicester University and described by Panter-Downes as 'a dark, serious young man'. Arriving at the crease late on Thursday, Hoggart called the novel not only 'not in any sense vicious', but instead 'highly virtuous and if anything, puritanical'. 'See old Baron Hoggart giving evidence for D.H.L.,' noted a sceptical Larkin that night. 'I suppose one ought really to save all the cuttings of the business. Nobody seems to think it will win. Certainly the witnesses as reported on the 10.30 news sound cracked enough.' Next morning, soon after observing how commonplace the word *fuck* had become ('fifty yards from this Court I heard a man say "fuck" three times as he passed me'), Hoggart received a lengthy cross-examination from Griffith-Jones. 'Is that a passage which you describe as puritanical?' the QC asked at one point after reading out a detailed account of the sexual act. 'Yes,' replied Hoggart, 'puritanical, and poignant, and tender, and moving, and sad, about two people who have no proper relationship.' There ensued a sequence of Griffith-Jones reading out erotic passages before asking, 'Is *that* puritanical?'; each time, Hoggart resolutely insisted that it was, in accordance with his definition of puritanism as 'an intense sense of responsibility for one's conscience'. 'Mr Griffith-Jones hammered at Mr Hoggart for over an hour,' noted Panter-Downes, 'with what seemed a strange and special ferocity. When this witness left the box – still calm, collected, and with intelligent arguments in hand – the sense of applause in court was deafening.'[17]

Any Questions? that evening came from St Mary's Hall, Arundel, with Gilbert Harding making his belated debut. Should the minimum age of criminal responsibility be raised from eight to twelve? 'It all depends surely on the child,' he answered. 'What we want are more intelligent magistrates – and that indeed we lack.' What was the best future for British Railways? 'People are just not any longer railway-minded. They're just put upon, and upset, and the sooner we get rid of them the better.' What about the overweight children of today? 'It's sweet-eating. It's encouraged by the commercial television, who say, "Don't forget the fruit gums, Mum." And there's also a terrible confection which is advertised expressly as something you can eat between meals without losing appetite.' Teenage vandalism? 'I've all the sympathy I have with young people, and I dislike very much the idea of saddling teenagers with all the damage that's done.' On Monday the 31st, the *Lady C* defence paraded 17 more witnesses, including Raymond Williams, Norman St John Stevas, Cecil Day Lewis and Noel Annan, with particular attention focused on the last and youngest, 21-year-old Bernardine Wall. Her credentials were impeccable – convent-educated, English at Cambridge, writing her first novel – and she insisted that Lawrence 'precisely does *not* put promiscuity on a pedestal', that indeed he treated sexual relations 'with great dignity'. Next day, Tuesday the 1st, a letter in *The Times* with 30 signatories

– including Harding and John Freeman as well as Kingsley Amis, Augustus John, Bertrand Russell, Richard Titmuss and Leonard Woolf – urged that Francis Forsyth, an 18-year-old found guilty of murder, should not be hanged 'in cold blood'; Gardiner and Griffith-Jones made their lengthy closing speeches, followed by the start of the judge's summing-up; and viewers flooded the BBC switchboard with calls, complaining about excessive bad language in a 45-minute TV excerpt from the West End production of *Billy Liar*.[18]

Wednesday, 2 November was decision day, with Sylvia Plath among those agog. 'Got a press ticket from Stephen Spender for the last day of the Lady Chatterley trial at the Old Bailey,' she reported home soon afterwards. 'Very exciting – especially with the surprising verdict of "not guilty"!' A surprise indeed, especially after the rest of Mr Justice Byrne's summing up had, observed Panter-Downes, 'cast gloom upon everyone from Penguin'. Having lost half a crown in a bet over the outcome, Larkin that evening took the big view:

> I must say I'm surprised they let it go. I thought the 3/6 element [the price at which Penguin intended to sell] would settle the issue, because the thing about pornography (I know it isn't pornography, but you know what I mean) is that it *isn't* cheap. If Baron Hoggart thinks you can buy 'pornography' in 'Charing Cross Road' for 3/6 he's mistaken. They ought to have called Robert Conquest, poet & editor: it's £3, 50/- on return, at the very least. Or £1, £2, and no return. Well, I feel I am out of touch with ordinary people . . . I shall put my copy on exhibition in the Library tomorrow – locked under glass, mind you.

Next morning not all the papers pronounced, but some did. The *Guardian* hailed 'a triumph of common sense'; the *Glasgow Herald* claimed that 'no reasonable person will quarrel with the decision'; *The Times* registered its 'dissent' on the grounds of 'decency and taste'; for the *Daily Express*, it was 'THIS FAR AND NO FURTHER!'; and the *Daily Sketch*'s editorial, printed in black type as a front-page 'Statement to Parents', accused the jury of having 'forced each one of us to make a choice whether or not we wish our children to buy sexual description at pocket money prices'.[19]

Predictably, the issue resonated over the next few days, pending

Penguin's imminent publication of the unexpurgated paperback. 'Well, I did attempt to procure a copy of this book, so that I should read it through *in case* anyone asked a question tonight,' Margaret Thatcher told the *Any Questions?* audience at the Women's Institute Hall, Dorchester on Friday evening. 'I got through it in three hours and twenty minutes. That was because I was not anxious to linger on it at all.' She added that in her view Lawrence's novel did 'offend against most of the ordinary standards of public taste'. Next day the Archbishop of Canterbury, Geoffrey Fisher, publicly condemned his errant Bishop of Woolwich, while in the Sunday press two commentators were in diametrical opposition. John Gordon in the *Sunday Express* described Penguin's Sir Allen Lane as 'the shrewd publisher who saw the golden beam of culture where others saw only dirt', but Kenneth Tynan in the *Observer* delighted in the defeat of Griffith-Jones – an Old Etonian with 'a voice passionate only in disdain, but barbed with a rabid belief in convention and discipline' – and cherished the moment when, having read out a passage, he had 'triumphantly' asked Hoggart whether a puritan would feel such reverence for a man's balls, to which Hoggart 'almost with compassion' had calmly replied in the affirmative. The evidence soon emerged from Gallup that public opinion was broadly on the jury's side, with only 20 per cent wanting *Lady C* banned and 53 per cent wanting the full version published. 'I am all for educated people in a free world, rather than half-educated people in a confined world,' asserted Dr Irene Green at a local 'Any Questions?' session in the Norfolk village of Horsford; her fellow-panellists, including a clergyman and a headmaster, agreed. Admittedly there was still the moral danger of stiletto heels – 'monstrosities', declared Green about that particular topic – but for the moment the centre of opinion had shifted a notch or two in the liberal direction.[20]

Life continued during the fortnight after the jury's epoch-defining verdict. On the 2nd itself, Anthony Heap complained in his diary about tailors increasingly selling single-breasted suits, not double; next day, Hugh Gaitskell defeated Harold Wilson's challenge for the Labour leadership by a convincing 166 votes to 81 (only MPs voting); on the 4th, after *Mirror* readers had given their verdict on Picasso's *The Man with the Red Glove* (70 per cent 'ridiculing' it), Madge Martin standing outside Oxford Town Hall was passed by the visiting royal couple

('When I bobbed my curtsey to the Queen, I suddenly saw Prince Philip turn to me with a smile and twinkle, and say, "You've dropped your hankie"'); on Guy Fawkes Night, Gyles Brandreth and his confrères at a prep school near Deal 'paraded out to the games pitch where we watched the "Burn the Bomb" Guy go on to the fire'; next evening, Heap found John Osborne's first TV play, *A Subject of Scandal and Concern*, starring Richard Burton as the Victorian atheist George Holyoake, 'drab and depressing'; on Monday morning the 18-year-old Hugo Williams started work at Simpson's in Piccadilly, theoretically working on its Christmas mail-order catalogue but mainly in the Gents reading J. D. Salinger's *For Esmé – with Love and Squalor*; by Tuesday the letters to the *Daily Mail* were running four to one in favour of hanging Francis Forsyth; next day, the news that John F. Kennedy had won the US presidential election was greeted enthusiastically by Kenneth Williams, inspired that 'a man of conscience, integrity, originality & quality *can* win through', while the result probably interested the 13-year-old David Jones (later Bowie), who about this time paid a visit to the American Embassy to find out more about his latest passion, American football. By now another young original, Alan Garner, was launched with *The Weirdstone of Brisingamen* – 'absolutely rum', according to one reviewer (Siriol Hugh-Jones), though 'maybe fine for all who like a really good shudder over the final digestives and hot milk'; on Thursday the 10th, Forsyth was hanged at Wandsworth Prison, Churchill made his last speech in public (telling the boys of Harrow School that he was 'always very glad when the day comes round for me to turn up here'), and William Burroughs in Cambridge told Allen Ginsberg in New York that he didn't think he could 'stick this English weather much longer', that 'as soon as I get some bread we'll split south'. Over the weekend, Eric Hobsbawm in the *New Statesman* welcomed the trad jazz phenomenon for at least replacing 'the rock-and-roll vogue' ('which is at last, thank God, fading away') but otherwise found its musical limitations 'only exceeded by the deficient amateurishness of many of its musicians'; a Sheffield MP (Fred Mulley) spent a disturbed night in a Park Hill flat hearing for himself the relentless noise of the hammers in a nearby forge; Macmillan stood next to the opposition leader at the Cenotaph ('poor Mr Gaitskell always seems a little conscious on these occasions that he has no medals'); and Gilbert Harding on *What's My Line?* remarked to a fellow-celebrity due to appear on *Juke Box Jury*, 'I do hope you can manage to keep awake.' Monday featured a despairing *Daily Telegraph* article by John Betjeman about the rapidly disappearing architectural heritage; Tuesday saw at the National Liberal Forum an early meeting between an architect (John Poulson) and a Tory politician (Reginald Maudling); and on Wednesday the 16th the latest issue of *Punch* included the racing driver Stirling Moss explaining how, if he was Minister of Transport and given dictatorial powers (not least 'over John Betjeman'), 'highway construction would be pushed hard, ruthlessly, 24 hours a day.'[21]

Early that evening, just after recording *Round Britain Quiz*, Gilbert Harding collapsed and died outside Broadcasting House, aged 53. 'A character in the great Johnsonian tradition,' reflected Heap next day, adding that 'we shall sadly miss his plump, delightfully grumpy presence on the "What's My Line" panel on Sunday evenings.' Another diarist, Nella Last, 'read Richard Dimbleby's pompous "eulogy"' in her *Daily Express* '& thought "you so silly fat man"'. Three days later, *What's My Line?* – the panel game that had brought Harding his greatest fame and at times notoriety – was replaced by a tribute programme, reckoned by the far-from-undiscerning Heap as 'the best thing of its kind I've yet seen on T.V.' But a more professional critic, Joanna Richardson, declined to be swayed by sentiment. 'Ham in the extreme,' she wrote in the *Listener*. 'The close-up of the empty chair, the slow movement from Mendelssohn Violin Concerto, the embarrassing hyperbole about Dr Johnson and fields of asphodel from Sir Compton Mackenzie: nothing had been wanting.'[22]

By this time Penguin Books were enjoying one of the great publishing triumphs. 'NOW YOU CAN READ IT' announced their posters barely a week after the trial's end, as an initial print run of 200,000 copies proved an instant sell-out. Many provincial bookshops retained a degree of circumspection – 'the book will not be on open display, but will be available on request' was the not untypical policy of Wildings in Shrewsbury – but for several weeks demand continued to exceed supply. On the 24th, Henry St John was in the bookshop at Gunnersbury in order to buy 'a strip-tease magazine "Play No 6"', also priced at 3s 6d. 'A woman came in for "Lady Chatterley's Lover," which she said she had ordered, but it seemed the boss had not. He gave her someone else's copy. Despite the flood of words poured out about this D.H. Lawrence novel it is for all practical purposes still unobtainable, as the numbers printed appear totally inadequate.' The Chief Constable of Lincolnshire was among those still holding out for the old standards. 'I hope you will not read this book even if you get the chance,' he told pupils and parents when presenting prizes at Brigg Glanford School, though refraining from mentioning the title. 'If you do get hold of it and feel ashamed after the first few pages, throw it away.' Gyles Brandreth at his prep school did not even get to first base: a parcel arrived for him, unfortunately with a Penguin label on it, and was immediately confiscated. Altogether, in what was still in many ways a deeply puritanical – and certainly prurient – society, it was an extraordinary episode, as Penguin sold more than two million copies within a year. 'I feel as if a window has been opened and fresh air has blown right through England,' joyously declared Lawrence's stepdaughter, Barbara Barr, after the jury's verdict, and of course at one level she was right. Yet there was truth also in Kate Paul's diary entry some two months later. 'The constant stream of jokes referring to the *Lady Chatterley* case makes me sick,' noted the anti-bomb, anti-apartheid, anti-capital-punishment twenty-year-old. 'People behave like children with curious, obscene, starved minds.'²³

There was no doubting the ubiquity. 'The references to homosexuality have sent nudges rippling up and down the rows of seats in school and village halls,' reported the *Guardian* about the Arts Council's touring production in Wales that autumn of Peter Shaffer's *Five Finger Exercise*, 'and has made a visit to the play the local equivalent of buying a copy of "Lady Chatterley's Lover".' Middle-class female dropouts were not yet common in Wales, but the phenomenon was just under way in London – caught by the novel of the autumn, Lynne Reid Banks's *The L-Shaped Room*. 'Where am I to find curry, for God's sake, in this benighted neighbourhood,' cries out the pregnant heroine Jane, living in a down-at-heel Fulham bedsit among prostitutes, a black musician and the inevitable struggling writer. The acclaim was instant and considerable for what became a bestseller, though Keith Waterhouse more sourly detected 'a conventional boarding-house saga, all baked beans and hearts of gold'. Annie Courtenay still badly missed the hearts of gold (and perhaps baser metals) she had known in her old home near the Fish Dock in Hull – 'I'll never feel at home in Longhill,' she wrote forlornly to her son Tom on 7 December from the new housing estate on the city's outskirts where she had been living for a year. On Friday the 9th, the day after Mike (later Mick) Jagger's end-of-term report at Dartford Grammar School had called him 'a lad of good general character', more than 2,000 people, many standing in the aisles, packed Westminster Cathedral for Gilbert Harding's requiem mass; among those attending were Nancy Spain, Eamonn Andrews, Hermione Baddeley, Brian Johnston and David Jacobs.[24]

Also in the congregation was Cliff Michelmore, and that evening *Tonight* found itself up against a newcomer on the other channel. Ray Chapman set the scene in the *TV Times*:

> 'Coronation Street' – four miles from Manchester in any direction – is a collection of seven terraced houses, an off-licence, a little general store on the corner, the back wall of a raincoat factory, a pub called 'The Rover's Return', and the Glad Tidings Mission Hall.
>
> The houses of 'Coronation Street' are representative – built more than 60 years ago, with no gardens. They have six rooms . . . parlour, living-room, scullery, and three bedrooms, one of which has been converted into a bathroom.
>
> Yet it is home to the 20 people who live there, and most of them would not like to change their warm surroundings for something new but less humanised.

Chapman got the backstory from the programme's creator Tony Warren, a 23-year-old former actor who had lived in Pendlebury (near Salford) for most of his life and whose idea for a serial set amid the northern working class had been curtly rejected by the BBC before being taken on by Manchester-based Granada. 'Apart from listening to people in pubs and clubs,' Warren explained about his two months of background research mainly in Manchester, 'I also "kept observation" in an off-licence, talked to people in buses and trains, wandered through street markets, made three trips to Blackpool illuminations and went on a "mystery" coach outing, which turned out to be a fourth visit to Blackpool.' 'I am *not*,' he stressed, 'having a joke at the expense of the people in the North. What I have aimed at is a true picture of life there and the people's basic friendliness and essential humour.'

Pat Phoenix as Elsie Tanner ('with the very battered remains of good looks and figure,' according to the script), William Roache as Ken Barlow ('little or no northern accent and looks faintly out of place'), Violet Carson as Ena Sharples (hair-netted caretaker of the hall, described by Chapman as a 'kindly ex-barmaid'), Jack Howarth as Albert Tatlock, Doris Speed as Annie Walker – some soon-to-be-famous characters were present from the first episode. 'With The Archers, Coronation St, Ward 10, This Week & Take Your Pick it was a pleasant enough programme,' noted Nella Last later that Friday evening, 'although I cannot see much entertainment value in the first named.' Next day, among *Coronation Street*'s few reviews in the national press, Mary Crozier in the *Guardian* praised 'something funny and forthright' about Warren's depiction of ordinary life, but the *Daily Mirror*'s Jack Bell found it 'hard to believe that viewers will want to put up with continuous slice-of-life domestic drudgery two evenings a week'. Among the provincial dailies, Peter Forth in the *Western Daily Press* conceded that it was 'no crowning achievement', but still felt it had 'started promisingly', while N.G.P. in the *Liverpool Daily Post* predicted 'entertaining possibilities'. The most resonant instant verdict came on Sunday from Maurice Wiggin. 'They undoubtedly have a winner coming up in the "Coronation Street" series,' he declared in the *Sunday Times* about 'the astute impresarios of Granada'. And he went on: 'This is "Emergency – Ward 10" and "Mrs Dale's Diary" and "The Grove Family" and Wilfred Pickles and Kipps and Armchair Theatre at its most socially-conscious all rolled into one great cosy Hall of Mirrors, in which the population can see itself, with the profound satisfaction of recognition, every Friday night for ever and ever.'

Wiggin got it in one. 'I actually remember the very first episode, because my dad was mending a puncture on his bike in our front room,' recalled Cilla Black 40 years later about that December evening in her working-class Liverpool home. 'The *Street* came on and we were all engrossed, and all of a sudden they were doing exactly the same thing. I think it was in the Barlows' household. We thought, "Wow, they're just as common as us".'[25]

PART TWO

6

Why Are We Falling Behind?

Over on BBC TV later that Friday evening in December 1960 was the second programme of a rather different new series: *Challenge to Prosperity*. 'Britain is raising her standard of living less quickly than any other European country,' explained the *Radio Times*. 'Must our rivals outstrip us?' The producer, Jack Ashley, further filled in the background:

> In less than ten years' time the people of Western Germany will be enjoying a standard of living twice as high as they have today. Yet it will be over thirty years before we double our standard – unless there is a radical change in British industry.
>
> It may be true that we have never had it so good. The luxuries of pre-war have become the necessities of today; business is booming and our major industries are among the best in the world. But, although we are increasing our material wealth, so are our major competitors, and they are doing so faster than we are. Why are we falling behind?

Accordingly, he and Christopher Chataway (athlete, broadcaster, Conservative MP) had been 'touring the country trying to find out'.

Michael Shanks, a *Financial Times* journalist, had even bigger questions on his mind, and by this time was writing at speed what became *The Stagnant Society* – a Penguin Special that on publication in summer 1961 made such an immediate impact that it was turned into a Pelican and altogether sold some 60,000 copies. 'The challenge is simply this,' Shanks declared at the outset:

> Can we allow the Soviet world to continue to enrich itself, by adding to its productive capacity, at a faster rate than ourselves? The two systems

are now on trial in the eyes of the world to see which can enrich itself fastest, and which can use its resources more effectively in promoting the happiness and well-being of its citizens. At present growth rates, one can foresee a point on the graph at which Soviet production per head will in fact surpass ours . . . How can we avert this danger? By establishing for ourselves the same sort of rate of growth as the Soviet countries – and some, but not many, advanced Western countries – have already achieved? In other words, how can we run our economic system more efficiently?

'A society which loses interest in material progress is a society on its way to the embalming chamber,' he went on. 'This is the great psychological danger facing the British people today – that we may bury ourselves under the rose-petals of a vast collective nostalgia, lost in a sweet sad love-affair with our own past.' Vigorous analysis followed of Britain's economic, political and social malaise, before Shanks reprised his dominant preoccupation:

What sort of an island do we want to be? This is the question to which we come back in the end. A lotus island of easy, tolerant ways, bathed in the golden glow of an imperial sunset, shielded from discontent by a threadbare welfare state and an acceptance of genteel poverty? Or the tough dynamic race we have been in the past, striving always to better ourselves, seeking new worlds to conquer in place of those we have lost, ready to accept growing pains as the price of growth?

'If we are to succeed,' insisted Shanks, 'it will be because we are determined as a nation to succeed, and because we are prepared to subordinate all other considerations – personal or sectional – to this national aim.' He added hopefully: 'If any people is capable of it, I believe we are.'[1]

Something was undeniably in the air: call it 'declinism'.[2] Inevitably, it was a moot point whether the economic facts at the start of the new decade justified the phenomenon. Britain's share of world manufactured exports had indeed declined from 22 per cent in 1950 to 16 per cent in 1960 (compared to West Germany's increase from 7 to 19 per cent), and the balance of payments was deteriorating quite rapidly. Even so, the British economy's annual rate of growth between 1957 and

1965 would be 3.2 per cent, the most impressive rate since the 1860s. Clearly, then, it was all about *relative* decline, particularly in relation to Europe (both West and East). And given, as Jack Ashley noted, the continuing never-had-it-so-good feeling amid inexorably spreading consumer affluence, it is far from clear that most people were really conscious of that relative decline, let alone cared about it. Nor was there necessarily unfailing interest or understanding even among the nation's opinion-formers. Anthony Sampson, working at the *Observer*, recalled how the eyes of his distinguished editor, David Astor, 'glazed over at the mention of economics and industry', being, along with 'most of the other pundits' around him, 'too preoccupied with Britain's responsibilities in the world to notice that she could not afford much of a role'. One day, added Sampson, the increasingly thorny problem of traffic came up – prompting the paper's main literary reviewer, Philip Toynbee, to ask why they didn't ban lorries from the new motorways.[3]

Associated Portland Cement, Bass, Bowater, British Motor Corporation, Coats Patons, Courtaulds, Distillers, Dunlop, EMI, GEC, GKN (Guest Keen & Nettlefolds), Hawker Siddeley, Alfred Herbert, House of Fraser, ICI, Imperial Tobacco, Lancashire Cotton, Leyland Motors, London Brick, Murex, P&O, Rolls-Royce, Spillers, Swan Hunter, Tate & Lyle, Tube Investments, United Steel, Vickers, Watney Combe & Reid, Woolworth's – these in the early 1960s were the proud constituents of the FT 30-Share Index, bellwether of the economy, and a list with a strongly manufacturing character. Nothing stands still, though, in the corporate landscape, and four distinct trends of long-term significance were already well under way: first, increasing size and concentration, typified by the rapid series of mergers and acquisitions in the brewing industry; second, increasing diversification, neatly exemplified by Guinness starting to sell butterscotch as well as stout; third, increasing foreign ownership, often American but not invariably, as when Nestlé in 1960 acquired Crosse & Blackwell; and fourth – arguably most resonant of all – the irresistible shift away from manufacturing and towards services, with employment in the latter sector (including distribution) now for the first time roughly equalling or even just exceeding employment in the former – a shift perhaps epitomised by jobs in the hairdressing sector hitting the six-figure mark. Even so, manufacturing remained central not only to the crucial exports performance but also, just as importantly, to national self-image; among the household names of the British economy *circa* 1960 were Accles & Pollock (based in Dudley and making steel tubes), Albright & Wilson (based in Oldbury and second only to ICI as a chemicals manufacturer), the match-makers Bryant & May, brake-lining specialists Ferodo (based in Chapel-en-le-Frith), and Britain's biggest toy-manufacturer, Liverpool-based Meccano, makers of Dinky cars and Hornby trains as well as of course Meccano itself.[4]

No sector of the economy would be more emblematic over the coming years than the motor industry. On the surface it seemed to be doing well enough at the start of the 1960s – with almost all of the major firms laying plans for future expansion – but there were troubling signs. Not only had West Germany's share of world car exports (an increasingly competitive marketplace) comfortably overtaken Britain's, but the industry was becoming increasingly strike-prone. 'There is now a total stoppage at Ford's Dagenham works – over 1 man!' despaired Macmillan in November 1960, adding that 'the T.U. leaders are doing their best, but the Communist shop stewards seem to be in control.' That year, over half a million working days were lost in the industry, followed in 1961 by another 350,000 plus, prompting Maurice Edelman to comment that 'the television comedian who says "Motor Shop Steward" can now count on a national guffaw'. But it was another Labour MP, Francis Noel-Baker, who offered in December 1961 the most rounded contemporary analysis of the industry's thinning slice of the world market. After accusing it of designing and making cars less well than foreign manufacturers, and not being helped by inferior after-sales service by local agents, he argued that 'perhaps at the bottom of this problem is the fact that the home market takes half and more of the output of many British motor firms, and is more profitable to them than struggling for exports – some leading men in the industry frankly admit as much in private.' Not that Noel-Baker played down the importance of what he called, with the notable exception of Vauxhall, 'an abominable record in industrial relations'. And he went on: 'Of course there are Communists, of course there are trouble-makers. But – equally of course – there are also managements who show no gleam of understanding for the strain and insecurity in which their employees work.'

The manager par excellence without a gleam of such understanding was undoubtedly the abrasive Sir Leonard Lord, chairman until 1961 of the British Motor Corporation (embracing both Cowley-based Morris and Longbridge-based Austin) and characterised by a biographer as 'a ruthless pursuer of efficiency and production goals, a strong opponent of organised labour and left-wing politics'. A less brutal if still driven approach came from the industry's rising man, Donald Stokes, whose resourcefulness in finding and exploiting new export markets had done much to establish a world-leading position in commercial vehicles for the Leyland Motor Corporation, which in 1961 expanded perhaps rashly into new territory by taking over the ailing Standard-Triumph (saloon and sports cars). But from whichever school, management now faced two huge challenges. F. Griffiths, BMC's chief production development engineer, spelled out the first in January 1961:

> What is required to be automated in the motor industry is the relationship of our processes with each other and to the production programme ... We are losing 20 per cent [of capacity] ... The cause of this will be found in the fact that the right material is not at the right place at the right time, and that the motor industry is really not in proper control of its business. The piecework systems which it has to use, its lack of immediate knowledge of its relationships between supply and what is required, all mean that its output is in the hands of a large number of people.

Or, as the economic historian Wayne Lewchuk has put it, the advent of new, American automated production techniques now enabled British managers – if they were up to it – 'to take direct responsibility for planning, maintenance and the organisation of shop floor activity' – a considerable ask, given that the unions (and especially the shop stewards) were becoming increasingly ambitious in their contesting of workplace control. The other challenge stemmed from the government's new attachment at the start of the decade to regional policy, leading during 1960 to a flurry of announcements, following government pressure and financial inducements. BMC and Rootes would be building new plants in Scotland (Bathgate and Linwood, respectively), while Ford, Standard-Triumph and Vauxhall would be doing the same on Merseyside (Halewood, Speke and Ellesmere Port, respectively), another area of high unemployment. Might these two new regional fronts help to improve labour relations? 'While shop stewards could not support anti-Scottish slogans being written on parts going from the Midlands,' noted a meeting in Coventry in early 1962 of the BMC Joint Shop Stewards Committee (reflecting on the so-far disappointing lack of interest by shop stewards at Bathgate in discussing rates of pay), 'the quick and sure way to get friendship with our colleagues at Bathgate is by personal contact.'[5]

Two-wheel manufacturing also had its problems. In 1959 the British motorcycle industry, still regarded as the world's number 1, produced 127,000 machines (excluding lightweight scooters etc), many for export; that, however, turned out to be the peak total, with significant defects by now becoming apparent. Not only had there been a serious failure to maximise the potential of the scooter phenomenon – certainly in comparison to Italian manufacturers – but too often the emphasis remained on targeting enthusiasts and promoting the motorbike as the winner of prestigious races rather than an object of everyday utility. By late 1961, the *Daily Mirror* was describing a deeply conservative industry facing a crisis, with the report noting that most British engines were still of basically pre-war design. Ominously, it quoted a director from the industry's dominant force, BSA: 'The Japanese Honda machines are quite frighteningly good – they are built like watches.' That of course was *the* threat, prompting one of the industry's participants (and later historians), Bert Hopwood, to argue in retrospect that in the early 1960s, before the Japanese invasion really got going in the area of heavyweight motorbikes, the Birmingham-based BSA group had 'the financial strength to lay the foundation for an operation to match many of its Japanese competitors', but that it lacked the drive and willpower to do so. Also on two wheels, these were qualities likewise largely lacking at Nottingham-based Raleigh, where the 1950s were characterised by production methods falling uneasily between mass and batch, a critical delay in diversifying into the rapidly growing moped market and, above all, a generally slow-moving culture (paternalistic and family-based) – all of which meant that in 1960 a one-time proud and independent world leader was forced, amid falling profit margins and increasing international competition, into absorption by Tube Investments.[6]

At this stage, though, there was little soul-searching outside Nottingham, though it could be a different matter elsewhere in the economy. 'Industry and the Prestige Cult' was the title of an *Observer* article in October 1959 by John Davy, a science correspondent who refreshingly saw the bigger picture:

> As the Empire and the Navy shrink, and other nations get better at football, British national pride has tended to identify itself increasingly with science and technology. Calder Hall, the Viscount, Zeta and the Hovercraft have become national idols. Each new scientific advance is hailed by the Press as 'another British first'. The laboratory bench is becoming the patriot's platform.
>
> This would not matter if the platform were solidly constructed – but in fact it has some alarming weaknesses. In particular, the two British industries on which most public money and scientific effort have been lavished are in trouble . . .

These, he explained, were 'the aircraft and the atomic industries'.

The facts, as Davy turned to the former, were damning enough: '£500 million of public money have been spent on aircraft research and development since 1949, involving over 3,000 of the highest-powered scientists and engineers (compared with seventy doing research and development in shipbuilding and marine engineering). Yet the Viscount is the only fully successful civil airliner which has been produced.' Within months of this piece – and in effect responding to the 1957 White Paper that had put the future defence emphasis on missiles not aircraft, itself followed by the demoralising realisation that the lengthy Comet hiatus in the mid-1950s had in practice allowed the Boeing 707 to become the world's jet aircraft of choice – the government reorganised the airframe part of the British aircraft industry into two main groups: the British Aircraft Corporation (including Vickers, English Electric and Bristol) and Hawker Siddeley (including also de Havilland and Blackburn). This was perhaps a logical step, notwithstanding predictable frictions within the groups, but in general most historians of the industry have been strongly critical of government's role during the two decades after the war. Overestimating the industry's capacity to manage a large number of projects, 'a clumsy approach to procurement', an unrealistic desire to compete across the board with the Americans – such, for instance, are the charges levelled by Geoffrey Owen in his dispassionate 1999 survey of post-war British industry. At the time, following rationalisation, perhaps the most unsparing assessment came in the *Spectator* (in September 1960) from Oliver Stewart, who argued that the Ministry of Aviation now had 'absolute power over all things aeronautical' – a power for which it was almost entirely unqualified, not least given how the government's technical officers had 'repeatedly shown that they are incapable of assessing correctly the potentialities of new designs', as well as the failure to do anything 'to prepare a British machine for the rapidly growing executive aircraft market'. Perhaps a world-defying lead in a supersonic airliner was the answer? 'Agitation persists,' noted John Davy, 'regardless of the fact that a British one would cost far more than it could hope to earn.' In 1960 the *New Statesman* contended that 'the government's decision to enter Britain in the race to produce a supersonic airliner should be examined critically.' But, as the Minister of Aviation, Churchill's son-in-law Duncan Sandys, urged the Cabinet, 'If we are not in the big supersonic airliner business, then it is really only a matter of time before the whole British aircraft industry packs up.'[7] The flight path, in other words, was clear for Concorde and the fateful Anglo-French agreement of late 1962.

On the nuclear front, Davy's correctly pessimistic assertion in 1959 was that 'while the atomic engineers have performed glittering feats of ingenuity, gloom is now seeping through the industry as export orders for nuclear power-stations fail to materialise.' In fact, an extraordinary story was continuing to unfold, in which so far there had been a handful of key landmarks: a reasonably modest civil nuclear-power programme announced in 1955; nuclear euphoria surrounding the Queen's opening of the power station at Calder Hall in October 1956; the Suez Crisis, which engendered a panic about the future security of oil supplies; a dramatically enhanced nuclear-power programme up to 1965 announced in April 1957; Sir Christopher Hinton, characterised by Richard Crossman as 'a striking, difficult, dominant engineer', not long afterwards leaving the Atomic Energy Authority (AEA) and becoming the first chairman of the Central Electricity Generating

Board, in effect the producer switching to the consumer; and the Hinton-influenced White Paper of June 1960, which not only found that the cost of electricity from the Magnox nuclear stations (due to start coming into operation shortly) would be significantly higher than originally estimated, but generally sought to trim nuclear aspirations. Hinton himself would offer in retirement a compelling perspective on the ill-conceived 1957 expansion (for which he had not been responsible):

> It condemned us to go on building bigger and bigger nuclear power plants, each cheaper than the last but all clumsy and each generating electricity more expensively than could be done in fossil fuel fired stations built concurrently. Supervision of these plants diverted scientific and engineering manpower from the rapid development of more advanced reactor systems. Yet I do not think that anyone could be blamed. The nuclear programme was the victim of circumstances, the victim of events that had moved with the uncontrollable recklessness of those in an Elizabethan tragedy.

Of course, nuclear's partial retreat from 1960 did not mean the end of that form of power, and already the AEA had in practice virtually decided on the successor to the Magnox reactors once it came in the mid-1960s to pushing on with a new generation of nuclear stations: the advanced gas-cooled reactor (AGR). Whatever its merits and flaws, at least one nuclear historian has concluded that a crucial fact in the AEA's eyes was that it was once again *British* technology, not American.[8] National pride and the prestige cult were, in short, all too alive and well.

In 1959, though, Davy did identify two other, lower-profile British industries which had invested heavily in research and were 'in a very healthy position' – namely, chemicals (including plastics) and electronics: 'The former has largely paid for its own research; the latter has been greatly stimulated by defence expenditure. There are no newspaper headlines for making a superb oscilloscope or developing a new method of making polystyrene – but the profits are often much larger.' Sadly, however, profits were seldom large, indeed sometimes non-existent, in one key branch of electronics: the nascent computer industry. British scientists and firms had been among the world's pioneers between the late 1940s and mid-1950s, but by around 1960 the picture was looking distinctly clouded. A significant technology gap had opened up between the UK and US computer industries, with the UK some two to three years behind; too many firms (principally International Computers and Tabulators (ICT), Elliott-Automation, Ferranti, LEO Computers and English Electric) were chasing too small a domestic market, with only about £15 million worth of computers sold during 1960–61; and case studies of Ferranti and LEO reveal a similar pattern of too much emphasis on technological excellence, too little on effective salesmanship. Then, in the early 1960s, the Americans moved forward decisively, above all IBM on the back of a huge, resources-generating domestic market, significant US government backing for R&D, and specifically its recently launched 1401. 'What grows faster than IBM?' rhetorically asked *Fortune* magazine in November 1960. Answer: 'IBM Abroad'. A single IBM 1401 could do the work of four conventional tabulators, and in the course of 1961–2, in a matter almost of months, it blew ICT's punched-card machine business out of the water. The only recourse for the British computer industry was to consolidate, but almost inevitably it was a case of too little, too late.[9]

In an altogether older sector, engineering, alarm bells were ringing by 1960, or should have been. Two especially ominous areas were textile machinery and machine tools – both traditional strengths, both by now seeing West Germany outstripping the UK in terms of share of world exports. Oldham-based Platt Brothers may have been the leading firm for textile machinery, but the historian D. A. Farnie argues that in these crucial years its management 'failed either to reduce costs of production or to diversify operations'. As for the machine-tool industry, Roger Lloyd-Jones and M. J. Lewis identify in their authoritative study a range of deficiencies in the 1950s – including poor productivity, an overly fragmented structure and a general failure to modernise – followed by only sluggish modernising efforts in the early 1960s. Easily the UK's biggest specialist machine-tool maker was the Coventry-based Alfred Herbert, and here Lloyd-Jones and Lewis find across the 1950s and 1960s much that was negative: 'limited organisational capabilities', 'capacity constraint', 'delays in developing a centralised design policy', failure to develop NC (numerical control) technology, persistence of 'learning by doing', and (in the early 1960s) a crucial delay, because of design problems, in developing the new Progmanto machine of advanced design. Alfred Herbert had once been the world's largest machine-tool business, but by the time its founder, Sir Alfred Herbert, died in 1957 (still in harness), it had become, observes Geoffrey Owen, 'a byword for ageing management, products and manufacturing methods'. Even by the mid-1960s, of its 1,500 machines in use, 70 were more than 50 years old and another 570 were over 30 years old, with the result, adds Owen, that 'many could be worked only by men who had the dying craft skills needed for precision work on antiquated plant.'[10]

Machine-tool making was a specialist world, little known to most outsiders, but there were three much more familiar industries that between them comprised the very heart of the British economy: textiles, steel and coal. Each had been a nineteenth-century 'staple' heavyweight, each had struggled between the wars, and by 1960 each was in a problematic place.

The setting for the Lancashire cotton industry was 'the great urban sprawl centred on Manchester, whose blackened houses and cobbled streets stretch with hardly a break for sixteen miles from Stockport in the south to Oldham and Rochdale in the north'. But, as the *Economist*'s special correspondent went on to explain in May 1960 (just as Blackburn Rovers were about to lose badly at Wembley), the industry's decline had been rapid over the past decade, notwithstanding eventual government efforts to help: 'Almost half the spinning and weaving industry on which it has traditionally depended has been closed down. Many mills, with their depressing look of Victorian workhouses, have closed for ever; others have only one of their former array of chimneys belching smoke into the greyish air.' What had gone wrong? One particularly well-informed historian, John Singleton, does not deny that the industry had plenty wrong with it – 'a workforce that viewed redeployment with suspicion, poor management, outmoded marketing arrangements, deficiencies in product design, and an atomistic industrial structure which militated against the co-ordination of the different stages in the production process' – but ultimately argues that sharp decline in the 1950s had probably been inevitable, especially given the 'devastating' competition of cheap imports from India, Hong Kong and elsewhere, which meant that the industry 'entered the 1960s in complete disarray'.

Across the Pennines, however, it was a significantly different picture. In Wool City, aka Bradford, local textile companies such as S. Jerome & Sons, a Bingley manufacturer of medium- and high-grade worsted fabrics, ended the 1950s at full stretch and often making record profits, as they 'struggled' (in the words of local historian Mark Keighley) 'to meet the universal demand for wool products'. The city's unemployment figure in early 1960 of 0.7 per cent was one of the lowest in the UK, and all seemed good; but, as Keighley also notes, the threat of rival fibres was already looming on the horizon.[11]

The glass was also at least half-full in nearby Steel City. The Sheffield special-steels industry, records its historian Geoffrey Tweedale, 'entered the decade on a confident note: order books were buoyant and production was at record levels after the advances [including continuous casting in the finishing processes] of the 1950s'. And, in the context of an expectation of ever-rising steel demand, significant further modernisation was soon under way, epitomised by United Steel's SPEAR project at Steel, Peech & Tozer, which 'replaced its old and now uneconomic open-hearth furnaces with electric arcs'. Steel City had a proud history – two centuries of 'the highest degree of metallurgical knowledge and practical skill', to quote a trade magazine – and a technical director at William Jessop & Co would recall a visit to Sheffield in the late 1950s by a Japanese delegation: 'We had a little giggle to ourselves after they had gone, their questions were naive and totally ill-informed.' Elsewhere, the sellers' market of the 1950s meant that the heavy-steel manufacturers were for the most part similarly sanguine, notwithstanding serious overmanning (especially at the Steel Company of Wales's showpiece Port Talbot works) and what Duncan Burn (in his magisterial 1961 account of the steel industry's recent history) called 'the slow advance of steelmaking techniques', notably 'the failure to increase and improve heavy plate production'. The industry was of course already a notorious political football – nationalised in 1950, largely denationalised in the course of the decade, the object of a nakedly political decision by Macmillan in 1958 (new strip mills at Ravenscraig *and* Llanwern), saved from renationalisation by Labour's defeat in 1959 – and Burn evocatively summarised what had become by the end of the 1950s its rather flabby and somewhat defensive underlying mentality:

The immunity to competition [ie, from abroad] which firms and groups of firms derived in varying degrees from the costliness and durability of the plant, the cost of transporting steel, their close contacts with local markets, development of profitable specialities, close links with consumers, including often complete integration in respect of part of their output, contacts through interlocking directorates with other steel companies and with banks and insurance companies, not to mention the strength some companies had through ownership of rights to work cheap home ore deposits, had if anything been increased. Moreover all the major firms still had plants of varying degrees of efficiency, and none had an undivided interest in seeing the most efficient production rise at the expense of the less efficient. Firms with a foot in different regions – it applied to all the firms with home ore based plants – did not, it was plain to see, feel impelled or compelled to concentrate developments where costs were or could be least. There was still no firm which would automatically devote all its resources single-mindedly to the further exploitation of home ore. On the contrary there was probably no firm which would not have thought it almost socially reprehensible to do so.

Overseeing the industry, and futilely trying to keep it out of politics, was the Iron and Steel Board. 'The case for central planning intervention,' judged Burn, 'was clearly strong', but so far the Board's contribution had been 'ineffective'.[12]

'South Wales Will Always Depend On COAL!' was the title of a National Coal Board recruitment pamphlet in around 1959, but the apparent confidence masked a rapidly deteriorating reality across the whole industry. Demand for coal slumped in the late 1950s as cheap oil imports rose sharply. By October 1959, a week after the election, the NCB's *Revised Plan for Coal* envisaged up to 240 pit closures over the next six years, manpower dropping by up to 11 per cent from its current 652,000, and capital expenditure to be focused mainly on the North-Eastern (including Yorkshire), South-Western (including Wales) and East Midlands coalfields. 'The Coal Board certainly does not take a faint-hearted view of the future,' declared the Minister of Power, Richard Wood, in a Commons debate soon afterwards. But William Stones, Labour MP for Consett, spoke on behalf of Durham miners when he related how that morning, on the bus to Newcastle, he had heard one miner say to another, 'I hear that 169 men are to finish at our pit,' to which the other responded, 'Aye, an' if things gan on we'll aal be finished.' The Tory MP Gerald Nabarro had no doubt where the blame lay for the industry's unpopularity, claiming that 'it has had a heritage over the past twelve years [ie, since nationalisation] of supplying much poor-quality material at a high price.' In practice, it was becoming increasingly clear that in the short to medium term a twin pattern lay ahead – contraction on the one hand, modernisation on the other, as a significantly smaller number of miners achieved significantly higher productivity. 'Mechanisation is being planned to a degree undreamed of 300 years ago,' the NCB's recently appointed chairman, the fluent, expansive, undeniably immodest former Labour politician Alf (now Lord) Robens told an interviewer in 1961. 'This year we'll install 400 power-loading machines. The miners, thank God, aren't Luddites: they don't mind machines, provided they get the money.'[13]

The problems arguably ran even deeper in another nationalised industry. 'In general, English trains are slow and unpunctual,' wrote Tony Mayer (a Frenchman who had worked in London for many years) in 1959. 'The stations and most of the rolling stock are in a truly appalling state of dirt and decay. The wooden carriages (sometimes without corridors), the waiting-rooms and the dismal buffets which in winter are ice-cold and smoky, the dining-cars with their chipped crockery, their grimy table-cloths and napkins, combine to make the traveller depressed and bewildered . . .' Soon afterwards, in the context of a threatened unofficial strike in early 1960, John Morgan took the pulse of British Railways – half a million employees, almost 5,000 stations (the densest network in the world), three out of four passenger seats unoccupied – for the *New Statesman*. 'To live a few days with railwaymen is to live in a world of disgruntlement,' he found, and he quoted a guard with 40 years' service: 'The public don't trouble a button whether they are polite to us or not. Before the war they used to think the world of the railwayman and now they don't give a fig.' The demoralisation was even greater in railway engineering plants, reflecting in part the clumsy handling of the transition from steam (the last locomotive was built in 1960) to diesel. In the Gorton district of east Manchester, the two main factories, Gorton Tank and Beyer Peacock, were being respectively closed and run down by the early 1960s, while the decline was equally sharp for the North British Locomotive Co in Springburn, Glasgow, once the second-largest of its type in the world. Certainly, for the railway industry as a whole, patchily attempting to modernise itself, there were few friends at court as losses mounted and the road lobby swept all before it. The transport minister was Ernest Marples, very much a roads man (not least because he owned a road-construction company), and in 1961 he put another unsentimental meritocrat, ICI's Richard Beeching, into the BR chair.[14]

If the railways were a world of their own, even more so were the docks. 'Between the British manufacturer and the foreign buyer stands the primeval jungle of dockland,' a rising young journalist, Peter Jenkins, wrote in early 1961 about the still very busy London docks. 'The tall elegant cranes tower above a thick undergrowth of warehouses, transit sheds and narrow winding road-ways; the natives are perpetually uneasy; predatory beasts are quick to pounce and strikes spread like a forest fire; many strange practices survive to confound the outside world; language is curious.' He went on to list some salient features: only about one-fifth of the workforce hired on a regular basis; 'the mentality of casual work' persisting; 'little personal contact' between the dockers and their employers; the nomadic docker tending to regard his union (usually the T&G) as a 'remote bureaucracy'; the strong influence of unofficial leaders like Jack Dash, the militant and 'dapper' chairman of the Royal Docks Liaison Committee; and 'one out, all out' as 'the unwritten law of dockland'. 1961 proved a year of trouble, including an absurd dispute that spring, the Lower Oliver's Wharf strike. There, the small manufacturer D. Cohen (Strawboards) Ltd had traditionally been permitted to use six of its own people to take monthly delivery by barge of strawboard; militants now objected, claiming that fully registered dock labour had to be used; the result was a widespread stoppage, lasting more than a week and involving some 15,000 men. A year later, in the context of a threatened national dock strike, a TV critic watching *Panorama* understandably found it hard to feel optimistic. 'The dockers, determined their sons should not work in the docks, saw no future for themselves elsewhere,' noted Arthur Calder-Marshall. 'Andrew Crichton for the employers and Frank Cousins for the dockers were at loggerheads because both were concerned with immediate problems ... seemingly unwilling to contemplate the mechanization necessary to decasualize dock labour.'[15]

And of course – long before Elvis Costello's song, long before Robert Wyatt's haunting version – there was shipbuilding: traditionally one of the British glories, but sadly much less so by the start of the 1960s. A decade earlier, the UK's share of world merchant-ship launchings had been 38 per cent; now it was down to 16 per cent. And in terms specifically of ships delivered to the UK-registered fleet, the proportion from foreign shipyards had (as measured by tonnage) grown from zero to 20 per cent. By July 1960, when the Labour MP and broadcaster Woodrow Wyatt visited Tyneside, the order book for the shipbuilding industry stood at less than four million tons, compared with seven million at the end of 1957:

> Inside, the quiet of generations. Outside, the deafening clank of construction. Superficially, in the shipyards of the North, the two seemed unrelated.
>
> How could one suppose that Colonel Eustace Smith, chairman of the dockyard that his family founded in 1756, was building tankers in desperate competition with the Japanese? The serenity of his manner, matched by that of his offices, was more that of a country gentleman discussing the management of his estates than of the conventional tough businessman.
>
> Stiff collars, well-cut dark suits. Charm, courtesy and dignity. Offices proudly lined with models of ships built by the yards – usually going back to sailing vessels. The atmosphere of an unhurried age.

Smith himself, who was then the president of the Shipbuilding Conference, assured Wyatt that 'Japan will soon be in great difficulties.'

That same month, an analysis by Nicholas Faith of the industry's failure 'to expand or to invest' plausibly argued that 'managerial ineptitude' had been 'matched by the failure of the unions to take anything but a narrowly craft and sectional view'. Later in 1960 a report by the Department of Scientific and Industrial Research was highly critical, finding no evidence that the industry was ahead of its major foreign competitors either technically or economically. The Colonel, though, was unperturbed. 'The British shipbuilding industry is as good, if not better, than that of any other country,' he insisted publicly the day after publication. 'Because we are in difficulties it does not mean that the rest of the world is all right.' Soon afterwards, the 'Waterfront' column in the Newcastle-based *Journal* backed him up: 'The report must be worth millions to foreign builders . . . No one in shipbuilding, or repairing, is complacent . . . Tyne, Tees, Wear, and Hartlepools have all produced their biggest ships this year . . . Technically, the north-east is second to none . . .'

Spring 1961 saw a further report on the industry, carried out under Ministry of Transport auspices, and again very critical. Managements at the 50 or so yards were urged to 'make the most strenuous efforts to improve labour relations', while union leaders 'should advise their members of the serious prospects facing the industry, and the need for the maximum possible co-operation between management and work people to achieve the most efficient methods of production'. Was that even-handedness fair enough? One not notably radical historian of the industry, Anthony Burton, makes the point that amid the much-trumpeted modernisation panacea of the early 1960s, above all of plant and if possible of working practices, 'the need to modernise management methods was scarcely considered at all.' By spring 1962, the order book was down to 2.5 million tons (330 ships), compared with 3.1 million tons (430 ships) a year earlier; also in 1962, the sight of the *Nissho Maru*, loading up at Kuwait with over 100,000 tons of crude oil, signalled the ominous arrival of the Japanese super-tanker – at a stroke upping the modernisation ante.[16]

Back in the 1930s, Nevil Shute had written a novel, *Ruined City*, about a merchant banker's attempt to rescue a failing shipyard in the north-east. The Square Mile itself had been part-ruined during the war, but now was on the cusp of starting to return to something like its pre-1914 pre-eminent position as an *international* financial centre. 'London – Centre of the Euro-Dollar Market', the title of a *Times* article by William Clarke in October 1960, was an early public sighting of the term *eurodollar*, while the market itself (with dealings on the telephone rather than face-to-face) owed much of its rapid growth in the early 1960s to the liberal attitude of the Bank of England. There, a youngish merchant banker, Lord (Rowley) Cromer, became Governor in 1961, after the City had followed Oxford's example and made a dead set against the more cerebral Sir Oliver Franks, former high-flying civil servant and, despite his chairmanship of Lloyds Bank, viewed as unsympathetic. Yet for all its openness to the Eurodollar market, the Bank of England remained in many ways a deeply conservative and somewhat introverted institution, characteristics broadly in line with the City as a whole at this time. In May 1962, two of the Bank's senior figures assembled a list of maxims, eloquently revealing of life's certainties as viewed from their Threadneedle Street fortress, a fortress seemingly far removed from the world of Coventry car-makers or Clydeside riveters:

> A central banker needs a sense of smell. Analysis is only theorising but may be encouraged when it confuses critics.
>
> No civil servant understands markets.
>
> Politicians do not sufficiently explain the facts of life to the electorate.
>
> Central bankers should always do what they say and never say what they do.
>
> Wave the big stick if you like, but never use it; it may break in your hand. Better still, try wagging your finger.
>
> Never spit into the wind.
>
> Always lean against the wind.[17]

————

Then as later, in what has inevitably been an intensive, ongoing historical debate about the scope and causes of British relative economic decline, the usual suspects were trotted out and fingered. In July 1961 an *FT* analysis of 'The Productivity Race' – in which Britain since 1953 had fallen behind all her competitors bar Sweden – identified, *inter alia*, the lack of planned targets; government not ensuring that investment was channelled into fast-growing industries; the multiplicity of craft unions, fighting to retain the status quo; complacent management, enjoying after the war 'a protected market at home and a largely "captive" market in many Commonwealth countries'; and – the joint fault of government and industry – a failure to increase the numbers of 'technical and scientific personnel', as evidenced by the current shortage of production engineers. 'What it all comes down to in the end,' concluded the analysis not unpersuasively, 'is that for a whole variety of reasons – institutional, social, political and economic – a psychological climate has been created in this country which is a powerful obstacle to change. This is true of management, the unions and the Government alike.'

One absentee from this particular list was perhaps a surprise. 'Disillusion has been mainly induced by the persistent denigration of the nationalised industries by the Press, by Conservative politicians both inside and outside Parliament, by leading business men, and by organs like the Federation of British Industries and the Institute of Directors,' observed William Robson in his magisterial 1960 survey *Nationalised Industry and Public Ownership*. 'For more than ten years a ceaseless campaign has been waged by the great majority of the daily newspapers to present a continuously unfavourable picture of the nationalised industries.' Of course, irrespective of those industries' actual shortcomings, the longstanding fuzziness about their purpose – economic? social? – did not help. When Robens in 1960 accepted Macmillan's offer to head the National Coal Board, he pointed out how hard it would be ever to make a genuine profit. 'Don't worry, dear boy,' responded Macmillan through drooping eyelids. 'Just blur the edges . . . Just blur the edges.' In fact, the government in 1961 did try to reduce the fuzziness, with a White Paper on *The Financial and Economic Obligations of the Nationalised Industries* setting out five-year targets for financial performance and explicitly acknowledging that 'the industries must have freedom to make upward price adjustments' – an approach typically welcomed by the *Economist* as 'not particularly impressive' but also 'not ill-intentioned'.

Yet arguably, even amid the fuzziness, the performance of the nationalised industries (comprising around one-fifth of the economy) had already been significantly better than its many critics allowed. Despite how 'the institutional arrangements from the very beginning contained inherent contradictions,' and despite, further, how 'those arrangements allowed governments to use the industries as an instrument of real income distribution,' including through cross-subsidy, the economic historians James Foreman-Peck and Robert Millward would claim that 'the underlying productivity growth of the industries compared favourably with private industry in the UK.' Their table shows the annual average percentage growth rates from 1951 to 1964:

	Output	Labour productivity	Total factor productivity
Manufacturing (private sector)	3.2	2.5	1.9
Public enterprise	2.7	3.3	2.4

How then to explain the fact that, taking the 1950s as a whole, the industries' average annual rate of profit was zero? Here, Foreman-Peck and Millward make two points: first, that although coal and rail were loss-makers, the new technology industries (electricity, airways, telecommunications) all earned significant profits; and second, with particular relevance to coal and rail, the industries were highly vulnerable to government intervention in terms of range of products and levels of service, quite apart from price considerations. Or, as the *FT* put it at the time of the White Paper, 'the fact of nationalisation has tended to arouse public expectation that the products and services of these industries should be provided cheaply', even when 'costs and prices elsewhere have been rising'. It was not, the paper hardly needed to add, an expectation likely to change overnight.[18]

What about government? Leaving aside for the moment industrial relations and macro-economic policy, and noting that regional-*cum*-industrial policy was still (with the odd exception) undeveloped, there were perhaps two areas in which by the early 1960s it should have been doing appreciably better. The first concerned the competitiveness of the economy. Admittedly the Restrictive Trade Practices Act of 1956 was a major step in reducing cartelisation, but otherwise, as Geoffrey Owen points out, 'the framework of regulation and [tariff] protection which had been in place since the 1930s was left largely untouched.' That framework included resale price maintenance (RPM), the practice covering most retail activities and defined by its historian as one 'whereby producers would dictate the price at which their goods could be sold by retailers, thereby ensuring that prices were "fixed" across the board'. RPM, declared the male-oriented *FT* in May 1962 as its possible abolition entered the mainstream political agenda at long last, 'tends to raise costs, hold up new methods of retailing and thus denies the consumer the opportunity – which he need not take – of buying cheap'. The other government failing concerned the whole difficult area of education and training. Success had been 'uneven', noted the *Economist* in December 1961, for the nine Colleges of Advanced Technology (CATs) so far set up in the wake of the 1956 White Paper on *Technical Education*, adding that it would be a help if they were given full university status. As for the effectiveness of the 1959 White Paper on *Better Opportunities in Technical Education* – calling for a broadened school curriculum, greater continuity between school and college, and an enhanced awareness of industry's needs – that was hugely blunted by government's unwillingness or inability to bang heads together in the education world and get it to agree on the most suitable provision for 15- to 18-year-olds. 'In my view the lack of urgency in implementing this White Paper,' reflected many years later the mandarin (Sir Antony Part) most intimately involved in its preparation, 'contributed in a significant way to the failure to raise the capability of our boys and girls to a level adequate for our economic needs in an increasingly competitive world.'[19]

Ultimately, though, what really mattered day-to-day were management and labour – and the relations between them.

Challenge to Prosperity on Corrie night, 9 December 1960, focused on the managers. 'Taking part,' noted a preview, 'are the assistant managing director of British Aluminium, who says that the best young men are not those who get to the top, and some young Oxford graduates who after taking jobs in industry left in disgust.' British management had, though, at least one defender. When Woodrow Wyatt had, earlier in the year on *Any Questions?*, castigated it as 'terribly complacent', a fellow-panellist had expressed her 'very strong objections to anyone who suggests that our exporters are complacent'. And Margaret Thatcher went on: 'I happen to be married to an exporter and know exactly how hard the work is to get orders and they're not in the least complacent.'[20]

Recent economic historians have tended to be on Wyatt's side of the argument and to offer largely critical appraisals of the quality of management through the 1950s and into the early 1960s. Cumulatively, their findings amount to a major indictment. Employers and managers had 'little or no interest in improving or transforming undeveloped management control systems towards the Fordist model'– ie, of mass standardised production; generally speaking, 'Americanisation' was viewed 'as a threat to established British production and management systems and markets'; by the mid-1960s, 'very few British firms had adopted the multi-divisional form of organisation' – ie, with the company separated into product divisions; progress towards enhanced management education was at best patchy, with the prominent industrialist Sir Norman Kipping observing in 1961 that 'it has to be proved that the leadership element in the manager is present before it is really worth spending any time on management training'; and, all too symptomatically, within the ranks of management there was a persistent downgrading of the status and power of production managers, compared with what Nick Tiratsoo calls the 'privileged "gin and tonic" specialisms like marketing and accountancy'. Or take the key, nuts-and-bolts question of handling materials, vital to productivity. 'For every commercial and industrial firm having a vigorous and continuously developing handling policy,' observed *Mechanical Handling* in 1959, 'there are a dozen more which have scarcely the haziest notion of the importance of the handling function from the viewpoint of time and cost.' Moreover, despite a big push by the British Productivity Council in the late 1950s, the application of statistical quality control (SQC) techniques seems actually to have been going backwards in the early 1960s.[21]

Further evidence stacks up on the negative side. 'They were very sleepy after 5 o'clock, perhaps because their rooms were well-furnished with drinks cabinets,' Lord (Arnold) Weinstock would recall in the 1990s about companies in the 1950s. 'The big wheels sat in their offices "making policy", lunching at the Savoy, going to trade associations, overseas tours, heaven knows what, but doing little that we would recognise as work. They weren't doing much to drum up business; and they weren't doing much to push ahead in technology.' In November 1961, reporting on the Scottish economy, the Toothill Committee found management there guilty of 'a tendency to over-caution', which meant that 'progress in modernising older Scottish industries has not been as fast as might be wished', and added that the ingrained belief among many industrialists that the best training for management was obtained on the shop floor was 'a dangerously limited attitude'. Two months later, a survey by the Aberdeen Productivity Committee of 252 firms in the district revealed that two-fifths thought that work-study was not applicable to them, and indeed that only three-fifths had bothered to reply. Arguably the most stultifying atmosphere was to be found in the really big companies, often appearing to observers like branches of the civil service. The historian Frank Mort, whose father worked for ICI in Runcorn as a cost accountant, evokes a world of 'exceptional formality', of 'bureaucratic attention to detail' and of 'a general culture of suspicion, which manifested itself through processes of complex monitoring extending from the top to the bottom of the management hierarchy'. Far more numerous, of course, were smaller, family-run firms, where almost invariably conservatism was deeply entrenched. One such was Briar & Peacock. In 1959, at a seminar series at the London School of Economics on 'Problems in Industrial Administration', Mr Briar described how quality control had worked in practice during his career:

> I tasted the golden syrup every day like my uncle before me. And if the flavour was off, 'Why?' During the war we had to change the process because of a shortage of something or other. And my cousin came back from the war and said, 'The flavour has altered. You've altered it!' And we said, 'Yes,' and he said, 'Don't f--- about! Bloody well go back to the original process.' 'It'll cost more.' 'It doesn't matter. Go back to the original recipe.'

'And,' added Briar, 'he was right. Only way to maintain the standard.'[22]

At least one prominent local industrialist missed *Coronation Street*'s launch. Instead, that Friday evening saw H. Hoyle of the Lancashire Footwear Manufacturers' Association speaking at a dinner (as reported by the *Bacup Times*) in honour of 75-year-old John Hollowood, until recently the long-serving leader of the Rossendale Union of Boot, Shoe and Slipper Operatives. Acknowledging that they had had their differences over the years, but also that there had been no major disputes for the last third of a century, Hoyle went on: 'I know of no one who evinces as he does the words of the Scottish poet, Robert Burns. "The rank is but the guinea stamp, the man's the gold for a' that." He has evinced that for the operatives of this trade throughout the forty years he has been working on their behalf.' Five of Hollowood's six sons were now in the slipper industry, and future harmony seemed assured. That was not quite, though, the perspective of *Challenge to Prosperity*, and a week later Christopher Chataway was looking critically at industrial relations, asking, 'Do workers devote too much energy to wage increases and too little to expanding production? Has the gulf between the trade unionist and his leaders affected industrial peace?'

Good questions, but in the early 1960s most managers in British industry were unwilling to get their hands dirty trying to resolve them and other such issues. A highly respected union leader, Sir Thomas Williamson of the General and Municipal Workers, summed up the attitude problem eloquently in a 1960 interview:

> The human element is treated in an astonishingly off-hand way. There are old-fashioned employers who believe the trade unions are just a damned nuisance and avoid any dealings with them for as long as possible. There are firms which tolerate and only just tolerate unions. There are firms which, at the first hearing of a workers' claim, say 'no' automatically. There are those which delay negotiations interminably ... Lack of communications between management and men, about reasons for changes in production methods, the transfer of workers, redundancy, and so on, provide the grounds for trouble. All these and other factors tend, rightly or wrongly, to create bloody-mindedness among the workers. The atmosphere is soured ...

Or, as an American academic, David Granick, found in Glasgow at about the same time, 'One managing director insisted in conversation with me that all management prerogatives were sacred. For example, if anyone from the union came asking to see his balance sheet, he would kick him out of the office.'

Yet it would be seriously misleading to suggest that the *prevailing* industrial-relations climate was adversarial. Full employment, strong demand, semi-captive markets, import penetration still within reasonable bounds, employers often divided among themselves and unable to put on a united front, paternalism anyway continuing to run deep in many corporate DNAs, the TUC a sufficient estate of the realm to be represented on almost a thousand tripartite public committees – unsurprisingly, management tended as often as not to be accommodating rather than confrontational. Sir Halford Reddish of non-unionised Rugby Portland Cement – 'prepared more than any other company chairman,' notes his biographer, to state publicly 'what many preferred to say privately' – undoubtedly wished it otherwise. 'All too often,' Reddish loudly complained in 1960, 'the employer meekly gives in, because he hasn't got the guts to stand up to the threat of the unofficial strike – engineered by the scheming few, acquiesced in by the unthinking many.' He added darkly: 'The blackmailer always comes back. The one who hasn't has yet to be born.'[23]

For a range of reasons – identified by the historian Howard Gospel as full employment, rising prices, greater expectations and a less deferential workforce, as well as 'the growing organisation and assertiveness of shop stewards and the weakness and inability of collective bargaining procedures to cope with the changed circumstances' – the frequency of strikes was undoubtedly greater between the mid-1950s and mid-1960s than it had been during the immediate post-war period. Between 1947 and 1954, the number of disputes beginning in each year was always below 2,000; from 1955 to 1964, it was always above 2,000, with 1957 (2,859) and 1960 (2,832) the two peak years, including 1960 as the first time that non-mining strikes exceeded 1,000. Of those strikes, by the early 1960s some 95 per cent were unofficial, with the average dispute involving some 500 workers and losing some 1,000 working days – ie, of only brief duration. A couple of other statistics add further perspective. Between 1952 and 1961, just one out of every 2,000 working days was lost through strikes; taking the 1950s as a whole, and comparing days lost per thousand workers in the Western industrial countries, the US, Finland, Belgium, Canada, Italy, Australia and France (but not West Germany) had appreciably higher rates than the UK. In short, any *I'm All Right, Jack* notion that Britain was uniquely strike-prone was at this stage a myth.

But what about more broadly? 'In industrial relations we are already out of date,' declared the *News Chronicle* in an economic leader shortly before its demise. 'Almost everywhere there are restrictive practices which make us a laughing stock abroad.' Not least of course in the newspaper industry itself, scrutinised in the early 1960s by a Royal Commission chaired by Lord Shawcross. The commission found, amid abundant evidence of management weakness in the face of the print unions, overmanning of the order of 34 per cent; excessive, even 'grotesque', demarcation; and, moving into Spanish practices territory, a whole host of 'house extras negotiated to meet special conditions', a 'substantial' number of which were 'based on reasons sometimes anachronistic and often fictitious'. Or, from a few years earlier, in another industry, take the *cri de coeur* of J. G. Stephen, of the Clydeside shipbuilders Alexander Stephens & Sons, about heavily demarcated existing practice:

> The clearest example perhaps is that of the Tack Welder who stands and watches a Plater position a bar. When it is in its place the Tack Welder then tacks it and the Plater stands and watches him, whereas the Plater, or his Helper, could perfectly well do the tack welding. If the Platers and the Shipwrights were allowed to do their own tack welding, our firm could dispense with 65 men the next day and probably increase the output as well . . .

That, though, was not a wholly attractive bargain. 'Every worker,' reflected the TUC's Vic Feather in 1959, 'has at least one concern at the back of his mind which is even more important than the size of the pay packet; that is, the regularity of his pay packets, the security of his employment.' Even so, the report of an American study group, doing its fieldwork the following year, suggests a rather more nuanced picture: 'The unions of Great Britain have generally welcomed technological development subject to full consultation about its effects and the maintenance of strict standards of safety. They believe that technological change opens the way to better pay and conditions for their members.' Indeed, the fullest survey of restrictive practices in British industry had already revealed something not altogether dissimilar. This was the National Joint Advisory Council's inquiry, whose 1959 report denied that industry was 'riddled' with restrictive practices, but instead expressed 'some satisfaction' that 'so many industries' were able to state that they were meeting, in their efforts to ensure the efficient use of manpower, 'no real difficulties'. To Robert Carr, Parliamentary Secretary to the Minister of Labour, the conclusion was clear after looking at that inquiry's evidence. Yes, it was 'undeniable' that there were 'difficulties in some industries', yet overall, the fact was that 'over much of industry' the 'two sides' were 'willing to tackle jointly any problems caused by restrictive practices'.[24]

Within trade unionism, by some way the most important development at this time was the rise of the shop steward – perhaps around 150,000 of them by the early 1960s, out of a total union membership of some 9.5 million – and accompanying workplace bargaining. In 1957 the industrial sociologist T. E. Stephenson gave a helpfully sober contextualisation to a phenomenon far from universally welcome:

> In many cases the shop stewards interpret the national agreements at local level, and whenever there is a dispute the shop stewards represent the workers. In some instances the shop stewards go still further and actually negotiate higher rates than those nationally agreed between unions and employers. They have been able to do this in a period of full employment and with a labour shortage in some industries, because the management has wanted to hold on to its labour force and avoid trouble with the stewards who often have considerable influence in a work place. Furthermore it is not only over wages that the shop stewards represent the workers to the local management, but also over the many problems that arise out of local working conditions and habits and customs. Hence the power of many shop stewards is great . . .

'With the depersonalisation of the unions,' he added about the erosion of central authority, 'the leadership's control over the members is more formalised, loyalty is weakened and with it the leaders' power.' Three years later, when Sir Miles Thomas penned a piece on trade unions for *Punch*, the humour came through rather clenched teeth. 'Someone once suggested that shop stewards should wear distinctive uniforms,' noted BOAC's former chairman. 'There is no need for that. Nature has cast them in distinctive moulds that make them recognisable a mile off . . . They are the militant ginger men, frequently a pain in the necks of the higher trades unionists, who prefer a quiet tempo of squabble-free industry to the brouhaha of stompings on the shop floor.' One of those ginger men was a toolmaker in an engineering firm in Glasgow's Govan district. 'I was a shop steward as an apprentice and led the apprentices' strike in '61,' recalled Sir Alex Ferguson half a century later. 'Later on, I became the shop steward of the toolroom when I was only 21. Looking after the workers' interests was why I became a shop steward.'

Significantly, it was not just politicians, industrialists and those at the top of the union hierarchies who demonised shop stewards – viewed as responsible for the proliferation of unofficial strikes – but even some academic experts on industrial relations. 'They think of the agreements negotiated by their unions at national level as no more than jumping-off points to be improved upon whenever possible by their own pressures,' noted Ben Roberts in 1962, regretfully adding that 'it is no longer felt to be morally improper to make such demands and to back them up by actions that are a violation of agreed procedure.' The temptation was to view the shop stewards' movement as a wilful and concerted power grab, possibly with sinister implications, yet the reality was usually more humdrum. 'Familiar as no outside negotiator could be with the maze of bargaining agreements peculiar to his own shop,' a writer on the car industry observed in 1960, 'the stewards have not usurped official power so often as they have been forced willy-nilly to accept responsibilities for which there is often no other immediate authority or substitute.' The historian Steven Tolliday fleshes out the picture in a pioneering study of Coventry's engineering (mainly car) workers and shop-floor bargaining between the 1940s and the 1970s. 'The shop steward system under piecework was fraught with inequity, lack of security, constant haggling and divisiveness,' he comments. 'The results of sectional, fragmented bargaining were only partly satisfactory to stewards. They recognised the bargaining advantages of piecework but were also critical of the system as dog-eat-dog and as vicious in dividing and driving the workers.' Accordingly, 'stewards were generally unable to develop broader strategic goals' – a conclusion notably at odds with some external perceptions over the years.[25]

The unions were undoubtedly in the spotlight. *Punch* during summer 1960 ran a seven-part series on 'State of the Unions', while in 1961 *The Times*'s labour correspondent Eric Wigham sought in a Penguin Special to answer the question *What's Wrong with the Unions?*. Among outsiders, a special status attached to Allan Flanders, co-editor of the 1954 classic *The System of Industrial Relations in Great Britain*, a study subsequently identified as a high-tide moment in the post-war consensus. The principle of industry-wide pay-fixing arrangements seemed then to be set in adamantine centralised stone, prompting Flanders to assert that 'there is not the slightest possibility of the clock being turned back to individual or to works bargaining over wage rates.' Barely half a decade later, things seemed less certain, and in August 1961, Flanders set out for *Socialist Commentary* his vision of 'Trade Unions in the Sixties'. Essentially his argument was that 'the spirit of materialism' had 'submerged the spirit of idealism' and that the unions needed to rediscover what he called their 'social purpose' – above all 'in the workshop, or whatever may be its equivalent, the colliery, the office, the site, the depot', where 'Britain's workers are still in many respects second-class citizens' and 'subjected to treatment which would be considered intolerable in any other walk of life'. Accordingly, over such issues as 'engagement, discipline, dismissal, promotion, training, welfare in many aspects, fair treatment on the job', he envisaged 'a struggle which the trade unions have to lead nationally, even if it is fought locally'.

As it happened, another front was already opening up which would soon engage Flanders deeply. This was the so-called 'Fawley experiment' – the productivity agreements reached in July 1960 between management and unions at the Esso Refinery at Fawley, near Southampton, by which (to quote Flanders from his 1964 Fawley study) 'the company agreed to provide large increases in its employees' rates of pay – of the order of 40 per cent – in return for the unions' consent to certain defined changes in working practices.' Was this the way ahead? The *Sunday Times*'s William Rees-Mogg certainly thought so – declaring in May 1962 that 'something like the Fawley experiment should be tried in the docks, a combined package of higher pay, de-casualisation and mechanisation' – but even by 1965 only a dozen or so 'productivity agreements' had been signed in British industry. This would not have surprised Michael Shanks, who in his 1961 *The Stagnant Society* had called for the movement at last to 'broaden its appeal to the dynamic element in modern society'. But he did so more in hope than expectation, given that the unions 'reflect the inhibitions and the conservatism of their members – particularly of the older, declining section of the working class'.[26]

It was a conservatism classically encouraged by top Conservatives. Many party members and even backbenchers may have hankered after a legislative salvo to curb what they saw as the twin evils of unofficial strikes and the closed shop, but senior figures were thoroughly aware of compelling reasons to leave well alone. The closed shop, they knew, was not only helpful to employers wanting to make collective bargaining stick but also served to increase union membership and thus lessen the internal influence of the left. At the same time, not picking a fight with the unions was entirely consistent with Macmillan's overriding wish to demonstrate that his party had learned the harsh lessons of the inter-war years. Inevitably, though, the temptation to go down the legislative route began to increase once the industrial-relations climate darkened – a temptation that pointed up the perennial Tory philosophical tension between control on the one hand and freedom on the other. A lecture by Edward Heath in March 1960 as Minister of Labour seemed to be moving in the former direction (as he emphasised the dangers of strikes and inflationary wage settlements), but ultimately veered away. 'It would,' he reminded his listeners, 'be unlike us as Conservatives to wish to impose some tidy plan on what has been a natural growth.' Within a year or so, however, such were economic circumstances (earnings increases outstripping price increases and a deteriorating balance of payments) that the possibility of a state-imposed policy of wage restraint was firmly on the agenda.

Undoubtedly the unions got largely negative coverage from the media. 'Suspicion of the press is ingrained and not unjustified,' observed Eric Wigham in his survey. 'There are papers which will seize on anything discreditable to the unions and magnify it out of all proportion to its news value. Some will misrepresent the union attitude and one or two, particularly during disputes, indulge in scurrilous personal attacks which do not spare a union leader's home or family. They do not treat employers in the same way.' Other papers, he added, were more balanced or even positive, but overall 'the weight of numbers is against the unions.' In the cinema, only months after *I'm All Right, Jack*, a key film of the early 1960s was *The Angry Silence*: a powerful drama (written by Bryan Forbes and starring Richard Attenborough) about a factory worker persecuted for not joining a strike. 'His colleagues are shown as being manipulated by skulking professional agitators,' recalled an obituarist of Forbes, 'and to some it seemed more like a political statement than a human story about the crushing of an individual.' The press loved it. 'Brave and important. A film that everyone must see' (*Daily Mail*). 'The clear ring of truth' (*The Times*). 'A story of our times' (*Daily Mirror*). Tom Stoppard, reviewing for Bristol's *Evening World*, joined the chorus: 'I stand on my tip-up seat to cheer . . . A cry from the dock on behalf of every stubborn, proud, infuriating little man who has ever committed the crime of preferring to do his own thinking for himself . . . A shout against the folly of our times.' *The Angry Silence* may or may not have been anti-union, but either way there was surely some justice to Ken Loach's retrospective verdict that 'although it had an arguable point, it was one that the film-makers should have hesitated to use to the disadvantage of working men so long as there were no other British films to espouse the workers' grievances with equal zeal.' What about TV? Coverage there was obviously more measured, including relative even-handedness in the BBC's 1961 sitcom *The Rag Trade*, with the grasping but ineffectual boss (Peter Jones) of a millinery basement sweatshop broadly balanced by the militant shop steward (Miriam Karlin) and her 'Everybody out!' catchphrase.[27]

Always there was the drip-drip of general discourse and background noise about the union 'question' or 'problem' (not least after the Communist-run Electrical Trades Union had in 1961 been found guilty of systematic ballot-rigging) as well as naturally about the 'laziness' of the working man. 'I think I do a good job,' a long-time Austin car worker, Harry Collins, told *TV Times* in April 1962, ahead of the latest television inquiry into Britain's economic future. 'It's darned hard work on the track. It's all very well for the Duke of Edinburgh to tell us to get our fingers out – let him come and work on the track for a few days!'

Gallup charted public attitudes. Back in 1954 – high-tide point – 71 per cent had considered trade unions 'a good thing', but by 1961 the figure was down to 57 per cent. As for the closed shop (applicable to some 35 to 40 per cent of trade unionists), Gallup in 1959 found 22 per cent of respondents defending the principle and 53 per cent disagreeing with it. An insight into working-class attitudes comes from the late 1950s and early 1960s fieldwork of Robert McKenzie and Allan Silver, who found that Conservative and Labour voters alike viewed unions as simultaneously inevitable, indispensable and imperfect – in fact somewhere, as one interviewee put it, between 'necessary' and 'necessary evil'. But among Sheffield's adolescents, it was more a case of an indifferent shrug of the shoulders. 'None were enthusiastic, they simply happened to be members, just as others happened not to be,' noted Michael Carter in his 1962 study of recent school-leavers (mainly working-class). He quoted some who had, as it happened, joined a union:

> If you are on strike they give you money.
>   Someone at the back to help you out.
>   My father made me join.
>   The bosses can't treat you just anyhow.
>   You can go on all machines if you are a member.
>   A man wanted me to fill a form in, so I thought I might as well.

Unsurprisingly, Carter found among these new members 'no understanding of the organisation, even at the branch level' – a lack of knowledge (and indeed interest) that was 'in many cases just another facet of lack of interest in work itself'. A girl and a boy agreed to enlighten him about their general attitude to unions. 'Don't be absurd,' declared the former, laughing. 'What have trade unions to do with life?' The boy agreed. 'You see about it in the papers, but I'm more interested in what United did on Saturday.'[28]

————

It is hard to avoid the cultural dimension. Anthony Crosland in 1961 termed 'typically British' what he convincingly identified as the 'lack of pride in *maximum professional achievement*, especially technical achievement'. For which, he went on, there were many long-term reasons:

> An aristocratic tradition, persisting strongly in the public schools, has bred a cult of the amateur, the gifted dilettante, the rounded and cultured Wykehamist who, patently superior to the drab, despised professional or technician, can turn his hand with marvellous facility to

anything. It has led also to a strong emphasis on 'liberal' as opposed to technical or scientific education. Again, the fact that we were for so long the world's first industrial and imperial power, and emerged relatively unscathed and apparent victors from two World Wars, created a sense that we should always triumph by a natural, effortless superiority, with no need to stoop to the humourless professionalism of Huns or Yanks; and so we stopped thinking in an original, professional way. We were saved, moreover, from detailed and therefore possibly odious comparisons by the existence of the British Channel and the absence of any large-scale wave of immigration. Lastly, a rather rigid class and status system, by inhibiting upward social movement, encouraged an accent on staying-put and family security rather than on personal drive for maximum achievement.

Crosland's analysis chimed with the findings of David Granick. 'Great Britain: The Home of the Amateur' was the title of his chapter on British management, based on 1959–60 comparative fieldwork across Europe, and he noted how 'even in the technical industries, the numbers of engineers and scientists who reach board level are seriously restricted.' The cult of the amateur was certainly alive and well in the club-like City of London, where to a large extent it still remained true that *who* one knew was more important that *what* one knew – and where an explicitly meritocratic stockbroking firm like Phillips & Drew, pioneers in the City of American-style investment analysis, was at best regarded as a regrettable necessity. Or take the world of government, where, broadly speaking, until at least the early 1960s, the generalist was prized above the specialist. Anthony Sampson described the Ministry of Aviation as being run by 'Latin and History scholars', while he found the Treasury's 'contact with any scientific project, from jet fighters to Blue Streaks, embarrassed by the fact that they have no scientists on their staff'. Such indeed had already been the conclusion of the Labour-supporting economist Thomas Balogh, who in a celebrated 1959 essay, 'The Apotheosis of the Dilettante', had given a scathing portrait of a conservative, entrenched and above all economics-averse Treasury. That prejudice was shared by its First Lord. 'Like anything that *Lombard* writes, it is interesting but exaggerated,' minuted Macmillan in 1961 on a ministerial letter enclosing an *FT* column about the failure since 1951 of monetary policy. 'Economists,' he added, 'are now worse than theologians.'[29]

Sampson and Balogh were writing at the time, but the most devastating analysis of the Treasury, applicable to the whole post-war period, was made retrospectively. In his bracingly polemical *The Wasting of the British Economy* (1982), the eminent economic historian Sidney Pollard identified 'the principle of concentrating first and foremost on symbolic figures and quantities, like prices, exchange rates and balances of payment, to the neglect of real quantities, like goods and services produced and traded', as lying at the heart of the failure of the British economy to grow as fast as other comparable economies. It was not, Pollard argued, that a concern with such issues as balance of payments or inflation was in itself wrong; it was rather that the Treasury's 'single-minded obsession' meant that 'real productive power and real goods and services available for consumption' – ie, the objectives that really mattered and could only be attained through higher investment – were 'repeatedly sacrificed for the sake of the symbols'. Ultimately, 'the attitude of the authorities can only be described as one of contempt for production and of the productive sectors of the economy.' Pollard spelled out the consequences:

> As a policy principle it proved to be thoroughly destructive. For it preferred the empty symbol to the living reality, and by utterly confusing ends and means, it lost both. Britain, sacrificing her productive power on the altar of monetary symbols, suffered not only in real welfare, but in the end damaged also the symbols for which it had been sacrificed; whereas the countries that got their priorities right and devoted their efforts to improving the productive base found that their symbols, the value of their currencies and the balance of their payments, also turned out successful and positive.

A specific example he gave of the skewed priorities in action was how the Treasury and other economic policy-makers 'failed to see that the cause of Britain's uncompetitive prices in world markets in the 1950s and 1960s was not that her wages were too high, as official opinion insisted throughout, but her rises in productivity too low'. How much, though, was the 'contempt for production' culturally determined?

Obviously it is easy to construct a picture of Oxbridge-educated, Latin-speaking mandarins finding the world of production essentially alien and outside their comfort zone. But there was also, Pollard suggested, a 'strongly moralistic element in the Treasury predilection for cuts', containing 'an appeal to the bourgeois/Puritan streak in all of us which believes that it is somehow wrong to spend and virtuous to refrain from spending'. This is surely plausible, as quite possibly also is the notion of a distinctively masochistic element in the national psyche more generally. 'The British public,' noted Pollard, 'was willing to suffer rationing and the petty tyrannies of shopkeepers much longer than citizens of other countries, including those who lost the war, for the sake of some moral comfort and perhaps a feeling of security.' Much of course changed in Britain after the 1940s, but an almost atavistic belief that, as Pollard put it, 'abstemiousness equates with good housekeeping and will ultimately bring its own reward' resolutely persisted, on the whole unhelpfully.

In 1960 itself, though, the most immediate macro-economic concern was the stop-go cycle and how to break out of it. Through the 1950s the traffic lights of economic policy had alternated with almost bewildering frequency – or, to apply another motoring metaphor, the economy had constantly oscillated between having its brakes on and off – and the new decade promised more of the same. Indeed, 1960 saw the Bank Rate zig-zagging around (with an inevitable impact on production and investment) amid competing judgements about the inflationary consequences of Macmillan's 1959 pre-election boom. Somewhat envious eyes were beginning to be cast at the French economy, with its impressive growth figures allied to a well-publicised central planning mechanism in the form of the Commissariat Général du Plan, which brought together ministers, civil servants, industrialists and trade unionists in an apparently successful attempt to achieve long-term modernisation. In November 1960, the Federation of British Industries (forerunner of the CBI) gathered at Brighton to discuss 'The Next Five Years'. There, the group addressing economic growth agreed that there was room for 'assessments of possibilities and expectations', which 'should be approached by Government and industry together'; and it called on government and industry to see 'whether it would be possible to agree on an assessment of expectations and intentions which should be before the country for the next five years'.³⁰ The new cry, in other words, was for greater planning, a desire unlikely to be ignored by a PM who, back in the 1930s, had made his intellectual 'Middle Way' reputation by repudiating naked laissez-faire.

There was perhaps one other big-picture element, though it did not often break cover. In essence, it was the question of whether Britain should go on discharging the necessary responsibilities in order still to be considered (at least in its own eyes) a top-table power.³¹ In practice, those responsibilities took two main forms: being one of the world's policemen, whether or not that was affordable; and upholding the prestige of sterling, even if the penalties for the domestic economy were artificially high interest rates and an overvalued exchange rate. It is true of course that in the early 1960s there took place a surprisingly rapid running down of the old British Empire, but the reason for that was primarily political rather than economic. Instead, as far as one can tell, the need to go on sustaining the twin burdens remained largely intact in the policy-making mind. It was almost as if, psychologically speaking, Suez had never happened. And as long as that continued to be the powerful, if seldom articulated, assumption, no national plan or productivity drive or management-education initiative or even trade union reform was likely to make all that much difference.

7

Working, Middle and Kidding Themselves

'Working-class life finds itself on the move towards new middle-class values and middle-class existence,' declared the enterprising, lone-wolf sociologist Ferdynand Zweig in the introduction to his 1961 study of *The Worker in an Affluent Society*. 'The change can only be described as a deep transformation of values, as the development of new ways of thinking and feeling, a new ethos, new aspirations and cravings.' The basis for these assertions, and the meat of the book, were the 672 interviews that he had conducted in 1958–9 with workers at the River Don Works (in Sheffield) of the English Steel Corporation, at the Workington Iron and Steel Co, at Vauxhall Motors (in Luton), at Dunlop (in Erdington, Birmingham) and at the Mullard Radio Valve Co (in Mitcham, Surrey). As usual with Zweig, the detail was remarkable and at times novelistic in its sensibility. 'The Father Image', 'Divorces and Separations', 'Acquisitive Tendencies', 'Home and Work Upsets', 'Pastimes', 'Hobbies and Sidelines', 'The Rewards of Temperance', 'Hedgehog Behaviour' – such were some of his chapter titles before, finally, in 'A New Mode of Life and a New Ethos', he pulled his material together. Specifically, he identified five main new tendencies on the part of the (predominantly male) British worker: increasing 'security-mindedness', including no longer letting tomorrow take care of itself; rising expectations ('he has a good life but wants more of it'); sharpening acquisitive instincts; growing 'family-mindedness and home-centredness', with the worker 'moving away from his mates' and the trade union 'taken for granted'; and, lastly, what Zweig called 'the process of greater individualization', as the worker thought of himself 'not as one of the mass but as an individual, a person'. Accordingly:

The worker wants little things instead of big things, he wants them for himself rather than for society at large, he wants better and wider opportunities for getting along. Old slogans, old loyalties tend to leave him cold. The class struggle interests him less and less. The idea of the working class as an oppressed or an exploited class or the romanticised idea of the working class as foremost in the struggle for progress and social justice, is fading from his mind and is more and more replaced by the idea of the working class as a class well established and well-to-do in its own right. 'Working-class but not poor' is his idea of himself. Class divisions are no longer marked out by hostility and segregation. They are still there, but class feelings are less active and less virulent . . .

'Large sections of the working classes are on the move,' reiterated Zweig in his closing sentences, 'not only to higher standards of living, but also to new standards of values and conduct and new social consciousness. The impact of these changes on social, political and economic life can hardly be foreseen. They are the augury of a new age, a new social horizon which is unfolding before our very eyes.'[1]

———————

Were working-class life and culture really changing fundamentally in the late 1950s and early 1960s? Certainly there is abundant evidence to suggest that something major was afoot, starting with the testimony of the workers themselves as quoted by Zweig:

I bought the car from overtime.
When I went on shifts I bought a car.
Since I had a car I gave up drinking; drinking and driving don't go together.
Since I had a car I gave up gambling; gambling became a mug's game.
The car's to take the family out.
My wife suffers from nerves but she is much better since I got T.V. for her.
T.V. kills the conversation. Nobody talks, we just listen.
It is the greatest hobby killer. Now you don't need to worry how you will spend your time.
A neighbour's conversation is uninteresting compared with T.V.

Keep apart from neighbours, but be friendly.
Mates [ie, at work] are not pals.
We like to forget work as soon as we are outside the gates.
I look after the money all right.
We both save and each of our children has a savings book.
I feel more independent since I got the house.
I am always improving or adding something in the house.
It's like heaven to settle down in one's own house.

In Zweig's five samples, the proportion of homeowners among working-class family men averaged 32 per cent (highest in Luton, lowest in Sheffield), while undoubtedly being a rising trend nationally. And of course, as he argued, so much followed, including domestic acquisitions, life insurance, a cheque book, and an enhanced concern with property values and respectable neighbours. Home ownership, in short, was 'certainly an important element in the new "gospel" of prosperity among the working classes'.

Some familiar staples of the working-class way of life were in palpable or seeming decline. Almost a pub a day closed during 1961, while beer consumption that year was down to twenty-four million barrels, six million fewer than during the war; circulation of the *News of the World* was by 1960 over 1.5 million less than at the paper's peak soon after the war; pawnshops in Bolton (Mass Observation's famous pre-war 'Worktown') were reduced by 1960 to a mere three; greyhound racing's peak annual attendance in the mid-1950s of some 25 million had shrunk by the early 1960s to some 16 million; the average rugby-league crowd declined from above 9,000 in 1950 to below 5,000 ten years later; the historian of the wakes week unhesitatingly pinpoints the end of that phenomenon's golden age 'to within a couple of years either side of 1960'; at the seaside, Morecambe's 1,300 boarding houses in 1956 were down only four years later to 927, while on a day-trip to Southend in 1958 the working-class writer Frank Norman lamented the new sobriety of a place where 'the Cockney mums and dads' of yesteryear used to go 'to have a good old-fashioned booze-up'; and a further lament came from the north-eastern writer Sid Chaplin, who on a Saturday afternoon in September 1960 counted only five cloth caps in Newcastle's Grainger Street – 'the victory', he feared, 'of Subtopia over the good old industrial common sense and the gaiety that often went with it'. No decline was more precipitate, of course, than that of the cinema, with admissions more than halving between 1950 and 1960 as at the same time more than a quarter of cinemas closed. Tellingly, the pace of closures was highest in the north and the Midlands, both predominantly working-class. The worst year was 1960 itself, typified by Derby's two oldest cinemas shutting their doors, while that November it was the same story in London's East End. 'I wouldn't be surprised if I have tears in my eyes,' confessed a former manager, Maurice Cheepen, ahead of the Troxy in Commercial Road closing. 'After all, the old Troxy has been quite a place in its time . . .'[2]

For the people's game, these were key years. 'Football must be given a new look,' urged the *News Chronicle* in February 1960, in the context of Football League attendances having declined from over 40 million a year in the late 1940s to under 30 million by the new decade. Later in 1960 some young Oxford graduates, calling themselves Group 60 and including Dennis Potter and Perry Anderson, investigated soccer's malaise. 'New tastes and habits' as well as 'dissatisfaction with cramped, dirty grounds, defeats abroad, dull games, allegations of bribery and the grey miseries of the British mid-winter' – such, they announced in the *Daily Herald*, were the reasons why 'the pull of football is slackening'. Undeniably there were grounds for complaint. Despite the magnificent North Stand at Sheffield Wednesday's Hillsborough, opened in August 1961, spectator facilities remained generally primitive, not least at Plymouth Argyle. A loyal but irate supporter wrote to the local paper in 1960, challenging the club's chairman 'to try watching Argyle from the "slag heap" at Barn Park end on a wet windy evening with water pouring around his feet through the wet cinders'.

Instead, it was in three other areas that a new football era was under way. One was player behaviour, with a member of the *Any Questions?* audience noting in January 1961 'a great deal of comment recently regarding the manner in which professional footballers are congratulated by their team-mates when scoring a goal' – an issue that prompted the panel's Colin MacInnes to declare how 'charming' he found 'all this kissing'. Another area was crowd behaviour. 1961 saw not only a televised pitch invasion at Sunderland but the pelting of the Leyton Orient goalkeeper at Huddersfield, prompting the local paper there to call on 'the more mature-minded, adult Soccer fan' to 'help the club keep law and order'. It was also about this time that the singing of 'Abide With Me' at the FA Cup Final began to lose its collective – and moving – discipline. The third area, though, was perhaps the most significant. 'Hill's Hour of Triumph' was the *Daily Mirror* headline in January 1961, marking Jimmy Hill's success (as chairman of the Professional Footballers' Association) in persuading the clubs to abandon the £20-a-week maximum wage. Unusually for a union campaign prepared to threaten strike action, Hill and his colleagues had been backed by much of the media, including the pro-market *Economist*. 'The day of the cloth-capped, faithful supporter of the local professional team has passed,' the paper observed without compunction about the dawning winner-takes-all world. And when Fulham's Johnny Haynes became soon afterwards English football's first £100-a-week player, it commented that this made him 'just like any other valuable entertainer'.[3]

The two dominant new factors of everyday life were of course the car (5.5 million in use in 1960, compared to 2.3 million in 1950) and television (in 82 per cent of homes by 1960, compared to 40 per cent in 1955), but in terms of working-class culture there were plenty of others. Two new trends in the early 1960s had an American flavour. 'Thumping with loud, bright, interior-decorated, Tannoy-guided, muzak-placated, electronically-operated life' was Tom Stoppard's impression in 1961 of the Kingswood Odeon (in Bristol) after its conversion from a cinema into a tenpin bowling alley; while on ITV on Saturday afternoons, the transatlantic voice of Kent Walton ('Greetings, grapple fans') signalled a hugely popular viewing slot somehow simultaneously exotic and homespun, with Jackie 'Mr TV' Pallo – gold-spangled boots, candy-striped Y-fronts, peroxided hair tied back with a black velvet ribbon – starting to become the wrestler millions loved to hate. Tastes were changing. Sales of filter-tipped cigarettes increased sixfold between 1955 and 1960; as for alcoholic drinks, not only was Ind Coope heavily promoting Skol lager, but pubs and restaurants were increasingly willing to sell wine by the glass. Almost everywhere, it appeared, were signs of a decisive shift upmarket. The Betting and Gaming Act of 1960 legalised off-course cash betting, leading to a rapid proliferation of high-street betting shops; a new breed of working men's clubs was springing up, described by one observer as 'ornate, chromium-plated with micro-phones and wurlitzers and white-coated waiters and chicken sand-wiches'; the public face of rugby league was now the cheerful commen-tator Eddie Waring, who reflected in 1962 that, since his *Grandstand* debut four years earlier, he had helped to make the game 'respectable', no longer perceived just as 'a working man's game, cloth caps and mufflers and that sort of thing'; and even Butlin's was changing its emphasis, with one camp having by 1959 as its main advertising slogan 'No loudspeakers, no regimentation'.[4]

The most sustained piece of reportage about all this came from the 26-year-old Dennis Potter, not yet a television playwright. *The Changing Forest*, published in spring 1962, anatomised the geographi-cally isolated, heavily working-class Forest of Dean, where he had grown up and which he still visited. There he found 'whole new roads of aerial-topped, flush-doored, nicely painted, flat-windowed build-ings with cars outside them and small pieces of lawn before you come to the front door'; older houses now changed by 'the pastel colour of the wallpaper, the bright paintwork, stripe of "contemporary" wallpa-per, tall flower vase, holding artificial blooms in winter, or the television aerial, the built-on lavatory, with coloured toilet roll, and the concreted path'; in Cinderford, the town's first supermarket (a Co-op), the district's first, belated Woolworth's and 'a new, candy-coloured shop called simply "Do It Yourself"'; in Coleford, two 'juke-box cafés' and an annual carnival becoming 'both more commercial and less spontan-eous'; in his home village of Berry Hill, just outside Coleford, an expanding Hawkins' Stores, 'serving the young families in new council houses up the road, offering Danish blue cheese, telly snacks, striped toothpaste and coloured toilet rolls'; at its pub, The Globe, 'the long tables and split benches put away or chopped up', now replaced by 'little tables with individual chairs, scattered around'; at Berry Hill Working Men's Club, a new 21-inch TV set, walls redecorated with high-gloss paint, and a noisy one-armed bandit; and, across the district as a whole, any number of 'new television and electrical goods shops' and 'new shop-fittings' and 'frozen-food counters' and 'record shops' and 'new garages'.

Yet at the same time, running through Potter's account was also a sense of the old, obdurate Forest, not quite yet out for the count. There were still 'older Foresters' who 'speak with a wide, beautiful splattering of chapel language and use a hundredfold country and coal-mining superstitions and prejudices' – Foresters who 'believe in God, in Britain, in the Forest and in the working class'. And he went on: 'Chapel (you can see one in each village, like a warehouse with tall, thin windows and a heavy door), rugby football, brass band, choir and pub: that's the old Forest, and, some will have it, that's the Forest now. All these things remain . . .' So they did. Even at The Globe, for all the physical changes, the atmosphere was 'much the same', with the talk still 'broad Forest', and strangers still looked at and discussed 'with the same faintly conspiratorial air'. In Berry Hill itself, 'it would still be unthinkable to be a homosexual or an adulterer, and wearing dirty clothes on a Sunday remains a bit suspect'.

Strong continuities existed elsewhere. Melanie Tebbutt's history-cum-memoir of her family in Northampton places that town's great cultural and environmental rupture in the 1970s, arguing that during the quarter-century after the war 'traditional patterns of behaviour, neighbourliness and respectability' continued to shape the experiences of her father Les (a fitter-welder) and his family. Meanwhile in Glasgow's East End, there still persisted almost endemic violence and feuding, to judge by the vivid but plausible recollections of Lulu (born 1948). Sociology's most suggestive contribution came from Peter Willmott, whose study of Dagenham between 1958 and 1961, *The Evolution of a Community*, found that in an almost entirely working-class, thirty-year-old settlement, London's East End had been largely 'reborn', notwithstanding the scarcity of pubs and corner shops. 'Local extended families, which hold such a central place in the older districts, have grown up in almost identical form on the estate, and so have local networks of neighbours – people living in the same street who help each other, mix together and are on easy-going terms.'

The fullest picture we have of continuity by the early 1960s, and indeed beyond, is set in the Black Country. The three predominantly working-class communities of Pensnett, Sedgley and Tipton are the focus for the historian Rosalind Watkiss Singleton, who in a path-breaking study – based largely on oral testimony, but supplemented by a wide range of other sources – shows how, between 1945 and 1970, 'growing affluence impacted only marginally upon the customary social mores.' Several key specific aspects emerge. The three main concepts underpinning day-to-day life were 'neighbourliness, pride and respectability'; there was instinctive suspicion, especially on the part of older people, of both owner-occupation (sometimes called a rope round the neck) and hire-purchase; the exchange of goods and services remained key to many family economies, as did the pawnshop; teenagers living at home seldom felt free to spend their disposable income as they wished; local shops continued to be valued for their credit facilities as well as the convenience of small quantities of non-pre-packaged food; the shift from keeping cash to building society or bank accounts was 'extremely gradual', while traditional types of savings clubs, such as 'diddlum' clubs run by charities, shops or individuals, remained popular; and the role of the Co-op was central, so that 'for affluent and poor alike, the divvy was anticipated with great pleasure.' Altogether, Singleton's study – consciously echoing and amplifying Richard Hoggart's observation about Hunslet in the mid-1950s that 'old habits persist' – takes us into an intensely local, intensely conservative and mutually self-sustaining ecology far, far removed from facile images of the 1960s. Mass Observation's Tom Harrisson, on the basis of 1960 fieldwork in both Bolton and London, concluded that, whatever the physical changes, 'the way you *behave* in the pub – the rounds you stand, the conversations you have, the games you play, the outings you go on, the raffles you join – is very little different from the way your dad and his friends carried on pre-war'; while even in a temple of modernism, Sheffield's brand-new Park Hill estate, a local journalist noted that same year how the living room of 42-year-old Mrs Dot Smith was in 'cosy red tones, red fitted carpet, regency striped curtains, red brocade three-piece suite and red fireside chairs."[5]

Football and holidays add to the picture of entrenched conservatism. 'The club was intensely local,' remembers Ian Jack about Dunfermline Athletic. 'The town's solicitors and owners of small businesses held the shares, and the players met most days for lunch in the City Hotel, where the proprietor was the team dietician. You would see them shopping in the high street and gripping a billiard cue at Joe Maloco's snooker hall or a glass in the East Port Bar. They took the bus. One or two readers among them borrowed books from the library I worked in and stood in the queue to have them stamped.' Elsewhere in Scotland, Ron Yeats combined playing for Dundee United with being a slaughterman, while

Motherwell's Ian St John had a day job at the local steelworks. 'If either of them didn't play well their mates were quick to tell them on the Monday,' note the football historians Andrew Ward and John Williams. 'They inherited a community responsibility.' In the north-west, the Blackburn Rovers pair of Ronnie Clayton and Bryan Douglas were classic local heroes, perceived as close to the supporters, with Clayton at one point combining the England captaincy with running his news-agent's business and going on holiday to Butlin's at Bognor Regis. That year, 1960, he and over two million others stayed at Butlin's or Pontin's holiday camps, with another half a million going to Warner's or smaller holiday camps; the following summer, at the start of August, the *Keighley News and Bingley Chronicle* was merely following time-honoured ritual when it reported that 'the people of Bingley' were taking 'full advantage of the annual holiday fortnight', with Cleethorpes, Skegness, Blackpool and Bridlington the most popular destinations, whether by train or coach. At Brid they found Jimmy Clitheroe starring in *It's a Grand Night* at the Grand Pavilion, a show prompting a heartfelt letter from Marjorie M. Durden. 'What a joy it is to have an entertainment to offer visitors of which we can be proud,' she wrote to the *Bridlington Free Press*. 'Every artiste is a professional, the show is beautifully dressed, and there is a harmony in the team which spills over into the audience.' The package holiday abroad, meanwhile, remained little more than a gleam in the tour operator's eye, certainly as far as the mass working-class market was concerned. Benidorm, explained a travel columnist in the *Blackpool Gazette* in 1961, was 'the name of a place and not a Spanish all-in wrestler'.[6] Change was coming, but as usual with change, some-what slower and somewhat later than often assumed.

The pace of change – and its implications – increasingly preoccupied Sid Chaplin. 'What I tried very hard to capture, in the Newcastle novels, is the strength of family life and street life, here in the town, and I tried to show how that was disappearing, going to waste,' he explained two decades later to Newcastle's evening paper. The novels were *The Day of the Sardine* (1961) and *The Watchers and the Watched* (1962). They not only made Chaplin's national reputation but indeed caught a city and its working-class inhabitants on the very cusp of transformational change. Clearly, whatever the considerable continuities, *something* was happening in early 1960s Britain; in April 1961, the editor of the *TV*

Times sought, on the basis of a national survey by the Institute of Practitioners in Advertising, to depict the 'typical family' watching ITV, by some margin the channel of working-class choice:

> Dad is in his early forties, smokes cigarettes, enjoys a glass of beer and an occasional glass of wine.
>
> He is skilled at his job, there's a good chance he owns a car and it's likely he has bought Mum a washing machine. He doesn't mind paper-hanging or a spot of painting. In fact, he likes do-it-yourself jobs and possibly reckons that doing jobs around the house helps him to put a bit of money away for the family's annual holiday which is, generally, spent away from home.
>
> Mum takes a pride in her appearance, spending more than average on cosmetics.
>
> The family are pet lovers. Their first choice is probably a budgerigar or a canary, with dogs and cats in second and third place.
>
> There are probably one or two children, over the age of five.
>
> It's a picture of comfortable, ordinary, hard-working people. In short, it's a picture of the backbone of Britain.

A modern, reasonably affluent family in a modern, reasonably affluent world. But a couple of months later, while in Manchester to take part in a Granada TV programme, Christopher Isherwood went into a chemist with Stephen Spender. 'He wanted a certain brand of mouthwash,' noted Isherwood. 'And the young lady behind the counter asked, "Is that for cleaning false teeth?" Never, never would you hear that in London, much less Los Angeles.'[7]

———

'The Social Barrier' was one of the chapter titles in Michael Shanks's *The Stagnant Society*, in which he lamented (in 1961) 'the distorting effect of the class system' on industrial relations and productivity. So too the following year Granada's *For Richer for Poorer* documentary series, which started at the workplace, prompting a reviewer to note 'the gulf in standards between the lavatories and canteens of the manual worker and those of the office worker'. And *Punch*'s unashamedly middle-class editor, Bernard Hollowood, went on: 'One set of workers is afforded British Railways and soccer-ground amenities; the other is recognised as coming from clean, comfortable homes. One set is paid by the week and is subject to almost instant dismissal; the other is paid by cheque and gets at least a month's notice. There are marked differences too in arrangements for sick pay and holidays.'

The fault lines between the two main classes continued to run deep. 'The middle classes live very differently from the working classes,' observed the sociologists Colin Rosser and Christopher Harris on the basis of extensive fieldwork in south Wales in the early 1960s:

> Any normally observant person in Swansea will detect without difficulty the continual sorting by social class that takes place in restaurants and cafés in the Town Centre, in the various bars of hotels and pubs (and from one pub to another), in shops of various types, in the membership of clubs and societies, in the audiences at various cultural events (from symphony concerts to bingo), in the crowds at various sporting events, in the holiday crushes on the beaches and bays of Gower (and from one bay to another), in the clothes they wear, in what they have to say and how they say it – and so on throughout the whole fabric of social living. Class is everywhere, pervasive, intangible, recognizable . . .

It was similar elsewhere. In the supposedly inclusive, egalitarian New Towns, the sociologist B. J. Heraud found, largely on the basis of early 1960s information, that 'different neighbourhoods have taken on distinctive class characteristics', while in and around Wetherby in Yorkshire, observes the historian Alan Simmonds about the housing situation by the end of the 1950s, 'the working classes were safely camped on estates such as Hallfields and Deighton Gates, enjoying panoramic views of the newly built by-pass, or tucked out of sight away behind the thatched cottages and greens of villages like Sicklinghall, or the expensively elegant properties of Boston Spa.' Or take the mass media: not only was the press for the most part segmented by content and allegiance along class lines but so in effect was television, with a 1961 survey predictably revealing that only 39 per cent of the professional and highly skilled watched ITV more than BBC, compared to 51 per cent of skilled, 65 per cent of moderately skilled,

67 per cent of semi-skilled and 74 per cent of unskilled. Likewise in sport. Lancashire in 1962 had its worst-ever cricket season under the captaincy of an amateur, J. F. Blackledge, who had no first-class experience, did not bowl and averaged 15.65 with the bat; that same year, English rugby union intensified its vendetta against the working-class code, with the RFU ruling that henceforth 'past or present rugby league players could not be admitted to membership of a rugby union club'; while an unlikely aficionado of motorcycle scrambling, John Berger, had already pointed out how this increasingly popular sport – reliant upon 'the willingness of hundreds of working-class lads throughout the country to save up their money and patiently work in sheds at night maintaining and perfecting their machines' – was virtually ignored by the mainstream press, whereas 'if Pat Smythe has a fall there is a paragraph in every paper'. Overall, whatever the increase in upward social mobility (largely caused by widening white-collar job opportunities), the broad sense remains of two classes largely separate from each other. And never more so than in relation to life's most important decision, with mid-century marriage surveys revealing an overwhelming preference to choose someone of roughly the same socio-economic status.[8]

There was no doubt where, relatively speaking, the wealth lay. Both classes may have aspired to acquire roughly the same consumer durables, but, as Mark Abrams stressed in 1962, 'for most working-class families even the modest contemporary middle-class style of life is still a very long way off.' More generally, after the very richest had taken a significant hit during the 1940s, income inequality across society as a whole seems to have remained broadly constant through the 1950s and early 1960s. 'The redistribution of wealth which took place in post-war Britain was not,' argued the sociologist W. G. Runciman in the mid-1960s after a grainy examination of the evidence, 'as extensive as was believed at the time.' *Some* skilled manual workers may apparently have been doing better by this time than *some* lower-grade non-manual workers, but, noted Runciman, a mixture of hours worked plus fringe benefits plus tax relief plus ownership of assets almost invariably meant that the total comparative picture was still markedly in favour of the middle-class worker, however lowly middle-class.

Moreover, even at the most fundamental level, life-chances were very different. Overall, the Standardised Mortality Ratio (SMR) decreased between the 1930s and the 1960s. Taking 1950–52 as the baseline (SMR = 100), it declined from 134 in the early 1930s to 91 by the early 1960s. People generally, in other words, were living longer. Yet, as this SMR table for males aged under 65 strikingly shows, the gap between the classes was widening, not narrowing:

Period	Social class				
	I	II	III	IV	V
1930–32	90	94	97	102	111
1949–53	86	92	101	104	118
1959–63	76	81	100	103	143

Analysis by the sociologist Barbara Preston in the 1970s found no single factor (occupational, housing or whatever) as being of decisive importance, and she was at pains to emphasise that 'these differences in mortality cannot be dismissed as only affecting the unskilled "problem families".'[9]

But what about the disadvantaged working class itself? How did it see things? How indeed did it see itself? Zweig in his five factories, Willmott in Dagenham, Rosser and Harris in Swansea, Runciman with his 1962 national survey – together they sought to provide answers about the class that still comprised some two-thirds of the population.[10]

Between them they drew a reasonably compatible, coherent picture. Zweig found evidence of diminishing class consciousness, with about 15 per cent of his sample, working-class by occupation, self-identifying themselves as middle-class. 'When speaking about classes,' he observed, 'a man would seem to be thinking primarily about himself, about the individual aspect of the problem, and not about the social situation or the social structure. The other classes were of little interest to him.' Willmott discovered something similar: almost the only residents of solidly working-class Dagenham ('The people here, they're the same as us, and we're the same as them,' said one) who were fussed about snobbish Ilford ('They're all fur coats and no drawers,' said another) were those living nearby. Not that working-class consciousness was notably strong even in

Dagenham, with 13 per cent of the working-class sample calling them-selves middle-class and 33 per cent declining to identify with any social class ('we're ordinary everyday types'). 'There is little proletarian resent-ment about the distribution of wealth,' Runciman reckoned, noting that when manual workers and their wives made comparisons, they 'referred more often to other manual jobs than to non-manual jobs of any kind'. What about the one-third of his sample who, though in theory working-class, identified themselves as middle-class? Were they succumbing to *embourgeoisement*? It was not, he argued, simply a case of newly affluent workers suddenly and wholesale switching classes. He cited one amply self-contradictory respondent: 'The wife of a hospital head porter who described herself as "middle-class" said that she meant by this people "kind of thoughtful, not stuck up and of reasonable income". But she described the working class as "people who do genuine jobs and not money on the fiddle", and gave as her reason for supporting the Labour Party "because they are for the working-class interest". When asked who she meant by "people like yourself", she replied "middle-class – working people".' Accordingly, Runciman went on, 'it would be wrong to infer from this person's description of herself as "middle-class" that she identi-fies herself with the non-manual class in any ideal-typical "bourgeois" way.' But equally, 'it would be wrong to suppose that her self-rating is therefore meaningless.' Perhaps, he speculated, at the core of this type of cross-class self-rating was an identification with a rather more 'priva-tised' way of life than that generally led by the traditional working class.

The most vivid testimony came from Swansea:

We're working-class, I suppose – at least that's where we came from. Perhaps we should say 'middle' now, though I'm no lady. It's very diffi-cult to say what we are. I have started going to the hairdresser's once a week if that means anything. (*29, daughter of a plumber, wife of a quan-tity surveyor, now living in a new house on a private estate*)

We are all working-class in Swansea – it's Sketty you find a different type of people, business people and doctors from the hospital. We don't mix with them of course. The dentist I work for, scrubbing and cleaning in the mornings before the surgery opens, lives over in West Cross and his wife thinks she's Lady Muck – though her father had a milk-round down in the town somewhere. (*55, wife of a bricklayer*)

Swansea has the usual three classes – working, middle and kidding themselves. I'd say we were all working-class here but there's plenty of showing off. If anybody does a bit of decorating or buys something new, they leave the lights on with the curtains open to make sure the neighbours get a good look. And the palaver with the dustbins when they are put out on the pavements for collection on a Tuesday morning is quite a sight – all the best tins, or bits of expensive vegetables or chicken bones or whatever, stuck prominently on the top where the neighbours can see how well-off the family is, or pretends to be. And then every Monday, though nobody admits it of course, we have the Battle of the Washing Lines . . . (*41, male nurse, living in a council house*)

Social class? If you get under £18 a week you are working-class, more than that and you're middle-class. That's all there is to it – it's just a matter of money. (*24, motor mechanic*)

We seem to live differently altogether from our parents – and it causes some trouble at times, I can tell you. We hardly ever speak Welsh now, and Sandra doesn't at all, and I'm not keen for her to learn either. I like to hear her speaking English properly. Some of the little girls down the road (in the private houses off the estate) speak beautifully. I think it makes all the difference if you can speak properly. (*33, daughter of a steelworker, wife of a local government clerk, with a six-year-old daughter*)

It is easy to sympathise with a retired railway shunter. 'There's only two classes – the employers and the employed,' the 69-year-old declared with seeming certainty. 'You can guess which one I belong to. At least that's how it used to be anyway. Nowadays I don't know what to make of it.'[11]

Wages mattered, working conditions mattered, but often so too did status – whether between classes or within the working class (above all the great 'respectability' divide). 'No daughter of mine is getting engaged to a British Railways waiter – get that bloody ring off your finger at once,' exploded the mother of a Fulham teenager, Janet Bull (later Street-Porter), and wife of an electrical engineer; in East Anglia, the Dagenham-born football manager Alf Ramsey had managed to acquire, by assiduously listening to BBC newsreaders, a more classless accent; and in the *Victor* – after transferring in 1960 from another boys' comic, the *Rover* – the ageless working-class athlete Alf Tupper, a welder by trade and known as 'The Tough of the Track', still fought the good fight against the blazered snobbery of officialdom.

Clearly one should not exaggerate: the ITV comedian Arthur Haynes may have been the archetypal belligerent working man (as created by Johnny Speight), but almost half the working-class respondents asked by Gallup in December 1961 whether there was still 'a class struggle in this country' declined to agree with the proposition. Even so, there was something emblematic about an episode the following spring in heavily working-class Salford, after the local paper had printed a letter from a 21-year-old 'playwright-typist', Myra Bassman, castigating the 'simple, insipid folk' around her: 'Speak to the average Salfordian of art, religion, any intellectual pursuit and they stare at you blankly. But speak the magic words, e.g. beer, bingo and "didya watch Ena on t'telly last night?" and they understand.' Letters of protest poured in, including from factory workers, and Bassman's mother was physically assaulted. None of which deterred the palpably middle-class 'Disgusted' from writing in soon afterwards to complain about 'the lack of amenities' in Salford. 'The town abounds in weird and noxious smells from the works and the Docks. Drunkenness is rife, not to mention other social disgraces. "Salt of the earth" my foot. These people deserve the decaying piles of masonry which form their burrow.'[12]

Indeed, it is probably a fair generalisation that often the real edge, even venom, tended to come from the middle class towards the working class rather than the other way round. Take a quartet of recollections. Rupert Christiansen's evocative memoir of growing up in a south London outer suburb describes how there were in effect two Petts Woods – one genteel and impeccably middle-class, the other (literally on the other side of the railway tracks) 'more densely and cheaply built', known as 'the tuppenny side' and 'considered a region where people were "common" and the source and cause of whatever minor frictions and infractions emerged'; near the Manchester Ship Canal, the young Frank Mort (son of an accountant) was told by his parents to stop playing in the street with children whose fathers ('big men in vests and braces, unshaven after getting up in the afternoon, silently drinking mugs of tea') worked on the tugs on the canal; at *Vogue*, recalled David Bailey, the refusal to use working-class models was justified by the invariable refrain, 'Oh no, we can't shoot her, have you heard her speak?'; and across the land, there persisted a distinct middle-class reluctance to give house-room to ITV (seen as council-estate fodder), in the case of W. Stephen Gilbert's family only overcome when he success-fully complained in 1961 that without it he was unable to play his part in school-break analysis of *77 Sunset Strip*.[13]

In sport the middle-class trenches were defended almost as doughtily in cricket as in rugby, with *Wisden*'s editor Norman Preston insistent in 1960 that English cricket 'cannot afford to lose the amateur', whose 'very independence contributes to the welfare of the game and there-fore to the well-being of the professional'. Elsewhere that year, a march along London's Oxford Street by Midland car-workers threatened by redundancy induced an angry response from a well-dressed female shopper ('nostrils flaring, face flushed') on the corner of Bond Street – 'You've had it so good all right! What have you done with all your money?' – while more generally a frequent flashpoint was housing. In the *Brighton Evening Argus* in May 1961, Gertrude Jordan of Hove claimed that 'working-class people, with their subsidised houses, free education, welfare services, new cars and televisions look down on us professional classes, who have to live in top-floor or basement flats for which we pay exorbitant rents, in order to keep them in the luxuries they demand.' A few months later, in a Manchester evening paper, 'Indignant' of Moston expressed her 'utter disgust' about the 'continu-ous moaning and protesting' of Manchester's slum tenants. 'If these people had anything like guts and ambition they could easily have done like hundreds of other families have done – save up a deposit and buy their own houses ... Why don't they give up their cigarettes, beer, perms, and bingo and stand on their own feet instead of whining to be kept in homes by the already overburdened ratepayers of this great city?'

Yet for many in the middle class, life still seemed so blessedly well-ordered that there was little need for resentments. Full employment, job security, hierarchical certainties – such was the unspoken backdrop in 1960 for Peter Bateman's Betjemanesque poem about Sanderstead, a prosperous suburb safely to the south of Croydon and not far from Selsdon:

Up past the Library grind the green buses.
With bowlers, umbrellas, and 'Financial Times'.
Through the dark cutting and out by the Rectory,
To stop by the pond just as six o'clock chimes.

Saturday's rugger match – Lime Meadow Avenue,
Old Mid-Whitgiftians sporting abode:
Striped scarves, duffle coats and rain on the windscreens
Of T.R.3s roaring up Purley Downs Road.

Gables and garages, drives full of Jaguars,
Fanciful flower-beds with sundials and gnomes;
Hundred-foot frontages facing the golf course –
No hawkers or circulars enter these homes.[14]

At the annual conference in 1960 of the Amalgamated Union of
Foundry Workers, the chairman, F. Hollingsworth, spoke bitterly of
how, out of the 2.5 million children in secondary schools, only 32,000
were aged 15 or over, with the rest sent into the world 'half-educated,
half-literate'. 'Such,' he went on, 'is the lot of the workers' children. No
self-respecting middle-class parent would dream of allowing his own
children to leave school at this age.'

Class and education: the two were inextricably linked whether in
terms of aspirations or of outcomes. A longitudinal survey of children
born in Newcastle in spring 1947 found that out of a possible 248 from
the social classes IV and V (the two lowest) who might in theory have
secured a grammar-school place, only six did so; that when the sample
as a whole were asked in 1959 about their preferred age for leaving
school, 20 per cent from social class V wanted to leave before the age of
14, compared to 4.8 per cent from social classes I and II; and that in the
event, only 24 out of 527 did stay at secondary moderns after their 15th
birthday (still the school-leaving age). More generally by the early
1960s, about 17 per cent of 18-year-olds from non-manual homes were
going to university – compared to fewer than 3 per cent from manual
homes.[15] Education was as ever a tangled picture, but the fundamental
fact remained the twin, class-determined apartheid: between the private

schools and the state schools, and, within the state system, between the grammar schools and the secondary moderns.

'Mr Attlee had three Old Etonians in his Cabinet,' observed Harold Macmillan in 1959. 'I have six. Things are twice as good under the Conservatives.' Not just in his party but across large swathes of national life, the privately educated continued into the 1960s to exercise a dominant influence. Over 50 per cent of admirals, generals and air chief marshals; over 60 per cent of physicians and surgeons at London teaching hospitals and on the General Medical Council; over 80 per cent of judges and QCs, of directors of prominent firms and the Bank of England, of Church of England bishops; and, among rugby-union players capped by England between 1956 and 1965, well over half were (as had always been the case since the 1870s) privately educated. Or take the undisputed top two universities: some 72 per cent of the intake elsewhere in 1961 may have been from maintained grammar schools, but at Oxbridge that year the figure was only 30 per cent, with instead 54 per cent coming from public (ie, private) schools and 16 per cent from direct-grant grammar schools (closer to the independent than to the state sector). The prevailing tone and ethos at Oxbridge remained, moreover, essentially public school – to the irritation of Kingsley Amis, who in 1961 left Swansea to go to Cambridge. 'He found the drunken and pretentious foibles of former public schoolboys hard to take,' notes a biographer, 'wistfully recalling the more straightforward excuse-making of Mr Cadwallader: "Sorry, Mr Amis, but I left my essay on King Lear on the bus, see, coming down from Fforestfach".'[16]

There were signs by this time that the whole issue of private education was starting to acquire some traction. A two-part article in *The Times* in September 1961, 'The Public Schools Are Not Static', generated correspondence lasting almost a month, including a memorable contribution from D. M. Wilkinson of York, who had recently left 'a major public school'. Arguing that these schools were essentially snobbish, and quoting as an 'extremely common' attitude what a school friend had said to him about a Cambridge college ('Oh, that's a good College; there are hardly any of those Grammar School types there'), he went on:

The inculcation of snobbery takes place not in the classroom (very much the reverse), but more subtly through the over-intimate and intolerant atmosphere that inevitably prevails among the younger boys. During this incubating period, the worst type of narrow-minded conservatism is rife. The prejudices learned so young die hard, if at all.

In spite of these disadvantages, I am convinced that I have received a better education than I should have at almost any other school. It is indefensible that, because our parents are rich, we should be privileged in such a manner . . .

I see only two alternatives: either the public schools must be greatly changed by the compulsory admission of the poorer classes or (reluctantly I admit it) they must be abolished altogether.

E. Liddall Armitage of Blenheim Crescent, W11 may or may not have agreed. 'The real reason,' he had asserted earlier that year in the *New Statesman*, 'why so many parents wish their offspring to go to public schools is because children who attend the ordinary state schools pick up a foul vocabulary and indecent behaviour.' To this, at least one state-educated reader took 'strong exception', prompting a finely calibrated response from Armitage: 'Personally I should like to see all the so-called Public schools taken over by the state, though I should like to see their historical associations remembered and old customs continued as far as practicable. I am only of middle-class origin, but in a long life I have noticed that very often people who seem of outstanding character were educated at Winchester. You can usually trust a Wykehamist.'

What about Labour? Ahead of the 1959 election, the party had reassuringly stated that 'no scheme for "taking over" or "democratising" the public schools shows sufficient merits to justify the large diversion of public money that would be involved'; but in summer 1961 its policy statement *Signposts for the Sixties* reflected an apparently significant shift, advocating 'integration' of the two systems – albeit integration to be achieved by what one of Hugh Gaitskell's biographers would describe as 'a rather shadowy educational trust'. As it happened, the House of Commons not long before had witnessed that rarest of things: a debate on the question of private education. Predictably, Labour's most fluent, articulate speaker was the privately educated Anthony Crosland. Although critical of the public schools on cultural grounds

– 'the emphasis on character and manners rather than brains; on the all-rounder and the amateur rather than the professional' – he stressed that such was the resources gap that 'I have no doubt that, educationally, the average public school is superior to the average maintained grammar school,' that indeed 'it simply teaches boys better, and that is that.' Of course, he went on, the overwhelming fact remained that 'a boy can get into a public school only if his parents are wealthy' – a 'painful denial of equal opportunity'. Who should those schools be educating instead? The brightest and the best among those children whose parents could not afford to send them there? Not in Crosland's eyes:

> I am utterly against a system of elite secondary education based on intellectual ability. I am completely against being governed by old Etonians and old Wykehamists because they are the most intellectual people in the country. I should prefer to be governed by hereditary old Wykehamists and old Etonians rather than those chosen for their brains . . . I want the public schools to be filled by a mixture and not by just the richest or just the cleverest children. That, in my opinion, must be one of the cardinal principles in selecting, and the selection should not be based on the grounds of ability to pass examinations.

Near the end, calling for up to 75 per cent of places at private schools to be allocated on a publicly subsidised basis, Crosland claimed that 'the tide of public opinion' was flowing in the direction of much greater integration between the two systems. But perhaps the most telling observation came at the start of his speech, as he confessed to 'a slight feeling of shame on behalf of my party at the fact that our benches are so nearly empty'.

Intriguingly, the debate had been initiated by a young Tory back-bencher. What public schools needed to do, asserted the Charterhouse-educated James Prior, was to broaden their basis of entry in order to guard against becoming 'irrelevant to the conditions of modern life at a time when the nation as a whole is drawing closer together'. But, given that there were some 55,000 places at public schools, his proposed scale of change was hardly huge, beginning with 500 state-subsidised places and 'rising up to 10 per cent of all places'. The debate ended with the education minister, Sir David Eccles. 'The only policy which is wise and just in our generation is to bring the two educational systems closer together,' he entirely agreed – though as a matter of strategy he explicitly *disagreed* with those who felt that 'if the Conservatives nationalised a good slice of Eton, then the Socialists who long to nationalise the whole of the school would be placated and abandon their attack.' Accordingly, he ruled out using government money 'to subsidise the transfer of boys from one system to the other', and instead urged the two systems 'to live alongside and to learn from each other'. Something, though, was apparently shifting. Later that year, Eccles strongly urged – though without any legislative stick – all children from five to eleven to be sent to state schools, prompting a classic Giles cartoon showing despondent top-hatted boys being transported to the guillotine on a tumbrel amidst pitchfork-waving working-class scamps.

The public schools themselves were divided. After observing that 'the time has come when people should think seriously about these schools and the way in which they fit into the social pattern,' Eton's head, Robert Birley, publicly proposed in April 1961 that 10 per cent of places should go to children from working-class homes, adding that at present 'we have too many boys from the same background.' That autumn, in the volley of *Times* correspondence, John Wilson of King's School, Canterbury declared that on finding a means of 'extending over the whole nation' the 'privilege' of a public-school education depended 'not only our educational future as a nation, but our social and moral future as well'. Yet when at about the same time the Headmasters' Conference considered Birley's suggestion that a national scheme be introduced for subsidising poorer boys at public schools, this was rejected. Instead, reported *The Times*, the heads 'reaffirmed belief in the value of independent schools'.[17]

For most people, of course, all this was a debate taking place on another planet, and the far more relevant divide was that within the state secondary system. There, the writ of social class continued to run wide and deep. The Nuffield Mobility Study of the early 1970s would find that boys born between 1943 and 1952 – ie, starting their secondary education between 1954 and 1963 – had a 22-per-cent chance of attending a selective (ie, grammar) school if they were from a working-class background and a 66-per-cent chance if they came from a professional or managerial background. Strikingly, reflecting the post-war growth of the 'service' class of professionals and managers, that 22-per-cent working-class chance was 5 per cent *less* than it had been for the cohort entering secondary schools between 1944 and 1953, in retro-spect the golden decade after the 1944 Education Act had opened up the grammars.[18] Working-class opportunities via education were, in short, narrowing by the early 1960s rather than expanding.

The annual focus – and defining moment in many lives – remained the 11-plus. 'It is all a matter of intelligent ability,' insisted Miss D. M. Hatch, headmistress of Derby High School, at the Junior School's speech day in July 1961, warning the children that they needed to be ready to 'take the knocks'. The realities were spelled out the following year by a primary teacher in a predominantly middle-class area. 'The fight for a grammar school place is a hot one,' s/he explained to the *New Statesman*, given the prevailing middle-class dread of 'that acad-emy for louts and layabouts, the secondary modern school'. Unsurprisingly, the local reputation of the primary school and its head was 'geared to shovelling into the grammar school every single remotely possible candidate'. Accordingly, 'an infant on his first day has hardly taken his coat off when he's handed a *Janet and John* Reading Book and bundled straight into the mysteries of tens, units, and the technique of learning to write on lined paper'; the end of the first term saw streaming into 'A' and 'B' classes; and, for a middle-class child in 'B', the inevit-able parental resort was to coaching – though 'it won't be called coach-ing, it'll be called "a bit of extra help".' Then came the day of the exam. 'I took one look at the paper and I just froze,' recalled Philip Gould, son of a primary-school headmaster near Woking. 'I went home to lunch, to be greeted by my parents – my mother in tears, my father ashen – telling me I had failed already.' For most, including Stephen Dixon, there followed the wait for the letter:

As the expected time drew nigh I raced out of bed and looked over the banister down the stairs to the mat behind the front door. Nothing! I walked the mile to school and asked a couple of likely exam-passers, 'Heard anything yet?' When they shook their heads my mood lifted for the rest of the day. And so it went on, probably for only a few days but it seemed an age – anticipation, despair, trepidation, relief – all for a boy who, being a July baby, hadn't even reached his eleventh birthday. Then

one morning, I looked down and there lay a small, brown envelope.
Euphoria! I still [in 2013] have that brown envelope and its typewritten
letter from the Grammar School headmaster, dated 6th June 1961 and
beginning, 'I rejoice with you that your son has been successful . . .'

'There was,' adds Dixon, 'rejoicing in seven households that morning
(six boys, one girl) as the class of 4A, Throston Junior (Mixed)
Hartlepool, learned their fates. We seven were to go to the Henry Smith
Grammar School on the Hartlepool Headland, separated by a few
hundred yards of Town Moor from the receptacle for all those who
didn't make it – Galleys Field Secondary Modern.' There was a nice
twist: 'Whilst six of us followed various anonymous paths in life, some
involving university, the one who gained the most celebrity was the boy
who ignored the grammar school headmaster's advice to "stop kicking
a ball around and concentrate on your studies" – John McGovern, who
later lifted the European Cup as captain of Nottingham Forest in 1979.'
That, though, was the rule-proving exception, and Dixon himself
reflects how in 1960s Hartlepool – a working-class town with the shipyards dying and the pits up the coast in decline – 'passing for the
Grammar School and the real possibility of a university education was
a ticket out to the rest of the world, an opportunity to escape the
poverty and living conditions which many of our parents had had to
endure.'[19]

The problem of course was that not all boats lifted equally. As had
been the case since the mid-1950s, there was an increasingly sharp
debate about the respective merits of grammars (approximately 1,200 of
them by 1961), secondary moderns (at least 3,800) and comprehensives
(only about 140 fully operational). 'Who in heaven's name wants "an
egalitarian educational system" anyway?' asked R. R. Pedley, headmaster of Chislehurst and Sidcup Grammar School for Boys, in response
to a pro-comp Listener article in 1960 by Michael Young. 'The electorate doesn't.' That same year, the educationalist Frances Stevens
published her defence of The Living Tradition – ie, the grammar school,
which for all its 'petty snobbery and priggishness' was 'at its best a
place of civilised relaxation as well as hard work, and an unrivalled
solvent of social prejudices and preparation for democratic living'.
Moreover, 'if selective maintained schools ceased to exist,' Stevens

warned, the probability was that 'even more parents than at present would make desperate efforts to send their children to public schools.'

From the left itself (with anti-selection, pro-comprehensive already entrenched as Labour policy), Anthony Crosland as usual had his take. Interestingly, his problem was less with the 11-plus exam itself – the strikingly different class outcomes, he wrote in 1961, 'accurately reflect the class distribution of measured intelligence at 11' – than with what happened at grammar school, where 'performance, length of school life, and academic promise at the time of leaving all deteriorate as one goes down the social scale.' The working-class experience at grammars was also the subject of Brian Jackson and Dennis Marsden's seminal Huddersfield-based study *Education and the Working Class*, published in February 1962 to considerable acclaim and attention. The *TLS* reviewer found 'deeply disturbing' the accumulated evidence of 'a mass of human suffering' caused through 'individual, familial and social strains and tensions'; for Raymond Williams, the book was further evidence that equality of educational opportunity remained an 'ill-founded' chimera; and David Marquand's perspective on this 'profoundly moving' book was that it revealed the grammars, with their honours boards, prefects and gowns, as transmitting 'a peculiarly hierarchic form of middle-class culture, in a rigidly dominative way', in effect aping the upper class. Jackson and Marsden themselves, in their closing pages, acknowledged their own 'large debt to grammar school education', but at the same time expressed the hope that 'our voice is the voice of the last grammar school generations'. That pointed in only one direction: 'We have come to that place where we must firmly accept the life of the majority and where we must be bold and flexible in developing the new forms – the "open" school which belongs to the neighbourhood, the "open" university [the term perhaps coined here] which involves itself in local life rather than dominates or defies it from behind college or red-brick walls. The first practical step is to abandon selection at 11, and accept the comprehensive principle.'[20]

It was a principle being wrestled with locally as well as nationally. In London by 1961, up to 60 schools were comprehensive, often viewed by critics as excessively large in size; in Bristol, the local Labour Party promised ahead of elections in 1962 to upgrade secondary moderns into comprehensives, but did nothing to dispel the illusion that those new schools could peacefully co-exist with grammar schools; at Ashby-de-la-Zouch in Leicestershire, the governors of the local boys' grammar protested in 1960 that 'to agree to the substitution of a scheme which is as yet unproven' was 'a complete abdication of responsibility'. In local practice, even if there was theoretical acceptance of the comprehensive principle, progress towards authentic comprehensivisation tended to be patchy and confusing. Coventry may have been one of the pioneer cities but in the 1960s, notes its educational historian, it 'still operated a selection examination at eleven, provided places at the Direct Grant schools for boys, and maintained two grammar schools for girls as well as allocating selected places within the comprehensive schools'. The issue itself, moreover, remained very alive in the public mind at the start of the decade, with a petition signed by 4,340 Coventrians demanding the retention of a mixed system of secondary education. In the city council's ensuing debate in April 1960, conciliatory words came from Labour's Alderman Callow, chair of the Education Committee: 'Our aim is to provide grammar schools for all, for make no mistake about it, our comprehensive schools have as much claim to be called grammar schools as any other institutions. Every child who goes to a comprehensive school carries a grammar school label with him.'

Over and above the question of structures, how realistic anyway was it to view education as the silver bullet for enhanced social mobility? Its importance was obvious to what was becoming an increasingly technocratic middle class, but what about the much more numerous working class? Ray Pahl's study in about 1962 of three commuter villages in Hertfordshire found the starkest of contrasts: 82 per cent of middle-class parents wanting their children to stay in full-time education until 18 or over, compared to 15 per cent of working-class parents. That same year, a reviewer of John Barron Mays's *Education and the Urban Child*, based on inner-city Liverpool, was struck by how, in terms of ability, 'quite a large number' of 'slum children' *could* take the 11-plus, but 'the trouble is that their parents are apathetic about education, they often prevent their children from sitting the examination at all because they want them to leave [school] as early as possible, and they provide a background which is not conducive to study.' The children, in turn, were 'not much bothered either'. Perhaps not everywhere was like that. Martin Johnes in his history of post-war Wales argues that 'despite the fact that education and university degrees were unlikely to solve the problems of an industrial town, out of a mix of idealism, pragmatism and snobbery, they were widely esteemed in all Wales' – but the probability is that working-class indifference was the overwhelming pattern.

The voices of the children themselves come through in Peter Willmott's study of adolescent boys in Bethnal Green, based on interviews done between 1959 and 1964. 'I didn't give it a thought,' said one secondary-modern boy about what had happened at 11. 'From my junior school you usually went on to the secondary modern around the corner, and that was that.' To which his friend chipped in: 'The 11-plus – the school never put me in for it. I didn't really know about it.' Yet not all the teenage boys were quite so retrospectively resigned to their fate. Willmott also recorded a suggestive – if ultimately futile – dialogue between three others at a secondary modern:

Jimmy: None of us went to those high schools, grammar schools, whatever you call them.
Alan: When you're in the junior school you're supposed to be able to choose out of three sorts of schools. But you can't really.
Ron: No, you can only go to crap schools.
Jimmy: They reckon you ain't got the brains for it, see.
Alan: They judge you at primary school. If you're no good at primary school they say, 'Right, you'll never be any good.' They don't give you a chance.[21]

As the working class seemingly inexorably in the late 1950s and early 1960s moved ever further towards the centre of the cultural frame – via sociology, literature, cinema, television and much else – so questions of class and culture became of increasingly paramount concern to the intelligentsia and indeed 'activators' as a whole – although not, of course, to all of them. 'Dewsbury, Batley, Birstall, Heckmondwike, Cleckheaton are all one – large textile mills huddling close together, workers' housing and little else,' observed in 1959 Nikolaus Pevsner, whose *The Buildings of England* barely managed to notice a football ground. In the middle of 1960, the as yet unpublished novelist John

Fowles – public school and Oxford – was engaging more fruitfully. 'All raw, bruised, harsh, ugly,' he recorded after reading David Storey's *This Sporting Life*. 'Absolutely devoid of beauty of feeling, mind and scene ... yet the whole has the paradoxical beauty of a Lowry painting.' Fowles then moved on to Alan Sillitoe's *Saturday Night and Sunday Morning*, provoking more general thoughts:

> I enjoyed reading this, though I had qualms. How true is Arthur Seaton of his class? No means of telling – the externals seem authentic, not the ideas (or lack of them?)? The violence and the hatred, the sheer brutishness, seem suspect – the pursuit of them too constant. All these beer-and-gut novels – Storey, Braine, Sillitoe – force the question – à quoi bon? They are sociological in intention, they criticise society (though each writer has the same love-hate for his hero), they are tacitly in defence of the 'good' working-class qualities; yet they all have the same inverted romanticism and sentimentality.

Sillitoe by the autumn of that year was undoubtedly the leader of the pack, with both film and best-selling paperback, the latter receiving a classically dusty and mandarin *TLS* review. 'Does Mr Sillitoe,' it asked, 'represent a significant new departure, the true voice of proletarian feeling coming at last after so many disgruntled arts-graduates fakes, or is it going to seem incredible in a few years' time that intelligent adults were ever persuaded to take his saga of beer, bed and brawls at all seriously?' Although conceding that Sillitoe's 'squalid story' included 'many good touches', the answer was essentially negative: 'His hero has the synthetic stamina of a comic-strip rather than real vitality or even plausibility. And does it not now seem that there is something altogether too calculated about his outbursts against authority in every shape or the complacent cynicism of the book's closing pages?' In sum: 'The fuss has not been altogether about nothing; but it seems a pity, not least for the author's sake, that uneven promise has been taken for solid achievement.'[22]

Cultural debate, often with an explicit or implicit class element, was ubiquitous that *Lady Chatterley* autumn. While a government-appointed committee under the chairmanship of the Lancashire glass-maker Sir Harry Pilkington began its job of assessing the quality of

British broadcasting and deciding who should operate a future third television channel, the National Union of Teachers sponsored a well-attended conference at Church Hall in Westminster on 'Popular Culture and Personal Responsibility' – or, more wordily, 'the impact of the media of mass communications on present-day moral and cultural standards'. Inevitably there was a strong focus on television, while Eric Hobsbawm (in relation to music) argued that 'the mass-media do debase the popular tradition.' But the most striking contributions had to do with the popular press. The spotlight fell on Cecil King, imperious chairman of the Mirror Newspaper Group, whose *Daily Mirror* was read each morning by around 40 per cent of the population. 'The trouble is,' he explained, 'the critics imagine the great British public is as educated as themselves and their friends, and that we ought to start where they are and raise the standard from there up. In point of fact it is only the people who conduct newspapers and similar organisations who have any idea quite how indifferent, quite how stupid, quite how uninterested in education of any kind the great bulk of the British public are.' After he had added that 'we insert in our paper as much education, uplift and information as we think the public will read, perhaps a little more,' a particularly trenchant attack on the *Mirror* came from the representative of the National Assembly of Women. 'The thing that shocks me is the way the writers talk down to the people as though they were readers of no intelligence,' declared Mrs Beatrice King. 'I have a particular phobia against Marjorie Proops who deals with quite important points like clothing and marriage and who should hold the purse strings and so on. The way she presents them is simply degrading. I think that applies to nearly the whole paper.' To which her namesake riposted, 'If you think the *Daily Mirror* writes down to its readers, you must think all our readers are extremely well-educated, high-brow people.' He signed off by noting that 'in the commercial world it does not matter whether you are selling a newspaper or a breakfast food, if you chase away customers you will be out of business.'

At one point the *Mirror*'s head honcho loftily referred to 'Mr Hoggart' as 'whoever he may be', but in reality there would have been few in the hall unaware of *The Uses of Literacy* and its author. Indeed, the fact of the conference itself directly reflected the huge influence already exercised by that 1957 book, and appropriately the delegates had circulated to them in advance a paper by Richard Hoggart on 'The quality of cultural life in mass society'. The other key recent book, second only to *Uses* in its sway, was *Culture and Society* (1958) by Raymond Williams, who at the conference spoke on 'The growth of communications in modern society' and was instantly commissioned to write a Penguin Special on the subject. Hoggart and Williams: not only were they the two intellectuals who (as Dick Taverne put it in a 1961 essay on the William Morris tradition) 'helped to make socialists direct their gaze once more at all the many varied aspects of our society that mould our attitudes and have a very direct bearing on politics'; they were also, crucially, two *working-class* intellectuals, who could apparently explain their class to the rest of the intelligentsia and mediate an often difficult, mutually uncomprehending relationship.

Uses, Hoggart's compelling evocation of working-class Hunslet, gave him abiding fame. 'Hoggartsville is by now familiar to us all,' claimed the young sociologist Hannah Gavron in May 1962. 'It is a world brimming over with extended family life, warmth and neighbourliness, and in this era of affluence, status seeking and acquisitiveness, it has come to be considered an oasis of calm if not quiet.' The problem was, she went on with particular reference to the recently published Jackson and Marsden study, that 'the deification of Hoggartsville is usually accompanied by arguments designed to show that for an individual to move from the working class to the middle class is for him to fall from grace.' Was it in fact possible, she wondered, to develop an educational system that embraced working-class culture and thereby enabled working-class children to be well educated but stay in Hoggartsville? Gavron was highly doubtful: 'The authors and their supporters feel that working-class culture is destroyed by middle-class values. I think this involves a romantic view of the working class (after all, no one, not even Hoggart, has ever really told us precisely what working-class culture really is), and is also based on a deliberate misrepresentation of middle-class values.' That same spring the unrepentant Hoggart himself was in Bradford, to give the keynote address at a conference on public culture being held to coincide with the city's ten-day Delius Festival. Sparking some local ill feeling, he likened the festival to pulling a cultural 'Christmas cracker' – all very fine, but only tangentially connecting with the lives and concerns of ordinary (ie, working-class) Bradfordians.[23]

Uses remained a stand-alone text, but *The Long Revolution*, Raymond Williams's 'continuation' of *Culture and Society*, was published in March 1961. Williams in his introduction made clear that he had in mind not only the ongoing 'democratic' and 'industrial' revolutions but just as much 'a cultural revolution', which he encapsulated as 'the aspiration to extend the active process of learning, with the skills of literacy and other advanced communication, to all people rather than to limited groups'. A series of discrete chapters, often with a historical dimension, put flesh on the bones, including a particularly notable one on the growth of the popular press, with Williams at pains to demolish the elitist conventional wisdom that 'with the entry of the masses on to the cultural scene [following the Education Act of 1870], the press became, in large part, trivial and degraded, where before, serving an educated minority, it had been responsible and serious.' Instead, he sought to demonstrate, what happened in the late nineteenth and early twentieth centuries – the 'Northcliffe Revolution' – was 'less an inno-vation in actual journalism than a radical change in the economic basis of newspapers, tied to the new kind of advertising'.

The book's final, lengthy chapter was on 'Britain in the 1960s', essentially an intricate disputation with another piece of conventional wisdom, namely that Britain entering the new decade was 'a country with a fairly obvious future: industrially advanced, securely demo-cratic, and with a steadily rising general level of education and culture'. Yet, claimed Williams, 'in deeper ways, that have perhaps not yet been articulated, this idea of a good society naturally unfolding itself may be exceptionally misleading.' His analysis of course included class, which he saw as increasingly based on money rather than birth and also increasingly corrosive: 'It is less the injustice of the British class system than its stupidity that really strikes one. People like to be respected, but this natural desire is now principally achieved by a system which defines respect in terms of despising someone else, and then in turn being inevitably despised.' As for the cultural state of play, Williams argued that 'the condition of cultural growth must be that varying elements are at least equally available, and that new and unfamiliar things must be offered steadily over a long period, if they are to have a reasonable chance of acceptance.' He additionally argued that, in a world where 'more is spent on advertising a new soap, and in printing a jingle attached to it, than on supporting an orchestra or a picture gallery', the sad truth was that 'policies of this degree of responsibility seem impossible in our present cultural organisation'. Might it be possible to organise culture on a different, non-capitalist basis? Williams believed it might be, suggesting various ways of applying 'public resources' to reduce the dependence of 'cultural producers' on 'dominant but essentially functionless financial groups'. He ended with a call not to allow 'the long revolution' – ultimately the evolution of a common, democratic, non-hierarchical culture – to be stalled by temporary setbacks. 'The nature of the process indicates a perhaps unusual revolutionary activity: open discussion, extending relationships, the practical shaping of institutions. But it indicates also a necessary strength: against arbitrary power whether of arms or of money, against all conscious confusion and weakening of this long and difficult human effort, and for and with the people who in many different ways are keeping the revolution going.'

The response was mixed, with Richard Crossman in a splash review in the *Guardian* the principal cheerleader. 'It is the book I have been waiting for since 1945,' he declared. 'Reading *The Long Revolution* I had the feeling that I was in at the birth, anxiously watching what was once an embryo now suddenly emerging, messily but triumphantly, as a new-born babe.' It was, in short, the first book 'to break through the thought barrier into a new epoch of socialist ideas'. Predictably, the main doubts came from the non-socialist intelligentsia. The *TLS* reviewer took strong exception to the style and tone ('maddening platitudes . . . over-solemn and frankly partisan pronouncements . . . utterly humourless textbook language'), while a supporting letter from Arthur Calder-Marshall grouped the writings of Williams and Hoggart as 'not works of scholarship but autobiographies of cultural displacement, disguised as objective studies'. P. N. Furbank in the *Listener*, after noting that Williams 'never seems in touch with English society at all' and 'is only seeing what he wants to see', called 'absurd' the notion that 'a working-class boy can adopt high culture without going through a radical transformation, without making himself in many respects a middle-class person'; while in *Encounter*, the take-few-prisoners

American critic Dwight Macdonald dismissed Williams as 'a preacher rather than a thinker, one more interested in exhorting than in analysing', least of all 'the awkward question why the masses prefer adulteration to the real thing, why the vast majority of the British people read the *News of the World* instead of the *Observer* and go to see *Carry On Nurse* instead of *L'Avventura*' – a question, according to Macdonald, that went beyond class, given that 'most people, of whatever education or social position, don't care very much about culture.' 'The fact is,' recalled Williams himself almost two decades later, 'that it was perceived as a much more dangerous book' – ie, than *Culture and Society*. 'Just at that time I came back to Cambridge. The spirit of the experience was like '39–'41 once again: there was a sense of really hard and bitter conflict.' Williams was indeed in 1961 returning to Cambridge (where he had been an undergraduate), as a lecturer in English; even before he took up his position, an *ad hominem* review in the *Cambridge Review* by one of Cambridge's Tory historians, Maurice Cowling, identified Williams as one of those 'English radicals, lapsed Stalinists, academic socialists and intellectual Trotskyites' whose true institutional home resided in 'the extra-mural boards, the community centres, and certain Northern universities'.[24]

The following spring, Williams's Penguin Special, *Communications*, came out. A pioneer text in media studies, and for the most part a careful exploration of the content of newspapers, women's magazines, advertising and television programmes (albeit he did not yet have a set himself), *Communications* reiterated his proposals for less paternalistic-*cum*-commercial, and instead more democratic, communication systems (including through new, publicly accountable bodies [a Books Council, an Advertising Council and a Broadcasting and TV Council, as well as a strengthened Press Council]), and 'the creation of genuinely independent programme companies'. Among reviewers, Kingsley Amis was appalled by the prospect of 'the entrenchment of a rigid self-perpetuating oligarchy' of cultural bureaucrats, but for the young critic John Gross the greater problem was what he saw as Williams's conventionally *de-haut-en-bas* attitude ('a kind of drug . . . an enervating and dangerous habit of mind') towards television. 'This kind of weary stock reaction,' observed Gross, 'is now so familiar that it has started to rebound on itself: the words look tired on the page.' And he continued:

Not only is it unfair to that proportion of television, low but not insignificant, which is genuinely worthwhile; it also implies an extraordinarily wooden view of human nature. Few of us are lucky enough to live night and day at the level of Mr Williams's 'great tradition'; and as drugs go, television has something to be said for it. Even bad television involves human beings, and may be interesting on account of its very badness. If Mr Williams finds that an arrogant attitude, I am afraid that I must shock him further by revealing that I have met a fair number of people who know a hawk from a handsaw – or a condor from a Conrad – and who nevertheless sometimes enjoy watching television programmes *while fully aware that they are trivial*. Such is human perversity.

Still, both men might have sympathised with Sid Chaplin's viewpoint. 'I love a good programme on TV but hate what it's doing to talk,' he had observed to a friend two years earlier. 'The other week my father and me visited two relatives in Shildon [the Durham town where Chaplin was born], two Uncles who were always good for salty tales and talks, and found them focused on a cheap police thriller.'[25]

One television programme increasingly fascinated both the working class and the intelligentsia. '*Coronation Street* goes into 7½ million homes,' noted Derek Hill in the *Spectator* in December 1961, as the soap entered its second year. 'It has an audience of between 22 and 23 million twice a week.' For Hill this popularity was entirely merited – 'consistently wittier, healthier and quite simply better than any of television's supposedly respectable series, not excluding *Monitor*' – and cause for a swipe at the intellectuals of the New Left: 'When anything is as impudently alive and kicking as *Coronation Street*, "popular" becomes a dirty word. It would be sad if the Clancy Sigals ("TV is a tragedy") and Doris Lessings ("The monster is too strong for the best of us") made us ignore the breakthrough which is under our noses until some future Hoggart resurrects it in fifty years' time for respectful minority nostalgia.' Sigal took the bait. Calling *Coronation Street* 'a lie from start to finish if it is supposed to represent any recognisable aspect of life', he launched (in the *New Statesman* in early 1962) a full-frontal assault:

It is false in the very orderliness and regularity of its working-class dialogue. It is false in never showing mitigating circumstances in character and incident. It is false in omitting the passion and joy and complexity of life. It is false in its avoidance of class-tensions such as I know, for example, to be alive between shop-keepers and street residents in the north. It is false in seducing our feelings of superiority and nostalgia by purporting to show us a contemporary cross-section of working-class life, while virtually everyone in it is poorer, in housing and wages, than he would be in real life. It is profoundly patronising in that it depicts working-class people as entirely and without qualification circumscribed and defined by the life of their simple-minded dialogue. All hostility in the script, all the natural and unnatural tensions behind the facts of social change in Northern society, are covered over with fraternal glue.

In short, claimed Sigal, 'life's dimensions are reduced to 21 inches of naturalistic puppetry.' For one reader, John Killeen, who now lived in Romford but who had spent 30 years in a Leeds back-to-back, Sigal was only betraying his woeful ignorance:

As long as people live in back-to-back terraces, sharing lavatories and washtime hooks, their lives will be intimate and shared. The Coronation Streets of the north are still characterised by social interdependence and by the feeling that it is natural to be curious about the lives of others, easy to find out and right to care. *Coronation Street* does give a reasonably convincing idea of what it feels like to live in the world of the as yet uncleared semi-slums, of the older districts of the cities and towns of the textile areas of Yorkshire and, I imagine, Lancashire. It is infinitely closer to reality than, for instance, *The Archers* with its absurd idealisation and music-hall yokels.

A sterling defence, and Killeen's letter ended with a sentiment of real resonance: 'It is probably too vain a hope to expect the modern town planner and builder to learn through *Coronation Street* that human happiness is destroyed through the seemingly deliberate erection of separateness and loneliness in a context of total visual monotony, but yet the lesson is instinct in the serial.'[26]

'Social Equality – The Class System' was the title for a Third Programme conversation recorded in July 1961, with Mark Abrams, Enoch Powell and Hugh Trevor-Roper among those joined by the now statutory presence of Richard Hoggart. Chaired by the philosopher Stuart Hampshire, it did not spark throughout but had its moments – Abrams insisting that in Britain the assumption remained that you would only get on 'if you know the right people, if you have the right backing'; Trevor-Roper relishing the artistic and cultural possibilities of 'a society full of complicated social anfractuosities rather than a blank, unanimous, flat, level plane'; Powell calling the 11-plus 'as near as we can get to equality of opportunity' and accusing Hoggart of 'a class grudge' against it; Hoggart himself asserting that 'whatever may be the aims and intentions of the 11-plus, what happens in thousands of homes is that the 11-plus examination is identified in the minds of parents, not with "our Jimmy is a clever lad and he's going to have his talents trained", but "our Jimmy is now going to move into another class, he's going to get a white-collar job" or something like that.' Again and again the focus returned to that life-defining event:

> *Abrams:* Some of us – Powell, for example – believe that the 11-plus is the beginning of setting up in this country some sort of contest society where ability is sorted out, and this in fact is not so. The outcome of the 11-plus is determined at the age of three, four, five, six, according to the child's parental background, home background. And this is an important explanation, I think, of why British society is so stable. The essence of the whole British class system is to stabilise it as early in life as possible, and the earlier you can do that the more stable, the more comfortable a class society you're going to have.
>
> *Hampshire:* Trevor-Roper, you're doubtful.
>
> *Trevor-Roper:* I am, yes, because I feel that supposing one has an entirely classless society, if such is conceivable, you are still going to have functional differences and intellectual differences. You are still going to have children who are brought up in homes where they have the disadvantage of being the children of unintelligent, uninterested, low-grade – if one may use that word – low-grade workers, and obviously those children are going to have a handicap when it comes to the 11-plus.

Inevitably the most deeply felt passages came from the Hunslet man, especially when near the end he explained why – if he had to choose – he would still privilege 'the old, habitual class system' over the 'merito-cratic' way of organising society. 'I'm thinking now of people I know best from my own district in Leeds, working-class people,' Hoggart began. And he went on:

It seemed to me that when one knew where one was this relieved a lot of anxiety, in a way, especially if you were a fairly intelligent working-class person, and I'm talking now not about the scholarship boys but about middle-aged railway drivers. That they had a nice kind of mickey-taking quality very often towards 'them outside', they weren't subservient, they weren't either particularly deferential. They lived in a society which assumed that they would get the dirty end of the stick most of the time, and they'd built up a whole lot of very good defences, very human defences in all sorts of ways ... It was claustrophobic, it was narrow, it was limiting, especially for the budding abstract thinker, but at the same time it had a lot of very strong human qualities, and in a way you knew what you were doing. You could grow as a person. Now, if you see some of those people, moving [ie, out of slums and into new estates], and thank goodness they do, it seems to me that you're faced with a society in which you're not sure. You look at the back page of *Woman*, if we can mention that, and it tells you that the young junior executive's wife, or the young electrician's grade three wife, is using such and such glassware, and so on, and you go round, spinning madly wondering about where you are and what you're doing . . .[27]

8

This Is My Work Now

'Big-time Bingo has hit Britain,' announced the *Daily Mirror* in March 1961, two months after the Betting and Gaming Act (1960) had come into force, permitting the start of commercial bingo. The craze was immediate. In the first half of the year, at least 40 of Mecca's dance halls and 15 of Rank's cinemas were converted into full-scale bingo clubs, with the Newcastle-based Essoldo cinema chain following suit. 'THE BINGO TIDAL WAVE' was the *Mirror*'s headline by September, the paper reporting that 'up and down the country' there were now an esti-mated 10,000 bingo clubs, with more than a million players. The chorus of noises off was entirely predictable. 'It is another sign of the moral decline of the nation,' responded a Congregationalist minister in Blackburn to the news that three local cinemas were to be converted to bingo; a vicar in Leeds called bingo clubs 'mental slums'; *The Times* thought it 'a cretinous pastime'; and by the end of the year the press was whipping up a moral panic about children being neglected by their bingo-addicted mothers.[1]

For that, crucially, was the point: bingo was not just the latest regret-table behaviour by the working class, but by the *female* working class, overwhelmingly the game's main constituency. 'Bingo, I was told,' noted a journalist after visiting the Mecca in Tottenham, 'was a nice change from sitting around the house, washing, ironing, talking to the wall, gave you a bit of company in the afternoon. Think of what you could do with 50 quid. No, the old man didn't mind, not that it mattered if he did . . .' Or, as Eva Hall from Stamford Hill, one of a syndicate of six, put it, 'There's not much for married women to do in their spare time. We think bingo is smashing fun.' No one followed the craze more closely than its mastermind, Mecca's Eric Morley, who in 1962 sought to set *Sunday Times* readers straight. 'Bingo,' he insisted, 'is not gambling.'

> It is a much-maligned form of social entertainment, with a flutter on the side. The most you could lose in a two and a half hour session is 8s. And the very most you *might* win would be the jackpot game, say about £80. No, bingo is a revolution, a turning against TV. People felt they were losing the power of the spoken word, of easy chit-chat. At a bingo session you spend more time having a cup of tea with your neighbours, having a talk, than you do actually playing. Another thing about bingo, it's a great social leveller. You require no special skill, no special knowledge, not a lot of money. You're all the same when you've got your cards in front of you.

Morley of course was talking his own book, but his words broadly convince. *Tonight*'s Fyfe Robertson may have grumbled about 'the most mindless ritual achieved in half a million years of human evolution', yet for a working-class woman (typically in her 40s or thereabouts), a pastime that was cheap, that was easy, that was friendly, that got her out of the home into a safe, uncensorious environment, was surely something positive. 'I come here once a week,' 48-year-old Mrs Ivy Johnson told the *Mirror* during a session at London's Lyceum. 'It's a real break and I feel part of the club. I'd go up the wall if it weren't for this outing.'[2]

'It's a man's world, my masters – after over forty years of franchise, as it always has been,' insisted the writer Elspeth Huxley in May 1962.

> Religion: no woman in the priesthood at all, let alone at the top. 'Trad' religion – Christianity – is now the faith of only about ten per cent of the British people, so perhaps this is marginal. What is the faith of the remaining ninety per cent? Materialism, undoubtedly. The high priests of materialism are the tycoons: controllers of industry, of banking, of insurance, of distribution: all, I think without exception, male. Any women on the Board of ICI? Are you trying to buy your daughter into Lloyd's?

Is your sister chairman of the National Provincial? Doing nicely on the Stock Exchange? A woman has no more chance of filling any of these positions than she has of becoming Archbishop of Canterbury . . .

Judges? Not on your life. I don't say there won't one day be a female judge or two. To give a little ground here and there takes the sting from enemy propaganda without jeopardising the position. After all there's not much men don't know about war.

Judges only administer law made by governments: that is the crucial thing. Here men have been obliged to give some ground, but only very little. Only about four and a half per cent of today's House of Commons is feminine. A very safe percentage – and as long as men continue to pick the candidates and finance the Parties, things are well under control. There is no woman Cabinet Minister and only a few top-ranking civil servants. Four out of the top 150 jobs in the BBC are held by women and of these one concerns wardrobes, another programmes for women. By and large the Establishment is safely and solidly trousered.

The occupations thought most suitable for females are those which administer either to the comfort or the recreation of the male. They are womaned by descendants of the dancing-girl and the slipper-warmer. Most branches of entertainment, deriving from the dancing-girl, are free of sex barriers. And in the slipper-warming derivatives – nursing, teaching, secretarial – women can rise to the summit, such as it is. These are all underpaid, depressed occupations compared with insurance, banking and sitting on boards. Let women become matrons of hospitals and head-mistresses of girls' schools – no man would want such exacting, ill-rewarded responsibilities.

Huxley was launching *Punch*'s all-women series on 'The Second Sex?' In later articles, the Tory politician Pat Hornsby-Smith called on women to 'stop carping' at other women ('How many times have you heard women say they'd rather "work for a man"?'); the sociologist Barbara Wootton highlighted the 'monstrous injustices' created by 'the practice – still widespread in industry, though fast disappearing from the professions – of simply paying lower rates to women than to men engaged on the same work'; and the journalist Siriol Hugh-Jones itemised some of the many 'man-made toys' designed to keep women 'deeply dazed and, it is hoped, more or less contented' – toys that included 'magazines constructed on fantasy, cheap lipsticks, off-the-peg clothes of amazing pushiness and no price at all, the whole armoury of kitchen gadgets, the availability of hairdressers and the magic combination of soothe and brace that is *Woman's Hour*, with its brief straight-from-the-shoulder yet somehow cosy talks on "My Recent Miscarriage" and "My First Arrest" (by a former policewoman)'.[3]

Even so, almost certainly there were more women in the late 1950s and early 1960s staking out distinctive ground for themselves compared to say a decade earlier. To mention just a few. Wootton herself, who back in 1921 had been the first woman to give university lectures in Cambridge, became in 1958 one of the first four female life peers; that same year, Hilda Harding was the first woman appointed to a full managerial position in an English clearing bank, Barclays; Nan Winton two years later became BBC TV's first female newsreader; among journalists, Sheila Black was storming the all-male bastion that was the *Financial Times*, Anne Sharpley (renowned for her coverage of royal tours) was the brightest star in the *Evening Standard* firmament, the *Guardian*'s Nesta Roberts became in 1961 the first woman on a national newspaper to take charge of a London news desk, and Marjorie Proops was limbering up for her full glory as the nation's agony aunt; in Whitehall, Evelyn Sharp remained the forthrightly dominant permanent secretary of the Ministry of Housing and Local Government; elsewhere, Irene Thomas was starting to make her mark on *Brain of Britain*, Ulrica Murray Smith was establishing herself as senior Joint Master of the Quorn hunt, the pioneer stockbroker Elisabeth Rivers-Bulkeley was educating women about investment, and Pat Moss and 'Tish' Ozanne were successful rally drivers competing with men on equal terms; while among those whose brilliant careers (as subsequently charted by Rachel Cooke) continued from the fifties into the sixties were the trouser-wearing writer-*cum*-personality Nancy Spain, the uncompromisingly modernist architect Alison Smithson, and of course Rose Heilbron QC, the most celebrated advocate since Norman Birkett's heyday.[4]

Were there also signs of a new assertiveness? 'Very much dominated by its womenfolk,' noted an early critic of *Coronation Street*, in which right from the start feckless men were played off against strong women. Or take football, with a spring 1962 survey into falling attendances identifying as a key reason the female pressure being applied on husbands and boyfriends to spend more time with their womenfolk on Saturday afternoons. Perhaps, revolutionary thought, those menfolk might even be inclusive about their pastime. 'Women don't like to be left out,' Joan Kennedy of Huyton wrote about the same time to the *Liverpool Echo*. 'Why not encourage the girls and women to go along and watch, instead of discouraging them? Girls can be just as enthusiastic as men about football.'

It could be uphill work. 'For a long time I've felt I'm a lone woman in a man's world,' Mrs Esme Griffith of Cobham's Summit Driving School told the *Surrey Comet* in 1961, 'but at last I feel I am being accepted and people are getting used to the idea of my being an instructor.' A man's world . . . Shortly before, in November 1960, an opinion poll had specifically asked hundreds of wives throughout the country whether they thought it was – and 62 per cent had answered in the affirmative.[5]

A handful of early 1960s snapshots helps to explain why. When Mary-Kay Wilmers, future editor of the *London Review of Books*, said to a female careers adviser to Oxford women graduates that she wanted to work in publishing, the adviser 'told me to run along and learn how to type with ten fingers and do shorthand and generally make myself useful'; when Antonia Byatt found herself an academic's wife at Durham, 'the only place where the university had any social life, as a university' was the elegant students' union on the Palace Green – but for men only; when radio's *Top of the Form* began a television version, the co-host alongside David Dimbleby was due to be Judith Chalmers, until vetoed (in favour of Geoffrey Wheeler) on the grounds that women lacked the gravitas to take charge of game shows, even junior ones; when the future crime writer Jessica Mann was about to have a caesarean, it was her husband, not she, who was requested to give permission and sign the consent form; and when Enid Blyton was asked to be a witness at the *Lady Chatterley* trial, she replied, 'I'd love to help Penguins but I don't see how I can. My husband says "No" at once. The thought of me standing up in court advocating a book like that . . . I'm awfully sorry but I don't see that I can go against my husband's most definitive wishes in this.'[6]

Not least because of the prominence of the Barclays branch

(Hanover Street in London's West End), Hilda Harding's appointment as manager provoked considerable publicity, not all of it favourable. 'Sir, a woman's place is in the home,' complained R. E. Hembling of Clapham Common to the *Daily Mail*. 'We don't want lady bank managers, prime ministers or lady executives in business. God made women for the home to be man's help-mate and comfort adviser.' Nor in general is it difficult to construct from the public domain a pattern of male-dominated societal stereotyping: among TV ads, from 1959 the phallic classic for Cadbury's Flake and from 1961 the 'hands that do dishes can be soft as your face' for Fairy Liquid; also in ad-land, the picture in 1962 of the husband behind the Kenwood Chef mixer with his wife leaning happily against him wearing a chef's hat ('The Chef does everything but cook – That's what wives are for!'); James Bond with his undeviating assumptions of gender hierarchy; the comic-postcard crudity ('dream breasts and nightmare bosoms', in Benny Green's phrase) of the depiction of women in the irresistibly popular *Carry On* films; and the sentiment, as favoured by Howard Jacobson and his youthful confrères in the Manchester of the late 1950s, that one wouldn't kick an attractive girl out of the Bedford Dormobile. Broadly speaking, moreover, the surging interest in the working class – whether through sociology, fiction, drama, film or TV – failed to break the mould. 'Neither traditional nor consumerist perspectives problematised the position of women as essentially wives, mothers and pivots of the family,' observes Stuart Laing. 'It was rather a case of two versions of the domestic role in contention: the Mum/children solidarity as the centre of the extendes family and working-class community against the affluent housewife leading the domestic revolution into the home-centred society.' There was also the casual, taken-for-granted, working-class misogyny, at its most full-bodied in Alan Sillitoe's Arthur Seaton. Or take politics. Labour was (in the words of Amy Black and Stephen Brooke) 'at best a reluctant attendant to women's concerns, whether feminist or traditional', indeed even 'a site of resistance to gender'; while although the Tories were more than happy to have the flourishing Young Conservatives (claiming at their height in the 1950s to be 'the largest voluntary political youth movement in the world'), it was a movement that was, as Lawrence Black puts it, 'attentive to women, but via a male gaze', with those women virtually powerless in internal party culture. 'A prerequisite for the success of any revue is a supply of attractive young ladies,' declared its magazine *Rightway*, praising Ilford's YCs as notably 'well off in this particular form of talent'.[7]

Among women themselves, the advice cascaded. Eleanor Brockett in *Choosing a Career* (1959) especially recommended the caring professions, where the 'essentially feminine' qualities of trust, confidence and personal integrity were at a premium; while among those writing career novels – a flourishing genre – Elizabeth Grey published between 1958 and 1961 *Pauline Becomes a Hairdresser*, *Pat Macdonald Sales Assistant* and *Jill Kennedy Telephonist*; Angela Mack's 1958 contribution was *Continuity Girl*; and Jane Sheridan chipped in with *Amanda in Floristry* (1959). In March 1960, a recently elected MP set out in the *Daily Express* 'What my daughter must learn for the next nine years'. A 'good education', yes, followed by a 'worthwhile career', but that was not all. 'I shall see that Carol learns the domestic arts at home,' added Margaret Thatcher. 'Teaching manners and the social graces to a child of six and a half gives rise to alternate hope and despair. The nagging seems endless . . .' Perhaps the answer was the Girl Guides. 'In a woman physical love is nearly always bound up with the longing for a home and companionship, whereas in a man the desire to settle down is not as a rule a fundamental need,' asserted Hilda Birkett and Hether Kay in a 1961 Girl Guides Association publication on marriage and the home, with the authors firmly warning their readers against extra-marital sex. Two high-profile brides also pointed the way. 'This is my work now,' declared the model Bronwen Pugh at her wedding in October 1960 to Viscount Astor, as she squeezed his arm. The following summer, when Katharine Worsley married the Duke of Kent, the *Daily Mirror* reported that 'Yes, it was "Obey,"' the submissive word apparently at her explicit wish.[8]

Crucial to self-image was appearance. A 1957 cosmetics survey revealed 88 per cent of middle-class women and 72 per cent of working-class women using face powder, while for lipstick the respective percentages were 85 and 72. For a 14-year-old girl, lipstick or not was not the only question. 'The lady told us,' noted Jacqueline Aitken in March 1960 after a visit to school from 'the fashion people, Simplicity', that 'we should wear bras to define and shape our figures (we already do wear them of course), that we should use deodorants (which I at any rate do), that we should pay attention to our deportment (which I try to do), that we should think carefully whether our lipsticks go with our dresses (which I do) etc., etc.' As for teenage girls generally, the educationalist Kathleen Ollerenshaw (a Conservative member of Manchester City Council) reflected in 1961 that it was 'a long time' since 'feminine traits' had been 'so widely flaunted' by them, and she expressed pleasure at how, on the part of single girls, 'flounced skirts, colourful coats and glamorous hair-dos brighten city streets during the lunch hour.' Pleasure too for Angela Carter, who in the 1970s remembered 'a giggling flock' of working-class girls at a south London tube station in 1959: 'They must have assembled there in order to go "up West". They were as weird and wonderful as humanoid flora from outer space, their hair backcombed into towering beehives, skirts so tight you could see the clefts between their buttocks, and shoes with pointed tips that stuck out so far in front they had to stand sideways on the escalators . . .' But it was not Gladys Langford's idea of femininity. 'Do dislike modern hair styles for women & the butter coloured and bright red dyed hair,' the septuagenarian diarist recorded in April 1962. And soon afterwards, when Burnley appeared at the Cup Final, there was no nonsense from the manager's wife as she led her WAGs to Wembley. 'It was hats, gloves, shoes,' recalled Margaret Potts almost half a century later, 'and what we called matching accessories.'

A survey in 1960 conducted by Bolton School Old Girls' Association touched little on dress, but the alumni's answers gave a sense of how a varying age range – albeit all grammar-educated – saw both themselves and women's place in society:

> I think women get very bored with housework. (*Left 1927*)
>
> A woman in general has to be far more capable than her male opposite number to get the same recognition that he gets, and any shortcomings are still criticised more sharply. The continuing prejudice against women drivers, in the face of evidence to the contrary gained by the Institute of Advanced Motorists, is an illustration of this. (*1929*)
>
> I am married to a man who has strong views that a wife's and mother's place is in the home and that for such a person to go out to work is tanta-

mount to casting aspersions on the husband's earning capacity. (*1939*)

I intend to return to teaching when my family is older, but only if able to be a proper mother too. (*1946*)

I think that any woman with a family is smaller-minded than a woman without one, whatever her education. (*1950*)

I would continue in my present work if I married, but if I had children I would give up my work no matter what extras and luxuries I had to give up as I feel that a woman's place is in the home. (*1953*)

It is up to a woman herself whether she becomes a vegetable after marriage. (*1954*)

Barrow-in-Furness *do not* employ any married women teachers in a permanent capacity. (*1955*)

I think graduate mothers, especially those who write to the *Observer*, get too sorry for themselves when bogged down by young children and suburbia. (*1957*)[9]

––––––––

'Is she lonely? Is she bored? Does she lack public spirit?' Such in January 1961 were the questions that BBC television's *Family Affairs* – a regular slot on Thursday afternoons – aimed to answer in the first of four programmes on 'The Married Woman's Place', with this one called 'The housewife at home'. The context, explained the *Radio Times*, was 'the changing social background of today', and those contributing included Claire Rayner, 'housewife'. About the same time, R.C.H. Webber, a Bristol-based building worker 'employed on interior maintenance work on a new, middle-class housing site', described in the *New Statesman* how he found himself 'daily confronted by exquisitely groomed and well-spoken housewives', with 'their peremptory commands and their sweeping generalisations about the British workers':

It does seem that people undergo considerable nervous strain while in the process of acquiring new property and status symbols and adapting themselves to new surroundings. Of the younger women on this small estate, it would be a fair generalisation to say that they are mainly occupied in elaborate self-grooming, press-button housewifery and subtly tyrannising their charladies. Ultra-smartness (fashionwise) seems to go with chain-smoking and poodle-cuddling. The more tenuous their contact with reality through gadgetry, glossy magazines and over-scrupulous hygiene, the more compulsive and idiosyncratic their behaviour.

Among the older section there are cases of ostentatious religiosity, invariably bound up with bitterness, ultra-conservatism, morbid accountancy and property embalming. I have glanced over bookshelves in vain for signs of social awareness and enlightenment.

Webber manfully refrained from using the n-word, but not long before a cinema news feature had boldly claimed that what it called 'suburban neurosis' was affecting 'one woman in four'.

The normative assumption remained that most married women – above all middle-class women – stayed at home. Judith Hubback may in 1957 have shown in *Wives Who Went to College* that, as she later put it, many graduate women did not want to be 'married to their homes', and Marguerite Patten may in 1962 have had her cookery programme axed by the BBC on the grounds that (in her paraphrasing words) 'women are now feeling that they want to spread their wings.' But this was still before Betty Friedan's groundbreaking, hugely influential *The Feminine Mystique* (1963) about the dissatisfaction of homemakers in the American suburbs – and well before Germaine Greer's *The Female Eunuch*. In early 1962, after a speaker in the House of Lords had argued that women should take advantage of labour-saving gadgets and go out to work, the widely syndicated columnist Gloria Gordon let rip. After insisting that 'it's just not true that a housewife vegetates while a working wife stays bright and well-informed,' she went on:

> For the woman who is prepared to be a full-time wife, there are three main jobs, looking after her husband, her children, and her home – in that order.
>
> For her husband, she must be a combination of wife, mistress, friend, cook and confidante.
>
> She has to keep herself looking attractive for him. She has to read and study enough to keep abreast of him intellectually. She has to find time to spoil him a little.
>
> For her children, she must be a mother, a nurse and a teacher all in one. Most important, she must just be there.
>
> To do all those jobs properly, as well as the shopping and housekeeping, leaves precious little time for any outside employment.

'Just about enough,' she added, 'to take a well-deserved nap every afternoon!'[10]

Seven and a half hours was the estimated time that women in 1961 spent each day on housework – a figure reflecting in part the still patchy spread of new domestic technology. 'Monday was wash day,' recalled one Barrow housewife (married in 1956, children born in 1958 and 1961). 'Of course with kiddies you have to wash every day but Monday was the main day. I don't know about Tuesday. Wednesday morning I used to go to the market. Thursday I always used to do my front. I did my window-sill and front door every morning and then on a Thursday I would give the windows and the front door and all the front a good wash. Sweep the front and then I used to wash right through, the tiles in the vestibule, the kitchen floor, then clean the windows and swill the yard out.'

Not all housewives did their washing at home. 'The "steamy"', remembered Lulu about her Glasgow childhood, was 'a big industrial wash-house where people from the tenements did their laundry', usually wheeled there in an old pram, and which 'looked like one of the underground scenes from the film *Metropolis*':

Steam billowed from large cauldrons and the machines hissed, gurgled and spluttered. Water sluiced down drains on the concrete floors and women screeched over the noise.

Sheets were washed in the cauldrons, but the rest of the clothes were scrubbed on washboards. Women dressed in aprons and boots hovered like witches over the metal tubs, scrubbing their husband's overalls. Cigarettes dangled from their lips and they had rollers in their hair covered by scarves tied at their foreheads. Steam was the enemy. It could turn a hairstyle into a lank, tired mess.

For most housewives, though certainly not all, a Puritan work ethic remained strong – so strong that Geoffrey Gorer's 1958 survey of TV-viewing habits revealed many women as unable to watch without also doing something else, usually knitting. 'I have little races with myself,' a 77-year-old woman told a journalist soon afterwards. 'I say, "Can you finish that pattern before the nine o'clock news?"' And when in 1962 a kitchen-designing firm commissioned a nationwide survey of housewives and their ideal kitchens, this found not only that 80 per cent voted against a heated draining board on the sink for drying crockery and that 58 per cent did not want a heated strip in the base of kitchen units for warming feet, but also that 'wholeheartedly, the housewives turned down a suggestion for a unit at which they could sit down to work.' The reason was obvious: 'Husbands and neighbours might take it as a sign of laziness.'[11]

How contented with their lot were stay-at-home housewives? 'I would like an occasional afternoon film during the coming months, when the winter weather means that many housewives, like myself, with young children, have to stay indoors,' Mrs I. Watt of Gateshead wrote in October 1959 to the Tyne Tees edition of the *TV Times*. 'A film now and again would certainly be a real treat.' Mrs E. Webster, in her 30s and living in Hornchurch, looked instead to 'Mr Music' – ie, the organist Reginald Dixon. 'We housewives get a pep pill when he broadcasts on Wednesday mornings,' she told the *Radio Times* in 1960. 'He never fails to cheer me up. A wonderful man and artist!' We also know that Tupperware parties, an American import, were first held in Britain in 1961. For a systematic survey, though, our main contemporary source is Hannah Gavron, who in 1960–1 interviewed 48 middle-class housewives (mainly from West Hampstead) and 48 working-class housewives (from Kentish Town) – the basis for what became her renowned 1966 book, *The Captive Wife: Conflicts of Housebound Mothers*. Gavron found a stark contrast between the two groups. Undeniably, many of the middle-class women did feel a sense of being tied down by having to be with their children all day – 'Of course I must be with them all the time,' a teacher's wife told her, 'though I must confess that sometimes I *long* to get away' – but Gavron's overall impression was that 'the majority' of those middle-class mothers were 'making a determined effort to keep up contact with the outside world' and that 'only a small minority seemed really isolated in the same way as were the majority of working-class mothers.' As for those working-class mothers, often in poor housing and with no live-in help or affordable nursery school, her conclusions were sombre: the prevailing atmosphere was one of 'confusion and muddling through'; family life was far more nuclear than extended; less than a third had any contact with their neighbours; and in general, their main contact with the outside world was via television. 'Alone with the gadgets' and 'Is your wife just a bird in a plastic cage?' were among the headlines that would greet the book's publication.

Gadgets were not enough for Betty Jerman. 'Home and childminding can have a blunting effect on a woman's mind,' the freelance journalist and mother of two small children declared in the *Guardian* in February 1960. 'But only she can sharpen it.' Her piece, called 'Squeezed in Like Sardines in Suburbia', spoke particularly loudly to one reader, Maureen Nicol, who had recently moved to the Wirral, knew no one, and was at home with a small baby and toddler. 'Perhaps,' she wrote to the paper, 'housebound wives with liberal interests and a desire to remain individuals could form a national register, so that whenever one moves, one can contact like-minded friends.' The suggestion snowballed, and the result, after over 2,000 had responded to Nicol, was the National Housewives' Register, which by the 1970s would have over 25,000 members. 'We were reasonably well educated,' recalled Nicol. 'We'd all had reasonably satisfying jobs. We never ever considered leaving the children and going back to work until they were at school at least. But we needed more stimulation. We needed to talk about things.' Essentially a network providing mutual support and sharing mutual interests, the NHR was, noted Elizabeth Wilson, 'neither political nor feminist', let alone anti-domesticity. But, she added, through being 'very loosely organised on the basis of small groups', it 'anticipated the women's liberation movement rather than copying the more committee-like campaigning organisations [such as the National Council of Women] in which women had hitherto organised themselves'.[12]

Articulation by full-time mothers and housewives of feelings of frustration was still relatively rare. In 1963 the pioneer editor of the *Guardian* women's page, Mary Stott, searched her files for the previous four years for 'letters from discontented mothers' and realised she had 'never received floods of such letters'. Instead, in her list of correspondents there was 'not one whom I took to be expressing discontent with her lot as housewife and mother'. How to explain the silence? The Cambridge-educated Jessica Mann, whose own experience of early motherhood after her 1959 marriage she vividly recalls in terms of feeling 'utterly bored and frustrated by full-time domesticity', argues that she was clearly at the time 'not the only young woman who did not feel able to admit her true feelings' – not least because, 'having achieved exactly what every girl was supposed to long for [ie, husband and children], I knew I ought to be satisfied' and not 'weeping into the nappy bucket'.

Yet of course, the counter-argument is that this discontent was seldom expressed because most women at home did not feel it sufficiently strongly, on the part anyway of the sort of middle-class women who wrote to the *Guardian*. That would seem to be the view of the historian Ali Haggett. On the basis of the oral testimony of some three dozen women, predominantly educated middle-class, who experienced domestic life during the 1950s and 1960s, she finds that 'the ups and downs of daily life were regarded as commonplace and were accepted as a normal facet of domestic life'; that 'the overwhelming majority made an explicit choice to explore other areas of creativity that did not necessarily involve paid employment'; and that 'most respondents expressed a general preference for activities [such as the NHR, the Townswomen's Guild, the Inner Wheel, the Church, the Women's Institute, the local choral society] that would reinforce the beliefs and values that underpinned family life and traditional gender roles.' Haggett does not deny that 'some wives understandably found their role isolating at times' – yet even so, 'by and large they did not feel it appropriate to aspire to a career outside the home until their children were much older.'[13] Those are conclusions broadly in line with Gavron's research into the middle-class housewives of West Hampstead. If there *were* desperate housewives, in other words, they may well have been mainly among the housewives of Kentish Town and many other working-class, pre-gentrified places. Their voices, however, remain mute and increasingly irrecoverable.

'How can she continue two jobs? Does her family suffer? Is she penalised legally and financially?' Those were the key questions when television's *Family Affairs* turned in January 1961 to 'The wife with a full-time job outside the home'. It was becoming an increasingly topical theme, with radio's *Home for the Day* (the Sunday version of *Woman's Hour*) having recently discussed 'Home and Office: The Dichotomy'. 'It gives the feeling of guilt and the feeling that you're not really doing the best for both jobs,' Thea Benson, a professional woman, told the interviewer Joan Yorke:

> I think this stems from the home side mainly. I know that my own husband, I'm sure subconsciously, seems to invent all sorts of chores for me to do. Generally these chores come about just at the moment when I've got a particularly difficult problem on my hands in the office, and I think that he expects that I shall put anything, however trivial, connected with the home before my business.
>
> *I imagine you aren't neglecting him, are you?*
>
> Not in the least. He has every care and attention. I do in fact rush home and do the major share of the cooking, and he is never neglected, and I make a point of being completely domestic over the weekend.
>
> *Is he interested in your job?*
>
> Not really. Polite questions are asked – I don't think he is really interested, but that is another point, that I have to show intense interest in his job. And of course I have to do a certain amount of secretarial work for him. I also have always got to change his library books and do any odd shopping.
>
> *I think every wife has to do that, don't you?*
>
> Yes, I do think so.

'What about the office?' asked Yorke later. 'Do you find that there is a dichotomy there?' 'Yes, I do,' replied Benson. 'I think that a lot of this feeling comes on in the morning when one is rushing, and I commute, so the train always seems to be late, I always seem to be late and I always get to this ghastly sense of guilt coming from the other side. I've left my home guilt now, now my guilt is towards the office . . .'[14]

The bottom-line facts, as revealed by the 1961 census, were that women now comprised 33 per cent of the total labour force (compared to 31 per cent in 1951); that among all women aged 20 to 64, some 42 per cent had paid employment (6 per cent up on 1951); and that 35 per cent of married women were in employment (a striking 9 per cent up on 1951), or about four million of them. Ministry of Labour figures for England and Wales in 1960 shed light on age and regional distribution: 16 per cent of 'occupied women' were aged 19 or under, 40 per cent were in the 20–39 age range, 38 per cent in the 40–59 range, and 6 per cent were 60 or over. As for regional differences, 38 per cent of the total labour force in the London area being female contrasted with the north (31 per cent) and Wales (29 per cent). What about the rewards? Equal pay was undoubtedly on the march – during 1961 alone, about half a million women achieved for the first time equal pay for equal work – but remained unusual in most sectors of private industry. And of course, not only were many women's jobs part-time, but there persisted a strong tendency in the main occupational groupings for women to be placed in lower grades than men. Thus among professional people in 1961, 93 per cent of women were only in 'minor' professions, compared to 42 per cent of men; in terms of those working in all non-manual (including professional) occupations, 70 per cent of women were in routine grades, compared to 40 per cent of men; and among those working in all manual (including personal-service) occupations, 80 per cent of women were in unskilled jobs, compared to 45 per cent of men.[15]

Education was inevitably part of the story. The Crowther Report, 15-18, took a gendered perspective. 'The prospect of courtship and marriage should rightly influence the education of the adolescent girl,' it recommended in 1959. 'Her direct interest in dress, personal appearance and in problems of human relations should be given a central place in her education.' Most adolescent girls were at (or had recently left) secondary moderns. 'They give a lively sense of purpose and reality,' the educational journalist Harold Dent found in 1958 about those schools' vocational courses. But, to judge by his lists, the courses themselves were strictly gendered, with girls assigned to such subjects as housecraft, cookery, retail shop work, secretarial work and nursing. The Newsom Committee would report on secondary moderns in 1963, and during its deliberations one member, the careers adviser Catherine Avent, was struck by how some of her fellow-members were unashamed 'misogynists', including one who saw women as 'either caterers or secretaries – the idea of girls being engineers was anathema to him'. Evidence to the committee included a memo from the National Association of Head Teachers. For the academically average girl, it argued, the aim of the secondary modern should be to offer a 'practical course' giving them 'opportunities to be socially acceptable', while at the same time linking their work to 'their future hope – marriage'.

What about the grammars? Some undoubtedly raised girls' aspirations, but strikingly, when in the early 1960s Kathleen Ollerenshaw talked with 15-year-olds at a large municipal girls' grammar, they 'clamoured almost unanimously for more housecraft and for the elimination from the time-table of subjects they deemed useless', by which they essentially meant academic subjects. She came across the odd exception – 'Why,' asked one, 'should girls who are interested in such subjects as physics and chemistry be forced to sew uninteresting tray-cloths or keep watch over the latest concoction in the cookery room?' – but the greater allure was overwhelmingly soft (ie, domestic) science rather than the hard stuff. Presumably, too, it was much the same in private and direct grant schools, given the gendered thrust of the Industrial Fund, set up by industry in the early 1960s to improve the facilities for science teaching in those sectors. Its initial disbursement was £3 million to 210 schools – of which 187 were boys' schools, 5 were co-eds, and a mere 18 were girls' schools. Nor was it necessarily so different even in higher education, where women in 1958 comprised 24 per cent of university student numbers, a ratio increasing only slowly over the next ten years to 28 per cent.[16]

Employers, unions, male workers and husbands all had their views on women working. 'Married women workers are considered to have disadvantages and many employers would not willingly engage them if alternative labour was available,' concluded Viola Klein on the basis of a 1960 survey of 120 firms employing an average of some 1,500 people, of whom almost a third were women. 'Other employers, while prepared to accept married women for unskilled jobs, will not readily provide them with skilled work or offer them opportunities for promotion. It may be suspected that prejudice is a factor in some of these attitudes . . .' So too in the male-dominated world of organised labour. In 1959 the National Society of Metal Mechanics grudgingly consented to admit women as 'half members'; two years later, at the large Coventry engineering firm Alfred Herbert, shop stewards proposed and carried that 'Re crane drivers we ask management to employ only male labour in future'; and in the Post Office, union resistance blocked management from employing more women to help reduce the queues at peak times.

In theory the trade-union movement was committed to the pursuit of equal pay, but in practice many male trade unionists had little or no appetite for the erosion, let alone the disappearance, of pay differentials.

Undoubtedly, here as elsewhere, there was a strong element of atavism as well as calculation. Likewise, many husbands instinctively adhered to the principle of separate spheres, not least because of a sense of stigma (among working-class as well as middle-class husbands) about the fact of a working wife apparently reflecting the husband's inability to support her. 'It's a poor man who cannot keep his wife,' one husband told Ferdynand Zweig.

Conversely, found Zweig, many husbands of wives who *did* work accepted the situation with a greater or lesser degree of enthusiasm. But that was certainly not true of all husbands everywhere, among them a Tipton husband in the Black Country who, his son recalled, became in 1961 'very angry when Mom started to work' – so angry indeed that he changed jobs 'and literally doubled his money overnight in an effort to stop Mom going to work'. 'But,' added the son, 'she still carried on.' Or take 'Doubtful'. 'My wife has a part-time job which doesn't interfere with the housekeeping nor mean leaving our daughter at home alone,' he wrote to the *Woman's Mirror* in 1960. 'She likes going out to work and, I must admit, she's much happier doing so. BUT, I don't really approve of wives working. Would it be wrong to stop her?' Most agony aunts would probably have played a dead bat, but not Marjorie Proops. 'If your wife prefers to work and still keeps her house in good order, why should you complain?' she answered. 'Sounds to me like you begrudge this bit of happiness and freedom your missus so enjoys. Selfish devil, aren't you?'[17]

Working married women were the subject of two major surveys in the late 1950s: one by Pearl Jephcott of the almost entirely working-class south London district of Bermondsey, the other by Zweig of the Mullard factory in Mitcham, in south-west London. Both found that although the economic motive was unsurprisingly paramount – 'To help to buy the car' and 'To help to buy a house' were favoured replies to Zweig's question 'What is your reason for working?' – it was relatively seldom the only one. Typical statements to Zweig included:

I would rather be here – the mind is occupied.

Housework does not satisfy me.

Keeps you young.

Would worry me more to be at home.

I've got to do something; I am too active.

Zweig was particularly struck by the frequency of outside contacts among the working women (far greater than in the case of working men). 'They go out shopping together, to cinemas, dance clubs and so on. They find great pleasure in companionship at work and they do not mind keeping it up outside.'

As for Bermondsey's working wives, Jephcott stressed that their non-economic motives for work were very different from those of a middle-class working wife. 'These working-class wives rode no feminist band-wagon. They seldom mentioned frustration over wasted talents, while few would think of claiming that their job was of any particular value to society. Nor did they reject domesticity. They appeared to be less in revolt against pots and pans, not quite sure how to fill in their day.' But, found Jephcott, it could also be a case of dispelling loneliness (especially for wives living in flats) and generally enlarging one's social life. 'To be able to exchange your "Tat-ah-love, see you tomorrow" with a heap of people, was a mark of status worth having.' Jephcott's most interesting point related further to status – namely her argument that, in the context of working-class mothers no longer having the same status *as mothers* that their own mothers had had (fewer children, fewer hazards, rather easier housework), going out to work helped to 'regain' some of that lost status. 'To add to the family's income showed that she cared about the proper things, like a lovely, modern home,' explained Jephcott about the working wife influenced, consciously or otherwise, by this consideration. 'The extra money meant she could dress better, wear her good clothes for part of every day, and be more of a credit to her husband when he took her out, a point often mentioned. To be able to hold down a job at all in the competitive outside world was reassuring and something that not every married woman would dare to tackle . . .'[18]

Of course, all working mothers had to make arrangements for childcare. Various contemporary studies of the subject – inevitably one with

emotive connotations – came to broadly similar conclusions: that relatively few mothers worked if they had a child or children under five;
that for those who did or might want/need to, there was a serious shortage of nursery schools and play facilities (prompting a letter to the
Guardian in 1961 from a young mother, Belle Tutaev, that led not only
to a mass petition to the minister of education but to the birth of the
Pre-school Playgroups Association); that in most cases, whether for
under- or over-fives, the key adult childcare role was played by the
maternal grandmother; and that, as a generalisation, it was difficult to
find convincing evidence that children were affected negatively by the
fact of their mothers working. 'Though they may be inconclusive,'
Simon Yudkin and Anthea Holme would write in 1963 after a dispassionate examination of studies since the mid-1950s, 'they provide no
support to the wilder statements about serious psychological trauma to
the children or to the production of a generation of juvenile delin-
quents.' Yet, they went on: 'The fact that a large number of schoolchildren
of all ages are left to manage on their own after school and during holidays, and the fact that many of the younger children are looked after by
their older brothers and sisters, suggests that we may be courting disaster if we continue to rely indefinitely on the resilience of the children
and their ability to cope with all the responsibilities that their enforced
independence brings.'

Among flesh-and-blood working mothers were a private heroine and
a public champion. 'Lily never stopped working,' recalls Alan Johnson
about his mother, married to the feckless Steve: 'cleaning and scrubbing' in a residential boarding house in South Kensington; 'up on a
chair, dusting lampshades' for a couple in Holland Park's Lansdowne
Crescent; 'polishing the furniture and disinfecting toilets' in the
spacious Notting Hill Gate flat of three young professionals; and in the
evenings 'often pressed into service at those dinners in the big houses
between Ladbroke Grove and Kensington Park Road'. When Steve
eventually left, it was 'yet more jobs':

> In spite of her illness, she never gave up cleaning. Her only concession to
> her GP's insistence that she must not work herself so hard was to try to
> find additional employment that was less physically demanding than yet
> more cleaning positions. Her CV soon incorporated the tobacco kiosk in

Ladbroke Grove, a newsagent's in North Pole Road and Harry's Café on Wormwood Scrubs. She also took up 'home work' – painting and varnishing wooden figures to go on toy roundabouts. The pieces were delivered in large crates, which Linda [Johnson's older sister, the other heroine of his childhood] and I would help to unpack. The extra money enabled Lily to rent a television, which took pride of place in our newly arranged living room alongside the Dansette.

The MP for Finchley would presumably have approved. 'I SAY A WIFE CAN DO TWO JOBS . . .' declared Margaret Thatcher in the *Evening News* in February 1960.

> It is possible, in my view, for a woman to run a home and continue with her career, provided two conditions are fulfilled.
>
> **First**, her husband must be in sympathy with her wish to do another job.
>
> **Secondly**, where there is a young family, the joint incomes of husband and wife must be sufficient to employ a first-class nannie-housekeeper to look after things in the wife's absence.

And as for the perennial nagging question: 'I think perhaps the real answer is that if a woman is going to be a bad mother she will be bad even though she is at home the whole time. Conversely if she is a good mother she will be good even though she is absent for part of the day.' She concluded: 'One last point. In an emergency the family comes first.'[19]

Undeniably, the phenomenon of the working woman was gaining visibility, and in 1962 Hannah Gavron had no doubts that it was all 'part of the wider process of social and economic emancipation for women that we have witnessed this century', and 'happily there can be no turning back of the clock'. But her north London friend Phyllis Willmott saw limits to that emancipation. 'I am pretty well certain,' she predicted in 1960, 'that "career women" as such – those who really wish to make work as large a part of their lives as home is – will remain relatively few. The New Woman is the one who wants enough but not too much of her interest and energies turned outwards.'

Perhaps the last word should go to the 1960 radio conversation between Joan Yorke and the conflicted professional woman Thea Benson. 'Do you think women have too much conscience?' wondered Yorke. 'I mean we all have super egos. We want to be perfect wives and mothers . . . Perhaps we should really make up our minds which it is we want to be.' With that proposition Benson apparently agreed, before going on:

> I'm not at all sure that the old-fashioned thing that the woman's place is in the home is not right. I have got a horribly sneaking feeling that it is . . . Of course the husband is really the key to all this. I think the younger men really are more used to this now than the older men. I think it's all accepted. I have a feeling that this problem won't arise at all in the next generation.[20]

––––––––––

Not all women were married, whether working or otherwise. The plight of the unmarried mother (probably 30 per cent or more living in poverty) was highlighted by Lynne Reid Banks's 1960 novel *The L-Shaped Room*. 'A lot of the women who come to me aren't just panic-stricken cowards trying to escape their just deserts, you know,' the Wimpole Street doctor tells the newly pregnant heroine. 'They have the sense to realize they're incapable of being mother *and* father, breadwinner *and* nursemaid, all at once. A lot of them have thought what the alternative means, of handing the child over to strangers who may or may not love it. And don't make the mistake of imagining the word bastard doesn't carry a sting any more . . .' About the same time, the *Daily Mirror*'s highly capable newsroom secretary, Gloria Crocombe, became pregnant by one of the paper's star reporters, the future BBC newsreader Peter Woods, and was sacked; while in its annual report for 1961–2, the National Council for the Unmarried Mother and her Child called for 'the lowering of the illegitimacy rate and a higher standard of moral responsibility throughout the country'. There was also the plight of the divorced wife, unless of course she remarried. 'Anger and shame became the two driving motives of my mother's life after my father left her,' wrote Rupert Christiansen in his poignant memoir about the aftermath of his journalist father abruptly walking out on the family in 1959. 'By shame,' Christiansen explained, 'I mean not only a head hung low, but also a fetid miasma of remorse, guilt and embarrassment, kept in circulation by the winds and tides of prevalent social attitudes.' After the divorce, the suburban vicar 'came round to commiserate and let slip that of course while she would be welcome at the church, the view of the diocesan bishop bla-bla-bla was that she could not take communion or – ahem! – belong to the Mothers' Union'. More often, 'she wasn't shunned or excluded, just subtly degraded – looked at, talked about, pitied from a distance and by tacit agreement marked down as a danger area'. In short, 'people in Petts Wood just didn't like divorced women, and my mother retaliated crisply by making it clear that she didn't like Petts Wood people either. Not so much a chip on her shoulder, one might say, as a bleeding chunk gouged out of it.'[21]

Marriage remained – as evidenced by the 1961 figures – overwhelmingly the norm. Out of every thousand women aged 21–39, the number married was 808 (compared to 572 30 years earlier); only 2.1 per thousand married people in England and Wales got divorced that year; only 6 per cent of births took place outside marriage; and less than 3 per cent of households were lone parents with dependent children. What, though, were the marriages themselves like? Still mainly on the familiar model, with the husband dominant and living in a largely separate sphere? Or rather, a companionate union of more or less equals?

Hard-and-fast answers to these intimate questions are impossible to determine, but it does seem clear that by the early 1960s the traditional style of marriage was far from dead. 'It is difficult to find many companionate marriages in this study up to 1970,' concluded Elizabeth Roberts on the basis of her extensive interviews of post-war women in north-west England; she particularly emphasised the strict gendering of most leisure activities, even in the home. This was especially true in coal-mining communities:

The relationship existing between a married couple is dominated by separateness [declared the sociologist Fernando Henriques in 1960] ... The cleavage between the two worlds means that husband and wife have little or no meeting ground. Talk in the home between men is pit or club talk. Between women, of children and the home. The most satisfactory marriages are those in the early stages where conflict and lack of interest in their partner's ideas can be solved by the bed. Custom demands that a

A *Vogue* model with schoolchildren, Bradford, 1960

Notting Hill, October 1960

Berwick Street Market, Soho, April 1961

Sea coalers collect coal, Hartlepool, 1961

Design studio, Crown Wallpapers, Cheshire, 1961

Science lesson, Surrey, 1961

Birmingham Reference Library, November 1961

Roy Thomson (*second from right*) addresses senior *Sunday Times* staff shortly after acquiring the paper, 1959

Sheep judging at the Royal Highland Show, Ingliston, Edinburgh, 1962

Early morning in Tipton, the Black Country, 1961

Park Hill, Sheffield, 1961

The Gorbals, Glasgow, 1962

Edmonton Green Market, Enfield, 1960

Supermarket shoppers, March 1962

Agatha Hart at Stockwell Bus Garage, March 1962

man provides a home, gives his wife a 'wage' to run it, and nothing else. If he does these things he is acting as a male should act. She on the other hand accepts the situation, for this is her customary role. We are a long way from sexual equality and the romanticism of the sexual partnership of the cinema.

So too in industrial Scotland. 'Men's definition of a good wife was not someone who was affectionate and loving, but simply someone who had your tea on the table and the house clean,' writes Carol Craig about Glasgow's traditional working-class male culture. 'There's little doubt that many women suffered terribly at the hands of selfish, uncaring and often violent men.' Growing up in nearby Paisley was Gerry Rafferty, whose father, an Irish-born miner and lorry driver, would until his death in 1963 regularly beat his wife and children when he returned home drunk. 'It was accepted,' recalls Ian Jack about the prevailing assumptions in and around Glasgow in the early 1960s, 'that men often came home drunk and sometimes assaulted their wives, and sometimes the wives deserved it. Outside the gossip of neighbours ("he gave her a good belting – I heard it through the wall") the crime had no public currency.' More generally, Jessica Mann notes that 'violence was not unknown in the posh households of the more educated classes, just better disguised'; she adds that her lawyer parents would tell her 'how many mild-looking middle-class men turned into wife-beating brutes in private, and also knew that their abused wives would go to any lengths to ensure that their sufferings remained secret', essentially because 'they were ashamed'. Was Mrs G. H. of London NW1 middle-class? Probably not. 'What a disgusting dress Elizabeth Taylor was wearing in the picture you published,' she complained to the *Daily Mirror* in 1961. 'I cannot understand how any woman could appear in public with half her bosom uncovered in this way ... My better half said he'd knock my block off if I ever wore a dress like that.'[22]

Class and region could make a difference, likewise age. 'Dad was very secretive about what he was earning'; 'Dad just gave mother what *he* thought' – such is typical Black Country oral testimony from respondents who in their own subsequent married lives adopted a much more open, equitable approach to the wage packet. The same may have been true about domestic tasks, where certainly the traditional marital model still largely prevailed in 1962. Well over a thousand adults were interviewed early that year, and the results – as measured by minutes spent per day – were striking:

	Women	Men
Preparing and eating meals	197	114
Housework	148	22
Knitting, sewing, childcare, laundry	77	4

Despite all this, the sociological evidence was mounting that marriages as a whole were becoming more companionate. Young and Willmott, fresh from having famously shown that the working-class husband in Bethnal Green took his turn wheeling the pram, now described Woodford men, of whichever class, as 'emphatically not absentee husbands', but instead as husbands who 'hurry back from their offices and factories' and 'share the work, worry and pleasure of the children'; Jephcott in working-class Bermondsey found that 'husbands and wives were aware of, and welcomed, a closer partnership' as well as greater 'joint decision-making, especially as regards the children's upbringing'; and among Gavron's samples, well over half the wives agreed with the proposition that their relationships with their husbands were more equal than those of their parents. Above all perhaps, there was Ferdynand Zweig, who in his inquiry at the Mullard factory asked 63 married men to respond to the statement 'Man is master in his own house' – to which around three-quarters of the sample claimed that that notion no longer applied, and that in their own homes there was absolute or near equality between themselves and their wives. Significantly, when he then separately asked Mullard wives, about two-thirds claimed that broadly the same principle applied. A newly married companionate-*cum*-egalitarian couple in the early 1960s were Hunter Davies and Margaret Forster, both from working-class Carlisle but now setting up home in London. 'My mother was most perturbed by the equality of our marriage,' recalls Forster. 'She saw that since we were both working, Hunter as a journalist and myself as a teacher, we should both share in the jobs which needed to be done ... My mother admitted the fairness of the arrangement, but she seemed unable fully to approve. Was her air of faint disapproval really a regret that these changes had come too late for her? It wasn't talked about. She went back to my father reluctantly . . .'[23]

Of course, 'companionate' did not *necessarily* mean 'equal'. 'Ask any couple who chooses the family car and most will agree that the husband decides on the model,' noted a columnist in the *Bolton Evening News* in 1962, though she did add that the wife got to choose the colour. Or take a butcher's observation two years earlier to the *Daily Mail* about a typical middle-class couple: 'They come in here together. She buys the meat, then he hands over the money. What's the matter? Can't he trust his wife with money?' Still, at a deeper level, it was clear that something of fundamental importance was happening – something that went far beyond the small change of day-to-day behaviour. The historian Claire Langhamer has charted an emotional revolution that, broadly speaking, seems to have unfolded through the 1950s and into the 1960s, a largely female-driven revolution that was less to do with sex as such than with idealised notions of marriage as an expression of love and a means of personal fulfilment. It was a revolution fuelled by popular magazines, by romantic literature, by films and crooners – but, emphasises Langhamer, 'the willingness to marry for love *above all else* was strongly linked to economic security' – in other words, would not have been possible without greater affluence and a full-employment economy. In the old, separate-spheres days, marriage had often been essentially a pragmatic bargain, with the wives usually even less romantic about the deal than the husbands. Now it was coming with a whole new baggage of shared expectations about entwined lives through to a glorious sunset. But as Langhamer observes, the problem was that 'people could fall out of love as readily as they could fall in love.'

The marriage of the Sheffield steelworker who for a week in May 1959 kept a diary for Zweig probably lay – like many others – somewhere between the traditional and the companionate:

Monday. 4.45 a.m. Up for work, enjoy double shift . . . Get home at 10.20 p.m., wife cooks supper, have words with the wife about daughter leaving school at midsummer, daughter wants to be tailoress, headteacher says she would do well in office. Bed 11.20. P.S. Wife has been busy washing, we have a washing machine.

Tuesday. I awoke 7.50, daughter crying Mam, Mam! I nudged the wife told her it was 7.50, she got up to get the children's breakfast, called the boy who was very tired, told him he would have to go to bed at 8.0 tomorrow. Got up myself at 8.30, sawn some wood then chop it. Had a shave, fetched the Express to read, daughter said she had fallen and hurt her shoulder playing rounders. She had fainted with the pain getting out of bed. Put some hardwood round the door to keep the draught out. Wife said she was fed up and browned off with the house, had an argument about her nerves, told her she should get out, said if she could go out she would go to work, but fear stopped her from going out, felt a bit down after that argument, had dinner of two eggs then work . . . Arrived home 10.20 took the watering can out as soon as I got in to water the lawn, washed, had my supper wrote this and then to bed. The wife says the boy ran in at 8.55 asked if his father had come home then washed and went straight to bed. The wife went to bed 10 minutes before me but she has just come down again sobbing saying she has been ill all day with her head.

Wednesday. I fetched the Express to read whilst the wife did some ironing, daughters shoulder a little better, a lot of wood to saw, off to work and feeling a lot better after the promise of some overtime, the day went very well at work, I also caught the 9.15 bus home. P.S. Wife and son had been in the garden from 6.0 to 9.30 and enjoyed it.

Thursday. Did not sleep too well, up at 4.45. Wife up at 6.50 messing about all day swapping and changing and cleaning carpets upstairs and downstairs, says she cannot explain how her nerves affect her, she has to go to the hospital tomorrow . . . I have had 3½ pints of beer today and enjoyed them.

Friday. Had a good nights sleep got up 8.5. Wife asked me what I was doing getting up at that time. Had a bit of breakfast wished the children good morning as they were going to school. Had a little chat with the wife, then helped her to shake a big carpet we both had a good 2 hours in the garden, it was now time for me to go to work, I bought a bottle of good sherry for the wife I have been told that with an egg in it it will help her nerves and also make her sleep better at night . . . I caught the 9.15 bus home. I told the wife I was going to have a bath the first thing but when I went up the bath was dirty so I had a few words with the wife about it because it was she who had left it like that so I had my supper in rather a gloomy manner.

'Today,' concluded that final entry, 'the wife went to the hospital the doctor asked her if she thought if she went to work in the company of other people it would help her to get better the wife said she would be alright there but it is the travelling there and back that she is afraid of.'[24]

Did the doctor also prescribe something for nerves? The historian Ali Haggett argues that following the discovery in 1952 of the anti-psychotic affects of chlorpromazine, which became the first major tran-quilliser and was marketed in Britain as Largactil, pharmaceutical companies did *not* particularly target women in their marketing of psychotropic drugs. Even so, it was striking that after early tests of the sedative Librium had been conducted in the late 1950s on some of the inmates at San Diego Zoo, the headline in one English paper was 'The Drug That Tames Tigers – What will it do for Nervous Women?' A few years later, in 1963, a much stronger type of benzodiazepine would be marketed as Valium, the proverbial mother's little helper. There was also the case of amphetamines. 'The reasons given by patients for taking amphetamines are relatively few,' reported the *British Medical Journal* in 1962 about the fact that in Newcastle the equivalent of 200,000 tablets was being prescribed monthly, overwhelmingly to women, especially middle-aged women. 'Depression, fatigue, obesity, and, surprisingly, anxiety are the most common . . .' As Richard Davenport-Hines notes on the basis of the report, 'several Newcastle women first received amphetamines from their hairdresser after complaining of depression or more commonly following a panic attack under a hairdrier.'[25]

One sort of pill would soon be getting a capital 'P'. 'Hard for the new generation to comprehend just how different life was in the late fifties, early sixties, pre-Pill, pre-coil, when the man not the woman was in charge of contraception,' recalled Fay Weldon in 2000. 'When the very word was still almost too rude and explicit to be mentioned, and body parts were a deep mystery to everyone except medical students. There were a few Marie Stopes "birth-control clinics" for women in the major cities, but you had to show a wedding ring to get access to one. Men had condoms, but often preferred not to use them. Abortion was frequent, dangerous and illegal.' In fact, the situation in relation to clinics was just starting to change for the better. In 1959 the Marie Stopes Clinic in central London held its first evening session for unmarried women, soon attracting women from all over the country, while two years later Helen Brook began the Brook Advisory Centre for Young People, albeit not yet admitting girls under 16. As for abortion, still illegally conducted in most cases, the *Daily Telegraph* estimated in April 1961 that there took place annually in England and Wales around 50,000 abortions for pregnant women who did not want to marry the father. 'We all know women, law-abiding citizens who, with no sense of crime, will "try everything" to end an unwanted pregnancy,' publicly declared the Labour MP Lena Jeger in 1958. Not long afterwards, she received a letter from a woman living in Newton Aycliffe, County Durham:

> I am writing on behalf of a large number of housewives on this new housing estate. We want abortion made legal (with no ties) and we want it now. I am going to send you a list of names and addresses of housewives here whose lives are just an agony of wondering if they are pregnant again, there is no happiness in any of these homes for these women and so it means the men can't be happy either. I myself have three young kiddies and can never afford to buy anything new for myself, and I live in constant fear of having any more children . . . One other friend has three kiddies and is very cold towards her husband. He in turn has turned to drink and bad temper. Yet another woman with three kiddies who swears she will commit suicide if she ever finds herself pregnant again.

'I could go on,' she added, 'but I am sure you have some idea just how unhappy we all are.'

In the event, although legalisation of abortion was still some way off, a new, more reliable form of contraception was on the immediate horizon. During 1961, the oral contraceptive pill, now already on sale in the US, was trialled in Britain, and that December the Health Minister, Enoch Powell, announced that GPs would henceforth be free to prescribe what the *Daily Mail* called 'the pink anti-birth pill', though as yet only to married women. It was undoubtedly a signal moment in women's modern history, even though the whole subject tended to be treated with kid gloves by the media. A refreshing exception was ITV's June 1961 documentary, *The Pill*:

There were [reported the *Daily Mirror*] more arguments in its favour than against – from the inventor, doctors, a sociologist, users and commentator Elaine Grand . . .

Miss Grand, the doctors and experts approached the subject calmly, and it was left to a group of Birmingham women who had experimented with the pill to make an emotional impact.

They all felt much happier, and one said it made for a more relaxed and natural marriage.

The religious viewpoint had only a brief say . . .[26]

In covering and exploring all this, the mainstream press tended to lag some way behind. 'One of the most uncompromisingly masculine institutions in the country' was Monica Furlong's apt description of *The Times* in her early 1962 survey of the fourth estate, noting also the 'coyness' of its recently introduced Monday women's page; turning to the *Daily Mirror*, where Marjorie Proops had not yet hit her full, authentic stride, Furlong observed that its three main topics remained sport, pets (especially budgies) and girls, while the letters conveyed a sense of husbands holding 'stoically to the view that the wife's place is in the home and that it is several paces behind and below that of her spouse'; even in the *Guardian*, where Mary Stott had been running its women's page since 1957, Furlong pointed out that although 'much space' was 'devoted to profiles of successful career women', this was accompanied by 'their writers often, in an unconscious defensive gesture, insisting that, despite intellectual or executive gifts, their subjects are feminine and attractive'. Arguably the most prominent female voice in Fleet Street belonged to Anne Scott-James of the *Daily Express*, but she was not really pushing back the boundaries. 'I PREDICT that career girls will become scarce as diamonds, and that employers will have to fight for their services,' she wrote in October 1959 about 'The 1960s Woman'. She gave two reasons for this 'strong reaction': 'One, jobs for women have proved pretty good hell. Two, there are now more young men than women, there's a glut of husbands, so why fend for yourself?' Waiting in the wings, ready to champion scepticism about the received wisdom of domesticity, was Katharine Whitehorn. Her celebrated *Observer* column would not start until

1963, but in a November 1960 *Spectator* piece, 'Nought for Homework', she reflected on behalf of herself 'and other sluts' that they were not willing to be 'finally judged as women by the way we run our houses'.[27]

'Sluts' were seldom allowed to sully the hottest market at the start of the new decade: the young female consumer. Magazines targeted at that readership were already flourishing – *Mirabelle*, *Romeo*, *Valentine*, *Roxy* and *Boyfriend* all began between 1956 and 1959 – but the early months of 1960 saw competition intensifying further. Newcomers included *Princess* ('A paper just like mummy's'), *Judy* (free bangle with first issue), *Marty* (named after Marty Wilde and claiming to be the 'first-ever photo romance weekly'), *Honey* ('Young, gay and get ahead!') and *Date* (absorbing the film fans' weekly, *Picturegoer*). Surveying the scene, Michael Frayn in the *Guardian* reckoned that the newly launched *Marty* was 'about the best of the bunch'. 'Even so,' he went on, 'the first story is about a girl who puts her boy-friend on the road to stardom as a rock 'n' roll singer. He callously forgets her – and simultaneously loses her grip on the cats. So he quickly remembers her again, marries her, and gets one of his records in the top twenty. Nice moral touch there.' As for the genre as a whole,

> *Mirabelle* carries a letter from an unmarried mother intended as a warning to other girls, but nowhere else do these strange magazines breathe a word about any of the problems their readers must really want help with.
>
> They hang suspended in a sexless limbo where 'hotly passionate kisses' (I quote) are just rungs on the ladder to marriage and where marriage means simply status and release from loneliness.

'These magazines,' concluded Frayn, 'return to the loneliness theme over and over again . . .'

A random 1961 dip, for the week ending 18 March, fills out the picture. 'Will El's loneliness never end?' asked *Mirabelle*'s front page about The King, while its 'romantic all-picture love stories' included 'Stars Look Down', 'Melody of Love' and 'Flatter Him My Heart'; *Boyfriend* kicked off with 'Flight of Fancy', the picture-story of an air hostess; *Cherie*'s letters included Lynda Rowe of Luton claiming to have 'exactly 621 pictures of Cliff'; and in *Marty* there were not only the usual clutch of stories ('Runaway Heart', 'Heart to Heart',

'Ginchytime Girls', 'This Must Be Love') and the special offer of a cut-out coupon to nominate a 'Disc to Remember' and send to Radio Luxembourg's Jimmy Savile, but also the last in a series by Jean Addams on 'ROMANCE ... and YOU'. Each of the previous weeks had included a behavioural quiz, and now she summed up. 'It's easy to see you'll make the grade as a boy's best girl,' she praised those who had scored high marks. 'You're a good mixer, a girl who joins clubs, social groups ... You're not a pushover for any old date because you don't want to be labelled a good-time girl ... You go Dutch when he's hard-up and you listen to his problems even when you don't understand them ... You've certainly got what it takes to win, and keep, a man's love.' But for those scoring under 15 marks:

I'm worried about you! You've so much to learn. Perhaps the best way is to take stock of your behaviour so far.

Are you an easy pick-up? Can any boy date you? Do you kiss freely and liberally, and boast about it afterwards? Do you lie about your job, your people, or your home? Do you try to impress not only the boy, but his folks? ...

Or are you, by any chance, the type who believes that if a fellow kisses you, even lightly, he must be ready to pop the ring on your finger? Are you possessive? Do you demand to know all his movements? Are you jealous (and show it) if he so much as looks at another girl? ...

In short: 'Just take a pull on yourself, honey – you've a long way to go.'[28]

The core market remained that for adult women, above all the mass-circulation weeklies – so much so that by the 1960s five out of six women were seeing at least one magazine per week. 'The social revolution has given women incomes beyond anything their mothers could have imagined,' declared an advertisement in March 1962 for the market leader, boasting some eight million readers. 'And *Woman* has played a major social role by training them in the wise use of that prosperity. Because of *Woman* they have new pride in their homes; in their house-keeping; in their personal appearance.' *Woman's Mirror*, advertising in February 1961 the two main features in its latest issue, staked rather lower ground:

The bride of the year? *Woman's Mirror* spotlights Henrietta Tiarks, most sought-after deb of 1957, now engaged to the Marquis of Tavistock, eldest son of the Duke of Bedford. Will her wedding be the most outstanding of 1961? Read the inspiring success story of this attractive young heiress . . . her family . . . her friends . . . her future . . .

HAPPY BIRTHDAY – PRINCE ANDREW! Here at last is the exclusive, behind-the-scenes story and wonderful pictures of 'the baby that nobody knows . . . The Secret Prince'. Already this 'chubby bundle of chuckles' is an engaging personality and, incredibly, an influential member of the Royal Family! For the first time ever, you can read about Prince Andrew's life – his playmates, his nursery, and the Queen's plans for his childhood . . .

More generally, it was probably true, as the historian Jeffrey Weeks has noted, that 'a well-established magazine like *Woman* was more sexually explicit in the 1960s than in the 1940s, but still found it difficult to handle sexual relations except on its problems page, or in relation to motherhood'; Weeks adds that 'it represented a particular type of femininity, more relaxed than a generation earlier but still domestic in its setting'; while Ali Haggett observes that it was not until the late 1960s that women's magazines began to tackle questions of depression and mental illness in any sustained way. Helpfully detailed analysis at the time came from Thena Heschel, who examined and compared 106 randomly selected stories that appeared in *Woman* and *Woman's Own* in 1952 and 1962. Over 80 were directly concerned with love; their heroes 'almost without exception' were professionals, independent businessmen or senior executives; among the heroines, 'the vast majority have no great interest in any career other than husband and children'; apart from the 'ever-popular hospital or surgery', only two stories were set in workplaces other than offices; and, perhaps most tellingly, 'on the whole there is very little difference in the stories published by the two magazines in 1952 and 1962', with 'no indication that the increasing vogue for social realism has produced any writers for the woman's magazine market'. It was all too much for the veteran campaigner Dora Russell. 'The main point about them is that they are not women's magazines but men's magazines,' she told the NUT's 1960 conference on popular culture, 'because first of all they are for the advertising firms who want to sell their products, among which cosmetics are not the least, and secondly they do present an image of women which is the kind of woman that men want to have, and unfortunately this kind of woman is expected to remain at home and take no interest in outside affairs' – a comment eliciting no response from the overwhelmingly male delegates.

Of course it is easy enough for the historian to cherry-pick quotes, and in the early 1960s *Woman's Own* (circulation second only to *Woman*) certainly obliged. In 1961 one of its star columnists, Monica Dickens, unambiguously informed her readers that 'you can't have deep and safe happiness in marriage and the exciting independence of a career as well,' that 'it isn't fair on your husband.' And in February 1962 a reader in her 50s, whose children were grown-up and who was thinking of leaving her husband ('he never takes me out or wants to talk and life is very dull'), did not get very far. 'Your problem is not unique by any means, but I do not think that leaving your husband is the solution,' replied the magazine's agony aunt Mary Grant. 'If every wife who found that her marriage had gone rather stale left her husband, the world would be a greater mess than it already is!'[29]

The random March 1961 sample, though, offers a fuller, perhaps more representative picture of the distinctive world and assumptions that these magazines inhabited and disseminated – to, it is worth repeating, five out of every six women.

Starting with some of the monthlies. In *Woman's Journal*, the wholly admiring profile was of 'the MAN of today', Prince Philip – 'no lover of tradition, a rejecter of sentiment', yet 'he preserves the receipted bill for his wife's wedding bouquet and on every anniversary sends her a replica of the white flowers she carried' – while in *Woman and Shopping*, Zita Alden's 'People' column featured Polly Elwes, the television personality married to Peter Dimmock, BBC TV Head of Outside Entertainment. 'She confessed that with her, marriage definitely came first. If there was the slightest suggestion that her work was taking up too much of her time – she would give it up immediately.' Perhaps surprisingly, the editorial diet was more intriguing in *Woman and Beauty*. The front page may have been 'Special Offer for 5/6: A Baroque Bracelet with the Golden Look', and the cookery column by radio's Jack de Manio may have been about giving dinner to the boss, but Dr

Eustace Chesser's regular column on sexual matters, this month 'Frigidity', was frank enough, albeit of arguable validity. 'Even today there is still often a false attitude of propriety in women. Many regard their husbands' sexual desires as coarse, gross and animalistic. And because they don't feel such desires themselves, they think that they are in some way superior. They may even care to look upon "that side" of marriage with a kind of smug contempt.' Such an attitude, Chesser added, could 'often be traced back to circumstances outside their control, to inhibitions implanted in their childhood, and perhaps ineradicable'. *Woman and Home* included an old standby's ineffable 'My World and Yours' monthly column: 'There is, of course, a way to make life appear more romantic and enjoyable. It is known as "gracious living". Here GODFREY WINN talks to you about it with his usual sensible charm.' The real interest, though, was in the ads. Gwen Berryman aka Mrs Doris Archer extolled Smith's crisps (only needing to be 'crushed to farthing size' to 'add crispy magic to the most ordinary dishes'); the Hovis ad evoked home as 'a pair of old slippers, a sleeping cat, the children arguing over their game of ludo'; and a full-page ad for Leisure kitchens, built by Allied Ironfounders 'in strong silent steel', spelled out a comprehensive domestic wish list:

I want . . . Leisure in my first kitchen. John and I are getting married, and we're going to have a super kitchen from the start.

I want . . . plenty of Leisure drawers and shelves. I want wall cupboards . . . and cupboards with swing-round shelves . . . and a special cupboard for dishes to drip themselves dry.

I want . . . colourful, easy-to-keep-clean Leisure in my kitchen. A built-to-last kitchen in silent steel . . . full of drawers that slide easily, doors that don't warp.

'And,' clinching the deal, 'I'd hang strings of onions and buy gay tea towels.'

Among those weeklies for week ending 18 March, two items stood out in *Woman's Day*. One was the new serial, *Doctor's Heartbreak* by Alex Stuart. Stuart was chairman of the recently founded Romantic Novelists Association – 'launching', explained the editor Mary Francis, 'a campaign against the sordid and salacious novels which are being published today'.

The other was a letter titled 'Home Cooking' from Mrs M. Beswick of Haltwhistle, Northumberland: 'For married bliss cake, take 1 lb love, 1 lb cheerfulness, pinch of unselfishness. Mix all together with 1 gill of sympathy and spice with a bright fireside. Put in a tin of contentment and bake well all your life.' *Woman's Mirror* started with seven pages of the continuing serialisation of 'My Story' by the Duchess of Argyll, but did have Marjorie Proops in vigorous agony-aunt action. 'Woo him,' she instructed 'Felice' about her hard-working but affection-lite husband. 'Be seductive. Be alluring. Slosh on the scent and wear tight form-fitting sweaters. Snuggle up.' And to 'Wanton', asking how a woman should keep her air of mystery: 'Talk less, think more . . . and let your neckline plunge at the back instead of the front.' The most down-to-earth weekly was as usual the highly successful relative newcomer, *Woman's Realm*. 'Sitting in my newly decorated kitchen,' related Mrs E. R. of Croydon in the letters page, 'I was horrified to see how badly out of place my old wooden clothes horse looked, so I went out and bought 1½ yards of self-adhesive plastic, in a gay contemporary pattern. I then covered the uprights and rungs of my clothes horse with this. What a difference it made!' Clare Shepherd ran the problems page, this week including a 22-year-old who had been married for three months: 'I get so miserable at times that I feel like crying. My husband doesn't help me very much. If we have company or go out anywhere, I am immediately forgotten, and if there happens to be a pretty girl there, all he seems to do is to try to impress her.' Shepherd's answer included practical advice, but not before some home truths:

> If the fact that your husband chose you out of all the other pretty girls and asked you to be his wife has not given you confidence, there seems little I can do to help. You have only been married for three months, and there should be a lot for you to be wonderfully happy about. It is possible you have not fully realised that whether a marriage is happy or not depends very much on what the wife puts into it. If a wife is warm and loving, it very seldom happens that a husband looks elsewhere.

That left the big two. In *Woman's Own*, that week's editorial column ('Between Friends') was in praise of marriage, its 'reward' defined as 'the true happiness that comes from doing what you love, and loving what you do, with all your heart'; while elsewhere, Roderick Wimpole wrote his 'Doctor's Diary', and on the letters page Mrs O. Moody of Southsea posed a question: 'Why is it, I wonder, that men cannot bear to be beaten at anything by a woman? I lost my first boyfriend by beating him at tennis, my second by winning a swimming race against him and my third by getting the prize at a fairground game of darts. It was then that I started to play the losing game. Soon afterwards I met my husband who, strangely enough, has always beaten me at everything!' Monica Dickens's column, 'Let's be frank about petting', was about a different type of pre-marital loss. 'Keeping your standards high never made anyone less desirable,' she insisted. 'Let down the bars once, and there is no reason why you shouldn't do it again. You'll want to do it again. Just petting isn't fun any more. Go on feeling like that, and you are well on the way to becoming a first-class promiscuous tramp. And people will know what you are. It shows.' For one protagonist in 'Mary Grant's Problems Page' it was already too late. 'My girl friend and I work in the same office. We are both in love with the manager and my friend finds she is expecting a baby, although she broke off the affair some weeks ago. I know he behaved badly, but I still love him and would like to help him if I could.' 'Surely,' replied Grant, 'it is your friend who needs help? If she has not confided in her mother, she should do so at once.' After recommending that the friend get in touch with the National Council for the Unmarried Mother and her Child, the agony aunt ended briskly: 'Do try to forget your feelings for the manager and stop wasting your sympathy on him; he has behaved so badly that he certainly does not deserve it.'

Woman's counter-attractions included four pieces of fiction ('Surgeon's Dilemma', 'Bride for a Bargain', 'The Happy Ending', 'Magic in Piccadilly'), the continuation of the series 'Happy Homecoming' about a real-life couple (Peggy and Tony) moving into a new home, the latest instalment of Dirk Bogarde's *My Life Story*, Ruth Morgan's cookery column ('Semolina at Your Service'), and Veronica Scott's 'The Three Faces of Fashion' (ie, sophisticated + casual + feminine). The stand-out ad was for Lux – as endorsed by 'a top top-model and a very nice person', Sandra Paul ('one marriage, one lifetime, she says') – while in his doctor's column Alan Lloyd was studiously neutral about the '"happiness" pills' now being popped, he estimated, at around a million a day: 'Such pills work on the emotions through the stem of the brain. Tranquillizers are designed to subdue the overwrought, while pep pills aim at lifting the depressed. Their job is to make you feel: "Gosh, life's better than I thought!".' Evelyn Home's remedy was different in her 'Talk It Over' problems page, responding to a reader with a shouting, bullying husband ('He's just the same even as a lover – no tender words or kisses, but because he is satisfied I must be as well'). The advice was seemingly timeless:

> Many men are boorish after work, and many are poor lovers; they need to be taught manners and tenderness by their wives.
>
> This is your job in future – the one you took on for better, for worse, remember? So don't waste time grumbling; start polishing your rough diamond into a perfect husband.[30]

––––––––

Just over a year later appeared memorable and long-lasting – but at this point still strictly minority – dispatches from an utterly different world. 'Mrs Doris Lessing,' began John Bowen's review in *Punch* in May 1962,

> is a novelist in her forties, whose first book, set in Africa, was a best-seller, but who has written no other best-sellers. She is a divorcée, and lives alone; she has one child. She has lived in Africa. Politically she is of the Left. She has written a novel, *The Golden Notebook*, of which the heroine is Anna, a novelist in her forties, who has written one best-selling novel, set in Africa, and can write no more novels. Anna is a divorcée with one child, and lives alone. Politically Anna is of the Left. She has spent some time in Africa. Anna is trying to write a novel about Ella, a novelist in her forties who has written one best-selling novel, and can write no more. Ella is a divorcée with one child, and lives alone. Politically she is of the Left . . .

Published the previous month, *The Golden Notebook* was a novel mainly about women that was reviewed largely by men. Peter Green in the *Daily Telegraph* acknowledged Lessing's 'capacity for realistic portrayal', but in its 568 'closely printed pages' was deterred by Anna Wulf's 'interminable ramblings' and 'altogether too much agonising and breast-beating, of the kind that invariably turns up when an intelligent artist breaks with the Communists'; in the *Listener*, the poet Vernon Scannell praised Lessing's 'courageous honesty, her intelligence and passion', but argued that 'the tone is too earnest and the women suffer too intensely', so that 'gradually a climate is engendered of thick, overheated solemnity'; and in the *TLS*, another poet, Randall Swingler, not only found Anna a 'drooling, exhibitionist hysteric' but reckoned that something had gone badly wrong artistically: 'It would seem that Mrs Lessing has attempted something here which she could not control. Her material has got badly out of hand and in desperation she has bundled the lot together and chucked it at the reader to make of it what he can.' The most perceptive reviewer in a socio-cultural sense was the *New Statesman*'s Robert Taubman. Calling the novel 'not a creation but a document', and asserting that 'simply as a record of how it is to be free and responsible, a woman in relation to men and to other women and the struggle to come to terms with one's self about these things and about writing and politics, it seems to me unique in its truthfulness and range,' he speculated that it might 'soon displace the Simone de Beauvoir paperbacks in the hands of all those who want what she is supposed to provide – a sort of intelligent woman's guide to the intelligent woman'. And, he added, 'Doris Lessing says far more of genuine interest, is less self-conscious and much less boring.'

One of the book's earliest female readers was Phyllis Willmott (who in November 2013 would die a fortnight before Lessing). 'Ralph [Samuel] very anxious to know what I will make of it,' she noted on 5 May. Some three weeks later, she had finished. 'It seems to me, in the summing up, to be an unnecessarily prolonged, involved and chaotic feat of imaginative usage of biographical material,' she reflected. 'Their way of life,' she observed about Anna and her circle, 'induces a feeling of horror for them rather than that they are unpleasant, nasty people. They seem intent on mucking their lives up. Her mistake is to "project" this style of life – which is undoubtedly hers and her friends – to be general . . .' Then came the crux:

> Why did she [Anna] need to be so aggressively feminist? Why did she need to act like a male sexually when it so clearly was known to her that it went against the feminine grain? Her assumption seemed to be that she was going to *force* her way through to a promiscuity, and enjoyment of it . . .
>
> All the same, there is some good good good stuff in it . . .[31]

PART THREE

9

Don't Hang Riley

'Very cold,' noted Dennis Dee's typically taciturn East Riding diary entry for Saturday, 10 December 1960. 'Neville came for some eggs. Busy with various jobs.' Next day, the *Sunday Express* exposed what it called 'the Lilac Establishment' (anti-capital punishment, pro-pornography, pro-homosexuality and exemplified by Henry Moore 'laying down his lucrative chisel in order to sign petitions'); Henry St John observed the demolition of 'the booking hall and entrance' of Ealing Broadway station ('there appeared to be about 3 negroes in the handful of workmen thus engaged'); and Adam Faith was on *Face to Face*. 'Agreeable surprise', reckoned viewers generally, though one found him 'a very ordinary fellow' and another thought it 'a waste of time for a man of John Freeman's calibre to interview a fledgling like Faith'. Two parliamentary assertions illuminated the 14th – the Postmaster-General, Reginald Bevins, stating that colour TV was unlikely in the near future, and the War Secretary, John Profumo, declaring in relation to *The Army Game* being banned in Pontefract Barracks that 'there are errors of judgement in all walks of life and some are fortunate in not having the spotlight turned on them' – while that evening Nella Last in Barrow 'didn't feel any interest in "Coronation St."' (the second episode). Even so, not only did the *Manchester Evening News*'s critic reckon that it 'has promise of a warm, homely series, bursting with feasible characters and such convincingly ungrammatical and slovenly speech', but the next episode (on Friday the 16th) saw the entrance of Arthur Lowe as teetotal Leonard Swindley, lay preacher at the Glad Tidings Mission. Another teetotaller spent that evening on the *Any Questions?* panel at the Memorial Hall in Pensford, Somerset. Would

Labour, it was asked, be able to supply an effective opposition? Undoubtedly, answered Anthony Wedgwood Benn, given that 'Eastern European advance' demonstrated that 'the idea of private enterprise offering any hope to a community like our own in the world today is gradually being realised to be out of date.' The run-up to Christmas suggested that capitalism still had a flicker of life left ('the shops – and the streets – are jammed,' noted the *FT*, adding that 'a record number of turkeys' had been sold), before (on the 27th) the Beatles, recently back from their first Hamburg stint, gave a storming performance in the ballroom of Litherland Town Hall, not far from the Mersey docks. 'People went crazy for their closing number, "What'd I Say",' recalled the prominent local DJ Bob Wooler. 'Paul took the mike off the stand, shed his guitar and did fantastic antics all over the stage. They were all stomping like hell and the audience went *mad* . . . That was the beginning of Beatlemania.' Four days later, things got even better for youth at large when National Service call-up formally ended, a liberating moment for a whole generation. But as that large door opened, a small one closed: New Year's Eve was also the last day of the farthing coin as legal tender, though in truth it was already several years since bus conductors had willingly accepted the jaunty little wren.[1]

'Some fearfully unfunny material,' according to the *Daily Mirror*'s Clifford Davis, marred Morecambe and Wise's New Year's Day appearance on *Sunday Night at the London Palladium*; three days later, as *Punch*'s Eric Keown criticised the Old Vic production of *A Midsummer Night's Dream* as too knockabout ('had she been a man, Judi Dench with her astonishing speed and agility would have been an England fly-half'), Beryl Bainbridge appeared on *Coronation Street* as a placard-carrying ban-the-bomb student friend of Ken Barlow; next evening, David Turner's notable debut TV play *The Train Set*, going out live and unrecorded, was about a Birmingham factory worker's relationship with his son and wife ('the reactions of the sample audience as a whole can hardly be described as enthusiastic,' noted a BBC report, with 'some marked disgust with the language by several of the characters in the factory scenes'); reviews continued to be dusty for Shelagh Delaney's recently opened second play, *The Lion in Love*, at the Royal Court ('her reach exceeds her grasp,' thought Alan Brien in the *Spectator*); and on Saturday, 7 January, at this stage with Ian Hendry in the main role,

Patrick Macnee's John Steed as his assistant, and no Cathy Gale let alone Emma Peel, *The Avengers* began – the same day that the police came knocking at an anonymous-looking bungalow in Cranleigh Drive, Ruislip, where Peter and Helen Kroger were running the communications centre of a huge Soviet spy ring. But at the start of 1961 this was all small beer compared to *The Archers*. 'The question whether Miss Carol Grey should or shouldn't marry Charles Grenville has been agitating the people of England more than the things that leader writers write about,' reflected one radio critic, just as a *Radio Times* letter from a Southport listener congratulated Grenville for his 'taming' of the 'shrewish' Grey ('it will be good to see her cut down to size'). On Tuesday the 10th, five-year-old Janice Galloway began primary school ('I wore a black blazer with a Saltcoats crest on a wavy line, a grey skirt, a vest, a shirt and long socks, none of it cheap,' plus of course 'brand-new flat, lace-up shoes'); two days later, T. Dan Smith set out in a Newcastle paper his personal credo ('it is *here* and *now* that the love one is admonished to feel for one's neighbour can be given positive expression – right *here* and *now*!!!'); and on Sunday the 15th, Noël Coward issued a blast in the *Sunday Times* against drama's new wave ('it is bigoted and stupid to believe that tramps and prostitutes and underprivileged housewives frying onions and using ironing boards are automatically the salt of the earth'), Henry St John dropped in at Ealing's A.B.C. ('a cup of coffee and a macaroon' for 1s 2d), and Harold Macmillan recorded that the outgoing Archbishop of Canterbury, the controlling Geoffrey Fisher, was '*violently*, even *brutally* opposed' to having the more congenial, bushy-eyebrowed Michael Ramsey as his successor. Next day, Madge Martin in Oxford went 'to the pictures after tea' to see the latest Norman Wisdom farce *The Bulldog Breed* ('not too good'); on Tuesday, after students at Hull had complained to a Sunday paper about the university, the Larkin verdict was that they were 'simply sodding little shop stewards'; on Thursday, Judy Haines in Chingford enjoyed a 'pleasant "Woman's Hour," knitting Pamela's golden cardigan the while'; and on Friday, typical viewer reaction to *Nina and Frederik* was that the Danish-Dutch singing duo were 'like a lovely fresh breeze', having 'no need for sequin suits, oversize jewellery or undersize garments'. Sunday the 22nd was a day for memories – Phyllis Willmott, back in respectable working-class south-east London, contrasting the 'quiet and very empty' streets with how before the war they had been full of unemployed men 'tramping' them 'in search of an extra shilling or two', and, in the doomed, soon-to-be submerged Tryweryn Valley, the last passenger train making its way on the winding track from Bala to Blaenau Ffestiniog and back again – before January ended with Ossie Clark and Celia Birtwell meeting for the first time on the 27th ('the night of the fifteenth episode of *Coronation Street*', as Clark later put it), Manchester City's Denis Law next day scoring six goals on a swamp at Luton before the match was abandoned, and *Housewives' Choice* on the Light Programme on the morning of the 31st coming up against a feature called *Two of a Kind* on the Home Service. One of the two, Ted, mentioned that at nine each morning he retreated to his room to work, but not so for the other Primrose Hill poet, Sylvia. 'I certainly,' she explained, 'have a life just like all the other housewives and mothers in our district: shopping, dishes and taking care of the baby and so forth. I think very few people have any idea I do anything at all except household chores.'[2]

Quite apart from ecclesiastical manoeuvres, the PM was in bullish mood at the start of 1961. 'We've got it good,' he told the *Daily Mail* about the Affluent Society. 'Let's keep it good. There is nothing to be ashamed of in that.' But everything, Macmillan well knew, depended upon the health of the economy – a cause of increasing concern. 'The situation could become most unattractive and cause unhappiness,' predicted the distinguished merchant banker Lionel Fraser in a letter to *The Times* in early January; and he demanded from government 'a Five-year Plan', to which 'the vast majority of the people would rise magnificently'. Ernest Skinner, in an earlier life Montagu Norman's faithful private secretary at the Bank of England, was appalled. 'One shudders to think,' he wrote to the paper, 'of the errors of judgement, political expedient, and bureaucratic authority that might be cemented into such a plan.' The force, though, was now seemingly with planning, and later that month the President of the Board of Trade, the ebullient Reginald Maudling, told the Merseyside branch of the National Union of Manufacturers that he had no doctrinal objection to the concept. What about the currency? About the same time, the National Institute of Economic and Social Research argued that devaluation of sterling was probably the only way to achieve a breathing space for the economy while more fundamental policy actions were taken. But again, an old Bank of England hand sought to reassert the ancient verities. 'Siren voices are heard once more,' began Harry Siepmann's mid-February letter to *The Times*, written from the Athenaeum and calling devaluation 'the forcible and unilateral denouncing of a hundred thousand honest contracts . . . a moral outrage'. Within weeks, with sterling under pressure, Selwyn Lloyd as Chancellor was compelled to provide a categorical public assurance that there would be no devaluation, but for Macmillan these were becoming increasingly difficult times. 'He says the £ will crash in the summer,' he noted after a visit from his trusted informal economic adviser Roy Harrod. 'We *must* restrict imports. Treasury and Board of Trade say the opposite. What is a poor Prime Minister to do?'

'An intellectual who looks like a sketch frugally executed in India ink – strong, thoughtful white face, black hair and neat moustache' was how Mollie Panter-Downes described Macmillan's least favourite Cabinet colleague, Enoch Powell, recently restored to the front bench as Minister of Health. On 1 February, he announced significantly raised NHS charges (including prescriptions doubling, to 2s), provoking a major political storm; later that day, Len Fairclough made his *Coronation Street* entrance; and the same evening, two note-taking gentlemen from the Lord Chamberlain's office attended *Fings Ain't Wot They Used T'Be* at the Garrick, leading to a series of cuts and changes that particularly affected Barbara Windsor's suggestive role. Taste was also in evidence at Bournemouth Town Hall on the 3rd, as the *Any Questions?* panel was asked to comment on 'the preponderance of kitchen sink playwrights these days'. 'I don't like 'em,' responded sturdy, commonsensical James Callaghan. 'I'm sick and tired of the BBC plays on Sunday night, of seeing the sort of thing we're getting.' Sunday the 5th saw the launch of the *Sunday Telegraph* – a dog's dinner, but notable for Nigel Lawson as trenchant City editor and the launch of Peregrine Worsthorne's 'Talking of Politics' column, acclaiming Powell as 'something new on the post-war political scene', namely 'a Tory minister of first-class intellectual calibre and of proved integrity who is passionately averse to the over-spending of public money' – before next day a live invitation from Eamonn Andrews to Danny Blanchflower to appear on *This Is Your Life* received a brusque refusal. 'I don't need to give any reason,' the Spurs captain told callers after returning home to Palmers Green. 'It was a matter of principle. My private life is my own.' Controversy too with the BBC's announcement on the 8th that the legendary *Children's Hour* was shortly to disappear from the radio, while that Wednesday evening – only a few weeks after the publication of Ludovic Kennedy's *10 Rillington Place* had thrown sharp doubt on the guilt of the hanged Timothy Evans – a haunting scene played out in Shrewsbury. For about an hour from 9.30, recorded the local paper, 'people living in Albert and Victoria Streets, adjoining the prison, were shocked and horrified by cries and chantings from the prisoners of "Don't hang Riley"' – the 21-year-old butcher's assistant George Riley, who on the basis of a confession which he later withdrew had been found guilty of murdering a widow, Adeline Mary Smith. Next morning, at 8.00 a.m., he was hanged. 'I knew the Riley boy; his family were patients of my father,' recalled John Ryle, eight at the time. 'I remember seeing the front page of the *Shrewsbury Chronicle* after the execution; and walking with my mother along the river, along the flooded towpath – swans sheltering among the osiers on half-submerged river islands – past the water gate, under the railway bridge to the prison, the site of one of Housman's threnodies: *They hang us now in Shrewsbury jail . . .*'[3]

At lunchtime on the day that Riley died, the still leather-jacketed Beatles made the first of their 292 appearances at the Cavern – alcohol-free, young office workers, no Teds. Over the next few days, the 14-year-old East Ender Helen Shapiro released her first single, 'Don't Treat Me Like a Child'; a frustrated Henry St John visited 'the pornographic shop' in Soho's Little Newport Street, where 'they too were displaying some magazines done up in transparent covers, so that they could not be opened'; Philip Larkin (who might have sympathised) had the first of his monthly jazz columns in the *Daily Telegraph*; a strike-enforced repeat of the first episode of *Coronation Street* prompted the *Daily Mirror*'s Jack Bell to call it a 'drab and doleful' series 'from which I would gladly have taken a rest'; John Bloom's wedding reception at the Savoy included two enormous wedding cakes in the shape of a washing-machine and a dishwasher; a talk on the Third Programme by Nikolaus Pevsner began with the assertion that 'queer things are happening in architecture today'; the latest *Black and White Minstrel*

Show was greeted by viewers as 'as usual, a tip-top show'; and the two records that Anthony Heap bought for his son's 12th birthday were a selection of songs from *Oliver!* and 'a currently popular comedy number "Goodness Gracious Me"'. There was also that mid-February a counter-cultural trio of events. 'Abstraction is "out", and a new manner, sharply flavoured with the signs, slogans and mordant humour of metropolitan life, is "in",' observed *The Times* about the quasi-annual *Young Contemporaries* exhibition in London, with the Royal College of Art student David Hockney among those identified as further adding 'a weird, satirical element' to what is often viewed as the start of British Pop art; some 5,000 people joined Bertrand Russell in the civil disobedience of a Whitehall sit-in against Polaris, the British nuclear deterrent; and at the Aldwych, John Whiting's *The Devils*, specially commissioned by Peter Hall for his Royal Shakespeare Company, had according to one critic 'speeches that for power have not been written by an Englishman in the English theatre since Webster'. None of this was Judy Haines's world. On the 20th she 'finished Pamela's v-necked cardigan', while her elder daughter Ione 'looked lovely going off in hers this morning' and was welcomed by a friend 'to the v-necked Club, for the "best people"'; three days later the girls 'stayed up for "Beyond our Ken"'; and on the 27th, after going to a matinee of Dirk Bogarde and John Mills in *The Singer Not the Song* ('quite good'), she returned to a disappointing sight: 'Washing soaking on line. I had hoped it would be rescued by a neighbour.' There was also disappointment in middle England – or, at the least, instinctive suspicion – about the eventual prospect of decimalisation. 'Do let us retain something British,' Mrs N. F. Bond of Cecil Road, NW10 wrote to the *Mirror*. 'The present system has been in use for a long time so why change it now?' And M.B. of Croydon agreed: 'A lot of mothers would find a new system a curse. It's worrying enough thinking what to get for dinner without having to work out how much to pay for it.'⁴

The major corporate story during the early months of 1961 concerned the *Daily Herald*. Owned 51 per cent by Odhams Press, 49 per cent by the TUC, the paper was an appreciably more faithful friend to the Labour party than the *Daily Mirror* was. But unfortunately, unlike the *Mirror*, the *Herald* had for a long time been struggling commercially, a process not significantly checked by an editorial move upmarket in the course of 1960. And now, to Hugh Gaitskell's considerable alarm, the Mirror Group under the overbearing leadership of Cecil King was making a strong bid to take over Odhams, less for the dubious prize of the *Herald* than for its range of successful magazines, including *Woman* and *Woman's Own*. In the event the government stood aside (kicking the monopoly issue into the long grass by setting up a royal commission on the press), Gaitskell and his colleagues were divided among themselves, King reluctantly promised to keep the *Herald* alive for a minimum of seven years, and eventually the bid triumphed. It happened to coincide with the formal opening in early March of the *Mirror*'s new building in Holburn Circus, described by Patrick Skene Catling in *Punch* as 'the world's most palatial, most magnificently equipped newspaper factory', with an 'overall appearance of orthodox modernity, of functional efficiency, brightness and colour'. Features included 3,170 fluorescent light fittings, seven automatic passenger lifts, the machine room in the basement like 'the empire room of an ocean liner' and, on the ninth floor, the boardroom chairs 'covered in purple leather'. 'Britain has known many powerful publishers,' declared a *New York Times* profile of King, 'but none has ever ruled such an empire as the one he heads.' A very minor outpost of that empire was the legendary children's comic the *Eagle*, itself only owned by Odhams since 1959: at its height in the early 1950s, it had sold some 800,000 copies, but now under the unsympathetic control of the Mirror Group's juvenile publications division it went into a precipitate fall, with square-jawed Colonel Dan Dare helpless to avert it. As for the reprieved *Herald*, the hope was that it could find its own distinctive, commercially viable market. 'The new "Daily Herald" differs greatly from its predecessor,' its promotion manager informed John Freeman at the *New Statesman* soon after the takeover. 'We are trying to make this a popular, radical, and responsible newspaper which appeals to both material and moral idealism.'[5]

Elsewhere during March, a month of exceptionally benign weather, 'Astonishing Mastery of Cello at 16' was *The Times*'s headline for Jacqueline du Pré's professional debut at the Wigmore Hall, including 'an account of Bach's C minor unaccompanied suite that thrilled the blood with its depth and intuitive eloquence'; Sylvia Plath, having had her appendix out, reflected how her fellow-patients in St Pancras

Hospital did not 'fuss or complain or whine, except in a joking way'; following a *Panorama* item on sex crimes, 'many viewers felt far too much was heard of psychiatric "mumbo jumbo"'; opening the annual conference of the National Association for Mental Health, Enoch Powell described the still operational asylums built by 'our forefathers' as 'isolated, majestic, imperious, brooded over by the gigantic water tower' – in effect, the start of the shift to care in the community; the Jaguar E-type was unveiled at the Geneva Motor Show; the third series of radio's *The Navy Lark* ended ('the dear old fruit getting hitched *was* a surprise,' noted a housewife); the consciously retro Temperance Seven, dressed in Edwardian style, released 'You're Driving Me Crazy', counter-intuitively but accurately predicted by the *Mirror*'s Patrick Doncaster to be 'a huge success' precisely 'because they are 40 YEARS OUT OF DATE'; Don Revie's first match in charge of struggling Leeds United ended in a 3–1 defeat at Portsmouth; viewer reaction to the Eurovision Song Contest and to John Mortimer's Hampstead-set Sunday-night play *The Wrong Side of the Park* was equally dismayed – 'Are You Sure?' by the Allisons (beaten into second place by the Luxembourg entry) was 'by far the best', while in NW3 the characters were 'tiresomely introspective' and 'their general behaviour either hysterical or obscure'; the decidedly non-introspective smallholder Dennis Dee had a good day when Nicolaus Silver became the second grey to win the Grand National ('I was lucky to pick him out'), with the two much-publicised Russian horses, Grifel and Reljef, failing to finish; and, on the Monday before Easter, the out-of-town run of the patchy revue *One Over the Eight* (largely written by Peter Cook) found Kenneth Williams in 'hateful, tasteless, witless, blank, boring, dirty, tat' Blackpool. He was probably never a candidate for *Coronation Street*, now establishing itself as a permanent fixture, going out nationally on Mondays and Wednesdays. David Jones – the future Monkee – took a part as Ena Sharples's grandson; Ena herself was sent to Coventry for spreading false rumours that the street was about to be slum-cleared; one viewer's letter praised 'a true picture of life', another's how 'it shows the selfish, the kind-hearted, and the nosy'; and Jack Rosenthal began writing scripts, the first one including some prize Ena dialogue: 'Folk round 'ere know nowt. One walk down t'canal bank and they think they're charting the Ganges.' The contrast was painfully stark with the Joan Littlewood production of *Sparrers Can't Sing*, transferring to the West End near the end of March. 'Sad to say,' noted *The Times*'s reviewer, 'most of the characters, despite the photographic realism of their talk, appear to have been taken not from contemporary life but from a long stage tradition of comic cockneys'; or, as Anthony Heap put it, 'mildly amusing', but 'no plot, no drama, no comedy, no nuffink!'[6]

The last day of March was Good Friday – 'suffering of the flesh and resurrection all in one day', recalled Margaret Drabble about childbirth at St George's, London. 'I found the hospital very authoritarian. I can remember the midwives telling me to shut up. I didn't see why I shouldn't yell.' That evening, *Any Questions?* came from Thorngate Hall, Gosport and included the 'practical farmer' Ted Moult, who had already introduced *Housewives' Choice* earlier in the day. 'I think it's a lot of bunk, bunk,' he declared about psychiatry to laughter and applause. And, in response to a question about marching with banners, he referred to the Aldermaston March: 'When this procession started several years ago, I had a good deal of sympathy with their point of view. Now, I am afraid to say that the sight of these marchers, and coupled with them the sort of beatnik element that they have dragged along with them, I am disgusted.' That year's CND march as usual started on Good Friday, and as usual was heading for Trafalgar Square on Easter Monday, but did not only come from Aldermaston. For instance, the Leicester contingent, among them A. R. Williams, a grammar-school sixth-former from Ashby-de-la-Zouch, travelled to Finchingfield in north-west Essex and began the march there:

After about an hour, a large open car with a jazz band perched on it crawled by and was greeted both with cheering and laughter since their enthusiasm far outweighed their skill. We marched in great form for the rest of the day with CND banners high and spirits even higher. The first night was spent at a Primary School at Braintree, where our group was personally welcomed by the Mayor.

The next morning, some of us were perhaps a little the worse for wear after singing and dancing well into the night . . . Easter Saturday was one long, hard, wet trudge and when we stopped for lunch I, for one, was thankful. Whilst we sat in the road eating and talking, television cameramen and reporters mingled with us trying to find the notorious 'beatnik' element. This was conspicuous by its absence, except for a small but lively group from Soho. These creatures in their black rags and with a huge sign with 'Soho says No' were strangely fascinating. The afternoon was wet and uneventful except for nagging feet. On and on we tramped, until we reached Brentwood where the programme was – a meal and to bed.

The still unpublished John Fowles was also in Essex that rainy weekend, staying with his parents at Leigh-on-Sea and finding it as hard as ever to control his irritation. 'Even the conversation about contemporary events seems peculiarly old-fashioned. This feeling of time past, of people absolutely based in the manners, attitudes, orders of thirty and forty years ago – peeping their horns out at today, like snails. But happier back in the shell. Snail-towns, these like Leigh.' One way and another, it was an apposite weekend for a television comedian's big-screen breakthrough. 'Went to Ritz, Leyton, to see Tony Hancock in "The Rebel",' recorded Judy Haines on Easter Monday. 'He, Liz Fraser, and Irene Handl extremely funny . . . Enjoyed other film in brilliant colour of Royal Tour of India.' As for the Leicester marchers, they had 'shuffled and limped' on Easter Sunday as far as West Ham, at one point being descended on by League of Empire Loyalists who 'hurled fireworks, smokebombs and yelled "Keep the Bomb" and "Tottenham for the Cup".' Then, 'Easter Monday – the last lap':

We hobbled off in heavy rain, still undaunted, and from then until lunch we sang and plodded, again aided by our unwilting jazz musicians. Lunch at Smithfield Market! then along the Embankment and we should be there.

Immediately after lunch, we were joined by the Aldermaston wing of the march, with its many and colourful foreign groups. We crammed into Trafalgar Square and I fought my way to the fountain where I soaked my tired feet as I listened to the speeches. Here to address us was the philosopher Bertrand Russell and many MPs and celebrities of public life. Actors and entertainers mingled among us. This at least showed the wide appeal of the campaign.

'Was it worth it?' wondered Williams. 'Did we achieve anything? I hope so! I think so.'

The *New Statesman* hoped so too, its current issue endorsing 'the healthy and vigorous motives of the Aldermaston marchers'. Those were not sentiments that Kingsley Amis, no unilateralist, could endorse, and on 5 April he informed the magazine's new literary editor Karl Miller that he would 'sooner not be tied up' with such a journal – a further significant step in his steady march rightwards. Another magazine, *Melody Maker*, featured on the 8th two notable interviewees. Interrupted at his 'elegant' Winchmore Hill home only by his mother coming in 'with tea and biscuits on an electronically-heated trolley', Cliff Richard confided that he did not want 'to make the same mistake as Tommy Steele', who 'went after the older audience and seems to have lost the following of the youngsters'; while 'handsome, blond, 20-year-old' Adam Faith, who 'runs an American Ford Galaxy car and has just bought his family a new luxury house in Sunbury-on-Thames', called himself 'a beat singer aiming mainly at the teenagers' and appeared 'unruffled' by the increasing popularity of the balladeers ('they'll never kill the beat idiom'). Seemingly unruffled too was Paul Raymond, whose trial began on Monday the 10th at Marlborough Street Magistrates' Court. The prosecution's case was that productions at his Soho strip club, the Revuebar, had gone too far; according to a police witness, this was typified by the obscene whipping sequence in 'Mutiny on the High Seas'. Next day, whipping was all but on the agenda of the Commons, as a Tory backbencher, Sir Thomas Moore, sought to insert a clause in the Criminal Justice Bill by which, 13 years after the abolition of judicial corporal punishment, violent young male offenders could be given a caning (up to the age of 17) or a birching (18 to 20). During the debate, Moore pointed to the sharp increase in crimes of violence (up from 2,800 in 1938 to 13,800 in 1958) and noted that of the 1,200 letters he had received, only 15 were opposed to his proposal. Another Tory backbencher, Gerald Nabarro, was likewise strongly in favour of 'thwacking the thugs', though calling himself a 'not indiscriminate flogger', while a third, Geoffrey Hirst, condemned the Home Secretary, Rab Butler, as 'deplorably out of touch' with public opinion. Moore failed to carry the day, with Labour MPs backing the government, but as many as 69 Tories – among them Sir Cyril Black, Cyril

Osborne, Wing Commander Bullus and, less predictably, the newly elected Peter Walker (future one-nation Conservative) – voted against the party whip. The rebels included Margaret Thatcher. 'It was the biggest Party revolt since we came to power in 1951,' she recalled without regret. 'It was also the only occasion in my entire time in the House of Commons when I voted against the Party line.'[7]

'It is nonsense to assume,' wrote Tom Stoppard in the *Western Daily Press* on the day Thatcher went rogue, 'that every time a coloured man fails to get or keep a job it is because he is black.' Even so, the young journalist, not yet a playwright, did not deny the existence of a colour bar in Bristol – most notoriously at the Bristol Omnibus Co, not employing a single black conductor or driver:

> On the Thursday before Easter a black friend of mine applied for a job as a conductor. He asked to see the personnel manager and was told to come back after the holidays, but, he told me, 'They said there were no vacancies anyway.'
>
> Five minutes later I applied for the same job. I was told that the conductors' 'school' was full but I could come back after the holiday when there would be vacancies, and I could then take the course.

Next day, 12 April, Stoppard turned to the housing aspect of Bristol's colour bar. One flat agency had told him that only 1 per cent of its clients would accept a non-white tenant, another that 25 per cent of landlords stipulated 'no coloured' without even being asked, while 'about half of the remainder would not accept a coloured tenant if one came along.' As for buying a house, he quoted an estate agent: 'We have never sold a house to a coloured man. They are not a good risk, and frankly we would never sell except for cash.' To which Stoppard added that 'however regrettable it may be, it is nevertheless true that when a coloured family moves into a house, then the house next door drops in price, and so on until a whole area takes the knock.' Near the end of his piece, he reflected that 'it is never the landlord who doesn't like coloured people. It's the other people in the house, or the other people in the street. No one you meet is guilty.'

It could be hard to be middle-class and qualm-free over the issue. 'The Johannson-Patterson fight – all along I have wanted Patterson (the negro) to win,' noted in March another writer-in-waiting, John Fowles. 'We woke up at 3.15 am to hear the commentary on the wireless; and I kept on finding myself wanting the Swede to win ... I loathe colour prejudice. But there it is.' Or take the experience shortly after Easter of a female diarist living in Barking. 'He overcharged me by 10d,' recorded Pat Scott about trouble with a bus conductor. 'I then caused a fuss about the charge but luckily an Inspector was on the bus. But unluckily the man was coloured. I didn't like causing a fuss but he was rather rude.' Even so, a couple of blasts earlier in 1961 to the *Listener* – normally an impeccably liberal organ – were strikingly qualm-free. 'I object to a sub-standard folk from another land "invading" in such numbers,' declared M. Blundell of London N22 in response to a fairly anodyne article on 'Britain's Colour Problem'. 'Anyone,' he went on, 'who has seen what Jamaicans especially can do within a few weeks to what was a neat and clean house ought not to be surprised at resentment ... It is the way of life that is objected to – the noisiness, the flamboyance ... They will take 100 years to catch up with us.' So too H. Russell Wakefield of London SW10, who on the basis of 'having seen what Jamaicans can do to a whole neighbourhood', endorsed Blundell 'heartily'. Calling himself 'a fanatical segregationist', he bluntly stated that 'these people should never be inflicted upon civilised persons.' As for public attitudes more generally, a revealing episode occurred when the Rev. Clifford Hill, a Congregationalist minister in Tottenham, was reported as saying on the radio in late May that he would not have a problem if his daughter married a black man. 'For the next seven days,' he recalled a few years later, 'an enormous flood of correspondence, mostly of a foul and abusive nature, poured through my letter box'; he gave some of the more printable examples:

A black blubber-lipped Negro on top of her and unending half castes year after year. Blacks breed and breed! What a fate! You are not fit to be a father at all. (*Woman in Brighton*)

I pity your poor little girl to be more or less married off to some great slob of a lazy ponce of a nigger. (*London man*)

It is not for you to tamper with God's handiwork! (*Middlesex man*)

'The climax of the avalanche of abuse that poured in from all quarters,' Hill added, 'came a week later when my house was attacked during the night. White paint was thrown over the doors and windows and outside walls, and such slogans as "NIGGER LOVER" and "RACE-MIXING PRIEST" were painted in huge letters along my fence and on the pavement outside the house.'

Soon afterwards, another clergyman, the Rev. Fred Milson, senior youth tutor at a Selly Oak training college, initiated a detailed six-week survey into the realities affecting Birmingham's 35,000 West Indians. Its key findings were that colour prejudice was almost entirely an adult phenomenon; that housing remained the biggest problem facing the immigrants; that the city was 'in danger of having "neighbourhood segregation"' – ie, between whites and non-whites; that it came across 'very few examples of informal integration', whether in churches or pubs or social life generally; and that outside the workplace (where relations were usually better), the prevailing attitude was 'tolerance without acceptance', in effect leaving the West Indians as 'a community within a community'. Looking ahead, Milson called on the immigrants to recognise that the English were 'at heart a neighbourly people' and not to mistake 'English reserve and reticence for race and colour discrimination'; while as for the English, on whom as hosts 'the greater responsibility for understanding' rested, 'we need, without fuss or patronage, to take the initiative in friendship', that in other words 'it is not enough to be "not against" the coloured immigrant'. In short: 'We must accept with our minds that there has come to Birmingham a common twentieth-century phenomenon – the multi-racial society.'[8]

Was restriction on numbers from the New Commonwealth a surer, more realistic route to improved relations? Milson recognised that this was becoming an increasingly hot political issue when he used the closing words of his report to assert that 'any control of West Indian immigration should be on the basis of availability of housing accommodation and general social amenities – not on the basis of race or colour.' The debate was keenest in the Conservative party, which traditionally had been wedded to free entry, largely for reasons of imperial sentiment. But by the end of 1960, and going into 1961, it was becoming increasingly hard to hold that line – 50,000 West Indian immigrants in 1960 alone, West Indian governments still refusing passport restrictions, the Indian and Pakistani governments under strong domestic pressure to relax theirs – with the result that by February 1961 even the reasonably liberal-minded Rab Butler had in effect accepted the principle of immigration controls and was turning his mind to the practicalities. In public, though, nothing changed. 'Latest immigration figures show that West Indians continue to flock into this overcrowded country at a higher rate than ever,' complained the impeccably bigoted Anthony Heap in early June. 'But does the Government heed the pleas from MPs, local authorities and other public bodies to restrict immigration on account of the acute housing and health problems created by this ever-increasing influx? No. Cravenly cowed by the leftist parrot cry of "no colour bar", they won't do a damned thing about it . . .' A few days later, a Gallup poll found only 11 per cent categorically saying they would move 'if coloured people came to live next door', but 67 per cent wanting restrictions on entry. And this two-thirds majority gave five main reasons: 'Too many coloured people here already [around 300,000]; the taxpayer has to support them; they are unhealthy; they should have jobs to go to; they lower our standards of living.'⁹

That was not the only time in the first half of 1961 that Gallup tested public opinion about race. Revealingly, in the wake of South Africa leaving the Commonwealth in March, it found that barely two in five wanted Britain to vote in the United Nations against apartheid, while one in ten actually wanted Britain to support South Africa. Mighty events were afoot elsewhere in Africa, with the key British player undoubtedly the brilliant, sometimes mercurial Colonial Secretary, Iain Macleod; he took the clear-sighted view, broadly backed by Macmillan (a year after his famous 'wind of change' speech in Cape Town), that, given the inevitability of decolonisation, there was no point in delaying. Under his predecessor, Alan Lennox-Boyd, the tentative British assumption had been that Tanganyika, Uganda and Kenya might each achieve independence during the first half of the 1970s. But thanks to Macleod's drive – in Timothy Raison's words, 'an astonishing display of tactical skill coupled with bravura and inspiration' – the actual respective dates were 1961, 1962 and 1963. Tory backbenchers could just about live with that. What they found much harder to stomach was the prospect of white surrender of power in the territories that comprised the Central African Federation (Southern and Northern Rhodesia and Nyasaland). 'Our Government and Party will be split in two,' privately predicted Macmillan in early February, if he and Macleod were to 'make a decision which, without satisfying African demands, goes in their general favour'. Mollie Panter-Downes's assessment at the start of March was that there were at least 90 Conservative MPs who believed that 'the Government is going ahead too fast in putting political power into the hands of the politically immature'; while in the Lords, the most bitter opposition to Macleod came from the Tory kingmaker Lord ('Bobbety') Salisbury, who on 7 March not only made a passionate defence of the white settlers ('these little communities, including wives and children, scattered about among primitive people') but accused the Colonial Secretary of being 'rather unscrupulous' and, still worse, 'too clever by half'. Later that month the Federation's Sir Roy Welensky, in many ways the orchestrator of Tory discord, addressed 200 of the party's backbenchers and was warmly received. Yet in practice that would prove to be the high-water mark for the refuseniks. 'That diehard groups found themselves unable to hold the centre of the Party for long,' argues the historian Nicholas Owen, 'is explained less by Macleod's ability to persuade MPs of the merits of his policies than by the size of Macmillan's majority, and the skill of his Party Whips at deploying persuasion, patronage and threats.' Which did not mean, as Owen rightly adds, that the Conservative Party as a whole, including its members, was suddenly converted to the principle of black majority rule.[10]

There is no evidence that any of this had significant traction in most people's minds. What about a much nearer continent? Almost four years after the Treaty of Rome and the start of the European Economic Community without British participation, Macmillan had formulated by the end of 1960 what he called 'The Grand Design' – in essence, an attempt 'to organise the great forces of the Free World – USA, Britain and Europe – economically, politically and militarily in a coherent effort to withstand the Communist tide all over the world'. In practice that meant, whatever the negative Commonwealth implications, a decision to attempt to join the Common Market, which it was also believed would stimulate the sluggish British economy. Formal announcement of an application still awaited. But by mid-May 1961, shortly after Edward Heath as the minister responsible for relations with Europe had called the issue the great challenge for 'our generation', Macmillan was noting that 'the European problem has held the attention of Parliament, the

Press and to some extent the public in the last few days.' 'The Press,' he added, 'is divided. Beaverbrook's papers – *Daily Express*, *Sunday Express*, *Evening Standard* – are already hysterical in opposition. Broadly speaking all the rest of the Press (*Times*, *Daily Telegraph*, *Daily Mail*, *Daily Mirror*) are sympathetic.' A month later, writing to her son, Lady Violet Bonham Carter referred to 'the *sudden* awakening "en sursaut" of the Govt & of the Press here to the importance of the Common Market' and, from the perspective of a veteran Liberal, summed up the political state of play: 'Both the major parties are split down the middle . . . Many Tories still don't realise that we have already lost "national sovereignty" – through NATO, UN, Gatt, IMF, etc, etc . . . The Labour Party are Jingo Little Englanders, economic Nationalists & xenophobes who dread the "foreigner" . . .' And public opinion? According to Gallup about the same time, just under one in two people offered approval of an application to join, one in five said they would disapprove, and the rest were unsure. The question was also asked: if Britain felt it had to join with other powers, would it be better to team up with Europe or America? Twenty-two per cent plumped for the former – and 55 per cent for Uncle Sam. We were not, in short, natural Europeans. Or, as a hostile cartoon in the *Mirror* in May put it, 'New German Arms Build-Up'.

One politician at this stage had relatively little to say about immigration or decolonisation or Europe. But he did in April, on St George's Day, give a speech to a dinner in London of the Royal Society of St George. In it, Enoch Powell recalled 'that incredible phase' during which 'the power and influence of England expanded with the force and speed of an explosion'; he acknowledged that 'that phase is ended, so plainly ended that even the generation born at its zenith, for whom the realisation is the hardest, no longer deceive themselves as to the fact'; and, after an eloquent disquisition about 'the unbroken life of the English nation over a thousand years and more', he looked ahead to the future with a sense of foreboding: 'The danger is not always violence and force; them we have withstood before and can again. The peril can also be indifference and humbug, which might squander the accumulated wealth of tradition and devalue our sacred symbolism to achieve some cheap compromise or some evanescent purpose.'[11]

'"MAN IN SPACE" screamed the inch-high banner headline across the front of the London "Evening News",' recorded Henry St John on Wednesday, 12 April, 'but the bowler-hatted man behind the paper in the train this evening was nodding off to sleep, and seemed in his oblivion the symbol of the age.' Next day, while the new Soviet hero rested up, the Paul Raymond trial ended with Raymond found guilty of keeping a disorderly house ('Your show can only be characterised as filthy, disgusting and beastly,' admonished the magistrate Reggie Seaton), before on the Friday came a coup for the BBC. 'Spent a lot of time looking at broadcast from Moscow [the first live one from there on British television] welcoming Gagarin the space flyer's return & welcome in Moscow,' noted another diarist, Florence Turtle. 'It started at 10.30 & I switched off at 12.30 & got my lunch.' Also on the TV front that day, Rab Butler wrote to the Independent Television Authority's Director-General Sir Robert Fraser complaining about the 'unhealthy amount of violence on the television screen, sometimes of a particularly vicious type', and a letter in the *TV Times* from W. Pepper of Leeds 8 wondered why 'so many contestants' on *Criss Cross Quiz* 'are bank clerks, teachers, managing directors, etc', while the next evening on *The Billy Cotton Band Show* viewers 'very much' enjoyed the Temperance Seven ('delightfully amusing') but far less so Alma Cogan ('harsh and tuneless'). By then, the Scotland goalkeeper Frank Haffey was reliving his Wembley nightmare: 9 goals conceded that hapless Saturday afternoon (in a 9–3 defeat to England, with a hat-trick for Chelsea's Jimmy Greaves), and already the cruel joke doing the rounds: 'What's the time? – Nearly 10 past Haffey'. Monday the 17th was Budget day, a lacklustre affair from Selwyn Lloyd, prompting Anthony Heap to register his 'despair of ever getting a Budget that will relieve in any appreciable degree the crushing burden of direct taxation on the likes of me'; and at last, the Electrical Trades Union trial got under way at the High Court. Two members of the Communist-run ETU were claiming that the union's leadership had over a period of several years permitted, and indeed encouraged, systematic fraud in the conduct of its elections. The trial would last 40 days, and, according to the biographers of Les Cannon, the most important non-Communist in the union, 'the most dramatic moment was evidence of extra ballot-papers being ordered from the printer and sent to St Pancras station "to be called for" whence they were collected by the Head Office of the union. What happened to the 26,000 spare ballot-papers? Mr Gardiner [Gerald Gardiner QC, for the prosecution] called for them. "They are not being produced," replied the Counsel for the defence.' At which point 'the judge allowed himself a little joke: "It may be they disappeared."' Proceedings ended in mid-June, with Mr Justice Winn reserving judgement.[12]

Back in April, the visiting Christopher Isherwood reflected on the 19th on his fortnight in London: 'The utter fatalistic patience of everyone when a line has to be formed or a train or bus waited for. You feel the wartime mentality still very strongly ... In general, life here seems tacky and lively and the people radiate a friendliness and willingness; all except for a shopkeeper or official type, which makes a face at you as if you had asked for the impossible and unspeakable.' Two days later, Miss M. Bird of Liverpool 17, a nurse in a casualty department, made her contribution to the *TV Times* debate about whether Ena should leave her hairnet off ('I can vouch that the Ena Sharples of Liverpool wear hair-nets, pins and rollers all day and every day'); David Marquand in the *New Statesman* reviewed A.J.P. Taylor's revisionist, instantly controversial *The Origins of the Second World War* (essentially arguing that Hitler in the 1930s had merely behaved as any rational German leader would) and acclaimed him as 'the only English historian now writing who can bend the bow of Gibbon and Macaulay'; and Hughie Green found himself 'besieged' at a large Newcastle furniture store by 'scores of frenzied, screaming, middle-aged women' who 'tore and plucked at his clothing'. Next day at the Scottish Cup Final at Hampden Park, where *The Times*'s correspondent noted 'the appalling experience of a continuous roar of cheering throughout the whole of the national anthem from the green end of the ground', an understandably shaky Haffey was back in the fray for Celtic, surprisingly held to a goalless draw by the underdogs, Jock Stein's Dunfermline Athletic. The replay, again at Hampden, was the following Wednesday afternoon (no floodlights there yet). Dunfermline's schools got the afternoon off, and 16-year-old Ian Jack and his friends 'stood in our school blazers among Celtic fans, men dressed with no intervening shirt between their vests and their jackets, flat caps, green and white scarves knotted as mufflers, large bottles of McEwan's Pale Ale to hand', and who 'pissed where they stood'. Dunfermline won 2–0, and that night 'the team appeared to wild noise on the balcony of the council chambers with the town's provost, wearing a high wing-collar and looking like Neville Chamberlain.' That same evening saw the start of the first series of Michael Bentine's *It's a Square World* (most viewers responding 'with somewhat guarded approval'), while next day the *Mirror*'s Richard Sear argued that 'the rocket success' of the 'women-dominated' *Coronation Street* owed much to its female appeal ('its clever, tangy dialogue, written at a trivial level, might have been gathered by women, for women, over any backyard fence') and Mrs N. M. Gibbs of Bideford complained in the *Radio Times* about 'the blight which has seemingly fallen upon *Mrs Dale's Diary*': 'Recently we have had nothing but unmitigated gloom – Mrs Freeman's serious illness and removal to hospital, then Captain being run over.' Over the last few days of the month, *The Ken Dodd Show* got a decent if unspectacular Reaction Index of 62 ('We can always be sure of a good laugh from him,' said one viewer); Richard Hoggart on BBC TV's *Bookstand* described Andy Capp as 'beautifully observed' and 'a piece of folk lore'; *Woman's Mirror* began the serialisation of the memoirs of Mrs Evelyn Yorke, for ten years a maid at Eton ('The most privileged boys in England are truly gentlemen in every sense of the word'); and Macmillan noted – possibly wistfully, possibly not – that 'there is no TV at Birch Grove [his Sussex home], except in Nanny's house at the Lodge gates.'[13]

May Day was the much-awaited day when off-course cash betting became legal, with that morning more than 150 betting shops opening in Liverpool alone and the street-runner (known on Merseyside as 'the back jigger-runner') facing extinction. In London, 21-year-old John McCririck climbed 'the rickety wooden stairs' to Jack Swift's smoke-filled first-floor premises in Dover Street, off Piccadilly. 'There was glorious bedlam in there,' he recalled; 'it was packed with punters shouting their horses home. Jim Joel's "Black Nanny" won the first race at Nottingham at 2–1 favourite.' Saturday the 6th also made sporting history. 'The Cup Final wasn't very rewarding, was it?' Larkin wrote to Monica Jones after Tottenham Hotspur had beaten injury-affected Leicester City 2–0 in a drab enough affair. But it meant that Tottenham had become the first club in the twentieth century to complete the League and FA Cup double. 'Now others may be tempted to imitate the Spurs concept in style and fluency,' speculated one football writer, Geoffrey Green. 'Their game is to decoy, create and destroy.' Later that weekend, on Sunday evening, Nella Last watched the ITV game show *For Love or Money*, noting gratefully that Des O'Connor as host had 'lost a lot of his silly facetiousness' and that 'the new hostess is a great improvement to the last sexy one, all wriggles & rolling eyes,' while on Monday she wondered whether it was time that *This is Your Life* 'had a rest': 'Sometimes there is a somewhat strained – artificial – air. My husband loves it – hates any change. Only one programme keeps its intense interest for me – Emergency Ward 10 – with Dixon of Dock Green a runner up.' A more enterprising couple, Madge Martin and her husband Robert, were in London on Tuesday looking for a chair that would be his retirement present as an Oxford clergyman. First came 'indifferent treatment' at Parker Knoll; then 'a look round Heals, too contemporary but fascinating'; and finally 'the palatial Maples in Tottenham Court Road', where they were treated 'with the utmost attention and interest'. The day's work done, they headed in the evening to Oxford Street's Studio One to see the newly released, 'perfectly enchanting' *101 Dalmatians*.[14]

Late April and early May was a particularly difficult time for one Home Counties writer. 'Save me,' declared Norman Shrapnel in his *Guardian* review of Elizabeth Taylor's Home Counties-set *In a Summer Season*, 'from the wise, witty, sensitive, accomplished, charming female novelist'; Richard Mayne in the *New Statesman* admitted to 'a brutish dislike for gracious upper-middle-class charm, at least in novels'; and John Weightman on radio's *The Critics* argued that Taylor's literary worth was seriously undermined by the fact that, in terms of her subject matter, 'we cannot be sure that she herself understands how marginal and decadent this part of English society has become.' Even *The Times* reviewer, albeit acknowledging Taylor's 'skilled craftsmanship', implicitly played the class card: 'Everything rings true. Yet the total is curiously disappointing. Perhaps the setting is too conventional. Perhaps the book is too much of a type.' Nor was the outlook auspicious for another established middle-class novelist who also wrote with sympathy and insight about the middle class. Barbara Pym's *No Fond Return of Love* had appeared earlier in the year and, notes her biographer, 'was not widely reviewed'. By contrast, a third female novelist was, in her unique way, altogether going with the larger flow. 'Entirely devoted to the bourgeois vices of a bourgeois world' was how in June one reviewer, Burns Singer in the *Listener*, encapsulated Iris Murdoch's *A Severed Head*, and he described admiringly its 'exquisitely formal game of unmusical beds in which adultery is accepted as the norm and incest is thrown in for good measure'.

The bourgeoisie were among the many targets of *Beyond the Fringe*. Given a more political edge since its Edinburgh debut the previous summer, the show went first to Cambridge and then, the week starting 1 May, to the Theatre Royal, Brighton. 'You young bounders don't know anything about it!' shouted one man in the audience at the 'Aftermyth of War' sketch (the RAF officer calling on the unfortunate Perkins to make 'a futile gesture' and be killed) as he ostentatiously got to his feet and stormed off. At the end of the week came the review by F.T.G. in the *Brighton and Hove Herald*, which was studded with phrases like 'absolutely infantile', 'full of smart prattle' and 'ingenuously cocksure', claimed that 'the satire has about as much sting as blanc-mange' and took the moral high ground: not only did it seem 'vaguely indecent for 20-year-olds to be making fun of Battle of Britain pilots' but 'a comic scene in a death cell to me was atrocious'. The London opening was at the Fortune on Wednesday the 10th, producing by contrast almost universally ecstatic reviews, typified by a punch-drunk Bernard Levin in the *Daily Express* calling it 'a revue so brilliant, adult, hard-boiled, accurate, merciless, witty, unexpected, alive, exhilarating, cleansing, right, true and good that my first conscious thought as I stumbled, weak and sick with laughter, up the stairs at the end was one of gratitude'. *The Times* entered a rare note of criticism – 'smacks a little of the Third Programme' – but the headline was admiring: 'Clowning with Distinction: Four Wrote Their Own Sketches'. As enthused as anyone that first night was Anthony Heap, who in his diary notice acclaimed 'this sparkling little revue, which mercilessly satirises the mad world of today and hits all its targets dead centre' – a revue performed by 'just four young men in grey suits, with no more props than a piano, a table, four chairs and a few period hats'. 'Hail to thee, blithe spirits,' ended his paean to Alan Bennett, Peter Cook, Jonathan Miller and Dudley Moore. 'The town is yours!'

Heap also noted that the show had been 'rapturously received' by the audience, but on the second night there was an interesting moment. 'The couple who sat behind me,' recalled Michael Frayn not long afterwards, 'honked happily away until they got to the middle of the Macmillan number [Cook playing him as a Scottish OAP], when the man suddenly turned to his girl-friend and said in an appalled whisper, "I say, this is supposed to be the Prime Minister", after which they sat in silence for the rest of the evening.' Such qualms did not stop the bandwagon rolling, and by the 20th the *Mail* was reporting that 'queues start to ring the theatre at 9.30 every morning'. A week later, the first of the political grandees attended. 'I sat & shook & writhed & shrieked & shouted with amusement for 2 hours,' recorded Lady Violet Bonham Carter. 'The targets were Macmillan, the Church, philosophers, & there were very good musical parodies ... a terribly funny one of some pansies with plucking gestures, dressing in sou'westers to do a terrifically virile hearty T.V. advertisement for something like Lifebouy Soap – & almost the funniest of all, 4 Clubmen meeting at their Club, making hearty gestures & quite inarticulate hearty noises, & finally sitting down together – to no food or drink.' Yet of course, in terms of raw numbers, *Beyond the Fringe* was seen by relatively few people (although an LP was almost instantly recorded), certainly compared to the doyens of the small screen. The start of the run at the Fortune coincided, for instance, with *Here's Harry* on the BBC. 'A great show with plenty of laughs which the whole family can enjoy because it's clean,' enthused a shop manager. 'We all like Harry Worth – what a terror! but so likeable – and so very funny.'[15]

'Just our cup of tea,' similarly found Madge Martin on 12 May after going to the recently released *The Greengage Summer* (Jane Asher as the younger sister). Three days later, Harold Wilson remarked to Labour colleagues that if the party was foolish enough in its next policy document to include a supportive passage about the Wolfenden recommendation to decriminalise homosexual behaviour, it would cost six million votes; while that evening at the Marlowe Theatre in Canterbury, as a huge power outage struck London and the south-east (mercifully just after the end of *Wagon Train*), 'a jazz band began to play "Twilight Time"' and 'teenagers jived in the aisles by candlelight'. Thursday the 18th saw the announcement that new universities were definitely to be built at Canterbury, Colchester and Coventry, in addition to those already being established at Brighton, Norwich and York, while that night the hills were alive at the Palace Theatre – but alive mainly, alas, to the sound not of music but of critics sharpening their pens. 'As sentimental as an Ivor Novello musical romance', 'The most predictable musical I have seen for a long time', 'The less said the better' – and Heap agreed, calling this final effort by Rodgers and Hammerstein 'cloying, meandering and lifeless'. On the 24th, England won a friendly in Italy (the decisive goal scored by Jimmy Greaves, about to move, amidst considerable ill-feeling, to AC Milan); next day, Totnes elected its 602nd Mayor, but only the second woman; the *East London Advertiser* on the 26th ran a story about 21-year-old Terence Stamp ('broad-shouldered, tousle-haired son of a Thames tugman') poised to get his big break on the film of *Billy Budd* ('All dad said to me was, "Don't get big-headed, son"'); and that Friday evening, the start of the ninth radio series of *Meet the Huggetts* (still starring Jack Warner and Kathleen Harrison as Joe and Ethel) was immediately followed on TV by the return of Tony Hancock, in a series simply called *Hancock*, a year after the comedian had controversially dispensed with Sid James. 'Ah yes, it's good-bye to all that black homburg hat and astrakhan collar rubbish,' he told the *Radio Times* about his move from East Cheam to Earl's Court. 'Knowledge and self-advancement are the things . . .' Above all in this first episode, performed solo, as he wrestled unavailingly in his bedsit with Bertrand Russell's *The History of Western Philosophy*. The audience was a massive 14.4 million, but the Reaction Index a relatively modest 64, well below the 80 and 77 averages for the last two series of *Hancock's Half Hour*. 'I think Hancock without James is like tea without milk,' commented an orderly, while according to a security officer's wife, 'he seemed lost all on his own.'[16]

A week later on 2 June, as Lady Violet was complaining on *Any Questions?* that modern elections had turned into 'a kind of scramble for a material hand-out in which victory will almost always go to the highest bidder', Hancock's RI was up to 67, on the back of an episode about 'The Bowmans' that, with Hancock as old Joshua Merryweather, took fairly amiable aim at radio's most popular soap. The following Tuesday evening in Hamburg, the visiting Malcolm Muggeridge 'dropped into a teenage rock-and-roll joint', the Top Ten Club:

The band were English, from Liverpool, and recognised me. Long-haired; weird feminine faces; bashing their instruments, and emitting nerveless sounds into microphones. In conversation rather touching in a way, their faces like Renaissance carvings of saints or Blessed Virgins. One of them [surely John Lennon?] asked me: 'Is it true that you're a Communist?' No, I said; just in opposition. He nodded understand-ingly; in opposition himself in a way. 'You make money out of it?' he went on. I admitted that this was so. He, too, made money. He hoped to take back £200 to Liverpool.

'As we sat waiting for the coach to return home,' noted the elderly Gladys Hague two days later about the end of the holiday she and her sister had had in Morecambe, 'we thought about the Duke of Kent's marriage to Katharine Worsley at York Minster.' The press gave it a moment's thought too, with *Daily Mirror* headlines next day including 'THE GAY YOUNG DUCHESS', 'DUKE "ATTACKS" THE ICING', 'YOU'VE SEEN NOTHING LIKE IT' (the bride's dress), 'KATE PAYS HER HOMAGE' (curtseying to the Queen) and 'GOOD LUCK!'. At Buckingham Palace on the 9th, the talented, well-connected osteopath Stephen Ward sketched a portrait of Prince Philip for the *Illustrated London News*, while Annie Courtenay sent her son Tom a sad letter from her lonely home on the outskirts of Hull ('I can't get used to Longhill . . . My head has been bothering me, my nerves aren't very good'). It was still upwards for *Hancock* – that Friday evening an RI of 71 for 'The Radio Ham' – and so too for Billy Fury, whose beat-ballad 'Halfway to Paradise' now entered the Top 10. On Monday the 12th, Tom Courtenay took over from Albert Finney as the star of *Billy Liar* in the West End (finding the speech about the 11-plus and family tensions 'very close to home'); next day, Christopher Isherwood and Don Bachardy visited E. M. Forster in Coventry, where two locals 'bored us nearly pissless talking about the wonders of Coventry and all the new building which is being done'; and on the 15th a distinguished Manchester doctor, Hugh Selbourne, tried to obtain a passport applica-tion form: 'Post Office girls told me to go to Withington Town Hall. The latter told me to go to the Ministry of National Insurance Offices in Wilbraham Road, and there they told me to go to their offices in Burton Road, and so on . . .'[17]

Next day, Hugh Gaitskell was in Sheffield officially opening the Park Hill redevelopment scheme – the famed streets in the sky. 'The flats are not the only things to have been built over the years,' insisted the introduction to the *Sheffield Telegraph*'s four-page supplement marking the occasion:

> There is a thriving, pulsing community spirit pervading the whole huge place – it is a spirit that has been evolved, tried and tested through the two years since the first tenants moved in. The spirit is no less – and possibly a good deal more – profound than that which existed among the terraced, begrimed and gloomy industrial revolution houses from whose ruins the mighty edifices of Park Hill rose. The architect's eye for shape, the builder's skill, the children's pleasures, their mother's peace of mind and the old folk's tranquillity have been carefully blended into a rich and telling example of progressive building for the community – with the community itself as one of the materials.

Friday's programme comprised a coach tour in the morning of the Council's new housing developments generally; luncheon at the Town Hall (melon – potted prawns salad – loin of lamb à la Delmonico, spring carrots, new potatoes, garden peas – strawberries and cream – bouchées – coffee – and of course plentiful wines); tour of inspection of the Park Hill scheme; and at 4.00, the official opening, followed by tea in the Tenants' Meeting Hall. 'I would agree that there are dangers in multi-storey development,' accepted Gaitskell in his speech at the opening ceremony.

> Sometimes, I must admit, blocks built up high remind me of nothing but barracks. Those, no doubt, are better than nothing, but not especially pleasant to live in or look at. But may I say how well you in Sheffield have avoided these dangers. You have combined in an extraordinarily successful manner a certain degree of uniformity, which you must have, with a proper degree of variety.

In short, he declared, the city had 'built something of beauty, dignity and harmony'.

That evening, 16 June, was the fourth *Hancock* – 'The Lift', RI of 74 – while next morning Henry St John had a somewhat Hancockian haircut experience ('3s 6d including tip') in Acton. 'For the first time in my experience of this saloon a radio was switched on, broadcasting the light programme. One reason why I do not go to a barber's on the other side of the road has been because they've always had a radio on. As last time, the barber who trimmed my hair lit a cigarette while doing it.' Philip Larkin and Judy Haines by now both had their eyes on the England v Australia Test, due to start at Lord's on Thursday the 22nd. 'Waiting for Benaud ogh ogh' was the former's response on Sunday to the news that Samuel Beckett was due to attend, while the latter on Monday noted that the in-form, fast-scoring Barry Knight (who played for her county, Essex) had been left out of the team. The Test itself coincided with the release of *The Guns of Navarone*, but there was all too little derring-do from the England cricketers. Friday evening brought solace with 'The Blood Donor' – RI of 77, and the imperishable apogee of Hancock's career – while early on the rest day, Sunday the 25th, a 61-year-old unmarried Glaswegian, Catherine McCardle of Maryhill, daubed with black paint the windows of a bookshop displaying *Lady Chatterley's Lover* ('offensive to the citizens of Glasgow', she subsequently told the court). Next day, England lost. 'Should have included Barry Knight,' reflected Haines, while from the ground itself, writing to a friend, the retired Eton schoolmaster George Lyttelton recorded mutterings in the Pavilion: 'The England side is giving no satisfaction – no guts, no concentration, not playing like a side etc etc, you hear all round. Cowdrey [the amateur captain, Colin Cowdrey] apparently melancholic at the wicket.' Beckett was presumably still around to watch that evening a performance of *Waiting for Godot* on BBC television. Fewer than three million tuned in, its RI of 32 was spectacularly low, and viewers 'reacted with feelings of frustration, sometimes expressed with humility – "the whole thing was much too abstract for my taste" – but more often with anger – "a lot of fatuous nonsense" and "I'm no royal courtier praising the Emperor's new clothes"'. On Tuesday, responding to the rise and rise of public relations, Malcolm Muggeridge in *The Times* noted of the PR man that 'his message is fed into the sausage machine of public affairs in the hope that it may reach the public stomach as normal nutriment' and called on him to have to identify himself 'by means of a clapper or bell such as lepers were forced to use in the Middle Ages'; the Queen Mother launched on the Tyne the liner *Northern Star*, declaring that 'the creative genius of our nation flowers as brightly as ever and British craftsmanship and skill cannot be rivalled anywhere in the world'; and on the Home Service the final took place of *Let The Peoples Sing*, the BBC's fifth annual amateur choral contest. 'Fine sunny day,' recorded Dennis Dee on Wednesday the 28th, a heatwave now under way. 'Started to make the hay stack, carried about 30 cocks on my fork, no transport.' And in London, Mr Justice Winn delivered his judgement, finding that the ETU's leadership had indeed been guilty of 'fraudulent and unlawful devices'. 'Not only,' he stated, 'was the Union managed and controlled by the Communist Party, but so run as to suit the ideals of the party.' Altogether the ballot-rigging case had, notes Francis Beckett in his history of the British Communist Party, 'received massive publicity', and it 'damaged the CP just as it was starting to recover from 1956'.[18]

Friday, the very hot last day of June, began with 16-year-old Carol Payne catching the train from Glasgow to London – and being waved off, reported Glasgow's *Evening Citizen*, by Dave 'Screaming Lord' Sutch (described as a £100-a-week singer currently touring Scotland) after Carol's mother had made an overnight dash to Scotland to prevent her marrying him. 'I don't even want to talk to David,' the mother told the paper. 'I don't like anything about him, particularly his long hair and the way he dresses.' The *Citizen*'s main headline, though, was 'THE QUEEN IN GORBALS', as that afternoon, between 3.45 and 4.35, the monarch, as the *Glasgow Herald* put it, 'saw both sides':

She visited six families in a blackened Victorian tenement in Sandyfoulds Street – a street where a family live in a single end with a bed recess, where there is no hot and cold running water, when they want a bath, they go to the public ones, and when they wash clothes they go to the 'steamies'. But even as she stood on the pavement, she also saw at the corner the tall towers of the first Hutchesontown-Gorbals redevelopment area, the gigantic 20-storey flats that are now nearing completion. Then she drove round the corner in a maroon plastic-topped Rolls-Royce and visited Ballater Street. She climbed to the second floor of a new maisonette block and spoke to three families living in new all-electric houses [ie, dwellings]: the contrast was complete.

The most emblematic moment of the tour – amid 'hoarse cheering, vast, dusty crowds and a million flags' – came as the Queen unveiled a commemorative plaque on 'one of four massive, wedge-shaped blocks which will one day grow into Queen Elizabeth Square, the centre-piece of Sir Basil Spence's "garden" scheme'; on being shown, together with Prince Philip, a model of the redevelopment, they 'asked many questions, and were interested to learn that every family will have a garden at their back door, even at 20-storey level'. That evening, as they prepared to leave Glasgow for Edinburgh, the Queen remarked that she had been overwhelmed by her reception in the Gorbals. 'I told her,' the Lord Provost revealed to the press afterwards, 'she should not be surprised, because they are a wholesome, generous, decent-living lot of people'; the Lord Provost added that the Queen had been 'amazed that four people could live in a small single end' and 'had commented on the amount of improvisation they must have to do'.

A different sort of end was at 8.00 p.m. on BBC television – the final *Hancock*. Called 'The Succession – Son and Heir', the episode had the anti-hero in search of a wife, ended with the words 'So exits the last of the Hancocks – good luck!', and gained an RI of 75, second only in the series to 'The Blood Donor'. 'Take back what I said earlier of Hancock,' reflected one viewer, an inspector. 'He does not now require James as a stooge – he progresses unattached by leaps and bounds.' 'Great fun for young and old alike,' declared another viewer, while a secretary spoke for millions: 'Bring him back – and quick! We shall miss the lad.'[19]

10

We'll All Be Uprooted

Summer 1961: ten years after the Festival of Britain and officially sanctioned modernity. That modernity – no longer 'soft', instead 'hard' – now unstoppable. Streets in the sky in Sheffield, London's Euston Arch and Coal Exchange poised to go, farewell the Victorian barracks of Aldershot, Birmingham's Inner Ring Road laying waste to all before it, T. Dan Smith ready to turn Newcastle into the Venice of the North (but ring roads, not canals), the firing gun started for Blackburn's comprehensive redevelopment, plans afoot for Glasgow's brutalist Red Road blocks (six point-blocks, two slab-blocks) to be the highest dwellings in Europe, the heart being ripped out of Bradford, slums being cleared that needed to be cleared, slums being cleared where there could have been renovation and human continuity, communities torn asunder, high-rise everywhere, old people trapped, mothers and small children trapped, an urban world of compulsory purchase and developers' boom time, of good intentions compromised by hubris, by greed, by the lure of size for size's sake, John Betjeman almost a lone voice of protest, most people shrugging their shoulders and mutely accepting destruction as the inevitable price of progress, you don't know what you've got . . . Summer 1961: a shake of the dice – and landing, who knew where?

That is the shorthand version. A fuller gazetteer of the seemingly ever-accelerating change to Britain's built environment, between roughly late 1960 and the summer of 1962, goes something like this:

In **Aldershot** work started on the new barracks for the Army School of Physical Training.

'SHOPWRECK' was a headline for 'the modernisation of the **Barnsley** Co-op', as a handsome piece of Victorian curtain walling was given the heave-ho.

In **Basingstoke** the Town Hall's clock tower was removed, the Alton Light Railway bridge was demolished, and the signing in October 1961 of the Town Development Scheme belatedly alerted locals to the utter change that lay ahead to the town's character.

Georgian **Bath** remained inviolable, but the closure of the Turkish baths ('Victorian, and retain much of their Victoriana,' observed Tom Stoppard) prompted a lament from Edward Hunt, who had run them since 1910: 'Of course they are a bit out of date. People like chromium and mirrors nowadays and they won't see much of that here.'

A massive rehousing programme was under way in **Birkenhead**, including three 14-storey blocks of flats on the Woodchurch estate and two 11-storey blocks on Sidney Road, Rock Ferry – all building done by George Wimpey & Co, all heating and hot water supplied by the North Western Gas Board. 'When you install Gas warm air central heating in your home, you *automatically* say goodbye to a whole lot of worry and drudgery,' promised an accompanying ad in the *Liverpool Echo*. 'There is no soot, smoke or dirt (and therefore no more money to be spent on chimney sweeps and having your upholstery and other furnishings cleaned after the sweep has been!). There are no fuel delivery or storage problems. No grates to be cleaned. And no heavy hods to be humped. Gas warm air central heating *frees* you from all these tiresome tasks – saves money into the bargain!'[1]

'Building Fever in **Birmingham**' proclaimed the *Financial Times* in May 1961 about the bold, can-do second city. 'Already the city centre is dominated by new buildings, and by the tower cranes helping to erect the still bigger ones in project; in another decade, when the plan nears completion, there will be scarcely a trace left of the nineteenth-century industrial complex which still thrives there.' All this development of the city centre was happening within the still-under-construction Inner Ring Road – 'the most drastically thorough example of traffic engineering yet seen on this scale in Britain' – and the correspondent noted how the process had already produced 'a tightly compressed mass of enormous buildings in which the ordinary pedestrian citizen may well feel lost'. The juggernaut's progress inevitably involved continual demolition work (that autumn, for example, around Masshouse Circus, in Suffolk Street and around Holloway Head), while across the city as a whole the car was now unambiguous king, with the council already agreeing in April 1961 to accelerate the road programme. March 1962 saw the much-publicised opening of the Perry Bar underpass on the busy, greatly widened Birmingham-to-Walsall road, prompting a local paper to note soon afterwards that 'little by little, Perry Bar is adjusting itself to the modern monster in its heart.' In the centre itself, of course, the emblematic feature would soon be the multi-level Bull Ring shopping and commercial centre, on which work by John Laing and Son started in May 1961. The architect, heavily influenced by American shopping centres, was Sydney Greenwood. 'People must not be allowed to take short cuts,' he told the *Architects' Journal*. 'The concourses they use cannot be more than 30 ft. wide and must have shops on both sides.' Nor was that all: the magazine noted that the Bull Ring's arcades would have 'the additional attraction of subdued lighting and piped music, which is expected to relax walkers down to a profitable pace of 1½ mph.' Birmingham's great emerging architect, though, was not Greenwood but John Madin, who in 1961 designed what became the eye-catching Birmingham Post and Mail building (podium plus 17 storeys) in Colmore Circus, according to Pevsner the 'finest commercial building of its time'.[2]

'The Mill Town Goes Modern', announced a May 1961 headline. That town was **Blackburn**, whose council had just approved an ambitious master plan, in liaison with Laings, for developing the centre: at its heart, replacing the old market (including a wonderful clock tower) and many buildings around it with a large, bang-up-to-date complex of shops, offices and flats, segregating pedestrians from traffic and providing generous car-parking facilities. 'INTO THE SPACE AND SPACIOUS AGE' declared the *Blackburn Times*. And it claimed that whereas 'other towns have embarked upon piecemeal schemes, nothing like Blackburn's complete reconstruction of a whole central area has ever been undertaken'.

Bradford's planners might have disputed that assertion and anyway were much further down the redevelopment road. 'Almost the whole of the original four-stage plan is now nearing completion, and the line of the new boulevard, Petergate, can be seen clearly to the right,' noted

the local *Telegraph & Argus* in February 1962 in relation to a front-page
aerial photo of the city's new centre. 'Towards the lower left can be seen
the site of the newest development, the demolition of shops around the
Ritz cinema, which will soon be enclosed by new buildings. Just above
is Swan Arcade, which is soon to be demolished and the block rebuilt
in keeping with the other developments.' A month later, and the headline was '"NEW LOOK" PLAN FOR FORSTER SQ.', as the paper
reported a big new development (a five-storey block of shops and
offices slap in front of the station) agreed between the Public Works
Committee and the developers Hammerson. That same day, photos
showed the ornate Swan Arcade – beloved by J. B. Priestley – in the
process of being demolished. 'Looking down on the inside, the skeletons of the old offices [before they became shops] can be clearly seen,'
explained the caption. 'The handsome gates are at the Charles Street
entrance, and the third picture shows one of the colonnades now
roofless.'[3]

In **Brighton**, note the historians of high-rise Miles Glendinning and
Stefan Muthesius, 'the powerful Conservative administration of
Councillor S.W. Theobald, "the King of Brighton", came under sudden
pressure in 1961–2 to increase output to cope with the problems caused
by the 1957 Act's decontrol of privately rented housing.' Accordingly,
he responded by unleashing 'a multi-storey crash drive'.

Bristol was maintaining what Timothy Mowl has called its 'largely
dreadful post-war planning record'. Accordingly, 'in 1961 the arcade of
a Norman town-house on Small Street, 900 years old, was pulled down
to widen a court room, and in 1962 the fifteenth-century St Augustine-
the-Less was demolished to make way for a hotel extension.' Meanwhile,
'the hanging gardens and ramshackle Georgian villas of Kingsdown',
looking down on the city centre, were being 'smashed to make room
for three fourteen-storey slabs housing only slightly more families than
had lived there before in poetic chaos'.

In Car City – Change City – the old continued to perish. Some 120
of **Coventry**'s timber houses had survived the German bombing; by
1958 100 remained. 'Two-thirds of these,' laments Gavin Stamp, 'would
disappear over the next few years as Arthur Ling, City Architect and
Planning Officer, pushed forward the construction of the Ring Road
and of new buildings like the Lanchester College of Technology. In

August 1961, as piles of old timbers from demolished houses in Little Park Street were burning, the *Coventry Standard* ran the front-page headline, "Demolition Recalls the Days of the Blitz".' The city that same year launched its first comprehensive development plan, for what the Corporation called the 'worn out' Hillfields area near the centre. The vision was largely high-rise, and the official description of the scheme conceded that it was 'considered economically impossible to re-locate all the existing shops' in the new Hillfields – 'a sad comment,' noted the *Guardian*, 'for an area where the little shop abounds.' Sad too was the 'sterile megaliths' reality of the 1961 scheme. 'Hillfields consists of a series of ten and seventeen-storey blocks of flats ranged in echelon and of identical design,' observed a 1969 architectural guide to Coventry. 'No attempt at human scaling appears to have been made, and the bull-dozer has been given free rein among the terraces.'⁴

'In an attempt to persuade local people to do their shopping in **Dalkeith**, Midlothian, instead of nearby Edinburgh, Dalkeith's town centre is to be given a £200,000 face-lift' was how an architectural maga-zine recorded in March 1961 what could hardly have been a more representative example of urban renewal. 'The scheme envisages a wider High Street and the provision, in three blocks, of 20 new shops, 33 maisonettes, extensive office accommodation and a tree-lined pedes-trian way.'

Dundee, under the sway of some powerful local Labour politicians, was poised to move big-time into high-rise living. By early 1962, a model was on display of four 23-storey blocks for the slum area of Maxwelltown; large-scale clearance was under way in the Hilltown area, where the Butterburn and Bucklemaker flats would become Dundee's highest; while to the north-west of the city, in Ardler, the golf club was being moved out and prefabs were being demolished, prior to the construction of what Glendinning and Muthesius call 'six mighty 17-storey slab blocks'.

'**Edinburgh** had been fairly cautious immediately after the war, but from the late 1950s plunged into peripheral development, area renewal, slum clearance and high-density building,' notes the Scottish housing historian Tom Begg about trends that were intensifying by the early 1960s. Little noticed by the media at the time, large new council schemes began to take shape on the city's southern edge, including at Oxgangs (three tower blocks built in 1961, demolished in 2005/6) and at Gracemount (three tower blocks built in 1962, demolished in 2009).

Soon to turn Fife into a dormitory for Edinburgh and invariably billed as 'the largest Scottish engineering project of the century', the **Forth Road Bridge** was by 1961 roughly halfway to completion. 'All around me, the landscape I'd grown up with was disappearing,' recalls Ian Jack, who lived in a nearby village, North Queensferry. 'Change was in full roar. Cuttings wide enough to fit four carriageways were driven through rock as earth-movers shaped embankments of fresh brown earth. Two 500-foot towers rose above the firth, soon to have steel cables suspended from them, spun on site from 30,000 miles of wire.'[5]

The story in **Glasgow** at this stage was partly about slum clearance (one issue alone of the *Glasgow Herald* in September 1960 had included four closely printed pages announcing the compulsory purchase in the Gorbals of over 60 tenements and many more individual properties), but above all about a great step-change in relation to high-rise starting to take effect – a step-change that went way beyond the well-publicised Hutchestown-Gorbals developments under the marque architects Basil Spence and Robert Matthew. A signal moment occurred in August 1961, some six weeks after the Queen's visit to the city, when at the opening ceremony for the three Wimpey-built 20-storey blocks at Royston (briefly the tallest blocks in Scotland), the Housing Convener, the impassioned David Gibson, 'said that, even allowing for overspill, Glasgow would have to build 500 of these multi-storey blocks in the next 20 years to help solve the housing problem'. Indeed, some important green lights had already been given. In February 1961 the Corporation's Housing Committee approved the building on the site of the condemned Maryhill Barracks of 12 high-rise blocks of flats, including five 26-storey point-blocks; two months later, the HC approved the plans for four 23-storey blocks in Sandyhills Road; and, that same April day, it gave the go-ahead to a mammoth scheme (some 16 25-storey blocks of flats) in the Sighthill area – a distinctly unpropitious 67-acre site known locally as 'the soda waste', having been used until about 1900 as a dump for chemical waste and subsequently, noted the *Glasgow Herald*, 'an eyesore for many years with stagnant ponds and derelict buildings'. The pace did not abate after Gibson's Royston pronouncement. In November 1961 the HC approved plans for five 18-storey tower blocks to 'rise up from the wooded hillside' at Broomhill, where five 'large old private houses' had recently been demolished; in early 1962, four or more blocks of at least 20 storeys were promised for the Townhead comprehensive development area, with the slum clearance involving 'a big loss of population'; that spring, Gibson gained approval for a major high-rise development at Toryglen North, on a site immediately next to railway sidings, clay workings and a refuse destructor. In terms of 1962 as a whole, almost gleefully note Glendinning and Muthesius about Gibson's relentless drive to turn the city into the European capital of high-rise, 'out of a UK cumulative total at that date of sixty-five blocks of 20 or more storeys, complete or under commencement, thirty-nine blocks were located in Glasgow!' The most emblematic scheme of all – even more so than Spence's development in the Gorbals – was also now starting to take shape, albeit not yet physically. The precise chronology is uncertain, but during the course of 1961–2 the way became clear for the Red Road scheme in the Balornock area: eight blocks, of up to 31 storeys each, that would be the tallest in Europe and, for half a century, the embodiment of a dream and what became of that dream.[6]

Jarrow from 1961 boasted a shopping centre – and what was more, the first Arndale Centre, although in this case called the Viking Precinct and open-air rather than a covered mall. The two men behind the Arndale Property Trust were both Yorkshiremen, Arnold Hagenbach and Sam Chippindale, who seven years earlier had acquired Bradford's Swan Arcade and would of course proceed to demolition once the leases expired. 'By the way,' explained Chippindale to an architectural magazine, 'we provide car parking in all our schemes, though the Jarrow people were amused at our providing a car park at all.'

The Empire Palace in **Leeds** bowed out in January 1961 with *Babes in the Wood* starring Nat Jackley and Ian Wallace. Demolition followed in 1962, with the site becoming the Empire Arcade and (eventually) Harvey Nichols.

Traditionally a reluctant moderniser, **Leicester** was getting into the swing of things by the early 1960s. Tesco's mammoth new store, on its opening in 1961 reputedly the largest of its type in Europe, was situated alongside a 36-lane bowling alley on the ground floor of Lee Circle, a six-tier concrete car park; at the university, the revolutionary Engineering Building, as designed by the young architects James Stirling and James Gowan, was starting to be erected ('That's a nice little toy that you've had made for yourself here, Jim,' said a friend of Stirling on first seeing it); and by the summer of 1962, the forceful Conservative local politician Kenneth Bowder, ambitious to transform Leicester along Coventrian lines, had recruited its first City Planning Officer, Konrad Smigielski, an ebullient Pole whose motto was that 'the only solution is complete clearance and redevelopment.'

Liverpool's commitment to high-rise living, already apparent for several years, intensified. In December 1960 the Housing Committee gave its endorsement to multi-storey development on the south side of the city; a year later it signalled the go-ahead for a 22-storey block in the cleared Harding Street area of Upper Parliament Street, prompting the headline 'The highest homes in Britain for Liverpool'; and in June 1962 a party of councillors, anxious to speed up completions, went to France to look at high-rise building systems there. The shabby, as yet barely touched city centre, meanwhile, was being closely scrutinised by the innovative London-based architect-planner Graeme Shankland, appointed in December 1961 as Liverpool's planning consultant. Only three months later, he and his team produced their first report. It was, according to the *Liverpool Daily Post*, a vision of 'pavements twenty feet above the road, special streets for buses and delivery vehicles only, shops with doors on the roof, car parks within easy reach of all strategic centres' – in short, a vision of Liverpool as 'Britain's first space-age city'.[7]

'New Flats Will Soar 300 ft Up' (in Latimer Road, near the Hammersmith/Kensington boundary), 'Flats of Thirteen Storeys' (on either side of Lewisham Road), '22-Storey Block On New Estate' (in Portland Grove, Lambeth) – those were typical **London** headlines in 1961–2. Or take East London. 'Jodrell Road with its two-storeyed little terrace cottages will be completely changed when the London County Council's new redevelopment scheme is carried out,' reported the *East London Advertiser* in February 1961 about the two 20-storey blocks shortly to tower over Victoria Park. While seven months later, Canning Town was 'rapidly getting a new look', not only with 'the giant Rathbone Street development scheme at last under way and work on the Adamson Road project nearing completion' but also with news that 'three giant, 15-storey skyscraper blocks are to go up on two island sites on either side of Fife Road near the junction with Beckton Road.' In terms of non-residential across the capital, a quartet of tall, landmark buildings was being completed or approaching completion – the Hilton Hotel, Millbank Tower (originally known as the Vickers Building), New Zealand House and the Shell Building – while one for the mid-1960s was Eric Bedford's 500-foot Post Office Tower, construction starting in the summer of 1961. Among office blocks, two emerging clusters stood out: those on London Wall (two completed by the spring of 1962, two well on the way, two in the pipeline) and those starting to mushroom in Croydon, including the unfortunate effort for General Accident – designed, thought Pevsner, 'so that the whole thing looks rather like folded paper . . . one feels like stretching the shape straight or squashing it'. An area by now on the cusp of root-and-branch change was the Elephant and Castle. The trio of Ernö Goldfinger towers that comprised Alexander Fleming House were on the verge of completion, work was about to start on a 25-storey LCC block of flats, and work had already begun on the much-trumpeted shopping centre (with the Elephant and Castle pub to be rebuilt at sunken-court level, 8 feet below the pavement and adjoining a pedestrian underpass). The most striking herald of modernity was Rodney Gordon's Michael Faraday Memorial – an electrical generator for the Tube, planted in 1961 in the middle of one of the Elephant's two new mega-roundabouts and consisting (in the words of Michael Collins, brought up locally) of 'an 80-foot-wide silver cube made up of 728 stainless-steel panels and rising 20 feet above pavement level'. Anthony Heap witnessed the changing urban scene with a keen eye. 'A number of main thoroughfares like Tottenham Court Road, Shaftesbury Avenue (part), Haymarket & Piccadilly have been turned into one-way streets,' he recorded in August 1961. 'As for Marble Arch and Hyde Park Corner, it is becoming hard to recognise them, so drastically have they been transformed.' Mollie Panter-Downes had already noted 'the scooping out of a large underpass beneath Hyde Park Corner'; in the event the twin tunnels opened for traffic in April 1962. To the west, Henry St John was also visually alert. 'The Hammersmith flyover has made progress since I last saw it,' he observed in February 1961. 'Part of it seems to be based on a central concrete spine, with concrete ribs on either side to support the roadway.' Nine months later, the traffic was flowing and the *Architects' Journal* was praising 'an exciting and elegant structure'. But it also asked a question: 'Why footpaths? A pedestrian was mown down within half an hour of opening.' The motor car's increasingly irresistible heft was displayed piquantly in the City. There, not long after the coming to Upper Thames Street of a steel-frame mechanised 'Zidpark' (one of London's first multi-storey car parks), the implacable requirement to widen Lower Thames Street finally (in the spring of 1962) spelled doom for the magnificent Coal Exchange, with demolition completed later that year. That would become a cause célèbre of vandalism, resonating down the years, but even more so was the sad story of the Euston Arch. 'By a ridiculous contrast with all this ultra-modern horror,' recorded Harold Macmillan on 24 October 1961 (as he considered among much else the implications of Russia having just exploded a 30-megaton bomb), 'I turned for ¾ hour to considering the fate of the doric Arch at Euston. The President of the Academy led a deputation of architects, artists, critics, & noblemen who all said this was a splendid – indeed a wonderful – work of art. It must not be lost, whatever the cost.' The scaffolding was already up; Macmillan (who according to one of the deputation sat listening with his eyes shut and asking no questions) promised nothing; a week later he gave his formal, wholly negative response; and within months the Euston Arch was no more. Half of the stones were dumped in a tributary of the River Lea, while the demolition contractor, Frank Valori, subsequently incorporated part of the arch into the stonework of the house which he had built for himself in Bromley.[8]

Construction began of the **M4** and **M5**. 'Due to open shortly,' noted the *Architects' Journal* in the summer of 1962 about the latter's first section, 'it will bring Ross-on-Wye to within an hour's run of the outskirts of Birmingham . . .'

The centre of modern **Manchester** continued to take shape during the early 1960s – the CIS tower (Europe's tallest office block on completion in 1962), the brash, sadly incoherent Piccadilly Plaza (not complete until 1965), M&S's biggest store in Lancashire – while outside the centre, the shift to high-rise was now becoming decisive. At the heart of the systematic new approach was the badly rundown district of

Hulme, specifically its St George's clearance area, where by early 1961 it was planned to build Manchester's first 16-storey block of flats, along with four 13-storey blocks. On top of the 16-storey block was to be a 'crow's nest' – or, as a housing department official explained, 'We thought it would be a good idea to give tenants, and their visitors, a chance to get a first-class panoramic view of the city and its surroundings.' Work started in July 1961, the topping-out ceremony took place that December, and the target date for completion was the spring of 1963. But by then, plans had already been announced (in March 1962) for a 20-storey block as part of the redevelopment of Hulme's Rutland Street area, where, altogether, 612 houses were to be cleared, with 362 new dwellings (including high-rise flats) built in their place – a fairly typical ratio.

'Slums are being torn down, crowded streets are disappearing, and in their place grow clean-cut modern flats' was how **Newcastle**'s evening paper described in October 1961 the rapidly transforming Scotswood Road Redevelopment Area. There was plenty else going on in T. Dan Smith's city. Basil Spence's eight-storey tower-and-podium Physics Building replaced the corporation tram depot; 'the area around the All Saints church,' recalled Terry Farrell about what happened 'immediately' after he left Newcastle for London in 1961, 'became the victim of an appalling piece of road planning', as 'a huge roundabout and three new office buildings [called Cuthbert, Bede and Aidan as a guilty nod to the church] were plonked there'; and, above all, Smith's right-hand man Wilfred Burns, the recently recruited City Planning Officer, unveiled in April 1961 his *Plan for the Centre of Newcastle*. 'IT'S THE MOTORWAY CITY' declared the *Evening Chronicle*, explaining how Burns envisaged a 'Central Motorway System' to 'completely surround the city centre', as well as 'skyscraper office blocks' and pedestrian shopping precincts. 'Because of the age of the City Centre,' pronounced Burns, 'a large-scale effort has now to be made in respect of redevelopment, and the process will be one of central area revolution rather than evolution.' Much flowed from this plan, perhaps not least the decision in 1962 to abandon Newcastle's trolley-bus system, one of the finest in the country.[9]

'A thing of great beauty' across 'a large open dank hummocky field': so in late 1960 the veteran town planner Thomas Sharp justified, to a public inquiry into **Oxford**'s severe traffic problems, his plan for a relief road across Christ Church Meadow. Much conflicting evidence was given, before eventually (in May 1961) the inquiry's chairman, Sir Frederick Armer, recommended in his report to government that such a road was 'inescapable'. The following year the minister, Charles Hill, upheld the report, and the landscape architect Geoffrey Jellicoe was commissioned to show how Sharp's vision could become reality.

Plymouth's most prominent new building was the multi-storey Civic Centre – well-appointed home from 1962 of the city council, with a water garden and rooftop restaurant as features, the whole effect curiously reminiscent of the UN headquarters in New York – while plans were under way for four tall blocks (one of 20 storeys, three of 17) on The Hoe, 'only a stone's throw from where Drake played bowls'.

The completion of Plymouth's Civic Centre roughly coincided with the demolition of **Preston**'s Town Hall, a magnificent 1860s Gothic Revival building that had been badly fire-damaged in 1947 but was still restorable. Elsewhere, in the Avenham district, slum clearance and redevelopment produced a notable housing scheme by Stirling and Gowan far removed from high-rise slab-blockery. 'We have tried here to maintain the vital spirit ("Saturday Night and Sunday Morning") of the alley, yard, and street houses that the new development is replacing, and from which its occupiers have recently moved,' the architects wrote in June 1961, not long before completion of 62 'working-class homes' situated in a maximum of four storeys. 'Whilst incorporating the essential improvements in space, light and convenience,' they added, 'we hope to perpetuate a familiar and vital environment.'

Ecclesiastical architecture had generally (apart from the odd high-profile exception) resisted twentieth-century modernism, which gave a particular impact to St George's Anglican Church in **Rugby**, consecrated in 1962. The architect (commissioned by a consciously progressive vicar) was Denys Hinton, whose obituarist describes 'a configuration of brick and glass boxes ... a series of horizontal spaces set at oblique angles' – and 'a font visible through the glass so that baptisms could be opened out and bathed in light'.[10]

'FORWARD TO THE CITY CENTRE BEAUTIFUL' was the bold headline in November 1961 of **Salford**'s weekly paper. That spring the city council had appointed the eminent architect Sir Robert Matthew to act as consultant to the Ellor Street/Broad Street comprehensive redevelopment scheme, so far making only destructive progress in transforming that 89-acre 'twilight' area in the centre of Salford. Now, Matthew's partner, the reliably visionary Percy Johnson-Marshall, had shown councillors a model of the new area and explained the key principles. 'Complete separation of pedestrians and traffic' plus 'provision of the maximum of open space' plus 'making the shopping centre an area of "bright lights", alive by day and night, with three tower blocks of maisonettes actually over the shops' plus 'getting a community feeling into the new residential development, even to the extent of providing the odd corner shop' – all these things, relayed the *Salford City Reporter*, made the planners 'confident that the new city centre will maintain Salford's individuality and dignity; that its housing and amenities will provide a warm and friendly neighbourhood unit; that its shops will attract people from all over the region, including Manchester'. Four months later, building work at last began on the first three blocks of flats, 16 storeys each, in the redevelopment area. Significantly, and adding a distinct tinge of bitterness to the occasion, it was (noted the paper) 'almost three years to the day since the Corporation started to move people out of the notorious "Hanky Park" slums' – a delay that led one councillor to reflect publicly how 'this desert of demolition' had been 'draining Salford's very life-blood'.

Across the Pennines, **Sheffield** was not just about Park Hill and electric milk-trolleys on wide decks. By 1962 three other ambitious housing schemes, all started by the Corporation in the mid-1950s, were complete or approaching completion: Greenhill, a garden city-style layout near the Derbyshire boundary but with three 13-storey point-blocks; Gleadless, mixed development in a woodland valley, but with another three 13-storey blocks crowning the hilltop; and Netherthorpe, in the valley near the city centre, with nine tower blocks and a further two under construction, as the process of slum clearance continued. There was also the small matter, literally looming on the horizon, of Park Hill II, also known as Hyde Park. This was the scheme for four monumental high-rise blocks of flats at the top of the hill immediately behind and above the now completed streets-in-the-sky Park Hill I – a scheme on which building work began at the start of 1962. 'To place buildings of this kind on such a dominant site will radically affect the visual aspect of the city,' claimed – or warned – the City Architect, Lewis Womersley, in advance. 'It is, therefore, considered essential to ensure that as far as possible the finished result will be worthy of the exceptional prominence which this scheme will have.'[11]

Down on the south coast, the first two of Basil Spence's buildings for the new University of **Sussex** were moving towards completion. That architect seldom came cheap – 'If only we could have looked after the Spences,' recalled a member of the University Grants Committee, 'the pounds would have taken care of themselves' – but there anyway he offered something distinctive and in tune with the venture. 'Concrete barrel-vaults and sensuous brickwork demonstrate the influence of Le Corbusier's Maisons Jaoul,' notes Brian Edwards. 'The choice of materials, the colour of the finishes and the relationship between buildings and landscape evoke the sense of a new university which is both traditional and progressive.' At a press conference in March 1962, Spence's assistant remarked that the inspiration for Falmer House and the School of Physics was the Colosseum – 'not as it was but as it is now'.

As dramatic a lurch to high-rise as anywhere took place in **Swansea**. By 1960 almost 8,000 new dwellings had been built since the war, entirely small houses and low-rise flats. Under a dynamic Housing Chairman, Councillor T. S. Harris, the local authority then changed direction completely, in 1961 alone commissioning 13 tower blocks.

'Massive scheme for **Wellingborough**' announced the local paper in November 1961. At its core was a new shopping centre in the heart of the town; three months later the *Wellingborough News* published an artist's impression of what it would look like when 'the existing buildings have been knocked down, the market stalls pushed over to the White Horse Yard car park, the traffic rerouted to the roof-tops, paving stones replaced by tarmac and a row of kiosk shops erected in the Market Place'.[12]

How and why was all this happening? What were the main forces at work? What was the debate? Was it ultimately a case of an irresistible zeitgeist?

At the level of national politics, it is fair to say that while there existed a broad consensus around the slum-clearance/high-rise/urban-redevel-opment orthodoxy, there was at this stage somewhat less zeal and a touch more scepticism on the Conservative side. 'The nineteenth century brought this country great good and great wealth, but some of its mistakes are with us yet,' reflected Henry Brooke in his New Year message for 1961 as Minister of Housing and Local Government. 'They were the mistakes of men who thought they saw opportunities and used them badly. Do not let us – perhaps through carelessness, perhaps through conceit – make new mistakes now which the twenty-first century will curse us for.' The minister also had an awareness of the complexities – including human sensitivities – of the process. 'I know there is a keen desire to see the out-of-date inner areas of the city rede-veloped,' Brooke told the Liverpool authorities later that year. 'But there will be no chance to do that properly until the slums can be cleared. All this needs popular support, based on good information and explanation.'

Indeed, slum-clearance rates, of around 60,000 houses a year being demolished or closed, were running by the early 1960s significantly behind the original mid-1950s targets – so much so that it was estimated that at the current rate it would take Liverpool another 94 years to clear its slums, Manchester another 46, Oldham another 41, Dundee another 36 and Birmingham another 33. All of those, and other Victorian indus-trial cities, tended to be Labour-run, and for that and other visceral reasons it was unsurprising that in this whole policy area the real passion usually came from Labour. 'It's a damned good job these houses are coming down,' Bermondsey's no-nonsense MP, Bob Mellish, told the press in May 1961 in the context of Princess Margaret's husband, John Betjeman and others seeking to prevent a riverside row of charming if dilapidated houses in Rotherhithe being demolished, to be replaced by a park and promenade. 'People come along trying to stop progress,' added Mellish, 'just because they like the look of a few old buildings. Mr Armstrong-Jones should try living there and see if it changes his attitude. The park is what the local people and the children want.' It was Labour that year that pushed unsuccessfully for new housing legis-lation to include a more generous subsidy for high flats, while in April (coinciding with Yuri Gagarin's exploits) the local MP, Edward Short, did not hold back when he spoke at the opening of three multi-storey blocks at Shieldfield, Newcastle: 'This surely is the dawn of a new epoch in the forward march of mankind, and it is perhaps appropriate and symbolic that these great, towering blocks of homes should be opened in the first few days of the space age.' Councillor T. Dan Smith, added Short, 'will surely rank with Dobson and Grainger as builders of the city', while the blocks themselves he hailed as 'almost the first fruits of Newcastle's great, new dynamic drive against squalor and degrading housing conditions'. A slightly more qualified perspective came from Short's leader. 'Mr Gaitskell agreed with Coun. Wright [chairman of the local Housing Committee] that a new kind of communal living was being developed, slowly but surely, in the multi-storey flats which were springing up in the industrial cities,' reported Salford's local paper in February 1962 about Hugh Gaitskell officially opening the Lower Kersal estate. 'The older people were bound to find it hard to adapt themselves from the life of the crowded cottages, but the younger generation already have no doubts at all – to them the flats were "smashing".'

That adjective of endorsement had come directly from 'the crowds of children who gave him an uproarious welcome', but of course for very young children – and their mothers – it might have been a different story. Here, it was Labour and not their opponents who were surely on the side of the angels: in May 1961, an Opposition attempt to compel authorities to provide adequate play facilities for pre-school children living in high-rise blocks foundered in the face of government resistance. Tellingly, the Commons debate does not seem to have been attended by Margaret Thatcher, the Conservative member of the steering committee that had overseen the background report into the problem of *Two to Five in High Flats*. But it is claimed that soon afterwards she was the author of an anonymous article in *The Times*, arguing that the problem would soon disappear if only mothers showed greater initiative and took their children out more.[13]

In a day-to-day sense, the local politicians probably mattered more. January 1961 saw two contrasting episodes. On the 19th an official luncheon in the tenants' meeting hall at Park Hill marked the completion of that scheme's first stage – ie, prior to the Hyde Park stage. Amid a perhaps understandable torrent of self-congratulation, Councillor Roy Hattersley, 29-year-old chairman of the Public Works Committee, 'said they have all in some way taken part in the building of the most ambitious and most comprehensive housing scheme in Europe', while the council's leader, Alderman C. W. Gascoigne, claimed that 'a squalid area has been transformed into an area where human beings can live in dignity.' Exactly a week later, a conference staged by the Society of Housing Managers at Church House, Westminster, heard the sociologist Edmund Cooney summarise his East London research about the effects of different kinds of housing, including the often negative effects of high-rise. Among those listening was Councillor W. W. Griffin, who, during the discussion, after noting how 'we in Bootle have done a tremendous amount of slum clearance', went on:

> When you tackle slum clearance in a place like Bootle you are dealing with 45 to 60 houses to the acre; and I mean houses, not people. When you re-build, if you are building houses, it is very, very difficult to get more than 24 to the acre. You can have your garden with the roses, but nobody looks after them. So therefore the large towns and cities must go into the air. People can live in the air if you make it suitable for them to live there. We have just built an estate with two eleven-storey blocks . . . What complaints have we had? Take this down, Mr Cooney. We have had no complaints . . .
>
> Mr Cooney, could I take the dockside industry out of Bootle to some place where I could put all the people in houses? Could I take 15,000 workers and put them on the outside? Oh, Mr Cooney, if only you were a member of our Housing Committee. I did not come here to make anybody laugh but to talk about a serious housing problem . . .

'We have to think of the appalling conditions that some of the young married people are living in, with one and sometimes two children in one room,' added Griffin. 'Look at that problem, Mr Cooney, if you are an economist. Study that problem. It is not only so in Bootle but in the whole country.'

Undoubtedly it was the pressure to do something substantive about dismal housing conditions, allied to housing shortages, that drove many local politicians. A 1960 survey published in March 1962 by members of the Ministry of Housing found that, across England and Wales, 'the problem of obsolescent housing extends well beyond the 850,000 dwellings recorded as unfit' – this despite the fact that during the 1950s well over two million new dwellings had been added to the national housing stock and almost 300,000 old houses demolished. Or take some specific places. 'I have been on the LCC housing list for ten years,' J. Cadden in Stepney wrote to the *East London Advertiser* just before Christmas 1960. 'I have a two-roomed flat, my wife and I sleeping in the living room, and my six children, including a boy aged 13 and a girl 15, share a bed in the bedroom.' In Birmingham by 1961, 15 per cent of households were still without exclusive use of a WC and 32 per cent without exclusive use of a fixed bath, while a survey that year of lodging houses revealed what the historians of the city have called 'some appalling conditions'. As for Manchester, nearly one-fifth of households were without the use of a hot-water tap, and a councillor, Bill Egerton, would recall how 'you were being pressurized by people who were living in crummy conditions, in houses they wanted to get out of' – and 'of course to get the maximum usage of any particular site, if you go up you get more personnel in per acre.' Such were exactly the pressures on David Gibson in Glasgow. 'Homes are what the people want,' a slum-dweller in the Whiteinch district implored him at the start of a new year. 'Let us see action in 1962 for God's sake and let mothers have peace of mind with a decent home. There would be less deaths and murders and mental patients.'[14]

There were other motives in play. 'Our future as a city stands or falls by Ellor Street, which will add 2,800 families to our population, revitalise our trade, and give our rateable value its first boost since the war,' declared a Salford councillor in March 1962 about the major redevelopment project there. Civic pride mattered. The 1961 edition of Salford's official handbook described it as 'one of the most exciting and forward-moving cities in the Britain of today', called the Lower Kersal estate 'an acknowledged triumph', and declared that 'under a vigorous and courageous City Council' there would be 'no faltering on the road to the creation of an ideal city'. In Sheffield, meanwhile, the Corporation's April 1962 publication, *Ten Years of Housing in Sheffield*, appeared in French and Russian as well as English, and claimed that 'the careful exploitation' of the city's topography was 'gradually producing something of the fascination of the Italian hill towns'.

Ultimately, nothing mattered more than being modern, being

up-to-date – and being seen to be so. 'They have been built for 70 years and Peel Park is now behind the times,' insisted Salford's Councillor S. Davies in March 1961 about the impending demolition of Peel Park College, the library and the art gallery, in order to make way for a Mechanical Engineering block at the new College of Advanced Technology. 'Perhaps there is a little nostalgia,' he conceded, 'but we cannot afford to have ancient monuments in Salford.' Was there also an element of being blinded by science? Possibly sometimes. 'Members were fascinated by a model of the new area which was on view,' noted the *Salford City Reporter* later in 1961 about the Planning and Development Committee having Percy Johnson-Marshall unfold his vision to them – a vision 'displaying a symmetry and sense of unity which suggested that a master mind was very much in charge of the master plan'.

Much of the process was broadly bipartisan, but even in T. Dan Smith's Newcastle there could be a degree of dissent. 'The plans for Scotswood Road are first-class – it will be a great thing for the people who live there,' freely admitted Councillor Wright for the Conservatives in November 1961. But at the same time, he called on Smith to be more open to criticism and to reflect on the need for 'a little more variety in new blocks of flats and new houses that we build', lest the city become 'soulless and lack character'. A colleague, Councillor Grey, added, 'There is far too much paternalism in housing design – far too much a belief that every tenant wants and needs the benefits of abstract sculpture, community centres, etc.' Argument was especially vigorous in Labour-run Smethwick, where also in 1961 the Liberals described the town's new high-rise blocks as 'monstrosities' and the Tories tried to block ambitious plans to redevelop Cape Hill into a bespoke shopping centre, on the grounds that extra shopping facilities were already available in nearby Birmingham, that most of the houses to be demolished were perfectly sound and habitable, and that compulsory purchase was in principle undesirable.[15]

A particularly suggestive squall was that in Glasgow *within* Labour's ranks. Jean Mann had not only been MP for Coatbridge but for ten years had represented (on the city council) the badly rundown, crime-ridden ward where the Royston Road 20-storey blocks of flats went up in 1960. 'Do social conditions not enter into the planning of high flats?' she asked at the end of that year. 'In these days of ever-increasing delinquency and crime, has no action ever been taken to discover whether its increased incidence has any connection with the trend throughout the cities of Britain to place youngsters in such close proximity in multi-storey dwellings? Certainly, neither councillors nor MPs will make application for these multi-storeyed flats.' And she declared that by loudly exalting the virtues of skyscraper flats on every postage-stamp site in the city, Glasgow's councillors had succumbed to 'panic planning' and 'stunt publicity'. Gibson's public riposte was instant. Mann, he asserted, was guilty of 'mistaking the sense of extreme emergency as panic'; 90,000 families in Glasgow still lived more than four to a room; and there were 'few planners' anywhere who had 'found it possible to omit multi-storey flats from town and city plans'.

Probably fairly typical, in terms of local politicians and other activators, was how the Blackburn story played out in 1961–2. 'We must plan big and boldly,' declared the council leader, Labour's Alderman George Eddie, shortly before the May 1961 unveiling of the proposed comprehensive redevelopment of the town centre. Alderman R. F. Mottershead, leader of the Conservative opposition, agreed – 'We have to look at the broad picture with vision and courage' – and the only councillor to dissent was Kenneth Culshaw, an Independent. 'This is not going to be our town when you have finished,' he predicted. 'It is not fair to let the big-money people [ie, Laings] come along and take it away . . . This town was built up by the small shopkeepers and we don't want to see them destroyed. I don't see why the Market Hall should come down at all.' Soon after the unveiling itself – at which Eddie hailed the prospect of a 'magnificent new shopping centre' on the market site and invoked William Blake's 'new' Jerusalem – strong support for the project came from the local chamber of trade, claiming that it would 'create in Blackburn a shopping Mecca which is bound – absolutely bound – to interest all and sundry round about and cause them to want to come to Blackburn to do their shopping'. Eddie did momentarily falter in June when he discovered that the master plan involved the flattening of 21 pubs ('I don't know what the lads are going to say'), but later that month he was boosted by a meeting of the local Trades Council and Labour Party. 'I personally can't see any architectural beauty in the building,' declared Councillor Tom Taylor about the Market Hall. 'In fact to me it is a monstrosity.' J. Mason agreed: 'If the people who are doing the shouting owned this building there is only one thing they would do and that is to pull it down because the site will make more money with something else on it.'

The decisive vote was in March 1962, as the town council decided whether to authorise progress on the master plan, and Eddie duly carried the day with a passionate oration:

In this space age, with its glamorous departmental stores and supermarkets, people will no longer be content to shop in shabby, inadequate buildings, or stand in an uncomfortable, cobbled market square buying goods from a rickety wooden stall with the rain dripping down the back of their necks from a canvas cover. There is no glamour or comfort in shopping under such conditions. Our critics must face the facts and realities.

The planned pedestrian shopping centre, insisted Eddie, was 'probably the finest example of a planned town centre in the whole country'. In short: 'Blackburn cannot mark time. It cannot afford to go on giving the impression of being a dull, shabby, sooty, uninteresting place. It must put on some glamorous war paint if it is going to succeed in selling itself.'[16]

What about the planners themselves? 'We are on the edge of a great job of urban renewal and a vast revolution in our industrial areas is taking place,' a junior housing minister, Sir Keith Joseph, told the Town Planning Institute's annual dinner, held at London's Trocadero, in March 1961. 'Heavy responsibility falls on the members of the planning profession. They are confronted with the challenge of not only filling in the void but of creating something out of existing disorder, and creating ordered beauty out of empty space.'

The planners were certainly busy: in May 1962 the TPI's annual conference at Worthing heard that more than 340 urban authorities in England and Wales were considering new central-area schemes. In terms of the core principles at work, especially in the major cities, these remained largely modernist: comprehensiveness, clearance, zoning, segregation. 'It is still essentially as the Victorians built it,' complained Manchester's veteran planner, Rowland Nicholas, in 1962:

> A new look for the City [ie, Manchester] has long been overdue ... Its unsightly areas of mixed industrial, commercial and residential develop-ment need to be systematically unravelled and redeveloped on compre-hensive lines ... One thing that should be obvious is the impossibility of achieving any satisfactory rearrangement of the highway pattern, pedes-trian access, re-allocation of space and improvement of buildings, daylighting and car parking, by the piecemeal development of small sites.

For Wilfred Burns in Newcastle, what mattered was 'a comprehensive plan, for redevelopment cannot seriously be called such unless it is on a substantial scale and is part of an overall plan, otherwise the process is mere rebuilding'; and for Percy Johnson-Marshall in Salford, his plan marked 'an unparalleled opportunity for Salford to think today what other cities would think tomorrow'. For all urban planners, an increas-ingly key concern was the motor car. 'My hunch is that people have taken the car to their hearts – I certainly have,' Colin Buchanan told a 'Rebuilding City Centres' conference in 1960. 'It's been a smashing success in every way, and I can't see anything to challenge this endear-ing though murderously destructive machine.' The danger, he added, was that city streets were being turned into 'simply traffic drains'; his solution was 'bold use of various levels with exciting architectural possibilities'. Buchanan himself, in his mid-50s, was rapidly emerging as the guru on all things to do with traffic and the urban environment, and in 1961 he was commissioned by the Transport Minister Ernest Marples to write a definitive report on the way ahead.[17]

More broadly, the planners themselves seem to have believed that, following a dip in their fortunes during much of the 1950s (compared to the heady, pro-planning mood – at activator level anyway – of the 1940s), the new decade represented a fresh golden opportunity. 'Planning,' the eminent town-planning academic Lewis Keeble assured the TPI in 1961, 'is important, it is beginning to recapture the public imagination.' Graeme Shankland in Liverpool agreed. 'The post-war epoch is over and so is that absurd brief flirtation with anarchy when frustrations with local bumbledom seemed to many to justify a final bonfire of what few planning controls we have left,' he argued in January 1962. 'Now planning, physical and economic, is back on the map.' None of which inclined those shaping the new tomorrow to take criticism kindly. 'He is completely ill-informed,' insisted Bradford's City Engineer and Surveyor, Stanley Wardley, in response in early 1962 to John Betjeman's disobliging verdict ('stamping out the individualism of the North . . . a sort of international nothingness') on the city's new buildings. When, some months earlier, Ian Nairn lamented the loss of much of Plymouth's character, Wardley's counterpart there hit back sharply: 'I hold the view that a major city should, at its centre, both look and function like a major city and not a whimsical amusement arcade.' Criticism, implicit in the form of a weighty warning, also came from a perhaps less predictable quarter. 'If you usurp a function which in the ultimate resort the ordinary citizen thinks should not be yours, you and all your works will be swept away,' T. Dan Smith candidly told the delegates at Worthing in May 1962. 'The planner's function is to advise and guide, not to decide. This means that ultimately he must accept the standards and values of the society he serves. Planning is a new profession, a young profession, and the public is afraid of its ambitions.'[18]

Unmentioned by Smith, however, were the property developers – arguably at least as important, if not more so, than either the politicians or the planners in determining what British cities would look like for the rest of the century and beyond. The journalist Sheila Lynd listened to some of them in early 1961. Arndale Property Trust's Sam Chippindale (then developing not only Jarrow but over two dozen shopping-centre schemes in the north of England) told her that his forte was persuading Woolworth's to move into the new centres and posited that whereas 'planners go in for research, we rely on experience – you've got to have a flair'; the bearded Felix Fenston (responsible for major London office blocks like BP House and Dunlop House) reflected that 'my interest in architecture has grown with the growth of what my other bearded friends call contemporary architecture' and asserted that 'some of the most outstanding buildings have been erected by developers'; Joe Levy, after explaining his scheme for (in Lynd's words) 'the comprehensive development of a nine-acre site bounded on the south by Euston Road and the west by Hampstead Road, which is to be combined [in liaison with the LCC] with a big road-widening scheme, including an under-pass', argued that, whether in the City or in the West End, the answer to shortage of office space was 'to pull down the acres and acres of low-standard buildings and replace them by modern office blocks with working conditions which will attract staff', adding that his personal motto was that 'it always pays to buy the best sites'; and Norwich Union's J. W. Draper, building high office blocks like Croydon's Norfolk House at a prodigious rate, had little patience for architectural individualism, noting that 'what a developer wants an architect to produce is something which is pleasing to look at and on completion will let – it must be functional.' Three particularly prominent developers not interviewed by Lynd were Charles Clore, Jack Cotton and Walter Flack. In 1960 the first two merged their property empires in what became a thoroughly uneasy marriage between chilly precision and off-the-cuff warmth, soon joined by Flack's Murrayfield Real Estate Co – an outfit that especially targeted potential new shopping centres in the Midlands and made profitable use of the articulate, energetic and flexible Birmingham Labour politician Frank Price. 'In negotiations always give it 'em straight,' the rags-to-riches Flack (son of a tailor) would say. 'The only trouble is that they often won't believe the truth.'

Perhaps unsurprisingly, given the intrinsically unlevel playing field of much urban redevelopment. 'If,' observed reluctantly but realistically the *Journal of the Town Planning Institute* in May 1961, 'the local authority attempts to drive a hard bargain which would reduce the profit – in the interests of good and beneficial overall design – then the development company concerned may take its capital elsewhere.' Speaking in early 1962 on the theme of 'urban renewal', the LCC's deputy town planner, Walter Bor, conceded that private developers could not just be dismissed as 'well-known and less-well-known bad eggs', but he contended that it would be much better, especially in central areas, if they operated 'on a lease basis' on land owned and planned, at least in outline, by the local authority. 'I do not see why,' he added, 'all the profit-making should be done by the private developer while all the unprofitable development is left to the local authority.' More generally, the developers may still have had some way to go before becoming national hate figures, but the signs were already there.

'If I had my way,' John Betjeman told the *Daily Mail*'s Vincent Mulchrone in August 1961, 'all "developers" would be put in prison for the crime of murdering our souls – which is far worse, after all, than murdering our bodies.' Four months later saw the release of *The Young Ones*. Cliff Richard plays Nicky, youth-club member and wannabe singer; he and his friends are trying to save their club from rich, ruthless London property developer Hamilton Black (Robert Morley), who wants to replace it with a large office block; Nicky keeps secret the fact that HB is his father – until, when some of his friends try to kidnap HB, he comes to the rescue. The film ends with honours shared as HB promises to build the young ones a new youth club.[19]

If the influence of the developer was on the up, so too was that of the contractor, against a background of building shortages and the start of a trend towards industrialised building methods. Glendinning and Muthesius trace in their history of the tower block the rise of the 'package-deal' contract, under which the contractor designed as well as built the development for the local authority; in one city, Birmingham, the Architect's Department was by the early 1960s almost frozen out of designing new blocks of dwellings. The coming of industrialisation accentuated the changing balance of power, with 1962 the key year, especially after the formation in May of a new company, Taylor Woodrow-Anglian Ltd, to produce factory-made dwellings. Nor, more generally, were the contractors shy in promoting themselves. Typically, the official opening in August 1961 of the Royston high-rise project saw Wimpey paying for an eight-page advertorial supplement in the *Glasgow Herald*. Not only did the development exemplify 'the higher standard of housing which Glasgow's citizens can expect to enjoy during the coming age', but across all of its Scottish high-rise developments Wimpey was ensuring that 'the experiences of tenants are recorded and analysed, and the experience thus accumulated is made available to local authorities contemplating multi-storeyed construction for the first time'.

Two increasingly ambitious contractors were Laing and Bovis. 'Blackburn,' declared the former in 1961, 'is going to have the sense and the courage to knock down its whole town centre, re-plan it, and build it in accordance with modern needs and ideas'; about the same time, the latter's Harry Vincent wrote glowingly in the *Architects' Journal* about the possibilities of 'very large imaginative' packaged deals, involving 'a new town hall, public library and bus garage, all the present ones being removed and rehoused so as to create a proper precinct shopping centre'. Vincent, though, did not rely just on words to get Bovis a satisfactory slice of the rapidly expanding 'urban renewal' market. Accordingly, by the first half of 1962 a three-way, mutually beneficial nexus was in place: Vincent as contractor; the northern eye-for-the-main-chance architect John Poulson; and the charismatic city boss with all the municipal contacts, one T. Dan Smith.[20]

That leaves, in terms of the main protagonists in this whole complex process, the architects. There is a clear sense in which they were starting by now to be marginalised – for example A. G. Sheppard Fidler as Birmingham's City Architect, arguably even Womersley in Sheffield – but they still mattered. Among a few of the better-known names, moreover, it is possible to detect some concern about the way things generally were going. After noting with satisfaction that almost all architects were committed to 'the search for acceptable forms of urban living', which in practice meant that 'high buildings are going to multiply', that conflicted progressive Lionel Brett went on in *The Times* in July 1961: 'British architects are well through the novelty phase of skyscraper building. Many are in fact alarmed at the effect on our old city silhouettes and open spaces of a proliferation of second-rate flat-tops, with off-the-peg curtain walls.' He called for different ways of achieving higher density, for instance 'the four-storey maisonette block, which is perfectly in scale with our Georgian streets and squares'. Few admired the Georgians more than Sir Albert Richardson, who later in 1961 attacked the plan to build five 25-storey blocks of flats in the St Leonard's area of Edinburgh. 'Clear the slums by all means,' Richardson argued, 'but don't congest. We must think of the visitors coming. They don't want to see an illogical imitation of New York.' Even Graeme Shankland (wearing his architect's rather than his planner's hat) had his doubts. Why, he asked in March 1962, had 'the image of the rectangular glass tower office' become so 'commonly acceptable'? The answer was economic: 'It is simply that in a modern western city it is the most easily lettable and vertically stackable unit that, therefore, yields the most ground-rent from a valuable central site.' Yet, he continued, this was not necessarily best for 'office efficiency and sociability'; he himself

found something 'disquieting' about 'the impersonality of this architectural expression, the calligraphy of whose windows seem a visual echo
of the calculating machine'.[21]

But the larger mood and forces were, of course, going the other way.
Denys Lasdun appeared on *Monitor* in April 1961 to talk about how his
Bethnal Green cluster blocks recreated the old street communities ('the
backyards have been transferred to the top floor; the building mothers
and encloses you'); soon afterwards, the Northern Architectural
Association intervened in the ongoing debate about Newcastle's
proposed Pilgrim Street roundabout, declaring that the Royal Arcade's
preservation 'could not be justified' if 'to any extent' it 'compromised
the large-scale and imaginative redevelopment which this main gateway
of the city demands'; and the following spring, asked by *TV Times* his
opinion of St Pancras station-*cum*-hotel, that supreme expression of the
Victorian Age, Sir Basil Spence replied, 'I don't admire this too much.'
Sam Bunton in Glasgow, meanwhile, was busy conceiving what would
become the Red Road flats, Europe's highest. It was a vision responding, yes, to a city's severe slum problem, but it was also predicated on
the unspoken assumption that Glasgow's traditional industrial economy still had a future as well as a past. 'It is interesting to consider how
Glasgow would have looked from the Red Road as Bunton worked at
his drawing board,' reflected Ian Jack half a century later. 'To the farther
west, the cranes of Clyde shipyards stretched several miles downriver;
to the closer west, the workshops of the North British Locomotive Co
still exported engines to Africa and Asia; to the south, steam rose night
and day from Parkhead's big iron forge; to the east, the chimneys of the
Lanarkshire rolling mills and the conical waste heaps of collieries
pricked the horizon.' All activators are creatures of their time, seldom
gifted with any special insight into what lies ahead. The idealistic,
gregarious Bunton, after the best part of a lifetime working towards
this supreme moment, was no exception.[22]

———

Press coverage of the great upheaval – actual and pending – tended to be
patchy but positive, relatively seldom questioning the need to embrace
the tide of modernity. 'How far are we, in this motor-packed island,'
asked *The Times* in December 1961 rhetorically and querulously, 'from

the style and planning that put Sweden twenty-six years ahead with Stockholm's Slussem Cloverleaf or its Tegelbacken Intersection?' For a *Daily Mail* journalist, inspecting Bradford's progress the following spring, paradise was already at hand. 'I drove up an electronically-warmed ramp to a rooftop car park,' he wrote with undisguised enthusiasm, 'drank coffee in a café with splendid city vistas, strolled through an air-conditioned supermarket, explored a semi-completed system of under-traffic tunnels for pedestrian moles.'

Closer to the action, the local press largely joined the chorus. 'Near-miracle of City Centre' trumpeted the *Western Morning News* about Plymouth's virtually completed shopping centre; 'a go-ahead town like Doncaster could be transformed in the space of a few years', urged the *Doncaster Gazette*; 'another demonstration of confidence in Bradford' the *Telegraph & Argus* greeted the Forster Square development plan; 'super-deluxe apartments' the Manchester-based *County Express* called Hulme's ongoing multi-storey St George's development. Or, at the western end of the East Lancs Road, take the *Liverpool Echo*'s coverage of the continuing Everton Heights redevelopment. 'Crying for the moon' was journalist George Cregeen's brisk verdict on slum-dwellers there obstinately refusing alternative accommodation. As for 'those who feel that with the disappearance of these communities, with their peculiarly local traditions and alliances, something of the heart of Liverpool will have been plucked out', the larger truth, according to Cregeen, was that 'it is a heart that is aged, wheezy and asthmatical, and a change of air can do no harm.' Sentiments were similar in Newcastle. 'A project of imagination, courage and forward-looking qualities' was the *Evening Chronicle*'s instant verdict on the Burns plan for the city centre; that same issue ran a 'Symbols of Hope' feature on the high-rise flats shortly to open at Shieldfield; while later in 1961, a feature by the paper's Joan Elliott on the imminent start of Byker's redevelopment sought to allay local fears that the area's 'close communities' would be 'broken up' as a result: 'Modern planning knows how to put the clock back wisely and Byker should enjoy in the future all the advantages of the best type of twentieth-century city life with the right of every man to breathe fresh air and to live in beautiful surroundings.'[23]

The treatment was sometimes more nuanced. In February 1961 the

Glasgow Herald asserted that 'tall buildings are imperative in Glasgow if the housing conditions are to be improved', but, seven months later, in a sceptical editorial on 'High Flats', reckoned that 'the prevailing fashion among municipalities for flats of 20 storeys and more' was 'a trend often followed more for reasons of civic pride than of housing need'. Furthermore: 'Building high into the air does not always save space on the ground. Scotland's present stock of multi-storey flats are insufficiently distinguished in architectural merit to qualify as prestige symbols.' The *Liverpool Daily Post* seems consciously to have allowed both sides of the argument to speak. On the one hand, George Eglin continued to hammer away, declaring in October 1961 that 'there are not just a few years of redevelopment ahead of Liverpool, but a programme that must go on for fifty years, a hundred years, a programme, in fact, without any end'. On the other hand, not only did the paper soon afterwards run a series of critical articles by J. R. Waddington on life in Liverpool Corporation's new multi-storey blocks (already showing signs of 'damage and neglect' as well as generally providing 'little scope for families to express any individuality'), but it had already (in November 1960) expressed concern about the failure to keep together communities of displaced slum-dwellers, perhaps through 'a sort of transit camp', so that when the new housing was ready, families might collectively 'return to the streets from whence they came, but with far better homes'. Even the *Blackburn Times*, after in May 1961 endorsing the master plan as undoubtedly necessary in order 'to eradicate the town's more ghastly features', and then in February 1962 reiterating that Blackburn would 'quickly become a back number' if it failed to keep up with its neighbours' plans, did implicitly come to concede a degree of anxiety, noting in March 1962 that 'we don't want a town centre full of chain stores exactly the same in appearance and customer-attraction as can be found in any other large town.'

Perhaps no local commentator was more conflicted than the *Wellingborough News*'s 'Redwell'. 'The people of the town must appreciate that it is essential that the town develop if it is to compete with neighbours,' the columnist wrote in November 1961. Yet at the same time: 'We must remember that once the town centre is knocked down and rebuilt, if we don't like it all the king's horses and all the king's men won't be able to put it together again.' Then, a week later: 'I still feel a tinge of regret at the possible mixture of ancient and modern buildings, but on reflection any modern development, even if it is in close proximity to Wellingborough's beautiful church, can hardly be worse than the jumble of backways which can be seen at present.' And finally, like a sore itch, looking ahead soon afterwards to 1962: 'Now there are plans laid to change the very heart and sometimes I fear the soul of the town. We may find we will have to make great sacrifices for the sake of the progress we wish to achieve.'[24]

The more specialist press and writers tended to go with the larger flow. Take the *Architects' Journal*, which, responding in May 1961 to Blackburn's comprehensive development plan, 'congratulated' the town 'on taking so bold a step', praised Councillor Eddie's 'dynamic leadership' and began one sentence with a hugely revealing assumption: 'One hesitates to criticise in any way so bold a slate wiping . . .' The *AJ* was certainly far from invariably uncritical – between February and May 1962, for instance, it vainly called it 'a sad and stupid thing' if Rotherhithe's old houses on the riverside were to be demolished, further along the Thames rated the huge new Shell building an 'abysmal architectural failure' and condemned out of hand the Marples 'lorry road' plan for Highgate – but its objections were almost always on an individual basis. Elsewhere, a writer somewhere in the middle of the broad progressive range was the *Guardian*'s architectural critic, Diana Rowntree, who in April 1962 offered a lengthy, mainly positive appraisal of developments in Sheffield. 'The city,' she declared, 'is making a bid to replace its nineteenth-century confusion with something planned specifically for today's needs.' Rowntree's greatest enthusiasm was for the plan 'to link the Markets with the lower decks of Park Hill, so that an upper pedestrian system of terraces and walkways operate across the whole area of the Sheaf Valley'. 'We have been waiting ever since the war,' she added, 'for some town to break through into this way of living.'[25]

In a class of his own was the shy, passionate, unpredictable Ian Nairn. A sample of his writings during 1961, partly for the architectural press but also for the *Listener*, brings out something of his love of vitality, a vitality with people at its centre. 'In ninety-nine per cent of cases,' he declared in March about the dire consequences of 'speculative building'

on subtopian housing estates, 'it creates a lowest common denomina-
tor, a collection of houses-with-gardens which are individually not
quite what anybody wants and collectively form little textbooks of
social sterility, endless windy lanes down which the prams trundle back
from the bus stop, whilst the ice-cream van chimes its weary way (those
chimes are often the only sign of life in a square mile or so and, dear
God, some people want to stop them).' The following month he was
travelling hopefully with the Burns plan for central Newcastle, which
provided 'the opportunity for showing that twentieth-century traffic
flow and a magnificent medieval and early-Victorian city can be harmo-
nised'. Then in June it was back to prams, with Nairn noting that in
reconstructed Plymouth the main shopping street, Royal Parade, faced
due west, was completely straight for 500 yards and offered no protection against the rain: 'Pushing a pram into wind in those conditions is
no advertisement for twentieth-century civilisation. Other centuries
knew better – but then they were just picturesque fuddy-duddies in a
pre-technological age.' By contrast, he observed in August, a new
Richard Seifert office block, Kellogg House in Baker Street, 'cheers you
up every time you see it'. Perhaps the most deeply felt contribution
came in November, when Nairn reviewed Lewis Mumford's massive,
magisterial *The City in History*. 'I gag on Mumford's turgid chapters
and intellectual abstractions the same way that I gag on D. H. Lawrence's
emotional abstractions,' he wrote. 'The protagonist of a humane city, he
puts people into compartments as fiercely as any zone-besotted planner.'
And Nairn offered his own credo: 'The really important thing in life as
in city planning is the "how", not the "what". If something – anything
– is done with love and true tolerance, not just freedom-to-like-what-I-
like, then it will be all right, even if it is cram-full of bric-à-brac and
oleographs. It is only the right "how" that will harmonise all the different "whats" that represent all the variety of human temperament.' As it
happened, a different American writer was already getting much closer
to Nairn's priorities. This was Jane Jacobs, whose *The Death and Life
of Great American Cities* was published in the US in 1961 and caused
immediate waves, but did not appear in Britain until the second half of
1962.[26]

Nairn would only become a national treasure posthumously, whereas
John Betjeman, 'as we all know, pedals about London on a bicycle,

finding sweetness in sooty railway stations, gathering treasured images in Victorian Gothic, and plucking poetic inspiration from other unlikely places'. That March 1961 profile in *Everywoman* magazine quoted Betjeman observing that he found himself unable 'to avoid battles to stop something or other being destroyed'. The two most famous battles, both unsuccessful and in both of which he played a leading role, were of course for the Euston Arch and the Coal Exchange. Over the former, it was much later claimed that at the crucial moment Betjeman had gone missing (with a five-week trip to Australia) – but by then, late October 1961, the battle was surely lost, little helped by *The Times* having pronounced in mid-October, 'Not Worth Saving'. As for the Coal Exchange, Betjeman's view was steely clear, telling a sympathiser in February 1961 that what was 'really behind its destruction' was not road-widening but 'a speculator who has his eye on the rest of the island site on which it stands'. There were other conservationist battles in these years, including a happier outcome in the City for the wonderful 1860s National Provincial building in Bishopsgate, but not so for Lewisham's Victorian town hall, to whose impending fate Betjeman had been alerted by a local 13-year-old schoolboy. He was also now using television as a campaigning medium, starting with *Steam and Stained Glass* on ITV in April 1962. 'A paean of praise for Victorian architecture,' noted the *Daily Mirror*'s Clifford Davis. 'He didn't win me over, but there was no denying his infectious enthusiasm.' What about 'the modern' itself? On the whole, Betjeman had by now few kind words, but in 1961 he was willing to see some potential good in Sheffield's Park Hill. Admittedly 'the first sight was terrifying and inhuman, tier on tier of concrete with ugly "contemprikit" detail rising on a steep slope', but after getting closer and walking about, he reckoned that 'the planning is thoughtful and ingenious and people do not much miss the gardens they never had.' Ultimately, reflecting on the city's new developments as a whole, his verdict was part-hopeful, part-disquieted: 'Who shall say what a race these new, churchless, communal blocks will breed? It is still too early to say . . . I believe they suit the rugged hills of Sheffield and its people. The question is, will they make a houseproud horizontal people apathetic and turn them into the machines they tend?'[27]

'When the bulldozers uproot the people' was the title of the Rev.

WE'LL ALL BE UPROOTED

Norman Power's *Birmingham Mail* article in July 1961, showing a photo of the wasteland in front of his Ladywood church. In the case of slum clearance, it seems at times to have been only clergymen who stood up for the powerless people whose lives were being turned upside-down by what was clearly all too often a blunt, inefficient and high-handedly insensitive process. After reflecting that 'when people are uprooted, they are uprooted from more than bricks and mortar,' and after noting that only about ten were left in the district out of his last hundred confirmation candidates ('these were our potential leaders'), Power wrote that 'we are begging our planners not to destroy the neighbourhood any more until more building has been done.' He concluded unforgivingly that 'the bulldozers have torn a living community to pieces. It could have been avoided.'

It was not so different in Liverpool, where a local paper in April 1962 identified Father George Earle of St Francis Xavier's Church as one of the few people concerned about 'the lonely people of Everton Brows'. 'The conditions they are living in,' he declared from that clearance zone, 'are appalling – not only in these derelict areas, but in the streets which are still intact.' Across in Manchester a few weeks earlier, the *County Express* had reported the Rev. Cecil Lewis from working-class Gorton joining forces with 'fellow churchmen in slum clearance areas who have forcibly criticised the Corporation's re-housing policy whereby families are being "uprooted" and found new homes in strange districts'. Lewis himself cited the recent wholesale redevelopment of the Bradford Road area of Ancoats and ensuing loss of the old community spirit: 'It is something which will take years to replace, if it ever can be.'[28]

It was not quite true that the public was never consulted. In T. Dan Smith's Newcastle, recalled the *Municipal Review* in 1974, public consultation (about the slum clearance and housing drive that he was pushing from the late 1950s) 'took place at crowded public meetings at a time when public participation was not a vogue catch-phrase'. Smith himself in 1964 reckoned that 'in three years I spoke to 30,000 people about our plans' and that this had been 'local democracy at work'. Or take another exemplar, Coventry. During the winter of 1961–2, not only did the city council arrange a series of 28 public meetings, covering every ward, to encourage feedback about the latest version of the Development Plan, but a television documentary showed people gathering round shop windows to examine models of the next stage – a sight prompting the *Architects' Journal* to reflect that 'there are not many towns where you would find the same knowledge among the people of what the local authority was trying to do.' That might have been true, and the relative apathy of the Glaswegian citizenry was probably more typical. There, the Corporation staged a week-long exhibition in March 1961 at the McLellan Galleries in order to publicise the city's quinquennial plan, setting out the strategy for a mixture of 'comprehensive redevelopment' and significant overspill. 'There was no crowd, no sign that it was "the thing" to attend the exhibition,' Elizabeth Mitchell observed in the next issue of *Town and Country Planning*. 'There is something strange in utter unconcern – unawareness even – about such vital matters.'[29]

On the actual frontline of slum clearance, whether happening or intended, attitudes varied. 'What the people in the area wanted, if any official had cared what they thought, was for their houses to be done up, bathrooms and proper lavatories put in, and the dangerous wiring replaced,' recalled Doris Lessing about London's Somers Town in the early 1960s. 'They were saying, "But we've all been living here for years. My mother was born here. My kids were born here."' So too in Frome, where ahead of the clearance of the town's Trinity Street area the *Western Daily Press*'s Bill Beckett found that the residents 'would rather stay than have their roots torn up to be transplanted on a modern foreign housing estate'. 'The council,' Mrs Gwen Latham told him, 'want it and they'll have it. Nobody wants to move but we'll all be uprooted and that will be it.' In Manchester a mass petition from private tenants living in atrocious conditions in Greenheys demanded that the council declare the district a slum-clearance area, but across the city as a whole, later in 1961, it was reported that the housing department was starting to adopt 'tough tactics' against 'people in condemned houses who refuse to leave', at least 'until they get the type of new home they want'. Or take Liverpool's Everton Heights, where the journalist George Cregeen came across not only refuseniks but also, at 59A William Henry Street, 'a very satisfied customer':

Mrs Mary McDonald was stacking all her household possessions on the balcony of her terraced home perched above a block of derelict shops. She was all smiles. 'We're moving tonight,' she told me. 'My three daughters aged ten, seven and 12 months, and my husband. We're all going to live in a council house at Norris Green. It's a re-let. The children are absolutely thrilled to bits. It will be much healthier for them out there.' She had lived in the area all her life and had mixed feelings about leaving it. 'You would go a long way to find people like those who lived around here,' she said. 'But they have gone to the four corners of Liverpool now.'

There were mixed feelings too in Coronation Street in Sunderland's East End, in the process of being cleared in April 1962. 'We would do anything to get a decent house,' 27-year-old Mrs June Price, a labourer's wife with three children, informed a journalist, while 37-year-old Mrs Elizabeth Taylor, a general dealer's wife, added, 'I can understand the street meaning a lot to the older folk, but I want to move out of it as soon as possible.' One of those older folk was 73-year-old Mrs Sarah Charlton, who had briefly left to live at the Thorney Close estate but was now back. 'I pined for the old sights and faces,' she explained, though most of the street's houses were now demolished and all but two of its dozen pubs. There was clearance and demolition too, perhaps more resonant than anywhere, in and just off Newcastle's Scotswood Road. 'The city was in their bones, they feared the wilderness of flats and isolated houses without a centre, they instinctively rejected amenities without that highway of shops and pubs which constitutes the ganglion of a living place,' wrote Sid Chaplin in *The Watchers and the Watched*. 'The Road was their life, and they clung to it. As long as they could, as long as they were allowed, they would stay. And yet their days were numbered. The Road was being demolished and the people were shifting. Some went, then returned from the desert, paying double the old rent rather than be dead, content to keep one wall between themselves and the demolition gang.'[30]

We also have for these years the occasional more systematic survey of attitudes to rehousing. The sociologists Dennis Marsden and Edmund Cooney, for instance, made a study of elderly people living in decaying housing in Stepney. 'You're not going to shift me, are you?'; 'Me fire's me comfort, me fire and me cup of tea, as long as I can get them I'm all right'; 'It'll last my time out' – all were typical of what Marsden and Cooney heard. One woman, fed up with her squalid living conditions and saying she would like 'a one-roomed flat' with 'a bath when you want', was asked whether she would, given the chance, move to a housing estate. 'Me, move out there?' she replied. 'No fear. I've been round here all my life. I'd be right out of it. I may as well die.' This strong attachment to Stepney, reflected Marsden, was not to 'the large, mixed administrative borough' but to 'the small area of intimately known streets "around here", where they had lived for so many years'. He further reflected that 'the old people's plea that the housing will last their time out is something deeper than mere inbred indifference to dirt and inconvenience: it is a challenge to the idea that their lives and their environment can be planned.'

By contrast, a major survey in Leeds of almost a thousand households in officially designated slum-clearance areas, carried out between May and July 1962 by the University of Leeds, was across the generations and yielded significantly different findings. Asked whether they wanted to move, 82 per cent of respondents said they did and only 16 per cent were opposed to the idea. Those in the latter camp tended, relative to the sample as a whole, to be older, poorer and have fewer children, while for those wanting to move, the inadequate condition of the house they were living in was the reason most commonly given. The university's R. K. Wilkinson and E. M. Sigsworth pondered the fact that 16 per cent non-movers was such a markedly lower proportion than in a similar survey undertaken some years earlier in a comparably inner-city part of Liverpool, where as many as 36 per cent had not wished to move. 'A relevant point may be the distance involved in a move,' they surmised. 'In Liverpool those who are moved are often rehoused in overspill areas, whereas in Leeds rehousing takes place within the city boundary.'[31] It was a plausible explanation, reaffirming again the supreme psychological importance of the local and the familiar.

In any case, irrespective of individual wishes and volition, the slum-clearance process itself could be (for adults anyway) an unutterably grim, bewildering experience. 'In the vicinity of Rokeby Street,' wrote George Cregeen in May 1961 about Everton Heights, 'I saw streets and streets of devastation – far worse than anything the German bombers could do even on the worst night of the May blitz.' Almost a year later, another Liverpool journalist wrote of how on Everton Brow 'single families live with acres of empty land all around them', some 'with a complete street to themselves', as 'children run wild over the area'. Sticking it out in Haigh Street were just two inhabitants: at number 139, where she had lived for 55 years, Mrs Mary Kempster, alone apart from her cat Nigger, her only running water a cold tap in the cellar, feeling forgotten ('I don't know why they're keeping us here ... Nobody seems to worry about us'), and at number 117, in a house flooding when it rained, no ceiling in the kitchen, the lavatory 'broken and useless', 77-year-old Mrs Catherine Hughes ('I'm afraid to go out, in case someone breaks up the house while I'm away').

It was little better in Bolton's Moncrieffe Street. 'Workmen have started to pull down terraced houses in a row in which three houses are still occupied,' reported the local paper in June 1961. 'It's terrible living here while the other houses are being demolished,' said the occupant of one of them, 82-year-old invalid Mrs Emily Phillips. 'We get a lot of people coming here thinking this house is also empty. They go in to take things from the empty houses.' In nearby Matthew Street there were also only three houses left occupied, including one by a pensioner who had lived in his for 40 years and now 'stood watching the bulldozers pull down the house next door'. 'I think,' he remarked, 'they could have at least left the houses on either side standing until I moved.' Salford may have been the worst of all. 'There was so much destruction,' recalled the photographer of slum clearance, Shirley Baker. 'A street would be half pulled down and the remnants set on fire while people were still living in the area. As soon as any houses were cleared, children would move in and break all the windows, starting the demolition process themselves.' In February 1962 one local paper reported (about the clearance area near Bury New Road) 'rats scurrying through the streets, children climbing on the roofs of partly demolished houses, indiscriminate tipping creating a health hazard', while another published a letter from 'A Resident':

Although what looks like half a square mile of devastated land lies awaiting the building of flats on the Broad Street side of Ellor Street, and it is going to take at least three years to do the building, the Corporation is knocking houses down on the opposite side of Ellor Street as fast as it can.

Why this panic? Why drive hundreds of families out of the district and in many cases out of the city when they could be left there for a couple of years at least without any delay to the rebuilding programme? It is not even as if they were very bad houses; many are quite good. It just doesn't make sense to any of us . . .

Why can't we be left here until the first set of flats are up, so that we can move straight into them and so continue living as neighbours? Isn't half the trouble in the new flats that families from all over the show are moved in, nobody knowing anybody else, and having slowly and painfully to build up community feeling from the very beginning?

'Perhaps,' the writer concluded, 'someone in authority will condescend to explain.'[32]

Many of Salford's slum-dwellers had gone, or would be going, to new overspill housing at Worsley, 8 miles away and intended by 1971 to be housing 18,000 people displaced by Salford's redevelopment. In 1960 the housing and planning expert Barry Cullingworth published his analysis of fieldwork from 1958 about how Worsley's new settlers were getting on; the following year he did much the same in relation to London's overspill population which had decanted to Swindon, this time based on 1959 fieldwork. His conclusions were broadly similar. In both cases the experience was largely – though far from uniformly – positive, including for many of those who had not wanted to move in the first place, and for most people the key plus was improved housing. 'We don't bother with relatives out here,' a Worsley interviewee explained. 'We live our own life. We've got a lovely house, a nice garden and a TV set. We're very happy.' The happiness quotient remained patchier in another, more-publicised overspill settlement, Kirkby, where the birth rate was eight times the national average. 'Older people are apt to feel a bit out of it all, especially if they are on their own,' Miss Margaret Lunt – disabled and living on the tenth floor of Cherryfield Heights – told the *Liverpool Echo* in May 1962. 'I think there should be little corner shops in Kirkby to make it more homely. Most of the people who came to live here are used to little corner shops.' Another insider account was in 1961 from the headmistress of a school on one of Newcastle's new housing estates, apparently some distance from the inner city. 'The estate,' she wrote, 'is a vast monotonous sprawl possessing the minimum of amenities and no charm; but an improvement on the areas from which the people come in that most for the first time have hot and cold water, baths, inside lavatories, a garden, and live in fresh air.' After describing some of her difficulties at the school, including how 'each year's intake throws up a leader of a small anti-social group,' she went on:

> The old areas from which the families came were settled, closely knit communities – where the family stuck together – where grandma was there with authority – to advise, to tell your troubles to, look after the baby, turn to in any emergency. She has stayed behind. From some parts of our estate there is a daily exodus back to her. The Welfare Officer was telling me how surprised she was to hear grown women talking about going back to 'me mum' . . .
>
> In that old world you could be your natural self – shout, laugh, quarrel, make love, get drunk, put up with things without that awful dread, 'What will the neighbours say – what will they think', for you knew your neighbours would be shouting, laughing, quarrelling, getting drunk too . . .
>
> Now, pitchforked into an entirely different neighbourhood, people are terribly lonely and insecure, old values are questioned, their actions are subject to criticism from neighbours, and even children come home from school with all sorts of fancy ideas, torn between two loyalties . . .

In short: 'I think our most pressing behaviour problems are understood better in the context of their previous environment, and the acute period of transition through which some section of the community is always moving.'[33]

Whether they stayed in their familiar district or went elsewhere (especially the former), many rehoused people finished up living in flats – often against their wishes. The 1962 survey of Leeds slum-dwellers showed, among those in the 20 to 49 age range, only 5 per cent wanting to move into a flat rather than a house. That same year, a survey of the St Mary's district of Oldham revealed that although 75 per cent wanted to be rehoused in the area, that preference rate halved if they were offered a flat, not a house. Local politicians were well aware of popular feeling on the subject. 'I know that many people do not like flats,' conceded Councillor Les Morris, chairman of the Housing Committee, in January 1961, 'but in a town like Smethwick it is the only way we have of giving people a home, and the sooner that is accepted by the townspeople, the happier they will be about it.' Across much of urban Britain, modernism was being imposed upon a deeply un-modernist populace. 'The more optimistic of the architects in London last week,' noted a journalist in July 1961 on the occasion of a major international architectural conference, 'would have done well to stand at the foot of one of the superb Roehampton blocks which overlook the hills of Richmond deer park; looking up he would have seen window upon window each heavily shrouded with patterned lace curtains.'[34]

Sometimes of course the experience could be good, especially in the early months, even years. 'It's like a palace when you've lived in a place like we came from,' Mrs Anne Knight told Newcastle's *Evening Chronicle* in April 1961 about the recently opened Heaton Park flats; and, according to the report, she 'could not say enough in praise of her new home and particularly about the gas appliances in it'. Eight months later and it was the turn of Liverpool's Garibaldi Street blocks to be unveiled, with one new resident, William McGowan, calling his flat 'a docker's paradise' after 23 years living in a 'hovel' in the city's Conway Street. By this time (between August 1961 and March 1962), the assistant estate manager at Sheffield's acclaimed Park Hill development was interviewing the households in every fifth dwelling. Although 72 of the 197 interviewed families complained of the noise (especially in relation to the main lifts and the laundry), the findings by Mrs Demers were otherwise generally positive: 86 per cent experiencing 'no difficulty with the lifts' (albeit they were 'often out of action as a result of abuse'); overall satisfaction with the revolutionary Garchey system of refuse disposal; only two families disappointed by the central heating system and preferring an open fire; only 20 per cent missing their garden and/ or wanting one; and 92 per cent feeling 'no loss of privacy', although Demers added that 'a visitor might well think on seeing a row of doors so close together that a lack of privacy was inherent in the design.'

'There can be no doubt,' she went on, 'as to the general feeling of approval for the decks themselves, which are appreciated for a great variety of reasons, for protection from weather, for cleanliness, for the view and for social contacts as well as for privacy.' Altogether, claimed the housing manager in his foreword to her report, 'the survey shows that Park Hill is a satisfactory "machine for living in", to use Le Corbusier's phrase.'

Too often, in too many multi-storey blocks, the experience was far from satisfactory. In September 1961 Salford Corporation was described as 'at its wits end' about how to stop 'mounting damage in its multi-storey flats', including 'windows broken, fire-hydrants damaged, lifts immobilised, refuse chutes blocked'; the following month, amid prolif-erating vandalism in Speke (complementing Kirkby as Liverpool's other major overspill location), Mrs Mabel Oakes, living in the large block on Central Way, frankly declared, 'It's murder living in these flats, we can't get any peace'; and in the Loxford Court flats in Hulme, elderly Mrs Dorothy Rowson wailed in May 1962, 'I would give anything to get away from here. During the day we get no peace from the children and late at night we suffer from rowdy teenagers.' Probably worst of all, though, was the plight of mothers looking after small chil-dren. 'THE SKY PRISONERS' was the *Daily Sketch*'s lurid but not inapposite headline in May 1961 for the survey conducted by Joan Maizels of 62 recently built council blocks in the London area, reveal-ing high levels of worry and isolation among the mothers ('a night-mare', according to one), with 52 per cent of two- to five-year-olds going out only to the shops and playing only in the flat. Nor was it just a London issue. 'I am a mother who lives in an eight-storey block of flats in Birmingham,' Mrs Bowratt of Kitts Green wrote soon after-wards to the *Daily Mirror*. 'I was nearly driven frantic trying to keep my little boy quiet when his daddy – who works nights – was sleeping during the day. Every toy that made a noise was taken away from him. The child could not go out to play because we live so high up and near a main road.' 'In desperation,' she added, 'I have put him in a nursery and now feel I am missing the best years of his life.'[35]

Specific reactions (in either direction) are somewhat harder to find in relation to city-centre/town-centre redevelopment; almost certainly the most common feeling among the inhabitants of those cities and towns was an assumption that it was going to happen anyway. Just occasionally there was strong support, as when D. Shaw (in a letter to the *Liverpool Echo* in August 1961) declared that 'whole areas of the city need sweeping away', condemned 'those black monstrosities of stone' opposite Lime Street station and urged city councillors to visit 'the beautiful city centre of Plymouth', which would 'shame them into quick action'. If there was support for major urban change, though, it was usually more muted, typified by the *Wellingborough News* noting in February 1962 that 'most seem to agree that, sometime, something had to be done.' Yet overall, the majority of identifiable reactions were essentially negative. Bristol in the spring of 1961 saw a mass petition (backed by the *Bristol Evening Post* and signed by 11,500 people) against the insensitive, piecemeal development (mainly by Norwich Union and the Bank of England) of the heavily bombed Wine Street area; about the same time, the *FT* wrote of 'bemused citizens' and 'disgruntled locals' calling the new Birmingham 'a concrete jungle'; in Devon that Christmas, another letter-writer, Miss Ada Watts, who had 'known and loved Torquay for the last 37 years', lamented the 'heartbreaking' sight of a new block of luxury flats 'ruining the exquisite wooded scenery' surrounding the town; and among the diarists, Kenneth Preston was in Bradford in the spring of 1962 and 'sadly' saw that 'almost the whole of that solid group of buildings constituting the Swan Arcade is now no more than a heap of rubble.' The sight prompted him to more general reflections: 'A surprising number of places now appear as though they have suffered a series of heavy air-raids. It would have saved a lot of work if they had it appears to me. Keighley [where he lived himself] presents a disgraceful sight. Great waste spaces have appeared. Everywhere buildings appear in ruins. I don't know why it must all be done at once. Why may one site not first be cleared and then built upon before another one is produced as an eye-sore?'

In one Lancashire town, almost all the changes were still to come. In 1961 the local paper published 'The Blackburn I Know: A Teenager's View of the Town Centre Controversy':

Blackburn [wrote J. A. Houghton] is not a pretty sight; in many ways it stinks. It is a collection of dirty, ugly factories and humble little houses that were thrown together as a result of the Industrial Revolution . . .

But Blackburn is changing; the Council say that they are going to tear down the town centre and build a new one with large gardens and supermarkets. They say that this will provide Blackburn with all the modern amenities and resultant civic pride that goes with a New Town. All that will happen, however, is that Blackburn will be destroyed. The bulldozers will cut out its heart and replace a supermarket, tear out its soul and substitute escalators . . .

Blackburn has character; it stinks but it has character, and that character depends on the town and on the town centre . . . If the town centre goes the only thing that Blackburn has to offer will go too, the character of the people . . .[36]

Those who believed in planned dispersion and low density found themselves badly on the defensive by the early 1960s. 'The advocates of high density, who usually have a visually aesthetic preoccupation,' complained Frederic Osborn in January 1961, 'persistently duck the evidence of popular preference as well as of cost'; that same month, writing to Lewis Mumford, he referred to the 'tacit unholy alliance' between 'the damned high-rise architects and the extreme countryside preservationists'; two months later, Wyndham Thomas, director of the Town and Country Planning Association, declared that 'the anti-dispersal flock of monumental architects, romantic sociologists, and the more selfish of countryside preservationists' comprised between them a 'gallimaufrous alliance' pushing 'prejudices disguised as arguments'; and in November 1961, addressing the Federation of Registered Housebuilders, Thomas spoke of 'an anti-social alliance of market pressures, aesthetic prejudices and preservationist sentiment' that was 'now forcing higher densities, higher costs and lower standards'.[37] Yet for all those protestations, and for all the validity of much of their case (especially in relation to high-rise), the mood music was pointing the other way. *Family and Kinship* (about lonely, fragmented Debden in comparison to warm, communal Bethnal Green), the new wave of working-class realism in novels and films, *Coronation Street*, the whole modernity zeitgeist – all these things gave urbanism, aka 'urban renewal', the critical momentum for the unfolding decade.

Much in the debate hinged on perceptions of the New Towns, those 'essays in civilisation' (as Lord Reith called them) that had been created after the war with such high expectations. By the early 1960s, with populations steadily expanding, most of their centres were at last complete or approaching completion, typified by Basildon's pedestrian-only Town Square, whose first shops opened in the Keay House block in 1959. The closest sociological study during these years was made by Peter Willmott in Stevenage. There, some 380 interviews in 1960 revealed almost all the employment (predominantly skilled manual) being local; 91 per cent saying they liked their homes ('It's a lovely modern house – ideal for a growing family'); and 60 per cent of wives using their local neighbourhood centres for weekday shopping. The whole question of neighbourhood was prominent in Willmott's mind, given the importance of the 'neighbourhood unit' – self-contained neighbourhoods around the town centre – in the original planning of the New Towns. Significantly, when asked where they lived, only 31 per cent gave the name of the neighbourhood (population of around 10,000), whereas most gave the name of one of the five or six housing estates (population nearer to 2,000) *within* the neighbourhood. As for visiting patterns, he found from detailed statistics that 'the physical boundaries of the neighbourhood itself are of no special significance in terms of informal social relationships.' Overall, concluded Willmott, 'the neighbourhoods seem to "work" well enough in functional terms, as areas for local amenities,' but 'there is no evidence that they do anything to create "community" or "neighbourliness", or indeed that they have any special *social* significance.'

Also on the hunt for New Town significance was the journalist Monica Furlong, who by 1960 had developed a love-hate fascination with another of the first wave, Harlow. 'All the buildings in the town centre are built with a feeling of airy grace,' she wrote in the *Spectator*, though not denying that during the winter 'the winds whip across the squares' – the price of 'a feeling of glass and straight lines and space'. More problematic was the human factor, notably the thin-on-the-ground professional class. 'I'm not a snob or anything like that,' one of the town's industrialists told her, 'it's just that these people here aren't our type. My wife felt she couldn't stand it any longer and we moved out to Bishop's Stortford. We made more friends in a month there than in four years here.' By contrast, Furlong was favourably struck by the 'kindly and paternalistic attitude' of the Development Corporation's staff, still motivated by 'intense idealism about the town', and she depicted the working-class population as by now thoroughly settled in its new environment, helped by 'an intense pride in their houses' and 'a passion for gardening' as well as 'a great pride in the schools their children are going to'. Altogether, her verdict on Harlow was that 'there is something fine and infinitely touching about the place'.[38]

Others were less generous to the New Towns. Although *The Times* in September 1960 broadly welcomed the prospect of three more, including Skelmersdale in Lancashire to help with the continuing Merseyside overspill problem, its tone was somewhat grudging. 'Is it necessary,' the paper asked, 'to perpetuate in new towns the desolate atmosphere of suburbs during the day by segregating industrial and residential areas?' The editorial also cited research in Crawley showing that most inhabitants there did not belong to a library, did not buy books and did not take part in any organisation. 'Over half of the adults spent three or more of the weekday evenings watching television,' it added. 'Are these the lineaments of Utopia?' As for the architectural quality of the New Towns, the progressive conventional wisdom was stated the following summer, also in *The Times*, by Graeme Shankland. His explicit yardstick was 'an environment that is as inspiring as it is clean', and he accused them of looking 'backwards' to the garden cities: 'Their housing, almost entirely of cottages and gardens, may satisfy their first young families; but does not constitute an environment for those who will follow.' Shankland was far more positive about the next New Town, the already designated Cumbernauld, planned as 'a compact hilltop town' whose centre, once built, 'should be one of Britain's few architectural wonders'. The most publicised critique of the New Towns already in existence came in August 1961 when the Ministry of Housing's annual report focused on progress so far and claimed that 'it is doubtful whether the neighbourliness and intimacy typical of urban life at its best can ever be reproduced within a framework of a housing layout based on the generous [ie, low] densities and living conditions inherent in the garden city idea.' The report then turned to the malady of the so-called 'New Town blues', arguing that though this had been considerably exaggerated by the press, it still undoubtedly existed: 'For those who are unable or unwilling to adapt themselves to completely new conditions, for those who are shy or worried by financial troubles and who miss the ready help of relatives and friends close by, life can be lonely and isolated.' That evening, the report and its conclusions featured on BBC Television's *Tonight*, in a way that thoroughly irritated 'Astragal', weekly columnist in the *Architects' Journal*: 'A combination of good scripting and good camerawork could say far more about the architecture of New Towns in a few minutes than any amount of interviewing of tenants.'[39]

The report was barely published before Victor Cull, community development officer for Hatfield New Town, vigorously denied the phenomenon of the 'New Town blues'. 'Some people from London feel there is too much space, and they've never had a garden,' he explained. 'Then they plant a couple of rose bushes and they say, "Look at this, Mr Cull – roses," as though they had sprouted coconuts. They feel a sense of creation for that sort of thing, if you see what I mean.' In fact, it was a phenomenon that in effect had already been explored by a New Town doctor, S. D. Coleman of East Kilbride, who in November 1959 visited half a dozen New Towns in England and took local soundings on the theme of mental health and social adjustment. In Stevenage, two doctors told him that they 'did not think there was an unusual incidence of neurosis'; in Harlow, a doctor stated that some patients 'felt quite uprooted at first, but later settled down'; in Crawley, a doctor noted that 'excessive demands for his services' were made by people, especially young married women, who had 'recently moved' there; in Basildon, a GP informed Coleman that 'for the first six or nine months, many people felt "quite lost," and pined away for familiar faces and places.' Coleman's own East Kilbride case notes were broadly in line with these findings. A 30-year-old married woman with two children, who had come from Edinburgh and been living there for four years, was still finding it difficult to come to terms with her new situation ('Everything is different . . . I feel trapped here'); a 22-year-old married woman with two children, living there for four months, had not yet begun to adjust ('It is quite lonely out here'); and a 25-year-old married woman, eight months there, was starting to accept her new life ('It is a much nicer place [than Glasgow], cleaner, and you feel as if you were somewhere, I feel as if I am abroad'). 'There is, in my opinion, no specific "New Town Neurosis",' concluded Coleman, 'as the symptoms complained of by patients in New Towns or Housing Estates are no different to those suffering from neurosis anywhere else. The name that I would suggest for neurosis of a temporary nature, due to or exacerbated by the social upheaval of re-housing, is "Transitional Neurosis".'

Even so, the tag stuck. Moreover, despite the BBC announcing in March 1962 that another doctor, Dr Dale, was moving with his wife, the country's best-known diarist, to a New Town called 'Exton', some 35 miles north of London, the shock of the new had largely gone. Once, the New Towns had been perhaps more emblematic than anything else of that unique '1945' moment: a healthy, egalitarian, herbivorous, planned future that would mark a clean break with all the old carnivorous urban horrors. But now, by the early 1960s, modernity had come to mean something different. 'Buildings like the Seagram in New York, cities like Brasilia, the work of men like Corbusier' – those were the exemplars held up for admiration by Princess Margaret's husband as he opened (at the Royal Festival Hall in July 1961) the Sixth Congress of the International Union of Architects. Britain itself, lamented Antony Armstrong-Jones, had 'of recent years been somewhat lacking in architectural inventiveness and the excitement that goes with it'. Accordingly, as he looked ahead to the rest of the 1960s and beyond, the photographer and designer (already planning his aviary for London Zoo) called on those present to bear two words in mind: 'calculated boldness'.[40]

11

Make Him Sir Yuri!

'The hottest day since 1947,' recorded Kenneth Williams in London on Saturday, 1 July 1961. 'Absolutely horrible and exhausting. Over 90°. All the nellies in the parks.' Hot too for the birth of the Queen's future hot-to-handle daughter-in-law, Diana Spencer, while Judy Haines in Chingford noted 'an absolute scorcher' for the fete at the County High School. 'Girls danced beautifully in broiling sun, and John snapped them in colour.' The family was shortly off for a fortnight's holiday, with Haines by Wednesday the 5th lamenting, 'I seem to be washing and ironing daily.' Another diarist, Madge Martin, that day had lunch with her husband in the new Grill Room at the Regent Palace Hotel near Piccadilly Circus: 'We had to admit, reluctantly, that the food (grilled chicken) was good, though we shall never like the modern surroundings, and do miss our dear old Grill Room in the basement.' Thursday saw the debut of *Mersey Beat* magazine – including 'Fashion Notes by Priscilla' by Cilla White, but from now called Cilla Black – while Haines allowed herself to listen to Britain's Angela Mortimer beating her South African opponent in the women's semi-finals at Wimbledon, and 'cried at the end of it'. Next day, the 7th, *TV Times* profiled 39-year-old Kingsley Amis ('the voice of youth, who shouts in protest against the failings of middle age and pomposity'); following a crisis meeting at Lyme Hall near Stockport of *New Left Review*'s board, editorial representatives and delegates from the clubs, the *NLR*'s editor Stuart Hall observed in a memo that 'the main complaint' had been that 'the style of the journal is pitched above the heads of the most active people in the movement'; and for Haines, it was 'more washing and ironing!!'[1]

It did not quite seem it at the time, but Saturday the 8th was one for the history books. Richard Crossman was in Workington ('a wholly working-class, dreary little place'); large queues formed ahead of the opening of the Soviet Exhibition at Earl's Court; a marriage guidance expert told a meeting at Keele of the National Association of Boys' Clubs that 'one of the major problems of young people in sex is how far they should go'; villagers at Iver in Buckinghamshire turned out in their hundreds ('despite a persistent drizzle') to welcome home the Duke and Duchess of Kent from their Majorca honeymoon; Britain's biggest jazz festival yet, in the grounds of Fulford Hall near Birmingham, was exclusively for 'traddies', starring Acker Bilk and his Paramount Jazz Band; Fred Trueman cleaned up against the Australians at Headingley; Stirling Moss won the main race of the day at Silverstone despite driving with a broken clutch; Angela Mortimer beat Christine Truman ('upset by a fall', noted Haines, 'but sportingly played on') in an all-British final at Wimbledon; a Russian crew (from the Central Sports Club, USSR Navy, Moscow, presumably watched by the embassy's assistant naval attaché, Yevgeny Ivanov) took the Grand Challenge Cup at Henley; Harrow thrashed Eton by an innings at Lord's ('a sea of grey toppers, cornstalks and multi-coloured hats and dresses surged out in front of the pavilion to greet the winning team'); and an Old Harrovian, now Secretary of State for War, that evening encountered a semi-naked Christine Keeler by a swimming pool at Cliveden. How two historians, with their fascination for the variousness of human behaviour, would have relished being on the inside track. Instead, the following evening, A.J.P. Taylor and Hugh Trevor-Roper jousted on television about Taylor's *The Origins of the Second World War*, condemned by Trevor-Roper in the current issue of *Encounter* as 'utterly erroneous' and the work of a historian who 'selects, suppresses, and arranges evidence on no principle other than the needs of his thesis' – so much so that 'it will do harm, perhaps irreparable harm, to Mr Taylor's reputation as a serious historian.' The debate itself, though, never quite fired, prompting an unimpressed Louis MacNeice to comment that the war 'was not fought out in a Senior Common Room where they had forgotten to open the windows'; or, as a local government officer put it after watching the programme (called *Did Hitler Cause the War?*), 'I do not think it much matters after 22 years if he did cause the war – it was enough that there was a war.'[2]

The *Daily Mirror*'s Clifford Davis kept up his campaign against *Coronation Street* on Tuesday the 11th ('nothing really changes and nobody does anything, except clack'), but next day's banner headline in the paper was altogether more positive: 'MAKE HIM SIR YURI!' The space pioneer was visiting, to a tumultuous welcome – 'his drive from London Airport to the Russian Embassy was a triumphal progress,' reported the *Evening Standard*, as 'crowds all along the route roared "Yuri" and "Well done"' – leaving Sir Harold Nicolson to reflect later in the week, after Gagarin had been interviewed on television, 'How can a country be a menace when it has as its hero a man with so entrancing a smile?' A less entrancing prospect to some was the imminent arrival in Pembrokeshire of West German Panzers, due to train on the ranges at Castlemartin. 'An insult to our dead and a betrayal of Britain and its people,' declared D. Ivor Davies in the *Pembroke County and West Wales Guardian* on Friday the 14th on behalf of protesting South Wales trades unionists. In Pembrokeshire that day to see for himself was the busy War minister, John Profumo, conceding that it was 'a very sensitive problem'. Next day, the Durham Miners Gala had a record number of arrests, mainly for drunkenness; on Sunday, Christopher Isherwood met Joan Littlewood ('a pretty bogus down-to-earther'), who had just announced her shock departure from Theatre Workshop and her intention to live abroad; on Tuesday a new accident wing opened at Oxbridge General; and on Wednesday, the Gentlemen met the Players in the annual encounter at Lord's, with the latter (including the always status-conscious Fred Trueman) making short work of two over-promoted young Cantabs, one of them J. M. Brearley. Two diarists gave the thumbs-down on Thursday the 20th – Kenneth Preston's son Allan to a 'typical' English meal at a Harrogate café ('nothing tasted of very much & there was not much of it'), Anthony Heap to the Anthony Newley musical vehicle *Stop the World, I Want to Get Off* ('its humour is crude, its satire heavy-handed') – before four days later saw the official launch of Arnold Wesker's Centre 42 movement, seeking to take culture to the people. 'Wouldn't going after this larger audience have an effect on the *content* of the art offered? asked someone,' recorded the *New Statesman*'s John Coleman about the management committee's informal press conference that evening at Wesker's house. 'What, anyway, *was* the art that the "working classes" (the phrase rang, undefined, throughout the discussion) were going to draw new life from? Examples, please? Early days for that, said some of the committee; the thing was to get things moving, to explore, not to dogmatise.' That same Monday evening, on a TV soap about a West End store called *Harpers West One*, the actor John Leyton, playing a pop singer, sung live his imminent new single 'Johnny Remember Me' – Victorian gothic for the early 1960s, as hauntingly evoked by the gifted producer Joe Meek – and at the last minute the line 'The girl I loved who died a year ago' changed at the BBC's request on the record itself to 'The girl I loved and lost a year ago'. A final word on the astronaut's visit – seen by some as excessively fawning on the part of the hosts – came in a letter to *The Times* on Tuesday the 25th. 'Was not Major Gagarin warmly welcomed in this country,' rhetorically asked G. R. Davies of Orpington, 'because he looked modest, handsome, sportsmanlike, and completely at ease – all essentially *English* qualities?'[3]

'No nation broker,' admitted Peter Cook's Macmillan in one of the *Beyond the Fringe* sketches, and the new Governor of the Bank of England, Lord (Rowley) Cromer, agreed. 'Sterling is under extreme pressure,' he informed the Chancellor, Selwyn Lloyd, in early July, as he demanded a comprehensive statement by the end of the month and set out his diagnosis of a sick economy: 'Wage and salary increases unrelated to increased productivity, sometimes even pre-empted on the conjecture of it'; 'restrictive practices on the part of labour'; 'complacency on the part of some employers'; too much 'non-productive investment' in public expenditure; and a defence policy that was still 'a heritage from the great days of our imperial past'. Lloyd's eventual package – 'the July measures' – was announced on the 25th: it included various personal credit and government expenditure restrictions, a 10 per cent increase in purchase tax, a hefty rise in the Bank Rate from 5 to 7 per cent and a call for a 'pay pause'. Taken as whole, the *FT* called them 'the toughest economic restraints since the austerity period of Sir Stafford Cripps'. Reaction was largely negative. *The Times* doubted whether 'the cautious and shrewd Swiss banker', that emblematic holder and seller of sterling, would see enough in Lloyd's measures 'to convince him that at last the British economy is going to stand on its feet'; the *Daily Mail* viewed 'the Chancellor's remedies' as 'designed to cure a recurrent tummy-ache but not to get at the seat of the trouble'; so too the City, where there was 'surprise and disappointment', with 'difficulty in seeing what long-term measures have been taken to tackle the basic defects in the economy'; while on the part of the trade unions, faced by the unusual sight of a peacetime government apparently aspiring to interfere comprehensively with free collective bargaining, they, 'in reply to Mr Lloyd's asking for a "pause" in the wages battle, did not pause an instant', noted Mollie Panter-Downes a week later, 'before informing him that raising the cost of living is no way to make men tuck pending wage claims back in their pockets, and that they will go ahead with them as though he had not uttered'. She added that 'a rain of strikes or threats of strikes is thus forecast as this autumn and winter's depressing weather.' Public opinion, as ever, focused on the essentials. 'On the bus to Marlborough,' recorded the holidaying Henry St John on the morning of the 26th as he travelled from Salisbury, 'a busman repeated like a parrot at least half a dozen times "You've never had it so good" . . . He and two other busmen talked about the increase of 4d on a packet of 20 cigarettes and the increase in the price of petrol, but not about the other aspects of the Chancellor of the Exchequer's speech.'[4]

Later on the 26th, Selwyn Lloyd – seldom viewed as an inspirational figure – sought to complement his short-term deflationary measures by setting out in the Commons how in the longer term the British economy might be enabled to grow on a sustainable basis and thus break out of its wretched stop-go cycle. 'The controversial matter of planning at once arises,' he noted. 'I am not frightened of the word.' He went on to explain his intention to achieve 'better co-ordination' with 'both sides of industry', specifically through 'a joint examination of the economic prospects of the country stretching five or more years into the future'. In short, 'I want both sides of industry to share with the Government the task of relating plans to the resources likely to be available.' Immediate reaction tended to be somewhat sceptical – the *FT* reflecting that 'planning will always suffer from one great disadvantage in a democracy', namely that 'there is no means of enforcing the plan', while the *Economist* predicted that the unions would 'scream blue murder',

given that 'the main thing that needs to be planned is that trade unionists and other earners should not annually get much more money before
they have earned it' – but Lloyd pressed on, asking on 8 August the
Federation of British Industries (FBI) and the TUC to come together in
a joint national forum.

'It had better be said straight away that the objective of planning
should not be to get some "representative" committee of trade union
leaders, large employers and establishment figures to sit down together,
air their mutual prejudices, and strike meaningless verbal compromises
with each other, in the hope that Britain's economic difficulties will
then somehow be rubbed away,' candidly warned the *Economist* later
that month. 'On the contrary, the purpose of any effective new planning machinery should be to diminish the practical power of some of
these organised groups, and to increase the influence of public policy
and attitudes of what might be called the economic technocrats.' Who
were these wonderful, disinterested people? The 'nearest equivalent' in
Britain, reckoned the paper, were 'some civil servants hidden from
public gaze in the Treasury and possibly some officials in the Bank of
England'; it also called for the Treasury to be split under two Cabinet
ministers, with the more senior one 'in charge of general economic
policy' and the other 'responsible for narrower financial operations'.
At the end the key, anti-corporatist argument was reiterated: 'It would
be a bad mistake to give too much planning power to those who, to
some extent, need to be planned against.' Still, however it was going to
be achieved, the planning moment was in the summer of 1961 apparently at hand, not only in relation to economic management, but there
most visibly. As the historian Glen O'Hara observes, 'If there was one
concept at the heart of the raised expectations and dashed hopes of
British politics in the 1960s, it was "planning"' – the concept that above
all 'held out the promise of a more modern Britain'.[5]

The intention to go down the planning road was not the last of the
major July pronouncements, for on Monday the 31st Macmillan made a
brief factual statement confirming that the British government did indeed
intend to make an application to join the European Economic Community,
aka the Common Market. Mollie Panter-Downes, watching from the
press gallery, was disappointed by the PM's deliberately low-key
approach – 'sounded and looked to many of us like a company chairman

badly in need of a holiday who was putting over with infinite caution the idea of a merger which might or might not come off' – over what she declared to be 'the most supremely important announcement delivered to Parliament and the country since the outbreak of the Second World War'. But two days later, as the Commons debated the issue, Macmillan did attempt to soar, claiming not only that 'our right place is in the vanguard of the movement towards the greater unity of the free world' but also that 'in the long run an island placed as ours is, where our need to export to other people will always be greater than their need to export to us, cannot maintain the high standards of life that we want for our people in an isolated protective system.' The press, apart of course from the Beaverbrook element, was still broadly supportive, including the *FT*'s strongly free-market columnist Harold Wincott, with a large following in the City. 'If by any other means we could get the necessary competition here in our own market, with compensating benefits and advantages for our exporters, we could afford to remain outside,' he argued the day after Macmillan's announcement. 'But we can't . . . Only the judgement and the cathartic properties of a market of 260 million people remain. But what a promise also resides in this new chapter of our economic history which we must pray is opening up.' What about public opinion? The most recent survey came from Gallup in July, finding that 38 per cent approved of an application to join, 22 per cent disapproved, and the rest – almost half – were undecided. *The Times* on 1 August called for a 'great national debate', but it was a debate missing some crucial information. Earlier in the summer, the Lord Chancellor, Lord Kilmuir, had sought to assess the impact of entry and had concluded:

(a) Parliament would be required to surrender some of its functions to the organs of the Community. (b) The Crown would be called on to transfer part of its treaty-making power to those organs. (c) Our courts of law would sacrifice some degree of independence by becoming subordinate in certain respects to the European Court of Justice. In the long run, we shall have to decide whether the economic factors require us to make some sacrifices of sovereignty. My concern is to ensure that we should see exactly what it is that we are being called on to sacrifice, and how serious our loss would be.

However, noted Andy Mullen and Brian Burkitt in the *Political Quarterly* in 2005, this assessment was 'never placed in the public domain'.[6]

A few hours after Macmillan had made his historic announcement, the penultimate day's play in the Fourth Test at Old Trafford ended with the match evenly poised, and, after the crowd had gone, the Australian captain Richie Benaud walking out in his blue suede shoes to inspect the wicket. Next afternoon, England were seemingly poised to win – 'yet nothing,' reported John Woodcock in *The Times*, 'would divert Benaud from his determination to attack ... chancing all on England's fallibility against flighted spin.' In under two hours, Benaud took 6 for 30, to win the game for Australia and retain the Ashes. 'A jolly good, exciting match,' graciously said England's amateur captain Peter May afterwards, but he himself had been bowled round his legs by Benaud for a second-ball duck; while from the professional camp, the Yorkshire all-rounder Brian Close had been little more successful in an innings that, complained E. W. Swanton in the *Daily Telegraph*, 'taxed credibility to behold'. Altogether, reflected Philip Larkin a couple of days later, it had been 'certainly an exasperating affair', in essence 'the same old story: they can do it, we can't'. Another poet, Alan Ross, broadly agreed, writing in the *Observer* the following Sunday that 'the best Australian characteristics, independence, generosity of endeavour, refusal to surrender, thrust and aggression, were displayed to the full like a spread peacock's tail.'[7] Put another way (as he did not add though might have done), a bold young country had defeated a rather tired old one. The embrace of modernity, including European modernity, was an attempt at reinvention. Whether it would succeed, and what the collateral damage would be, remained to be seen.

'Determined to use washing machine till it drops,' noted Judy Haines, back from her West Country holiday, on 2 August. 'I stuck broken piece of shaft back on and washed a blanket most satisfactorily.' That evening, Anthony Heap saw the new Brian Rix farce, *One for the Pot* ('never has a Whitehall first night audience been more continuously convulsed with laughter'); while over the next few days, the military historian Michael Howard laid into Alan Clark's *The Donkeys* (his

Listener review criticising Clark's attack on the First World War generals as full of 'personal bitterness', 'slovenly scholarship' and 'petulant caricatures'); *Melody Maker* acclaimed Chubby Checker's new single 'Let's Twist Again' as 'juke-box material with tremendous urge against a potent beat'; and at the Loders Fete in Dorset on Saturday the 5th 'the highlight of the afternoon,' reported the Rev. Oliver Willmott, 'was the adjudication by the stage and television star, Vic Oliver, of a competition for glamorous grandmothers.' 'Nobody,' he added, 'envied the judge his job. Never before has mutton looked so lamb-like. His choice was Mrs Thomas, the wife of our worthy sacristan, whom he gallantly kissed.' Over the next ten days or so, the *Daily Mirror* printed a letter from D.L. of Orpington about how some German friends recently on holiday in Britain had been especially impressed by 'the orderly queues at bus stops, people taking newspapers from unattended stands and leaving the correct money, the quiet of our parks'; officers from the 84th Panzer Division arrived in Pembrokeshire; Margaret Thatcher told her Finchley constituents that 'sovereignty and independence are not ends in themselves' and that it was time for Britain to follow the French example of sinking 'political differences' with Germany and working for 'a united Europe'; a BBC survey of the popularity of its television sports commentators found Peter West ('exceptionally versatile') coming out on top, with E. W. Swanton ('rather a patronising manner') well down the field; and on Wednesday the 16th, Judy Haines was at Broadcasting House with her children. 'They waited in foyer while I was interviewed by Mollie Lee on Mother and Daughter Relationship. The atmosphere was velvety, and I enjoyed speaking, which was recorded. I agreed to suggestion I use a fictitious name, and Mollie Lee suggested Barnes – Pauline Barnes.' The programme was Haines's favourite, *Woman's Hour*, and as Lee explained to listeners, 'Some time ago, we received a letter from a listener who seemed to be worried by her own relationship with her mother. "Are all mothers saintly?" was the question she was putting to herself. We invited her to the studio . . .' Haines's mother had died in January, and in front of the microphone she spoke (as revealed by the transcript) quite candidly about her mother's possessiveness and lack of humour, and how she as a mother herself was now trying to bring up her own daughters differently ('they're individuals, to live their own lives and to be free'). 'You see,' concluded Haines, 'my mother was a good woman but I didn't love her and I don't think she loved me and she expected a lot of me and I never felt I came up to scratch.' Meanwhile, noted her diary, 'nothing exciting had happened in the foyer', and 'in desperation' Ione, Pamela and their friend John 'asked me for *my* autograph'.[8]

Two days later, Friday the 18th, the radio ballad *The Big Hewer* (including Ewan MacColl's song of the same name) gave the heroic treatment to the coal miner; Anthony Heap on holiday with his son at Butlin's in Pwllheli reflected that 'the young yobs and chits here seem less addicted to the portable radio mania than they were at Filey last year, but tend to be much rowdier late at night'; Isabel Quigly in the *Spectator* reviewed *The Parent Trap* (a 'shamelessly sentimental film' in which Hayley Mills 'justifies the overworked word infectious'); and two very different observers of the contemporary scene vented their feelings. 'Gloom and despondency,' the Manchester physician Hugh Selbourne wrote in his diary. 'Berlin crisis [the Wall now being built], Rhodesians' clash, salaries of £12,000 being paid to railways executives in England, Macmillan grouse-shooting.' The other lament, very much public, was John Osborne's instantly notorious open letter 'Damn you, England' in the left-wing weekly *Tribune*. 'This is a letter of hate,' he began. 'It is for you, my countrymen. I mean those men of my country who have defiled it. The men with manic fingers leading the sightless, feeble, betrayed body of my country to its death. You are its murderers.' Osborne's attack was not, as was often lazily assumed at the time, a general state-of-the-nation polemic; rather, it was a savage verbal assault by a ban-the-bomber against the keep-the-bombers. 'There is murder in my brain,' he declared, 'and I carry a knife in my heart for every one of you. Macmillan, and you, Gaitskell, you particularly.' The *Sunday Times* took the immediate pulse. 'He expresses exactly what I feel when I think of Gaitskell, Macmillan and the whole horrible crew, it's impossible not to feel too violently,' said the novelist John Braine. 'I know what he feels and so do hundreds of thousands of others,' broadly agreed Arnold Wesker. 'I haven't read the whole thing, but is it all that important?' wondered J. B. Priestley. 'Ludicrous – a wild, pathetic letter,' responded the artist John Bratby. 'I might read it if it were translated into English,' half-promised Hugh Trevor-Roper. And from the most renowned arbiter of the moment, Richard Hoggart, just two words: 'Oh, dear!'[9]

That weekend saw the first major race riot since Notting Hill three years earlier. Perhaps surprisingly, it did not happen in Smethwick, where during July the already heated temperature had gone up a few further degrees with the Price Street rent strike, attracting national attention. The episode began when a Pakistani family of five (Mr and Mrs Sardar Mohammed, their two children and a nephew), their present house due for demolition, were allocated a council flat in Price Street's hitherto all-white block; the tenants there refused to pay rent; and the strike collapsed only when Smethwick Town Council gave non-payers four weeks' notice to quit. The council's action was unanimous, though with Alderman George Aldridge publicly warning that 'while it is our moral obligation to rehouse this family, we should remember that cleanliness is next to Godliness and insist that council regulations are observed.' Soon afterwards, investigating 'Smethwick's "Little Asia"' for the *Sunday Times*, Tom Stacey sat in a local pub – where 'six dingy streets' met, five leading in from factories ('glass-works, screws, motor parts'), one from the Price Street block – and heard the views of local whites. From a 'red-eyed foreman': 'Send the sluggers back. Put 'em on the Queen Mary and sink it 'arf way.' From a 20-year-old electrical apprentice in a narrow tie: 'Bloodshed, that's what's going to 'appen. The young people won't stand much more.' And from a 'brooched lady': 'They breed like rabbits . . . They're real smelly, I'll tell you that . . . You've only got to black your face to pick up four or five pound National Assistance.' 'In the pub,' reflected Stacey about the impact of the town's mainly Asian 'coloured immigrants' (some 5,000 out of an 80,000 population), 'the symptoms were accumulating – of the gravity of the challenge to the fragile but intensely precious homogeneity of a sparingly-educated urban community; of the profound insecurity worked by an intrusion unfathomably alien . . .'

In fact the race riot, over the weekend of 19–20 August, was in Middlesbrough (estimated non-white population of 3,000, again mainly Asian, out of a total of nearly 160,000). On Friday night a white youth was fatally stabbed, with an Arab from the Aden Protectorate being arrested and charged on Saturday. The trouble, reported the *Guardian*, began that night:

After public-house closing time, a crowd of several hundred people congregated in Cannon Street. Stones and bottles were hurled through the windows of the cafe [the Taj Mahal] run by coloured people and an ugly situation developed. Large numbers of police were rushed to the area and there were numerous outbreaks of fighting. At the height of the disturbance the fire brigade received a call to the cafe where a table was set on fire . . .

There was some trouble yesterday [Sunday] afternoon when youths threw stones at a shop owned by an Indian in Boundary Road. More stone-throwing took place in the market place area and a cafe window there was broken. A large crowd, including many women and children, collected in Cannon Street and police reinforcements stood by in cars and vans in side streets.

Several Pakistanis and Arabs yesterday moved with their families to friends living well away from the Cannon Street area. Crowds gathered and there were one or two shouts and catcalls as the coloured residents loaded their suitcases into taxis and drove off.

In the confusion yesterday a Methodist church was holding its service as normal but the hymns were almost drowned by the shouting outside.

'POLICE FIGHT MOB OF 500 IN RACE RIOT TOWN' was the *Daily Mirror*'s headline, but the town's Chief Constable, Ralph Davison, sought to play down the race aspect: 'I don't feel it is a true racial dispute in the sense that the majority of the people of Middlesbrough are hostile to coloured people. A small minority has seized on recent incidents to settle old scores.' That, though, was probably wishful thinking, with the historian Panikos Panayi finding in his detailed study of these events and their local context that 'the disturbance of August 1961 was not an isolated example of racial prejudice,' that indeed 'it brought to the surface the subconscious racial hostility of white Middlesbrough which found an outlet for its prejudice.' Still, whatever the motivation, a riot was not quite a war. On the Monday the *Northern Echo* (the Darlington-based regional paper where the youngish Harold Evans had just arrived as editor) gratefully observed how 'to their credit the coloured people have suffered the present provocations without retaliating in kind.'[10]

That evening, as Madge Martin sat in a 'packed' house at the Palace Theatre to see *The Sound of Music* ('strangely popular in these days of

smart, unhappy stage shows . . . the audience rapturous'), the National
Gallery's recently acquired Goya portrait of the Duke of Wellington
went missing – stolen, it eventually turned out, by an unemployed
Newcastle man, Kempton Bunton, whose 'sole object', he would
explain, was 'to set up a charity to pay for television licences for old and
poor people who seem to be neglected in our affluent society'. On
Tuesday the 22nd, Dick Etheridge, leading shop steward at the Austin
car plant at Longbridge, curtly informed Selwyn Lloyd that he had 'the
cheek of the devil asking us to agree to a wage increase pause' and that
Lloyd could expect 'the uttermost opposition' to his policies; that evening, Michael Caine had a starring role ('marvellous . . . perfect . . . never
seen such acting,' according to viewers), as a young man who eventually pulls a gun, in Johnny Speight's television play *The Compartment*;
and at around 6.45 on Wednesday morning, a Bedfordshire farm
labourer called Sidney Burton was walking along the Deadman's Hill
stretch of the A6, near the village of Clophill, when he came across,
parked in a lay-by, a grey 1956 Morris Minor – in which he found the
dead Michael Gregsten, a scientist at the Road Research Laboratory
near Slough, and his semi-conscious mistress, Valerie Storie, who had
been raped, shot and left paralysed. Within hours a manhunt was under
way. Three days later on the 26th, while Declan MacManus (later Elvis
Costello) watched the day after his seventh birthday his first match at
Anfield (Liverpool crushing Leeds 5–0) and became a lifelong Red, the
14-year-old Jonathan Meades was stuck in a classic summer Saturday
traffic jam on the notorious Exeter bypass, this one 20 miles long. The
radio played the grimly atmospheric 'Johnny Remember Me' (by now
supplanting Helen Shapiro's second single, 'You Don't Know', as
number 1), then gave the latest on the A6 murder, and Meades would
spend a lifetime 'failing to dissociate the song from the news report
which followed it'.

The summer was almost over. On Wednesday the 30th, the Gentlemen
of England took on the Australians in front of a thin crowd (but including this 10-year-old boy) at Lord's; next day, as Pat Hornsby-Smith
resigned as a junior minister in order to pursue her business interests
and thereby put herself out of contention as a future female PM, Bob
Wooler's first column in *Mersey Beat* hailed 'A Phenomenon called The
Beatles!' ('musically authoritative and physically magnetic . . . the stuff

that screams are made of'); and on Friday, 1 September, Hampshire beat Derbyshire at Bournemouth to win the county championship for the first time. 'I always insist on the boys being in bed by dawn,' the team's bold Old Etonian captain Colin Ingleby-Mackenzie told a BBC reporter when asked about the secret of their success: seemingly a last hurrah, in an increasingly professionalised age, for the old-style amateur.[11]

12

The Immigrants Are Human

Some advertisements from 1961 and the first half of 1962: Nimble was 'The Lighter Bread That Keeps You Fit'; Eskimo offered 'the most modern, up-to-date line in frozen foods'; Crosse & Blackwell's Double Soups were '*condensed* modern-style to give you double the quantity!'; Kraft's Philadelphia Cream Cheese Spread was 'going to be as popular as it is in the States!'; the Milky Bars were on the Milky Bar Kid (a pale, freckly boy with NHS glasses); Mackintosh's 'Week-End' selection of chocolates brought the flavour home to you; Heinz Spaghetti Bolognese was the 'EXCITING NEW ITALIAN DISH'; Skol was 'the light dry lager' brewed 'IN THE CONTINENTAL MANNER'; the Consul Capri was the 'FIRST PERSONAL CAR FROM FORD OF BRITAIN' ('a sleek and elegant extension of your own personality'); Ford's two new Zephyrs were the 4 and 6 ('Value never looked so good . . . Comfort never had such power!'); 'Square Deal Surf' promised 18 per cent more washing powder for the same price; for children there were 'The Newsiest Fashions Chosen by C&A for Young Moderns'; and at Victor Value supermarket in Romford, the come-on was not only 'money-saving one-stop shopping' but also 'free gifts', such as a 'beautiful Contemporary Italian Table Lamp designed for modern living'. The new retained its premium, and more. A women's-page editor referred to 'the growing popularity of contact lenses as an alternative to spectacles'; another noted how 'more and more people are becoming "frying fiends" since the introduction of vegetable oil on the British market' (as a healthier alternative to animal fats); Rowntree's launched (initially in Scotland) the After Eight Mint as an upmarket after-dinner treat; Imperial Tobacco's Golden Wonder brought in the first flavoured crisps (cheese and onion), bad news for Smith's Crisps and the little blue bag of salt; the first Cranks vegetarian restaurant (in Covent Garden) was complemented by the rapid rise of London Steak Houses (the first one opening in Baker Street); the electric toothbrush, fruit yoghurts and aluminium foil were all newcomers; a factory opened in Newport, Shropshire to wash, grade and pre-pack potatoes, the first of its kind in Britain; and, almost simultaneously, in September 1961, the first 21 Shop opened in Knightsbridge (interior design by Terence Conran, clothes by Mary Quant, Jean Muir and others) and the pioneer Mother-and-Child Centre, in effect the first Mothercare, opened in Kingston, Surrey (selling not just children's clothes and equipment but also 'Paris Maternity Fashions – At Practical Prices'). The new had certainly appealed the previous month to the 16-year-old Ian Jack, down from Scotland and taken by his older brother to a Chinese restaurant on Shaftesbury Avenue to try sweet-and-sour pork: 'The taste and texture of the crisp little golden balls and their sauce were sensational.'[1]

What about shopping itself? By 1961, although still taking only 11 per cent of all retail sales, there were well over 6,000 self-service stores in Britain, of which at least 500 were supermarkets; that spring, a detailed survey of housewives' attitudes to supermarket shopping was conducted in various 'good' parts of London and the Home Counties, including Harrow, Wimbledon, Maidenhead and Bromley. Called *Shopping in Suburbia* on publication in 1963, it featured a range of housewives' voices:

> I like to wander round and not be restricted and you can take what you want and then put it back and they don't seem to mind how long you spend there. I think you get everything fresh and wrapped and it's not handled by people's fingers. That's a good point. Then you get a penny off this and that and it all helps to pay your fare to the shop – you get all your shopping there in the one shop and that's what I like about it. Then you have finished and can go home. They're awfully polite, too. The queuing up is the biggest disadvantage – and then when they're open at weekends some of the women push and push with wire baskets ... (*Working-class, age 47*)
>
> Of course, you can go from shop to shop but most women like me

think shopping is all very well but not food shops. We'd much rather look in dress shops. Still, the supermarket can give you some ideas. You have to watch prices, though. In the supermarket they're not always cut-price. At another shop luncheon meat is 9d a quarter but at the supermarket it's 10½d. It's best if you can dodge about ... (*Lower middle-class, 48*)

I expect I'll get the habit – like everybody else when there are more of them. And I do rather like the wide variety you can choose from and the spaciousness when there aren't too many people there! (*Middle-class, 35*)

You've got everything under the one roof and there is everything you can think of there. The working housewife who's out all day finds it much quicker and more helpful. (*Working-class, 60*)

You sort of learn what to get and not get as you go. (*Middle-class, 20*)

When you first start going you do feel lost but you get used to it. (*Middle-class, 39*)

Cheeses are well displayed and I tried some I have never tried before because I see them cut up and ready to take away. (*Working-class, 29*)

I'm not so keen on some wrapped things. I wouldn't buy potatoes or greens because although they have air-holes they sweat a lot and smell musty. (*Lower middle-class, 47*)

Packaging is a good thing really. You don't get flies on it. It's very hygienic. (*Working-class, 45*)

Chickens haven't the flavour as you buy in the butcher's. When I buy meat I like the atmosphere in a butcher's shop but it does take more time. (*Middle-class, 35*)

There is too much persuasion to buy – voices speaking and loudspeakers telling you to buy. They do press you. I think they're a step in the wrong direction but I feel I'm in the minority – wanting to shop with the small retailers. (*Lower middle-class, 57*)

It *is* an American idea, isn't it? I believe some people go to America to get ideas sometimes. (*Working-class, 50*)

The main conclusions reached by the survey were that the housewife was far likelier to go to the supermarket for soap and detergents or canned goods than for meat or fruit and veg, where the traditional butcher and greengrocer still retained her trust and custom; that 'there is, so far, no obvious sign of supermarket inroads into *non-food* markets'; that younger housewives were more likely to find supermarket shopping 'fun'; and that, despite some housewives missing 'the homeliness and security of small shops', the overall view across the age spectrum was 'largely favourable'. Specifically, in addition to 'speed, variety and price range', interviewees identified three main pluses: the ability to go at one's own pace; 'freedom from embarrassment' when confronted by new or unfamiliar products; and, perhaps most suggestively, that it was easier in a supermarket for the shopper to start experimenting and thereby, in the report's words, to 'build up a satisfying image of herself as a housewife'.

Not all supermarkets were the same. Whereas Sainsburys adopted in 1961 a strictly regulated five-day week ('morally and socially right', declared Robert Sainsbury, adding that 'the anarchy of late shopping hours is precisely what we want to avoid'), Tesco under the buccaneering Jack Cohen pushed ahead on all possible fronts: not only the opening in December 1961 of its huge Leicester flagship store but a sustained guerrilla campaign against the system of fixed retail prices as legally embodied in Resale Price Maintenance. 'We are not attacking the small trader,' declared Cohen at the Leicester opening (after Sid James had cut the tape). 'It is the manufacturer we are after. We are fighting for the right of every believer in free retail enterprise to expect keen prices and greater choice.' Consumer protection, meanwhile, was slowly advancing. The Molony Committee (1959–62) barely gave a voice to the actual consumer, let alone the female consumer, but did point the way to the creation in 1963 of the Consumer Council; *Which?* magazine started in January 1962 a quarterly supplement on cars, earning the instant dislike of British manufacturers after the first issue placed the Volkswagen as best in its group; and, the following month, the BBC nervously dipped its toes in the consumer water with the start of a TV series, fronted by Richard Dimbleby, called *Choice*. 'Trying too hard to keep on the right side of all the interested parties who might have objected,' complained one critic, adding that it was 'so cluttered with information that no clear conclusions could be drawn' – in short, 'no way to perform a public service'. Probably indifferent to these concerns, one poet and one future poet were viewing the unfolding consumer revolution in a positive light. In 1961, after his library colleague and now lover Maeve Brennan had acquired a new handbag in Hull's Marks and Spencer, Philip Larkin paid a visit himself and wrote admiringly of 'The large cool store selling cheap clothes/Set out in simple sizes plainly'. That same year, the 16-year-old Carol Rumens was in George Street, Croydon:

> It was my first time in a Wimpy Bar, my first time in any café by myself. I did not order a Wimpy; the red plastic tomato on my table, with its stem oozing half-dried ketchup, was not encouraging. But I had coffee in a tall, hexagonal melamine mug, and an aluminium tray of flapjacks with maple syrup and a blob of sweetish, cold, synthetic cream. Delicious! I was alone in the café. Perhaps no other Croydon teenagers had yet discovered the Wimpy Bar, or perhaps I was Wimpishly early and it was still only teatime. I felt lonely, but good, and meditated on Man's lofty but probably abandoned status in the universe.[2]

The Panzer troops were nicely bedded in on their South Pembrokeshire range when on Saturday, 9 September 1961 some 30 coaches, full of protesters from all over Britain, arrived in Pembroke itself – to be greeted, according to one pro-protest eyewitness, by 'a pack of irresponsible, gum-chewing, ill-bred youths (most of whom were not born when Pembroke Dock was bombed), backed by their girl friends and a few middle-aged women,' who 'pelted' the coaches 'with eggs, tomatoes, bottles, earth and anything they could lay hands on'. The protest march still went ahead, amid much heckling from the locals and a party of schoolgirls holding a banner aloft saying, 'Leave the Germans alone, you big-heads and trouble-makers'. Among those heckled was Leo Abse, the flamboyant Labour MP for Pontypool. 'We understand there are temptations when you find there are a large number of troops with spending power in your area,' he told the crowd. 'But this we must tell you – that merely to pander to the Panzers because they are spending money in the town can be likened to the rewards that fall to "camp followers".' Yet almost certainly the local impatience with censorious, interfering outsiders was not just about the economic aspect, in the case of some of the younger people anyway. 'Smashing' was how 14-year-old Colin Rogers described the Panzers to a reporter, adding that he had collected 121 of their autographs; soon afterwards, the *Pembroke*

County and West Wales Guardian printed a letter from 'An Angry Panzer Girl', who identified herself as one of the egg-throwers, declared that 'we love the troops (only as friends) and have nothing against them training here,' and finished with two questions to the older generation: 'Surely it is up to everyone to accept these "boys" now? How can we expect a world peace when so many want to live in the past and not the future?'

The other major Welsh story that autumn was the vote on 8 November to determine which parts of the principality would henceforth be permitted to have pubs opening on Sundays – a concept that was in effect a direct assault on the sway of Welsh Nonconformity and its chapels. Many meetings were held during the weeks ahead of the poll. 'I do not want to see the Sunday nights of Aberystwyth and Wales becoming Saturday nights,' Professor R. I. Aaron from the chair told Cardiganshire's pro-retentionists; on the other side of the argument, also at an Aberystwyth meeting, the Rhondda MP Iorwerth Thomas complained sarcastically about how 'these brave nonconformists want to thrust their morality on other people.' Or take Glamorgan, where at a Maesteg gathering the veteran Presbyterian deacon J. Kirkhouse Williams condemned 'the age of bingo, booze and betting shops' as 'the decadent age', to be countered soon afterwards by Cliff Jones, chairman of the Bridgend and District Licensed Victuallers' Association, accusing Williams of a 'dog-in-the-manger, dictator-like attitude'. On a 47 per cent turnout, the eventual vote revealed 454,720 in favour of Sunday opening and 382,059 against. Put more locally, which is what mattered, four county boroughs and five counties decided to go wet, and eight counties – in west and north Wales, the Welsh-speaking heartlands, with the biggest majority in Carmarthenshire – decided to stay dry, at least until the next referendum in seven years' time. 'The women of Pembrokeshire won the day for Sunday closing,' commented Major Tom George, President of Haverfordwest and District Licensed Victuallers' Association, about the reluctance there and elsewhere in rural Wales to embrace change. 'Having been around a few of the polling stations during the day it was obvious that from 8 am to 4 pm, 90 per cent of voters were women, who in my opinion looked chapel or church.'[3]

For Macmillan's increasingly criticised government, it was an autumn of industrial troubles. The PM's diary on 8 October noted the imminent promotion to ministerial rank (as Parliamentary Under-secretary at the Ministry of Pensions and National Insurance) of 'Mrs Thatcher, a clever young woman MP'. But in this entry two days after the start of BBC's sitcom *The Rag Trade*, he was more concerned about the threat of public-sector strikes against Selwyn Lloyd's 'pay pause' policy, about the already deeply entrenched strike at a Rootes subsidiary (British Light Steel Pressings at Acton) that was 'causing a complete hold-up of all Rootes factories, involving all their car production and thousands of men', and about the incendiary effects of employees seeking to count tea breaks as paid time, especially in the building industry and in Ford's at Dagenham. 'Meanwhile,' he added, 'our French, German and other European competitors are hard at work.' Attention particularly focused on the Acton strike – 'the agitators pounce on grievances, exploit them, blow them up, and strive to prevent a reasoned settlement,' declared the *Daily Mail* on 24 October, before asking, 'What are the Special Branch up to?' – but Macmillan two days later was by now more worried about how 'the likelihood of a strike in the Power Stations is growing', with the union demanding a substantial wage rise in explicit defiance of the pay pause. 'This is intolerable,' he reflected. 'But these 150,000 [electricity supply workers] have the whole country in pawn.' Three weeks later, the Electricity Board surrendered, leaving the pay pause apparently in tatters and earning for the Minister of Power, the unfortunate Richard Wood, a public rebuke from Macmillan. The press had the proverbial field day – the *Daily Telegraph* comparing the PM to Lewis Carroll's Bellman (in blundering search of the Snark), the *Economist* preferring the analogy of 'an impotent Pontius Pilate', *The Times* stating frankly that 'Britain lacks the nerve to master her destiny' – but as an unnamed union leader in the electricity-supply industry calmly explained, 'Pay pause? I do not recognise it. We have come to a satisfactory conclusion and we think it will suit the Chancellor not to have a strike. We think he will be pleased.'

How to untie this Gordian knot? Selwyn Lloyd himself hoped that planning might be the answer, having told the Cabinet shortly before the July announcements that 'in the long run we must try to link consideration of wages with the problem of economic growth.' But as discussions took place during the autumn to prepare the way for what ultimately became the National Economic Development Council (Neddy), it became clear that there were serious reservations on the part of five principal players. 'The pay pause must go' was the essence of the TUC's attitude about any invitation to join a government-sponsored body; elements at the FBI (Federation of British Industries), the original pusher of planning, were getting cold feet, with Maurice Laing warning of the danger that a future Labour government might utilise Neddy 'to impose on the country a full "planned economy" which could include full-scale Socialism'; the City at this stage did not want to know; the Treasury was at best divided, with little appetite for modish, turf-threatening institutional initiatives that might compromise the defence of sterling and the balance of payments; and among Lloyd's fellow ministers, even the generally go-ahead Charles Hill and Reginald Maudling were sceptical, fearing (in the Chancellor's disappointed words to Macmillan) 'the creation of a new monster which would embarrass us in the future'. The planning moment, in short, looked as if it had arrived more in theory than in practice. Still, perhaps some of the blame attached to Lloyd himself. 'Rather like an encounter between a whale and an elephant,' recalled his economic adviser Alec Cairncross about Lloyd's meetings with trade union leaders, adding that the Chancellor was unable to enter into their psychology or even 'to communicate to them his own ideas'.[4]

That autumn, Battle of Britain Day fell on Sunday, 17 September – the day that the anti-bomb Committee of 100 (the radical outgrowth from the CND) chose to organise a mass sit-in at Trafalgar Square. The near-nonagenarian Bertrand Russell could not be present, imprisoned at Brixton as a precautionary measure, while in the days before Kenneth Williams would be among those weighing up whether to attend, finally deciding on the Friday that despite feeling 'frightened inside' about possible consequences, the cause was just and he had no alternative but to 'join the demonstration and run the risk of being arrested'. Then on Sunday itself:

> The Police [recorded Williams] used filthy methods of removing limp, passive people – a man dragged by one arm with his head on the ground . . . a woman thrown bodily against a wall . . . The entire crowd that I was in was anti-Police – I did not hear, for two hours, one dissident voice.

One thing became abundantly clear. They hated the bomb, and they hated the corrupt government that didn't ban it, and they hated the uniformed bullies that enforce an unjust law. Leaders arrested were John Osborne, Shelagh Delaney, and Vanessa Redgrave. All I seem to be able to do is send me miserable donation and pray for them all.

The police had forbidden the use of the square, but altogether some 12,000 took part and over 1,000 arrests were made. 'There seemed,' noted the *Economist*, 'to be a genuine wish even among some of the most extreme to remove the impression of unwashed artiness that the movement has in the public mind. Not a few young women sat on, and ruined, their skirts rather than turn up in the blue jeans that would have caused them to be classed as "beatniks".' It would need more than that, though, to shift public opinion as a whole on the larger issue. Just over a fortnight later, at its annual conference at Blackpool, the Labour party realigned itself with the majority view by rejecting unilateralism (an about-turn from a year earlier) and, by a huge majority, neutralism. 'A great & deserved triumph for Gaitskell & will increase his stature in the country,' privately admitted Macmillan. 'He has been very persistent & courageous.'

It was generally a good conference for the Gaitskellites (and their Campaign for Democratic Socialism). Not only did it endorse the recent policy document *Signposts for the Sixties*, generally seen as a pragmatic, carefully targeted approach that helped to reconcile the party's two wings after the acrimonious post-election debate, but Roy Jenkins, who had been dreading his stay in Britain's favourite resort ('it takes a long time to get there, the sea front is hideous, the hotels are inadequate'), was pleasantly surprised ('slightly more agreeable than I had remembered it . . . the food was better . . . the illuminated tramcars were most impressive'). Even so, despite all that and despite the welcome votes, he found himself still disquieted by 'the general tone of the debates', in particular by how 'farragos of half-baked semi-Marxist nonsense' were 'cheered by what appeared to be most of the delegates'. Jenkins was also struck by the reaction during the defence debate to the unsuccessful attempt by the T&G's Frank Cousins to hold the unilateralist line: 'By any standards, for both content and form, this was one of the worst speeches which I have ever heard. Yet it was greeted, by perhaps 100 delegates and by a claque in the gallery, with an almost Nuremberg-like reception.' In short, concluded Jenkins, there now undeniably existed in the party a 'vociferous extremism'. The *New Statesman*'s young, razor-sharp political correspondent Anthony Howard – also not wholly relishing Blackpool's 'creaking Big Wheel, its clanking trams, its barn-like pubs and its hideously archaic hotels' – likewise identified Cousins as the Labour left's new hero and 'the spectre at the feast' for the Gaitskellites. But to the public at large, when Cousins appeared on *Face to Face* later in October, the dominant union leader of the day came across, noted an audience research report, 'in a new light, as a man of transparent honesty and sincerity, dedicated in the service of his fellow men and intolerant of injustice in any form'. At one point, Cousins told John Freeman that he had 'no intention or wish to be in Parliament' – a perspective probably sympathetic to the New Left intellectual Ralph Miliband, who in his new book *Parliamentary Socialism* delivered a sustained, historically based attack on the Labour party (left as well as right) for having over the years refused to embrace extra-parliamentary action as the means to achieving socialism as opposed to mere social reform. The final chapter was called 'The Sickness of Labourism', and Miliband ended by predicting that, unless Labour fundamentally altered and became 'the political instrument of radical change', what lay ahead was 'the kind of slow but sure decline which – deservedly – affects parties that have ceased to serve any distinctive political purpose'.[5]

The Saturday after the Battle of Trafalgar Square was when Keith Nicholson's numbers came up. A young miner, living in Castleford and married to Vivian (miner's daughter, 25 years old, blonde, outgoing), he checked his Littlewoods pools coupon and found he had eight draws. Two days later, just before the train reached London, an accompanying Littlewoods representative told them that they had won over £150,000 (at least £5 million in 2014 terms). 'It was then,' related Gordon Burn in 1976 after interviewing her, 'as she alighted at King's Cross, to be immediately mobbed by reporters, that Vivian, remembering the newsreels of Jayne Mansfield that she'd seen, uttered the words that were going to make her famous. "I'm going to spend," she said, intoxicated by the attention, "and spend – and spend!"' Soon they were at the Dorchester, receiving a cheque from Bruce Forsyth, and the centre of intense media attention. 'Does the team think the reaction of "spend, spend, spend" is the best one for the winner of a large sum in the football pools?' was the inevitable question at the following Friday's *Any Questions?* from the Memorial Hall at Portscatho, Cornwall. 'I find it's very refreshing,' said Ted Moult; 'don't spend it on having a spree with your friends because you're never going to have them off your necks,' warned the writer and broadcaster Brian Inglis; while the view of Lady Isobel Barnett was that 'it'll go jolly quickly, but let her enjoy it while it's there.' Letters soon afterwards in the *Daily Mirror* broadly agreed: although 'Retired Schoolmaster' of Cardiff professed himself 'disgusted' at a woman 'whose idea seems to be spending on herself', the consensus was with Slough's Mrs B. Henton, who called it 'a joy' to read about Viv's unabashed attitude instead of the usual 'money will make no difference' protestations. The mood was different nearer to home, after the winners had flown from Luton back to Yorkshire. By the second day, recalled Viv, 'the bitterness started creeping in: "Why them, they're so bloody young, we've been filling the pools in for years," "I've worked all my life." They wouldn't speak to us, we were literally ignored all the time by people that you pass the time of day with or say good morning to. But winning the pools – I had to say, "Why didn't you speak to me the other day, have I got the plague or something?" "Well, if I speak, people will think I'm after something."' Within a few weeks, the couple had moved to the show house on a new, middle-class estate in Garforth, 5 miles from Castleford. 'I try to make friends but the women won't accept it,' Viv told a newspaper soon afterwards. 'If I go out in ordinary clothes they say: "Look at her – all that money and wearing those things." If I wear any of my new cocktail dresses they say: "She must think she's somebody now." That's why I tint my hair mauve and green and pink sometimes and put my new clothes on and go dancing. The more they talk, the more I do to give them something to natter about.'[6]

The diarists that autumn had other things on their minds. Florence Turtle was in a thin audience at the unheated Wimbledon Theatre to see Robert Bolt's *A Man for All Seasons* ('had a large Scotch, the barmaid said the only thing that seemed to fill the theatre was ballet or the pantomime'); Anthony Heap admired the RSC's production of *The Taming of the Shrew* (Vanessa Redgrave 'a rare combination of charm and artistry'); Judy Haines listened to her *Woman's Hour* broadcast ('sounded quite satisfactory'), but not long afterwards was reflecting, 'I always get depressed when John says I'm lucky to be able to stay at home so much,' adding, 'I think one has to be very strong-minded not to go crackers'; Harold Macmillan in late September contrasted the popular press having 'hardly a word about Congo crisis, Berlin crisis or even general Home affairs' with its lavish treatment of the pursuit of the A6 murderer (with James Hanratty, a petty thief from north London, being arrested in Blackpool on 11 October); John Fowles and his smartly dressed wife took a walk around old, working-class Southwark ('two boys on bicycles stare at us hostilely – they see I have Pevsner and the A-to-Z in my hand'); Nella Last one Thursday evening viewed *Tonight* and *Double Your Money*, but then 'came gladly to bed, the thought alone of a "variety" show of Morecambe & Wise made me curl at the edges'; Allan Preston experienced the new diesel rail cars on the Leeds-to-Scarborough line ('five-abreast seating to gangway makes it much too cramped'); Madge Martin in Bayswater one Friday 'looked in at the strangely old-fashioned Whiteley's [department store], which doesn't seem to have changed since we first knew it, in 1916'; Hugh Selbourne watched Lord Hailsham on *Face to Face* ('strikes me now as a complacent member of the blimpish Tory establishment, of some degree of mediocrity'); and Henry St John had an unsatisfactory lunch in the Ministry of Labour canteen ('the meat in what was sold as steak and kidney pie had no recognisable taste and consisted of dark amorphous lumps').[7]

The diarists' most-watched movie was Tony Richardson's *A Taste of Honey*, a naturalistic, Salford-filmed version of the Shelagh Delaney play. Haines, who enjoyed it, thought Rita Tushingham in the central role was 'very like Princess Margaret'; Martin found it 'much better' than the original, calling it 'a splendid, touching, sordid, beautifully actual film'; and Kenneth Williams was struck by its 'brilliant' and 'breathtaking' beginning (including in the opening scene Hazel Blears as a five-year-old street urchin wearing her mother's best shoes). *The Times* praised especially the living feel of its northern industrial backdrop – 'the shabby streets and wet pavements, the school playgrounds, the public monuments and the rubbish-strewn canals' – as well as Tushingham's 'moving and eloquent performance' in what was in effect her acting debut. 'A garlic of a girl' was the approbatory phrase of another critic, but not everyone immediately bought into the vulnerable, huge-eyed 19-year-old Liverpudlian. 'This apparently ugly duckling,' retorted a furious John Osborne (the film's co-producer), 'has more expression and beauty when she crooks her little finger than most of these damned starlets have if they waggled their oversized bosoms and bottoms from here to eternity.' Among the movie's warm admirers was Monica Jones. 'At last to see *A Taste of Honey*, as much to rest my brains and because you'd praised it as anything,' Larkin wrote to her a few months after its release. 'I much enjoyed it at the time: it seemed very stirring and touching. In retrospect it fades a bit. All the children seemed a bit *voulu*.'

The autumn's other landmark film left Kenneth Williams underwhelmed from the first: 'To see Dirk Bogarde play the homosexual barrister fighting a blackmail ring in *Victim* – it was all v. slick, superficial and never knocking the real issues.' Most reviewers, though, were more positive about what after all was the courageous storyline of a homosexual being blackmailed because of his sexual orientation (and which was the first English-language film to use the actual word *homosexual*). '*Victim* may not say a great deal about this difficult problem,' reflected *The Times* in comments that were about par for the course, 'but what it does say is reasoned and just; and it does invite a compassionate consideration of this particular form of human bondage.' The director, Basil Dearden, originally wanted the square-jawed, ultra-masculine Jack Hawkins to play the lead role, but eventually Hawkins declined – because, commented Bogarde subsequently, it might have 'prejudiced his chances of a knighthood'. Bogarde himself, renowned through the 1950s as a matinee idol, spoke revealingly to the press at the time of the film's release. After acknowledging that 'some people would rather see you kill your wife on the screen than play a role like this,' he went on: 'It's about a real man and a very, very real problem. He is a barrister, about to take silk. Successful, apparently happily married. He has a fine house. But he has this weakness – sickness if you like. He has managed to overcome it for a long time. But one day he gives a lift to a young man who works on a building site . . .' What did audiences make of it? Simon Raven saw it in Deal, where a largely working-class, message-resistant audience watched quietly and attentively enough – until 'the characters started piously intoning "white paper" extracts about protecting juveniles from marauding homosexuals'. The future film director Terence Davies, then a 15-year-old clerk in a shipping office, saw it in Liverpool at the Odeon. 'Alright – alright, you want to know, I'll tell you – you won't be content until I tell you will you – until you've ripped it out of me – I stopped seeing him because I *wanted* him,' the barrister tells his beautiful wife in the climactic scene. 'Can you understand – because I *wanted* him.' At which point, recalls Davies, 'you could have heard a feather drop' – as he and others in the audience realised that they were not alone in their sexual orientation.[8]

Both films were on release in September, the month that Georg Solti, a Hungarian, uneasily took over as musical director at the Royal Opera House ('a small anonymous group engaged in booing from the amphitheatre,' recalled his chairman, Lord Drogheda, 'and he used to find things like "Solti must go" written on the windscreen of his car'), that the photographer David Bailey made his name in *Vogue* (having successfully faced down the fashion editor Lady Rendlesham, by insisting that a young graduate of the Lucie Clayton modelling school, Jean Shrimpton, be his model), and that Violet Carson, accompanied by the rest of the *Coronation Street* cast, switched on the Blackpool Illuminations amidst hugely enthusiastic crowd scenes. *Dixon of Dock Green* returned for a new series ('about real people and their problems', explained the writer Ted Willis, 'without murder or mayhem to jazz it up'); Bruce Forsyth, after a year's absence through illness, was back in charge of *Sunday Night at the London Palladium*; Malcolm Muggeridge provoked mixed feelings when he took on a PR man, Alan Eden-Green, in a TV debate ('the word "off" used so many times and pronounced "orf" or "awf" really niggled me,' complained a life-assurance representative); Alan Freeman took over radio's *Pick of the Pops*; the BBC's new Sunday-afternoon serial *Stranger on the Shore*, about a young French *au pair* in Brighton, had 'music composed and played by Mr Acker Bilk'; and, reviewing two new books, *The Times* praised John Prebble's demythologising, history-from-below *Culloden* ('where most other accounts are romantic in tone, his is as realistic as he can make it'), but stuck the knife into *The Old Men at the Zoo*, a liberal humanist's critical, allegorical novel about the English ruling class ('Mr Angus Wilson possesses almost every literary virtue except a heart').[9]

October came in with the start of two new TV programmes – *Songs of Praise* (from the Tabernacle Baptist Chapel, Cardiff) on BBC and the much shorter-lived, fortnightly *Tempo* on ITV (edited by Kenneth Tynan, introduced by the Earl of Harewood, and, according to one critic, the discussion on the artist and politics 'just getting going, and Lindsay Anderson on the point of losing his temper with the egregious Mr Auberon Waugh, when we were moved on to the next item') – not to mention Juliette Greco on BBC singing from the Left Bank. 'She looked like a beatnik, could not sing – in fact, she would rather put one off going to Paris', 'we were not very interested in hearing so many songs of this type in a foreign language' and 'the whole thing irritated me' were typical viewers' reactions. Over the rest of the month, Plymouth had its Shopping Festival ('a dazzling display of the latest, the gayest, and the best value in everything, from boats and coats to cosmetics and photography'); the BBC's science-fiction thriller series *A for Andromeda*, set in the Yorkshire Dales in 1970 and co-written by the astronomer Fred Hoyle, introduced Julie Christie (as a brunette); Antony Armstrong-Jones became Lord Snowdon; correspondence raged on *Woman's Hour* about the serialisation of *Moll Flanders* ('What type of people do you cater for?' asked a listener from Bourne End, adding, 'Please take it off and keep *Woman's Hour* clean,' while from Halifax the demand was simple: 'Put her on the Welfare State and get finished with her'); Peter Cook's satirical nightclub The Establishment began in Soho ('nobody is going to go out into Greek Street feeling more revolutionary than when they went in,' reckoned George Melly, describing the audience as 'nice clean ladies and gentlemen of impeccable liberal principles and good SW addresses'); Graham Greene wrote to the *Spectator* pointing out that 'somebody should surely tell Lord Home [the Foreign Secretary] not to lick his lips continually in front of a television camera as he did on the last *Panorama*'; the Methodist church in Hunslet Carr, Leeds had its final service, membership having more than halved since 1953; BBC TV began a series of Friday-night plays 'that treat adult themes frankly', providing 'greater freedom of subject and treatment than is available on Sundays, when the plays are designed for family viewing'; hours after Rediffusion's new Record Bar had opened in Beeston, two 'Teddy Boy types' ran amok in the town's newly opened Fine Fare supermarket, as 'they grabbed bottles of salad cream and tomato sauce from the window display and splattered it over the shop interior'; Cyril Connolly, in his *Sunday Times* review of Alan Sillitoe's new novel *Key to the Door*, evinced little enthusiasm for a return to the Seaton family and their 'small, closed world' in which people worked in factories, drank in pubs and frequently 'copulated'; a last-minute intervention from the Lord Chamberlain's office cut to ribbons a student revue sketch in Newcastle about 'a royal personage' and class barriers; three female undergraduates gate-crashed an all-male Cambridge Union debate ('Union members jumped to their feet and shouted "Out! Out!" at the girls'); only 'rather guarded approval' greeted *Dr Kildare*'s TV debut ('Perhaps when I get used to the extra-ordinary way they go about things in American hospitals it will grow on me,' thought a secretary); the first issue of *Private Eye* came out on the 25th (yellow paper, six pages, mainly the work of Christopher Booker and Willie Rushton, with Mr Punch of the eponymous maga-zine as first 'Bore of the Week'), the same day the British Library acquired its copy of R. D. Laing's *The Self and Others* ('the reader should remember,' he warned, 'that I am not saying that other people *cause* madness'); and Arnold Wesker addressed a meeting in Kingsley Hall, Bristol about his Centre 42 movement, as observed by a sceptical Tom Stoppard, who believed the playwright guilty of 'incredible naivety' in assuming that the TUC's support the previous year for Resolution 42 was proof that 'the millions' were dissatisfied with their staple culture of 'football, films, telly, bingo and pools', with Stoppard adding that 'the masses have no monopoly on unenlightenment'.[10]

The scepticism seemed justified during the first few days of November, as Centre 42 put on a cultural festival and art exhibition at Wellingborough to which the public response was, according to a local trade unionist, 'disappointing and meagre', with folksingers drafted in from Birmingham touring the pubs to sparse audiences and some of the paintings on show 'so abstract as to be a source of bewilderment to the beholders'. Meanwhile, Winston Churchill was spotted lightly tapping his foot in time with the Twist at the coming-out dance of his grand-daughter; Rudolf Nureyev, having fled from Soviet Russia, made his London debut; and Princess Margaret gave birth by Caesarean section, not on medical grounds but because of her anxiety that babies born 'naturally' came out blemished. November also saw a notably high

Reaction Index of 74 for the BBC's coverage of Miss World 1961, won by the Marks and Spencer counter-girl Rosemarie Frankland, whose reward would be a 20-year affair with Bob Hope and a tragic life ended by a drugs overdose; three Mersey poets – Roger McGough, Adrian Henri and Brian Patten – met for the first time in a basement coffee bar on Mount Pleasant; Pauline Tilston's wedding to her merchant seaman beau John Prescott was ruined by her industrial-strength hairspray melting the diamante on her tiara; Jeremy Maas's exhibition of *The Pre-Raphaelites and their Contemporaries* in London was those Victorians' first major outing for many years; a new series began of Harry Worth's *Here's Harry* (described in the *Radio Times* as looking like a suburban commuter but in fact 'a twentieth-century knight errant' who 'sallies forth from his semi-detached castle and goes out to do battle against the dragons and giants of today', which 'have awe-inspiring names like Bureaucracy and Regulation, Restriction and Red Tape, and lurk around us everywhere'); the start of a winter-long strike by Equity reduced *Coronation Street*'s cast to the 13 actors on long-term contracts; Benny Hill's impersonation of Ena Sharples was acclaimed by viewers as 'a real riot'; E. H. Carr's pugnacious *What is History?* was making an immediate impact and anticipated much that lay ahead ('the more sociological history becomes, and the more histor-ical sociology becomes, the better for both'); Jimmy Hill as Coventry City's new manager initiated the 'Sky Blue revolution', repackaging football as more upmarket but still affordable family entertainment, while the Spurs captain Danny Blanchflower began writing for the *Observer*; and Raymond Williams, reviewing a history of Fabian social-ism, argued that that incremental, top-down approach, concentrating on building organisations rather than changing people, was no longer relevant ('We look like a branch line, with the stations closed and the people gone away, but with the machine we have built still running through our lives, whether it serves us or not').[11]

December began with the *TLS* welcoming John Rowe Townsend's *Gumble's Yard*, set in 'a Northern city slum', as refreshingly different from 'the usual middle-class, country-holiday-with-ponies back-ground' of children's books; the piano-playing Mrs Mills – comfortably built, middle-aged, virtually unknown – appeared on the *Billy Cotton Band Show* ('a charmer', noted one critic) and found instant fame; on

Sunday Night at the London Palladium, the Equity strike left Bruce Forsyth and Norman Wisdom to fill the whole hour, which they managed with aplomb; the Royal Society for the Prevention of Accidents launched the Tufty Club; and the first series of *The Rag Trade* came to an end on the 8th. 'This has been an excellent series,' declared a physicist. 'We shall miss them all – they cheered us up no end. "Everybody out!" is now part of the English language.'[12]

The 'problem of youth' seemed that autumn an especially problematic problem. 'All the aberrations of today are, I think, uncharacteristic of England,' the Isle of Ely's MP, Sir Harry Legge-Bourke, told the Wisbech Institute Brotherhood's annual harvest festival in September. 'The fire of resentment may blaze fiercely for a while in the heads of the beatniks and the angry young men, but will, I believe, flicker out eventually – leaving those of us, who meanwhile have exercised our national steadiness, to pick up the threads again and weave a tapestry in accordance with our heritage.' Was Blackpool part of that heritage? Hugh Selbourne visited the resort a few days later to see the 'garish' illuminations: 'The town was crowded with youths; all beer and bingo, their behaviour rough, and deteriorating.' *The Times*, meanwhile, was running a sustained, largely grumpy correspondence about 'A Nation in Danger', after the Rev. Leslie Weatherhead had complained in a letter that 'the very word "discipline" is universally hated by the young' and noted that 'your paper, Sir, reported the habit of teenage girls wearing a yellow golliwog, not as a sign of academic or athletic distinction, but as a sign that the wearer had had sexual intercourse.' Two sociologists, E. M. and M. Epple, responded to the correspondence by sending questionnaires about the state of adolescent morality to almost 600 magistrates, probation officers and youth leaders, eliciting a 23-per-cent completion rate. The general view was that young people were more engaged in sexual activity than in the previous generation ('chastity is a hardly understood virtue'); that there was not necessarily any significant change in attitudes to authority, although a substantial minority of respondents thought there was; that there existed greater frankness and intellectual honesty ('no longer the shabby pretence that once prevailed'); and that the crucial influence was home background ('thirty years ago we were just as keen on the latest dance records by the band leader of the moment, but most of us had a stable home and only one

Mum and Dad, and Mum was always there when we got home – instead of going out to work to pay the H.P.'). The young themselves were more directly scrutinised in a two-year Gallup investigation into 16- to 18-year-olds reporting in December. The poll found them likelier to have good relations with their mother than their father; regular working habits (after three years, more than half still in the same job as when they started); many 'severely critical' of their schooling, not least the 'lack of discipline'; one-third as regular attenders at church; only one in ten not looking forward to getting married; 85 per cent disagreeing with the assertion that it did not matter very much whether or not a marriage worked out well; Churchill as easily their most-respected adult; parents, then sportsmen, as their most respected type of person, with 'statesmen and film stars far behind, teachers nowhere at all'; and only 9 per cent disagreeing with the opinion that the world would be a better place to live in in ten years' time. 'In many ways,' reflected the *Daily Telegraph* (in a summary of the survey, called 'The Not-So-Lost Generation'), 'the image of an unstable and feckless generation pales, the further one goes from adult guesses and the nearer one comes to facts.'[13]

Two-thirds of Gallup's teenage sample listened to popular music, and during 1961 almost 55 million singles (going round the turntable at 45 rpm) were sold, double the total three years earlier. Single of the autumn was the cloudlessly optimistic 'Walkin' Back to Happiness' by Helen Shapiro ('Walk down any London high street on a Saturday afternoon,' noted Jonathan Miller in October, 'and you will hear her voice float out on the Delphic breath of the local electric stores'); ITV's *Thank Your Lucky Stars*, which had begun in April, was now nationally networked, hosted by the (in Dave McAleer's words) 'amiable if patronising' Brian Matthew; and Anthony Heap moaned that 'one can seldom go into a roadside café without finding an infernal slot machine called a "juke box" into which some half-witted oaf must ever be inserting the coin necessary to make the thing churn out some horrible "pop disc" and so inflict it on everyone in the place.' Perhaps it was not as bad as all that. The trad jazz boom was cheerfully approaching its commercial peak, with Acker Bilk in a magazine article plaintively asking the jazz police, 'Is It A Crime To Be Successful?'; the charts that autumn featured such reassuring names as Shirley Bassey, Connie Francis, Frank Sinatra and

Frankie Vaughan, not to mention a novelty hit for Charlie Drake with 'My Boomerang Won't Come Back'; and Mrs Alice Stirrup of Blackburn expressed her satisfaction to the *Radio Times* that 'at last Mummy, who has hitherto been regarded as a "square", is coming into her own!', given that 'many of the latest "pops" are the songs of twenty or more years ago – perhaps with a new rhythm, but the same good old songs.' It was time for a chance encounter on platform 2 at Dartford station. Mike (but soon Mick) Jagger was on his way on Tuesday, 17 October to the London School of Economics, carrying Chuck Berry and Muddy Waters albums under his arm; Keith Richards, apparently also holding a Chuck Berry record, was on his way to Sidcup Art College; and the two, friends at primary school before the 11-plus sundering, now reconnected.

First, though, the Mersey sound – and of course one beat group in particular of the 500 or so playing in the Merseyside area during the late 1950s and early 1960s. On Saturday, 9 December the Beatles – newly under the management of the perceptive, socially accomplished Brian Epstein, but fulfilling a previously arranged commitment – spent much of the day travelling to Aldershot in order to play for the first time in the south of England. They were still on the road as the *Aldershot News* held its annual Christmas tea party for the borough's elderly people. 'You've never seen a happier crowd,' wrote the paper's tame reporter:

> Gay and high-spirited they were singing the carols and all the old songs, laughing at the jokes with tears streaming down their faces, wishing one another a Happy Christmas and almost falling over themselves to express their pleasure at being invited. And what a cheeky lot they were in their saucy paper hats – heart-shaped, and gay little trilbies for the men. It did you good just to look at them.

Unfortunately, the *Aldershot News*'s generosity stopped there, for the current issue had failed to insert the advertisement for the Palais Ballroom. In the event, just 18 people watched the Beatles play for almost four hours. Alan Freeman, Jane Asher, Acker Bilk and the singer Julie Wilson were doing *Juke Box Jury* service that evening, the Tubby Hayes Quartet was at London's Marquee Club, Humphrey Lyttelton and his Band were at the Spa Ballroom in Scarborough – but it was in

Thomas Hardy's *Quartershot* that a bathetic slice of cultural history was made, a year exactly since the start of *Coronation Street*.[14]

'You must be in no doubt that you are watching one of the great dramas of history, as so many countries thrust forwards through nationalism towards their independence,' the outgoing Colonial Secretary – removed by Macmillan because he was making too many enemies – told the Conservative annual conference in Brighton on the morning of 11 October. And, in what was a very consciously valedictory speech, Iain Macleod not only strongly defended the policy of rapid decolonisation he had set in train, but stated his fundamental belief in 'the brotherhood of man' and ended by declaring that 'the task of bringing these countries towards their destiny of free and equal partners and friends with us in the Commonwealth of Nations can be a task as exciting, as inspiring and as noble as the creation of empire itself.' A standing ovation duly followed, 'but,' observed the *Economist*, 'it was an ovation still noticeably led by a minority claque, in which the rank and file of Tuscany eventually joined because it seemed impossible not to do so'. Afterwards, in the hotel bar, one delegate was heard to say, 'Beautiful phrases Macleod has, but they mean nothing. I still wouldn't like to be a white man in Africa.' There were other signs, moreover, of a reluctance to accept man's indivisible brotherhood. The Monday Club was by now in operation, at this stage essentially a ginger group of young Tories hostile to majority black rule and whose first pamphlet was *Wind of Change or Whirlwind?*; while when the Central African Federation's embattled Sir Roy Welensky spoke on 8 November at the Institute of Directors' annual conference – calling nationalism in Africa 'among the tragedies of this age . . . that has made a mockery of liberty and enslaved thousands upon thousands of its own people in dictatorships and in the thraldom of poverty and chaos' – he, noted *The Times*, 'sat down to an ovation which vibrated the Albert Hall'. What about Macleod's successor? 'He is a man of integrity, has a first-class brain, is willing to listen and will, I think, do an excellent job,' a right-wing Tory MP, Patrick Wall, had reassured Welensky the day after Macmillan's reshuffle had been announced. 'The new appointment,' he had added, 'will certainly mean a modification of the ruthless pro-African Nationalist line which has been pursued recently.' Wall, though, called it wrong, for in practice Reginald Maudling essentially continued Macleod's policy – so much so that Macmillan by early 1962 was finding him 'more difficult & intransigent than his predecessor'. According to Maudling's biographer Lewis Baston, the 'awful comparison' in his calm, pragmatic mind 'was the doomed French resistance to Algerian independence. To cling on, to spit in the wind of change, was inconceivable. Maudling was the ideal man to come to terms with necessity, and to do it with dignity.'[15]

The brotherhood of man continued to falter on the home front. In Bristol for instance, a local paper took soundings in September 1961 in the St Paul's district. 'There is colour prejudice here,' said a black man, Basil Simpson. 'Sure there is. Some people think we just aren't human.' Even so, he added, 'This is my country, and I'm staying.' A white woman, living in a house with Jamaicans, agreed: 'There's definitely a colour bar in Martin Street. Live with coloured people and they say you're a prostitute straight away. I've got two half-caste children. You should hear what's said when I take them to school. "Nigger's children" is what's shouted . . . Lots of people have been really nasty to me.' But in nearby Bishop Street, 'a massively genial, bearded and turbaned Sikh', J. S. Patel, disagreed: 'I've been in England 26 years. No trouble with white people. I play darts with them, eat, drink. No trouble. Everything fine.' Later that month, in Bradford, a council meeting featured some sharp exchanges:

COUN R.N.W. BISHOP asked what connotation in Minute 3 (Proposed Special Classes for Coloured Children) the word 'coloured' had in that context.

ALD WOODGATE said the answer was that the children who it was proposed would form those classes were coloured children, chiefly Pakistanis and West Indians.

COUN BISHOP said it was an excellent scheme to bring a bit of English education to immigrants to this country. He deprecated, however, the use of the term 'coloured' which in that context to his mind bore no proper meaning insofar as they were all coloured. Some who had been on holiday were tanned brown; others looked blotchy and pink like himself who had not had the pleasure of a holiday. To call someone coloured was not the happiest way of phrasing that particular resolution. He would have been happier to see the phrase 'new immigrants' used.

ALD R.C. RUTH said it would have been better if some other adjective could be found but it was not easy and he was sure it was with the best intentions it had been used in the descriptive sense. He thought the motive of those special classes was a very good one. *(Hear, hear)*

COUN E.W. MOULSON said he thought they were getting very very fancy and supercilious. What were those children other than coloured children? One could not make them any other. It was all right Coun Bishop trying to bring a fancy word but they remained coloured people. He would like to go a step further. The Minute as it stood would do a useful job of work, but he had worked in industrial premises where parents of that type of coloured children were employed and the Minute as it stood was only the beginning of something which they did not know where it would finish. Those children from birth had not been brought up to living in the English way of life. They would probably finish up wanting a new canteen and feeding centre . . . Some thought he was talking out of the top of his hat but he worked in industrial premises where thousands of pounds had been spent on toilet facilities for them. They had a different way of life. *(Laughter)*

'He was no colour bar merchant,' insisted Moulson, 'but they did not know what they were letting themselves in for – new toilets for them, new school feeding centres and a lot more.'

By now the larger politics of uncontrolled immigration from the New Commonwealth were about to come to a head. At the Tories' seaside gathering, the morning of 11 October was notable not only for Macleod's memorable oration, and for the *Daily Express* snapping a front-page photograph of Lady Antonia Fraser taking a chilly plunge with her politician-husband, but for the staunchly pro-restriction back-bencher Sir Cyril Osborne handing out to delegates a copy of his just-published letter ('IMMIGRATION LUNACY: Ever Nearer an Afro-Asian Britain') in the *Daily Telegraph*. That afternoon saw a full-scale debate on the immigration issue, during which (in the *Economist*'s words) 'speaker after speaker said that he felt no colour prejudice, and then proceeded to show shamefacedly that he did.' One watching journalist, Bernard Levin, was less restrained – 'some of the nastiest sights and sounds I have ever seen on the daylight side of a large, flat stone' – but fully agreed about the hypocrisy of those who pretended that support for immigration controls had nothing to do with colour or race. As an example of 'the sort of muck' that was 'indistinguishable from the harangues of Mosley's corner-boys in Notting Hill', he cited the decidedly un-shamefaced Frank Taylor, a delegate from Manchester's Moss Side:

> 'The immigrants are human,' he said, beaming broadly about him; 'They get married and have children. Some of them are very human and have lots of children ... who can blame them for clubbing to buy houses, very often over the heads of English residents ... driving out the English people and eventually becoming owners of residences in whole streets ... we have leprosy in the country 150 per cent more than ten years ago. That must be something to do with immigration ... Some – a minority, I agree – do not really want to do an awful lot of work. I was on a doorstep last week, and a gentleman came to the door ... ladies and gentlemen, you and I are keeping him and his wife and about six delightful little piccaninnies round his knees.'

The final speech came from the Home Secretary, Rab Butler, generally viewed as in the liberal camp. 'It may be,' he conceded, 'that we can work out a system which is humane, unprejudiced and sensible and which meets some of the undoubted rising social and economic problems which otherwise may become too much for certain parts of our country.' Minutes later, the resolution demanding that the government 'take action quickly' over 'the uncontrolled number of immigrants flowing into the United Kingdom' was passed by a large majority.[16]

'WHILE THE DOOR IS STILL OPEN...' was the *Daily Mail*'s headline five days later, a reporter having met the 3.33 'immigrant train' at Waterloo station the previous foggy afternoon – on board, some 980 West Indians whose smiles 'flash all the warmth of their native Caribbean sunshine'. Some increasingly familiar statistics were trotted out: 'There are 400,000 coloured people in Britain, almost half being West Indians. Last year 52,000 West Indians poured in; last month 5,000 came. And a record 80,000 expected to flood in during the whole of this year. Indians and Pakistanis are also arriving here in spectacularly higher numbers

– 16,700 in the first six months this year, against 2,500 in the same period in 1960.' On 1 November, the day after the Queen's Speech had explicitly anticipated the measure, Butler's bill was duly published, enabling immigration officers to refuse entry to anyone from the Commonwealth (in effect the New Commonwealth – ie, non-white) without the means of actual or prospective support. Opinion-polling evidence had long suggested overwhelming public backing for such a measure, but the *Daily Mirror* that day took a contrary stand, declaring it 'fundamentally WRONG' to impose restrictions on entry from the Commonwealth. Not only would they amount to 'a colour bar' but 'coloured immigrants' amounted to less than 1 per cent of the population and 'the overwhelming majority do useful jobs here'.

The Commonwealth Immigrants Bill had its second reading on the evening of 16 November, producing a heated Commons debate. Butler, observed Mollie Panter-Downes, 'introduced it with the evident acute distaste of a man of strong liberal principles being forced by party pressure to act against them'; much was made of the decision to exempt the Irish from immigration controls; and Gaitskell, in Panter-Downes's words, 'raked the uncomfortable-looking front bench [not least Macleod, now party chairman] with scorn in what many people felt was one of the finest speeches of his career' – a speech that memorably characterised the bill as a 'miserable, shameful, shabby' surrender to 'the crudest clamour'. With Tory imperialists as well as liberals deeply unhappy, the party's whips at one point were seriously worried about securing a convincing majority, but in the end managed 84. Even from the right, press reaction was largely hostile. The Irish exemption, reflected *The Times*, removed any doubts that the bill was 'racially discriminatory'; the *Daily Mail* likewise detected 'an unhealthy whiff of hypocrisy', depicted government handling of the whole immigration issue as 'labouring under a feeling of guilt', admitted 'we are a crowded island' but emphasised 'there is not a shortage of work for the West Indians who come here', and altogether concluded that 'the whole edifice' of the Commonwealth would 'tremble' if free entry was 'swept away'. The writer Colin MacInnes was also unimpressed. 'Willy-nilly,' he wrote to *The Times*, 'we created, or enforced, an international, inter-racial community of millions. Must we destroy it through hasty inane fear?' Anthony Heap was disappointed only by the delay of 'some months yet' before the bill became law ('in the meantime, beat-the-ban blacks will continue to flock to this overcrowded and underhoused country in their tens of thousands'); Macmillan on the 30th noted with relief rather than satisfaction that the latest Gallup had shown over-whelming support; and soon afterwards Cyril Osborne (described by one parliamentary correspondent as 'the spirit, if not the architect, of the Bill') treated *Guardian* readers to 'The case for immigration control'. Conceding that 'unfortunately' the proposed legislation did indeed 'look like colour discrimination', he went on:

> Nine-tenths of the Commonwealth are coloured. They are also the poor-est. They are naturally attracted by our affluent society. It is their vast numbers and their awful poverty that make it impossible for us to accept indefinitely all who would like to come. It is therefore not colour, or race, but numbers and poverty that make action unavoidable.
>
> It is strange the Labour Party, which claims especially to represent the working man, has totally ignored the unfortunate English family which has had to bear the social stresses which unlimited immigration has brought. Has the Englishman no rights in his own country? Scarcely one Socialist MP has raised his voice in answer to the appeal for protection that has come from the workers in our big cities where the immigrants have settled.

'The Socialists,' in short, 'seem to be so obsessed by the rights of the immigrants they cannot hear the cries of their own supporters.'[17]

In fact, Labour's opposition to the bill significantly softened over the next few months, with the party's front-bench spokesman on colonial affairs, Denis Healey, declining to promise that a future Labour govern-ment would repeal the legislation. The final Commons vote in February 1962 saw a comfortable majority of 101 ('after all the threat of opposi-tion from our side and of abstention', recorded Macmillan), Royal Assent was given in April, and the Act took effect at the start of July. There was certainly, as Heap had feared, a beat-the-ban rush, typified by many Pakistani women and children arriving in Bradford to join their menfolk; overall, between January 1961 and June 1962 net inward migration from India, Pakistan and the West Indies was over 190,000 – only some 20,000 fewer than for the six years from 1955 to 1960. If the government was ever tempted to drop the bill, events in West Yorkshire at the start of 1962 probably stiffened its resolve. 'Hey, dig the plague in Bradford,' Philip Larkin wrote to Monica Jones on 13 January. 'What lunacy our immigration laws are.' The 'plague' was smallpox, involving several deaths, and a Leeds paper reported how 'all over' the rival city, 'in public houses, clubs and on the buses, there was open evidence that the public as a whole were blaming the Pakistani population', with 'conversation mainly centred on the lines of "Send them home"'. An editorial ('Without Anger') in Bradford's *Telegraph & Argus* sought to play down the racial aspect, insisting that 'the present need is for calm and tolerance', but readers' letters in response were far from calm or tolerant:

> People I have spoken to are angry. (*'ENOUGH IS ENOUGH'*, *Bradford 9*)
>
> My wife, myself and lots of other people we know, agree with the report in the Leeds morning paper about 'sending them home'. All the mothers about these parts are frightened . . . (*'WINDY'*, *Shipley*)
>
> The stupid and irrational policy of uncontrolled mass entry by coloured immigrants has brought its terrible reward . . . I am not in favour of any colour bar, only common sense. (*H.T. Mudd, Bradford 5*)
>
> As far as we are concerned this smallpox outbreak has been the last straw. (*'SIX SOBER HOUSEWIVES'*, *Bradford 5*)
>
> England is like a pawn-shop and will take anything in. (*'Bradford born and bred'*)

More generally, the imminent introduction of immigration controls seemed to do little at this stage to ameliorate feelings. The elderly Keighley diarist Gladys Hague may have reflected at the end of 1961 that 'coloured people can be just as charming as white people when you get to know them and much more polite', but when in April 1962 a national sample survey asked 1,254 respondents in England and Wales whether they agreed with the opinion that 'foreign immigrants to this country' were 'doing too well at the expense of the British people', 71 per cent answered 'yes'. That majority view was more or less equally shared among men and women, and among Conservative and Labour voters, but was less common among under-45s than over-45s, with hostility rates exceeding 80 per cent for those in their 60s and 70s. Perhaps inevitably, the survey threw up three other variables. 'The less educated are more frequently hostile to immigrants than the better educated,' summarised the sociologists W. G. Runciman and C. R. Bagley, 'the less well-paid more frequently hostile than the better-paid, and those in manual occupations more frequently hostile than those in non-manual occupations.'

Of course, the immigrants themselves had their own backstories and experiences. Take two young men. Darcus Howe landed at Southampton on 11 April 1962 from Trinidad and Tobago. 'On arrival at Waterloo station,' he recalled, 'a friend who came to meet me warned that I must not under any circumstances walk alone at night because I would face arrest by the police and a beating from white racists. I contemplated returning home almost at once. During the first eighteen months or so, loneliness never left me alone even though I lived with five others in a rented flat atop a car showroom.' Abdul Ghani Javid was already in England, having arrived at London Airport in 1961 with just a pound note in his pocket – all that he would need, his father in Pakistan had hopefully calculated, to get him through his first month. Javid found his way to Rochdale, starting work in a cotton mill before becoming a bus conductor and driver, earning the nickname 'Mr Night and Day' from his colleagues. Just over half a century later, in April 2014, his son Sajid became the first Asian man in the British Cabinet.[18]

13

That First Small Cheer

On Monday, 11 December 1961, with the Beatles safely back in Liverpool and playing the Cavern that lunchtime, 60,000 at Twickenham saw Cambridge beat Oxford (by 9–3, high-scoring for the era) to go through the whole season unbeaten; the *Lincolnshire Echo*'s 'Stylus' reviewed the latest records ('Billy Fury and his ilk do not sing so much as whine,' unlike the 'cosy treat' of listening to 'that familiar round and warm tone' of Donald Peers); and Peter Noone made his *Coronation Street* debut as Stanley Fairclough, son of Len. Later in the week, an *Any Questions?* discussion about decimalisation gave Harold Wilson the chance to make an emotional plea to keep 'the pound and the pound sterling', because 'not only Britain and the sterling area, but the world will lose something if the pound disappears from the markets of the world'; David Mercer's first television play *Where the Difference Begins* – about an engine driver's family, set in his hometown of Wakefield and portraying radicalism betrayed by affluence – got from viewers a very high Reaction Index of 78 ('this was sheer drama of life and *real* people') but a going-over from the *Spectator*'s Peter Forster ('a big theme tackled with insufficient talent'); and the bowler-hatted Acker Bilk, whose 'Stranger on the Shore' was in its melancholic way storming up the charts, was asked by an interviewer whether he was 'in favour of the public school system'. 'None of my kids is going away from home,' he replied. 'That's like the army. Money makes all the difference. People who have it get all the training and education and others don't. So I'm against public schools.' Soon afterwards, two big economic stories broke almost simultaneously: ICI's announcement of a giant takeover bid for Courtaulds (the *FT* immediately wondering 'whether such a

merger does not create a group too large to be in the national interest')
and Selwyn Lloyd announcing decimalisation of the coinage by around
1966 (warmly greeted by the *Daily Mail* on the grounds that 'decimal
coinage is modern'). *The Young Ones* was about to go on general release
for the Christmas holidays (one critic acclaiming Cliff Richard as 'still
as dewy as he was in *Expresso Bongo*, still as apparently unslicked and
unspoiled'), while just before Christmas the Advisory County Cricket
Committee agreed to inaugurate in 1963 a one-day knock-out competition, prompting the commentator Rex Alston to speculate, 'Will some
crafty captain keep his fast bowlers on and spread the field defensively?'
Christmas Day itself saw the BBC getting a two-thirds share of the TV
audience (but *Coronation Street* besting *This Is Your Life*); on Boxing
Day, Madge Martin in Oxford went to the panto (including 'a funny
"Dame," Terry Scott'), while Phyllis Willmott that night at Mavis
Nicholson's north London party re-encountered Kingsley Amis and
'was struck again by his capacity to control his drunkenness'; and on
the 27th, the stand-out programme on the Home Service was Charles
Chilton's moving one-hour documentary *The Long, Long Trail:
Soldiers' Songs of the First World War*. 1962 came in chilly. 'The coldest
New Year's Day for 75 years,' noted Anthony Heap, 'with yesterday's
snow (London's heaviest fall since records began in 1940) frozen into
ice on slippery pavements, rail, tube and bus services in a state of chaos
and everyone coming in late at the TH [ie, Finsbury Town Hall] – the
last arriving at 11.0.' Eleven o'clock as it happened was when, after a
dreadful overnight journey, the Beatles were sitting uneasily in reception at Decca's West Hampstead recording studios, about to be audi-
tioned. It did not go well, with John underused, Paul palpably nervous,
Pete Best on drums having a nightmare and the atmosphere generally
downbeat. Gloom also at Accrington, where financially troubled
Stanley entered the year next to bottom in Division Four and the local
paper observed that 'it has been the Peel Park club's misfortune that if
anything possible can go wrong to make their plight worse it usually
does.' Little optimism too from the PM. 'The Post Office workers are
"working to rule" & this (with the ice & snow) has produced a rather
bad situation,' recorded Macmillan on the 5th. 'Everything turns on a)
holding on to the wage *pause* for 2 or 3 more months, b) being able to
slide into "wage restraint", c) getting started the machinery for a

long-term policy.' Still, behind the headlines, nothing could apparently stop the steady, inexorable drift upmarket. Amidst the snow and cold that first week of January, the International Boat Show at Earl's Court saw £200,000 worth of orders taken in its opening four days, while at the end of the week, the *East London Advertiser*'s women's page announced the passing of the 'char' and the arrival of the 'domestic help' – gadget-conscious, 'often young' and usually wearing 'trim nylon house overalls instead of a floral wrap-around apron'.[1]

The *Radio Times* covering this week's television (BBC only) was a lips-licking affair: on Tuesday the 2nd, 7.30–8.00, a new twice-weekly soap set in the offices of 'The Magazine for the Busy Woman'; half an hour later, 8.30–9.15, the first episode of a police drama set 'in the North of England overspill estate called Newtown'; and on Friday the 5th, 8.45–9.15, 'The Offer', the latest in Ray Galton and Alan Simpson's *Comedy Playhouse* series. Written and created by Hazel Adair and Peter Ling, the magazine-*cum*-soap was called *Compact*, and it got a critical mauling, largely for lack of credibility, with Forster declaring that 'the only people I really believed in were the bloody-minded telephone engineers'. By contrast, 'The Offer' provoked more mixed feelings for the *Listener*'s Frederick Laws: positive in that it 'established a couple of characters very pleasantly and hinted at a situation', but less so in that 'the miserly father of the rag-and-bone-man business became so dislikeable that one wanted his exploited but undeceived son to get away and found his frustration and defeat painful.' The father (Albert) was played by Wilfrid Brambell, the son (Harold) by one of Joan Littlewood's Theatre Workshop finest, Harry H. Corbett, and the family firm was called Steptoe and Son. For the largely appreciative viewers (RI of 74), noted the audience-research report, 'tears were never far from laughter', while there was 'a considerable amount of praise for the "incredibly realistic" setting'.[2] In the event, of course, 'The Offer' would not be the only visit to that Shepherd's Bush junkyard. But the real waves were made by the week's other new programme, *Z Cars*.

The police by early 1962 were undergoing scrutiny – albeit rather tame scrutiny – by a Royal Commission, which the government had reluctantly set up two years earlier largely because of the Podola episode of 1959, involving a murder suspect receiving severe, much-publicised injuries as a result of eight hours of questioning in a London police station. Exemplar of the tough policeman on a tough beat using tough methods was Detective Sergeant Harry Challenor, the Soho-based SAS war hero. 'Many of those he helped put behind bars,' his obituarist would note, 'complained that he had planted evidence on them and used his fists, but if his superiors and the courts had misgivings they took no action.' The Royal Commission, when it reported later in 1962, found that the public still broadly trusted the police, but two observers that year offered more critical perspectives. C.G.L. Du Cann, a barrister specialising in criminal law, wrote damningly about the police's role in the justice system, especially in relation to taking bribes from criminals ('there is big money to be made by the police officer who is willing to be "fair" and say a few kind words when he is asked to "tell the court what you know about the prisoner"') and to perjury ('the policeman's familiarity with the witness-box breeds contempt of its obligations'); in the same volume, *The Police and the Public*, the working-class writer Frank Norman, himself a prisoner four times, put it bluntly enough: 'The truth is coppers are just geezers doing a job. Some like doing it; some don't; some are bent and some are straight . . . Some of them use the power given them by being rude to people and looking for trouble and others just want a quiet life, but whichever way you look at it the romantic idea of "the good old London bobby being wonderful" is nothing but a load of old moody. If you want to know the time, look at your watch.'

The best-known – and hugely popular – bobby remained the reassuring, imperturbable, rock-solid-incorruptible George Dixon. 'Evening all,' he announced himself as usual to viewers at the start of an episode in December 1961. 'You know, I expect you remember the cafuffle there was when the Ministry of Transport introduced their ten-year test for cars . . . Well, the fact is with the traffic and the danger on the roads these days it's absolutely vital to keep a car a hundred per cent up to scratch – as we found out ourselves not long back . . .' In fact, popular representations of the police were already starting to change. In two films, Joseph Losey's *Blind Date* (1959) and Val Guest's *Hell Is a City* (in this case Manchester, 1960), the working-class actor Stanley Baker played troubled policemen who were, in Andrew Roberts's words, 'a far cry from the trilby-hatted automaton of the second-feature

CID man'; while on television, not only did ITV's long-running *No Hiding Place* (starting in 1959, with Raymond Francis as the dapper, clip-voiced Inspector Lockhart) have a harder edge than *Dixon of Dock Green*, but the BBC in late 1961 ran a four-part drama series called *Jacks and Knaves* that was Liverpool-set and prompted a youngish Tory MP, Nicholas Ridley, to complain to the Corporation that one of his constituents, a Major Neal, believed it to be showing the police 'in an unfortunate light, making them out to be fools lacking in discipline'.[3]

Even so, there was still plenty of scope for the step-change that was *Z Cars*. Essentially the creation of Troy Kennedy Martin and John McGrath, and set partly in 'Newtown' (based on Kirkby) and partly in 'Seaport' ('based on the Crosby-Waterloo water front', recalled McGrath), it was previewed by the *Liverpool Echo* on 2 January, a few hours before 'Four of a Kind', the first episode: 'Drama documentary series on the day to day work of the crime patrol cars of a County Police Force. The cars, each manned by two young constables selected for their ability to deal effectively with trouble on the spot, are constantly on patrol day and night.' The episode itself, ushered in by a jaunty flutes-and-drums arrangement of the Liverpool-Irish skipping tune 'Johnny Todd', began with the abrasive Detective Chief Inspector Barlow and the milder Detective Sergeant John Watt smoking cigarettes near the grave of a murdered colleague; PC Bob Steele arguing with his facially bruised wife; and his partner in Z-Victor 2, PC Bert Lynch, betting on the horses. Unfortunately, burst pipes that Tuesday evening meant that the *Echo*'s TV reviewer was unable to watch, but next day Richard Sear in the *Daily Mirror* declared that whereas *Compact* had been 'as superficial as powder on the puff', *Z Cars* was 'much more realistic and went straight to the heart of the story'. Then came the complaints. 'It was nowhere near the class of *Dixon of Dock Green*,' the chairman of the Police Federation told the press, adding that 'it showed the police in a pretty poor light'; a spokesman for Preston CID claimed that 'the police were made to look a lot of gormless numskulls'; and, having initially co-operated with the programme, Colonel Eric St Johnston, Chief Constable of Lancashire, now very publicly wanted it taken off. Nor, calling it 'completely inaccurate', was Kirkby Urban District Council enthusiastic – unsurprisingly, given that Kennedy

Martin on an exploratory field trip had privately described Kirkby as 'one of the black spots of England, where 50,000 displaced and truculent Merseysiders carry out a continuous war against authority and where crime and adolescent terror incubate'. As for viewers at large, 'many' were positive, with praise for a portrayal of the police that was 'neither brutal nor benign, but thoroughly human and down-to-earth'. The audience-research report, however, showed a significant minority dissenting: 'It was hardly likely, they maintained, that many real policemen would behave so unattractively, and therefore the whole thing seemed unbelievable and false.'[4]

Over the course of 1962's next four months or so, the *People* put the question 'TOUGHEN HIM UP?' as its contribution to the national debate about whether the 13-year-old Prince Charles should go to Eton (his mother's choice) or Gordonstoun (his father's); the annual hedging competition at Eardisley in Herefordshire 'attracted only a few competitors, but judges were unanimous in their admiration of the skilled craftsmanship of those who built good hedges in a bitter wind'; amidst a storm of press criticism about the cost of Princess Margaret's Kensington Palace apartments, the Queen (recorded Macmillan after a visit to Sandringham) 'showed me a very intimate & moving letter from her sister, wh. revealed how distressed the Princess was at this fickleness, wh. made her feel uncertain of the future'; at blustery Twickenham, England and Wales ground out an attritional o–o draw; Enoch Powell, four years after resigning from the government as a champion of fiscal parsimony, published a White Paper detailing a hugely ambitious hospital-building plan; the *Sunday Times* launched on 4 February its pioneering colour magazine (editor Mark Boxer, artistic adviser Snowdon, photos on the cover of Jean Shrimpton in a Mary Quant dress and Burnley's stylish inside-forward Jimmy McIlroy, the whole billed as 'a sharp glance at the mood of Britain' and, after a shaky start, a lucrative magnet for socially aspirational colour advertising); on *Any Questions?*, Mark Abrams and Michael Foot wanted the national anthem dropped at cinemas and theatres, but not so Lady Isobel Barnett and Gerald Nabarro ('should be played on all public occasions and as frequently as possible'); Labour's Eirene White promised that a future

Labour government would not abolish public schools ('it is foolish to destroy something that has virtue'); a playground fight at Bromley Tech left David Jones (later Bowie) with a permanently dilated left pupil; reviewing the latest *Young Contemporaries* show, *The Times* identified David Hockney as the 'star turn' of 'the raspberry-blowing "new surrealist school" (for want of a better name) at the Royal College of Art'; Albert Finney appeared on *Face to Face* ('pleasant, modest, and talkative – but alas, not an inch larger than life', noted John Gross); vast numbers thronged the National Gallery to see the Da Vinci cartoon under threat of export to America; Cyril Osborne led Tory backbenchers talking out Leo Abse's bill which aimed to curb the excesses of homophobic chief constables; the Duke of Edinburgh called the *Daily Express* 'a bloody awful newspaper . . . full of lies, scandal and imagination'; Express Dairies announced that it was stopping 7-days-a-week milk deliveries in London; the 12-year-old Kilmore came in at 28 to 1 in the Grand National; 45 experimental 'Panda' pedestrian crossings opened on 2 April in over 20 towns, amidst widespread confusion; Glasgow's North British Locomotive Co ('too "steam-minded",' according to its chairman) announced it was to go into liquidation; James Hanratty was hanged at Bedford Prison for the A6 murder; Robert Fraser, son of the merchant banker Lionel Fraser and not quite yet 'Groovy Bob', opened his gallery in Duke Street off Grosvenor Square ('I will be dealing entirely in modern paintings and sculpture'); at a housing conference in Sutton Coldfield organised by the West Midlands Old People's Welfare Committee, an 80-year-old 'amused the Delegates by remarking that it was time Local Councils in the design of toilets would raise the height of the pan level as old ladies like herself had great difficulty in getting up from the low-down position of present-day toilets'; David Hockney went home to Bradford for Easter ('he looks well,' noted his mother in her diary, 'but I'm not keen on his blond hair'); Stirling Moss almost died on Easter Monday in a career-ending crash at Goodwood; a magazine advertisement for the *Daily Herald* took the form of an interview with Tony Hancock, an admirer of its content rather than of its 'a bit grave-looking' appearance ('It still reminds you a bit of words like *Labour*. Terrible word, that. Breaking stones in a quarry . . . done more harm to socialism, that word has . . .'); in football's closing weeks, Don Revie at relegation-threatened Leeds

tried to bribe a fellow-manager to 'take it easy', Bill Shankly's Liverpool
achieved their long-awaited return to the top division as the Kop found
its spontaneous singing voice, Ipswich in a last blow for egalitarianism
in football's brave new world Mark One won the League Championship
(the habitually taciturn manager Alf Ramsey admitting that he felt like
'jumping over the moon'), and Spurs beat Burnley 3–1 in the Cup Final
(a young Burnley supporter, Blake Morrison, straight afterwards taking
his ball out on the front lawn and re-enacting the match, 'with certain
crucial adjustments to the scoreline'); Hugh Trevor-Roper's review of
E. H. Carr's *What is History?* in the May issue of *Encounter* expanded
into a general attack on the 'dogmatic ruthlessness' of Carr's multi-
volume history of Soviet Russia ('the "might-have-beens", the devia-
tionists, the rivals, the critics of Lenin are reduced to insignificance,
denied justice, or hearing, or space, because they backed the wrong
horse'); Charles started at spartan Gordonstoun (shorts whatever the
weather, cold showers at 7 am); Joe Orton (29) and Kenneth Halliwell
(35) were found guilty of stealing over 70 books from north London
public libraries and 'wilfully' defacing them – 'in a sense', commented
the senior probation officer, 'both defendants are frustrated authors' –
with the upshot a six-month sentence; and London's last trolleybus,
from Wimbledon to Fulwell depot, ran in the early hours of 9 May.[5]

   Easily the biggest corporate story of these months was ICI's
protracted attempt to gain control over Courtaulds. The pre-Christ-
mas announcement of the bid had, observes John Littlewood in his
history of the modern stock market, 'aroused strong emotions across
the marketplace. It was perceived as breathtaking in size and outra-
geous in concept because ICI was the fourth-largest company after
Shell, Unilever and BP, and Courtaulds was not far behind in thir-
teenth place. It was barely within most people's perception that bids
could happen for companies the size of Courtaulds.' Nor just the
stock market as a keenly contested battle unfolded, with Mollie
Panter-Downes noting in February that it had 'shaken the business
world and the public as both parties have roared ever louder bids to
the shareholders'. Labour's call was for government intervention.
'The public at the moment,' declared Douglas Jay, 'are confronted
with the spectacle of two giant companies, supposed to be models of
enlightened private enterprise, suddenly grappling in a financial fight

to the finish in which either short-term profits or megalomania will decide the issue, with the national interest nowhere considered.' 'Shd the govt intervene?' Macmillan asked himself in late January. 'It has *no* powers. Shd it use its influence? I think the answer really is that ICI are more intelligent & more efficient than Courtaulds as regards management.' Most observers shared that expectation of an ICI victory, but over the next six weeks or so, the balance shifted in Courtaulds's favour, in large part due to the determination and drive of its rapidly emerging future leader, Frank Kearton. 'The great ICI-Courtauld battle is drawing to its inglorious close,' recorded Macmillan on 10 March. 'It looks as if the majority of Courtaulds shareholders will decide to refuse ICI's offer & be loyal to their own board. So all the damage to the reputation of ICI will have been in vain, not to speak of the damage to "capitalism" & the Conservative party. Mr Paul Chambers (Chairman of ICI) is clever, but brash; full of vigour & energy, but lacking in judgement & clumsy in execution.'

Courtaulds indeed lived to fight another day, duly marked by a solemn thanksgiving service for the staff at St Vedast's in the City. Would it, though, have been in the national interest if the contest had gone the other way and a new single combine had come to control some 90 per cent of the UK man-made fibre market? Littlewood argues that it would have been positive, seeing Chambers as ahead of his time in his rationale (as explained to the American Chamber of Commerce during the bid) that 'much of modern industry is bound to be concentrated into big units as the requirements of capital, research and development increase the optimum size of the economic unit.' Against that, Geoffrey Owen in his study of Courtaulds contends that an amalgamation would have inherently posed 'big risks' and is sceptical whether ICI would have 'benefited from having a full hand of fibres, adding acrylic, viscose, and acetate to polyester and nylon'. Where Littlewood is surely right, though, is in his assertion that the broader culture remained instinctively resistant to ambitious corporate restructuring, especially if resulting in large-scale concentrations of economic power. 'A good deal of applause,' noted the *Economist*, greeted a revealing statement that it quoted by a female shareholder at ICI's extraordinary general meeting later in March: 'There is nothing worse than trying to be too clever . . .

ICI and Mr Chambers were too clever and I think they deserved defeat ... They were covetous about Courtaulds and they got a slap in the face.'[6]

Britain was still a land of smokers (almost three-quarters of men, almost half of women), and that spring saw the publication by the Royal College of Physicians of an important report, *Smoking and Health*, that attracted considerable attention and sold well over 20,000 copies in a matter of weeks. Heavy smokers, it explained in authoritative detail, were 30 times likelier than non-smokers to get lung cancer. The report also spelled out smoking's causal link with chronic bronchitis, gastric and duodenal ulcers, and coronary heart disease. The RCP made seven recommendations 'to curb the present rising consumption of tobacco': more public education on smoking's risks; more restrictions on the sale of tobacco to children; restrictions on tobacco advertising; restrictions on smoking in public places; increased tax on cigarettes; information on tar and nicotine content; and anti-smoking clinics. Press reaction to the report was predictably mixed. The *Guardian* called the RCP's case 'overwhelming' and provided sustained, sympathetic coverage; *The Times* was less convinced, arguing that for the 'moderate smoker' the 'hazard is not of an order that seems to call for intervention'; the *Daily Mirror* for a few weeks colourfully highlighted the 'cigarette peril', but then dropped the subject; while the *Daily Express* was sure that 'people who want to smoke will continue to do so,' adding that 'the vast majority of them, being reasonable in their use of cigarettes, will live long and healthy lives.' Equally predictably, government reaction was, as the historian Virginia Berridge puts it, 'muted'. The main emphasis would be on health education – even though the Health minister Enoch Powell, when shown a draft of the report the previous autumn, had expressed the view that 'health education is merely humbug' and that it had 'already gone a long way without producing the slightest effect'. Nor did Powell believe that restrictions on advertising would 'make any difference one way or the other', though in the event the ITA soon after the report did tighten up on television advertising, including insisting that smoking must no longer be connected with social success, manliness or romance. Instead, the crux, as Powell recognised in advance, was whether the government was willing substantially to increase duty 'for explicitly public health reasons' and thereby reduce consumption. This, in the report's wake, it was not beyond a certain point prepared to do, especially given Treasury resistance to the very principle of differential taxation, as well as of course the obvious attendant unpopularity. And the smokers themselves? 'Quite honestly,' a 20-to-25-a-day man told *Tonight* on the day the report came out, 'I think that the end of one's life is probably in the hands of almighty God, you know, than in my own hands or the hands of the tobacco manufacturers.' Another stated frankly, 'If I'm going to die, I'm going to die, so I might as well enjoy life.' That specialist in enjoying life, Philip Larkin, was less fatalistic. 'I have temporarily given up,' he wrote to Monica Jones in early May, two months after the report. He added about a university colleague and his wife, heavier smokers, who had also given up: 'Their tobacconist's receipts have fallen dramatically. Social history.'[7]

The PM had an even keener eye for the historic moment. 'It's a changed Stockton – poverty has been left behind,' he announced in early April on returning to the north-eastern constituency he had represented during the slump of the 1930s. In fact, what would be called by the mid-1960s the 'rediscovery of poverty' was just starting. 'Poverty in Britain today – the Evidence' was the title of the paper read by the Cambridge economist Dorothy Wedderburn in March to the British Sociological Association, meeting at Brighton:

Although [she concluded] there are some people, mostly old, actually living below National Assistance levels, the main effect of the 1948 legislation and subsequent amendments has been to build in a floor in real terms at a little above the subsistence levels of the 'thirties. Memories of the 'thirties remain alive, however, particularly among that group, the old, who are the main sufferers from poverty and this may lower the line by which they define poverty. In many quarters on the other hand the balance of opinion seems to be in favour of raising the level.

If being at current subsistence levels is being in poverty, there are many people in poverty who are not receiving National Assistance. We estimate that there are 6 per cent of households living long-term on Assistance. Another 4 per cent are at equivalent financial levels, that is below or not more than 25 per cent above scale rates excluding rent but without Assistance. Most of these are old. If one takes as the poverty line

50 per cent instead of 25 per cent above present scale rates, one increases the percentage of households by half, and brings in many more households where the main source of income is earnings.

The single-minded sociologist Peter Townsend, out of the Institute of Community Studies stable and now very much his own man, was also on the case; his *New Statesman* piece of 20 April on 'The Meaning of Poverty' argued that poverty was appreciably more widespread than generally assumed. 'Of course we are more prosperous than our grandparents were,' he wrote. 'That is a claim that can be made by each generation. Yet we speak of the "affluent" society. This fine adjective will ring a little hollow in the ears of our grandchildren 50 years from now. They will probably describe the Britain of today, just as we do the Britain of 50 years ago, as a society which tolerated poverty among its aged, its disabled and its large families, and in important sectors of its public services.' Getting across the true situation, though, was not going to be easy – as, the following week, the magazine's 'Charon' demonstrated with some informal fieldwork in relation to the recent assertion in *The Times* by the left-wing Labour MP Frank Allaun that upwards of 15 million people still lived in houses without baths:

> I decided to try this revelation out in a saloon bar of a typical suburban pub which I sometimes use as a sounding board. The opinions held here are invariably representative of the admass: e.g. total apathy towards the prospect of the Common Market, ditto towards the international situation in general; little enthusiasm ever expressed for any public issue except possible retention of capital punishment. I was met on this occasion with total incredulity. I must have made a mistake, added on a nought; the Welfare State took care of all that sort of thing nowadays . . .

'It just didn't occur to them,' concluded the columnist, 'that their own conditions of life weren't thoroughly representative.'

Accrington Stanley's tragedy probably did not much touch the saloon bars either. On Saturday, 13 January, a week after the Twist had reached the Lancashire mill town, the team went bottom of the Fourth Division with a 4–0 defeat at home to Colchester – despite for an hour, according to Bill Hay's match report in the *Accrington Observer*, 'a snap and crackle in their play'. Results over the next month were dismal, apart from a 'heartening' draw at Aldershot, and by 17 February, amidst a rapidly deteriorating financial situation and just before a 'debatable' 2–1 defeat at home to Stockport, the bleak headline was 'STANLEY ON THE BRINK OF A PRECIPICE: Only a miracle can save Peel Park club'. An apparent saviour now came forward in the shape of Bob Lord, the Burnley butcher who doubled as the bullying, bigoted chairman of the Turf Moor club, less than 10 miles away from Accrington. But as Hay noted, many Stanley supporters were reserving judgement on his motives for offering to help what had become a severely depleted board. Almost 2,700 turned up on Saturday the 24th, but unfortunately they saw a 2–0 defeat at home to Rochdale in which 'Stanley were made to look like a team of cart-horses against thoroughbreds.' Then came a creditable 1–1 draw at Doncaster before losing 4–0 at Crewe on Friday, 2 March in a snowstorm, as 'the forwards once again lacked punch'. Three days later, on Monday the 5th, the crunch finally arrived. 'STANLEY – THE END' announced the local paper next morning:

> A Football Club died last night.
>   And with its demise, League football in the town, which Accrington helped to pioneer in 1888, died too.

The club was some £60,000 in debt, a creditors' meeting had been held the previous evening, and Lord had led the way in recommending liquidation. 'I just cannot see any ray of hope,' he declared. 'It's a shame, but I'm afraid this is only the first of many.' Accrington now resigned from the Football League – and when, later in the week, the board desperately tried to withdraw its resignation, the league (under the autocratic, unforgiving Alan Hardaker) refused any reprieve to one of its founder members. In the event, it would be a full 30 years before another club, also beginning with 'A', was compelled for financial reasons to leave the league in mid-season. In Accrington itself, a last word at the time went to Miss Ellen Rishton, who on that dismal Tuesday came out of Queen's Mill in her overalls and clogs to tell a reporter, 'It's like a death . . . I can't understand anybody who isn't loyal to their home-town team. I've often been despairing and sometimes I say I won't go to watch them, but I live near the ground, and when I hear that first small cheer I get my coat on. I just don't know what I'll do now . . .'[8]

Elsewhere in Lancashire, a few weeks earlier on 12 February, there had been serious trouble on the *Street*. 'Kenneth Barlow, 24-year-old schoolmaster of 3 Coronation Street, jeered at the simple pleasures of his homely neighbours in a scathing 2,000 word attack in the left-wing political review *Survival*' ran a local paper's story ('Ex-student Slams Neighbours') that could hardly have been more incendiary. 'Summing up the attitude of the people he lives and works among, Barlow described them as "lazy-minded, politically ignorant, starved of a real culture and stubbornly prejudiced against any advance in human insight, and scientific progress".' The rugged Len Fairclough took particular exception. 'He might be a walkin', flamin' dictionary, but 'e 'asn't the guts of a louse,' he said to a friend; and to Ken himself, as the two men (both in jackets and ties) squared up in the Rover's Return, 'Look, if there's one thing wrong with Coronation Street it's because it sometimes throws up nasty, snivelling, clever dicks like you.' A brawl ensued, finishing with Len delivering a knockout punch on behalf of loyalty to the working class that both came from.

Meanwhile, it was not only in highbrow London weeklies that the debate continued about the authenticity of a programme that was now regularly top or second in the TAM ratings (some 7.7 million homes watching the Barlow/Fairclough fight). 'I must confess,' wrote Guy Williams in Newcastle's *Sunday Sun* in early March, 'to a sneaking regard and affection for those quaint characters who have tenancies in the street – dear old Ena Sharples, the baggage with the whiplash tongue; layabout young Dennis Tanner; and his tart of a mother called Elsie.' Even so, he went on, *Coronation Street* was not in fact a realistic portrayal of working-class life: 'The truth is, of course, that the "Enas" in real life are scorpion-tongued bitches who make the Sharples woman sound like a tinkling-voiced angel by comparison. And you wouldn't find, in real life, the neighbours being so friendly with the Dennis Tanners who simply refuse to work. They'd be much more likely badgering him to follow some worthwhile occupation instead of sponging on the State and National Assistance.' Williams listed other ways in which the soap fell short, including its absence of real drunkenness, of wife-beating husbands, of 'sloppy, ill-kempt wives who slouch around houses that are nauseating to the sight and nostrils', and of malevolent neighbours who 'resent and despise each other so much that they almost delight in others' misfortunes, and would never offer a helping hand'. Why, then, the popularity?

> The upper classes indulgently smile at the quirks of behaviour of the lower classes. The middle classes silently thank their lucky stars that they proved able enough to lift themselves from such an unenterprising and tedious existence. And the humble working folk are faintly flattered by this spotlight of publicity, and amused and almost comforted at the way the unpleasantness of their existence has been wiped out by the script-writers.
>
> It's fine to be amused but they shouldn't delude themselves. *Coronation Street* may be a pleasant attempt at entertainment. But authentic? – phooey!

'I disagree entirely,' responded 'Admirer' from Newcastle's Heaton district. 'The reason for the programme's immense popularity is simply because it IS so "human" and true to life.' Mrs L. Burdon of Sunderland, however, declared that Ena Sharples was simply 'too bad to be true', that 'I've been in business all my life, but I've yet to come across a person like Ena.' And she asked, 'How about someone giving her the telling off she deserves?'[9]

There was by now a rival TV debate. 'While I admire the smoothness, the variety, and the timing of *Dixon of Dock Green*, it is sugary nonsense,' asserted the *Listener*'s Frederick Laws in mid-January. He compared its recent episode 'The Battle of Bellamy Court' ('dodged all the realities of housing problems, rent riots and evictions, and ended in a maddeningly soapy compromise') unfavourably to the second *Z Cars* episode 'Limping Rabbit' ('a good betting-shop squabble, an excellent genteel monster of a grandmother, and a fair hunt round the docks'). A month later *The Times* agreed – calling *Z Cars* 'realistic to a fault' – before March saw a split among *Radio Times* letter-writers. 'The actors in *Z Cars* are good, but they never for one moment give me the impression that they are anything but actors, whereas the cast in *Dock Green* seem to be utterly and entirely genuine policemen,' insisted Lady Savile of London SW7. But for 17-year-old B. E. Fargher of Birmingham 23, the plaudits belonged to 'pulsating, lively, and above all genuine'

Z Cars. 'The rough tongue, the occasional display of bad temper, and the crafty "drag" at a cigarette all tend to reassure me that policemen can be portrayed as human beings with the same frailties as the rest of us.' The respective audience figures suggested that Lady S in South Ken had already lost the battle, as *Z Cars* climbed rapidly through January and February from 9 million viewers to 15 million, in the end overtaking *Dixon*. 'This is the best series of its kind we have ever seen,' declared a plumber in early March about the bumptious upstart. 'These characters seem to have flesh on their bones and blood in their veins.'

The first series proper of *Z Cars* ended with its 13th episode at the end of March, but such had been its success that it went straight on into a further 18 episodes (seven written by the brilliant John Hopkins), which ran through until the end of July. It remained, as it had started, not everyone's favourite. 'The constant belittling and ridiculing of police officers may create a wrong image in the minds of some,' publicly argued the West Riding's chief constable, George Scott, at the end of April. 'But depicting them as they really are can do nothing but good. *Z Cars* is a typical bad example. *Dixon of Dock Green* and *The Blue Lamp* are good examples.' At about the same time, from a rather different angle, the great Methodist moral warrior Donald Soper claimed that '*Z Cars* destroys genuine respect for the law by blurring the real divisions between right and wrong,' as typified by Barlow's brutal methods of interrogation and the police assault on a child-murder suspect. The *Listener*'s Derek Hill, in his column soon afterwards on TV drama, had none of it: not only did the *Z Cars* characters 'live within shouting distance of people rather than in a writer's no-man's land' but the series as a whole 'has broken with the bland traditions of Ted Willis the policeman's P.R.O., and shows both sides of the law as equally human'. That was too much for *Dixon*'s creator and writer, who in a dignified response argued that much of the difference was down to scheduling, with *Dixon* going out at 6.30 on Saturday evenings, and that accordingly 'at least 70 per cent of the material used in *Z Cars* could not be used in our programme.' Yet strikingly – despite the critical acclaim, despite the ratings triumph – the two creators of *Z Cars*, Troy Kennedy Martin and John McGrath, were about to jump ship. 'After the cops kept appearing week after week people began to fall in love with them, and they became stars,' recalled McGrath. 'So the pressure was on to make them the subjects, rather than the device. And when the BBC finally decided that's what they were going to do, then Troy and I decided we'd had enough.'[10]

TV by this time occupied a central part in Nella Last's diary and perhaps life. Take January alone: 'such interesting types of people' (*Compact*); 'it's rare to see a plain or "ugly" face' (*Juke Box Jury*); 'a somewhat childish party game' (*Play Your Hunch*); 'Bootsie and Snudge I could NOT take'; 'even the Beat The Clock lost any "fun"' (*Sunday Night at the London Palladium* in the absence of Bruce Forsyth); 'we were so very happy for the young student who won through to £1,000' (*Double Your Money*). Other viewers had other perspectives. Sid Ward of Sheffield 11 wrote to *TV Times* to praise ITN's 'wonderful' news-reader Reginald Bosanquet ('no mistakes, coughing or mannerisms – and his English is perfectly spoken'); an industrial chemist enjoyed Danny Blanchflower on *Face to Face* ('he is a personality – so many "personalities" aren't!'); a housewife found 'far too much flashing here and there' in Ken Russell's *Monitor* film 'Pop Goes the Easel' on four young artists, including Pauline Boty; and Dennis Potter, during a stint in May as the *Daily Herald*'s TV critic, broadly welcomed *Emergency – Ward 10*'s return after the Equity strike ('a heady pill of concentrated hokum, guaranteed to anaesthetise the credulous, but harmless in small doses'), had little time for Peter Dimmock's 'aloof' presentation of *Sportsview* ('somehow manages to reduce the tingling passion of sport to the teatime comments of a retired insurance clerk') and condemned *Double Your Money* ('"Isn't that won-der-ful?" Mr Green kept saying as he radiated a distressing sincerity') for being 'a 17-inch manifesto for all that is shoddy on TV'. There was also during these months a major row. Having started in January, the BBC's Sunday-afternoon adaptation of *Oliver Twist* was nearing its end when on 18 March it showed Bill Sikes (played by Peter Vaughan) clubbing Nancy to death with a few-holds-barred realism that many viewers apparently found shocking, not helped by a cutaway shot of a trickle of water mingling with her blood. Among those shocked were the Postmaster-General's wife and 12-year-old son, prompting Reginald Bevins (supported by MPs on both sides) to condemn the scene as 'brutal and quite inexcusable' and to protest to the BBC. The direct upshot was that for the final episode, going out on 1 April, the BBC eliminated the scene showing the shadow of Sikes's body hanging from a rope. The controversy filled the correspondence pages, with perhaps the testimony of 'Mother' from Sheldon, writing to the *Birmingham Mail*, having a particular weight: 'When my children (age 10 and seven years) read about the criticisms of brutality in TV's "Oliver Twist" they commented: "Why all the fuss? We didn't see anything to worry about."'[11]

In cinema the British New Wave continued with John Schlesinger's adaptation of Stan Barstow's *A Kind of Loving* – just needing 'an ounce more courage', according to Penelope Gilliatt in the *Observer*, in order to spell out candidly that 'its real theme is not social discontent but the misogyny that has been simmering under the surface of half the inter-esting plays and films in England since 1956' – but the main action was in the theatre. Vanessa Redgrave's Rosalind in the RSC's *As You Like It* at the Aldwych not only seduced both Anthony Heap ('divinely tall and fair, well graced and eloquently poetic') and John Fowles ('better than one could imagine ... makes the role scramble up to her') but was all part of Peter Hall's increasingly irresistible footprint ('We have plans,' John Wells by the spring had him say in a spoof *Private Eye* interview, 'to build a new theatre on the South Bank which will prob-ably be called Peter Hall'); Heap was also at the Apollo to see the first night of the farce *Boeing-Boeing* ('I don't suppose it will please many of the critics,' he accurately predicted, 'but it did me and I think it will a multitude of others'); and Ann Jellicoe's *The Knack* got a mixed recep-tion, but with consistent praise for Rita Tushingham ('a gay, yelping performance') and James Bolam ('clowns with remarkable spirited authority').

For two youngish men of the theatre, both of whom had surfed the zeitgeist to remarkable effect in recent years, it was an important spring. Arnold Wesker's class-conscious National Service drama *Chips with Everything* opened at the Royal Court on 27 April (amidst, according to Heap, his 'faithful following of weirdies and ardent leftists') and was hailed by Kenneth Tynan in the *Observer* as 'furious, compassionate and unforgiving', and by Harold Hobson in the *Sunday Times* as 'the first anti-Establishment entertainment of which the Establishment need be afraid'. Not every critic joined the chorus – Bamber Gascoigne in the *Spectator* condemning Wesker's 'over-simplified sociology', Eric Keown in *Punch* arguing that he 'loads his play so heavily that deep feelings are not engaged' – but it was undoubtedly a moment, signalled by Mollie Panter-Downes writing with perhaps surprising admiration of the 'savagery' of Wesker's treatment of 'the enormous gulf that in the much-advertised new Britain still in reality yawns between the rulers and the ruled; the failure to communicate across it, even with good will on both sides; and the inevitable flattening out of the apathetically resigned and the rebellious alike in the caste machine'. Just over a week later, it was the turn of Lionel Bart at the Adelphi. *Blitz!*, his new, expensively staged musical set in the East End during the six months beginning in September 1940, received huge publicity ahead of the opening, but did not quite prove to be the 'whacking, whopping, walloping hit' that the *Daily Telegraph*'s W. A. Darlington forecast. 'A tawdry, ramshackle show,' scribbled Heap; 'the plot woofles and splutters along like a dud incendiary,' thought the *Daily Herald*; Milton Shulman in the *Evening Standard* condemned Bart's 'lush sentimentality'; Gascoigne found 'no scene touched with imagination'; 'frankly a tin-pan-alley musical', reckoned the *New Statesman*; and for Noël Coward, connoisseur of patriotic corn, it was 'as long as the real thing, and twice as noisy'.[12]

Pop music remained in a state – at least as viewed in retrospect from a particular vantage point – of suspended animation, though of course little-noticed things were happening. In early April the 20-year-old Brian Jones (middle-class from Cheltenham, a letter just published in *Disc* praising authentic American rhythm and blues) met Mick Jagger and Keith Richards at the Ealing Club; while on the Beatles front, Decca predictably turned them down, Brian Epstein got the boys into suits, EMI (in the form of Parlophone) at last came through with a recording contract – and the group appeared on national radio. *Teenagers Turn* was on the Light Programme on Thursday, 8 March at five o'clock for half an hour; top of the bill were The Trad Lads; and the rival attraction on BBC television was *Crackerjack*, with Ronnie Carroll as guest star, ten days before coming fourth-equal in the Eurovision Song Contest with 'Ring-a-Ding Girl'. Generally, it was not a radio scene that enthused a Cambridge 16-year-old. '"Whirling around the kitchen," I should think,' Syd Barrett wrote in February to his girlfriend as he lay in bed with glandular fever listening to Desmond Carrington presenting *Housewives' Choice*. 'Just imagine all the great fat old housewives jumping around the kitchen table!' The two main television options were still *Juke Box Jury* and *Thank Your Lucky Stars* (where from February a Birmingham teenager, Janice Nicholls, was giving it 'foive'), with a BBC report on the former finding that over-30s especially disliked 'moronic faces' in the audience and that the main gripe for under-30s was those jury members who 'don't know anything about pop music, criticise harshly, are facetious, wordy, rude or ill-mannered, or try to steal the show', with Katie Boyle and Nancy Spain particularly disliked. Soon afterwards, *Melody Maker* readers chose their ideal jury, with Helen Shapiro ('charming – and she knows pop tastes') and Jane Asher ('represents the teenage point of view and talks sense') as especially favoured, though with one or two plumping for Fidel Castro ('because he's a bit of a rebel'). Cliff Richard and the Shadows, meanwhile, continued in their pomp: Cliff's 36-day sell-out tour early in the year caused pandemonium everywhere, and the Shads released the chart-topping 'Wonderful Land' – 'probably written as a hymn to America, its glamour, its colour and its endless skies', reckons Bob Stanley, but to his ears 'a British dream of the future, the primary-coloured optimism of post-war Britain, people moving to the new towns ringing London, the space and light in the bright open spaces of Crawley and Stevenage . . .' Inevitably it was Cliff who topped the male-singer category in *Melody Maker*'s 1962 Pop Poll, alongside Helen Shapiro (female singer), the Springfields (vocal group) and David Jacobs (disc jockey). No category alas for novelty artists, but the genre still flourished, with Mike Sarne's 'Come Outside' the latest contender. 'One of the most interesting comedy discs for ages by a British artist,' declared *MM* in early May. 'An ingenious laugh featuring Wendy Richard "feeding" Sarne with Cockney jargon.'[13]

The timing was getting interesting. 'Contemporary poetry began in 1962 – in April to be precise – with the publication of A. Alvarez's Penguin anthology *The New Poetry*, the first two volumes of the Penguin Modern Poets series, and the first number of Ian Hamilton's little magazine, the *Review*,' observed William Wootten exactly half a century later. He pointed to a particular aspect of that celebrated inter-val between the end of the *Lady Chatterley* ban (November 1960) and the arrival of the first Beatles LP (March 1963): 'On the one hand, sales of D.H. Lawrence's book had greatly enriched Penguin Books, which allowed the recently appointed chief editor, Tony Godwin, to pursue ambitious new projects; on the other, the Fab Four had yet to ensure that the new and relevant would be more culturally synonymous with Pop than with Lawrentian intensities and critical seriousness.' Hamilton's emphasis was on tough-mindedness, and the first half-dozen PMPs (three in each volume) included Lawrence Durrell, Elizabeth Jennings, R. S. Thomas and Kingsley Amis, but most attention at the time was focused on Al Alvarez's anthology – partly on the weighting of its selection, heavily playing up Ted Hughes and Thom Gunn (thirty-eight poems between them) and heavily playing down the so-1950s 'Movement' poets (Larkin doing best with eight), but above all on the editor's combative introduction, entitled 'The New Poetry, *or* Beyond the Gentility Principle'. 'The concept of gentility still reigns supreme,' declared Alvarez of most contemporary poets, specifically mentioning Larkin as a main culprit. 'And gentility is a belief that life is always more or less orderly, people always more or less polite, their emotions and habits more or less decent and more or less controllable; that God, in short, is more or less good.' At the end, after comparing Larkin's 'At Grass' unfavourably to Hughes's 'A Dream of Horses' ('unlike Larkin's, Hughes's horses have a violent, impending presence'), he called on English poets to seek to combine 'the openness to experience, the psychological insight and integrity of D.H. Lawrence' with 'the technical skill and formal intelligence of T.S. Eliot'. The anthology itself, all-male, wilfully excluded Elizabeth Jennings, who in her *Listener* review, after noting Alvarez was 'most interested in the sort of poetry which is rough in texture and which communicates a sense of tamed violence or disturbance', asserted that 'his dogmatism, when carefully analysed, proves to be little more than a collection of emotionally charged prejudices.' There were some harsh words too, a little later in the spring, for Anthony Burgess's short novel *A Clockwork Orange*, whose conception had been inspired, he would recall, by returning to England from Malaya, living in Hove and finding on the south coast 'a new British phenomenon – the violence of teenage gangs'. For the *TLS* it was all in 'questionable taste', for Jeremy Brooks in the *Sunday Times* it was 'a very ordinary, brutal and psychologically shallow story', for Penelope Mortimer in the *Daily Express* it was simply 'incomprehensible'. But one young novelist and critic saw it differently. 'What is remarkable is the incredible teenage argot that Mr Burgess invents to tell the story in,' proclaimed Malcolm Bradbury in *Punch*. 'All Mr Burgess's powers as a comic writer, which are considerable, have gone into this rich language of his inverted Utopia. If you can stomach the horrors, you'll enjoy the manner.'[14]

Verbal dexterity was not F. R. Leavis's kind of thing. On 28 February, almost three years since C. P. Snow had delivered his famous Cambridge lecture calling for the literary and scientific cultures to come closer together and viewing them as equally indispensable, the hugely influential Cambridge critic – inspiring more than one generation of English teachers – used another lecture, also in Cambridge, to seek to demolish Snow's reputation. 'If confidence in oneself as a master-mind, qualified by capacity, insight and knowledge to pronounce authoritatively on the frightening problems of our civilisation, is genius,' Leavis began, 'then there can be no doubt about Sir Charles Snow's.' There followed a relentless barrage of abuse. Snow was 'portentously ignorant', indeed 'intellectually as undistinguished as it is possible to be'; *The Two Cultures* itself, which Leavis had read in book form only the previous summer, 'exhibits an utter lack of intellectual distinction and an embarrassing vulgarity of style'; while as for Snow the novelist, 'he can't be said to know what a novel is . . . never was dialogue more inept . . . he is utterly without a glimmer of what creative literature is, or why it matters.' The lecture was printed in full on 9 March in the *Spectator*, which over the next few weeks printed an avalanche of responses, mainly hostile to Leavis:

Such a silly exhibition. (*Dame Edith Sitwell*)

Barren . . . malevolent. (*Lord Boothby*)

Leavis has not given me one single, valid reason for lowering my opinion of Snow. (*Susan Hill*)

The boomerang of the year. (*Ronald Millar*)

A man may be ignorant of history and slipshod in his mode of expression, as C.P. Snow often is, and yet be able to state an important truth. (*Peter Jay*)

Snow is right; there *are* two cultures; no amount of clichés can disguise the fact. (*Gavin Ewart*)

'I say, Leavis!' the retired Eton schoolmaster George Lyttelton wrote to the publisher Rupert Hart-Davis on the 28th. 'Have you ever known opinion so unanimous about a man's spite, bad manners, injustice, bad English and conceit?' Perhaps the most damning verdict came from the young, rapidly rising George Steiner in May's *Encounter*. It had been 'an ignoble performance' in which Leavis had 'yielded entirely to a streak of shallow, arrogant cruelty'; the blunt repetitiveness of the charges had evoked 'the shadow of a grotesque, intellectual McCarthyism'; and in terms of the positive message, it all amounted to little more than an already over-familiar 'ceremonial dance before the dark god, D.H. Lawrence'. Yet there was a defence. Leavis's opponents, his publisher Ian Parsons observed in the *Spectator*, had over the years been doing to him much what he was now doing to Snow: 'Almost any literary luncheon, poetry prize-giving, public lecture or critical review has been seized upon by them as an opportunity for "having a go" at Leavis.' In essence, that was probably true. 'Many years ago – it must have been in the late 1950s – I attended a literary function somewhere in Mayfair,' recalled the writer Dan Jacobson in 1995.

> Many publishers were there, together with a good sprinkling of literary journalists and editors: soft-faced men who looked as though they had done well out of culture. Someone made a speech. What was said would long since have gone out of my mind, were it not that at one point the speaker referred to an issue or problem on which, he said, everyone was agreed – 'except of course for the *egregious* Dr Leavis in Cambridge'. At this there rose from the glass-clutching throng, into the gin-scented air, a sound I had last heard in the junior quad of my school, when the boys turned in a gang against some wretch who had said or done the wrong thing, or was wearing the wrong kind of socks. Between a jeer and a prolonged, self-satisfied snigger, it was not a pleasant sound.

'For those moments,' added Jacobson, 'the party came close to turning itself into an incarnation of "the London literary scene" that Leavis referred to so often in his writing: as a malign coven of enemies, a corrupt clique or claque, an insidious, powerful conspiracy united against him.'[15]

Cliques and claques too in the somewhat febrile world of the New

Left. 'Early in 1962, when the affairs of the *New Left Review* were in some confusion,' wrote one of the movement's founding fathers, E. P. Thompson, three years later, 'the New Left Board invited an able contributor, Perry Anderson, to take over the editorship.' Anderson himself was a wealthy, manifestly intelligent, Eton-and-Oxford 22-year-old, and a classic Thompsonian passage explained what happened next:

> We found (as we had hoped) in Comrade Anderson the decision and the intellectual coherence necessary to ensure the review's continuance. More than that, we discovered that we had appointed a veritable Dr Beeching of the socialist intelligentsia. All the uneconomic branch-lines and socio-cultural sidings of the New Left which were, in any case, carrying less and less traffic, were abruptly closed down. The main lines of the review underwent an equally ruthless modernisation. Old Left steam-engines were swept off the tracks; wayside halts ('Commitment,' 'What Next for C.N.D.?', 'Women in Love') were boarded up; and the lines were electrified for the speedy traffic from the marxistentialist Left Bank.

Soon, added Thompson, 'the founders of the review discovered, to their chagrin, that the Board lived on a branch-line which, after rigorous intellectual costing, had been found uneconomic.' And, 'finding ourselves redundant we submitted to dissolution.' Had it in effect been a coup? That over the years would be the version propagated by Thompson and his supporters, a version strongly denied by Anderson – who, given that Thompson privately conceded in March 1962 that 'the Board should cease to pretend that it "leads" in any way a new left movement since it has proved itself incompetent to do so,' may well be right. In any case, what mattered more was the fundamentally changed nature and feel of the *NLR* itself. Phyllis Willmott, on being shown by Raphael (as he now was) Samuel in April 1962 a copy of the latest issue (only part-edited by Anderson and including a detailed study by Samuel of the slum-clearance programme), thought it 'quite different, quite excitingly good and a real "break-through" to something better than the old verbose mixture of "depth" and confusion'; yet as Anderson proceeded to put his stamp on the magazine, it is unlikely that she would have remained so positive. 'Anderson had flinty views on what to do with the *Review*,' reflects Fred Inglis, a reader through it all:

> He would ditch the uneasy mixture of up-to-date journalism, CND and anti-Tory polemics, investigative exposures and movie reviews, *ULR* moralising and *New Reasoner* economics. The new version of the *Review* would be a trans-continental and trans-Atlantic journal of neo-Marxist theory with a strongly revisionist turn, taking its lead from Sartre and Louis Althusser, a name then barely known in Britain, from early Marx and the unheard-of Italian, Antonio Gramsci. It would keep faith with the cultural emphasis that had made its signature, but attach it to a more exigent and rigorous sociology than the old Marxist historians had ever read. Weber would be as much cited as Bernstein, Lévi-Strauss as Engels.[16]

It is a fair characterisation. In its first two years the *NLR* had been empirically grounded and closely in touch with what was actually happening in the Britain of the early 1960s; that grounding subsequently almost entirely disappeared, as theory supplanted practice and Britain itself no longer had priority in the New Left world-view. Something may have been gained as a result, but undeniably something precious was lost.

The diarists for their part remained grounded in the day-to-day empirical:

> Took myself off to Bearman's for their remnant sale. Bought two pieces for shirt and blouse for Ione. Hope they will do. Not very experienced at that. Clothes are so dear, if I succeed in my needlework I am pounds in. Waited ages at Green Man, Leytonstone, in wind while traffic oozed fumes all into me, for a bus to Bakers Arms, and decided it was not worth it. Joined a great queue at Bakers Arms for Chingford bus. 'On top only.' The cigarette smoke! (*Judy Haines, 12 January*)
>
> Quite reasonable food – English and Chinese (we chose moderately – Chinese dishes – not daring to try the exciting-sounding real ones). Spotless service, and charming – even beautiful – white-coated Chinese waiters. (*Madge Martin, 3 February, Chinese restaurant in Ship Street, Oxford*)

At 8.31 we had the last of present series of 'Beyond Our Ken' with Kenneth Horne. I like Rodney and Charles, two wags. (*Judy Haines, 22 February*)

Left 19 bus at Holborn. Walked thro' Drury Lane. Asked a woman to see me across the road but she ignored me, an elderly man came to the rescue. Walked through Long Acre into Bow Street, a policeman saw me across. Went thro' Covent Garden very doddery, Teddy boy with beat-nik girl left his canoodling to see me across another road, slipped on a cabbage leaf and lay helpless covered with mud. Man hauled me up & raised his hat & departed. So shaken asked a very young policeman to call a taxi. He hurried round the streets searching for one. Taxi-driver was Jewish & talked to me thro' sliding panel. Was held up so long meter cost soared yet he refused to accept anything but 5/-. I urged him to accept 2/- tip but he would NOT take it. He told me he had lived in Stoke Newington but now has a house in Edgware. (*Gladys Langford, 23 March*)

Phoned Gas Board yet again; rude and uncouth response. (*Hugh Selbourne, 26 March*)

What a treat to have a fire after days without even if it is in the new smokeless grate. (*Gladys Hague, 31 March*)

8.28 a.m. I walked to Lion Gate, Kew Gardens. At the school near the north end of Acton Lane, the Scottish contingent of the ban-the-bomb marchers was assembling; others were walking south down Acton Lane and several others assembling on Acton Green, including the Young Communists' League. I heard 2 women talking, apparently about the marchers. One described them as 'a lot of scum'; she said they drank cider from bottles in the street. On Acton Green a lad was trying to sell the 'Guardian'. (*Henry St John, 23 April*)

As the forecast was not too good and we take no notice of it anyhow, we decided we would go to Bradford and have a look at the Spring exhi-bition of 'art' in the Cartwright Hall. We very soon finished with that. I think this is one of the maddest exhibitions we have ever seen since we started to go. There are not half-a-dozen pictures that we could under-stand at all, and the so-called 'sculpture' has to be seen to be believed. I could find as effective pieces in the coal-cellar. I wonder how long people will put up with the spending of money on such nonsense. (*Kenneth Preston, 5 May*)

I love coming out at Archway and getting on the bus up the hill with the feeling of having reached the freshness of the 'heights'. Almost – dare I admit it – a feeling of reaching the 'haven' of suburbia? (*Phyllis Willmott, 8 May*)

Haines was one of the more tolerant diarists, but even she came close to losing it on Saturday the 19th. 'Embarrassed by greengrocer delivering my Wednesday eggs today,' she recorded. 'I am fed up with him, especially as he left me 2lbs greens instead of "green apples" just before hols. and had the cheek to charge them. I showed him them rotten in dustbin, too.'[17]

The diarists also recorded a still difficult industrial scene, as Selwyn Lloyd's 'pay pause' morphed into the 'guiding light' policy of more modified wage restraint. 'Much industrial unrest,' noted Selbourne on 19 January. 'Postman, GPO engineers, Equity actors, coal-miners, redundancies on Railways etc.' Ten days later a Tube strike managed, in Anthony Heap's words, 'to jam all the main roads leading into and through central London with cars'. In February the railwaymen settled, on terms which allowed Macmillan to reflect that 'three hours' talk' and 'much consumption of whisky' had been worth it, not least to banish at least temporarily the press's depiction of 'the ageing and feeble Premier'. From a government perspective, however, the terms were much less good in mid-May, when the Transport and General Workers' Union's Frank Cousins managed to secure from the port employers a 9-per-cent deal for the dockers, way above the 2½-per-cent guiding-light recommendation. 'Incomes policy has come a crasher,' noted Alec Cairncross, the government's economic adviser, who soon afterwards had lunch with Selwyn Lloyd and the editor of *The Times*. 'He said public would have felt more favourable to pay pause had they seen some prospect of useful results,' Cairncross recorded Sir William Haley as remarking. 'But idea that prices might stop rising still seems implausible to them.' The *Economist*'s predictable headline was 'Surrender at the Docks', the paper adding that 'the one sensible remark made after this disaster was Mr Enoch Powell's observation that when the line of incomes policy has been breached in one sector, this makes it all the more necessary to hold the line with redoubled vigour in other sectors.' Powell himself as Minister of Health had been successfully holding the line against the pay claim of the nurses, possessed of far less industrial muscle than the dockers, and Mollie Panter-Downes was not alone in observing that 'this all looks unpleasantly like one wage scale for the strong, who can strike, and another for dedicated public servants, who cannot or will not' – and that 'the contrast has been damaging for the Government.' Still, as Macmillan reflected in his memoirs, 'I could not help noticing that while berating the concession to the dockers, everybody was, in fact, delighted with the fact that the strike was off.'

The other half of Lloyd's economic strategy was apparently making some belated progress. In January the unions finally agreed to join the employers on the National Economic Development Council ('Neddy', though at this stage sometimes known as 'Ned'), which held its first meeting in March. 'Loud cheers for Ned!' acclaimed the *Economist* two months later about the new body's commitment to achieving a growth rate of 4 per cent per annum over the next five years; while in the *Sunday Times*, hailing a 'realistic growth policy', William Rees-Mogg expressed satisfaction that, after a long period of adherence to the primacy of stability, British economic policy had now 'moved into a new and definitely more optimistic phase'. At least one politician and one economist had their doubts. 'Mrs Thatcher warned,' noted the *Coventry Evening Telegraph* in February about her address at a wine-and-cheese-tasting party organised by local female Tories, 'that this Council [ie, Neddy] would not be a panacea for all their troubles.' And, talking in the spring on the Third Programme, a former economic adviser to the Treasury, John Brunner, argued that the new cult of planning and growth was 'really just a form of wishful thinking' and that, 'rather than recognise that a higher rate of growth represents a serious challenge to deeply held values and customs, we prefer the easy way out apparently offered by the N.E.D.C.' He elaborated:

> To do significantly better calls for little short of a revolution in our attitudes, customs, values, and institutions. We would have to create a much more ruthless, competitive, materialistic society. We are fully entitled to say we do not want such a society. We are not entitled to demand faster growth and expect business, and indeed life, to continue as usual.

In short, 'as Mr Forster would say, let us "only connect".'[18]

The Tories by this time, after their golden run in the 1950s, were struggling to connect. 'This evening watched Harold Macmillan on TV,' noted Hugh Selbourne in late January. 'He made an empty speech, full of platitudes and drivel.' By early February the inevitable was happening. 'All the Sunday press,' recorded Macmillan himself, 'is full of gossip about the attacks on me by Tory back-benchers. It is an obscure and may become a dangerous situation, but I hope to ride this storm.' There followed on 14 March perhaps the most famous by-election result of the century, and the moment that marked the beginning of the end of the two-party monopoly, as the Liberal candidate Eric Lubbock (local, a palpable gent, an effective campaigner) at the Kent commuter seat of Orpington overturned a Conservative majority of almost 15,000 into a stunning Liberal victory of almost 8,000. Macmillan's public take was the familiar Edwardian imperturbability – 'If it is due to temporary emotion it will pass like the wearing of the type of trousers I wore when I was eighteen years old' – but later in March he set down his real thoughts:

It is the revolt of the middle classes or lower middle classes, who resent the vastly improved conditions of the working classes, and are envious of the apparent prosperity and luxury of the 'rich' – whether they live on office expenses, capital gains, or capital. These white collar 'little men' – clerks, civil servants, etc., have [in the past] voted Conservative 'to keep Labour out'. Now (especially at by-elections) they are voting Liberal to 'give the Government a smack in the eye'.

Then there is fashion. It is getting dull to be a young Conservative. It is not at all smart to go Labour. Liberal is not in the Establishment; has a flavour of 'something different'.

Most of all, it is a revolt against all the unsolved problems. The Bomb (it favours the abolition of the British independent deterrent); relations with Russia; NATO; Berlin; Rhodesia . . . But it springs most from the Government's inability to keep the economy on an even course of continuous progress. It deplores 'Stop and Go' or 'Acceleration and Brake'. It wants enormously *increased* expenditure, and *reduced* taxation. It wants a larger army, without conscription. It wants wage stability, without any restraint. In a word, it wants what we all want and know we can't have.

The Pay Pause – the Government's policy – has offended dons, school-masters, school-teachers, civil servants, clerks, nurses, public utility workers, railwaymen, and all the rest. But perhaps it is most resented by the doctors, dons, nurses, etc., who feel that they are *relatively* ill paid, compared to the high wages which they hear about coming in to the ordinary artisans' household. Anyway, it is a portent, and the Tories are very worried . . .

Soon afterwards, on the 28th, the *Daily Mail* published the sensational National Opinion Poll (NOP) news that the Liberals were now ahead nationally, with the Tories in third place. At this point the pressure on Selwyn Lloyd to produce a sparkling, politically uplifting Budget, due on 9 April, was intense, but despite a sweetener to owner-occupiers through the promise to abolish Schedule A taxation he failed to deliver. 'The government,' notes the historian of Gallup, 'was thought to be doing too much for the well-to-do, too little for the working class and for people living on small pensions or on small incomes, and on balance doing too little to level up the classes.' At this point there was still a potential two and a half years to go before the next election, but later in the spring the Shadow Chancellor, James Callaghan, started making regular trips to Nuffield College, Oxford in order to become better versed in fiscal, industrial and monetary matters. 'I still do not have clear in my head,' he wrote to an Oxford economist ahead of the first seminar about the apparently insoluble 'stop-go' problem, 'how we can run British industry on a high level and still pay our way overseas.'[19]

There were moments during the first half of 1962 when old England seemed under serious attack. Macmillan and the Queen both gamely attended, on separate evenings, *Beyond the Fringe* ('When I've a spare evening,' said Peter Cook's PM in a late addition to the script for the benefit of the real PM, 'there's nothing I like better than to wander over to a theatre and sit there listening to a group of sappy, urgent, vibrant young satirists, with a stupid great grin spread all over my silly old face'); the American comedian Lenny Bruce ('a staccato of reminiscence and fantasy', noted Tom Stoppard, 'mowing down conventional barriers of language and subject until the unspeakable has become eminently, hilariously speakable') spent a month at The Establishment club in Soho becoming a hate figure for much of the press; and *Private Eye* started to take off, announcing in early April what it fundamentally believed in: 'Balls to the lot of them.' Pearson Phillips, a *Daily Mail* feature writer, used the occasion of the royal visit to try to see the bigger picture and in so doing part-reassure his paper's readers:

> The Queen at *Beyond the Fringe* – in a way this is the unkindest cut of all, the last twist of the knife. The *Fringe* men were to have been the satirical stormtroopers on the wing of Britain's post-war rebellion. They were to have drawn blood. Instead, they have been assimilated. Court jesters, by appointment. No wonder our British rebels are sad and disillusioned. From John Osborne to Lord Russell the whole glumly articulate group are showing signs of discouragement, despair, and general intellectual wear and tear.
>
> Who can blame them? For the past six years – ever since *Look Back in Anger* – they have been mounting a powerful assault on what they see as the flabby, self-satisfied face of the well-bred philistines who preside over the destiny of Great Britain and the Commonwealth. It would be very wrong to underestimate the power of this artistic, social and intellectual cleansing operation. And yet, what has it achieved?
>
> Nothing, they feel. Nothing at all. The same kind of people are still on top and show no signs of budging or being budged. Damn you, England.

Yet, argued Phillips, the 'vague, flabby jelly-fish of opinion and power' *was* shifting, 'imperceptibly but inexorably like a glacier', as Britain made its uneasy transition 'from a rich imperial Power to a medium poor one':

> You can detect the shift in all sorts of ways. Go to the City and see what the climate of opinion is on the question of State control compared with what it was five years ago. Go to a meeting of headmasters and see how they have quietly shifted their ground on the role and function of the public schools in the last few years. Look how the Labour Party – for that matter – has picked up the right direction on the role of nationalisation. See what a shift there has been in thought on capital punishment . . .

The Crazy Gang (Bud Flanagan et al) were never going to be part of that shift. On Saturday, 19 May at London's Victoria Palace, they gave their farewell performance, televised the following evening. A packed-out theatre included John Betjeman ('a very sad evening'), Noël Coward ('a horrid, sad evening – I shall miss them dearly'), Peter Sellers and Ingrid Bergman; all the familiar, intensely nostalgic routines and songs (including 'Underneath the Arches', 'Run Rabbit Run' and 'Maybe It's Because I'm a Londoner') were performed; and at the end, reported *The Times*, 'a beautifully worded telegram from Sir Laurence Olivier was read out.'[20]

———

Six days later, over twenty years since its medieval predecessor had been destroyed, the new Coventry Cathedral was consecrated. The architectural critics delivered their judgement: to Kenneth Robinson, 'a great and humbling building', albeit 'a box of functional tricks'; to the out-and-out modernist Reyner Banham, 'a traditional cathedral re-styled', involving 'no reassessment of cathedral functions', that altogether amounted to 'the worst set-back to English church architecture for a very long time'; and to Ian Nairn (calling himself 'a disillusioned though still firm believer in modern architecture') 'a terrible disappointment', essentially because 'the enthusiasm which is the mainspring of Sir Basil Spence's architecture may here have outrun his technique'. The service itself on Friday the 25th had its drama. 'The Queen's yellow outfit clashed with John Piper's new canary-yellow copes,' notes the obituarist of the Bishop of Coventry, Cuthbert Bardsley. 'The Lord Mayor fainted with a terrible clatter of municipal chains and had to be revived by the Bishop of Birmingham. As the sidesman attempted to pile the collection on to gold salvers there was a continual cascade of coins to the floor in front of the stony gaze of the Queen.' Both television channels covered the event – 'the long service was beautiful, moving and dignified,' thought Madge Martin (watching it at a friend's house in Oxford), 'except for the dull sermon by the Archbishop of Canterbury' – and the critic Maurice Wiggin observed that Sir Kenneth Clark on ITV 'had the courage to acknowledge a fact which the BBC would not face – the fact that just possibly a new cathedral is difficult to design because it simply is not wanted by the mass of the people'. That evening, after all the dignitaries had left, some 20,000 Coventrians and others filed through, with queues stretching back 300 yards, and a local paper gathered some vox pop:

> I think it is really lovely. The building is splendid. But the fleche still reminds me of a wireless mast. (*Mr G.R. Johnson, lecturer in telecommunications at the local Lanchester College of Technology*)
>
> It is so different, to one as old as I am. I am so used to the old cathedrals. (*Miss F. E. Butterfield, 86, from Brighton*)
>
> Very fabulous – the most fabulous place I have ever known. (*Margaret West, 14, from Rugby*)
>
> A very nice building. I have seen temples in Delhi, and I would compare it with them. (*Mr P. D. Patel, 24, from India*)
>
> The old cathedrals are out-dated, in my opinion. We are now living in a modern age. I think this cathedral is wonderful. (*Mr J. Williams, 68, retired commercial traveller from Preston*)

Five days after the consecration, on Wednesday the 30th, the new building's complementary set piece took place: the first performance, broadcast live on the Home Service, of Benjamin Britten's *War Requiem*. 'Surely a masterpiece of our time,' proclaimed one critic, Desmond Shawe-Taylor, while Mollie Panter-Downes found Britten's 'warning' about the folly (and pity) of war 'infinitely more shattering than any marches to Aldermaston'. And she went on: 'It seemed fitting that Coventry should be the first to hear such a passionate denunciation of what killed its cathedral and many of its citizens and remains the adversary that no splendid, straggling archangel, even St Michael, has yet properly finished off for us. But we will try, says the new cathedral, and it is this spirit, perhaps, that is making the world beat a path to its door.'[21]

Of course, it was not only bombs that destroyed the old and beautiful. On 28 May, Newcastle's Town Planning Committee took 19 minutes to decide to demolish much of Eldon Square – designed by John Dobson and developed by Richard Grainger in the 1820s – in order to build a new shopping centre. 'Gain and Loss' was the local *Journal*'s judicious editorial the next morning: 'reluctant agreement' that the proposed redevelopment was 'justifiable' in terms of 'a hard business appraisal', and also that it would be hailed as a great improvement by 'most citizens'; yet, 'for our part, we just hate the involved demolition of the Dobson terraces, and the inevitable loss of a dignity of form and character the architect created for us.' Later on the 29th, a prominent local Tory and former Lord Mayor, William McKeag, came out fighting:

> The disciples of destruction have been on the march for some time. We must try to prevent the present trend from developing into an uncontrollable orgy . . . The decision of the planning committee to destroy Eldon Square shocks me beyond measure. I say 'shocks,' not 'surprises,' because I have almost ceased to be surprised at the enormities our so-called planners are prepared to perpetrate in the sacred name of progress.

The *Evening Chronicle* also quoted one of the square's residents, Mrs Sarah Sutherland: 'I wonder what will happen to all the old people who sit in the square. It is the only place in the city centre they can rest.' The controversy continued over the next week or so. A letter to the *Journal* from Veronica Nisbet of Newcastle 2 called the news 'a bombshell to an unsuspecting public'; Labour's local leader, T. Dan Smith, justified the decision at a meeting of the city council ('If we failed to achieve this stage of redevelopment, then the whole conception of the central area would be incapable of achievement. This is not out of spite . . .'); and in a television debate with McKeag, a proponent of the redevelopment, Dr Henry Russell, claimed – with a large degree of exaggeration – that the square was a 'rabbit warren of tenements'.[22] Not that any of this really signified: some 140 years on, the die had been cast.

'The ageless, classless, nostalgic appeal of the whole thing is quite irresistible,' noted Anthony Heap on 25 May (the same day as Coventry Cathedral's consecration) after going to the first night of *The Black and White Minstrel Show*, now replacing the Crazy Gang at the Victoria Palace. Next day, Labour's Barbara Castle revealed that the Minister of Works had agreed to her request to have the lavatory turnstiles in the royal parks removed forthwith; on Monday the 28th, Macmillan told the Cabinet about his intention to go full steam ahead for reflation, and Stephen Spender had a pub lunch with Ray Gosling ('teddy-boy appearance . . . exaggerated gestures . . . lively and observant . . . on the whole, I didn't feel too optimistic about Ray G.'); and on Tuesday, the *FT*'s headline about the new exhibition at the Tate was 'Francis Bacon – Too Shrill a Cry?', the Manchester authorities unveiled their vision for the comprehensive redevelopment of Hulme (including the number of pubs to go down from fourteen to two) and a meeting at Lord's of MCC's Cricket Enquiry Committee decided 'to retain the status quo of the amateur'. The round of county fixtures starting on Wednesday the 30th saw two debuts: at Gravesend, Henry Blofeld's as a cricket reporter ('glorious day . . . drying wicket . . . splendidly aggressive innings . . .'), followed by a pub in Rochester where he had 'a filthy dinner of brown Windsor soup and very old mutton with underboiled potatoes'; and at Liverpool, the West Ham footballer Geoff Hurst playing his only match for Essex and being caught off Ken Higgs for 3. Perhaps he should have been in Chile, where 'the Nelson spirit was not enough' as England went down 2–1 to Hungary in their opening World Cup match. Over the early days of June, as the warm weather continued after a very cold spring, *Private Eye*'s Willie Rushton had some cruel fun with his depiction of 'Tony Halfcock' as an egocentric comedian who had abandoned everyone around him ('I like God, but it's time for us to go our separate ways'); Judy Haines went to *A Kind of Loving* ('not the sort of subject for filming, I reckon'); Harold Wilson pronounced at the Worthing conference of the Boilermakers' Society that 'the Labour Party is a moral crusade or it is nothing'; England beat Argentina 3–1 ('young' Bobby Moore, on his third appearance, showing 'courage and rare intelligence in his use of the ball'); the Football League voted in Oxford United to replace Accrington Stanley; and a full-page, Beaverbrook-funded statement by Field Marshal Viscount Montgomery appeared in the daily press ('I say we must not join Europe . . . Let us rather continue to rely on our own strength and judgement'). On Wednesday the 6th, by-elections at West Derbyshire and Middlesbrough West produced poor results for the Tories, seven horses fell in chaotic scenes at the Derby, and the Beatles had their first recording session with George Martin ('Let me know if there's anything you don't like,' he said helpfully, getting the response from the other George, 'Well, for a start, I don't like your tie'). Next day, England managed an 'insipid' goalless draw against Bulgaria to edge through to the quarter-finals; at the Arts Theatre, David Rudkin's brutal *Afore Night Come* (set in a Midlands pear orchard) generated predictable complaints about 'meaningless violence' and 'tedious bestiality' but powerfully conveyed the native workers' atavistic hatred of outsiders; and on TV the judging panel for *Miss Interflora-G.P.O. 1962* comprised the Countess of Longford, 'A Psychiatrist' and Mr C. W. Davies (Telephone Manager, Centre Area). Friday the 8th began with Ronald Bryden in the *Spectator* acclaiming Iris Murdoch's new novel *An Unofficial Rose* ('with each book she moves forward in mastery, setting herself and encompassing larger goals, advancing steadily towards the great, deep comic classic she is surely going to write within our lifetimes') and *The Times*'s Scottish correspondent reporting, six days ahead of polling, on the West Lothian by-election. There he found Labour's 29-year-old Old Etonian candidate, Tam Dalyell, 'already moving at a good gallop' and 'calling at scores of houses each day'; while on going into the committee rooms in Bathgate of the Scottish Nationalist candidate William Wolfe, seeking to revive his party's fortunes after a decade or more in the doldrums, he heard the recorded voice of Andy Stewart singing 'Tunes of Glory'. That evening, David Turner's Jonsonian *Semi-Detached*, arguably the great modern play (understanding, not condemnatory) about the suburban lower middle class, had its premiere at Coventry's Belgrade Theatre, in the process launching the career of Leonard Rossiter; and on the radio, the *Any Questions?* panel was asked about the ethics of going on holiday to Spain. 'I think it is a mistake when we appear to be giving support to Franco and his hideous regime, but I'm all in favour of English people going on holiday and seeing for themselves,' replied a youngish Labour MP, John Stonehouse. 'What I am opposed to are these coach tours, these packaged holidays. I mean, people go with groups of other English, they stay in hotels which are catering with English breakfasts, English lunches, English dinners, cups of tea whenever they're required. The people who go on these package tours hardly ever see the people in the countries that they visit. I'm all opposed to them . . .'[23]

Saturday, 9 June – the culmination of a week of celebrations of the centenary of the Tyneside anthem, 'The Blaydon Races' – was T. Dan Smith's day. A mass parade, with 120 decorated floats and 20 brass bands (including the Cowpen and Crofton Workmen's Band, the Dawdon Lodge Band and the Hetton Silver Band) made its way along the 5 miles from the city centre to Blaydon; much of that route was along the Scotswood Road, with 'many people' living in streets off it 'celebrating with street parties'; and generally there was music, fireworks and – almost unthinkably – all-day drinking in the pubs. A celebration of a hundred years of materially impoverished but emotionally largely stable working-class life? Or a celebration of the slum clearance and large-scale redevelopment that was now happening and the promise of what lay ahead? For Smith himself, who had pushed through the lavish celebrations against bitter local Conservative opposition, it was overwhelmingly the latter. Sloping up on the north side of Scotswood Road was his cherished, Swedish-inspired Cruddas Park development: six 15-storey blocks of flats in varying states of construction, with the first completed one, The Willows, to be officially opened that day by the Labour leader Hugh Gaitskell. This Gaitskell duly did, accompanied by Smith, as well as unveiling a modernist, 13-foot-high sculpture by Kenneth Ford (young and bearded) that had been commissioned by Smith to mark the 'rebirth' of Scotswood Road. Next day, Newcastle's Sunday paper described all the events of a special day that most people seem to have hugely enjoyed. It also ran an interview with 15-year-old Helen Shapiro, who had been appearing all week at the Empire Sunderland on a bill that included Lenny the Lion, Dave Allen and an animal act called Captain Fleming's Chimpanzees. 'She is a typical modern teenager with little knowledge of the past (the war is just a vague bit of history to her),' observed the interviewer. 'She has no sentimental feelings about anything that has happened before her own life.'[24]

Afterword

A few weeks later, one of the emblematic books of the era appeared: Anthony Sampson's *Anatomy of Britain*. Britain, argued Sampson in his closing pages, had been through two distinct phases since the war, the first of them essentially static: 'The social revolution of 1945, though profound, took ten years to show its effects on spending. London's skyline, broken by bomb damage, remained almost unchanged. Newspapers rationed their newsprint. The BBC was unchallenged . . .' The second phase, he went on, started in 1957: 'Within two years, the credit squeeze ended, skyscrapers rushed up, supermarkets spread over cities, newspapers became fatter or died, commercial television began making millions, shops, airlines, even coal had to fight for their lives. After the big sleep many people welcomed any novelty . . .' Not everyone, it is clear, was quite so welcoming, but about the overwhelming fact of change in the late 1950s going into the early 1960s, and the broad post-war periodisation, Sampson from his 1962 vantage point was surely correct. What, though, was now the most propitious way ahead? Sampson had no doubts about where (so far) there had been a seriously damaging absence of change: 'The old privileged values of aristocracy, public schools and Oxbridge which still dominate government today have failed to provide the stimulus, the purposive policies and the keen eye on the future which Britain is looking for, and must have . . . The old fabric of the British governing class, while keeping its social and political hold, has failed to accommodate or analyse the vast forces of science, education or social change which (whether they like it or not) are changing the face of the country.'[1] It was time, in short, for tomorrow's new men, and perhaps even the odd new woman, to be allowed to step up to the plate. Or, put another way, modernity Britain, yes; but also – at long last – opportunity Britain.

Notes

Abbreviations

Abrams	Mark Abrams Papers (Churchill Archives Centre, Churchill College, Cambridge)
Amis	Zachary Leader (ed), *The Letters of Kingsley Amis* (2000)
BBC WA	BBC Written Archives Centre (Caversham)
Benn	Ruth Winstone (ed), Tony Benn, *Years of Hope: Diaries, Letters and Papers, 1940–1962* (1994)
Chaplin	Sid Chaplin Papers (Special Collections, University of Newcastle)
Crossman	Janet Morgan (ed), *The Backbench Diaries of Richard Crossman* (1981)
Crossman	Diary of Richard Crossman (Modern Records Centre, University of Warwick)
Daly	Lawrence Daly Papers (Modern Records Centre, University of Warwick)
Dee	Diary of Dennis Dee (East Riding of Yorkshire Archives, Beverley)
Fowles	Charles Drazin (ed), John Fowles, *The Journals: Volume 1* (2003)
Fowles	John Fowles Papers (Special Collections, University of Exeter)
Gorer	Geoffrey Gorer Papers (Special Collections, University of Sussex)
Hague	Frances and Gladys Hague Papers (Keighley Library)
Haines	Diary of Alice (Judy) Haines (Special Collections, University of Sussex)
Heap	Diary of Anthony Heap (London Metropolitan Archives)
Langford	Diary of Gladys Langford (Islington Local History Centre)
Larkin	Anthony Thwaite (ed), Philip Larkin, *Letters to Monica* (2010)
Larkin	Unpublished Letters of Philip Larkin to Monica Jones (Bodleian Library, Oxford)
Last	Diary of Nella Last (Mass-Observation Archive, Special Collections, University of Sussex)
Lewis	Diary of Frank Lewis (Glamorgan Archives, Cardiff)
Macmillan (1)	Harold Macmillan, *Riding the Storm: 1956–1959* (1971)
Macmillan (2)	Harold Macmillan, *Pointing the Way: 1959–61* (1972)
Macmillan (3)	Harold Macmillan, *At the End of the Day: 1961–63* (1973)
Macmillan	Harold Macmillan Papers (Bodleian Library, Oxford)
Martin	Diary of Madge Martin (Oxfordshire History Centre, Oxford)
M-O A	Mass-Observation Archive (Special Collections, University of Sussex)
Osborn	Michael Hughes (ed), *The Letters of Lewis Mumford and Frederic J. Osborn* (Bath, 1971)
Preston	Diary of Kenneth Preston (Bradford Archives, Bradford Central Library)
Raynham	Diary of Marian Raynham (Special Collections, University of Sussex)
St John	Diary of Henry St John (Ealing Local History Centre)
Turtle	Diary of Florence Turtle (Wandsworth Heritage Service)
Willmott	Diary of Phyllis Willmott (Churchill Archives Centre, Churchill College, Cambridge)
Wilson	Jacqueline Wilson, *My Secret Diary* (2009)

All books are published in London unless otherwise stated.

Opening the Box

1 Isn' 'e Smashin'?

1. The Society of Housing Managers, *Report of Conference, Housing Management, Thursday and Friday 10th and 11th January 1957* (1957), pp 5, 18, 49; Haines, 12 Jan 1957; Preston, 12 Jan 1957; BBC WA, R9/19/2, Viewer Research Newsletters, Jan 1957 (II); Richard Webber, *Fifty Years of Hancock's Half Hour* (2004), p 214; Larkin, Ms Eng. c. 7415, 13 Jan 1957, fol 61.
2. Iverach McDonald, *The History of The Times, Volume V* (1984), p 319; Macmillan, dep.d.28, 3 Feb 1957, fol 13; Michael Cockerell, *Live from Number 10* (1988), pp 54–5; Nigel Jones, *Through a Glass Darkly* (1991), pp 354–5; Last, 18 Jan 1957; Benn, p 226; Richard Ingrams, *Muggeridge* (1995), p 187.
3. Spencer Leigh, 'Alan Sytner', *Independent*, 13 Jan 2006; *Liverpool Echo*, 17 Jan 1957; St John, 19 Jan 1957; *Listener*, 7 Feb 1957; Aurelia Schober Plath (ed), Sylvia Plath, *Letters Home* (1976), p 293; Heap, 24 Jan 1957; *Sunday Times*, 27 Jan 1957.
4. John McIlroy, '"Every Factory Our Fortress"', Pt 2, *Historical Studies in Industrial Relations* (Autumn 2001), p 75; H. A. Turner et al, *Labour Relations in the Motor Industry* (1967), p 276; Richard Etheridge Papers (Modern Records Centre, University of Warwick), 202/S/J/3/2/19, 28 Jan 1957; *Daily Mail*, 12–13 Feb 1957; Turner et al, p 277; *Barking, East Ham and Ilford Advertiser*, 16 Feb 1957.
5. Last, 30 Jan 1957; *Educating Archie*, 30 Jan 1957; Muir and Norden Archive (Special Collections, University of Sussex), Box 19, *Take It From Here*, 30 Jan 1957; *Daily Mirror*, 30–31 Jan 1957.
6. BBC WA, R9/7/26 – VR/57/66; *News Chronicle*, 5 Feb 1957; Joanna Moorhead, *New Generations* (Cambridge, 1996), pp 7–10; *Daily Sketch*, 6 Feb 1957.
7. *Picture Post*, 25 Feb 1957; *Leicester Mercury*, 4 Feb 1957, 6–7 Feb 1957; *Picture Post*, 25 Feb 1957; *News Chronicle*, 6 Feb 1957; Bill Law, 'The Boys Who Got Us Swinging', *Guardian*, 7 Mar 1997; Ray Gosling, *Personal Copy* (Five Leaves edn, 2010), pp 42–3.
8. *East London Advertiser*, 8 Feb 1957; *Architects' Journal*, 14 Feb 1957; *Glasgow Herald*, 9 Feb 1957; *East London Advertiser*, 15 Feb 1957.
9. *New Statesman*, 9 Feb 1957; *Sunday Times*, 17 Feb 1957; *Birmingham Mail*, 14 Feb 1957; Last, 11 Feb 1957.
10. Last, 11 Feb 1957; *Daily Mirror*, 11–12 Feb 1957; Heap, 15 Feb 1957; *Daily Mirror*, 18 Feb 1957; *Sunday Express*, 17 Feb 1957.
11. John Hill, 'Television and Pop', in John Corner (ed), *Popular Television in Britain* (1991), p 90; *Daily Sketch*, 11 Dec 1956; Hill, p 90; *Radio Times*, 8 Feb 1957.
12. Pete Frame, *The Restless Generation* (2007), p 219; Hill, p 93; *Sunday Times*, 17 Feb 1957; BBC WA, R9/7/26 – VR/57/95; *News Chronicle*, 18 Feb 1957; *Daily Telegraph*, 18 Feb 1957; *Daily Mail*, 18 Feb 1957.
13. *Radio Times*, 15 Feb 1957; *Daily Mirror*, 18 Feb 1957; *Sunday Times*, 24 Feb 1957; *Daily Mail*, 19 Feb 1957; *Radio Times*, 15 Feb 1957.
14. *New Statesman*, 23 Feb 1957; *Daily Mirror*, 19 Feb 1957; *Daily Telegraph*, 19 Feb 1957; *Daily Mail*, 19 Feb 1957; BBC WA, R9/7/26 – VR/57/110; Leonard Miall, 'Donald Baverstock', *Independent*, 18 Mar 1995; Alasdair Milne, *DG* (1988), p 15; Asa Briggs, *The History of Broadcasting in the United Kingdom, Volume V* (Oxford, 1995), pp 161–4; Andrew Crisell, 'Filth, Sedition and Blasphemy', in Corner, *Popular Television*, p 149.
15. http://www.televisionheaven.co.uk/ward.htm; *Sunday Times*, 24 Feb 1957.

2 A Lot of Mums

1. Alan Bennett, *Untold Stories* (2005), p 402; Chas Critcher, 'Sociology, Cultural Studies and the Post-war Working Class', in John Clarke et al (eds), *Working-Class Culture* (1979), p 17; *Guardian*, 7 Feb 2004; *New Statesman*, 2 Mar 1957 (Chatto & Windus advertisement); *Manchester Guardian*, 23 Feb 1957; Richard Johnson, 'Culture and the Historians', in Clarke et al, *Working-Class Culture*, p 59.

2. Peter Townsend Collection (Qualidata, University of Essex), Box 60, File B, Michael Young memorandum, 8 Jan 1956; *Star*, 23–7 Apr 1957; *Daily Herald*, 26 Apr 1957; *Daily Mirror*, 26 Apr 1957; *News Chronicle*, 27 Apr 1957; *Daily Telegraph*, 26 Apr 1957; *The Times*, 26 Apr 1957; *Daily Mail*, 30 Apr 1957; *Financial Times*, 13 May 1957.

3. *Spectator*, 1 Mar 1957, 21 Jun 1957; Nick Tiratsoo and Mark Clapson, 'The Ford Foundation and Social Planning in Britain', in Giuliana Gemelli (ed), *American Foundations and Large-Scale Research* (Bologna, 2001), p 212; *Listener*, 30 May 1957; *Encounter* (Sep 1957), p 84; *Times Literary Supplement*, 25 Oct 1957; *Case Conference* (May 1957), pp 24–5.

4. Michael Young Papers (Churchill Archives Centre, Churchill College, Cambridge), 5/23, 28 Apr 1957; Dartington Hall Trust Archives, DWE/G/11/C, 5 May 1957.

5. *Encounter*, Apr 1955, p 14; John Vaizey, *In Breach of Promise* (1983), p 119; David Marquand, *Britain since 1918* (2008), pp 246–7; Lawrence Black, *The Political Culture of the Left in Affluent Britain, 1951–64* (Basingstoke, 2003), pp 85–6; Michael Young and Peter Willmott, *Family and Kinship in East London* (Penguin edn, 1986), p xvii; Young and Willmott, *Family and Kinship* (Pelican edn, 1962), pp 197–8; Young and Willmott, *Family and Kinship* (1986), p xix.

6. *Spectator*, 20 Jan 1956; *Architects' Journal*, 31 Jan 1957.

7. Margot Jefferys, 'Londoners in Hertfordshire', in Ruth Glass et al, *London: Aspects of Change* (1964), pp 239–43; J. B. Cullingworth, 'The Social Implications of Overspill', *Sociological Review* (Jul 1960), pp 77–96; J. B. Cullingworth, 'The Swindon Social Survey', *Sociological Review* (Jul 1961), pp 151–66; *Royal Society for the Promotion of Health Journal* (Mar–Apr 1959), pp 206–8.

8. Maurice Broady Collection (Special Collections, University of Glasgow), uncatalogued red-and-green box, interview with Mrs Stewart, Craigbank, 20 Feb 1957.

3 Never Had It So Good

1. *Daily Mail*, 4 Mar 1957; David Jeremiah, *Architecture and Design for the Family, 1900–70* (Manchester, 2000), pp 167–8; *New Statesman*, 9 Mar 1957; Robert J. Wybrow, *Britain Speak Out, 1937–87* (Basingstoke, 1989), p 49; *Punch*, 13 Mar 1957; Anne Hardy, 'Reframing Disease', *Historical Research* (Nov 2003), p 540; Simon Berry and Hamish Whyte (eds), *Glasgow Observed* (Edinburgh, 1987), p 239; *Fowles*, p 388.

2. Deborah Geller, *The Brian Epstein Story* (2000), pp 18–21; *Guardian*, 20 Feb 2010 (David Lacey); *Daily Telegraph*, 14 Dec 2007 (Jim White); Macmillan, dep.d.29, 4 May 1957, fol 18; Anthony Thwaite (ed), *Selected Letters of Philip Larkin, 1940–1985* (1992), p 276.

3. *Economist*, 2 Mar 1957; Huw Beynon, *Working for Ford* (1984 edn), p 61; Steven Tolliday, 'Ford and "Fordism" in Postwar Britain', in Steven Tolliday and Jonathan Zeitlin (eds), *The Power to Manage?* (1991), p 88; *The Times*, 12 Apr 1957; H. A. Turner et al, *Labour Relations in the Motor Industry* (1967), p 277; John McIlroy, '"Every Factory Our Fortress"', Pt 2, *Historical Studies in Industrial Relations* (Autumn 2001), p 75.

4. Raynham, 16 Mar 1957; Heap, 20 Mar 1957; John Bright-Holmes (ed), *The Diaries of Malcolm Muggeridge* (1981), p 473; *Observer*, 24 Mar 1957; Macmillan, dep.d.28, 15 Mar 1957, fol 81; George H. Gallup, *The Gallup International Public Opinion Polls: Great Britain 1937–1975: Volume 1* (New York, 1976), p 408; Robert Shepherd, *Iain Macleod* (1994), pp 124, 126–7; *New Yorker*, 13 Apr 1957; Shepherd, *Iain Macleod*, pp 127–8. For a full account of the strikes, see Nina Fishman, '"The Most Serious Crisis since 1926"', in Alan Campbell et al (eds), *British Trade Unions and Industrial Politics, Volume One* (Aldershot, 1999), pp 242–67.

5. *Evening Standard*, 4 Apr 1957; Ferdinand Mount, *Cold Cream* (2008), p 200; *Evening Standard*, 4 Apr 1957; Jim Tomlinson, 'Inventing "Decline"', *Economic History Review*, Nov 1996, p 747; Jim Tomlinson, 'Economic Growth, Economic Decline', in Kathleen Burk (ed), *The British Isles since 1945* (Oxford, 2003), p 70; D. M. Ashford, 'Critical Comets', *Times Literary Supplement*, 18 Mar 2011; Cambridge Union Society: Record of Debates, 7 May 1957 (Cambridge University Library); Lord Moran, *Winston Churchill* (1966), p 726.

6. Colin Clark, *Younger Brother, Younger Son* (1997), p 105; Heap, 10 Apr 1957; Dominic Shellard (ed), Kenneth Tynan, *Theatre Writings* (2007), p 169; *Listener*, 2 May 1957; John Heilpern, *John Osborne* (2006), pp 215–16.

7. Richard Bradford, *Lucky Him* (2001), p 156; Kingsley Amis, *Socialism and the Intellectuals* (1957), p 13; *Universities and Left Review* (Spring 1957), pp ii, 3, 1, 32, 44–8; (Summer 1957), pp 29–34, 39–40; *New Reasoner* (Summer 1957), pp 2, 132, 141–2.

8. Alan Bold, *MacDiarmid* (1988), pp 410–11; *Daily Worker*, 22 Apr 1957; Paul Routledge, *Scargill* (1993), p 26; *Daily Worker*, 23 Apr 1957; Malcolm MacEwen, *The Greening of a Red* (1991), pp 198–9.

9. *Daily Worker*, 7 Jun 1957; Matthew Hilton, *Smoking in British Popular Culture, 1800–2000* (Manchester, 2000), p 185; Jeremy Laurance, 'Scientists Lament 40 Fatal Years of Smoking', *Independent*, 8 Mar 2002; Hilton, *Smoking*, p 229; *Manchester Guardian*, 2 Jul 1957; *Salford City Reporter*, 29 Mar 1957; Janet Frame, *The Envoy from Mirror City* (1985), pp 96–7; Martin, 24 May 1957.

10. David Bernstein, 'The Television Commercial', in Brian Henry (ed), *British Television Advertising* (1986), p 261; Adam Sisman, *Hugh Trevor-Roper* (2010), p 283; *News Chronicle*, 1 Apr 1957; Leonard Miall (ed), *Richard Dimbleby, Broadcaster* (1966), p 106; *Daily Mail*, 2 Apr 1957; Leonard Miall, 'Charles de Jaeger', *Independent*, 29 May 2000.

11. BBC WA, R9/13/142, 12 Mar 1957, 22 Mar 1957; *Financial Times*, 13 Jul 1957; Mark Lewisohn, *Radio Times Guide to TV Comedy* (2003 edn), pp 49–50; *Spectator*, 12 Apr 1957 (John Beavon); Anthony Hayward, 'Edward Evans', *Independent*, 4 Jan 2002.

12. *Radio Times*, 24 May 1957; Larkin, Ms Eng. c. 7416, 8 Jun 1957, fol 38; *Guardian*, 2 Jun 1997 (Frank Keating); C.L.R. James, *Beyond a Boundary* (Serpent's Tail edn,

1994), pp 216–17; Rupert Hart-Davis (ed), *The Lyttelton Hart-Davis Letters, Volume Two* (1979), p 120.

13. D. R. Thorpe, *Supermac* (2010), p 328; *Independent*, 30 Oct 2006 (David Prosser); Macmillan, dep.d.29, 1 Jun 1957, fol 50; Heap, 22 May 1957; Katherine Whitehorn, *Selective Memory* (2007), p 84; Francis Wheen, *Television* (1985), p 77; Vanessa Redgrave, *An Autobiography* (1991), pp 68, 76; *Sunday Pictorial* file, box 18, John Hilton Bureau Archive, News Group Newspapers Ltd Archive, News International.

14. Mark Norton, *Birmingham Past & Present* (Stroud, 2006), pp 8–9; *Yorkshire Post*, 26 Mar 1957; *Architects' Journal*, 28 Mar 1957; *Liverpool Daily Post*, 9 Apr 1957, 12 Apr 1957, 15 Apr 1957; Graeme Shankland, 'The Crisis in Town Planning', *Universities and Left Review* (Spring 1957), p 39.

15. John R. Gold, *The Practice of Modernism* (Abingdon, 2007), p 170; *Architects' Journal*, 7 Mar 1957, 14 Mar 1957; *Birmingham Mail*, 20 Mar 1957, 28 Mar 1957; *The Times*, 8 May 1957, 11 May 1957; Patrick Dunleavy, *The Politics of Mass Housing in Britain, 1945–1975* (Oxford, 1981), p 143.

16. *Manchester Guardian*, 6 Jun 1957; *Builder*, 21 Jun 1957; *Liverpool Echo*, 5 Jul 1957.

17. Ninian Johnston, 'Miracle in the Gorbals?', *Architectural Prospect* (Spring 1957), p 18; *Architects' Journal*, 18 Apr 1957; Tom Brennan, 'Gorbals: A Study in Redevelopment', *Scottish Journal of Political Economy* (Jun 1957), pp 122–6.

18. *Town and Country Planning* (May 1957), p 204; *Architects' Journal*, 4 Apr 1957; *Evening Express* (Liverpool), 22 Mar 1957; *Coventry Standard*, 17 May 1957; *Barking, East Ham & Ilford Advertiser*, 2 Mar 1957, 20 Apr 1957.

19. *Architects' Journal*, 7 Mar 1957, 13 Jun 1957; *Spectator*, 17 May 1957; *Punch*, 19 Jun 1957.

20. Haines, 6 Jul 1957; Turtle, 6 Jul 1957; Martin, 6 Jul 1957; Last, 6 Jul 1957; *Larkin*, p 223; *Liverpool Echo*, 6 Jul 1957; *Evening Express* (Liverpool), 6 Jul 1957; *Liverpool Echo*, 6 Jul 1957; Mark Lewisohn, *The Complete Beatles Chronicle* (1996 edn), p 14; Philip Norman, *John Lennon* (2008), pp 105–6; *The Beatles Press Conferences 1964–1966* (*Uncut* magazine CD, 2005), Track 21, 'John, New York City, December 8, 1980'.

21. *Vauxhall Mirror*, Jul 1957; *East Essex Gazette*, 19 Jul 1957; *Guardian*, 22 Jul 1997 (Richard Williams); Heap, 20 Jul 1957; Haines, 22 Jul 1957; *Durham Chronicle*, 26 Jul 1957.

22. *Radio Times*, 12 Jul 1957; *Bedford Record*, 16 Jul 1957, 23 Jul 1957; Macmillan, dep.c. 740; *People's Friend*, 20 Jul 1957.

4 Catch a Falling Sputnik

1. *Financial Times*, 14 Nov 1957; *Observer*, 23 Oct 1960 (Mark Abrams); *Never Had It So Good?*, BBC Four, 10 Dec 2007; *Liverpool Echo*, 16 Sep 1957; *Financial Times*, 6 Sep 1957; Abrams, Box 81, 'L.P.E. Merchandising Bulletin No. 3'; Lucy Ward, 'Forget Filling the Coal Shed', *Guardian*, 29 Jan 2008; *Woman's Own*, 18 Jul 1957, 30 May 1957.

2. Derek J. Oddy, *From Plain Fare to Fusion Food* (Woodbridge, 2003), p 185; Peter Bird, *The First Food Empire* (Chichester, 2000), p 226; *Woman's Own*, 18 Jul 1957;

James Obelkevich, 'Consumption', in James Obelkevich and Peter Catterall (eds), *Understanding Post-War British Society* (1994), p 148; David L. Wakefield, *The Hoover Story in Merthyr Tydfil* (Merthyr Tydfil, c. 1977), p 7; *Financial Times*, 12 Oct 1959; *Reynolds News*, 24 Feb 1957; Rhys David, 'Cyril Lord', *Dictionary of Business Biography, Volume 3* (1985), p 853; David Hunt, 'Cyril Lord', *Oxford Dictionary of National Biography* (Oxford, 2004), vol 34, p 437; Douglas Lowndes, 'Norman Parkinson', *Independent*, 20 Feb 1990; Ralph Harris and Arthur Seldon, *Advertising in Action* (1962), pp 272, 80–81.

3. Subrata Dasgupta, *Salaam Stanley Matthews* (2006), p 179; Mick Grabham, 'Low Fidelity', *Mojo* (Aug 1997).

4. Paul Levy, 'Egon Ronay', *Independent*, 14 Jun 2010; Matthew Hilton, 'The Fable of the Sheep, or, Private Virtues, Public Vices', *Past & Present* (Aug 2002), p 229; Elizabeth Dunn, 'The Quiet Man of Change', *Sunday Times*, 30 January 1977; Dartington Hall Trust Archives, LKE/G/35, Michael Young to Dorothy and Leonard Elmhurst, 10 Oct 1957.

5. Asa Briggs, *Michael Young* (Basingstoke, 2001), p 150; *The Times*, 8 Oct 1957; BBC WA, *Woman's Hour*, 11 Oct 1957; *Independent*, 3 Jul 1997 (Jack O'Sullivan); *Which?* (Winter 1957), p 20; Maurice Healy, 'Eirlys Roberts', *Guardian*, 22 Mar 2008; *Which?* (Autumn 1957), pp 3–6; Gorer, Box 103, Michael Young to Geoffrey Gorer, 14 Oct 1957; Lawrence Black, *Redefining British Politics* (Basingstoke, 2010), pp 16–25; M-O A, TC78/3/EF.

6. *Manchester Guardian*, 23 Jul 1957; Stephen Chalke, 'Peter Loader', *Independent*, 21 Mar 2011; *Larkin*, p 227; William Smethurst, *The Archers* (1996), pp 59–72; Turtle, 29 Jul 1957; Macmillan, dep.d.29, 29 Jul 1957, fol 106.

7. Elizabeth Longford, *Elizabeth R* (1983), p 182; *New Statesman*, 10 Aug 1957 (Francis Williams); Jeremy Paxman, 'Hard-pressed Royalty', *Daily Telegraph*, 19 Aug 1996; Macmillan, dep.d.29, 8 Aug 1957, fol 116; *New Statesman*, 17 Aug 1957 (Francis Williams); Robert Lacey, *Majesty* (1978 edn), p 320; *New Yorker*, 7 Sep 1957; Macmillan, dep.d.29, 1 Sep 1957, fol 137.

8. *Spectator*, 4 Oct 1957; *Sunday Dispatch*, 6 Oct 1957; Richard Ingrams, *Muggeridge* (1995), p 182; *Sunday Express*, 13 Oct 1957; Last, 13 Oct 1957; *People*, 13 Oct 1957 (Leonard Coulter); *Daily Mirror*, 15 Oct 1957; Asa Briggs, *The History of Broadcasting in the United Kingdom, Volume V* (Oxford, 1995), pp 145–6; 'Lieutenant-General Sir Ian Jacob', *The Times*, 26 Apr 1993.

9. *Financial Times*, 22 Dec 2007 (John Lloyd); Martin, 16 Aug 1957; *Liverpool Echo*, 13–14 Sep 1957.

10. Spencer Leigh, 'Alan Sytner', *Independent*, 13 Jan 2006; *Mojo* (Oct 1997), p 38 (Paul Du Noyer); *Guardian*, 20 Feb 2004 (Will Hodgkinson); Lorna Sage, *Bad Blood* (2000), p 193; Lewis, 2 Sep 1957.

11. Frank Mort, *Capital Affairs* (2010), p 194; *New Yorker*, 28 Sep 1957; *Manchester Guardian*, 5 Sep 1957; Matt Houlbrook, *Queer London* (Chicago, 2005), p 261; *Daily Mirror*, 6 Sep 1957.

12. *Daily Express*, 5 Sep 1957; Richard Davenport-Hines, *Sex, Death and Punishment* (1990), p 322; Adrian Bingham, *Family Newspapers* (Oxford, 2009), p 189; *Spectator*, 6 Sep 1957; Roger Davidson and Gayle Davis, '"A Field for Private Members"', *Twentieth Century British History*, 15/2 (2004), p 194; *Daily Mirror*, 10–11 Sep 1957; George H. Gallup, *The Gallup International Public Opinion Polls: Great*

Britain 1937–1975, Volume One (New York, 1976), pp 426–8; *New Yorker*, 28 Sep 1957. In general on press reaction, including for some of the quotations, see *New Statesman*, 14 Sep 1957 (Francis Williams).

13. Humphrey Carpenter, *Dennis Potter* (1998), p 67; Anthony Howard, *RAB* (1987), pp 264–5; 'Lord Denning', *The Times*, 6 Mar 1999; Ben Pimlott, *Hugh Dalton* (1985), pp 627–8; Peter Townsend, 'Professor Brian Abel-Smith', *Independent*, 9 Apr 1996; Liz Homans, 'Swinging Sixties', *History Today* (Dec 2008), pp 46–7.

14. Macmillan, dep.d.29, 17 Sep 1957, fol 153; *Evening Standard*, 19 Sep 1957; Forrest Capie, *The Bank of England: 1950s to 1979* (New York, 2010), p 93; *Crossman*, p 607; *Spectator*, 27 Sep 1957; *Financial Times*, 21 Sep 1957.

15. *Macmillan (1)*, p 417; David Kynaston, *The City of London, Volume 4* (2001), pp 88, 98; Gary Burn, 'The State, the City and the Euromarkets', *Review of International Political Economy* (Summer 1999), pp 234–5.

16. *New Statesman*, 28 Sep 1957; *Spectator*, 11 Oct 1957, 4 Oct 1957; *New Statesman*, 5 Oct 1957; Turtle, 25 Sep 1957; Heap, 28 Sep 1957; BBC WA, R9/19/2, Nov 1957; *The Times*, 15 Jun 1998 (Tim Jones); Denis Gifford, 'Reg Smythe', *Independent*, 15 Jun 1998.

17. John Bright-Holmes (ed), *Like It Was: The Diaries of Malcolm Muggeridge* (1981), p 479; *New Yorker*, 2 Nov 1957; John Campbell, *Nye Bevan* (1997 edn), p 337; D. B. Smith, 'Michael Foot on Aneurin Bevan', *Llafur* (May 1974), p 24; Campbell, p 338; Crossman, Ms 154/8/26, 8 Feb 1961, fol 1315.

18. Haines, 4 Oct 1957; *The Times*, 8 Mar 2008 (Erica Wagner); *Financial Times*, 5 Oct 1957; Frances Partridge, *Everything to Lose* (1999 edn), p 285; Doris Lessing, *Walking in the Shade* (1997), p 277; *Evening Standard*, 7 Oct 1957; *Financial Times*, 11 Oct 1957; *New Statesman*, 12 Oct 1957; John Callaghan, 'The Left and the "Unfinished Revolution"', *Contemporary British History* (Autumn 2001), pp 74–5; Martin Gilbert, *'Never Despair'* (1988), p 1,252; *New Yorker*, 23 Nov 1957 (Panter-Downes); *Punch*, 23 Oct 1957.

19. Lewis Baston, *Reggie* (Stroud, 2004), pp 120–21; David Lowry, 'Tom Tuohy', *Guardian*, 7 May 2008; Jean McSorley, 'Contaminated Evidence', *Guardian*, 10 Oct 2007; Lord Hinton of Bankside Papers (Institution of Mechanical Engineers), 'Autobiography', chap XXIV; Last, 12 Oct 1957; *Western Daily Press*, 15 Oct 1957; *New Yorker*, 2 Nov 1957; Last, 17 Oct 1957; D. R. Thorpe, *Supermac* (2010), pp 396–7; *News Chronicle*, 9 Nov 1957; Tony Hall, *Nuclear Politics* (1986), p 63; Lorna Arnold, *Windscale* (Basingstoke, 1992), p 71; email to author from Jenny Uglow, 29 Jul 2011.

20. *Spectator*, 9 Aug 1957, 11 Oct 1957; Bevis Hillier, *John Betjeman: New Fame, New Love* (2002), pp 567–9; *Spectator*, 20 Dec 1957.

21. *Architects' Journal*, 11 Apr 1957; Peter Self, *Cities in Flood* (1957), p 166; *Architects' Journal*, 1 Aug 1957; *Listener*, 5 Sep 1957.

22. *Liverpool Daily Post*, 3 Sep 1957, 20 Sep 1957; *Liverpool Echo*, 24 Sep 1957; *Liverpool Daily Post*, 1 Oct 1957, 3 Oct 1957; John English et al, *Slum Clearance* (1976), p 156.

23. *Yorkshire Post*, 12–13 Nov 1957; *Yorkshire Evening News*, 12 Nov 1957; *Yorkshire Post*, 13 Nov 1957; Colin Ward and Dennis Hardy, *Goodnight Campers!* (1986), pp 125–7; *Bognor Regis Post*, 28 Sep 1957, 12 Oct 1957.

24. *Quarterly Bulletin of the Society of Housing Managers* (Jan 1958), p 11; *Liverpool Echo*, 13 Sep 1957; N. S. Power, *The Forgotten People* (Evesham, 1965), pp 13–14, 37–8; *Salford City Reporter*, 6 Dec 1957; John Winstone, *Bristol As It Was, 1963–1975* (Bristol, 1990), p 36; Patrick Dunleavy, *The Politics of Mass Housing in Britain, 1945–1975* (Oxford, 1981), p 312; *Architects' Journal*, 24 Oct 1957, 26 Dec 1957; *Kensington News and West London Times*, 15 Nov 1957; *Architects' Journal*, 14 Nov 1957.

25. *Architects' Journal*, 16 Jan 1958; *Sunday Times*, 1 Dec 1957, 8 Dec 1957, 15 Dec 1957; Adrian Smith, 'The Coventry Factor', *Literature & History* (Spring 1999), pp 34–5; Heap, 17 Nov 1957.

26. Haines, 12 Oct 1957; *New Statesman*, 19 Oct 1957 (Francis Williams); *New Yorker*, 2 Nov 1957; *Sunday Times*, 13 Oct 1957; *New Statesman*, 19 Oct 1957; *Macmillan (1)*, pp 419–20; Michael Bentley, 'Maurice Cowling', *Independent*, 6 Sep 2005; *Listener*, 31 Oct 1957.

27. Tom Maschler (ed), *Declaration* (1957), pp 23, 76, 120, 155, 159, 166; *Sunday Times*, 13 Oct 1957; *Observer*, 13 Oct 1957; *Listener*, 7 Nov 1957; Humphrey Carpenter, *The Angry Young Men* (2002), p 183.

28. *Glasgow Herald*, 21 Oct 1957; *The Times*, 12 Nov 2002 (John Goodbody); Daly, Mss 302/2/1, 31 Oct 1957, 302/3/12, 8 Oct 1957.

29. 'Lawrence Daly', *Daily Telegraph*, 1 Jun 2009; Philip Norman, *John Lennon* (2008), pp 122–3; Pete Frame, *The Restless Generation* (2007), p 267; *Radio Times*, 8 Nov 1957; Owen Adams, 'The 2i's and the Birth of British Rock', *Record Collector*, Jan 2007, pp 35–6; Anne de Courcy, *Snowdon* (2008), p 52; *Yorkshire Post*, 19 Nov 1957; *News Chronicle*, 19 Nov 1957; Colin MacInnes, *England, Half English* (1986 edn), pp 11–16; Langford, 28 Nov 1957.

30. Hague, 3 Nov 1957; Macmillan, dep.d.30, 5 Nov 1957, fol 52; *New Yorker*, 23 Nov 1957; Partridge, p 290; Benn, p 251; *Yorkshire Post*, 13 Nov 1957; David Kynaston, *The Financial Times* (1988), p 261; *New Yorker*, 23 Nov 1957; *New Statesman*, 14 Dec 1957 (Francis Williams); Iona and Peter Opie, *The Lore and Language of Schoolchildren* (1959), p 106.

31. 'John Sandoe', *The Times*, 9 Jan 2008; *Yorkshire Evening News*, 12 Nov 1957; Haines, 12 Nov 1957; Derrik Mercer (ed), *20th Century Day by Day* (Dorling Kindersley edn, 1999), p 1,140; *Wisden Cricketers' Almanack, 1958* (1958), p 1,004; Mercer, *20th Century*, p 1,140; *Guardian*, 3 Sep 2011 (Fiona MacCarthy).

32. *Yorkshire Evening News*, 12 Nov 1957; Benn, p 253; *Spectator*, 29 Nov 1957; BBC WA, R9/19/2, Jan 1958; *Spectator*, 27 Dec 1957; *Daily Telegraph*, 10 Dec 1957; Lawrence Black, '"Sheep May Safely Gaze"', in idem et al, *Consensus or Coercion?* (Cheltenham, 2001), p 36; Gorer, Box 45, 'Institute of Community Studies' file, Young to Gorer, 31 Jan 1958.

33. Gorer, Box 4, file 4/A, Box 2, file 2/B, Box 4, file 4/A; *Manchester Guardian*, 20 Dec 1957; Briggs, *History of Broadcasting*, pp 222–3; *Guardian*, 9 Oct 1997 (John Dugdale); Briggs, *History of Broadcasting*, p 222; BBC WA, R9/9/21, 14 Jan 1958.

34. Haines, 30 Nov 1957; *Manchester Guardian*, 5 Dec 1957; Mercer, *20th Century*, p 1,141; Barbara Weinberger, *The Best Police in the World* (Aldershot, 1995), p 198; Brian Cathcart, 'The Police Punch that Troubled Parliament', *Independent on Sunday*, 19 Jun 1994; Olga Cannon and J.R.L. Anderson, *The Road from Wigan Pier* (1973), pp 163–8; Hansard, *House of Commons Debates*, 19 Dec 1957, cols 717–38; *Listener*, 12 Dec 1957; Sage, p 212; Cliff Goodwin, *When the Wind*

Changed (1999), pp 234–5; *Spectator*, 20 Dec 1957; Stephen F. Kelly, *Bill Shankly* (1996), pp 109–10.

35. Kynaston, *City*, p 90; Macmillan, dep.30, 12 Dec 1957, fol 78; Kynaston, *City*, pp 91–2; *New Yorker*, 4 Jan 1958.

36. *Listener*, 2 Jan 1958; BBC WA, R9/19/2, Feb 1958; Haines, 27 Dec 1957; Dee, 1–4 Jan 1958; Martin, 4 Jan 1958; Robert Ross, *The Complete Frankie Howerd* (Richmond, 2001), p 35; Heap, 5 Jan 1958; *Merthyr Express*, 11 Jan 1958, 18 Jan 1958.

5 Not a Matter of Popularity

1. Dee, 6 Jan 1958; Martin, 6 Jan 1958; Haines, 6 Jan 1958; *Daily Telegraph*, 7 Jan 1958.

2. Helpful accounts include: John Hunt, 'Much More than a "Little Local Difficulty"', *Financial Times*, 3 Jan 1989; Robert Shepherd, *Enoch Powell* (1996), pp 159–84; Simon Heffer, *Like the Roman* (1998), pp 217–41; Mark Jarvis, 'The 1958 Treasury Dispute', *Contemporary British History* (Summer 1998), pp 22–50; E.H.H. Green, 'The Treasury Resignations of 1958', *Twentieth Century British History*, 11/4 (2000), pp 409–30; D. R. Thorpe, *Supermac* (2010), pp 401–7; Chris Cooper, 'Little Local Difficulties Revisited', *Contemporary British History* (Jun 2011), pp 227–50.

3. 'Lord Thorneycroft', *The Times*, 6 Jun 1994; Cooper, 'Little Local Difficulties', p 231; David Kynaston, *Family Britain* (2009), p 447; Shepherd, *Enoch Powell*, pp 160, 194; *The Times*, 12 Feb 1998; Heffer, *Like the Roman*, p 215.

4. Cooper, 'Little Local Difficulties', p 236; Green, 'Treasury', p 416; Jarvis, '1958', p 27; Green, 'Treasury', pp 417, 420–211; Jarvis, '1958', p 31; Green, 'Treasury', p 420; Thorpe, *Supermac*, pp 400–401; Cooper, 'Little Local Difficulties', p 236.

5. Green, 'Treasury', p 419; David Kynaston, *City of London, Volume 4* (2001), pp 42–3, 77; *Listener*, 24 Nov 1957; *News Chronicle*, 18 Nov 1957; *Economist*, 21 Dec 1957; Kynaston, *City*, p 105.

6. Macmillan, dep.d.30, 22 Dec 1957, fol 95, 6 Jan 1958, fols 100–101, 104; Hunt, 'Much More'; Cooper, 'Little Local Difficulties', p 240.

7. *The Times*, 7 Jan 1958; Michael Cockerell, *Live from Number 10* (1988), pp 56–7; Macmillan, dep.d.30, 7 Jan 1958, fol 110.

8. *Daily Telegraph*, 7 Jan 1958; *Financial Times*, 8 Jan 1958; *Daily Express*, 7 Jan 1958; *Daily Sketch*, 8 Jan 1958; *Daily Mail*, 7 Jan 1958; *Spectator*, 10 Jan 1958; *Sunday Times*, 12 Jan 1958; *Economist*, 11 Jan 1958; *The Times*, 7–8 Jan 1958.

9. *Kent & Sussex Courier*, 10 Jan 1958; *Yorkshire Post*, 9 Jan 1958; *Financial Times*, 14 Jan 1958.

10. *New Statesman*, 11 Jan 1958; Preston, 7 Jan 1958; *News Chronicle*, 21 Jan 1958.

11. *News Chronicle*, 8 Jan 1958; *Spectator*, 10 Jan 1958; Hunt, 'Much More'.

12. *The Times*, 8 Jan 1958; *Daily Express*, 8 Jan 1958; Hunt, 'Much More'; *New Yorker*, 25 Jan 1958, 8 Feb 1958; *Financial Times*, 25 Jan 1958; *Daily Mirror*, 24 Jan 1958; Alan Howarth, 'Lord Thorneycroft', *Independent*, 6 Jun 1994.

13. Alan Booth, 'Inflation, Expectations and the Political Economy of Conservative Britain, 1951–1964', *Historical Journal* (Sep 2000), pp 832–4; *Independent*, 2 Jan 1989 (Anthony Bevins and Colin Hughes); *Independent*, 2 Feb 1988; 'Arthur Seldon', *Daily Telegraph*, 13 Oct 2005.

6 A Worried Song

1. BBC WA, R9/10/5 – VR/58/214; Turtle, 11 Jan 1958; Willmott, 14 Jan 1958; Denis Healey, *The Time of My Life* (1989), p 72; Willmott, 14 Jan 1958.

2. Sue Harper and Vincent Porter, *British Cinema of the 1950s* (Oxford, 2003), p 72; Haines, 16 Jan 1958; Denis Gifford, *Complete Catalogue of British Comics* (1985), pp 129, 191; *New Statesman*, 1 Mar 1958 (Francis Williams); *Woman's Realm*, 22 Feb 1958; Cynthia L. White, *Women's Magazines, 1693–1968* (1970), pp 170–71.

3. Langford, 18 Feb 1958; *Spectator*, 28 Mar 1958; Pat Thane, *Old Age in English History* (Oxford, 2000), pp 447–8.

4. David Kynaston, *The City of London, Volume 4* (2001), p 93; *Financial Times*, 22 Jan 1958; *New Yorker*, 8 Feb 1958 (Mollie Panter-Downes); Ben Pimlott, *Harold Wilson* (1992), pp 216–17; Kynaston, *City*, p 94; Forrest Capie, *The Bank of England: 1950s to 1979* (New York, 2010), p 99.

5. Gordon Burn, *Best and Edwards* (2006), pp 101–4; 'Peter Jackson', *Daily Telegraph*, 24 Mar 2004; *The Times*, 25 Mar 2004; *Financial Times*, 9 Sep 1995 (Christopher Dunkley); *New Statesman*, 8 Feb 1958 (Tom Driberg); Paul Ferris, *Sir Huge* (1990), p 144; BBC WA, R9/19/2, Jul 1958; *Brighton and Hove Herald*, 1 Feb 1958, 8 Mar 1958; *The Times*, 3–5 Feb 1958; *Daily Mirror*, 5 Feb 1958; Heap, 5 Feb 1958; Dee, 6 Feb 1958; Mark Lewisohn, *The Complete Beatles Chronicle* (1996 edn), p 16; *Independent*, 31 Jan 1998 (John Roberts).

6. *Guardian*, 2 Feb 2008 (Richard Williams); Preston, 6 Feb 1958; Last, 7 Feb 1958; Diary of Vincent Walmsley (Special Collections, University of Sussex), 7 Feb 1958; *Independent on Sunday*, 30 Jan 1994 (Brian Cathcart); *New Statesman*, 15 Feb 1958; *Salford City Reporter*, 14 Feb 1958; *The Times*, 1 Feb 2008 (Matt Dickinson).

7. Michael Cockerell, *Live from Number 10* (1988), pp 58–9; Bernard Sendall, *Independent Television in Britain, Volume 1* (1982), p 351; 'Sir Cyril Smith', *The Times*, 4 Sep 2010; David Steel, 'Sir Ludovic Kennedy', *Guardian*, 20 Oct 2009; BBC WA, R9/10/5 – VR/58/79; Macmillan, dep.d.30, 10 Feb 1958, fol 137; Crossman, Ms 154/8/21, 12 Feb 1958, fol 1,073; Last, 12 Feb 1958; BBC WA, *Any Questions?*, 14 Feb 1958; Cockerell, *Live*, p 59.

8. Anthony Howard, *RAB* (1987), pp 261–2; Robin Day, *Television* (1961), p 161; Sir Robin Day, *Grand Inquisitor* (1989), p 1; Sir Robin Day, *... But With Respect* (1993), p 25; Day, *Television*, pp 162–4; Macmillan, dep.d.31, 23 Feb 1958, fol 13.

9. Mark Pottle (ed), *Daring to Hope: The Diaries and Letters of Violet Bonham Carter, 1946–1969* (2000), p 196; Macmillan, dep.d.31, 13 Mar 1958, fol 33; Crossman, p 663; *The Times*, 6 Jun 1958.

10. John Campbell, *Margaret Thatcher, Volume One* (2000), pp 110–11; Pete Frame, *The Restless Generation* (2007), p 323; Derek A. J. Lister, *Bradford's Rock 'n' Roll* (Bradford, 1991), p 95; Christopher Sandford, *Mick Jagger* (1999 edn), p 29.

11. Dee, 29 Mar 1958; Archie Burnett (ed.), *The Complete Poems of Philip Larkin* (2012), p 409; Larkin, Ms Eng. c. 7418, 31 Mar 1958, fols 5–6; Simon Reynolds, 'Sorcerers of Sound', *Guardian*, 20 Sep 2008; Richard Webber, *Fifty Years of Hancock's Half Hour* (2004), pp 223–4.

12. *Punch*, 2 Apr 1958; *New Statesman*, 5 Apr 1958; David Stafford, 'Fleming's Lament for Britain', *The Times*, 18 Nov 1999; Simon Winder, *The Man Who Saved Britain* (2006), p 103.

13. Helpful accounts of CND's background and early history include: Richard Taylor and Colin Pritchard, *The Protest Makers* (Oxford, 1980), pp 5–7; Meredith Veldman, *Fantasy, the Bomb and the Greening of Britain* (Cambridge, 1994), pp 131–40; Mervyn Jones, *Michael Foot* (1994), pp 225–31; Kathleen Burk, *Troublemaker* (2000), pp 211–17.

14. *New Statesman*, 2 Nov 1957; Jones, *Foot*, pp 227–8; *The Times*, 18 Feb 1958; Day, *Respect*, p 26; Jad Adams, *Tony Benn* (1992), pp 135–6; *New Statesman*, 29 Mar 1958; BBC WA, *Any Questions?*, 4 Apr 1958.

15. *Guardian*, 10 Dec 2011 (Albert Beale); *Manchester Guardian*, 5 Apr 1958; *Observer*, 6 Apr 1958; David V. Barratt, 'John Brunner', *Independent*, 31 Aug 1995; Kathleen Tynan, *The Life of Kenneth Tynan* (1987), p 142; Veldman, *Fantasy*, pp 139–40; 'Norris McWhirter', *Daily Telegraph*, 21 Apr 2004.

16. Benn, p 272; Healey, *Time*, p 241; Julia Langdon, 'Lord Marsh', *Guardian*, 3 Aug 2011; Veldman, *Fantasy*, p 153; Peter Webb, *Portrait of David Hockney* (1988), pp 13, 18; Stephen Woodhams, *History in the Making* (2001), p 193; *Socialist Commentary* (May 1958), p 14 ('Lupus'); *New Statesman*, 21 Jun 1958; Adam Sisman, *A.J.P. Taylor* (1994), pp 276–7; *Guardian*, 30 Apr 2008 (Julie Bindel); Amis, p 521; Willmott, 9 Apr 1958; *New Yorker*, 3 May 1958; Lawrence Black, '"The Bitterest Enemies of Communism"', *Contemporary British History* (Autumn 2001), p 52; *Observer*, 6 Apr 1958.

17. *Coventry Standard*, 10 Jan 1958, 17 Jan 1958; *The Times*, 25 Oct 1957; *Observer*, 18 May 1958; Carole Newbiggin, 'The Development of Blackbird Leys', http://www.bbc.co.uk/news/england/oxford/, 'Memoryshare'; *The Times*, 9 Jun 1994 (Alan Franks); Frances Reynolds, *The Problem Housing Estate* (Aldershot, 1986), pp 15–17.

18. *Architects' Journal*, 5 Jun 1958; Andrew Homer, 'Administrative and Social Change in the Post-War British New Towns', PhD diss, University of Luton, 1999, pp 168, 170; *Architectural Review* (Jun 1958), p 422; A.G.V. Simmonds, 'Conservative Governments and the Housing Question, 1951–59', PhD diss, University of Leeds, 1995, pp 412–16; *Daily Mail*, 25 Aug 1958; *Architects' Journal*, 5 Jun 1958.

19. *Architects' Journal*, 20 Mar 1958; *Observer*, 30 Mar 1958; *New Statesman*, 21 Jun 1958; *Sunday Times*, 22 Jun 1958; *Architects' Journal*, 24 Apr 1958, 26 Jun 1958; William Whyte, 'The Modernist Moment at the University of Leeds, 1957–1977', *Historical Journal* (Mar 2008), pp 173–8.

20. *The Times*, 6 Feb 1958; Joe Moran, *On Roads* (2009), pp 23–4; Simon Jenkins, 'From Green Belt to Rust Belt: How the Queen of the Midlands Was Throttled', *Guardian*, 20 Oct 2006; John R. Gold, *The Practice of Modernism* (Abingdon, 2007), p 134; *Evening Chronicle* (Newcastle), 31 May 1958; Gordon E. Cherry, *Birmingham* (Chichester, 1994), p 213; Simmonds, 'Conservative Governments', p 206; *Architects' Journal*, 6 Feb 1968; *Independent*, 26 Feb 1992 (Lucy Musgrove); *East London Advertiser*, 28 Mar 1958, 8 Aug 1958, 15 Aug 1958; Gold, *Practice*, pp 208–9.

21. Kynaston, *City*, p 130; *Guardian*, 20 Aug 2009 (Gavin Stamp); Kynaston, *City*, p 130; Nicholas Bullock, *Building the Post-War World* (2002), pp 258–9. For suggestive accounts of why conditions were so propitious by the late 1950s for a speculative property boom, above all in offices, see: Oliver Marriott, *The Property Boom* (1967), chaps 1, 3; Charles Gordon, *The Two Tycoons* (1984), chaps 2, 5; Peter

Mandler, 'New Towns for Old', in Becky Conekin et al (eds), *Moments of Modernity* (1999), pp 215–20; Gold, *Practice*, pp 84–6.

22. Interview with Richard Seifert (National Life Story Collection, National Sound Archive), C467/75, p 22; 'Richard Seifert', *The Times*, 27 Oct 2001; Martin Pawley, 'Richard Seifert', *Guardian*, 29 Oct 2001; 'Richard Seifert', *Daily Telegraph*, 29 Oct 2001.

23. *Star*, 25 Mar 1958; *Listener*, 17 Apr 1958; *New Statesman*, 19 Apr 1958; Fowles, EUL MS 102/1/10, 20 Apr 1958; *Listener*, 24 Apr 1958; Heap, 23 Jun 1958; *Architectural Review*, Jul 1958, pp 7–8.

24. *News Chronicle*, 28 Jan 1958; *Western Daily Press*, 14 Feb 1958; *Salford City Reporter*, 21 Mar 1958; *Architects' Journal*, 10 Apr 1958.

25. *Architects' Journal*, 17 Apr 1958; *Kensington News and West London Times*, 11 Apr 1958; *Salford City Reporter*, 9 May 1958; Raynham, 14 Jun 1958; *Architectural Review*, Jul 1958, p 58; *Evening News*, 9 Jul 1958; N. Tiratsoo, *Reconstruction, Affluence and Labour Politics* (1990), pp 96–7; Crossman, Ms 154/8/23, 17 Oct 1958, fols 1,215–6.

26. *Salford City Reporter*, 28 Mar 1958, 4 Apr 1958; *Manchester Guardian*, 19 Jul 1958; *East London Advertiser*, 28 Mar 1958; *Reynolds News*, 20 Apr 1958; *News Chronicle*, 7 May 1958; Bryan Appleyard, *Richard Rogers* (1986), pp 87–8.

27. Gold, *Practice*, pp 212–15; *Sheffield Telegraph*, 26 Apr 1958; *Star* (Sheffield), 25 Apr 1958; *Listener*, 8 May 1958.

28. *Surveyor*, 5 Jul 1958; *Architects' Journal*, 3 Jul 1958; Brian Edwards, *Basil Spence, 1907–1976* (Edinburgh, 1995), pp 82–4; Miles Horsey, *Tenements and Towers* (Edinburgh?, 1990), p 39; *Glasgow Herald*, 28 Aug 1958; *Architects' Journal*, 4 Sep 1958; *People*, 7 Sep 1958, 31 Aug 1958, 7 Sep 1958.

7 Stone Me

1. *New Statesman*, 12 Apr 1958; *Accrington Observer*, 19 Apr 1958; Phil Whalley, *Accrington Stanley* (Cheltenham, 2006), pp 20–25; *Evening News* (Portsmouth), 31 May 1958.

2. John Fisher, *Tony Hancock* (2008), p 164; Robert J. Wybrow, *Britain Speaks Out, 1937–87* (Basingstoke, 1989), p 54.

3. Frank Mort, *Capital Affairs* (2010), pp 247–8, 267–70; *People*, 27 Apr 1958; Mort, *Capital Affairs*, pp 276–7; *Independent*, 6 Apr 1992 (Danny Danziger). In general on Raymond, see Paul Willetts, *Members Only* (2010).

4. Crossman, Ms 154/8/21, 6 May 1958, fol 1,109; Arnold Wesker, *As Much As I Dare* (1994), p 556; Crossman, Ms 154/8/21, 6 May 1958, fol 1,109; *Universities and Left Review* (Summer 1958), p 3; *Manchester Guardian*, 18 Aug 1958.

5. Heap, 25 Feb 1958; *Observer*, 2 Mar 1958; 'Wolf Mankowitz', *The Times*, 22 May 1998; Michael Coveney, 'Julian More', *Guardian*, 3 Mar 2010; Heap, 23 Apr 1958, 30 Apr 1958; *Financial Times*, 1 May 1958; *Sunday Times*, 4 May 1958; BBC WA, *Any Questions?*, 9 May 1958.

6. Geoffrey Wansell, *Terence Rattigan* (1995), pp 295–6; Heap, 8 May 1958; *News Chronicle*, 10 May 1958.

7. *The Times*, 20 May 1958; *Crewe Chronicle*, 24 May 1958; Heap, 19 May 1958;

Michael Billington, *The Life and Work of Harold Pinter* (1996), p 74; *Daily Telegraph*, 20 May 1958; *News Chronicle*, 20 May 1958; *Daily Mail*, 20 May 1958; John Walsh, 'That Nice Mr Pinter', *Independent*, 8 Feb 1999; Billington, *Pinter*, pp 84–5; *Sunday Times*, 25 May 1958.

8. John Russell Taylor, *Anger and After* (1969 edn), p 131; *New Statesman*, 26 May 2008 (Antonia Quirke); *Daily Mail*, 27–8 May 1958; *The Times*, 28 May 1958; *Sunday Times*, 1 Jun 1958; *Observer*, 1 Jun 1958; *Spectator*, 6 Jun 1958; Wesker, *As Much*, p 667.

9. *Coventry Standard*, 4 Jul 1958; *Coventry Evening Telegraph*, 7 Jul 1958; *Coventry Standard*, 11 Jul 1958; *Coventry Evening Telegraph*, 8 Jul 1958, 11 Jul 1958; Wesker, *As Much*, p 636; *Spectator*, 18 Jul 1958; *Punch*, 23 Jul 1958; *Sunday Times*, 20 Jul 1958; Wesker, *As Much*, p 638; *Observer*, 20 Jul 1958.

10. *Punch*, 14 May 1958, 18 Jun 1958; *Spectator*, 23 May 1958; *Punch*, 11 Jun 1958; Mark Lewisohn, *Radio Times Guide to TV Comedy* (2003 edn), p 49; BBC WA, R9/19/2, May 1958; Mark Lewisohn, *Funny, Peculiar* (2002), pp 253–5; *Listener*, 29 May 1958 (Ivor Brown); *New Statesman*, 21 Jun 1958; BBC WA, R9/19/2, Sep 1958.

11. Gorer, 'Television and the English' Survey, Box 1, C(i) file, Enid Blyton to Geoffrey Gorer, 13 Apr 1958; Jeffrey Milland, 'Courting Malvolio', *Contemporary British History* (Summer 2004), pp 79–80; Gorer, 'Television and the English' Survey, Box 1, C(i) file, William Empson to Geoffrey Gorer, 14 Apr 1958.

12. Gorer, 'Television and the English' Survey, Box 1, C(i) file, Enid Blyton to Geoffrey Gorer, 5 May 1958; Hilde Himmelweit, *Television and the Child* (1958), pp 40, 49; *Sociological Review* (Dec 1959), pp 273–4 (Edward Blishen); *Spectator*, 26 Dec 1958 (Geoffrey Nicholson); *Listener*, 25 Dec 1958; Abrams, Box 88, 'Working Papers on TV, 1954–65' file, 'A Study of Children's Television', Jun 1958.

13. Haines, 1–6 Jun 1958; Dave Russell, *Looking North* (Manchester, 2004), p 253; Leo McKinstry, *Jack & Bobby* (2002), pp 105–7; Stephen Wagg, *The Football World* (Brighton, 1984), p 130; *Daily Express*, 18 Jun 1958; *Observer*, 22 Jun 1958; *Financial Times*, 26 Jun 2010 (Simon Kuper); Ian Chadband, 'Sweden, Skegness and the "First" Sven', *Evening Standard*, 27 May 2002; Matthew Taylor, *The Association Game* (Harlow, 2008), p 213.

14. Helpful accounts of the strike include: Geoffrey Goodman, *The Awkward Warrior* (1979), pp 164–99; Robert Shepherd, *Iain Macleod* (1994), pp 134–42; Nina Fishman, '"Spearhead of the Movement"?', in Alan Campbell et al (eds), *British Trade Unions and Industrial Politics, Volume One* (Aldershot, 1999), pp 268–92.

15. *Observer*, 9 Feb 1958; *Daily Mail*, 13 Jan 1958; Macmillan, dep.d.31, 29 Apr 1958, fol 90; Goodman, *Awkward Warrior*, pp 173–4; *Observer*, 4 May 1958.

16. *New Statesman*, 10 May 1958, 14 Jun 1958 (Francis Williams); Haines, 11 May 1958; Shepherd, *Iain Macleod*, p 139; Macmillan, dep.d.31, 31 May 1958, fol 135; Langford, 1 Jun 1958; *Evening News*, 3 Jun 1958; Goodman, *Awkward Warrior*, pp 187–8; Heap, 20 Jun 1958; *New Yorker*, 12 Jul 1958; Goodman, *Awkward Warrior*, p 194; BBC WA, *Any Questions?*, 14 Feb 1958; *Punch*, 14 May 1958; Turtle, 11 Jun 1958.

17. Macmillan, dep.d.31, 11 May 1958, fol 99, 10 Apr 1958, fol 69, 11 Apr 1958, fol 70; Colin Crouch, *The Politics of Industrial Relations* (1982 edn), p 40; John Campbell, *Margaret Thatcher, Volume One* (2000), p 108; Shepherd, *Iain Macleod*, p 148; Michael Kandiah, 'Conservative Leaders, Strategy – And "Consensus"?,

1945–1964', in Harriet Jones and Michael Kandiah (eds), *The Myth of Consensus* (Basingstoke, 1996), p 62.

18. Russell Bretherton, *The Control of Demand 1958–1964* (1999), pp 6–7; *Financial Times*, 4 Jul 1958; Macmillan, dep.d.32, 31 Jul 1958, fol 91.

19. Macmillan, dep.d.32, 14 Jun 1958, fol 22; Wybrow, *Britain Speaks*, p 54; *News Chronicle*, 9 Jul 1958; *New Statesman*, 19 Jul 1958; Campbell, *Margaret Thatcher*, pp 113–15; Goodman, *Awkward Warrior*, pp 240–41; Crossman, pp 687–9.

20. *Independent*, 18 Jun 1999 (Robert Hanks); Alun Howkins, 'History and the *Radio Ballads*', *Oral History* (Autumn 2000), pp 89–93; Paul Leslie Long, 'The Aesthetics of Class in Post-War Britain', Phd diss, University of Warwick, 2001, p 196; *New Statesman*, 12 Jul 1958; BBC WA, R9/6/79 – LR/58/1051; *Sunday Times*, 13 Jul 1958; H. E. Bates, *The World in Ripeness* (1972), p 150; *Punch*, 20 Aug 1958 (R.G.G. Price).

21. Lawrence Black, *Redefining British Politics* (Basingstoke, 2010), p 54; idem, *The Political Culture of the Left in Affluent Britain, 1951–64* (Basingstoke, 2003), p 115; Kevin Jefferys, *Anthony Crosland* (1999 edn), p 65; *The Times*, 28 Jul 1958.

22. *Financial Times*, 14 Aug 1958; *Independent*, 29 Sep 1999 (Ian Herbert); *News Chronicle*, 19 Aug 1958; *Daily Mail*, 22 Jul 1958; Dennis Barker, 'Richard Tompkins', *Guardian*, 11 Dec 1992; 'Lawrence Batley', *Daily Telegraph*, 27 Aug 2002; Turtle, 6 Jun 1958; *Kentish Mercury*, 7 Mar 1958; *Drapers Weekly*, 1 Feb 1959; Tom Courtenay, *Dear Tom* (2000), p 133.

23. *Financial Times*, 1 Jun 1959; ITC material at British Film Institute, Audience Research boxes, 1958 box, 'Public Standing Index', Jun 1958; Ralph Harris and Arthur Seldon, *Advertising in Action* (1962), pp 317, 277–81, 82; Mark Robinson, *100 Greatest TV Ads* (2000), pp 31, 86.

24. Jan Boxshall, *Every Home Should Have One* (1997), p 72; John Orbell, 'The Development of Office Technology', in Alison Turton (ed), *Managing Business Archives* (1991), p 63; *Spectator*, 2 May 1958 (Leslie Adrian); William Osgerby, '"One For the Money, Two For the Show"', PhD diss, University of Sussex, 1992, p 265; *Independent*, 16 Jun 1997 (Nic Cicutti), 23 Nov 2002 (Howard Jacobson); Frances Woodsford, *Dear Mr Bigelow* (2009), p 279.

25. Nicholas Ind, *Terence Conran* (1995), pp 118–19; *Daily Herald*, 10 Jul 1958; *Guardian*, 4 Jan 2007 (Simon Bowers and Julia Kollewe).

26. *New Yorker*, 16 Aug 1958; *Radio Times*, 25 Jul 1958; *The Times*, 26 Mar 2009 (Valentine Low); *Daily Mirror*, 28 Jul 1958, 31 Jul 1958.

27. Patricia Greene et al, *The Book of The Archers* (1994), pp 39, 164; David Marr (ed), Patrick White, *Letters* (1994), pp 145–6; Carl Chinn, *Better Betting with a Decent Feller* (2004 edn), p 238; *The Times*, 26 Aug 1958; Martin, 27 Aug 1958; Langford, 27 Aug 1958; *Listener*, 4 Sep 1958 (Philip Henderson); Larkin, Ms Eng. c. 7418, 27 Aug 1958, fol 88.

28. http://www.theclitheroekid.org.uk; John Hudson, *Wakes Week* (Stroud, 1992), p 145; Macmillan, dep.d.33, 20 Aug 1958, fol 8; *Coventry Standard*, 25 Jul 1958; Haines, 3 Aug 1958; Sue Read, *Hallo Campers!* (1986), pp 163, 166. For a fuller version of Cliff-at-Clacton, see Pete Frame, *The Restless Generation* (2007), p 334.

29. *Sunday Times*, 1 Sep 1958; *Evening News* (Portsmouth), 23 Aug 1958, 1 Sep 1958.

8 Get the Nigger

1. *Guardian Journal* (Nottingham), 25 Aug 1958; *Manchester Guardian*, 25 Aug 1958; Ruth Glass, *Newcomers* (1960), p 131; *Manchester Guardian*, 26 Aug 1958; Glass, *Newcomers*, p 132; *The Times*, 1 Sep 1958; *Manchester Guardian*, 27 Aug 1958; Glass, *Newcomers*, p 135; *Kensington News and West London Times*, 29 Aug 1958, 5 Sep 1958.

2. *Daily Express*, 1 Sep 1958; Mike Phillips and Trevor Phillips, *Windrush* (1998), p 174; Glass, *Newcomers*, pp 136–7; *Kensington News and West London Times*, 5 Sep 1958; *Manchester Guardian*, 5 Sep 1958.

3. *Daily Express*, 2 Sep 1958; *Manchester Guardian*, 2 Sep 1958; *Scotsman*, 2 Sep 1958; *Kensington News and West London Times*, 5 Sep 1958; Phillips, *Windrush*, pp 175–6; *Daily Express*, 2 Sep 1958; Benn, p 286; Glass, *Newcomers*, p 140; *The Times*, 3 Sep 1958; Glass, *Newcomers*, p 141.

4. Michael Banton, *White and Coloured* (1959), p 159; *City and Suburban News* (Manchester), 11 Oct 1957; *Spectator*, 5 Sep 1958 (Eleanor Ettlinger); Glass, *Newcomers*, p 81; *Observer*, 22 Jun 1958; *Coventry Standard*, 1 Aug 1958; *Birmingham Mail*, 30 Aug 1958.

5. *Kensington News and West London Times*, 22 Aug 1958; Glass, *Newcomers*, p 60; *Manchester Guardian*, 23 Nov 1957; Sheila Patterson, *Dark Strangers* (1963), pp 179–84; Glass, *Newcomers*, p 76; *Manchester Guardian*, 4 Mar 1957.

6. Glass, *Newcomers*, p 86; *Big Issue*, 26 Apr 2004; *Radio Times*, 6 Jun 1958; *Punch*, 27 Aug 1958.

7. BBC WA, *Any Questions?*, 12 Sep 1958.

8. *The Times*, 4 Sep 1958; *Observer*, 7 Sep 1958; D. W. Dean, 'Conservative Governments and the Restriction of Commonwealth Immigration in the 1950s', *Historical Journal* (Mar 1992), p 189; *Smethwick Telephone*, 12 Sep 1958; Glass, *Newcomers*, pp 153, 155; Simon Heffer, 'What Enoch Was Really Saying', *Spectator*, 24 Nov 2001.

9. Paul Foot, *Immigration and Race in British Politics* (Harmondsworth, 1965), p 169; Arthur Marwick, *The Sixties* (Oxford, 1998), p 235; *Daily Mail*, 2 Sep 1958; *Daily Mirror*, 3 Sep 1958; Ken Lunn, 'Complex Encounters: Trade Unions, Immigration and Racism', in John McIlroy et al (eds), *British Trade Unions and Industrial Politics, Volume Two* (Aldershot, 1999), p 80; *Reynolds News*, 7 Sep 1958; Dean, 'Conservative Governments', p 192; *The Times*, 29 Sep 1958.

10. Heap, 1 Sep 1958; Maurice Edelman Papers (Modern Records Centre, University of Warwick), Ms 125/1/3/33; *News Chronicle*, 8 Sep 1958; Glass, *Newcomers*, p 123; Turtle, 17 Sep 1958; Colin MacInnes, *England, Half English* (1986 edn), p 39; BBC WA, R9/19/2, Oct–Nov 1958; Glass, *Newcomers*, p 247.

11. *Listener*, 11 Sep 1958 (Philip Henderson); *Kensington News and West London Times*, 12 Sep 1958; *Express and Star* (Wolverhampton), 4 Sep 1958, 6 Sep 1958, 8–9 Sep 1958, 11 Sep 1958; *Guardian Journal* (Nottingham), 13 Sep 1958; *The Times*, 18 Sep 1958; *North London Press*, 19 Sep 1958, 26 Sep 1958; *The Times*, 19 Sep 1958, 22 Sep 1958; *North London Press*, 3 Oct 1958; Emily Green, 'Sylvester Hughes', *Independent*, 23 Jul 1991.

12. *Evening Standard*, 4 Sep 1958; Frank Cousins Papers (Modern Records Centre, University of Warwick), Ms 282/8/3/1, Sep 1958; Olga Cannon and J.R.L.

Anderson, *The Road from Wigan Pier* (1973), pp 192–6; *Billingham Post*, 11 Sep 1958; David Kynaston, *The City of London, Volume 4* (2001), p 153.

13. Michael Hellicar, 'The First TV Set', *Daily Mail*, 14 Sep 2002; *Daily Mirror*, 15 Sep 1958, 29 Sep 1958, 6 Oct 1958, 19 Sep 1958; Morris Bright and Robert Ross, *Carry On Uncensored* (1999), pp 8, 10; Sue Harper and Vincent Porter, *British Cinema of the 1950s* (Oxford, 2003), p 193.

14. Muriel Beadle, *These Ruins Are Inhabited* (1961), pp 15–17; *Daily Mirror*, 24 Sep 1958; John Bloom, *It's No Sin to Make a Profit* (1971), pp 14–15, 21–32; T.A.B. Corley, *Domestic Electrical Appliances* (1966), p 55.

15. *Daily Mirror*, 15 Sep 1958; *The Times*, 21 Jul 2008 (Mick Hume); Joe Moran, 'Milk Bars, Starbucks and The Uses of Literacy', *Cultural Studies* (Nov 2006), p 564; Willmott, 1 Oct 1958.

16. Raymond Williams, *Politics and Letters* (1979), p 132; John Mullan, 'Rebel in a Tweed Suit', *Guardian*, 28 May 2005; Raymond Williams, *Culture and Society, 1780–1950* (1958), pp 205–6; Raphael Samuel, '"Philosophy Teaching By Example": Past and Present in Raymond Williams', *History Workshop* (Spring 1989), p 146; Williams, *Culture and Society*, pp 327–8; *New Statesman*, 27 Sep 1958; *Spectator*, 10 Oct 1958; *Times Literary Supplement*, 26 Sep 1958; *Encounter*, Jan 1959, pp 86–8; Samuel, 'Past and Present', p 142; Fred Inglis, *Raymond Williams* (1995), p 146.

17. Norman MacKenzie (ed), *Conviction* (1958), pp 92, 138, 230; *Socialist Commentary*, Nov 1958, pp 29; Noel Annan, *Our Age* (1990), p 596.

18. *Architects' Journal*, 25 Sep 1958; Turtle, 21 Sep 1958; *Daily Telegraph*, 26 Sep 1958; Benn, p 289; *Sheffield Telegraph*, 24 Sep 1958; *Architectural Review* (Oct 1958), p 282; Bevis Hillier, *Betjeman: The Bonus of Laughter* (2004), pp 167–8; *Lost City*, BBC TV, 26 Oct 1958 (TV Heaven at National Media Museum, Bradford); Dan Smith, *An Autobiography* (Newcastle upon Tyne, 1970), pp 48, 61–5.

19. Spencer Leigh, 'Halfway to Paradise', *Record Collector* (Feb 2008), p 59; *Observer Music Monthly* (May 2004), p 25 (Simon Napier-Bell); Spencer Leigh, 'Ian Samwell', *Independent*, 17 Mar 2003; *Guardian*, 26 Sep 2008 (John Pidgeon); *The Times*, 25 Jun 2004 (Lisa Verrico).

20. *The Times*, 4 Oct 2008 (David Robertson); *Guardian*, 23 Jun 2007 (Ian Jack); Ronald Miller and David Sawers, *The Technical Development of Modern Aviation* (1968), pp 179–82; Clive Jenkins, 'BOAC: The Anatomy of a Strike', *Universities and Left Review* (Spring 1959), pp 30–34.

21. Peter Weiler, 'The Rise and Fall of the Conservatives' "Grand Design for Housing", 1951–64', *Contemporary British History* (Spring 2000), p 132; Hilary Spurling, *Secrets of a Woman's Heart* (1984), p 245; Richard Davenport-Hines, 'Peter Rachman', in *Oxford Dictionary of National Biography*, vol 45 (Oxford, 2004), p 716. In general on the Rent Act's background and implementation, see (in addition to Weiler's 'Rise and Fall'): John Davis, 'Rent and Race in 1960s London: New Light on Rachmanism', *Twentieth Century British History*, 12/1 (2001), pp 69–92; Alan G. V. Simmonds, 'Raising Rachman: The Origins of the Rent Act, 1957', *Historical Journal* (Dec 2002), pp 843–68.

22. *Guardian*, 11 Oct 2008 (Bobby Smith); Garry Whannel, '"Grandstand", the Sports Fan and the Family Audience', in John Corner (ed), *Popular Television in Britain* (1991), p 188; *Radio Times*, 3 Oct 1958; Larkin, Ms Eng. c.7418, 16 Oct 1958, fol 120; Martin Bauml Duberman, *Paul Robeson* (1989), p 471.

23. Alan Sillitoe, *Saturday Night and Sunday Morning* (Pan edn, 1960), p 5; Richard
    Bradford, *The Life of a Long-Distance Writer* (2008), p 152; *New Statesman*, 25
    Oct 1958.
24. Turtle, 16 Oct 1958; *Radio Times*, 10 Oct 1958; Biddy Baxter, 'Christopher Trace',
    Independent, 8 Sep 1992; Lawrence Black, *Redefining British Politics* (Basingstoke,
    2010), p 87; BBC WA, R9/7/36 – VR/58/558; *Guardian*, 28 Oct 2008 (Frank
    Keating), 15 Sep 2009 (Richard Williams); *News Chronicle*, 21 Oct 1958; *New
    Yorker*, 1 Nov 1958; *Daily Mirror*, 20 Oct 1958, 22 Oct 1958.
25. Macmillan, dep.d.33, 4 Oct 1958, fol 60, 18 Oct 1958, fol 74; Neil Rollings,
    'Butskellism, the Postwar Consensus and the Managed Economy', in Harriet Jones
    and Michael Kandiah (eds), *The Myth of Consensus* (Basingstoke, 1996), p 111;
    Macmillan, dep.d.33, 22 Oct 1958, fols 80–81; *Manchester Guardian*, 28 Oct 1958;
    George H. Gallup, *The Gallup International Public Opinion Polls: Great Britain
    1937–1975, Volume One* (New York, 1976), p 482.
26. Jonathan Dimbleby, *Richard Dimbleby* (1975), p 342; Langford, 28 Oct 1958;
    Heap, 28 Oct 1958; *TV Times*, 26 Oct 1958; Tony Jasper, *The Top Twenty Book*
    (1994 edn), p 42; *Radio Times*, 24 Oct 1958, 31 Oct 1958; *Oldie*, Sep 2000, p 59
    (Frank Keating); Jim White, 'And Coleman is 70', *Independent*, 26 Apr 1996;
    Dennis Barker, 'Bryan Cowgill', *Guardian*, 18 Jul 2008.

9 Parity of Esteem

1. *Socialist Commentary* (May 1956), p 13; Michael Young, *The Rise of the Meritocracy,
   1870–2033* (Penguin edn, 1961), pp 94, 169.
2. Paul Barker, 'A Tract for the Times', in Geoff Dench (ed), *The Rise and Rise of
   Meritocracy* (Oxford, 2006), pp 44, 40; *Spectator*, 21 Nov 1958; *The Times*, 30 Oct
   1958; Barker, 'Tract', p 39; *Encounter*, Feb 1959, pp 68–72.
3. Harry Ritchie, *Success Stories* (1988), p 79; Humphrey Carpenter, *The Angry Young
   Men* (2002), p 153; *Crossman*, p 598; *Daily Sketch*, 25 Jan 1958; David Edgerton,
   Warfare State (Cambridge, 2006), p 180; Joe Moran, *On Roads* (2009), pp 20, 34;
   'Sir Denis Rooke, OM', *Daily Telegraph*, 6 Sep 2008; Tam Dalyell, 'Sir Denis
   Rooke', *Independent*, 8 Sep 2008.
4. Nicholas Faith, 'Lord Weinstock', *Independent*, 24 Jul 2002; D. C. Coleman,
   Courtauld's: III (Oxford, 1980), pp 141–2, 327; David Kynaston, *The City of
   London, Volume 4* (2001), p 78.
5. Michael Leapman, 'Robert Robinson', *Independent*, 15 Aug 2011; Michael
   Leapman, 'Brian Redhead', *Independent*, 24 Jan 1994; Harold Evans, *My Paper
   Chase* (2009), p 208; 'Jean Rook', *Daily Telegraph*, 6 Sep 1991; Michael Leapman,
   'Keith Waterhouse', *Independent*, 8 Sep 2009; Peter Guttridge, 'Professor Sir
   Malcolm Bradbury', *Independent*, 29 Nov 2000; Jonathan Coe, *Like a Fiery
   Elephant* (2004), p 82; Lucasta Miller, 'John Carey', *Guardian*, 4 Jun 2005; *Ian
   Hamilton in Conversation with Dan Jacobson* (2002), pp 13, 113; Tony
   Richardson, *Long Distance Runner* (1993); Stephen Fay, *Power Play* (1995);
   'John Thaw', *Daily Telegraph*, 23 Feb 2002; Peter Stead, *Film and the Working
   Class* (1989), pp 190–91; Val Williams, 'Terence Donovan', *Independent*, 25 Nov
   1996; Tim Cumming, 'Shooting Stars', *Independent*, 7 Aug 2002; Pierre Perrone,

'Brian Duffy', *Independent*, 17 Jun 2010; *Financial Times*, 3 Nov 2007 (Julian Flanagan); Natalie Rudd, *Peter Blake* (2003), pp 7, 25; Tim Marlow, 'Bryan Robertson', *Independent*, 26 Nov 2002; Wikipedia, 'Zandra Rhodes'; *Independent*, 9 Jan 2009 (Michael Coveney); John Repsch, *The Legendary Joe Meek* (1989), pp 52, 63.

6. *Encounter*, Feb 1958, p 60, Apr 1958, p 70; Humphrey Carpenter, *Dennis Potter* (1998), pp 55–98; Margaret Forster, *Hidden Lives* (1995), pp 244–9; *Daily Telegraph*, 31 May 2003; *Guardian*, 10 Oct 1998.

7. *Sunday Times*, 11 Oct 1959; Anton Rippon, *A Derby Boy* (Stroud, 2007), chap 6; Mary Evans, *A Good School* (1991), pp 91, 9, 83–5, 101, 4, 10–11, 41, 120; Roy Greenslade, *Goodbye to the Working Class* (1976), pp 23, 151–9; *The Ashbeian*, 1957–8, pp 28–9.

8. *Spectator*, 28 Jun 1957; Jacqueline Wilson, *Jacky Daydream* (2007), pp 285–7; Haines, 24 Jan 1958; Wilson, *Jacky*, pp 287–90; Haines, 24–5 Apr 1958; Ken Blakemore, *Sunnyside Down* (Stroud, 2005), pp 145–6; Greenslade, *Goodbye*, pp 20–21; Kevin Cann, *Any Day Now* (2010), p 18.

9. Peter Willmott, 'Some Social Trends', in J. B. Cullingworth (ed), *Problems of an Urban Society, Volume III* (1973), p 96; *News Chronicle*, 21–3 Apr 1958; *Listener*, 24 Oct 1957; Roy Lewis and Rosemary Stewart, *The Boss* (1958), p 99.

10. J. E. Floud et al, *Social Class and Educational Opportunity* (1956), p 42; William Taylor, *The Secondary Modern School* (1963), pp 51, 156, 47; Michael Sanderson, *Educational Opportunity and Social Change in England* (1987), p 56; William Liversidge, 'Life Chances', *Sociological Review* (Mar 1962), pp 21–2, 33; M. P. Carter, *Home, School and Work* (Oxford, 1962), pp 71, 79.

11. Sanderson, *Educational Opportunity*, p 52; Alan Little and John Westergaard, 'The Trend of Class Differentials in Educational Opportunity in England and Wales', *British Journal of Sociology* (Dec 1964), p 303; Eva Bene, 'Some Differences between Middle-Class and Working-Class Grammar School Boys in their Attitudes towards Education', *British Journal of Sociology* (Jun 1959), p 151.

12. Sanderson, *Educational Opportunity*, p 71; Brian Simon, *Education and the Social Order, 1940–1990* (1991), pp 201–2; *Observer*, 4 Sep 1960; Willmott, 'Social Trends', p 96; *New Statesman*, 30 Aug 1958 (K. W. Wedderburn); *Sunday Times*, 29 Dec 1957; *Observer*, 4 Sep 1960.

13. Floud et al, *Social Class*, p 81; Abrams, Box 85, file '1 of 3', Research Services Ltd, 'A Pilot Enquiry into Some Aspects of Working-Class Life in London' (1957); Peter Willmott, *The Evolution of a Community* (1963), pp 115–16; Brian Jackson and Dennis Marsden, *Education and the Working Class* (1962), pp 103–23, 237; Carter, *Home*, pp 118–19.

14. *Daily Mail*, 1 Aug 1958, 4–5 Aug 1958; *Wisden Cricketers' Almanack, 1958* (1958), pp 111–12; Michael Marshall, *Gentlemen and Players* (1987), pp 253–4.

15. Gerald Aylmer, 'Lord James of Rusholm', *Independent*, 21 May 1992; George Perry, *The Great British Picture Show* (1985 edn), pp 200–201; Basil Bernstein, *Class, Codes and Control, Volume 1* (1971), pp 43–61; Anne de Courcy, *Snowdon* (2008), p 57; John Moynihan, 'Sunday Soccer', in Ian Hamilton (ed), *The Faber Book of Soccer* (1992), pp 76–86.

16. *Radio Times*, 15 Aug 1958; BBC WA, R9/2/10, week 17–23 Aug 1958; Kynaston, *City*, p 212.

17. Turtle, 15 Sep 1958; *New Statesman*, 23 Aug 1958; Anthony Crosland, *The Future of Socialism* (2006 edn), p 218; *Spectator*, 4 Jan 1957; Dennis Dean, 'Preservation or Renovation? The Dilemmas of Conservative Educational Policy 1955–1960', *Twentieth Century British History*, 3/1 (1992), pp 28–9; *Daily Mail*, 20 May 1958.

18. *New Statesman*, 30 Aug 1958, 20 Sep 1958, 27 Sep 1958, 11 Oct 1958; *Socialist Commentary*, Oct 1958, p 26; Muriel Beadle, *These Ruins are Inhabited* (1961), pp 148–51; Crosland, *Future*, p 218; BBC WA, R9/7/26 – VR/57/66.

19. Sanderson, *Educational Opportunity*, p 47; Robin Pedley, *Comprehensive Education* (1956), p 41; Simon, *Education*, p 209; P. E. Vernon, *Secondary School Selection* (1957), pp 169, 177; Harry Judge, *A Generation of Schooling* (Oxford, 1984), pp 47–8; *New Statesman*, 25 May 1957; *News Chronicle*, 5 Feb 1957; *Daily Express*, 8 May 1957.

20. Taylor, *Secondary Modern*, p 34; *Sunday Times*, 21 Apr 1957; *Spectator*, 14 Jun 1957; Carter, *Home*, p 5; Gary McCulloch, *Failing the Ordinary Child?* (Buckingham, 1998), p 89; Taylor, *Secondary Modern*, p 50.

21. Taylor, *Secondary Modern*, p 37; *New Statesman*, 21 Sep 1957; H. C. Dent, *Secondary Modern School* (1958), pp 14, 42, 152; Melissa Benn, *School Wars* (2011), pp 45–7; John Lanchester, *Family Romance* (2007), pp 234–5.

22. Taylor, *Secondary Modern*, pp 106–7, 110; Rhodes Boyson, *Speaking My Mind* (1995), p 52; Taylor, *Secondary Modern*, p 118; Brian Simon, 'The Tory Government and Education, 1951–60', *History of Education* (Dec 1985), p 293; *Economist*, 6 Dec 1958.

23. George H. Gallup, *The Gallup International Public Opinon Polls: Great Britain, 1937–1975, Volume One* (New York, 1976), p 470; Melissa Benn, 'Allen Clarke', *Guardian*, 25 Aug 2007; *Economist*, 6 Dec 1958.

24. *Sunday Times*, 27 Jan 1957; *Times Educational Supplement*, 15 Feb 1957; *Economist*, 22 Jun 1957; *Spectator*, 12 Dec 1958; Brian Simon, 'Harry Rée', *Independent*, 21 May 1991; Simon, *Education*, p 210; *New Statesman*, 12 Oct 1957, 18 Oct 1958; *Listener*, 11 Jul 1957; *New Statesman*, 21 Feb 1959, 25 May 1957; Vernon, *Secondary School Selection*, p 50; Raymond Williams, *Culture and Society, 1780–1950* (1958), pp 331–2.

25. David Crook, 'The Disputed Origins of the Leicestershire Two-Tier Comprehensive Schools Plan', *History of Education Society Bulletin* (Autumn 1992), pp 55–8; *Observer*, 19 Oct 1958; *Times Educational Supplement*, 12 Apr 1957; Leicestershire RO, DE 3627/207, Oadby Gartree School minutes, 23 Sep 1957, 21 Jan 1958; Gerald T. Rimmington, *The Comprehensive Issue in Leicester 1945–1974 and Other Essays* (Peterborough, 1984), pp 8–9.

26. *Western Daily Press*, 12 Oct 1957; Simon, *Education*, pp 206, 219; *Western Daily Press*, 14 Oct 1957, 18 Oct 1957; *Northern Despatch*, 3 Oct 1958, 8 Nov 1958, 23 Oct 1958; Richard Batley et al, *Going Comprehensive* (1970), pp 36–9, 98.

27. City of Bradford, *Official Records of Council Meetings, 1957–8* (Bradford, 1958), pp 148, 151, *1958–9* (Bradford, 1959), pp 142–5.

28. *Socialist Commentary*, Apr 1957, p 9; Labour Party Archives (People's History Museum, Manchester), 'Study Group on Education: Minutes and Papers: 27 March 1957–8 Jan 1958', 'Study Group on Education: Minutes and Papers: 20 Jan 1958–4 Feb 1959'; Crossman, Ms 154/8/21, 10 Feb 1958, fols 1,070–72.

29. *Spectator*, 20 Jun 1958; Robin Pedley, *The Comprehensive School* (Penguin edn, 1969), p 180; *New Yorker*, 6 Sep 1958; Beverley Shaw, *Comprehensive Schooling* (Oxford, 1983), pp 56–7; *New Statesman*, 28 Jun 1958, 5 Jul 1958.
30. *The Times*, 30 Sep 1958; *Journal* (Newcastle), 30 Sep 1958; *New Statesman*, 4 Oct 1958; Philip M. Williams, *Hugh Gaitskell* (1979), pp 468, 896; *Sociological Review* (Dec 1959), pp 269–70.

10 Unnatural Practices

1. *TV Times*, 31 Oct 1958; *Spectator*, 21 Nov 1958 (Peter Forster); *Radio Times*, 7 Nov 1958; Tony Jasper, *The Top Twenty Book* (1994 edn), p 42; *New Statesman*, 8 Nov 1958, 22 Nov 1958; Charles Marowitz et al (eds), *The Encore Reader* (Methuen pbk edn, 1970), pp 96–103; *Larkin*, p 244; Fowles, EUL Ms 102/1/10, 9 Nov 1958; *News Chronicle*, 17 Nov 1958; Raynham, 8 Nov 1958; Haines, 17 Nov 1958; Heap, 28 Nov 1958.
2. Ian Harvey, *To Fall like Lucifer* (1971), pp 105–13; *The Times*, 21 Nov 1958, 25 Nov 1958; Macmillan, dep.d.33, 21 Nov 1958, fol 106; *The Times*, 30 Jul 2002.
3. *The Times*, 19 Oct 1995 (William Rees-Mogg); *New Yorker*, 13 Dec 1958 (Mollie Panter-Downes); *Hansard*, House of Commons Debates, 26 Nov 1958, cols 417, 428–9, 465; Trevor Fisher, 'Permissiveness and the Politics of Morality', *Contemporary Record* (Summer 1993), p 161; George H. Gallup, *The Gallup International Public Opinon Polls: Great Britain, 1937–1975, Volume One* (New York, 1976), p 487; *Encounter* (Feb 1959), p 62 (Peter Wildeblood); *Spectator*, 26 Dec 1958 (letters); Gordon Westwood, *A Minority* (1960), pp ix, 182–90.
4. Fisher, 'Permissiveness', pp 159, 161–2; Tanya Evans, 'The Other Woman and Her Child', seminar at Institute of Historical Research, London, 20 Feb 2008.
5. Peter Pagnamenta and Richard Overy, *All Our Working Lives* (1984), pp 93–4; Stephen Wilks, *Industrial Policy and the Motor Industry* (Manchester, 1984), p 77; Peter Scott, 'The Worst of Both Worlds', *Business History* (Oct 1996), p 54; Michael P. Jackson, *The Price of Coal* (1974), pp 100–101; *Listener*, 13 Nov 1958; *The Times*, 4 Dec 1958; Geoffrey Owen, *From Empire to Europe* (1999), pp 66–7; John Singleton, *Lancashire on the Scrapheap*, (Oxford, 1991), p 160.
6. A.G.V. Simmonds, 'Conservative Governments and the Housing Question', PhD diss, University of Leeds, 1995, p 41; Chris Maume, 'Sir Lawrie Barratt', *Independent*, 21 December 2012; John Turner, 'A Land Fit for Tories to Live In', *Contemporary European History* (Jul 1995), p 201; *Hansard*, House of Commons Debates, 15 Dec 1958, col 892.
7. *New Statesman*, 6 Nov 1958; Geoffrey Goodman, *The Awkward Warrior* (1979), pp 205–6; *Crossman*, p 726; Anthony Howard, *Crossman* (1990), p 214; *Financial Times*, 14 Nov 1958; *Evening Standard*, 21 Jan 1959; *Crossman*, p 726.
8. Benn, pp 294–5; *Universities and Left Review* (Autumn 1958), p 66; Eric Hobsbawm, *Interesting Times* (2002), pp 212–14; Willmott, 3 Jan 1959, 29 Jan 1959.
9. Joe Moran, *On Roads* (2009), p 20; *The Times*, 6 Dec 1958; Michael Bond, *A Bear Called Paddington* (Young Lions edn, 1971), p 9; *The Times*, 6 Apr 1998 (Dalya Alberge); *Times Literary Supplement*, 21 Nov 1958; Michael Bond, *Bears & Forebears* (1996), p 159; Bevis Hillier, *John Betjeman: New Fame, New Love* (2002),

pp 605–11; *New Statesman*, 6 Dec 1958; *Listener*, 11 Dec 1958; Rupert Hart-Davis (ed), *The Lyttelton Hart-Davis Letters: Volume Three* (1981), p 176.

10. *New Statesman*, 13 Dec 1958; *New Musical Express*, 19 Dec 1958; Spencer Leigh, 'Tito Burns', *Independent*, 17 Sep 2010; 'John Koon', *Daily Telegraph*, 12 Feb 1997; Heap, 18 Dec 1958; *Spectator*, 2 Jan 1959; *TV Times*, 26 Dec 1958; BBC WA, R9/7/38 – VR/59/6.

11. *News Chronicle*, 17 Nov 1958; *Financial Times*, 24 Dec 1958; *New Statesman*, 3 Jan 1959 (Francis Williams); *Financial Times*, 1 Jan 1959; *Economist*, 3 Jan 1959; Gerold Krozewski, *Money and the End of Empire* (Basingstoke, 2001), p 150; *Listener*, 12 Feb 1959.

12. For the fullest recent account of the Aluminium War, see Niall Ferguson, *High Financier* (2010), pp 183–99, though see also Tim Congdon's review in *Times Literary Supplement*, 30 Jul 2010.

13. David Kynaston, *The City of London, Volume 4* (2001), pp 107–14.

14. Larkin, Ms Eng. c.7419, 27 Dec 1958, fol 43; *News of the World*, 4 Jan 1959; *Sunday Express*, 4 Jan 1959; Jim Laker, *Over To Me* (1960), p 53.

11 Morbid Sentimentality

1. *The Times*, 3 Jan 1959, 7 Jan 1959; *Sunday Express*, 4 Jan 1959; Heap, 6 Jan 1959; 'Edwin Brock', *The Times*, 26 Sep 1997; Anthony Thwaite, 'Edwin Brock', *Independent*, 10 Sep 1997; Larkin, Ms Eng. c. 7419, 12 Jan 1959, fol 51; *The Times*, 13 Jan 1959; D. R. Thorpe, *Supermac* (2010), p 424; *Spectator*, 24 May 1963; *The Times*, 16 Jan 1959.

2. *New Yorker*, 7 Mar 1959; *Birmingham Post*, 25 Feb 1959; Michael Frostick and Mark Pottle, 'Michael Hawthorn', *Oxford Dictionary of National Biography*, vol 25 (Oxford, 2004), p 977; Preston, 23 Jan 1959; Haines, 29–30 Jan 1959; *Radio Times*, 23 Jan 1959; *Guardian Weekend*, 17 Aug 2002 (Gary Younge); Colin Prescod, 'Carnival', in Marika Sherwood (ed), *Claudia Jones* (1999), pp 151–8.

3. *Spectator*, 6 Feb 1959; *Daily Mirror*, 6 Feb 1959; *New Statesman*, 7 Feb 1959; Benn, p 298; Macmillan, dep.d.34, 6 Feb 1959, fol 76; Brian McHugh, 'The Saturday after Buddy Holly Died', *Guardian*, 8 Jan 2011; BBC WA, R9/7/38 – VR/59/68.

4. *Vogue* (Feb 1959), p 98; David Hendy, 'Bad Language and BBC Radio Four in the 1960s and 1970s', *Twentieth Century British History*, 17/1 (2006), p 76; *Spectator*, 30 Jan 1959; *New Statesman*, 31 Jan 1959; John Hill, *Sex, Class and Realism* (1986), p 191; Paddy Whannel, 'Room at the Top', *Universities and Left Review* (Spring 1959), p 24; Dave Russell, *Looking North* (Manchester, 2004), pp 184–5; *Birmingham Mail*, 27 Feb 1959.

5. http://www.youtube.com/watch?v=Dictn9woAve; Dave Rolinson, '"If They Want Culture, They Pay"', in Ian MacKillop and Neil Sinyard (eds), *British Cinema of the 1950s* (Manchester, 2003), p 91; Vincent Porter, 'The Hegemonic Turn', *Journal of Popular British Cinema* (2001), p 91; Hill, *Sex*, pp 192–3; Heap, 26 Mar 1959; Dennis Barker, 'Peter Rogers', *Guardian*, 16 Apr 2009.

6. Alan Strachan, 'Willis Hall', *Independent*, 12 Mar 2005; Dennis Barker, 'Willis Hall', *Guardian*, 12 Mar 2005; *Spectator*, 16 Jan 1959; *Birmingham Mail*, 8 Jan 1959; Michael Billington, *The Life and Work of Harold Pinter* (1996), p 106;

Birmingham Mail, 13 Jan 1959; *Birmingham Post*, 13 Jan 1959; Stuart Laing, *Representations of Working-Class Life, 1957–1964* (Basingstoke, 1986), p 106; *Spectator*, 27 Feb 1959.

7. *News Chronicle*, 11 Feb 1959; Heap, 10 Feb 1959; *News Chronicle*, 11 Feb 1959, 13–14 Feb 1959; *Sunday Times*, 15 Feb 1959; *Observer*, 15 Feb 1959; *Sunday Express*, 15 Feb 1959; *News Chronicle*, 16 Feb 1959, 19 Feb 1959; *New Statesman*, 21 Feb 1959, 28 Feb 1959; Graham Payn and Sheridan Morley (eds), *The Noël Coward Diaries* (1982), p 408.

8. *TV Times*, 12 Sep 1958; Leonard Miall, 'Sydney Newman', *Independent*, 4 Nov 1997; *Spectator*, 27 Mar 1959; Derrik Mercer (ed), *20th Century Day by Day* (Dorling Kindersley edn, 1999), p 1,144; 'The Army Game' (TV Heaven fact sheet); BBC WA, R9/7/38 – VR/59/52; Richard Webber, *Fifty Years of Hancock's Half Hour* (2004), p 267; Geoff Phillips, *Memories of Tyne Tees Television* (Durham City, 1998), pp 116–17; Dave Nicholson, *Bobby Thompson* (1996 edn), pp 19–20, 27–8, 43, 109–10, 118–19, 130–31, 139–40.

9. BBC WA, R9/7/39 – VR/59/145; *Listener*, 19 Mar 1959; *Radio Times*, 27 Feb 1959; *New Statesman*, 21 Mar 1959; *Punch*, 11 Feb 1959, 18 Mar 1959; Leo McKinstry, *Jack & Bobby* (2002), pp 159–60; *Oxford Mail*, 6 Mar 1959.

10. *Neath Guardian*, 27 Feb 1959; Cy Young, 'The Rise and Fall of the News Theatres', *Journal of British Cinema and Television*, 2/2 (2005), p 238; Holbeck Working Men's Club Centenary Brochure (Leeds Central Library, Local Studies, PLH69 (367)); *Romford Times*, 4 Mar 1959; *Oxford Mail*, 9 Mar 1959; Turtle, 11 Mar 1959; *Scunthorpe and Frodingham Star*, 13 Mar 1959; Wikipedia, 'Eurovision Song Contest 1959'.

11. *TV Times*, 6 Mar 1959; Larkin, Ms Eng. c. 7419, 15 Mar 1959, fols 93–4; *Herts Advertiser*, 20 Mar 1959; *The Times*, 26 Aug 2003 (Roger de Mercado); Martin, 20 Mar 1959; *Daily Mirror*, 23 Mar 1959.

12. *New Yorker*, 4 Apr 1959; *Crossman*, p 742; Steven Fielding, 'Activists Against "Affluence"', *Journal of British Studies* (Apr 2001), p 251; *Socialist Commentary* (Mar 1959), pp 15–17; *New Statesman*, 21 Mar 1959 (Francis Williams); *Woman*, 14 Mar 1959.

13. *Woman's Mirror*, 3 Apr 1959, 10 Apr 1959, 17 Apr 1959, 24 Apr 1959, 1 May 1959; Abrams, Box 54, Industrial Welfare Society, 'What I Expect from Work', May 1959.

14. *Observer*, 22 Mar 1959; http://garydexter.blogspot.com, 7 Oct 2009; Wikipedia, 'Ernö Goldfinger'; *Hampstead & Highgate Express*, 14 Nov 1958; *Architects' Journal*, 12 Mar 1959; Nigel Warburton, *Ernö Goldfinger* (2004), p 142.

15. *Architects' Journal*, 12 Mar 1959; *East London Advertiser*, 19 Dec 1958; Paul Barker, 'London Witness', *Prospect* (Apr 2005), p 44; *The Times*, 10 Apr 1959; David Kynaston, *The City of London, Volume 4* (2001), pp 131–2; *New Yorker*, 4 Apr 1959.

16. *Independent*, 21 Feb 1990 (James Dunnett); *Vogue* (Feb 1959), pp 100–101; 'David Pearce', *The Times*, 17 Oct 2001; *Architects' Journal*, 22 Jan 1959; *New Yorker*, 4 Apr 1959.

17. *Birmingham Mail*, 25 Feb 1959, 5 Mar 1959; Anthony Sutcliffe and Roger Smith, *Birmingham, 1939–1970* (1974), p 445; *Birmingham Mail*, 26–7 Feb 1959, 5 Mar 1959, 27 Feb 1959, 5 Mar 1959, 19 Feb 1959, 25 Feb 1959; David Harvey, *Birmingham Past and Present: The City Centre: Volume 2* (Kettering, 2003), p 69;

Radio Times, 20 Feb 1959; *Who Cares?* ('Never Had It So Good' evening, BBC Parliament, 10 Oct 2009).

18. *Radio Times*, 30 Jan 1959; *Listener*, 12 Feb 1959 (K. W. Gransden); BBC WA, R9/7/38 – VR/59/77; Miles Glendinning and Stefan Muthesius, *Tower Block* (1994), pp 220–24; *Times Literary Supplement*, 4 Sep 1959; T. Brennan, *Reshaping a City* (Glasgow, 1959), p 200; Alec Cairncross, *Living with the Century* (1998), pp 178–9.

19. *Liverpool Echo*, 14 Nov 1958, 24 Nov 1958; Benn, pp 299–300.

20. *Architectural Review* (Jan 1959), pp 71–2; Benwell Community Project, Final Report Series no 4, 'Slums on the Drawing Board' (Newcastle upon Tyne, 1978), pp 8–10; *Proceedings of the Council of the City and County of Newcastle upon Tyne for 1958–1959* (Newcastle upon Tyne, 1959), pp 743–9; *Architects' Journal*, 23 Apr 1959; Clare Hartwell, *Manchester* (2001), pp 35–6, 240–41, 189–90; *Manchester Evening News*, 28 Nov 1958; *Salford City Reporter*, 3 Apr 1959, 10 Apr 1959.

21. *Derbyshire Times*, 30 Jan 1959, 6 Feb 1959; *Oxford Mail*, 5 Mar 1959; *Wigan Examiner*, 20 Mar 1959.

22. *Journal of the Royal Institute of British Architects* (Dec 1958), p 48; *Architects' Journal*, 6 Nov 1958; David Watkin, 'Quinlan Terry', *Standpoint* (Jul 2008), p 81; *Listener*, 12 Feb 1959; Kenneth Powell, 'Geoffrey Powell', *Independent*, 7 Feb 2000; *Architects' Journal*, 19 Mar 1959; *Encounter* (Feb 1959), pp 54–6.

23. N. Tiratsoo, *Reconstruction, Affluence and Labour Politics* (1990), pp 86, 97; *Birmingham Mail*, 16 Feb 1959; *Socialist Commentary* (Apr 1959), pp 12–14; *Spectator*, 1 May 1959.

24. St John, 30 Mar 1959; *Guardian*, 10 Dec 2011 (Albert Beale); *Architects' Journal*, 9 Apr 1959; Simon Gunn and Rachel Bell, *Middle Classes* (2002), p 111; *New Statesman*, 4 Apr 1959; *Ayr Advertiser*, 2 Apr 1959.

25. Last, 4 Apr 1959; *Radio Times*, 27 Mar 1959; *Listener*, 9 Apr 1959; Anthony Thwaite (ed), *Selected Letters of Philip Larkin, 1940–1985* (1992), p 301; Joanna Moorhead, *New Generations* (Cambridge, 1996), p 23.

26. Macmillan, dep.d.35, 7 Apr 1959, fol 71; Heap, 7 Apr 1959; *Financial Times*, 8 Apr 1959; *The Times*, 8 Apr 1959; *Hansard*, House of Commons Debates, 8 Apr 1959, cols 233–4; *Crossman*, pp 744–5; Macmillan, dep.d.35, 9 Apr 1959, fol 72.

27. Peter Willmott and Michael Young, *Family and Class in a London Suburb* (1960), pp 1, 13–14, 112–13, 117–22; *Hansard*, House of Lords Debates, 8 Apr 1959, col 490; *Woman's Mirror*, 3 Apr 1959; *Weekly News*, 4 Apr 1959, 18 Apr 1959.

28. 'Russ Conway', *The Times*, 17 Nov 2000; Spencer Leigh, 'Russ Conway', *Independent*, 18 Nov 2000; Pete Frame, *The Restless Generation* (2007), p 309; *Daily Mirror*, 28 Mar 1959; *New Musical Express*, 24 Apr 1959; *Derby Evening Telegraph*, 20 Apr 1959; Frame, *Restless*, p 373; *Hansard*, House of Commons Debates, 22 Apr 1959, cols 381–2; *Derby Evening Telegraph*, 23–4 Apr 1959, 27 Apr 1959; *New Musical Express*, 1 May 1959; Frame, *Restless*, pp 360–61.

29. Heap, 26 Apr 1959; Gyles Brandreth, *Something Sensational to Read in the Train* (2009), p 4; *Accrington Observer*, 21 Apr 1959, 2 May 1959; Haines, 30 Apr 1959; *South London Press*, 5 May 1959; *Hants and Berks Gazette*, 8 May 1959; Last, 1 May 1959; Crossman, Ms 154/8/24, 6 May 1959, fol 1304; *The Times*, 4 May 1959.

30. Raynham, 4 May 1959; Crossman, Ms 154/8/24, 6 May 1959, fols 1304–5; *The Times*, 4 May 1959; *Neath Guardian*, 8 May 1959; *Aldershot News*, 8 May 1959.

31. *Sunday Express*, 3 May 1959; *Radio Times*, 24 Apr 1959; *TV Times*, 24 Apr 1959; *The Times*, 4 May 1959; Crossman, Ms 154/8/24, 6 May 1959, fol 1,305; *Nottingham Evening News*, 4–5 May 1959. In general on Forest's triumph, see Gary Imlach, *My Father and Other Working-Class Football Heroes* (2005), pp 110–34, 224–31.

12 A Merry Song of Spring

1. *Daily Sketch*, 5 May 1959; Peter Willmott and Michael Young, *Family and Class in a London Suburb* (1960), p 113; Haines, 5 May 1959; Tom Courtenay, *Dear Tom* (2000), pp 196–8; John Heilpern, *John Osborne* (2006), p 252; Graham Payn and Sheridan Morley (eds), *The Noël Coward Diaries* (1982), p 409; *Larkin*, p 249; *New Yorker*, 20 Jun 1959; Michael Billington, *State of the Nation* (2007), p 122.

2. *New Statesman*, 6 Oct 1956; Labour Party Archives (People's History Museum, Manchester), 'Study Group on Education Minutes and Papers: 27 Mar 1957–8 Jan 1958'; Guy Ortolano, 'Two Cultures, One University', *Albion* (Spring 2003), pp 607–9; C. P. Snow, *The Two Cultures* (Cambridge University Press pbk edn, 1969), pp 11, 14, 36–7, 50.

3. *Economist*, 16 May 1959; Russell Davies (ed), *The Kenneth Williams Diaries* (1993), p 150; Lawrence Black, '"Sheep May Safely Gaze"', in Lawrence Black et al, *Consensus or Coercion?* (Cheltenham, 2001), p 37; *Daily Mirror*, 5 May 1959; *The Times*, 2 May 1959; *Daily Express*, 10 Jun 1959; *Punch*, 13 May 1959; Robert Ross, *The Complete Frankie Howerd* (Richmond, 2001), p 166; Graham McCann, *Frankie Howerd* (2004), p 164; Courtenay, *Dear Tom*, pp 198–9.

4. *The Times*, 8 May 1959, 11 May 1959; Richard Bradford, *The Life of a Long-Distance Writer* (2008), p 169; *Kensington News and West London Times*, 22 May 1959; Jerry White, 'Evening All', *Times Literary Supplement*, 13 Nov 2009; *Observer*, 24 May 1959. See also: Mark Olden, *Murder in Notting Hill* (Alresford, 2011).

5. *Observer*, 24 May 1959; *The Times*, 25 May 1959; Mike Phillips and Trevor Phillips, *Windrush* (1998), pp 184–5; *Kensington News and West London Times*, 12 Jun 1959; Yasmin Alibhai-Brown, '50 Years of Race', *Independent*, 11 May 2000; Anthony Sutcliffe and Roger Smith, *Birmingham 1939–1970* (1974), pp 375–6; *Birmingham Mail*, 16 May 1959.

6. Stephen Wagg, *The Football World* (Brighton, 1984), pp 90–91; *Aldershot News*, 29 May 1959; *The Times*, 25 May 1959; *New Statesman*, 6 Jun 1959; Langford, 31 May 1959; David Clutterbuck and Marion Devine, *Clore* (1987), pp 81–3; *Punch*, 10 Jun 1959; E. P. Thompson 'The New Left', *New Reasoner*, Summer 1959, p 16; *Observer*, 31 May 1959.

7. *Listener*, 21 May 1959; John Hill, *Sex, Class and Realism* (1986), p 196; Peter Stead, *Film and the Working Class* (1989), pp 188–9; *Guardian*, 26 Sep 2008 (John Pidgeon); John Hill, 'Television and Pop', in John Corner (ed), *Popular Television in Britain* (1991), pp 101–3; *Radio Times*, 29 May 1959; *Star* (Sheffield), 1 Jun 1959; *Daily Sketch*, 29 May 1959; *Daily Mirror*, 29–30 May 1959, 2–3 Jun 1959.

8. John Hudson, *Wakes Week* (Stroud, 1992), pp 65–6; Aubrey Jones, *Britain's Economy* (Cambridge, 1985), p 80; *New Statesman*, 13 Jun 1959; Martin, 19 Jun

1959, 24 Jun 1959; Patricia Greene et al, *The Book of The Archers* (1994), p 227; Rupert Hart-Davis, *The Lyttelton Hart-Davis Letters: Volume Four* (1982), p 78; Heap, 9 Jun 1959; Macmillan, dep.d.36, 13 Jun 1959, fol 8; *Daily Mirror*, 18 Jun 1959; Paul Bailey, 'Hokum Writ Large', *Times Literary Supplement*, 5 Mar 2004; Richard Roberts, 'Regulatory Responses to the Rise of the Market for Corporate Control in Britain in the 1950s', *Business History* (Jan 1992), pp 193–4; *The Times*, 25 Jun 1959; R. A. Leeson, *Strike* (1973), p 189.

9. Gordon Bowker, *Through the Dark Labyrinth* (1996), p 274; *Daily Express*, 9 Jun 1959; *Crossman*, pp 764, 759; Macmillan, dep.d.36, 25 Jun 1959, fol 32; Geoffrey Goodman, *The Awkward Warrior* (1979), pp 217, 219–21.

10. Arnold Wesker, *Roots* (Harmondsworth, 1959), p 16; Heap, 30 Jun 1959; *Spectator*, 10 Jul 1959; Willmott, 15 Jul 1959; Paul Leslie Long, 'The Aesthetics of Class in Post-War Britain', PhD diss, University of Warwick, 2001, pp 205–6; *Noël Coward Diaries*, p 412.

11. *The Times*, 7 Jul 1959; *Architects' Journal*, 4 Jun 1959; Graeme Shankland, 'Barbican and the Elephant', *Architectural Design* (Oct 1959), p 416; *Architects' Journal*, 17 Sep 1959, 27 Aug 1959; Maxwell Hutchinson, 'Back in the High Life Again', *Independent*, 23 Feb 1994; *Architects' Journal*, 13 Aug 1959; Nigel Warburton, *Ernö Goldfinger* (2004), p 147; *East London Advertiser*, 4 Sep 1959; *Architectural Review* (Apr 1962), p 236.

12. Elain Harwood, 'White Light/White Heat', *Twentieth Century Architecture* (2002), p 61; *Guardian*, 26 Aug 1959; *Birmingham Mail*, 19 Aug 1959; Andrew Motion, *Philip Larkin* (1993), pp 293–4; *Larkin*, p 252.

13. Candida Lycett Green (ed), John Betjeman, *Coming Home* (1997), p 333; *East London Advertiser*, 19 Jun 1959; *Observer*, 14 Jun 1959; *Architects' Journal*, 21 May 1959; Rodney Gordon, 'Modern Architecture for the Masses', *Twentieth Century Architecture* (2002), pp 73–4; Nikolaus Pevsner, 'Roehampton LCC Housing and the Picturesque Tradition', *Architectural Review* (Jul 1959), pp 21–35.

14. *Shrewsbury Chronicle*, 11 Sep 1959; *Hampstead & Highgate Record*, 28 Aug 1959; *Hampstead & Highgate Express*, 4 Sep 1959, 18 Sep 1959, 25 Sep 1959.

15. *Manchester Guardian*, 17 Jun 1959; *New Statesman*, 8 Aug 1959; *Sheffield Telegraph*, 9 Jun 1959; *Birmingham Post*, 20 May 1959.

13 We're All Reaching Up

1. Last, 3 Jul 1959; Tim McDonald, 'Cliff Adams', *Guardian*, 1 Nov 2001; Last, 7 Jul 1959, 10 Jul 1959; Frances Partridge, *Everything to Lose* (1985), p 332; BBC WA, R9/41 – VR/59/428, T16/439/1.

2. Geoffrey Goodman, *The Awkward Warrior* (1979), p 224; Brian Brivati, *Hugh Gaitskell* (1996), pp 320–21; George Cyriax and Robert Oakeshott, *The Bargainers* (1960), p 129; *Courier and Advertiser*, 4 Jul 1959; *Oxford Mail*, 21 Jul 1959, 12 Aug 1959; Alan Thornett, *From Militancy to Marxism* (1987), p 26; *News Chronicle*, 7 Sep 1959; Peter Stead, 'A Paradoxical Turning Point', in Sheila Rowbotham and Huw Beynon (eds), *Looking at Class* (2001), p 48; Alexander Walker, *Peter Sellers* (1981), pp 87–9, 92; Geoffrey Macnab, 'Strikes . . . Camera, Action', *Independent*,

17 Sep 2010; Tony Shaw, *British Cinema and the Cold War* (2001), p 160; *Daily Mirror*, 14 Aug 1959; Shaw, *British Cinema*, p 159; D. R. Thorpe, *Supermac* (2010), pp 441, 767.

3. Macmillan, dep.d.36, 30 Jul 1959, fol 103, 5–6 Aug 1959, fols 112–14; Nigel Nicolson (ed), Harold Nicolson, *Diaries and Letters, Volume III* (1968), p 369; *New Yorker*, 29 Aug 1959.

4. Ben Pimlott, *Hugh Dalton* (1985), pp 630–31; *Grimsby Evening Telegraph*, 22 Aug 1959; *Crossman*, pp 769–70; *New Statesman*, 27 Mar 1998 (Peter Hennessy); Richard Hoggart and Raymond Williams, 'Working Class Attitudes', *New Left Review* (Jan–Feb 1960), pp 28–30.

5. Hague, Box 2 (green notebook), Bridlington diary, 1–3 Aug 1959; *Glasgow Herald*, 4 Aug 1959; Hague, Box 2 (green notebook), Bridlington diary, 8 Aug 1959; Pete Frame, *The Restless Generation* (2007), p 399; Chris Bryant, *Glenda Jackson* (1999), pp 39–40; Frame, *Restless*, p 429; *Evening Sentinel* (Stoke), 7 Sep 1959; Trina Beckett, 'Our Beach Hut on the South Coast', *Guardian*, 26 Nov 2011.

6. Dee, 15 Aug 1959; Jerry White, *London in the Twentieth Century* (2001), p 323; *East London Advertiser*, 14 Aug 1959; *Evening Sentinel* (Stoke), 21 Aug 1959; Dee, 22 Aug 1959; *Manchester Guardian*, 22 Aug 1959; *Liverpool Echo*, 26 Aug 1959, 31 Aug 1959; Mark Lewisohn, *The Complete Beatles Chronicle* (1996 edn), p 13; Chris Salewicz, *McCartney* (1986), p 79; *Liverpool Echo*, 31 Aug 1959.

7. Martin, 31 Aug 1959; Turtle, 31 Aug 1959; Michael Cockerell, *Live from Number 10* (1988), p 67; *New Yorker*, 12 Sep 1959; *Oxford Mail*, 1 Sep 1959; Russell Davies (ed), *The Kenneth Williams Diaries* (1993), p 154.

8. *Times Literary Supplement*, 4 Sep 1959; *Spectator*, 4 Sep 1959; *New Statesman*, 5 Sep 1959; *Times Literary Supplement*, 4 Sep 1959; *New Statesman*, 12 Sep 1959; Dave Russell, *Looking North* (Manchester, 2004), p 105; *Spectator*, 11 Sep 1959.

9. Larkin, Ms Eng. c. 7420, 2 Sep 1959, fol 34; *Sunday Pictorial*, 6 Sep 1959; *Radio Times*, 28 Aug 1959; *Spectator*, 18 Sep 1959; *New Statesman*, 12 Sep 1959; *Hackney Gazette*, 11 Sep 1959; *East London Advertiser*, 4 Sep 1959, 11 Sep 1959.

10. David Goodway, seminar at Institute of Historical Research, London, 1 Feb 1994; Daly, Ms 302/3/13, 31 Aug 1959, 2 Sep 1959, 8 Sep 1959; *News Chronicle*, 8 Sep 1959.

11. Sources for this collage include: *Liverpool Echo*, 27 Aug 1959; *Woman*, 20 Jun 1959; *Stores and Shops*, Jul 1959; *TV Times*, 20 Jun 1959, 5 Sep 1959.

12. *Daily Mail*, 25 Jun 1960; *Daily Express*, 4 Sep 1959.

13. *Financial Times*, 25 Jul 1959; *New Statesman*, 5 Sep 1959 (Tom Driberg); *Financial Times*, 29 Aug 1959; *Liverpool Echo*, 24 Aug 1959; *Financial Times*, 29 Aug 1959; *Manchester Evening News*, 1 Jul 1959; *Essex & Thurrock Gazette*, 8 May 1959.

14. Jan Boxshall, *Every Home Should Have One* (1997), p 73; *Financial Times*, 31 Jul 1959, 15 May 1959, 2 Feb 1960; *Guardian*, 14 Jun 1961.

15. *Manchester Evening News*, 15 Jul 1959, 21 Jul 1959; Ian Allan, *abc Scooters & Light Cars* (1959); Peter Evans, 'Mario Cassandro', *Guardian*, 10 Aug 2011; Frank Mort, 'Retailing, Commercial Culture and Masculinity in 1950s Britain', *History Workshop* (Autumn 1994), p 122; Roger Tredre, 'Willie Gertler', *Independent*, 21 Aug 1991; *Spectator*, 13 Feb 1959 (Leslie Adrian); Susan Bowden, 'Sir Charles Colston', *Dictionary of Business Biography, Volume 1* (1984), p 757; *Daily Mirror*, 28 May 1959; Ralph Harris and Arthur Seldon, *Advertising in Action* (1962), p 82.

16. Giles Chapman, 'Harry Webster', *Independent*, 17 Feb 2007; *Daily Mirror*, 26 Aug 1959; Simon Garfield, *Mini* (2009), p 40; *The Times*, 26 Aug 1959; Garfield, *Mini*, pp 78–9; *Autosport*, 28 Aug 1959; Garfield, *Mini*, p 84; *New Yorker*, 12 Sep 1959.

17. Catherine Ellis, 'The Younger Generation', *Journal of British Studies* (Apr 2002), p 211; Mark Abrams, *The Teenage Consumer* (1959), pp 10–22; M. P. Carter, *Home, School and Work* (Oxford, 1962), pp 284–5, 298–9.

18. Maggie Urry, 'Woolies Gets into Shape for the 1990s', *Financial Times*, 6 Nov 1989; *Oxford Mail*, 19 Aug 1959; *Scunthorpe and Frodingham Star*, 2 Oct 1959; *Stores and Shops*, May 1959, p 47; *The Times*, 9 Mar 1959; 'Frank Brierley', *Daily Telegraph*, 28 Jul 1999; Mort, 'Retailing', pp 122–3; Harris and Seldon, *Advertising*, pp 304–6; *Stores and Shops*, May 1959, p 17.

19. *Coventry Evening Telegraph*, 11 Aug 1959; *Daily Mail*, 11 Mar 1959; *Retail News Letter*, Sep 1959, p 9.

20. *News Chronicle*, 10 Mar 1959; *The Times*, 11 Mar 1959; Gorer, 'Television and the English', Box 1, file 1/C1; *New Statesman*, 21 Mar 1959; Last, 11 Jul 1959; Fowles, EUL Ms 102/1/11, 14–22 Aug 1959, fol 35.

21. Lawrence Black, *The Political Culture of the Left in Affluent Britain, 1951–64* (Basingstoke, 2003), p 100; Stefan Schwarzkopf, 'They Do It with Mirrors', *Contemporary British History* (Jun 2005), p 136; Dave Rolinson, '"If They Want Culture, They Pay"', in Ian MacKillop and Neil Sinyard (eds), *British Cinema of the 1950s* (Manchester, 2003), p 94; Ferdynand Zweig, *The Worker in an Affluent Society* (1961), pp 9–10, 105–6; Peter Willmott, *The Evolution of a Community* (1963), pp 99–100; *Hampstead & Highgate Express*, 21 Aug 1959.

14 Beastly Things, Elections

1. *Middlesex County Times and West Middlesex Gazette*, 19 Sep 1959; *Grimsby Evening Telegraph*, 18 Sep 1959; D. E. Butler and Richard Rose, *The British General Election of 1959* (1960), p 24; *Listener*, 1 Oct 1959; *New Yorker*, 2 Aug 1958; D. R. Thorpe, *Supermac* (2010), p 447; Julian Critchley, *A Bag of Boiled Sweets* (1994), p 67; *The Times*, 9 Sep 1959.

2. Paul Routledge, *Madam Speaker* (1995), p 77; *Listener*, 1 Oct 1959; *Luton News*, 24 Sep 1959.

3. Michael Foot, *Aneurin Bevan: Volume 2* (1973), p 622; *Daily Herald*, 24 Sep 1959; Geoffrey Goodman, *From Bevan to Blair* (2003), pp 81–2; Foot, *Bevan*, pp 624–6.

4. Butler and Rose, *General Election*, pp 124, 126, 138; John Campbell, *Margaret Thatcher: Volume One* (2000), pp 119–20; Michael Crick, *Michael Heseltine* (1997), p 89; Joan Lestor, 'Lord Pitt of Hampstead', *Independent*, 20 Dec 1994; *Southampton Evening Echo*, 25 Sep 1959; Tom Bower, *Maxwell* (1988), pp 89–93; *Grimsby Evening Telegraph*, 17 Sep 1959; Daly, Ms 302/3/13, *c* 22 Sep 1959; *Evening Times* (Glasgow), 25 Sep 1959; Bernard Bergonzi, *No Lewisham Concerto* (privately published, 1997; University of Warwick Library), p 240; *New Statesman*, 13 Feb 1998.

5. Butler and Rose, *General Election*, p 81; *Spectator*, 11 Sep 1959; John Campbell, *Nye Bevan* (1997 edn), p 358; *Kensington News and West London Times*, 2 Oct 1959; Asa Briggs, *The History of Broadcasting in the United Kingdom, Volume 5*

(Oxford, 1995), p 249; BBC WA, R9/13/182; Lawrence Black, *The Political Culture of the Left in Affluent Britain, 1951–64* (Basingstoke, 2003), p 181; BBC WA, R9/9/23 – LR/59/1597; Michael Cockerell, *Live from Number 10* (1988), p 70; *Spectator*, 9 Oct 1959 (Peter Forster); 'Never Had It So Good' evening, BBC Parliament, 10 Oct 2009; *The Times*, 22 Sep 1959; Benn, p 313; Harold Macmillan, *Pointing the Way, 1959–1961* (1972), p 8.

6. David Kynaston, *The City of London, Volume 4* (2001), p 243; Butler and Rose, *General Election*, p 55; *Crossman*, pp 779-80; Larkin, Ms Eng. c. 7420, 26 Sep 1959, fos 49-50; *Spectator*, 9 Oct 1959; Philip M. Williams, *Hugh Gaitskell* (1979), p 526; Macmillan, *Pointing*, pp 9-10; Williams, *Gaitskell*, p 526; Butler and Rose, *General Election*, p 63; *Crossman*, p 780; Benn, p 314; Butler and Rose, *General Election*, p 85.

7. *The Times*, 19 Sep 1959; Last, 18 Sep 1959, 27 Sep 1959; *New Yorker*, 10 Oct 1959; Ian S. MacNiven (ed), *The Durrell–Miller Letters 1935–80* (1988), p 360.

8. *The Times*, 19 Sep 1959; *Romford Recorder*, 18 Sep 1959; Wikipedia, 'Gerard Hoffnung'; *The Times*, 8 Oct 1959; Russell Davies (ed), *The Kenneth Williams Diaries* (1993), p 155; *Radio Times*, 4 Sep 1959; *Listener*, 24 Sep 1959; Larkin, Ms Eng. c. 7420, 10 Sep 1959, fol 36, 23 Sep 1959, fol 46; *Hackney Gazette*, 18 Sep 1959, 22 Sep 1959, 25 Sep 1959.

9. Ralph Harris and Arthur Seldon, *Advertising in Action* (1962), pp 67–70; *Grimsby Evening Telegraph*, 24 Sep 1959; *Shrewsbury Chronicle*, 25 Sep 1959; Martin, 1 Oct 1959; *The Times*, 7 Oct 1959; *Architects' Journal*, 1 Oct 1959; Malcolm MacEwen, *The Greening of a Red* (1991), pp 213–14; *Architects' Journal*, 1 Oct 1959; *Liverpool Daily Post*, 16 Sep 1959; Candida Lycett Green (ed), John Betjeman, *Letters: Volume Two* (1995), p 177.

10. *Daily Herald*, 29 Sep 1959; *The Times*, 29 Sep 1959; Ian Gilmour and Mark Garnett, *Whatever Happened to the Tories?* (1997), p 151; Geoffrey Goodman, *The Awkward Warrior* (1979), p 237; *The Times*, 30 Sep 1959; *Kensington News and West London Times*, 2 Oct 1959.

11. *Northern Echo*, 1 Oct 1959; Harry Mount, *How England Made the English* (2012), p 190; *Daily Sketch*, 1 Oct 1959; *The Times*, 1 Oct 1959; *Daily Herald*, 1 Oct 1959; *Middlesex Independent*, 9 Oct 1959; *Hampstead & Highgate Express*, 2 Oct 1959.

12. Last, 1 Oct 1959; Benn, p 314; Butler and Rose, *General Election*, p 62; *Daily Herald*, 2–3 Oct 1959; *Spectator*, 2 Oct 1959; *New Statesman*, 10 Oct 1959.

13. Heap, 3 Oct 1959; *Grimsby Evening Telegraph*, 5 Oct 1959; Benn, pp 312, 314; *News Chronicle*, 5 Oct 1959; Butler and Rose, *General Election*, p 66; *Crossman*, p 785; Butler and Rose, *General Election*, p 66; *Crossman*, p 788; Last, 5 Oct 1959.

14. *Daily Sketch*, 6 Oct 1959; *The Times*, 7 Oct 1959; *Luton News*, 8 Oct 1959; *Southampton Evening Echo*, 7 Oct 1959; Benn, p 316; Butler and Rose, *General Election*, p 67; BBC WA, R9/13/182; *Daily Telegraph*, 7 Oct 1959; *Daily Sketch*, 8 Oct 1959; *Radio Times*, 2 Oct 1959; Mervyn Jones, *Michael Foot* (1994), p 240; Preston, 7 Oct 1959.

15. Benn, p 316; Preston, 8 Oct 1959; Willmott, 8 Oct 1959; *The Times*, 8 Oct 1959; Butler and Rose, *General Election*, p 105; Benn, p 316; *Hampstead & Highgate Express*, 9 Oct 1959; *Grimsby Evening Telegraph*, 8 Oct 1959; Larkin, Ms Eng. c.

7420, 7–8 Oct 1959, fol 60; Lewis, 8 Oct 1959; *Daily Mirror*, 8 Oct 1959; Roy Greenslade, *Press Gang* (2003), p 117; Last, 8 Oct 1959.

16. Last, 8 Oct 1959; George H. Gallup, *The Gallup International Public Opinion Polls: Great Britain 1937–1975, Volume One* (New York, 1976), p 543; Briggs, *History of Broadcasting*, p 253; *Spectator*, 16 Oct 1959 (Peter Forster); *New Yorker*, 24 Oct 1959; *Billericay Times*, 7 Oct 1959, 14 Oct 1959; Ben Pimlott (ed), *The Political Diary of Hugh Dalton* (1986), p 693; David Childs, 'Geoffrey Johnson Smith', *Independent*, 26 Aug 2010; Heap, 8 Oct 1959; *Kenneth Williams Diaries*, p 156; *Grimsby Evening Telegraph*, 9 Oct 1959; Margaret Thatcher, *The Path to Power* (1995), pp 100–101; Roy Hattersley, *Who Goes Home?* (1995), p 23; Foot, *Bevan*, p 627; Benn, p 316.

17. Butler and Rose, *General Election*, pp 189–90; Kevin Jefferys, *Retreat from New Jerusalem* (Basingstoke, 1997), p 81; N. Tiratsoo, *Reconstruction, Affluence and Labour Politics* (1990), p 99; Lewis Baston, *Reggie* (Stroud, 2004), p 135; Roy Jenkins, *A Life at the Center* (New York, 1991), p 122; Butler and Rose, *General Election*, p 216; Routledge, *Madam Speaker*, p 79; Bower, *Outsider*, p 93; Butler and Rose, *General Election*, pp 184–5 (Keith Kyle); Kynaston, *City*, p 244; Norman Sherry, *The Life of Graham Greene, Volume 3* (2004), p 215; *Larkin*, p 260; Larkin, Ms Eng. c. 7420, 9 Oct 1959, fol 62; Turtle, 9 Oct 1959; Last, 10 Oct 1959; Tom Courtenay, *Dear Tom* (2000), p 244; *Daily Sketch*, 10 Oct 1959.

18. *Crossman*, p 786; *Fowles*, p 431; David Owen, *Time to Declare* (1991), p 54; Butler and Rose, *General Election*, p 201; *The Times*, 10 Oct 1959; Macmillan, *Pointing*, p 15; *Viewer*, 29 Aug 1959.

A Shake of the Dice

1 Sure as Progress Itself

1. Haines, 16 Oct 1959; John Fisher, *Tony Hancock* (2008), pp 270–1; BBC WA, *Any Questions?*, 16 Oct 1959; *Times*, 10 Oct 1959; Gorer, Box 45, Young to Gorer, 19 Oct 1959; *Daily Mirror*, 28 Oct 1959; *Times*, 29 Oct 1959; *Daily Mirror*, 29 Oct 1959.

2. Michael Billington, *State of the Nation* (2007), pp 115–17; *New Statesman*, 31 Oct 1959; *Times*, 19 Oct 1959; *Liverpool Echo*, 22 Oct 1959; *Listener*, 12 Nov 1959 (James Reeves); *Times*, 5 Nov 1959; Iona and Peter Opie, *The Lore and Language of Schoolchildren* (1959), pp vii, 356; Macmillan, dep.37, 1 Nov 1959, fol 60.

3. *Hants and Berks Gazette*, 16 Oct 1959; *Times*, 28 Oct 1959; *Daily Mirror*, 28 Oct 1959; Martin, 23 Oct 1959; *East London Gazette*, 9 Oct 1959; *New Yorker*, 24 Oct 1959 (Stephen Watts); *Paisley Daily Express*, 23 Oct 1959, 26 Oct 1959; Osborn, p 293.

4. *Daily Herald*, 28 Oct 1959; *Evening Standard*, 28 Oct 1959; *Liverpool Weekly News*, 12 Nov 1959; J. F. Demers, 'Community and Park Hill' in The Society of Housing Managers, *Quarterly Journal*, Oct 1963, p 2; *Star* (Sheffield), 20 Oct 1959, 21 Oct 1959, 23 Oct 1959; *Sheffield Telegraph*, 9 Nov 1959.

5. *Melody Maker*, 17 Oct 1959, 31 Oct 1959; *Times*, 2 Nov 1959; *Luton News*, 22 Oct 1959; *Daily Sketch*, 3 Nov 1959.

6. BBC WA, R9/74/2, Nov 1959; *Daily Express*, 19 Oct 1959; *Daily Sketch*, 14 Oct 1959; *East London Advertiser*, 30 Oct 1959, 13 Nov 1959.

2 A Real Love Match

1. Kingsley Amis, *Memoirs* (1991), pp 187–90; Anne de Courcy, *Snowdon* (2008); *Daily Express*, 2 Nov 1959, 10 Nov 1959; A.C.H. Smith, *Paper Voices* (1975), pp 217–22; *New Statesman*, 12 Dec 1959 (Jeremy Sandford).

2. 'Alan Keith', *Times*, 19 Mar 2003; *Manchester Evening News*, 21 Nov 1959; Asa Briggs, *The History of Broadcasting in the United Kingdom: Volume V* (Oxford, 1995), p 209; *Spectator*, 4 Dec 1959; Spencer Leigh, 'Adam Faith', *Independent*, 10 Mar 2003; Jonathan Margolis, *Bernard Manning* (1996), pp 74–5; Brian Jackson Collection at Qualidata, University of Essex, 'Working-Class Community' Papers, File (i.e. Box) C1, 13 Dec 1959.

3. Heap, 24 Nov 1959; BBC WA, R9/9/23 – LR/59/1963; Last, 10 Feb 1960; Martin, 3 Dec 1959; *Punch*, 31 Dec 1959; Sylvie Simmons, *I'm Your Man* (2012), p 72; *Guardian*, 3 Oct 2009 (Jenny Diski); *Spectator*, 1 Jan 1960; BBC WA, R9/74/2, Feb 1960; Richard Webber, *Fifty Years of Hancock's Half Hour* (2004), p 238.

4. *News Chronicle*, 28 Dec 1959; David Blunkett, *On a Clear Day* (2002 edn), pp 42–3; Margaret Drabble, *Angus Wilson* (1995), pp 259–63.

5. Rick Rogers, *Crowther to Warnock* (1980), p 13; *Times*, 29 Jan 1960, 4 Feb 1960; *Socialist Commentary*, May 1960, p 22; A. Crichton *et al*, 'Youth and leisure in Cardiff, 1960', *Sociological Review*, Jul 1962, pp 218–19; Wilson, pp 66, 131, 72, 144, 168, 77, 184–5.

6. Norma Farnes (ed), *The Goons* (1997), p 138; Hugh Carleton Greene, *The Third Floor Front* (1969), p 13; BBC WA, *Any Questions?*, 8 Jan 1960; *Guardian*, 29 Oct 2011 (Jeanette Winterson); *Sunday Express*, 24 Jan 1960; *Observer*, 24 Jan 1960, 4 Nov 2001 (Oliver James); www.britishpathe.com/video/ten-pin-bowling; John Tilbury, *Cornelius Cardew* (Harlow, 2008), p 82; BBC WA, R9/7/44 – VR/60/60; *Hansard*, House of Commons, 5 Feb 1960, cols 1350–8, 1366; *Times*, 8 Feb 1960; *Sunday Times*, 14 Feb 1960 (John Raymond); John Cole, 'Bruce Hobbs', *Independent*, 17 Nov 2004; 'John May', *Daily Telegraph*, 21 Mar 2002.

7. *Times*, 12 Feb 1960; *Observer*, 14 Feb 1960; John Ramsden, 'Refocusing "The People's War"', *Journal of Contemporary History*, Jan 1998, pp 41–2; Tom Vallance, 'James Booth', *Independent*, 13 Aug 2005; Heap, 11 Feb 1960; *Sunday Times*, 14 Feb 1960; *Punch*, 17 Feb 1960, 10 Aug 1960; *East London Advertiser*, 28 Oct 1960.

8. *Times Literary Supplement*, 11 Mar 1960; *Observer*, 28 Feb 1960; *Times Literary Supplement*, 26 Feb 1960; *New Statesman*, 13 Feb 1960; Chaplin, 7/3/1, 29 Feb 1960.

9. *Guardian*, 8 Jul 2011 (Esther Addley); *News of the World*, 24 Jan 1960, 31 Jan 1960, 7 Feb 1960; Last, 7 Feb 1960; *Sunday Express*, 7 Feb 1960; Last, 7 Feb 1960; BBC WA, R9/7/44 – VR/60/80; *Punch*, 2 Mar 1960; Olga Cannon & J.R.L. Anderson, *The Road from Wigan Pier* (1973), pp 225–6; *Times*, 27 Feb 1960, 1 Mar 1960.

10. *New Yorker*, 20 Feb 1960; Turtle, 11 Feb 1960; *Times*, 13 Feb 1960; John Campbell, *Edward Heath* (1993), p 109; *Daily Mail*, 13 Feb 1960; *Economist*, 20 Feb 1960; William Maxwell (ed), Sylvia Townsend Warner, *Letters* (1982), p 181.

11. Raynham, 18 Feb 1960; *New Left Review*, May–Jun 1960, pp 63–4; Haines, 19 Feb 1960; Raynham, 19 Feb 1960; Martin, 19 Feb 1960; Last, 19 Feb 1960; *New Statesman*, 27 Feb 1960 (Francis Williams); *Listener*, 3 Mar 1960; Macmillan, dep.d. 38, 16 Feb 1960, fol 20.

12. Diary of Jennie Hill (Hampshire Record Office, Winchester), 26 Feb 1960; Haines, 26 Feb 1960; Martin, 26 Feb 1960; Amis, *Memoirs*, p 190; Turtle, 26 Feb 1960; Last, 26 Feb 1960; *New Statesman*, 5 Mar 1960 (Francis Williams); Heap, 3 Mar 1960.

13. *New Statesman*, 28 Nov 1959, 5 Dec 1959; *TV Times*, 18 Mar 1960; *Punch*, 24 Feb 1960.

14. *Spectator*, 20 Nov 1959; *Architectural Design*, Apr 1960, p 140; *Official Architecture and Planning*, Apr 1960, p 157; *Architectural Review*, May 1960, pp 338–43 (Kenneth Browne); *Architects' Journal*, 7 Jan 1960; *Punch*, 6 Apr 1960.

15. *Architects' Journal*, 5 Nov 1959; Malcolm MacEwen, *The Greening of a Red* (1991), pp 215–16; *New Yorker*, 30 Jan 1960; *Town Planning Review*, Jan 1960, p 273; Oliver Marriott, *The Property Boom* (1967), p 143; Bevis Hillier, *Betjeman: The Bonus of Laughter* (2004), p 130; Susie Harries, *Nikolaus Pevsner* (2011), p 622; Elain Harwood, *Chamberlin, Powell & Bon* (2011), pp 112–13; *Architectural Review*, May 1960, pp 304–12.

16. *Architects' Journals*, 4 Feb 1960; David Harvey, *Birmingham Past and Present: The City Centre: Volume 2* (Kettering, 2003), p 71; *Liverpool Daily Post*, 2 Mar 1960; Pat Rogan, 'Rehousing the Capital', in Miles Glendinning (ed), *Rebuilding Scotland* (East Linton, 1997), p 71; *New Statesman*, 26 Dec 1959; George Hume, 'Finance & Development', in Helen Peacock (ed), *The Unmaking of Edinburgh* (Edinburgh, 1976), p 31; *Glasgow Herald*, 12 Mar 1960; Miles Glendinning, '1945–75: An Architectural Introduction', in Glendinning, *Rebuilding*, p 16; *Architects' Journal*, 10 Mar 1960; *Glasgow Herald*, 19 Feb 1960, 22 Feb 1960.

17. *Guardian*, 19 Feb 1960; *Salford City Reporter*, 26 Feb 1960, 22 Apr 1960; *Sheffield Telegraph*, 5 Jan 1960, 22 Mar 1960.

18. Miles Glendinning and Stefan Muthesius, *Tower Block* (1994), p 65; Tom Begg, *Housing Policy in Scotland* (Edinburgh, 1996), p 144; A.G.V. Simmonds, 'Conservative governments and the housing question, 1951–59' (University of Leeds PhD, 1995), pp 226–7; Leeds City Council, *Agenda and Verbatim Reports, 1959–60* (1960), p 145.

19. *Liverpool Echo*, 8 Apr 1960; Patrick Dunleavy, *The Politics of Mass Housing in Britain, 1945–1975* (Oxford, 1981), p 41; *Evening News*, 26 Feb 1960, 7 Apr 1960, 29 Apr 1960.

20. The Society of Housing Managers, *Report of Conference: "Living in Council Houses"* (1960), pp 20–5; *Evening Advertiser* (Swindon), 21 Mar 1960; *Liverpool Daily Post*, 13 Jan 1960; Tom Courtenay, *Dear Tom* (2000), pp 261–7, 293.

21. BBC WA, R9/7/44-VR/60/121; *TV Times*, 26 Feb 1960, 18 Mar 19; *Guardian*, 5 Mar 2010 (Richard Williams); *Times*, 3 Mar 1960; Henry Hardy and Jennifer Holmes (eds), Isaiah Berlin, *Enlightening: Letters 1946–1960* (2009), p 731; Dilwyn Porter, '"Play It Safe or Think Big?"' (Business History Unit Occasional Paper, 2000), p 9; David Kynaston, *The Financial Times* (1988), p 283; D. R. Thorpe, *Supermac* (2010), p 462; Macmillan, dep.d.38, 5 Mar 1960, fols 44–5.

22. Macmillan, dep.d.38, 26 Feb 1960, fols 39–40, 11 Mar 1960, fol 49; Alan Booth, 'New revisionists and the Keynesian era in British economic policy', *Economic History Review*, May 2001, p 353; *Macmillan (2)*, p 225; 'Leo Abse', *Times*, 21 Aug 2008; *Punch*, 13 Apr 1960 ('Lombard Lane'); Sir Gerald Nabarro, *Nab 1* (Oxford, 1969), pp 169–83; Larkin, Ms. Eng. C. 7421, 17 Apr 1960, fol 67; BBC WA, *Any Questions?*, 8 Apr 1960; David Cannadine, *In Churchill's Shadow* (2002), p 305;

Robin Jones, *Beeching* (2011), p 24; *Times*, 7 Apr 1960; Bank of England Archives, G3/89, 16 Nov 1960, Cobbold to Sir Frank Lee.

23. *Guardian*,19 Apr 1960; *Spectator*, 22 Apr 1960; Aurelia Schober Plath (ed), *Letters Home by Sylvia Plath* (1976), p 378; Benn, p 329; *New Statesman*, 23 Apr 1960 (Francis Williams); BBC WA, *Any Questions?*, 22 Apr 1960.

24. Larkin, Ms. Eng. C. 7421, 4 Feb 1960, fol 20; Heap, 14 Mar 1960; Robert J. Wybrow, *Britain Speaks Out, 1937–87* (Basingstoke, 1989), p 60; *New Yorker*, 23 Apr 1960; Peter Oborne, *Basil D'Oliveira* (2004), chap 5; John Arlott, *Cricket on Trial* (1960), pp 18–19.

25. *Sheffield Telegraph*, 22 Mar 1960; *Observer*, 10 Apr 1960; *New Statesman*, 9 Apr 1960; *Evening World* (Brisol), 10 May 1960; Sue Harper and Vincent Porter, *British Cinema of the 1950s* (Oxford, 2003), p 194; *Guardian*, 19 Nov 2010 (Xan Brooks); Heap, 14 Apr 1960; *Listener*, 17 Mar 1960 (Irving Wardle); *New Statesman*, 2 Apr 1960 (Francis Williams); *Spectator*, 22 Apr 1960; Joan Barrell and Brian Braithwaite, *The Business of Women's Magazines* (1988 edn), pp 41–5; Wilson, p 117; Haines, 18 Apr 1960; *Mojo*, Dec 1993; 'Dave Dee', *Times*, 10 Jan 2009.

26. N. Tiratsoo, *Reconstruction, Affluence and Labour Politics* (1990), p 100; *Coventry Evening Telegraph*, 1 Mar 1960, 8 Mar 1960; *Times*, 5 Apr 1960; *Coventry Evening Telegraph*, 5 Apr 1960; Michael Billington, *The Life and Work of Harold Pinter* (1996), p 110; *Times*, 22 Mar 1960; *TV Times*, 8 Apr 1960; Billington, *Pinter*, p 111; *Times*, 23 Apr 1960; *Guardian*, 16 May 2005 (Maggie Brown); Billington, *Pinter*, p 127; *Financial Times*, 28 Apr 1960; *New Statesman*, 7 May 1960; Graham Payn and Sheridan Morley (eds), *The Noël Coward Diaries* (1982), p 436; Heap, 30 May 1960; *Independent*, 15 Nov 2000.

27. Billington, *Pinter*, p 118; *Wisden Cricketers' Almanack, 1961* (1961), pp 310, 632, 271; *Lancashire Evening Post*, 30 Apr 1960; Ivan Ponting, 'Harry Potts', *Independent*, 22 Jan 1996; Ivan Ponting, 'Brian Miller', *Independent*, 12 Apr 2007; *Sunday Times*, 28 Dec 2003 (Greg Struthers); Philip Norman, *Shout* (1981), pp 77–8; Mark Lewisohn, *The Complete Beatles Chronicle* (1996 edn), p 18; Philip Norman, *John Lennon* (2008), pp 176–7; Larkin, Ms Eng. C. 7421, 4 May 1960, fol 78; Geoff Phillips, *Memories of Tyne Tees Television* (Durham City, 1998), pp 122–3.

28. De Courcy, *Snowdon* (2008), pp 90–1; Amis, p 572; Andrew Barrow, *Gossip* (1980 edn), p 214; *Coward Diaries*, p 437.

29. BBC WA, R9/74/2, Jul 1960; Jonathan Dimbleby, *Richard Dimbleby* (1975), p 256; Barrow, p 214; Haines, 6 May 1960; Diary of May Marlor, 6 May 1960; Martin, 6 May 1960; Last, 6 May 1960; Turtle, 6 May 1960; Macmillan, dep.d.38, 6 May 1960, fol 127; *Guardian*, 7 May 1960; Last, 6 May 1960; John Fisher, *Tony Hancock* (2008), pp 282–90.

3 To the Rear of the Column

1. Heap, 9 Oct 1959. In general for the Clause 4 story, see: Philip M. Williams, *Hugh Gaitskell* (1979), pp 537–73; Brian Brivati, *Hugh Gaitskell* (1996), pp 330–48; Tudor Jones, '"Taking Genesis out of the Bible",' *Contemporary British History*, Summer 1997, pp 1–23; Catherine Ellis, 'Letting it Slip', *Contemporary British History*, March 2012, pp 47–71.

2. *Times*, 15 Jun 1998; *New Statesman*, 17 Oct 1959 (Francis Williams); James Thomas, 'Reflections on the Broken *Mirror*', *Media History*, Aug 2003, p 111.

3. Ben Pimlott (ed), *The Political Diary of Hugh Dalton* (1986), pp 694–5; Benn, pp 317–18; Douglas Jay, *Change and Fortune* (1980), pp 271–5; Frances Partridge, *Everything to Lose* (1999 Phoenix edn), p 340; *New Yorker*, 21 Nov 1959.

4. Brivati, *Gaitskell*, p 330; Chaplin, 7/3/1, 11 Jun 1957; Ina Zweiniger-Bargielowska, 'South Wales Miners' Attitudes towards Nationalisation', *Llafur*, 1994 (6/3), p 78; *Universities & Left Review*, Autumn 1959, p 75; Lawrence Black, *The Political Culture of the Left in Affluent Britain, 1951–64* (Basingstoke, 2003), pp 173–4; *New Statesman*, 17 Oct 1959, 31 Oct 1959; Frank Cousins papers (Modern Records Centre, University of Warwick), Ms 282/8/1/1, 23 Nov 1959.

5. Jay, *Change*, pp 276, 278; Williams, *Gaitskell*, pp 553–5; *Spectator*, 4 Dec 1959 (Bernard Levin); Benn, p 320; *Spectator*, 4 Dec 1959; Williams, *Gaitskell*, p 557; *Spectator*, 4 Dec 1959.

6. *Spectator*, 22 Jan 1960; R.H.S. Crossman, *Labour in the Affluent Society* (1960), pp 9, 22; *New Statesman*, 19 Mar 1960; *Encounter*, Mar 1960, pp 6–7.

7. *New Statesman*, 19 Mar 1960; Benn, p 333; Geoffrey Goodman, *The Awkward Warrior* (1979), p 245; *New Yorker*, 23 Jul 1960 (Panter-Downes); Ralph Miliband, *Parliamentary Socialism* (1972 Merlin edn), p 346; Peter Patterson, *Tired and Emotional* (1993), p 94; Kevin Jefferys, *Anthony Crosland* (2000 Politico's edn), p 74; Radhika Desai, *Intellectuals and Socialism* (1994), pp 105–6; David Howell, '"Shut Your Gob!",' in Alan Campbell *et al* (eds), *British Trade Unions and Industrial Politics: Volume One* (Aldershot, 1999), p 133; A. J. Davies, *To Build a New Jerusalem* (1992), p 207; Ben Pimlott, *Harold Wilson* (1992), p 227.

8. *Encounter*, Sep 1959, pp 11–19; Brivati, *Gaitskell*, p 343–4; *Encounter*, Mar 1960, p 11.

9. *New Statesman*, Dec 1959; *New Left Review*, Jan–Feb 1960, pp 1, 9, 25, 52, 54; Fred Inglis, *Radical Earnestness* (Oxford, 1982), p 177; *New Left Review*, May–Jun 1960, pp 68–9.

10. Michael Kenny, *The First New Left* (1995), p 34; E. P. Thompson *et al*, *Out of Apathy* (1960), pp 95–6, 235, 15, 192, 286, 298–308; *New Statesman*, 4 Jun 1960; *Spectator*, 17 Jun 1960; *Times Literary Supplement*, 2 Sep 1960; *Political Quarterly*, Jul–Sep 1960, pp 371–2.

11. *New Left Review*, Jan–Feb 1960, p 2, Mar–Apr 1960, p 71, May–Jun 1960, p 2; *Socialist Commentary*, Jul 1960, p 17; Michael Newman, *Ralph Miliband and the Politics of the New Left* (2002), p 98; *Socialist Commentary*, Oct 1960, p 30.

12. D. E. Butler and Richard Rose, *The British General Election of 1959* (1960), pp 11–16; Anthony Crosland, *Can Labour Win?* (1960), p 23; *Socialist Commentary*, May 1960, pp 4–9, Jun 1960, pp 5–11, July 1960, pp 5–12, Aug 1960, pp 5–10; *New Left Review*, Sep–Oct 1960, pp 2–9.

13. *Architects' Journal*, 16 Jan 1958; *Listener*, 26 Nov 1959; Benn, p 333; Michael Young, *The Chipped White Cups of Dover* (1960), pp 20, 11–13, 17, 19; Benn, p 333.

4 Some Fearful Risks

1. *Observer*, 8 May 1960; Andrew Taylor, *20th Century Blackburn* (Barnsley, 2000), p 91; *Punch*, 18 May 1960; Heap, 9–10 May 1960; Robert J. Wybrow, *Britain Speaks Out, 1937–87* (Basingstoke, 1989), p 61; Diary of Jennie Hill (Hampshire Record Office, Winchester), 17 May 1960; Kate Paul, *Journal: Volume One, 1958–1963* (Hay-on-Wye, 1997), p 94; Leila Berg, *Risinghill* (1968), p 61; *Guardian*, 15 May 2002 (Frank Keating), 16 Oct 2010 (Richard Williams); Wilson, p 79; *Spectator*, 20 May 1960; *New Statesman*, 21 May 1960; Liverpool Local Studies Library, 780.42 CUT (Cavern Club cuttings, 1957–77); Dave Russell, *Football and the English* (Preston, 1997), pp 152–3.
2. Last, 22 May 1960; *East London Advertiser*, 27 May 1960; *Highland News*, 20 May 1960; Mark Lewisohn, *The Complete Beatles Chronicle* (1996 edn), pp 19–20, 26–7; *Forres News*, 28 May 1960; *Northern Chronicle*, 25 May 1960; *Banffshire Herald*, 28 May 1960.
3. BBC WA, R9/7/46 – VR/60/314; A. Silver, 'Angels in Marble' collection (interview files) at UK Data Archive, University of Essex.
4. Alan Bennett, *Untold Stories* (2005), pp 501–2; Robert Brown, *Basingstoke* (Chichester, 1994), unpaginated; David Harvey, *Birmingham Past and Present: The City Centre, Volume 2* (Kettering, 2003), p 67; Elain Harwood, 'White Light/White Heat', *Twentieth Century Architecture*, 2002, p 62; Kathryn A. Morrison, *English Shops and Shopping* (New Haven, 2003), p 107; *Derby Evening Telegraph*, 30 Nov 1983; Lionel Esher, *A Broken Wave* (1981), p 248; *Leeds Weekly Citizen*, 29 Jul 1960; *Liverpool Daily Post*, 18 Nov 1960; *Architects' Journal*, 28 Jul 1960; *Guardian*, 16 Jun 1960, 20 May 2006 (Ian Jack); *Architectural Design*, Dec 1960, p 486; *East London Advertiser*, 22 Jul 1960; Richard Davenport-Hines, *An English Affair* (2013), p xiii; *Architectural Review*, Oct 1960, p 302; *Official Architecture and Planning*, Aug 1960, pp 346–9; John R. Gold, *The Practice of Modernism* (Abingdon, 2007), pp 117–18; Harwood, p 69; *Architects' Journal*, 4 Aug 1960; Carole Newbigging, 'The Development of Blackbird Leys', BBC Oxford website, 'Memoryshire', 2007; *Western Evening Herald*, 30 Dec 1960; *RIBA Journal*, Dec 1962, p 456 (Jack Lynn); *Star* (Sheffield), 10 Oct 1960; *Glasgow Herald*, 18 Jun 1960; Miles Glendinning and Stefan Muthesius, *Tower Block* (New Haven, 1994), p 238; *Glasgow Herald*, 23 Jun 1960; *Tower Block*, p 224; *Town and Country Planning*, Dec 1960, p 397 (Elizabeth B. Mitchell).
5. *Yorkshire Post*, 9 Nov 1960; *Guardian*, 30 Aug 1960; Simon Gunn, 'The Buchanan Report, Environment and the Problem of Traffic in 1960s Britain', *Twentieth Century British History*, 2011 (22/4), p 528; *Sunday Times*, 10 Jul 1960; *Lennox Herald*, 9 Jul 1960; *Peckham & Dulwich Advertiser & News*, 23 Jul 1960; *Listener*, 13 Oct 1960.
6. *Evening Chronicle* (Newcastle), 7 Mar 1960; Archie Potts, 'T. Dan Smith', *North East Labour History*, 1994 (Bulletin no 28), p 11; *Evening Chronicle* (Newcastle), 7 Mar 1960; James Elliott, 'The Politics of Planning' (M.Lit thesis, Newcastle upon Tyne, 1972), p 13; *Journal of the Town Planning Institute*, Jul–Aug 1960, pp 195–200; *Sunday Times*, 24 Jul 1960; *Star* (Sheffield), 19 May 1960, 30 Aug 1960, 9 Sep 1960; *Middleton Guardian*, 22 Apr 1960; Patrick Dunleavy, *The Politics of Mass Housing in Britain, 1945–1975* (Oxford, 1981), pp 313–23; *Salford City Reporter*, 12 Aug 1960.

7. *Glasgow Herald*, 24 Jun 1960; *Lennox Herald*, 25 Jun 1960; *News Chronicle*, 22 Sep 1960; *Architectural Design*, Oct 1960, p 395; *Birmingham Mail*, 24 Oct 1960, 26 Oct 1960; *Daily Telegraph*, 23 Nov 1960.

8. *Bury Free Press*, 13 Nov 1959, 27 Nov 1959, 22 Apr 1960, 15 Jul 1960, 14 Oct 1960, 21 Oct 1960, 28 Oct 1960; *Listener*, 30 Jun 1960, 28 Jul 1960, 29 Sep 1960, 27 Oct 1960; *Architectural Review*, Aug 1960, pp 111–12.

9. J. B. Cullingworth, 'Some Implications of Overspill', *Sociological Review*, Jul 1960, p 77; *New Society*, 22 Aug 1963; *Liverpool Echo*, 23 Sep 1960, 28 Sep 1960.

10. This summary of the findings of the Kirkby survey is based on: *New Society*, 22 Aug 1963 (John Barron Mays); N. H. Rankin, 'Social Adjustment in a North-West Newtown', *Sociological Review*, Nov 1963, pp 289–302; Kathleen G. Pickett and David K. Boulton, *Migration and Social Adjustment* (Liverpool, 1974), especially chaps 3 and 5.

11. 'Social Adjustment at Kirkby' survey (Special Collections and Archives, University of Liverpool), D416/4/1–17.

12. *Twentieth Century*, Jul 1960, p 73; Douglas Jay, *Change and Fortune* (1980), p 279; Paul, *Journal*, p 102; Wilson, p 38; *Surrey Comet*, 15 Jun 1960; *Times Educational Supplement*, 17 Jun 1960.

13. Sir Jimmy Young, *Forever Young* (2003), pp 59–62; Rupert Hart-Davis (ed), *The Lyttelton Hart-Davis Letters: Volume Five* (1983), p 92; Andrew Motion, *Philip Larkin* (1993), p 302; *Financial Times*, 24 Jun 1960; Haines, 24 Jun 1960; Selbourne, p 40; *Radio Times*, 24 Jun 1960; *Glasgow Herald*, 28 Jun 1960; *South Wales Echo*, 28–9 Jun 1960.

14. *Hansard*, House of Commons, 29 Jun 1960, cols, 1453, 1474, 1490–4, 1510; *Spectator*, 8 Jul 1960 (Roy Jenkins); *Star* (Sheffield), 30 Jun 1960; Richard Davenport-Hines, *Sex, Death and Punishment* (1990), pp 325–6; *Spectator*, 15 Jul 1960, 22 Jul 1960.

15. Heap, 30 Jun 1960; Bevis Hillier, *Betjeman: The Bonus of Laughter* (2004), p 207; *Sunday Times*, 3 Jul 1960; *Spectator*, 8 Jul 1960; Tom Vallance, 'Lionel Bart', *Independent*, 5 Apr 1999; Michael Billington, *State of the Nation* (2007), pp 156–7; Dominic Shellard (ed), Kenneth Tynan, *Theatre Writings* (2007), pp 211–12; *Sunday Times*, 3 Jul 1960; *New Statesman*, 8 Aug 1960; *Spectator*, 5 Aug 1960; *Daily Mail*, 30 Jun 1960; *Times Literary Supplement*, 8 Jul 1960; Stan Barstow, *In My Own Good Time* (Otley, 2001), p 78; *New Statesman*, 30 Jul 1960; *Times Literary Supplement*, 5 Aug 1960.

16. *Encounter*, Jul 1960, p 8, Sep 1960, p 87; Turtle, 6 Jul 1960; *New Yorker*, 23 Jul 1960; John Campbell, *Nye Bevan* (1997 edn), p xiv; *Crossman*, p 863; Crossman, Ms 154/8/25, 4 Aug 1960, fols 1254–5; *Crossman*, p 867.

17. Diary of May Marlor, 16 Jul 1960; Philip Norman, *John Lennon* (2008), pp 187–8; *Sunday Telegraph*, 28 Mar 1993 (Frances Welch); *Financial Times*, 28 Jul 1960; Martin, 29 Jul 1960; Dee, 29 Jul 1960; *Listener*, 4 Aug 1960; Michael Willmott (ed), Reverend Oliver Willmott, *The Parish Notes of Loders, Dottery & Askerswell: Volume I* (Shrewsbury, 1996), Sep 1960.

18. John Clay, *R.D. Laing* (1996), p 117; *New Statesman*, 16 Jul 1960; *Listener*, 28 Jul 1960; *Guardian*, 25 Aug 1989; Tony Jasper, *The Top Twenty Book* (1994 edn), pp 58–9; Spencer Leigh, 'Tony Meehan', *Independent*, 30 Nov 2005; *Record Collector*, Aug 2006, p 75 (Spencer Leigh); Steve Humphries *et al*, *A Century of Childhood*

(1988), p 32; *Observer*, 19 Jun 2005 (Stuart Nicholson); *Radio Times*, 12 Aug 1960 (Ernest Bradbury); BBC WA, R9/9/24 – LR/60/1775, R9/7/48 – VR/60/154.

19. Haines, 2 Aug 1960; Macmillan, dep.d.40, 12 Aug 1960, fol 15, 15 Aug 1960, fol 19; Haines, 16 Aug 1960; Macmillan, dep.d.40, 18 Aug 1960, fol 24; Haines, 19 Aug 1960.

5 An Act of Holy Communion

1. *London Review of Books*, 2 Jan 2003 (Alan Bennett); Humphrey Carpenter, *That Was Satire That Was* (2000), p 106; Tom Courtenay, *Dear Tom* (2000), pp 304–24; Carpenter, pp 107–8; *Punch*, 7 Sep 1960; *Spectator*, 2 Sep 1960; Harry Thompson, *Peter Cook* (1997), p 97; Michael Billington, *State of the Nation* (2007), p 127.

2. David Brett, *George Formby* (1999), pp 215–18; *Southend Standard*, 25 Aug 1960; Bob Mee, 'Dick Richardson', *Independent*, 16 Jul 1999; Aurelia Schober Plath (ed), Sylvia Plath, *Letters Home* (1976), p 391.

3. *Daily Herald*, 3 Sep 1960, 9 Sep 1960; Lawrence Black, *Redefining British Politics* (Basingstoke, 2010), p 149; *Daily Herald*, 9 Sep 1960; Macmillan, dep.d.40, 9 Sep 1960, fol 39; St John, 10 Sep 1960; Paul Morley, *The North* (2013), pp 46–7; Gary Imlach, *My Father and Other Working-Class Football Heros* (2005), pp 152–3; *Daily Mail*, 12 Sep 1960; David Ayerst, *Guardian* (1971), p 628; *Radio Times*, 9 Sep 1960; Turtle, 14 Sep 1960; Selbourne, p 54.

4. Heap, 13 Sep 1960; *Punch*, 21 Sep 1960; *Spectator*, 30 Sep 1960; Dominic Shellard (ed), Kenneth Tynan, *Theatre Writings* (2007), pp 213–1.

5. *Radio Times*, 16 Sep 1960; Joe Moran, *Armchair Nation* (2013), pp 134–5; BBC WA, R9/7/48 – VR/60/550; Andy Medhurst, 'Every Wart and Postule', in John Corner (ed), *Popular Television in Britain* (1991), pp 66–7; *Radio Times*, 16 Sep 1960, 26 Aug 1960; Joe Moran, 'The Big Ben dissidents', *Guardian*, 11 May 2009; *Radio Times*, 13 Oct 1960.

6. *Punch*, 19 Oct 1960 (Patrick Ryan); Stuart Laing, *Representations of Working Class Life, 1957–1964* (Basingstoke, 1986), p 151; *Radio Times*, 23 Sep 1960; Zachary Leader, *The Life of Kingsley Amis* (2006), pp 437–8; Larkin, Ms. Eng. c. 7422, 26 Sep 1960, fol 10; *TV Times*, 16 Sep 1960; Mark Lewisohn, *Radio Times to TV Comedy* (2003 edn), pp 109–10; *Times*, 4 Mar 2010.

7. *Fowles*, p 443; Philip M. Williams, *Hugh Gaitskell* (1979), pp 574–610; *New Yorker*, 22 Oct 1960; *New Statesman*, 8 Oct 1960; Williams, *Gaitskell*, p 612; Benn, p 343; George H. Gallup, *The Gallup International Public Opinion Polls: Great Britain, 1937–1975, Volume One* (New York, 1976), p 554; Ronald W. Clark, *The Life of Bertrand Russell* (1975), pp 573–84.

8. St John, 16 Oct 1960; *Spectator*, 21 Oct 1960; *News Chronicle*, 17 Oct 1960; Roy Greenslade, *Press Gang* (2003), pp 98–104; *New Yorker*, 5 Nov 1960 (Panter-Downes); *Listener*, 27 Oct 1960; *Daily Mail*, 18 Oct 1960, 20 Oct 1960.

9. *Manchester Evening News*, 2 Aug 1960; Andrew Thompson, *The Empire Strikes Back?* (Harlow, 2005), p 217; Randall Hansen, *Citizenship and Immigration in Post-war Britain* (Oxford, 2000), pp 96–7; Anthony Howard, *RAB* (1987), pp 280–1; *West Indian Gazette and Afro-Asian-Caribbean News*, Jun 1960, p 7; *New*

Statesman, 9 Jan 1960; *Times Literary Supplement*, 1 Aug 2003; Floella Benjamin, *Coming to England* (1995), pp 69, 80, 89, 92, 113; *Independent*, 15 Jun 1998 (Randeep Ramesh); V. S. Naipaul, *The Middle Passage* (1962), p 12; *Birmingham Mail*, 13 Oct 1960; Anthony Sutcliffe and Roger Smith, *Birmingham 1939–1970* (1974), pp 373–4; Paul Foot, *Immigration and Race in British Politics* (Harmondsworth, 1965), p 197; Kate Paul, *Journal* (Hay-on-Wye, 1997), pp 154–5.

10. *Daily Mail*, 29 Feb 1960; Ralph Harris and Arthur Seldon, *Advertising in Action* (1962), pp 93–5; *Daily Telegraph*, 10 Jan 2006 (Harry Wallop); *Times*, 21 May 2012 (Diamond Jubilee supplement); Jan Boxshall, *Every Home Should Have One* (1997), p 83; Paul Levy, 'Kenneth Wood', *Independent*, 24 Oct 1997; Stephen Bayley, 'Kenneth Wood', *Guardian*, 23 Oct 1997; Boxshall, p 83; David L. Wakefield, 'The Hoover Story in Merthyr Tydfil' (*circa* 1977), p 7; David Kynaston, 'John Bloom' (unpublished obituary for *Financial Times*).

11. *Observer*, 23 Oct 1960 (Mark Abrams); Wilson, pp 154–5; Turtle, 23 Sep 1960; Haines, 18–20 Jun 1960.

12. Anthony Sampson, *Anatomy of Britain* (1962), p 590; ITC records, 3995938/9014, Research Services Ltd, 'Attitudes to Advertising – ITV Programmes (Oct 1960); *Spectator*, 22 Apr 1960; *TV Times*, 8 Jul 1960; David Powell, *Counter Revolution* (1991), p 74; *News Chronicle*, 9 Mar 1960; *Radio Times*, 15 Dec 1960 ('Bookshelf'); *Guardian*, 13 Mar 2010 (Sally Jaine); *Spectator*, 4 Nov 1960 (Leslie Adrian); Heap, 25 Jan 1960; Carol Kennedy, *ICI* (1986), p 110; Larkin, Ms. Eng. c. 7421, 11 Aug 1960, fol 114.

13. Market Investigations Ltd, *Mrs Housewife and Her Grocer* (1961); *Spectator*, 9 Sep 1960; Kathryn A. Morrison, *English Shops and Shopping* (New Haven, 2003), p 207; Turtle, 14 Jul 1960.

14. Powell, *Counter Revolution*, p 75; *Southend Standard*, 1 Sep 1960; Gareth Shaw *et al*, 'Selling Self-Service and the Supermarket', *Business History*, Oct 2004, p 575; Martin, 24 Sep 1960; *Southend Standard*, 29 Sep 1960; *Observer*, 2 Oct 1960 (John Gale).

15. *Daily Mail*, 20 Oct 1960; *New Yorker*, 19 Nov 1960; *Guardian*, 2 Oct 2010 (Simon Hoggart); C. H. Rolph (ed), *The Trial of Lady Chatterley* (1990 edn), pp 9–22; *New Yorker*, 19 Nov 1960.

16. Peter Stead, 'A Paradoxical Turning Point', in Sheila Rowbotham and Huw Beynon (eds), *Looking at Class* (2001), p 53; Arthur Marwick, '*Room at the Top*, *Saturday Night and Sunday Morning*, and the "Cultural Revolution" in Britain', *Journal of Contemporary History*, Jan 1984, p 145; Sheridan Morley, *Dirk Bogarde* (1996), p 77; Sue Harper and Vincent Porter, *British Cinema of the 1950s* (Oxford, 2003), p 184; *Financial Times*, 31 Oct 1960; *Daily Mail*, 29 Oct 1960, 1 Nov 1960.

17. Rolph, pp 68, 71, 22, 113, 92; *New Yorker*, 19 Nov 1960; Larkin, Ms. Eng. c. 7422, 27 Oct 1960, fol 30; Rolph, pp 100, 102; *New Yorker*, 19 Nov 1960.

18. BBC WA, *Any Questions?*, 28 Oct 1960; Rolph, pp 171–2; *Times*, 1 Nov 1960; *Daily Mail*, 2 Nov 1960.

19. Plath, *Letters*, p 399; *New Yorker*, 19 Nov 1960; Larkin, Ms. Eng. c. 7422, 2 Nov 1960, fols 34–5; *Guardian*, 3 Nov 1960; *Glasgow Herald*, 3 Nov 1960; *Times*, 3 Nov 1960, *Daily Express*, 3 Nov 1960; *Daily Sketch*, 3 Nov 1960.

20. BBC WA, *Any Questions?*, 4 Nov 1960; *Kentish Observer*, 10 Nov 1960; *Sunday*

Express, 6 Nov 1960; *Observer*, 6 Nov 1960; *Gallup*, p 571; *Eastern Daily Press*, 8 Nov 1960.

21. Heap, 2 Nov 1960; Ben Pimlott, *Harold Wilson* (1992), p 245; *Daily Mirror*, 4 Nov 1960; Martin, 4 Nov 1960; Gyles Brandreth, *Something Sensational to Read in the Train* (2009), p 15; Heap, 6 Nov 1960; *Times Literary Supplement*, 22 Oct 1999; *Daily Mail*, 8 Nov 1960; Russell Davies (ed), *The Kenneth Williams Dairies* (1993), p 166; Kevin Cann, *Any Day Now* (2010), p 20; *Punch*, 9 Nov 1960; *Times*, 11 Nov 1960; Martin Gilbert, *'Never Despair'* (1988), p 1316; Bill Morgan (ed), *Rub Out the Words* (2012), pp 58–9; *New Statesman*, 12 Nov 1960; *Star* (Sheffield), 11 Nov 1960, 14 Nov 1960; Macmillan, dep.d.40, 13 Nov 1960, fol 99; *Shrewsbury Chronicle*, 18 Nov 1960 (Jack Cater); *Daily Telegraph*, 14 Nov 1960; Michael Gillard and Martin Tomkinson, *Nothing to Declare* (1980), p 178; *Punch*, 16 Nov 1960.

22. *Daily Mail*, 17 Nov 1960; Heap, 17 Nov 1960; Last, 17 Nov 1960; Heap, 20 Nov 1960; *Listener*, 1 Dec 1960.

23. *Eastern Daily Press*, 4 Nov 1960; *Guardian*, 29 Oct 2010 (Peter Stansill); *Shrewsbury Chronicle*, 11 Nov 1960; St John, 24 Nov 1960; *Grimsby Evening Telegraph*, 17 Nov 1960; Brandreth, p 15; Alan Travis, *Bound and Gagged* (2000), p 163; Paul, *Journal*, p 178.

24. *Guardian*, 3 Dec 1960; *Times*, 9 Aug 1997; *Times Literary Supplement*, 7 Dec 2001 (John Gross); *New Statesman*, 12 Nov 1960; Courtenay, p 334; Christopher Sandford, *Mick Jagger* (New York, 1999 edn), p 35; *Daily Mail*, 10 Dec 1960; *Times*, 10 Dec 1960.

25. *TV Times*, 2 Dec 1960; Graham Nown (ed), *Coronation Street: 25 Years* (1985), pp 72–91; Last, 9 Dec 1960; *Guardian*, 10 Dec 1960; *Daily Mirror*, 10 Dec 1960; *Western Daily Press*, 10 Dec 1960; *Liverpool Daily Post*, 10 Dec 1960; *Sunday Times*, 11 Dec 1960; *Radio Times*, 9 Dec 2000.

6 Why Are We Falling Behind?

1. *Radio Times*, 1 Dec 1960, 24 Nov 1960; Matthew Grant, 'Historians, the Penguin Specials and the "State-of-the-Nation" Literature, 1958–1964', *Contemporary British History*, autumn 2003, p 29; Michael Shanks, *The Stagnant Society* (Harmondsworth, 1961), pp 28–9, 232–3.

2. Jim Tomlinson, 'Inventing "decline"', *Economic History Review*, Nov 1996, pp 731–57; Jim Tomlinson, *The Politics of Decline* (Harlow, 2000).

3. George L. Bernstein, *The Myth of Decline* (2004), p 163; R. F. Bretherton, *Demand Management 1958–1964* (1999), pp 21–2; Ian Budge, 'Relative Decline as a Political Issue', *Contemporary Record*, summer 1993, p 10; *Observer*, 9 Dec 2001.

4. Nicholas Comfort, *The Slow Death of British Industry* (2013), pp 5, 9; T. R. Gourvish and R. G. Wilson, *The British Brewing Industry 1830–1980* (Cambridge, 1994), pp 452–65; Anthony Sampson, *Anatomy of Britain* (1962), pp 496–7; Frances Bostock and Geoffrey Jones, 'Foreign Multinationals in British Manufacturing, 1850–1962', *Business History*, Jan 1994, p 105; Sampson, *Anatomy of Britain*, p 499; Comfort, pp 324–30.

5. Geofffrey Owen, *From Empire to Europe* (1999), pp 221–2; Steven Tolliday,

'Government, employers and shop floor organisation in the British motor industry, 1939–69', in Steven Tolliday and Jonathan Zeitlin (eds), *Shop Floor Bargaining and the State* (Cambridge, 1985), p 131; Macmillan, dep.d.40, 19 Nov 1960, fol 108; *New Statesman*, 10 Nov 1961; *Spectator*, 8 Dec 1961; Richard Overy, 'Leonard Percy Lord', in *Dictionary of Business Biography, Vol 3* (1985), p 858; C. Gulvin, 'Donald Gresham Stokes', in *Dictionary of Business Biography, Vol 5* (1986), pp 347–55; Wayne Lewchuk, *American Technology and the British Vehicle Industry* (Cambridge, 1987), p 195; Tolliday, *Government*, p 132; Stephen Wilks, *Industrial Policy and the Motor Industry* (Manchester, 1984), pp 75–8; Les Gurl papers (Oxfordshire History Centre), Acc 5639, 1962 file, 17 Feb 1962.

6. Comfort, p 37; Steve Koener, *The Strange Death of the British Motor Cycle Industry* (Lancaster, 2012), pp 119–20, 125, 134–5; *Daily Mirror*, 30 Nov 1961; Bert Hopwood, *Whatever Happened to the British Motorcycle Industry?* (Yeovil, 1981), p 185; Roger Lloyd-Jones *et al*, 'Culture as Metaphor', *Business History*, Jul 1989, pp 93–133.

7. *Observer*, 18 Oct 1959; Keith Hayward, *The British Aircraft Industry* (Manchester, 1989), pp 74–8; Owen, *Empire to Europe*, pp 310–11; *Spectator*, 2 Sep 1960; *Observer*, 18 Oct 1959; *New Statesman* 27 Feb 1960; Owen, *Empire to Europe*, p 309.

8. *Observer*, 18 Oct 1959; Crossman, Ms 154/8/27, 17 Jul 1963, fol 50; Lord Robens, *Ten Year Stint* (1972), pp 179–80; Tony Hall, *Nuclear Politics* (1986), p 71; Lord Hinton papers (Institution of Mechanical Engineers), 'The Memoirs of Christopher Hinton', p 313; Andrew Massey, *Technocrats and Nuclear Politics* (1988), pp 109–10.

9. *Observer*, 18 Oct 1959; Martin Campbell-Kelly, *ICL* (Oxford, 1989), pp 207–8, 215; Geoffrey Tweedale, 'Marketing in the Second Industrial Revolution', *Business History*, Jan 1992, p 116; John Hendry, 'The Teashop Computer Manufacturer', *Business History*, Jan 1987, p 96; Campbell-Kelly, pp 201–5; Owen, *Empire to Europe*, pp 203–4.

10. Owen, *Empire to Europe*, p 188; D.A. Farnie, 'The Textile Machine-Making Industry and the World Market, 1870–1960', *Business History*, Oct 1990, p 163; Roger Lloyd-Jones and M. J. Lewis, *Alfred Herbert Ltd and the British Machine Tool Industry, 1887–1983* (Aldershot, 2006), chaps 7–9; *Financial Times*, 15 Dec 1990 (Geoffrey Owen).

11. *Economist*, 7 May 1960; John Singleton, 'Lancashire's Last Stand', *Economic History Review*, Feb 1986, p 107; John Singleton, 'Showing the White Flag', *Business History*, Oct 1990, pp 129–30; John Singleton, *Lancashire on the Scrapheap* (Oxford, 1991), pp 126, 137, 140; Mark Keighley, *Wool City* (Ilkley, 2007), pp 129–34.

12. Geoffrey Tweedale, *Steel City* (Oxford, 1995), pp 1, 331–4; Owen, *Empire to Europe*, pp 127–8; Duncan Burn, *The Steel Industry 1939–1959* (Cambridge, 1961), pp 558, 674–5, 678–9.

13. S. O. Davies papers (South Wales Coalfield Archive, University of Swansea), F33; Tony Hall, *King Coal* (Harmondsworth, 1981), pp 106–8; *Times*, 16 Oct 1959; *Hansard*, House of Commons, 23 Nov 1959, cols 56, 81, 114; William Ashworth, *The History of the British Coal Industry: Volume 5* (Oxford, 1986), p 668; 'Lord Robens of Woldingham', *Times*, 29 Jun 1999; Sampson, *Anatomy of Britain*, pp 540–1.

14. Tony Mayer, *La Vie Anglaise* (1960), p 95; *Guardian*, 23 Feb 2013 (Ian Jack); Sampson, *Anatomy of Britain*, p 541; *New Statesman*, 16 Jan 1960; 'Gorton', *Wikipedia*; Christopher Harvie, *Scotland and Nationalism* (1998 edn), p 123; Charles Loft, 'The Beeching Myth', *History Today*, Apr 2003, p 39; Nicholas Faith, 'Lord Beeching', *Independent*, 29 Dec 1990.

15. *Time and Tide*, 24 Feb 1961; David F. Wilson, *Dockers* (1972), p 158; *New Statesman*, 5 May 1961 (J.P.W. Mallalieu); *Listener*, 10 May 1962.

16. Owen, *Empire to Europe*, p 99; E. Lorenz and F. Wilkinson, 'The Shipbuilding Industry, 1880–1965', in Bernard Elbaum and William Lazonick (eds), *The Decline of the British Economy* (Oxford, 1986), p 117; *Sunday Times*, 17 Jul 1960; *New Left Review*, Jul–Aug 1960, p 58; *Glasgow Herald*, 16 Dec 1960; *Journal* (Newcastle), 17 Dec 1960, 22 Dec 1960; *Glasgow Herald*, 20 Apr 1961; *Evening Chronicle* (Newcastle), 19 Apr 1961; Anthony Burton, *The Rise and Fall of British Shipbuilding* (1994), p 215; *Liverpool Daily Post*, 25 Apr, 1962; Burton, p 216.

17. David Kynaston, *The City of London, Volume 4* (2001), pp 268–70, 252–3, 202.

18. *Financial Times*, 31 Jul 1961 ('Our Diplomatic Correspondent', probably Fredy Fisher); William A. Robson, *Nationalized Industry and Public Ownership* (1960), p 479; Geoffrey Goodman, 'Lord Robens of Woldingham', *Guardian*, 28 Jun 1999; *Economist*, 15 Apr 1961; James Foreman-Peck and Robert Millward, *Public and Private Ownership of British Industry, 1820–1990* (Oxford, 1994), pp 300–14; *Financial Times*, 12 Apr 1961.

19. Owen, *Empire to Europe*, p 449; Richard Findley, 'The Conservative Party and Defeat', *Twentieth Century British History*, 2001 (12/3), p 327; *Financial Times*, 29 May 1962; *Economist*, 2 Dec 1961; Peter Hennessy, 'Practical lesson in training the young', *Independent*, 18 Jun 1990.

20. *Glasgow Herald*, 9 Dec 1960; BBC WA, *Any Questions?*, 8 Jan 1960.

21. This paragraph on management weaknesses is based on: Ian Clark, 'Employer Resistance to the Fordist Production Process', *Contemporary British History*, summer 2001, pp 30, 34; Howard F. Gospel, *Markets, Firms and the Management of Labour in Modern Britain* (Cambridge, 1992), p 110; Nick Tiratsoo and Jim Tomlinson, *The Conservatives and Industrial Efficiency, 1951–64* (1998), pp 72, 56–7; Nick Tiratsoo, '"Cinderellas at the Ball"', *Contemporary British History*, autumn 1999, p 105.

22. *Financial Times*, 31 Dec 1996; *Glasgow Herald*, 22 Nov 1961, 16 Jan 1962; Frank Mort, 'Social and Symbolic Fathers and Sons in Postwar Britain', *Journal of British Studies*, Jul 1999, p 369; Michael Roper, *Masculinity and the British Organization Man* (Oxford, 1994), p 59.

23. *Bacup Times*, 17 Dec 1960; *Radio Times*, 8 Dec 1960; Eric Wigham, *What's Wrong with the Unions?* (Harmondsworth, 1961), p 189; David Granick, *The European Executive* (1962), p 234; Alan Campbell *et al*, 'The Post-War Compromise', in Alan Campbell *et al* (eds), *British Trade Unions and Industrial Politics: Volume One* (Aldershot, 1999), pp 72–4; *Financial Times*, 9 Jun 1992 (Geoffrey Owen); *London Review of Books*, 10 May 1990 (Jose Harris); Fred Wellings, 'Sir Halford Walter Luckton Reddish', in *Dictionary of Business Biography, Volume 4* (1985), p 860; Wigham, p 187.

24. Howard Gospel, 'The Management of Labour' in Chris Wrigley (ed), *A History of British Industrial Relations, 1939–1979* (Cheltenham, 1996), p 90; David Gilbert,

'Strikes in postwar Britain', in Wrigley, *History*, pp 134–5; Gospel, 'Management', p 89; J.E.T. Eldridge and G. C. Cameron, 'Unofficial Strikes', *British Journal of Sociology*, Mar 1964, p 29; Sampson, *Anatomy of Britain*, pp 568–9; *News Chronicle*, 15 Oct 1960; David Kynaston, *The Financial Times* (1988), pp 292–3; Burton, pp 204–5; Mark W. Bufton, *Britain's Productivity Problem, 1948–1990* (Basingstoke, 2004), pp 44, 53; Nick Tiratsoo and Jim Tomlinson, 'Restrictive Practices on the Shopfloor in Britain, 1945–60', *Business History*, Apr 1994, pp 74–7.

25. Campbell *et al*, 'Post-War Compromise', p 94; Chris Wrigley, 'Trade union development, 1945–79', in Wrigley, *History*, p 63; T. E. Stephenson, 'The Changing Role of Local Democracy', *Sociological Review*, Jul 1957, pp 33, 40; *Punch*, 10 Feb 1960; John Bew, 'The last great Briton', *New Statesman*, 13 Dec 2013; *Times*, 22 May 2009; Eldridge and Cameron, p 33, quoting B. C. Roberts; *New Left Review*, May–Jun 1960, p 14 (Denis Butt); Stephen Tolliday, 'High Tide and After', in Bill Lancaster and Tony Mason (eds), *Life and Labour in a Twentieth Century City* (Warwick, 1986), pp 229–30.

26. William Brown, 'The High Tide of Consensus', *Historical Studies in Industrial Relations*, Sep 1997, p 141; *Socialist Commentary*, Aug 1961, pp 10–15; Allan Flanders, *The Fawley Productivity Agreements* (1966 ppk edn), p 13; *Sunday Times*, 13 May 1962; Flanders, *Fawley*, p 9 (Aubrey Jones); Shanks, *Stagnant*, pp 74, 138. In general on Flanders, see: John Kelly, *Ethical Socialism and the Trade Unions* (Abingdon, 2010).

27. Peter Dorey, *British Conservatism and Trade Unionism, 1945–1964* (Farnham, 2009), pp 63, 82; John Campbell, *Edward Heath* (1993), p 111; Wigham, p 169; Dennis Barker, 'Bryan Forbes', *Guardian*, 10 May 2013; *Daily Mail*, 11 Mar 1960; *Times*, 14 Mar 1960; *Daily Mirror*, 11 Mar 1960; *Evening World* (Bristol), 15 Mar 1960; Tony Shaw, *British Cinema and the Cold War* (2001), p 166; Anthony Hayward, 'Ronald Wolfe', *Guardian*, 22 Dec 2011.

28. *TV Times*, 13 Apr 1962; Robert J. Wybrow, *Britain Speaks Out, 1937–87* (Basingstoke, 1989), p 160; W.E.J. McCarthy, *The Closed Shop in Britain* (Oxford, 1964), pp 3, 28, 79; Robert McKenzie and Allan Silver, *Angels in Marble* (1968), pp 128–30; M.P. Carter, *Home, School and Work* (Oxford, 1962), pp 269–75.

29. *Encounter*, Apr 1961, p 67; Granick, pp 242–3; W. J. Reader and David Kynaston, *Phillips & Drew* (1998), chaps 3–4; Sampson, *Anatomy of Britain*, pp 227, 278; Scott Newton and Dilwyn Porter, *Modernization Frustrated* (1988), p 138; National Archives, PREM 11/3756, Macmillan minute on Eccles letter, 1 Nov 1961.

30. Sidney Pollard, *The Wasting of the British Economy* (Beckenham, 1984 edn), pp 72–90; Newton and Porter, pp 133–5; *Times*, 28 Nov 1960.

31. See in general on this whole question of sterling: Tiratsoo and Tomlinson, *Conservatives*, pp 22, 163; Newton and Porter, pp 132–4; Bernstein, *Myth*, pp 670–1; Susan Strange, *Sterling and British Policy* (1971), chaps 3 and 10.

7 Working, Middle and Kidding Themselves

1. Ferdynand Zweig, *The Worker in an Affluent Society* (1961), pp ix, 205–12.

2. Zweig, *Worker*, pp 104–29; *Sunday Times*, 16 Sep 1962 (magazine); *New Statesman*, 20 Aug 1960 (Francis Williams); Tom Harrisson, *Britain Revisited* (1961), p 35;

Sunday Times, 16 Sep 1962 (magazine); Tony Collins, *Rugby League in Twentieth Century Britain* (Abingdon, 2006), p 89; John Hudson, *Wakes Weeks* (Stroud, 1992), p 145; Roger K. Bingham, *Lost Resort?* (Milnthorpe, 1990), p 287; Frank Norman, *Norman's London* (1969), pp 25–7; Sid Chaplin, *The Smell of Sunday Dinner* (1971), pp 113–14; *Socialist Commentary*, Apr 1962, p 27; Barry Doyle, 'The Geography of Cinemagoing in Great Britain, 1934–1994', *Historical Journal of Film, Radio and Television*, Mar 2003, p 61; Ashley Franklin, *A Cinema Near You* (Derby, 1996), p 147; *East London Advertiser*, 18 Nov 1960.

3. *News Chronicle*, 8 Feb 1960; Matthew Taylor, *The Association Game* (Harlow, 2008), pp 192–5; Humphrey Carpenter, *Dennis Potter* (1998), p 115; Simon Inglis, *The Football Grounds of England and Wales* (1983), pp 90–1; *Western Evening Herald*, 23 Nov 1960; BBC WA, *Any Questions?*, 27 Jan 1961; Stephen Wagg, *The Football World* (1984), p 195; Brian Jackson, *Working Class Community* (1968), p 114; *Huddersfield Daily Examiner*, 30 Sep 1961; Hudson, p 63; *Daily Mirror*, 19 Jan 1961; *Times*, 18 Jan 2011 (Matt Dickinson); Dilwyn Porter, 'British Sport Transformed' in Richard Coopey and Peter Lyth (eds), *Business in Britain in the Twentieth Century* (Oxford, 2009), p 337.

4. Julian Demetriadi, 'The golden years', in Gareth Shaw and Allan Williams (eds), *The Rise and Fall of British Coastal Resorts* (1997), p 61; Roy Wallis, 'Moral Indignation and the Media', *Sociology*, May 1976, p 287; *Western Daily Press*, 12 Oct 1961; *Spectator*, 6 Sep 2003 (Michael Henderson); 'Jackie Pallo', *Daily Telegraph*, 16 Feb 2006; *Economist*, 16 Apr 1960, 18 Jun 1960, 28 May 1960; Keith Leybourn, *Working-Class Gambling in Britain, c. 1906–1960s* (Lampeter, 2007), pp 132–3; *Time and Tide*, 13 Apr 1961 (Jack Braithwaite); Tony Hannan, *Being Eddie Waring* (Edinburgh, 2008), p 237; *Financial Times*, 31 Jul 1959.

5. Dennis Potter, *The Changing Forest* (1996 Minerva edn), pp 2–5, 14–16, 37, 64–5, 79–81, 99; Melanie Tebbutt, 'Imagined Families and Vanished Communities', *History Workshop Journal*, spring 2012, p 161; Lulu, *I Don't Want to Fight* (2002), pp 38–41; Peter Willmott, *The Evolution of a Community* (1963), p 109; Rosalind Watkiss Singleton, '"Old Habits Persist": Change and Continuity in Black Country Communities: Pensnett, Sedgley and Tipton, 1945–c.1970' (University of Wolverhampton PhD, 2010), *passim*; Harrisson, *Britain*, p 184; *Sheffield Telegraph*, 19 May 1960.

6. *Guardian*, 1 Dec 2012 (Ian Jack); *Big Issue*, 16 Aug 2010 (Andrew Ward and John Williams); Gavin Mellor, 'Post-war Lancastrian Football Heroes', *North West Labour History*, 1999/2000, pp 48–50; Ivan Ponting, 'Ronnie Clayton', *Independent*, 2 Nov 2010; *Guardian*, 6 Nov 2010 (Jim Whelan); Sandra Trudgen Dawson, *Holiday Camps in Twentieth-Century Britain* (Manchester, 2011), p 212; *Keighley News and Bingley Chronicle*, 5 Aug 1961; *Bridlington Free Press*, 4 Aug 1961; John Benson, *The Rise of Consumer Society in Britain, 1880–1980* (Harlow, 1994), p 87; John K. Walton, *The Blackpool Landlady* (Manchester, 1978), p 193.

7. *Evening Chronicle* (Newcastle), 29 Dec 1984; D. J. Taylor, 'Key to the Sardine Can', *Guardian*, 30 Apr 2005; *TV Times*, 21 Apr 1961; Katherine Bucknell (ed), Christopher Isherwood, *The Sixties* (2010), p 79.

8. Michael Shanks, *The Stagnant Society* (Harmondsworth, 1961), p 52; *Punch*, 2 May 1962; Colin Rosser and Christopher Harris, *The Family and Social Change* (1965), p 115; B. J. Heraud, 'Social Class and the New Towns', *Urban Studies*, Feb 1968,

p 53; A.G.V. Simmonds, 'Conservative governments and the housing question, 1951–59' (University of Leeds PhD, 1995), pp 327–8; BBC WA, R9/9/25 – VR/61/598; *Independent*, 19 Sep 2007 (Paul Newman); *Wisden Cricketers' Almanack, 1963* (1963), p 485; Tony Collins, *A Social History of English Rugby Union* (Abingdon, 2009), pp 118–19; *New Statesman*, 14 Nov 1959; Claire Langhamer, *The English in Love* (Oxford, 2013), pp 57–8.

9. *Financial Times*, 5 Dec 1962; Paul Johnson, 'The welfare state, income and living standards', in Roderick Floud and Paul Johnson, *The Cambridge Economic History of Modern Britain, Volume III* (Cambridge, 2004), p 230; W. G. Runciman, *Relative Deprivation and Social Justice* (1966), pp 82–9; Barbara Preston, 'Statistics of Inequality', *Sociological Review*, Feb 1974, pp 103–18.

10. Peter Willmott, 'Some Social Trends', in J. B. Cullingworth (ed), *Problems of an Urban Society, Vol III* (1973), p 95. For an illuminating survey of sociologists at work, see: Mike Savage, *Identities and Social Change in Britain since 1940* (Oxford, 2010).

11. Zweig, *Worker*, pp 134–6; Willmott, *Evolution*, pp 101–3; W. G. Runciman, 'Towards a classless society?', *Listener*, 15 Jul 1965; W. G. Runciman, '"Enlightenment," Self-Rated Class and Party Preference', *Sociological Review*, Jul 1964, pp 141, 146–7; Rosser and Harris, *Family*, pp 82–5.

12. Janet Street-Porter, *Baggage* (2004), p 132; *Sir Alf* (Channel Four, 29 Jun 2002); Jeffery Hill, '"I'll Run Him"', *Sport in History*, Dec 2006, pp 502–19; Mark Lewisohn, *Radio Times Guide to TV Comedy* (2003 edn), p 51; George H. Gallup, *The Gallup International Public Opinion Polls: Great Britain, 1937–1975, Volume One* (New York, 1976), p 613; *Salford City Reporter*, 16 Mar 1962, 23 Mar 1962, 30 Mar 1962, 13 Apr 1962.

13. Rupert Christiansen, *I Know You're Going To Be Happy* (2013), p 68; Frank Mort, 'Social and Symbolic Fathers and Sons in Postwar Britain', *Journal of British Studies*, Jul 1999, pp 375–6; *Observer*, 16 Feb 2014; *Independent*, 21 Oct 1995.

14. *Wisden Cricketers' Almanack, 1960* (1960), pp 125–6; *Daily Express*, 15 Nov 1960; Ben Jones, *The Working Class in Mid-Twentieth-Century England* (Manchester, 2012), p 182; *Manchester Evening News*, 25 Sep 1961; *The Bridge* (Southwark Diocese), Feb 2000.

15. *Star* (Sheffield), 30 May 1960; F.J.W. Miller *et al*, *The School Years in Newcastle-upon-Tyne, 1952–62* (1974), pp 258–69; Willmott, 'Social Trends', p 96.

16. Sampson, *Anatomy of Britain*, p 175; Michael Sanderson, *Educational Opportunity and Social Change in England* (1987), p 69; Collins, *Rugby Union*, p 215; Anthony Sampson, *Anatomy of Britain Today* (1965), p 223; Neil Powell, *Amis & Son* (2008), p 128.

17. *Times*, 25–7 Sep 1961; *New Statesman*, 27 Jan 1961, 3 Feb 1961, 10 Feb 1961; Nicholas Hillman, 'The Public Schools Commission', *Contemporary British History*, Dec 2010, pp 513–14; Philip M. Williams, *Hugh Gaitskell* (1979), p 659; *Hansard*, House of Commons, 16 Jun 1961, cols 828–36, 809–16, 884–99; *Times*, 14 Oct 1961; Peter Tory, *The Ultimate Giles* (1995), p 295; *Daily Mail*, 26 Apr 1961; *Times*, 2 Oct 1961; Sampson, *Anatomy of Britain*, p 182; *Times*, 30 Sep 1961.

18. Sanderson, *Educational Opportunity*, pp 46–7; Robert M. Blackburn and Catherine Marsh, 'Education and social class', *British Journal of Sociology*, Dec 1991, pp 507–36.

19. *Derby Evening Telegraph*, 8 Jul 1961; *New Statesman*, 16 Mar 1962; *Independent*, 3 Dec 1998; Stephen Dixon, letter to author, 11 Sep 2013.

20. William Taylor, *The Secondary Modern School* (1963), p 156; *Listener*, 9 Jun 1960; Frances Stevens, *The Living Tradition* (1960), pp 9, 260; *Encounter*, Jul 1961, p 51; *Times Literary Supplement*, 23 Feb 1962; *Sunday Times*, 4 Feb 1962; *New Statesman*, 16 Feb 1962; Brian Jackson and Dennis Marsden, *Education and the Working Class* (1962), pp 224–5; Kit Hardwick, *Brian Jackson* (Cambridge, 2003), p 23.

21. Alan Kerckhoff *et al*, *Going Comprehensive in England and Wales* (1996), pp 65, 89, 126; Robert G. Burgess, 'Changing Concepts of Secondary Education', in Bill Lancaster and Tony Mason (eds), *Life and Labour in a Twentieth Century City* (Warwick, 1986), p 303; *Coventry Evening Telegraph*, 5–6 Apr 1960; Savage, *Identities*, pp 232–3; R.E. Pahl, 'Education and Social Class in Commuter Villages', *Sociological Review*, Jul 1963, p 242; *Listener*, 13 Sep 1962 (W.J.H. Sprott); Martin Johnes, *Wales Since 1939* (Manchester, 2012), p 135; Peter Willmott, *Adolescent Boys of East London* (1966), p 76.

22. Nikolaus Pevsner, *Yorkshire: The West Riding* (Harmondsworth, 1959), p 178; *Spectator*, 21 May 2005 (Frank Keating); Fowles, EUL Ms 102/1/11, ? late Jul 1960, fol 81, Aug 1960, fol 85; *Times Literary Supplement*, 2 Sep 1960.

23. National Union of Teachers, *Popular Culture and Personal Responsibility* (1961), pp 124, 253, 278, 286, 259; Stuart Laing, *Representations of Working-Class Life, 1957–1964* (Basingstoke, 1986), p 194; Fred Inglis, *Raymond Williams* (1995), p 173; *Socialist Commentary*, Oct 1961, p 27; May 1962, pp 19–21; Dave Russell, *Looking North* (Manchester, 2004), p 229.

24. Raymond Williams, *The Long Revolution* (1961), pp ix–x, 174, 202, 293–4, 321, 337–8, 345–6, 355; *Guardian*, 9 Mar 1961; *Times Literary Supplement*, 10 Mar 1961, 7 Apr 1971; *Listener*, 20 Jul 1961; *Encounter*, Jun 1961, pp 79–84; Raymond Williams, *Politics and Letters* (1979), p 134; Inglis, *Williams*, p 177.

25. Nicolas Tredell, 'Uncancelled Challenge', *PN Review*, 1989 (15/5), pp 36–7; *Spectator*, 27 Apr 1962; *New Statesman*, 4 May 1962; Chaplin, 7/3/1, letter to John Bate, 14 Sep 1960.

26. *Spectator*, 29 Dec 1961; *New Statesman*, 12 Jan 1962, 26 Jan 1962.

27. Abrams, box 83, 'Class Stratification, 1910–67', file 2, 'Social Equality – The Class System', 27 Jul 1961.

8 This Is My Work Now

1. *Daily Mirror*, 2 Mar 1961; Carolyn Downs, *A Social, Economic and Cultural History of Bingley, 1906–2005* (Saarbrücken, 2009), p 153; *Daily Mirror*, 5–6 Sep 1961; *Blackburn Times*, 16 Jun 1961; *Daily Mirror*, 5 Sep 1961; *Times*, 14 Sep 1961; Downs, p 184.

2. Rachael Dixey, *Women, Leisure and Bingo* (Leeds, 1982), p 112; *New Statesman*, 7 Jul 1961 (John Morgan); *Daily Mirror*, 2 Mar 1961; *Sunday Times Magazine*, 16 Sep 1962; *Eyes Down!* (BBC Four, 30 Jan 2013); *Daily Mirror*, 6 Sep 1961.

3. *Punch*, 2 May 1962, 9 May 1962, 30 May 1962, 6 Jun 1962.

4. Anne Oakley, *A Critical Woman* (2011), pp 1, 15; David Lascelles, *Other People's Money* (2005), p 99; Jessica Mann, *The Fifties Mystique* (Cornovia Press edn, Sheffield, 2013), p 182; *Financial Times*, 22 Dec 2007 (Sue Cameron); Charles Wintour, 'Anne Sharpley', *Independent*, 17 Apr 1989; Geoffrey Taylor, 'Nesta

Roberts', *Guardian*, 19 Jan 2009; Penny Vincenzi, 'Marjorie Proops', *Independent*, 12 Nov 1996; Kevin Theakston, 'Evelyn Sharp (1903–85)', *Contemporary Record*, summer 1993, pp 132–3; Dennis Barker, 'Irene Thomas', *Guardian*, 4 Apr 2001; 'Ulrica Murray Smith', *Times*, 12 Feb 1999; 'Elisabeth Rivers-Bulkely', *Times*, 12 Feb 2007; 'Pat Moss', *Times*, 18 Oct 2008; 'Patricia Ozanne', *Times*, 7 Mar 2009; Rachel Cooke, *Her Brilliant Career* (2013), chaps 2, 3, 7.

5. *Liverpool Daily Post*, 22 Dec 1960; John Williams, *Red Men* (Edinburgh, 2010), p 319; *Surrey Comet*, 8 Jul 1961; *Daily Mail*, 21 Nov 1960.

6. *Guardian*, 17 May 1999; Simon Farquhar, 'Geoffrey Wheeler', *Independent*, 2 Jan 2014; Mann, p 131; *Spectator*, 4 Sep 2010 (Kate Chisholm).

7. Lascelles, p 100; Mark Robinson, *Hundred Greatest TV Ads* (2000), pp 82, 36; *East London Advertiser*, 9 Mar 1962; David Cannadine, *In Churchill's Shadow* (2002), pp 297–8; Marion Jordan, 'Carry On... Follow that Stereotype', in James Curran and Vincent Porter (eds), *British Cinema History* (1983), pp 312–27; *Independent*, 10 Mar 2001; Stuart Laing, *Representations of Working-Class Life, 1957–1964* (Basingstoke, 1986), p 221; John Hill, *Sex, Class and Realism* (1986), pp 156–68; D. J. Taylor, *After the War* (1993), pp 224–8; Amy Black and Stephen Brooke, 'The Labour Party, Women and the Problem of Gender, 1951–1966', *Journal of British Studies*, Oct 1997, p 452; Lawrence Black, *Redefining British Politics* (Basingstoke, 2010), p 85.

8. Stephanie Spencer, *Gender, Work and Education in Britain in the 1950s* (Basingstoke, 2005), pp 91–3, 125–6; *Daily Express*, 4 Mar 1960; Jim Gledhill, 'White Heat, Guide Blue', *Contemporary British History*, Mar 2013, p 76; *News Chronicle*, 15 Oct 1960; *Daily Mirror*, 9 Jun 1961.

9. *Punch*, 21 Dec 1960 (Patrick Skene Catling); Wilson, p 28; Kathleen Ollerenshaw, *Education for Girls* (1961), pp 17, 40; Jenny Uglow (ed), Angela Carter, *Shaking a Leg* (1997), p 178; Langford, 26 Apr 1962; *Guardian*, 31 Oct 2006 (Frank Keating); Bolton School Old Girls' Association, *Learning and Living* (Bolton, 1960), pp 33–48.

10. *Radio Times*, 12 Jan 1961; *New Statesman*, 31 Jan 1961; Christina Hardyment, *Slice of Life* (1995), pp 68, 70; *Accrington Observer*, 20 Feb 1962.

11. Ben Jones, *The Working Class in Mid-Twentieth-Century England* (Manchester, 2012), pp 177–8; Elizabeth Roberts, *Women and Families* (Oxford, 1995), pp 30–2; Lulu, *I Don't Want to Fight* (2002), pp 36–7; Joe Moran, *Armchair Nation* (2013), p 113; *Smethwick Telephone*, 8 Jun 1962 (Mary Browne).

12. *The Viewer*, 17 Oct 1959; *Radio Times*, 12 Aug 1960; *Guardian*, 24 Jan 2003 (Julia Finch); Hannah Gavron, *The Captive Wife* (1966), pp 69–72, 88–94; Bill Williamson, *The Temper of the Times* (Oxford, 1990), p 154; Angela Holdsworth, *Out of the Doll's House* (1988), p 31; Michael McNay, 'Betty Jerman', *Guardian*, 26 Jul 2010; Holdsworth, pp 31–2; Elizabeth Wilson, *Only Halfway to Paradise* (1980), p 183.

13. Mann, p 179; Jessica Mann, 'What good old days?', *Guardian*, 28 Apr 2012; Ali Haggett, *Desperate Housewives, Neuroses and the Domestic Environment, 1945–1970* (2012), pp 64, 67.

14. *Radio Times*, 19 Jan 1961; BBC WA, *Woman's Hour*, 23 Jan 1961, report of conversation originally transmitted on *Home for the Day*, 11 Dec 1960.

15. Roberts, p 118; Jane Lewis, *Women in Britain since 1945* (Oxford, 1992), p 74; Edw. James, 'Women at Work in Twentieth Century Britain', *Manchester School*, Sep

1962, pp 288, 294; John Westergaard and Henrietta Resler, *Class in a Capitalist Society* (Aldershot, 1975), pp 101–3.

16. Spencer, pp 78, 59; Gary McCulloch, *Failing the Ordinary Child?* (Buckingham, 1998), pp 121–2; Ollerenshaw, p 24; Barry Turner, *Equality for Some* (1974), p 208; Carol Dyhouse, 'Education', in Ina Zweiniger-Bargielowska (ed), *Women in Twentieth-Century Britain* (Harlow, 2001), pp 124, 127.

17. Viola Klein, *Britain's Married Women Workers* (1965), pp 133, 89, 91; Alan Campbell *et al*, 'The Post-War Compromise', in Alan Campbell *et al* (eds), *British Trade Unions and Industrial Politics, Volume One* (Aldershot, 1999), p 93; Ken Grainger, 'Management Control and Labour Quiescence', in Michael Terry and P. K. Edwards (eds), *Shopfloor Politics and Job Controls* (Oxford, 1988), p 99; Joe Moran, 'Queuing Up in Post-War Britain', *Twentieth Century British History*, 2005 (16/3), p 290; Williamson, p 111; Chris Wrigley, 'Women in the Labour Market and in the Unions', in John McIlroy *et al* (eds), *British Trade Unions and Industrial Politics, Volume Two* (Aldershot, 1999), p 54; Ferdynand Zweig, *The Worker in an Affluent Society* (1961), pp 44–5; Rosalind Watkiss Singleton, '"Old Habits Persist"' (University of Wolverhampton PhD, 2010), p 152; *Woman's Mirror*, 1 Oct 1960.

18. Zweig, pp 172–5, 118; Pearl Jephcott, *Married Women Working* (1962), pp 106–11.

19. Ann Cartwright and Margot Jefferys, 'Married Women Who Work', *British Journal of Preventive and Social Medicine*, Oct 1958, pp 159–71; Jephcott, chap 9; Barbara Thompson and Angela Finlayson, 'Married Women who Work in Early Motherhood', *British Journal of Sociology*, Jun 1963, pp 150–68; Simon Yudkin and Anthea Holme, *Working Mothers and their Children* (1963), chaps 2–6; *Guardian*, 25 Aug 2010 (Jill Faux); Yudkin and Holme, p 104; Alan Johnson, *This Boy* (2013), pp 42, 97; *Evening News*, 25 Feb 1960. For two helpful overviews on working mothers, see: Roberts, *Women and Families*, chap 7; Dolly Smith Wilson, 'A New Look at the Affluent Worker: The Good Working Mother in Post-War Britain', *Twentieth Century British History*, 2006 (17/2), pp 206–29.

20. *Socialist Commentary*, Aug 1962, p 34; Willmott, 21 Nov 1960; BBC WA, *Woman's Hour*, 23 Jan 1961, report of conversation originally transmitted on *Home for the Day*, 11 Dec 1960.

21. Lewis, p 103; Lynne Reid Banks, *The L-Shaped Room* (1960), p 32; *Independent*, 18 Jan 2011 (Ian Burrell); Pat Thane and Tanya Evans, *Sinners? Scroungers? Saints?* (Oxford, 2012), p 132; Rupert Christiansen, *I Know You're Going to be Happy* (2013), pp 76–89.

22. Jeffery Weeks, *Sex, Politics and Society* (Harlow, 2nd edn, 1989), pp 256–7; Lewis, p 45; Howard Glennerster, *British Social Policy since 1945* (Oxford, 1995), p 163; Roberts, pp 99–105; *Twentieth Century*, May 1960, pp 409–10; Carol Craig, *The Tears that made the Clyde* (Glendarvel, 2010), p 172; Pierre Perrone, 'Gerry Rafferty', *Independent*, 6 Jan 2011; *Guardian*, 12 Mar 2011; Mann, pp 133–4; *Daily Mirror*, 23 May 1961.

23. Watkiss Singleton, p 144; Nick Tiratsoo, 'Popular politics, affluence and the Labour party in the 1950s', in Anthony Gorst *et al* (eds), *Contemporary British History, 1931–1961* (1991), p 51; Peter Willmott and Michael Young, *Family and Class in a London Suburb* (1960), pp 21–2; Jephcott, p 134; Gavron, p 57; Zweig, pp 31, 181; Margaret Forster, *Hidden Lives* (1995), p 255.

24. *Bolton Evening News*, 17 Feb 1962; *Daily Mail*, 21 Nov 1960; Claire Langhamer, *The English in Love* (Oxford, 2013), pp 170, 186–7; Zweig, pp 221–3.

25. Haggett, pp 55, 57; Richard Davenport-Hines, *The Pursuit of Oblivion* (2001), pp 259, 249.

26. *Radio Times*, 25 Nov 2000; *Guardian*, 3 Jan 1991 (Rebecca Abrams); Barbara Brookes, *Abortion in England, 1900–1967* (Beckenham, 1988), p 154; Stephen Brooke, *Sexual Politics* (Oxford, 2011), p 144; *Daily Mail*, 5 Dec 1961; *Daily Mirror*, 29 Jun 1961.

27. *Punch*, 7 Feb 1962, 17 Jan 1962, 24 Jan 1962; Lena Jeger, 'Mary Stott', *Guardian*, 18 Sep 2002; *Daily Express*, 13 Oct 1959; Katharine Whitehorn, *Selective Memory* (2007), p 139; *Spectator*, 25 Nov 1960.

28. Joan Barrell and Brian Braithwaite, *The Business of Women's Magazines* (1988 edn), p 26; *Financial Times*, 27 Jan 1960; Barrell and Braithwaite, p 45; *Guardian*, 20 Jan 1960 (Michael Frayn); *Mirabelle*, 18 Mar 1961; *Boyfriend*, 18 Mar 1961; *Cherie*, 18 Mar 1961; *Marty*, 18 Mar 1961.

29. Penny Summerfield, 'Women in Britain since 1945', in James Obelkevich and Peter Catterall (eds), *Understanding post-war British society* (1994), p 61; *Times*, 22 Mar 1962; *Daily Mirror*, 14 Feb 1961; Weeks, p 258; Haggett, pp 115–16; *New Society*, 3 Oct 1962; Laing, p 205; Cynthia L. White, *Women's Magazines, 1693–1968* (1970), p 166; *Woman's Own*, 3 Feb 1962.

30. *Woman's Journal*, Mar 1961; *Woman and Shopping*, Mar–Apr 1961; *Woman and Beauty*, Mar 1961; *Woman and Home*, Mar 1961; *Woman's Day*, 18 Mar 1961; *Woman's Mirror*, 18 Mar 1961; *Woman's Realm*, 18 Mar 1961; *Woman's Own*, 18 Mar 1961; *Woman*, 18 Mar 1961.

31. *Punch*, 9 May 1962; *Daily Telegraph*, 19 Apr 1962; *Listener*, 3 May 1962; *Times Literary Supplement*, 27 Apr 1962; *New Statesman*, 20 Apr 1962; Willmott, 5 May 1962, 31 May 1962.

9 Don't Hang Riley

1. Dee, 10 Dec 1960; *Sunday Express*, 11 Dec 1960; St John, 11 Dec 1960; BBC WA, R9/7/49 – VR/60/725; *Western Daily Press*, 15 Dec 1960; *Times*, 15 Dec 1960; Last, 14 Dec 1960; *Manchester Evening News*, 15 Dec 1960; *TV Times*, 9 Dec 1960; Graham Nown (ed), *Coronation Street* (1985), p 102; BBC WA, *Any Questions?*, 16 Dec 1960; *Financial Times*, 24 Dec 1960; Mark Lewisohn, *All These Years, Volume One* (2013), p 406; David Pritchard and Alan Lysaght, *The Beatles* (Hyperion edn, New York, 1998), p 55; *History Today*, Dec 2010, p 9.

2. *Daily Mirror*, 2 Jan 1961; *Punch*, 4 Jan 1961; Beryl Bainbridge, *English Journey* (1984), p 80; Don Taylor, 'David Turner', *Guardian*, 20 Dec 1990; BBC WA, R9/7/50 – VR/61/13; *Spectator*, 6 Jan 1961; Wikipedia, 'List of *The Avengers* episodes'; *Daily Telegraph*, 20 May 2000 (Roger Wilkes); *Listener*, 5 Jan 1961; *Radio Times*, 5 Jan 1961; Janice Galloway, *This is Not About Me* (2008), p 113; *Journal* (Newcastle), 12 Jan 1961; *Sunday Times*, 15 Jan 1961; St John, 15 Jan 1961; Macmillan, dep.d.41, 15 Jan 1961, fol 45; Martin, 16 Jan 1961; Larkin, Ms Eng. c.7422, 17 Jan 1961, fol 74; Haines, 19 Jan 1961; BBC WA, R9/7/50 – VR/61/42; Willmott, 23 Jan 1961; *Y Cyfnod*, 27 Jan 1961; Lady Henrietta Rous (ed), *The Ossie*

Clark Diaries (1998), p lii; *Guardian*, 27 Jan 2007; J.C., 'Sylvia's Pig', *Times Literary Supplement*, 2 Apr 2010.

3. *Daily Mail*, 10 Jan 1961; *Times*, 5 Jan 1961, 7 Jan 1961; *Spectator*, 27 Jan 1961 (Nicholas Davenport); *Financial Times*, 1 Feb 1961; *Times*, 13 Feb 1961, 9 Mar 1961; *Macmillan (2)*, p 371; *New Yorker*, 25 Feb 1961; Simon Heffer, *Like the Roman* (1998), pp 278–82; Anthony Hayward, 'Peter Adamson', *Independent*, 21 Jan 2002; *Spectator*, 17 Feb 1961 (Bamber Gascoigne); *East London Advertiser*, 7 Feb 1961; BBC WA, *Any Questions?*, 3 Feb 1961; Roy Greenslade, *Press Gang* (2004 revised edn), pp 150–2; *Sunday Telegraph*, 5 Feb 1961; *Daily Mail*, 7 Feb 1961; Asa Briggs, *The History of Broadcasting in the United Kingdom, Volume V* (Oxford, 1995), p 342; *New Yorker*, 1 Feb 1961 (Panter-Downes); *Shrewsbury Chronicle*, 10 Feb 1961; *Guardian*, 8 Mar 1996.

4. Lewisohn, *Years*, pp 426–8; *East London Advertiser*, 10 Feb 1961; St John, 10 Feb 1961; Andrew Motion, *Philip Larkin* (1993), p 308; *Daily Mirror*, 11 Feb 1961; Andrew Barrow, *Gossip* (1980 edn), p 219; *Radio Times*, 9 Feb 1961; BBC WA, R9/7/50 – VR/61/89; Heap, 13 Feb 1961; *Times*, 13 Feb 1961; Peter Webb, *Portrait of David Hockney* (1988), p 31; Elizabeth Nelson, *The British Counter-Culture, 1966–1973* (Basingstoke, 1989), p 35; *New Statesman*, 24 Feb 1961 (H.A.L. Craig); Haines, 20 Feb 1961, 23 Feb 1961, 27 Feb 1961; *Daily Mirror*, 28 Feb 1961.

5. *Punch*, 8 Mar 1961; Ruth Dudley Edwards, *Newspapermen* (2003), p 272; Steve Holland, 'Derek Lord', *Guardian*, 30 Sep 2004; *Independent*, 20 Jan 1998 (Jennifer Rodger); New Statesman papers (Special Collections, University of Sussex), Box 20, John Freeman, Editorial Correspondence, 1960–64, A-L. For fuller accounts of the Mirror/Odhams story, see: Philip M. Williams, *Hugh Gaitskell* (1979), pp 667–8; Huw Richards, *The Bloody Circus* (1997), p 176; Adrian Smith, 'The Fall and Fall of the Third *Daily Herald*, 1930–64', in Peter Catterall *et al* (eds), *Northcliffe's Legacy* (2000), pp 186–7.

6. *Daily Telegraph*, 5 Mar 2011 (Philip Eden); *Times*, 2 Mar 1961; Aurelia Schober Plath (ed), *Letters Home by Sylvia Plath* (1976), p 412; BBC WA, R9/7/51 – VR/61/132; *Times*, 10 Mar 1961, 15 Mar 1961; BBC WA, R9/74/2, May 1961; *Daily Mirror*, 16 Mar 1961; Rob Bagchi and Paul Rogerson, *The Unforgiven* (2002), p 32; BBC WA, R9/7/51 – VR/61/162, 164; Dee, 25 Mar 1961; Reg Green, *National Heroes* (Edinburgh, 1999 edn), p 167; Russell Davies (ed), *The Kenneth Williams Diaries* (1993), p 171; Chris Welch, 'Davy Jones', *Independent*, 2 Mar 2012; Graeme Kay, *Life in the Street* (1991), p 90; *TV Times*, 24 Mar 1961, 18 Mar 1961; *Guardian*, 30 Apr 2005 (Michael Coveney); *Times*, 30 Mar 1961; Heap, 29 Mar 1961.

7. *Independent*, 11 Mar 1997 (Margaret Drabble); BBC WA, *Any Questions?*, 31 Mar 1961; *Ashbeian*, 1960–1, p 40; *Fowles*, p 459; Haines, 3 Apr 1961; *Ashbeian*, pp 40–1; *New Statesman*, 31 Mar 1961; Amis, p 587; *Melody Maker*, 8 Apr 1961; Paul Willetts, *Members Only* (2010), p 143; *Times*, 12–13 Apr 1961; Margaret Thatcher, *The Path to Power* (1995), p 117.

8. *Western Daily Press*, 11–12 Apr 1961; Fowles, EUL Ms 102/1/11, 8 Mar 1961, fol 123; Diaries of Patricia (Pat) Scott (Special Collections, University of Sussex), '1957' Diary, 5 Apr 1961; *Listener*, 5 Jan 1961, 12 Jan 1961; Clifford Hill, *How Colour Prejudiced is Britain?* (1965), pp 218–20; Fred Milson, *Operation Integration* (Birmingham, 1961), pp 1–7; *Evening Despatch* (Birmingham), 17 Aug 1961.

9. Milson, p 7; Randall Hansen, *Citizenship and Immigration in Post-war Britain* (Oxford, 2000), pp 96–7, 102; Heap, 8 Jun 1961; *Scotsman*, 13 Jun 1961.

10. Robert J. Wybrow, *Britain Speaks Out, 1937–87* (Basingstoke, 1989), pp 62–3; Timothy Raison, 'Macleod and Howe', *Twentieth Century British History*, 1997 (8/1), p 103; *Macmillan (3)*, p 309; *New Yorker*, 11 Mar 1961; Anthony Sampson, *Anatomy of Britain* (1962), pp 80–1; Robert Shepherd, *Iain Macleod* (1994), p 228; Bill Schwarz, *Memories of Empire, Volume 1* (Oxford, 2011), p 383; Nicholas Owen, 'Decolonisation and Postwar Consensus', in Harriet Jones and Michael Kandiah (eds), *The Myth of Consensus* (Basingstoke, 1996), pp 173–4.

11. Andrew Thompson, *The Empire Strikes Back?* (Harlow, 2005), pp 215–16; D. R. Thorpe, *Supermac* (2010), p 514; John Campbell, *Edward Heath* (1993), p 119; *Macmillan (3)*, p 8; Mark Pottle (ed), *Daring to Hope: The Diaries and Letters of Violet Bonham Carter, 1946–1969* (2000), p 240; Wybrow, p 63; *Daily Mirror*, 26 May 1961; *Daily Telegraph*, 9 Feb 1998.

12. St John, 12 Apr 1961; Willetts, pp 149–50; Turtle, 14 Apr 1961; IBA Audience Research material (Independent Television Commission), Television Research Committee (Noble Committee), 3995533/3088; *TV Times*, 14 Apr 1961; BBC WA, R9/7/51 – VR/61/214; Tam Dalyell, 'Jim Baxter', *Independent*, 16 Apr 2001; Heap, 17 Apr 1961; C. H. Rolph, *All Those in Favour?* (1962); Olga Cannon and J.R.L. Anderson, *The Road from Wigan Pier* (1973), p 234.

13. Katherine Bucknell (ed), Christopher Isherwood, *The Sixties* (2010), p 62; *TV Times*, 21 Apr 1961; *New Statesman*, 21 Apr 1961; *Evening Chronicle* (Newcastle), 21 Apr 1961; *Times*, 24 Apr 1961; Ian Jack, *The Country Formerly Known as Great Britain* (2009), pp 80–1; BBC WA, R9/7/51 – VR/61/237; *Daily Mirror*, 27 Apr 1961; *Radio Times*, 27 Apr 1961; BBC WA, R9/7/51 – VR/61/245; *Daily Mirror*, 1 May 1961; *Woman's Mirror*, 29 Apr 1961; Macmillan, dep.d.42, 29 Apr 1961, fol 13.

14. *Liverpool Daily Post*, 1 May 1961; *Independent*, 27 Apr 2001 (Stan Hey); Larkin, Ms Eng. c.7423, 6 May 1961, fol 26; 'Bill Nicholson', *Times*, 25 Oct 2004; Last, 7–8 May 1961; Martin, 9 May 1961.

15. Nicola Beauman, *The Other Elizabeth Taylor* (2009), p 335; *Times*, 11 May 1961; Hazel Holt, *A Lot to Ask* (1990), p 183; *Listener*, 15 Jun 1961; Humphrey Carpenter, *That Was Satire That Was* (2000), pp 110–24; Harry Thompson, *Peter Cook* (1997), pp 107–8; *Brighton and Hove Herald*, 6 May 1961; *Daily Express*, 11 May 1961; *Times*, 11 May 1961; Heap, 10 May 1961; *Twentieth Century*, autumn 1961, p 181 (Michael Frayn); *Daily Mail*, 20 May 1961; *Daring to Hope*, p 239; BBC WA, R9/7/52 – VR/61/255.

16. Martin, 12 May 1961; *Crossman*, p 944; Joe Moran, *Armchair Nation* (2013), p 140; *Times* 16 May 1961; *Guardian*, 19 May 1961; *Times*, 19 May 1961; *Sunday Telegraph*, 21 May 1961 (Alan Brien); *New Statesman*, 26 May 1961 (Roger Gellert); Heap, 18 May 1961; *Independent*, 10 Oct 1997 (Ken Jones); *New Statesman*, 7 Sep 1962 (Danny Blanchflower); *Totnes Times*, 27 May 1961; *East London Advertiser*, 26 May 1961; *Radio Times*, 18 May 1961; John Fisher, *Tony Hancock* (2008), p 314; BBC WA, R9/7/52 – VR/61/291.

17. BBC WA, *Any Questions?*, 2 Jun 1961; BBC WA, R9/7/52 – VR/61/353 (this includes Reaction Index figures for 2–5 of *Hancock*); *Independent*, 27 May 2000 (David Aaronovitch); John Bright-Holmes (ed), *Like It Was: The Diaries of Malcolm Muggeridge* (1981), pp 524–5; Hague, 8 Jun 1961; *Daily Mirror*, 9 Jun

1961; *Evening Standard*, 3 Oct 2011; Tom Courtenay, *Dear Tom* (2000), pp 344–6; Spencer Leigh, 'Pre-Fab Britain', *Record Collector*, Aug 2006, p 75; Courtenay, pp 347–50; Isherwood, *Sixties*, p 71; Selbourne, p 87.

18. *Sheffield Telegraph*, 16 Jun 1961; Local Studies Library, Sheffield, MP 1117 M; *Sheffield Telegraph*, 17 Jun 1961; St John, 17 Jun 1961; Larkin, Ms Eng. c.7423, 18 Jun 1961, fol 58; Haines, 19 Jun 1961; *Evening Citizen* (Glasgow), 3 Jul 1961; Haines, 26 Jun 1961; Rupert Hart-Davis (ed), *The Lyttelton Hart-Davis Letters: Volume Six* (1984), p 76; BBC WA, R9/74/2, Aug 1961; *Times*, 27 Jun 1961; *Glasgow Herald*, 28 Jun 1961; *Radio Times*, 22 Jun 1961; Dee, 28 Jun 1961; Sampson, *Anatomy*, pp 567–8; Francis Beckett, *Enemy Within* (1998 Merlin Press edn, Woodbridge), p 151.

19. *Evening Citizen* (Glasgow) 30 Jun 1961; *Glasgow Herald*, 1 Jul 1961; Fisher, *Hancock*, p 326; BBC WA, R9/7/52 – VR/61/353.

10 We'll All Be Uprooted

1. *Architectural Review*, Jan 1961, pp 42–3; *Architects' Journal*, 30 Aug 1961; Robert Brown, *Basingstoke* (Chichester, 1994); *Western Daily Press*, 14 Jun 1961; *Liverpool Echo*, 27 Apr 1961.

2. *Financial Times*, 31 May 1961; *Birmingham Post*, 4 Sep 1961; Anthony Sutcliffe and Roger Smith, *Birmingham, 1939–1970* (1974), p 410; *Sunday Mercury*, 15 Apr 1962; *Architects' Journal*, 18 May 1961; Alan Clawley, *John Madin* (2011), p 54; 'John Madin', *Times*, 24 Jan 2012.

3. *Liverpool Daily Post*, 5 May 1961; Derek Beattie, *Blackburn* (Halifax, 1992), p 171; *Official Architecture and Planning*, Jul 1961, pp 315–16; *Blackburn Times*, 5 May 1961; *Telegraph & Argus* (Bradford), 6 Feb 1962, 13 Mar 1962; Michael Birdsall *et al*, *A Century of Bradford* (Stroud, 2000), p 81.

4. Miles Glendinning and Stefan Muthesius, *Tower Block* (1994), p 263; *Times Literary Supplement*, 4 Feb 2005 (Timothy Mowl); Gavin Stamp, *Britain's Lost Cities* (2007), p 53; *Guardian*, 3 Mar 1961; Grant Lewison and Rosalind Billingham (eds), *Coventry New Architecture* (Warwick, 1969), p 60.

5. *Official Architecture and Planning*, Mar 1961, p 142; *Tower Block*, p 241; *Architectural Design*, Jan 1962, p 17; *Wikipedia*, 'Ardler'; *Tower Block*, p 241; Tom Begg, *Housing Policy in Scotland* (Edinburgh, 1996), p 154; *Wikipedia*, 'Oxgangs High Rise Flats'; edinburghguide.com, 'Gracemount Tower Blocks Hit the Dust', 26 Oct 2009; *Guardian*, 5 Jan 2008 (Ian Jack).

6. John Grindrod, *Concretopia* (Brecon, 2013), pp 152–3; *Glasgow Herald*, 11 Aug 1961, 11 Feb 1961, 20 Apr 1961, 2 Nov 1961; *Official Architecture and Planning*, Feb 1962, p 96; *Tower Block*, pp 235, 65; Miles Horsey, 'Multi-storey council housing in Britain', *Planning Perspectives*, 1988, pp 183–4.

7. David Bean, *Tyneside* (1971), p 155; 'Arnold Haggenbach', *Times*, 8 Apr 2005; *Architects' Journal*, 19 Jan 1961; arthurlloyd.co.uk, 'The Empire Palace Theatre, Leeds'; Kathryn A. Morrison, *English Shops and Shopping* (2003), p 284; Ben Beazley, *Postwar Leicester* (Stroud, 2006), pp 67–9; Mark Girouard, *Big Jim* (1998), pp 106–15; *Tower Block*, p 263; David Nash and David Reeder, *Leicester in the Twentieth Century* (Stroud, 1993), p 30; *Liverpool Daily Post*, 16 Dec 1960, 12 Dec

1961; John R. Gold, *The Practice of Modernism* (Abingdon, 2007), pp 185, 128; *Liverpool Daily Post*, 21 Dec 1961, 27 Mar 1962.

8. *Evening Standard*, 7 Dec 1961; *Evening News*, 12 Apr 1962, 13 May 1962; *East London Advertiser*, 17 Feb 1961, 15 Sep 1961; Jay Merrick, 'Tower Power', *Independent*, 14 Aug 2001; *Architectural Review*, Mar 1962, pp 190–6; Oliver Harris, *Cranes, Critics and Croydonisation* (Croydon, 1993), p 20; *Evening News*, 7 Jan 1963; *Architectural Review*, Jan 1961, pp 54–5; Michael Collins, *The Likes of Us* (2004), pp 141–2; Heap, 10 Aug 1961; *New Yorker*, 21 Jan 1961; St John, 19 Feb 1961; *Architects' Journal*, 22 Nov 1961, 1 Nov 1961; David Kynaston, *The City of London, Volume 4* (2001), pp 133–4; Macmillan, dep.d.44, 24 Oct 1961, fol 3; Gavin Stamp, *Lost Victorian Britain* (2010), p 21; 'The Euston Murder', *Architectural Review*, Apr 1962, pp 234–8; *Sunday Telegraph*, 22 Oct 1995 (Peter Elson); *Wikipedia*, 'Euston Arch'.

9. *Architects' Journal*, 11 Jul 1962; John J. Parkinson-Bailey, *Manchester* (Manchester, 2000), p 181; Clare Hartwell, *Manchester* (2001), p 36; *Evening Chronicle* (Manchester), 4 May 1961; *Guardian*, 10 Jan 1961; *County Express*, 28 Dec 1961; *Manchester Evening News*, 15 Mar 1962; Anthony Flowers and Derek Smith, *Out of One Eye* (Newcastle, 2002), p 18; Elain Harwood, 'White Light/White Heat', *Twentieth Century Architecture*, 2002, p 68; Terry Farrell, *Place* (2004), p 57; *Evening Chronicle* (Newcastle), 12 Apr 1961; James Elliott, 'The Politics of Planning' (M.Lit Thesis, University of Newcastle, 1972), p 104; Noel Hanson, 'Getting About', in Anna Flowers and Vanessa Histon, *Water under the Bridges* (Newcastle, 1999), p 64.

10. *Architects' Journal*, 12 Jan 1961, 25 May 1961; *Oxford Times*, 25 Oct 2013 (Damian Fantato); *Western Morning News*, 11 Nov 1961; Grindrod, p 124; *Architectural Design*, Mar 1962, p 104; Stamp, *Lost*, pp 124–5; David Hunt, *A History of Preston* (Preston, 1992), p 260; Fred Inglis, 'Nation and Community', *Sociological Review*, Aug 1977, pp 503–4; *Architects' Journal*, 8 Jun 1961; 'Professor Denys Hinton', *Times*, 3 Apr 2010.

11. *Salford City Reporter*, 3 Nov 1961; *Official Architecture and Planning*, Aug 1963, p 753; *Salford City Reporter*, 16 Mar 1962; The Housing Development Committee of the Corporation of Sheffield, *Ten Years of Housing in Sheffield* (Sheffield, 1962), pp 9–37; *Sheffield Telegraph*, 3 Jan 1961.

12. Stefan Muthesius, *The Postwar University* (2000), p 114; Brian Edwards, *Basil Spence, 1907–1976* (Edinburgh, 1995), pp 68–70; *Architects' Journal*, 4 Apr 1962; *Tower Block*, p 263; *Wellingborough News*, 3 Nov 1961, 9 Feb 1962.

13. *Architects' Journal*, 19 Jan 1961; *Liverpool Daily Post*, 16 Sep 1961; *Daily Telegraph*, 5 Jun 1962; Raphael Samuel *et al*, 'But Nothing Happens', *New Left Review*, Jan–Apr 1962, pp 38–69; *Daily Mail*, 17 May 1961; Patrick Dunleavy, *The Politics of Mass Housing in Britain, 1945–1975* (Oxford, 1981), pp 154–6; *Evening Chronicle* (Newcastle), 14 Apr 1961; *Salford City Reporter*, 2 Feb 1962; Dunleavy, pp 149–50, 156, 384.

14. *Sheffield Telegraph*, 20 Jan 1961; The Society of Housing Managers, *Report of Conference: "Housing in the Welfare State – An Assessment"* (1961), p 24; F. T. Burnett and Sheila F. Scott, 'A Survey of Housing Conditions in the Urban Areas of England and Wales', *Sociological Review*, Mar 1962, pp 76–7; *East London Advertiser*, 23 Dec 1960; Sutcliffe and Smith, pp 236, 242; Claire Langhamer, 'The

Meanings of Home in the Postwar Britain', *Journal of Contemporary History*, Apr 2005, p 350; Peter Shapely *et al*, 'Civic Culture and Housing Policy in Manchester, 1945–79', *Twentieth Century British History*, 2004 (15/4), p 422; Strathclyde Education, *Housing in 20th century Glasgow* (Glasgow, 1993), p 154.

15. *Salford City Reporter*, 16 Mar 1962, 21 Jul 1961; Corporation of Sheffield, p 3; *Salford City Reporter*, 24 Mar 1961, 3 Nov 1961; *Proceedings of the Council of the City and County of Newcastle upon Tyne for 1961–1962* (Newcastle upon Tyne, 1962), pp 519, 523; *Smethwick Telephone*, 6 Jan 1961; *Time and Tide*, 9 Mar 1961 (Richard West).

16. *Town and Country Planning*, Jan 1961, pp 11–14; *Evening Citizen* (Glasgow), 26 Dec 1960; *Blackburn Times*, 7 Apr 1961, 5 May 1961, 12 May 1961, 2 Jun 1961, 30 Jun 1961, 23 Feb 1962, 23 Mar 1962.

17. *Journal of the Town Planning Institute*, Apr 1961, p 91; *Architect's Journal*, 6 Jun 1962; Parkinson-Bailey, p 180; Elliott, p 96; *Guardian*, 1 Nov 1961; *Architects' Journal*, 21 Jul 1960; 'Professor Sir Colin Buchanan', *Times*, 10 Dec 2001.

18. *Architects' Journal*, 22 Jun 1961, 17 Jan 1962; *Telegraph & Argus* (Bradford), 12 Jan 1962; *Listener*, 15 Jun 1961; *Architects' Journal*, 6 Jun 1962.

19. *Architects' Journal*, 19 Jan 1961; Oliver Marriott, *The Property Boom* (1967), chaps 9–10; Charles Gordon, *The Two Tycoons* (1984), chaps 10 ff; *Twentieth Century*, Jul 1961, p 164 (Kenneth J. Robinson); *Architects' Journal*, 7 Feb 1962; *Daily Mail*, 25 Aug 1961; *Wikipedia*, 'The Young Ones'.

20. *Tower Block*, pp 200–4; Sutcliffe and Smith, p 436; Dunleavy, pp 115–16; *Glasgow Herald*, 10 Aug 1961; James Schmiechen and Kenneth Carls, *The British Market Hall* (1999), p 219; Gold, p 106; Michael Gillard and Martin Tomkinson, *Nothing To Declare* (1980), pp 62–3.

21. Gold, pp 72, 74–6; *Times*, 3 Jul 1961; *Official Architecture and Planning*, Nov 1961, p 473; *Architectural Review*, Mar 1962, p 196.

22. *Architects' Journal*, 27 Apr 1961, 6 Sep 1961; *TV Times*, 30 Mar 1962; *Guardian*, 13 Mar 2010 (Ian Jack); Miles Glendinning, '"Public Building": Sam Bunton and Scotland's Modern Housing Revolution', *Planning History*, 1992 (14/3), pp 13–22.

23. Joe Moran, *On Roads* (2009), p 40; Simon Gunn, 'The Rise and Fall of British Urban Modernism', *Journal of British Studies*, Oct 2010, p 861; *Western Morning News*, 14 Dec 1961; *Doncaster Gazette*, 9 Mar 1961; *Telegraph & Argus* (Bradford), 14 Mar 1962; *County Express*, 28 Dec 1961; *Liverpool Echo*, 23 May 1961; *Evening Chronicle* (Newcastle), 12 Apr 1961; Flowers and Smith, p 18; *Evening Chronicle* (Newcastle), 10 Nov 1961.

24. *Glasgow Herald*, 11 Feb 1961, 25 Sep 1961; *Liverpool Daily Post*, 6 Oct 1961, 1 Dec 1961, 24 Nov 1960; *Blackburn Times*, 5 May 1961, 16 Feb 1962, 2 Mar 1962; *Wellingborough News*, 10 Nov 1961, 17 Nov 1961, 29 Dec 1961.

25. *Architects' Journal*, 25 May 1961, 7 Feb 1962, 4 Apr 1962, 16 May 1962; *Guardian*, 17 Apr 1962.

26. *Architectural Review*, Mar 1961, p 164; *Architects' Journal*, 20 Apr 1961; *Listener*, 1 Jun 1961, 3 Aug 1961; *Listener*, 23 Nov 1961; *Architects' Journal*, 2 May 1962, 22 Aug 1962.

27. *Everywoman*, Mar 1961, pp 42–5; *Times*, 23 Aug 2006, 17 Oct 1961; Candida Lycett Green (ed), John Betjeman, *Letters, Volume Two* (1995), p 213; Bevis Hillier,

Betjeman: The Bonus of Laughter (2004), pp 37, 261–3; *Daily Mirror*, 3 Apr 1962; Candida Lycett Green (ed), John Betjeman, *Coming Home* (1997), pp 400–1.

28. *Birmingham Mail*, 8 Jul 1961; *Liverpool Weekly News*, 26 Apr 1962; *County Express* (South Manchester edn), 29 Mar 1962.

29. *Municipal Review*, May 1974, p 66; *Daily Herald*, 1 May 1964; *Birmingham Post*, 10 Jul 1962; *Architects' Journal*, 22 Nov 1961; *Town and Country Planning*, May 1961, pp 214–15.

30. Doris Lessing, *Walking in the Shade* (1997), p 358; *Western Daily Press*, 13 Feb 1962; Peter Shapely, *The Politics of Housing* (Manchester, 2007), p 167; *Manchester Evening News*, 29 Dec 1961; *Liverpool Echo*, 23 May 1961; *Sunday Sun* (Newcastle), 15 Apr 1962; Sid Chaplin, *The Watchers and the Watched* (1989 edn, Buckhurst Hill), p 156.

31. Brian Jackson Collection (Qualidata, University of Essex), 'Working-Class Community' papers, File (i.e. box) C1, Dennis Marsden, 'Can Old People Be Rehoused?'; R. K. Wilkinson and E. M. Sigsworth, 'Slum Dwellers of Leeds', *New Society*, 4 Apr 1963; R. Wilkinson, 'A Statistical Analysis of Attitudes to Moving', *Urban Studies*, May 1965, pp 1–14.

32. *Liverpool Echo*, 23 May 1961; *Liverpool Weekly News*, 26 Apr 1962; *Bolton Evening News*, 30 Jun 1961; *Guardian*, 2 Feb 2012; *Manchester Evening News*, 27 Feb 1962; *Salford City Reporter*, 25 May 1962.

33. *Town and Country Planning*, Sep 1961, p 375; J. B. Cullingworth, 'Social Implications of Overspill', *Sociological Review*, Jul 1960, pp 77–96; J. B. Cullingworth, 'The Swindon Social Survey', *Sociological Review*, Jul 1961, pp 151–66; Cullingworth, 'Social Implications', p 89; *Liverpool Echo*, 30 May 1962; F.J.W. Miller *et al*, *The School Years in Newcastle upon Tyne, 1952–62* (1974), pp 243–5, 293.

34. *Architects' Journal*, 18 Sep 1963 (E. M. Sigsworth); J. A. Yelling, 'Residents' Reactions to Post-War Slum Clearance in England', *Planning History*, 1999, p 8; *Smethwick Telephone*, 6 Jan 1961; *Time and Tide*, 13 Jul 1961 (Giles Wordsworth).

35. *Evening Chronicle* (Newcastle), 14 Apr 1961; *Liverpool Daily Post*, 5 Dec 1961; City of Sheffield Housing Department, 'Park Hill Survey', Sep 1962 (at Sheffield Local Studies Library); *Manchester Evening News*, 27 Sep 1961; *Liverpool Echo*, 26 Oct 1961; *County Express*, 1 Jun 1962; *Daily Sketch*, 12 May 1961; *Daily Mirror*, 24 May 1961.

36. *Liverpool Echo*, 16 Aug 1961; *Wellingborough News*, 9 Feb 1962; *Architects' Journal*, 4 May 1961; *Financial Times*, 31 May 1961; *Western Morning News*, 22 Dec 1961; Preston, 5 May 1962; *Blackburn Times*, 15 Sep 1961.

37. *Official Architecture and Planning*, Jan 1961, p 47; Osborn, p 301; *Town and Country Planning*, Mar 1961, p 134; *Guardian*, 3 Nov 1961.

38. *Economist*, 3 Aug 2013 ('Paradise lost'); Peter Lucas, *Basildon: Birth of the City* (Wickford, 1986), p 88; Peter Lucas, *Basildon* (Chichester, 1991), p 78; Peter Willmott, 'Housing Density and Town Design in a New Town', *Town Planning Review*, Jul 1962, pp 115–27; *Spectator*, 30 Sep 1960.

39. *Times*, 17 Sep 1960, 3 Jul 1961; *Guardian*, 4 Aug 1961; *Architects' Journal*, 16 Aug 1961.

40. *Times*, 4 Aug 1961; S. D. Coleman, *Mental Health and Social Adjustment in a New Town* (nd), pp 42–5, 67, 73, 78; Mark Clapson, *Invincible Green Suburbs, Brave*

New Towns (Manchester, 1998), pp 138–9; *Town and Country Planning*, Apr 1962, p 143; email to author from Erin O'Neill (BBC Written Archives), 1 Feb 2005; *Journal of the Royal Institute of British Architecture*, Aug 1961, p 379.

11 Make Him Sir Yuri!

1. Russell Davies (ed), *The Kenneth Williams Diaries* (1993), p 174; Haines, 1 Jul 1961, 5 Jul 1961; Martin, 5 Jul 1961; Paul Morley, *The North* (2013), p 417; Haines, 6 Jul 1961; *TV Times*, 7 Jul 1961; Michael Kenny, *The First New Left* (1995), pp 28–9; Daly, Ms 302/3/3, memo by Stuart Hall, 7 Jul 1961; Haines, 7 Jul 1961.
2. Crossman, Ms 154/8/26, 13 Jul 1961, fol 1367; *Evening Sentinel* (Stoke), 8 Jul 1961; *Melody Maker*, 15 Jul 1961; Haines, 8 Jul 1961; *Sunday Times*, 9 Jul 1961; Richard Davenport-Hines, *An English Affair* (2013), p 247; *Encounter*, Jul 1961, p 95; *New Statesman*, 21 Jul 1961; BBC WA, R9/7/53 – VR/61/368.
3. *Daily Mirror*, 11–12 Jul 1961; *Evening Standard*, 11 Jul 1961; Nigel Nicolson (ed), *Harold Nicolson, The Later Years* (1968), p 396; *Pembroke County and West Wales Guardian*, 14 Jul 1961, 21 Jul 1961; *Northern Echo*, 18 Jul 1961; Katherine Bucknell (ed), Christopher Isherwood, *The Sixties* (2010), p 85; *East London Advertiser*, 14 Jul 1961; *TV Times*, 14 Jul 1961; Michael Marshall, *Gentlemen and Players* (1987), p 244; Diary of Allan Preston, 20 Jul 1961; Heap, 20 Jul 1961; Jonathon Green, *All Dressed Up* (1998), p 152; Edward Hyams (ed), *New Statesmanship* (1963), pp 278–9; Rob Bradford, 'Joe Meek', *Record Collector*, Feb 2007, p 35; *Times*, 25 Jul 1961.
4. Humphrey Carpenter, *That Was Satire That Was* (2000), p 103; David Kynaston, *The City of London, Volume 4* (2001), pp 258–9; *Daily Mail*, 26 Jul 1961; *Times*, 26 Jul 1961; Stephen Fay, *Measure for Measure* (1970), p 18; *New Yorker*, 12 Aug 1961; St John, 26 Jul 1961.
5. Richard Bailey, *Managing the British Economy* (1968), pp 10–11; *Financial Times*, 27 Jul 1961; *Economist*, 29 Jul 1961; D. R. Thorpe, *Selwyn Lloyd* (1989), p 327; *Economist*, 26 Aug 1961; Glen O'Hara, *From Dreams to Disillusionment* (Basingstoke, 2007), pp 1, 35.
6. *New Yorker*, 12 Aug 1961; *Macmillan (3)*, pp 20, 22; *Financial Times*, 1 Aug 1961; George H. Gallup, *The Gallup International Public Opinion Polls: Great Britain, 1937–1975, Volume One* (New York, 1976), p 590; *Times*, 1 Aug 1961; Andy Mullen and Brian Burkitt, 'Spinning Europe', *Political Quarterly*, Jan–Mar 2005, pp 102–3.
7. *Times*, 1–2 Aug 1961; *Evening Chronicle* (Manchester), 2 Aug 1961; *Daily Telegraph*, 2 Aug 1961; Larkin, Ms Eng. c.7423, 3 Aug 1961, fol 74; *Observer*, 6 Aug 1961.
8. Haines, 2 Aug 1961; Heap, 2 Aug 1961; *Listener*, 3 Aug 1961; *Melody Maker*, 5 Aug 1961; Michael Willmott (ed), Rev. O. L. Willmott, *The Parish Notes of Loders, Dottery and Askerswell, Dorset: Volume I, 1948–1965* (Shrewsbury, 1996), Sep 1961; *Daily Mirror*, 8 Aug 1961, 11 Aug 1961; John Campbell, *Margaret Thatcher, Volume One* (2000), pp 138–40; BBC WA, R9/10/8 – VR/61/427; Haines, 16 Aug 1961; BBC WA, *Woman's Hour*, 2 Oct 1961; Haines, 16 Aug 1961.
9. Vic Gammon, '"Two for the Show"', *History Workshop*, spring 1986, pp 150–1; Heap, 18 Aug 1961; *Spectator*, 18 Aug 1961; Selbourne, p 98; John Heilpern, *John Osborne* (2006), pp 239–41; *Sunday Times*, 20 Aug 1961.

10. *Smethwick Telephone*, 28 Jul 1961; *Sunday Times*, 30 Jul 1961; *Guardian*, 21 Aug 1961; *Daily Mirror*, 21 Aug 1961; Panikos Panayi, 'Middlesbrough 1961: A British Race Riot of the 1960s?', *Social History*, May 1991, p 151; Harold Evans, *My Paper Chase* (2009), pp 214–24; *Northern Echo*, 21 Aug 1961.

11. Martin, 21 Aug 1961; James Whitfield, 'The Duke Disappears', *History Today*, Aug 2011, pp 43–9; Richard Etheridge papers (Modern Records Centre), Ms 202/S/J/3/2/39, 22 Aug 1961; BBC WA, R9/7/53 – VR/61/447; Paul Foot, *Who Killed Hanratty?* (1988 Penguin edn), pp 25–32; *Times*, 11 May 2001; *Listener*, 31 Aug 1961; Jonathan Meades, *An Encyclopaedia of Myself* (2014), p 310; *Times*, 31 Aug 1961, 1 Sep 1961; Mark Lewisohn, *All These Years, Volume 1* (2013), pp 491–2; Marshall, pp 205–6.

12 The Immigrants Are Human

1. *Woman's Own*, 18 Mar 1961; *Woman*, 18 Mar 1961; Mark Robinson, *Hundred Greatest TV Acts* (2000), p 81; *Daily Express*, 17 May 1962; *Radio Times*, 20 Apr 1961; *Daily Mirror*, 22 Jun 1961; *Listener*, 4 Jan 1962; *Spectator*, 4 May 1962; Ralph Harris and Arthur Seldon, *Advertising in Action* (1962), pp 152–3; *Evening Chronicle* (Manchester), 5 May 1961; *Romford Recorder*, 9 Feb 1962; *Liverpool Daily Post*, 4 Jan 1962 (Diana Pulson); *East London Advertiser*, 16 Mar 1962 (Valerie Carter); Martin Childs, 'Brian Sollit', *Independent*, 19 Sep 2013; Robert Fitzgerald, *Rowntree and the Marketing Revolution, 1862–1969* (Cambridge, 1995), pp 465–6; *Financial Times*, 7 Mar 2006 (John Kay); *Daily Telegraph*, 1 Jun 2002 (Max Davidson); Peter Bird, *The First Food Empire* (Chichester, 2000), pp 196–7; Jan Boxshall, *Every Home Should Have One* (1997), p 83; *Shrewsbury Chronicle*, 8 Sep 1961; Kate McIntyre, 'The Most "In" Shops for Gear', *Twentieth Century Architecture*, 2002, p 38; *Surrey Comet*, 13 Sep 1961; *Guardian*, 24 Apr 2004.

2. British Market Research Bureau, *Shopping in Suburbia* (1963), p 45; Dawn Nell *et al*, 'Investigating Shopper Narratives of the Supermarket in Early Post-War England, 1945–75', *Oral History*, spring 2009, p 64; *Shopping in Suburbia*, pp 8–32; Christine Shaw, 'Alan John Sainsbury and Sir Robert Sainsbury', in *Dictionary of Business Biography, Vol 5* (1986), pp 5–6; David Powell, *Counter-Revolution* (1991), pp 96–9; Matthew Hilton, 'The Female Consumer and the Politics of Consumption in Twentieth-Century Britain', *Historical Journal*, Mar 2002, pp 121–6; Eirlys Roberts, *Which? 25: Consumers' Association, 1957–1982* (1982), p 42; *Spectator*, 23 Feb 1962 ('Leslie Adrian'); Andrew Motion, *Philip Larkin* (1993), p 316; Archie Burnett (ed), Philip Larkin, *The Complete Poems* (2012), p 61; *Times Literary Supplement*, 1 Sep 2000.

3. *Pembroke County and West Wales Guardian*, 15 Sep 1961, 22 Sep 1961; *Cambrian News*, 20 Oct 1961, 13 Oct 1961; *Glamorgan Gazette*, 27 Oct 1961, 3 Nov 1961; *Cambrian News*, 17 Nov 1961; *Carmarthen Journal*, 17 Nov 1961. In general on this episode, see: Martin Johnes, *Wales Since 1939* (Manchester, 2012), pp 166–8.

4. Macmillan, dep.d.43, 8 Oct 1961, fol 100; *Macmillan (3)*, p 38; *Daily Mail*, 24 Oct 1961; *Macmillan (3)*, p 44; John Barnes, 'Lord Holderness', *Independent*, 16 Aug 2002; *New Yorker*, 9 Dec 1961 (Panter-Downes); Ronald S. Edwards and R.D.V. Roberts, *Status, Productivity and Pay* (1971), p 53; Glen O'Hara, *From Dreams to*

Disillusionment (Basingstoke, 2007), pp 45–8; Keith Middlemas, 'Sir Robert Shone', *Independent*, 30 Dec 1992; Astrid Ringe and Neil Rollings, 'Responding to relative decline', *Economic History Review*, May 2000, pp 344–7; O'Hara, p 45; Sir Alec Cairncross, *Diaries: The Radcliffe Committee and the Treasury, 1961–64* (1999), p 47.

5.　*Times Literary Supplement*, 2 Jan 1998 (Nicolas Walter); Russell Davies (ed), *The Kenneth Williams Diaries* (1993), pp 176–7; Jonathon Green, *All Dressed Up* (1998), p 22; *Economist*, 23 Sep 1961; Philip M. Williams, *Hugh Gaitskell* (1979), pp 651–2; Macmillan, dep.d.43, 8 Oct 1961, fol 102; Williams, *Gaitskell*, pp 658–64; Stuart Middleton, '"Affluence" and the Left in Britain, c.1958–1974', *English Historical Review*, Feb 2014, p 119; *Spectator*, 29 Sep 1961, 13 Oct 1961; *New Statesman*, 6 Oct 1961; BBC WA, R9/7/54 – VR/61/555; *Listener*, 26 Oct 1961; Michael Newman, *Ralph Miliband and the Politics of the New Left* (2002), pp 73–7; Ralph Miliband, *Parliamentary Socialism* (1972 Merlin Press edn), pp 348–9.

6.　*Sunday Times Magazine*, 28 Nov 1976 (Gordon Burn); BBC WA, *Any Questions?*, 29 Sep 1961; Selina Todd, *The People* (2014), p 251; Stephen Smith and Peter Razzell, *The Pools Winners* (1975), p 42; *Sunday Times Magazine*, 28 Nov 1976.

7.　Turtle, 19 Oct 1961; Heap, 13 Sep 1961; Haines, 2 Oct 1961, 17 Oct 1961; Macmillan, dep.d.43, 23 Sep 1961, fols 84–5; Paul Foot, *Who Killed Hanratty?* (1988 Penguin edn), p 97; Fowles, EUL Ms 102/1/11, 29 Oct 1961, fol 168; Last, 26 Oct 1961; Diary of Allan Preston, 2 Sep 1961; Martin, 20 Oct 1961; Selbourne, p 114; St John, 18 Oct 1961.

8.　Haines, 13 Oct 1961; Martin, 6 Nov 1961; *Kenneth Williams*, p 178; *Times*, 4 Jul 2008 (Anne Ashworth and Judith Heywood), 13 Sep 1961; *New Statesman*, 15 Sep 1961; *Independent*, 19 Aug 2002 (John Walsh); Larkin, Ms Eng.c.7424, 31 Jan 1961, fol 79; *Kenneth Williams*, p 175; *Times*, 24 Sep 2003 (Stephen Dalton), 30 Aug 1961; John Coldstream, *Dirk Bogarde* (2004), p 268; *Oldham Evening Chronicle*, 9 Sep 1961; *Spectator*, 24 Nov 1961; Coldstream, *Bogarde*, pp 280, 270; *Spectator*, 3 Sep 2011 (John Coldstream).

9.　Lord Drogheda, *Double Harness* (1978), p 284; *Guardian Weekend*, 17 Mar 2007 (Robin Muir); Darran Little, *The Coronation Street Story* (1995), pp 35–6; *Radio Times*, 7 Sep 1961; *TV Times*, 25 Aug 1961; BBC WA, R9/7/54 – VR/61/493; *Radio Times*, 21 Sep 1961; *Times*, 28 Sep 1961; *Guardian*, 26 May 1995 (James Wood).

10.　*Radio Times*, 28 Sep 1961; *TV Times*, 29 Sep 1961; *Spectator*, 6 Oct 1961 (Guy Gisbourne); BBC WA, R9/7/54 – VR/61/527; *Western Morning News*, 3 Oct 1961; *Radio Times*, 28 Sep 1961, 5 Oct 1961; BBC WA, *Woman's Hour*, 4 Oct 1961; *New Statesman*, 13 Oct 1961; *Spectator*, 6 Oct 1961; R.G.G. Stevenson, *The Methodist Church, Hunslet Carr, Leeds, 1842–1961* (Leeds, 1962), pp 17–18; *Radio Times*, 5 Oct 1961; *Beeston Gazette & Echo*, 13 Oct 1961, 20 Oct 1961; Harry Ritchie, *Success Stories* (1988), pp 200–1; *Times*, 17 Oct 1961; *Daily Express*, 18 Oct 1961; BBC WA, R9/7/54 – VR/61/560; Adam Macqueen, *Private Eye* (2011), pp 36, 96–7; R. D. Laing, *The Self and Others* (1961), p ix; *Western Daily Press*, 30 Oct 1961.

11.　Alan Fox, 'Two Worlds in Collision', *Socialist Commentary*, Mar 1962, pp 26–7; Martin Gilbert, *"Never Despair"* (1988), p 1331; *Times*, 3 Nov 1961; *New Statesman*, 3 Nov 1961; Tim Heald, *Princess Margaret* (2007), pp 140–1; BBC WA, R9/7/55 – VR/61/594; *Daily Telegraph*, 18 Dec 2000 (Richard Alleyne); *Uncut*, Jul 2011

(Mick Houghton); *Observer*, 14 Mar 2010 (Rachel Cooke); Nicolas Barker, 'Jeremy Maas', *Independent*, 31 Jan 1997; *Radio Times*, 9 Nov 1961; Jack Tinker, *Coronation St.* (1985), pp 30–1; BBC WA, R9/7/55 – VR/61/628; E. H. Carr, *What is History?* (1961), p 66; Adrian Smith, *The City of Coventry* (2006), pp 26–7; *Observer*, 26 Nov 1961; *Listener*, 30 Nov 1961.

12. *Times Literary Supplement*, 1 Dec 1961; *Listener*, 7 Dec 1961 (Frederick Laws); *TV Times*, 15 Dec 1961; *Western Morning News*, 5 Dec 1961; BBC WA, R9/7/55 – VR/61/653.

13. *Isle of Ely and Wisbech Advertiser*, 27 Sep 1961; Selbourne, p 104; *Times*, 20 Sep 1961; E. M. and M. Epple, '"Connotations of Morality"', *British Journal of Sociology*, Sep 1962, pp 243–63; *Daily Telegraph*, 27 Dec 1961 (Ian Colquhoun).

14. *Daily Telegraph*, 27 Dec 1961; *Times*, 10 Oct 2009 (Bob Stanley); *New Statesman*, 20 Oct 1961; Dave McAleer, *Hit Parade Heroes* (1993), pp 111–12; Heap, 14 Sep 1961; *Melody Maker*, 9 Sep 1961; Tony Jasper, *The Top Twenty Book* (6th edn, 1994), pp 69–71; *Radio Times*, 28 Sep 1961; Christopher Sandford, *Primitive Cool* (1999 edn, New York), pp 38–9; Keith Richards, *Life* (2010), pp 77–9; Keith Gildart, *Images of England through Popular Music* (Basingstoke, 2013), p 63; *Aldershot News*, 15 Dec 1961; *Radio Times*, 7 Dec 1961; *Melody Maker*, 2 Dec 1961, 9 Dec 1961. For the fullest account of the Aldershot gig and its context, see: Mark Lewisohn, *All These Years, Volume 1* (2013), pp 544–5.

15. Robert Shepherd, *Iain Macleod* (1994), pp 253–5; *Economist*, 14 Oct 1961; Patrick Seyd, 'Factionalism within the Conservative Party', *Government and Opposition*, 1972 (7/4), pp 468–9, 479; *Times*, 9 Nov 1961; Lewis Baston, *Reggie* (Stroud, 2004), p 153; Macmillan, dep.d.44, 10 Jan 1962, fol 107; Baston, p 171.

16. *Western Daily Press*, 15 Sep 1961; City of Bradford, *Official Records of Council Meetings, 1961–2* (Bradford, 1962), pp 78–80; *Daily Express*, 12 Oct 1961; Paul Foot, *Immigration and Race in British Politics* (Harmondsworth, 1965), p 137; *Economist*, 14 Oct 1961; *Spectator*, 20 Oct 1961; Randall Hansen, *Citizenship and Immigration in Post-war Britain* (Oxford, 2000), p 108.

17. *Daily Mail*, 16 Oct 1961; Foot, p 139; Michael Dawswell, 'The Pigmentocracy of Citizenship', in Lawrence Black *et al*, *Consensus or Coercion?* (Cheltenham, 2001), p 73; *Daily Mirror*, 1 Nov 1961; *New Yorker*, 9 Dec 1961; Williams, *Gaitskell*, pp 676–9; Hansen, pp 115–16; *Times*, 17 Nov 1961; *Daily Mail*, 18 Nov 1961; *Times*, 22 Nov 1961; Heap, 20 Nov 1961; Macmillan, dep.d.44, 30 Nov 1961, fol 62; *Times*, 17 Nov 1961; *Guardian*, 4 Dec 1961.

18. Foot, pp 172–4; Macmillan, dep.d.45, 27 Feb 1962, fol 41; Dervla Murphy, *Tales from Two Cities* (1987), p 10; G. J. Dear, 'Coloured Immigrant Communities and the Police', *Police Journal*, Apr 1972, p 130; Larkin, Ms Eng.c.7424, 13 Jan 1962, fol 62; *Telegraph & Argus* (Bradford), 15 Jan 1962, 17 Jan 1962; Hague, 30 Dec 1961; W. G. Runciman and C. R. Bagley, 'Status Consistency, Relative Deprivation, and Attitudes to Immigrants', *Sociology*, Sep 1969, pp 366–70; *Observer*, 11 Mar 2012; *Daily Telegraph*, 10 Apr 2014.

13 That First Small Cheer

1. Mark Lewisohn, *The Complete Beatles Chronicle* (1996 edn), p 51; *Guardian*, 7 Dec 2011 (Frank Keating); *Lincolnshire Echo*, 11 Dec 1961; coronationstreet.wikia. com/wiki; BBC WA, *Any Questions?*, 15 Dec 1961; *Radio Times*, 7 Dec 1961; BBC WA, R9/7/55 – VR/61/668; *Spectator*, 22 Dec 1961; *Melody Maker*, 16 Dec 1961; *Financial Times*, 19 Dec 1961; *Daily Mail*, 20 Dec 1961; *Spectator*, 22 Dec 1961 (Isabel Quigly); *Wisden Cricketers' Almanack, 1962* (1962), p 1031; *Listener*, 4 Jan 1962; BBC WA, R9/74/2, Feb 1962; Martin, 26 Dec 1961; Willmott, 28 Dec 1961; Cy Young, 'Charles Chilton', *Independent*, 5 Jan 2013; Heap, 1 Jan 1962; Lewisohn, *Complete*, p 52; Mark Lewisohn, *All These Years, Volume 1* (2013), pp 558–62; *Accrington Observer & Times*, 2 Jan 1962; Macmillan, dep.d.44, 5 Jan 1962, fol 103; *Sunday Times*, 7 Jan 1962; *East London Advertiser*, 5 Jan 1962.

2. *Radio Times*, 28 Dec 1961; *Spectator*, 12 Jan 1962; *Listener*, 11 Jan 1962; BBC WA, R9/7/56 – VR/62/14.

3. Barbara Weinberger, *The Best Police in the World* (Aldershot, 1995), p 199; Donald Thomas, *Villains' Paradise* (2005), pp 451–3; David McKittrick, 'Harry Challenor', *Independent*, 23 Sep 2008; *Times*, 1 Jun 1962; C.G.L. Du Cann, 'Police and the Advocate', in C. H. Rolph (ed), *The Police and the Public* (1962), pp 146–7; Frank Norman, 'The Kite Man', in Rolph, *Police*, pp 78–9; *Radio Times*, 14 Dec 1961; *Guardian*, 12 Aug 2011 (Andrew Roberts); Edward Durham Taylor, 'Raymond Francis', *Independent*, 3 Nov 1987; Susan Sydney-Smith, *Beyond Dixon of Dock Green* (2002), pp 137–43.

4. Stuart Laing, *Representations of Working-Class Life, 1957–1964* (Basingstoke, 1986), pp 169–70; *Liverpool Echo*, 2 Jan 1962; Martin Anderson, 'Fritz Spiegl', *Independent*, 31 Mar 2003; TV Heaven (National Media Museum), 'Z Cars' factsheet (2008); Dennis Barker, 'James Ellis', *Guardian*, 10 Mar 2014; *Liverpool Echo*, 10 Jan 1962; *Daily Mirror*, 3–4 Jan 1962; Asa Briggs, *The History of Broadcasting in the United Kingdom, Volume V* (Oxford, 1995), pp 427–8; *Liverpool Echo*, 4 Jan 1962; Briggs, p 428; BBC WA, R9/7/56 – VR/62/10.

5. *People*, 7 Jan 1962; *Hereford Times*, 19 Jan 1962; Macmillan, dep.d.44, 15 Jan 1962, fol 110; Tony Collins, *A Social History of English Rugby Union* (Abingdon, 2009), p 130; Nicholas Timmins, *The Five Giants* (2001 edn), p 209; Mark Amory, 'Mark Boxer', *Independent*, 21 Jul 1988; Nick Clarke, *The Shadow of a Nation* (2003), p 72; *Sunday Times Magazine*, 4 Feb 1962; Roy Greenslade, *Press Gang* (2004 edn), pp 147–8; BBC WA, *Any Questions?*, 9 Feb 1962; *Daily Sketch*, 12 Feb 1962; Kevin Cann, *Any Day Now* (2010), pp 22–3; *Times*, 13 Feb 1962; *New Statesman*, 9 Mar 1962; *Independent on Sunday*, 6 Nov 2011 (Richard Cork); Adam Carr, 'Leo Abse', in Robert Aldrich and Garry Wotherspoon (eds), *Who's Who in Contemporary Gay and Lesbian History: From World War II to the Present Day* (2001), p 2; *Daily Mirror*, 22 Mar 1962 ('Cassandra'); *Daily Express*, 28 Mar 1962; Reg Green, *National Heroes* (1999 edn, Edinburgh), pp 168–9; *Birmingham Mail*, 2 Apr 1962; Joe Moran, 'Crossing the Road in Britain, 1931–1976', *Historical Journal*, Jun 2006, pp 488–9; *Times*, 4 Apr 1962; Paul Foot, *Who Killed Hanratty?* (Penguin 1988 edn, Harmondsworth), p 299; Harriet Vyner, *Groovy Bob* (1999), p 68; Les Gurl papers (Oxfordshire History Centre), Acc 5639, 1962 file; Christopher Simon Sykes, *Hockney, Volume 1* (2011), p 108; 'Autosport's 50 years', *Autosport*, 13 Jul 2000, pp 104–5; *New Statesman*, 27 Apr 1962;

Leo McKinstry, *Jack & Bobby* (2002), p 121; Stephen F. Kelly, *Bill Shankly* (1996), pp 169–72; McKinstry, p 170; Blake Morrison, 'Turf Moor and Other Fields of Dreams', in Ian Hamilton (ed), *The Faber Book of Soccer* (1992), p 136; *Encounter*, May 1962, p 76; *Daily Mail*, 2 May 1962; John Lahr, *Prick Up Your Ears* (2002 edn), pp 80–3; Mark Davison and Ian Currie, *Surrey in the Sixties* (Coulsdon, 1994), p 56.

6. John Littlewood, *The Stock Market* (1998), p 114; *New Yorker*, 10 Feb 1962; William Davis, *Merger Mania* (1970), p 49; Macmillan, dep.d.44, 24 Jan 1962, fol 122; Davis, pp 44–6; Macmillan, dep.d.45, 10 Mar 1962, fol 61; *Punch*, 28 Mar 1962 (B. A. Young); Littlewood, p 115; Geoffrey Owen, *The Rise and Fall of Great Companies* (Oxford, 2010), pp 58–9; Littlewood, p 115; *Economist*, 24 Mar 1962.

7. *Independent*, 8 Mar 2002 (Jeremy Laurance); Matthew Hilton, *Smoking in British Popular Culture, 1800–2000* (Manchester, 2000), pp 202, 182–3; *Independent*, 8 Mar 2002; Hilton, pp 202–3; Virginia Berridge, 'The Policy Response to the Smoking and Lung Cancer Connection in the 1950s and 1960s', *Historical Journal*, Dec 2006, pp 1206, 1204; Winston Fletcher, *Powers of Persuasion* (Oxford, 2008), p 81; Berridge, pp 1204–5; www.bbc.co.uk/news/health, 6 Mar 2012; *Larkin*, p 296.

8. *Economist*, 7 Apr 1962; Dorothy Cole Wedderburn, 'Poverty in Britain Today – The Evidence', *Sociological Review*, Nov 1962, pp 279–80; *New Statesman*, 20 Apr 1962, 27 Apr 1962; *Accrington Observer & Times*, 9 Jan 1962, 16 Jan 1962, 13 Feb 1962, 17 Feb 1962, 20 Feb 1962; *Guardian*, 26 Jan 2008 (David Lacey); *Accrington Observer & Times*, 24 Feb 1962, 27 Feb 1962, 3 Mar 1962, 6 Mar 1962, 13 Mar 1962; *Guardian*, 7 Mar 1962. For a full account of Accrington Stanley's demise, see: Phil Whalley, *Accrington Stanley* (Cheltenham, 2006), chap 1.

9. coronationstreet.wikia.com/wiki/Episode 122; *Sunday Sun* (Newcastle), 4 Mar 1962, 18 Mar 1962.

10. *Listener*, 18 Jan 1962; Stuart Laing, 'Banging In Some Reality', in John Corner (ed), *Popular Television in Britain* (1991), p 130; *Radio Times*, 8 Mar 1962, 29 Mar 1962; Briggs, p 432; BBC WA, R9/7/57 – VR/62/137; Sydney-Smith, p 254; *Western Daily Press*, 30 Apr 1962; *Listener*, 3 May 1962; Laing, 'Banging', pp 131–3.

11. Last, 11 Jan 1962, 13 Jan 1962, 17 Jan 1962, 18 Jan 1962, 21 Jan 1962, 25 Jan 1962; *TV Times*, 26 Jan 1962; BBC WA, R9/7/57 – VR/62/159, 170; *Daily Herald*, 9–11 May 1962; *Independent*, 2 Nov 1994 (Kevin Jackson); *Daily Mail*, 28 Mar 1962; *Daily Express*, 31 Mar 1962; *Birmingham Mail*, 7 Apr 1962.

12. John Hill, *Sex, Class and Realism* (1986), p 210; Heap, 10 Jan 1962; Fowles, EUL Ms 102/1/11, 16 Feb 1962, fol 209; *Vogue*, Jun 1962, p 76 (Mary Holland); Heap, 20 Feb 1962; *New Statesman*, 13 Apr 1962 (Roger Gellert); Heap, 27 Apr 1962; *Observer*, 6 May 1962; *Sunday Times*, 6 May 1962; *Spectator*, 11 May 1962; *Punch*, 9 May 1962; *New Yorker*, 12 May 1962; *Daily Telegraph*, 9 May 1962; Heap, 8 May 1962; *Daily Herald*, 9 May 1962 (David Nathan); *Evening Standard*, 9 May 1962; *Spectator*, 18 May 1962; *New Statesman*, 25 May 1962 (Roger Gellert); *Times Literary Supplement*, 18 Oct 2013 ('J.C.').

13. Lewisohn, *Years*, pp 610, 576–83, 602–4, 619–20, 646–9; *Radio Times*, 1 Mar 1962; Paul Gambaccini *et al*, *The Complete Eurovision Song Contest Companion* (1998), pp 25–7; Rob Chapman, *Syd Barrett* (2010), p 34; *Radio Times*, 1 Feb 1962; ABC Television, *Thank Your Lucky Stars* (1962, unpaginated); BBC WA, R9/10/9 – VR/62/58; *Melody Maker*, 7 Apr 1962, 3 Feb 1962; Bob Stanley, *Yeah Yeah Yeah* (2013), p 82; *Melody Maker*, 14 Apr 1962, 5 May 1962.

14. *Times Literary Supplement*, 27 Apr 2012; A. Alvarez (ed), *The New Poetry* (1966 edn, Harmondsworth), pp 25, 29–32; *Listener*, 3 May 1962; Anthony Burgess, *You've Had Your Time* (1990), p 26; *Times Literary Supplement*, 25 May 1962; *Sunday Times*, 13 May 1962; *Daily Express*, 17 May 1962; *Punch*, 16 May 1962.

15. *Spectator*, 9 Mar 1962, 16 Mar 1962; Rupert Hart-Davis (ed), *The Lyttelton Hart-Davis Letters: Volume Six* (1984), p 179; *Encounter*, May 1962, pp 42–3; *Spectator*, 23 Mar 1962; *Times Literary Supplement*, 4 Aug 1995.

16. E. P. Thompson, *The Poverty of Theory* (1978), p 35; Michael Kenny, *The First New Left* (1995), pp 29–31; Daly, Ms 302/3/4, E. P. Thompson to John Rex and Lawrence Daly, 16 Mar 1962; Willmott, 8 Apr 1962; Fred Inglis, *Raymond Williams* (1995), p 185. (The copy that Willmott was shown was almost certainly the issue dated January–April 1962, which only reached the LSE library on 10 April.)

17. Haines, 12 Jan 1962; Martin, 3 Feb 1962; Haines, 22 Feb 1962; Langford, 23 Mar 1962; Selbourne, 26 Mar 1962; Hague, 31 Mar 1962; St John, 23 Apr 1962; Preston, 5 May 1962; Willmott, 8 May 1962; Haines, 19 May 1962.

18. Selbourne, p 120; Heap, 29 Jan 1962; *Macmillan (3)*, p 53; Sir Alec Cairncross, *Diaries: The Radcliffe Committee and the Treasury, 1961–64* (1999), pp 48–9; *Economist*, 19 May 1962; *New Yorker*, 2 Jun 1962; *Macmillan (3)*, p 66; *Economist*, 12 May 1962; *Sunday Times*, 13 May 1962; *Coventry Evening Telegraph*, 10 Feb 1962; *Listener*, 10 May 1962, 17 May 1962.

19. Selbourne, p 121; Macmillan, dep.d.45, 4 Feb 1962, fol 12; D. R. Thorpe, *Supermac* (2010), pp 516–18; *Punch*, 28 Mar 1962; *Macmillan (3)*, pp 58–9; *Daily Mail*, 28 Mar 1962; D. R. Thorpe, *Selwyn Lloyd* (1989), p 334; Robert J. Wybrow, *Britain Speaks Out, 1937–87* (Basingstoke, 1989), p 64; Kenneth O. Morgan, *Callaghan* (Oxford, 1997), pp 173–4.

20. Harry Thompson, *Peter Cook* (1997), p 114; *Western Daily Press*, 30 Apr 1962; Humphrey Carpenter, *That Was Satire That Was* (2000), pp 186–7, 183; *Daily Mail*, 1 Mar 1962; *Sunday Times*, 20 May 1962; *Times*, 21 May 1962.

21. *Spectator*, 25 May 1962; *New Statesman*, 25 May 1962; *Daily Telegraph*, 18 May 1962; Michael De-La-Noy, 'The Right Rev Cuthbert Bardsley', *Independent*, 11 Jan 1991; Martin, 25 May 1962; *Sunday Times*, 27 May 1962; *Coventry Evening Telegraph*, 26 May 1962; *Sunday Times*, 3 Jun 1962; *New Yorker*, 30 Jun 1962.

22. *Journal* (Newcastle), 29 May 1962; *Evening Chronicle* (Newcastle), 29 May 1962; *Journal*, 5 Jun 1962; *Evening Chronicle*, 7 Jun 1962; *Journal*, 8 Jun 1962.

23. Heap, 25 May 1962; *Times*, 28 May 1962; Richard Shepherd, *Enoch Powell* (1996), pp 244–5; Lara Feigel and John Sutherland (eds), Stephen Spender, *New Selected Journals, 1939–1995* (2012), p 292; *Financial Times*, 29 May 1962; Peter Shapely, *The Politics of Housing* (Manchester, 2007), p 163; Charles Williams, *Gentlemen & Players* (2012), pp 166–7; Henry Blofeld, *A Thirst for Life* (2000), pp 60–3; *Times*, 31 May 1962, 1 Jun 1962; John Fisher, *Tony Hancock* (2008), p 348; Haines, 1 Jun 1962; *Daily Herald*, 2 Jun 1962; *Times*, 4 Jun 1962; Robert Shepherd, *Iain Macleod* (1994), p 277; *Times*, 7 Jun 1962; Chris Welsh, 'George Harrison', *Independent*, 1 Dec 2001; *Times*, 8 Jun 1962; *New Statesman*, 15 Jun 1962 (Roger Gellert); Michael Billington, *State of the Nation* (2007), pp 152–4; *Radio Times*, 31 May 1962; *Spectator*, 8 Jun 1962; *Times*, 8 Jun 1962; John Russell Taylor, *Anger and After* (1969 edn), pp 193–7; 'David Turner', *Times*, 13 Dec 1990; BBC WA, *Any Questions?*, 8 Jun 1962.

24. *Journal* (Newcastle), 11 Jun 1962; *Sunday Sun* (Newcastle), 10 Jun 1962. See also: Bill Lancaster, 'Sociability and the City', in Robert Colls and Bill Lancaster (eds), *Newcastle upon Tyne* (Chichester, 2001), pp 319–20; Natasha Vall, 'Northumbria in north-east England during the Twentieth Century', in Robert Colls (ed), *Northumbria* (Chichester, 2007), pp 285–6, 289; John Grindrod, *Concretopia* (Brecon, 2013), pp 213–16.

Afterword

1. Anthony Sampson, *Anatomy of Britain* (1962), pp 636–8.

Acknowledgements

The following kindly gave me permission to reproduce copyright material: Evelyn Abrams (Mark Abrams); The Agency (London) Ltd (extracts from the writing of Arnold Wesker; extract from *As Much As I Dare* © Arnold Wesker, 1994; extract from Wesker's piece in Charles Marowitz et al, *The Encore Reader* © Arnold Wesker 1970; letter to New Statesman © Arnold Wesker, 1959; letter to Charles Parker © Arnold Wesker, 2001, as quoted in Paul Leslie Long, 'The Aesthetics of Class in Post-War Britain'. All rights reserved); Aitken Alexander Associates (extracts from the diaries of John Fowles © J. R. Fowles Ltd); Lady Diana Baer (Mollie Panter-Downes); BBC Written Archives Centre (BBC copyright material reproduced courtesy of the British Broadcasting Corporation. © BBC. All rights reserved); Ken Blakemore (*Sunnyside Down*); Alan Brodie Representation Ltd (extracts from *The Noël Coward Diaries* copyright © NC Aventales AG 1982); Michael Chaplin (Sid Chaplin); Rupert Christiansen; Kate Clarke (Kate Paul); Jonathan Clowes Ltd (extract from *Walking in the Shade* © Doris Lessing 1997; extract from 'The Small Personal Voice' by Doris Lessing in *Declaration*, ed Tom Maschler 1957; extract from *The Four-Gated City* copyright © Doris Lessing 1969); John Cousins (Frank Cousins); Virginia Crossman (Richard Crossman); Curtis Brown Group Ltd, London (on behalf of the Trustees of the Mass-Observation Archive, copyright © Trustees of the Mass-Observation Archive); The Dartington Hall Trust Archive; Stephen Dixon; Mary Evans, Centennial Professor, London School of Economics (*A Good School*); Faber and Faber Ltd (extract from *Untold Stories* by Alan Bennett; extracts from *Selected Letters 1940–85* and *Letters to Monica* by Philip Larkin, edited by Anthony Thwaite; extract from *Letters Home* by Sylvia Plath, edited by Aurelia Schober Plath;); Ray Galton and Alan Simpson (extract from the opening sequence from *Hancock's Half Hour,* 'Sunday Afternoon at Home'); Roy Greenslade (*Goodbye to the Working Class*); Rachel Gross (Geoffrey Gorer); Merryn Hemp (Raymond Williams); Pamela Hendicott and Ione Lee (Judy Haines); Islington Local History Centre (Gladys Langford); the *Liverpool Echo*; The Trustees of the Harold Macmillan Book Trust (extracts from the late Harold Macmillan's diaries); Duncan Marlor (May Marlor); Sally Muggeridge and the Malcolm Muggeridge Society (Malcolm Muggeridge); Jamie Muir and Denis Norden (Frank Muir and Denis Norden Archive); News Group Newspapers Ltd Archive (John Hilton Bureau); Allan Preston (Kenneth Preston); Random House Children's Books (extracts from *My Secret Diary* by Jacqueline Wilson); The Random House Group Limited (extracts from *Years of Hope: Diaries, Letters and Papers 1940–1962* by Tony Benn, published by Hutchinson; extracts from *Dear Tom: Letters from Home* by Tom Courtenay, published by Doubleday; extract from *This Boy* by Alan Johnson, published by Bantam Press, extract from *The Changing Forest* by Dennis Potter, published by Secker & Warburg; extracts from *Culture and Society 1780–1950* by Raymond Williams, published by Chatto & Windus); Marian Ray and Robin Raynham (Marian Raynham); Rogers, Coleridge and White Ltd (*Diaries 1939–1972* by Frances Partridge Copyright © Frances Partridge 1985); David Selbourne (Hugh Selbourne) The Society of Authors as the Literary Representative of the Estate of Philip Larkin (extracts from the unpublished letters of Philip Larkin); Tanya Stobbs (extract from a letter by Sylvia Townsend Warner taken from *Letters,* edited by William Maxwell); Roxana and Matthew Tynan (*Theatre Writings* and extract from *Observer* writings by Kenneth Tynan); United Agents LLP (extracts from *The Kenneth Williams Diaries* © The Estate of Kenneth Williams); Lewis and Michael Willmott (Phyllis Willmott, The Wylie Agency (UK) Ltd (extracts from reviews published in the *Spectator* of *The Uses of Literacy* and *Family and Kinship in East London,* and extracts from *Socialism and the Intellectuals* and *The Letters of Kingsley Amis,* all © Kingsley Amis); Toby Young (Michael Young).

Many people helped to make *Modernity Britain* happen – some in relatively small ways, others in much larger – and to all I am grateful. They include (with apologies for any inadvertent omissions): Mark Aston; Joe Bailey; Michael Banton; Andrea Belloli; Catherine Best; Libby Bishop; Sophie Bridges; Mike Burns; Nigel Cochrane; James Codd; Nick Corbo-Stuart; Fiona Courage; Richard Davenport-Hines; Patric Dickinson; Jill Faux; Helen Ford; Juliet Gardiner; John Gold; Ali Haggett; Adam Harwood; Antony Jay; Helen Langley; Rose Lock; Sandy Macmillan; Duncan Marlor; Nick Mays; David Milner; Louise North; Jonathan Oates; Stanley Page; Christopher Phipps; Dil Porter; Harry Ricketts; Jessica Scantlebury; Allan Silver; Alan Simmonds; John Southall; John Symons; Sue Taylor; Richard Thorpe; Lisa Towner; Jenny Uglow; Andy Ward; David Warren; Karen Watson; Annalisa Zisman (Back to Balance).

To Amanda Howard (Superscript Editorial Services), at the coalface transcribing my tapes, a huge and heartfelt 'thank you'.

I am fortunate to be represented by Rogers, Coleridge & White and am grateful for all the support I have received from Georgia Garrett, Mohsen Shah, Peter Straus and Matt Turner. The death of Deborah Rogers in April 2014 was a grievous blow to all her authors, and we remember her fondly.

I am fortunate also to be published by Bloomsbury and would like to express my thanks to Imogen Corke, Jude Drake, Ros Ellis, Oliver Holden-Rea and Anna Simpson. I am especially grateful to Bill Swainson and Nick Humphrey for all their hard work, perceptiveness and unfailing patience.

My debt to my family is enormous: to my wife Lucy; to our no-longer-children Laurie, George and Michael; to my son-in-law Graham; and to little Wolfie.

My final debt is rather different. In 2012 I was diagnosed with a non-Hodgkins lymphoma when I was just over halfway through writing this volume. It would not have been completed without the care and dedication of Dr Ruth Pettengell and all her colleagues at St George's Hospital, Tooting.

New Malden
August 2014

Picture Credits

The Bradford Empire just before demolition, 1957 (*Picture courtesy of Telegraph & Argus, Bradford*)

Birmingham, May 1957: Aston Villa players and mascot parade the FA Cup at Villa Park (*photographer unknown*)

Unrationed sweets: London, 1957 (*Popperfoto/Getty Images*)

Clarendon Crescent, Paddington, 1957 (*Mary Evans Picture Library ROGER MAYNE*)

Notting Hill at night, 1958 (*Getty Images*)

Fishermen carry coracles to the River Teifi in Cardiganshire, March 1958 (*Getty Images*)

Cherry-picking: West Malling, Kent, July 1958 (*The Times/NI Syndication*)

Redevelopment in Everton Heights, Liverpool, 1959 (*Courtesy of the Liverpool Echo*)

Youth club float, New Malden, Surrey, July 1959 (*Courtesy of the Kingston Heritage Service Picture Collection*)

St George's Day parade, St Helier Estate, South London, 1959 (*Photo taken by a photographer from the Croydon Times, now incorporated in the Croydon Advertiser. Image courtesy of Sutton Local Studies & Archives Service*)

Harold Macmillan in the north-east, January 1959 (*Jim Pringle/AP/Press Association Images*)

Hugh Gaitskell at the Midland Area Miners' Gala, June 1959 (*Mirrorpix*)

Election night, October 1959 (*Copyright BBC Photo Library*)

A *Vogue* model with schoolchildren, Bradford, 1960 (*©Frank Horvat*)

Notting Hill, October 1960 (*Terence Donovan/Getty Images*)

Berwick Street Market, Soho, April 1961 (*Photo by Archive Photos/Getty Images*)

Sea coalers collect coal, Hartlepool, 1961 (*Photograph by John Bulmer*)

Design studio, Crown Wallpapers, Cheshire, 1961 (*Photograph courtesy of the family of Marie McCormick*)

Science lesson, Surrey, 1961 (*Roger Mayne/Mary Evans Picture Library*)

Birmingham Reference Library, November 1961 (*Photograph courtesy of Mirrorpix*)

Roy Thomson addresses senior *Sunday Times* staff shortly after acquiring the paper, 1959 (*The Times/News Syndication*)

Sheep judging at the Royal Highland Show, Ingliston, Edinburgh, 1962 (*Photograph by Oscar Marzaroli. © Anne Marzaroli*)

Early morning in Tipton, the Black Country, 1961 (*Photograph by John Bulmer*)

Park Hill, Sheffield, 1961 (*Photographic courtesy of Architectural Review*)

The Gorbals, Glasgow, 1962 (*Courtesy of Herald and Times Group*)

Edmonton Green Market, Enfield, 1960 (*Courtesy of Enfield Local Studies & Archive*)

Supermarket shoppers, March 1962 (*Photo by Bert Hardy Advertising Archive/Getty Images*)

Agatha Hart at Stockwell Bus Garage, March 1962 (*Copyright TfL from the London Transport Museum collection*)

Index